r_t	Expected rate of return (or cost of capital) in period t. We omit the subscript where the expected return is identical in each period. Sometimes we use a *second* subscript to define the date at which the investment is made. Thus, $_{t-1}r_t$ is the (spot) rate of return on an investment made at $t-1$ and paying off at time t.
$\tilde{r}_t$	Uncertain actual rate of return in period t
r_D	Rate of return on firm's debt
r_E	Expected rate of return on firm's equity
r_f	Risk-free interest rate
r_m	Expected rate of return on the market portfolio
$r_\$$	Dollar rate of interest
r^*	Adjusted cost of capital
$s_{\text{SFr}/\$}$	Spot rate of exchange between Swiss francs and dollars
t	Time
T_c	Rate of corporate income tax
T_p	Rate of personal income tax
V	Market value of firm: $V = D + E$
β	Beta: A measure of market risk
δ	Delta: hedge ratio
λ	Lambda: Market price of risk $= \dfrac{r_m - r_f}{\sigma_m^2}$
ρ_{12}	Rho: Correlation coefficient between investments 1 and 2
σ	Sigma: Standard deviation
σ_{12}	Sigma: Covariance of investment 1 with investment 2
σ^2	Sigma squared: Variance
Σ	Capital sigma: "The sum of"

Ignatios Alexander   241-8950 (H)
    Fall 1996   268-7258 (W)
    Financial Mgt.

PRINCIPLES OF CORPORATE FINANCE

MCGRAW-HILL SERIES IN FINANCE

FIFTH EDITION

PRINCIPLES

OF

CORPORATE

FINANCE

RICHARD A. BREALEY
Tokai Bank Professor of Finance
London Business School

STEWART C. MYERS
Gordon Y Billard Professor of Finance
Sloan School of Management
Massachusetts Institute of Technology

The McGraw-Hill Companies, Inc.
New York   St. Louis   San Francisco   Auckland   Bogotá   Caracas
Lisbon   London   Madrid   Mexico City   Milan   Montreal   New Delhi
San Juan   Singapore   Sydney   Tokyo   Toronto

McGraw-Hill
A Division of the **McGraw-Hill** Companies

Principles of Corporate Finance

This book is printed on acid-free paper.

1234567890 DOC DOC 909876

ISBN 0-07-007417-8

This book was set in Janson by York Graphic Services, Inc.
The editors were Michelle E. Cox and Elaine Rosenberg; the production supervisor was Kathryn Porzio.
The design manager was Charles Carson.
The text was designed by Blake Logan.
The cover was designed by Danielle Conlon.
New drawings were done by Dartmouth Publishing, Inc.
R. R. Donnelley & Sons Company was printer and binder.

Cover photograph by Joshua Sheldon.
Library of Congress Cataloging-in-Publication Data is available:
LC Card # 96-76441.

When ordering this title, use ISBN 0-07-114053-0.

About the Authors

RICHARD A. BREALEY

London Business School. Tokai Bank Professor of Finance. Past President of European Finance Association and Director of the American Finance Association. Current research interests include portfolio theory and international finance. Member of editorial board of *Journal of Applied Corporate Finance*. Other books include *Introduction to Risk and Return from Common Stocks*. Director of Sun Life Assurance Company of Canada UK Holdings PLC and Tokai Derivative Products Ltd.

STEWART C. MYERS

Gordon Y Billard Professor of Finance at the Massachusetts Institute of Technology's Sloan School of Management. Research Associate of the National Bureau of Economic Research and past President and Director of the American Finance Association. His research is primarily concerned with the valuation of real and financial assets, corporate financial policy, and financial aspects of government regulation of business. Director of CAT Limited and The Brattle Group. Coauthor of *Optimal Financing Decisions* (with A. A. Robichek) and editor of *Modern Developments in Financial Management*.

To Our Parents

Contents

Preface

This book describes the theory and practice of corporate finance. We hardly need to explain why financial managers should master the practical aspect of their job, but a word on the role of theory may be helpful.

Managers learn from experience how to cope with routine problems. But the best managers are also able to respond rationally to change. To do this you need more than time-honored rules of thumb; you must understand *why* companies and financial managers behave the way they do. In other words, you need a *theory* of corporate finance.

Does that sound intimidating? It shouldn't. Good theory helps you understand what is going on in the world around you. It helps you ask the right questions when times change and new problems must be analyzed. It also tells you what things you do *not* need to worry about.

Throughout the book we show how to use financial theory to solve practical problems, and also to illuminate the facts and institutional material that students of corporate finance must absorb.

Of course, the theory presented in this book is not perfect and complete—no theory is. There are some famous controversies in which financial economists cannot agree on what firms ought to do. We have not glossed over these controversies. We set out the main arguments for each side and tell you where we stand.

There are also a few cases where theory indicates that the practical rules of thumb employed by today's managers are leading to poor decisions. Where financial managers appear to be making mistakes, we say so, while admitting that there may be hidden reasons for their actions. In brief, we have tried to be fair but to pull no punches.

Once understood, good theory is common sense. Therefore we have tried to present it at a commonsense level. We have avoided abstract proofs and heavy mathematics. However, parts of the book may require a significant intellectual effort for those unused to economic reasoning. We have marked the most difficult sections with asterisks, and suggest that you skim these sections on the first reading.

A WORD ABOUT LEARNING AIDS

There are no ironclad prerequisites for reading this book except algebra and the English language. An elementary knowledge of accounting, statistics, and microeconomics is helpful, however.

Each chapter of the book closes with a summary, an annotated list of suggestions for further reading, a quick and easy quiz, and some more challenging questions and problems. Answers to the quiz questions may be found at the end of the book, along with present value and option tables and a glossary.

The study guide for this book (Stewart D. Hodges, *Study Guide to Accompany Principles of Corporate Finance*, *McGraw-Hill, New York, 1997*) includes chapter summaries, additional illustrations, problems, and other useful material.

McGraw-Hill will make available a microcomputer software package that uses Lotus 1-2-3 or Excel templates to undertake a variety of financial calculations. In addition, a stand-alone PC package (*PCF Toolkit*) can be used to solve a variety of practical finance problems or be used as a learning aid.

For teachers who are using the book, there is an *Instructor's Manual*, a *Test Bank* with approximately 900 multiple-choice and true-false questions, and a comprehensive set of 400 overhead acetates which can also be displayed as a "Powerpoint" presentation. An additional 1700 Powerpoint slides will be made available to adopters.

We should mention two matters of style now to prevent confusion later. First, you will notice that the most important financial terms are set in boldface type the first time they appear. Second, most algebraic symbols representing dollar values are capital letters. Other symbols are generally lowercase letters. Thus the symbol for a dividend payment is "DIV," and the symbol for a percentage rate of return is "r."

CHANGES IN THE FIFTH EDITION

Readers of the fourth edition of this book may be interested to know what's different about the fifth edition, apart from polishing. First, we have substantially rewritten chapters or sections where we felt that we could make the ideas easier to follow. For example, there are important expository changes to the basic chapters on valuation and capital budgeting. We have reordered the material on the valuation of bonds and equities, and we have introduced an explanation of inflation and the distinction between nominal and real interest rates in Chapter 3. In Chapter 5 we have brought together the discussions of the profitability index and capital rationing. Later material which we believe is substantially improved and simplified includes the discussions of the weighted-average cost of capital in Chapter 19 and of risk management in Chapter 25.

Updating was needed for all but the most basic material. For example, our review of the capital asset pricing model covers recent controversies and empirical evidence. Similarly, the chapter on market efficiency now contains a brief survey of market anomalies.

Throughout the book we have added new, real-world examples. For instance, Chapter 4's discussion of the dividend discount model includes new estimates of the cost of capital for electric utilities. In Chapter 8 we show how arbitrage pricing theory has been used to derive the cost of capital for the same utilities. In Chapter 10 we describe how Merck uses simulation to analyze its investment in research and development.

Since financial managers increasingly need to understand other countries' financial systems, in Chapter 14 we compare ownership and corporate governance in Germany, Japan, and the United States. This is also one example of this edition's greater emphasis on agency issues.

Finally, we have added a large number of questions and problems. There are now about a thousand questions in all, an increase of 40 percent over the fourth edition.

Of course, one cannot always add and never subtract. Some examples become dated and are natural candidates for removal. But from time to time it is necessary to do more drastic pruning. Therefore, in this edition we have reduced the number of chapters by dropping the material on pensions. Instructors who would like to assign the material on pension schemes may obtain a revised version of the pension chapter from McGraw-Hill.

ACKNOWLEDGMENTS

We have a long list of people to thank for their helpful criticism of earlier editions or drafts of this edition: Lynda Borucki, The Brattle Group; Charles D'Ambrosio, University of Washington, Seattle; Carolyn Dorsa, Merck & Company, Inc.; Ahmad Etebari, University of New Hampshire; Thomas Eyssel, University of Missouri; Donald Fehrs, University of Notre Dame; Michael Hemler, University of Notre Dame; Leo Herzel, Mayer, Brown & Platt; Stewart Hodges, University of Warwick; Christopher Howe, MIT; Costas Kaplanis, Salomon Brothers; Evi Kaplanis, London Business School; A. Lawrence Kolbe, The Brattle Group; John Lightstone, SUNY Albany; Terence Lim, MIT; Surendra Mansinghka, San Francisco State University; Michael Mazzeo, Michigan State University; Hun Park, University of Illinois; Philip Perry, SUNY Buffalo; Richard Ruback, Harvard Business School; Richard Shepro, Mayer, Brown & Platt; Kevin Stephenson, Middlebury College; and Emery Trahan, Northeastern University.

This list is almost surely incomplete. We know how much we owe to our colleagues at the London Business School and MIT's Sloan School of Management. In many cases, the ideas that appear in this book are as much theirs as ours. Finally, we record the thanks due to our wives, Diana and Maureen, who were unaware when they married us that they were also marrying *The Principles of Corporate Finance*.

Richard A. Brealey
Stewart C. Myers

PRINCIPLES OF CORPORATE FINANCE

VALUE

1

Why Finance Matters

This book is about financial decisions by corporations. We should start by saying what these decisions are and why they are important.

The financial manager has two broad responsibilities, which we can boil down to two simple questions: What investments should the firm make? How should it pay for those investments? The first question involves spending money; the second involves raising it.

The secret of success in financial management is to increase value. That is a simple statement, but not a very helpful one. It is like advising an investor in the stock market to "buy low, sell high." The problem is how to do it.

There may be a few activities in which one can read a textbook and then "do it," but financial management is not one of them. That is why finance is worth studying. Who wants to work in a field where there is no room for experience, creativity, judgment, and a pinch of luck? Although this book cannot supply any of these items, it does present the concepts and information on which good financial decisions are based, and it shows you how to use the tools of the trade of finance.

Financial decisions are crucial. Investments made today have long-term fundamental effects on the business. So most senior managers are to some degree involved in financial decisions. However, some managers specialize in finance. In this chapter we describe their responsibilities. We also explain how corporations are organized and how they differ from other forms of business. We conclude the chapter with a brief survey of the topics that are covered in this book.

1-1 THE ROLE OF THE FINANCIAL MANAGER

To carry on business, companies need an almost endless variety of **real assets.** Many of these assets are tangible, such as machinery, factories, and offices; others are intangible, such as technical expertise, trademarks, and patents. All of them need to be paid for. To obtain the necessary money, the company sells pieces of paper called **financial assets,** or **securities.** These pieces of paper have value because they are claims on the firm's real assets and the cash that they produce. For example, if the company borrows money from the bank, the bank has a financial asset. That financial asset gives the bank a claim to a stream of interest payments and to repayment of the loan. The company's real assets need to produce enough cash to satisfy these claims. Financial assets include not only bank loans but also shares of stock, bonds, lease financing obligations, and so on.

Figure 1-1 Flow of cash between financial markets and the firm's operations. Key: (1) Cash raised by selling financial assets to investors; (2) cash invested in the firm's operations and used to purchase real assets; (3) cash generated by the firm's operations; (4a) cash reinvested; (4b) cash returned to investors. (*Source:* Adapted from S. C. Myers, ed., *Modern Developments in Financial Management,* New York, Praeger Publishers, Inc., Fig. 1, p. 5.)

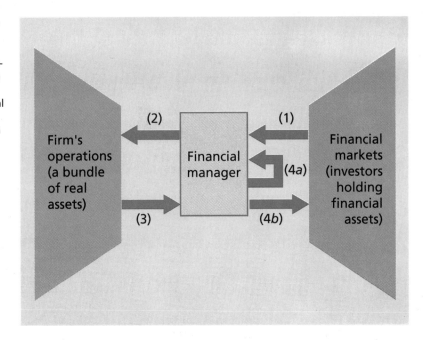

The financial manager stands between the firm's operations and the **financial markets,** where investors hold the financial assets issued by the firm.[1] The financial manager's role is shown in Figure 1-1, which traces the flow of cash from investors to the firm and back to investors again. The flow starts when securities are issued to raise cash (arrow 1 in the figure). The cash is used to purchase real assets used in the firm's operations (arrow 2). (You can think of the firm's operations as a bundle of real assets.) Later, if the firm does well, the real assets generate cash inflows which more than repay the initial investment (arrow 3). Finally, the cash is either reinvested (arrow 4a) or returned to the investors who purchased the original security issue (arrow 4b). Of course, the choice between arrows 4a and 4b is not completely free. For example, if a bank lends money at stage 1, the bank has to be repaid the money plus interest at stage 4b.

Our diagram takes us back to the financial manager's two basic questions. First, what real assets should the firm invest in? Second, how should the cash for the investment be raised? The answer to the first question is the firm's **investment,** or **capital budgeting, decision.** The answer to the second is the **financing decision.**

Financial managers ultimately answer to shareholders, who are the owners of the company. Shareholders are made better off by any decision which increases the value of their stake in the firm. Thus, you might say that a good capital budgeting decision is one that results in the purchase of a real asset that is worth more than it costs—an asset that makes a net contribution to value.

If successful investments are ones that increase a firm's value, the financial manager needs to know how investors value a firm. The analysis of even the most routine investment—the purchase of a new delivery truck, say—must logically flow from an understanding of how financial markets work.

---

[1]You will hear financial managers use the terms *financial markets* and *capital markets* almost synonymously. But *capital markets* are the source of long-term financing only. We use the term *financial markets* to refer to all sources of financing.

Financing decisions cannot be separated from financial markets either. For example, suppose a firm chooses to finance a major expansion program by borrowing money. The financial manager must have asked whether the value of the firm would be increased more by an issue of debt than by an issue of shares to stockholders. That required a theory of how the choice of financing affects value. Also, the financial manager must have considered the interest rate on the loan and concluded that it was not too high. That required an understanding of how interest rates are set and loans are priced.

The financial manager cannot avoid coping with time and uncertainty. Firms often have the opportunity to invest in assets which cannot pay their way in the short run and which expose the firm and its stockholders to considerable risk. The investment, if undertaken, may have to be financed by debt which cannot be fully repaid for many years. The firm cannot walk away from such choices—someone has to decide whether the opportunity is worth more than it costs and whether the debt burden can be safely borne.

1-2 ORGANIZING A BUSINESS

All businesses face the basic problems of what investments to make and how to pay for them, but these decisions tend to be more complex in large corporations than in small one-person businesses. Since this book is about the principles of *corporate* finance, we should explain briefly how corporations are organized and how they differ from other forms of business such as sole proprietorships and partnerships.

Sole Proprietorships

In 1901 pharmacist Charles Walgreen bought the drugstore in which he worked on the south side of Chicago. Today Walgreen's is the largest drugstore chain in the United States. If, like Charles Walgreen, you start on your own, with no partners or stockholders, you are said to be a **sole proprietor.** You bear all the costs and keep all the profits—after the Internal Revenue Service has taken its cut in taxes, of course.

As sole proprietor, you have *unlimited liability.* This means that you are personally responsible for all the business's debts. If you borrow money for the business and cannot repay the loan, you may be forced into personal bankruptcy. One interesting group of sole proprietors are the "Names" who provide the insurance at Lloyd's of London. If there are large insurance claims, each Name is individually liable "down to the last collar stud."

Partnerships

Instead of starting on your own, you may wish to pool your money or expertise with friends or business associates. If so, a sole proprietorship is obviously inappropriate. Instead, you can form a **partnership.** Your *partnership agreement* will set out how management decisions are to be made and the proportion of profits to which each partner is entitled. The partners then pay personal income tax on their share of the profits.

Partners, like sole proprietors, have the disadvantage of unlimited liability. If the business runs into financial heavy weather, each partner has unlimited liability for *all* the business's debts, not just his or her share.[2] The moral is clear and simple: "Know thy partner."

---

[2]Larger businesses can be set up as *limited partnerships.* In this case partners are classified as "general" or "limited." General partners manage the business and have unlimited personal liability for the business's debts. Limited partners usually have a restricted role in management, but their liability is confined to the money they contribute to the business. They can lose everything they put in, but no more.

Many professional businesses are organized as partnerships. They include the large accounting, legal, and management consulting firms. Most large investment banks, such as Morgan Stanley, Salomon Brothers, Merrill Lynch, First Boston, and Goldman Sachs, started life as partnerships. So did many well-known companies, such as Microsoft and Apple Computer. But eventually these companies and their financing needs grew too large for them to continue as partnerships.[3]

Corpora-tions

As your firm grows, you may decide to *incorporate*. Unlike a proprietorship or partnership, a **corporation** is legally distinct from its owners. It is based on *articles of incorporation* that set out the purpose of the business, how many shares can be issued, the number of directors to be appointed, and so on. These articles must conform to the laws of the state in which the business is incorporated.[4] For many legal purposes, the corporation is considered a resident of its state. For example, it can borrow or lend money, and it can sue or be sued. It pays its own taxes (but cannot vote!).

Unlike proprietorships and partnerships, corporations have **limited liability,** which means that the stockholders cannot be held personally responsible for the firm's debts. If, say, IBM were to fail, no one could demand that its shareholders put up more money to pay off its debts. The most a stockholder can lose is the amount invested in the stock.

While the stockholders own their corporation, they do not manage it. Instead, they elect a *board of directors.* Some of these directors may be drawn from the firm's management, but others are nonexecutive directors, who are not employed by the firm. The board of directors is the representative of the shareholders. It appoints the top managers and is supposed to ensure that management acts in the shareholders' best interests.

This *separation of ownership and management* is one distinctive feature of corporations. In other forms of business organization, such as proprietorships and partnerships, the owners are the managers. The separation between ownership and management gives a corporation more flexibility and permanence than a partnership. Even if managers of a corporation quit or are dismissed and replaced by others, the corporation can survive. Similarly, today's shareholders may sell all their shares to new investors without affecting the business.

By organizing as a corporation, a business may be able to attract a wide variety of investors. The shareholders may include individuals who hold only a single share worth a few dollars, receive only a single vote, and are entitled to only a tiny proportion of the profits. Shareholders may also include giant pension funds and insurance companies, whose investment in the firm may run into millions of shares and who are entitled to a correspondingly large number of votes and proportion of the profits.

Given these advantages, you might be wondering why anyone forms a partnership. One reason is the time and cost required to manage a corporation's legal machinery. There is also an important tax drawback to corporations in the United States. Because the corporation is a separate legal entity, it is taxed separately. So corporations pay tax on their profits, and, in addition, shareholders pay tax on any dividends that they receive from the company.[5] By contrast, income received by partners is taxed only once, as personal income.

---

[3]Goldman Sachs is the only large investment bank still organized as a partnership.

[4]Delaware has a well-developed and supportive system of corporate law. A high proportion of U.S. corporations are incorporated in Delaware, even though they may do relatively little business in that state.

[5]The United States is unusual in its taxation of corporations. To avoid taxing the same income twice, most other countries give shareholders at least some credit for the taxes that their company has already paid.

When you first establish a corporation, the shares may all be held by a small group, perhaps the company's managers and a small number of backers who believe the business will grow into a profitable investment. The shares are not publicly traded and your company is *closely held*. Eventually, when the firm grows and new shares are issued to raise additional capital, the shares will be widely traded. Such corporations are known as *public companies*. Most well-known corporations are public companies.

Notice that a corporation has many choices open to it that are not open to other forms of business. It can raise money by selling new shares to shareholders, and it can pay back the money by declaring a dividend. Shareholders can vote in a new management team, and one corporation can make a takeover bid for another.

1-3 WHO IS THE FINANCIAL MANAGER?

In this book we will use the term *financial manger* to refer to anyone responsible for a significant corporate investment or financing decision. But except in the smallest firms, no *single* person is responsible for all the decisions discussed in this book. Responsibility is dispersed throughout the firm. Top management is of course continuously involved in financial decisions. But the engineer who designs a new production facility is also involved: The design determines the kind of real asset the firm will hold. The marketing manager who commits to a major advertising campaign is also making an important investment decision. The campaign is an investment in an intangible asset that will pay off in future sales and earnings.

Nevertheless, there are managers who specialize in finance. The **treasurer** is usually the person most directly responsible for obtaining financing, managing the firm's cash account and its relationships with banks and other financial institutions, and making sure the firm meets its obligations to the investors holding its securities. Typical responsibilities of the treasurer are listed in the left-hand column of Table 1-1.

For small firms, the treasurer is likely to be the only financial executive. Larger corporations usually also have a **controller.** The right-hand column of Table 1-1 lists the typical controller's responsibilities. Notice the difference between the two jobs. The treasurer obtains and manages the company's capital. By contrast, the controller

TABLE 1-1

Some typical responsibilities of the treasurer and controller

Treasurer	Controller
Banking relationships	Accounting
Cash management	Preparation of financial statements
Obtaining financing	Internal auditing
Credit management	Payroll
Dividend disbursement	Custody of records
Insurance	Preparing budgets
Pensions management	Taxes

Note: This table is not an exhaustive list of tasks treasurers and controllers may undertake.

checks that the money is used efficiently. The controller manages budgeting, accounting, and auditing.

The largest firms usually appoint a **chief financial officer (CFO)** to oversee both the treasurer's and the controller's work. The CFO is deeply involved in financial policymaking and corporate planning. Often he or she will have general managerial responsibilities beyond strictly financial issues and may also be a member of the board of directors.

Major capital investment projects are so closely tied to plans for product development, production, and marketing that managers from these areas are inevitably drawn into planning and analyzing the projects. If the firm has staff members specializing in corporate planning, they are naturally involved in capital budgeting too. Usually the treasurer, controller, or CFO is responsible for organizing and supervising the capital budgeting process.

Because of the importance of many financial issues, ultimate decisions often rest by law or by custom with the board of directors. For example, only the board has the legal power to declare a dividend or to sanction a public issue of securities. Boards usually delegate decision-making authority for small- or medium-size investment outlays, but the authority to approve large investments is almost never delegated.

1-4 TOPICS COVERED IN THIS BOOK

This book covers investment decisions first, then financing decisions, and finally a series of topics in which investment and financing decisions interact and cannot be made separately.

In Parts One, Two, and Three we look at different aspects of the investment decision. The first is the problem of how to value assets, the second is the link between risk and value, and the third is the management of the investment process. Our discussion of these topics occupies Chapters 2 through 12.

Eleven chapters devoted to the simple problem of "finding real assets that are worth more than they cost" may seem excessive, but that problem is not so simple in practice. We will require a theory of how long-lived, risky assets are valued, and that requirement will lead us to basic questions about financial markets. For example:

- How are corporate bonds and stocks valued in financial markets?
- What risks are borne by investors in corporate securities? How can these risks be measured?
- What compensation do investors demand for bearing risk?
- What rate of return can investors in common stocks reasonably expect to receive?

Intelligent capital budgeting and financing decisions require answers to these and other questions about how financial markets work.

Financing decisions occupy Parts Four through Seven. We begin in Chapter 13 with another basic question about financial markets: Do security prices reflect the fair value of the underlying assets? This question is crucially important because the financial manager must know whether securities can be issued at a fair price. The remaining chapters in Part Four describe the kinds of securities corporations use to raise money and explain how and when they are issued.

Parts Five, Six, and Seven continue the analysis of the financing decision, covering dividend policy, debt policy, risk management, and the alternative forms of debt. Literally dozens of different financial instruments are described and analyzed, including debentures, convertibles, leases, eurobonds, financial futures, and many other exotic beasts. We will also describe what happens when firms find themselves in financial distress because of poor operating performance, excessive borrowing, or both. Furthermore, we will show how financing considerations sometimes affect capital budgeting decisions.

Part Eight covers financial planning. Decisions about investment, dividend policy, debt policy, and other financial issues cannot be reached independently. They have to add up to a sensible overall financial plan for the firm, one which increases the value of the shareholders' investment yet still retains enough flexibility for the firm to avoid financial distress and to pursue unexpected new opportunities.

Part Nine is devoted to decisions about the firm's short-term assets and liabilities. There are separate chapters on three topics: channels for short-term borrowing or investment, management of liquid assets (cash and marketable securities), and management of accounts receivable (money lent by the firm to its customers).

Part Ten covers two important problems which require decisions about both investment and financing. First we look at mergers and acquisitions. Then we consider international financial management. All the financial problems of doing business at home are present overseas, but the international financial manager faces the additional complications created by multiple currencies, different tax systems, and special regulations imposed by foreign institutions and governments.

Part Eleven is our conclusion. It also discusses some of the things that we *don't* know about finance. If you can be the first to solve any of these puzzles, you will be justifiably famous.

1-5   SUMMARY

In Chapter 2 we will begin with the most basic concepts of asset valuation. However, let us first sum up the principal points made in this introductory chapter.

A business may be organized in one of several ways. For example, it may be owned by a sole proprietor, who bears all the costs and keeps all the profits, or a number of business associates may combine together to form a partnership. Large businesses are usually organized as corporations. Corporations differ from proprietorships and partnerships in several important ways: First, they are legally distinct from their owners, and they pay their own taxes. Second, unlike proprietorships and partnerships, corporations have limited liability, which means that the stockholders who own the corporation cannot be held responsible for the firm's debts. Third, the owners of a corporation are not usually the managers.

The overall task of the financial manager can be broken down into (1) the investment, or capital budgeting, decision and (2) the financing decision. In other words, the firm has to decide (1) how much to invest and what assets to invest in and (2) how to raise the necessary cash. The objective is to increase the value of the shareholders' stake in the firm.

One final word of advice: In small companies there is often only one financial executive. However, the larger corporation usually has both a treasurer and a controller. The treasurer's job is to obtain and manage the company's financing. By contrast, the controller's job is one of inspecting to see that the money is used correctly. In large firms there may also be a financial vice-president who acts as the firm's chief financial officer.

Of course all managers, not just finance specialists, face financial problems. In this book we will use the term *financial manager* to refer to any person confronted with a corporate financing or investment decision.

Financial managers read *The Wall Street Journal (WSJ), The Financial Times (FT),* or both daily. You should too. *The Financial Times* is published in Britain, but there is a North American edition. *The New York Times* and a few other big-city newspapers have good business and financial sections, but they are no substitute for the *WSJ* or *FT*. The business and financial sections of most local United States dailies are, except for local news, nearly worthless for the professional financial manager.

Several magazines specialize in finance and financial management. These include *Euromoney, Corporate Finance, Journal of Applied Corporate Finance, Risk*, and *CFO Magazine*. This list does not include research journals such as the *Journal of Finance, Journal of Financial Economics*, and *Financial Management*. Following chapters give specific references to pertinent research.

Quiz

1. Read the following passage: "Companies usually buy ___(a)___ assets. These include both tangible assets such as ___(b)___ and intangible assets such as ___(c)___. In order to pay for these assets, they sell ___(d)___ assets such as ___(e)___. The decision regarding which assets to buy is usually termed the ___(f)___ or ___(g)___ decision. The decision regarding how to raise the money is usually termed the ___(h)___ decision."
   Now fit each of the following terms into the most appropriate space: *financing, real, bonds, investment, executive airplanes, financial, capital budgeting, brand names.*

2. Which of the following statements more accurately describe the treasurer rather than the controller?
   (*a*) Likely to be the only financial executive in small firms
   (*b*) Monitors capital expenditures to make sure that they are not misappropriated
   (*c*) Responsible for investing the firm's spare cash
   (*d*) Responsible for arranging any issue of common stock
   (*e*) Responsible for the company's tax affairs

3. Which of the following are real assets, and which are financial?
   (*a*) A share of stock
   (*b*) A personal IOU
   (*c*) A trademark
   (*d*) A truck
   (*e*) Undeveloped land
   (*f*) The balance in the firm's checking account
   (*g*) An experienced and hardworking sales force
   (*h*) A corporate bond

4. What are the advantages and disadvantages of setting up a business as:
   (*a*) A sole proprietor?
   (*b*) A partnership?
   (*c*) A corporation?

5. Match each of the following characteristics with one of the two types of organization listed after each statement:
   (*a*) Ownership and management are distinct. (*sole proprietorship, corporation*)
   (*b*) Owners have unlimited liability for the business's debts. (*sole proprietorship, corporation*)
   (*c*) Income of the business and that of its owners are taxed separately. (*partnership, corporation*)
   (*d*) Ownership of the business can be transferred without affecting its operations. (*sole proprietorship, corporation*)
   (*e*) Shares in the business are widely traded. (*partnership, public company*)

2

Present Value and the Opportunity Cost of Capital

Companies invest in a variety of real assets. These include tangible assets such as plant and machinery and intangible assets such as management contracts and patents. The object of the investment, or capital budgeting, decision is to find real assets which are worth more than they cost. In this chapter we will show what this objective means in a country with extensive and well-functioning financial markets. At the same time we will take the first, most basic steps toward understanding how assets are valued. It turns out that if there is a good market for an asset, its value is exactly the same as the market price.

There are a few cases in which it is not that difficult to estimate asset values. In real estate, for example, you can hire a professional appraiser to do it for you. Suppose you own an apartment building. The odds are that your appraiser's estimate of its value will be within a few percent of what the building would actually sell for.[1] After all, there is continuous activity in the real estate market, and the appraiser's stock-in-trade is knowledge of the prices at which similar properties have recently changed hands.

Thus the problem of valuing real estate is simplified by the existence of an active market in which all kinds of properties are bought and sold. For many purposes no formal theory of value is needed. We can take the market's word for it.

But we have to go deeper than that. First, it is important to know how asset values are reached in an active market. Even if you can take the appraiser's word for it, it is important to understand *why* that apartment building is worth, say, $250,000 and not a higher or lower figure. Second, the market for most corporate assets is pretty thin. Look in the classified advertisements in *The Wall Street Journal:* It is not often that you see a blast furnace for sale.

Companies are always searching for assets that are worth more to them than to others. That apartment house is worth more to you if you can manage it better than others. But in that case, looking at the price of similar buildings will not tell you what your apartment house is worth under your management. You need to know how asset prices are determined. In other words, you need a theory of value.

We start to build that theory in this chapter. We will stick to the simplest problems and examples in order to make basic ideas clear. Readers with a taste for more complication will find plenty to satisfy them in later chapters.

---

[1]Needless to say, there are some kinds of properties that appraisers find really difficult to value—for example, nobody knows the potential selling price of the Taj Mahal or the Parthenon or Windsor Castle. If you own such a place, we congratulate you.

2-1 INTRODUCTION TO PRESENT VALUE

Later in this chapter we will prove why the concept of present value is useful. However, that concept will go down more easily if you first acquire an intuitive understanding of it.

Suppose your apartment house burns down, leaving you with a vacant lot worth $50,000 and a check for $200,000 from the fire insurance company. You consider rebuilding, but your real estate adviser suggests putting up an office building instead. The construction cost would be $300,000, and there would also be the cost of the land, which might otherwise be sold for $50,000. On the other hand, your adviser foresees a shortage of office space and predicts that a year from now the new building would fetch $400,000 if you sold it. Thus you would be investing $350,000 now in the expectation of realizing $400,000 a year hence. You should go ahead if the **present value** of the expected $400,000 payoff is greater than the investment of $350,000. Therefore, you need to ask yourself, "What is the value today of $400,000 one year from now, and is that present value greater than $350,000?"

....

Calculating Present Value

The present value of $400,000 one year from now must be less than $400,000. After all, *a dollar today is worth more than a dollar tomorrow*, because the dollar today can be invested to start earning interest immediately. This is the first basic principle of finance.

Thus, the present value of a delayed payoff may be found by multiplying the payoff by a **discount factor** which is less than 1. (If the discount factor were more than 1, a dollar today would be worth *less* than a dollar tomorrow.) If C_1 denotes the expected payoff at time period 1 (1 year hence), then

$$\text{Present value (PV)} = \text{discount factor} \times C_1$$

This discount factor is expressed as the reciprocal of 1 plus a *rate of return*:

$$\text{Discount factor} = \frac{1}{1 + r}$$

The rate of return r is the reward that investors demand for accepting delayed payment.

Let us consider the real estate investment, assuming for the moment that the $400,000 payoff is a sure thing. The office building is not the only way to obtain $400,000 a year from now. You could invest in United States government securities maturing in a year. Suppose these securities yield 7 percent interest. How much would you have to invest in them in order to receive $400,000 at the end of the year? That's easy: You would have to invest $400,000/1.07, which is $373,832. Therefore, at an interest rate of 7 percent, the present value of $400,000 one year from now is $373,832.

Let's assume that, as soon as you've committed the land and begun construction on the building, you decide to sell your project. How much could you sell it for? That's another easy question. Since the property produces $400,000, investors would be willing to pay $373,832 for it. That's what it would cost them to get a $400,000 payoff from investing in government securities. Of course you could always sell your property for less, but why sell for less than the market will bear? The $373,832 present value is the only feasible price that satisfies both buyer and seller. Therefore, the present value of the property is also its market price.

To calculate present value, we discount expected future payoffs by the rate of return offered by comparable investment alternatives. This rate of return is often referred to as the **discount rate, hurdle rate,** or **opportunity cost of capital.** It is called the *opportunity cost* because it is the return forgone by investing in the project rather than investing in securities. In our example the opportunity cost was 7 percent. Present value was obtained by dividing $400,000 by 1.07:

$$PV = \text{discount factor} \times C_1 = \frac{1}{1+r} \times C_1 = \frac{400,000}{1.07} = \$373,832$$

Net Present Value

The building is worth $373,832, but this does not mean that you are $373,832 better off. You committed $350,000, and therefore your **net present value (NPV)** is $23,832. Net present value is found by subtracting the required investment:

$$NPV = PV - \text{required investment} = 373,832 - 350,000 = \$23,832$$

In other words, your office development is worth more than it costs—it makes a *net* contribution to value. The formula for calculating NPV can be written as

$$NPV = C_0 + \frac{C_1}{1+r}$$

remembering that C_0, the cash flow at time period 0 (that is, today) will usually be a negative number. In other words, C_0 is an investment and therefore a cash *outflow*. In our example, $C_0 = -\$350,000$.

A Comment on Risk and Present Value

We made one unrealistic assumption in our discussion of the office development: Your real estate adviser cannot be *certain* about future values of office buildings. The $400,000 figure represents the best *forecast*, but it is not a sure thing.

Therefore, our conclusion about how much investors would pay for the building is wrong. Since they could achieve $400,000 with certainty by buying $373,832 worth of United States government securities, they would not buy your building for that amount. You would have to cut your asking price to attract investors' interest.

Here we can invoke a second basic financial principle: *A safe dollar is worth more than a risky one.* Most investors avoid risk when they can do so without sacrificing return. However, the concepts of present value and the opportunity cost of capital still make sense for risky investments. It is still proper to discount the payoff by the rate of return offered by a comparable investment. But we have to think of *expected* payoffs and the *expected* rates of return on other investments.

Not all investments are equally risky. The office development is riskier than a government security but is probably less risky than drilling a wildcat oil well. Suppose you believe the project is as risky as investment in the stock market and that you forecast a 12 percent rate of return for stock market investments. Then 12 percent becomes the appropriate opportunity cost of capital. That is what you are giving up by not investing in comparable securities. You can now recompute NPV:

$$PV = \frac{400,000}{1.12} = \$357,143$$

$$NPV = PV - 350,000 = \$7143$$

If other investors agree with your forecast of a $400,000 payoff and with your assessment of a 12 percent opportunity cost of capital, then your property ought to be worth $357,143 once construction is under way. If you tried to sell it for more than that, there would be no takers, because the property would then offer an expected rate of return lower than the 12 percent available in the stock market. The office building still makes a net contribution to value, but it is much smaller than our ear-lier calculations indicated.

In Chapter 1 we said that the financial manager must be concerned with time and uncertainty and their effects on value. This is clearly so in our example. The $400,000 payoff would be worth exactly that if it could be realized instantaneously. If the office building is as risk-free as government securities, the 1-year delay reduces value to $373,832. If the office building is as risky as investment in the stock market, then uncertainty reduces value by a further $16,689 to $357,143.

Unfortunately, adjusting asset values for time and uncertainty is often more complicated than our example suggests. Therefore, we will take the two effects separately. For the most part, we will dodge the problem of risk in Chapters 2 through 6, either treating all payoffs as if they were known with certainty or talking about expected cash flows and expected rates of return without worrying how risk is defined or measured. Then in Chapter 7 we will turn to the problem of understanding how capital markets cope with risk.

Present Values and Rates of Return

We have decided that construction of the office building is a smart thing to do, since it is worth more than it costs—it has a positive net present value. To calculate how much it is worth, we worked out how much one would have to pay to achieve the same income by investing directly in securities. The project's present value is equal to its future income discounted at the rate of return offered by these securities.

We can reexpress our criterion by saying that our property venture is worth undertaking because the return exceeds the cost of capital. The return on the capital invested is simply the profit as a proportion of the initial outlay:

$$\text{Return} = \frac{\text{profit}}{\text{investment}} = \frac{400,000 - 350,000}{350,000} = .14, \text{ or } 14\%$$

The cost of capital invested is once again just the return forgone by *not* investing in securities. In our present case, if the office building is about as risky as investing in the stock market, the return forgone is 12 percent. Since the 14 percent return on the office building exceeds the 12 percent cost, we should start digging the foundations of the building.

Here then we have two equivalent decision rules for capital investment.[2]

1. *Net present value rule*. Accept investments that have positive net present values.

2. *Rate-of-return rule*. Accept investments that offer rates of return in excess of their opportunity costs of capital.[3]

The Opportunity Cost of Capital

The opportunity cost of capital is such an important concept that we will give one more example.

You are offered the following opportunity: Invest $100,000 today, and, depending on the state of the economy at the end of the year, you will receive one of the following payoffs:

---

[2]You might check for yourself that these are equivalent rules. In other words, if the return 50,000/350,000 is greater than r, then the net present value $-350,000 + [400,000/(1 + r)]$ *must* be greater than 0.

[3]The two rules can conflict when there are cash flows in more than two periods. We address this problem in Chapter 5.

Slump	Normal	Boom
80,000	110,000	140,000

If there is an equal chance of each outcome, the expected payoff on your project is simply the average of the three possible payoffs:

$$\text{Expected payoff} = C_1 = \frac{80,000 + 110,000 + 140,000}{3} = \$110,000$$

The *expected* payoff is $110,000, but of course it is by no means certain. The payoff could be $30,000 more or less than the expected level. You need to decide whether the present value of this payoff is greater than the up-front investment.

Suppose you determine that the stock of company X has equally uncertain prospects. X's current stock price is $95.65, and, depending on the state of the economy at the end of the year, the price will be as follows:

Slump	Normal	Boom
80	110	140

Since the three states of the economy are equally likely, the expected payoff from company X's stock is

$$\text{Expected payoff} = \frac{80 + 110 + 140}{3} = \$110$$

Thus, if you invest in the stock, you are laying out $95.65 today with an expected payoff of $110 at the end of the year. The expected return on the stock is

$$\text{Expected return} = \frac{\text{expected profit}}{\text{investment}} = \frac{110 - 95.65}{95.65} = .15, \text{ or } 15\%$$

This is the expected return that you are giving up by investing in the project rather than the stock market. In other words, it is the project's opportunity cost of capital.

To value the project, you need to discount the expected cash flow by the opportunity cost of capital:

$$PV = \frac{110,000}{1.15} = \$95,650$$

This is the amount it would cost investors in the stock market to buy an expected cash flow of $110,000. (They could do so by buying 1000 shares of the stock X.) It is, therefore, also the sum that investors would be prepared to pay for your project.

To calculate net present value, you need to deduct the initial investment:

$$NPV = 95,650 - 100,000 = -\$4350$$

The project is worth $4350 less than it costs and is not worth undertaking.

Notice that you come to a similar conclusion if you compare the expected project return with the cost of capital:

$$\text{Expected return on project} = \frac{\text{expected profit}}{\text{investment}}$$

$$= \frac{110,000 - 100,000}{100,000} = .10, \text{ or } 10\%$$

The expected return on the project is less than the 15 percent investors could expect to earn by investing in the stock market, and so the project is not worthwhile.

Of course in real life it's impossible to restrict the future states of the economy to just "slump," "normal," and "boom." We have also simplified by assuming a perfect match between the payoffs of 1000 shares of stock X and the payoffs to the investment project. The main point of the example does carry through to real life, however. Remember this: The opportunity cost of capital for an investment project is the expected rate of return demanded by investors in common stocks or other securities subject to the same risks as the project. When you discount the project's expected cash flow at its opportunity cost of capital, the resulting present value is the amount investors—including your company's stockholders—would be willing to pay for the project. Any time you find and launch a positive-NPV project—a project with present value exceeding its required cash outlay—you have made your company's stockholders better off.

Two Sources of Confusion

The $110,000 project payoff is not a single-point estimate. It is an average, or expected, cash flow. We averaged in the upside (boom) payoff of $140,000 and the downside (slump) payoff of $80,000.[4]

Sometimes people say that explicit recognition of upside and downside payoffs completely "takes care of" uncertainty. Then they slide into the idea that expected cash flows can be discounted at risk-free rates, such as the 7 percent return on government securities. Of course discounting at 7 percent would make the project worth 110,000/1.07 = $102,800 and give it a positive NPV.

Wait a minute! That can't be right. If you can buy an expected payoff of $110,000 for $95,650 in the stock market, why would you or anybody pay $102,800 for the project?

Stock X is not a government security; it's risky. That's why investors demand a 15 percent expected return to put their money in it. (They are equally content to lend money to the government at 7 percent because that investment is risk-free.) Your project is risky, not safe. No investor will accept less than 15 percent from the project when stock X is a freely available alternative.

Now here is another possible source of confusion. Suppose a banker approaches. "Your company is a fine and safe business with few debts," she says. "My bank will lend you the $100,000 that you need for the project at 8 percent." Does that mean the cost of capital for the project is 8 percent? If so, the project would be above water, with PV at 8 percent = 110,000/1.08 = $101,852 and NPV = 101,852 − 100,000 = $1852.

That can't be right either. First, the interest rate on the loan has nothing to do with the risk of the project: It reflects the good health of your existing business. Second, whether you take the loan or not, you still face the choice between the project, which offers an expected return of only 10 percent, or the equally risky stock, which gives an expected return of 15 percent. A financial manager who borrows at 8

---

[4]In this example the expected payoff is the same as the payoff in a "normal" economy. This need not be the case. If the boom payoff were $150,000, for example, the expected payoff would be *higher* than the intermediate, "normal" payoff.

percent and invests at 10 percent is not smart, but stupid, if the company or its share-holders can borrow at 8 percent and buy an equally risky investment offering 15 percent. That is why the 15 percent expected return on the stock is the opportunity cost of the capital for the project.

*2-2 FOUNDATIONS OF THE NET PRESENT VALUE RULE[5]

So far our discussion of net present value has been rather casual. Increasing NPV *sounds* like a sensible objective for a company, but it is more than just a rule of thumb. We need to understand why the NPV rule makes sense and why we look to the bond and stock markets to find the opportunity cost of capital.

Figure 2-1 illustrates the problem of choosing between spending today and spending in the future. Assume that you have a cash inflow of B today and F in a year's time. Unless you have some way of storing or anticipating income, you will be compelled to consume it as it arrives. This could be inconvenient or worse. If the bulk of your cash flow is received next year, the result could be hunger now and gluttony later. This is where the capital market comes in. It allows the transfer of wealth across time, so that you can eat moderately both this year and next.

The capital market is simply a market where people trade between dollars today and dollars in the future. The downward-sloping line in Figure 2-1 represents the rate of exchange in the capital market between today's dollars and next year's dollars; its slope is $1 + r$, where r denotes the 1-year rate of interest. By lending all your present cash flow, you could increase your *future* consumption by $(1 + r)B$ or FH. Alternatively, by borrowing against your future cash flow, you could increase your *present* consumption by $F/(1 + r)$ or BD.

Let us put some numbers into our example. Suppose that your prospects are as follows:

- Cash on hand: $B = \$20{,}000$
- Cash to be received 1 year from now: $F = \$25{,}000$

If you do not want to consume anything today, you can invest $20,000 in the capital market at, say, 7 percent. The rate of exchange between dollars next year and dollars today is 1.07: This is the slope of the line in Figure 2-1. If you invest $20,000 at 7 percent, you will obtain $20,000 × 1.07 = $21,400. Of course, you also have $25,000 coming in a year from now, so you will end up with $46,400. This is point H in Figure 2-1.

What if you want to cash in the $25,000 future payment and spend everything today on some ephemeral frolic? You can do so by borrowing in the capital market. The present value formula tells us how much investors would give you today in return for the promise of $25,000 next year:

$$PV = \frac{C_1}{1 + r} = \frac{25{,}000}{1.07} = \$23{,}364$$

This is the distance BD. The total present value of the current and future cash flows (point D in the future) is found by adding this year's flow:

$$C_0 + \frac{C_1}{1 + r} = 20{,}000 + \frac{25{,}000}{1.07} = \$43{,}364$$

---

[5]Sections marked with an asterisk contain more difficult material and may be skipped on a first reading.

Figure 2-1 Notice how borrowing and lending enlarge the individual's choice. By borrowing against future cash flow *F*, an individual can consume an extra *BD* today; by lending current cash flow *B*, the individual can consume an extra *FH* tomorrow.

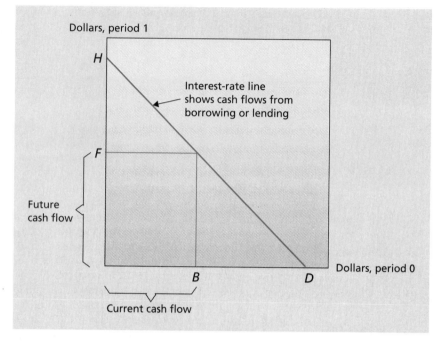

This is the formula that we used before to calculate net present value (except that in this case C_0 is positive).

What if you cash in but then change your mind and want to consume next year? Can you get back to point *H*? Of course—just invest the net present value at 7 percent:

$$\text{Future value} = 43,364 \times 1.07 = \$46,400$$

As a matter of fact, you can end up anywhere on the straight line connecting *D* and *H* depending on how much of the $43,364 current wealth you choose to invest. Figure 2-1 is actually a graphical representation of the link between present and future value.

*How the Capital Market Helps to Smooth Consumption Patterns

Few of us save all our current cash flow or borrow fully against our future cash flow. We try to achieve a balance between present and future consumption. But there is no reason to expect that the best balance for one person is best for another.

Suppose, for example, that you have a prodigal disposition and favor present over future consumption. Your preferred pattern might be indicated by Figure 2-2: You choose to borrow *BC* against future cash flow and consume *C* today. Next year you are obliged to repay *EF* and, therefore, can consume only *E*. By contrast, if you have a more miserly streak, you might prefer the policy shown in Figure 2-3: You consume *A* today and lend the balance *AB*. In a year's time you receive a repayment of *FG* and are therefore able to indulge in consumption of *G*.[6]

---

[6]The exact balance between present and future consumption that each individual will choose depends on personal taste. Readers who are familiar with economic theory will recognize that the choice can be represented by superimposing an indifference map for each individual. The preferred combination is the point of tangency between the interest-rate line and the individual's indifference curve. In other words, each individual will borrow or lend until 1 plus the interest rate equals the marginal rate of time preference (i.e., the slope of the indifference curve).

Figure 2-2 The prodigal chooses to borrow *BC* against tomorrow's cash flow, in order to consume *C* today and *E* tomorrow.

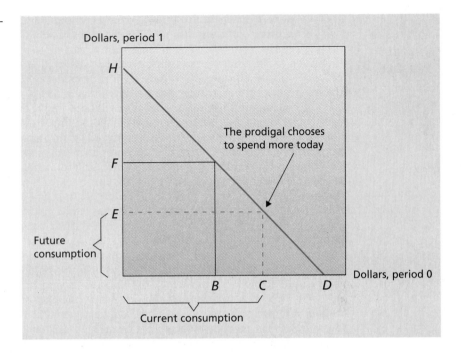

Both the miser and the prodigal *can* choose to spend cash only as it is received, but in these examples both prefer to do otherwise. By opening up borrowing and lending opportunities, the capital market removes the obligation to match consumption and cash flow.

Figure 2-3 The miser chooses to lend *AB*, in order to consume *A* today and *G* tomorrow.

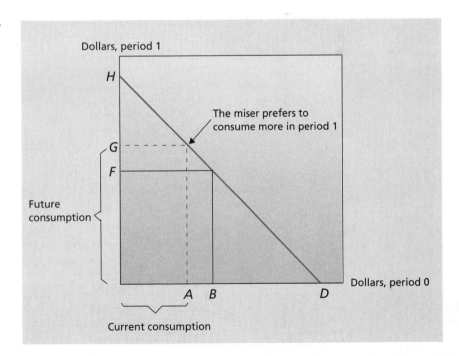

*Now We Introduce Productive Opportunities

In practice individuals are not limited to investing in capital market securities: They may also acquire plant, machinery, and other real assets. Thus, in addition to plotting the returns from buying securities, we can also plot an investment-opportunities line which shows the returns from buying real assets. The return on the "best" project may well be substantially higher than returns in the capital market, so that the investment-opportunities line may be initially very steep. But, unless the individual is a bottomless pit of inspiration, the line will become progressively flatter. This is illustrated in Figure 2-4, where the first $10,000 of investment produces a subsequent cash flow of $20,000, whereas the next $10,000 offers a cash flow of only $15,000. In the jargon of economics, there is a declining marginal return on capital.

We can now return to our hypothetical example and inquire how your welfare would be affected by the possibility of investing in real assets. The solution is illustrated in Figure 2-5. To keep our diagram simple, we shall assume that you have maximum initial resources of D. Part of this may come from borrowing against future cash flow; but we do not have to worry about that, because, as we have seen, the amount D can always be deployed into future income. If you choose to invest any part of this sum in the capital market, you can attain any point along the line DH.

Now let us introduce investment in *real assets* by supposing that you can retain J of your initial resources and invest the balance JD in plant and machinery. We can see from the curved investment-opportunities line that such an investment would produce a future cash flow of G. This is all very well, but maybe you do not want to consume J today and G tomorrow. Fortunately you can use the capital market to adjust your spending pattern as you choose. By investing the whole of J in the capital market, you can increase *future* income by GM. Alternatively, by borrowing against your entire future earnings of G, you can increase *present* income by JK. In other words, by *both* investing JD in *real assets* and borrowing or lending in the capital market, you can obtain any point along the line KM. Regardless of whether you are a

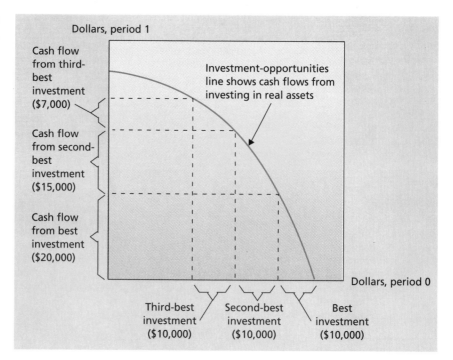

Figure 2-4 The effect of investment in real assets on cash flows in periods 0 and 1. Notice the diminishing returns on additional units of investment.

Figure 2-5 Both the prodigal and the miser have initial wealth of D. They are better off if they invest *JD* in real assets and then borrow or lend in the capital market. If they could invest *only* in the capital market, they would be obliged to choose a point along *DH*; if they could invest *only* in real assets, they would be obliged to choose a point along *DL*.

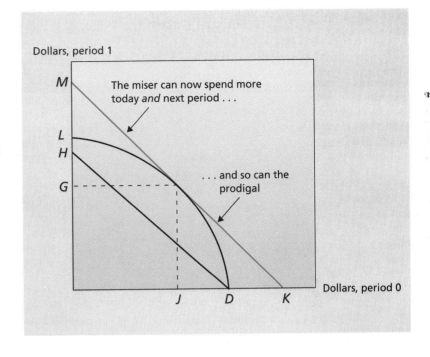

prodigal or a miser, you have more to spend either today or next year than if you invest *only* in the capital market (i.e., choose a point along the line *DH*). You also have more to spend either today or next year than if you invest *only* in real assets (i.e., choose a point along the curve *DL*).

Let us look more closely at the investment in *real assets*. The maximum sum that could be realized today from the investment's future cash flow is *JK*. This is the investment's *present value*. Its cost is *JD*, and the difference between its present value and its cost is *DK*. This is its *net present value*. Net present value is the addition to your resources from investing in *real assets*.

Investing the amount *JD* is a smart move—it makes you better off. In fact it is the smartest possible move. We can see why if we look at Figure 2-6. If you invest *JD* in real assets, the net present value is *DK*. If you invest, say, *ND* in real assets, the net present value declines to *DP*. In fact investing either more or less than *JD* in real assets *must* reduce net present value.

Notice also that by investing *JD*, you have invested up to the point at which the investment-opportunities line just touches and has the same slope as the interest-rate line. Now the slope of the investment-opportunities line represents the return on the marginal investment, so that *JD* is the point at which the return on the marginal investment is exactly equal to the rate of interest. In other words, you will maximize your wealth if you invest in *real* assets until the marginal return on investment falls to the rate of interest. Having done that, you will borrow or lend in the capital market until you have achieved the desired balance between consumption today and consumption tomorrow.

We now have a logical basis for the two equivalent rules that we proposed so casually at the end of Section 2-1. We can restate the rules as follows:

1. *Net present value rule*. Invest so as to maximize the net present value of the investment. This is the difference between the discounted, or present, value of the future income and the amount of the initial investment.

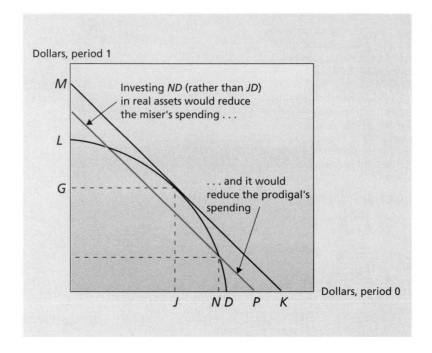

Figure 2-6 If the prodigal or the miser invested *ND* in real assets, the NPV of the investment would be only *DP*. The investor would have less to spend both today and tomorrow.

Dollars, period 1

Investing *ND* (rather than *JD*) in real assets would reduce the miser's spending . . .

. . . and it would reduce the prodigal's spending

Dollars, period 0

2. *Rate-of-return rule.* Invest up to the point at which the marginal return on the investment is equal to the rate of return on equivalent investments in the capital market. This is the point of tangency between the interest-rate line and the investment-opportunities line.

*A Crucial Assumption

In our examples, the miser and the prodigal placed an identical value on the firm's investment. They agreed because they faced identical borrowing and lending opportunities. Whenever firms discount cash flows at capital market rates, they are implicitly making some assumptions about their shareholders' opportunities to borrow and lend. Strictly speaking, they are assuming:

1. That there are no barriers preventing access to the capital market and that no participant is sufficiently dominant as to have a significant effect on price

2. That access to the capital market is costless and that there are no "frictions" preventing the free trading of securities

3. That relevant information about the price and quality of each security is widely and freely available

4. That there are no distorting taxes

In sum, they are assuming a perfectly competitive capital market. Clearly this is at best an approximation, but it may not be too bad a one. First, there are nearly 50 million stockholders in the United States. Even a giant institution like Calpers (the California employee pension fund) controls less than 2 percent of publicly traded stocks. Second, the costs of trading in securities are generally small both in absolute terms and relative to the costs of trading in real assets such as office buildings and

Figure 2-7 Here there are separate borrowing and lending rates. The steep line represents the interest rate for a borrower; the flatter line represents the rate for a lender. In this case the prodigal and the miser prefer different levels of capital investment.

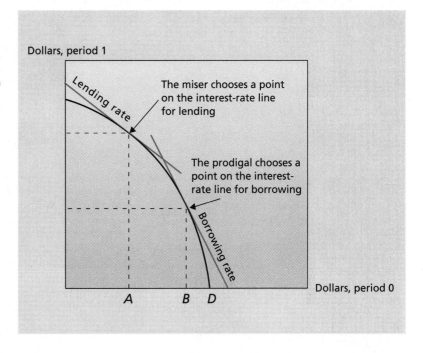

Dollars, period 1

Lending rate

The miser chooses a point on the interest-rate line for lending

The prodigal chooses a point on the interest-rate line for borrowing

Borrowing rate

A   B   D

Dollars, period 0

blast furnaces. Finally, though there obviously are cases in which investors have possessed privileged information, the mighty power of avarice and the Securities and Exchange Commission ensure that potentially profitable information seldom remains for long the property of one individual.[7]

Even though our conditions are not fully satisfied, there is considerable evidence that security prices behave almost as if they were. This evidence is presented and discussed in Chapter 13.

*Imperfect Capital Markets

Suppose that we did not have such a well-functioning capital market. How would this damage our net present value rule?

As an example, Figure 2-7 shows what happens if the borrowing rate is substantially higher than the lending rate. This means that when you want to turn period-0 dollars into period-1 dollars (i.e., lend), you move *up* a relatively flat line; when you want to turn period-1 dollars into period-0 dollars (i.e., borrow), you move *down* a relatively steep line. You can see that would-be borrowers (who must move down the steep line) prefer the company to invest only *BD*. In contrast, would-be lenders (who must move *up* the relatively flat line) prefer the company to invest *AD*. In this case the two groups of shareholders want the manager to use different discount rates. The manager has no simple way to reconcile their differing objectives.

No one believes that the competitive market assumption is fully satisfied. Later in this book we will discuss several cases in which differences in taxation, transaction costs, and other imperfections must be taken into account in financial decision making. However, we will also discuss research which indicates that, in general, capital markets

---

[7]Avarice helps because any other individual who can obtain this information can use it to make trading profits.

function fairly well. That is one good reason for relying on net present value as a corporate objective. Another good reason is that net present value makes common sense; we will see that it gives obviously silly answers less frequently than its major competitors. But for now, having glimpsed the problems of imperfect markets, we shall, like an economist in a shipwreck, simply *assume* our life jacket and swim safely to shore.

2-3 A FUNDAMENTAL RESULT

The present value rule really dates back to the work of the great American economist Irving Fisher, in 1930.[8] What was so exciting about Fisher's analysis was his discovery that the capital investment criterion has nothing to do with the individual's preferences for current versus future consumption. The prodigal and the miser are unanimous in the amount that they want to invest in real assets. Because they have the same investment criterion, they can cooperate in the same enterprise and can safely delegate the operation of that enterprise to a professional manager. Managers do not need to know anything about the personal tastes of their shareholders and should not consult their own tastes. Their task is to maximize net present value. If they succeed, they can rest assured that they have acted in the best interest of their shareholders.

Our justification of the net present value rule has been restricted to two periods and to certain cash flows. However, the rule also makes sense for cases in which the cash flows extend beyond the next period. The argument goes like this:

1. A financial manager should act in the interest of the firm's stockholders.
2. Each stockholder wants three things:
   (*a*) To be as rich as possible, that is, to maximize current wealth
   (*b*) To transform that wealth into whatever time pattern of consumption he or she most desires
   (*c*) To choose the risk characteristics of that consumption plan
3. But stockholders do not need the financial manager's help to reach the best time pattern of consumption. They can do that on their own, providing they have free access to competitive capital markets. They can also choose the risk characteristics of their consumption plan by investing in more or less risky securities.
4. How then can the financial manager help the firm's stockholders? By increasing the market value of each stockholder's stake in the firm. The way to do that is to seize all investment opportunities that have a positive net present value.

This gives us the fundamental condition for the successful operation of a capitalist economy. Separation of ownership and management is a practical necessity for large organizations. Many corporations have hundreds of thousands of shareholders, no two with the same tastes, wealth, or personal opportunities. There is no way for all the firm's owners to be actively involved in management: It would be like running New York City through a series of town meetings for all its citizens. Therefore, authority has to be delegated. The remarkable thing is that managers of firms can all be given one simple instruction: Maximize net present value.

---

[8]I. Fisher, *The Theory of Interest*, Augustus M. Kelley, Publishers, New York, 1965 (reprinted from the 1930 edition). Our graphical illustration closely follows the exposition in E. F. Fama and M. H. Miller, *The Theory of Finance*, Holt, Rinehart and Winston, New York, 1972.

**Other
Corporate
Goals**

Sometimes you hear managers speak as if the corporation has other goals. For example, they may say that their job is to maximize profits. That sounds reasonable. After all, don't shareholders prefer to own a profitable company rather than an unprofitable one? But, taken literally, profit maximization doesn't make sense as a corporate objective. Here are three reasons:

1. "Maximizing profits" leaves open the question of "Which year's profits?" Shareholders might not want a manager to increase next year's profits at the expense of profits in later years.

2. A company may be able to increase future profits by cutting its dividend and investing the cash. That is not in the shareholders' interest if the company earns only a low rate of return on the investment.

3. Different accountants may calculate profits in different ways. So you may find that a decision which improves profits in one accountant's eyes will reduce them in the eyes of another.

Do Managers Maximize Net Present Value?   Do real managers really maximize net present value? Some idealists say that managers should not be obliged to act in the selfish interests of their stockholders. Some realists argue that, regardless of what managers ought to do, they in fact look after themselves.

Let us respond to the idealists first. Does a focus on value mean that managers must act as greedy mercenaries riding roughshod over the weak and helpless? Most of this book is devoted to financial policies that increase a firm's value. None of these policies requires gallops over the weak and helpless. In most instances there is little conflict between doing well (maximizing value) and doing good.

We are reminded here of a survey of businesspeople that inquired whether they attempted to maximize profits. They indignantly rejected the notion, protesting that they were responsible, God-fearing, and so on: Their responsibilities went far beyond the narrow profit objective. But when the question was reformulated and they were asked whether they could increase profits by raising or lowering their selling price, they replied that neither policy would do so.[9] In a rather similar vein, we suspect that many managers do not have an explicit objective of maximizing net present value and yet can think of no action that would do other than to reduce it.

Of course, ethical issues do arise in business as in other walks of life, and therefore when we say that the objective of the firm is to maximize shareholder wealth, we do not mean that anything goes. In part, the law deters managers from making blatantly dishonest decisions, but most managers are not simply concerned with observing the letter of the law or with keeping to written contracts. In business dealings, as in other day-to-day dealings, there are also unwritten or implicit rules of behavior. To work efficiently together, we need to trust each other. Thus huge deals are regularly completed on a handshake, and each side knows that the other will not renege later if things turn sour. Whenever anything happens to weaken this trust, we are all a little worse off.[10]

Managers play fair partly because they know that doing so is in the general interest. But good managers also know that their firm's reputation is one of its most

---

[9]Cited in G. J. Stigler, *The Theory of Price*, 3d ed., Macmillan Company, New York, 1966.

[10]For a discussion of this issue, see A. Schleifer and L. H. Summers, "Breach of Trust in Corporate Takeovers," in A. J. Auerbach (ed.), *Corporate Takeovers: Causes and Consequences*, University of Chicago Press, 1988.

important assets and therefore that playing fair and keeping one's word are simply good business practices. Johnson and Johnson is an example of a firm that places a very high value on its reputation. When it discovered in 1986 that capsules of Tylenol had been tampered with, it withdrew all bottles immediately from the shops. This move cost $140 million, but the company knew that it would be more costly in the end to downplay the risk or cover it up.

In many financial transactions one party has more information than the other. This opens up plenty of opportunities for sharp practice and outright fraud, and, because the activities of rogues are more entertaining than those of honest people, bookshelves are packed with accounts of financial fraudsters. What is the reaction of honest financial firms? It is to build long-term relationships with customers and establish a name for fair dealing and financial integrity. Major banks and securities firms know that their most valuable asset is their reputation; when seeking new customers, they emphasize their long history and their responsible behavior. When something happens to undermine that reputation, the cost can be enormous.

Consider the case of the Salomon Brothers bidding scandal in 1991.[11] A Salomon trader tried to evade rules limiting the firm's participation in auctions of U.S. Treasury bonds by submitting bids in the names of the company's customers without the customers' knowledge. When this was discovered, Salomon settled the case by paying almost $200 million in fines and establishing a $100 million fund for payments of claims from civil lawsuits. Yet the value of Salomon Brothers stock fell by far more than $300 million. In fact the price dropped by about a third, representing a $1.5 billion decline in the company's market value.

Why did the value of the firm drop so dramatically? Largely because investors were worried that Salomon would lose business from customers that now distrusted the company. The damage to Salomon's reputation was far greater than the explicit costs of the scandal and was hundreds or thousands of times as costly as the potential gains Salomon could have reaped from the illegal trades.

DO MANAGERS LOOK AFTER THEIR OWN INTERESTS?   Now, how about the realists who say that managers look after their own interests rather than those of their shareholders?

Think of the company's net revenue as a pie that is divided among a number of claimants. These include the management and the workforce as well as the lenders and shareholders who have put up the money to establish and maintain the business. The government is a claimant, too, since it gets to tax the profits of the enterprise.

All these claimants are bound together in a complex web of contracts and understandings. For example, when banks lend money to the firm, they insist on a formal contract stating the rate of interest and repayment dates, perhaps placing restrictions on dividends or additional borrowing, and so on. But you can't devise written rules to cover every possible future event. So the written contracts are supplemented by understandings. For example, managers understand that in return for a fat salary they are expected to work hard and not to snaffle part of the pie for unwarranted personal luxuries.

---

[11]This discussion is based on Clifford W. Smith, Jr., "Economics and Ethics: The Case of Salomon Brothers," *Journal of Applied Corporate Finance*, **5**:23–28 (Summer 1992).

What enforces this understanding? Is it realistic to expect financial managers always to act on behalf of the shareholders? The shareholders can't spend their lives watching through binoculars to check that managers are not shirking. A closer look reveals institutional arrangements that help to ensure that the shareholders' pockets are close to the managers' hearts:

- Managers are subject to the scrutiny of specialists. Their actions are monitored by the board of directors; managers are also reviewed by banks, which keep an eagle eye on the progress of firms receiving their loans.

- Shirkers are likely to find that they are ousted by more energetic managers. This competition may arise within the firm, but poorly performing companies are also more likely to be taken over. That sort of takeover typically brings in a fresh management team, and the old team finds itself on the street.

- Finally, managers are spurred on by incentive schemes, such as stock options, which pay off big if shareholders gain but are valueless if they do not.

Thus few managers at the top of major United States corporations are lazy or inattentive to stockholders' interests. On the contrary, the pressure to perform can be intense. Just ask Robert Stempel, former president of General Motors; John Akers, former chairman of IBM; Kay Whitmore, former chairman of Eastman Kodak; and Kenneth Olsen, founder and former chairman of Digital Equipment Corporation. All left their posts at the urging of investors and the company's board of directors. None was lazy or inattentive, but each was forced to step aside when the company's profitability and competitiveness deteriorated and the need for new strategies became clear.

We do not want to leave the impression that corporate life is a rat race or a series of squabbles. It isn't, because practical corporate finance has evolved to reconcile personal and corporate interests—to keep everyone working together to increase the value of the whole pie, not merely the size of each person's slice.

2-4 SUMMARY

In this chapter we have introduced the concept of present value as a way of valuing assets. Calculating present value is easy. Just discount future cash flow by an appropriate rate, usually called the *opportunity cost of capital*, or *hurdle rate*:

$$\text{Present value (PV)} = \frac{C_1}{1 + r}$$

Net present value is present value plus any immediate cash flow:

$$\text{Net present value (NPV)} = C_0 + \frac{C_1}{1 + r}$$

Remember that C_0 is negative if the immediate cash flow is an investment, that is, if it is a cash outflow.

The discount rate is determined by rates of return prevailing in capital markets. If the future cash flow is absolutely safe, then the discount rate is the interest rate on safe securities such as United States government debt. If the size of the future cash flow is uncertain, then the expected cash flow should be discounted at the expected rate of return offered by equivalent-risk securities. We will talk more about this in Chapter 7.

Cash flows are discounted for two simple reasons: first, because a dollar today is worth more than a dollar tomorrow, and second, because a risky dollar is worth less than a safe one. Formulas for PV and NPV are numerical expressions of these ideas. We look to rates of return prevailing in capital markets to determine how much to discount for time and for risk. By calculating the present value of an asset, we are in effect estimating how much people will pay for it if they have the alternative of investing in the capital markets.

The concept of net present value allows efficient separation of ownership and management of the corporation. A manager who invests only in assets with positive net present values serves the best interests of each one of the firm's owners—regardless of differences in their wealth and tastes. This is made possible by the existence of the capital market which allows each shareholder to construct a personal investment plan that is custom-tailored to his or her own needs. For example, there is no need for the firm to arrange its investment policy to obtain a sequence of cash flows that matches shareholders' preferred time patterns of consumption. The shareholders can shift funds forward or back over time perfectly well on their own, provided they have free access to competitive capital markets. In fact, their plan for consumption over time is constrained by only two things: their personal wealth (or lack of it) and the interest rate at which they can borrow and lend. The financial manager cannot affect the interest rate but can increase stockholders' wealth. The way to do so is to invest in assets having positive net present values.

Further Reading

The pioneering works on the net present value rule are:

I. Fisher: *The Theory of Interest*, Augustus M. Kelley, Publishers. New York, 1965. Reprinted from the 1930 edition.

J. Hirschleifer: "On the Theory of Optimal Investment Decision," *Journal of Political Economy*, **66:**329–352 (August 1958).

For a more rigorous textbook treatment of the subject, we suggest:

E. F. Fama and M. H. Miller: *The Theory of Finance*, Holt, Rinehart and Winston, New York, 1972.

If you would like to dig deeper into the question of how managers may be motivated to maximize shareholder wealth, we suggest:

M. C. Jensen and W. H. Meckling: "Theory of the Firm: Managerial Behavior, Agency Costs, and Ownership Structure," *Journal of Financial Economics*, **3:**305–360 (October 1976).

E. F. Fama: "Agency Problems and the Theory of the Firm," *Journal of Political Economy*, **88:**288–307 (April 1980).

M. C. Jensen: "The Modern Industrial Revolution, Exit, and the Failure of Internal Control Systems," *Journal of Applied Corporate Finance*, **6:**4–24 (Winter 1994).

Quiz

1. C_0 is the initial cash flow on an investment, and C_1 is the cash flow at the end of 1 year. The symbol r is the discount rate.
   (*a*) Is C_0 usually positive or negative?
   (*b*) What is the formula for the present value of the investment?
   (*c*) What is the formula for the net present value?

(**d**) The symbol r is often termed the *opportunity cost of capital*. Why?

(**e**) If the investment is risk-free, what is the appropriate measure of r?

2. If the present value of $150 paid at the end of 1 year is $130, what is the 1-year discount factor? What is the discount rate?

3. Calculate the 1-year discount factor DF_1 for discount rates of (**a**) 10 percent, (**b**) 20 percent, and (**c**) 30 percent.

4. A merchant pays $100,000 for a load of grain and is certain that it can be resold at the end of 1 year for $132,000.

(**a**) What is the return on this investment?

(**b**) If this return is *lower* than the rate of interest, does the investment have a positive or a negative net present value?

(**c**) If the rate of interest is 10 percent, what is the present value of the investment?

(**d**) What is the net present value?

5. What is the net present value rule? What is the rate-of-return rule? Do the two rules give the same answer?

6. For an outlay of $8 million you can purchase a tanker load of bucolic acid delivered in Rotterdam 1 year hence. Unfortunately the net cash flow from selling the tanker load will be very sensitive to the growth rate of the world economy:

Slump	Normal	Boom
8 million	12 million	16 million

(**a**) What is the expected cash flow? Assume the three outcomes for the economy are equally likely.

(**b**) What is the expected rate of return on the investment in the project?

(**c**) One share of stock Z is selling for $10. The stock has the following payoffs after 1 year:

Slump	Normal	Boom
8	12	16

Calculate the expected rate of return offered by stock Z. Explain why this is the opportunity cost of capital for your bucolic acid project.

(**d**) Calculate the project's net present value. Is the project a good investment? Explain why.

*7. In Figure 2-8, the sloping line represents the opportunities for investment in the capital market and the solid curved line represents the opportunities for investment in plant and machinery. The company's only asset at present is $2.6 million in cash.

(**a**) What is the interest rate?

(**b**) How much should the company invest in plant and machinery?

(**c**) How much will this investment be worth next year?

(**d**) What is the average rate of return on the investment?

(**e**) What is the marginal rate of return?

(**f**) What is the present value of this investment?

(**g**) What is the net present value of this investment?

(**h**) What is the total present value of the company?

Figure 2-8 See
Quiz question 7.

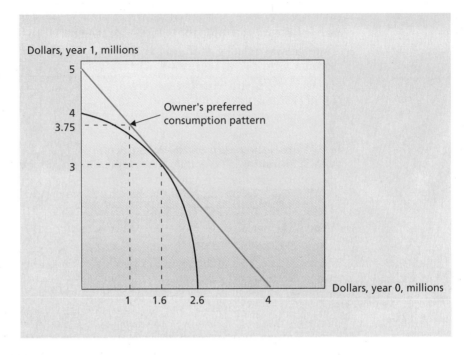

(*i*) How much will the individual consume today?

(*j*) How much will he or she consume tomorrow?

8. We can imagine the financial manager doing several things on behalf of the firm's stockholders. For example, the manager might:

(*a*) Make shareholders as wealthy as possible by investing in real assets with positive net present values.

(*b*) Modify the firm's investment plan to help shareholders achieve a particular time pattern of consumption.

(*c*) Choose high- or low-risk assets to match shareholders' risk preferences.

(*d*) Help balance shareholders' checkbooks.

But in well-functioning capital markets, shareholders will vote for *only one* of these goals. Which one? Why?

Questions and Problems

· ·

1. In Section 2-1, we analyzed the possible construction of an office building on a plot of land appraised at $50,000. We concluded that this investment had a positive NPV of $7143.

Suppose E. Coli Associates, a firm of genetic engineers, offers to purchase the land for $60,000, $30,000 paid immediately and $30,000 after 1 year. United States government securities maturing in 1 year yield 7 percent.

(*a*) Assume E. Coli is sure to pay the second $30,000 installment. Should you take its offer or start on the office building? Explain.

(*b*) Suppose you are *not* sure E. Coli will pay. You observe that other investors demand a 10 percent return on their loans to E. Coli. Assume that the other investors have correctly assessed the risks that E. Coli will not be able to pay. Should you accept E. Coli's offer?

2. Write down the formulas for an investment's net present value and rate of return. Prove that NPV is positive *only* if the rate of return exceeds the opportunity cost of capital.

3. What is the net present value of a *firm's* investment in a U.S. Treasury security yielding 6 percent and maturing in 1 year? *Hint:* What is the opportunity cost of capital? Ignore taxes.

4. Calculate the NPV and rate of return for each of the following investments. The opportunity cost of capital is 20 percent for all four investments.

Investment	Initial Cash Flow, C_0	Cash Flow in Year 1, C_1
1	−10,000	+20,000
2	−5,000	+12,000
3	−5,000	+5,500
4	−2,000	+5,000

(*a*) Which investment is most valuable?

(*b*) Suppose each investment would require use of the same parcel of land. Therefore you can take only one. Which one? *Hint:* What is the firm's objective? To earn a high rate of return? Or to increase firm value?

5. In real life the future health of the economy cannot be reduced to three equally probable states like "slump," "normal," and "boom." But we'll keep that simplification for one or two more examples.

Your company has identified two more projects, B and C. Each will require a $5 million outlay immediately. The possible payoffs at year 1 are, in millions:

	Slump	Normal	Boom
B	4	6	8
C	5	5.5	6

You have identified the possible payoffs to investors in three stocks, X, Y, and Z:

	Current Price per Share	PAYOFF AT YEAR 1		
		Slump	Normal	Boom
X	95.65	80	110	140
Y	40	40	44	48
Z	10	8	12	16

(*a*) What are the expected cash inflows of projects B and C?

(*b*) What are the expected rates of return offered by stocks X, Y, and Z?

(*c*) What are the opportunity costs of capital for projects B and C? *Hint:* Calculate the percentage differences, slump versus normal and boom versus normal, for stocks X, Y, and Z. Match up to the percentage differences in B's and C's payoffs.

(*d*)   What are the NPVs of projects B and C?

(*e*)   Suppose B and C are launched and $5 million is invested in each. How much will they add to the total market value of your company's shares?

6. Answer the following conceptual questions after you have completed the calculations for question 5.

    (*a*)   Explain why projects B and C have the *same* NPV (zero) even though B has the higher expected rate of return.

    (*b*)   Your company has invested last year's profits in U.S. Treasury debt yielding a 7 percent rate of return. Suppose projects B and C are to be funded by selling $10 million of these securities. A marketing manager claims that B and C must both be *great* projects, since their rates of return clearly exceed the 7 percent return on Treasuries. Explain why the marketing manager is wrong.

    (*c*)   Suppose instead that the cash parked in Treasuries is earmarked for a hostile takeover of the Harvard Business School. Projects B and C have to be financed with borrowed money. Your company's Director of Information Technology argues that the cost of capital for *both* B and C is the 8 percent interest rate paid on the borrowing. Explain why this manager is wrong. Be sure to stress the difference between the cost of borrowing and the opportunity cost of capital.

*7. Redraw Figure 2-5 to scale to represent the following situation:

    (*a*)   A firm starts out with $10 million in cash.

    (*b*)   The rate of interest r is 10 percent.

    (*c*)   To maximize NPV the firm invests today $6 million in real assets ($C_0 = -6$ million). This leaves $4 million which can be paid out to the shareholders.

    (*d*)   The NPV of the investment is $2 million.

When you have finished, answer the following questions:

    (*e*)   How much cash is the firm going to receive in year 1 from its investment?

    (*f*)   What is the marginal return from the firm's investment?

    (*g*)   What is the present value of the shareholders' investment after the firm has announced its investment plan?

    (*h*)   Suppose shareholders want to spend $6 million today. How can they do this?

    (*i*)   How much will they then have to spend next year? Show this on your drawing.

*8. Resketch Figure 2-5 to show how the firm's investment plan should be affected by a decline in the interest rate. Mark the NPV of the revised investment plan. Show whether the miser or the prodigal would be better off.

*9. Look again at Figure 2-5. Suppose the firm decides to invest *more* than JD in real assets. Redraw the interest-rate line to show the NPV of the revised investment plan. Show that both the miser *and* the prodigal are worse off.

*10. The interest-rate line in our diagrams always has a slope greater than 1. Why?

11. "The discount rate is the rate at which the company will be able to reinvest its cash flows." Is that right? Discuss.

12. Respond to the following comment: "It's all very well telling companies to maximize net present value, but 'net present value' is just an abstract notion.

What I tell my managers is that profits are what matters and it's profits that we're going to maximize."

13. Respond to the following comment: "It's no good just telling me to maximize my stock price. I can easily take a short view and maximize today's price. What I would prefer is to keep it on a gently rising trend."

14. Here's a harder question. It is sometimes argued that the net present value criterion is appropriate for corporations but not for governments. First, governments must consider the time preferences of the community as a whole rather than those of a few wealthy investors. Second, governments must have a longer horizon than individuals, for governments are the guardians of future generations. What do you think?

15. Give examples of potential conflicts of interest between managers and shareholders. Why do managers generally work hard to make the firm successful?

16. When a company's stock is widely held, it may not pay an individual shareholder to spend time monitoring the managers' performance and trying to replace poor management. Explain why. Do you think that a bank that has made a large loan to the company is in a different position?

17. As you drive down a deserted highway, you are overcome with a sudden desire for a hamburger. Fortunately, just ahead are two hamburger outlets: One is owned by a national chain; the other appears to be owned by "Joe." Which outlet has the greater incentive to serve you catmeat? Why? What lessons does your answer have for financial institutions?

18. Sometimes lawyers work on a contingency basis. They collect a percentage of their client's settlement instead of receiving a fixed fee. Why might clients prefer this arrangement? Would this sort of arrangement be more appropriate for clients who use lawyers regularly or for those who use them infrequently?

19. Discuss which of the following forms of compensation is most likely to align the interests of managers and shareholders:
    (*a*) A fixed salary
    (*b*) A salary linked to company profits
    (*c*) A salary paid partly in the form of the company's shares
    (*d*) An option to buy the company's shares at an attractive price

3

How to Calculate Present Values

In Chapter 2 we learned how to work out the value of an asset that produces cash exactly 1 year from now. But we did not explain how to value assets that produce cash 2 years from now or in several future years. That is the first thing that we must do in this chapter. We will then have a look at some shortcut methods for calculating present values and at some specialized present value formulas. We will consider how inflation affects the purchasing power of future cash payments.

By then you will deserve some payoff for the mental investment you have made in learning about present values. Therefore, we will try out the concept on bonds. In Chapter 4 we will look at the valuation of common stocks, and after that we will tackle the firm's capital investment decisions at a practical level of detail.

3-1 VALUING LONG-LIVED ASSETS

Do you remember how to calculate the present value PV of an asset that produces a cash flow (C_1) 1 year from now?

$$PV = DF_1 \times C_1 = \frac{C_1}{1 + r_1}$$

The discount factor for the year-1 cash flow is DF_1, and r_1 is the opportunity cost of investing your money for 1 year. Suppose you will receive a certain cash inflow of $100 next year ($C_1 = 100$) and the rate of interest on 1-year U.S. Treasury bills is 7 percent ($r_1 = .07$). Then present value equals

$$PV = \frac{C_1}{1 + r_1} = \frac{100}{1.07} = \$93.46$$

The present value of a cash flow 2 years hence can be written in a similar way as

$$PV = DF_2 \times C_2 = \frac{C_2}{(1 + r_2)^2}$$

C_2 is the year-2 cash flow, DF_2 is the discount factor for the year-2 cash flow, and r_2 is the annual rate of interest on money invested for 2 years. Continuing with our example, suppose you get another cash flow of $100 in year 2 ($C_2 = 100$). The rate of interest on 2-year Treasury notes is 7.7 percent per year ($r_2 = .077$); this means that a dollar invested in 2-year notes will grow to $1.077^2 = \$1.16$ by the end of 2 years. The present value of your year-2 cash flow equals

$$PV = \frac{C_2}{(1 + r_2)^2} = \frac{100}{(1.077)^2} = \$86.21$$

Valuing Cash Flows in Several Periods

One of the nice things about present values is that they are all expressed in current dollars—so that you can add them up. In other words, the present value of cash flow $A + B$ is equal to the present value of cash flow A plus the present value of cash flow B. This happy result has important implications for investments that produce cash flows in several periods.

We calculated above the value of an asset that produces a cash flow of C_1 in year 1, and we calculated the value of another asset that produces a cash flow of C_2 in year 2. Following our additivity rule, we can write down the value of an asset that produces cash flows in *each* year. It is simply

$$PV = \frac{C_1}{1 + r_1} + \frac{C_2}{(1 + r_2)^2}$$

We can obviously continue in this way and find the present value of an extended stream of cash flows:

$$PV = \frac{C_1}{1 + r_1} + \frac{C_2}{(1 + r_2)^2} + \frac{C_3}{(1+r_3)^3} + \cdots$$

This is called the **discounted cash flow** (or **DCF**) formula. A shorthand way to write it is

$$PV = \sum \frac{C_t}{(1 + r_t)^t}$$

where Σ refers to the sum of the series. To find the *net* present value we add the (usually negative) initial cash flow, just as in Chapter 2:

$$NPV = C_0 + PV = C_0 + \sum \frac{C_t}{(1 + r_t)^t}$$

***Why the Discount Factor Declines as Futurity Increases—And a Digression on Money Machines**

If a dollar tomorrow is worth less than a dollar today, one might suspect that a dollar the day after tomorrow should be worth even less. In other words, the discount factor DF_2 should be less than the discount factor DF_1. But is this *necessarily* so, when there is a different interest rate r_t for each period?

Suppose r_1 is 20 percent and r_2 7 percent. Then

$$DF_1 = \frac{1}{1.20} = .83$$

$$DF_2 = \frac{1}{(1.07)^2} = .87$$

Apparently the dollar received the day after tomorrow is *not* necessarily worth less than the dollar received tomorrow.

But there is something wrong with this example. Anyone who could borrow and lend at these interest rates could become a millionaire overnight. Let us see how such a "money machine" would work. Suppose the first person to spot the opportunity is Hermione Kraft. Ms. Kraft first lends $1000 for 1 year at 20 percent. That is an attractive enough return, but she notices that there is a way to earn an *immediate* profit on her investment and be ready to play the game again. She reasons as follows. Next year she will have $1200 which can be reinvested for a further year. Although she does not know what interest rates will be at that time, she does know that she can always put the money in a checking account and be sure of having $1200 at the end of year 2. Her next step, therefore, is to go to her bank and borrow the present value of this $1200. At 7 percent interest this present value is

$$PV = \frac{1200}{(1.07)^2} = \$1048$$

Thus Ms. Kraft invests $1000, borrows back $1048, and walks away with a profit of $48. If that does not sound like very much, remember that the game can be played again immediately, this time with $1048. In fact it would take Ms. Kraft only 147 plays to become a millionaire (before taxes).[1]

Of course this story is completely fanciful. Such an opportunity would not last long in capital markets like ours. Any bank that would allow you to lend for 1 year at 20 percent and borrow for 2 years at 7 percent would soon be wiped out by a rush of small investors hoping to become millionaires and a rush of millionaires hoping to become billionaires. There are, however, two lessons to our story. The first is that a dollar tomorrow *cannot* be worth less than a dollar the day after tomorrow. In other words, the value of a dollar received at the end of 1 year (DF_1) must be greater than the value of a dollar received at the end of 2 years (DF_2). There must be some extra gain[2] from lending for 2 periods rather than 1: $(1 + r_2)^2$ must be greater than $1 + r_1$.

Our second lesson is a more general one and can be summed up by the precept "There is no such thing as a money machine."[3] In well-functioning capital markets, any potential money machine will be eliminated almost instantaneously by investors who try to take advantage of it. Therefore, beware of self-styled experts who offer you a chance to participate in a "sure thing."

Later in the book we will invoke the *absence* of money machines to prove several useful properties about security prices. That is, we will make statements like "The prices of securities X and Y must be in the following relationship—otherwise there would be a money machine and capital markets would not be in equilibrium."

How Present Value Tables Help the Lazy

In principle there can be a different interest rate for each future period. This relationship between the interest rate and the maturity of the cash flow is called the **term structure of interest rates.** We are going to look at term structure in Chapter 23, but for now we will finesse the issue by assuming that the term structure is "flat"—in other words, the interest rate is the same regardless of the date of the cash flow. This means that we can replace the series of interest rates $r_1, r_2, \ldots, r_t$, etc., with a single rate r and that we can write the present value formula as

---

[1]That is, $1000 \times (1.04813)^{147} = \$1,002,000$.

[2]The extra return for lending 2 years rather than 1 is often referred to as a *forward rate of return.* Our rule says that the forward rate cannot be negative.

[3]The technical term for money machine is **arbitrage.** There are no opportunities for arbitrage in well-functioning capital markets.

$$PV = \frac{C_1}{1 + r} + \frac{C_2}{(1 + r)^2} + \cdots$$

So far all our examples can be worked out fairly easily by hand. Real problems are often much more complicated and require the use of an electronic calculator that is specifically programmed for present value calculations, a spreadsheet program on a personal computer, or present value tables. Here is a somewhat complex example which illustrates how such tables are used.

You have some bad news about your office building venture (the one described at the start of Chapter 2). The contractor says that construction will take 2 years instead of 1 and requests payment on the following schedule:

1. A $100,000 down payment now. (Note that the land, worth $50,000, must also be committed now.)

2. A $100,000 progress payment after 1 year.

3. A final payment of $100,000 when the building is ready for occupancy at the end of the second year.

Your real estate adviser maintains that despite the delay the building will be worth $400,000 when completed.

All this yields a new set of cash-flow forecasts:

Period	$t = 0$	$t = 1$	$t = 2$
Land	−50,000		
Construction	−100,000	−100,000	−100,000
Payoff			+400,000
Total	$C_0 = -150{,}000$	$C_1 = -100{,}000$	$C_2 = +300{,}000$

If the interest rate is 7 percent, then NPV is

$$NPV = C_0 + \frac{C_1}{1 + r} + \frac{C_2}{(1 + r)^2}$$

$$= -150{,}000 - \frac{100{,}000}{1.07} + \frac{300{,}000}{(1.07)^2}$$

Table 3-1 shows how to set up the calculations and how to get NPV. The discount factors can be found in Appendix Table 1 at the end of the book. Look at the first two entries in the column headed 7 *percent*. The top one is .935 and the second is .873. Thus you do not have to compute 1/1.07 or 1/(1.07)²—you can pull the figures from the present value table. (Notice that the other entries in the 7 *percent* column give discount factors out to 30 years and the other columns cover a range of discount rates from 1 to 30 percent.)

Fortunately the news about your office venture is not all bad. The contractor is willing to accept a delayed payment; this means that the present value of the contractor's fee is less than before. This partly offsets the delay in the payoff. As Table 3-1 shows, the net present value is $18,400—not a substantial decrease from the $23,800 calculated in Chapter 2. Since the net present value is positive, you should still go ahead.

TABLE 3-1
· ·

Present value worksheet

Period	Discount Factor	Cash Flow	Present Value
0	1.0	−150,000	−150,000
1	$\dfrac{1}{1.07} = .935$	−100,000	− 93,500
2	$\dfrac{1}{(1.07)^2} = .873$	+300,000	+261,900
			Total = NPV = $18,400

3-2 LOOKING FOR SHORTCUTS—PERPETUITIES AND ANNUITIES

Sometimes there are shortcuts that make it very easy to calculate the present value of an asset that pays off in different periods. Let us look at some examples.

Among the securities that have been issued by the British government are so-called **perpetuities**. These are bonds that the government is under no obligation to repay but that offer a fixed income for each year to perpetuity. The rate of return on a perpetuity is equal to the promised annual payment divided by the present value:[4]

$$\text{Return} = \frac{\text{cash flow}}{\text{present value}}$$

$$r = \frac{C}{\text{PV}}$$

We can obviously twist this around and find the present value of a perpetuity given the discount rate r and the cash payment C. For example, suppose that some worthy person wishes to endow a chair in finance at a business school. If the rate of interest

---

[4]You can check this by writing down the present value formula

$$\text{PV} = \frac{C}{1+r} + \frac{C}{(1+r)^2} + \frac{C}{(1+r)^3} + \cdots$$

Now let $C/(1 + r) = a$ and $1/(1 + r) = x$. Then we have

$$\text{PV} = a(1 + x + x^2 + \cdots) \tag{1}$$

Multiplying both sides by x, we have

$$\text{PV}x = a(x + x^2 + \cdots) \tag{2}$$

Subtracting (2) from (1) gives us

$$\text{PV}(1 - x) = a$$

Therefore, substituting for a and x,

$$\text{PV}\left(1 - \frac{1}{1+r}\right) = \frac{C}{1+r}$$

Multiplying both sides by $(1 + r)$ and rearranging gives

$$r = \frac{C}{\text{PV}}$$

is 10 percent and if the aim is to provide $100,000 a year in perpetuity, the amount that must be set aside today is

$$\text{Present value of perpetuity} = \frac{C}{r} = \frac{100,000}{.10} = \$1,000,000$$

How to Value Growing Perpetuities

Suppose now that our benefactor suddenly recollects that no allowance has been made for growth in salaries, which will probably average about 4 percent a year. Therefore, instead of providing $100,000 a year in perpetuity, the benefactor must provide $100,000 in year 1, $1.04 \times \$100,000$ in year 2, and so on. If we call the growth rate in salaries g, we can write down the present value of this stream of cash flows as follows:

$$PV = \frac{C_1}{1 + r} + \frac{C_2}{(1 + r)^2} + \frac{C_3}{(1 + r)^3} + \cdots$$

$$= \frac{C_1}{1 + r} + \frac{C_1(1 + g)}{(1 + r)^2} + \frac{C_1(1 + g)^2}{(1 + r)^3} + \cdots$$

Fortunately, there is a simple formula for the sum of this geometric series.[5] If we assume that r is greater than g, our clumsy-looking calculation simplifies to

$$\text{Present value of growing perpetuity} = \frac{C_1}{r - g}$$

Therefore, if our benefactor wants to provide perpetually an annual sum that keeps pace with the growth rate in salaries, the amount that must be set aside today is

$$PV = \frac{C_1}{r - g} = \frac{100,000}{.10 - .04} = \$1,666,667$$

How to Value Annuities

An **annuity** is an asset that pays a fixed sum each year for a specified number of years. The equal-payment house mortgage or installment credit agreement are common examples of annuities.

Figure 3-1 illustrates a simple trick for valuing annuities. The first row represents a *perpetuity* that produces a cash flow of C in each year *beginning in year 1*. It has a present value of

$$PV = \frac{C}{r}$$

The second row represents a second *perpetuity* that produces a cash flow of C in each year *beginning in year $t + 1$*. It *will* have a present value of C/r in year t and it therefore has a present value today of

$$PV = \frac{C}{r(1 + r)^t}$$

Both perpetuities provide a cash flow from year $t + 1$ onward. The only difference between the two perpetuities is that the first one *also* provides a cash flow in each of the years 1 through t. In other words, the difference between the two perpetuities is

---

[5] We need to calculate the sum of an infinite geometric series $PV = a(1 + x + x^2 + \cdots)$ where $a = C_1/(1 + r)$ and $x = (1 + g)/(1 + r)$. In footnote 4 we showed that the sum of such a series is $a/(1 - x)$. Substituting for a and x in this formula we find that

$$PV = \frac{C_1}{r - g}$$

Figure 3-1 An annuity that makes payments in each of years 1 to *t* is equal to the difference between two perpetuities.

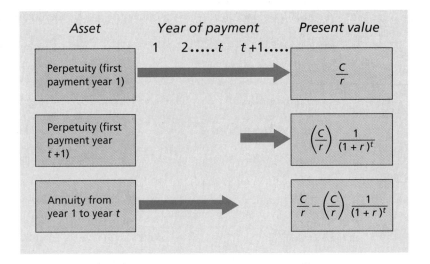

an annuity of C for t years. The present value of this annuity is, therefore, the difference between the values of the two perpetuities:

$$\text{Present value of annuity} = C\left[\frac{1}{r} - \frac{1}{r(1 + r)^t}\right]$$

The expression in brackets is the *annuity factor*, which is the present value at discount rate r of an annuity of $1 paid at the end of each of t periods.[6]

Suppose, for example, that our benefactor begins to vacillate and wonders what it would cost to endow a chair providing $100,000 a year for only 20 years. The answer calculated from our formula is

$$PV = 100,000\left[\frac{1}{.10} - \frac{1}{.10(1.10)^{20}}\right] = 100,000 \times 8.514 = \$851,400$$

Alternatively, we can simply look up the answer in the annuity table in the Appendix at the end of the book (Appendix Table 3). This table gives the present value of a dollar to be received in each of t periods. In our example $t = 20$ and the interest rate $r = .10$, and therefore we look at the twentieth number from the top in

------

[6]Again we can work this out from first principles. We need to calculate the sum of the finite geometric series

$$PV = a(1 + x + x^2 + \cdots + x^{t-1}) \qquad (1)$$

where $a = C/(1 + r)$ and $x = 1/(1 + r)$. Multiplying both sides by x, we have

$$PVx = a(x + x^2 + \cdots + x^t) \qquad (2)$$

Subtracting (2) from (1) gives us

$$PV(1 - x) = a(1 - x^t)$$

Therefore, substituting for a and x,

$$PV\left(1 - \frac{1}{1 + r}\right) = C\left[\frac{1}{1 + r} - \frac{1}{(1 + r)^{t+1}}\right]$$

Multiplying both sides by $(1 + r)$ and rearranging gives

$$PV = C\left[\frac{1}{r} - \frac{1}{r(1 + r)^t}\right]$$

the *10 percent* column. It is 8.514. Multiply 8.514 by $100,000, and we have our answer, $851,400.

You should always be on the lookout for ways in which you can use these formulas to make life easier. For example, we sometimes need to calculate how much a series of annual payments earning a fixed annual interest would amass to by the end of t periods. In this case it is easiest to calculate the *present* value and then multiply it by $(1 + r)^t$ to find the future value.[7] Thus suppose our benefactor wished to know how much wealth $100,000 would produce if it were invested each year instead of being given to those no-good academics. The answer would be

$$\text{Future value} = \text{PV} \times 1.10^{20} = \$851,400 \times 6.727 = \$5.73 \text{ million}$$

How did we know that 1.10^{20} was 6.727? Easy—we just looked it up in Appendix Table 2 at the end of the book: "Future Value of $1 at the End of t Periods."

3-3 COMPOUND INTEREST AND PRESENT VALUES

There is an important distinction between **compound interest** and **simple interest.** When money is invested at compound interest, each interest payment is reinvested to earn more interest in subsequent periods. In contrast, the opportunity to earn interest on interest is not provided by an investment that pays only simple interest.

Table 3-2 compares the growth of $100 invested at compound versus simple interest. Notice that in the simple interest case, *the interest is paid only on the initial investment of $100.* Your wealth therefore increases by just $10 a year. In the compound interest case, you earn 10 percent on your initial investment in the first year, which gives you a balance at the end of the year of $100 \times 1.10 = \$110$. Then in the second year you earn 10 percent on this $110, which gives you a balance at the end of the second year of $100 \times 1.10^2 = \$121$.

Table 3-2 shows that the difference between simple and compound interest is nil for a 1-period investment, trivial for a 2-period investment, but overwhelming for an investment of 20 years or more. A sum of $100 invested during the American Revolution and earning compound interest of 10 percent a year would now be worth $80 billion. Don't you wish your ancestors had shown rather more foresight?

The two top lines in Figure 3-2 compare the results of investing $100 at 10 percent simple interest and at 10 percent compound interest. It looks as if the rate of growth is constant under simple interest and accelerates under compound interest. However, this is an optical illusion. We know that under compound interest our wealth grows at a *constant* rate of 10 percent. Figure 3-3 is in fact a more useful presentation. Here the numbers are plotted on a semilogarithmic scale and the constant compound growth rates show up as straight lines.

Problems in finance generally involve compound interest rather than simple interest, and therefore financial people always assume that you are talking about compound interest unless you specify otherwise. Discounting is a process of compound interest. Some people find it intuitively helpful to replace the question "What is the present value of $100 to be received 10 years from now, if the opportunity cost of

---

[7]For example, suppose you receive a cash flow of C in year 6. If you invest this cash flow at an interest rate of r, you will have by year 10 an investment worth $C(1 + r)^4$. You can get the same answer by calculating the *present value* of the cash flow $\text{PV} = C/(1 + r)^6$ and then working out how much you would have by year 10 if you invested this sum today:

$$\text{Future value} = \text{PV}(1 + r)^{10} = \frac{C}{(1 + r)^6}(1 + r)^{10} = C(1 + r)^4$$

TABLE 3-2

· ·

Value of $100 invested at 10 percent simple and compound interest

| | SIMPLE INTEREST | | | | COMPOUND INTEREST | | | | |
Year	Starting Balance	+	Interest	=	Ending Balance	Starting Balance	+	Interest	=	Ending Balance
1	100	+	10	=	110	100	+	10	=	110
2	110	+	10	=	120	110	+	11	=	121
3	120	+	10	=	130	121	+	12.1	=	133.1
4	130	+	10	=	140	133.1	+	13.3	=	146.4
10	190	+	10	=	200	236	+	24	=	259
20	290	+	10	=	300	612	+	61	=	673
50	590	+	10	=	600	10,672	+	1,067	=	11,739
100	1,090	+	10	=	1,100	1,252,783	+	125,278	=	1,378,061
200	2,090	+	10	=	2,100	17,264,116,042	+	1,726,411,604	=	18,990,527,646
215	2,240	+	10	=	2,250	72,116,497,132	+	7,211,649,713	=	79,328,146,845

capital is 10 percent?" with the question "How much would I have to invest now in order to receive $100 after 10 years, given an interest rate of 10 percent?" The answer to the first question is

$$PV = \frac{100}{(1.10)^{10}} = \$38.55$$

And the answer to the second question is

$$\text{Investment} \times (1.10)^{10} = \$100$$

$$\text{Investment} = \frac{100}{(1.10)^{10}} = \$38.55$$

Figure 3-2 Compound interest versus simple interest. The top two ascending lines show the growth of $100 invested at simple and compound interest. The longer the funds are invested, the greater the advantage with compound interest. The bottom line shows that $38.55 must be invested now to obtain $100 after 10 periods. Conversely, the present value of $100 to be received after 10 years is $38.55.

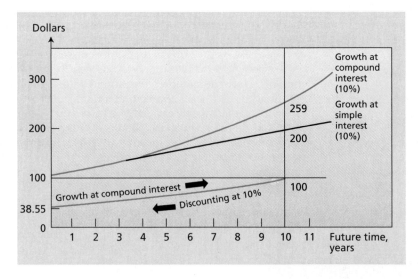

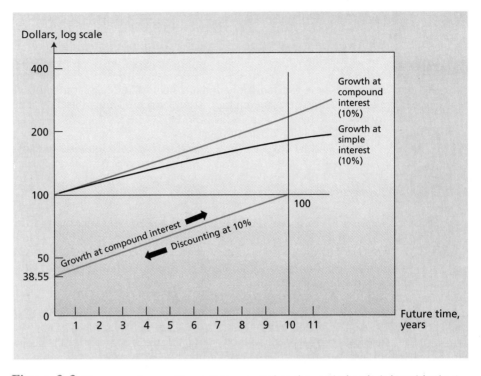

Figure 3-3 The same story as Figure 3-2, except that the vertical scale is logarithmic. A constant compound rate of growth means a straight ascending line. This graph makes clear that the growth rate of funds invested at simple interest actually *declines* as time passes.

The bottom lines in Figures 3-2 and 3-3 show the growth path of an initial investment of $38.55 to its terminal value of $100. One can think of discounting as traveling *back* along the bottom line, from future value to present value.

*A Note on Compounding Intervals

So far we have implicitly assumed that each cash flow occurs at the end of the year. This is sometimes the case. For example, in France and Germany most corporations pay interest on their bonds annually. However, in the United States and Britain most pay interest semiannually. In these countries, the investor will be able to earn an additional 6 months' interest on the first payment, so that an investment of $100 in a bond that paid interest of 10 percent per annum compounded semiannually would amount to $105 after the first 6 months, and by the end of the year it would amount to $1.05^2 \times 100 = 110.25. In other words, 10 percent compounded semiannually is equivalent to 10.25 percent compounded annually. More generally, an investment of $1 at a rate of r per annum compounded m times a year amounts by the end of the year to $[1 + (r/m)]^m$, and the equivalent annually compounded rate of interest is $[1 + (r/m)]^m - 1$.

The attractions to the investor of more frequent payments did not escape the attention of the savings and loan companies. Their rate of interest on deposits was traditionally stated as an annually compounded rate. The government used to stipulate a maximum annual rate of interest that could be paid but made no mention of the compounding interval. When interest ceilings began to pinch, savings and loan companies changed progressively to semiannual and then to monthly compounding.

Therefore the equivalent annually compounded rate of interest increased first to $[1 + (r/2)]^2 - 1$ and then to $[1 + (r/12)]^{12} - 1$.

Eventually one company quoted a **continuously compounded rate,** so that payments were assumed to be spread evenly and continuously throughout the year. In terms of our formula, this is equivalent to letting m approach infinity.[8] This might seem like a lot of calculations for our savings and loan companies. Fortunately, however, someone remembered high school algebra and pointed out that as m approaches infinity $[1 + (r/m)]^m$ approaches $(2.718)^r$. The figure 2.718—or e, as it is called—is simply the base for natural logarithms.

The sum \$1 invested at a continuously compounded rate of r will, therefore, grow to $e^r = (2.718)^r$ by the end of the first year. By the end of t years it will grow to $e^{rt} = (2.718)^{rt}$. Appendix Table 4 at the end of the book is a table of values of e^{rt}. Let us practice using it.

Example 1: Suppose you invest \$1 at a continuously compounded rate of 10 percent ($r = .10$) for 1 year ($t = 1$). The end-year value is simply $e^{.10}$, which you can see from the second row of Appendix Table 4 is \$1.105. In other words, investing at 10 percent a year *continuously* compounded is exactly the same as investing at 10.5 percent a year *annually* compounded.

Example 2: Now suppose you invest \$1 at a continuously compounded rate of 11 percent ($r = .11$) for 1 year ($t = 1$). The end-year value is now $e^{.11}$, which you can see from the second row of Appendix Table 4 is \$1.116. In other words, investing at 11 percent a year *continuously* compounded is exactly the same as investing at 11.6 percent a year *annually* compounded.

Example 3: Finally, suppose you invest \$1 at a continuously compounded rate of 11 percent ($r = .11$) for 2 years ($t = 2$). The final value of the investment is $e^{rt} = e^{.22}$. You can see from the third row of Appendix Table 4 that $e^{.22}$ is \$1.246.

There is a particular value to continuous compounding in capital budgeting, where it may often be more reasonable to assume that a cash flow is spread evenly over the year than that it occurs at the year's end. It is easy to adapt our previous formulas to handle this. For example, suppose that we wish to compute the present value of a perpetuity of C dollars a year. We already know that if the payment is made at the end of the year, we divide the payment by the *annually* compounded rate of r:

$$PV = \frac{C}{r}$$

If the same total payment is made in an even stream throughout the year, we use the same formula but substitute the *continuously* compounded rate.

For any other continuous payments, we can always use our formula for valuing annuities. For instance, suppose that our philanthropist has thought more seriously and decided to found a home for elderly donkeys, which will cost \$100,000 a year,

---

[8]When we talk about *continuous* payments, we are pretending that money can be dispensed in a continuous stream like water out of a faucet. One can never quite do this. For example, instead of paying out \$10,000 every year, our benefactor could pay out \$100 every 8¾ hours or \$1 every 5¼ minutes or 1 cent every 3⅙ seconds but could not pay it out *continuously.* Financial managers *pretend* that payments are continuous rather than hourly, daily, or weekly because (1) it simplifies the calculations, and (2) it gives a *very* close approximation to the NPV of frequent payments.

starting immediately, and spread evenly over 20 years. Previously, we used the annually compounded rate of 10 percent; now we must use the continuously compounded rate of $r = 9.53$ percent ($e^{.0953} = 1.10$). To cover such an expenditure, then, our philanthropist needs to set aside the following sum:[9]

$$PV = C\left(\frac{1}{r} - \frac{1}{r} \times \frac{1}{e^{rt}}\right)$$

$$= 100,000\left(\frac{1}{.0953} - \frac{1}{.0953} \times \frac{1}{6.727}\right) = 100,000 \times 8.932 = \$893,200$$

Alternatively, we could have cut these calculations short by using Appendix Table 5. This shows that, if the annually compounded return is 10 percent, then $1 a year spread over 20 years is worth $8.932.

If you look back at our earlier discussion of annuities, you will notice that the present value of $100,000 paid at the *end* of each of the 20 years was $851,406. Therefore, it costs the philanthropist $41,800—or 5 percent—more to provide a continuous payment stream.

Often in finance we need only a ballpark estimate of present value. An error of 5 percent in a present value calculation may be perfectly acceptable. In such cases it doesn't usually matter whether we assume that cash flows occur at the end of the year or in a continuous stream. At other times precision matters, and we do need to worry about the exact frequency of the cash flows.

3-4 NOMINAL AND REAL RATES OF INTEREST

If you invest $1000 in a bank deposit offering an interest rate of 10 percent, the bank promises to pay you $1100 at the end of the year. But it makes no promises about what the $1100 will buy. That will depend on the rate of inflation over the year. If the prices of goods and services increase by more than 10 percent, you have lost ground in terms of the goods that you can buy.

Several indexes are used to track the general level of prices. The best known is the Consumer Price Index, or CPI, which measures the number of dollars that it takes to pay for a typical family's purchases. The change in the CPI from one year to the next measures the rate of inflation. Figure 3-4 shows the rate of inflation in the United States since 1926. During the Great Depression there was actual *deflation*; prices of goods on average fell. Inflation touched a peak just after World War II, when it reached 18 percent. This figure, however, pales into insignificance com-

---

[9]Remember that an annuity is simply the difference between a perpetuity received today and a perpetuity received in year t. A continuous stream of C dollars a year in perpetuity is worth C/r, where r is the continuously compounded rate. Our annuity, then, is worth

$$PV = \frac{C}{r} - \text{present value of } \frac{C}{r} \text{ received in year } t$$

Since r is the continuously compounded rate, C/r received in year t is worth $(C/r) \times (1/e^{rt})$ today. Our annuity formula is therefore

$$PV = \frac{C}{r} - \frac{C}{r} \times \frac{1}{e^{rt}}$$

sometimes written as

$$\frac{C}{r}(1 - e^{-rt})$$

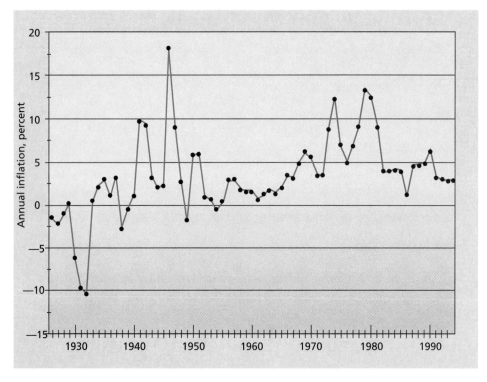

Figure 3-4 Annual rates of inflation in the United States from 1926 to 1994. (*Source:* Ibbotson Associates, Inc., *Stocks, Bonds, Bills, and Inflation, 1995 Yearbook,* Chicago, 1995.)

pared with inflation in Yugoslavia in 1993, which at its peak was almost 60 percent *a day*.

Economists sometimes talk about current, or nominal, dollars versus constant, or real, dollars. For example, the *nominal* cash flow from your 1-year bank deposit is $1100. But suppose prices of goods rise over the year by 6 percent; then each dollar will buy you 6 percent less goods next year than it does today. So at the end of the year $1100 will buy the same quantity of goods as $1100/1.06 = $1037.74 today. The nominal payoff on the deposit is $1100, but the *real* payoff is only $1037.74.

The general formula for converting nominal cash flows at a future period to real cash flows is

$$\text{Real cash flow} = \frac{\text{nominal cash flow}}{(1 + \text{inflation rate})^t}$$

For example, if you were to invest that $1000 for 20 years at 10 percent, your future nominal payoff would be $1000 \times 1.1^{20} = \$6727.50$, but with an inflation rate of 6 percent a year, the real value of that payoff would be $6727.50/1.06^{20} = \$2097.67$. In other words, you will have roughly six times as many dollars as you have today, but you will be able to buy only twice as many goods.

When the bank quotes you a 10 percent interest rate, it is quoting a nominal interest rate. The rate tells you how rapidly your money will grow:

Invest Current Dollars		Receive Period-1 Dollars	Result
1,000	$\rightarrow$	1,100	10% *nominal* rate of return

However, with an inflation rate of 6 percent you are only 3.774 percent better off at the end of the year than at the start:

Invest Current Dollars		Expected Real Value of Period-1 Receipts	Result
1,000	$\rightarrow$	1,037.74	3.774% expected *real* rate of return

Thus, we could say, "The bank account offers a 10 percent nominal rate of return," *or* "It offers a 3.774 percent expected real rate of return." Note that the nominal rate is certain but the real rate is only expected. The actual real rate cannot be calculated until the end of the year arrives and the inflation rate is known.

The 10 percent nominal rate of return, with 6 percent inflation, translated into a 3.774 percent real rate of return. The formula for calculating the real rate of return is

$$1 + r_{nominal} = (1 + r_{real})(1 + \text{inflation rate})$$

$$= 1 + r_{real} + \text{inflation rate} + (r_{real})(\text{inflation rate})$$

In our example,

$$1.10 = 1.03774 \times 1.06$$

3-5 USING PRESENT VALUE FORMULAS TO VALUE BONDS

When governments or companies borrow money, they often do so by issuing bonds. A bond is simply a long-term debt. If you own a bond, you receive a fixed set of cash payoffs: Each year until the bond matures, you collect an interest payment; then at maturity, you also get back the face value of the bond.[10]

If you want to buy or sell a bond, you simply contact a bond dealer, who will quote a price at which he or she is prepared to buy or sell. Suppose, for example, that in September 1994 you invested in a 6 percent 1999 U.S. Treasury bond. The bond has a coupon rate of 6 percent and a face value of $1000. This means that each year until 1999 you will receive an interest payment of .06 × 1000 = $60. The bond matures in August 1999: At that time, the Treasury pays you the final $60 interest, plus the $1000 face value. So the cash flows from owning the bond are as follows:

---

[10]The face value of the bond is known as the *principal.* Therefore, when the bond matures, the government pays you principal and interest.

Cash Flows, Dollars

1995	1996	1997	1998	1999
60	60	60	60	1,060

What is the present value of these payoffs? To determine that, we need to look at the return provided by similar securities. Other medium-term U.S. Treasury bonds in fall 1994 offered a return of about 6.9 percent. That is what investors were giving up when they bought the 6 percent Treasury bonds. Therefore, to value the 6 percent bonds, we need to discount the cash flows at 6.9 percent:

$$PV = \frac{60}{1.069} + \frac{60}{(1.069)^2} + \frac{60}{(1.069)^3} + \frac{60}{(1.069)^4} + \frac{1060}{(1.069)^5} = \$963$$

Bond prices are usually expressed as a percentage of the face value. Thus, we can say that our 6 percent Treasury bond is worth $963, or 96.3 percent.

You may have noticed a shortcut way to value the Treasury bond. The bond is like a package of two investments: The first investment consists of five annual coupon payments of $60 each, and the second investment is the payment of the $1000 face value at maturity. Therefore, you can use the annuity formula to value the coupon payments and add on the present value of the final payment:

PV(bond) = PV(coupon payments) + PV(final payment)

$$= (\text{coupon} \times 5\text{-year annuity factor}) + (\text{final payment} \times \text{discount factor})$$

$$= 60 \left[\frac{1}{.069} - \frac{1}{.069(1.069)^5} \right] + \frac{1000}{1.069^5}$$

$$= 246.67 + 716.33 = \$963$$

Any bond can be valued as a package of an annuity (the coupon payments) and a single payment (the final payment).

Rather than asking the value of the bond, we could have phrased our question the other way around: If the price of the bond is $963, what return do investors expect? In that case, we need to find the value of r that solves the following equation:

$$963 = \frac{60}{1 + r} + \frac{60}{(1 + r)^2} + \frac{60}{(1 + r)^3} + \frac{60}{(1 + r)^4} + \frac{1060}{(1 + r)^5}$$

The rate r is often called the bond's **yield to maturity** or **internal rate of return.** In our case r is 6.9 percent. If you discount the cash flows at 6.9 percent, you arrive at the bond's price of $963. As we will see in Chapter 5, the only *general* procedure for calculating r is trial and error. But specially programmed electronic calculators can be used to calculate r, or you can use a book of bond tables that show values of r for different coupon levels and different maturities.

You may have noticed that the formula that we used for calculating the present value of 6 percent Treasury bonds was slightly different from the general present value formula that we developed in Section 3-1, where we allowed r_1, the rate of return offered by the capital market on 1-year investments, to differ from r_2, the rate of return offered on 2-year investments. Then we finessed this problem by assuming that r_1 is the same as r_2. In valuing our Treasury bond, we again assume that investors use the same rate to discount cash flows occurring in different years. That does not matter as long as short-term rates are approximately the same as long-term rates. But often when we value bonds, we should discount each cash flow at a different rate. There will be more about that in Chapter 23.

What Happens When Interest Rates Change?

Interest rates fluctuate. In 1945 United States government bonds were yielding less than 2 percent. By 1981 yields were a touch under 15 percent. How would the price of our 5-year Treasuries be affected by such changes in interest rates? With a yield of 2 percent the price of the Treasuries would be

$$PV = \frac{60}{1.02} + \frac{60}{(1.02)^2} + \frac{60}{(1.02)^3} + \frac{60}{(1.02)^4} + \frac{1060}{(1.02)^5} = \$1188.54$$

If yields jumped to 15 percent, the price would fall to

$$PV = \frac{60}{1.15} + \frac{60}{(1.15)^2} + \frac{60}{(1.15)^3} + \frac{60}{(1.15)^4} + \frac{1060}{(1.15)^5} = \$698.31$$

Not surprisingly, the higher the interest rate that investors demand, the less that they will be prepared to pay for the bond.

Some bonds are more affected than others by a change in the interest rate. A change may have a substantial effect on bond value when the cash flows on the bond last for many years. It will have a trivial effect if the bond matures tomorrow.

*Compounding Intervals and Bond Prices

In calculating the value of the 6 percent Treasury bonds, we made two approximations. First, we assumed that interest payments occurred annually. In practice, most U.S. bonds make coupon payments *semiannually*, so that, instead of receiving $60 every year, an investor holding 6 percent bonds would receive $30 every *half* year. Second, yields on U.S. bonds are usually quoted as semiannually compounded yields. Therefore, if the semiannually compounded yield is 6.9 percent, the yield over 6 months is 6.9/2 = 3.45 percent.

Now we can recalculate the value of the 6 percent Treasury bonds, recognizing that there are ten 6-month coupon payments of $30 and a final payment of $1000:

$$PV = \frac{30}{1.0345} + \frac{30}{(1.0345)^2} + \cdots + \frac{30}{(1.0345)^9} + \frac{1030}{(1.0345)^{10}} = \$962.48$$

3-6 SUMMARY

The difficult thing in any present value exercise is to set up the problem correctly. Once you have done that, you must be able to do the calculations, but they are not difficult. Now that you have worked through this chapter, all you should need is a little practice.

The basic present value formula for an asset that pays off in several periods is the following obvious extension of our 1-period formula:

$$PV = \frac{C_1}{1 + r_1} + \frac{C_2}{(1 + r_2)^2} + \cdots$$

You can always work out any present value using this formula, but when the interest rates are the same for each maturity, there may be some shortcuts that can reduce the tedium. We looked at three such cases. First, there was the case of an asset that pays C dollars a year in perpetuity. Its present value is simply

$$PV = \frac{C}{r}$$

Second, there was the case of an asset whose payments increase at a steady rate g in perpetuity. Its present value is

$$PV = \frac{C_1}{r - g}$$

Third, there was the case of an annuity that pays C dollars a year for t years. To find its present value we take the difference between the values of two perpetuities:

$$PV = C \left[\frac{1}{r} - \frac{1}{r(1 + r)^t} \right]$$

Our next step was to show that discounting is a process of compound interest. It is the amount that we would have to invest now at compound interest r in order to produce the cash flows C_1, C_2, etc. When someone offers to lend us a dollar at an annual rate of r, we should always check how frequently the interest is to be compounded. If the compounding interval is annual, we will have to repay $(1 + r)^t$ dollars; on the other hand, if the compounding is continuous, we will have to repay 2.718^{rt} (or, as it is usually expressed, e^{rt}) dollars. Very often in capital budgeting we are willing to assume that the cash flows occur at the end of each year, and therefore we discount them at an annually compounded rate of interest. Sometimes, however, it may be fairer to assume that they are spread evenly over the year; in this case we must make use of continuous compounding.

Present value tables will help us to perform many of these calculations. You have been introduced now to tables that show:

1. Present value of $1 received at the end of year t
2. Future value of $1 by the end of year t
3. Present value of $1 received at the end of each year until year t
4. Future value of $1 invested at a continuously compounded rate of interest
5. Present value of $1 received continuously for t years when the annually compounded interest rate is r

It is important to distinguish between *nominal* cash flows (the actual number of dollars that you will pay or receive) and *real* cash flows, which are adjusted for inflation. Similarly, an investment may promise a high *nominal* interest rate, but, if inflation is also high, the *real* interest rate may be low or even negative.

We concluded the chapter by applying discounted cash flow techniques to value United States government bonds with fixed annual coupons.

We introduced in this chapter two very important ideas which we will come across several times again. The first is that you can add present values: If your formula for the present value of $A + B$ is not the same as your formula for the present value of A plus the present value of B, you have made a mistake. The second is the notion that there is no such thing as a money machine: If you think you have found one, go back and check your calculations.

Further Reading

The material in this chapter should cover all you need to know about the mathematics of discounting; but if you wish to dig deeper, there are a number of books on the subject. Try, for example:

R. Cissell, H. Cissell, and D. C. Flaspohler: *The Mathematics of Finance,* 8th ed., Houghton Mifflin Company, Boston, 1990.

Quiz

1. At an interest rate of 12 percent, the 6-year discount factor is .507. How many dollars is $.507 worth in 6 years if invested at 12 percent?

2. If the present value of $139 is $125, what is the discount factor?

3. If the 8-year discount factor is .285, what is the present value of $596 received in 8 years?

4. If the cost of capital is 9 percent, what is the present value of $374 paid in year 9?

5. A project produces the following cash flows:

Year	Flow
1	432
2	137
3	797

If the cost of capital is 15 percent, what is the project's present value?

6. If you invest $100 at an interest rate of 15 percent, how much will you have at the end of 8 years?

7. An investment of $232 will produce $312.18 in 2 years. What is the annual interest rate?

8. An investment costs $1548 and pays $138 in perpetuity. If the interest rate is 9 percent, what is the net present value?

9. It costs $2590 to insulate your home. Next year's fuel saving will be $220. If the interest rate is 12 percent, what percentage growth rate in fuel prices is needed to justify insulation? Assume fuel prices will grow in perpetuity at the rate g.

10. A common stock will pay a cash dividend of $4 next year. After that, the dividends are expected to increase indefinitely at 4 percent per year. If the discount rate is 14 percent, what is the present value of the stream of dividend payments?

11. If you invest $502 at the end of each of the next 9 years at an interest rate of 13 percent, how much will you have at the end?

12. Harold Filbert is 30 years of age and his salary next year will be $20,000. Harold forecasts that his salary will increase at a steady rate of 5 percent per annum until his retirement at age 60.
    (*a*) If the discount rate is 8 percent, what is the present value of these future salary payments?
    (*b*) If Harold saves 5 percent of his salary each year and invests these savings at an interest rate of 8 percent, how much will he have saved by age 60?
    (*c*) If Harold plans to spend these savings in even amounts over the subsequent 20 years, how much can he spend each year?

13. A factory costs $400,000. You reckon that it will produce an inflow after operating costs of $100,000 in year 1, $200,000 in year 2, and $300,000 in year 3. The opportunity cost of capital is 12 percent. Draw up a worksheet like that shown in Table 3-1 and use tables to calculate the net present value.

14. Do not use tables for these questions. The interest rate is 10 percent.
    (*a*) What is the present value of an asset that pays $1 a year in perpetuity?
    (*b*) The value of an asset that appreciates at 10 percent per annum approximately doubles in 7 years. What is the approximate present value of an asset that pays $1 a year in perpetuity beginning in year 8?
    (*c*) What is the approximate present value of an asset that pays $1 a year for each of the next 7 years?
    (*d*) A piece of land produces an income that grows by 5 percent per annum. If the first year's flow is $10,000, what is the value of the land?

15. Use the tables at the end of the book for each of the following calculations:
    (*a*) The cost of a new automobile is $10,000. If the interest rate is 5 percent, how much would you have to set aside now to provide this sum in 5 years?
    (*b*) You have to pay $12,000 a year in school fees at the end of each of the next 6 years. If the interest rate is 8 percent, how much do you need to set aside today to cover these bills?
    (*c*) You have invested $60,476 at 8 percent. After paying the above school fees, how much would remain at the end of the 6 years?
    *(*d*) You have borrowed $1000 and in return have agreed to pay back $1762 in 5 years. What is the *annually* compounded rate of interest on the loan? What is the *continuously* compounded rate of interest?

Questions and Problems

1. Use the *discount factors* shown in Appendix Table 1 at the end of the book to calculate the present value of $100 received in:
   (*a*) Year 10 (at a discount rate of 1 percent).
   (*b*) Year 10 (at a discount rate of 13 percent).
   (*c*) Year 15 (at a discount rate of 25 percent).
   (*d*) Each of years 1 through 3 (at a discount rate of 12 percent).

2. Use the *annuity factors* shown in Appendix Table 3 to calculate the present value of $100 in each of:
   (*a*) Years 1 through 20 (at a discount rate of 23 percent).
   (*b*) Years 1 through 5 (at a discount rate of 3 percent).
   (*c*) Years 3 through 12 (at a discount rate of 9 percent).

3. (*a*) If the 1-year discount factor is .88, what is the 1-year interest rate?
   (*b*) If the 2-year interest rate is 10.5 percent, what is the 2-year discount factor?
   (*c*) Given these 1- and 2-year discount factors, calculate the 2-year annuity factor.
   (*d*) If the present value of $10 a year for 3 years is $24.49, what is the 3-year annuity factor?
   (*e*) From your answers to (*c*) and (*d*), calculate the 3-year discount factor.

 4. A factory costs $800,000. You reckon that it will produce an inflow after operating costs of $170,000 a year for 10 years. If the opportunity cost of capital is 14 percent, what is the net present value of the factory? What will the factory be worth at the end of 5 years?[11]

---

[11]Where a question is marked with the picture of a floppy disk, you can use the lotus spreadsheet templates prepared for this book. (See Preface.)

5. Halcyon Lines is considering the purchase of a new bulk carrier for $8 million. The forecast revenues are $5 million a year and operating costs are $4 million. A major refit costing $2 million will be required after both the fifth and tenth years. After 15 years, the ship is expected to be sold for scrap at $1.5 million. If the discount rate is 8 percent, what is the ship's NPV?

6. As winner of a breakfast cereal competition, you can choose one of the following prizes:
   (*a*) $100,000 now
   (*b*) $180,000 at the end of 5 years
   (*c*) $11,400 a year forever
   (*d*) $19,000 for each of 10 years
   (*e*) $6500 next year and increasing thereafter by 5 percent a year forever
   If the interest rate is 12 percent, which is the most valuable prize?

7. Refer back to the story of Ms. Kraft in Section 3-1.
   (*a*) If the 1-year interest rate were 25 percent, how many plays would Ms. Kraft require to become a millionaire? (*Hint:* You may find it easier to use a calculator and a little trial and error.)
   (*b*) What does the story of Ms. Kraft imply about the relationship between the 1-year discount factor, DF_1, and the 2-year discount factor, DF_2?

 8. Siegfried Basset is 65 years of age and has a life expectancy of 12 years. He wishes to invest $20,000 in an annuity that will make a level payment at the end of each year until his death. If the interest rate is 8 percent, what income can Mr. Basset expect to receive each year?

9. James and Helen Turnip are saving to buy a boat at the end of 5 years. If the boat costs $20,000 and they can earn 10 percent a year on their savings, how much do they need to put aside at the end of years 1 through 5?

 10. Kangaroo Autos is offering free credit on a new $10,000 car. You pay $1000 down and then $300 a month for the next 30 months. Turtle Motors next door does not offer free credit but will give you $1000 off the list price. If the rate of interest is 10 percent a year, which company is offering the better deal?

11. Recalculate the net present value of the office building venture in Section 3-1 at interest rates of 5, 10, and 15 percent. Plot the points on a graph with NPV on the vertical axis and the discount rates on the horizontal axis. At what discount rate (approximately) would the project have zero NPV? Check your answer.

12. (*a*) How much will an investment of $100 be worth at the end of 10 years if invested at 15 percent a year simple interest?
    (*b*) How much will it be worth if invested at 15 percent a year compound interest?
    (*c*) How long will it take your investment to double its value at 15 percent compound interest?

13. You own an oil pipeline which will generate a $2 million cash return over the coming year. The pipeline's operating costs are negligible, and it is expected to last for a very long time. Unfortunately, the volume of oil shipped is declining, and cash flows are expected to decline by 4 percent per year. The discount rate is 10 percent.
    (*a*) What is the present value of the pipeline's cash flows if its cash flows are assumed to last forever?
    (*b*) What is the present value of the cash flows if the pipeline is scrapped after 20 years?

[*Hint* for part (**b**): Start with your answer to part (**a**), then subtract the present value of a declining perpetuity starting in year 21. Note that the forecasted cash flow for year 21 will be much less than the cash flow for year 1.]

*14. If the interest rate is 7 percent, what is the value of the following three investments?
   (**a**) An investment that offers you $100 a year in perpetuity with the payment at the *end* of each year
   (**b**) A similar investment with the payment at the *beginning* of each year
   (**c**) A similar investment with the payment spread evenly over each year

*15. Refer back to Section 3-2. If the rate of interest is 8 percent rather than 10 percent, how much would our benefactor need to set aside to provide each of the following?
   (**a**) $100,000 at the end of each year in perpetuity
   (**b**) A perpetuity that pays $100,000 at the end of the first year and that grows at 4 percent a year
   (**c**) $100,000 at the end of each year for 20 years
   (**d**) $100,000 a year spread evenly over 20 years

*16. For an investment of $1000 today, the Tiburon Finance Company is offering to pay you $1600 at the end of 8 years. What is the annually compounded rate of interest? What is the continuously compounded rate of interest?

*17. How much will you have at the end of 20 years if you invest $100 today at 15 percent *annually* compounded? How much will you have if you invest at 15 percent *continuously* compounded?

18. You have just read an advertisement stating, "Pay us $100 a year for 10 years and we will pay you $100 a year thereafter in perpetuity." If this is a fair deal, what is the rate of interest?

*19. Which would you prefer?
   (**a**) An investment paying interest of 12 percent compounded annually.
   (**b**) An investment paying interest of 11.7 percent compounded semiannually.
   (**c**) An investment paying 11.5 percent compounded continuously.
   Work out the value of each of these investments after 1, 5, and 20 years.

*20. Here are two useful rules of thumb. The "Rule of 72" says that with discrete compounding the time it takes for an investment to double in value is roughly 72/interest rate (in percent). The "Rule of 69" says that with continuous compounding the time that it takes to double is *exactly* 69.3/interest rate (in percent).
   (**a**) If the annually compounded interest rate is 12 percent, use the Rule of 72 to calculate roughly how long it takes before your money doubles. Now work it out exactly.
   (**b**) Can you prove the rule of 69?

21. In 1880 five aboriginal trackers were each promised the equivalent of 100 Australian dollars for helping to capture the notorious outlaw Ned Kelley. In 1993 the granddaughters of two of the trackers claimed that this reward had not been paid. The prime minister of Victoria stated that, if this was true, the government would be happy to pay the $100. However, the granddaughters also claimed that they were entitled to compound interest. How much was each entitled to if the interest rate was 5 percent? What if it was 10 percent?

22. A leasing contract calls for an immediate payment of $100,000 and nine subsequent $100,000 semiannual payments at 6-month intervals. What is the present value of these payments if the *annual* discount rate is 8 percent?

23. Use a spreadsheet program to construct your own set of annuity tables.

 24. A famous quarterback just signed a $15 million contract providing $3 million a year for 5 years. A less famous receiver signed a $14 million 5-year contract providing $4 million now and $2 million for 5 years. Who is better paid? The interest rate is 10 percent.

 25. In August 1994 *The Wall Street Journal* reported that the winner of the Massachusetts State Lottery prize had the misfortune to be both bankrupt and in prison for fraud. The prize was $9,420,713, to be paid in 19 equal annual installments.[12] The bankruptcy court judge ruled that the prize should be sold off to the highest bidder and the proceeds used to pay off the creditors. If the interest rate was 8 percent, how much would you have been prepared to bid for the prize? Enhance Reinsurance Company was reported to have offered $4.2 million. Use the annuity table to find (approximately) the return that the company was looking for.

26. You estimate that by the time you retire in 35 years, you will have accumulated savings of $2 million. If the interest rate is 8 percent and you live 15 years after retirement, what annual level of expenditure will those savings support?

    Unfortunately, inflation will eat into the value of your retirement income. Assume a 4 percent inflation rate and work out a spending program for your retirement that will allow you to maintain a level *real* expenditure during retirement.

27. An oil well now produces 100,000 barrels per year. The well will last forever, but production will decline by 4 percent per year. Oil prices, however, will increase by 2 percent per year. The discount rate is 8 percent. What is the present value of the well's production if today's price is $20 per barrel?

28. An oil production platform in Alaska's Cook Inlet will operate for 15 more years. At the end of that time environmental regulations require dismantlement and removal. The current cost of this would be $10 million, but the cost is expected to increase by 5 percent per year.
    (*a*) What is the present value of the future cost? Assume a discount rate of 11 percent.
    (*b*) Suppose new regulations require the oil platform's owner to contribute an equal annual nominal amount to build up a trust fund sufficient to cover dismantlement and removal at year 15. The trust fund has to be invested in U.S. Treasury bonds yielding 6.5 percent. How much will the oil company have to put in each year?

29. You are considering the purchase of an apartment complex that will generate a net cash flow of $400,000 per year. You normally demand a 10 percent rate of return on such investments. Future cash flows are expected to grow with inflation at 4 percent per year. How much would you be willing to pay for the complex if it:
    (*a*) Will produce cash flows forever?
    (*b*) Will have to be torn down in 20 years? Assume that the site will be worth $5 million at that time net of demolition costs. (The $5 million includes 20 years' inflation.)

---

[12]There were 20 installments, but the winner had already received the first payment.

Now calculate the real discount rate corresponding to the 10 percent nominal rate. Redo the calculations for parts (*a*) and (*b*) using real cash flows. (Your answers should not change.)

30. The following table shows recent rates of inflation in a sample of countries belonging to the Organization for Economic Cooperation and Development (OECD):

	Annual Inflation, Percent per Year
France	2.8
Germany	3.7
Greece	17.6
Japan	2.5
Switzerland	4.9
Turkey	68.0
United Kingdom	4.8
United States	3.6

If recent inflation rates persist in the future, how long will it take for price levels to double in each of these countries? (*Hint:* Check back to question 20 and use the Rule of 69 or 72.)

31. Vernal Pool, a self-employed herpetologist, wants to put aside a fixed fraction of her annual income as savings for retirement. Ms. Pool is now 40 years old and makes $40,000 a year. She expects her income to increase by 2 percentage points over inflation (e.g., 4 percent inflation means a 6 percent increase in income). She wants to accumulate $500,000 in real terms to retire at age 70. What fraction of her income does she need to set aside? Assume her retirement funds are conservatively invested at an expected real rate of return of 5 percent a year. Ignore taxes.

32. Calculate the real cash flows on the 6 percent U.S. Treasury bond (see Section 3-5) assuming annual interest payments and an inflation rate of 5 percent. Now show that by discounting these real cash flows at the real interest rate, you get the same PV that you get when you discount the nominal cash flows at the nominal interest rate.

33. Use a spreadsheet program to construct a set of bond tables that show the present value of a bond given the coupon rate, maturity, and yield to maturity. Assume that coupon payments are semiannual and yields are compounded semiannually. Use your bond table to check the yields on a couple of Treasury bonds quoted in *The Wall Street Journal*.

4

The Value of Common Stocks

We should warn you that being a financial expert has its occupational hazards. One is being cornered at cocktail parties by people who are eager to explain their system for making creamy profits by investing in common stocks. Fortunately, these bores go into temporary hibernation whenever the market goes down.

We may exaggerate the perils of the trade. The point is that there is no easy way to ensure superior investment performance. Later in the book we will show that changes in security prices are fundamentally unpredictable and that this result is a natural consequence of well-functioning capital markets. Therefore, in this chapter, when we propose to use the concept of present value to price common stocks, we are not promising you a key to investment success; we simply believe that the idea can help you to understand why some investments are priced higher than others.

Why should you care? If you want to know the value of a firm's stock, why can't you look up the stock price in the newspaper? Unfortunately, that is not always possible. For example, you may be the founder of a successful business. You currently own all the shares but are thinking of "going public" by selling off shares to other investors. You and your advisers need to estimate the price at which those shares can be sold. Or suppose that Establishment Industries is proposing to sell its concatanator division to another company. It needs to figure out the value of this mini-firm.

There is also another, deeper reason why managers need to understand how shares are valued. We have stated that a firm which acts in its shareholders' interest should accept those investments which increase the value of their stake in the firm. But in order to do this, it is necessary to understand what determines the shares' value.

We start the chapter with a brief look at how shares are traded. Then we explain the basic principles of share valuation. We look at the fundamental difference between growth stocks and income stocks and the significance of earnings per share and price-earnings multiples. Finally, we discuss some of the special problems managers and investors encounter when they calculate the present values of entire businesses.

A word of caution before we proceed. Everybody knows that common stocks are risky and that some are more risky than others. Therefore, investors will not commit funds to stocks unless the expected rates of return are commensurate with the risks. The present value formulas we have discussed so far can take account of the effects of risk on value, but we have not yet told you exactly *how* to do so. Recognize, therefore, that risk comes into the following discussion in a loose and intuitive way. A more careful treatment of risk starts in Chapter 7.

4-1 HOW COMMON STOCKS ARE TRADED

There are a billion shares of Ford Motor Company, and at last count these shares were owned by about a quarter of a million shareholders. They included large pension funds and insurance companies that own several million shares, as well as individuals who own a handful of shares. If you owned one Ford share, you would own one-billionth of the company and have a claim on a billionth of the profits. Of course, the more shares you own, the larger your "share" of the company.

If Ford wishes to raise additional capital, it may do so by either borrowing or selling new shares to investors. Sales of new shares to raise new capital are said to occur in the *primary market*. But most trade in Ford shares takes place in existing shares, which investors buy from each other, and therefore does not raise new capital for the firm. This market for secondhand shares is known as the *secondary market*. The principal secondary marketplace for Ford shares is the New York Stock Exchange (NYSE).[1] This is the largest stock exchange in the world and trades, on an average day, 265 million shares in some 2400 companies.

Suppose that you are the head trader for a pension fund that wishes to buy 100,000 Ford shares. You contact your broker, who then relays the order to the floor of the NYSE. Trading in each stock is the responsibility of a specialist, who keeps a record of orders to buy and sell. When your order arrives, the specialist will check this record to see if an investor is prepared to sell at your price. Alternatively, the specialist may be able to get you a better deal from one of the brokers who are gathered around or may sell you some of his or her own stock. If no one is prepared to sell at your price, the specialist will make a note of your order and execute it as soon as possible.

The NYSE is not the only stock market in the United States. For example, many stocks are traded "over the counter" by a network of dealers, who display the prices at which they are prepared to trade on a system of computer terminals known as NASDAQ (National Association of Securities Dealers Automated Quotations System). If you like the price that you see on the NASDAQ screen, you simply call the dealer and strike a bargain.

The prices at which stocks trade are summarized in the daily press. Here, for example, is how *The Wall Street Journal* recorded the day's trading in Ford on February 15, 1995:

| 52 Week | | | | Yld | | Vol | | | | Net |
High	Low	Stock	Div	%	PE	100s	Hi	Lo	Close	Chg.
33⁷⁄₁₆	24¼	FordMotor	1.04	4.0	5	40143	26⅜	26	26¼	+⅛

You can see that on this day investors traded a total of 40,143 × 100 = 4,014,300 shares of Ford stock. The stock price reached a high during the day of $26⅜ and a low of $26. By the close of the day the stock traded at $26¼ a share, up ⅛ from the

---

[1]Ford shares are also traded on several regional stock exchanges as well as a number of overseas exchanges.

day before. Since there are about 1 billion shares of Ford outstanding, investors were placing a total value on the stock of $26¼ billion.

Buying stocks is a risky occupation. You can see that by looking at the yearly high and low for Ford's stock price. An unfortunate investor who bought at the high of $33⅞₆ and sold at the low of $24¼ would have lost over a quarter of his or her investment. Of course, you don't come across such people at cocktail parties; they either keep quiet or aren't invited.

The Wall Street Journal also provides three other facts about Ford's stock. Ford pays an annual dividend of $1.04 a share, the yield on the stock is 4 percent, and the ratio of the stock price to the earnings (P/E ratio) is 5. We will explain shortly why investors pay attention to these figures.

4-2 HOW COMMON STOCKS ARE VALUED

Think back to the last chapter, where we described how to value future cash flows. The discounted-cash-flow (DCF) formula for the present value of a stock is just the same as it is for the present value of any other asset. We just discount the cash flows by the return that can be earned in the capital market on securities of comparable risk. Shareholders receive cash from the company in the form of a stream of dividends. So

$$PV(stock) = PV(expected \ future \ dividends)$$

At first sight this statement may seem surprising. When investors buy stocks, they usually expect to receive a dividend, but they also hope to make a capital gain. Why does our formula for present value say nothing about capital gains? As we now explain, there is no inconsistency.

Today's Price

The cash payoff to owners of common stocks comes in two forms: (1) cash dividends and (2) capital gains or losses. Suppose that the current price of a share is P_0, that the expected price at the end of a year is P_1, and that the expected dividend per share is DIV_1. The rate of return that investors expect from this share over the next year is defined as the expected dividend per share DIV_1 plus the expected price appreciation per share $P_1 - P_0$, all divided by the price at the start of the year P_0:

$$Expected \ return = r = \frac{DIV_1 + P_1 - P_0}{P_0}$$

This return that is expected by investors is often called the **market capitalization rate.**

Suppose Fledgling Electronics stock is selling for $100 a share ($P_0 = 100$). Investors expect a $5 cash dividend over the next year ($DIV_1 = 5$). They also expect the stock to sell for $110 a year hence ($P_1 = 110$). Then the expected return to the stockholders is 15 percent:

$$r = \frac{5 + 110 - 100}{100} = .15, \ or \ 15\%$$

Correspondingly, if you are given investors' forecasts of dividend and price and the expected return offered by other equally risky stocks, you can predict today's price:

$$Price = P_0 = \frac{DIV_1 + P_1}{1 + r}$$

For Fledgling Electronics $DIV_1 = 5$ and $P_1 = 110$. If r, the expected return on securities in the same "risk class" as Fledgling, is 15 percent, then today's price should be $100:

$$P_0 = \frac{5 + 110}{1.15} = \$100$$

How do we know that $100 is the right price? Because no other price could survive in competitive capital markets. What if P_0 were above $100? Then Fledgling stock would offer an expected rate of return that was *lower* than other securities of equivalent risk. Investors would shift their capital to the other securities and in the process would force down the price of Fledgling stock. If P_0 were less than $100, the process would reverse. Fledgling's stock would offer a higher rate of return than comparable securities. In that case, investors would rush to buy, forcing the price up to $100.

The general conclusion is that at each point in time *all securities in an equivalent risk class are priced to offer the same expected return*. This is a condition for equilibrium in well-functioning capital markets. It is also common sense.

But What Determines Next Year's Price?

We have managed to explain today's stock price P_0 in terms of the dividend DIV_1 and the expected price next year P_1. Future stock prices are not easy things to forecast directly. But think about what determines next year's price. If our price formula holds now, it ought to hold then as well:

$$P_1 = \frac{DIV_2 + P_2}{1 + r}$$

That is, a year from now investors will be looking out at dividends in year 2 and price at the end of year 2. Thus we can forecast P_1 by forecasting DIV_2 and P_2, and we can express P_0 in terms of DIV_1, DIV_2, and P_2:

$$P_0 = \frac{1}{1 + r}(DIV_1 + P_1) = \frac{1}{1 + r}\left(DIV_1 + \frac{DIV_2 + P_2}{1 + r}\right) = \frac{DIV_1}{1 + r} + \frac{DIV_2 + P_2}{(1 + r)^2}$$

Take Fledgling Electronics. A plausible explanation why investors expect its stock price to rise by the end of the first year is that they expect higher dividends and still more capital gains in the second. For example, suppose that they are looking today for dividends of $5.50 in year 2 and a subsequent price of $121. That would imply a price at the end of year 1 of

$$P_1 = \frac{5.50 + 121}{1.15} = \$110$$

Today's price can then be computed either from our original formula

$$P_0 = \frac{DIV_1 + P_1}{1 + r} = \frac{5.00 + 110}{1.15} = \$100$$

or from our expanded formula

$$P_0 = \frac{DIV_1}{1 + r} + \frac{DIV_2 + P_2}{(1 + r)^2} = \frac{5.00}{1.15} + \frac{5.50 + 121}{(1.15)^2} = \$100$$

We have succeeded in relating today's price to the forecasted dividends for 2 years (DIV_1 and DIV_2) plus the forecasted price at the end of the *second* year (P_2). You will probably not be surprised to learn that we could go on to replace P_2 by $(DIV_3 + P_3)/(1 + r)$ and relate today's price to the forecasted dividends for 3 years

(DIV$_1$, DIV$_2$, and DIV$_3$) plus the forecasted price at the end of the *third* year (P_3). In fact we can look as far out into the future as we like, removing P's as we go. Let us call this final period H. This gives us a general stock price formula:

$$P_0 = \frac{DIV_1}{1 + r} + \frac{DIV_2}{(1 + r)^2} + \cdots + \frac{DIV_H + P_H}{(1 + r)^H}$$

$$= \sum_{t=1}^{H} \frac{DIV_t}{(1 + r)^t} + \frac{P_H}{(1 + r)^H}$$

The expression $\sum_{t=1}^{H}$ simply means the sum of the discounted dividends from year 1 to year H.

Table 4-1 continues the Fledgling Electronics example for various time horizons, assuming that the dividends are expected to increase at a steady 10 percent compound rate. The expected price P_t increases at the same rate each year. Each line in the table represents an application of our general formula for a different value of H. Figure 4-1 provides a graphical representation of the table. Each column shows the present value of the dividends up to the time horizon and the present value of the price at the horizon. As the horizon recedes, the dividend stream accounts for an increasing proportion of present value, but the *total* present value of dividends plus terminal price always equals $100.

How far out could we look? In principle the horizon period H could be infinitely distant. Common stocks do not expire of old age. Barring such corporate hazards as bankruptcy or acquisition, they are immortal. As H approaches infinity, the present value of the terminal price ought to approach zero, as it does in the final column of Figure 4-1. We can, therefore, forget about the terminal price entirely and express today's price as the present value of a perpetual stream of cash dividends. This is usually written as

TABLE 4-1
· ·

Applying the stock valuation formula to Fledgling Electronics

| Horizon Period (H) | EXPECTED FUTURE VALUES | | PRESENT VALUES | | |
	Dividend (DIV$_t$)	Price (P_t)	Cumulative Dividends	Future Price	Total
0	—	100	—	100.00	100
1	5.00	110	4.35	95.65	100
2	5.50	121	8.51	91.49	100
3	6.05	133.10	12.48	87.52	100
4	6.66	146.41	16.29	83.71	100
10	11.79	259.37	35.89	64.11	100
20	30.58	672.75	58.89	41.11	100
50	533.59	11,739.09	89.17	10.83	100
100	62,639.15	1,378,061.23	98.83	1.17	100

Assumptions:
1. Dividends increase at 10 percent per year, compounded.
2. Capitalization rate is 15 percent.

Figure 4-1 As your horizon recedes, the present value of the future price (shaded area) declines but the present value of the stream of dividends (unshaded area) increases. The *total* present value (future price and dividends) remains the same.

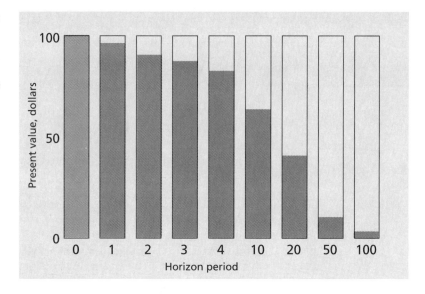

$$P_0 = \sum_{t=1}^{\infty} \frac{\text{DIV}_t}{(1 + r)^t}$$

where the sign ∞ is used to indicate infinity.

This discounted-cash-flow (DCF) formula for the present value of a stock is just the same as it is for the present value of any other asset. We just discount the cash flows—in this case the dividend stream—by the return that can be earned in the capital market on securities of comparable risk. Some find the DCF formula implausible because it seems to ignore capital gains. But we know that the formula was *derived* from the assumption that price in any period is determined by expected dividends *and* capital gains over the next period.

4-3   A SIMPLE WAY TO ESTIMATE THE CAPITALIZATION RATE

In Chapter 3 we encountered some simplified versions of the basic present value formula. Let us see whether they offer any insights into stock values. Suppose, for example, that we forecast a constant growth rate for a company's dividends. This does not preclude year-to-year deviations from the trend: It means only that *expected* dividends grow at a constant rate. Such an investment would be just another example of the growing perpetuity that we helped our fickle philanthropist to evaluate in the last chapter. To find its present value we must divide the annual cash payment by the difference between the discount rate and the growth rate:

$$P_0 = \frac{\text{DIV}_1}{r - g}$$

Remember that we can use this formula only when g, the anticipated growth rate, is less than r, the discount rate. As g approaches r, the stock price becomes infinite. Obviously r must be greater than g if growth really is perpetual.

Our growing perpetuity formula explains P_0 in terms of next year's expected dividend DIV_1, the projected growth trend g, and the expected rate of return on other securities of comparable risk r. Alternatively, the formula can be used to obtain an estimate of r from DIV_1, P_0, and g:

$$r = \frac{DIV_1}{P_0} + g$$

The market capitalization rate equals the **dividend yield** (DIV_1/P_0) plus the expected rate of growth in dividends (g).

These two formulas are much easier to work with than the general statement that "price equals the present value of expected future dividends."[2] Here is a practical example.

Using the DCF Model to Set Gas and Electricity Prices

The prices charged by local electric and gas utilities are regulated by state commissions. The regulators try to keep consumer prices down but are supposed to allow the utilities to earn a fair rate of return. But what is "fair"? It is usually interpreted as r, the market capitalization rate for the firm's common stock. That is, the fair rate of return on equity for a public utility ought to be the rate offered by securities that have the same risk as the utility's common stock.[3]

Small variations on estimates of a utility's cost of equity capital can have a substantial effect on the prices charged to the customers and on the firm's profits. So both utilities and regulators devote considerable resources to estimating r. They call r the **cost of equity capital.** Utilities are mature, stable companies which ought to offer tailor-made cases for application of the constant-growth DCF formula. So let us look at how one study used the formula to estimate the cost of equity capital.

Suppose you wished to estimate the cost of equity for Duke Power in September 1992, when its stock was selling for $36 a share. Dividend payments for the next year were expected to be $1.87 a share. Thus it was a simple matter to calculate the first half of the DCF formula:

$$\text{Dividend yield} = \frac{DIV_1}{P_0} = \frac{1.87}{36} = .052$$

The hard part was estimating g, the expected rate of dividend growth. One option was to consult the views of security analysts who study the prospects for each company. Analysts are rarely prepared to stick their necks out by forecasting dividends to kingdom come, but they often forecast growth rates over the next 5 years, and these estimates may provide an indication of the expected long-run growth path. In the case of Duke Power, analysts in 1992 were forecasting an annual growth of 4.1 percent.[4] This, together with the dividend yield, gave an estimate of the cost of equity capital:

---

[2] These formulas were first developed in 1938 by Williams and were rediscovered by Gordon and Shapiro. See J. B. Williams, *The Theory of Investment Value*, Harvard University Press, Cambridge, Mass., 1938; and M. J. Gordon and E. Shapiro, "Capital Equipment Analysis: The Required Rate of Profit," *Management Science*, **3**:102–110 (October 1956).

[3] This is the accepted interpretation of the U.S. Supreme Court's directive in 1944 that "the returns to the equity owner [of a regulated business] should be commensurate with returns on investments in other enterprises having corresponding risks." *Federal Power Commission v. Hope Natural Gas Company*, 302 U.S. 591 at 603.

[4] This was an average of several analysts' earnings forecasts. Earnings and dividends do not always grow in lockstep, but in this study future dividend and earnings growth rates were equated. The earnings forecasts were provided by I/B/E/S, a company which compiles and publishes analysts' forecasts.

$$r = \frac{DIV_1}{P_0} + g = .052 + .041 = .093, \text{ or } 9.3\%$$

An alternative approach to estimating long-run growth starts with the **payout ratio,** the ratio of dividends to earnings per share (EPS). For Duke Power, this has generally been around 70 percent. In other words, each year the company plows back into the business about 30 percent of earnings per share:

$$\text{Plowback ratio} = 1 - \text{payout ratio} = 1 - \frac{DIV}{EPS} = 1 - .70 = .30$$

Also, Duke Power's ratio of earnings per share to book equity per share has been about 12.5 percent. This is its **return on equity,** or **ROE:**

$$\text{Return on equity} = \text{ROE} = \frac{EPS}{\text{book equity per share}} = .125$$

Duke Power has always been a stable company. Assume that these relationships will continue. If the company earns 12.5 percent of book equity and reinvests 30 percent of that, then book equity will increase by $.30 \times .125 = .0375$, or 3.75 percent. Earnings and dividends per share will also increase by 3.75 percent:

$$\text{Dividend growth rate} = g = \text{plowback ratio} \times \text{ROE} = .30 \times .125 = .0375$$

That gives a second estimate of the market capitalization rate:

$$r = \frac{DIV_1}{P_0} + g = .052 + .0375 = .0895, \text{ or about } 9\%$$

Although this estimate of the market capitalization rate for Duke Power stock seems reasonable enough, there are obvious dangers in analyzing any single firm's stock with such simple rules of thumb as the constant-growth DCF formula. First, the underlying assumption of regular future growth is at best an approximation. Second, even if it is an acceptable approximation, errors inevitably creep into the estimate of g.

Remember, Duke Power's cost of equity is not its personal property. In well-functioning capital markets investors capitalize the dividends of all securities in Duke Power's risk class at exactly the same rate. But any estimate of r for a single common stock is noisy and subject to error. Good practice does not put too much weight on single-company cost-of-equity estimates. It collects samples of similar companies, estimates r for each, and takes an average. The average gives a more reliable benchmark for decision making.

Figure 4-2 shows DCF cost-of-equity estimates for two samples, one comprising 9 New York utilities, the other 17 similar, or "comparable," companies from other states.[5] Duke Power is part of the second sample. The dashed line indicates the median cost-of-equity estimates, which seem to lie about 4 percentage points above the 10-year Treasury bond yield. The dots show the scatter of individual estimates. Most of this scatter is probably "noise." Thus the median estimates are the most useful benchmark estimates for costs of equity capital for typical utilities. Of course, riskier utilities had costs of equity higher than the benchmark; safer utilities, lower.

---

[5] These estimates were prepared for the New York State Public Service Commission. See S. C. Myers and L. S. Borucki, "Discounted Cash Flow Estimates of the Cost of Equity Capital—A Case Study," *Financial Markets, Institutions and Instruments*, **3**:9–45 (August 1994).

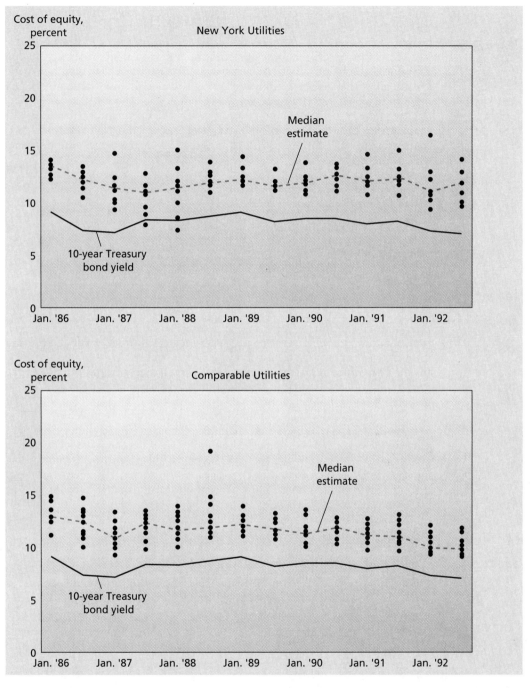

Figure 4-2 DCF cost-of-equity estimates for samples of 9 New York State utilities and 17 utilities operating in other states. The median estimates (dashed line) track long-term interest rates fairly well. (The solid line is the 10-year Treasury yield.) The dots show the scatter of the cost-of-equity estimates for individual companies. [*Source:* S. C. Myers and L. S. Borucki, "Discounted Cash Flow Estimates of the Cost of Equity Capital—A Case Study," *Financial Markets, Institutions and Investments,* **3:**9–45 (August 1994).]

The simple constant-growth DCF formula is an extremely useful rule of thumb, but no more than that. Naive trust in the formula has led many financial analysts to silly conclusions.

We have stressed the difficulty of estimating r by analysis of one stock only. Try to use a large sample of equivalent-risk securities. Even that may not work, but at least it gives the analyst a fighting chance, because the inevitable errors in estimating r for a single security tend to balance out across a broad sample.

In addition, resist the temptation to apply the formula to firms having high current rates of growth. Such growth can rarely be sustained indefinitely, but the constant-growth DCF formula assumes it can. This erroneous assumption leads to an overestimate of r.

Consider Growth-Tech, Inc., a firm with $DIV_1 = \$.50$ and $P_0 = \$50$. The firm has plowed back 80 percent of earnings and has had a return on equity (ROE) of 25 percent. This means that *in the past*

$$\text{Dividend growth rate} = \text{plowback ratio} \times \text{ROE} = .80 \times .25 = .20$$

The temptation is to assume that the future long-term growth rate (g) also equals .20. This would imply

$$r = \frac{.50}{50.00} + .20 = .21$$

But this is silly. No firm can continue growing at 20 percent per year forever, except possibly under extreme inflationary conditions. Eventually, profitability will fall and the firm will respond by investing less.

In real life the return on investment will decline *gradually* over time, but for simplicity let's assume it suddenly drops to 16 percent at year 3 and the firm responds by plowing back only 50 percent of earnings. Then g drops to $.50(.16) = .08$.

Table 4-2 shows what's going on. Growth-Tech starts year 1 with assets of $10.00. It earns $2.50, pays out 50 cents as dividends, and plows back $2. Thus it starts year 2 with $10 + 2 = \$12$. After another year at the same ROE and payout, it starts year 3 with equity of $14.40. However, ROE drops to .16, and the firm earns only $2.30. Dividends go up to $1.15, because the payout ratio increases, but the firm has only $1.15 to plow back. Therefore subsequent growth in earnings and dividends drops to 8 percent.

Now we can use our general DCF formula to find the capitalization rate r:

$$P_0 = \frac{DIV_1}{1 + r} + \frac{DIV_2}{(1 + r)^2} + \frac{DIV_3 + P_3}{(1 + r)^3}$$

Investors in year 3 will view Growth-Tech as offering 8 percent per year dividend growth. We will apply the constant-growth formula:

$$P_3 = \frac{DIV_4}{r - .08}$$

$$P_0 = \frac{DIV_1}{1 + r} + \frac{DIV_2}{(1 + r)^2} + \frac{DIV_3}{(1 + r)^3} + \frac{1}{(1 + r)^3} \frac{DIV_4}{r - .08}$$

$$= \frac{.50}{1 + r} + \frac{.60}{(1 + r)^2} + \frac{1.15}{(1 + r)^3} + \frac{1}{(1 + r)^3} \frac{1.24}{r - .08}$$

We have to use trial and error to find the value of r that makes P_0 equal $50. It turns out that the r implicit in these more realistic forecasts is approximately .099, quite a difference from our "constant-growth" estimate of .21.

TABLE 4-2

....

Forecasted earnings and dividends for Growth-Tech. Note the changes in year 3: ROE and earnings drop, but payout ratio increases, causing a big jump in dividends. However, subsequent growth in earnings and dividends falls to 8 percent per year. Note that the increase in equity equals the earnings not paid out as dividends.

	Year 1	Year 2	Year 3	Year 4
Book equity	10.00	12.00	14.40	15.55
Earnings per share, EPS	2.50	3.00	2.30	2.49
Return on equity, ROE	.25	.25	.16	.16
Payout ratio	.20	.20	.50	.50
Dividends per share, DIV	.50	.60	1.15	1.24
Growth rate of dividends	—	.20	.92	.08

A final warning: Do not use the simple constant-growth formula to test whether the market is correct in its assessment of a stock's value. If your estimate of the value is different from that of the market, it is probably because you have used poor dividend forecasts. Remember what we said at the beginning of this chapter about simple ways of making money on the stock market. There aren't any.

4-4 THE LINK BETWEEN STOCK PRICE AND EARNINGS PER SHARE

Investors often use the terms *growth stocks* and *income stocks*. They seem to buy growth stocks primarily for the expectation of capital gains, and they are interested in the future growth of earnings rather than in next year's dividends. On the other hand, they buy income stocks primarily for the cash dividends. Let us see whether these distinctions make sense.

Imagine first the case of a company that does not grow at all. It does not plow back any earnings and simply produces a constant stream of dividends. Its stock would be rather like the perpetual bond described in the last chapter. Remember that the return on a perpetuity is equal to the yearly cash flow divided by the present value. The expected return on our share would thus be equal to the yearly dividend divided by the share price (i.e., the dividend yield). Since all the earnings are paid out as dividends, the expected return is also equal to the earnings per share divided by the share price (i.e., the earnings-price ratio). For example, if the dividend is $10 a share and the stock price is $100, we have

$$\text{Expected return} = \text{dividend yield} = \text{earnings-price ratio}$$

$$= \frac{\text{DIV}_1}{P_0} \qquad = \frac{\text{EPS}_1}{P_0}$$

$$= \frac{10.00}{100} \qquad = .10$$

The price equals

$$P_0 = \frac{DIV_1}{r} = \frac{EPS_1}{r} = \frac{10.00}{.10} = \$100$$

The expected return for growing firms can also equal the earnings-price ratio. The key is whether earnings are reinvested to provide a return greater or less than the market capitalization rate. For example, suppose our monotonous company suddenly hears of an opportunity to invest $10 a share next year. This would mean no dividend at $t = 1$. However, the company expects that in each subsequent year the project would earn $1 per share, so that the dividend could be increased to $11 a share.

Let us assume that this investment opportunity has about the same risk as the existing business. Then we can discount its cash flow at the 10 percent rate to find its net present value at year 1:

$$\text{Net present value per share at year 1} = -10 + \frac{1}{.10} = 0$$

Thus the investment opportunity will make no contribution to the company's value. Its prospective return is equal to the opportunity cost of capital.

What effect will the decision to undertake the project have on the company's share price? Clearly none. The reduction in value caused by the nil dividend in year 1 is exactly offset by the increase in value caused by the extra dividends in later years. Therefore, once again the market capitalization rate equals the earnings-price ratio:

$$r = \frac{EPS_1}{P_0} = \frac{10}{100} = .10$$

Table 4-3 repeats our example for different assumptions about the cash flow generated by the new project. Note that the earnings-price ratio, measured in terms of EPS_1, next year's expected earnings, equals the market capitalization rate (r) *only* when the new project's NPV = 0. This is an extremely important point—managers frequently make poor financial decisions because they confuse earnings-price ratios with the market capitalization rate.

In general, we can think of stock price as the capitalized value of average earnings under a no-growth policy, plus PVGO, the **present value of growth opportunities:**

TABLE 4-3
....

Effect on stock price of investing an additional $10 in year 1 at different rates of return. Notice that the earnings-price ratio overestimates r when the project has negative NPV and underestimates it when the project has positive NPV.

Project Rate of Return	Incremental Cash Flow, C	Project NPV in Year 1*	Project's Impact on Share Price in Year 0†	Share Price in Year 0, P_0	$\dfrac{EPS_1}{P_0}$	r
.05	$ .50	−$ 5.00	−$ 4.55	$ 95.45	.105	.10
.10	1.00	0	0	100.00	.10	.10
.15	1.50	+ 5.00	+ 4.55	104.55	.096	.10
.20	2.00	+ 10.00	+ 9.09	109.09	.092	.10
.25	2.50	+ 15.00	+ 13.64	113.64	.088	.10

*Project costs $10.00 ($EPS_1$). NPV $= -10 + C/r$, where $r = .10$.
†NPV is calculated at year 1. To find the impact on P_0, discount for 1 year at $r = .10$.

$$P_0 = \frac{EPS_1}{r} + PVGO$$

The earnings-price ratio, therefore, equals

$$\frac{EPS}{P_0} = r\left(1 - \frac{PVGO}{P_0}\right)$$

It will underestimate r if PVGO is positive and overestimate it if PVGO is negative. (The latter case is less likely, since firms are rarely *forced* to take projects with negative net present values.)

> ***Calculating the Present Value of Growth Opportunities for Fledgling Electronics**

In our last example both dividends and earnings were expected to grow, but this growth made no net contribution to the stock price. The stock was in this sense an "income stock." Be careful not to equate firm performance with the growth in earnings per share. A company that reinvests earnings at below the market capitalization rate may increase earnings but will certainly reduce the share value.

Now let us turn to that well-known *growth stock*, Fledgling Electronics. You may remember that Fledgling's market capitalization rate, r, is 15 percent. The company is expected to pay a dividend of $5 in the first year, and thereafter the dividend is predicted to increase indefinitely by 10 percent a year. We can, therefore, use the simplified constant-growth formula to work out Fledgling's price:

$$P_0 = \frac{DIV_1}{r - g} = \frac{5}{.15 - .10} = \$100$$

Suppose that Fledgling has earnings per share of $8.33. Its payout ratio is then

$$\text{Payout ratio} = \frac{DIV_1}{EPS_1} = \frac{5.00}{8.33} = .6$$

In other words, the company is plowing back $1 - .6$, or 40 percent of earnings. Suppose also that Fledgling's ratio of earnings to book equity is ROE = .25. This explains the growth rate of 10 percent:

$$\text{Growth rate} = g = \text{plowback ratio} \times ROE = .4 \times .25 = .10$$

The capitalized value of Fledgling's earnings per share if it had a no-growth policy would be

$$\frac{EPS_1}{r} = \frac{8.33}{.15} = \$55.56$$

But we know that the value of Fledgling stock is $100. The difference of $44.44 must be the amount that investors are paying for growth opportunities. Let's see if we can explain that figure.

Each year Fledgling plows back 40 percent of its earnings into new assets. In the first year Fledgling invests $3.33 at a permanent 25 percent return on equity. Thus the cash generated by this investment is $.25 \times 3.33 = \$.83$ per year starting at $t = 2$. The net present value of the investment as of $t = 1$ is

$$NPV_1 = -3.33 + \frac{.83}{.15} = \$2.22$$

Everything is the same in year 2 except that Fledgling will invest $3.67, 10 percent more than in year 1 (remember $g = .10$). Therefore at $t = 2$ an investment is made with a net present value of

$$NPV_2 = -3.33 \times 1.10 + \frac{.83 \times 1.10}{.15} = \$2.44$$

Thus the payoff to the owners of Fledgling Electronics stock can be represented as the sum of (1) a level stream of earnings, which could be paid out as cash dividends if the firm did not grow, and (2) a set of tickets, one for each future year, representing the opportunity to make investments having positive NPVs. We know that the first component of the value of the share is

$$\text{Present value of level stream of earnings} = \frac{EPS_1}{r} = \frac{8.33}{.15} = \$55.56$$

The first ticket is worth \$2.22 in $t = 1$, the second is worth $\$2.22 \times 1.10 = \$2.44$ in $t = 2$, the third is worth $\$2.44 \times 1.10 = \$2.69$ in $t = 3$. These are the forecasted cash values of the tickets. We know how to value a stream of future cash values that grows at 10 percent per year: Use the simplified DCF formula, replacing the forecasted dividends with forecasted ticket values:

$$\text{Present value of growth opportunities} = PVGO = \frac{NPV_1}{r - g} = \frac{2.22}{.15 - .10}$$
$$= \$44.44$$

Now everything checks:

$$\begin{aligned}\text{Share price} &= \text{present value of level stream of earnings} \\ &\quad + \text{present value of growth opportunities} \\ &= \frac{EPS_1}{r} + PVGO \\ &= \$55.56 + \$44.44 \\ &= \$100\end{aligned}$$

Why is Fledgling Electronics a growth stock? Not because it is expanding at 10 percent per year. It is a growth stock because the net present value of its future investments accounts for a significant fraction (about 44 percent) of the stock's price.

Stock prices today reflect investors' expectations of future operating *and investment* performance. Growth stocks sell at high price-earnings ratios because investors are willing to pay now for expected superior returns on investments that have not yet been made.[6]

Some Examples of Growth Opportunities?

Stocks like Hewlett-Packard, Merck, Microsoft, and Wal-Mart are often described as growth stocks, while those of mature firms like AT&T, Conagra, Exxon, and International Paper are regarded as income stocks. Let us check it out. The first column of Table 4-4 shows the stock price for each of these companies in March 1995. The remaining columns estimate PVGO as a proportion of the stock price.

Remember, if there are no growth opportunities, present value equals the average future earnings from existing assets discounted at the market capitalization rate. We averaged security analysts' forecasts for 1995 and 1996 to provide a measure of the earning power of existing assets. You can see that most of the value of the growth

---

[6]Michael Eisner, the chairman of Walt Disney Productions, made the point this way: "In school you had to take the test and then be graded. Now we're getting graded, and we haven't taken the test." This was in late 1985, when Disney stock was selling at nearly 20 times earnings. See Kathleen K. Wiegner, "The Tinker Bell Principle," *Forbes*, December 2, 1985, p. 102.

TABLE 4-4

●●

Estimated PVGOs

Stock	Stock Price, P_0	EPS*	Market Capitalization Rate, $r^\dagger$	PVGO $= P_0 - \dfrac{EPS}{r}$	PVGO, Percent of Stock Price
Income stocks:					
AT&T	$51.13	$3.76	.136	$23.48	46
Conagra	32.88	2.16	.139	17.34	53
Duke Power	38.25	3.10	.097	6.29	16
Exxon	64.00	4.42	.109	23.45	37
International Paper	72.75	8.51	.143	13.24	18
Growth stocks:					
Genzyme	$ 39.00	$2.09	.244	$30.43	78
Hewlett-Packard	118.50	9.33	.214	74.90	63
Merck	42.50	2.84	.152	23.82	56
Microsoft	64.38	2.57	.165	48.80	76
Wal-Mart	24.38	1.54	.153	14.31	59

*Average earnings under a no-growth policy were estimated as the average of 1995 and 1996 forecasted earnings. (*Source:* I/B/E/S.)

$\dagger$The market capitalization rate was estimated using the capital asset pricing model. We describe this model and how to use it in Section 8-2.

stocks comes from the expectation that the companies will be able to earn more than the cost of capital on their future investments. But AT&T and Conagra, though usually regarded as income stocks, do pretty well on the PVGO scale.

Some companies have such extensive growth opportunities that they prefer to pay no dividends for long periods of time. When we wrote the last edition of this book, we pointed out that Digital Equipment Corporation (DEC) had never paid dividends but had reinvested all its earnings in its rapidly growing minicomputer business. But DEC's common stock price was nevertheless based on the present value of *expected future* dividends. Investors were prepared to forgo immediate cash dividends in the hope that DEC would be in a position to pay high dividends when growth and the need for new capital slowed down.

Unfortunately, growth companies don't always live up to expectations. As demand for its computers slumped, DEC's rapid growth not only slowed down but went into sharp reverse. As we write this, DEC still does not pay dividends; it needs all its cash to survive. The company reported losses of $251 million in 1993 and $2.1 billion in 1994. Needless to say, investors were not happy about this turnaround. The total market value of DEC's outstanding shares fell from a high of $27 billion in 1987 to less than $5 billion in 1994.

●●●●●●●●●●●●●●●●●●●●

Free Cash Flow

Zeus made a habit of appearing in unusual disguises to unsuspecting maidens. The general DCF formula for valuing stocks is rather like that: It keeps cropping up in different forms. Here is another useful version of the formula.

Cash not retained and reinvested in the business is often known as **free cash flow:**

$$\text{Free cash flow} = \text{revenue} - \text{costs} - \text{investment}$$

But cash that is not reinvested in the business is paid out as dividends. So dividends per share are the same as free cash flow per share, and the general DCF formula can be written in terms of per share revenues, costs, and investment:

$$P_0 = \sum_{t=1}^{\infty} \frac{(\text{Free cash flow per share})_t}{(1+r)^t}$$

Notice that it is *not* correct to say that a share's value is equal to the discounted stream of its future earnings per share. That would recognize the *rewards* of investment (in the form of increased revenues) but not the *sacrifice* (in the form of investment). The correct formulation states that share value is equal to the discounted stream of free cash flow per share.

To summarize, we can think of a stock's value as representing either (1) the present value of the stream of expected future dividends, or (2) the present value of free cash flow, or (3) the present value of average future earnings under a no-growth policy plus the present value of growth opportunities.

What Do Price-Earnings Ratios Mean?

The **price-earnings ratio** is part of the everyday vocabulary of investors in the stock market. People casually refer to a stock as "selling at a high P/E." You can look up P/Es in stock quotations given in the newspaper. (However, the newspaper gives the ratio of current price to the most recent earnings. Investors are more concerned with price relative to *future* earnings.) Unfortunately, some financial analysts are confused about what price-earnings ratios really signify and often use the ratios in odd ways.

Should the financial manager celebrate if the firm's stock sells at a high P/E? The answer is usually yes. The high P/E shows that investors think that the firm has good growth opportunities (high PVGO), that its earnings are relatively safe and deserve a low capitalization rate (low r), or both. However, firms can have high price-earnings ratios not because price is high but because earnings are low. A firm which earns *nothing* (EPS = 0) in a particular period will have an *infinite* P/E as long as its shares retain any value at all.

Are relative P/Es helpful in evaluating stocks? Sometimes. Suppose you own stock in a family corporation whose shares are not actively traded. What are those shares worth? A decent estimate is possible if you can find traded firms that have roughly the same profitability, risks, and growth opportunities as your firm. Multiply your firm's earnings per share by the P/E of the counterpart firms.

Does a high P/E indicate a low market capitalization rate? No. There is *no* reliable association between a stock's price-earnings ratio and the capitalization rate r. The ratio of EPS to P_0 measures r only if PVGO = 0 and only if reported EPS is the average future earnings the firm could generate under a no-growth policy.

What Do Earnings Mean?

Another reason P/Es are hard to interpret is the difficulty of interpreting and comparing earnings per share, the denominator of the price-earnings ratio. What do earnings per share mean? They mean different things for different firms. For some firms they mean more than for others.

The problem is that the earnings that firms report are book, or accounting, figures, and as such reflect a series of more or less arbitrary choices of accounting methods. Almost any firm's reported earnings can be changed substantially by adopting different accounting procedures. A switch in the depreciation method used for reporting purposes directly affects EPS, for example. Yet it has *no* effect on cash flow, since depreciation is a noncash charge. (The depreciation method used for tax purposes *does* affect cash flow.) Other accounting choices which affect reported earnings are the valuation of inventory, the procedures by which the accounts of two merging firms are combined, the choice between expensing or capitalizing research and development, and the way the tax liabilities of the firm are reported. The list could go on and on.

We shall discuss the biases in accounting income and profitability measures in Chapter 12, after we have used present value concepts to develop measures of true, economic income. For the moment, we just want you to remember that accounting earnings are slippery animals.

4-5 VALUING A BUSINESS BY DISCOUNTED CASH FLOW

Investors routinely buy and sell shares of common stock. Companies frequently buy and sell entire businesses. For example, when Eastman Kodak sold its medical and pharmaceutical business to SmithKline Beecham for $2.9 billion in 1994, you can be sure that both companies burned a lot of midnight oil to make sure that the deal was fairly priced.

Do the discounted-cash-flow formulas we presented in this chapter work for entire businesses as well as for shares of common stock? Sure: It doesn't matter whether you forecast dividends per share or the total free cash flow of a business. Value today always equals future cash flow discounted at the opportunity cost of capital.

Remembering our rule about adding present values, you may be tempted to think that the *total* value of a firm's outstanding common stock is equal to the discounted stream of *all* future dividends. But be a little careful here: You must include only dividends to be paid on *existing* stock. The company may at some future date decide to sell more stock, which will then be entitled to its share of the future dividend stream. The total value of the company's *existing* stock is equal to the discounted value of that *portion* of the total dividend stream which will be paid to the stock outstanding today.

There is another approach to this issue. You could assume that existing shareholders buy any new shares the company issues. In this case, shareholders would bear *all* the costs of future investments and receive *all* the rewards. In other words, existing shareholders would receive every penny of free cash flow. Company value can therefore be calculated as

$$PV(\text{firm}) = PV(\text{free cash flow}) = PV(\text{revenues} - \text{costs} - \text{investment})$$

Example: Icarus Air has 1 million shares outstanding and expects to earn a constant $10 million per year on its existing assets. All earnings will be paid out as dividends, so

$$\text{Earnings per share} = \text{dividends per share}$$

$$\text{EPS} = \text{DIV} = \frac{\$10 \text{ million}}{1 \text{ million shares}} = \$10$$

If investors' opportunity cost of capital is 10 percent,

$$P_0 = \frac{\text{DIV}_1}{r} = \frac{\text{EPS}_1}{r} = \frac{10}{.10} = \$100$$

Suppose that next year Icarus plans to double in size by issuing an additional 1 million shares at $100 a share. Everything is the same as before but twice as big. Thus from year 2 onward the company earns a constant $20 million, all of which is paid out as dividends on the 20 million shares.

What is the value of Icarus Air? With our first approach we simply discount the total dividends that are expected to be paid on *existing* shares. These are unaffected by next year's expansion, which is entirely paid for by investors in the newly issued shares. These investors get the extra profits and dividends, too.[7]

The second approach discounts the net cash flow to *existing* shareholders if they buy the additional shares that Icarus plans to issue. In this case they will receive the entire profits *less* the cost of the investments to generate those profits:

Cash Flows, Millions of Dollars

	Year 1	Year 2	Year 3	Year 4	Etc.
Total profits	10	20	20	20	...
Less investments	−100				
Free cash flow	−90	20	20	20	...

Now discount the free cash flows at 10 percent:

$$PV = -\frac{90}{1.1} + \frac{20}{(1.1)^2} + \frac{20}{(1.1)^3} + \frac{20}{(1.1)^4} + \cdots$$

This series includes a perpetuity of $20 million per year starting in year 2:

$$PV = -\frac{90}{1.1} + \frac{1}{1.1}\left(\frac{20}{.10}\right) = \$100 \text{ million}$$

The two methods give exactly the same answer.[8]

<table>
<tr><td>

Valuing the Concatenator Business

</td><td>

Of course, things are never as easy in practice as they seem in principle. However, smart application of some basic financial concepts can make discounted cash flow less mechanical and more trustworthy. We can illustrate how to apply the concepts by walking you through a practical example.

</td></tr>
</table>

Rumor has it that Establishment Industries is interested in buying your company's concatenator manufacturing operation. Your company is willing to sell if it can get the full value of this rapidly growing business. The problem is to figure out what its true present value is.

Table 4-5 gives a forecast of free cash flow.[9] The table is similar to Table 4-2, which forecasted earnings and dividends per share for Growth-Tech, based on assumptions about Growth-Tech's assets per share, return on equity, and the growth of its business. For the concatenator business, we also have assumptions about assets, profitability—in this case, after-tax operating earnings relative to assets—and growth. Growth starts out at a rapid 20 percent per year, then falls in two steps to a moderate

---

[7]The new stockholders will demand only a fair rate of return on their investment. If Icarus's expansion had a positive NPV, the company's *current* stock price would increase, due to positive PVGO, and new shares could be sold at a higher price. With fewer new shares issued, the "old" shareholders would receive part of the profits from the expansion.

[8]They have to as long as the company is expected to issue shares at fair value. The new shares cost $100 million. They are expected to provide dividends worth $100 million. Subtracting the cost of the shares and recognizing the dividends they generate does not affect value.

[9]Since the concatenator division will have only one shareholder, which receives all the profits and bears the cost of all investments, it is natural to forecast and value the division's free cash flow.

TABLE 4-5

●●

Forecasts of free cash flow, in millions of dollars, for the Concatenator Manufacturing Division. Rapid expansion in years 1–6 means that free cash flow is negative, because required additional investment outstrips earnings. Free cash flow turns positive when growth slows down after year 6.

	YEAR									
	1	2	3	4	5	6	7	8	9	10
Asset value	10.00	12.00	14.40	17.28	20.74	23.43	26.47	28.05	29.73	31.51
Earnings	1.20	1.44	1.73	2.07	2.49	2.81	3.18	3.36	3.57	3.78
Investment	2.00	2.40	2.88	3.46	2.69	3.04	1.59	1.68	1.78	1.89
Free cash flow	–.80	–.96	–1.15	–1.39	–.20	–.23	1.59	1.68	1.79	1.89
Earnings growth from previous period (percent)	20	20	20	20	20	13	13	6	6	6

Notes:
1. Starting asset value is $10 million. Assets required for the business grow at 20 percent per year to year 4, at 13 percent in years 5 and 6, and at 6 percent afterward.
2. Profitability is constant at 12 percent.
3. Free cash flow equals earnings minus net investment. Net investment equals total capital expenditures less depreciation. Note that earnings are also calculated net of depreciation.

6 percent rate for the long run. The growth rate determines the net additional investment required to expand assets, and the profitability rate determines the earnings thrown off by the business.[10]

It turns out that free cash flow, the next to last line in Table 4-5, is negative in years 1 through 6. The concatenator business is paying a negative dividend to the parent company; it is absorbing more cash than it is throwing off.

Is that a bad sign? Not really: The business is running a cash deficit not because it is unprofitable, only because it is growing so fast. Rapid growth is good news, not bad, so long as the business is earning more than the opportunity cost of capital. Your company, or Establishment Industries, will be happy to invest an extra $800,000 in the concatenator business next year, so long as the business offers a superior rate of return.

●●●●●●●●●●●●●●●●●

Valuation Format

The value of a business is usually computed as the discounted value of free cash flows out to a **valuation horizon** (H), plus the forecasted value of the business at the horizon, also discounted back to present value. That is,

$$PV = \underbrace{\frac{FCF_1}{1+r} + \frac{FCF_2}{(1+r)^2} + \cdots + \frac{FCF_H}{(1+r)^H}}_{PV(\text{free cash flow})} + \underbrace{\frac{PV_H}{(1+r)^H}}_{PV(\text{horizon value})}$$

---

[10]Table 4-5 shows *net* investment, which is total investment less depreciation. We are assuming that investment for replacement of existing assets is covered by depreciation, and that net investment is devoted to growth.

We could have reported gross investment in Table 4-5. However, that would have required adding depreciation back to earnings to get operating cash flow. The bottom line, free cash flow, would be the same.

Of course, the concatenator business will continue after the horizon, but it's not practical to forecast free cash flow year by year to infinity. PV_H stands in for free cash flow in periods $H + 1$, $H + 2$, etc.

Valuation horizons are often chosen arbitrarily. Sometimes the boss tells everybody to use 10 years because that's a round number. We will try year 6, because growth of the concatenator business seems to settle down to a long-run trend in year 7.

Estimating Horizon Value

There are several common formulas or rules of thumb for estimating horizon value. First, let us try the constant-growth formula. This requires free cash flow for year 7, which we have from Table 4-5, a long-run growth rate, which appears to be 6 percent, and a discount rate, which some high-priced consultant has told us is 10 percent. Therefore,

$$PV(\text{horizon value}) = \frac{1}{(1.1)^6}\left(\frac{1.59}{.10 - .06}\right) = 22.4$$

The present value of the near-term free cash flows is

$$PV(\text{cash flows}) = -\frac{.80}{1.1} - \frac{.96}{(1.1)^2} - \frac{1.15}{(1.1)^3} - \frac{1.39}{(1.1)^4}$$
$$- \frac{.20}{(1.1)^5} - \frac{.23}{(1.1)^6}$$
$$= -3.6$$

and therefore, the present value of the business is

$$PV(\text{business}) = PV(\text{free cash flow}) + PV(\text{horizon value})$$
$$= -3.6 \qquad\qquad + 22.4$$
$$= \$18.8 \text{ million}$$

Now, are we done? Well, the mechanics of this calculation are perfect. But doesn't it make you just a little nervous to find that 119 percent of the value of the business rests on the horizon value? Moreover, a little checking shows that the horizon value can change dramatically in response to apparently minor changes in assumptions. For example, if the long-run growth rate is 8 percent rather than 6 percent, the value of the business increases from \$18.8 to \$26.3 million.[11]

In other words, it's easy for a discounted cash flow business valuation to be mechanically perfect and practically wrong. Smart financial managers try to check their results by calculating horizon value in several different ways.

Suppose you can observe stock prices for mature manufacturing companies whose scale, risk, and growth prospects today roughly match those projected for the concatenator business in year 6. Suppose further that these companies tend to sell at price-earnings ratios of about 11. Then you could reasonably guess that the price-earnings ratio of a mature concatenator operation will likewise be 11. That implies:

---

[11]If long-run growth is 8 rather than 6 percent, an extra 2 percent of period-7 assets will have to be plowed back into the concatenator business. This reduces free cash flow by \$.53 to \$1.06 million. So,

$$PV(\text{horizon value}) = \frac{1}{(1.1)^6}\left(\frac{1.06}{.10 - .08}\right) = \$29.9$$

$$PV(\text{business}) = -3.6 + 29.9 = \$26.3 \text{ million}$$

$$PV(\text{horizon value}) = \frac{1}{(1.1)^6}(11 \times 3.18) = 19.7$$

$$PV(\text{business}) = -3.6 + 19.7 = \$16.1 \text{ million}$$

Suppose also that the market-book ratios of the sample of mature manufacturing companies tend to cluster around 1.4. (The market-book ratio is just the ratio of stock price to book value per share.) If the concatenator business's market-book ratio is 1.4 in year 6,

$$PV(\text{horizon value}) = \frac{1}{(1.1)^6}(1.4 \times 23.43) = 18.5$$

$$PV(\text{business}) = -3.6 + 18.5 = \$14.9 \text{ million}$$

It's easy to poke holes in these last two calculations. Book value, for example, often is a poor measure of the true value of a company's assets. It can fall far behind actual asset values when there is rapid inflation, and it often entirely misses important intangible assets, such as your patents for concatenator design. Earnings may also be biased by inflation and a long list of arbitrary accounting choices. Finally, you never know when you have found a sample of truly similar companies.

But remember, the purpose of discounted cash flow is to estimate market value—to estimate what investors would pay for a stock or business. When you can *observe* what they actually pay for similar companies, that's valuable evidence. Try to figure out a way to use it. One way to use it is through valuation rules of thumb, based on price-earnings or market-book ratios. A rule of thumb, artfully employed, sometimes beats a complex discounted cash flow calculation hands down.

A Further Reality Check

Here is another approach to valuing a business. It is based on what you have learned about price-earnings ratios and the present value of growth opportunities.

Suppose the valuation horizon is set not by looking for the first year of stable growth, but by asking when the industry is likely to settle into competitive equilibrium. You might go to the operating manager most familiar with the concatenator business and ask:

> Sooner or later you and your competitors will be on an equal footing when it comes to major new investments. You may still be earning a superior return on your core business, but you will find that introductions of new products or attempts to expand sales of existing products trigger intense resistance from competitors who are just about as smart and efficient as you are. Give a realistic assessment of when that time will come.

"That time" is the horizon after which PVGO, the net present value of subsequent growth opportunities, is zero. After all, PVGO is positive only when investments can be expected to earn more than the cost of capital. When your competition catches up, that happy prospect disappears.[12]

We know that present value in any period equals the capitalized value of next period's earnings, plus PVGO:

$$PV_t = \frac{\text{earnings}_{t+1}}{r} + PVGO$$

---

[12] We cover this point in more detail in Chapter 11.

But what if PVGO = 0? At the horizon period H, then,

$$PV_H = \frac{earnings_{H+1}}{r}$$

In other words, when the competition catches up, the price-earnings ratio equals $1/r$, because PVGO disappears.

Suppose competition is expected to catch up by period 8. We can recalculate the value of the concatenator business as follows:[13]

$$PV(\text{horizon value}) = \frac{1}{(1 + r)^8} \left(\frac{\text{earnings in period 9}}{r} \right)$$

$$= \frac{1}{(1.1)^8} \left(\frac{3.57}{.10} \right)$$

$$= \$16.7 \text{ million}$$

$$PV(\text{business}) = -2.0 + 16.7 = \$14.7 \text{ million}$$

We now have four estimates of what Establishment Industries ought to pay for the concatenator business. The estimates reflect four different methods of estimating horizon value. There is no "best" method, although in many cases we put most weight on the last method, which sets the horizon date at the point when management expects PVGO to disappear. The last method forces managers to remember that sooner or later competition catches up.

Our calculated values for the concatenator business range from \$14.7 to \$18.8 million, a difference of about \$4 million. The width of the range may be disquieting, but it is not unusual. Discounted cash flow formulas only estimate market value, and the estimates change as forecasts and assumptions change. Managers cannot know market value until an actual transaction takes place.

4-6 SUMMARY

In this chapter we have used our newfound knowledge of present values to examine the market price of common stocks. The value of a stock is equal to the stream of cash payments discounted at the rate of return that investors expect to receive on comparable securities.

Common stocks do not have a fixed maturity; their cash payments consist of an indefinite stream of dividends. Therefore, the present value of a common stock is

$$PV = \sum_{t=1}^{\infty} \frac{DIV_t}{(1 + r)^t}$$

However, we did not *derive* our DCF formula just by substituting DIV_t for C_t. We did not just *assume* that investors purchase common stocks solely for dividends. In fact, we began with the assumption that investors have relatively short horizons and invest for both dividends and capital gains. Our fundamental valuation formula is, therefore,

$$P_0 = \frac{DIV_1 + P_1}{1 + r}$$

---

[13] The present value of free cash flow before the horizon improves to $-\$2.0$ million because inflows in years 7 and 8 are now included.

This is a condition of market equilibrium: If it did not hold, the share would be overpriced or underpriced, and investors would rush to sell or buy it. The flood of sellers or buyers would force the price to adjust so that the fundamental valuation formula holds.

This formula will hold in each future period as well as the present. That allowed us to express next year's forecasted price in terms of the subsequent stream of dividends $DIV_1, DIV_2, \ldots$.

We also made use of the formula for a growing perpetuity presented in Chapter 3. If dividends are expected to grow forever at a constant rate of g, then

$$P_0 = \frac{DIV_1}{r - g}$$

We showed how it is often helpful to twist this formula around and use it to estimate the capitalization rate r, given P_0 and estimates of DIV_1 and g.

The general DCF formula can be transformed into a statement about earnings and growth opportunities:

$$P_0 = \frac{EPS_1}{r} + PVGO$$

The ratio EPS_1/r is the capitalized value of the earnings per share that the firm would generate under a no-growth policy. PVGO is the net present value of the investments that the firm will make in order to grow. A "growth" stock is one for which PVGO is large relative to the capitalized value of EPS. Most growth stocks are stocks of rapidly expanding firms, but expansion alone does not create a high PVGO. What matters is the profitability of the new investments.

The same formulas that are used to value a single share can also be applied to valuing the total package of shares that a company has issued. In other words, we can use them to value an entire business. Applying our present value formulas to a firm or line of business is easy in principle but messy in application. That is why we concluded the chapter with a practical valuation problem.

In earlier chapters you should have acquired—we hope painlessly—a knowledge of the basic principles of valuing assets and a facility with the mechanics of discounting. Now you know something of how common stocks are valued and market capitalization rates estimated. In Chapter 5 we can begin to apply all this knowledge in a more specific analysis of capital budgeting decisions.

Further Reading

There are a number of discussions of the valuation of common stocks in investment texts. We suggest:
Z. Bodie, A. Kane, and A. J. Marcus: *Investments*, 2d ed., Richard D. Irwin, Inc., Homewood, Ill., 1992.
W. F. Sharpe and G. J. Alexander: *Investments*, 4th ed., Prentice-Hall, Inc., Englewood Cliffs, N.J., 1989.

J. B. Williams's original work remains very readable. See particularly Chapter V of:
J. B. Williams: *The Theory of Investment Value*, Harvard University Press, Cambridge, Mass., 1938.

The following articles provide important developments of Williams's early work. We suggest, however, that you leave the third article until you have read Chapter 16:
D. Durand: "Growth Stocks and the Petersburg Paradox," *Journal of Finance*, **12**:348–363 (September 1957).

M. J. Gordon and E. Shapiro: "Capital Equipment Analysis: The Required Rate of Profit," *Management Science*, **3**:102–110 (October 1956).

M. H. Miller and F. Modigliani: "Dividend Policy, Growth and the Valuation of Shares," *Journal of Business*, **34**:411–433 (October 1961).

Leibowitz and Kogelman call PVGO the "franchise factor." They analyze it in detail in:

M. L. Leibowitz and S. Kogelman: "Inside the P/E Ratio: The Franchise Factor," *Financial Analysts Journal*, **46**:17–35 (November–December 1990).

Myers and Borucki cover the practical problems encountered in estimating DCF costs of equity for regulated companies; Harris and Marston report DCF estimates of rates of return for the stock market as a whole:

S. C. Myers and L. S. Borucki: "Discounted Cash Flow Estimates of the Cost of Equity Capital—A Case Study," *Financial Markets, Institutions and Instruments*, **3**:9–45 (August 1994).

R. S. Harris and F. C. Marston: "Estimating Shareholder Risk Premia Using Analysts' Growth Forecasts," *Financial Management*, **21**:63–70 (Summer 1992).

Quiz

1. Company X is expected to pay an end-of-year dividend of $10 a share. After the dividend its stock is expected to sell at $110. If the market capitalization rate is 10 percent, what is the current stock price?

2. Company Y does not plow back any earnings and is expected to produce a level dividend stream of $5 a share. If the current stock price is $40, what is the market capitalization rate?

3. Company Z's dividends per share are expected to grow indefinitely by 5 percent a year. If next year's dividend is $10 and the market capitalization rate is 8 percent, what is the current stock price?

4. Company Z-prime is like Z in all respects save one: Its growth will stop after year 4. In year 5 and afterward, it will pay out all earnings as dividends. What is Z-prime's stock price? Assume next year's EPS is $15.

5. If company Z (see question 3) were to distribute all its earnings, it could maintain a level dividend stream of $15 a share. How much, therefore, is the market actually paying per share for growth opportunities?

6. Which of the following statements are correct?
   (*a*) The value of a share equals the discounted stream of future earnings per share.
   (*b*) The value of a share equals the present value of earnings per share assuming the firm does not grow, plus the net present value of future growth opportunities.
   (*c*) The value of a share equals the discounted stream of future dividends per share.

7. Under what conditions does r, a stock's market capitalization rate, equal its earnings-price ratio EPS_1/P_0?

8. What do financial managers mean by "free cash flow"? How is free cash flow related to dividends paid out? Briefly explain.

9. Consider three investors:
   (*a*) Mr. Single invests for 1 year.
   (*b*) Ms. Double invests for 2 years.
   (*c*) Mrs. Triple invests for 3 years.

Assume each invests in company Z (see question 3). Show that each expects to earn an expected rate of return of 8 percent per year.

Questions and Problems

1. Rework Table 4-1 under the assumption that the dividend on Fledgling Electronics is $10 next year and that it is expected to grow by 5 percent a year. The capitalization rate is 15 percent.

2. In the late 1980s, Japanese price-earnings ratios were much higher than those in the United States, and Japanese dividend yields were much lower. Long-term nominal interest rates in Japan were about 4 percent lower than those in the United States; real interest rates were estimated to be about 1 percent lower.[14]

	Japan	United States
Price-earnings ratio	32.1	11.7
Dividend yield (percent)	0.6	3.0
Nominal interest rate (percent)	4.8	9.2
Estimated real interest rate (percent)	3.0	4.1

Does this information suggest or imply that expected rates of return demanded by investors were lower in the Japanese market than in the U.S. market? Before you answer, be sure to think through the possible explanations of the Japanese market's higher price-earnings ratio and lower dividend yield.

3. Look in a recent issue of *The Wall Street Journal* at "NYSE-Composite Transactions."
   (*a*) What is the latest price of IBM stock?
   (*b*) What are the annual dividend payment and the dividend yield on IBM stock?
   (*c*) What would the yield be if IBM changed its yearly dividend to $8?
   (*d*) What is the P/E ratio on IBM stock?
   (*e*) Use the P/E ratio to calculate IBM's earnings per share.
   (*f*) Is IBM's P/E higher or lower than that of Exxon?
   (*g*) What are the possible reasons for the difference in P/E?

4. P/E ratios reported in *The Wall Street Journal* use the latest closing prices and the last 12 months' reported earnings per share. Explain why the corresponding earnings-price ratios (the reciprocals of reported P/Es) are *not* accurate measures of the expected rates of return demanded by investors.

5. In March 1995, International Paper's stock sold for about $73. Security analysts were forecasting a long-term earnings growth rate of 8.5 percent. The company was paying dividends of $1.68 per share.

---

[14]These figures were calculated for the NRI 350 index (Japan) and the Standard and Poor's industrials (United States) by K. R. French and J. M. Poterba, "Are Japanese Stock Prices Too High?" *Journal of Financial Economics*, **29**:337–363 (1991). Poterba and French adjusted for accounting differences that make commonly reported Japanese price-earnings ratios artificially high. The unadjusted Japanese 1988 price-earnings ratio was 54!

(*a*) Assume dividends are expected to grow along with earnings at $g = 8.5$ percent per year in perpetuity. What rate of return r were investors expecting?

(*b*) International Paper was expected to earn about 12 percent on book equity and to pay out about 50 percent of earnings as dividends. What do these forecasts imply for g? For r? Use the perpetual-growth DCF formula.

6. Crecimiento S.A. currently plows back 40 percent of its earnings and earns a return of 20 percent on this investment. The dividend yield on the stock is 4 percent.

(*a*) Assuming that Crecimiento can continue to plow back this proportion of earnings and earn a 20 percent return on the investment, how rapidly will earnings and dividends grow? What is the expected return on Crecimiento stock?

(*b*) Suppose that management suddenly announces that future investment opportunities have dried up. Now Crecimiento intends to pay out all its earnings. How will the stock price change?

(*c*) Suppose that management simply announces that the expected return on new investment would in the future be the same as the market capitalization rate. Now what is Crecimiento's stock price?

7. Consider the following three stocks:

(*a*) Stock A is expected to provide a dividend of $10 a share forever.

(*b*) Stock B is expected to pay a dividend of $5 next year. Thereafter, dividend growth is expected to be 4 percent a year forever.

(*c*) Stock C is expected to pay a dividend of $5 next year. Thereafter, dividend growth is expected to be 20 percent a year for 5 years (i.e., until year 6) and zero thereafter.

If the market capitalization rate for each stock is 10 percent, which stock is the most valuable? What if the capitalization rate is 7 percent?

8. You believe that next year the Dong Lumination Company will pay a dividend of $2 on its common stock. Thereafter you expect dividends to grow at a rate of 4 percent a year in perpetuity. If you require a return of 12 percent on your investment, how much should you be prepared to pay for the stock?

*9. Rework the analysis of the present value of the growth opportunities for Fledgling Electronics, assuming (i) that the dividend is $10 next year, (ii) that it is expected to grow by 5 percent a year, (iii) that it plows back a constant 20 percent of earnings, and (iv) that the market capitalization rate is 14 percent.

(*a*) What is next year's expected earnings per share (EPS_1)?

(*b*) What is the return on book equity (ROE)?

(*c*) What is PVGO?

10. Explain carefully why different stocks may have different P/Es. Show how the price-earnings ratio is related to growth, dividend payout, and the required return.

11. Look one more time at Table 4-1, which applies the DCF stock valuation formula to Fledgling Electronics. The CEO, having just learned that stock value is the present value of future dividends, proposes that Fledgling pay a bumper dividend of $15 a share in period 1. The extra cash would have to be raised by an issue of new shares. Recalculate Table 4-1 assuming that profits and payout ratios in all subsequent years are unchanged. You should find that the total present value of dividends *per existing share* is unchanged at $100. Why?

12. The constant-growth DCF formula

$$P_0 = \frac{DIV_1}{r - g}$$

is sometimes written as

$$P_0 = \frac{ROE(1 - b)BVPS}{r - bROE}$$

where BVPS is book equity value per share, b the plowback ratio, and ROE the ratio of earnings per share to BVPS. Use this equation to show how the price-to-book ratio varies as ROE changes. What is price-to-book when ROE $= r$?

13. Each of the following formulas for determining shareholders' required rate of return can be right or wrong depending on the circumstances:

(a) $r = \dfrac{DIV_1}{P_0} + g$

(b) $r = \dfrac{EPS_1}{P_0}$

For each formula construct a *simple* numerical example showing that the formula can give wrong answers and explain why the error occurs. Then construct another simple numerical example for which the formula gives the right answer.

14. Phoenix Motor Corporation has pulled off a miraculous recovery. Four years ago, it was near bankruptcy. Now its charismatic leader, a corporate folk hero, may run for president.

    Phoenix has just announced a $1 per share dividend, the first since the crisis hit. Analysts expect an increase to a "normal" $3 as the company completes its recovery over the next 3 years. After that, dividend growth is expected to settle down to a moderate long-term growth rate of 6 percent.

    Phoenix stock is selling at $50 per share. What is the expected long-run rate of return from buying the stock at this price? Assume dividends of $1, $2, and $3 for years 1, 2, 3. A little trial and error will be necessary to find r.

*15. Look again at the financial forecasts for Growth-Tech given in Table 4-2. This time assume you *know* that the opportunity cost of capital is $r = .12$ (discard the .099 figure calculated in the text). Assume you do *not* know Growth-Tech's stock value. Otherwise follow the assumptions given in the text.
    (a) Calculate the value of Growth-Tech stock.
    (b) What part of that value reflects the discounted value of P_3, the price forecasted for year 3?
    (c) What part of P_3 reflects the present value of growth opportunities (PVGO) after year 3?
    (d) Suppose that competition will catch up with Growth-Tech by year 4, so that it can earn only its cost of capital on any investments made in year 4 or subsequently. What is Growth-Tech stock worth now under this assumption? (Make additional assumptions if necessary.)

16. Consider a firm with existing assets that generate an EPS of $5. If the firm does not invest except to maintain existing assets, EPS is expected to remain constant at $5 a year. However, starting next year the firm has the chance to invest $3 per share a year in developing a newly discovered geothermal steam source for electricity generation. Each investment is expected to generate a

permanent 20 percent return. However, the source will be fully developed by the fifth year. What will be the stock price and earnings-price ratio assuming investors require a 12 percent rate of return? Show that the earnings-price ratio is .20 if the required rate of return is 20 percent.

17. Compost Science, Inc. (CSI), is in the business of converting Boston's sewage sludge into fertilizer. The business is not in itself very profitable. However, to induce CSI to remain in business, the Metropolitan District Commission (MDC) has agreed to pay whatever amount is necessary to yield CSI a 10 percent book return on equity. At the end of the year CSI is expected to pay a $4 dividend. It has been reinvesting 40 percent of earnings and growing at 4 percent a year.

    (*a*) Suppose CSI continues on this growth trend. What is the expected long-run rate of return from purchasing the stock at $100? What part of the $100 price is attributable to the present value of growth opportunities?

    (*b*) Now the MDC announces a plan for CSI to treat Cambridge sewage. CSI's plant will, therefore, be expanded gradually over 5 years. This means that CSI will have to reinvest 80 percent of its earnings for 5 years. Starting in year 6, however, it will again be able to pay out 60 percent of earnings. What will be CSI's stock price once this announcement is made and its consequences for CSI are known?

18. Look back at our valuation of the concatenator division in Section 4-5. Since the division is owned by a single shareholder, it was natural to think of that shareholder as receiving all the profits and paying for all the investments. This question is designed to show that you get the same answer if you value the dividends on the existing shares. Think of the concatenator division as a separate company financed by 1000 shares. After year 6 all free cash flows are paid out as dividends, but in each of years 1 through 6 the company has no cash to pay dividends and finances the deficits by selling new shares.

    (*a*) Suppose that our $18.8 million valuation using the constant-growth formula is correct. (Actually the value is $18.85 million. We rounded.) Given that the market capitalization rate is 10 percent, what is the expected value of existing shares in year 1?

    (*b*) Concatenator now needs to issue new shares to finance the year-1 deficit of $.80 million. Suppose that it offers them to investors. How many shares does it need to issue? (Remember, you have just calculated the price per share.)

    (*c*) Now calculate the expected share price in year 2. How many new shares need to be issued to finance the year-2 deficit of $.96 million?

    (*d*) Repeat the exercise for each year through year 6. After financing the deficit in year 6, what is the total number of shares outstanding? What proportion of the company is owned by the initial shareholders?

    (*e*) Now calculate the stream of dividends beginning in year 7 that goes to *initial* shareholders and discount at 10 percent. The answer should be $18.85 million, the same figure as we got by discounting free cash flow.

19. Portfolio managers are frequently paid a proportion of the funds under management. Suppose you manage a $100 million equity portfolio offering a dividend yield (DIV_1/P_0) of 5 percent. Dividends and portfolio value are expected to grow at a constant rate. Your annual fee for managing this portfolio is .5 percent of portfolio value and is calculated at the end of each year. Assuming that you will continue to manage the portfolio from now to eternity, what is the present value of the management contract?

5

Why Net Present Value Leads to Better Investment Decisions than Other Criteria

In the first four chapters we introduced, at times surreptitiously, most of the basic principles of the investment decision. In this chapter we begin by consolidating that knowledge. We then take a critical look at three other criteria that companies sometimes use to make investment decisions—the payback rule, the average-return-on-book rule, and the internal-rate-of-return rule. The first two are ad hoc rules and may lead to silly decisions. If correctly used, the internal-rate-of-return rule should always select those projects that increase shareholder wealth, but we shall see that there are also a number of traps for the unwary.

We conclude the chapter by showing how to cope with situations when the firm has only limited capital or other resources. There are two aspects to this problem. One is computational. In simple cases we just choose those projects that give the highest NPV per dollar of investment. But resource constraints and project interactions often create problems of such complexity that linear programming is needed to solve this problem and help the financial manager handle some project interactions at the same time. The other part of the problem is to decide whether capital rationing really exists and whether it invalidates net present value as a criterion for capital budgeting.[1]

5-1 A REVIEW OF THE BASICS

Vegetron's financial manager is wondering how to analyze a proposed $1 million investment in a new venture called project X. He asks what you think.

Your response should be as follows: "First, forecast the cash flows generated by project X over its economic life. Second, determine the appropriate opportunity cost of capital. This should reflect both the time value of money and the risk involved in project X. Third, use this opportunity cost of capital to discount the future cash flows of project X. The sum of the discounted cash flows is called present value (PV). Fourth, calculate *net* present value (NPV) by subtracting the $1 million investment from PV. Invest in project X if its NPV is greater than zero."

---

[1] Guess what? NPV, properly interpreted, wins out in the end.

However, Vegetron's financial manager is unmoved by your sagacity. He asks why NPV is so important.

You reply: "Let us look at what is best for Vegetron stockholders. They want you to make their Vegetron shares as valuable as possible.

"Right now Vegetron's total market value (price per share times the number of shares outstanding) is $10 million. That includes $1 million cash we can invest in project X. The value of Vegetron's other assets and opportunities must therefore be $9 million. We have to decide whether it is better to keep the $1 million cash and reject project X or to spend the cash and accept project X. Let us call the value of the new project PV. Then the choice is as follows:

	MARKET VALUE, MILLIONS OF DOLLARS	
Asset	Reject Project X	Accept Project X
Cash	1	0
Other assets	9	9
Project X	0	PV
	10	9 + PV

"Clearly project X is worthwhile if its present value, PV, is greater than $1 million—that is, if net present value is positive."

Financial manager: "How do I know that the PV of project X will actually show up in Vegetron's market value?"

Your reply: "Suppose we set up a new, independent firm X, whose only asset is project X. What would be the market value of firm X?

"Investors would forecast the dividends firm X would pay and discount those dividends by the expected rate of return of securities having risks comparable to firm X. We know that stock prices are equal to the present value of forecasted dividends.

"Since project X is firm X's only asset, the dividend payments we would expect firm X to pay are exactly the cash flows we have forecasted for project X. Moreover, the rate investors would use to discount firm X's dividends is exactly the rate we should use to discount project X's cash flows.

"I agree that firm X is entirely hypothetical. But if project X is accepted, investors holding Vegetron stock will really hold a portfolio of project X and the firm's other assets. We know the other assets are worth $9 million considered as a separate venture. Since asset values are additive, we can easily figure out the portfolio value once we calculate the value of project X as a separate venture.

"By calculating the present value of project X, we are replicating the process by which the common stock of firm X would be valued in capital markets."

Financial manager: "The one thing I don't understand is where the discount rate comes from."

Your reply: "I agree that the discount rate is difficult to measure precisely. But it is easy to see what we are *trying* to measure. The discount rate is the opportunity cost of investing in the project rather than in the capital market. In other words, instead of accepting a project, the firm can always give the cash to the shareholders and let them invest it in financial assets.

"Figure 5-1 shows the trade-off. The opportunity cost of taking the project is the return shareholders could have earned had they invested the funds on their own. When we discount the project's cash flows by the expected rate of return on compa-

Figure 5-1 The firm can either keep and reinvest cash or return it to investors. (Arrows represent possible cash flows or transfers.) If cash is reinvested, the opportunity cost is the expected rate of return that shareholders could have obtained by investing in financial assets.

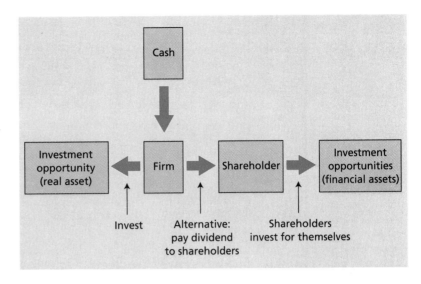

rable financial assets, we are measuring how much investors would be prepared to pay for your project."

"But which financial assets?" Vegetron's financial manager queries. "The fact that investors expect only 12 percent on AT&T stock does not mean that we should purchase Fly-by-Night Electronics if it offers 13 percent."

Your reply: "The opportunity-cost concept makes sense only if assets of equivalent risk are compared. In general, you should identify financial assets with risks equivalent to the project under consideration, estimate the expected rate of return on these assets, and use this rate as the opportunity cost."

5-2 NET PRESENT VALUE'S COMPETITORS

Let us hope that the financial manager is by now convinced of the correctness of the net present value rule. But it is possible that the manager has also heard of some alternative investment criteria and would like to know why you do not recommend any of them. Just so that you are prepared, we will now look at the three most popular alternatives to the NPV rule. These are:

1. Payback

2. Average return on book value

3. Internal rate of return

Later in the chapter we shall come across one further investment criterion. There are circumstances in which this measure has some special advantages.

As we look at these alternative criteria, it is worth keeping in mind the following key features of the net present value rule. First, the NPV rule recognizes that *a dollar today is worth more than a dollar tomorrow*, because the dollar today can be invested to start earning interest immediately. Any investment rule which does not recognize the *time value of money* cannot be sensible. Second, net present value depends solely on the *forecasted cash flows* from the project and the *opportunity cost of capital*.

Any investment rule which is affected by the manager's tastes, the company's choice of accounting method, the profitability of the company's existing business, or the profitability of other independent projects will lead to inferior decisions. Third, *because present values are all measured in today's dollars, you can add them up.* Therefore, if you have two projects A and B, the net present value of the combined investment is

$$NPV(A + B) = NPV(A) + NPV(B)$$

This additivity property has important implications. Suppose project B has a negative NPV. If you tack it onto project A, the joint project (A + B) will have a lower NPV than A on its own. Therefore, you are unlikely to be misled into accepting a poor project (B) just because it is packaged with a good one (A). As we shall see, the alternative measures do not have this additivity property. If you are not careful, you may be tricked into deciding that a package of a good and a bad project is better than the good project on its own.

5-3 PAYBACK

Companies frequently require that the initial outlay on any project should be recoverable within some specified cutoff period. The **payback** period of a project is found by counting the number of years it takes before cumulative forecasted cash flows equal the initial investment. Consider projects A and B:

CASH FLOWS, DOLLARS

Project	C_0	C_1	C_2	C_3	Payback Period, Years	NPV at 10%
A	−2,000	+2,000	0	0	1	−182
B	−2,000	+1,000	+1,000	+5,000	2	+3,492

Project A involves an initial investment of $2000 ($C_0 = -2000$) followed by a single cash inflow of $2000 in year 1. Suppose the opportunity cost of capital is 10 percent. Then project A has an NPV of −$182:

$$NPV(A) = -2000 + \frac{2000}{1.10} = -\$182$$

Project B also requires an initial investment of $2000 but produces a cash inflow of $1000 in years 1 and 2 and $5000 in year 3. At a 10 percent opportunity cost of capital project B has an NPV of +$3492:

$$NPV(B) = -2000 + \frac{1000}{1.10} + \frac{1000}{(1.10)^2} + \frac{5000}{(1.10)^3} = +\$3492$$

Thus the net present value rule tells us to reject project A and accept project B.

The Payback Rule

Now let us look at how rapidly each project pays back its initial investment. With project A you take 1 year to recover your $2000; with project B you take 2 years. If the firm used the payback *rule* with a cutoff period of 1 year, it would accept only project A; if it used the payback rule with a cutoff period of 2 or more years, it would accept both A and B. Therefore, regardless of the choice of cutoff period, the payback rule gives a different answer from the net present value rule.

The reason for the difference is that payback gives equal weight to all cash flows before the payback date and no weight at all to subsequent flows. For example, the following three projects all have a payback period of 2 years:

CASH FLOWS, DOLLARS

Project	C_0	C_1	C_2	C_3	NPV at 10%	Payback Period, Years
B	−2,000	+1,000	+1,000	+5,000	3,492	2
C	−2,000	0	+2,000	+5,000	3,409	2
D	−2,000	+1,000	+1,000	+100,000	74,867	2

The payback rule says that these projects are all equally attractive. But project B has a higher NPV than project C for *any* positive interest rate ($1000 in each of years 1 and 2 is more valuable than $2000 in year 2). And project D has a higher NPV than either B or C.

In order to use the payback rule a firm has to decide on an appropriate cutoff date. If it uses the same cutoff regardless of project life, it will tend to accept too many short-lived projects and too few long-lived ones. If, on average, the cutoff periods are too long, it will accept some projects with negative NPVs; if, on average, they are too short, it will reject some projects that have positive NPVs.

Many firms that use payback choose the cutoff period essentially by guesswork. It is possible to do better than that. If you know the typical pattern of cash flows, then you can find the cutoff period that would come closest to maximizing net present value.[2] However, this "optimal" cutoff point works only for those projects that have "typical" patterns of cash flows. So it is still better to use the net present value rule.

Discounted Payback

Some companies discount the cash flows before they compute the payback period. The **discounted-payback rule** asks, "How many periods does the project have to last in order to make sense in terms of net present value?" This modification to the payback rule surmounts the objection that equal weight is given to all flows before the cutoff date. However, the discounted-payback rule still takes no account of any cash flows after the cutoff date.

Discounted payback is a whisker better than undiscounted payback. It recognizes that a dollar at the beginning of the payback period is worth more than a dollar at the end of the payback period. This helps, but it may not help much. The discounted-payback rule still depends on the choice of an arbitrary cutoff date and it still ignores all cash flows after that date.

---

[2]If the inflows are, on average, spread evenly over the life of the project, the optimal cutoff for the payback rule is

$$\text{Optimal cutoff period} = \frac{1}{r} - \frac{1}{r(1+r)^n}$$

where n denotes the project life. This expression for the optimal payback was first noted in M. J. Gordon, "The Pay-Off Period and the Rate of Profit," *Journal of Business*, **28**:253–260 (October 1955).

5-4 AVERAGE RETURN ON BOOK VALUE

Some companies judge an investment project by looking at its **book rate of return.**
To calculate book rate of return it is necessary to divide the average forecasted profits of a project after depreciation and taxes by the average book value of the investment. This ratio is then measured against the book rate of return for the firm as a
whole or against some external yardstick, such as the average book rate of return for
the industry.

Table 5-1*a* shows projected income statements for project A over its 3-year life.
Its average net income is $2000 per year (we assume for simplicity that there are no
taxes). The required investment is $9000 at $t = 0$. This amount is then depreciated
at a constant rate of $3000 per year. So the book value of the new investment will
decline from $9000 in year 0 to zero in year 3:

	Year 0	Year 1	Year 2	Year 3
Gross book value of investment	$9,000	$9,000	$9,000	$9,000
Accumulated depreciation	0	3,000	6,000	9,000
Net book value of investment	$9,000	$6,000	$3,000	$ 0
		Average net book value = $4,500		

The average net income is $2000, and the average net investment is $4500. Therefore,
the average book rate of return is 2000/4500 = .44. Project A would be undertaken
if the firm's target book rate of return were less than 44 percent.[3]

This criterion suffers from several serious defects. First, because it considers only
the *average* return on book investment, there is no allowance for the fact that immediate receipts are more valuable than distant ones. Whereas payback gives no weight
to the more distant flows, return on book gives them too much weight. Thus in Table
5-1*b* we can introduce two projects, B and C, which have the same average book investment, the same average book income, and the same average book profitability as
project A. Yet A clearly has a higher NPV than B or C because a greater proportion
of the cash flows for project A occur in the early years.

Notice also that the average return on book depends on accounting income; it is
not based on the cash flows of a project. Cash flows and accounting income are often very different. For example, the accountant labels some cash outflows *capital investment* and others *operating expenses.* The operating expenses are, of course, deducted immediately from each year's income. The capital expenditures are depreciated
according to an arbitrary schedule chosen by the accountant. Then the depreciation
charge is deducted from each year's income. Thus the average return on book depends on which items the accountant treats as capital investments and how rapidly
they are depreciated. However, the accountant's decisions have nothing to do with
the cash flow[4] and therefore should not affect the decision to accept or reject.

A firm that uses average return on book has to decide on a yardstick for judging
a project. This decision is also arbitrary. Sometimes the firm uses its current book re-

---

[3]There are many variants on this rule. For example, some companies measure the *accounting return on cost,*
that is, the ratio of average profits before depreciation but after tax to the initial cost of the asset.

[4]Of course, the depreciation method used for tax purposes does have cash consequences which should be
taken into account in calculating NPV.

TABLE 5-1*a*

Computing the average book rate of return on an investment of $9000 in project A

	CASH FLOWS, DOLLARS		
Project A	Year 1	Year 2	Year 3
Revenue	12,000	10,000	8,000
Out-of-pocket cost	6,000	5,000	4,000
Cash flow	6,000	5,000	4,000
Depreciation	3,000	3,000	3,000
Net income	3,000	2,000	1,000

$$\text{Average book rate of return} = \frac{\text{average annual income}}{\text{average annual investment}} = \frac{2,000}{4,500} = .44$$

TABLE 5-1*b*

Projects A, B, and C all cost $9000 and produce an average income of $2000. Therefore, they all have a 44 percent book rate of return

	CASH FLOWS, DOLLARS		
Project	Year 1	Year 2	Year 3
A Cash flow	6,000	5,000	4,000
Net income	3,000	2,000	1,000
B Cash flow	5,000	5,000	5,000
Net income	2,000	2,000	2,000
C Cash flow	4,000	5,000	6,000
Net income	1,000	2,000	3,000

turn as a yardstick. In this case companies with high rates of return on their existing business may be led to reject good projects, and companies with low rates of return may be led to accept bad ones.

Payback is a bad rule. Average return on book is probably worse. It ignores the opportunity cost of money and is not based on the cash flows of a project, and the investment decision may be related to the profitability of the firm's existing business.

5-5 INTERNAL (OR DISCOUNTED-CASH-FLOW) RATE OF RETURN

Whereas payback and average return on book are ad hoc rules, internal rate of return has a much more respectable ancestry and is recommended in many finance texts. If, therefore, we dwell more on its deficiencies, it is not because they are more numerous but because they are less obvious.

In Chapter 2 we noted that net present value could also be expressed in terms of rate of return, which would lead to the following rule: "Accept investment opportunities offering rates of return in excess of their opportunity costs of capital." That statement, properly interpreted, is absolutely correct. However interpretation is not always easy for long-lived investment projects.

There is no ambiguity in defining the true rate of return of an investment that generates a single payoff after one period:

$$\text{Rate of return} = \frac{\text{payoff}}{\text{investment}} - 1$$

Alternatively, we could write down the NPV of the investment and find that discount rate which makes NPV = 0.

$$\text{NPV} = C_0 + \frac{C_1}{1 + \text{discount rate}} = 0$$

implies

$$\text{Discount rate} = \frac{C_1}{-C_0} - 1$$

Of course C_1 is the payoff and $-C_0$ the required investment, and so our two equations say exactly the same thing. *The discount rate that makes NPV = 0 is also the rate of return.*

Unfortunately, there is no wholly satisfactory way of defining the true rate of return of a long-lived asset. The best available concept is the so-called **discounted-cash-flow (DCF) rate of return** or **internal rate of return (IRR).** The internal rate of return is used frequently in finance. It can be a handy measure, but, as we shall see, if can also be a misleading measure. You should, therefore, know how to calculate it and how to use it properly.

The internal rate of return is defined as the rate of discount which makes NPV = 0. This means that to find the IRR for an investment project lasting T years, we must solve for IRR in the following expression:

$$\text{NPV} = C_0 + \frac{C_1}{1 + \text{IRR}} + \frac{C_2}{(1 + \text{IRR})^2} + \cdots + \frac{C_T}{(1 + \text{IRR})^T} = 0$$

Actual calculation of IRR usually involves trial and error. For example, consider a project which produces the following flows:

	Cash Flows, Dollars	
C_0	C_1	C_2
−4,000	+2,000	+4,000

The internal rate of return is IRR in the equation

$$\text{NPV} = -4000 + \frac{2000}{1 + \text{IRR}} + \frac{4000}{(1 + \text{IRR})^2} = 0$$

Let us arbitrarily try a zero discount rate. In this case NPV is not zero but +$2000:

$$NPV = -4000 + \frac{2000}{1.0} + \frac{4000}{(1.0)^2} = +\$2000$$

The NPV is positive; therefore, the IRR must be greater than zero. The next step might be to try a discount rate of 50 percent. In this case net present value is $-\$889$:

$$NPV = -4000 + \frac{2000}{1.50} + \frac{4000}{(1.50)^2} = -\$889$$

The NPV is negative; therefore, the IRR must be less than 50 percent. In Figure 5-2 we have plotted the net present values implied by a range of discount rates. From this we can see that a discount rate of 28 percent gives the desired net present value of zero. Therefore IRR is 28 percent.

The easiest way to calculate IRR, if you have to do it by hand, is to plot three or four combinations of NPV and discount rate on a graph like Figure 5-2, connect the points with a smooth line, and read off the discount rate at which NPV = 0. It is of course quicker and more accurate to use a computer or a specially programmed calculator, and this is what most companies do.

Now, the internal rate of return *rule* is to accept an investment project if the opportunity cost of capital is less than the internal rate of return. You can see the reasoning behind this idea if you look again at Figure 5-2. If the opportunity cost of capital is less than the 28 percent IRR, then the project has a *positive* NPV when discounted at the opportunity cost of capital. If it is equal to the IRR, the project has a *zero* NPV. And if it is greater than the IRR, the project has a *negative* NPV. Therefore, when we compare the opportunity cost of capital with the IRR on our project, we are effectively asking whether our project has a positive NPV. This is

Figure 5-2 This project costs $4000 and then produces cash inflows of $2000 in year 1 and $4000 in year 2. Its internal rate of return (IRR) is 28 percent, the rate of discount at which NPV is zero.

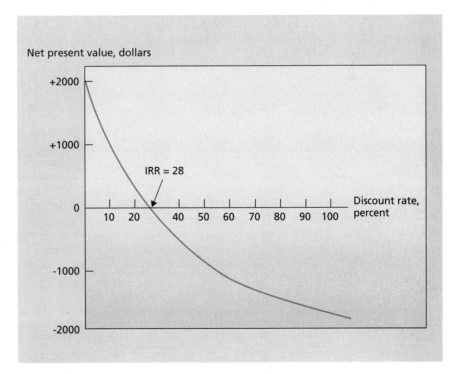

true not only for our example. The rule will give the same answer as the net present value rule *whenever the NPV of a project is a smoothly declining function of the discount rate.*[5]

Many firms use internal rate of return as a criterion in preference to net present value. We think that this is a pity. Although, properly stated, the two criteria are formally equivalent, the internal rate of return rule contains several pitfalls.

Pitfall 1— Lending or Borrowing?

Not all cash-flow streams have NPVs that decline as the discount rate increases. Consider the following projects A and B:

CASH FLOWS,
DOLLARS

Project	C_0	C_1	IRR, Percent	NPV at 10%
A	−1,000	+1,500	+50	+364
B	+1,000	−1,500	+50	−364

Each project has an IRR of 50 percent. (In other words, $-1000 + 1500/1.50 = 0$ *and* $+1000 - 1500/1.50 = 0$.)

Does this mean that they are equally attractive? Clearly not, for in the case of A, where we are initially paying out $1000, we are *lending* money at 50 percent; in the case of B, where we are initially receiving $1000, we are *borrowing* money at 50 percent. When we lend money, we want a *high* rate of return; when we borrow money, we want a *low* rate of return.

If you plot a graph like Figure 5-2 for project B, you will find that NPV increases as the discount rate increases. Obviously the internal rate of return rule, as we stated it above, won't work in this case; we have to look for an IRR *less* than the opportunity cost of capital.

This is straightforward enough, but now look at project C:

CASH FLOWS, DOLLARS

Project	C_0	C_1	C_2	C_3	IRR, Percent	NPV at 10%
C	+1,000	−3,600	+4,320	−1,728	+20	−.75

It turns out that project C has zero NPV at a 20 percent discount rate. If the opportunity cost of capital is 10 percent, that means the project is a good one. Or does it? In part, project C is like borrowing money, because we receive money now and pay it out in the first period; it is also partly like lending money because we pay out

---

[5] Here is a word of caution: Some people confuse the internal rate of return and the opportunity cost of capital because both appear as discount rates in the NPV formula. The internal rate of return is a *profitability measure* which depends solely on the amount and timing of the project cash flows. The opportunity cost of capital is a *standard of profitability* for the project which we use to calculate how much the project is worth. The opportunity cost of capital is established in capital markets. It is the expected rate of return offered by other assets equivalent in risk to the project being evaluated.

Figure 5-3 The net present value of project C increases as the discount rate increases.

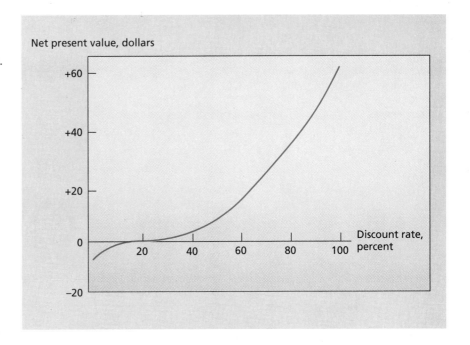

money in period 1 and recover it in period 2. Should we accept or reject? The only way to find the answer is to look at the net present value. Figure 5-3 shows that the NPV of our project *increases* as the discount rate increases. If the opportunity cost of capital is 10 percent (i.e., less than the IRR), the project has a very small negative NPV and we should reject.

Pitfall 2— Multiple Rates of Return

In most countries there is usually a short delay between the time that a company receives income and the time it pays tax on the income. Consider the case of Herbie Vore, who needs to assess a proposed advertising campaign by the vegetable canning company of which he is financial manager. The campaign involves an initial outlay of $1 million but is expected to increase pretax profits by $300,000 in each of the next five periods. The tax rate is 50 percent, and taxes are paid with a delay of one period. Thus the expected cash flows from the investment are as follows:

Cash Flows, Thousands of Dollars

	PERIOD						
	0	1	2	3	4	5	6
Pretax flow	−1,000	+300	+300	+300	+300	+300	
Tax		+500	−150	−150	−150	−150	−150
Net flow	−1,000	+800	+150	+150	+150	+150	−150

Note: The $1 million outlay in period 0 *reduces* the company's taxes in period 1 by $500,000; thus we enter +500 in year 1.

Figure 5-4
The advertising
campaign has
two internal
rates of return.
NPV = 0 when
the discount
rate is −50 per-
cent and when
it is +15.2 per-
cent.

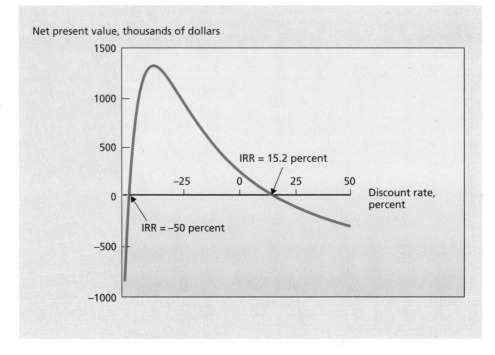

Mr. Vore calculates the project's IRR and its NPV as follows:

IRR, Percent	NPV at 10%
−50 *and* 15.2	74.9 or $74,900

Note that there are *two* discount rates that make NPV = 0. That is, *each* of the following statements holds:

$$\text{NPV} = -1000 + \frac{800}{.50} + \frac{150}{(.50)^2} + \frac{150}{(.50)^3} + \frac{150}{(.50)^4} + \frac{150}{(.50)^5} - \frac{150}{(.50)^6} = 0$$

and

$$\text{NPV} = -1000 + \frac{800}{1.152} + \frac{150}{(1.152)^2} + \frac{150}{(1.152)^3} + \frac{150}{(1.152)^4} + \frac{150}{(1.152)^5} - \frac{150}{(1.152)^6} = 0$$

In other words, the investment has an IRR of both −50 *and* 15.2 percent. Figure 5-4 shows how this comes about. As the discount rate increases, NPV initially rises and then declines. The reason for this is the double change in the sign of the cash-flow stream. There can be as many different internal rates of return for a project as there are changes in the sign of the cash flows.[6]

---

[6]By Descartes' "rule of signs" there can be as many different solutions to a polynomial as there are changes of sign. For a discussion of the problem of multiple rates of return, see J. H. Lorie and L. J. Savage, "Three Problems in Rationing Capital," *Journal of Business,* **28**:229–239 (October 1955); and E. Solomon, "The Arithmetic of Capital Budgeting," *Journal of Business,* **29**:124–129 (April 1956).

In our example the double change in sign was caused by a lag in tax payments, but this is not the only way that it can occur. For example, many projects involve substantial decommissioning costs. If you strip-mine coal, you may have to invest large sums to reclaim the land after the coal is mined. Thus a new mine creates an initial investment (negative cash flow up front), a series of positive cash flows, and an ending cash outflow for reclamation. The cash-flow stream changes sign twice, and mining companies typically see two IRRs.

As if this is not difficult enough, there are also cases in which *no* internal rate of return exists. For example, project D has a positive net present value at all discount rates:

CASH FLOWS, DOLLARS

Project	C_0	C_1	C_2	IRR, Percent	NPV at 10%
D	+1,000	−3,000	+2,500	None	+339

A number of adaptations of the IRR rule have been devised for such cases. Not only are they inadequate, they are unnecessary, for the simple solution is to use net present value.

Pitfall 3—Mutually Exclusive Projects

Firms often have to choose from among several alternative ways of doing the same job or using the same facility. In other words, they need to choose from among **mutually exclusive projects**. Here too the IRR rule can be misleading.

Consider projects E and F:

CASH FLOWS, DOLLARS

Project	C_0	C_1	IRR, Percent	NPV at 10%
E	−10,000	+20,000	100	+8.182
F	−20,000	+35,000	75	+11,818

Perhaps project E is a manually controlled machine tool and project F is the same tool with the addition of computer control. Both are good investments, but F has the higher NPV and is, therefore, better. However, the IRR rule seems to indicate that if you have to choose, you should go for E since it has the higher IRR. If you follow the IRR rule, you have the satisfaction of earning a 100 percent rate of return; if you follow the NPV rule, you are $11,818 richer.

You can salvage the IRR rule in these cases by looking at the internal rate of return on the incremental flows. Here is how to do it: First, consider the smaller project (E in our example). It has an IRR of 100 percent, which is well in excess of the 10 percent opportunity cost of capital. You know, therefore, that E is acceptable. You now ask yourself whether it is worth making the additional $10,000 investment in F. The incremental flows from undertaking F rather than E are as follows:

Figure 5-5 The IRR
of project G exceeds
that of project H, but
the net present value
of project G is higher
only if the discount
rate is greater than
15.6 percent.

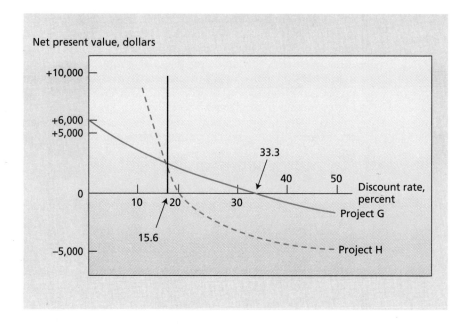

CASH FLOWS,
DOLLARS

Project	C_0	C_1	IRR, Percent	NPV at 10%
F–E	−10,000	+15,000	50	+3,636

The IRR on the incremental investment is 50 percent, which is also well in excess of the 10 percent opportunity cost of capital. So you should prefer project F to project E.[7]

Unless you look at the incremental expenditure, IRR is unreliable in ranking projects of different scale. It is also unreliable in ranking projects which offer different patterns of cash flow over time. For example, suppose the firm can take project G *or* project H but not both (ignore I for the moment):

CASH FLOWS, DOLLARS

Project	C_0	C_1	C_2	C_3	C_4	C_5	Etc.	IRR, Percent	NPV at 10%
G	−9,000	+6,000	+5,000	+4,000	0	0	. . .	33	3,592
H	−9,000	+1,800	+1,800	+1,800	+1,800	+1,800	. . .	20	9,000
I		−6,000	+1,200	+1,200	+1,200	+1,200	. . .	20	6,000

Project G has a higher IRR, but project H has the higher NPV. Figure 5-5 shows why the two rules give different answers. The solid line gives the net present value

---

[7] You may, however, find that you have jumped out of the frying pan into the fire. The series of incremental cash flows may involve several changes in sign. In this case there are likely to be multiple IRRs and you will be forced to use the NPV rule after all.

of project G at different rates of discount. Since a discount rate of 33 percent produces a net present value of zero, this is the internal rate of return for project G. Similarly, the dashed line shows the net present value of project H at different discount rates. The IRR of project H is 20 percent. (We assume project H's cash flows continue indefinitely.) Note that project H has a higher NPV so long as the opportunity cost of capital is less than 15.6 percent.

The reason that IRR is misleading is that the total cash inflow of project H is larger but tends to occur later. Therefore, when the discount rate is low, H has the higher NPV; when the discount rate is high, G has the higher NPV. (You can see from Figure 5-5 that the two projects have the *same* NPV when the discount rate is 15.6 percent.) The internal rates of return on the two projects tell us that at a discount rate of 20 percent H has a zero NPV (IRR = 20 percent) and G has a positive NPV. Thus if the opportunity cost of capital were 20 percent, investors would place a higher value on the shorter-lived project G. But in our example the opportunity cost of capital is not 20 percent but 10 percent. Investors are prepared to pay relatively high prices for longer-lived securities, and so they will pay a relatively high price for the longer-lived project. At a 10 percent cost of capital, an investment in G has an NPV of $9000 and an investment in H has an NPV of only $3592.[8]

This is a favorite example of ours. We have gotten many businesspeople's reaction to it. When asked to choose between G and H, many choose G. The reason seems to be the rapid payback generated by project G. In other words, they believe that if they take G, they will also be able to take a later project like I (note that I can be financed using the cash flows from G), whereas if they take H, they won't have money enough for I. In other words they implicitly assume that it is a *shortage of capital* which forces the choice between G and H. When this implicit assumption is brought out, they usually admit that H is better if there is no capital shortage.

But the introduction of capital constraints raises two further questions. The first stems from the fact that most of the executives preferring G to H work for firms that would have no difficulty raising more capital. Why would a manager at G.M., say, choose G on the grounds of limited capital? G.M. can raise plenty of capital and can take project I regardless of whether G or H is chosen; therefore I should not affect the choice between G and H. The answer seems to be that large firms usually impose capital budgets on divisions and subdivisions as a part of the firm's planning and control system. Since the system is complicated and cumbersome, the budgets are not easily altered, and so they are perceived as real constraints by middle management.

The second question is this. If there is a capital constraint, either real or self-imposed, should IRR be used to rank projects? The answer is no. The problem in this case is to find that package of investment projects which satisfies the capital constraint and has the largest net present value. The IRR rule will not identify this package. As we will show in the next section, the only practical and general way to do so is to use the technique of linear programming.

When we have to choose between projects G and H, it is easiest to compare the net present values. But if your heart is set on the IRR rule, you can use it as long as you look at the internal rate of return on the incremental flows. The procedure is exactly the same as we showed above. First, you check that project G has a satisfactory IRR. Then you look at the return on the additional investment in H.

---

[8]It is often suggested that the choice between the net present value rule and the internal rate of return rule should depend on the probable reinvestment rate. This is wrong. The prospective return on another *independent* investment should *never* be allowed to influence the investment decision. For a discussion of the reinvestment assumption see A. A. Alchian, "The Rate of Interest, Fisher's Rate of Return over Cost and Keynes' Internal Rate of Return." *American Economic Review*, **45**:938–942 (December 1955).

CASH FLOWS, DOLLARS

Project	C_0	C_1	C_2	C_3	C_4	C_5	Etc.	IRR, Percent	NPV at 10%
H–G	0	−4,200	−3,200	−2,200	+1,800	+1,800	. . .	15.6	+5,408

The IRR on the incremental investment in H is 15.6 percent. Since this is greater than the opportunity cost of capital, you should undertake H rather than G.

Pitfall 4— What Happens When We Can't Finesse the Term Structure of Interest Rates?

We have simplified our discussion of capital budgeting by assuming that the opportunity cost of capital is the same for all the cash flows, C_1, C_2, C_3, etc. Now this is not the right place to discuss the term structure of interest rates, but we must point out certain problems with the IRR rule that crop up when short-term interest rates are different from long-term rates.

Remember our most general formula for calculating net present value:

$$\text{NPV} = C_0 + \frac{C_1}{1 + r_1} + \frac{C_2}{(1 + r_2)^2} + \cdots$$

In other words, we discount C_1 at the opportunity cost of capital for 1 year, C_2 at the opportunity cost of capital for 2 years, and so on. The IRR rule tells us to accept a project if the IRR is greater than the opportunity cost of capital. But what do we do when we have several opportunity costs? Do we compare IRR with r_1, r_2, r_3, . . . ? Actually we would have to compute a complex weighted average of these rates to obtain a number comparable to IRR.

What does this mean for capital budgeting? It means trouble for the IRR rule whenever the term structure of interest rates becomes important.[9] In a situation where it is important, we have to compare the project IRR with the expected IRR (yield to maturity) offered by a traded security that (1) is equivalent in risk to the project and (2) offers the same time pattern of cash flows as the project. Such a comparison is easier said than done. It is much better to forget about IRR and just calculate NPV.

Many firms use the IRR, thereby implicitly assuming that there is no difference between short-term and long-term rates of interest. They do this for the same reason that we have so far finessed the term structure: simplicity.[10]

The Verdict on IRR

We have given four examples of things that can go wrong with IRR. We gave only one example of what could go wrong with payback or return on book. Does this mean that IRR is four times worse than the other two rules? Quite the contrary. There is little point in dwelling on the deficiencies of payback or return on book. They are clearly ad hoc rules which often lead to silly conclusions. The IRR rule has a much more respectable ancestry. It is a less easy rule to use than NPV, but, used properly, it gives the same answer.

---

[9]The source of the difficulty is that the IRR is a derived figure without any simple economic interpretation. If we wish to define it, we can do no more than say that it is the discount rate which applied to all cash flows makes NPV = 0. The IRR is a complex average of the separate interest rates. The problem here is not that the IRR is a nuisance to calculate but that it is not a very useful number to have.

[10]In Chapter 9, we will look at some other cases in which it would be misleading to use the same discount rate for both short-term and long-term cash flows.

5-6 CHOOSING THE CAPITAL EXPENDITURE PROGRAM WHEN RESOURCES ARE LIMITED

Our entire discussion of methods of capital budgeting has rested on the proposition that the wealth of a firm's shareholders is highest if the firm accepts *every* project that has a positive net present value. Suppose, however, that there are limitations on the investment program that prevent the company from undertaking all such projects. Economists call this *capital rationing*. When capital is rationed, we need a method of selecting the package of projects that is within the company's resources yet gives the highest possible net present value.

An Easy Problem in Capital Rationing

Let us start with a simple example. The opportunity cost of capital is 10 percent, and our company has the following opportunities:

	CASH FLOWS, MILLIONS OF DOLLARS			
Project	C_0	C_1	C_2	NPV at 10%
A	−10	+30	+5	21
B	−5	+5	+20	16
C	−5	+5	+15	12

All three projects are attractive, but suppose that the firm is limited to spending $10 million. In that case, it can invest *either* in project A *or* in projects B and C, but it cannot invest in all three. Although individually B and C have lower net present values than project A, when taken together they have the higher net present value. Here we cannot choose between projects solely on the basis of net present values. When funds are limited, we need to concentrate on getting the biggest bang for our buck. In other words, we must pick the projects that offer the highest net present value per dollar of initial outlay. This ratio is known as the **profitability index:**[11]

$$\text{Profitability index} = \frac{\text{net present value}}{\text{investment}}$$

For our three projects the profitability index is calculated as follows:[12]

Project	Investment, Millions of Dollars	NPV, Millions of Dollars	Profitability Index
A	10	21	2.1
B	5	16	3.2
C	5	12	2.4

---

[11]If a project requires outlays in two or more periods, the denominator should be the present value of the outlays. (Some companies do not discount the benefits or costs before calculating the profitability index. The less said about these companies the better.)

[12]Sometimes the profitability index is defined as the ratio of present value to initial outlay—that is, as PV/investment. This measure is also known as the benefit-cost ratio. To calculate the benefit-cost ratio, we simply add 1.0 to each profitability index. Project rankings are unchanged.

Project B has the highest profitability index and C the next highest. Therefore, if our budget limit is $10 million, we should accept these two projects.[13]

Unfortunately, there are some limitations to this simple ranking method. One of the most serious is that it breaks down whenever more than one resource is rationed. For example, suppose that the firm can raise $10 million for investment in *each* of years 0 and 1 and that the menu of possible projects is expanded to include an investment next year in project D:

CASH FLOWS, MILLIONS OF DOLLARS

Project	C_0	C_1	C_2	NPV at 10%	Profitability Index
A	−10	+30	+5	21	2.1
B	−5	+5	+20	16	3.2
C	−5	+5	+15	12	3.4
D	0	−40	+60	13	0.4

One strategy is to accept projects B and C; however, if we do this, we cannot also accept D, which costs more than our budget limit for period 1. An alternative is to accept project A in period 0. Although this has a lower net present value than the combination of B and C, it provides a $30 million positive cash flow in period 1. When this is added to the $10 million budget, we can also afford to undertake D next year. A and D have *lower* profitability indexes than B and C, but they have a *higher* total net present value.

The reason that ranking on the profitability index fails in this example is that resources are constrained in each of two periods. In fact, this ranking method is inadequate whenever there is *any* other constraint on the choice of projects. This means that it cannot cope with cases in which two projects are mutually exclusive or in which one project is dependent on another.

....

*Some More Elaborate Capital Rationing Models

The simplicity of the profitability-index method may sometimes outweigh its limitations. For example, it may not pay to worry about expenditures in subsequent years if you have only a hazy notion of future capital availability or investment opportunities. But there are also circumstances in which the limitations of the profitability-index method are intolerable. For such occasions we need a more general method for solving the capital rationing problem.

We begin by restating the problem just described. Suppose that we were to accept proportion x_A of project A in our example. Then the net present value of our investment in the project would be $21x_A$. Similarly, the net present value of our investment in project B can be expressed as $16x_B$, and so on. Our objective is to select the set of projects with the highest *total* net present value. In other words we wish to find the values of x that maximize

---

[13]If a project has a positive profitability index, it must also have a positive NPV. Therefore, firms sometimes use the profitability index to select projects when capital is *not* limited. However, like the IRR, the profitability index can be misleading when used to choose between mutually exclusive projects. For example, suppose you were forced to choose between (1) investing $100 in a project whose payoffs have a present value of $200, or (2) investing $1 million in a project whose payoffs have a present value of $1.5 million. The first investment has the higher profitability index; the second makes you richer.

$$NPV = 21x_A + 16x_B + 12x_C + 13x_D$$

Our choice of projects is subject to several constraints. First, total cash outflow in period 0 must not be greater than $10 million. In other words,

$$10x_A + 5x_B + 5x_C + 0x_D \leq 10$$

Similarly, total outflow in period 1 must not be greater than $10 million:

$$-30x_A - 5x_B - 5x_C + 40x_D \leq 10$$

Finally, we cannot invest a negative amount in a project, and we cannot purchase more than one of each. Therefore we have

$$0 \leq x_A \leq 1, \qquad 0 \leq x_B \leq 1, \ldots$$

Collecting all these conditions, we can summarize the problem as follows:

- Maximize $21x_A + 16x_B + 12x_C + 13x_D$
- Subject to

$$10x_A + 5x_B + 5x_C + 0x_D \leq 10$$
$$-30x_A - 5x_B - 5x_C + 40x_D \leq 10$$
$$0 \leq x_A \leq 1, \qquad 0 \leq x_B \leq 1, \ldots$$

One way to tackle such a problem is to keep selecting different values for the x's, noting which combination both satisfies the constraints and gives the highest net present value. But it's smarter to recognize that the equations above constitute a linear programming (LP) problem. It can be handed to a computer equipped to solve LPs.

The answer given by the LP method is somewhat different from the one we obtained earlier, Instead of investing in one unit of project A and one of project D, we are told to take half of project A, all of project B, and three-quarters of D. The reason is simple. The computer is a dumb, but obedient, pet, and since we did not tell it that the x's had to be whole numbers, it saw no reason to make them so. By accepting "fractional" projects, it is possible to increase NPV by $2.25 million. For many purposes this is quite appropriate. If project A represents an investment in 1000 square feet of warehouse space or in 1000 tons of steel plate, it might be feasible to accept 500 square feet or 500 tons, and quite reasonable to assume that cash flow would be reduced proportionately. If, however, project A is a single crane or oil well, such fractional investments make little sense.

When fractional projects are not feasible, we can use a form of linear programming known as *integer* (or *zero-one*) *programming*, which limits all the x's to integers. Unfortunately, integer programs are less common and more awkward to use.

Uses of Capital Rationing Models

Linear programming models seem tailor-made for solving capital budgeting problems when resources are limited. Why then are they not universally accepted either in theory or in practice? One reason is that these models are often not cheap to use. We know of an oil company that spent over $4 million in 1 year on an investment planning model using integer programming. While linear programming is considerably cheaper in terms of computer time, it cannot be used when large, indivisible projects are involved.

Second, as with any sophisticated long-range planning tool there is the general problem of getting good data. It is just not worth applying costly, sophisticated methods to poor data. Furthermore, these models are based on the assumption that all future investment opportunities are known. In reality, the discovery of investment ideas is an unfolding process.

Our most serious misgivings center on the basic assumption that capital is limited. When we come to discuss company financing, we shall see that most firms do not face capital rationing and can raise very large sums of money on fair terms. Why then do many company presidents tell their subordinates that capital is limited? If they are right, the capital market is seriously imperfect. What then are they doing maximizing NPV?[14] We might be tempted to suppose that if capital is not rationed, they do not *need* to use the LP model and, if it is rationed, then surely they *ought* not to use it. But that would be too quick a judgment. Let us look at this problem more deliberately.

SOFT RATIONING.   Many firms' capital constraints are "soft." They reflect no imperfections in capital markets. Instead they are provisional limits adopted by management as an aid to financial control.

Some ambitious divisional managers habitually overstate their investment opportunities. Rather than trying to distinguish which projects really are worthwhile, headquarters may find it simpler to impose an upper limit on divisional expenditures and thereby force the divisions to set their own priorities. In such instances budget limits are a rough but effective way of dealing with biased cash-flow forecasts. In other cases management may believe that very rapid corporate growth could impose intolerable strains on management and the organization. Since it is difficult to quantify such constraints explicitly, the budget limit may be used as a proxy.

Because such budget limits have nothing to do with any inefficiency in the capital market, there is no contradiction in using an LP model in the division to maximize net present value subject to the budget constraint. On the other hand, there is not much point in elaborate selection procedures if the cash-flow forecasts of the division are seriously biased.

Even if capital is not rationed, other resources may be. The availability of management time, skilled labor, or even other capital equipment often constitutes an important constraint on a company's growth. In the Appendix to this chapter we show you how the programming model that we have described can be extended to incorporate such constraints. And we also show how they may be used to cope with project interactions.

HARD RATIONING.   Soft rationing should never cost the firm anything. If capital constraints become tight enough to hurt—in the sense that projects with significant positive NPVs are passed up—then the firm raises more money and loosens the constraint. But what if it *can't* raise more money—what if it faces *hard* rationing?

Hard rationing implies market imperfections, but that does not necessarily mean we have to throw away net present value as a criterion for capital budgeting. It depends on the nature of the imperfection.

Arizona Aquaculture, Inc. (AAI), borrows as much as the banks will lend it, yet it still has good investment opportunities. This is not hard rationing so long as AAI can issue stock. But perhaps it can't. Perhaps the founder and majority shareholder vetoes the idea from fear of losing control of the firm: Perhaps a stock issue would bring costly red tape or legal complications.[15]

---

[14]Don't forget that we had to assume perfect capital markets to derive the NPV rule.

[15]A majority owner who is "locked in" and has much personal wealth tied up in AAI may be effectively cut off from capital markets. The NPV rule may not make sense to such an owner, though it will to the other shareholders.

This does not invalidate the NPV rule. AAI's *shareholders* can borrow or lend, sell their shares, or buy more. They have free access to security markets. The type of portfolio they hold is independent of AAI's financing or investment decisions. The only way AAI can help its shareholders is to make them richer. Thus AAI should invest its available cash in the package of projects having the largest aggregate net present value.

A barrier between the firm and capital markets does not undermine net present value so long as the barrier is the *only* market imperfection. The important thing is that the firm's *shareholders* have free access to well-functioning capital markets.

The method of net present value *is* undermined when imperfections restrict shareholders' portfolio choice. Suppose that Nevada Aquaculture, Inc. (NAI), is solely owned by its founder, Alexander Turbot. Mr. Turbot has no cash or credit remaining, but he is convinced that expansion of his operation is a high-NPV investment. He has tried to sell stock but has found that prospective investors, skeptical of prospects for fish farming in the desert, offer him much less than he thinks his firm is worth. For Mr. Turbot capital markets hardly exist. It makes little sense for him to discount the prospective cash flows at a market opportunity cost of capital.

5-7 SUMMARY

If you are going to persuade your company to use the net present value rule, you must be prepared to explain why other rules do *not* give correct decisions. That is why we have examined three alternative investment criteria in this chapter.

Some companies use the payback method to make investment decisions. In other words, they accept only those projects that recover their initial investment within some specified period. Payback is an ad hoc rule. It ignores the order in which cash flows come within the payback period, and it ignores subsequent cash flows entirely. It therefore takes no account of the opportunity cost of capital.

The simplicity of payback makes it an easy device for *describing* investment projects. Managers talk casually about "quick-payback" projects in the same way that investors talk about "high-P/E" common stocks. The fact that managers talk about the payback periods of projects does not mean that the payback rule governs their decisions. Some managers *do* use payback in judging capital investments. Why they rely on such a grossly oversimplified concept is a puzzle.

Some firms use average return on book value. In this case the company must decide which cash payments are capital expenditures and must pick appropriate depreciation schedules. It must then calculate the ratio of average income to the average book value of the investment and compare it with the company's target return. Average return on book is another ad hoc method. Since it ignores whether the income occurs next year or next century, it takes no account of the opportunity cost of money.

The internal rate of return (IRR) is defined as the rate of discount at which a project would have zero NPV. It is a handy measure and widely used in finance; you should therefore know how to calculate it. The IRR rule states that companies should accept any investment offering an IRR in excess of the opportunity cost of capital. The IRR rule is, like net present value, a technique based on discounted cash flows. It will, therefore, give the correct answer if properly used. The problem is that it is easily misapplied. There are four things to look out for:

1. *Lending or borrowing?* If a project offers positive cash flows followed by negative flows, NPV *rises* as the discount rate is increased. You should accept such projects if their IRR is *less* than the opportunity cost of capital.

2. *Multiple rates of return.* If there is more than one change in the sign of the cash flows, the project may have several IRRs or no IRR at all.

3. *Mutually exclusive projects.* The IRR rule may give the wrong ranking of mutually exclusive projects that differ in economic life or in scale of required investment. If you insist on using IRR to rank mutually exclusive projects, you must examine the IRR on each additional unit of investment.

4. *Short-term interest rates may be different from long-term rates.* The IRR rule requires you to compare the project's IRR with the opportunity cost of capital. But sometimes there is an opportunity cost of capital for 1-year cash flows, a different cost of capital for 2-year cash flows, and so on. In these cases there is no simple yardstick for evaluating the IRR of a project.

If you are going to the expense of collecting cash-flow forecasts, you might as well use them properly. Ad hoc criteria should therefore have no role in the firm's decisions, and the net present value rule should be employed in preference to other techniques. Having said that, we must be careful not to exaggerate the payoff of proper technique. Technique is important, but it is by no means the only determinant of the success of a capital expenditure program. If the forecasts of cash flows are biased, even the most careful application of the net present value rule may fail.

In developing the NPV rule, we assumed that the company can maximize shareholder wealth by accepting every project that is worth more than it costs. But, if capital is strictly limited, then it may not be possible to take every project with a positive NPV. If capital is rationed in only one period, then the firm should follow a simple rule: Calculate each project's profitability index, which is the project's net present value per dollar of investment. Then pick the projects with the highest profitability indexes until you run out of capital. Unfortunately, this procedure fails when capital is rationed in more than one period or when there are other constraints on project choice. The only general solution is linear or integer programming.

"Hard" capital rationing always reflects a market imperfection—a barrier between the firm and capital markets. If that barrier also implies that the firm's shareholders lack free access to a well-functioning capital market, the very foundations of net present value crumble. Fortunately, hard rationing is rare for corporations in the United States. Many firms do use "soft" capital rationing, however. That is, they set up self-imposed limits as a means of financial planning and control.

APPENDIX: SOME EMBELLISHMENTS TO THE CAPITAL RATIONING MODEL

In Section 5-6 we showed that when capital is rationed you can set up the investment decision as a linear programming problem. In this appendix we describe some embellishments to these models, and we show how you can use them to cope with other resource constraints and project interactions.

Cash Carry-Forward

A plant manager who is forced to return the unspent part of an annual capital allocation may be goaded into a substantial year-end investment in pink carpeting for the foundry floor or other equally silly assets. (How can you argue for a high budget next year if there's money left over this year?) Headquarters can alleviate this problem by permitting the manager to carry forward any unspent balance. (Then the manager could at least wait until January and get a better selection of carpet colors.) Let us take the sample problem that we described in Section 5-6. To incorporate the possibility of cash carry-forward, we simply need to add another term to our spending constraint. Let s denote funds transferred from year 0 to year 1 and let them earn interest at the rate r. Then we can rewrite our constraint for year 0 as

$$10x_A + 5x_B + 5x_C + 0x_D + s = 10$$

Similarly, the constraint for year 1 becomes

$$-30x_A - 5x_B - 5x_C + 40x_D \leq 10 + (1 + r)s$$

Since carrying forward a negative amount is equivalent to borrowing, we will probably wish to add the constraint $s \geq 0$.

Mutually Exclusive and Contingent Projects

Suppose now that projects B and C are mutually exclusive. We can take care of this in an *integer* program by specifying that our *total* investment in the two projects cannot be greater than 1:

$$x_B + x_C \leq 1, \qquad x_B, x_C = 0 \text{ or } 1$$

In other words, if x_B is 1, x_C must be 0; if x_C is 1, x_B must be 0.

Suppose next that project D is an attachment to project A, and we cannot accept D *unless* we also accept A. In this case we need to add

$$x_D - x_A \leq 0 \qquad x_D, x_A = 0 \text{ or } 1$$

In other words, if x_A is 1, x_D can be 0 *or* 1; but if x_A is 0, x_D must likewise be 0.

Constraints on Non-financial Resources

Money may not be the only scarce resource. Each of our projects may require services from a 12-person technical design department. If project A would employ three designers, project B two, and so on, we would need to add a constraint like

$$3x_A + 2x_B + 8x_C + 3x_D \leq 12$$

Sometimes it is appropriate to place constraints on the total increase in physical capacity. Suppose that projects A and C produce four and three units, respectively, of the same product. If the company is unable to sell more than five units, it is necessary to add

$$4x_A + 3x_C \leq 5$$

We could go on—but you get the idea.

Further Reading

Most capital budgeting texts contain a discussion of alternative budgeting criteria. See, for example:
H. Bierman, Jr., and S. Smidt: *The Capital Budgeting Decision*, 8th ed., Macmillan Company, New York, 1992.

Classic articles on the internal rate of return rule include:
J. H. Lorie and L. J. Savage: "Three Problems in Rationing Capital," *Journal of Business*, **28**:229–239 (October 1955).
E. Solomon: "The Arithmetic of Capital Budgeting Decisions," *Journal of Business*, **29**:124–129 (April 1956).
A. A. Alchian: "The Rate of Interest, Fisher's Rate of Return over Cost and Keynes' Internal Rate of Return," *American Economic Review*, **45**:938–942 (December 1955).

The classic treatment of linear programming applied to capital budgeting is:
H. M. Weingartner: *Mathematical Programming and the Analysis of Capital Budgeting Problems*, Prentice-Hall, Inc., Englewood Cliffs, N.J., 1963.

There is a long scholarly controversy on whether capital constraints invalidate the NPV rule. Weingartner has reviewed this literature:

H. M. Weingartner: "Capital Rationing: *n* Authors in Search of a Plot," *Journal of Finance,* **32**:1403–1432 (December 1977).

Quiz

1. What is the opportunity cost of capital supposed to represent? Give a concise definition.

2. (*a*) What is the payback period on each of the following projects?

CASH FLOWS, DOLLARS

Project	C_0	C_1	C_2	C_3	C_4
A	−5,000	+1,000	+1,000	+3,000	0
B	−1,000	0	+1,000	+2,000	+3,000
C	−5,000	+1,000	+1,000	+3,000	+5,000

   (*b*) *Given* that you wish to use the payback rule with a cutoff period of 2 years, which projects would you accept?

   (*c*) If you use a cutoff period of 3 years, which projects would you accept?

   (*d*) If the opportunity cost of capital is 10 percent, which projects have positive NPVs?

   (*e*) "Payback gives too much weight to cash flows that occur after the cutoff date." True or false?

   (*f*) "If a firm uses a single cutoff period for all projects, it is likely to accept too many short-lived projects." True or false?

   (*g*) If the firm uses the discounted-payback rule, will it accept any negative-NPV projects? Will it turn down positive-NPV projects? Explain.

3. A machine costs $8000 and is expected to produce profit before depreciation of $2500 in each of years 1 and 2 and $3500 in each of years 3 and 4. Assuming that the machine is depreciated at a constant rate of $2000 a year and that there are no taxes, what is the average return on book?

4. True or false? Why?

   (*a*) "The average return on book rule gives too much weight to the later cash flows."

   (*b*) "If companies use their existing return on book as a yardstick for new investments, successful companies will tend to undertake too much investment."

5. (*a*) Calculate the net present value of the following project for discount rates of 0, 50, and 100 percent:

Cash Flows, Dollars

C_0	C_1	C_2
−6,750	+4,500	+18,000

   (*b*) What is the IRR of the project?

6. Consider projects A and B:

CASH FLOWS, DOLLARS

Project	C_0	C_1	C_2	IRR, Percent
A	−4,000	+2,410	+2,930	21
B	−2,000	+1,310	+1,720	31

(*a*) The opportunity cost of capital is less than 10 percent. Use the IRR rule to determine which project or projects you should accept (i) if you can undertake both, and (ii) if you can undertake only one.

(*b*) Suppose that project A has an NPV of $690 and project B has an NPV of $657. What is the NPV of the $2000 incremental investment in A?

7. Projects C and D both involve the same outlay and offer the same IRR, which exceeds the opportunity cost of capital. The cash flows generated by project C are larger than those of D but tend to occur later. Which project has the higher NPV?

8. You have the chance to participate in a project that produces the following cash flows:

Cash Flows, Dollars

C_0	C_1	C_2
+5,000	+4,000	−11,000

The internal rate of return is 13 percent. If the opportunity cost of capital is 10 percent, would you accept the offer?

9. Suppose you have the following investment opportunities, but only $100,000 available for investment. Which projects should you take?

Project	NPV	Investment
1	5,000	10,000
2	5,000	5,000
3	10,000	90,000
4	15,000	60,000
5	15,000	75,000
6	3,000	15,000

10. What is the difference between "hard" and "soft" capital rationing? Does soft rationing mean the manager should stop trying to maximize NPV? How about hard rationing?

Questions and Problems

· ·

1. Consider the following projects:

CASH FLOWS, DOLLARS

Project	C_0	C_1	C_2	C_3	C_4	C_5
A	−1,000	+1,000	0	0	0	0
B	−2,000	+1,000	+1,000	+4,000	+1,000	+1,000
C	−3,000	+1,000	+1,000	0	+1,000	+1,000

(a) If the opportunity cost of capital is 10 percent, which projects have a positive NPV?

(b) Calculate the payback period for each project.

(c) Which project(s) would a firm using the payback rule accept if the cutoff period were 3 years?

2. Project A (shown in Table 5-1a) has undergone some revisions. The initial investment has been reduced to $6,000, and the firm proposes to depreciate this investment by $2000 a year. Operating costs unfortunately have increased by $1000 a year. If the opportunity cost of capital is 7 percent, how do these changes alter the NPV of the project? How do they affect the average return on book?

3. Consider a project with the following cash flows:

C_0	C_1	C_2
−100	+200	−75

(a) How many internal rates of return does this project have?

(b) The opportunity cost of capital is 20 percent. Is this an attractive project? Briefly explain.

4. Respond to the following comments:

(a) "We like to use payback principally as a way of coping with risk."

(b) "The great merit of the IRR rule is that one does not have to think about what is an appropriate discount rate."

5. The payback rule is still used by many firms despite its acknowledged theoretical shortcomings. Why do you think this is so?

6. Unfortunately, your chief executive officer refuses to accept any investments in plant expansion that do not return their original investment in 4 years or less. That is, he insists on a *payback rule* with a *cutoff period* of 4 years. As a result, attractive long-lived projects are being turned down.

The CEO is willing to switch to a *discounted payback rule* with the same 4-year cutoff period. Would this be an improvement? Explain.

7. Consider the following two mutually exclusive projects:

CASH FLOWS, DOLLARS

Project	C_0	C_1	C_2	C_3
A	−100	+60	+60	0
B	−100	0	0	+140

(a) Calculate the NPV of each project for discount rates of 0, 10, and 20 percent. Plot these on a graph with NPV on the vertical axis and discount rate on the horizontal.
(b) What is the approximate IRR for each project?
(c) In what circumstances should the company accept project A?
(d) Calculate the NPV of the incremental investment (B − A) for discount rates of 0, 10, and 20 percent. Plot these on your graph. Show that the circumstances in which you would accept A are also those in which the IRR on the incremental investment is less than the opportunity cost of capital.

8. Mr. Cyrus Clops, the president of Giant Enterprises, has to make a choice between two possible investments:

CASH FLOWS,
THOUSANDS OF DOLLARS

Project	C_0	C_1	C_2	IRR, Percent
A	−400	+241	+293	21
B	−200	+131	+172	31

The opportunity cost of capital is 9 percent. Mr. Clops is tempted to take B, which has the higher IRR.
(a) Explain to Mr. Clops why this is not the correct procedure.
(b) Show him how to adapt the IRR rule to choose the best project.
(c) Show him that this project also has the higher NPV.

9. The Titanic Shipbuilding Company has a noncancelable contract to build a small cargo vessel. Construction involves a cash outlay of $250,000 at the end of each of the next 2 years. At the end of the third year the company will receive payment of $650,000. The company can speed up construction by working an extra shift. In this case there will be a cash outlay of $550,000 at the end of the first year followed by a cash payment of $650,000 at the end of the second year. Use the IRR rule to show the (approximate) range of opportunity costs of capital at which the company should work the extra shift.

10. Look again at projects E and F in Section 5-5. Assume that the projects are mutually exclusive and that the opportunity cost of capital is 10 percent.
(a) Calculate the profitability index for each project.
(b) Show how the profitability-index rule can be used to select the superior project.

11. In 1983 wealthy investors were offered a scheme that would allow them to postpone taxes. The scheme involved a debt-financed purchase of a fleet of beer delivery trucks, which were then leased to a local distributor. The cash flows were as follows:

Year	Cash Flow	
0	−21,750	
1	+7,861	
2	+8,317	
3	+7,188	Tax savings
4	+6,736	
5	+6,231	
6	−5,340	
7	−5,972	More tax paid later
8	−6,678	
9	−7,468	
10	+12,578	Salvage value

Calculate the approximate IRRs. Is the project attractive at a 14 percent opportunity cost of capital?

12. Borghia Pharmaceuticals has $1 million allocated for capital expenditures. Which of the following projects should the company accept to stay within the $1 million budget? How much does the budget limit cost the company in terms of its market value? The opportunity cost of capital for each project is 11 percent.

Project	Investment, Thousands of Dollars	NPV, Thousands of Dollars	IRR, Percent
1	300	66	17.2
2	200	−4	10.7
3	250	43	16.6
4	100	14	12.1
5	100	7	11.8
6	350	63	18.0
7	400	48	13.5

6

Making Investment Decisions with the Net Present Value Rule

We hope that by now you are convinced that wise investment decisions are based on the net present value rule. In this chapter we can think about how to apply the rule to practical investment problems. Our task is twofold. The first issue is to decide what should be discounted. We know the answer in principle: discount cash flows. But useful forecasts of cash flows do not arrive on a silver platter. Often the financial manager has to make do with raw data supplied by specialists in product design, production, marketing, and so on, and must check such information for relevance, completeness, consistency, and accuracy and then pull everything together into a usable forecast.

Our second task is to explain how the net present value rule should be used when there are project interactions. These occur when a decision about one project cannot be separated from a decision about another. Project interactions can be extremely complex. We will make no attempt to analyze every possible case. But we will work through most of the simple cases, as well as a few examples of medium complexity.

6-1 WHAT TO DISCOUNT

Up to this point we have been concerned mainly with the mechanics of discounting and with the various methods of project appraisal. We have had almost nothing to say about the problem of *what* one should discount. When you are faced with this problem, you should always stick to three general rules:

1. Only cash flow is relevant.
2. Always estimate cash flows on an incremental basis.
3. Be consistent in your treatment of inflation.

We will discuss each of these rules in turn.

Only Cash Flow Is Relevant

The first and most important point is that the net present value rule is stated in terms of cash flows. Cash flow is the simplest possible concept; it is just the difference between dollars received and dollars paid out. Many people nevertheless confuse cash flow with accounting profits.

Accountants *start* with "dollars in" and "dollars out," but in order to obtain accounting income they adjust these data in two important ways. First, they try to show profit as it is *earned* rather than when the company and the customer get around to paying their bills. Second, they sort cash outflows into two categories: current expenses and capital expenses. They deduct current expenses when calculating profit but do *not* deduct capital expenses. Instead they "depreciate" capital expenses over a number of years and deduct the annual depreciation charge from profits. As a result of these procedures, profits include some cash flows and exclude others, and they are reduced by depreciation charges, which are not cash flows at all.

It is not always easy to translate the customary accounting data back into actual dollars—dollars you can buy beer with. If you are in doubt about what is a cash flow, simply count the dollars coming in and take away the dollars going out. Don't assume without checking that you can find cash flow by simple manipulation of accounting data.

You should always estimate cash flows on an after-tax basis. Some firms do not deduct tax payments. They try to offset this mistake by discounting the cash flows before taxes at a rate higher than the opportunity cost of capital. Unfortunately, there is no reliable formula for making such adjustments to the discount rate.

You should also make sure that cash flows are recorded *only when they occur* and not when the work is undertaken or the liability incurred. For example, taxes should be discounted from their actual payment date, not from the time when the tax liability is recorded in the firm's books.

Estimate Cash Flows on an Incremental Basis

The value of a project depends on *all* the additional cash flows that follow from project acceptance. Here are some things to watch for when you are deciding which cash flows should be included:

DO NOT CONFUSE AVERAGE WITH INCREMENTAL PAYOFFS.   Most managers naturally hesitate to throw good money after bad. For example, they are reluctant to invest more money in a losing division. But occasionally you will encounter "turnaround" opportunities in which the *incremental* NPV on investment in a loser is strongly positive.

Conversely, it does not always make sense to throw good money after good. A division with an outstanding past profitability record may have run out of good opportunities. You would not pay a large sum for a 20-year-old horse, sentiment aside, regardless of how many races that horse had won or how many champions it had sired.

Here is another example illustrating the difference between average and incremental returns: Suppose that a railroad bridge is in urgent need of repair. With the bridge the railroad can continue to operate; without the bridge it can't. In this case the payoff from the repair work consists of all the benefits of operating the railroad. The incremental NPV of the investment may be enormous. Of course, these benefits should be net of all other costs and all subsequent repairs; otherwise the company may be misled into rebuilding an unprofitable railroad piece by piece.

INCLUDE ALL INCIDENTAL EFFECTS.   It is important to include all incidental effects on the remainder of the business. For example, a branch line for a railroad may have a negative NPV when considered in isolation, but still be a worthwhile investment when one allows for the additional traffic that it brings to the main line.

DO NOT FORGET WORKING CAPITAL REQUIREMENTS.   **Net working capital** (often referred to simply as *working capital*) is the difference between a company's short-term assets and liabilities. The principal short-term assets are cash, accounts receivable (customers' unpaid bills), and inventories of raw materials and finished goods. The principal short-term liabilities are accounts payable (bills that *you* have not paid). Most projects entail an additional investment in working capital. This investment should, therefore, be recognized in your cash-flow forecasts. By the same token, when the project comes to an end, you can usually recover some of the investment. This is treated as a cash inflow.

FORGET SUNK COSTS.   Sunk costs are like spilled milk: They are past and irreversible outflows. Because sunk costs are bygones, they cannot be affected by the decision to accept or reject the project, and so they should be ignored.

This fact is often forgotten. For example, in 1971 Lockheed sought a federal guarantee for a bank loan to continue development of the TriStar airplane. Lockheed and its supporters argued it would be foolish to abandon a project on which nearly $1 billion had already been spent. Some of Lockheed's critics countered that it would be equally foolish to continue with a project that offered no prospect of a satisfactory return on that $1 billion. Both groups were guilty of the *sunk-cost fallacy*; the $1 billion was irrecoverable and, therefore, irrelevant.[1]

INCLUDE OPPORTUNITY COSTS.   The cost of a resource may be relevant to the investment decision even when no cash changes hands. For example, suppose a new manufacturing operation uses land which could otherwise be sold for $100,000. This resource is not free: It has an opportunity cost, which is the cash it could generate for the company if the project were rejected and the resource sold or put to some other productive use.

This example prompts us to warn you against judging projects on the basis of "before versus after." The proper comparison is "with or without." A manager comparing before versus after might not assign any value to the land because the firm owns it both before and after:

Before	Take Project	After	Cash Flow, Before versus After
Firm owns land	$\longrightarrow$	Firm still owns land	0

The proper comparison, which is with or without, is as follows:

---

[1]U. E. Reinhardt provides an analysis of the value of the TriStar in 1971: "Break-Even Analysis for Lockheed's TriStar: An Application of Financial Theory," *Journal of Finance*, **28**:821–838 (September 1973). Reinhardt does not fall into the sunk-cost fallacy.

Before	Take Project	After	Cash Flow, with Project
Firm owns land	$\longrightarrow$	Firm still owns land	0
	Do Not Take Project	After	Cash Flow, without Project
	$\longrightarrow$	Firm sells land for $100,000	$100,000

Comparing the two possible "afters," we see that the firm gives up $100,000 by undertaking the project. This reasoning still holds if the land will not be sold but is worth $100,000 to the firm in some other use.

Sometimes opportunity costs may be very difficult to estimate;[2] however, where the resource can be freely traded, its opportunity cost is simply equal to the market price? Why? It cannot be otherwise. If the value of a parcel of land to the firm is less than its market price, the firm will sell it. On the other hand, the opportunity cost of using land in a particular project cannot exceed the cost of buying an equivalent parcel to replace it.

BEWARE OF ALLOCATED OVERHEAD COSTS. We have already mentioned that the accountant's objective in gathering data is not always the same as the investment analyst's. A case in point is the allocation of overhead costs. Overheads include such items as supervisory salaries, rent, heat, and light. These overheads may not be related to any particular project, but they have to be paid for somehow. Therefore, when the accountant assigns costs to the firm's projects, a charge for overhead is usually made. Now our principle of incremental cash flows says that in investment appraisal we should include only the *extra* expenses that would result from the project. A project may generate extra overhead expenses—and then again it may not. We should be cautious about assuming that the accountant's allocation of overheads represents the true extra expenses that would be incurred.

Treat Inflation Consistently

As we pointed out in Chapter 3, interest rates are usually quoted in *nominal* rather than *real* terms. For example, if you buy a 1-year 8 percent Treasury bond, the government promises to pay you $1080 at the end of the year, but it makes no promises of what that $1080 will buy. Investors take inflation into account when they decide what is a fair rate of interest.

Suppose that the yield on the Treasury bond is 8 percent and that next year's inflation is expected to be 6 percent. If you buy the bond, you get back $1080 in year-1 dollars, which are worth 6 percent less than current dollars. The nominal payoff is $1080, but the expected *real* value of your payoff is 1080/1.06 = $1019. Thus we could say, "The *nominal* rate of interest on the bond is 8 percent," *or* "The expected *real* rate of interest is 1.9 percent." Remember that the formula linking the nominal interest rate and the real rate is

---

[2] They may be so difficult to estimate that it is often preferable just to note their existence rather than attempt to quantify them.

$$1 + r_{\text{nominal}} = (1 + r_{\text{real}})(1 + \text{inflation rate})$$

If the discount rate is stated in nominal terms, then consistency requires that cash flows be estimated in nominal terms, taking account of trends in selling price, labor and materials cost, etc. This calls for more than simply applying a single assumed inflation rate to all components of cash flow. Labor cost per hour of work, for example, normally increases at a faster rate than the consumer price index because of improvements in productivity and increasing real wages throughout the economy. Tax shields on depreciation do not increase with inflation; they are constant in nominal terms because tax law in the United States allows only the original cost of assets to be depreciated.

Of course, there is nothing wrong with discounting real cash flows at a real discount rate, although this is *not* commonly done. Here is a simple example showing the equivalence of the two methods.

Suppose your firm usually forecasts cash flows in nominal terms and discounts at a 15 percent nominal rate. In this particular case, however, you are given project cash flows estimated in real terms, that is, current dollars:

Real Cash Flows,
Thousands of Dollars

C_0	C_1	C_2	C_3
-100	$+35$	$+50$	$+30$

It would be inconsistent to discount these real cash flows at 15 percent. You have two alternatives: Either restate the cash flows in nominal terms and discount at 15 percent, or restate the discount rate in real terms and use it to discount the real cash flows. We will now show you that both methods produce the same answer.

Assume that inflation is projected at 10 percent a year. Then the first cash flow for year 1, which is $35,000 in current dollars, will be $35,000 \times 1.10 = \$38,500$ in year-1 dollars. Similarly the cash flow for year 2 will be $50,000 \times (1.10)^2 = \$60,500$ in year-2 dollars, and so on. If we discount these nominal cash flows at the 15 percent nominal discount rate, we have

$$\text{NPV} = -100 + \frac{38.5}{1.15} + \frac{60.5}{(1.15)^2} + \frac{39.9}{(1.15)^3} = 5.5, \text{ or } \$5500$$

Instead of converting the cash-flow forecasts into nominal terms, we could convert the discount rate into real terms by using the following relationship:

$$\text{Real discount rate} = \frac{1 + \text{nominal discount rate}}{1 + \text{inflation rate}} - 1$$

In our example this gives

$$\text{Real discount rate} = \frac{1.15}{1.10} - 1 = .045, \text{ or } 4.5\%$$

If we now discount the real cash flows by the real discount rate, we have an NPV of $5500, just as before:

$$\text{NPV} = -100 + \frac{35}{1.045} + \frac{50}{(1.045)^2} + \frac{30}{(1.045)^3} = 5.5, \text{ or } \$5500$$

Note that the real discount rate is approximately equal to the *difference* between the nominal discount rate of 15 percent and the inflation rate of 10 percent. Discounting at 5 percent would give NPV = $4600—not exactly right, but close.

The message of all this is quite simple. Discount nominal cash flows at a nominal discount rate. Discount real cash flows at a real rate. Obvious as this rule is, it is sometimes violated. For example, in 1974 there was a political storm in Ireland over the government's acquisition of a stake in Bula Mines. The price paid by the government reflected an assessment of £40 million as the value of Bula Mines; however, one group of consultants thought that the company's value was only £8 million and others thought that it was as high as £104 million. Although these valuations used different cash-flow projections, a significant part of the difference in views seemed to reflect confusion about real and nominal discount rates.[3]

6-2 EXAMPLE—IM&C PROJECT

As the newly appointed financial manager of International Mulch and Compost Company (IM&C), you are about to analyze a proposal for marketing guano as a garden fertilizer. (IM&C's planned advertising campaign features a rustic gentleman who steps out of a vegetable patch singing, "All my troubles have guano way.")[4]

You are given the forecasts shown in Table 6-1. The project requires an investment of $10 million in plant and machinery (line 1). This machinery can be dismantled and sold for net proceeds estimated at $1 million in year 7 (line 1, column 7). This amount is the plant's *salvage value*.

Whoever prepared Table 6-1 depreciated the capital investment over 6 years to an arbitrary salvage value of $500,000, which is less than your forecast of salvage value. *Straight-line depreciation* was assumed. Under this method annual depreciation equals a constant proportion of the initial investment less salvage value ($9.5 million). If we call the depreciable life T, then the straight-line depreciation in year t is

$$\text{Depreciation in year } t = \frac{1}{T} \times \text{depreciable value} = \frac{1}{6} \times 9.5 = \$1.583 \text{ million}$$

Lines 6 to 12 in Table 6-1 show a simplified income statement for the guano project. This might be taken as a starting point for estimating cash flow. However, you discover that all figures submitted to you are based on costs and selling prices prevailing in year zero. IM&C's production managers realize there will be inflation, but they have assumed that prices can be raised to cover increasing costs. Thus they claim that inflation won't affect the real value of the project.

Though this line of argument sounds plausible, it will get you into trouble. First, opportunity costs of capital are usually expressed as *nominal* rates. You cannot use a nominal rate to discount real cash flows. Second, not all prices and costs increase at the same rate. For example, the tax savings provided by depreciation are unaffected by inflation, since the Internal Revenue Service allows you to depreciate only the original cost of the equipment regardless of what happens to prices after the invest-

---

[3]In some cases it is unclear what procedure was used. At least one expert seems to have discounted nominal cash flows at a real rate. For a review of the Bula Mines controversy see E. Dimson and P. R. Marsh, *Cases in Corporate Finance*, Wiley International, London, 1987.

[4]Sorry.

TABLE 6-1

IM&C's guano project—initial projections (figures in thousands of dollars)

| | PERIOD | | | | | | |
	0	1	2	3	4	5	6	7
1. Capital investment	10,000							−1,000*
2. Accumulated depreciation		1,583	3,167	4,750	6,333	7,917	9,500	0
3. Year-end book value	10,000	8,417	6,833	5,250	3,667	2,083	500	0
4. Working capital		500	1,065	2,450	3,340	2,225	1,130	0
5. Total book value (3 + 4)	10,000	8,917	7,898	7,700	7,007	4,308	1,630	0
6. Sales		475	10,650	24,500	33,400	22,250	11,130	
7. Cost of goods sold		761	6,388	14,690	20,043	13,345	6,678	
8. Other costs†	4,000	2,000	1,000	1,000	1,000	1,000	1,000	
9. Depreciation		1,583	1,583	1,583	1,583	1,583	1,583	
10. Pretax profit (6 − 7 − 8 − 9)	−4,000	−3,869	1,679	7,227	10,774	6,322	1,869	500‡
11. Tax at 35%	−1,400	−1,354	588	2,529	3,771	2,213	654	175
12. Profit after tax	−2,600	−2,515	1,091	4,698	7,003	4,109	1,215	325

*Salvage value.
†Start-up costs in years 0 and 1, and general and administrative costs in years 1 through 6.
‡The difference between the salvage value and the ending book value of $500 is a taxable profit.

ment is made. On the other hand, wages generally increase faster than the inflation rate. Labor cost per ton of guano will rise in real terms unless technological advances allow more efficient use of labor.

Assume that future inflation is forecasted at 10 percent a year. Table 6-2 restates Table 6-1 in nominal terms assuming just for simplicity that sales, investment, operating costs, and required working capital appreciate at this general rate. You can see, however, that depreciation is not affected by inflation.

Table 6-3 derives cash-flow forecasts from the investment and income data given in Table 6-2. Cash flow from operations is defined as sales less cost of goods sold, other costs, and taxes.[5] The remaining cash flows include the changes in working capital, the initial capital investment, and the final recovery of salvage value. If, as you expect, the salvage value turns out higher than the depreciated value of the machinery, you will have to pay tax on the difference. So you must also include this figure in your cash-flow forecast.

IM&C estimates the nominal opportunity cost of capital for projects of this type as 20 percent. When all cash flows are added up and discounted, the guano project is seen to offer a net present value of about $3.5 million:

[5] Sales revenue may not represent actual cash inflow. Costs may not represent cash outflows. This is why change in working capital must be taken into account, as it is in Table 6-3. The "Further Note on Estimating Cash Flow" in this section discusses the relationship between operating cash flow and change in working capital in more detail.

TABLE 6-2

IM&C's guano project—revised projections reflecting inflation (figures in thousands of dollars)

				PERIOD				
	0	1	2	3	4	5	6	7
1. Capital investment	10,000							−1,949*
2. Accumulated depreciation		1,583	3,167	4,750	6,333	7,917	9,500	0
3. Year-end book value	10,000	8,417	6,833	5,250	3,667	2,083	500	0
4. Working capital		550	1,289	3,261	4,890	3,583	2,002	0
5. Total book value (3 + 4)	10,000	8,967	8,122	8,511	8,557	5,666	2,502	0
6. Sales		523	12,887	32,610	48,901	35,834	19,717	
7. Cost of goods sold		837	7,729	19,552	29,345	21,492	11,830	
8. Other costs	4,000	2,200	1,210	1,331	1,464	1,611	1,772	
9. Depreciation		1,583	1,583	1,583	1,583	1,583	1,583	
10. Pretax profit (6 − 7 − 8 − 9)	−4,000	−4,097	2,365	10,144	16,509	11,148	4,532	1,449†
11. Tax at 35%	−1,400	−1,434	828	3,550	5,778	3,902	1,586	507
12. Profit after tax (10 − 11)	−2,600	−2,663	1,537	6,594	10,731	7,246	2,946	942

*Salvage value.

†The difference between the salvage value and the ending book value of $500 is a taxable profit.

$$\text{NPV} = -12,600 - \frac{1630}{1.20} + \frac{2381}{(1.20)^2} + \frac{6205}{(1.20)^3} + \frac{10,685}{(1.20)^4} + \frac{10,136}{(1.20)^5}$$

$$+ \frac{6110}{(1.20)^6} + \frac{3444}{(1.20)^7} = +3519, \text{ or } \$3,519,000$$

Separating Investment and Financing Decisions

Our analysis of the guano project takes no notice of how that project is financed. It may be that IM&C would decide to finance partly by debt, but if it did, we would not subtract the debt proceeds from the required investment, nor would we recognize interest and principal payments as cash outflows. We would treat the project as if it were all equity-financed, treating all cash outflows as coming from stockholders and all cash inflows as going to them.

We approach the problem in this way so that we can separate the analysis of the investment decision from the financing decision. Then, when we have calculated NPV, we can undertake a separate analysis of financing. Financing decisions and their possible interaction with investment decisions are covered later in the book.

*A Further Note on Estimating Cash Flow

Now here is an important point. You can see from line 6 of Table 6-3 that working capital increases in the early and middle years of the project. "What is working capital?" you may ask, "and why does it increase?"

Working capital summarizes the net investment in short-term assets associated with a firm, business, or project. Its most important components are *inventory, ac-*

TABLE 6-3

IM&C's guano project—cash-flow analysis (figures in thousands of dollars)

				PERIOD				
	0	1	2	3	4	5	6	7
1. Sales		523	12,887	32,610	48,901	35,834	19,717	
2. Cost of goods sold		837	7,729	19,552	29,345	21,492	11,830	
3. Other costs	4,000	2,200	1,210	1,331	1,464	1,611	1,772	
4. Tax on operations	−1,400	−1,434	828	3,550	5,778	3,902	1,586	
5. Cash flow from operations (1 − 2 − 3 − 4)	−2,600	−1,080	3,120	8,177	12,314	8,829	4,529	
6. Change in working capital		−550	−739	−1,972	−1,629	1,307	1,581	2,002
7. Capital investment and disposal	−10,000							1,442*
8. Net cash flow (5 + 6 + 7)	−12,600	−1,630	2,381	6,205	10,685	10,136	6,110	3,444
9. Present value at 20%	−12,600	−1,358	1,654	3,591	5,153	4,074	2,046	961
Net present value = +3,519								

*Salvage value of $1949 less tax of $507 on the difference between salvage value and ending book value.

counts receivable, and *accounts payable*. The guano project's requirements for working capital in year 2 might be as follows:

Working capital	=	inventory	+	accounts receivable	−	accounts payable
$1289	=	635	+	1030	−	376

Why does working capital increase? There are several possibilities:

1. Sales recorded on the income statement overstate actual cash receipts from guano shipments because sales are increasing and customers are slow to pay their bills. Therefore, accounts receivable increase.

2. It takes several months for processed guano to age properly. Thus, as projected sales increase, larger inventories have to be held in the aging sheds.

3. An offsetting effect occurs if payments for materials and services used in guano production are delayed. In this case accounts payable will increase.

The changes in working capital from year 2 to 3 might be

Change in working capital	=	increase in inventory	+	increase in accounts receivable	−	increase in accounts payable
$1972	=	972	+	1500	−	500

A detailed cash-flow forecast for year 3 would look like Table 6-4.

TABLE 6-4

· ·

Details of cash-flow forecast for IM&C's guano project in year 3 (figures in thousands of dollars)

Cash Flows	Data from Forecasted Income Statement		Working-Capital Changes
Cash inflow	=	Sales	− Increase in accounts receivable
$31,110	=	32,610	− 1,500
Cash outflow	=	Cost of goods sold, other costs, and taxes	+ Increase in inventory net of increase in accounts payable
$24,905	=	(19,552 + 1,331 + 3,550)	+ (972 − 500)

Net cash flow = cash inflow − cash outflow
$6,205   = 31,110   − 24,905

Instead of worrying about changes in working capital, you could estimate cash flow directly by counting the dollars coming in and taking away the dollars going out. In other words,

1. If you replace each year's sales with that year's cash payments received from customers, you don't have to worry about accounts receivable.

2. If you replace cost of goods sold with cash payments for labor, materials, and other costs of production, you don't have to keep track of inventory or accounts payable.

However, you would still have to construct a projected income statement to estimate taxes.
We discuss the links between cash flow and working capital in much greater detail in Chapter 29.

A Further Note on Depreciation

Depreciation is a noncash expense; it is important only because it reduces taxable income. It provides an annual *tax shield* equal to the product of depreciation and the marginal tax rate:

$$\text{Tax shield} = \text{depreciation} \times \text{tax rate}$$
$$= 1583 \times .35 = 554, \text{ or } \$554,000$$

The present value of the tax shields ($554,000 for 6 years) is $1,842,000 at a 20 percent discount rate.[6]

Now if IM&C could just get those tax shields sooner, they would be worth more, right? Fortunately tax law allows corporations to do just that: It allows *accelerated depreciation*.

The current rules for tax depreciation were set by the Tax Reduction Act of 1986, which established a modified accelerated cost recovery system. Table 6-5 summarizes

---

[6]By discounting the depreciation tax shields at 20 percent, we assume that they are as risky as the other cash flows. Since they depend only on tax rates, depreciation method, and IM&C's ability to generate taxable income, they are probably less risky. In some contexts—the analysis of financial leases, for example— depreciation tax shields are treated as safe, nominal cash flows and discounted at an after-tax borrowing or lending rate. See Chapter 26.

TABLE 6-5

Tax depreciation allowed under the modified accelerated cost recovery system (figures in percent of depreciable investment)

Tax Depreciation Schedules by Recovery-Period Class

Year(s)	3-Year	5-Year	7-Year	10-Year	15-Year	20-Year
1	33.33	20.00	14.29	10.00	5.00	3.75
2	44.45	32.00	24.49	18.00	9.50	7.22
3	14.81	19.20	17.49	14.40	8.55	6.68
4	7.41	11.52	12.49	11.52	7.70	6.18
5		11.52	8.93	9.22	6.93	5.71
6		5.76	8.93	7.37	6.23	5.28
7			8.93	6.55	5.90	4.89
8			4.45	6.55	5.90	4.52
9				6.55	5.90	4.46
10				6.55	5.90	4.46
11				3.29	5.90	4.46
12					5.90	4.46
13					5.90	4.46
14					5.90	4.46
15					5.90	4.46
16					2.99	4.46
17–20						4.46
21						2.25

Notes:
1. Tax depreciation is lower in the first year because assets are assumed to be in service for only 6 months.
2. Real property is depreciated straight-line over 27.5 years for residential property and 31.5 years for nonresidential property.

the tax depreciation schedules. Note that there are six schedules, one for each recovery period class. Most industrial equipment falls into the 5- and 7-year classes. To keep things simple, we will assume that all the guano project's investment goes into 5-year assets. Thus, IM&C can write off 20 percent of its depreciable investment in year 1, as soon as the assets are placed in service, then 32 percent of depreciable investment in year 2, and so on. Here are the tax shields for the guano project:

	YEAR					
	1	2	3	4	5	6
Tax depreciation (ACRS percentage × depreciable investment)	2,000	3,200	1,920	1,152	1,152	576
Tax shield (tax depreciation × tax rate, $T = .35$)	700	1,120	672	403	403	202

The present value of these tax shields is $2,174,000, about $331,000 higher than under the straight-line method.

Table 6-6 recalculates the guano project's impact on IM&C's future tax bills, and Table 6-7 shows revised after-tax cash flows and present value. This time we have incorporated realistic assumptions about taxes as well as inflation. We of course arrive at a higher NPV than in Table 6-3, because that table ignored the additional present value of accelerated depreciation.

There is one possible additional problem lurking in the woodwork behind Table 6-6: It is the *alternative minimum tax*, which can limit or defer the tax shields of accelerated depreciation or other *tax preference* items. Because the alternative minimum tax can be a motive for leasing, we discuss it in Chapter 26, rather than here. But make a mental note not to sign off on a capital budgeting analysis without checking whether your company is subject to the alternative minimum tax.

A Final Comment on Taxes

Almost every large corporation keeps two separate sets of books, one for its stockholders and one for the Internal Revenue Service. It is common to use straight-line depreciation on the stockholder books and accelerated depreciation on the tax books. The IRS doesn't object to this, and it makes the firm's reported earnings higher than if accelerated depreciation were used everywhere. There are many other differences between tax books and shareholder books.

The financial analyst must be careful to remember which set of books he or she is looking at. In capital budgeting only the tax books are relevant, but to an outside analyst only the shareholder books are available.

A Final Comment on Project Analysis

Let's review. Several pages ago, you embarked on an analysis of IM&C's guano project. It appeared, at first, that you had all the facts you needed in Table 6-1, but many of those numbers had to be thrown away because they didn't reflect expected inflation. So you worked out revised projections and calculated project net present value.

TABLE 6-6

Tax payments on IM&C's guano project (figures in thousands of dollars)

					PERIOD			
	0	1	2	3	4	5	6	7
1. Sales*		523	12,887	32,610	48,901	35,834	19,717	
2. Cost of goods sold*		837	7,729	19,552	29,345	21,492	11,830	
3. Other costs*	4,000	2,200	1,210	1,331	1,464	1,611	1,772	
4. Tax depreciation		2,000	3,200	1,920	1,152	1,152	576	
5. Pretax profit (1 − 2 − 3 − 4)	−4,000	−4,514	748	9,807	16,940	11,579	5,539	1,949[†]
6. Taxes at 35%[‡]	−1,400	−1,580	262	3,432	5,929	4,053	1,939	682

*From Table 6-2.
[†]Salvage value is zero, for tax purposes, after all tax depreciation has been taken. Thus, IM&C will have to pay tax on the full salvage value of $1949.
[‡]A negative tax payment means a cash *inflow*, assuming IM&C can use the tax loss on its guano project to shield income from other projects.

TABLE 6-7

IM&C's guano project—revised cash-flow analysis (figures in thousands of dollars)

	PERIOD						
	0	1	2	3	4	5	6	7
1. Sales*		523	12,887	32,610	48,901	35,834	19,717	
2. Cost of goods sold*		837	7,729	19,552	29,345	21,492	11,830	
3. Other costs*	4,000	2,200	1,210	1,331	1,464	1,611	1,772	
4. Tax†	−1,400	−1,580	262	3,432	5,929	4,053	1,939	682
5. Cash flow from operations (1 − 2 − 3 − 4)	−2,600	−934	3,686	8,295	12,163	8,678	4,176	−682
6. Change in working capital		−550	−739	−1,972	−1,629	1,307	1,581	2,002
7. Capital investment and disposal	−10,000							1,949*
8. Net cash flow (5 + 6 + 7)	−12,600	−1,484	2,947	6,323	10,534	9,985	5,757	3,269
9. Present value at 20%	−12,600	−1,237	2,047	3,659	5,080	4,013	1,928	912
Net present value = +3,802								

*From Table 6-2.
†From Table 6-6.

However, then you remembered accelerated depreciation; you turned wearily back to your worksheets and finally obtained decent estimates of cash flow and NPV.

You were lucky to get away with just two NPV calculations. In real situations, it often takes several tries to purge all inconsistencies and mistakes. Then there are "what if" questions. For example: What if inflation rages at 15 percent per year, rather than 10? What if technical problems delay start-up to year 2? What if gardeners prefer chemical fertilizers to your natural product?

You won't truly understand the guano project until these questions are answered. *Project analysis* is more than one or two NPV calculations, as we will see in Chapter 10.

However, before you become too deeply immersed in guano, we should now turn to the subject of project interactions.

6-3 PROJECT INTERACTIONS

Almost all decisions about capital expenditure involve "either-or" choices. The firm can build either a 90,000-square-foot warehouse in northern South Dakota or a 100,000-square-foot warehouse in southern North Dakota. It can heat it either by oil or natural gas, and so on. These mutually exclusive options are simple examples of *project interactions.*

Project interactions can arise in countless ways. The literature of operations research and industrial engineering sometimes addresses cases of extreme complexity and difficulty. We will concentrate on five simple but important cases.

The fact that a project has a positive NPV does not mean that it is best undertaken now. It might be even more valuable if undertaken in the future. Similarly, a project with a currently negative NPV might become a valuable opportunity if we wait a bit. Thus *any* project has two mutually exclusive alternatives: Do it now, or wait and invest later.

The question of optimal timing of investment is not difficult under conditions of certainty. We first examine alternative dates (t) for making the investment and calculate its net *future* value as of each date. Then, in order to find which of the alternatives would add most to the firm's *current* value, we must work out

$$\frac{\text{Net future value as of date } t}{(1 + r)^t}$$

For example, suppose you own a large tract of inaccessible timber. In order to harvest it, you have to invest a substantial amount in access roads and other facilities. The longer you wait, the higher the investment required. On the other hand, lumber prices will rise as you wait, and the trees will keep growing, although at a gradually decreasing rate.

Let us suppose that the net value of the harvest at different future dates is as follows:

	YEAR OF HARVEST					
	0	1	2	3	4	5
Net *future* value, thousands of dollars	50	64.4	77.5	89.4	100	109.4
Change in value from previous year, percent		+28.8	+20.3	+15.4	+11.9	+9.4

As you can see, the longer you defer cutting the timber, the more money you will make. However, your concern is with the date that maximizes the net *present* value of your investment. You therefore need to discount the net future value of the harvest back to the present. Suppose the appropriate discount rate is 10 percent. Then if you harvest the timber in year 1, it has a net *present* value of $58,500:

$$\text{NPV if harvested in year 1} = \frac{64.4}{1.10} = 58.5, \text{ or } \$58,500$$

The net present value (at $t = 0$) for other harvest dates is as follows:

	YEAR OF HARVEST					
	0	1	2	3	4	5
Net present value, thousands of dollars	50	58.5	64.0	67.2	68.3	67.9

The optimal point to harvest the timber is year 4 because this is the point that maximizes NPV.

Notice that before year 4 the net future value of the timber increases by more than 10 percent a year: The gain in value is greater than the cost of the capital that is tied up in the project. After year 4 the gain in value is still positive but less than the cost of capital. You maximize the net present value of your investment if you harvest your timber as soon as the rate of increase in value drops below the cost of capital.[7]

The problem of optimal timing of investment under uncertainty is, of course, much more complicated. An opportunity not taken at $t = 0$ might be either more or less attractive at $t = 1$; there is rarely any way of knowing for sure. Perhaps it is better to strike while the iron is hot even if there is a chance it will become hotter. On the other hand, if you wait a bit you might obtain more information and avoid a bad mistake.[8]

Case 2— Choosing between Long- and Short- Lived Equipment

Suppose the firm is forced to choose between two machines, A and B. The two machines are designed differently but have identical capacity and do exactly the same job. Machine A costs $15,000 and will last 3 years. It costs $4000 per year to run. Machine B is an "economy" model costing only $10,000, but it will last only 2 years and costs $6000 per year to run. These are real cash flows: The costs are forecasted in dollars of constant purchasing power.

Because the two machines produce exactly the same product, the only way to choose between them is on the basis of cost. Suppose we compute the present value of cost:

| | COSTS, THOUSANDS OF DOLLARS | | | | Present Value at 6%, |
Machine	C_0	C_1	C_2	C_3	Thousands of Dollars
A	+15	+5	+5	+5	28.37
B	+10	+6	+6		21.00

Should we take machine B, the one with the lower present value of costs? Not necessarily, because B will have to be replaced a year earlier than A. In other words, the timing of a future investment decision is contingent on today's choice of A or B.

So, a machine with total PV(costs) of $21,000 spread over 3 years (0, 1, and 2) is not necessarily better than a competing machine with PV(costs) of $25,690 spread over 4 years (0 to 3). Somehow we have to convert total PV(costs) to a cost *per year*.

Suppose the financial manager is asked to *rent* machine A to the plant manager actually in charge of production. There will be three equal rental payments starting

---

[7]Our timber-cutting example conveys the right idea about investment timing, but it misses an important practical point: The sooner you cut the first crop of trees, the sooner the second crop can start growing. Thus, the value of the second crop depends on when you cut the first. This more complex and realistic problem might be solved in one of two ways:

1. Find the cutting dates that maximize the present value of a series of harvests, taking account of the different growth rates of young and old trees.
2. Repeat our calculations, counting the future market value of cut-over land as part of the payoff to the first harvest. The value of cut-over land includes the present value of all subsequent harvests.

The second solution is far simpler if you can figure out what cut-over land will be worth.

H. Bierman and S. Smidt discuss the tree-cutting problem in *The Capital Budgeting Decision*, 8th ed., Macmillan Company, New York, 1992.

[8]We return to optimal investment timing under uncertainty in Chapter 21.

in year 1. The three payments must recover both the original cost of Machine A in year 0 and the cost of running it in years 1 to 3. Therefore the financial manager has to make sure that the rental payments are worth $28,370, the total PV(costs) of machine A. This fair rental payment, which is usually called the **equivalent annual cost,** turns out to be 10.61, or $10,610 per year:

| | COSTS, THOUSANDS OF DOLLARS | | | | Present Value at 6%, |
	C_0	C_1	C_2	C_3	Thousands of Dollars
Machine A	+15	+5	+5	+5	28.37
Equivalent annual cost		+10.61	+10.61	+10.61	28.37

The fair rental payment, or equivalent annual cost, is an annuity which has exactly the same life and present value as machine A. How did we know that the right cash flow from the annuity was 10.61? It was easy! We set the PV of the annuity equal to the present value of A and solved for the payment of the annuity:

PV of annuity = PV of cash outflows of A = 28.37
= annuity payment × 3-year annuity factor

Therefore the annuity payment equals the present value divided by the annuity factor, which is 2.673 for 3 years and a 6 percent real cost of capital:

$$\text{Annuity payment} = \frac{28.37}{2.673} = 10.61$$

If we make a similar calculation for machine B, we get:

| | COSTS, THOUSANDS OF DOLLARS | | | Present Value at 6%, |
	C_0	C_1	C_2	Thousands of Dollars
Machine B	+10	+6	+6	21.00
Equivalent annual cost		+11.45	+11.45	21.00

We see that machine A is better, because its equivalent annual cost is less ($10,610 versus $11,450 for machine B). In other words, machine A could be rented to the production manager for less than machine B.

Our rule for comparing assets of different lives is, therefore, as follows. Select the machine that has the lowest equivalent annual cost. The equivalent annual cost is simply the present value of all costs divided by the annuity factor.

EQUIVALENT ANNUAL COST AND INFLATION. The equivalent annual costs we just calculated are *real* annuities based on forecasted *real* costs and a 6 percent *real* discount rate. We could, of course, restate the annuities in nominal terms. Suppose the expected inflation rate is 5 percent; we multiply the first cash flow of the annuity by 1.05, the second by $(1.05)^2 = 1.105$, and so on.

	C_0	C_1	C_2	C_3
A Real annuity		10.61	10.61	10.61
Nominal cash flow		11.14	11.70	12.28
B Real annuity		11.45	11.45	
Nominal cash flow		12.02	12.62	

Note that B is still inferior to A. Of course the present values of the nominal and real cash flows are identical. Just remember to discount the real annuity at the real rate and the equivalent nominal cash flows at the consistent nominal rate.[9]

When you use equivalent annual costs simply for comparison of costs per period, as we did for machines A and B, then we strongly recommend doing the calculations in real terms.[10] But if you actually rent out the machine to the plant manager, or anyone else, be careful to specify that the rental payments be "indexed" to inflation. If inflation runs on at 5 percent per year and rental payments do not increase proportionally, then the real value of the rental payments must decline and will not cover the full cost of buying and operating the machine.

EQUIVALENT ANNUAL COST AND TECHNOLOGICAL CHANGE. So far we have the following simple rule: Two or more streams of cash outflows with different lengths or time patterns can be compared by converting their present values to equivalent annual costs. Just remember to do the calculations in real terms.

Now any rule this simple cannot be completely general. For example, it would not make sense to compare the current annual costs for renting machines A and B if the rent on machine A is likely to leap in year 3 after machine B has worn out in year 2. When we compare the equivalent annual real costs, we are implicitly assuming that the real rental for machine A will *continue* to be $10,610. This will be so only if the *real* costs of buying and operating the machine stay the same.

Suppose that this is not the case. Specifically, suppose that thanks to technological improvements new machines each year cost 20 percent less in real terms to buy and operate. In this case future owners of brand-new, lower-cost machines will be able to cut the rental cost by 20 percent, and owners of old machines will be forced to match this reduction. Thus, we now need to ask: If the real level of rents declines by 20 percent a year, how much will it cost to rent each machine?

If the rent for year 1 is $rent_1$, rent for year 2 is $rent_2 = .8 \times rent_1$. $Rent_3$ is $.8 \times rent_2$, or $.64 \times rent_1$. The owner of each machine must set the rent sufficiently high to recover the present value of the costs. In the case of machine A,

---

[9]The nominal discount rate is

$$r_{nominal} = (1 + r_{real})(1 + \text{inflation rate}) - 1$$
$$= (1.06)(1.05) - 1 = .113, \text{ or } 11.3\%$$

Discounting the nominal annuities at this rate gives the same present values as discounting the real annuities at 6 percent.

[10]Do *not* calculate equivalent annual costs as level nominal annuities. This procedure can give incorrect rankings of true equivalent annual costs at high inflation rates. See problem 10 at the end of this chapter for an example.

$$\text{PV of renting machine A} = \frac{\text{rent}_1}{1.06} + \frac{\text{rent}_2}{(1.06)^2} + \frac{\text{rent}_3}{(1.06)^3} = 28.37$$

$$= \frac{\text{rent}_1}{1.06} + \frac{.8(\text{rent}_1)}{(1.06)^2} + \frac{.64(\text{rent}_1)}{(1.06)^3} = 28.37$$

$$\text{rent}_1 = 12.94, \text{ or } \$12,940$$

and for machine B,

$$\frac{\text{rent}_1}{1.06} + \frac{.8(\text{rent}_1)}{(1.06)^2} = 21.00$$

$$\text{rent}_1 = 12.69, \text{ or } \$12,690$$

The merits of the two machines are now reversed. Once we recognize that technology is expected to reduce the real costs of new machines, then it pays to buy the shorter-lived machine B rather than become locked into an aging technology for year 3.

You can imagine other complications. Perhaps machine C will arrive in year 1 with an even lower equivalent annual cost. You would then need to consider scrapping or selling machine B at year 1 (more on this decision below). The financial manager could not choose between machines A and B in year 0 without taking a detailed look at what each machine could be replaced with.

Our point is a general one: Comparing equivalent annual costs should never be a mechanical exercise; always think about the assumptions that are implicit in the comparison. Finally, remember why equivalent annual costs are necessary in the first place. The reason is that A and B will be replaced at different future dates. The choice between them therefore affects future investment decisions. If subsequent decisions are not affected by the initial choice—for example, because neither machine will be replaced—then we do *not need to take future decisions into account.*[11]

Case 3—Deciding When to Replace an Existing Machine

The previous example took the life of each machine as fixed. In practice the point at which equipment is replaced reflects economic considerations rather than total physical collapse. *We* must decide when to replace. The machine will rarely decide for us.

Here is a common problem. You are operating an elderly machine that is expected to produce a net cash *inflow* of $4000 in the coming year and $4000 next year. After that it will give up the ghost. You can replace it now with a new machine, which costs $15,000 but is much more efficient and will provide a cash inflow of $8000 a year for 3 years. You want to know whether you should replace your equipment now or wait a year.

We can calculate the NPV of the new machine and also its equivalent annual cash flow, that is, the 3-year annuity that has the same net present value:

	CASH FLOWS, THOUSANDS OF DOLLARS				NPV at 6%, Thousands of Dollars
	C_0	C_1	C_2	C_3	
New machine	−15	+8	+8	+8	6.38
Equivalent 3-year annuity		+2.387	+2.387	+2.387	6.38

---

[11]However, if neither machine will be replaced, then we have to consider the extra revenue generated by machine A in its third year, when it will be operating but B will not.

In other words, the cash flows of the new machine are equivalent to an annuity of $2387 per year. So we can equally well ask at what point we would want to replace our old machine with a new one producing $2387 a year. When the question is put this way, the answer is obvious. As long as your old machine can generate a cash flow of $4000 a year, who wants to put in its place a new one that generates only $2387 a year?

It is a simple matter to incorporate salvage values into this calculation. Suppose that the current salvage value is $8000 and next year's value is $7000. Let's see where you come out next year if you wait and then sell. On one hand, you gain $7000, but you lose today's salvage value *plus* a year's return on that money. That is, 8000 × 1.06 = $8480. Your net loss is 8480 − 7000 = $1480, which only partly offsets the operating gain. You should not replace yet.

Remember that the logic of such comparisons requires that the new machine be the best of the available alternatives and that it in turn be replaced at the optimal point.

Case 4— Cost of Excess Capacity

Any firm with a computer encounters many proposals for using it. Recently installed computers tend to have excess capacity, and, since the immediate marginal cost of using such computers seems to be negligible, management often encourages new uses. Sooner or later, however, the load on the machine will increase to a point at which management must either terminate the uses it originally encouraged or invest in another computer several years earlier than it had planned. Such problems can be avoided if a proper charge is made for the use of spare capacity.

Suppose we have a new investment project which requires heavy use of the computer. The effect of adopting the project is to bring the purchase date of a new computer forward from year 4 to year 3. This new computer has a life of 5 years, and at a discount rate of 6 percent the present value of the cost of buying and operating it is $500,000.

We begin by converting the $500,000 present value of cost of the computer to an equivalent annual cost of $118,700 for each of 5 years.[12] Of course, when the new computer in turn wears out, we will replace it with another. So we face the prospect of computing expenses of $118,700 a year. If we undertake the new project, the series of expenses begins in year 4; if we do not undertake it, the series begins in year 5. The new project, therefore, results in an *additional* computing cost of $118,700 in year 4. This has a present value of $118,700/(1.06)^4$, or about $94,000. This cost is properly charged against the new project. When we recognize it, the NPV of the project may prove to be negative. If so, we still need to check whether it is worthwhile undertaking the project now and abandoning it later, when the excess capacity of the present computer disappears.

Case 5— Fluctua- ting Load Factors

Although a $10 million warehouse may have a positive net present value, it should be built only if it has a higher NPV than a $9 million alternative. In other words, the NPV of the $1 million *marginal* investment required to buy the more expensive warehouse must be positive.

One case in which this is easily forgotten is when equipment is needed to meet fluctuating demand. Consider the following problem: A widget manufacturer oper-

---

ates two machines, each of which has a capacity of 1000 units a year. They have an indefinite life and no salvage value, and so the only costs are the operating expenses of $2 per widget. Widget manufacture, as everyone knows, is a seasonal business, and widgets are perishable. During the fall and winter, when demand is high, each machine produces at capacity. During the spring and summer, each machine works at 50 percent of capacity. If the discount rate is 10 percent and the machines are kept indefinitely, the present value of the costs is $30,000:

	Two Old Machines
Annual output per machine	750 units
Operating cost per machine	$2 \times 750 = \$1,500$
PV operating cost per machine	$1,500/.10 = \$15,000$
PV operating cost of two machines	$2 \times 15,000 = \$30,000$

The company is considering whether to replace these machines with newer equipment. The new machines have a similar capacity, and so two would still be needed to meet peak demand. Each new machine costs $6000 and lasts indefinitely. Operating expenses are only $1 per unit. On this basis the company calculates that the present value of the costs of two new machines would be $27,000:

	Two New Machines
Annual output per machine	750 units
Capital cost per machine	$6,000
Operating cost per machine	$1 \times 750 = \$750$
PV total cost per machine	$6,000 + 750/.10 = \$13,500$
PV total cost of two machines	$2 \times 13,500 = \$27,000$

Therefore, it scraps both old machines and buys two new ones.

The company was quite right in thinking that two new machines are better than two old ones, but unfortunately it forgot to investigate a third alternative; to replace just one of the old machines. Since the new machine has low operating costs, it would pay to operate it at capacity all year. The remaining old machine could then be kept simply to meet peak demand. The present value of the costs under this strategy is $26,000:

	One Old Machine	One New Machine
Annual output per machine	500 units	1,000 units
Capital cost per machine	0	$6,000
Operating cost per machine	$2 \times 500 = \$1,000$	$1 \times 1,000 = \$1,000$
PV total cost per machine	$1,000/.10 = \$10,000$	$6,000 + 1,000/.10 = \$16,000$
PV total cost of both machines	$26,000	

Replacing one machine saves $4000; replacing two machines saves only $3000. The net present value of the *marginal* investment in the second machine is $-\$1000$.

6-4 SUMMARY

By now present value calculations should be a matter of routine. However, forecasting cash flows will never be routine. It will always be a skilled, hazardous occupation. Mistakes can be minimized by following three rules.

1. Concentrate on cash flows after taxes. Be wary of accounting data masquerading as cash-flow data.

2. Always judge investments on an incremental basis. Tirelessly track down all cash-flow consequences of your decision.

3. Treat inflation consistently. Discount nominal cash-flow forecasts at nominal rates and real forecasts at real rates.

We might add a fourth rule: Recognize project interactions. Decisions involving only a choice of accepting or rejecting a project rarely exist, since capital projects can rarely be isolated from other projects or alternatives. The simplest decision normally encountered is accept or reject or delay. A project having a positive NPV if undertaken today may have a still higher NPV if undertaken tomorrow.

Projects also interact because they are mutually exclusive. You can install machine A or B, for example, but not both. When mutually exclusive choices involve different lengths or time patterns of cash outflows, comparison is difficult unless you convert present values to equivalent annual costs. Think of the equivalent annual cost as the period-by-period rental payment necessary to cover all the cash outflows. Choose A over B, other things equal, if it has the lower equivalent annual cost. Remember, though, to calculate equivalent annual costs in real terms and adjust for technological change if necessary.

This chapter is concerned with the mechanics of applying the net present value rule in practical situations. All our analysis boils down to two simple themes. First, be careful about the definition of alternative projects. Make sure you are comparing like with like. Second, make sure that your calculations include all incremental cash flows.

Further Reading

· ·

There are several good general texts on capital budgeting that cover project interactions. Two examples are:
E. L. Grant, W. G. Ireson, and R. S. Leavenworth: *Principles of Engineering Economy*, 8th ed., Ronald Press, New York, 1990.
H. Bierman and S. Smidt: *The Capital Budgeting Decision*, 8th ed., Macmillan Company, New York, 1992.

Reinhardt provides an interesting case study of a capital investment decision in:
U. E. Reinhardt: "Break-Even Analysis for Lockheed's TriStar: An Application of Financial Theory," *Journal of Finance*, **32**:821–838 (September 1973).

Quiz

· ·

1. Which of the following should be treated as incremental cash flows when deciding whether to invest in a new manufacturing plant? The site is already owned by the company, but existing buildings would need to be demolished.

(a) The market value of the site and existing buildings
(b) Demolition costs and site clearance
(c) The cost of a new access road put in last year
(d) Lost earnings on other products due to executive time spent on the new facility
(e) A proportion of the cost of leasing the president's jet airplane
(f) Future depreciation of the new plant
(g) The reduction in the corporation's tax bill resulting from tax depreciation of the new plant
(h) The initial investment in inventories of raw materials
(i) Money already spent on engineering design of the new plant

2. M. Loup Garou will be paid 100,000 French francs 1 year hence. This is a nominal flow, which he discounts at a 15 percent nominal discount rate:

$$PV = \frac{100,000}{1.15} = 86,957 \text{ francs}$$

The inflation rate is 10 percent.

   Calculate the present value of M. Garou's payment using the equivalent *real* cash flow and *real* discount rate. (You should get exactly the same answer as he did.)

3. "Those egghead finance MBAs make everything too complicated. Take inflation, for example. We don't worry about it. We just take today's selling prices, less labor, raw material, and other unit manufacturing costs, and multiply by forecasted unit sales. Who cares what inflation turns out to be? It doesn't matter because costs and revenues will rise or fall together."

   Could this be true? Does the net present value of a typical capital investment project not depend on whether forecasted future inflation is high or low? Explain briefly. (*Hint:* Compare Tables 6-1 and 6-2. Does inflation affect all of each year's entries proportionally?)

4. How does the present value of depreciation tax shields vary across the recovery-period classes shown in Table 6-5? Give a general answer; then check it by calculating the present values of depreciation tax shields in the 5-year and 7-year classes. The tax rate is 35 percent. Use any reasonable discount rate.

5. Each of the following statements is true. Explain why they are consistent.
   (a) When a company introduces a new product, or expands production of an existing product, investment in net working capital is usually an important cash outflow.
   (b) Forecasting changes in net working capital is not necessary if the timing of *all* cash inflows and outflows is carefully specified.

6. When appraising mutually exclusive projects, many companies calculate the projects' equivalent annual costs and rank the projects on this basis. Why is this necessary? Why not just compare the projects' NPVs? Explain briefly.

7. Machines A and B are mutually exclusive and are expected to produce the following cash flows:

CASH FLOWS, THOUSANDS OF DOLLARS

Machine	C_0	C_1	C_2	C_3
A	−100	+110	+121	
B	−120	+110	+121	+133

The opportunity cost of capital is 10 percent.
(*a*) Calculate the NPV of each machine.
(*b*) Use present value tables to calculate the equivalent annual cash flow from each machine.
(*c*) Which machine should you buy?

8. Machine C was purchased 5 years ago for $200,000 and produces an annual cash flow of $80,000. It has no salvage value but is expected to last another 5 years. The company can replace machine C with machine B (see question 7 above) *either* now *or* at the end of 5 years. Which should it do?

Questions and Problems

1. Restate the cash flows for the guano project in real terms. (See Table 6-7.) Discount the restated cash flows at a real discount rate. Assume a 20 percent *nominal* rate and 10 percent expected inflation. Net present value should be unchanged at +3,802, or $3,802,000.

2. Calculate the NPV of some personal investment decision, such as buying a washing machine instead of using the laundromat, insulating the attic, or re-placing the car. Ignore the extra convenience of the new asset. Just focus on the cash costs and benefits.

3. Discuss the following statement: "We don't want individual plant managers to get involved in the firm's tax position. So instead of telling them to discount after-tax cash flows at 10 percent, we just tell them to take the pretax cash flows and discount at 15 percent. With a 35 percent tax rate, 15 percent pretax generates approximately 10 percent after tax."

4. What do you think of the following statement: "We like to do all our capital budgeting calculations in real terms. It saves making any forecasts of the infla-tion rate."

5. A project requires use of spare computer capacity. If the project is not termi-nated, the company will need to buy an additional disk at the end of year 2. If it is terminated, the disk will not be required until the end of year 4. If disks cost $10,000 and last 5 years, and if the opportunity cost of capital is 10 percent, what is the present value of the cost of this extra usage if the project is terminated at the end of year 2? What if the project continues indefinitely?

6. Mrs. T. Potts, the treasurer of Ideal China, has a problem. The company has just ordered a new kiln for $400,000. Of this sum, $50,000 is described by the supplier as "installation cost." Mrs. Potts does not know whether the Internal Revenue Service will permit the company to treat this cost as a tax-deductible current expense or as a capital investment. In the latter case, the company could depreciate the $50,000 using the 5-year tax depreciation schedule. If the tax rate is 35 percent and the opportunity cost of capital is 5 percent, what is the present value of the tax shield in either case?

7. You own 500 acres of timberland, with young timber worth $40,000 if logged now. This represents 1000 cords of wood worth $40 per cord net of costs of cutting and hauling. A paper company has offered to purchase your tract for $140,000. Should you accept the offer? You have the following information:

Years	Yearly Growth Rate of Cords per Acre
1–4	16%
5–8	11
9–13	4
14 and subsequent years	1

You expect price per cord to increase at 4 percent per year indefinitely.
The cost of capital is 9 percent. Ignore taxes.
The market value of your land would be $100 per acre if you cut and removed the timber this year. The value of cut-over land is also expected to grow at 4 percent per year indefinitely.

8. The Borstal Company has to choose between two machines which do the same job but have different lives. The two machines have the following costs:

Year	Machine A	Machine B
0	$40,000	$50,000
1	10,000	8,000
2	10,000	8,000
3	10,000 + replace	8,000
4		8,000 + replace

These costs are expressed in real terms.
(a) Suppose you are Borstal's financial manager. If you had to buy one or the other machine, and rent it to the production manager for that machine's economic life, what annual rental payment would you have to charge? Assume a 6 percent real discount rate and ignore taxes.
(b) Which machine should Borstal buy?
(c) Usually the rental payments you derived in part (a) are just hypothetical—a way of calculating and interpreting equivalent annual cost. Suppose you actually do buy one of the machines and rent it to the production manager. How much would you actually have to charge in each future year if there is steady 8 percent per year inflation? (Note: The rental payments calculated in part (a) are real cash flows. You would have to mark those payments up to cover inflation.)

9. Look again at your calculations for problem 8. Suppose that technological change is expected to reduce costs by 10 percent per year. There will be new machines in year 1 that cost 10 percent less to buy and operate than A and B. In year 2 there will be a second crop of new machines incorporating a further 10 percent reduction—and so on. How does this change the equivalent annual costs of machines A and B?

10. We warned that equivalent annual costs should be calculated in real terms. We did not fully explain why. This problem will show you.
    Look back to the cash flows for machines A and B (in "Case 2—Choosing between Long- and Short-Lived Equipment"). The present values of purchase and operating costs are 28.37 (over 3 years for A) and 21.00 (over 2 years for B). The real discount rate is 6 percent, and the inflation rate is 5 percent.

(*a*) Calculate the 3- and 2-year *level nominal* annuities which have present values of 28.37 and 21.00. Explain why these annuities are *not* realistic estimates of equivalent annual costs. (*Hint:* In real life machinery rentals increase with inflation.)

(*b*) Suppose the inflation rate increases to 25 percent. The real interest rate stays at 6 percent. Recalculate the level nominal annuities. Note that the *ranking* of machines A and B appears to change. Why? (*Hint:* Think of renting out machines A and B. Suppose you are locked into level nominal rental payments, with no increase to cover inflation at 25 percent. You then suffer more from inflation over the 3-year life of A than over the 2-year life of B. Therefore the required immediate payment for A goes up more than for B, and A *appears* more expensive.)

11. As a result of improvements in product engineering, United Automation is able to sell one of its two milling machines. Both machines perform the same function but differ in age. The newer machine could be sold today for $50,000. Its operating costs are $20,000 a year, but in 5 years the machine will require a $20,000 overhaul. Thereafter operating costs will be $30,000 until the machine is finally sold in year 10 for $5000.

    The older machine could be sold today for $25,000. If it is kept, it will need an immediate $20,000 overhaul. Thereafter operating costs will be $30,000 a year until the machine is finally sold in year 5 for $5000.

    Both machines are fully depreciated for tax purposes. The company pays tax at 35 percent. Cash flows have been forecasted in real terms. The real cost of capital is 12 percent.

    Which machine should United Automation sell? Explain the assumptions underlying your answer.

12. Hayden Inc. has a number of copiers that were bought 4 years ago for $20,000. Currently maintenance costs $2000 a year, but the maintenance agreement expires at the end of 2 years and thereafter the annual maintenance charge will rise to $8000. The machines have a current resale value of $8000, but at the end of year 2 their value will have fallen to $3500. By the end of year 6 the machines will be valueless and would be scrapped.

    Hayden is considering replacing the copiers with new machines that would do essentially the same job. These machines cost $25,000, and the company can take out an 8-year maintenance contract for $1000 a year. The machines have no value by the end of the 8 years and would be scrapped.

    Both machines are depreciated by using 7-year ACRS, and the tax rate is 35 percent. Assume for simplicity that the inflation rate is zero. The real cost of capital is 7 percent.

    When should Hayden replace its copiers?

13. The *Financial Analysts Journal* has offered the following subscription options: 1 year, $150; 2 years, $260; 3 years, $345. These rates are expected to increase at the general rate of inflation. What is your optimal strategy assuming you intend to be a permanent subscriber? Make other assumptions as appropriate.

14. The president's executive jet is not fully utilized. You judge that its use by other officers would increase direct operating costs by only $20,000 a year and would save $100,000 a year in airline bills. On the other hand, you believe that with the increased use the company will need to replace the jet at the end of 3 years rather than 4. A new jet costs $1.1 million and (at its current low rate of use) has

a life of 6 years. Assume that the company does not pay taxes. All cash flows are forecasted in real terms. The real opportunity cost of capital is 8 percent. Should you try to persuade the president to allow other officers to use the plane?

15. A project requires an initial investment of $100,000 and is expected to produce a cash inflow before tax of $26,000 per year for 5 years. Company A has substantial accumulated tax losses and is unlikely to pay taxes in the foreseeable future. Company B pays corporate taxes at a rate of 35 percent and can depreciate the investment for tax purposes using the 5-year tax depreciation schedule.

    Suppose the opportunity cost of capital is 8 percent. Ignore inflation.
    (*a*) Calculate project NPV for each company.
    (*b*) What is the IRR of the after-tax cash flows for each company? What does comparison of the IRRs suggest is the effective corporate tax rate?

16. A widget manufacturer currently produces 200,000 units a year. It buys widget lids from an outside supplier at a price of $2 a lid. The plant manager believes that it would be cheaper to make these lids rather than buy them. Direct production costs are estimated to be only $1.50 a lid. The necessary machinery would cost $150,000. This investment could be written off for tax purposes using the 7-year tax depreciation schedule. The plant manager estimates that the operation would require additional working capital of $30,000 but argues that this sum can be ignored since it is recoverable at the end of the 10 years. If the company pays tax at a rate of 35 percent and the opportunity cost of capital is 15 percent, would you support the plant manager's proposal? State clearly any additional assumptions that you need to make.

17. Reliable Electric is considering a proposal to manufacture a new type of industrial electric motor which would replace most of its existing product line. A research breakthrough has given Reliable a 2-year lead on its competitors. The project proposal is summarized in Table 6-8.
    (*a*) Read the notes to the table carefully. Which entries make sense? Which do not? Why or why not?
    (*b*) What additional information would you need to construct a version of Table 6-8 that makes sense?
    (*c*) Construct such a table and recalculate NPV. Make additional assumptions as necessary.

18. United Pigpen is considering a proposal to manufacture high-protein hog feed. The project would make use of an existing warehouse, which is currently rented out to a neighboring firm. The next year's rental charge on the warehouse is $100,000, and thereafter the rent is expected to grow in line with inflation at 4 percent a year. In addition to using the warehouse the proposal envisages an investment in plant and equipment of $1.2 million. This could be depreciated for tax purposes straight-line over 10 years. However, Pigpen expects to terminate the project at the end of 8 years and to resell the plant and equipment in year 8 for $400,000. Finally, the project requires an initial investment in working capital of $350,000. Thereafter, working capital is forecast to be 10 percent of sales in each of years 1 through 7.

    Year 1 sales of hog feed are expected to be $4.2 million, and thereafter sales are forecast to grow by 5 percent a year, slightly faster than the inflation rate. Manufacturing costs are expected to be 90 percent of sales, and profits are subject to tax at 35 percent. The cost of capital is 12 percent.

    What is the net present value of Pigpen's project?

TABLE 6-8

Cash flows and present value of Reliable Electric's proposed investment (figures in thousands of dollars). See problem 17.

	1995	1996	1997	1998–2005
1. Capital expenditure	−10,400			
2. Research and development	−2,000			
3. Working capital	−4,000			
4. Revenue		8,000	16,000	40,000
5. Operating costs		−4,000	−8,000	−20,000
6. Overhead		−800	−1,600	−4,000
7. Depreciation		−1,040	−1,040	−1,040
8. Interest		−2,160	−2,160	−2,160
9. Income	−2,000	0	3,200	12,800
10. Tax	0	0	420	4,480
11. Net cash flow	−16,400	0	2,780	8,320
Net present value = +13,932				

Notes:
1. *Capital expenditure:* $8 million for new machinery and $2.4 million for a warehouse extension. The full cost of the extension has been charged to this project, although only about half of the space is currently needed. Since the new machinery will be housed in an existing factory building, no charge has been made for land and building.
2. *Research and development:* $1.82 million spent in 1994. This figure was corrected for 10 percent inflation from the time of expenditure to date. Thus 1.82 × 1.1 = $2 million.
3. *Working capital:* Initial investment in inventories.
4. *Revenue:* These figures assume sales of 2000 motors in 1996, 4000 in 1997, and 10,000 per year from 1998 through 2005. The initial unit price of $4000 is forecast to remain constant in real terms.
5. *Operating costs:* These include all direct and indirect costs. Indirect costs (heat, light, power, fringe benefits, etc.) are assumed to be 200 percent of direct labor costs. Operating costs per unit are forecasted to remain constant in real terms at $2000.
6. *Overhead:* Marketing and administrative costs, assumed equal to 10 percent of revenue.
7. *Depreciation:* Straight-line for 10 years.
8. *Interest:* Charged on capital expenditure and working capital at Reliable's current borrowing rate of 15 percent.
9. *Income:* Revenue less the sum of research and development, operating costs, overhead, depreciation, and interest.
10. *Tax:* 35 percent of income. However, income is negative in 1995. This loss is carried forward and deducted from taxable income in 1997.
11. *Net cash flow:* Assumed equal to income less tax.
12. *Net present value:* NPV of net cash flow at a 15 percent discount rate.

19. In the International Mulch and Compost example (Section 6-2), we assumed that losses on the project could be used to offset taxable profits elsewhere in the corporation. Suppose that the losses had to be carried forward and offset against future taxable profits from the project. How would the project NPV change? What is the value of the company's ability to use the tax deductions immediately?

20. In 2009 Peter Handy, the finance director of New Economy Transport Company (NETCO), was evaluating a proposed $610,000 outlay for an overhaul of its dry cargo boat, the Vital Spark. Estimated costs were as follows:

1. Install new engine	$250,000
2. New navigation system	200,000
3. Repair hull	160,000
	$610,000

The hull repair was chargeable against taxable profits in year 0. Items 1 and 2 were regarded as capital expenditure and could be depreciated for tax purposes straight-line over years 1 to 5.

NETCO's chief engineer, McPhail, had estimated post-overhaul operating costs as $985,000 per annum. However, the company could decide not to go ahead with the navigation system, in which case operating costs would rise to $1,181,000.

The Vital Spark is fully depreciated, and even if rehabilitated, it could not last more than 10 years. Instead of overhauling the Vital Spark, NETCO could sell it as is for $140,000 and invest in a new boat. The new boat would cost $2,000,000, and this expenditure could be depreciated straight-line over 10 years. The new boat would have an economic life of 15 years and would cost only $900,000 a year to operate.

The cost of capital is 10 percent and the company tax rate is 40 percent. Inflation was eliminated when the United States returned to the gold standard in 2006. What should NETCO do?

PART two

RISK

7

Introduction to Risk, Return, and the Opportunity Cost of Capital

We have managed to go through six chapters without directly addressing the problem of risk, but now the jig is up. We can no longer be satisfied with vague statements like "The opportunity cost of capital depends on the risk of the project." We need to know how risk is defined, what the links are between risk and the opportunity cost of capital, and how the financial manager can cope with risk in practical situations.

In this chapter we concentrate on the first of these issues and leave the other two to Chapters 8 and 9. We start by summarizing nearly 70 years of evidence on rates of return in capital markets. Then we take a first look at investment risks and show how they can be reduced by portfolio diversification. We introduce you to **beta**, the standard risk measure for individual securities.

The themes of this chapter, then, are portfolio risk, security risk, and diversification. For the most part, we take the view of the individual investor. But at the end of the chapter we turn the problem around and ask whether diversification makes sense as a *corporate* objective.

7-1 SIXTY-NINE YEARS OF CAPITAL MARKET HISTORY IN ONE EASY LESSON

Financial analysts are blessed with an enormous quantity of data on security prices and returns. For example, the University of Chicago's Center for Research in Security Prices (CRSP) has developed a file of prices and dividends for each month since 1926 for every stock that has been listed on the New York Stock Exchange (NYSE). Other files give data for stocks that are traded on the American Stock Exchange and the over-the-counter market, data for bonds, for options, and so on. But this is supposed to be one easy lesson. We, therefore, concentrate on a study by Ibbotson Associates which measures the historical performance of five portfolios of securities:

1. A portfolio of Treasury bills, i.e., United States government debt securities maturing in less than 1 year
2. A portfolio of long-term United States government bonds

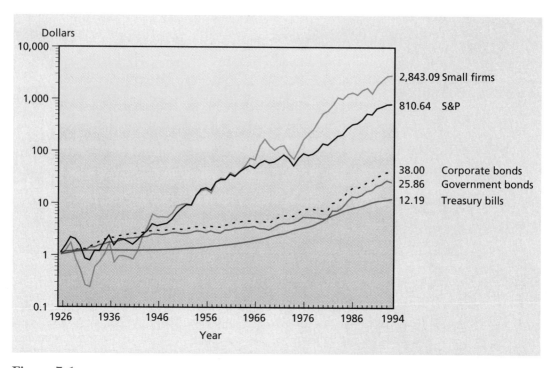

Figure 7-1 How an investment of $1 at the start of 1926 would have grown, assuming reinvestment of all dividend and interest payments. (*Source:* Ibbotson Associates, Inc., *Stocks, Bonds, Bills, and Inflation, 1995 Yearbook,* Chicago, 1995; cited hereafter in this chapter as the *1995 Yearbook.*)

3. A portfolio of long-term corporate bonds[1]

4. Standard and Poor's Composite Index, which represents a portfolio of common stocks of 500 large firms (Although only a small proportion of the 7000 or so publicly traded companies are included in the "S&P," these companies account for roughly 70 percent of the *value* of stocks traded.)

5. A portfolio of the common stocks of small firms

    These investments offer different degrees of risk. Treasury bills are about as safe an investment as you can make. There is no risk of default, and their short maturity means that the prices of Treasury bills are relatively stable. In fact, an investor who wishes to lend money for, say, 3 months can achieve a perfectly certain payoff by purchasing a Treasury bill maturing in 3 months. However, the investor cannot lock in a *real* rate of return: There is still some uncertainty about inflation.

    By switching to long-term government bonds, the investor acquires an asset whose price fluctuates as interest rates vary. (Bond prices fall when interest rates rise and rise when interest rates fall.) An investor who shifts from government to corporate bonds accepts an additional *default* risk. An investor who shifts from corporate bonds to common stocks has a direct share in the risks of the enterprise.

    Figure 7-1 shows how your money would have grown if you had invested $1 at the start of 1926 and reinvested all dividend or interest income in each of the five

---

[1]The two bond portfolios were revised each year in order to maintain a constant maturity.

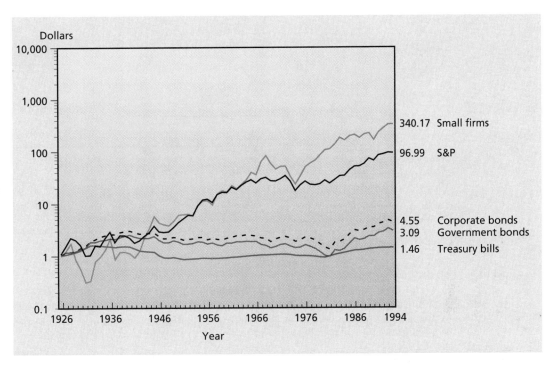

Figure 7-2 How an investment of $1 at the start of 1926 would have grown in real terms, assuming reinvestment of all dividend and interest payments. Compare this plot to Figure 7-1, and note how inflation has eroded the purchasing power of returns to investors. (*Source:* Ibbotson Associates, Inc., *1995 Yearbook.*)

portfolios.[2] Figure 7-2 is identical except that it depicts the growth in the *real* value of the portfolio. We will focus here on nominal values.

Portfolio performance coincides with our intuitive risk ranking. A dollar invested in the safest investment, Treasury bills, would have grown to just over $12 by 1994, barely enough to keep up with inflation. An investment in long-term Treasury bonds would have produced $26, and corporate bonds a pinch more. Common stocks were in a class by themselves. An investor who placed a dollar in the stocks of large U.S. firms would have received $811. The jackpot, however, went to investors in stocks of small firms, who walked away with $2843 for each dollar invested.

Ibbotson Associates also calculated the rate of return from these portfolios for each year from 1926 to 1994. This rate of return reflects both cash receipts—dividends or interest—and the capital gains or losses realized during the year. Averages of the 69 annual rates of return for each portfolio are shown in Table 7-1.

Since 1926 Treasury bills have provided the lowest average return—3.7 percent per year in *nominal* terms and .6 percent in *real* terms. In other words, the average rate of inflation over this period was just over 3 percent per year. Common stocks were again the winners. Stocks of major corporations provided on average a *risk premium* of 8.4 percent a year over the return on Treasury bills. Stocks of small firms offered an even higher premium.

---

[2]Portfolio values are plotted on a log scale. If they were not, the ending values for the two common stock portfolios would run off the top of the page.

TABLE 7-1
· ·

Average rates of return on Treasury bills, government bonds, corporate bonds, and common stocks, 1926–1994 (figures in percent per year)

Portfolio	AVERAGE ANNUAL RATE OF RETURN		Average Risk Premium (Extra Return versus Treasury Bills)
	Nominal	Real	
Treasury bills	3.7	.6	0
Government bonds	5.2	2.1	1.4
Corporate bonds	5.7	2.7	2.0
Common stocks (S&P 500)	12.2	8.9	8.4
Small-firm common stocks	17.4	13.9	13.7

Source: Ibbotson Associates, Inc., *1995 Yearbook.*

You may ask why we look back over such a long period to measure average rates of return. The reason is that annual rates of return for common stocks fluctuate so much that averages taken over short periods are meaningless. Our only hope of gaining insights from historical rates of return is to look at a very long period.[3]

Arithmetic Averages and Compound Annual Returns
Notice that the average returns shown in Table 7-1 are arithmetic averages. In other words, Ibbotson Associates simply added the 69 annual returns and divided by 69. The arithmetic average is higher than the compound annual return over the period. The 69-year compound annual return for the S&P index was 10.2 percent.[4]

The proper uses of arithmetic and compound rates of return from past investments are often misunderstood. Therefore, we call a brief time-out for a clarifying example.

Example: Suppose that the price of Big Oil's common stock is $100. There is an equal chance that at the end of the year the stock will be worth $90, $110, or $130. Therefore, the return could be −10 percent, +10 percent, or +30 percent (we assume that Big Oil does not pay a dividend). The *expected* return is $\frac{1}{3}(-10 + 10 + 30) = +10$ percent.

If we run the process in reverse and discount the expected cash flow by the expected rate of return, we obtain the value of Big Oil's stock:

---

[3]Even with 69 years of data we cannot be sure that this period is truly representative and that the average is not distorted by a few unusually high or low returns. The reliability of an estimate of the average is usually measured by its *standard error.* For example, the standard error of our estimate of the average risk premium on common stocks is 2.5 percent. There is a 95 percent chance that the *true* average is within plus or minus 2 standard errors of the 8.4 percent estimate. In other words, if you said that the true average was between 3.5 and 13.4 percent, you would have a 95 percent chance of being right. (*Technical note:* The standard error of the mean is equal to the standard deviation divided by the square root of the number of observations. In our case the standard deviation is 20.6 percent, and therefore the standard error is $20.6/\sqrt{69} = 2.5$.)

[4]This was calculated from $(1 + r)^{69} = 811$, which implies $r = .102$. (*Technical note:* For lognormally distributed returns the annual compound return is equal to the arithmetic average return minus half the variance. For example, the annual standard deviation of returns on the U.S. market was about .20, or 20 percent. Variance was therefore $.20^2$, or .04. The compound annual return is $.04/2 = .02$, or 2 percentage points less than the arithmetic average.)

$$PV = \frac{110}{1.10} = \$100$$

The expected return of 10 percent is therefore the correct rate at which to discount the expected cash flow from Big Oil's stock. It is also the opportunity cost of capital for investments which have the same degree of risk as Big Oil.

Now suppose that we observe the returns on Big Oil stock over a large number of years. If the odds are unchanged, the return will be −10 percent in a third of the years, +10 percent in a further third, and +30 percent in the remaining years. The arithmetic average of these yearly returns is

$$\frac{-10 + 10 + 30}{3} = +10\%$$

Thus the arithmetic average of the returns correctly measures the opportunity cost of capital for investments of similar risk to Big Oil stock.

The compound annual return on Big Oil stock is

$$(.9 \times 1.1 \times 1.3)^{\frac{1}{3}} - 1 = .088, \text{ or } 8.8\%,$$

less than the opportunity cost of capital. Investors would not be willing to invest in a project that offered an 8.8 percent expected return if they could get an expected return of 10 percent in the capital markets. The net present value of such a project would be

$$NPV = 100 + \frac{108.8}{1.1} = -1.1$$

Moral: If the cost of capital is estimated from historical returns or risk premiums, use arithmetic averages, not compound annual rates of return.

<h3>Using Historical Evidence to Evaluate Today's Cost of Capital</h3>

Suppose there is an investment project which you *know*—don't ask how—has the same risk as Standard and Poor's Composite Index. We will say that it has the same degree of risk as the *market portfolio*, although this is speaking somewhat loosely, because the index does not include all risky securities. What rate should you use to discount this project's forecasted cash flows?

Clearly you should use the currently expected rate of return on the market portfolio; that is the return investors would forgo by investing in the proposed project. Let us call this market return r_m. One way to estimate r_m is to assume that the future will be like the past and that today's investors expect to receive the same "normal" rates of return revealed by the averages shown in Table 7-1. In this case, you would set r_m at 12.2 percent, the average of past market returns.

Unfortunately, this is *not* the way to do it: r_m is not likely to be stable over time. Remember that it is the sum of the risk-free interest rate r_f and a premium for risk. We know that r_f varies. For example, as we finish this chapter in early 1995, Treasury bills yield about 6 percent, more than 2 percentage points above the 3.7 percent average return of Treasury bills.

What if you were called upon to estimate r_m in 1995? Would you have said 12.2 percent? That would have squeezed the risk premium by 2.2 percentage points. A more sensible procedure takes the current interest rate on Treasury bills plus 8.4 percent, the average *risk premium* shown in Table 7-1. With a rate of 6 percent for Treasury bills, that gives

$$r_m(1995) = r_f(1995) + \text{normal risk premium}$$
$$= .06 + .084 = .144, \text{ or } 14.4\%$$

Figure 7-3 Expected market returns estimated using the constant-growth DCF formula. The spread between these estimates and Treasury bill yields varies, but it is consistent with the long-run average risk premium of 8.4 percent shown in Table 7-1. [*Source:* R. S. Harris and F. C. Marston, "Estimating Shareholder Risk Premia Using Analysts' Growth Forecasts," *Financial Management,* 21:63–70 (Summer 1992).]

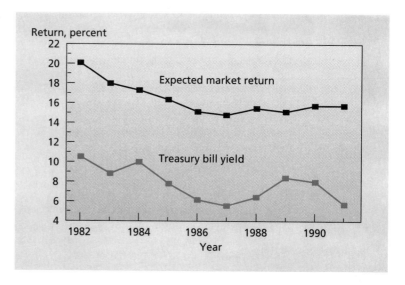

The crucial assumption here is that there is a normal, stable risk premium on the market portfolio, so that the expected *future* risk premium can be measured by the average past risk premium. One could quarrel with this assumption, but at least it does yield estimates of r_m that seem sensible.

Even with nearly 70 years of data, we can't estimate the market risk premium exactly; nor can we be sure that today investors are demanding the same reward for risk that they were 70 years ago. So it would be good to have a check that our figures are at least in the right ballpark. Robert Harris and Felicia Marston have used the constant-growth DCF formula to estimate average rates of return that security analysts expected on a large sample of common stocks.[5] Their findings are summarized by Figure 7-3. Over the period 1982 to 1991 analysts appeared to be forecasting a market return about 8½ percent above the Treasury bill rate.

7-2 MEASURING PORTFOLIO RISK

You now have a couple of benchmarks. You know the discount rate for safe projects, and you know the rate for "average-risk" projects. But you *don't* know yet how to estimate discount rates for assets that do not fit these simple cases. To do that, you have to learn (1) how to measure risk and (2) the relationship between risks borne and risk premiums demanded.

Figure 7-4 shows the 69 annual rates of return calculated by Ibbotson Associates for Standard and Poor's Composite Index. The fluctuations in year-to-year returns are remarkably wide. The highest annual return was 54.0 percent in 1933—a partial rebound from the stock market crash of 1929–1932. However, there were losses exceeding 25 percent in 4 years, the worst being the −43.3 percent return in 1931.

---

[5]See R. S. Harris and F. C. Marston, "Estimating Shareholder Risk Premia Using Analysts' Growth Forecasts," *Financial Management,* 21:63–70 (Summer 1992). Harris and Marston used 5-year earnings forecasts regularly published by I/B/E/S. See Section 4-3.

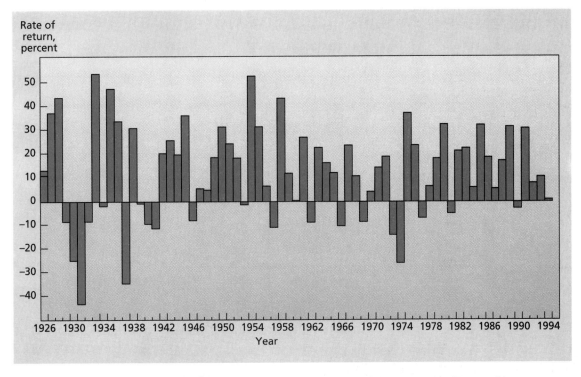

Figure 7-4 The stock market has been a profitable but extremely variable investment. (*Source:* Ibbotson Associates, Inc., *1995 Yearbook.*)

Another way of presenting these data is by a histogram or frequency distribution. This is done in Figure 7-5, where the variability of year-to-year returns shows up in the wide "spread" of outcomes.

Variance and Standard Deviation

The standard statistical measures of spread are **variance** and **standard deviation.** The variance of the market return is the expected squared deviation from the expected return. In other words,

$$\text{Variance } (\tilde{r}_m) = \text{the expected value of } (\tilde{r}_m - r_m)^2$$

where $\tilde{r}_m$ is the actual return and r_m is the expected return.[6] The standard deviation is simply the square root of the variance:

$$\text{Standard deviation of } \tilde{r}_m = \sqrt{\text{variance } (\tilde{r}_m)}$$

Standard deviation is often denoted by σ and variance by σ^2.

---

[6]One more technical point: When variance is estimated from a sample of *observed* returns, we add the squared deviations and divide by $N - 1$, where N is the number of observations. We divide by $N - 1$ rather than N to correct for what is called *the loss of a degree of freedom.* The formula is

$$\text{Variance } (\tilde{r}_m) = \frac{1}{N-1} \sum_{t=1}^{N} (\tilde{r}_{mt} - r_m)^2$$

where $\tilde{r}_{mt}$ = market return in period t
r_m = mean of the values of $\tilde{r}_m$

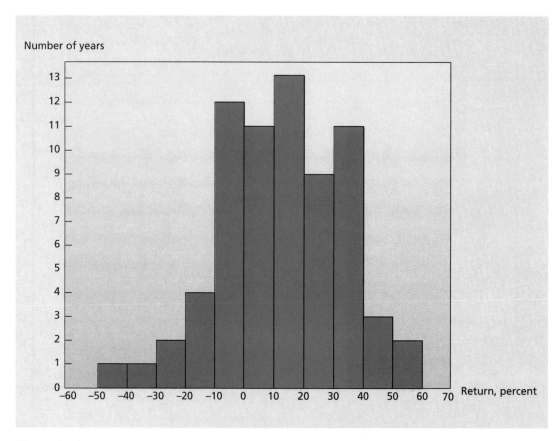

Figure 7-5 Histogram of the annual rates of return from the stock market in the United States, 1926–1988, showing the wide spread of returns from investment in common stocks. (*Source:* Ibbotson Associates, Inc., *1995 Yearbook.*)

Example: Here is a very simple example showing how variance and standard deviation are calculated. Suppose that you are offered the chance to play the following game. You start by investing $100. Then two coins are flipped. For each head that comes up you get back your starting balance *plus* 20 percent, and for each tail that comes up you get back your starting balance *less* 10 percent. Clearly there are four equally likely outcomes:

- Head + head: You gain 40 percent.
- Head + tail: You gain 10 percent.
- Tail + head: You gain 10 percent.
- Tail + tail: You lose 20 percent.

There is a chance of 1 in 4, or .25, that you will make 40 percent; a chance of 2 in 4, or .5, that you will make 10 percent; and a chance of 1 in 4, or .25, that you will lose 20 percent. The game's expected return is, therefore, a weighted average of the possible outcomes:

TABLE 7-2

The coin-tossing game: calculating variance and standard deviation

(1) Percent Rate of Return ($\tilde{r}$)	(2) Deviation from Expected Return ($\tilde{r} - r$)	(3) Squared Deviation $[(\tilde{r} - r)^2]$	(4) Probability	(5) Probability $\times$ Squared Deviation
+40	+30	900	.25	225
+10	0	0	.5	0
−20	−30	900	.25	225

$$\text{Variance} = \text{expected value of } (\tilde{r} - r)^2 = 450$$
$$\text{Standard deviation} = \sqrt{\text{variance}} = \sqrt{450} = 21$$

$$\text{Expected return} = (.25 \times 40) + (.5 \times 10) + (.25 \times -20) = +10\%$$

Table 7-2 shows that the variance of the percentage returns is 450. Standard deviation is the square root of 450, or 21. This figure is in the same units as the rate of return, so we can say that the game's variability is 21 percent.

One way of defining uncertainty is to say that more things can happen than will happen. The risk of an asset can be completely expressed, as we did for the coin-tossing game, by writing all possible outcomes and the probability of each. For real assets this is cumbersome and often impossible. Therefore we use variance or standard deviation to summarize the spread of possible outcomes.[7]

These measures are natural indexes of risk.[8] If the outcome of the coin-tossing game had been certain, the standard deviation would have been zero. The actual standard deviation is positive because we *don't* know what will happen.

Or think of a second game, the same as the first except that each head means a 35 percent gain and each tail means a 25 percent loss. Again, there are four equally likely outcomes:

- Head + head: You gain 70 percent.
- Head + tail: You gain 10 percent.
- Tail + head: You gain 10 percent.
- Tail + tail: You lose 50 percent.

For this game the expected return is 10 percent, the same as that of the first game. But its standard deviation is double that of the first game, 42 versus 21 percent. By this measure the second game is twice as risky as the first.

---

[7] Which of the two we use is solely a matter of convenience. Since standard deviation is in the same units as the rate of return, it is generally more convenient to use standard deviation. However, when we are talking about the *proportion* of risk that is due to some factor, it is usually less confusing to work in terms of the variance.

[8] As we explain in Chapter 8, standard deviation and variance are the correct measures of risk if the returns are normally distributed.

In principle, you could estimate the variability of any portfolio of stocks or bonds by the procedure just described. You would identify the possible outcomes, assign a probability to each outcome, and grind through the calculations. But where do the probabilities come from? You can't look them up in the newspaper; newspapers seem to go out of their way to avoid definite statements about prospects for securities. We once saw an article headlined "Bond Prices Possibly Set to Move Sharply Either Way." Stockbrokers are much the same. Yours may respond to your query about possible market outcomes with a statement like this:

> *The market currently appears to be undergoing a period of consolidation. For the intermediate term, we would take a constructive view, provided economic recovery continues. The market could be up 20 percent a year from now, perhaps more if inflation moderates. On the other hand, . . .*

The Delphic oracle gave advice, but no probabilities.

Most financial analysts start by observing past variability. Of course, there is no risk in hindsight, but it is reasonable to assume that portfolios with histories of high variability also have the least predictable future performance.

The annual standard deviations and variances observed for our five portfolios over the period 1926–1994 were:[9]

Portfolio	Standard Deviation (σ)	Variance (σ^2)
Treasury bills	3.3	10.7
Long-term government bonds	8.7	75.5
Corporate bonds	8.3	69.7
Common stocks (S&P 500)	20.2	408.0
Small-firm common stocks	34.3	1177.4

As expected, Treasury bills were the least variable security, and small-firm stocks were the most variable. Government and corporate bonds hold the middle ground.[10]

You may find it interesting to compare the coin-tossing game and the stock market as alternative investments. The stock market generated an average annual return of 12.2 percent with a standard deviation of 20.2 percent. The game offers 10 and 21 percent, respectively—slightly lower return and about the same variability. Your gambling friends may have come up with a crude representation of the stock market.

---

[9]Ibbotson Associates, Inc., *1995 Yearbook*. In discussing the riskiness of *bonds*, be careful to specify the time period and whether you are speaking in real or nominal terms. The *nominal* return on a long-term government bond is absolutely certain to an investor who holds on until maturity; in other words, it is risk-free if you forget about inflation. After all, the government can always print money to pay off its debts. However, the real return on Treasury securities is uncertain because no one knows how much each future dollar will buy.

The bond returns reported by Ibbotson Associates were measured annually. The returns reflect year-to-year changes in bond prices as well as interest received. The *1-year* returns on long-term bonds are risky in *both* real and nominal terms.

[10]You may have noticed that corporate bonds come in just ahead of government bonds in terms of low variability. You shouldn't get excited about this. The problem is that it is difficult to get two sets of bonds that are alike in all other respects. For example, most corporate bonds are *callable* (i.e., the company has an option to repurchase them for their face value). Government bonds are not callable. Also interest payments are higher on corporate bonds. Therefore, investors in corporate bonds get their money sooner. As we will see in Chapter 25, this also reduces the bond's variability.

Of course, there is no reason to believe that the market's variability should stay the same over nearly 70 years. For example, it is clearly less now than in the Great Depression of the 1930s. Here are standard deviations of the returns on the S&P index for successive periods starting in 1926:

Period	Market Standard Deviation (σ_m)
1926–1939	33.6
1940–1949	15.8
1950–1959	11.8
1960–1969	12.1
1970–1979	15.9
1980–1994	15.2

These figures do not support the widespread impression of especially volatile stock prices during the 1980s and early 1990s. These years were below average on the volatility front.

However, there were brief episodes of extremely high volatility. On Black Monday, October 19, 1987, the market index fell by 23 percent *on a single day*. The standard deviation of the index for the week surrounding Black Monday was equivalent to 89 percent per year. Fortunately, volatility dropped back to normal levels within a few weeks after the crash.

How Diversification Reduces Risk

We can calculate our measures of variability equally well for individual securities and portfolios of securities. Of course, the level of variability over 69 years is less interesting for specific companies than for the market portfolio—it is a rare company that faces the same business risks today as it did in 1926.

Table 7-3 presents estimated standard deviations for 10 well-known common stocks for a recent 5-year period.[11] Do these standard deviations look high to you? They should. Remember that the market portfolio's standard deviation was about 20 percent over the entire 1926–1994 period and somewhat less in later years. Of our individual stocks only Exxon had a standard deviation significantly less than 20 percent, though two others just creep in under the bar. Most stocks are substantially more variable than the market portfolio; only a handful are less variable.

This raises an important question: The market portfolio is made up of individual stocks, so why doesn't its variability reflect the average variability of its components? The answer is that *diversification reduces variability*.

Even a little diversification can provide a substantial reduction in variability. Suppose you calculate and compare the standard deviations of randomly chosen one-stock portfolios, two-stock portfolios, five-stock portfolios, etc. You can see from Figure 7-6 that diversification can cut the variability of returns about in half. But you

---

[11]These estimates are derived from *monthly* rates of return. Five annual observations are insufficient for estimating variability. We converted the monthly variance to an annual variance by multiplying by 12. That is, the variance of the monthly return is one-twelfth of the annual variance. The longer you hold a security or portfolio, the more risk you have to bear.

This conversion assumes that successive monthly returns are statistically independent. This is, in fact, a good assumption, as we will show in Chapter 13.

Because variance is approximately proportional to the length of time interval over which a security or portfolio return is measured, *standard deviation* is proportional to the square root of the interval.

TABLE 7-3

· ·

Standard deviations for selected common stocks, 1989–1994 (figures in percent per year)

Stock	Standard Deviation	Stock	Standard Deviation
AT&T	21.4	Exxon	12.1
Biogen	51.5	Ford Motor	28.0
Bristol-Myers Squibb	18.6	General Electric	19.6
Coca-Cola	21.6	McDonald's	21.7
Compaq	43.5	Microsoft	53.6

Figure 7-6 Diversification reduces risk (standard deviation) rapidly at first, then more slowly.

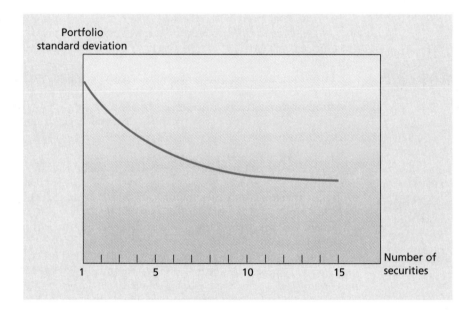

can get most of this benefit with relatively few stocks: The improvement is slight when the number of securities is increased beyond, say, 20 or 30.

Diversification works because prices of different stocks do not move exactly together. Statisticians make the same point when they say that stock price changes are less than perfectly correlated. Look, for example, at Figure 7-7. You can see that an investment in *either* Coca-Cola *or* Compaq would have been very variable. But on many occasions a decline in the value of one stock was canceled by a rise in the price of the other.[12] Therefore there was an opportunity to reduce your risk by diversification. Figure 7-7 shows that if you had divided your funds evenly between the two stocks, the variability of your portfolio would have been substantially less than the average variability of the two stocks.[13]

---

[12]Over this period the correlation between the returns on the two stocks was .24.

[13]For the five years from 1989 to 1994, the standard deviations of Coca-Cola and Compaq were 21.6 and 43.5 percent, respectively. The standard deviation of a portfolio with half invested in each was 26.5 percent.

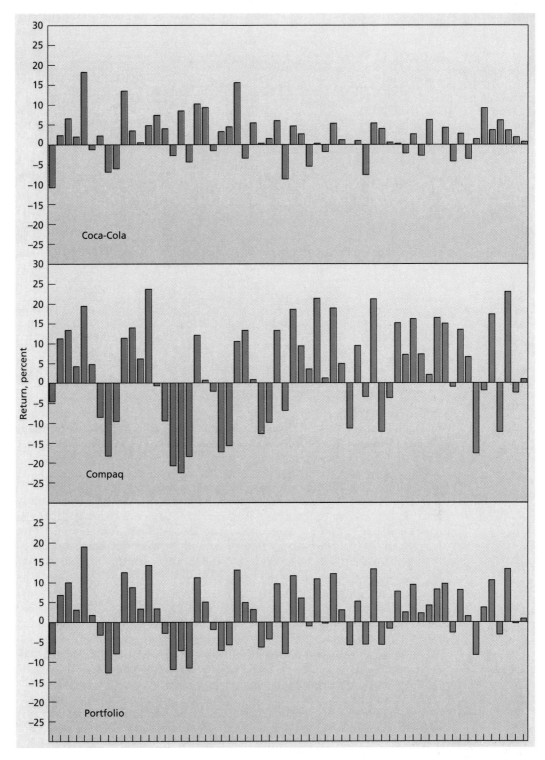

Figure 7-7 The variability of a portfolio with equal holdings in Coca-Cola and Compaq would have been less than the average variability of the individual stocks. These returns run from July 1989 to June 1994.

Figure 7-8 Diversification eliminates unique risk. But there is some risk that diversification *cannot* eliminate. This is called *market risk.*

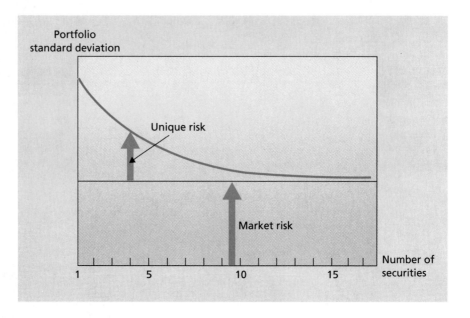

The risk that potentially can be eliminated by diversification is called **unique risk.**[14] Unique risk stems from the fact that many of the perils that surround an individual company are peculiar to that company and perhaps its immediate competitors. But there is also some risk that you can't avoid, regardless of how much you diversify. This risk is generally known as **market risk.**[15] Market risk stems from the fact that there are other economywide perils which threaten all businesses. That is why stocks have a tendency to move together. And that is why investors are exposed to "market uncertainties," no matter how many stocks they hold.

In Figure 7-8 we have divided the risk into its two parts—unique risk and market risk. If you have only a single stock, unique risk is very important; but once you have a portfolio of 20 or more stocks, diversification has done the bulk of its work. For a reasonably well-diversified portfolio, only market risk matters. Therefore, the predominant source of uncertainty for a diversified investor is that the market will rise or plummet, carrying the investor's portfolio with it.

*7-3 CALCULATING PORTFOLIO RISK

We have given you an intuitive idea of how diversification reduces risk, but to understand fully the effect of diversification, you need to know how the risk of a portfolio depends on the risk of the individual shares.

Suppose that 60 percent of your portfolio is invested in the shares of Bristol-Myers Squibb and the remainder in Ford Motor. You expect that over the coming year Bristol-Myers will give a return of 15 percent and Ford 21 percent. The ex-

[14]Unique risk may be called *unsystematic risk, residual risk, specific risk,* or *diversifiable risk.*

[15]Market risk may be called *systematic risk* or *undiversifiable risk.*

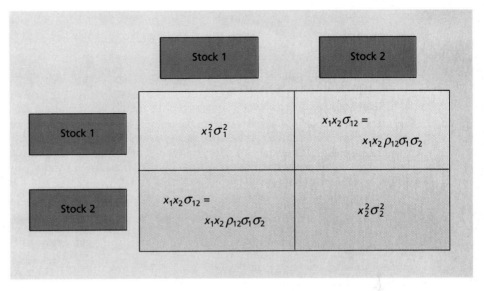

Figure 7-9 The variance of a two-stock portfolio is the sum of these four boxes. x_i = proportion invested in stock i; σ_i^2 = variance of return on stock i; σ_{ij} = covariance of returns on stocks i and j ($\rho_{ij}\sigma_i\sigma_j$); ρ_{ij} = correlation between returns on stocks i and j.

pected return on your portfolio is simply a weighted average of the expected returns on the individual stocks:[16]

$$\text{Expected portfolio return} = (0.60 \times 15) + (0.40 \times 21) = 17.4\%$$

Calculating the expected portfolio return is easy. The hard part is to work out the risk of your portfolio. In the past the standard deviation of returns was about 18.6 percent for Bristol-Myers and 28.0 percent for Ford. You believe that these figures are a fair measure of the spread of possible *future* outcomes. Your first inclination may be to assume that the standard deviation of the returns on your portfolio is a weighted average of the standard deviations on the individual holdings, that is, $(0.60 \times 18.6) + (0.40 \times 28.0) = 22.4$ percent. That would be correct *only* if the prices of the two stocks moved in perfect lockstep. In any other case, diversification would reduce the risk below this figure.

The exact procedure for calculating the risk of a two-stock portfolio is given in Figure 7-9. You need to fill in four boxes. To complete the top left box, you weight the variance of the returns on stock 1 (σ_1^2) by the *square* of the proportion invested in it (x_1^2). Similarly, to complete the bottom right box, you weight the variance of the returns on stock 2 (σ_2^2) by the *square* of the proportion invested in stock 2 (x_2^2).

The entries in these diagonal boxes depend on the variances of stocks 1 and 2; the entries in the other two boxes depend on their *covariance*. As you might guess, the covariance is a measure of the degree to which the two stocks "covary." The co-

---

[16]Let's check this. Suppose you invest $60 in Bristol-Myers and $40 in Ford. The expected dollar return on your Bristol-Myers is .15(60) = $9.00, and on Ford it is .21(40) = $8.40. The expected dollar return on your portfolio is 9.00 + 8.40 = $17.40. The portfolio *rate* of return is 17.40/100 = 0.174, or 17.4 percent.

variance can be expressed as the product of the correlation coefficient ρ_{12} and the two standard deviations: [17]

$$\text{Covariance between stocks 1 and 2} = \sigma_{12} = \rho_{12}\sigma_1\sigma_2$$

For the most part stocks tend to move together. In this case the correlation coefficient ρ_{12} is positive, and therefore the covariance σ_{12} is also positive. If the prospects of the stocks were wholly unrelated, both the correlation coefficient and the covariance would be zero; and if the stocks tended to move in opposite directions, the correlation coefficient and the covariance would be negative. Just as you weighted the variances by the square of the proportion invested, so you must weight the covariance by the *product* of the two proportionate holdings x_1 and x_2.

Once you have completed these four boxes, you simply add the entries to obtain the portfolio variance:

$$\text{Portfolio variance} = x_1^2\sigma_1^2 + x_2^2\sigma_2^2 + 2(x_1x_2\rho_{12}\sigma_1\sigma_2)$$

The portfolio standard deviation is, of course, the square root of the variance.

Now you can try putting in some figures for Bristol-Myers and Ford Motor. We said earlier that if the two stocks were perfectly correlated, the standard deviation of the portfolio would lie 40 percent of the way between the standard deviations of the two stocks. Let us check this out by filling in the boxes with $\rho_{12} = +1$.

	Bristol-Myers	Ford Motor
Bristol-Myers	$x_1^2\sigma_1^2 = (.60)^2 \times (18.6)^2$	$x_1x_2\rho_{12}\sigma_1\sigma_2 = .60 \times .40 \times 1$ $\times 18.6 \times 28.0$
Ford Motor	$x_1x_2\rho_{12}\sigma_1\sigma_2 = .60 \times .40 \times 1$ $\times 18.6 \times 28.0$	$x_2^2\sigma_2^2 = (.40)^2 \times (28.0)^2$

The variance of your portfolio is the sum of these entries:

$$\begin{aligned}
\text{Portfolio variance} &= [(.60)^2 \times (18.6)^2] + [(.40)^2 \times (28.0)^2] \\
&\quad + 2(.60 \times .40 \times 1 \times 18.6 \times 28.0) \\
&= 500
\end{aligned}$$

The standard deviation is $\sqrt{500} = 22.4$ percent, or 40 percent of the way between 18.6 and 28.0.

Bristol-Myers and Ford do not move in perfect lockstep. If past experience is any guide, the correlation between the two stocks is about .2. If we go through the same exercise again with $\rho_{12} = +.2$, we find

$$\begin{aligned}
\text{Portfolio variance} &= [(.60)^2 \times (18.6)^2] + [(.40)^2 \times (28.0)^2] \\
&\quad + 2(.60 \times .40 \times .2 \times 18.6 \times 28.0) \\
&= 300
\end{aligned}$$

---

[17]Another way to define the covariance is as follows:

$$\text{Covariance between stocks 1 and 2} = \sigma_{12} = \text{expected value of } (\tilde{r}_1 - r_1) \times (\tilde{r}_2 - r_2)$$

Note that any security's covariance with itself is just its variance:

$$\begin{aligned}
\sigma_{11} &= \text{expected value of } (\tilde{r}_1 - r_1) \times (\tilde{r}_1 - r_1) \\
&= \text{expected value of } (\tilde{r}_1 - r_1)^2 = \text{variance of stock 1}
\end{aligned}$$

The standard deviation is $\sqrt{300} = 17.3$ percent. The risk is now *less* than 40 percent of the way between 18.6 and 28.0—in fact, it is less than the risk of investing in Bristol-Myers alone.

The greatest payoff to diversification comes when the two stocks are *negatively* correlated. Unfortunately, this almost never occurs with real stocks, but just for illustration, let us assume it for Bristol-Myers and Ford. And as long as we are being unrealistic, we might as well go whole hog and assume perfect negative correlation ($\rho_{12} = -1$). In this case,

$$\text{Portfolio variance} = [(.60)^2 \times (18.6)^2] + [(.40)^2 \times (28.0)^2]$$
$$+ 2[.60 \times .40 \times (-1) \times 18.6 \times 28.0]$$
$$= 0$$

When there is perfect negative correlation, there is always a portfolio strategy (represented by a particular set of portfolio weights) which will completely eliminate risk.[18] It's too bad perfect negative correlation doesn't really occur between common stocks.

*General Formula for Computing Portfolio Risk

The method for calculating portfolio risk can easily be extended to portfolios of three or more securities. We just have to fill in a larger number of boxes. Each of those down the diagonal—the shaded boxes in Figure 7-10—contains the variance weighted by the square of the proportion invested. Each of the other boxes contains the covariance between that pair of securities, weighted by the product of the proportions invested.[19]

Did you notice in Figure 7-10 how much more important the covariances became as we added more securities to the portfolio? When there are just two securities, there are equal numbers of variance boxes and of covariance boxes. When there are many securities, the number of covariances is much larger than the number of variances. Thus the variability of a well-diversified portfolio reflects mainly the covariances.

*Limits to Diversification

Suppose we are dealing with portfolios in which equal investments are made in each of N stocks. The proportion invested in each stock is, therefore, $1/N$. So in each variance box we have $(1/N)^2$ times the variance, and in each covariance box we have $(1/N)^2$ times the covariance. There are N variance boxes and $N^2 - N$ covariance boxes. Therefore,

$$\text{Portfolio variance} = N\left(\frac{1}{N}\right)^2 \times \text{average variance}$$
$$+ (N^2 - N)\left(\frac{1}{N}\right)^2 \times \text{average covariance}$$
$$= \frac{1}{N} \times \text{average variance} + \left(1 - \frac{1}{N}\right) \times \text{average covariance}$$

Notice that as N increases, the portfolio variance steadily approaches the average covariance. If the average covariance were zero, it would be possible to eliminate *all* risk by holding a sufficient number of securities. Unfortunately common stocks move to-

---

[18] Since the standard deviation of Ford is 1.5 times that of Bristol-Myers, you need to invest 1.5 times as much in Bristol-Myers to eliminate risk in this two-stock portfolio.

[19] The formal equivalent to "add all the boxes" is

$$\text{Portfolio variance} = \sum_{i=1}^{N} \sum_{j=1}^{N} x_i x_j \sigma_{ij}$$

Notice that when $i = j$, σ_{ij} is just the variance of stock i.

Figure 7-10 To find the variance of an *N*-stock portfolio, we must add the entries in a matrix like this. The diagonal boxes contain variance terms $(x_i^2\sigma_i^2)$, and the off-diagonal boxes contain covariance terms $(x_i x_j \sigma_{ij})$.

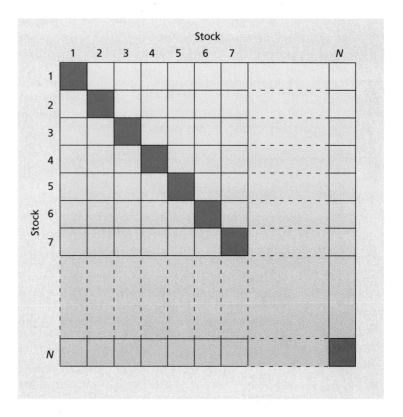

gether, not independently. Thus most of the stocks that the investor can actually buy are tied together in a web of positive covariances which set the limit to the benefits of diversification. Now we can understand the precise meaning of the market risk portrayed in Figure 7-8. It is the average covariance which constitutes the bedrock of risk remaining after diversification has done its work.

7-4 HOW INDIVIDUAL SECURITIES AFFECT PORTFOLIO RISK

We presented earlier some data on the variability of 10 individual securities. Biogen had the highest standard deviation and Exxon the lowest. If you had held Biogen on its own, the spread of possible returns would have been four times greater than if you had held Exxon on its own. But that is not a very interesting fact. Wise investors don't put all their eggs into just one basket: They reduce their risk by diversification. They are therefore interested in the effect that each stock will have on the risk of their portfolio.

This brings us to one of the principal themes of this chapter: *The risk of a well-diversified portfolio depends on the market risk of the securities included in the portfolio.* Tattoo that statement on your forehead if you can't remember it any other way. It is one of the most important ideas in this book.

Market Risk Is Measured by Beta

If you want to know the contribution of an individual security to the risk of a well-diversified portfolio, it is no good thinking about how risky that security is if held in isolation—you need to measure its *market* risk, and that boils down to measuring how sensitive it is to market movements. This sensitivity is called **beta** (β).

TABLE 7-4
• •

Betas for selected common stocks, 1989–1994

Stock	Beta	Stock	Beta
AT&T	.92	Exxon	.51
Biogen	2.20	Ford Motor	1.12
Bristol-Myers Squibb	.97	General Electric	1.22
Coca-Cola	1.12	McDonald's	1.07
Compaq	1.18	Microsoft	1.23

Stocks with betas greater than 1.0 tend to amplify the overall movements of the market. Stocks with betas between 0 and 1.0 tend to move in the same direction as the market, but not as far. Of course, the market is the portfolio of all stocks, so the "average" stock has a beta of 1.0. Table 7-4 reports betas for the 10 well-known common stocks we referred to earlier.

Biogen, a rapidly growing biotech company, had a beta of 2.20 over the 5 years from mid-1989 to mid-1994. If the future resembles the past, this means that *on average* when the market rises an extra 1 percent, Biogen's stock price will rise by an extra 2.20 percent. When the market falls an extra 2 percent, Biogen will fall an extra 4.40 percent. Thus a line fitted to a plot of Biogen's returns versus market returns has a slope of 2.20. See Figure 7-11.

Of course, Biogen's stock returns are not perfectly correlated with market returns. The company is also subject to unique risk, so the actual returns will be scattered about the fitted line in Figure 7-11. Sometimes Biogen will head south while the market goes north, or vice versa.

Figure 7-11 The return on Biogen stock changes on average by 2.20 percent for each additional 1 percent change in the market return. Beta is therefore 2.20.

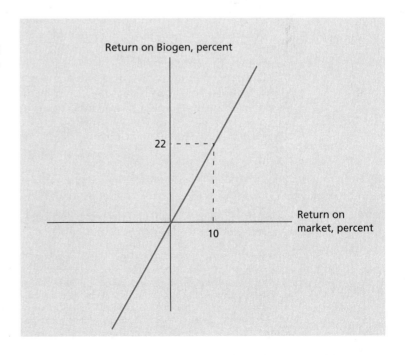

Of all the stocks in Table 7-4 Biogen stands out as unusually sensitive to market movements. Exxon is at the other extreme. A line fitted to a plot of Exxon's returns versus market returns would be much less steep: Its gradient would be only .51.

Why Security Betas Determine Portfolio Risk

Let's review the two crucial points about security risk and portfolio risk:

- Market risk accounts for most of the risk of a well-diversified portfolio.
- The beta of an individual security measures its sensitivity to market movements.

It's easy to see where we are headed: In a portfolio context, a security's risk is measured by beta. Perhaps we could just jump to that conclusion, but we'd rather explain it. In fact, we'll offer two explanations.

EXPLANATION 1: WHERE'S BEDROCK?   Look back to Figure 7-8, which shows how the standard deviation of portfolio return depends on the number of securities in the portfolio. With more securities, and therefore better diversification, portfolio risk declines until all unique risk is eliminated and only the bedrock of market risk remains.

Where's bedrock? It depends on the average beta of the securities selected.

Suppose we constructed a portfolio containing a large number of stocks—500, say—drawn randomly from the whole market. What would we get? The market itself, or a portfolio *very* close to it. The portfolio beta would be 1.0, and the correlation with the market would be 1.0. If the standard deviation of the market were 20 percent (roughly its average for 1926–1994), then the portfolio standard deviation would also be 20 percent.

But suppose we constructed the portfolio from a large group of stocks with an average beta of 1.5. Again we would end up with a 500-stock portfolio with virtually no unique risk—a portfolio that moves almost in lockstep with the market. However, *this* portfolio's standard deviation would be 30 percent, 1.5 times that of the market.[20] A well-diversified portfolio with a beta of 1.5 will amplify every market move by 50 percent and end up with 150 percent of the market's risk.

Of course, we could repeat the same experiment with stocks with a beta of .5 and end up with a well-diversified portfolio half as risky as the market. Figure 7-12*a*, *b*, and *c* shows these three cases.

The general point is this: The risk of a well-diversified portfolio is proportional to the portfolio beta, which equals the average beta of the securities included in the portfolio. This shows you how portfolio risk is driven by security betas.

*EXPLANATION 2: BETAS AND COVARIANCES.   A statistician would define the beta of stock *i* as

$$\beta_i = \frac{\sigma_{im}}{\sigma_m^2}$$

where σ_{im} is the covariance between stock i's return and the market return, and σ_m^2 is the variance of the market return.

---

[20]A 500-stock portfolio with $\beta = 1.5$ would still have some unique risk because it would be unduly concentrated in high-beta industries. Its actual standard deviation would be a bit higher than 30 percent. If that worries you, relax; we will show you in Chapter 8 how you can construct a fully diversified portfolio with a beta of 1.5 by borrowing and investing in the market portfolio.

Figure 7-12 (a) A randomly selected 500-stock portfolio ends up with $\beta = 1$ and a standard deviation equal to the market's—in this case 20 percent. (b) A 500-stock portfolio constructed with stocks with average $\beta = 1.5$ has a standard deviation of about 30 percent—150 percent of the market's. (c) A 500-stock portfolio constructed with stocks with average $\beta = .5$ has a standard deviation of about 10 percent—half the market's.

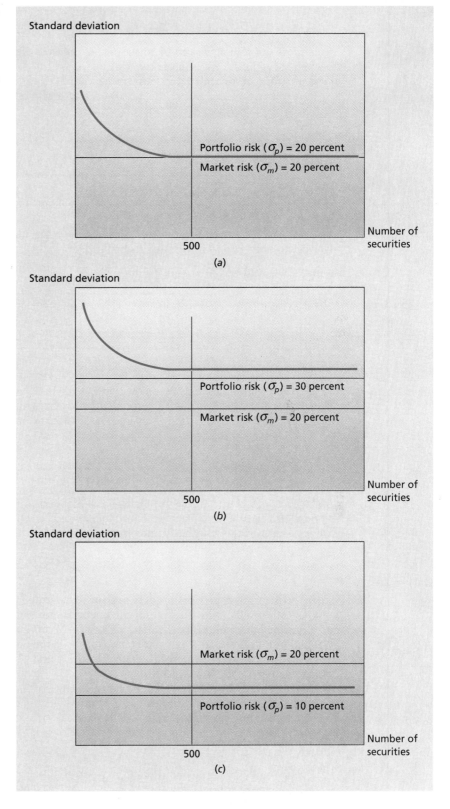

It turns out that this ratio of covariance to variance measures a stock's contribution to portfolio risk. You can see this by looking back at our calculations for the risk of the portfolio of Bristol-Myers Squibb and Ford Motor.

Remember that the risk of this portfolio was the sum of the following boxes:

	Bristol-Myers	Ford Motor
Bristol-Myers	$(.60)^2 \times (18.6)^2$	$.60 \times .40 \times .2 \times 18.6 \times 28.0$
Ford Motor	$.60 \times .40 \times .2 \times 18.6 \times 28.0$	$(.40)^2 \times (28.0)^2$

If we add each *row* of boxes, we can see how much of the portfolio's risk comes from Bristol-Myers and how much from Ford:

Stock	Contribution to Risk
Bristol-Myers	$.60 \times \{[.60 \times (18.6)^2] + (.40 \times .2 \times 18.6 \times 28.0)\} = .60 \times 249$
Ford	$.40 \times \{(.60 \times .2 \times 18.6 \times 28.0) + [.40 \times (28.0)^2]\} = .40 \times 376$
Total portfolio	300

Bristol-Myers's contribution to portfolio risk depends on its relative importance in the portfolio (.60) and its average covariance with the stocks in the portfolio (249). (Notice that the average covariance of Bristol-Myers with the portfolio includes its covariance with itself, i.e., its variance.) The *proportion* of the risk that comes from the Bristol-Myers holding is

$$\text{Relative market value} \times \frac{\text{average covariance}}{\text{portfolio variance}} = .60 \times \frac{249}{300} = .60 \times .83 = .5$$

Similarly, Ford's contribution to portfolio risk depends on its relative importance in the portfolio (.40) and its average covariance with the stocks in the portfolio (376). The *proportion* of the risk that comes from the Ford holding is also .5:

$$.40 \times \frac{376}{300} = .40 \times 1.25 = .5$$

In each case the proportion depends on two numbers—the relative size of the holding (.60 or .40) and a measure of the effect of that holding on portfolio risk (.83 or 1.25). The latter values are the betas of Bristol-Myers and Ford *relative to that portfolio*. On average, an extra 1 percent change in the value of the portfolio would be associated with an extra .83 percent change in the value of Bristol-Myers and a 1.25 percent change in the value of Ford.

To calculate Bristol-Myers's beta relative to the portfolio, we simply take the covariance of Bristol-Myers with the portfolio and divide by the portfolio variance. The idea is exactly the same if we wish to calculate the beta of Bristol-Myers *relative to the market portfolio*. We just calculate its covariance with the market portfolio and divide by the variance of the market:

$$\begin{array}{c}\text{Beta relative to market portfolio} \\ \text{(or, more simply, beta)}\end{array} = \frac{\text{covariance with market}}{\text{variance of market}} = \frac{\sigma_{im}}{\sigma_m^2}$$

7-5   DIVERSIFICATION AND VALUE ADDITIVITY

We have seen that diversification reduces risk and, therefore, makes sense for investors. But does it also make sense for the firm? Is a diversified firm more attractive to investors than an undiversified one? If it is, we have an *extremely* disturbing result. If diversification is an appropriate corporate objective, each project has to be analyzed as a potential addition to the firm's portfolio of assets. The value of the diversified package would be greater than the sum of the parts. So present values would no longer add.

Diversification is undoubtedly a good thing, but that does not mean that firms should practice it. If investors were *not* able to hold a large number of securities, then they might want firms to diversify for them. But investors *can* diversify.[21] In many ways they can do so more easily than firms. Individuals can invest in the steel industry this week and pull out next week. A firm cannot do that. To be sure, the individual would have to pay brokerage fees on the purchase and sale of steel company shares, but think of the time and expense for a firm to acquire a steel company or to start up a new steel-making operation.

You can probably see where we are heading. If investors can diversify on their own account, they will not pay any *extra* for firms that diversify. And if they have a sufficiently wide choice of securities, they will not pay any *less* because they are unable to invest separately in each factory. Therefore, in countries like the United States, which have large and competitive capital markets, diversification does not add to a firm's value or subtract from it. The total value is the sum of its parts.

This conclusion is important for corporate finance, because it justifies adding present values. The concept of *value additivity* is so important that we will give a formal definition of it. If the capital market establishes a value PV(A) for asset A and PV(B) for B, the market value of a firm that holds only these two assets is

$$PV(AB) = PV(A) + PV(B)$$

A three-asset firm combining assets A, B, and C would be worth PV(ABC) = PV(A) + PV(B) + PV(C), and so on for any number of assets.

We have relied on intuitive arguments for value additivity. But the concept is a general one that can be proved formally by several different routes.[22] The concept of value additivity seems to be widely accepted, for thousands of managers add thousands of present values daily, usually without thinking about it.

7-6   SUMMARY

Our review of capital market history showed that the returns to investors have varied according to the risks they have borne. At one extreme, very safe securities like U.S. Treasury bills have provided an average return over more than half a century of only 3.7 percent a year. The riskiest securities that we looked at were common stocks. The stock market provided an average return of 12.2 percent, a premium of more than 8 percent over the safe rate of interest.

---

[21]One of the simplest ways for an individual to diversify is to buy shares in a mutual fund which holds a diversified portfolio.

[22]You may wish to refer to the Appendix to Chapter 33, which discusses diversification and value additivity in the context of mergers.

This gives us two benchmarks for the opportunity cost of capital. If we are evaluating a safe project, we discount at the current risk-free rate of interest. If we are evaluating a project of average risk, we discount at the expected return on the average common stock, which historical evidence suggests is about 8 percent above the risk-free rate. That still leaves us with a lot of assets that don't fit these simple cases. Before we can deal with them, we need to learn how to measure risk.

Risk is best judged in a portfolio context. Most investors do not put all their eggs into one basket: They diversify. Thus the effective risk of any security cannot be judged by an examination of that security alone. Part of the uncertainty about the security's return is "diversified away" when the security is grouped with others in a portfolio.

Risk in investment means that future returns are unpredictable. This spread of possible outcomes is usually measured by standard deviation. The standard deviation of the *market portfolio*—generally represented by the Standard and Poor's Composite Index—is around 20 percent a year.

Most individual stocks have higher standard deviations than this, but much of their variability represents *unique* risk that can be eliminated by diversification. Diversification cannot eliminate *market* risk. Diversified portfolios are exposed to variations in the general level of the market.

A security's contribution to the risk of a well-diversified portfolio depends on how the security is liable to be affected by a general market decline. This sensitivity to market movements is known as *beta* (β). Beta measures the amount that investors expect the stock price to change for each additional 1 percent change in the market. The average beta of all stocks is 1.0. A stock with a beta greater than 1 is unusually sensitive to market movements; a stock with a beta below 1 is unusually insensitive to market movements. The standard deviation of a well-diversified portfolio is proportional to its beta. Thus a diversified portfolio invested in stocks with a beta of 2.0 will have twice the risk of a diversified portfolio with a beta of 1.0.

One theme of this chapter is that diversification is a good thing *for the investor*. This does not imply that *firms* should diversify. Corporate diversification is redundant if investors can diversify on their own account. Since diversification does not affect the firm value, present values add even when risk is explicitly considered. Thanks to *value additivity*, the net present value rule for capital budgeting works even under uncertainty.

Further Reading

A very valuable record of the performance of United States securities since 1926 is:
Ibbotson Associates, Inc.: *Stocks, Bonds, Bills, and Inflation, 1995 Yearbook*, Ibbotson Associates, Chicago, 1995.

Merton discusses the problems encountered in measuring average returns from historical data:
R. C. Merton: "On Estimating the Expected Return on the Market: An Exploratory Investigation," *Journal of Financial Economics*, **8**:323–361 (December 1980).

Most investment texts devote a chapter or two to the distinction between market and unique risk and to the effect of diversification on risk. See, e.g.,
Z. Bodie, A. Kane, and A. J. Marcus: *Investments*, 2d ed., Richard D. Irwin, Inc., Homewood, Ill., 1992.
W. F. Sharpe and G. J. Alexander: *Investments*, 4th ed., Prentice-Hall, Inc., Englewood Cliffs, N.J., 1989.

The classic analysis of the degree to which stocks move together is:
B. F. King: "Market and Industry Factors in Stock Price Behavior," *Journal of Business, Security Prices: A Supplement*, **39**:179–190 (January 1966).

There have been several studies of the way that standard deviation is reduced by diversification, including:

M. Statman: "How Many Stocks Make a Diversified Portfolio?" *Journal of Financial and Quantitative Analysis*, **22**:353–364 (September 1987).

Formal proofs of the value additivity principle can be found in:

S. C. Myers: "Procedures for Capital Budgeting under Uncertainty," *Industrial Management Review*, **9**:1–20 (Spring 1968).

L. D. Schall: "Asset Valuation, Firm Investment and Firm Diversification," *Journal of Business*, **45**:11–28 (January 1972).

Quiz

1. (*a*) What was the average annual return on United States common stocks from 1926 to 1994 (approximately)?
   (*b*) What was the average difference between this return and the return on Treasury bills?
   (*c*) What was the average return on Treasury bills in real terms?
   (*d*) What was the standard deviation of returns on the market index?
   (*e*) Was this standard deviation more or less than on most individual stocks?

2. Fill in the missing words:
   Risk is usually measured by the variance of returns or the _____, which is simply the square root of the variance. As long as the stock price changes are not perfectly _____, the risk of a diversified portfolio is _____ than the average risk of the individual stocks.
   The risk that can be eliminated by diversification is known as _____ risk. But diversification cannot remove all risk; the risk that it cannot eliminate is known as _____ risk.

3. A game of chance offers the following odds and payoffs. Each play of the game costs $100, so the net profit per play is the payoff less $100.

Probability	Payoff	Net Profit
.10	$500	$400
.50	100	0
.40	0	−100

   What are the expected cash payoff and expected rate of return? Calculate the variance and standard deviation of this rate of return.

4. Lawrence Interchange, ace mutual fund manager, produced the following percentage rates of return from 1990 to 1994. Rates of return on the S&P 500 are given for comparison.

	1990	1991	1992	1993	1994
Mr. Interchange	+2.0	+25.1	+10.0	−2.3	−5.0
S&P 500	−3.2	+30.6	+7.7	+10.0	+1.3

   Calculate the average return and standard deviation of Mr. Interchange's mutual fund. Did he do better or worse than the S&P by these measures?

TABLE 7-5

See Quiz question 6

	EXPECTED STOCK RETURN IF MARKET RETURN IS:	
Stock	-10%	$+10\%$
A	0	$+20$
B	-20	$+20$
C	-30	0
D	$+15$	$+15$
E	$+10$	-10

5. True or false?
   (a) Investors prefer diversified companies because they are less risky.
   (b) If stocks were perfectly positively correlated, diversification would not reduce risk.
   (c) The contribution of a stock to the risk of a well-diversified portfolio depends on its market risk.
   (d) A well-diversified portfolio with a beta of 2.0 is twice as risky as the market portfolio.
   (e) An undiversified portfolio with a beta of 2.0 is less than twice as risky as the market portfolio.

6. What is the beta of each of the stocks shown in Table 7-5?

7. Suppose the standard deviation of the market return is 20 percent.
   (a) What is the standard deviation of returns on a well-diversified portfolio with a beta of 1.3?
   (b) What is the standard deviation of returns on a well-diversified portfolio with a beta of 0?
   (c) A well-diversified portfolio has a standard deviation of 15 percent. What is its beta?
   (d) A poorly diversified portfolio has a standard deviation of 20 percent. What can you say about its beta?

8. A portfolio contains equal investments in 10 stocks. Five have a beta of 1.2; the remainder have a beta of 1.4. What is the portfolio beta?
   (a) 1.3
   (b) Greater than 1.3 because the portfolio is not completely diversified
   (c) Less than 1.3 because diversification reduces beta

9. In which of the following situations would you get the largest reduction in risk by spreading your investment across two stocks?
   (a) The two shares are perfectly correlated.
   (b) There is no correlation.
   (c) There is modest negative correlation.
   (d) There is perfect negative correlation.

10. To calculate the variance of a three-stock portfolio, you need to add nine boxes:

Use the same symbols that we used in this chapter; for example, x_1 = proportion invested in stock 1 and σ_{12} = covariance between stocks 1 and 2. Now complete the nine boxes.

11. True or false? Why? "Diversification reduces risk. Therefore corporations ought to favor capital investments with low correlations with their existing lines of business."

Questions and Problems

1. Here are inflation rates and stock market and Treasury bill returns between 1990 and 1994:

Year	Inflation	S&P 500 Return	T-Bill Return
1990	+6.1%	−3.2%	+7.8%
1991	+3.1	+30.6	+5.6
1992	+2.9	+7.7	+3.5
1993	+2.8	+10.0	+2.9
1994	+2.8	+1.3	+3.9

(*a*) What was the real return on the S&P 500 in each year?
(*b*) What was the average real return?
(*c*) What was the risk premium in each year?
(*d*) What was the average risk premium?
(*e*) What was the standard deviation of the risk premium?

2. You toss a die. If the number on the die is less than 3, you receive $10. If it is greater than 4, you pay $20. Otherwise you call it quits. What is the expected payoff? What is the standard deviation?

3. Each of the following statements is dangerous or misleading. Explain why.
(*a*) A long-term United States government bond is always absolutely safe.
(*b*) All investors should prefer stocks to bonds because stocks offer higher long-run rates of return.
(*c*) The best practical forecast of future rates of return on the stock market is a 5- or 10-year average of historical returns.

4. There are few, if any, real companies with negative betas. But suppose you found one with $\beta = -.25$.
(*a*) How would you expect this stock's price to change if the overall market rose by an extra 5 percent? What if the market fell by an extra 5 percent?
(*b*) You have $1 million invested in a well-diversified portfolio of stocks. Now you receive an additional $20,000 bequest. Which of the following actions will yield the safest overall portfolio return?
(**i**) Invest $20,000 in Treasury bills (which have $\beta = 0$).
(**ii**) Invest $20,000 in stocks with $\beta = 1$.
(**iii**) Invest $20,000 in the stock with $\beta = -.25$.
Explain your answer.

TABLE 7-6
• •

Standard deviations and correlation coefficients for a sample of seven stocks

| | | | Correlation Coefficients | | | | |
	AT&T	Biogen	Coca-Cola	Compaq	General Electric	McDonald's	McGraw-Hill	Standard Deviation
AT&T	1	.13	.40	.08	.42	.27	.26	21%
Biogen		1	.22	.34	.45	.28	.18	51
Coca-Cola			1	.24	.48	.34	.32	22
Compaq				1	.17	.14	.17	44
General Electric					1	.48	.54	20
McDonald's						1	.39	22
McGraw-Hill							1	19

5. Lonesome Gulch Mines has a standard deviation of 42 percent per year and a beta of +.10. Amalgamated Copper has a standard deviation of 31 percent a year and a beta of +.66. Explain why Lonesome Gulch is the safer investment for a diversified investor.

*6. Table 7-6 shows standard deviations and correlation coefficients for seven stocks. Calculate the variance of a portfolio invested 40 percent in Compaq, 40 percent in McDonald's, and 20 percent in McGraw-Hill.

*7. Look back at your calculations for question 6. Calculate each stock's contribution to the overall portfolio variance. What is each stock's beta relative to the three-stock portfolio?

*8. Your eccentric Aunt Claudia has left you $50,000 in General Electric shares plus $50,000 cash. Unfortunately her will requires that the General Electric stock not be sold for 1 year, and the $50,000 cash must be entirely invested in one of the stocks shown in Table 7-6. What is the safest attainable portfolio under these restrictions?

*9. Suppose that Treasury bills offer a return of about 6 percent and the expected market risk premium is 8.5 percent. The standard deviation of Treasury-bill returns is zero and the standard deviation of market returns is 20 percent. Use the formula for portfolio risk to calculate the standard deviation of portfolios with different proportions in Treasury bills and the market. (Note that the covariance of two rates of return must be zero when the standard deviation of one return is zero.) Graph the expected portfolio returns and standard deviations.

10. Hippique s.a., which owns a stable of racehorses, has just invested in a mysterious black stallion with great form but disputed bloodlines. Some experts in horseflesh predict the horse will win the coveted Prix de Bidet; others argue that it should be put out to grass. Is this a risky investment for Hippique shareholders? Explain.

11. "The variance of a stock has *no* effect whatsoever on portfolio risk, providing the portfolio is diversified." Is that correct? Explain.

12. "There's upside risk and downside risk. Standard deviation doesn't distinguish between them." Do you think the speaker has a fair point?

13. Respond to the following comments:
    (*a*) "Risk is not variability. If I know a stock is going to fluctuate between $10 and $20, I can make myself a bundle."
    (*b*) "There are all sorts of risk in addition to beta risk. There's the risk that we'll have a downturn in demand, there's the risk that my best plant manager will drop dead, there's the risk of a hike in steel prices. You've got to take all these things into consideration."
    (*c*) "Risk to me is the probability of loss."
    (*d*) "Those guys who suggest beta is a measure of risk make the big assumption that betas don't change."

*14. Here are some historical data on the risk characteristics of MCI and Polaroid:

	MCI	Polaroid
β (beta)	1.24	.99
Yearly standard deviation of return	34	28

Assume that the standard deviation of the return on the market was 20 percent.
    (*a*) The correlation coefficient of MCI's return versus Polaroid's is .20. What is the standard deviation of a portfolio half invested in MCI and half in Polaroid?
    (*b*) What is the standard deviation of a portfolio one-third invested in MCI, one-third in Polaroid, and one-third in Treasury bills?
    (*c*) What is the standard deviation if the portfolio is split evenly between MCI and Polaroid and is financed at 50 percent margin, i.e., the investor puts up only 50 percent of the total amount and borrows the balance from the broker?
    (*d*) What is the *approximate* standard deviation of a portfolio composed of 100 stocks with betas of 1.24 like MCI? How about 100 stocks like Polaroid? [*Hint*: Part (*d*) should not require anything but the simplest arithmetic to answer.]

*15. You believe that there is a 40 percent chance that stock A will decline by 10 percent and a 60 percent chance that it will rise by 20 percent. Correspondingly, there is a 30 percent chance that stock B will decline by 10 percent and a 70 percent chance that it will rise by 20 percent. The correlation coefficient between the two stocks is .7. Calculate the expected return, the variance, and the standard deviation for each stock. Then calculate the covariance between their returns.

*16. An individual invests 60 percent of her funds in stock I and the balance in stock J. The standard deviation of returns on I is 10 percent, and on J it is 20 percent. Calculate the variance of portfolio returns, assuming
    (*a*) The correlation between the returns is 1.0.
    (*b*) The correlation is .5.
    (*c*) The correlation is 0.

*17. (*a*) How many variance terms and how many covariance terms do you need to calculate the risk of a 100-share portfolio?
    (*b*) Suppose all stocks had a standard deviation of 30 percent and a correlation with each other of .4. What is the standard deviation of the returns on a portfolio that has equal holdings in 50 stocks?

(*c*) What is the standard deviation of a fully diversified portfolio of such stocks?

*18. Suppose that the standard deviation of returns from a typical share is about .40 (or 40 percent) a year. The correlation between the returns of each pair of shares is about .3. Calculate the variance and standard deviation of the returns on a portfolio that has equal investments in two shares, three shares, and so on, up to 10 shares.

(*a*) Use your estimates to draw two graphs like Figure 7-8 (one for variance, the other for standard deviation). How large is the underlying market risk that cannot be diversified away?

(*b*) Now repeat the problem, assuming that the correlation between each pair of stocks is zero.

*19. The market portfolio has a standard deviation of 20 percent, and the covariance between the returns on the market and those on stock Z is 800.

(*a*) What is the beta of stock Z?

(*b*) What is the standard deviation of a fully diversified portfolio of such stocks?

(*c*) What is the average beta of all stocks?

(*d*) If the market portfolio gave an extra return of 5 percent, how much extra return can you expect from stock Z?

*20. It is often useful to know how well your portfolio is diversified. Two measures have been suggested:

(*a*) The variance of the returns on a fully diversified portfolio as a proportion of the variance of returns on *your* portfolio

(*b*) The number of shares in a portfolio that (i) has the same risk as yours, (ii) is invested in "typical" shares, and (iii) has equal amounts invested in each share.

Suppose that you hold eight stocks. All are fairly typical—they have a standard deviation of .40 a year, and the correlation between each pair is .3. Of your fund, 20 percent is invested in one stock, 20 percent in a second stock, and the remaining 60 percent is spread evenly over a further six stocks.

Calculate each of the above two measures of portfolio diversification.

21. Diversification has enormous value to investors, yet opportunities for diversification should not sway capital investment decisions by corporations. How would you explain this apparent paradox?

8

Risk and Return

In Chapter 7 we began to come to grips with the problem of measuring risk. Here is the story so far.

The stock market is risky because there is a spread of possible outcomes. The usual measure of this spread is the standard deviation or variance. The risk of any stock can be broken down into two parts. There is the *unique risk* that is peculiar to that stock, and there is the *market risk* that is associated with marketwide variations. Investors can eliminate unique risk by holding a well-diversified portfolio, but they cannot eliminate market risk. *All* the risk of a fully diversified portfolio is market risk.

A stock's contribution to the risk of a fully diversified portfolio depends on its sensitivity to market changes. This sensitivity is generally known as *beta*. A security with a beta of 1.0 has average market risk—a well-diversified portfolio of such securities has the same standard deviation as the market index. A security with a beta of .5 has below-average market risk—a well-diversified portfolio of these securities tends to move half as far as the market moves and has half the market's standard deviation.

In this chapter we use this new-found knowledge to develop some theories linking risk and return in a competitive economy, and we show you how to use these theories to estimate the return that investors require in different stock market investments. Then in Chapter 9 we look at how these ideas can help the financial manager cope with risk in practical capital budgeting situations.

8-1 HARRY MARKOWITZ AND THE BIRTH OF PORTFOLIO THEORY

Most of the ideas in Chapter 7 date back to an article written in 1952 by Harry Markowitz.[1] Markowitz drew attention to the common practice of portfolio diversification and showed exactly how an investor can reduce the standard deviation of portfolio returns by choosing stocks that do not move exactly together. But Markowitz did not stop there—he went on to work out the basic principles of portfolio construction. These principles are the foundation for much of what has been written about the relationship between risk and return.

We begin with Figure 8-1, which shows a histogram of the daily returns on IBM stock for 18 months ending March 1995. On this histogram we have superimposed a bell-shaped normal distribution. The result is typical: When measured over some

---

[1] H. M. Markowitz, "Portfolio Selection," *Journal of Finance*, **7**:77–91 (March 1952).

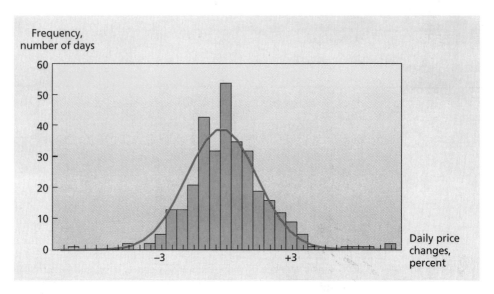

Figure 8-1 Daily price changes for IBM are approximately normally distributed.

fairly short interval, the past rates of return on any stock conform closely to a normal distribution.[2]

Normal distributions can be completely defined by two numbers. One is the average or "expected" return; the other is the variance or standard deviation. Now you can see why in Chapter 7 we discussed the calculation of expected return and standard deviation. They are not just arbitrary measures: If returns are normally distributed, they are the *only* two measures that an investor need consider.

Figure 8-2 pictures the distribution of possible returns from two investments. Both offer an expected return of 10 percent, but A has much the wider spread of possible outcomes. Its standard deviation is 30 percent; the standard deviation of B is 15 percent. Most investors dislike uncertainty and would therefore prefer B to A.

Figure 8-3 pictures the distribution of returns from two other investments. This time both have the *same* standard deviation, but the expected return is 20 percent from stock C and only 10 percent from stock D. Most investors like high expected return and would therefore prefer C to D.

Combining Stocks into Portfolios

Suppose that you are wondering whether to invest in shares of Bristol-Myers Squibb or Ford Motor Company. You decide that Ford offers an expected return of 21 percent and Bristol-Myers an expected return of 15 percent. After looking back at the past variability of the two stocks, you also decide that the standard deviation of returns is 18.6 percent for Bristol-Myers and 28 percent for Ford. Ford offers the higher expected return, but it is considerably more risky.

Now there is no reason to restrict yourself to holding only one stock. For example, in Section 7-3 we analyzed what would happen if you invested 60 percent of

---

[2]If you were to measure returns over a *long* interval, the distribution would be skewed. For example, you would encounter returns greater than 100 percent but none *less* than −100 percent. The distribution of returns over a period of, say, one year would be better approximated by a *lognormal* distribution. The lognormal distribution, like the normal, is completely specified by its mean and standard deviation.

Figure 8-2 These two investments both have an *expected* return of 10 percent; but because investment A has the greater spread of *possible* returns, it is more risky than B. We can measure this spread by the standard deviation. Investment A has a standard deviation of 30 percent; B, 15 percent. Most investors would prefer B to A.

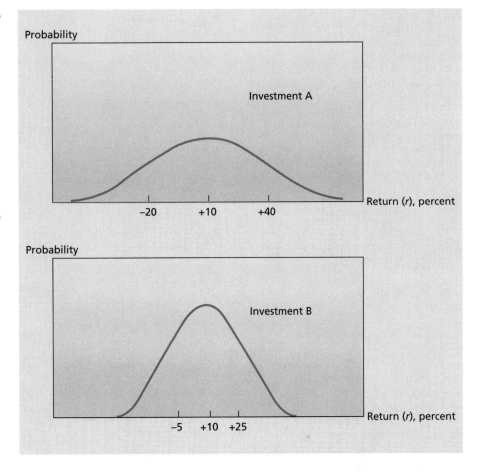

your money in Bristol-Myers and 40 percent in Ford. The expected return on this portfolio is 17.4 percent, which is simply a weighted average of the expected returns on the two holdings. What about the risk of such a portfolio? We know that thanks to diversification the portfolio risk is less than the average of the risks of the separate stocks. In fact, on the basis of past experience the standard deviation of this portfolio is 17.3 percent.[3]

In Figure 8-4 we have plotted the expected return and risk that you could achieve by different combinations of the two stocks. Which of these combinations is best? That depends on your stomach. If you want to stake all on getting rich quickly, you will do best to put all your money in Ford. If you want a more peace-

---

[3]We pointed out in Section 7-3 that the correlation between the returns of Bristol-Myers and Ford has been about .2.

The variance of a portfolio which is invested 60 percent in Bristol-Myers and 40 percent in Ford is

$$\text{Variance} = x_1^2\sigma_1^2 + x_2^2\sigma_2^2 + 2x_1x_2\rho_{12}\sigma_1\sigma_2$$
$$= [(.60)^2 \times (18.6)^2] + [(.40)^2 \times (28.0)^2] + 2(.60 \times .40 \times .2 \times 18.6 \times 28.0)$$
$$= 300$$

The portfolio standard deviation is $\sqrt{300} = 17.3$ percent.

Figure 8-3 The
standard deviation
of possible returns
is 15 percent for
both these invest-
ments, but the ex-
pected return from
C is 20 percent
compared with an
expected return
from D of only 10
percent. Most in-
vestors would pre-
fer C to D.

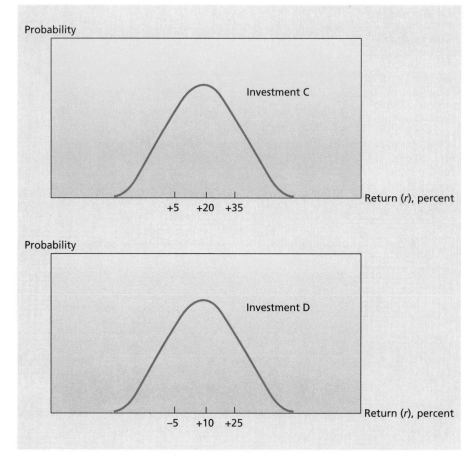

Figure 8-3 The standard deviation of possible returns is 15 percent for both these investments, but the expected return from C is 20 percent compared with an expected return from D of only 10 percent. Most investors would prefer C to D.

ful life, you should invest most of your money in Bristol-Myers—to minimize risk you should keep a small investment in Ford.[4]

In practice, you are unlikely to be limited to investing in only two stocks. Figure 8-5 shows what happens when you have a larger choice of securities. Each cross represents the combination of risk and return offered by a different individual security. By mixing these securities in different proportions you can obtain an even wider selection of risk and expected return. For example, the range of attainable combinations might look something like the broken-egg-shaped area in Figure 8-5. Since you wish to increase expected return and to reduce standard deviation, you will be interested in only those portfolios that lie along the heavy solid line. Markowitz called them **efficient portfolios.** Once again, whether you want to choose the minimum-risk portfolio (portfolio A) or the maximum-expected-return portfolio (portfolio B) or some other efficient portfolio depends on how much you dislike taking risk.

The problem of finding these efficient portfolios is rather similar to a problem that we encountered in Section 5-6. There we wanted to deploy a limited amount of capital in a mixture of projects to give the highest total NPV. Here we want to

[4]The portfolio with the minimum risk has 26.2 percent in Ford.

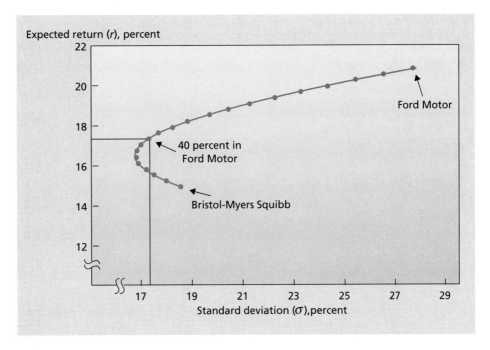

Figure 8-4 The curved line illustrates how expected return and standard deviation change as you hold different combinations of two stocks. For example, if you invest 40 percent of your money in Ford and the remainder in Bristol-Myers, your expected return is 17.4 percent, which is 40 percent of the way between the expected returns on the two stocks. The standard deviation is 17.3 percent, which is *much less* than 40 percent of the way between the standard deviations on the two stocks. This is because diversification reduces risk.

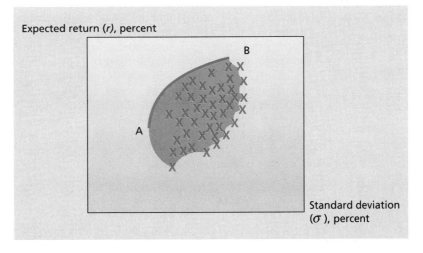

Figure 8-5 Each cross shows the expected return and standard deviation from investing in a single stock. The broken-egg-shaped area shows the possible combinations of expected return and standard deviation if you invest in a *mixture* of stocks. If you like high expected returns and dislike high standard deviations, you will prefer portfolios along the heavy line. These are *efficient* portfolios.

Figure 8-6 Lending and borrowing extend the range of investment possibilities. If you invest in portfolio S and lend or borrow at the risk-free interest rate, r_f, you can achieve any point along the straight line from r_f through S. This gives you a higher expected return for any level of risk than if you just invest in common stocks.

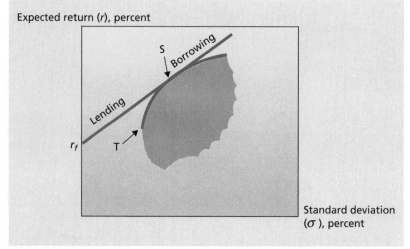

deploy a limited amount of capital to give the highest expected return for a given standard deviation. In principle, both problems can be solved by a hunt-and-peck procedure—but only in principle. To solve the capital rationing problem in practice, we can employ linear programming techniques; to solve the portfolio problem, we can employ a variant of linear programming known as *quadratic programming*. If we estimate the expected return and standard deviation for each stock in Figure 8-5, as well as the correlation between each pair of stocks, then we can use a standard computer quadratic program to calculate the set of efficient portfolios.

We Introduce Borrowing and Lending

Now we introduce yet another possibility. Suppose that you can also lend and borrow money at some risk-free rate of interest r_f. If you invest some of your money in Treasury bills (i.e., lend money) and place the remainder in common stock portfolio S, you can obtain any combination of expected return and risk along the straight line joining r_f and S in Figure 8-6.[5] Since borrowing is merely negative lending, you can extend the range of possibilities to the right of S by borrowing funds at an interest rate of r_f and investing them as well as your own money in portfolio S.

Let us put some numbers on this. Suppose that portfolio S has an expected return of 15 percent and a standard deviation of 16 percent. Treasury bills offer an interest rate (r_f) of 5 percent and are risk-free (i.e., their standard deviation is zero). If you invest half your money in portfolio S and lend the remainder at 5 percent, the expected return on your investment is halfway between the expected return on S and the interest rate on Treasury bills:

$$r = (\tfrac{1}{2} \times \text{expected return on S}) + (\tfrac{1}{2} \times \text{interest rate})$$
$$= 10\%$$

---

[5] If you want to check this, write down the formula for the standard deviation of a two-stock portfolio:

$$\text{Standard deviation} = \sqrt{x_1^2 \sigma_1^2 + x_2^2 \sigma_2^2 + 2x_1 x_2 \rho_{12} \sigma_1 \sigma_2}$$

Now see what happens when security 2 is riskless, i.e., when $\sigma_2 = 0$.

And the standard deviation is halfway between the standard deviation of S and the standard deviation of Treasury bills:

$$\sigma = (\tfrac{1}{2} \times \text{standard deviation of S}) + (\tfrac{1}{2} \times \text{standard deviation of bills})$$
$$= 8\%$$

Or suppose that you decide to go for the big time: You borrow at the Treasury bill rate an amount equal to your initial wealth, and you invest everything in portfolio S. You have twice your own money invested in S, but you have to *pay* interest on the loan. Therefore your expected return is

$$r = (2 \times \text{expected return on S}) - (1 \times \text{interest rate})$$
$$= 25\%$$

And the standard deviation of your investment is

$$\sigma = (2 \times \text{standard deviation of S}) - (1 \times \text{standard deviation of bills})$$
$$= 32\%$$

You can see from Figure 8-6 that when you lend a portion of your money, you end up partway between r_f and S; if you can borrow money at the risk-free rate, you can extend your possibilities beyond S. You can also see that regardless of the level of risk you choose, you can get the highest expected return by a mixture of portfolio S and borrowing or lending. There is no reason ever to hold, say, portfolio T.

This means that we can separate the investor's job into two stages. First, the "best" portfolio of common stocks must be selected—S in our example.[6] Second, this portfolio must be blended with borrowing or lending to obtain an exposure to risk that suits the particular investor's taste. Each investor, therefore, should put money into just two benchmark investments—a risky portfolio S and a risk-free loan (borrowing or lending).[7]

What does portfolio S look like? If you have better information than your rivals, you will want the portfolio to include relatively large investments in the stocks you think are undervalued. But in a competitive market you are unlikely to have a monopoly of good ideas. In that case there is no reason to hold a different portfolio of common stocks from anybody else. In other words, you might just as well hold the market portfolio. That is why many professional investors invest in a market-index portfolio and why most others hold well-diversified portfolios.

8-2 THE RELATIONSHIP BETWEEN RISK AND RETURN

In Chapter 7 we looked at the returns on selected investments. The least risky investment was U.S. Treasury bills. Since the return on Treasury bills is fixed, it is unaffected by what happens to the market. In other words, Treasury bills have a beta of 0. We also considered a much riskier investment, the market portfolio of common stocks. This has average market risk: Its beta is 1.0.

---

[6] Portfolio S is the point of tangency to the set of efficient portfolios. It offers the highest expected risk premium $(r - r_f)$ per unit of standard deviation (σ).

[7] This *separation theorem* was first pointed out by J. Tobin in "Liquidity Preference as Behavior toward Risk," *Review of Economic Studies*, **25**:65–86 (February 1958).

Figure 8-7 The capital
asset pricing model states
that the expected risk premium on each investment
is proportional to its beta.
This means that each in-
vestment should lie on the
sloping security market
line connecting Treasury
bills and the market portfolio.

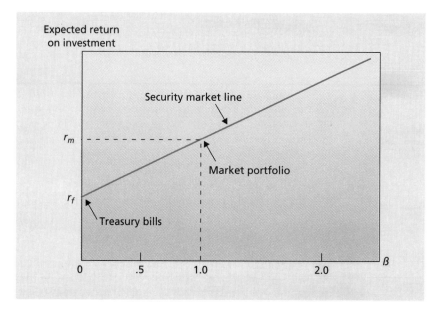

Wise investors don't take risks just for fun. They are playing with real money. Therefore, they require a higher return from the market portfolio than from Treasury bills. The difference between the return on the market and the interest rate is termed the *market risk premium*. Over a period of 69 years the market risk premium $(r_m - r_f)$ has averaged 8.4 percent a year.

In Figure 8-7 we have plotted the risk and expected return from Treasury bills and the market portfolio. You can see that Treasury bills have a beta of 0 and a risk premium of 0.[8] The market portfolio has a beta of 1.0 and a risk premium of $r_m - r_f$. This gives us two benchmarks for the expected risk premium. But what is the expected risk premium when beta is not 0 or 1?

In the mid-1960s three economists—William Sharpe, John Lintner, and Jack Treynor—produced an answer to this question.[9] Their answer is known as the **capital asset pricing model,** or **CAPM.** The model's message is both startling and simple. In a competitive market, the expected risk premium varies in direct proportion to beta. This means that in Figure 8-7 all investments must plot along the sloping line, known as the **security market line.** The expected risk premium on an investment with a beta of .5 is, therefore, *half* the expected risk premium on the market; and the expected risk premium on an investment with a beta of 2.0 is *twice* the expected risk premium on the market. We can write this relationship as

Expected risk premium on stock = beta × expected risk premium on market

$$r - r_f = \beta(r_m - r_f)$$

---

[8]Remember that the risk premium is the difference between the investment's expected return and the risk-free rate. For Treasury bills, the difference is zero.

[9]W. F. Sharpe, "Capital Asset Prices: A Theory of Market Equilibrium under Conditions of Risk," *Journal of Finance,* **19**:425–442 (September 1964); J. Lintner, "The Valuation of Risk Assets and the Selection of Risky Investments in Stock Portfolios and Capital Budgets," *Review of Economics and Statistics,* **47**:13–37 (February 1965); Treynor's article has not been published.

TABLE 8-1

. . . .

These estimates of the returns *expected* by investors in early 1995 were based on the capital asset pricing model. We assumed that the interest rate $r_f = 6$ percent and that the expected market premium $r_m - r_f = 8.4$ percent.

Stock	Beta (β)	Expected Return $[r_f + \beta(r_m - r_f)]$
AT&T	.92	13.7%
Biogen	2.20	24.5
Bristol-Myers Squibb	.97	14.1
Coca-Cola	1.12	15.4
Compaq	1.18	15.9
Exxon	.51	10.3
Ford Motor	1.12	15.4
General Electric	1.22	16.2
McDonald's	1.07	15.0
Microsoft	1.23	16.3

. . . .

Some Estimates of Expected Returns

Before we tell you where this formula comes from, let us use it to figure out what returns investors are looking for from particular stocks. To do this, we need three numbers: r_f, $r_m - r_f$, and β. In early 1995 the interest rate on Treasury bills was about 6 percent. From past evidence we would judge that $r_m - r_f$ is about 8.4 percent. Finally, in Table 7-4 we gave you estimates of the betas of 10 stocks. Table 8-1 puts these numbers together to give an estimate of the expected return on each stock. The least risky stock in our sample is Exxon. Our estimate for the expected return from Exxon is 10.3 percent. The *most* risky stock is Biogen. Our estimate of the expected return from Biogen is 24.5 percent, 18.5 percent more than the interest rate on Treasury bills.

You can also use the capital asset pricing model to find the discount rate for a new capital investment. For example, suppose that you are analyzing a proposal by Compaq to expand its capacity. At what rate should you discount the forecast cash flows? According to Table 8-1, investors are looking for a return of 15.9 percent from businesses with the risk of Compaq. So the cost of capital for a further investment in the same business is 15.9 percent.[10]

In practice, choosing a discount rate is seldom so easy. (After all, you can't expect to be paid a fat salary just for plugging numbers into a formula.) For example, you must learn how to adjust for the extra risk caused by company borrowing and how to estimate the discount rate for projects that do not have the same risk as the company's existing business. There are also tax issues. But these refinements can wait until later.[11]

---

[10]Remember that instead of investing in plant and machinery, the firm could return the money to the shareholders. The opportunity cost of investing is the return that shareholders could expect to earn by buying financial assets. This expected return depends on the market risk of the assets.

[11]Tax issues arise because a corporation must pay tax on income from an investment in Treasury bills or other interest-paying securities. It turns out that the correct discount rate for risk-free investments is the *after-tax* Treasury bill rate. We come back to this point in Chapters 19 and 26.

   Various other points on the practical use of betas and the capital asset pricing model are covered in Chapter 9.

A Proof of the Capital Asset Pricing Model

Let's review four basic principles of portfolio selection:

1. Investors like high expected return and low standard deviation. Common stock portfolios that offer the highest expected return for a given standard deviation are known as *efficient portfolios.*

2. If you want to know the marginal impact of a stock on the risk of a portfolio, you must look not at the risk of that stock in isolation, but at its contribution to the portfolio risk. That contribution depends on the stock's sensitivity to changes in the value of the portfolio.

3. A stock's sensitivity to changes in the value of the *market* portfolio is known as *beta.* Beta, therefore, measures the marginal contribution of a stock to the risk of the market portfolio.

4. If investors can borrow and lend at the risk-free rate of interest, then they should always hold a mixture of the risk-free investment and one particular common stock portfolio. The composition of this stock portfolio depends only on investors' assessment of the prospects for each stock and not on their attitude to risk. If they have no superior information, investors should hold the same stock portfolio as everybody else—in other words, they should hold the market portfolio.

Now if everyone holds the market portfolio, and if beta measures each security's contribution to the market portfolio risk, then it's no surprise that the risk premium demanded by investors is proportional to beta.

Risk premiums always reflect the contribution to portfolio risk. Suppose you are constructing a portfolio. Some stocks will add to the risk of the portfolio, and so you will buy them only if they also increase the expected return. Other stocks will reduce portfolio risk, and you may, therefore, be prepared to buy them even if they also reduce the portfolio's expected return. If the portfolio you have chosen is efficient, each of your investments must be working equally hard for you. So if one stock has a greater marginal effect on portfolio risk than another stock, it must also have proportionately greater expected return. This means that if you plot each stock's expected return against its marginal contribution to the risk of your efficient portfolio, you will find that the stocks lie along a straight line, as in Figure 8-8. This is *always* the case: If a portfolio is efficient, there must be a straight-line relationship between each stock's expected return and its marginal contribution to portfolio risk. The converse is also true: If there is not a straight-line relationship, the portfolio is not efficient.

Now you can see that Figures 8-7 and 8-8 are identical *if* the efficient portfolio in Figure 8-8 is the market portfolio. (Remember that the beta of a stock measures its marginal contribution to the risk of the market portfolio.) So the capital asset pricing model boils down to the statement that the market portfolio is efficient. As we have already seen, this will be so if each investor has the same information and faces the same opportunities as everyone else. In these circumstances, each investor should hold the same portfolio as everyone else—in other words, each should hold the market portfolio.

What if a Stock Did *Not* Lie on the Security Market Line?

Imagine that you encounter stock A in Figure 8-9. Would you buy it? We hope not[12]—if you want an investment with a beta of .5, you could get a higher expected return by investing half your money in Treasury bills and half in the market portfo-

---

[12]Unless, of course, we were trying to sell it.

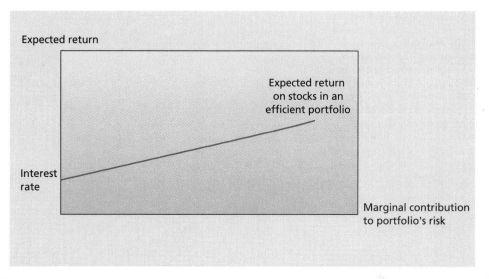

Figure 8-8 If a portfolio is efficient, each stock should lie along a straight line linking the stock's expected return with its marginal contribution to the portfolio's risk.

lio. If everybody shares your view of the stock's prospects, the price of A will have to fall until the expected return matches what you could get elsewhere.

What about stock B in Figure 8-9? Would you be tempted by its high return? You wouldn't if you were smart. You could get a higher expected return for the same beta by borrowing 50 cents for every dollar of your own money and investing in the market portfolio. Again, if everybody agrees with your assessment, the price of stock B cannot hold. It will have to fall until the expected return on B is equal to the expected return on the combination of borrowing and investment in the market portfolio.

We have made our point. An investor can always obtain an expected risk premium of $\beta(r_m - r_f)$ by holding a mixture of the market portfolio and a risk-free loan. So in well-functioning markets nobody will hold a stock that offers an expected risk premium of *less* than $\beta(r_m - r_f)$. But what about the other possibility? Are there stocks that offer a higher expected risk premium? In other words, are there any that lie above the security market line in Figure 8-9? If we take all stocks together, we have the market portfolio. Therefore, we know that stocks *on average* lie on the line. Since none lies *below* the line, then there also can't be any that lie *above* the line. Thus each and every stock must lie on the security market line and offer an expected risk premium of

$$r - r_f = \beta(r_m - r_f)$$

8-3 VALIDITY AND ROLE OF THE CAPITAL ASSET PRICING MODEL

Any economic model is a simplified statement of reality. We need to simplify in order to interpret what is going on around us. But we also need to know how much faith we can place in our model.

Let us begin with some matters about which there is broad agreement. First, few people quarrel with the idea that investors require some extra return for taking on risk. That is why common stocks have given on average a higher return than U.S. Treasury bills. Who would want to invest in risky common stocks if they offered only the *same* expected return as bills? We wouldn't, and we suspect you wouldn't either.

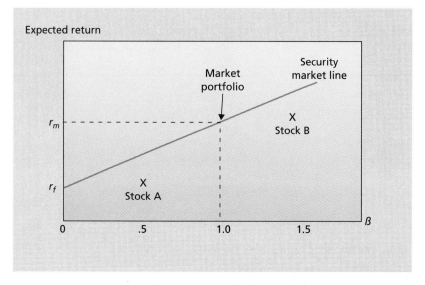

Figure 8-9 In equilibrium no stock can lie below the security market line. For example, instead of buying stock A, investors would prefer to lend part of their money and put the balance in the market portfolio. And instead of buying stock B, they would prefer to borrow and invest in the market portfolio.

Second, investors do appear to be concerned principally with those risks that they cannot eliminate by diversification. If this were not so, we should find that stock prices increase whenever two companies merge to spread their risks. And we should find that investment companies which invest in the shares of other firms are more highly valued than the shares they hold. But we don't observe either phenomenon. Mergers undertaken just to spread risk don't increase stock prices, and investment companies are no more highly valued than the stocks they hold.

The capital asset pricing model captures these ideas in a simple way. That is why many financial managers find it the most convenient tool for coming to grips with the slippery notion of risk. And it is why economists often use the capital asset pricing model to demonstrate important ideas in finance even when there are other ways to prove these ideas. But that doesn't mean that the capital asset pricing model is ultimate truth. We will see later that it has several unsatisfactory features, and we will look at some alternative theories. Nobody knows whether one of these alternative theories is eventually going to come out on top or whether there are other, better models of risk and return that have not yet seen the light of day.

Tests of the Capital Asset Pricing Model

Imagine that in 1931 ten investors gathered together in a Wall Street bar to discuss their portfolios. Each agreed to follow a different investment strategy. Investor 1 opted to buy the 10 percent of New York Stock Exchange stocks with the lowest estimated betas; investor 2 chose the 10 percent with the next-lowest betas; and so on, up to investor 10, who agreed to buy the stocks with the highest betas. They also undertook that at the end of every year they would reestimate the betas of all NYSE stocks and reconstitute their portfolios.[13] Finally, they promised that they would return 60 years later to compare results, and so they parted with much cordiality and good wishes.

In 1991 the same 10 investors, now much older and wealthier, met again in the same bar. Figure 8-10 shows how they had fared. Investor 1's portfolio turned out to be much less risky than the market; its beta was only .49. However, investor 1 also realized the

---

[13]Betas were estimated using returns over the previous 60 months.

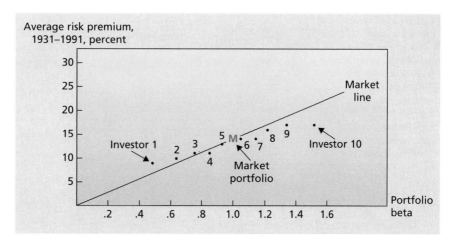

Figure 8-10 The capital asset pricing model states that the expected risk premium from any investment should lie on the market line. The dots show the actual average risk premiums from portfolios with different betas. The high-beta portfolios generated higher average returns, just as predicted by the CAPM. But the high-beta portfolios plotted below the market line, and four of the five low-beta portfolios plotted above. A line fitted to the 10 portfolio returns would be "flatter" than the market line. [*Source:* F. Black, "Beta and Return," *Journal of Portfolio Management,* **20:**8–18 (Fall 1993).]

lowest return, 9 percent above the risk-free rate of interest. At the other extreme, the beta of investor 10's portfolio was 1.52, about three times that of investor 1's portfolio. But investor 10 was rewarded with the highest return, averaging 17 percent a year above the interest rate. So over this 60-year period returns did indeed increase with beta.

As you can see from Figure 8-10, the market portfolio over the same 60-year period provided an average return of 14 percent above the interest rate[14] and (of course) had a beta of 1.0. The CAPM predicts that the risk premium should increase in proportion to beta, so that the returns of each portfolio should lie on the upward-sloping security market line in Figure 8-10. Since the market provided a risk premium of 14 percent, investor 1's portfolio, with a beta of .49, should have provided a risk premium of a shade under 7 percent and investor 10's portfolio, with a beta of 1.52, should have given a premium of a shade over 21 percent. You can see that, while high-beta stocks performed better than low-beta stocks, the difference was not as great as the CAPM predicts.

Figure 8-10 provides broad support for the CAPM, though it suggests that the line relating return to beta has been "too flat." But the model has come under fire on two fronts. First, the slope of the line has been particularly flat in recent years. For example, Figure 8-11 shows how our 10 investors fared between 1966 and 1991. Now it's less clear who is buying the drinks: The portfolios of investors 1 and 10 had very different betas but both earned the same average return over these 25 years. Of course, the line was correspondingly steeper before 1966. This is also shown in Figure 8-11.

---

[14]In Figure 8-10 the stocks in the "market portfolio" are weighted equally. Since the stocks of small firms have provided higher average returns than those of large firms, the risk premium on an equally weighted index is higher than on a value-weighted index. This is one reason for the difference between the 14 percent market risk premium in Figure 8-10 and the 8.4 percent premium reported in Table 7-1.

Figure 8-11 The re-
lationship between
beta and actual aver-
age return has been
much weaker since the
mid-1960s. Compare
Figure 8-10. [*Source:*
F. Black, "Beta and
Return," *Journal of
Portfolio Management,*
20:8–18 (Fall 1993).]

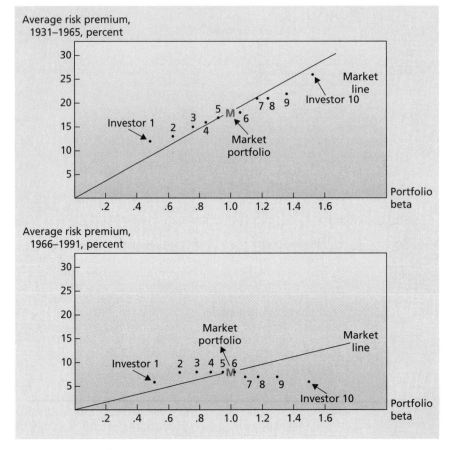

Second, critics of the CAPM point out that, while return has not risen with beta in recent years, it has been related to other measures. For example, Figure 8-12*a* and *b* shows that from 1963 to 1990 small-company stocks performed substantially better than large-company stocks[15] and that stocks with low ratios of market value to book value performed much better than stocks with a high ratio of market to book.[16] Apparently, stocks of small companies and companies with low market-to-book ratios were exposed to risks not captured in the CAPM; this could account for their higher returns.

But the CAPM predicts that beta is the *only* reason that expected returns differ. If investors *expected* the returns to depend on firm size or market-to-book ratio, then the simple version of the CAPM cannot be the whole truth. Such findings have prompted headlines like "Is Beta Dead?" in the business press.[17]

---

[15]We pointed out in Section 7-1 that since the mid-1960s the stocks of small firms have provided higher average returns than those of large firms.

[16]Small-firm stocks have higher betas, but the difference in betas is not sufficient to explain the difference in returns. There is no simple relationship between market-to-book ratios and beta.

[17]A. Wallace, "Is Beta Dead?" *Institutional Investor,* **14**:22–30 (July 1980). Similar obituaries have been circulating for many years. Perhaps this goes to the CAPM's credit: Only a strong theory can survive several funerals.

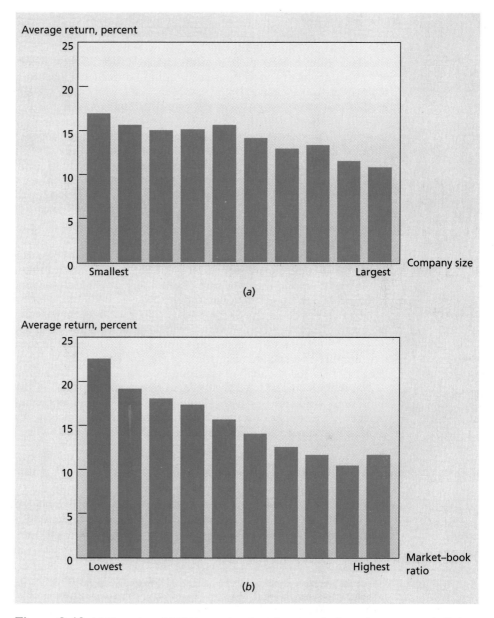

Figure 8-12 (*a*) Since the mid-1960s, stocks of small companies have done systematically better than stocks of large companies. (*b*) Stocks with low ratios of price to book value per share have done better than stocks with high price-to-book ratios. [*Source:* G. Fama and K. French, "The Cross-Section of Expected Stock Returns," *Journal of Finance*, **47**:427–465 (June 1992).]

What's going on here? It is hard to say. Defenders of the capital asset pricing model emphasize that it is concerned with *expected* returns, whereas we can observe only *actual* returns. Actual stock returns reflect expectations, but they also embody lots of "noise"—the steady flow of surprises that conceal whether on average investors have received the returns that they expected. This noise may make it impossible to judge whether the model holds better in one period than another.[18] Perhaps the best that we can do is to focus on the longest period for which there is reasonable data. This would take us back to Figure 8-10, which suggests that expected returns do indeed increase with beta, though less rapidly than the simple version of the CAPM predicts.[19]

What about the anomalous relationship between stock returns and firm size or the market-to-book ratio? Both have been well documented, yet if you look long and hard at past stock returns, you are bound to find some strategy that just by chance would have worked in the past. This practice is known as "data mining" or "data snooping." Maybe the size and market-to-book effects are simply chance results, the effect of data snooping. If so, they should vanish now that they have been discovered.[20]

One thing is for sure: It will be very hard to reject the CAPM beyond all reasonable doubt. Data and statistics will probably not give final answers soon, so the plausibility of the CAPM *theory* will have to be weighed along with the "facts."

Assumptions behind the Capital Asset Pricing Model

The capital asset pricing model rests on several assumptions that we did not fully spell out. For example, we assumed that investment in U.S. Treasury bills is risk-free. It is true that there is little chance of default, but they don't guarantee a *real* return. There is still some uncertainty about inflation. Another assumption was that investors can *borrow* money at the same rate of interest at which they can lend. Generally borrowing rates are higher than lending rates.

It turns out that many of these assumptions are not crucial, and with a little pushing and pulling it is possible to modify the capital asset pricing model to handle them. The really important idea is that investors are content to invest their money in a limited number of benchmark portfolios. (In the basic CAPM these benchmarks are Treasury bills and the market portfolio.)

In these modified CAPMs expected return still depends on market risk, but the definition of market risk depends on the nature of the benchmark portfolios.[21] In practice, none of these alternative capital asset pricing models is as widely used as the standard version.

*8-4 SOME ALTERNATIVE THEORIES

Consumption Betas versus Market Betas

The capital asset pricing model pictures investors as solely concerned with the level and uncertainty of their future wealth. But for most people wealth is not an end in itself. What good is wealth if you can't spend it? People invest now to provide future

---

[18]A second problem with testing the model is that the market portfolio should contain all risky investments, including stocks, bonds, commodities, real estate—even human capital. Most market indexes contain only a sample of common stocks. See, for example, R. Roll, "A Critique of the Asset Pricing Theory's Tests; Part 1: On Past and Potential Testability of the Theory," *Journal of Financial Economics*, **4**:129–176 (March 1977).

[19]We say "simple version" because Fischer Black has shown that if there are borrowing restrictions, there should still exist a positive relationship between expected return and beta, but the security market line would be less steep as a result. See F. Black, "Capital Market Equilibrium with Restricted Borrowing," *Journal of Business*, **45**:444–455 (July 1972).

[20]For example, there is some evidence that the size effect has become less important since it was first discovered by Rolf Banz in 1981. See R. Banz, "The Relationship between Return and Market Values of Common Stock," *Journal of Financial Economics*, **9**:3–18 (March 1981).

[21]For example, see M. C. Jensen (ed.), *Studies in the Theory of Capital Markets*, Frederick A. Praeger, Inc., New York, 1972. In the introduction Jensen provides a very useful summary of some of these variations on the capital asset pricing model.

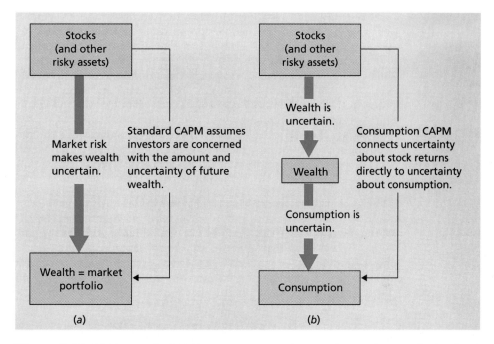

Figure 8-13 (a) The standard CAPM concentrates on how stocks contribute to the level and uncertainty of investor's wealth. Consumption is outside the model. (b) The consumption CAPM defines risk as a stock's contribution to uncertainty about consumption. Wealth (the intermediate step between stock returns and consumption) drops out of the model.

consumption for themselves or for their families and heirs. The most important risks are those which might force a cutback of future consumption.

Douglas Breeden has developed a model in which a security's risk is measured by its sensitivity to changes in investors' consumption. If he is right, a stock's expected return should move in line with its *consumption beta* rather than its market beta. Figure 8-13 summarizes the chief differences between the standard and consumption CAPMs. In the standard model investors are concerned exclusively with the amount and uncertainty of their future wealth. Each investor's wealth ends up perfectly correlated with the return on the market portfolio; the demand for stocks and other risky assets is thus determined by their market risk. The deeper motive for investing—to provide for consumption—is outside the model.

In the consumption CAPM, uncertainty about stock returns is connected directly to uncertainty about consumption. Of course, consumption depends on wealth (portfolio value), but wealth does not appear explicitly in the model.

The consumption CAPM has several appealing features. For example, you don't have to identify the market or any other benchmark portfolio. You don't have to worry that Standard and Poor's Composite Index doesn't track returns on bonds, commodities, and real estate.

However, you do have to be able to measure consumption. *Quick:* How much did you consume last month? It's easy to count the hamburgers and movie tickets, but what about the depreciation on your car or washing machine or the daily cost of your homeowner's insurance policy? We suspect that your estimate of total consumption will rest on rough or arbitrary allocations and assumptions. And if it's hard for you to put a dollar value on your total consumption, think of the task facing a government statistician asked to estimate month-by-month consumption for all of us.

Compared to stock prices, estimated aggregate consumption changes smoothly and gradually over time. Changes in consumption often seem to be out of phase with the stock market. Individual stocks seem to have low or erratic consumption betas. Moreover, the volatility of consumption appears too low to explain the past average rates of return on common stocks unless one assumes unreasonably high investor risk aversion.[22] These problems may reflect our poor measures of consumption or perhaps poor models of how individuals distribute consumption over time. It seems too early for the consumption CAPM to see practical use.

Arbitrage Pricing Theory

The capital asset pricing theory begins with an analysis of how investors construct efficient portfolios. Steven Ross's **arbitrage pricing theory,** or **APT,** comes from a different family entirely. It does not ask which portfolios are efficient. Instead, it starts by *assuming* that each stock's return depends partly on pervasive macroeconomic influences or "factors" and partly on "noise"—events that are unique to that company. Moreover, the return is assumed to obey the following simple relationship:

$$\text{Return} = a + b_1(r_{\text{factor 1}}) + b_2(r_{\text{factor 2}}) + b_3(r_{\text{factor 3}}) + \cdots + \text{noise}$$

The theory doesn't say what the factors are: There could be an oil price factor, an interest-rate factor, and so on. The return on the market portfolio *might* serve as one factor, but then again it might not.

Some stocks will be more sensitive to a particular factor than other stocks. Exxon would be more sensitive to an oil factor than, say, Coca-Cola. If factor 1 picks up unexpected changes in oil prices, b_1 will be higher for Exxon.

For any individual stock there are two sources of risk. First is the risk that stems from the pervasive macroeconomic factors which cannot be eliminated by diversification. Second is the risk arising from possible events that are unique to the company. Diversification *does* eliminate unique risk, and diversified investors can therefore ignore it when deciding whether to buy or sell a stock. The expected risk premium on a stock is affected by "factor" or "macroeconomic" risk; it is *not* affected by unique risk.

Arbitrage pricing theory states that the expected risk premium on a stock should depend on the expected risk premium associated with each factor and the stock's sensitivity to each of the factors (b_1, b_2, b_3, etc.). Thus the formula is[23]

$$\begin{aligned}\text{Expected risk premium} \\ \text{on investment}\end{aligned} \begin{aligned}&= r - r_f \\ &= b_1(r_{\text{factor 1}} - r_f) + b_2(r_{\text{factor 2}} - r_f) + \cdots\end{aligned}$$

Notice that this formula makes two statements:

---

[22]See R. Mehra and E. C. Prescott, "The Equity Risk Premium: A Puzzle," *Journal of Monetary Economics,* **15**:145–161 (1985).

[23]There may be some macroeconomic factors that investors are simply not worried about. (For example, some macroeconomists believe that money supply doesn't matter and therefore investors are not worried about inflation.) Such factors would not command a risk premium. They would drop out of the APT formula for expected return.

1. If you plug in a value of zero for each of the *b*'s in the formula, the expected risk premium is zero. A diversified portfolio that is constructed to have zero sensitivity to each macroeconomic factor is essentially risk-free and therefore must be priced to offer the risk-free rate of interest. If the portfolio offered a higher return, investors could make a risk-free (or "arbitrage") profit by borrowing to buy the portfolio. If it offered a lower return, you could make an arbitrage profit by running the strategy in reverse—in other words, you would *sell* the diversified "zero-sensitivity" portfolio and *invest* the proceeds in U.S. Treasury bills.

2. A diversified portfolio that is constructed to have exposure to, say, factor 1, will offer a risk premium, which will vary in direct proportion to the portfolio's sensitivity to that factor. For example, imagine that you construct two portfolios, A and B, which are affected only by factor 1. If portfolio A is twice as sensitive to factor 1 as portfolio B, portfolio A must offer twice the risk premium. Therefore, if you divided your money equally between U.S. Treasury bills and portfolio A, your combined portfolio would have exactly the same sensitivity to factor 1 as portfolio B and would offer the same risk premium.

Suppose that the arbitrage pricing formula did *not* hold. For example, suppose that the combination of Treasury bills and portfolio A offered a higher return. In that case investors could make an arbitrage profit by selling portfolio B and investing the proceeds in the mixture of bills and portfolio A.

The arbitrage that we have described applies to well-diversified portfolios, where the unique risk has been diversified away. But if the arbitrage pricing relationship holds for all diversified portfolios, it must generally hold for the individual stocks. Each stock must offer an expected return commensurate with its contribution to portfolio risk. In the ATP, this contribution depends on the sensitivity of the stock's return to unexpected changes in the macroeconomic factors.

A Comparison of the Capital Asset Pricing Model and Arbitrage Pricing Theory

Like the capital asset pricing model, arbitrage pricing theory stresses that expected return depends on the risk stemming from economywide influences and is not affected by unique risk. You can think of the factors in arbitrage pricing as representing special portfolios of stocks that tend to be subject to a common influence. If the expected risk premium on each of these portfolios is proportional to the portfolio's market beta, then the arbitrage pricing theory and the capital asset pricing model will give the same answer. In any other case they won't.

How do the two theories stack up? Arbitrage pricing has some attractive features. For example, the market portfolio that plays such a central role in the capital asset pricing model does not feature in arbitrage pricing theory.[24] So we don't have to worry about the problem of measuring the market portfolio, and in principle we can test the arbitrage pricing theory even if we have data on only a sample of risky assets.

Unfortunately you win some and lose some. Arbitrage pricing theory doesn't tell us what the underlying factors are—unlike the capital asset pricing model, which collapses *all* macroeconomic risks into a well-defined *single* factor, the return on the market portfolio.

---

[24]Of course, the market portfolio *may* turn out to be one of the factors, but that is not a necessary implication of arbitrage pricing theory.

Arbitrage pricing theory will provide a good handle on expected returns only if we can (1) identify a reasonably short list of macroeconomic factors,[25] (2) measure the expected risk premium on each of these factors, and (3) measure the sensitivity of each stock to these factors. Let us look briefly at how Elton, Gruber, and Mei tackled each of these issues and estimated the cost of equity for a group of nine New York utilities.[26]

STEP 1: IDENTIFY THE MACROECONOMIC FACTORS. Although APT doesn't tell us what the underlying economic factors are, Elton, Gruber, and Mei identified five principal factors that could affect either the cash flows themselves or the rate at which they are discounted. These factors are:

Factor	Measured by
Yield spread	Return on long government bond *less* return on 30-day Treasury bills
Interest rate	Change in Treasury bill return
Exchange rate	Change in value of dollar relative to basket of currencies
Real GNP	Change in forecasts of real GNP
Inflation	Change in forecasts of inflation

To capture any remaining pervasive influences, Elton, Gruber, and Mei also included a sixth factor, the portion of the market return that could not be explained by the first five.

STEP 2: ESTIMATE THE RISK PREMIUM FOR EACH FACTOR. Some stocks are more exposed than others to a particular factor. So we can estimate the sensitivity of a sample of stocks to each factor and then measure how much extra return investors would have received in the past for taking on factor risk. The results are shown in Table 8-2.

For example, stocks with positive sensitivity to real GNP tended to have higher returns when real GNP increased. A stock with an average sensitivity gave investors an additional return of .49 percent a year compared with a stock that was completely unaffected by changes in real GNP. In other words, investors appeared to dislike "cyclical" stocks, whose returns were sensitive to economic activity, and demanded a higher return from these stocks.

By contrast, Table 8-2 shows that a stock with average exposure to *inflation* gave investors .83 percent a year *less* return than a stock with no exposure to inflation. Thus investors seemed to prefer stocks that protected them against inflation (stocks that did well when inflation accelerated), and they were willing to accept a lower expected return from such stocks.

STEP 3: ESTIMATE THE FACTOR SENSITIVITIES. The estimates of the premiums for taking on factor risk can now be used to estimate the cost of equity for the group

---

[25]Some researchers have argued that there are four or five principal pervasive influences on stock prices, but others are not so sure. They point out that the more stocks you look at, the more factors you need to take into account. See, for example, P. J. Dhrymes, I. Friend, and N. B. Gultekin, "A Critical Reexamination of the Empirical Evidence on the Arbitrage Pricing Theory," *Journal of Finance*, **39**:323–346 (June 1984).

[26]See E. J. Elton, M. J. Gruber, and J. Mei, "Cost of Capital Using Arbitrage Pricing Theory: A Case Study of Nine New York Utilities," *Financial Markets, Institutions, and Instruments*, **3**:46–73 (August 1994). The study was prepared for the New York State Public Utility Commission. We described a parallel study in Chapter 4 which used the discounted-cash-flow model to estimate the cost of equity capital for the same group of firms.

TABLE 8-2
• •

Estimated risk premiums for taking on factor risks, 1978–1990

Factor	Estimated Risk Premium $(r_{factor} - r_f)^*$
Yield spread	5.10%
Interest rate	−.61
Exchange rate	−.59
Real GNP	.49
Inflation	−.83
Market	6.36

*The risk premiums have been scaled to represent the annual premiums for the average industrial stock in the Elton-Gruber-Mei sample.
Source: E. Elton, M. Gruber, and J. Mei, "Cost of Capital Using Arbitrage Pricing Theory: A Case Study of Nine New York Utilities," *Financial Markets, Institutions, and Instruments,* **3**:46–73 (August 1994).

of New York State utilities. Remember, APT states that the risk premium for any asset depends on its sensitivities to factor risks (b) and the expected risk premium for each factor ($r_{factor} - r_f$). In this case there are six factors, so

$$r - r_f = b_1(r_{factor\ 1} - r_f) + b_2(r_{factor\ 2} - r_f) + \cdots + b_6(r_{factor\ 6} - r_f)$$

The first column of Table 8-3 shows the factor risks for the portfolio of utilities, and the second column shows the required risk premium for each factor (taken from

TABLE 8-3
• •

Using APT to estimate the expected risk premium for a portfolio of nine New York State utility stocks

Factor	Factor Risk (b)	Expected Risk Premium $(r_{factor} - r_f)^*$	Factor Risk × Risk Premium $[b(r_{factor} - r_f)]$
Bond maturity	1.04	5.10%	5.30%
Interest rate	−2.25	−.61	1.37
Exchange rate	.70	−.59	−.41
GNP	.17	.49	.08
Inflation	−.18	−.83	.15
Market	.32	6.36	2.04
Total			8.53%

*Risk premiums have been restated as approximate annual rates.
Source: E. Elton, M. Gruber, and J. Mei, "Cost of Capital Using Arbitrage Pricing Theory: A Case Study of Nine New York Utilities," *Financial Markets, Institutions, and Instruments,* **3**:46–73 (August 1994), tables 3 and 4.

Table 8-2). The third column is simply the product of these two numbers. It shows how much return investors demanded for taking on each factor risk. To find the expected risk premium, just add the figures in the final column:

$$\text{Expected risk premium} = r - r_f = 8.53\%$$

The 1-year Treasury bill rate in December 1990, the end of the Elton-Gruber-Mei sample period, was about 7 percent, so the APT estimate of the expected return on New York State utility stocks was[27]

$$\begin{aligned}\text{Expected return} &= \text{risk-free interest rate} + \text{expected risk premium}\\ &= 7 + 8.53\\ &= 15.53, \text{ or about } 15.5\%\end{aligned}$$

8-5 SUMMARY

The basic principles of portfolio selection boil down to a commonsense statement that investors try to increase the expected return on their portfolios and to reduce the standard deviation of that return. A portfolio that gives the highest expected return for a given standard deviation, or the lowest standard deviation for a given expected return, is known as an *efficient portfolio*. To work out which portfolios are efficient, an investor must be able to state the expected return and standard deviation of each stock and the degree of correlation between each pair of stocks.

Investors who are restricted to holding common stocks should choose efficient portfolios that suit their attitudes to risk. But investors who can also borrow and lend at the risk-free rate of interest should choose the "best" common stock portfolio *regardless* of their attitudes to risk. Having done that, they can then set the risk of their overall portfolio by deciding what proportion of their money they are willing to invest in stocks. For an investor who has only the same opportunities and information as everybody else, the best stock portfolio is the same as the best stock portfolio for other investors. In other words, he or she should invest in a mixture of the market portfolio and a risk-free loan (i.e., borrowing or lending).

A stock's marginal contribution to portfolio risk is measured by its sensitivity to changes in the value of the portfolio. If a portfolio is efficient, there will be a straight-line relationship between each stock's expected return and its marginal contribution to the risk of the portfolio. The marginal contribution of a stock to the risk of the *market portfolio* is measured by *beta*. So if the market portfolio is efficient, there will be a straight-line relationship between the expected return and beta of each stock. That is the fundamental idea behind the capital asset pricing model, which concludes that each security's expected risk premium should increase in proportion to its beta:

$$\text{Expected risk premium} = \text{beta} \times \text{market risk premium}$$
$$r - r_f = \beta(r_m - r_f)$$

The capital asset pricing theory is the best-known model of risk and return. It is plausible and widely used but far from perfect. Actual returns are related to beta over the long run, but the relationship is not as strong as the CAPM predicts, and other factors seem to explain returns better since the mid-1960s. Stocks of small compa-

---

[27]This estimate rests on risk premiums actually earned from 1978 to 1990, an unusually rewarding period for common stock investors. Estimates based on long-run market risk premiums would be lower. See Elton, Gruber, and Mei, op. cit., p. 61.

nies, and stocks with low market prices relative to book value per share, appear to have risks not captured by the CAPM.

The CAPM has also been criticized for its strong simplifying assumptions. A new theory called the *consumption* capital asset pricing model suggests that security risk reflects the sensitivity of returns to changes in investors' *consumption*. This theory calls for a consumption beta rather than a beta relative to the market portfolio.

The arbitrage pricing theory offers an alternative theory of risk and return. It states that the expected risk premium on a stock should depend on the stock's exposure to several pervasive macroeconomic factors that affect stock returns:

$$\text{Expected risk premium} = b_1(r_{\text{factor 1}} - r_f) + b_2(r_{\text{factor 2}} - r_f) + \cdots$$

Here b's represent the individual security's sensitivities to the factors, and $r_{\text{factor}} - r_f$ is the risk premium demanded by investors who are exposed to this factor.

Arbitrage pricing theory does not say what these factors are. It asks for economists to hunt for unknown game with their statistical tool kits. The hunters have returned with several candidates, including unanticipated changes in:

- The level of industrial activity
- The rate of inflation
- The spread between short- and long-term interest rates

Each of these different models of risk and return has its fan club. However, all financial economists agree on two basic ideas: (1) Investors require extra expected return for taking on risk, and (2) they appear to be concerned predominantly with the risk that they cannot eliminate by diversification.

Further Reading

The pioneering article on portfolio selection is:
H. M. Markowitz: "Portfolio Selection," *Journal of Finance*, **7**:77–91 (March 1952).

There are a number of textbooks on portfolio selection which explain both Markowitz's original theory and some ingenious simplified versions. See, e.g.:
E. J. Elton and M. J. Gruber: *Modern Portfolio Theory and Investment Management*, 4th ed., John Wiley & Sons, New York, 1991.

Of the three pioneering articles on the capital asset pricing model, Jack Treynor's has never been published. The other two articles are:
W. F. Sharpe: "Capital Asset Prices: A Theory of Market Equilibrium under Conditions of Risk," *Journal of Finance*, **19**:425–442 (September 1964).
J. Lintner: "The Valuation of Risk Assets and the Selection of Risky Investments in Stock Portfolios and Capital Budgets," *Review of Economics and Statistics*, **47**:13–37 (February 1965).

The subsequent literature on the capital asset pricing model is enormous. The following book provides a collection of some of the more important articles plus a very useful survey by Jensen:
M. C. Jensen (ed.): *Studies in the Theory of Capital Markets*, Frederick A. Praeger, Inc., New York, 1972.

There have been a number of tests of the capital asset pricing model. Some of the more important are:
E. F. Fama and J. D. MacBeth: "Risk, Return and Equilibrium: Empirical Tests," *Journal of Political Economy*, **81**:607–636 (May 1973).
F. Black, M. C. Jensen, and M. Scholes: "The Capital Asset Pricing Model: Some Empirical Tests," in M. C. Jensen (ed.), *Studies in the Theory of Capital Markets*, Frederick A. Praeger, Inc., New York, 1972.

M. R. Gibbons: "Multivariate Tests of Financial Models," *Journal of Financial Economics*, **10**:3–27 (March 1982).

For a critique of empirical tests of the model, see:
R. Roll: "A Critique of the Asset Pricing Theory's Tests; Part I: On Past and Potential Testability of the Theory," *Journal of Financial Economics*, **4**:129–176 (March 1977).

Much of the recent controversy about the performance of the capital asset pricing model was prompted by Fama and French's paper. The paper by Black takes issue with Fama and French and updates the Black, Jensen, and Scholes test of the model:
E. F. Fama and K. R. French: "The Cross-Section of Expected Stock Returns," *Journal of Finance*, **47**:427–465 (June 1992).
F. Black, "Beta and Return," *Journal of Portfolio Management*, **20**:8–18 (Fall 1993).

Breeden's 1979 article describes the consumption asset pricing model, and the Breeden, Gibbons, and Litzenberger paper tests the model and compares it with the standard CAPM:
D. T. Breeden: "An Intertemporal Asset Pricing Model with Stochastic Consumption and Investment Opportunities," *Journal of Financial Economics*, **7**:265–296 (September 1979).
D. T. Breeden, M. R. Gibbons, and R. H. Litzenberger: "Empirical Tests of the Consumption-Oriented CAPM," *Journal of Finance*, **44**:231–262 (June 1989).

Arbitrage pricing theory is described in Ross's 1976 paper. The other papers test the model and attempt to identify the principal factors:
S. A. Ross: "The Arbitrage Theory of Capital Asset Pricing," *Journal of Economic Theory*, **13**:341–360 (December 1976).
R. Roll and S. A. Ross: "An Empirical Investigation of the Arbitrage Pricing Theory," *Journal of Finance*, **35**:1073–1103 (December 1980).
N-F Chen, R. Roll, and S. A. Ross: "Economic Forces and the Stock Market," *Journal of Business*, **59**:383–403 (July 1986).

The most accessible recent implementation of APT is:
E. Elton, M. Gruber, and J. Mei, "Cost of Capital Using Arbitrage Pricing Theory: A Case Study of Nine New York Utilities," *Financial Markets, Institutions, and Instruments*, **3**:46–73 (August 1994).

Quiz
....

1. Figures 8-14 and 8-15 purport to show the range of attainable combinations of expected return and standard deviation.
   (*a*) Which diagram is incorrectly drawn and why?
   (*b*) Which is the efficient set of portfolios?
   (*c*) If r_f is the rate of interest, mark with an X the optimal stock portfolio.

2. For each of the following pairs of investments, state which would always be preferred by a rational investor (assuming that these are the *only* investments available to the investor):
   (*a*) Portfolio A $r = 18$ percent $\sigma = 20$ percent
          Portfolio B $r = 14$ percent $\sigma = 20$ percent
   (*b*) Portfolio C $r = 15$ percent $\sigma = 18$ percent
          Portfolio D $r = 13$ percent $\sigma = 8$ percent
   (*c*) Portfolio E $r = 14$ percent $\sigma = 16$ percent
          Portfolio F $r = 14$ percent $\sigma = 10$ percent

3. Consider the following four portfolios:
   (*a*) 50 percent in Treasury bills, 50 percent in share W
   (*b*) 50 percent in share W, 50 percent in share X, where the returns are perfectly positively correlated

Figure 8-14 See Quiz question 1.

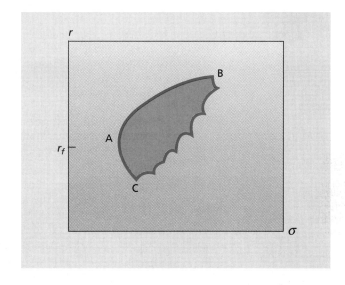

Figure 8-15 See Quiz question 1.

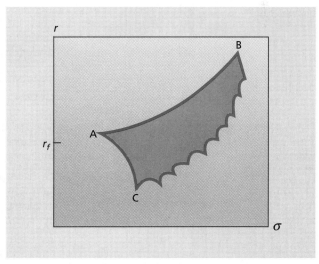

(*c*) 50 percent in share X, 50 percent in share Y, where the returns are uncorrelated

(*d*) 50 percent in share Y, 50 percent in share Z, where the returns are perfectly negatively correlated

In which of these cases would the standard deviation of the portfolio lie exactly midway between that of the two securities?

4. (*a*) Plot the following risky portfolios on a graph:

	PORTFOLIO							
	A	B	C	D	E	F	G	H
Expected return (*r*), percent	10	12.5	15	16	17	18	18	20
Standard deviation (σ), percent	23	21	25	29	29	32	35	45

(b) Five of these portfolios are efficient, and three are not. Which are *in-efficient* ones?

(c) Suppose you can also borrow and lend at an interest rate of 12 percent. Which of the above portfolios is best?

(d) Suppose you are prepared to tolerate a standard deviation of 25 percent. What is the maximum expected return that you can achieve if you cannot borrow or lend?

(e) What is your optimal strategy if you can borrow or lend at 12 percent and are prepared to tolerate a standard deviation of 25 percent? What is the maximum expected return that you can achieve?

5. True or false?

(a) The capital asset pricing model implies that if you could find an investment with a negative beta, its expected return would be less than the interest rate.

(b) The expected return on an investment with a beta of 2.0 is twice as high as the expected return on the market.

(c) If a stock lies below the security market line, it is undervalued.

6. Suppose that the Treasury bill rate is 4 percent and the expected return on the market is 10 percent. Use the betas in Table 8-1.

(a) Calculate the expected return from General Electric.

(b) Find the highest expected return that is offered by one of these stocks.

(c) Find the lowest expected return that is offered by one of these stocks.

(d) Would Compaq offer a higher or lower expected return if the interest rate were 6 rather than 4 percent? Assume that the expected return on the market stays at 10 percent.

(e) Would AT&T offer a higher or lower expected return if the interest rate were 6 percent?

7. The capital asset pricing model states that a stock has the same market risk and expected return as:

(a) A portfolio with proportion β invested in Treasury bills and $1 - \beta$ in the market.

(b) A portfolio with β invested in the market and $1 - \beta$ in Treasury bills.

(c) A portfolio evenly divided between the market and Treasury bills. Which is the correct answer?

*8. By 2005, after 2 years of frenzied merger activity, only two giant conglomerates remain on the New York Stock Exchange. For convenience, we will label these firms A and B. Each accounts for half the value of the market portfolio. You are given the following data:

	Firm A	Firm B
Expected rate of return (r)	23	13
Standard deviation of return (σ), percent per year	40	24

The correlation coefficient of A and B is $\rho_{AB} = .8$.

(a) What is the expected rate of return on the market portfolio (r_m)?

(b) What is the standard deviation of the market portfolio (σ_m)?

(c) What are the betas of stocks A and B with respect to the market portfolio?

(d) Assume the risk-free rate is 10 percent. Are the expected rates of return on A and B consistent with the capital asset pricing model?

*9. Write out the APT equation for the expected rate of return on a risky stock. Identify and interpret each of the variables entering the equation.

*10. Consider a three-factor APT model. The factors and associated risk premiums are:

Factor	Risk Premium
Change in GNP	5%
Change in energy prices	−1
Change in long-term interest rates	+2

Calculate expected rates of return on the following stocks. The risk-free interest rate is 7 percent.
(*a*) A stock whose return is uncorrelated with all three factors
(*b*) A stock with average exposure to each factor (i.e., with $b = 1$ for each)
(*c*) A pure-play energy stock with high exposure to the energy factor ($b = 2$) but zero exposure to the other two factors
(*d*) An aluminum company stock with average sensitivity to changes in interest rates and GNP, but negative exposure of $b = -1.5$ to the energy factor. (The aluminum company is energy-intensive and suffers when energy prices rise.)

Questions and Problems

1. True or false? Explain or qualify as necessary.
   (*a*) Investors demand higher expected rates of return on stocks with more variable rates of return.
   (*b*) The capital asset pricing model predicts that a security with a beta of 0 will offer a zero expected return.
   (*c*) An investor who puts $10,000 in Treasury bills and $20,000 in the market portfolio will have a beta of 2.0.
   (*d*) Investors demand higher expected rates of return from stocks with returns that are highly exposed to macroeconomic changes.
   (*e*) Investors demand higher expected rates of return from stocks with returns that are very sensitive to fluctuations in the stock market.

2. "There may be some truth in these CAPM and APT theories, but last year some stocks did much better than these theories predicted, and other stocks did much worse." Is this a valid criticism?

3. Here are betas estimated from 1990 to 1994 for several well-known common stocks:

Stock	Beta
Hewlett-Packard	1.81
Thermo Electron	1.29
Niagara Mohawk	.69
Merrill Lynch	1.81
Tyson Foods	1.04

(*a*) Estimate the expected rate of return using the CAPM formula. The risk-free rate was 6 percent.

(*b*) The standard deviation of Tyson Foods' stock was about 26 percent per year. Thermo Electron's standard deviation was about 24 percent. Yet the CAPM says Tyson Foods was the safer investment. Explain why this makes sense.

4. Sketch the efficient set of common stock portfolios. Show the combinations of expected return and risk that you could achieve if you could borrow and lend at the same risk-free rate of interest. Now show the combinations of expected return and risk that you could achieve if the rate of interest is higher for borrowing than for lending.

5. Look back at the calculation for Bristol-Myers and Ford in Section 8-1. Recalculate the expected portfolio return and standard deviation for different values of x_1 and x_2, assuming $\rho_{12} = 0$. Plot the range of possible combinations of expected return and standard deviation as in Figure 8-4. Repeat the problem for $\rho_{12} = +1$ and for $\rho_{12} = -1$.

6. Mark Harrywitz proposes to invest in two shares, X and Y. He expects a return of 12 percent from X and 8 percent from Y. The standard deviation of returns is 8 percent for X and 5 percent for Y. The correlation coefficient between the returns is .2.

(*a*) Compute the expected return and standard deviation of the following portfolios:

Portfolio	Percentage in X	Percentage in Y
1	50	50
2	25	75
3	75	25

(*b*) Sketch the set of portfolios composed of X and Y.
(*c*) Suppose that Mr. Harrywitz can also borrow or lend at an interest rate of 5 percent. Show on your sketch how this alters his opportunities. Given that he can borrow or lend, what proportions of the common stock portfolio should be invested in X and Y?

7. Hilda Hornbill has invested 60 percent of her money in share A and the remainder in share B. She assesses their prospects as follows:

	A	B
Expected return, percent	15	20
Standard deviation, percent	20	22
Correlation between returns	.5	

(*a*) What are the expected return and the standard deviation of returns on her portfolio?
(*b*) How would your answer change if the correlation coefficient were 0 or −.5?
(*c*) Is Ms. Hornbill's portfolio better or worse than one invested entirely in share A, or is it not possible to say?

8. The Treasury bill rate is 4 percent, and the expected return on the market portfolio is 12 percent. On the basis of the capital asset pricing model:
(*a*) Draw a graph similar to Figure 8-7 showing how the expected return varies with beta.

(**b**) What is the risk premium on the market?

(**c**) What is the required return on an investment with a beta of 1.5?

(**d**) If an investment with a beta of .8 offers an expected return of 9.8 percent, does it have a positive NPV?

(**e**) If the market expects a return of 11.2 percent from stock X, what is its beta?

9. Estimate the returns expected by investors *today* for the 10 stocks in Table 8-1. Plot the expected returns against beta as in Figure 8-7.

10. A company is deciding whether to issue stock to raise money for an investment project which has the same risk as the market and an expected return of 20 percent. If the risk-free rate is 10 percent and the expected return on the market is 15 percent, the company should go ahead:

(**a**) Unless the company's beta is greater than 2.0.

(**b**) Unless the company's beta is less than 2.0.

(**c**) Whatever the company's beta.

Which answer is correct? Say briefly why.

11. The stock of United Merchants has a beta of 1.0 and very high unique risk. If the expected return on the market is 20 percent, the expected return on United Merchants will be:

(**a**) 10 percent if the interest rate is 10 percent.

(**b**) 20 percent.

(**c**) More than 20 percent because of the high unique risk.

(**d**) Indeterminate unless you also know the interest rate.

Which is the right answer? Explain *briefly* why.

12. The expected return on a stock is frequently written as $r = \alpha + \beta r_m$, where r_m is the expected return on the market. The capital asset pricing model says that in equilibrium:

(**a**) $\alpha = 0$.

(**b**) $\alpha = r_f$ (the risk-free rate of interest).

(**c**) $\alpha = (1 - \beta)r_f$.

(**d**) $\alpha = (1 - r_f)$.

Which is correct?

13. Suppose that there is *no* relationship between beta and expected returns. Does that mean that beta is an uninteresting statistic? What would you do as an investor? What strategies should a corporation adopt?

 14. Table 7-6 gave some data on the standard deviation of returns for a sample of stocks and on the correlation between the returns. Suppose that you undertake an intense investigation and forecast the following returns for these stocks:

Stock	Expected Return
AT&T	10.4%
Biogen	22.7
Coca-Cola	11.9
Compaq	18.2
General Electric	12.5
McDonald's	11.7
McGraw-Hill	10.6

(*a*) Calculate the set of efficient portfolios.
(*b*) What is the portfolio with the highest expected return?
(*c*) What is the minimum risk portfolio?

*15. Look again at Question 14. Take one of the efficient portfolios (other than the minimum-variance portfolio), and calculate the beta of each holding relative to that portfolio. Show that there is a straight-line relationship between the expected returns on the stocks held and their betas *relative to the efficient portfolio*.

16. In footnote 4 we noted that the minimum-risk portfolio contained an investment of 26.2 percent in Ford and thus 73.8 percent in Bristol-Myers. Prove it. (*Hint:* You need a little calculus to do so.)

*17. The following question illustrates the arbitrage pricing theory. Imagine that there are only two pervasive macroeconomic factors. Investments X, Y, and Z have the following sensitivities to these two factors:

Investment	b_1	b_2
X	1.75	.25
Y	−1.00	2.00
Z	2.00	1.00

We assume that the expected risk premium is 4 percent on factor 1 and 8 percent on factor 2. Treasury bills obviously offer zero risk premium.
(*a*) According to arbitrage pricing theory, what is the risk premium on each of the three stocks?
(*b*) Suppose you buy $200 of X and $50 of Y and sell $150 of Z. What is the sensitivity of your portfolio to each of the two factors? What is the expected risk premium?
(*c*) Suppose you buy $80 of X and $60 of Y and sell $40 of Z. What is the sensitivity of your portfolio to each of the two factors? What is the expected risk premium?
(*d*) Finally, suppose you buy $160 of X and $20 of Y and sell $80 of Z. What is your portfolio's sensitivity now to each of the two factors? And what is the expected risk premium?
(*e*) Suggest two possible ways that you could construct a fund that had a sensitivity of .5 to factor 1 only. Now compare the expected risk premiums on each of these investments.

(*f*) Suppose that the arbitrage pricing relationship did *not* hold and that X offered a risk premium of 8 percent, Y offered a premium of 14 percent, and Z a premium of 16 percent. Devise an investment that has zero sensitivity to each factor and that offers a positive risk premium.

*18. Some true or false questions about the APT:
(*a*) The APT factors cannot reflect diversifiable risks.
(*b*) The market rate of return cannot be an APT factor.
(*c*) Each APT factor must have a positive risk premium associated with it—otherwise the model is inconsistent.
(*d*) There is no theory that specifically identifies the APT factors.
(*e*) The APT model could be true but not very useful, for example, if the relevant factors change unpredictably.

* 19. "Suppose you could forecast the behavior of APT factors, such as industrial production, interest rates, etc. You could then identify stocks' sensitivities to these factors, pick the right stocks, and make lots of money." Is this a good argument favoring the APT? Explain why or why not.

20. Percival Hygiene has $10 million invested in long-term corporate bonds. This bond portfolio's expected annual rate of return is 9 percent, and the annual standard deviation is 10 percent.

   Amanda Reckonwith, Percival's financial adviser, recommends that Percival consider investing in an index fund which closely tracks the Standard and Poor's 500 index. The index has an expected return of 14 percent, and its standard deviation is 16 percent.

   (*a*) Suppose Percival puts all his money in a combination of the index fund and Treasury bills. Can he thereby improve his expected rate of return without changing the risk of his portfolio? The Treasury bill yield is 6 percent.

   (*b*) Could Percival do even better by investing equal amounts in the corporate bond portfolio and the index fund? The correlation between the bond portfolio and the index fund is +.1.

9

Capital Budgeting and Risk

Long before the development of modern theories linking risk and expected return, smart financial managers adjusted for risk in capital budgeting. They realized intuitively that, other things being equal, risky projects are less desirable than safe ones. Therefore financial managers demanded a higher rate of return from risky projects, or they based their decisions on conservative estimates of the cash flows.

Various rules of thumb are often used to make these risk adjustments. For example, many companies estimate the rate of return required by investors in their securities and use the **company cost of capital** to discount the cash flows on all new projects. Since investors require a higher rate of return from a very risky company, such a firm will have a higher company cost of capital and will set a higher discount rate for its new investment opportunities. For example, in Table 8-1 we estimated that investors expected a rate of return of .163 or about 16.5 percent from Microsoft common stock. Therefore, according to the company cost of capital rule, Microsoft should have been using a 16.5 percent discount rate to compute project net present values.[1]

This is a step in the right direction. Even though we can't measure risk or the expected return on risky securities with absolute precision, it is still reasonable to assert that Microsoft faced more risk than the average firm and, therefore, should have demanded a higher rate of return from its capital investments.

But the company cost of capital rule can also get a firm into trouble if the new projects are more or less risky than its existing business. Each project should be evaluated at its *own* opportunity cost of capital. This is a clear implication of the value-additivity principle introduced in Chapter 7. For a firm composed of assets A and B, the firm value is

Firm value = PV(AB) = PV(A) + PV(B) = sum of separate asset values

Here PV(A) and PV(B) are valued just as if they were mini-firms in which stockholders could invest directly. Investors would value A by discounting its forecasted cash flows at a rate reflecting the risk of A. They would value B by discounting at a rate reflecting the risk of B. The two discount rates will, in general, be different.

---

[1]Microsoft did not use any significant amount of debt financing. Thus its cost of capital is the rate of return investors expect on its common stock. The complications caused by debt are discussed later in this chapter.

Figure 9-1 A comparison between the company cost of capital rule and the required return under the capital asset pricing model. Microsoft's company cost of capital is about 16.5 percent. This is the correct discount rate only if the project beta is 1.23. In general, the correct discount rate increases as project beta increases. Microsoft should accept projects with rates of return above the security market line relating required return to beta.

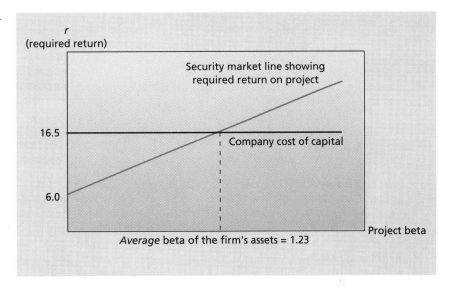

If the firm considers investing in a third project C, it should also value C as if C were a mini-firm. That is, the firm should discount the cash flows of C at the expected rate of return that investors would demand to make a separate investment in C. *The true cost of capital depends on the use to which the capital is put.*

This means that Microsoft should accept any project that more than compensates for the *project's beta.* In other words, Microsoft should accept any project lying above the upward-sloping line that links expected return to risk in Figure 9-1. If the project has a high risk, Microsoft needs a higher prospective return than if the project has a low risk. Now contrast this with the company cost of capital rule, which is to accept any project *regardless of its risk* as long as it offers a higher return than the *company's* cost of capital. In terms of Figure 9-1, the rule tells Microsoft to accept any project above the horizontal cost-of-capital line, i.e., any project offering a return of more than 16.5 percent.

It is clearly silly to suggest that Microsoft should demand the same rate of return from a very safe project as from a very risky one. If Microsoft used the company cost of capital rule, it would reject many good low-risk projects and accept many poor high-risk projects. It is also silly to suggest that just because Duke Power has a low company cost of capital, it is justified in accepting projects that Microsoft would reject. If you followed such a rule to its seemingly logical conclusion, you would think it possible to enlarge the company's investment opportunities by investing a large sum in Treasury bills. That would make the common stock safe and create a low company cost of capital.[2]

The notion that each company has some individual discount rate or cost of capital is widespread, but far from universal. Many firms require different returns from different categories of investment. For example, discount rates might be set as follows:

---

[2]If the present value of an asset depended on the identity of the company that bought it, present values would not add up. Remember, a good project is a good project is a good project.

Category	Discount Rate
Speculative ventures	30%
New products	20%
Expansion of existing business	15% (company cost of capital)
Cost improvement, known technology	10%

The capital asset pricing model is widely used by large corporations to estimate the discount rate. It states

$$\text{Expected project return} = r = r_f + (\text{project beta})(r_m - r_f)$$

To calculate this, you have to figure out the project beta. Before thinking about the betas of individual projects, we will look at some problems you would encounter in using beta to estimate a company's cost of capital. It turns out that beta is difficult to measure accurately for an individual firm: Much greater accuracy can be achieved by looking at an average of similar companies. But then we have to define *similar*. Among other things, we will find that a firm's borrowing policy affects its stock beta. It would be misleading, e.g., to average the betas of Chrysler, which has been a heavy borrower, and General Motors, which has generally borrowed less.

The company cost of capital is the correct discount rate for projects that have the same risk as the company's existing business but *not* for those projects that are safer or riskier than the company's average. The problem is to judge the relative risks of the projects available to the firm. To handle that problem, we will need to dig a little deeper and look at what features make some investments riskier than others. After you know *why* AT&T stock has less market risk than, say, Ford Motor, you will be in a better position to judge the relative risks of capital investment opportunities.

There is still another complication: Project betas can shift over time. Some projects are safer in youth than in old age; others are riskier. In this case, what do we mean by *the* project beta? There may be a separate beta for each year of the project's life. To put it another way, can we jump from the capital asset pricing model, which looks out one period into the future, to the discounted-cash-flow formula that we developed in Chapters 2 and 6 for valuing long-lived assets? Most of the time it is safe to do so, but you should be able to recognize and deal with the exceptions.

We will use the capital asset pricing model, or CAPM, throughout this chapter. But don't infer that the CAPM is the last word on risk and return. The principles and procedures covered in this chapter work just as well with other models such as arbitrage pricing theory (APT). For example, we could have started with an APT estimate of the expected rate of return on Microsoft stock; the discussion of company and project costs of capital would have followed exactly.

9-1   MEASURING BETAS

Suppose that you were considering an across-the-board expansion by your firm. Such an investment would have about the same degree of risk as the existing business. Therefore you should discount the projected flows at the company cost of capital. To estimate that, you could begin by estimating the beta of the company's stock.

An obvious way to measure the beta of the stock is to look at how its price has responded in the past to market movements. For example, in Figure 9-2*a* and *b* we have plotted monthly rates of return from AT&T and Hewlett-Packard against market returns for the same months. In each case we have fitted a line through the points. Beta is the slope of the line. It varied from one period to the other, but there is little doubt that Hewlett-Packard's beta was greater than AT&T's. If you had used the past beta of either stock to predict its future beta, you wouldn't have been too far off in most cases, though both companies' betas increased in the last measurement period.

Using a Beta Book

Because of the investment community's interest in market risk, beta estimates of varying quality are regularly published by a number of brokerage and advisory services. Table 9-1, page 210, shows an extract from one of the better-known services. Look more closely at Minnesota Mining and Manufacturing (MMM), one of the stocks in Table 9-1. Merrill Lynch recorded the change in the price of MMM stock and in the level of the market (represented by Standard and Poor's Composite Index) in each month during a 5-year period. That made 60 monthly observations. MMM's beta of .71 was estimated by "straight" regression, i.e., by using a standard least-squares regression program to find the line of "best fit."[3]

The other information in Table 9-1 is also interesting.

ALPHA. Figure 9-3 shows the line that Merrill Lynch's regression program fitted to the plot of price changes of MMM and the market. Beta is the slope of the line, and alpha (α) is the intercept. MMM's alpha was .22.

Alpha is a rate of price change. Its units are percent per period (in this case percent per month since the line was fitted to monthly data). MMM's positive alpha tells us that the company's stock did reasonably well from 1989 through 1995. From Figure 9-3 we see that MMM stock appreciated on average by + .22 percent per month (about $12 \times .22 = 2.6$ percent per year) when investors in the market as a whole earned nothing. Investors in some other stocks in Table 9-1 were less fortunate. What about the future? Will MMM continue to perform well? Possibly, but you should not bet on it. The most likely outcome is that the return (price change plus dividend yield) will simply compensate for the market risk.

R-SQUARED AND RESIDUAL STANDARD DEVIATION. In Table 9-1, the column headed *R-SQR* shows the proportion of the total variance of MMM stock price changes that can be explained by market movements. That is, 37 percent of its risk is market risk, and 63 percent is unique risk. The next column is the amount of unique or diversifiable risk, measured as a standard deviation: 3.29 percent per month for MMM, equivalent to 11.4 percent per year. This is the standard deviation of the unique price change, that part of the actual change that was not explained by the change in the market index.[4]

STANDARD ERRORS OF ALPHA AND BETA. Merrill Lynch's betas are simply *estimates* based on 60 particular months. Therefore, we would like to have an idea of the extent of the possible error in these estimates. The column labeled *STD. ERR. OF BETA* provides this information. Statisticians set up a *confidence interval* of the esti-

---

[3]Although it is easy in principle to find a line of best fit, there are some tricks to finding the best time period over which to measure returns, to dealing with stocks that trade only infrequently, and so on. Some "beta services" are much more careful than others.

[4]From these two columns we can figure out the *total* risk of MMM stock. The unique variance is the square of the unique standard deviation: $(3.29)^2 = 10.8$ per month. We know this amounts to 63 percent of the total variance, so total variance must be $10.8/.63 = 17.2$ per month. The total variance per year is therefore $17.2 \times 12 = 206.2$, and the standard deviation is $\sqrt{206.2} = 14.4$ percent.

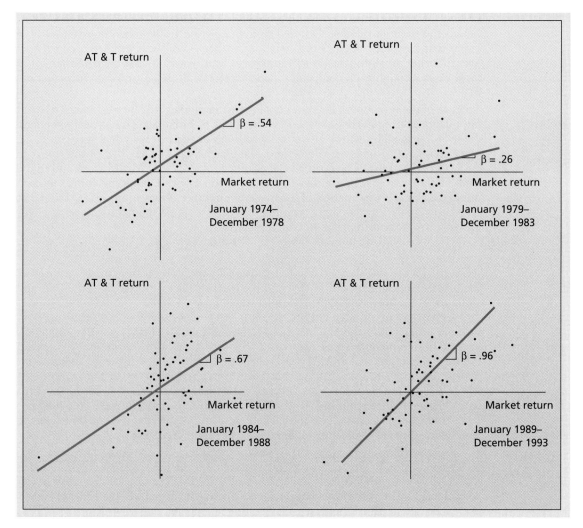

Figure 9-2a We can use data on past prices to obtain an estimate of AT&T's beta. Notice that it is consistently less than 1.

mated value plus or minus two standard errors. Thus the confidence interval for MMM's beta is .71 plus or minus 2 × .12. If you state that the *true* beta for MMM was between .47 and .95, you have a 95 percent chance of being right. You have to do the best you can when estimating risk, but never forget the large margin for error when estimating beta for individual stocks.

Similarly, the standard error of alpha tells us to be cautious about inferring anything as to MMM's "true" or "normal" alpha. All we can say is that MMM's stockholders did well in this particular period.

ADJUSTED BETA.   Merrill Lynch uses an adjustment formula which gives better predictions than the unadjusted figures listed under *BETA*. The formula pushes low betas up toward 1.0. MMM's adjusted beta is .81.

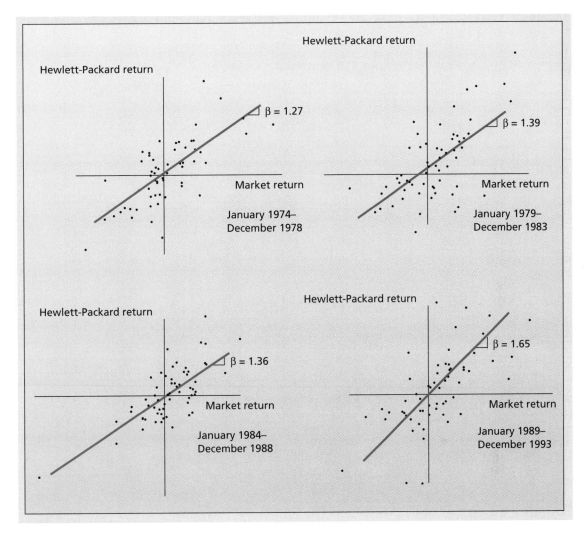

Figure 9-2b Here is a similar exercise for Hewlett-Packard. Notice that Hewlett-Packard's beta is consistently greater than AT&T's.

The Bayesian statistics needed to understand adjusted betas are beyond the scope of this book. We will stick to "raw" betas.

Industry Betas and the Divisional Cost of Capital

That concludes our lesson on how to estimate and predict betas for individual stocks. You should now understand how to estimate a stock's beta by fitting a line to past data, and you should be able to read and understand a publication like Merrill Lynch's "beta book." Bear in mind that such estimates do not allow you to draw fine distinctions. You are exposed to potentially large estimate errors when you estimate betas of individual stocks from a limited sample of data. Fortunately these errors tend to cancel when you estimate betas of *portfolios*. Suppose that you were to compute the average of the betas of 100 common stocks. The standard error of the average

TABLE 9-1

A page from Merrill Lynch's "beta book"

MLPF&S, INC.—MARKET SENSITIVITY STATISTICS

TICKER SYMBOL	SECURITY NAME		94/12 CLOSE PRICE	BETA	ALPHA	R-SQR	RESID STD DEV-N	−STD OF BETA	ERR.− OF ALPHA	ADJUSTED BETA	NUMBER OF OBSERV
MILW	MILWAUKEE INS GROUP INC		10.250	0.46	0.22	0.02	9.13	0.33	1.19	0.64	60
MNES	MINE SAFETY APPLIANCES CO		45.000	0.49	−0.51	0.12	4.39	0.16	0.57	0.66	60
MTX	MINERALS TECHNOLOGIES		29.250	1.06	1.91	0.09	6.76	0.56	1.34	1.04	26
MNBC	MINERS NATL BANCORP INC		25.375	0.03	0.76	0.02	2.69	0.10	0.35	0.36	60
MSIX	MINING SVCS INTL CORP		2.750	−0.68	3.03	0.00	20.77	0.75	2.71	−0.11	60
MBRW	MINNESOTA BREWING CO		4.438	−1.38	−1.26	0.10	8.96	0.87	2.40	−0.57	14
MMM	MINNESOTA MNG & MFG CO		53.375	0.71	0.22	0.37	3.29	0.12	0.43	0.81	60
MPL	MINNESOTA PWR & LT CO		25.250	0.60	−0.33	0.23	3.84	0.14	0.50	0.73	60
MPL PA	MINNESOTA PWR & LT CO	PFD 5%	56.000	0.37	−0.19	0.11	3.59	0.13	0.47	0.58	60
MPL PB	MINNESOTA PWR & LT CO	PFD $7.36	86.250	0.15	−0.02	0.04	2.40	0.09	0.31	0.44	60
MNTX	MINNTECH CORP		15.750	1.67	1.53	0.28	9.54	0.35	1.24	1.45	60
MNRCY	MINORCO	SPONSORED ADR	23.750	0.10	0.81	0.01	6.38	0.23	0.83	0.41	60
MMAN	MINUTEMAN INTL INC		10.375	0.25	0.30	0.01	9.57	0.35	1.25	0.51	60
MIR	MIRAGE RESORTS INC		20.500	2.25	0.83	0.33	11.25	0.41	1.47	1.83	60
MSON	MISONIX INC		0.781	−0.12	−3.78	0.03	20.35	1.50	3.48	0.26	35
MSW	MISSION WEST PPTYS		6.500	−0.20	0.47	0.01	11.11	0.40	1.45	0.20	60
MP PB	MISSISSIPPI POWER CO	PFD DEP 1/4 SH	19.000	−0.18	−1.81	0.06	3.59	0.35	0.96	0.22	14
MP PA	MISSISSIPPI POWER CO	PFD DP 7.25%	20.625	0.95	−0.81	0.48	2.36	0.20	0.47	0.97	26
MVBI	MISSISSIPPI VY BANCSHARES IN		17.375	0.76	1.18	0.02	7.48	0.68	1.82	0.84	17
MRJY	MISTER JAY FASHIONS INTL INC		19.500	0.73	5.69	0.03	14.17	1.21	3.03	0.82	22
MND A	MITCHELL ENERGY & DEV CORP	CLASS A	16.250	1.35	0.11	0.12	7.71	0.60	1.43	1.23	30
MND B	MITCHELL ENERGY & DEV CORP	CLASS B	18.750	1.75	0.76	0.15	9.06	0.70	1.68	1.50	30
MITK	MITEK SYS INC		1.000	0.41	0.82	0.01	21.40	0.78	2.79	0.61	60
MLT	MITEL CORP		3.500	2.43	1.75	0.11	23.60	0.86	3.08	1.95	60
MYTK	MITEK SURGICAL PRODS INC		24.750	1.53	0.32	0.07	14.11	0.78	2.32	1.35	38
MBK	MITSUBISHI BK LTD JAPAN	SPONSORED ADR	24.125	0.84	0.19	0.09	9.06	0.33	1.18	0.89	60
MITSY	MITSUI & CO LTD	ADR	171.500	0.87	−0.13	0.08	9.59	0.35	1.25	0.91	60
MOB	MOBIL CORP		84.250	0.64	0.27	0.26	3.80	0.14	0.50	0.76	60
MAME	MOBILE AMER CORP FLA		5.500	−0.11	2.66	0.02	10.87	0.39	1.42	0.26	60
MBLE	MOBILE GAS SVC CORP		19.250	0.20	0.13	0.01	4.41	0.16	0.57	0.47	60

BASED ON S&P 500 INDEX, USING STRAIGHT REGRESSION

Note: "PFD" refers to preferred stock; "class A" and "class B" refer to two different types of common stock, usually differing in voting rights, issued by the same company. (See Chapter 14.) "ADR" stands for American Depositary Receipt, a device allowing foreign shares to trade on U.S. exchanges.
Source: Merrill Lynch, Pierce, Fenner & Smith, Inc., "Security Risk Evaluation," January 1995.

Figure 9-3 Results of regressing MMM's price changes on the market changes for 60 months ending in January 1994. The slope of the fitted line is beta. The intercept is alpha.

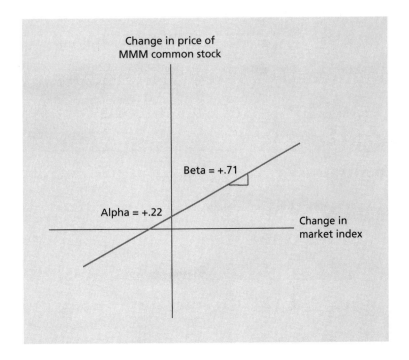

would be much less than the average standard error of the 100 individual betas.[5] That is why it is often easier to estimate *industry betas* than betas for individual firms.

Here are two examples. The first is drawn from a study of the cost of capital of large, mostly successful pharmaceutical companies in 1990. Table 9-2 shows estimated betas for individual companies and also for an "industry" portfolio of all the companies' stocks.[6] Notice the much lower standard error of the industry beta.

Put yourself in the shoes of the chief financial officer of Eli Lilly & Company, in 1990. According to Table 9-2, your *estimated* company cost of capital is 17.6 percent; the estimated industry cost of capital is 15.4 percent.[7] Which is the better benchmark for Lilly's capital investment decisions? If you believe that Lilly's business is substantially the same as the business of the other companies in the industry sample, you should use the industry number. The differences between Lilly's beta and the industry beta are probably just noise. However, if you have reason to believe that Lilly is really riskier, then the company's estimated beta (1.24) and cost of capital (17.6 percent) deserve more weight.[8]

---

[5]If the observations are independent, the standard error of the estimated mean declines in proportion to the square root of the number of observations.

[6]Hypothetical portfolios were formed assuming investments proportional to the aggregate market values of the companies' stocks. Monthly portfolio returns were calculated. These returns were used to estimate portfolio betas and the corresponding standard errors. This is generally the most reliable way of "averaging" individual company betas.

[7]These are actually costs of *equity* capital, which differ from the true opportunity cost of capital to the extent that debt financing is used. But most of these pharmaceutical companies had very little debt outstanding.

[8]In this case, you could try to repeat the analysis for a redefined industry group of truly similar companies.

TABLE 9-2

• •

Estimated betas and costs of (equity) capital (r) for large pharmaceutical companies and for a portfolio of these companies. The precision of the portfolio beta is much better than that of betas for individual companies—note the lower standard error for the portfolio.

	β_{equity}	Standard Error	Cost of Capital
Abbot Laboratories	1.01	.13	15.6%
American Home Products	.89	.11	14.6
Bristol-Myers	.81	.10	13.9
Johnson & Johnson	.93	.11	14.9
Lilly, Eli, & Company	1.24	.12	17.6
Merck & Company	.85	.12	14.2
Pfizer	1.02	.14	15.7
Rorer Group	1.18	.23	17.1
Schering-Plough	.84	.11	14.1
Smith Kline-Beecham	.93	.16	14.9
Squibb	1.18	.20	17.1
Syntex	1.41	.15	19.1
Upjohn	1.19	.18	17.2
Warner-Lambert	1.05	.13	16.0
Market value–weighted industry portfolio	.98	.07	15.4

Source: S. C. Myers and L. Shyam-Sunder, "Cost of Capital Estimates for Investment in Pharmaceutical Research and Development," in R. B. Helms (ed.), *Competitive Strategies in the Pharmaceutical Industry,* American Enterprise Institute, Washington, D.C., 1995.

The second example is given in Figure 9-4, which shows betas estimated for a sample of the common stocks of large oil companies from 1965 to 1992.[9] Such long industry time series inspire more confidence than "spot" estimates based on a few years' data. With hindsight the high oil company betas of the early 1980s are revealed as an aberration. We suspect the fall in estimated betas in the early 1990s will likewise prove temporary.

Warning: Oil companies are not financed solely with common stock. They also use many billions of dollars of debt financing. Estimates of company or industry costs of capital must take returns on debt as well as equity into account. We will get to this shortly.

Perfect Pitch and the Cost of Capital

Why is so much time spent estimating company and industry costs of capital? The true cost of capital depends on project risk, not on the company undertaking the project.

There are two reasons. First, many, maybe most, projects can be treated as average risk, that is, no more or less risky than the average of the company's other assets. For these projects the company cost of capital is the right discount rate. Second, the company cost of capital is a useful starting point for setting discount rates for un-

---

[9]We thank Brattle/IRI, Inc., for supplying these estimates.

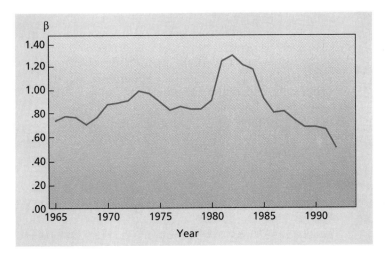

Figure 9-4 Betas of a portfolio of common stocks of large oil companies. (*Source:* Brattle/IRI, Inc.)

usually risky or safe projects. It is easier to add to, or subtract from, the company cost of capital than to estimate each project's cost of capital from scratch.

There is a good musical analogy here.[10] Most of us, lacking perfect pitch, need a well-defined reference point, like middle C, before we can sing on key. But anyone who can carry a tune gets *relative* pitches right. Businesspeople have good intuition about *relative* risks, at least in industries they are used to, but not about absolute risk or required rates of return. Therefore, they set a company- or industrywide cost of capital as a benchmark. This is not the right hurdle rate for everything the company does, but adjustments can be made for more or less risky ventures.

9-2 CAPITAL STRUCTURE AND THE COMPANY COST OF CAPITAL

The cost of capital is a hurdle rate for capital budgeting decisions. It depends on the *business risk* of the firm's investment opportunities. The risk of a common stock reflects the business risk of the real assets held by the firm. But shareholders also bear *financial risk* to the extent that the firm issues debt to finance its real investments. The more a firm relies on debt financing, the riskier its common stock is.

We did not have to worry about this in Microsoft's case, because Microsoft had essentially no debt, but Microsoft is unusual. Many companies' debt is worth more than their equity.

Borrowing is said to create *financial leverage* or *gearing*. Financial leverage does not affect the risk or the expected return on the firm's assets, but it does push up the risk of the common stock and lead the stockholders to demand a correspondingly higher return.

---

[10]The analogy is borrowed from S. C. Myers and L. S. Borucki, "Discounted Cash Flow Estimates of the Cost of Equity Capital—A Case Study," *Financial Markets, Institutions, and Investments*, **3**:18 (August 1994).

How
Changing
Capital
Structure
Affects
Expected
Returns

Think again of what the *company* cost of capital is and what it is used for. We *define* it as the opportunity cost of capital for the firm's existing assets; we *use* it to value new assets which have the same risk as the old ones.

If you owned a portfolio of all the firm's securities—100 percent of the debt and 100 percent of the equity—you would own the firm's assets lock, stock, and barrel. You wouldn't share the cash flows with anyone; every dollar of cash the firm paid out would be paid to you.

You can think of the company cost of capital as the expected return on this hypothetical portfolio. To calculate it, you just take a weighted average of the expected returns on the debt and the equity:

$$\text{Company cost of capital} = r_{\text{assets}} = r_{\text{portfolio}}$$

$$= \frac{\text{debt}}{\text{debt} + \text{equity}} r_{\text{debt}} + \frac{\text{equity}}{\text{debt} + \text{equity}} r_{\text{equity}}$$

For example, suppose that the firm's market value balance sheet is as follows:

Asset value	100	Debt value (D)	40
		Equity value (E)	60
Asset value	100	Firm value (V)	100

Note that the values of debt and equity add up to the firm value ($D + E = V$) and that the firm value equals the asset value. (These figures are *market* values, not *book* values: The market value of the firm's equity is often substantially different from its book value.)

If investors expect a return of 8 percent on the debt and 15 percent on the equity, then the expected return on the assets is

$$r_{\text{assets}} = \frac{D}{V} r_{\text{debt}} + \frac{E}{V} r_{\text{equity}}$$

$$= \left(\frac{40}{100} \times 8\right) + \left(\frac{60}{100} \times 15\right) = 12.2\%$$

If the firm is contemplating investment in a project that has the same risk as the firm's existing business, the opportunity cost of capital for this project is the same as the firm's cost of capital; in other words, it is 12.2 percent.

What would happen if the firm issued an additional 10 of equity and used the cash to repay 10 of its debt? The revised market value balance sheet is:

Asset value	100	Debt value (D)	30
		Equity value (E)	70
Asset value	100	Firm value (V)	100

The change in financial structure does not affect the amount or risk of the cash flows on the total package of the debt and the equity. Therefore, if investors require a return of 12.2 percent on the total package before the refinancing, they must require a 12.2 percent return on the firm's assets afterward.

Although the required return on the *package* of the debt and equity is unaffected, the change in financial structure does affect the required return on the individual securities. Since the company has less debt than before, the debtholders are likely to be satisfied with a lower return. We will suppose that the expected return on the debt falls to 7.3 percent. Now you can write down the basic equation for the return on assets:

$$r_{assets} = \frac{D}{V} r_{debt} + \frac{E}{V} r_{equity}$$

$$= \left(\frac{30}{100} \times 7.3\right) + \left(\frac{70}{100} \times r_{equity}\right) = 12.2\%$$

and solve for the return on equity:

$$r_{equity} = 14.3\%$$

Reducing the amount of debt reduced debtholder risk and led to a fall in the return that debtholders required (r_{debt} fell from 8 to 7.3 percent). The lower leverage also made the equity safer and reduced the return that shareholders required (r_{equity} fell from 15 to 14.3 percent). The weighted average return on debt and equity remained at 12.2 percent:

$$r_{assets} = (.3 \times r_{debt}) + (.7 \times r_{equity})$$

$$= (.3 \times 7.3) + (.7 \times 14.3) = 12.2\%$$

Suppose that the company issues enough equity to repay all the debt. In that case all the cash flows will go to the equity holders. The firm cost of capital, r_{assets}, stays at 12.2 percent, and r_{equity} is also 12.2 percent.

How Changing Capital Structure Affects Beta

We have looked at how changes in financial structure affect expected return. Let us now look at the effect on beta.

The stockholders and debtholders both receive a share of the firm's cash flows, and both bear part of the risk. For example, if the firm's assets turn out to be worthless, there will be no cash to pay stockholders *or* debtholders. But debtholders bear much less risk than stockholders. Debt betas of large blue-chip firms are typically close to zero—close enough that for such companies many financial analysts just assume that $\beta_{debt} = 0$.[11]

If you owned a portfolio of all the firm's securities, you wouldn't share the cash flows with anyone. You wouldn't share the risks with anyone either; you would bear them all. Thus the firm's asset beta is equal to the beta of a portfolio of all the firm's debt and its equity.

The beta of this hypothetical portfolio is just a weighted average of the debt and equity betas:

$$\beta_{assets} = \beta_{portfolio} = \frac{D}{V} \beta_{debt} + \frac{E}{V} \beta_{equity}$$

Think back to our example. If the debt before the refinancing has a beta of .2 and the equity a beta of 1.2, then

$$\beta_{assets} = (.4 \times .2) + (.6 \times 1.2) = .8$$

What happens after the refinancing? The risk of the total package is unaffected, but both the debt and the equity are now less risky. Suppose that debt beta falls to .1. We can work out the new equity beta:

---

[11]This assumption should be challenged in periods of volatile interest rates, when prices of long-term corporate and government bonds can fluctuate dramatically. There were such periods in the early 1980s when bond betas were as high as .3 to .4. Recent bond betas have been roughly .2.

Figure 9-5 Expected returns and betas before refinancing. The expected return and beta of the firm's assets are weighted averages of the expected return and betas of the debt and equity.

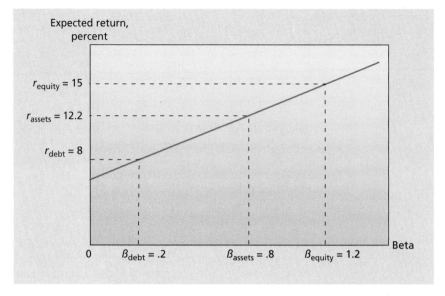

$$\beta_{assets} = \frac{D}{V} \beta_{debt} - \frac{E}{V} \beta_{equity}$$

$$.8 = (.3 \times .1) + (.7 \times \beta_{equity})$$

$$\beta_{equity} = 1.1$$

Figure 9-5 shows the expected return and beta of the firm's assets. It also shows how expected return and risk are shared between the debtholders and equity holders before the refinancing. Figure 9-6 shows what happens after the refinancing. Both debt and equity are less risky, and therefore investors are satisfied with a lower expected return. But equity now accounts for a larger proportion of firm value than before. As a result, the weighted average of both the expected return and beta on the two components is unchanged.

Now you can see how to *unlever* betas, that is, how to go from an observed β_{equity} to β_{assets}. You have the equity beta, say, 1.1. You also need the debt beta, say, .1, and the relative market values of debt (D/V) and equity (E/V). If debt accounts for 30 percent of overall value V,

$$\beta_{assets} = (.3 \times .1) + (.7 \times 1.1) = .8$$

This runs the previous example in reverse. Just remember the basic relationship:

$$\beta_{assets} = \beta_{debt}D/V + \beta_{equity}E/V$$

A Word of Caution and a Few Observations

In many ways we have given an oversimplified version of how financial leverage affects equity risks and returns. For example, later we will need to amend our formulas to recognize the fact that interest can be deducted from taxable income. These finer points can wait.[12] for now, there are just a few points to remember:

---

[12]In fact, they will have to wait until Chapters 18 and 19.

Figure 9-6 Expected returns and betas after refinancing.

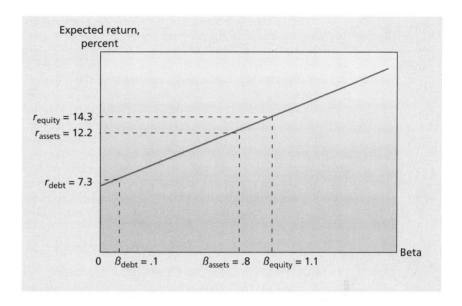

- It is the company cost of capital that is relevant in capital budgeting decisions, not the expected return on the common stock.
- The company cost of capital is a weighted average of the returns that investors expect from the various debt and equity securities issued by the firm.
- The company cost of capital is related to the firm's asset beta, not to the beta of the common stock.
- The asset beta can be calculated as a weighted average of the betas of the various securities.
- When the firm changes its financial leverage, the risk and expected returns of the individual securities change. The asset beta and the company cost of capital do *not* change.

9-3 HOW TO ESTIMATE DUKE POWER'S COST OF CAPITAL—AN EXAMPLE

The Expected Return on Duke Power's Common Stock

Suppose that in early 1995 you were asked to estimate the company cost of capital of Duke Power. Remember, the company cost of capital is the expected return on a portfolio of all the firm's securities. Thus it can be calculated as a weighted average of the returns on the separate parts.

The tough part of the weighted average is finding the expected rate of return on Duke Power's common stock. In Chapter 4 we used the constant-growth DCF formula to estimate the expected rates of return for Duke Power and a sample of 17 utility stocks. We now try out the capital asset pricing model on these same companies.

Table 9-3 shows estimates of beta and the standard errors of these estimates for the common stocks of the 17 large utilities. Most of the standard errors are less than .15, but they are still large enough to preclude a precise estimate of any particular utility's beta. Our confidence about the average beta of the 17 utilities is somewhat better.

Are these utility stocks really equivalent-risk securities? Judging from Table 9-3, that appears to be a reasonable assumption. Much of the spread of estimated betas could be attributed to random measurement errors. It would be hard to reject the hypothesis that the "true" beta was the same for each of the firms.

You now have two clues about the true beta of Duke Power: the direct estimate of .48 and the average estimate for the industry of .47.[13] Fortunately, these two pieces of evidence agree, so let us use .47. In early 1995 the risk-free rate of interest r_f was about 6 percent. Therefore, if you accept our estimate of 8.4 percent for the risk premium on the market, you will conclude that the expected return on Duke Power's stock was about 10 percent:[14]

$$r_{\text{equity}} = r_f + \beta_{\text{equity}}(r_m - r_f)$$

$$= .06 + .47(.084) = .099, \text{ or about } 10\%$$

We have focused on using the capital asset pricing model to estimate the expected return on Duke Power's common stock. But it would be useful to get a check on this figure. We have already mentioned one possibility, the constant-growth DCF formula. You could also use DCF models with varying future growth rates, or perhaps arbitrage pricing theory (APT). We applied APT to another group of utilities in Section 8-4.

Estimating Duke Power's Company Cost of Capital

If Duke Power were financed only by common stock, the company cost of capital would be the same as the expected return on its stock. In early 1995 common stock accounted for about 65 percent of the market value of the company's securities. Debt accounted for 29 percent, and preferred stock make up for the remaining 6 percent.[15] To keep matters simple, we will just lump the preferred stock in with the debt.

---

[13]Comparing the betas of Duke Power with those of the other 16 utilities in the sample would be misleading if Duke Power had a materially higher or lower debt ratio. A more complete analysis would relever the betas of the utility sample to Duke Power's debt-to-value ratio. We discussed the relationship between leverage and beta in the last section.

[14]This is really a discount rate for near-term cash flows, since it rests on a risk-free rate measured by the yield on Treasury bills with maturities less than 1 year. Is this, you may ask, the right discount rate for cash flows from an asset with, say, a 10- or 20-year expected life?

Well, now that you mention it, possibly not. In early 1995 longer-term Treasury bonds yielded about 7.5 percent, i.e., about 1.5 percent above the Treasury bill rate.

The risk-free rate could be defined as a long-term Treasury bond yield. If you do this, however, you should subtract the risk premium of Treasury bonds over bills, which we gave as 1.4 percent in Table 7-1. This gives a rough-and-ready estimate of the expected yield on short-term Treasury *bills* over the life of the bond:

$$\text{Expected average T-bill rate} = \frac{\text{T-bond}}{\text{yield}} - \frac{\text{premium of}}{\text{bonds over bills}}$$

$$= .075 - .014 = .061, \text{ or about } 6\%$$

The expected average future Treasury bill rate should be used in the capital asset pricing model if a discount rate is needed for an extended stream of cash flows. But in early 1995 this "long-term r_f" was almost exactly the same as the Treasury bill rate.

[15]We will discuss preferred stock in Chapter 14. For now all you need to know is that it is less risky than common stock but more risky than debt.

TABLE 9-3

· ·

Betas for 17 large utilities, 1990–1994. The average beta was calculated from the monthly rates of return on a portfolio of the 17 companies.

	Beta	Standard Error
Allegheny Power Systems	.38	.11
Central Main Power	.43	.14
Duke Power	.48	.11
Houston Industries	.25	.13
IPALCO Enterprises	.63	.16
Minnesota Power & Light	.49	.13
Northeast Utilities	.37	.13
Northern States Power	.64	.13
Pacific Gas & Electric	.46	.11
Potomac Electric Power	.37	.10
Public Service of Colorado	.57	.11
Puget Sound Power & Light	.43	.13
SCE	.60	.12
Southern	.41	.13
Southwestern Public Service	.56	.12
Texas Utilities	.35	.10
Wisconsin Energy	.53	.14
Portfolio	.47	.09

We estimated the expected return from Duke Power's common stock at 10 percent. The yield on the company's debt was about 8 percent.[16] To find the company cost of capital, just calculate a weighted average of the expected returns on the different securities:[17]

---

[16]This is a *promised* yield; i.e., it is the yield if Duke Power makes all the promised payments. Since there is some risk of default, the *expected* return is less than the promised yield. For a blue-chip company like Duke Power, the difference is small. But for a company that is hovering on the brink of bankruptcy, it can be important.

[17]Note that you get exactly the same result by estimating the asset beta and plugging it into the capital asset pricing model:

$$r_{debt} = r_f + \beta_{debt}(r_m - r_f)$$
$$.08 = .06 + \beta_{debt}(.084)$$
$$\beta_{debt} = .24$$

Now calculate the beta of the firm's assets:

$$\beta_{assets} = \beta_{debt}\frac{D}{V} + \beta_{equity}\frac{E}{V}$$
$$= .35(.24) + .65(.47) = .39$$

Finally, use the capital asset pricing model to calculate r_{assets}:

$$r_{assets} = r_f + \beta_{assets}(r_m - r_f)$$
$$= .06 + .39(.084) = .093, \text{ or } 9.3\%$$

$$\text{Company cost of capital} = r_{\text{assets}} = \frac{D}{V} r_{\text{debt}} + \frac{E}{V} r_{\text{equity}}$$

$$= .35(.08) + .65(.10)$$

$$= .093, \text{ or } 9.3\%$$

9-4 SETTING DISCOUNT RATES WHEN YOU CAN'T USE A BETA BOOK

Stock or industry betas provide a rough guide to the risk encountered in various lines of business. But an asset beta for, say, the steel industry can take us only so far. Not all investments made in the steel industry are "typical." What other kinds of evidence about business risk might a financial manager examine?

In some cases the asset is publicly traded. If so, we can simply estimate its beta from past price data. For example, suppose a firm wants to analyze the risks of holding a large inventory of copper. Because copper is a standardized, widely traded commodity, it is possible to calculate rates of return from holding copper and to calculate a beta for copper.

What should a manager do if the asset has no such convenient price record? What if the proposed investment is not close enough to business as usual to justify using a company or divisional cost of capital?

These cases clearly call for judgment. For managers making that kind of judgment, we offer two pieces of advice.

1. *Avoid fudge factors.* Don't give in to the temptation to add fudge factors to the discount rate to offset things that could go wrong with the proposed investment. Adjust cash-flow forecasts first.

2. *Think about the determinants of asset betas.* Often the characteristics of high- and low-beta assets can be observed when the beta itself cannot be.

Let us expand on these two points.

Avoiding Fudge Factors in Discount Rates

We have defined risk, from the investor's viewpoint, as the standard deviation of portfolio return or the beta of a common stock or other security. But in everyday usage *risk* simply equals "bad outcome." People think of the risks of a project as a list of things that can go wrong. For example,

- A geologist looking for oil worries about the risk of a dry hole.

- A pharmaceutical manufacturer worries about the risk that a new drug which cures baldness may not be approved by the Food and Drug Administration.

- The owner of a hotel in a politically unstable part of the world worries about the "political risk" of expropriation.

Managers often add fudge factors to discount rates to offset worries such as these.

This sort of adjustment makes us nervous. First, the bad outcomes we cited appear to reflect unique (i.e., diversifiable) risks which would not affect the expected rate of return demanded by investors. Second, the need for a discount rate adjustment usually arises because managers fail to give bad outcomes their due weight in cash-flow forecasts. The managers then try to offset that mistake by adding a fudge factor to the discount rate.

Example: Project Z will produce just one cash flow, forecasted at $1 million at year 1. It is regarded as average risk, suitable for discounting at a 10 percent company cost of capital:

$$PV = \frac{C_1}{1+r} = \frac{1,000,000}{1.1} = \$909,100$$

But now you discover that the company's engineers are behind schedule in developing the technology required for the project. They're "confident" it will work, but they admit to a small chance that it won't. You still see the *most likely* outcome as $1 million, but you also see some chance that project Z will generate *zero* cash flow next year.

Now the project's prospects are clouded by your new worry about technology. It must be worth less than the $909,100 you calculated before that worry arose. But how much less? There is *some* discount rate (10 percent plus a fudge factor) which will give the right value, but we don't know what that adjusted discount rate is.

We suggest you reconsider your original $1 million forecast for project Z's cash flow. Project cash flows are supposed to be *unbiased* forecasts, which give due weight to all possible outcomes, favorable and unfavorable. Managers making unbiased forecasts are correct on average. Sometimes their forecasts will turn out high, other times low, but their errors will average out over many projects.

If you forecast cash flow of $1 million for projects like Z, you will overestimate the average cash flow, because every now and then you will hit a zero. Those zeros should be "averaged in" to your forecasts.

For many projects, the most likely cash flow is also the unbiased forecast. If there are three possible outcomes with the probabilities shown below, the unbiased forecast is $1 million. (The unbiased forecast is the sum of the probability-weighted cash flows.)

Possible Cash Flow	Probability	Probability-Weighted Cash Flow	Unbiased Forecast
1.2	.25	.3	1.0, or
1.0	.50	.5	$1 million
.8	.25	.2	

This might describe the initial prospects of project Z. But if technological uncertainty introduces the chance of a zero cash flow, the unbiased forecast could drop to $833,300:

Possible Cash Flow	Probability	Probability-Weighted Cash Flow	Unbiased Forecast
1.2	.25	.3	
1.0	.333	.333	.833,
.8	.25	.2	or $833,000
0	.167	0	

The present value is

$$PV = \frac{.833}{1.1} = .757, \text{ or } \$757,000$$

Now, of course, you can figure out the right fudge factor to add to the discount rate to apply to the original $1 million forecast to get the correct answer. But you have to think through possible cash flows in order to get that fudge factor; and once you have thought through the cash flows, you don't *need* the fudge factor.

Managers often work out a range of possible outcomes for major projects, sometimes with explicit probabilities attached. We give more elaborate examples and further discussion in Chapter 10. But even when a range of outcomes and probabilities is not explicitly written down, the manager can still consider the good and bad outcomes as well as the most likely one. When the bad outcomes outweigh the good, the cash-flow forecast should be reduced until balance is regained.

Step 1, then, is to do your best to make unbiased forecasts of a project's cash flows. Step 2 is to consider whether *investors* would regard the project as more or less risky than typical for a company or division. Here our advice is to search for characteristics of the asset that are associated with high or low betas. We wish we had a more fundamental scientific understanding of what these characteristics are. We see business risks surfacing in capital markets, but as yet there is no satisfactory theory describing how these risks are generated. Nevertheless, some things are known.

What Determines Asset Betas?

CYCLICALITY.   Many people intuitively associate risk with the variability of book, or accounting, earnings. But much of this variability reflects unique or diversifiable risk. Lone prospectors in search of gold look forward to extremely uncertain future earnings, but whether they strike it rich is not likely to depend on the performance of the market portfolio. Even if they do find gold, they do not bear much market risk. Therefore, an investment in gold has a high standard deviation but a relatively low beta.

What really counts is the strength of the relationship between the firm's earnings and the aggregate earnings on all real assets. We can measure this either by the *accounting beta* or by the *cash-flow beta*. These are just like a real beta except that changes in book earnings or cash flow are used in place of rates of return on securities. We would predict that firms with high accounting or cash-flow betas should also have high stock betas—and the prediction is correct.[18]

This means that cyclical firms—firms whose revenues and earnings are strongly dependent on the state of the business cycle—tend to be high-beta firms. Thus you should demand a higher rate of return from investments whose performance is strongly tied to the performance of the economy.

*OPERATING LEVERAGE.   We have already seen that financial leverage—in other words, the commitment to fixed debt charges—increases the beta of an investor's portfolio. In just the same way, operating leverage—in other words, the commitment to fixed *production* charges—must add to the beta of a capital project. Let's see how this works.

The cash flows generated by any productive asset can be broken down into revenue, fixed costs, and variable costs:

$$\text{Cash flow} = \text{revenue} - \text{fixed cost} - \text{variable cost}$$

Costs are variable if they depend on the rate of output. Examples are raw materials, sales commissions, and some labor and maintenance costs. Fixed costs are cash out-

---

[18]For example, see W. H. Beaver and J. Manegold, "The Association between Market-Determined and Accounting-Determined Measures of Systematic Risk: Some Further Evidence," *Journal of Financial and Quantitative Analysis*, **10**:231–284 (June 1975).

flows that occur regardless of whether the asset is active or idle—e.g., property taxes or the wages of workers under contract.

We can break down the asset's present value in the same way:

$$PV(\text{asset}) = PV(\text{revenue}) - PV(\text{fixed cost}) - PV(\text{variable cost})$$

Or equivalently:

$$PV(\text{revenue}) = PV(\text{fixed cost}) + PV(\text{variable cost}) + PV(\text{asset})$$

Those who *receive* the fixed costs are like debtholders in the project—they simply get a fixed payment. Those who receive the net cash flows from the asset are like holders of common stock—they get whatever is left after payment of the fixed costs.

We can now figure out how the asset's beta is related to the betas of the values of revenue and costs. We just use our previous formula with the betas relabeled:

$$\beta_{\text{revenue}} = \beta_{\text{fixed cost}} \frac{PV(\text{fixed cost})}{PV(\text{revenue})}$$

$$+ \beta_{\text{variable cost}} \frac{PV(\text{variable cost})}{PV(\text{revenue})} + \beta_{\text{asset}} \frac{PV(\text{asset})}{PV(\text{revenue})}$$

In other words, the beta of the value of the revenues is simply a weighted average of the beta of its component parts. Now the fixed-cost beta is zero by definition: Whoever receives the fixed costs holds a safe asset. The betas of the revenues and variable costs should be approximately the same, because they respond to the same underlying variable, the rate of output. Therefore, we can substitute $\beta_{\text{variable cost}}$ and solve for the asset beta. Remember that $\beta_{\text{fixed cost}} = 0$.

$$\beta_{\text{asset}} = \beta_{\text{revenue}} \frac{PV(\text{revenue}) - PV(\text{variable cost})}{PV(\text{asset})}$$

$$= \beta_{\text{revenue}} \left[1 + \frac{PV(\text{fixed cost})}{PV(\text{asset})} \right]$$

Thus, given the cyclicality of revenues (reflected in β_{revenue}), the asset beta is proportional to the ratio of the present value of fixed costs to the present value of the project.

Now you have a rule of thumb for judging the relative risks of alternative designs or technologies for producing the same project. Other things being equal, the alternative with the higher ratio of fixed costs to project value will have the higher project beta. Empirical tests confirm that companies with high operating leverage actually do have high betas.[19]

Searching for Clues

Recent research suggests a variety of other factors that affect an asset's beta.[20] But going through a long list of these possible determinants would take us too far afield.

You cannot hope to estimate the relative risk of assets with any precision, but good managers examine any project from a variety of angles and look for clues as to

[19]See B. Lev, "On the Association between Operating Leverage and Risk," *Journal of Financial and Quantitative Analysis*, **9**:627–642 (September 1974); and G. N. Mandelker and S. G. Rhee, "The Impact of the Degrees of Operating and Financial Leverage on Systematic Risk of Common Stock," *Journal of Financial and Quantitative Analysis*, **19**:45–57 (March 1984).

[20]This work is reviewed in G. Foster, *Financial Statement Analysis*, 2d ed., Prentice-Hall, Inc., Englewood Cliffs, N.J., 1986, chap. 10.

its riskiness. They know that high market risk is a characteristic of cyclical ventures and of projects with high fixed costs. They think about the major uncertainties affecting the economy and consider how projects are affected by these uncertainties.[21]

*9-5   ANOTHER LOOK AT RISK AND DISCOUNTED CASH FLOW

In practical capital budgeting, a single discount rate is usually applied to all future cash flows. For example, an expected return may be calculated from the capital asset pricing model:

$$r = r_f + \beta(r_m - r_f)$$

The resulting r would be plugged directly into the standard discounted-cash-flow formula:

$$PV = \sum_{t=1}^{T} \frac{C_t}{(1 + r)^t}$$

Among other things, this procedure assumes that beta is constant over the project's entire life.[22] Here is an example which shows what that assumption really means.

EXAMPLE: Project A is expected to produce a cash inflow of $100 million for each of 3 years. The risk-free interest rate is 6 percent, the market risk premium is 8 percent, and project A's beta is .75. You therefore calculate A's opportunity cost of capital as follows:

$$r = r_f + \beta(r_m - r_f)$$
$$= 6 + .75(8) = 12\%$$

Discounting at 12 percent gives the following present value for each cash flow:

Project A

Year	Cash Flow	PV at 12%
1	100	89.3
2	100	79.7
3	100	71.2
	Total PV	240.2

Now compare these figures with the cash flows of project B. Notice that B's cash flows are lower than A's; but B's flows are safe, and therefore they are discounted at the risk-free interest rate. The *present value* of each year's cash flow is identical for the two projects.

---

[21]Sharpe's article on a "multibeta" interpretation of market risk offers a useful way of thinking about these uncertainties and tracing their impact on a firm's or project's risk. See W. F. Sharpe, "The Capital Asset Pricing Model: A 'Multi-Beta' Interpretation," in H. Levy and M. Sarnat (eds.), *Financial Decision Making under Uncertainty*, Academic Press, New York, 1977.

[22]See E. F. Fama, "Risk-Adjusted Discount Rates and Capital Budgeting under Uncertainty," *Journal of Financial Economics*, **5**:3–24 (August 1977); or S. C. Myers and S. M. Turnbull, "Capital Budgeting and the Capital Asset Pricing Model: Good News and Bad News," *Journal of Finance*, **32**:321–332 (May 1977).

	Project B	
Year	Cash Flow	PV at 6%
1	94.6	89.3
2	89.6	79.7
3	84.8	71.2
	Total PV	240.2

In year 1 project A has a risky cash flow of 100. This has the same present value as the safe cash flow of 94.6 from project B. Economists would describe the 94.6 as the **certainty equivalent** of 100. Since the two cash flows have the same present value, investors are willing to give up $100 - 94.6 = 5.4$ in expected year-1 income in order to get rid of the uncertainty.

In year 2 project A has a risky cash flow of 100, and B has a safe cash flow of 89.6. Again both flows have the same present value. Thus to eliminate the uncertainty in year 2, investors are prepared to give up $100 - 89.6 = 10.4$ of future income. And to eliminate uncertainty in year 3, they are willing to give up $100 - 84.8 = 15.2$ of future income.

To value project A, you discounted each cash flow at the same risk-adjusted discount rate of 12 percent. Now you can see what is implied when you did that. By using a constant rate, you effectively made a larger deduction for risk from the later cash flows:

Year	Forecasted Flow for Project A	Certainty-Equivalent Cash Flow	Deduction for Risk
1	100	94.6	5.4
2	100	89.6	10.4
3	100	84.8	15.2

The second cash flow is riskier than the first because it is exposed to 2 years of market risk. The third cash flow is riskier still because it is exposed to 3 years of market risk. You can see this increased risk reflected in the steadily declining certainty equivalents.

In the first year, investors would be willing to accept a 5.4 percent lower cash flow if it were risk-free:

$$\text{Risky cash flow}/1.054 = \text{certainty-equivalent cash flow}$$

$$100/1.054 = 94.6$$

Later years' certainty equivalents decrease by 5.4 percent per year:

Second year: $100/(1.054)^2 = 89.6$

Third year: $100/(1.054)^3 = 84.8$

There's no law of nature stating that certainty equivalents have to decrease in this smooth and regular way. In just a moment we'll sketch a real example in which they did not. But first let's formalize and review the concept of certainty equivalents.

Valuing Certainty-Equivalent Flows

Let us start again with a single future cash flow C_1. If C_1 is certain, its present value is found by discounting at the risk-free rate r_f:

$$PV = \frac{C_1}{1 + r_f}$$

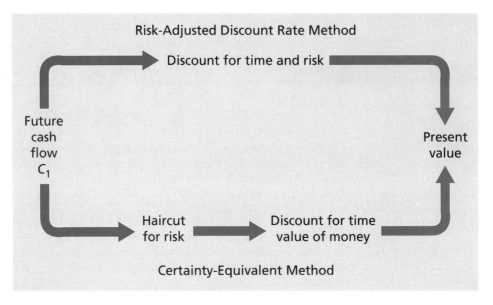

Figure 9-7 Two ways to calculate present value.

If the cash flow is risky, the normal procedure is to discount its forecasted (expected) value at a *risk-adjusted discount rate r* which is greater than r_f.[23] The risk-adjusted discount rate adjusts for both time and risk. This is illustrated by the clockwise route in Figure 9-7.

The alternative certainty-equivalent method makes separate adjustments for risk and time. This is illustrated by the counterclockwise route in Figure 9-7. When you use this method, you should ask, "What is the smallest *certain* payoff for which I would exchange the risky cash flow C_1?" This is called the *certainty equivalent* of C_1, denoted by CEQ_1.[24]

Since CEQ_1 is the value equivalent of a safe cash flow, it is discounted at the risk-free rate r_f. Thus we have two identical expressions for PV:

$$PV = \frac{C_1}{1 + r} = \frac{CEQ_1}{1 + r_f}$$

For cash flows 2, 3, or t years away,

$$PV = \frac{C_t}{(1 + r)^t} = \frac{CEQ_t}{(1 + r_f)^t}$$

But if we are to use the same discount rate for every future cash flow, then the certainty equivalents must decline steadily as a fraction of the cash flow. We saw this with project A, where the ratio of the certainty-equivalent cash flow to the forecasted flow declined by 5.4 percent a year:

---

[23]The quantity r can be less than r_f for assets with negative betas. But the betas of the assets which corporations hold are almost always positive.

[24]CEQ_1 can be calculated directly from the capital asset pricing model. The formula is given in the Appendix to this chapter.

Year	Forecasted Flow for Project A (C_t)	Certainty-Equivalent Cash Flow (CEQ_t)	Ratio of CEQ_t to C_t
1	100	94.6	.946
2	100	89.6	$.896 = .946^2$
3	100	84.8	$.848 = .946^3$

When You Cannot Use a Single Risk-Adjusted Discount Rate for Long-Lived Assets

Here is a disguised, simplified, and somewhat exaggerated version of an actual project proposal that one of the authors was asked to analyze. The scientists at Vegetron have come up with an electric mop, and the firm is ready to go ahead with pilot production and test marketing. The preliminary phase will take 1 year and cost $125,000. Management feels that there is only a 50 percent chance that pilot production and market tests will be successful. If they are, then Vegetron will build a $1 million plant which would generate an expected annual cash flow in perpetuity of $250,000 a year after taxes. If they are not successful, the project will have to be dropped.

The expected cash flows (in thousands of dollars) are

$$C_0 = -125$$

$$C_1 = 50\% \text{ chance of } -1000 \text{ and } 50\% \text{ change of } 0$$

$$= .5(-1000) + .5(0) = -500$$

$$C_t \text{ for } t \text{ for } 2, 3, \ldots = 50\% \text{ chance of } 250 \text{ and } 50\% \text{ chance of } 0$$

$$= .5(250) + .5(0) = 125$$

Management has little experience with consumer products and considers this a project of extremely high risk.[25] Therefore management discounts the cash flows at 25 percent, rather than at Vegetron's normal 10 percent standard:

$$\text{NPV} = -125 - \frac{500}{1.25} + \sum_{t=2}^{\infty} \frac{125}{(1.25)^t} = -125, \text{ or } -\$125,000$$

This seems to show that the project is not worthwhile.

Management's analysis is open to criticism if the first year's experiment resolves a high proportion of the risk. If the test phase is a failure, then there's no risk at all—the project is *certain* to be worthless. If it is a success, there could well be only normal risk from there on. That means there is a 50 percent chance that in 1 year Vegetron will have the opportunity to invest in a project of *normal* risk, for which the *normal* discount rate of 10 percent would be appropriate. Thus the firm has a 50 percent chance to invest $1 million in a project with a net present value of $1.5 million:

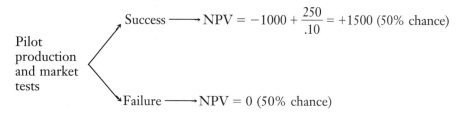

$$\text{Success} \longrightarrow \text{NPV} = -1000 + \frac{250}{.10} = +1500 \ (50\% \text{ chance})$$

Pilot production and market tests

$$\text{Failure} \longrightarrow \text{NPV} = 0 \ (50\% \text{ chance})$$

---

[25]We will assume that they mean high *market* risk and that the difference between 25 and 10 percent is *not* a fudge factor introduced to offset optimistic cash-flow forecasts.

Thus we could view the project as offering an expected payoff of .5(1500) + .5(0) = 750, or $750,000, at $t = 1$ on a $125,000 investment at $t = 0$. Of course, the certainty equivalent of the payoff is less than $750,000, but the difference would have to be very large to justify rejecting the project. For example, if the certainty equivalent is half the forecasted cash flow and the risk-free rate is 7 percent, the project is worth $225,500:

$$\text{NPV} = C_0 + \frac{\text{CEQ}_1}{1 + r_f}$$

$$= -125 + \frac{.5(750)}{1.07} = 225.5, \text{ or } \$225,500$$

This is not bad for a $125,000 investment—and quite a change from the negative NPV that management got by discounting all future cash flows at 25 percent.

A Common Mistake

You sometimes hear people say that because distant cash flows are "riskier," they should be discounted at a higher rate than earlier cash flows. That is quite wrong: Using the same risk-adjusted discount rate for each year's cash flow implies a larger deduction for risk from the later cash flows. The reason is that the discount rate compensates for the risk borne *per period*. The more distant the cash flows, the greater the number of periods and the larger the *total* risk adjustment.

It makes sense to use a single risk-adjusted discount rate as long as the project has the same market risk at each point in its life. But look out for exceptions like the electric mop project, where market risk changes as time passes.

9-6 SUMMARY

In Chapter 8 we set out some basic principles for valuing risky assets. In this chapter we have shown you how to apply these principles to practical situations.

The problem is easiest when you believe that the project has the same market risk as the company's existing assets. In this case, the required return equals the required return on a portfolio of the company's securities. This is called the *company cost of capital*.

Capital asset pricing theory states that the required return on any asset depends on its risk. In this chapter we have defined risk as beta and used the capital asset pricing model to calculate expected returns.

The most common way to estimate the beta of a stock is to figure out how the stock price has responded to market changes in the past. Of course, this will give you only an estimate of the stock's true beta. You may get a more reliable figure if you calculate an industry beta for a group of similar companies.

Suppose that you now have an estimate of the stock's beta. Can you plug that into the capital asset pricing model to find the company's cost of capital? No, the stock beta may reflect both business and financial risk. Whenever a company borrows money, it increases the beta (and the expected return) of its stock. Remember, the company cost of capital is the expected return on a portfolio of all the firm's securities, not just the common stock. You can calculate it by estimating the expected return on each of the securities and then taking a weighted average of these separate returns. Or you can calculate the beta of the portfolio of securities and then plug this *asset beta* into the capital asset pricing model.

The company cost of capital is the correct discount rate for projects that have the same risk as the company's existing business. Many firms, however, use the company cost of capital to discount the forecasted cash flows on all new projects. This is a dangerous procedure. In principle, each project should be evaluated at its own opportunity cost of capital; the true cost of capital depends on the use to which the capital is put. If we wish to estimate the cost of capital for a particular project, it is *project risk* that counts. Of course the company cost of capital is fine as a discount rate for average-risk projects. It is also a useful starting point for estimating discount rates for safer or riskier projects.

We cannot give you a neat formula that will allow you to estimate project betas, but we can give you some clues. First, avoid adding fudge factors to discount rates to offset worries about bad project outcomes. Adjust cash-flow forecasts to give due weight to bad outcomes as well as good; *then* ask whether the chance of bad outcomes adds to the project's market risk. Second, you can often identify the characteristics of a high- or low-beta project even when the project beta cannot be calculated directly. For example, you can try to figure out how much the cash flows are affected by the overall performance of the economy: Cyclical investments are generally high-beta investments. You can also look at the project's operating leverage: Fixed production charges work like fixed debt charges; i.e., they increase beta.

There is one more fence to jump. Most projects produce cash flows for several years. Firms generally use the same risk-adjusted rate r to discount each of these cash flows. When they do this, they are implicitly assuming that cumulative risk increases at a constant rate as you look further into the future. That assumption is usually reasonable. It is precisely true when the project's future beta will be constant, i.e., when risk *per period* is constant.

But exceptions sometimes prove the rule. Be on the alert for projects where risk clearly does *not* increase steadily. In these cases, you should break the project into segments within which the same discount rate can be reasonably used. Or you should use the certainty-equivalent version of the DCF model, which allows separate risk adjustments to each period's cash flow.

APPENDIX: USING THE CAPITAL ASSET PRICING MODEL TO CALCULATE CERTAINTY EQUIVALENTS

When calculating present value, you can take account of risk in either of two ways. You can discount the expected cash flow C_1 by the risk-adjusted discount rate r:

$$PV = \frac{C_1}{1 + r}$$

Alternatively, you can discount the certainty-equivalent cash flow CEQ_1 by the risk-free rate of interest r_f:

$$PV = \frac{CEQ_1}{1 + r_f}$$

In this appendix we show how you can derive CEQ_1 from the capital asset pricing model.

We know from our present value formula that $1 + r$ equals the expected dollar payoff on the asset divided by its present value:

$$1 + r = \frac{C_1}{PV}$$

The capital asset pricing model also tells us that $1 + r$ equals

$$1 + r = 1 + r_f + \beta(r_m - r_f)$$

Therefore,

$$\frac{C_1}{PV} = 1 + r_f + \beta(r_m - r_f)$$

In order to find beta, we calculate the covariance between the asset return and the market return and divide by the market variance:

$$\beta = \frac{\text{cov }(\tilde{r}, \tilde{r}_m)}{\sigma_m^2} = \frac{\text{cov }(\tilde{C}_1/PV - 1, \tilde{r}_m)}{\sigma_m^2}$$

The quantity $\tilde{C}_1$ is the future cash flow and is, therefore, uncertain. But PV is the asset's present value: It is *not* unknown and, therefore, does not "covary" with $\tilde{r}_m$. Therefore, we can rewrite the expression for beta as

$$\beta = \frac{\text{cov }(\tilde{C}_1, \tilde{r}_m)}{PV \, \sigma_m^2}$$

Substituting this expression back into our equation for C_1/PV gives

$$\frac{C_1}{PV} = 1 + r_f + \frac{\text{cov }(\tilde{C}_1, \tilde{r}_m)}{PV} \cdot \frac{r_m - r_f}{\sigma_m^2}$$

The expression $(r_m - r_f)/\sigma_m^2$ is the expected risk premium on the market per unit of variance. It is often known as the *market price of risk* and is written as λ (lambda). Thus

$$\frac{C_1}{PV} = 1 + r_f + \frac{\lambda \, \text{cov }(\tilde{C}_1, \tilde{r}_m)}{PV}$$

Multiplying through by PV and rearranging give

$$PV = \frac{C_1 - \lambda \, \text{cov }(\tilde{C}_1, \tilde{r}_m)}{1 + r_f}$$

This is the certainty-equivalent form of the capital asset pricing model. It tells us that, if the asset is risk-free, cov $(\tilde{C}_1 \tilde{r}_m)$ is zero and we simply discount C_1 by the risk-free rate. But, if the asset is risky, we must discount the certainty equivalent of C_1. The deduction that we make from C_1 depends on the market price of risk and on the covariance between the cash flows on the project and the return on the market.

Further Reading

····································

There is a good review article by Rubinstein on the application of the capital asset pricing model to capital investment decisions:

M. E. Rubinstein: "A Mean-Variance Synthesis of Corporate Financial Theory," *Journal of Finance,* **28**:167–182 (March 1973).

There have been a number of studies of the relationship between accounting data and beta. Many of these are reviewed in:

G. Foster: *Financial Statement Analysis,* 2d ed., Prentice-Hall, Inc., Englewood Cliffs, N.J., 1986.

For some ideas on how one might break down the problem of estimating beta, see:
W. F. Sharpe: "The Capital Asset Pricing Model: A 'Multi-Beta' Interpretation," in H. Levy and M. Sarnat (eds.), *Financial Decision Making under Uncertainty*, Academic Press, New York, 1977.

The assumptions required for use of risk-adjusted discount rates are discussed in:
E. F. Fama: "Risk-Adjusted Discount Rates and Capital Budgeting under Uncertainty," *Journal of Financial Economics*, **5**:3–24 (August 1977).
S. C. Myers and S. M. Turnbull: "Capital Budgeting and the Capital Asset Pricing Model: Good News and Bad News," *Journal of Finance*, **32**:321–332 (May 1977).

The relationship between the certainty-equivalent and risk-adjusted discount rate valuation formulas was first discussed by:
A. A. Robichek and S. C. Myers: "Conceptual Problems in the Use of Risk-Adjusted Discount Rates," *Journal of Finance*, **21**:727–730 (December 1966).

Quiz

1. Suppose a firm uses its company cost of capital to evaluate all capital projects. What kinds of mistakes will it make?

2. A project costs $100,000 and offers a single $150,000 cash flow 1 year hence. The project beta is 2.0, and the market risk premium $(r_m - r_f)$ is 8.5 percent. Look up current risk-free interest rates in *The Wall Street Journal* or another newspaper. Use the capital asset pricing model to find the opportunity cost of capital and the present value of the project.

3. Look again at Table 9-1 and the row of statistics shown for Milwaukee Insurance Group. Define and interpret each of these statistics.

4. A company is financed 40 percent by risk-free debt. The interest rate is 10 percent, the expected market return is 18 percent, and the stock's beta is .5. What is the company cost of capital?

5. The total market value of the common stock of the Okefenokee Real Estate Company is $6 million, and the total value of its debt is $4 million. The treasurer estimates that the beta of the stock is currently 1.5 and that the expected risk premium on the market is 9 percent. The Treasury bill rate is 8 percent.
   (*a*) What is the required return on Okefenokee stock?
   (*b*) What is the beta of the company's existing portfolio of assets?
   (*c*) Estimate the company's cost of capital.
   (*d*) Estimate the discount rate for an expansion of the company's present business.
   (*e*) Suppose the company wants to diversify into the manufacture of rose-colored spectacles. The beta of unleveraged optical manufacturers is 1.2. Estimate the required return on Okefenokee's new venture.

6. An oil company is drilling a series of new wells on the perimeter of a producing oil field. About 20 percent of the new wells will be dry holes. Even if a new well strikes oil, there is still uncertainty about the amount of oil produced: Forty percent of new wells which strike oil produce only 1000 barrels a day. Sixty percent produce 5000 barrels per day.
   (*a*) Forecast the annual cash revenues from a new perimeter well. Use a future oil price of $18 per barrel.
   (*b*) A geologist proposes to discount the cash flows of the new wells at 30 percent to offset the risk of dry holes. The oil company's normal cost of capital is 10 percent. Does this proposal make sense? Briefly explain why or why not.

*7. Which of these companies is likely to have the higher cost of capital?
   (*a*) A's sales force is paid a fixed annual rate; B's is paid on a commission basis.
   (*b*) C produces machine tools; D produces breakfast cereal.

*8. Select the appropriate phrase from within each pair of brackets:
   "In calculating PV there are two ways to adjust for risk. One is to make a deduction from the expected cash flows. This is known as the *certainty-equivalent method*. It is usually written as $PV = [CEQ_t/(1 + r_f)^t; CEQ_t/(1 + r_m)^t]$. The certainty-equivalent cash flow, CEQ_t, is always [more than; less than] the forecasted risky cash flow. Another way to allow for risk is to discount the expected cash flows at a rate of r. If we use the capital asset pricing model to calculate r, then r is $[r_f + \beta r_m; r_f + \beta(r_m - r_f); r_m + \beta(r_m - r_f)]$. This method is exact only if the ratio of the certainty-equivalent cash flow to the forecasted risky cash flow [is constant; declines at a constant rate; increases at a constant rate]. For the majority of projects, the use of a single discount rate, r, is probably a perfectly acceptable approximation."

*9. A project has a forecasted cash flow of $110 in year 1 and $121 in year 2. The interest rate is 5 percent, the estimated risk premium on the market is 10 percent, and the project has a beta of .5. If you use a constant risk-adjusted discount rate, what is:
   (*a*) The present value of the project?
   (*b*) The certainty-equivalent cash flow in year 1 and year 2?
   (*c*) The ratio of the certainty-equivalent cash flows to the expected cash flows in years 1 and 2?

Questions and Problems

1. Look at Table 9-1.
   (*a*) How much did Minuteman International's stock price tend to change in an unchanged market?
   (*b*) Which stock had price changes that were most closely related to the market? What proportion of the stock's risk was market risk, and what proportion was unique risk?
   (*c*) What is the confidence interval on Mobil's beta?
   (*d*) What is the total risk of Mitel's stock *per year*?

2. Explain the estimate of alpha for Minnesota Power and Light's stock in Table 9-1. Why is this not a good guide to the stock's future alpha? What is your best forecast of alpha?

3. It appears from Table 9-1 that six companies have *negative* betas. What do you make of that? (*Hint*: Look at the standard errors of the beta estimates for these companies.)

4. Look again at the estimates for Mobil common stock in Table 9-1.
   (*a*) Calculate the expected rate of return on Mobil stock assuming the capital asset pricing model is correct. Use current 1-year Treasury rates and a reasonable forecast of the expected market risk premium. How much confidence would you have in this estimate?
   (*b*) What are the pros and cons of using an oil industry cost of capital as a benchmark discount rate for Mobil?

5. "The cost of capital always depends on the risk of the project being evaluated. Therefore company costs of capital are useless." Is that correct? Evaluate the statement.

6. (**a**) Nero Violins has the following capital structure:

Security	Beta	Total Market Value, Millions of Dollars
Debt	0	100
Preferred stock	.20	40
Common stock	1.20	200

What is the firm's asset beta (i.e., the beta of a portfolio of all the firm's securities)?

(**b**) How would the asset beta change if Nero issued an additional $140 million of common stock and used the cash to repurchase all the debt and preferred stock?

(**c**) Assume that the capital asset pricing model is correct. What discount rate should Nero set for investments that expand the scale of its operations without changing its asset beta? Assume any new investment is all equity-financed. Plug in numbers that are reasonable today.

7. You are given the following information for Lorelei Motorwerke:

- Long-term debt outstanding: $300,000
- Current yield to maturity (r_D): 8 percent
- Number of shares of common stock: 10,000
- Price per share: $50
- Book value per share: $25
- Expected rate of return on stock (r_E): 15 percent

(**a**) Calculate Lorelei's weighted-average cost of capital.

(**b**) How would r_E and the weighted-average cost of capital change if Lorelei's stock price falls to 25 due to declining profits? Business risk is unchanged.

8. Amalgamated Products has three operating divisions:

Division	Percentage of Firm Value
Food	50
Electronics	30
Chemicals	20

To estimate the cost of capital for each division, Amalgamated has identified the following three principal competitors:

	Estimated Equity Beta	Debt/(Debt + Equity)
United Foods	.8	.3
General Electronics	1.6	.2
Associated Chemicals	1.2	.4

Assume these betas are accurate estimates and that the capital asset pricing model is correct.

(*a*) Assuming that the debt of these firms is risk-free, estimate the asset beta for each of Amalgamated's divisions.

(*b*) Amalgamated's ratio of debt to debt plus equity is .4. If your estimates of divisional betas are right, what is Amalgamated's equity beta?

(*c*) Assume that the risk-free interest rate is 7 percent and that the expected return on the market index is 15 percent. Estimate the cost of capital for each of Amalgamated's divisions.

(*d*) How much would your estimates of each division's cost of capital change if you assumed that debt has a beta of .2?

9. "The errors in estimating beta are so great that you might just as well assume that all betas are 1.0." Do you agree?

10. Assume you have identified a group of six food companies with similar products and operating strategies. Explain how you would calculate an industry beta and cost of capital for this sample of companies. Assume for simplicity that the companies have no debt outstanding. How would you check the range of potential error in the industry beta?

11. Mom and Pop Groceries has just dispatched a year's supply of groceries to the government of the Central Antarctic Republic. Payment of $250,000 will be made 1 year hence after the shipment arrives by snow train. Unfortunately there is a good chance of a coup d'etat, in which case the new government will not pay. Mom and Pop's controller therefore decides to discount the payment at 40 percent, rather than at the company's 12 percent cost of capital.

(*a*) What's wrong with using a 40 percent rate to offset "political risk"?

(*b*) How much is the $250,000 payment really worth if the odds of a coup d'etat are 25 percent?

12. Here is a more challenging problem involving cash-flow forecasts, discount rates, and fudge factors. An oil company executive is considering investing $10 million in one or both of two wells: Well 1 is expected to produce oil worth $3 million a year for 10 years; well 2 is expected to produce $2 million for 15 years. These are *real* (inflation-adjusted) cash flows.

The beta for *producing wells* is .9. The market risk premium is 8 percent, the nominal risk-free interest rate is 6 percent, and expected inflation is 4 percent.

The two wells are intended to develop a previously discovered oil field. Unfortunately there is still a 20 percent chance of a dry hole in each case. A dry hole means zero cash flows and a complete loss of the $10 million investment.

Ignore taxes and make further assumptions as necessary.

(*a*) What is the correct real discount rate for cash flows from developed wells?

(*b*) The oil company executive proposes to add 20 percentage points to the real discount rate to offset the risk of a dry hole. Calculate the NPV of each well with this adjusted discount rate.

(*c*) What do *you* say the NPVs of the two wells are?

(*d*) Is there any *single* fudge factor that could be added to the discount rate for developed wells that would yield the correct NPV for both wells? Explain.

13. "For a high-beta project, you should use a high discount rate to value positive cash flows and a low discount rate to value negative cash flows." Is this statement correct? Should the sign of the cash flow affect the appropriate discount rate?

*14. A project has the following forecasted cash flows:

Cash Flows, Thousands of Dollars			
C_0	C_1	C_2	C_3
-100	$+40$	$+60$	$+50$

The estimated project beta is 1.5. The market return r_m is 16 percent, and the risk-free rate r_f is 7 percent.
   (a) Estimate the opportunity cost of capital and the project's present value (using the same rate to discount each cash flow).
   (b) What are the certainty-equivalent cash flows in each year?
   (c) What is the ratio of the certainty-equivalent cash flow to the expected cash flow in each year?
   (d) Explain why this ratio declines.

*15. Look back at project A in Section 9-5. Now assume that:
   (a) Expected cash flow is $150 per year for 5 years.
   (b) The risk-free rate of interest is 5 percent.
   (c) The market risk premium is 9 percent.
   (d) The estimated beta is 1.2.
   Recalculate the certainty-equivalent cash flows, and show that the ratio of these certainty-equivalent cash flows to the risky cash flows declines by a constant proportion each year.

*16. The McGregor Whisky Company is proposing to market diet scotch. The product will first be test-marketed for 2 years in southern California at an initial cost of $500,000. This test launch is not expected to produce any profits but should reveal consumer preferences. There is a 60 percent chance that demand will be satisfactory. In this case, McGregor will spend $5 million to launch the scotch nationwide and will receive an expected annual profit of $700,000 in perpetuity. If demand is not satisfactory, diet scotch will be withdrawn.
   Once consumer preferences are known, the product will be subject to an average degree of risk, and, therefore, McGregor requires a return of 12 percent on its investment. However, the initial test-market phase is viewed as much riskier, and McGregor demands a return of 40 percent on this initial expenditure.
   What is the NPV of the diet scotch project?

*17. Use past stock price data to estimate the betas of a sample of common stocks. Plug these betas into the capital asset pricing model to estimate the return that investors require on these stocks today. Now use a different sample period to reestimate the betas of each stock. How much difference would it have made to your estimates of the required return if you had used these betas?

PART three

PRACTICAL PROBLEMS IN CAPITAL BUDGETING

A Project Is Not a Black Box

A *black box* is something that we accept and use but do not understand. For most of us a computer is a black box. We may know what it is supposed to do, but we do not understand how it works and, if something breaks, we cannot fix it.

We have been treating capital projects as black boxes. In other words, we have talked as if managers are handed unbiased cash-flow forecasts and their only task is to assess risk, choose the right discount rate, and crank out net present value. Actual financial managers won't rest until they understand what makes the project tick and what could go wrong with it. Remember Murphy's law, "If anything can go wrong, it will," and O'Reilly's corollary, "at the worst possible time."

Even if the project's risk is wholly diversifiable, you still need to understand why the venture could fail. Once you know that, you can decide whether it is worth trying to resolve the uncertainty. Maybe further expenditure on market research would clear up these doubts about acceptance by consumers, maybe another drill hole would give you a better idea of the size of the ore body, and maybe some further work on the test bed would confirm the durability of those welds. If the project really has a negative NPV, the sooner you can identify it, the better. And even if you decide that it is worth going ahead on the basis of present information, you do not want to be caught by surprise if things subsequently go wrong. You want to know the danger signals and the actions you might take.

In short, managers avoid black boxes whenever they can, and they reward whoever can help them look inside. Consequently, consultants and academics have developed procedures for what we will call *project analysis*. We will discuss several of the procedures in this chapter, mainly sensitivity analysis, break-even analysis, Monte Carlo simulation, and decision trees. There is no magic in these techniques, just computer-assisted common sense. You don't need a license to use them.

Some analysts have proposed these techniques not only for project analysis but also as a supplement or replacement for net present value. You can imagine our reaction to that. Their proposals seem to reflect a belief that net present value cannot cope with risk. But we have seen that it can cope. At the end of the day, after project analysis is complete, the final decisions should flow from NPV.

TABLE 10-1

$\cdots\cdots\cdots\cdots\cdots\cdots\cdots\cdots\cdots\cdots\cdots\cdots\cdots\cdots\cdots\cdots\cdots\cdots\cdots\cdots\cdots\cdots\cdots\cdots\cdots\cdots\cdots\cdots\cdots\cdots\cdots$

Preliminary cash-flow forecasts for Jalopy Motor's electric scooter project (figures in millions of dollars)

	Year 0	Years 1–10
Investment	150	
1. Revenue		375
2. Variable cost		300
3. Fixed cost		30
4. Depreciation		15
5. Pretax profit (1 − 2 − 3 − 4)		30
6. Tax		15
7. Net profit (5 − 6)		15
8. Operating cash flow (4 + 7)		30
Net cash flow	−$150	+$30

Assumptions:
1. Investment is depreciated over 10 years straight-line.
2. Income is taxed at a rate of 50 percent.

10-1 SENSITIVITY ANALYSIS

Uncertainty means that more things can happen than will happen. Whenever you are confronted with a cash-flow forecast, you should try to discover what else can happen.

Put yourself in the well-heeled shoes of the treasurer of the Jalopy Motor Company. You are considering the introduction of an electrically powered motor scooter for city use. Your staff members have prepared the cash-flow forecasts shown in Table 10-1. Since NPV is positive at the 10 percent opportunity cost of capital, it appears to be worth going ahead.

$$\text{NPV} = -150 + \sum_{t=1}^{10} \frac{30}{(1.10)^t} = +\$34.3 \text{ million}$$

Before you decide, you want to delve into these forecasts[1] and identify the key variables that determine whether the project succeeds or fails. It turns out that the marketing department has estimated revenue as follows:

Unit sales = new product's share of market × size of scooter market

$$= .1 \times 1 \text{ million} = 100,000 \text{ scooters}$$

Revenue = unit sales × price per unit

$$= 100,000 \times 3750 = \$375 \text{ million}$$

---

[1]Bear in mind, when you are working with cash-flow forecasts, the distinction between the expected value and the most likely (or modal) value. Present values are concerned with *expected* cash flows—i.e., the probability-weighted average of the possible future cash flows. If the distribution of possible outcomes is skewed, the expected cash flow will not be the same as the most likely cash flow.

The production department has estimated variable costs per unit as $3000. Since projected volume is 100,000 scooters per year, *total* variable cost is $300 million. Fixed costs are $30 million per year. The initial investment can be depreciated on a straight-line basis over the 10-year period, and profits are taxed at a rate of 50 percent.

These seem to be the important things you need to know, but look out for unidentified variables. Perhaps there are patent problems, or perhaps you will need to invest in service stations that will recharge the scooter batteries. The greatest dangers often lie in these *unknown* unknowns, or "unk-unks," as scientists call them.

Having found no unk-unks (no doubt you'll find them later), you conduct a **sensitivity analysis** with respect to market size, market share, and so on. In order to do this, the marketing and production staffs are asked to give optimistic and pessimistic estimates for the underlying variables. These are set out in the left-hand columns of Table 10-2. The right-hand side shows what happens to the project's net present value if the variables are set *one at a time* to their optimistic and pessimistic values. Your project appears to be by no means a sure thing. The most dangerous variables appear to be market share and unit variable cost. If market share is only .04 (and all other variables are as expected), then the project has an NPV of −$104 million. If unit variable cost is $3600 (and all other variables are as expected), then the project has an NPV of −$150 million.

Value of Information

Now you can check whether an investment of time or money could resolve some of the uncertainty *before* your company parts with the $150 million investment. Suppose that the pessimistic value for unit variable cost partly reflects the production department's worry that a particular machine will not work as designed and that the operation will have to be performed by other methods at an extra cost of $200 per unit. The chance that this will occur is only 1 in 10. But, if it did occur, the extra $200 unit cost would reduce after-tax cash flow by

TABLE 10-2

To undertake a sensitivity analysis of the electric scooter project, we set each variable *in turn* at its most pessimistic or optimistic value and recalculate the net present value of the project

Variable	RANGE			NET PRESENT VALUE, MILLIONS OF DOLLARS		
	Pessimistic	Expected	Optimistic	Pessimistic	Expected	Optimistic
Market size	.9 million	1 million	1.1 million	+11	+34	+57
Market share	.04	.1	.16	−104	+34	+173
Unit price	$3,500	$3,750	$3,800	−42	+34	+50
Unit variable cost	$3,600	$3,000	$2,750	−150	+34	+111
Fixed cost	$40 million	$30 million	$20 million	+4	+34	+65

Unit sales $\times$ additional unit cost $\times$ (1 $-$ tax rate)

$$= 100,000 \times 200 \times .50 = \$10 \text{ million}$$

It would reduce the net present value of your project by

$$\sum_{t=1}^{10} \frac{10}{(1.10)^t} = \$61.4 \text{ million},$$

putting the NPV of the scooter project underwater at $+34 - 61.4 = -\$27.4$ million.

Suppose further that a \$100,000 pretest of the machine will reveal whether it will work or not and allow you to clear up the problem. It clearly pays to invest \$100,000 to avoid a 10 percent probability of a \$61.4 million fall in NPV. You are ahead by $-100,000 + .10 \times 61,400,000 = +\$6,040,000$.

On the other hand, the value of additional information about market size is small. Because the project is acceptable even under pessimistic assumptions about market size, you are unlikely to be in trouble if you have misestimated that variable.[2]

Limits to Sensitivity Analysis

Sensitivity analysis boils down to expressing cash flows in terms of key project variables and then calculating the consequences of misestimating the variables. It forces the manager to identify the underlying variables, indicates where additional information would be most useful, and helps to expose confused or inappropriate forecasts.

One drawback to sensitivity analysis is that it always gives somewhat ambiguous results. For example, what exactly does *optimistic* or *pessimistic* mean? The marketing department may be interpreting the terms in a different way from the production department. Ten years from now, after hundreds of projects, hindsight may show that the marketing department's pessimistic limit was exceeded twice as often as the production department's; but what you may discover 10 years hence is no help now. One solution is to ask the two departments for a *complete* description of the various odds. However, it is far from easy to extract a forecaster's subjective notion of the complete probability distribution of possible outcomes.[3]

Another problem with sensitivity analysis is that the underlying variables are likely to be interrelated. What sense does it make to look at the effect in isolation of an increase in market size? If market size exceeds expectations, it is likely that demand will be stronger than you anticipated and unit prices will be higher. And why look in isolation at the effect of an increase in price? If inflation pushes prices to the upper end of our range, it is quite probable that costs will also be inflated.

Sometimes the analyst can get around these problems by defining underlying variables so that they are roughly independent. But you cannot push *one-at-a-time* sensitivity analysis too far. It is impossible to obtain expected, optimistic, and pessimistic values for total *project* cash flows from the information in Table 10-2.

Examining the Project under Different Scenarios

If the variables are interrelated, it may help to consider some alternative plausible combinations. For example, perhaps the company economist is worried about the possibility of another sharp rise in world oil prices. The direct effect of this would

---

[2]Of course, these are very simple examples. The derivation of optimal rules for investing in information is a well-developed part of Bayesian statistics. See H. Raiffa, *Decision Analysis: Introductory Lectures on Choices under Uncertainty*, Addison-Wesley Publishing Company, Inc., Reading, Mass., 1968.

[3]If you doubt this, try some simple experiments. Ask the person who repairs your television to state a numerical probability that your set will work for at least 1 more year. Or construct your own subjective probability distribution of the number of telephone calls you will receive next week. That ought to be easy. Try it.

be to encourage the use of electrically powered transportation. The popularity of "compacts" after the oil price increases in the 1970s leads you to estimate that an immediate 20 percent price rise in oil would enable you to capture an extra 3 percent of the scooter market. On the other hand, the economist also believes that higher oil prices would prompt a world recession and at the same time stimulate inflation. In that case, market size might be in the region of 8 million scooters and both prices and cost might be 15 percent higher than your initial estimates. Table 10-3 shows that this scenario of higher oil prices and recession would on balance help your new venture. Its net present value would increase to $65 million.

Managers often find it helpful to look at how their project would fare under different scenarios. It allows them to look at different but *consistent* combinations of variables. Forecasters generally prefer to give an estimate of revenues or costs under a particular scenario than to give some absolute optimistic or pessimistic value.

Break-Even Analysis

When we undertake a sensitivity analysis of a project or when we look at alternative scenarios, we are asking how serious it would be if sales or costs turned out to be worse than we forecasted. Managers sometimes prefer to rephrase this question and ask how bad sales can get before the project begins to lose money. This exercise is known as **break-even analysis.**

TABLE 10-3

How the net present value of the electric scooter project would be affected by higher oil prices and a world recession

	CASH FLOWS, YEARS 1–10, MILLIONS OF DOLLARS	
	Base Case	High Oil Prices and Recession Case
1. Revenue	375	449
2. Variable cost	300	359
3. Fixed cost	30	35
4. Depreciation	15	15
5. Pretax profit (1 − 2 − 3 − 4)	30	40
6. Tax	15	20
7. Net profit (5 − 6)	15	20
8. Net cash flow (4 + 7)	30	35
Present value of cash flows	+184	+215
Net present value	+34	+65

	ASSUMPTIONS	
	Base Case	High Oil Prices and Recession Case
Market size	1 million	.8 million
Market share	.1	.13
Unit price	$3,750	$4,313
Unit variable cost	$3,000	$3,450
Fixed cost	$30 million	$35 million

TABLE 10-4

NPV of electric scooter project under different assumptions about unit sales (figures in millions of dollars except as noted)

| | INFLOWS | OUTFLOWS | | | | | | |
| | | YEAR 0 | YEARS 1–10 | | | | | |
Unit Sales, Thousands	Revenue, Years 1–10	Investment	Variable Costs	Fixed Costs	Taxes	PV Inflows	PV Outflows	NPV
0	0	150	0	30	−22.5	0	196	−196
100	375	150	300	30	15	2,304	2,270	34
200	750	150	600	30	52.5	4,608	4,344	264

In the left-hand portion of Table 10-4 we set out the revenues and costs of the electric scooter project under different assumptions about annual sales.[4] In the right-hand portion of the table we discount these revenues and costs to give the *present value* of the inflows and the *present value* of the outflows. *Net* present value is of course the difference between these numbers.

You can see that NPV is strongly negative if the company does not produce a single scooter. It is just positive if (as expected) the company sells 100,000 scooters and

---

[4]Notice that if the project makes a loss, this loss can be used to reduce the tax bill on the rest of the company's business. In this case the project produces a tax saving—the tax outflow is negative.

Figure 10-1 A break-even chart showing the present value of Jalopy's cash inflows and outflows under different assumptions about unit sales. NPV is zero when sales are 85,000.

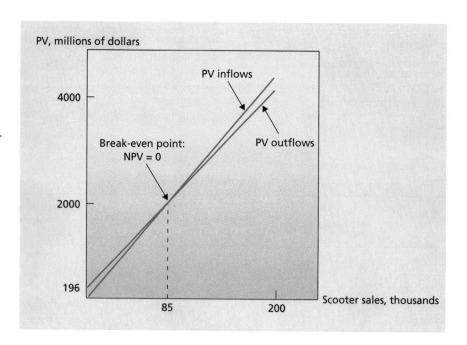

TABLE 10-5

· ·

The electric scooter project's accounting profit under different assumptions about unit sales (figures in millions of dollars except as noted)

Unit Sales, Thousands	Revenue	Variable Costs	Fixed Costs	Depreciation	Taxes	Total Costs	Profit after Tax
0	0	0	30	15	−22.5	22.5	−22.5
100	375	300	30	15	15	360	15
200	750	600	30	15	52.5	697.5	52.5

is strongly positive if it sells 200,000. Clearly the *zero*-NPV point occurs at a little under 100,000 scooters.

In Figure 10-1 we have plotted the present value of the inflows and outflows under different assumptions about annual sales. The two lines cross when sales are 85,000 scooters. This is the point at which the project has zero NPV. As long as sales are greater than 85,000, the project has a positive NPV.[5]

Managers frequently calculate break-even points in terms of accounting profits rather than present values. Table 10-5 shows Jalopy's after-tax profits at three levels of scooter sales. Figure 10-2 once again plots revenues and costs against sales. But the story this time is different. Figure 10-2, which is based on accounting profits, suggests a break-even of 60,000 scooters. Figure 10-1, which is based on present values, shows a break-even at 85,000 scooters. Why the difference?

When we work in terms of accounting profit, we deduct depreciation of $15 million each year to cover the cost of the initial investment. If Jalopy sells 60,000 scooters a year, revenues will be sufficient both to pay operating costs and to recover the initial outlay of $150 million. But they will *not* be sufficient to repay the *opportunity cost of capital* on that $150 million. If we allow for the fact that the $150 million could have been invested elsewhere to earn 10 percent, the equivalent annual cost of the investment is not $15 million but $24.4 million.[6]

Companies that break even on an accounting basis are really making a loss—they are losing the opportunity cost of capital on their investment. Reinhardt has described a dramatic example of this mistake.[7] In 1971 Lockheed managers found themselves

---

[5]We could also calculate break-even sales by plotting equivalent annual costs and revenues. Of course, the break-even point would be identical at 85,000 scooters.

[6]To calculate the equivalent annual cost of the initial $150 million investment, we divide by the 10-year annuity factor for a 10 percent discount rate:

$$\text{Equivalent annual cost} = \frac{\text{investment}}{\text{10-year annuity factor}}$$

$$= \frac{150}{6.145} = \$24.4 \text{ million}$$

See Section 6-3.

The annual revenues at 85,000 scooters per year are about $319 million. You can check that this is sufficient to cover variable costs, fixed costs, and taxes and still leave $24.4 million per year to recover the $150 million initial investment and a 10-percent return on that investment.

[7]U. E. Reinhardt, "Break-Even Analysis for Lockheed's TriStar: An Application of Financial Theory," *Journal of Finance,* **28**:821–838 (September 1973).

Figure 10-2
Sometimes break-even charts are constructed in terms of accounting numbers. After-tax profit is zero when sales are 60,000.

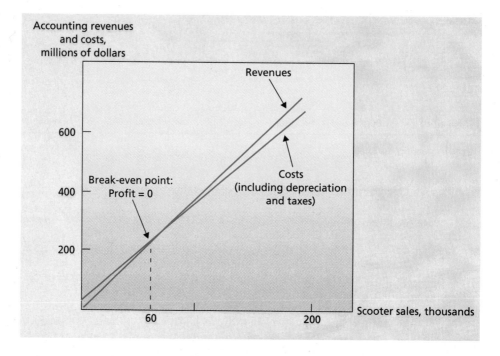

having to give evidence to Congress on the viability of the company's L-1011 TriStar program. They argued that the program appeared to be "commercially attractive" and that TriStar sales would eventually exceed the break-even point of about 200 aircraft. But in calculating this break-even point, Lockheed appears to have ignored the opportunity cost of the huge $1 billion capital investment on this project. Had it allowed for this cost, the break-even point would probably have been nearer to 500 aircraft.

Operating Leverage and Break-Even Points

Break-even charts like Figure 10-1 help managers appreciate *operating leverage*—that is, project exposure to fixed costs. Remember from Section 9-4 that high operating leverage means high risk, other things equal, of course.

The electric scooter project had low fixed costs, only $30 million against projected revenues of $375 million. But suppose Jalopy Motors now considers a different production technology with lower variable costs of only $1200 per unit (versus $3000 per unit) but higher fixed costs of $190 million. Total forecasted production costs are lower (120 + 190 = $310 million versus $330 million), so profitability improves—compare Table 10-6 to Table 10-1. Project NPV increases to $96 million.

Figure 10-3 is the new break-even chart. Break-even sales have *increased* to 88,000 (that's bad), even though total production costs have *fallen*. A new sensitivity analysis would show that project NPV is much more exposed to changes in market size, market share, or unit price. All of these differences can be traced to the higher fixed costs of the alternative production technology.

Is the alternative technology better than the original one? The financial manager would have to consider the alternative technology's higher business risk, and perhaps recompute NPV at a higher discount rate, before making a final decision.[8]

---

[8]He or she could use the procedures outlined in Section 9-4 to recalculate beta and come up with a new discount rate.

TABLE 10-6

Cash-flow forecasts and present value for the electric scooter project, here assuming a production technology with high fixed costs but low total costs (figures in millions of dollars). Compare Table 10-1.

	Year 0	Years 1–10
Investment	150	
1. Revenue		375
2. Variable costs		120
3. Fixed cost		190
4. Depreciation		15
5. Pretax profit (1 − 2 − 3 − 4)		50
6. Tax		25
7. Net profit (5 − 6)		25
8. Operating cash flow (4 + 7)		40
Net cash flow	−$150	+$40

$$\text{Net present value} = -150 + \sum_{t=1}^{10} \frac{40}{(1.1)^t} = +\$96 \text{ million}$$

10-2 MONTE CARLO SIMULATION

Sensitivity analysis allows you to consider the effect of changing one variable at a time. By looking at the project under alternative scenarios, you can consider the effect of a *limited number* of plausible combinations of variables. **Monte Carlo simulation** is a tool for considering *all* possible combinations. It therefore enables you to inspect the entire distribution of project outcomes. Its use in capital budgeting was first advocated by David Hertz[9] and McKinsey and Company, the management consultants.

Imagine that you are a gambler at Monte Carlo. You know nothing about the laws of probability (few casual gamblers do), but a friend has suggested to you a complicated strategy for playing roulette. Your friend has not actually tested the strategy but is confident that it will *on the average* give you a 2½ percent return for every 50 spins of the wheel. Your friend's optimistic estimate for any series of 50 spins is a profit of 55 percent; your friend's pessimistic estimate is a loss of 50 percent. How can you find out whether these really are the odds? An easy but possibly expensive way is to start playing and record the outcome at the end of each series of 50 spins. After, say, 100 series of 50 spins each, plot a frequency distribution of the outcomes and calculate the average and upper and lower limits. If things look good, you can then get down to some serious gambling.

An alternative is to tell a computer to simulate the roulette wheel and the strategy. In other words, you could instruct the computer to draw numbers out of its hat

---

[9]See D. B. Hertz, "Investment Policies that Pay Off," *Harvard Business Review*, **46**:96–108 (January–February 1968).

Figure 10-3
Break-even chart for an alternative production technology with higher fixed costs. Notice that break-even sales increase to 88,000. Compare Figure 10-1.

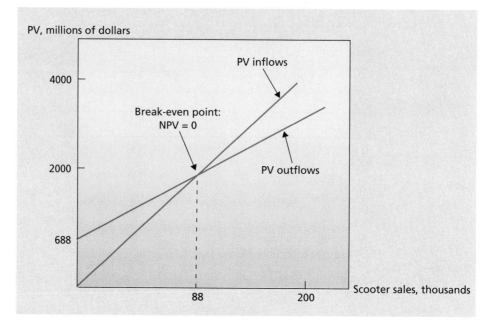

to determine the outcome of each spin of the wheel and then to calculate how much you would make or lose from the particular gambling strategy.

That would be an example of Monte Carlo simulation. In capital budgeting we replace the gambling strategy with a model of the project, and the roulette wheel with a model of the world in which the project operates. Let's see how this might work with our project for an electrically powered scooter.

Simulating the Electric Scooter Project

STEP 1: MODELING THE PROJECT. The first step in any simulation is to give the computer a precise model of the project. For example, the sensitivity analysis of the scooter project was based on the following implicit model of cash flow:

Cash flow = (revenues − costs − depreciation) × (1 − tax rate)
            + depreciation

Revenues = market size × market share × unit price

Costs = (market size × market share × variable unit cost) + fixed cost

This model of the project was all that you needed for the simpleminded sensitivity analysis that we described above. But if you wish to simulate the whole project, you need to think about how the variables are interrelated.

For example, consider the first variable—market size. The marketing department has estimated a market size of 1 million scooters in the first year of the project's life, but of course you do not know how things will work out. Actual market size will exceed or fall short of expectations by the amount of the department's forecast error:

$$\text{Market size, year 1} = \text{expected market size, year 1} \times \left(1 + \dfrac{\text{forecast error,}}{\text{year 1}}\right)$$

You *expect* the forecast error to be zero, but it could turn out to be positive or negative. Suppose, for example, that the actual market size turns out to be 1.1 million. That means a forecast error of 10 percent, or +.1:

$$\text{Market size, year 1} = 1 \times (1 + .1) = 1.1 \text{ million}$$

You can write the market size in the second year in exactly the same way:

$$\text{Market size, year 2} = \text{expected market size, year 2} \times \left(1 + \frac{\text{forecast error, year 2}}{}\right)$$

But at this point you must consider how the expected market size in year 2 is affected by what happens in year 1. If scooter sales are below expectations in year 1, it is likely that they will continue to be below in subsequent years. Suppose that a shortfall in sales in year 1 would lead you to revise down your forecast of sales in year 2 by a like amount. Then

$$\text{Expected market size, year 2} = \text{actual market size, year 1}$$

Now you can rewrite the market size in year 2 in terms of the actual market size in the previous year plus a forecast error:

$$\text{Market size, year 2} = \text{market size, year 1} \times \left(1 + \frac{\text{forecast error, year 2}}{}\right)$$

In the same way you can describe the expected market size in year 3 in terms of market size in year 2 and so on.

This set of equations illustrates how you can describe interdependence between different *periods*. But you also need to allow for interdependence between different *variables*. For example, the price of electrically powered scooters is likely to increase with market size. Suppose that this is the only uncertainty and that a 10 percent shortfall in market size would lead you to predict a 3 percent reduction in price. Then you could model the first year's price as follows:

$$\text{Price, year 1} = \text{expected price, year 1} \times \left(1 + \frac{.3 \times \text{error in market size forecast, year 1}}{}\right)$$

Then, if variations in market size exert a permanent effect on price, you can define the second year's price as

$$\text{Price, year 2} = \text{expected price, year 2} \times \left(1 + \frac{.3 \times \text{error in market size forecast, year 2}}{}\right)$$

$$= \text{actual price, year 1} \times \left(1 + \frac{.3 \times \text{error in market size forecast, year 2}}{}\right)$$

The complete model of your project would include a set of equations for each of the variables—market size, price, market share, unit variable cost, and fixed cost. Even if you allowed for only a few interdependencies between variables and across time, the result would be quite a complex list of equations.[10] Perhaps that is not a bad thing if it forces you to understand what the project is all about. Model building is like spinach: You may not like the taste, but it is good for you.

STEP 2: SPECIFYING PROBABILITIES.   Remember the procedure for simulating the gambling strategy? The first step was to specify the strategy, the second was to specify the numbers on the roulette wheel, and the third was to tell the computer to select these numbers at random and calculate the results of the strategy:

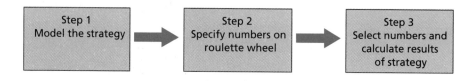

The steps are just the same for your scooter project:

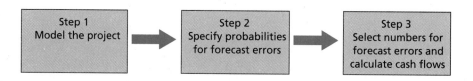

Figure 10-4 illustrates how you might go about specifying your possible errors in forecasting market size. You *expect* market size to be 10 million scooters. You obviously don't think that you are underestimating or overestimating market size; therefore your expected forecast error is zero. On the other hand, the marketing department has given you a range of possible estimates. Market size could be as low as .85 million scooters or as high as 1.15 million scooters. Thus the forecast error has an expected value of 0 and a range of plus or minus 15 percent.[11] You need to draw up similar patterns of the possible forecast errors for each of the other variables that are in your model.

STEP 3: SIMULATE THE CASH FLOWS.   The computer now *samples* from the distribution of the forecast errors, calculates the resulting cash flows for each period, and records them. After many iterations you begin to get accurate estimates of the probability distributions of the project cash flows—accurate, that is, only to the extent that

---

[10]Specifying the interdependencies is the hardest and most important part of a simulation. If all components of project cash flows were unrelated, simulation would rarely be necessary.

[11]An error of plus or minus .15 is three standard deviations away from the mean. Larger errors are possible, given the normal distribution in Figure 10-4, but extremely improbable.

Other distributions could, of course, be used. For example, the marketing department may view any market size between .9 and 1.1 million scooters as equally likely. In that case the simulation would require a uniform (rectangular) distribution of forecast errors, with a range of −.10 to +.10.

Figure 10-4
Distribution of forecast errors for market size. The expected error is 0, but extreme errors could be as large as plus or minus .15. We have assumed a normal, bell-shaped distribution with a standard deviation of .05.

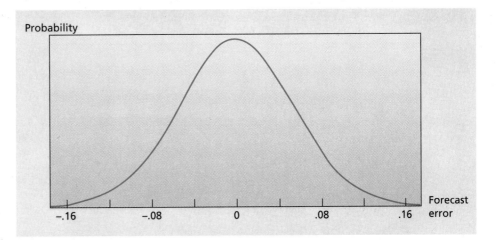

your model and the probability distributions of the forecast errors are accurate. Remember the GIGO principle: "Garbage in, garbage out."

Figure 10-5 shows some of the outputs from an actual simulation of the electric scooter project.[12] The mean cash flow is about $31 million for both years shown, but the range of possible outcomes is considerably higher in year 10 than in year 5. Note also the positive skewness of the outcomes—very large outcomes are somewhat more likely than very small ones. This is common, and realistic, when forecast errors accumulate over time. Because of the skewness the average cash flow is somewhat higher than the most likely outcome—in other words, a bit to the right of the peak of the distribution.

Simulation of Pharmaceutical Research and Development

Simulation, though sometimes costly and complicated, has the obvious merit of compelling the forecaster and the decision maker to face up to uncertainty and to interdependencies. By constructing a detailed Monte Carlo simulation model, you will gain a better understanding of how the project works and what could go wrong with it. You will have confirmed, or improved, your forecasts of future cash flows, and your calculations of project NPV will be more confident.

Several large pharmaceutical companies have used Monte Carlo simulation to analyze investments in research and development (R&D) of new drugs. These companies spend billions of dollars annually on R&D, in the face of massive uncertainty. Figure 10-6 sketches the life cycle of a new drug from its infancy, when it is identified as a promising chemical compound, to old age, when the drug's patents expire and "generic" competitors enter and drive down selling prices. The R&D phase may last 10 to 12 years before the federal Food and Drug Administration (FDA) approves the new drug and the company begins to market it. The total life cycle may span 25 to 30 years.

The pharmaceutical companies' scientists and marketing and financial managers face three kinds of uncertainty:

---

[12]These are actual outputs from Crystal Ball™ software used with an EXCEL spreadsheet program. The simulation ran through 10,000 trials. We thank Christopher Howe for running the simulation.

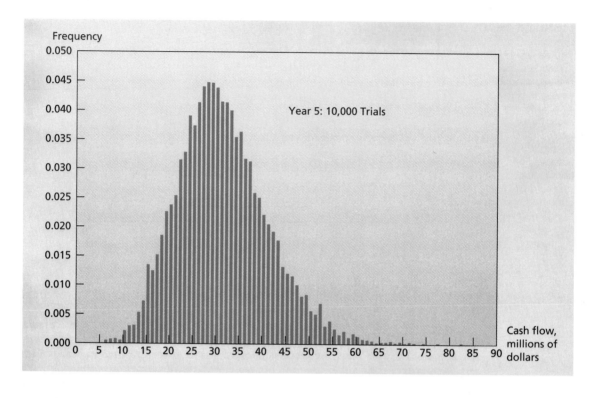

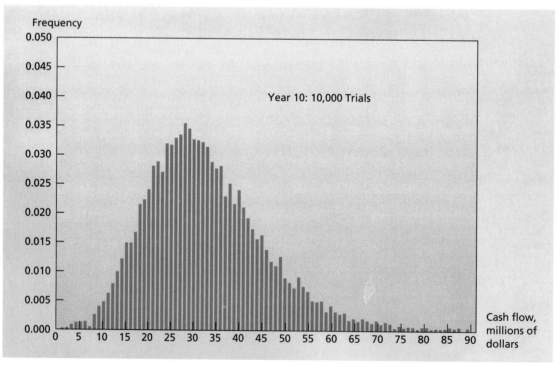

Figure 10-5 Simulations of cash flows in years 5 and 10 for the electric scooter project.

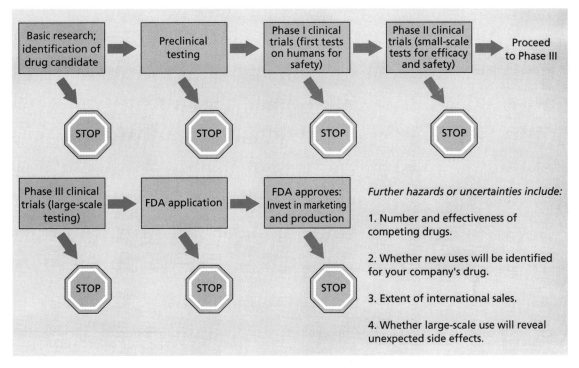

Figure 10-6 Research and testing of a potential new drug from discovery to initial sales. This figure concentrates on the odds that the drug will pass all required clinical tests and be approved by the Food and Drug Administration (FDA). Some of the hazards or uncertainties facing an approved drug are listed at bottom right. Only a small fraction of drug candidates identified in basic research prove safe and effective and achieve profitable production. The "Stop" signs indicate failure and abandonment of the candidate.

1. *Scientific and clinical.* Will the compound work? Will it have harmful side effects? Will it ultimately gain FDA approval? (Most drugs do not: Of 10,000 promising compounds, only 1 or 2 may ever get to market. The 1 or 2 that are marketed have to generate enough cash flow to make up for the 9,999 or 9,998 that fail.)

2. *Production and distribution.* Heavy investments in R&D have to be made with only a vague idea of costs of production and distribution.

3. *Market success.* FDA approval does not guarantee that a drug will sell. A competitor may be there first with a similar (or better) drug. The company may or may not be able to sell the drug worldwide. Selling prices and marketing costs are unknown.

   Imagine that you are standing at the top left of Figure 10-6. A proposed research program will investigate a promising class of compounds. Could you write down the expected cash inflows and outflows of the program up to 25 or 30 years in the future? We suggest that no mortal could do so without a model to help.

   Figure 10-7 reproduces a flowchart for a Monte Carlo simulation model used by Merck & Company. This "Research Planning Model" has been used for more than 10 years and is "integral to [Merck's] strategic decision making process."[13]

---

[13]N. A. Nichols, "Scientific Management at Merck: An Interview with CFO Judy Lewent," *Harvard Business Review,* **72**:91 (January–February 1994).

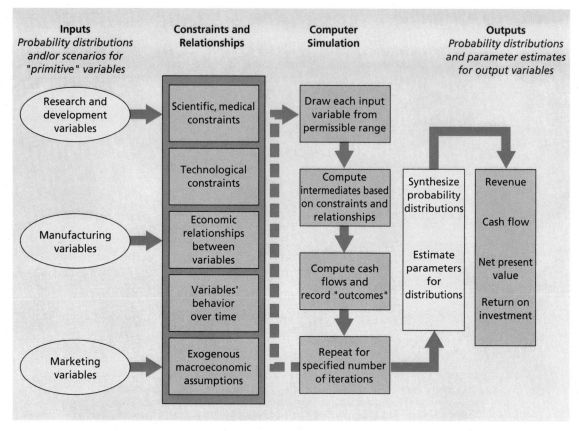

Figure 10-7 Flowchart of a simulation model used by Merck & Company to analyze investments in pharmaceutical R&D. [Reprinted by permission of *Harvard Business Review*. An exhibit from "Scientific Management at Merck: An Interview with CFO Judy Lewent," by N. A. Nichols, **72**:95 (January–February 1994). Copyright © 1994 by the President and Fellows of Harvard College; all rights reserved.]

Simulation may sound like a panacea for the world's ills, but, as usual, you pay for what you get. Sometimes you pay for more than you get. It is not just a matter of the time and money spent in building the model. It is extremely difficult to estimate interrelationships between variables and the underlying probability distributions, even when you are trying to be honest.[14] But in capital budgeting, forecasters are seldom impartial and the probability distributions on which simulations are based can be highly biased.

In practice, a simulation that attempts to be realistic will also be complex. Therefore the decision maker may delegate the task of constructing the model to management scientists or consultants. The danger here is that, even if the builders understand their creation, the decision maker cannot and therefore does not rely on it. This is a common but ironic experience: The model that was intended to open up black boxes ends up creating another one.

---

[14]These difficulties are less severe for the pharmaceutical industry than for most other industries. Pharmaceutical companies have accumulated a great deal of information on the probabilities of scientific and clinical success and on the time and money required for clinical testing and FDA approval.

Misusing Simulation

The financial manager, like a detective, must use every clue. Simulation should be regarded as one of several ways to obtain information about expected cash flows and risk. But the final investment decision involves only one number, net present value.

Some of the early champions of simulation made much greater claims for the method. They started with the premise that net present value cannot in itself reflect risk properly and, therefore, they bypassed that last crucial step.

In this alternative approach the financial manager is given distributions not of cash flows but of NPVs or internal rates of return. Now that may sound attractive—isn't a whole distribution of NPVs better than a single number? But we shall see that this "more is better" reasoning leads the financial manager into a trap.

First, we should explain what is meant by a distribution of NPVs. The cash flows for each iteration of the simulation model are translated into a net present value by *discounting at the risk-free rate*. Why are they not discounted at the opportunity cost of capital? Because, if you know what that is, you don't need a simulation model, except perhaps to help forecast cash flows. The risk-free rate is used to avoid prejudging risk.

A project's "risk" is then reflected in the dispersion of its NPV distribution. Thus the term *net present value* takes on a very different meaning from the usual one. If an asset has a number of possible "present values," it makes little sense to associate NPV with *the* price the asset would sell at in a competitive capital market.[15]

The "risk" of this distribution ignores the investors' opportunity to diversify. Moreover, it is sensitive to the definition of the project. If two unrelated projects are combined, the "risk" of the NPV of the combined projects will be less than the average "risk" of the NPVs of the two separate projects. That not only offends the value-additivity principle, but it also encourages sponsors of marginal projects to beat the system by submitting joint proposals.

Finally, it is very difficult to interpret a distribution of NPVs. Since the risk-free rate is not the opportunity cost of capital, there is no economic rationale for the discounting process. Because the whole edifice is arbitrary, managers can only be told to stare at the distribution until inspiration dawns. No one can tell them how to decide or what to do if inspiration never dawns.

Don't use simulation just to generate distribution of NPVs. Use it to understand the project, forecast its expected cash flows, and assess its risk. Then calculate NPV the old-fashioned way, by discounting expected cash flows at a discount rate appropriate for the project's risk.

10-3   DECISION TREES AND SUBSEQUENT DECISIONS

If financial managers treat projects as black boxes, they may be tempted to think only of the first accept-reject decision and to ignore the subsequent investment decisions that may be tied to it. But if subsequent investment decisions depend on those made today, then today's decision may depend on what you plan to do tomorrow.

---

[15] The only interpretation we can put on these bastard NPVs is the following: Suppose all uncertainty about the project's ultimate cash flows were resolved the day after the project was undertaken. On that day the project's opportunity cost of capital would fall to the risk-free rate. The distribution of NPVs represents the distribution of possible project values on that second day of the project's life.

An Example: Vegetron

We have already solved in the last chapter a simple sequential decision problem, Vegetron's electric mop project. The problem was the following one:

> *The scientists at Vegetron have come up with an electric mop and the firm is ready to go ahead with pilot production and test marketing. The preliminary phase will take a year and cost $125,000. Management feels that there is only a 50-50 chance that the pilot production and market tests will be successful. If they are, then Vegetron will build a $1 million plant which will generate an expected annual cash flow in perpetuity of $250,000 a year after taxes. If they are not successful, Vegetron will not continue with the project.*

Of course Vegetron *could* go ahead even if the tests fail. Let's suppose that in that case the $1 million investment would generate only $75,000 per year.

Financial managers often use **decision trees** for analyzing projects involving sequential decisions. Figure 10-8 displays the electric mop problem as a decision tree. You can think of it as a game between Vegetron and fate. Each square represents a separate decision point for Vegetron; each circle represents a decision point for fate. Vegetron starts the play at the left-hand box. If Vegetron decides to test, then fate casts the enchanted dice and decides the result of the tests. If the tests are successful—there is a probability of ½ that they will be—then the firm faces a second

Figure 10-8
The electric mop example from Chapter 9 expressed as a decision tree. This is a project involving sequential decisions. The investment in testing generates the opportunity to invest in full-scale production. (All figures are in thousands; probabilities are in parentheses.)

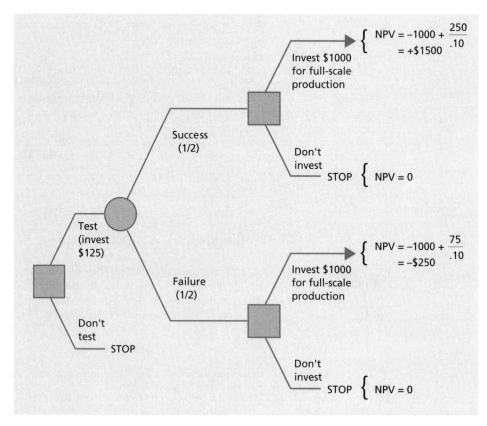

$$NPV = -1000 + \frac{250}{.10}$$
$$= +\$1500$$

Invest $1000 for full-scale production

Success (1/2)

Don't invest
STOP $\quad NPV = 0$

Test (invest $125)

Don't test
STOP

Failure (1/2)

Invest $1000 for full-scale production

$$NPV = -1000 + \frac{75}{.10}$$
$$= -\$250$$

Don't invest
STOP $\quad NPV = 0$

decision: Invest $1 million in a project offering a $1.5 million net present value or stop. If the tests fail, Vegetron has a similar choice but the investment yields a net present value of −$250,000.

It is obvious what the second-stage decisions will be: Invest if the tests are successful and stop if they fail. The net present value of stopping is zero, so the decision tree boils down to a simple problem: Should Vegetron invest $125,000 now to obtain a 50 percent chance of $1.5 million a year later?

....

*A Tougher Example: Magna Charter

Magna Charter is a new corporation formed by Agnes Magna to provide an executive flying service for the southeastern United States. The founder thinks there will be a ready demand from businesses that cannot justify a full-time company plane but nevertheless need one from time to time. However, the venture is not a sure thing. There is a 40 percent chance that demand in the first year will be low. If it is low, there is a 60 percent chance that it will remain low in subsequent years. On the other hand, if the initial demand is high, there is an 80 percent chance that it will stay high.

The immediate problem is to decide what kind of plane to buy. A turboprop costs $550,000. A piston-engine plane costs only $250,000 but has less capacity and customer appeal. Moreover, the piston-engine plane is an old design and likely to depreciate rapidly. Ms. Magna thinks that next year secondhand piston aircraft will be available for only $150,000.

That gives Ms. Magna an idea: Why not start out with one piston plane and buy another if demand is still high? It will cost only $150,000 to expand. If demand is low, Magna Charter can sit tight with one small, relatively inexpensive aircraft.

Figure 10-9 displays these choices. The square on the left marks the company's initial decision to purchase a turboprop for $550,000 or a piston aircraft for $250,000. After the company has made its decision, fate decides on the first year's demand. You can see in parentheses the probability that demand will be high or low, and you can see the expected cash flow for each combination of aircraft and demand level. At the end of the year the company has a second decision to make if it has a piston-engine aircraft: It can either expand or sit tight. This decision point is marked by the second square. Finally fate takes over again and selects the level of demand for year 2. Again you can see in parentheses the probability of high or low demand. Notice that the probabilities for the second year depend on the first-period outcomes. For example, if demand is high in the first period, then there is an 80 percent chance that it will also be high in the second. The chance of high demand in *both* the first and second periods is .6 × .8 = .48. After the parentheses we again show the profitability of the project for each combination of aircraft and demand level. You can interpret each of these figures as the present value at the end of year 2 of the cash flows for that and all subsequent years.

The problem for Ms. Magna is to decide what to do today. We solve that problem by thinking first what she would do next year. This means that we start at the right side of the tree and work backward to the beginning on the left.

The only decision that Ms. Magna needs to make next year is whether to expand if purchase of a piston-engine plane is succeeded by high demand. If she expands, she invests $150,000 and receives a payoff of $800,000 if demand continues to be high and $100,000 if demand falls. So her *expected* payoff is

(Probability high demand × payoff with high demand)

$$+ \text{(probability low demand} \times \text{payoff with low demand)}$$

$$= (.8 \times 800) + (.2 \times 100) = \$660,000$$

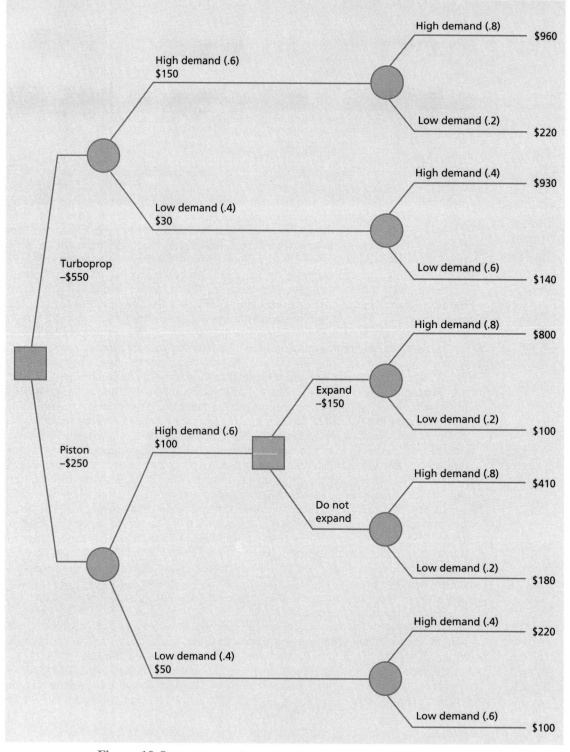

Figure 10-9 Decision tree for Magna Charter. Should it buy a turboprop or a smaller piston-engine plane? A second piston plane can be purchased in year 1 if demand turns out to be high. (All figures are in thousands.)

If the opportunity cost of capital for this venture is 10 percent,[16] then the net present value of expanding, computed as of year 1, is

$$\text{NPV} = -150 + \frac{660}{1.10} = +450, \text{ or } \$450,000$$

If Ms. Magna does *not* expand, the expected payoff is

(Probability high demand × payoff with high demand)

$$+ \text{ (probability low demand} \times \text{payoff with low demand)}$$

$$= (.8 \times 410) + (.2 \times 180) = \$364,000$$

The net present value of *not* expanding, computed as of year 1, is

$$\text{NPV} = 0 + \frac{364}{1.10} = +331, \text{ or } \$331,000$$

Expansion obviously pays if market demand is high.

Now that we know what Magna Charter ought to do if faced with the expansion decision, we can "roll back" to today's decision. If the first piston-engine plane is bought, Magna can expect to receive cash worth $550,000 in year 1 if demand is high and cash worth $185,000 if it is low:

High demand (.6) → $550,000 $\left\{\begin{array}{l}\text{\$100,000 cash flow}\\\text{plus \$450,000 net}\\\text{present value}\end{array}\right.$

Invest $250,000

Low demand (.4) → $185,000 $\left\{\begin{array}{l}\text{\$50,000 cash flow}\\\text{plus net present value of}\\\dfrac{(.4 \times 220) + (.6 \times 100)}{1.10}\\= \$135,000\end{array}\right.$

The net present value of the investment in the piston-engine plane is therefore $117,000:

$$\text{NPV} = -250 + \frac{.6(550) + .4(185)}{1.\ 10} = +117, \text{ or } +\$117,000$$

If Magna buys the turboprop, there are no future decisions to analyze, and so there is no need to roll back. We just calculate expected cash flows and discount:

$$\text{NPV} = -550 + \frac{.6(150) + .4(30)}{1.10}$$

$$+ \frac{.6[.8(960) + .2(220)] + .4[.4(930) + .6(140)]}{(1.10)^2}$$

$$= -550 + \frac{102}{1.10} + \frac{670}{(1.10)^2} = +96, \text{ or } \$96,000$$

---

[16]We are guilty here of assuming away one of the most difficult questions. Just as in the Vegetron mop case, the most risky part of Ms. Magna's venture is likely to be the initial prototype project. Perhaps we should use a lower discount rate for the second piston-engine plane than for the first.

Thus the investment in the piston-engine plane has an NPV of $117,000; the investment in the turboprop has an NPV of $96,000. The piston-engine plane is the better bet. Note, however, that the choice would be different if we forgot to take account of the option to expand. In that case the NPV of the piston-engine plane would drop from $117,000 to $52,000:

$$\text{NPV} = -250 + \frac{.6(100) + .4(50)}{1.10}$$

$$+ \frac{.6[.8(410) + .2(180)] + .4[.4(220) + .6(100)]}{(1.10)^2}$$

$$= +52, \text{ or } \$52,000$$

The value of the *option to expand* is, therefore,

$$117 - 52 = +65, \text{ or } \$65,000$$

....
*Bailing Out

If the option to expand has value, how about the option to *contract* or to abandon the venture entirely?

We have assumed that Magna Charter can buy a secondhand piston-engine plane for $150,000 in year 1. We can also assume that it could sell one for the same amount. That is exactly what it should do if it buys the piston-engine plane and encounters low demand: $150,000 cash received from the sale of the plane now is obviously better than a 40 percent chance of $220,000 a year later and a 60 percent chance of $100,000.

Let's suppose that the turboprop could be sold for $500,000 in year 1. Again, it makes sense to sell if demand is low.

But now we must think again about the decision to buy the piston-engine plane. If Magna Charter can "bail out" of either investment, why not take the turboprop and shoot for the big payoff?

Figure 10-10 represents Magna Charter's decision problem with the abandonment options included. First, we figure out the net present value of buying the turboprop. This reduces to a simple one-period problem:

High demand (.6) → $888,000	$150,000 cash flow plus $738,000 net present value
Invest $550,000	
Low demand (.4) → $530,000	$30,000 cash flow plus 500,000 from sale of plane

$$\text{NPV} = -550 + \frac{.6(888) + .4(530)}{1.10} = +127, \text{ or } \$127,000$$

Thus, when we allow for the possibility of abandonment, the net present value of the turboprop investment increases from $96,000 to $127,000. The value of the *option to abandon* is

$$\text{Value of abandonment option} = \text{NPV with abandonment} - \frac{\text{NPV without}}{\text{abandonment}}$$

$$= 127 - 96$$

$$= 31, \text{ or } \$31,000$$

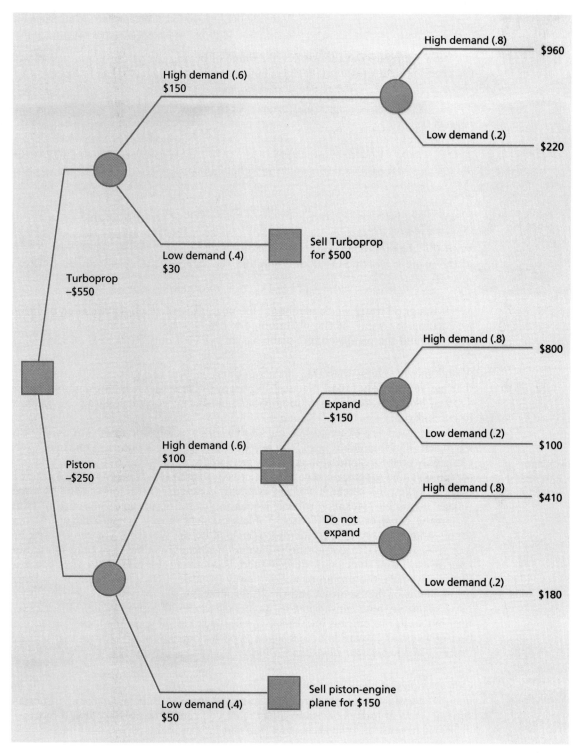

Figure 10-10 Revised decision tree for Magna Charter, taking account of the possibility of abandoning the business if demand turns out to be low. (All figures are in thousands.)

Now we figure out the net present value of buying the piston-engine plane with the abandonment option included. The payoffs for this plane are as follows:

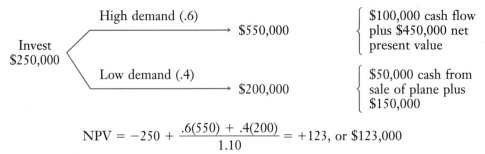

High demand (.6) → $550,000 {$100,000 cash flow plus $450,000 net present value}

Invest $250,000

Low demand (.4) → $200,000 {$50,000 cash from sale of plane plus $150,000}

$$NPV = -250 + \frac{.6(550) + .4(200)}{1.10} = +123, \text{ or } \$123,000$$

With the abandonment option the piston-engine plane is worth $123,000; without it, the plane is worth $117,000. Therefore the value of the abandonment option is

$$123 - 117 = 6, \text{ or } \$6000$$

It is a good thing we remembered the possibility of reselling the aircraft. When we include the value of the abandonment option, the turboprop has an NPV of $127,000 and the piston-engine plane has an NPV of only $123,000.

Abandonment Value and Capital Budgeting

Abandonment value—the value of the option to bail out of a project—is a simple idea that has surprisingly broad practical implications. In a way it is just common sense; disaster, like a cat, is always waiting to pounce, and so you must always be prepared to cut and run.

Some assets are easier to bail out of than others: Tangible assets are usually easier to sell than intangible ones.[17] It helps to have active secondhand markets, which really only exist for standardized, widely used items. Real estate, airplanes, trucks, and certain machine tools are likely to be relatively easy to sell. The knowledge accumulated by Vegetron's research and development program, on the other hand, is a specialized intangible asset and probably would not have a significant abandonment value.

In the worst case a firm's stockholders can bail out by going bankrupt. It may sound strange to say that an investor is helped by the possibility of bankruptcy, but it is true. Investors in corporations have *limited liability:* They risk only the money they invest. From their point of view there is a limit to the money the firm can lose; they always have the option of walking away from the firm and leaving its problems in the hands of the creditors and the bankruptcy courts.[18]

Expansion value can be just as important as abandonment value. When things turn out well, the quicker and easier the business can be expanded, the better. The best of all possible worlds occurs when good luck strikes and you find that you can expand quickly *but your competitors cannot.*

Pro and Con Decision Trees

Our examples of abandonment and expansion are extreme simplifications of the sequential decision problems that financial managers face. But they make an important general point. If today's decisions affect what you can do tomorrow, then tomorrow's decisions have to be analyzed before you can act rationally today.

---

[17]This is, of course, not always the case. Some tangible assets you have to *pay* to get rid of—worn-out refrigerators, for instance.

[18]We will discuss bankruptcy in Chapter 18.

Any cash-flow forecast rests on some assumption about the firm's future investment and operating strategy. Often that assumption is implicit. Decision trees force the underlying strategy into the open. By displaying the links between today's and tomorrow's decisions, they help the financial manager to find the strategy with the highest net present value.[19]

The trouble with decision trees is that they get so _____ complex so _____ quickly (insert your own expletives). What will Magna Charter do if demand is neither high nor low but just middling? In that event Ms. Magna might sell the turboprop and buy a piston-engine plane, or she might defer expansion and abandonment decisions until year 2. Perhaps middling demand requires a decision about a price cut or an intensified sales campaign.

There are other possibilities. Perhaps there is uncertainty about future prices of secondhand aircraft. If so, abandonment will depend not just on the level of demand but also on the level of secondhand prices. What is more, secondhand prices are likely to be depressed if demand is low and buoyant if demand is high.

We could draw a new decision tree covering this expanded set of events and decisions. Try it if you like: You'll see how fast the circles, squares, and branches accumulate.

Life is complex, and there is very little we can do about it. It is therefore unfair to criticize decision trees because they can become complex. Our criticism is reserved for analysts who let the complexity become overwhelming. The point of decision trees is to allow explicit analysis of possible future events and decisions. They should be judged not on their comprehensiveness but on whether they show the most important links between today's and tomorrow's decisions. Decision trees used in real life will be more complex than Figures 10-9 and 10-10, but they will nevertheless display only a small fraction of possible future events and decisions. Decision trees are like grapevines: They are productive only if they are vigorously pruned.

Our analysis of the Magna Charter project begged an important question. The option to expand enlarged the spread of possible outcomes and therefore increased the risk of investing in a piston aircraft. Conversely, the option to bail out narrowed the spread of possible outcomes. So it reduced the risk of investment. We should have used different discount rates to recognize these changes in risk, but decision trees do not tell us how to do this. In fact, decision trees don't tell us how to value options at all; they are just a convenient way to summarize cash-flow consequences. But the situation is not hopeless. Modern techniques of option valuation are beginning to help value these investment options. We will describe these techniques in Chapters 20 and 21.

Decision Trees and Monte Carlo Simulation

We have said that any cash-flow forecast rests on assumptions about future investment and operating strategy. Think back to the Monte Carlo simulation model that we constructed for the Jalopy Motor Company. What strategy was that based on? We don't know. Inevitably Jalopy will face decisions about pricing, production, expansion, and abandonment, but the model builder's assumptions about these decisions are buried in the model's equations. The model builder may have implicitly identified a future strategy for Jalopy, but it is clearly not the optimal one. There will be some runs of the model when nearly everything goes wrong and when in real life Jalopy would abandon to cut its losses. Yet the model goes on period after period, heedless

---

[19]Some analysts go further than that. Like the early advocates of simulation models, they start with the premise that net present value cannot take account of risk. They, therefore, propose that the decision tree be used to calculate a *distribution* of "NPVs" or internal rates of return for each possible sequence of company decisions. That may sound like a gingerbread house, but you should know by now that there is a witch inside.

of the drain on Jalopy's cash resources. The most unfavorable outcomes reported by the simulation model would never be encountered in real life.

On the other hand, the simulation model probably understates the project's potential value if nearly everything goes right: There is no provision for expanding to take advantage of good luck.

Most simulation models incorporate a "business as usual" strategy, which is fine as long as there are no major surprises. The greater the divergence from expected levels of market growth, market share, cost, etc., the less realistic is the simulation. Therefore the extreme high and low simulated values—the "tails" of the simulated distributions—should be treated with extreme caution. Don't take the area under the tails as realistic probabilities of disaster or bonanza.

10-4 SUMMARY

There is more to capital budgeting than grinding out calculations of net present value. If you can identify the major uncertainties, you may find that it is worth undertaking some additional preliminary research that will *confirm* whether the project is worthwhile. And even if you decide that you have done all you can to resolve the uncertainties, you still want to be aware of the potential problems. You do not want to be caught by surprise if things go wrong: You want to be ready to take corrective action.

There are three ways in which companies try to identify the principal threats to a project's success. The simplest is to undertake a sensitivity analysis. In this case the manager considers in turn each of the determinants of the project's success and estimates how far the present value of the project would be altered by taking a very optimistic view or a very pessimistic view of that variable.

Sensitivity analysis of this kind is easy, but it is not always helpful. Variables do not usually change one at a time. If costs are higher than you expect, it is a good bet that prices will be higher also. And if prices are higher, it is a good bet that sales volume will be lower. If you don't allow for the dependencies between the swings and the merry-go-rounds, you may get a false idea of the hazards of the fairground business. Many companies try to cope with this problem by examining the effect on the project of alternative plausible combinations of variables. In other words, they will estimate the net present value of the project under different scenarios and compare these estimates with the base case.

In a sensitivity analysis you change variables one at a time: When you analyze scenarios, you look at a limited number of alternative combinations of variables. If you want to go whole hog and look at *all* possible combinations of variables, then you will probably need to use Monte Carlo simulation to cope with the complexity. In that case you must construct a complete model of the project and specify the probability distribution of each of the determinants of cash flow. You can then ask the computer to select a random number for each of these determinants and work out the cash flows that would result. After the computer has repeated this process a hundred or so times, you should have a fair idea of the expected cash flow in each year and the spread of possible cash flows.

Simulation can be a very useful tool. The discipline of building a model of the project can in itself lead you to a deeper understanding of the project. And once you have constructed your model, it is a simple matter to see how the outcomes would be affected by altering the scope of the project or the distribution of any of the variables. There are of course limits to what you can learn from simulations. A marine engineer uses a tank to simulate the performance of alternative hull designs but knows that it is impossible to fully replicate the conditions that the ship will encounter. In the same way, the financial manager can learn a lot from "laboratory" tests but cannot hope to build a model that accurately captures all the uncertainties and interdependencies that really surround a project.

Books about capital budgeting sometimes create the impression that, once the manager has made an investment decision, there is nothing to do but sit back and watch the cash flows unfold. In practice, companies are constantly modifying their operations. If cash flows are better than anticipated, the project may be expanded; if they are worse, it may be contracted or abandoned altogether. Good managers take account of these options when they value a project. One convenient way to analyze them is by means of a decision tree. You identify the principal things that could happen to the project and the main counteractions that you might take. Then, working back from the future to the present, you can calculate which action you *should* take in each case. Once you know that, it is easy to work out how much the value of the project is increased by these opportunities to react to changing circumstances.

Many of the early articles on simulation and decision trees were written before we knew how to introduce risk into calculations of net present value. Their authors believed that these techniques might allow the manager to make investment decisions without estimating the opportunity cost of capital and calculating net present value. Today we know that simulation and decision analysis cannot save you from having to calculate net present value. The value of these techniques is to help the manager get behind the cash-flow forecast; they help the manager to understand what could go wrong and what opportunities are available to modify the project. That is why we described them as tools to open up black boxes.

Further Reading
••••••••••••••••••••••••••••••••••••

For an excellent case study of break-even analysis, see:
U. E. Reinhardt: "Break-Even Analysis for Lockheed's TriStar: An Application of Financial Theory," *Journal of Finance,* **28:**821–838 (September 1973).

The first advocate of simulation was David Hertz. See:
D. B. Hertz: "Investment Policies That Pay Off," *Harvard Business Review,* **46:**96–108 (January–February 1968).
D. B. Hertz: "Risk Analysis in Capital Investment," *Harvard Business Review,* **42:**95–106 (January–February 1964).

Merck's use of Monte Carlo simulation is discussed in:
N. A. Nichols: "Scientific Management at Merck: An Interview with Judy Lewent," *Harvard Business Review,* **72:**89–99 (January–February 1994).

Myers discusses the interpretation and use of simulations in:
S. C. Myers: "Postscript: Using Simulation for Risk Analysis," in S. C. Myers (ed.), *Modern Developments in Financial Management,* Praeger Publishers, Inc., New York, 1976.

The use of decision trees in investment appraisal was first discussed in:
J. Magee: "How to Use Decision Trees in Capital Investment," *Harvard Business Review,* **42:**79–96 (September–October 1964).

Hax and Wiig discuss how Monte Carlo simulation and decision trees were used in an actual capital budgeting decision:
A. C. Hax and K. M. Wiig: "The Use of Decision Analysis in Capital Investment Problems," *Sloan Management Review,* **17:**19–48 (Winter 1976).

The abandonment option in capital budgeting was first analyzed by:
A. A. Robichek and J. C. Van Horne: "Abandonment Value in Capital Budgeting," *Journal of Finance,* **22:**577–590 (December 1967).

Quiz

1. Define and briefly explain each of the following terms or procedures:
   (*a*) Project analysis
   (*b*) Sensitivity analysis
   (*c*) Break-even analysis
   (*d*) Monte Carlo simulation
   (*e*) Decision tree
   (*f*) Abandonment value
   (*g*) Expansion value

2. What is the NPV of the electric scooter project under the following scenario?

   - Market size: 1.1 million
   - Market share: .1
   - Unit price: $4000
   - Unit variable cost: $3600
   - Fixed cost: $20 million

3. Jalopy Motor is considering still another production method for its electric scooter. It would require an additional investment of $150 million but would reduce variable costs by $40 million a year. Other assumptions follow Table 10-1.
   (*a*) What is the NPV of this alternative scheme?
   (*b*) Draw break-even charts for this alternative scheme along the lines of Figure 10-1.
   (*c*) Explain how you would interpret the break-even figure.

4. Summarize the problems that a manager would encounter in interpreting a standard sensitivity analysis, such as the one shown in Table 10-2. Which of these problems are alleviated by examining the project under alternative scenarios?

5. True or false?
   (*a*) Project analysis is unnecessary for projects with asset betas that are equal to zero.
   (*b*) Sensitivity analysis can be used to identify the variables most crucial to a project's success.
   (*c*) Sensitivity analysis gives "optimistic" and "pessimistic" values for project cash flow and NPV.
   (*d*) The break-even sales level of a project is higher when *break-even* is defined in terms of NPV rather than accounting income.
   (*e*) Monte Carlo simulation can be used to help forecast cash flows.
   (*f*) Monte Carlo simulation eliminates the need to estimate a project's opportunity cost of capital.
   (*g*) Decision trees are useful when future investment decisions may depend on today's decision.
   (*h*) High abandonment value increases NPV, other things being equal.

6. Suppose a manager has already estimated a project's cash flows, calculated its NPV, and done a sensitivity analysis like the one shown in Table 10-2. List the additional steps required to carry out a Monte Carlo simulation of project cash flows.

7. Use a decision tree to show that it pays Jalopy Motor to conduct a pretest of the suspect machine (see Section 10-1).

8. Big Oil is wondering whether to drill for oil in Westchester County. The prospects are as follows:

Depth of Well, Feet	Total Cost, Millions of Dollars	Cumulative Probability of Finding Oil	PV of Oil (if Found), Millions of Dollars
1,000	2	.5	5
2,000	2.5	.6	4.5
3,000	3	.7	4

Draw a decision tree showing the successive drilling decisions to be made by Big Oil. How deep should it be prepared to drill?

Questions and Problems

1. Your staff has come up with the following revised estimates for the electric scooter project:

	Pessimistic	Expected	Optimistic
Market size	.8 million	1.0 million	1.2 million
Market share	.04	.1	.16
Unit price	$3,000	$3,750	$4,000
Unit variable cost	$3,500	$3,000	$2,750
Fixed cost	$50 million	$30 million	$10 million

Conduct a sensitivity analysis. What are the principal uncertainties in the project?

2. The Goodyear Welt Company is proposing to replace its old welt-making machinery with more modern equipment. The new equipment costs $10 million and the company expects to sell its old equipment for $1 million. The attraction of the new machinery is that it is expected to cut manufacturing costs from their current level of $8 a welt to $4. However, as the following table shows, there is some uncertainty both about future sales and about the performance of the new machinery:

	Pessimistic	Expected	Optimistic
Sales, millions of welts	.4	.5	.7
Manufacturing cost with new machinery, dollars per welt	6	4	3
Economic life of new machinery, years	7	10	13

Conduct a sensitivity analysis of the replacement decision, assuming a discount rate of 12 percent. Goodyear Welt does not pay taxes.

3. Goodyear Welt could commission engineering tests to determine the actual improvement in manufacturing costs generated by the proposed new welt ma-

TABLE 10-7

• •

Projected investment and cash flows for the Downeast Tourist Mall (figures in millions of dollars)

	YEAR					
	0	1	2	3	4	5–17
Investment:						
Land	15					
Construction	10	15	5			
Operations:						
Rentals				6	6	6
Share 5% of retail sales				12	12	12
Operating and maintenance costs	1	2	2	5	5	5
Real estate taxes	1	1	1.5	2	2	2

chines. (See problem 2 above.) The study would cost $450,000. Would you advise the company to go ahead with the study?

4. Waldo County, the well-known real estate developer, plans to build still another shopping mall designed to intercept tourists heading downeast toward Maine. Table 10-7 shows Mr. County's projections. Note that the mall's revenues come from two sources: Mr. County will (1) charge retail stores for the space they occupy and (2) receive 5 percent of each store's gross sales.

Construction costs can be depreciated over 15 years starting in year 3. For simplicity you can assume straight-line depreciation. Land cannot be depreciated. The tax rate is 35 percent, and the cost of capital is 9 percent. Assume zero inflation.

Mr. County believes that the shopping mall will have to be rebuilt in year 17. The $30 million construction cost outlay will have no value at that time. The land should retain its value, however.

(a) What is the net present value of Mr. County's project?
(b) The mall's sales are highly uncertain. They could be as much as 40 percent higher or lower than forecast. Do a sensitivity analysis for this variable.
(c) Calculate the break-even level of sales for the project.
(d) Calculate the sales level for which the project breaks even in terms of accounting profits. Explain why this sales level is lower than your answer to (c).
(e) Mr. County worries that rapid growth in the mall's sales would mean higher costs and taxes. Calculate the project's net present value for a scenario with 20 percent higher sales, 15 percent higher operating and maintenance costs, and 20 percent higher real estate taxes.
(f) Mr. County also worries about construction cost overruns and delays due to required zoning changes and environmental approvals. He's seen cases of 25 percent cost overruns and delays up to 12 months. What effect would this scenario have on the project's net present value? On its break-even revenue level?

5. Waldo County has received a brochure from Hotshot Consultants advocating Monte Carlo simulation. Mr. County is intrigued and wants to try the method out on the Downeast Tourist Mall described in problem 4.
   (*a*) Outline the steps required to set up and run the Monte Carlo simulation for this project. Which key uncertainties would you advise Mr. County to concentrate on?
   (*b*) What would the output of the simulation be? What could Mr. County learn from it?
   (*c*) The brochure from Hotshot Consultants says that the most important simulation output is the probability distribution of project NPVs. Hotshot implies that projects should not be accepted unless the probability of negative NPVs (as calculated by the simulation) is small. What do you think of this? Explain.

*6. Agnes Magna has found some errors in her data (see Section 10-3). The corrected figures are as follows:

   - Price of turbo, year 0: $350,000
   - Price of piston, year 0: $180,000
   - Price of turbo, year 1: $300,000
   - Price of piston, year 1: $150,000
   - Discount rate: 8 percent

   Redraw the decision tree with the changed data. Calculate the value of the option to expand. Recalculate the value of the abandonment option. Which plane should Ms. Magna buy?

*7. Ms. Magna has thought of another idea. Perhaps she should buy a piston-engine plane now. Then, if demand is high in the first year, she can sell it and buy a turboprop. Redraw Figure 10-9 to incorporate this possibility. What should Ms. Magna do?

8. For what kinds of capital investment projects do you think Monte Carlo simulation would be most useful? For example, can you think of some industries in which this technique would be particularly attractive? Would it be more useful for large-scale investments than small ones? Discuss.

9. You own an unused gold mine that will cost $100,000 to reopen. If you open the mine, you expect to be able to extract 1000 ounces of gold a year for each of 3 years. After that, the deposit will be exhausted. The gold price is currently $500 an ounce, and each year the price is equally likely to rise or fall by $50 from its level at the start of the year. The extraction cost is $460 an ounce and the discount rate is 10 percent.
   (*a*) Should you open the mine now or delay 1 year in the hope of a rise in the gold price?
   (*b*) What difference would it make to your decision if you could costlessly (but irreversibly) shut down the mine at any stage?

10. Read and criticize the Hax-Wiig article mentioned in the "Further Reading" for this chapter. Are all their recommendations consistent with finance theory?

11. You are considering a new consulting service. There is a 60 percent chance the demand will be high in the first year. If it is high, there is an 80 percent chance that it will continue high indefinitely. If demand is low in the first year, there is a 60 percent chance that it will continue low indefinitely.

If demand is high, forecasted revenue is $90,000 a year; if demand is low, forecasted revenue is $70,000 a year. You can cease to offer the service at any point, in which case, of course, revenues are zero. Costs other than computing are forecasted at $50,000 a year regardless of demand. These costs also can be terminated at any point. You have a choice on computing costs. One possibility is to buy your own minicomputer. This involves an initial outlay of $200,000 and no subsequent expenditure. It has an economic life of 10 years and no salvage value. The alternative is to rent computer time as you need it. In this case computer costs are 40 percent of revenues.

Assume that the computing decision cannot be reversed (i.e., if you buy a computer, you cannot resell it; if you do *not* buy it today, you cannot do so later).

There are no taxes, and the opportunity cost of capital is 10 percent.

Draw a decision tree showing the alternatives. Is it better to buy a computer or rent?

State clearly any additional assumptions that you need to make.

11

Where Positive Net Present Values Come From

Why is an M.B.A. student who has learned about DCF like a baby with a hammer? Answer: Because to a baby with a hammer, everything looks like a nail.

Our point is that you should not focus on the arithmetic of DCF and thereby ignore the forecasts that are the basis of every investment decision. Senior managers are continuously bombarded with requests for funds for capital expenditures. All these requests are supported with detailed DCF analyses showing that the projects have positive NPVs.[1] How, then, can managers distinguish the NPVs that are truly positive from those that are merely the result of forecasting errors? We suggest that they should ask some probing questions about the possible sources of economic gain.

The first section in this chapter reviews certain common pitfalls in capital budgeting, notably the tendency to apply DCF when market values are already available and no DCF calculations are needed. The second section covers the *economic rents* that underlie all positive-NPV investments. The third section presents a case study describing how Marvin Enterprises, the gargle blaster company, analyzed the introduction of a radically new product.

11-1 LOOK FIRST TO MARKET VALUES

Let us suppose that you have persuaded all your project sponsors to give honest forecasts. Although those forecasts are unbiased, they are still likely to contain errors, some positive and others negative. The average error will be zero, but that is little consolation because you want to accept only projects with *truly* superior profitability.

Think, for example, of what would happen if you were to jot down your estimates of the cash flows from operating various items of equipment. You would probably find that about half *appeared* to have positive NPVs. This may not be because you personally possess any superior skill in operating jumbo jets or running a chain of laundromats but because you have inadvertently introduced large errors into your

---

[1]Here is another riddle. Are projects proposed because they have positive NPVs, or do they have positive NPVs because they are proposed? No prizes for the correct answer.

estimates of the cash flows. The more projects you contemplate, the more likely you are to uncover projects that *appear* to be extremely worthwhile. Indeed, if you were to extend your activities to making cash-flow estimates for various companies, you would also find a number of *apparently* attractive takeover candidates. In some of these cases you might have genuine information and the proposed investment really might have a positive NPV. But in many other cases the investment would look good only because you made a forecasting error.

What can you do to prevent forecast errors from swamping genuine information? We suggest that you begin by looking at market values.

The Cadillac and the Movie Star

The following parable should help to illustrate what we mean. Your local Cadillac dealer is announcing a special offer. For $35,001 you get not only a brand new Cadillac but also the chance to shake hands with your favorite movie star. You wonder how much you are paying for that handshake.

There are two possible approaches to the problem. You could evaluate the worth of the Cadillac's power steering, disappearing windshield wipers, and other features and conclude that the Cadillac is worth $36,000. This would seem to suggest that the dealership is willing to pay $999 to have a movie star shake hands with you. Alternatively, you might note that the market price for Cadillacs is $35,000, so that you are paying $1 for the handshake. As long as there is a competitive market for Cadillacs, the latter approach is more appropriate.

Security analysts face a similar problem whenever they value a company's stock. They must consider the information that is already known to the market about a company, *and* they must evaluate the information that is known only to them. The information that is known to the market is the Cadillac; the private information is the handshake with the movie star. Investors have already evaluated the information that is generally known. Security analysts do not need to evaluate this information again. They can *start* with the market price of the stock and concentrate on valuing their private information.

While lesser mortals would instinctively accept the Cadillac's market value of $35,000, the financial manager is trained to enumerate and value all the costs and benefits from an investment and is therefore tempted to substitute his or her own opinion for the market's. Unfortunately this approach increases the chance of error. Many capital assets are traded in a competitive market, and so it makes sense to *start* with the market price and then ask why these assets should earn more in your hands than your rivals.

Example: Investing in a New Department Store

We encountered a department store chain that estimated the present value of the expected cash flows from each proposed store, including the price at which it could eventually sell the store. Although the firm took considerable care with these estimates, it was disturbed to find that its conclusions were heavily influenced by the forecasted selling price of each store. Management disclaimed any particular real estate expertise, but it discovered that its investment decisions were unintentionally dominated by its assumptions about future real estate prices.

Once the financial managers realized this, they always checked the decision to open a new store by asking the following question: "Let us assume that the property is fairly priced. What is the evidence that it is best suited to one of our department stores rather than to some other use?" In other words, *if an asset is worth more to others than it is to you, then beware of bidding for the asset against them.*

Let us take the department store problem a little further. Suppose that the new store costs $100 million.[2] You forecast that it will generate after-tax cash flow of $8 million a year for 10 years. Real estate prices are estimated to grow by 3 percent a year, so the expected value of the real estate at the end of 10 years is $100 \times (1.03)^{10}$ = $134 million. At a discount rate of 10 percent, your proposed department store has an NPV of $1 million:

$$\text{NPV} = -100 + \frac{8}{1.10} + \frac{8}{(1.10)^2} + \cdots + \frac{8 + 134}{(1.10)^{10}} = \$1 \text{ million}$$

Notice how sensitive this NPV is to the ending value of the real estate. For example, an ending value of $120 million implies an NPV of −$5 million.

It is helpful to imagine such a business as divided into two parts—a real estate subsidiary which buys the building and a retailing subsidiary which rents and operates it. Then figure out how much rent the real estate subsidiary would have to charge, and ask whether the retailing subsidiary could afford to pay the rent.

In some cases a fair market rental can be estimated from real estate transactions. For example, we might observe that similar retail space recently rented for $10 million a year. In that case we would conclude that our department store was an unattractive use for the site. Once the site had been acquired, it would be better to rent it out at $10 million than to use it for a store generating only $8 million.

Suppose, on the other hand, that the property could be rented for only $7 million per year. The department store could pay this amount to the real estate subsidiary and still earn a net operating cash flow of $8 - 7 = \$1$ million. It is therefore the best *current* use for the real estate.[3]

Will it also be the best *future* use? Maybe not, depending on whether retail profits keep pace with any rent increases. Suppose that real estate prices and rents are expected to increase by 3 percent per year. The real estate subsidiary must charge $7 \times 1.03 = \$7.21$ million in year 2, $7.21 \times 1.03 = \$7.43$ million in year 3, and so on.[4] Figure 11-1 shows that the store's income fails to cover the rental after year 5.

If these forecasts are right, the store has only a 5-year economic life; from that point on the real estate is more valuable in some other use. If you stubbornly believe that the department store is the best long-term use for the site, you must be ignoring potential growth in income from the store.[5]

---

[2]For simplicity we assume all the $100 million goes to real estate. In real life there would also be substantial investments in fixtures, information systems, training, and start-up costs.

[3]The fair market rent equals the profit generated by the real estate's *second*-best use.

[4]This rental stream yields a 10 percent rate of return to the real estate subsidiary. Each year it gets a 7 percent "dividend" and 3 percent capital gain. Growth at 3 percent would bring the value of the property to $134 million by year 10.

The present value (at $r = .10$) of the growing stream of rents is

$$\text{PV} = \frac{7}{r - g} = \frac{7}{.10 - .03} = \$100 \text{ million}$$

This PV is the initial market value of the property.

[5]Another possibility is that real estate rents and values are expected to grow at less than 3 percent a year. But in that case the real estate subsidiary would have to charge more than $7 million rent in year 1 to justify its $100 million real estate investment (see footnote 4 above). That would make the department store even less attractive.

Figure 11-1
Beginning in year 6, the department store's income fails to cover the rental charge.

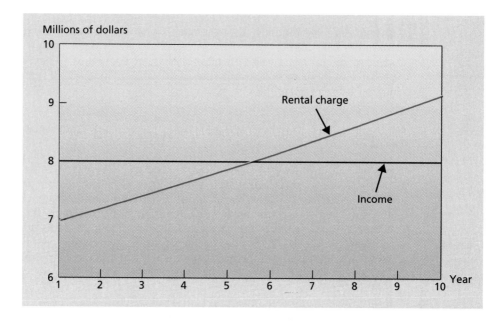

There is a general point here. Whenever you make a capital investment decision, think what bets you are placing. Our department store example involved at least two bets—one on real estate prices and another on the firm's ability to run a successful department store. But that suggests some alternative strategies. For instance, it would be foolish to make a lousy department store investment just because you are optimistic about real estate prices. You would do better to buy real estate and rent it out to the highest bidders. The converse is also true. You shouldn't be deterred from going ahead with a profitable department store because you are pessimistic about real estate prices. You would do better to sell the real estate and *rent* it back for the department store. We suggest that you separate the two bets by first asking "Should we open a department store on this site, assuming that the real estate is fairly priced?" and then deciding whether you also want to go into the real estate business.

Another Example: Opening a Gold Mine

Here is another example of how market prices can help you make better decisions. Kingsley Solomon is considering a proposal to open a new gold mine. He estimates that the mine will cost $200 million to develop and that in each of the next 10 years it will produce .1 million ounces of gold at a cost, after mining and refining, of $200 an ounce. Although the extraction costs can be predicted with reasonable accuracy, Mr. Solomon is much less confident about future gold prices. His best guess is that the price will rise by 5 percent per year from its current level of $400 an ounce. At a discount rate of 10 percent, this gives the mine an NPV of −$10 million:

$$\text{NPV} = -200 + \frac{.1(420 - 200)}{1.10} + \frac{.1(441 - 200)}{(1.10)^2} + \cdots + \frac{.1(652 - 200)}{(1.10)^{10}}$$

$$= -\$10 \text{ million}$$

Therefore the gold mine project is rejected.

Unfortunately, Mr. Solomon did not look at what the market was telling him. What is the present value of an ounce of gold? Clearly, if the gold market is functioning properly, it is the current price—$400 an ounce. Gold does not produce any income, so $400 is the discounted value of the expected future gold price.[6] Since the mine is expected to produce a total of 1 million ounces (.1 million ounces per year for 10 years), the present value of the revenue stream is $1 \times 400 = \$400$ million.[7] We assume that 10 percent is an appropriate discount rate for the relatively certain extraction costs. Thus

$$NPV = \frac{-\text{initial}}{\text{investment}} + PV \text{ revenues} - PV \text{ costs}$$

$$= -200 + 400 - \sum_{t=1}^{10} \frac{.1 \times 200}{(1.10)^t} = \$77 \text{ million}$$

It looks as if Kingsley Solomon's mine is not such a bad bet after all.[8]

Mr. Solomon's gold was just like anyone else's gold. So there was no point in trying to value it separately. By taking the present value of the gold sales as given, Mr. Solomon was able to focus on the crucial issue: Were the extraction costs sufficiently low to make the venture worthwhile? That brings us to another of those fundamental truths: If others are producing an article profitably and (like Mr. Solomon) you

---

[6]Investing in an ounce of gold is like investing in a stock that pays no dividends: The investor's return comes entirely as capital gains. Look back at Section 4-2, where we showed that P_0, the price of the stock today, depends on DIV_1 and P_1, the expected dividend and price for next year, and the opportunity cost of capital r:

$$P_0 = \frac{DIV_1 + P_1}{1 + r}$$

But for gold $DIV_1 = 0$, so

$$P_0 = \frac{P_1}{1 + r}$$

In words, *today's price is the present value of next year's price.* Therefore, we don't have to know either P_1 or r to find the present value. Also since $DIV_2 = 0$,

$$P_1 = \frac{P_2}{1 + r}$$

and we can express P_0 as

$$P_0 = \frac{P_1}{1 + r} = \frac{1}{1 + r}\left(\frac{P_2}{1 + r}\right) = \frac{P_2}{(1 + r)^2}$$

In general,

$$P_0 = \frac{P_t}{(1 + r)^t}$$

This holds for any asset which pays no dividends, is traded in a competitive market, and costs nothing to store. Storage costs for gold or common stocks are very small compared to asset value.

We also assume that guaranteed future delivery of gold is just as good as having gold in hand today. This is not quite right. As we will see in Chapter 25, gold in hand can generate a small "convenience yield."

[7]We assume that the extraction rate does not vary. If it can vary, Mr. Solomon has a valuable operating option to increase output when gold prices are high or to cut back when prices fall. Option pricing techniques are needed to value the mine when operating options are important. See Chapters 20 and 21.

[8]As in the case of our department store example, Mr. Solomon is placing two bets—one on his ability to mine gold at a low cost and the other on the price of gold. Suppose that he really does believe that gold is overvalued. That should not deter him from running a low cost gold mine as long as he can place separate bets on gold prices. For example, he might be able to enter into a long term contract to sell the mine's output or he could sell gold futures. (We explain *futures* in Chapter 25.)

can make it more cheaply, then you don't need any NPV calculations to know that you are probably onto a good thing.

We confess that our example of Kingsley Solomon's mine is somewhat special. Unlike gold, most commodities are not kept solely for investment purposes, and therefore you cannot automatically assume that today's price is equal to the present value of the future price.[9] But when you do have the market value of an asset, *use it*, at least as a starting point for your analysis.

One more example. Suppose that an oil company is contemplating an additional investment in tankers. Tankers are freely traded in a competitive market. Therefore the present value of a tanker to the oil company is equal to the tanker's price *plus* any extra gains that are likely to come from having the oil company, rather than another owner, operate the vessel.

11-2 FORECASTING ECONOMIC RENTS

We recommend that financial managers ask themselves whether an asset is more valuable in their hands than in another's. A bit of classical microeconomics can help to answer that question. When an industry settles into long-run competitive equilibrium, all its assets are expected to earn their opportunity costs of capital—no more and no less. If the assets earned more, firms in the industry would expand or firms outside the industry would try to enter it.

Profits that *more* than cover the opportunity cost of capital are known as *economic rents*. These rents may be either temporary (in the case of an industry that is not in long-run equilibrium) or persistent (in the case of a firm with some degree of monopoly or market power). The NPV of an investment is simply the discounted value of the economic rents that it will produce. Therefore when you are presented with a project that appears to have a positive NPV, don't just accept the calculations at face value. They may reflect simple estimation errors in forecasting cash flows. Probe behind the cash-flow estimates, and *try to identify the source of economic rents*. A positive NPV for a new project is believable only if *you* believe that your company has some special advantage.

Such advantages can arise in several ways. You may be smart or lucky enough to be first to the market with a new, improved product for which customers are prepared to pay premium prices (until your competitors enter and squeeze out excess profits). You may have a patent, proprietary technology, or production cost advantage that competitors cannot match, at least for several years. You may have some valuable contractual advantage, e.g., the distributorship for gargle blasters in France (see Section 11-3).

Thinking about competitive advantage can also help ferret out negative-NPV calculations that are negative by mistake. If you are the lowest-cost producer of a

---

[9]However, Hotelling has pointed out that if there are constant returns to scale in mining any mineral, the expected rise in the price of the mineral *less* extraction costs should equal the cost of capital. If the expected growth were faster, everyone would want to postpone extraction; if it were slower, everyone would want to exploit the resource today. In this case the value of a mine would be independent of when it was exploited, and you could value it by calculating the value of the mineral at today's price less the current cost of extraction. If (as is usually the case) there are declining returns to scale, then the expected price rise net of costs must be less than the cost of capital. For a review of Hotelling's Principle, see S. Devarajan and A. C. Fisher, "Hotelling's 'Economics of Exhaustible Resources': Fifty Years Later," *Journal of Economic Literature*, **19**:65–73 (March 1981). And for an application to the problem of valuing mineral deposits, see M. H. Miller and C. W. Upton, "A Test of the Hotelling Valuation Principle," *Journal of Political Economy*, **93**:1–25 (1985).

TABLE 11-1

● ●

NPV calculation for proposed investment in polyzone production by a U.S. chemical company (figures in millions of dollars except as noted)

	Year 0	Year 1	Year 2	Years 3–10
Investment	100			
Production, millions of pounds per year*	0	0	40	80
Spread, dollars per pound	1.20	1.20	1.20	1.20
Net revenues	0	0	48	96
Production costs†	0	0	30	30
Transport‡	0	0	4	8
Other costs	0	20	20	20
Cash flow	−100	−20	−6	+38

NPV (at $r = 8\%$) = $63.6 million

Note: For simplicity, we assume no inflation and no taxes. Plant and equipment have no salvage value after 10 years.
*Production capacity is 80 million pounds per year.
†Production costs are $.375 per pound after start-up ($.75 per pound in year 2, when production is only 40 million pounds).
‡Transportation costs are $.10 per pound to European ports.

profitable product in a growing market, then you should invest to expand along with the market. If your calculations show a negative NPV for such an expansion, then you have probably made a mistake.

How One Company Avoided a $100 Million Mistake

A U.S. chemical producer was about to modify an existing plant to produce a specialty product, polyzone, which was in short supply on world markets.[10] At prevailing raw material and finished-product prices the expansion would have been strongly profitable. Table 11-1 shows a simplified version of management's analysis. Note the NPV of about $64 million at the company's 8 percent real cost of capital—not bad for a $100 million outlay.

Then doubt began to creep in. Notice the outlay for transportation costs. Some of the project's raw materials were commodity chemicals, largely imported from Europe, and much of the polyzone production was exported back to Europe. Moreover, the U.S. company had no long-run technological edge over potential European competitors. It had a head start perhaps, but was that really enough to generate a positive NPV?

---

[10]This is a true story, but names and details have been changed to protect the innocent.

Notice the importance of the price spread between raw materials and finished product. The analysis in Table 11-1 forecasted the spread at a constant $1.20 per pound of polyzone for 10 years. That had to be wrong: European producers, who did not face the U.S. company's transportation costs, would see an even larger NPV and expand capacity. Increased competition would almost surely squeeze the spread. The U.S. company decided to calculate the competitive spread—the spread at which a European competitor would see polyzone capacity as zero NPV. Table 11-2 shows management's analysis. The resulting spread of 95 cents per pound was the best *long-run* forecast for the polyzone market, other things constant of course.

How much of a head start did the U.S. producer have? How long before competitors forced the spread down to $.95? Management's best guess was 5 years. It prepared Table 11-3, which is identical to Table 11-1 except for the forecasted spread, which would shrink to $.95 by the start of year 5. Now the NPV was negative.

The project might have been saved if production could have been started in year 1 rather than 2 or if local markets could have been expanded, thus reducing transportation costs. But these changes were not feasible, so management canceled the project, albeit with a sigh of relief that its analysis hadn't stopped at Table 11-1.

This is a perfect example of the importance of thinking through sources of economic rents. Positive NPVs are suspect without some long-run competitive advantage. When a company contemplates investing in a new product or expanding production of an existing product, it should specifically identify its advantages or disadvantages over its most dangerous competitors. It should calculate NPV from those competitors' points of view. If competitors' NPVs come out strongly positive, the company had better expect decreasing prices (or spreads) and evaluate the proposed investment accordingly.

TABLE 11-2

What's the competitive spread to a European producer? About $.95 per pound of polyzone. Note that European producers face no transportation costs. Compare Table 11-1 (figures in millions of dollars except as noted).

	Year 0	Year 1	Year 2	Years 3–10
Investment	100			
Production, millions of pounds per year	0	0	40	80
Spread, dollars per pound	.95	.95	.95	.95
Net revenues	0	0	38	76
Production costs	0	0	30	30
Transport	0	0	0	0
Other costs	0	20	20	20
Cash Flow	−100	−20	−12	+26

NPV (at $r = 8\%$) = 0

TABLE 11-3

· ·

Recalculation of NPV for polyzone investment by U.S. company (figures in millions of dollars except as noted). If expansion by European producers forces competitive spreads by year 5, the U.S. producer's NPV falls to −$10.3 million. Compare Table 11-1.

	YEAR					
	0	1	2	3	4	5–10
Investment	100					
Production, millions of pounds per year	0	0	40	80	80	80
Spread, dollars per pound	1.20	1.20	1.20	1.20	1.10	.95
Net revenues	0	0	48	96	88	76
Production costs	0	0	30	30	30	30
Transport	0	0	4	8	8	8
Other costs	0	20	20	20	20	20
Cash flow	−100	−20	−6	+38	+30	+18

NPV (at $r = 8\%$) = −$10.3

*11-3 EXAMPLE—MARVIN ENTERPRISES DECIDES TO EXPLOIT A NEW TECHNOLOGY

To illustrate some of the problems involved in predicting economic rents, let us leap forward to the twenty-first century and look at the decision by Marvin Enterprises to exploit a new technology.[11]

One of the most unexpected developments of these years was the remarkable growth of a completely new industry. By 2013, annual sales of gargle blasters totaled $1.68 billion, or 240 million units. Although it controlled only 10 percent of the market, Marvin Enterprises was among the most exciting growth companies of the decade. Marvin had come late into the business, but it had pioneered the use of integrated microcircuits to control the genetic engineering processes used to manufacture gargle blasters. This development had enabled producers to cut the price of gargle blasters from $9 to $7 and had thereby contributed to the dramatic growth in the size of the market. The estimated demand curve in Figure 11-2 shows just how responsive demand is to such price reductions.

Table 11-4 summarizes the cost structure of the old and new technologies. While companies with the new technology were earning 20 percent on their initial invest-

---

[11]We thank Stewart Hodges for permission to adapt this example from a case prepared by him, and we thank the BBC for permission to use the term *gargle blasters*.

Figure 11-2 The demand "curve" for gargle blasters shows that for each $1 cut in price there is an increase in demand of 80 million units.

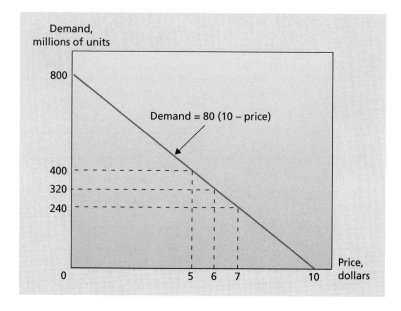

ment, those with first-generation equipment had been hit by the successive price cuts. Since all Marvin's investment was in the 2009 technology, it had been particularly well placed during this period.

Rumors of new developments at Marvin had been circulating for some time, and the total market value of Marvin's stock had risen to $460 million by January 2014. At that point Marvin called a press conference to announce another technological breakthrough. Management claimed that its new third-generation process involving mutant neurons enabled the firm to reduce capital costs to $10 and manufacturing costs to $3 per unit. Marvin proposed to capitalize on this invention by embarking on a huge $1 billion expansion program that would add 100 million units to capacity. The company expected to be in full operation within 12 months.

TABLE 11-4

Size and cost structure of the gargle blaster industry before Marvin announced its expansion plans

Technology	CAPACITY, MILLIONS OF UNITS		Capital Cost per Unit, Dollars	Manufacturing Cost per Unit, Dollars	Salvage Value per Unit, Dollars
	Industry	Marvin			
First generation (2001)	120	—	17.50	5.50	2.50
Second generation (2009)	120	24	17.50	3.50	2.50

Note: Selling price is $7 per unit. One "unit" means one gargle blaster.

Before deciding to go ahead with this development, Marvin had undertaken extensive calculations on the effect of the new investment. The basic assumptions were as follows:

1. The cost of capital was 20 percent.
2. The production facilities had an indefinite physical life.
3. The demand curve and the costs of each technology would not change.
4. There was no chance of a fourth-generation technology in the foreseeable future.
5. The corporate income tax, which had been abolished in 2004, was not likely to be reintroduced.

Marvin's competitors greeted the news with varying degrees of concern. There was general agreement that it would be 5 years before any of them would have access to the new technology. On the other hand, many consoled themselves with the reflection that Marvin's new plant could not compete with fully depreciated existing plant.

Suppose that you were Marvin's financial manager. Would you have agreed with the decision to expand? Do you think it would have been better to go for a larger or smaller expansion? How do you think Marvin's announcement is likely to affect the price of its stock?

You have a choice. You can go on *immediately* to read *our* solution to these questions. But you will learn much more if you stop and work out your own answer first. Try it.

*Forecasting Prices of Gargle Blasters

Up to this point in any capital budgeting problem we have always given you the set of cash-flow forecasts. In the present case you have to *derive* those forecasts.

The first problem is to decide what is going to happen to the price of gargle blasters. Marvin's new venture will increase industry capacity to 340 million units. From the demand curve in Figure 11-2, you can see that the industry can sell this number of gargle blasters only if the price declines to $5.75:

$$\text{Demand} = 80(10 - \text{price})$$

$$= 80(10 - 5.75) = 340 \text{ million units}$$

If the price falls to $5.75, what will happen to companies with the 2001 technology? They also have to make an investment decision: Should they stay in business, or should they sell their equipment for its salvage value of $2.50 per unit? With a 20 percent opportunity cost of capital, the NPV of staying in business is

$$\text{NPV} = -\text{investment} + \text{PV(price} - \text{manufacturing cost)}$$

$$= -2.50 + \frac{5.75 - 5.50}{.20} = -\$1.25 \text{ per unit}$$

Smart companies with 2001 equipment will, therefore, see that it is better to sell off capacity. No matter what their equipment originally cost or how far it is depreciated, it is more profitable to sell the equipment for $2.50 per unit than to operate it and lose $1.25 per unit.

As capacity is sold off, the supply of gargle blasters will decline and the price will rise. An equilibrium is reached when the price gets to $6. At this point 2001 equipment has a zero NPV:

$$\text{NPV} = -2.50 + \frac{6.00 - 5.50}{.20} = \$0 \text{ per unit}$$

How much capacity will have to be sold off before the price reaches \$6? You can check that by going back to the demand curve:

$$\text{Demand} = 80(10 - \text{price})$$

$$= 80(10 - 6) = 320 \text{ million units}$$

Therefore Marvin's expansion will cause the price to settle down at \$6 a unit and will induce first-generation producers to withdraw 20 million units of capacity.

But after 5 years Marvin's competitors will also be in a position to build third-generation plants. As long as these plants have positive NPVs, companies will increase their capacity and force prices down once again. A new equilibrium will be reached when the price reaches \$5. At this point, the NPV of new third-generation plants is zero, and there is no incentive for companies to expand further:

$$\text{NPV} = -10 + \frac{5.00 - 3.00}{.20} = \$0 \text{ per unit}$$

Looking back once more at our demand curve, you can see that with a price of \$5 the industry can sell a total of 400 million gargle blasters:

$$\text{Demand} = 80(10 - \text{price}) = 80(10 - 5) = 400 \text{ million units}$$

The effect of the third-generation technology is, therefore, to cause industry sales to expand from 240 million units in 2013 to 400 million 5 years later. But that rapid growth is no protection against failure. By the end of 5 years any company that has only first-generation equipment will no longer be able to cover its manufacturing costs and will be *forced* out of business.

*The Value of Marvin's New Expansion

We have shown that the introduction of third-generation technology is likely to cause gargle blaster prices to decline to \$6 for the next 5 years and to \$5 thereafter. We can now set down the expected cash flows from Marvin's new plant:

	Year 0 (Investment)	Years 1–5 (Revenue – Manufacturing Cost)	Year 6, 7, 8, . . . (Revenue – Manufacturing Cost)
Cash flow, per unit, dollars	−10	6 − 3 = 3	5 − 3 = 2
Cash flow, 100 million units, millions of dollars	−1,000	600 − 300 = 300	500 − 300 = 200

Discounting these cash flows at 20 percent gives us

$$\text{NPV} = -1000 + \sum_{t=1}^{5} \frac{300}{(1.20)^t} + \frac{1}{(1.20)^5}\left(\frac{200}{.20}\right) = \$299 \text{ million}$$

It looks as if Marvin's decision to go ahead was correct. But there is something we have forgotten. When we evaluate an investment, we must consider *all* incremental cash flows. One effect of Marvin's decision to expand is to reduce the value of its existing 2009 plant. If Marvin decided not to go ahead with the new technology, the $7 price of gargle blasters would hold until Marvin's competitors started to cut prices in 5 years' time. Marvin's decision, therefore, leads to an immediate $1 cut in price. This reduces the present value of its 2009 equipment by

$$24 \text{ million} \times \sum_{t=1}^{5} \frac{1.00}{(1.20)^t} = \$72 \text{ million}$$

Considered in isolation, Marvin's decision has an NPV of $299 million. But it also reduces the value of existing plant by $72 million. The net present value of Marvin's venture is, therefore, $299 - 72 = \$227$ million.

*Alternative Expansion Plans

Marvin's expansion has a positive NPV, but perhaps Marvin could do better to build a larger or smaller plant. You can check that by going through the same calculations as above. First you need to estimate how the additional capacity will affect gargle blaster prices. Then you can calculate the net present value of the new plant and the change in the present value of the existing plant. The total NPV of Marvin's expansion plan is

Total NPV = NPV of new plant + change in PV of existing plant

We have undertaken these calculations and plotted the results in Figure 11-3. You can see how total NPV would be affected by a smaller or larger expansion.

When the new technology becomes generally available in 2019, firms will construct a total of 280 million units of new capacity.[12] But Figure 11-3 shows that it would be foolish for Marvin to go that far. if Marvin added 280 million units of new capacity in 2014, the discounted value of the cash flows from the new plant would be zero *and* the company would have reduced the value of its old plant by $144 million. To maximize NPV, Marvin should construct 200 million units of new capacity and set the price just below $6 to drive out the 2001 manufacturers. Output is, therefore, less and price is higher than either would be under free competition.[13]

*The Value of Marvin Stock

Let us think about the effect of Marvin's announcement on the value of its common stock. Marvin has 24 million units of second-generation capacity. In the absence of any third-generation technology, gargle blaster prices would hold at $7 and Marvin's existing plant would be worth

$$\text{PV} = 24 \text{ million} \times \frac{7.00 - 3.50}{.20}$$
$$= \$420 \text{ million}$$

Marvin's new technology reduces the price of gargle blasters initially to $6 and after 5 years to $5. Therefore the value of existing plant declines to

---

[12]Total industry capacity in 2019 will be 400 million units. Of this, 120 million units are second-generation capacity, and the remaining 280 million units are third-generation capacity.

[13]Notice that we are assuming that all customers have to pay the same price for their gargle blasters. If Marvin could charge each customer the maximum price which that customer would be willing to pay, output would be the same as under free competition. Such direct price discrimination is illegal and in any case difficult to enforce. But firms do search for indirect ways to differentiate between customers. For example, stores often offer free delivery which is equivalent to a price discount for customers who live at an inconvenient distance. Publishers differentiate their products by selling hardback copies to libraries and paperbacks to impecunious students. In the early years of electronic calculators, manufacturers put a high price on their product. Although buyers knew that the price would be reduced in a year or two, the additional outlay was more than compensated for by the convenience of having the machines for the extra time.

Figure 11-3
Effect on net present value of alternative expansion plans. Marvin's 100-million-unit expansion has a total NPV of $227 million (total NPV = NPV new plant + change in PV existing plant = 299 − 72 = 227). Total NPV is maximized if Marvin builds 200 million units of new capacity. If Marvin builds 280 million units of new capacity, total NPV is −$144 million.

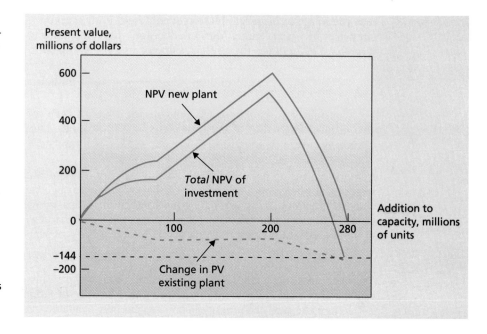

$$PV = 24 \text{ million} \times \left[\sum_{t=1}^{5} \frac{6.00 - 3.50}{(1.20)^t} + \frac{5.00 - 3.50}{.20 \times (1.20)^5} \right]$$

$$= \$252 \text{ million}$$

But the *new* plant makes a net addition to shareholders' wealth of $299 million. So after Marvin's announcement its stock will be worth

$$252 + 299 = \$551 \text{ million}[14]$$

Now here is an illustration of something we talked about in Chapter 4: Before the announcement, Marvin's stock was valued in the market at $460 million. The difference between this figure and the value of the existing plant represented the present value of Marvin's growth opportunities (PVGO). The market valued Marvin's ability to stay ahead of the game at $40 million even before the announcement. After the announcement PVGO rose to $299 million.[15]

The Lessons of Marvin Enterprises

Marvin Enterprises may be just a piece of science fiction, but the problems that it confronts are very real. Whenever Intel considers developing a new microprocessor or Genentech a new drug, these firms must face up to exactly the same issues as Marvin. We have tried to illustrate the *kind* of questions that you should be asking

---

[14]In order to finance the expansion, Marvin is going to have to sell $1000 million of new stock. Therefore the *total* value of Marvin's stock will rise to $1551 million. But investors who put up the new money will receive shares worth $1000 million. The value of Marvin's old shares after the announcement is therefore $551 million.

[15]Notice that the market value of Marvin stock will be greater than $551 million if investors expect the company to expand again within the 5-year period. In other words, PVGO after the expansion may still be positive. Investors may expect Marvin to stay one step ahead of its competitors or to successfully apply its special technology in other areas.

when presented with a set of cash-flow forecasts. Of course, no economic model is going to predict the future with accuracy. Perhaps Marvin can hold the price above $6. Perhaps competitors will not appreciate the rich pickings to be had in the year 2019. In that case, Marvin's expansion would be even more profitable. But would you want to bet $1 billion on such possibilities? We don't think so.

Investments often turn out to earn far more than the cost of capital because of a favorable surprise. This surprise may in turn create a temporary opportunity for further investments earning more than the cost of capital. But anticipated and more prolonged rents will naturally lead to the entry of rival producers. That is why you should be suspicious of any investment proposal that predicts a stream of economic rents into the indefinite future. Try to estimate *when* competition will drive the NPV down to zero, and think what that implies for the price of your product.

Many companies try to identify the major growth areas in the economy and then concentrate their investment in these areas. But the sad fate of first-generation gargle blaster manufacturers illustrates how rapidly existing plants can be made obsolete by changes in technology. It is fun being in a growth industry when you are at the forefront of the new technology, but a growth industry has no mercy on technological laggards.

You can expect to earn economic rents only if you have some superior resource such as management, sales force, design team, or production facilities. Therefore, rather than trying to move into growth areas, you would do better to identify your firm's comparative advantages and try to capitalize on them. Unfortunately, superior profits will not accrue to the firm unless it can also avoid paying the full value of the superior resources. For example, the Boeing 777 is a much more efficient plane to operate than older aircraft. But that does not mean that the airlines which operate the 777 can expect to earn supernormal profits. The greater efficiency is likely to be reflected in the price that Boeing charges for the 777. An airline will earn superior profits (i.e., economic rents) only if the 777 is more valuable to it than to other operators.[16]

We do not wish to imply that good investment opportunities don't exist. For example, such opportunities frequently arise because the firm has invested money in the past which gives it the option to expand cheaply in the future. Perhaps the firm can increase its output just by adding an extra production line, whereas its rivals would need to construct an entire new factory. In such cases, you must take into account not only *whether* it is profitable to exercise your option, but also *when* it is best to do so.

Marvin also reminded us of project interactions, which we first discussed in Chapter 6. When you estimate the incremental cash flows from a project, you must remember to include the project's impact on the rest of the business. By introducing the new technology immediately, Marvin reduced the value of its existing plant by $72 million. Sometimes the losses on existing plants may completely offset the gains from a new technology. That is why we sometimes see established, technologically advanced companies deliberately slowing down the rate at which they introduce new products.

Notice that Marvin's economic rents were equal to the difference between its costs and those of the marginal producer. The costs of the marginal 2001-generation

---

[16] The rent that you earn because equipment is worth more to you than to your rivals is known as *consumer surplus*. If Boeing were able to charge each customer the maximum price that it was prepared to pay, no airline could expect to earn a consumer surplus from operating the 777, and Boeing would capture all the benefits.

plant consisted of the manufacturing costs plus the opportunity cost of not selling the equipment. Therefore, if the salvage value of the 2001 equipment were higher, Marvin's competitors would incur higher costs and Marvin could earn higher rents. We took the salvage value as given, but it in turn depends on the cost savings from substituting outdated gargle blaster equipment for some other asset. In a well-functioning economy, assets will be used so as to minimize the *total* cost of producing the chosen set of outputs. The economic rents earned by any asset are equal to the total extra costs that would be incurred if that asset were withdrawn.

Here's another point about salvage value which takes us back to our discussion of Magna Charter in the last chapter: A high salvage value gives the firm an option to abandon a project if things start to go wrong. However, if competitors *know* that you can bail out easily, they are more likely to enter your market. If it is clear that you have no alternative but to stay and fight, they will be more cautious about competing.

When Marvin announced its expansion plans, many owners of first-generation equipment took comfort in the belief that Marvin could not compete with their fully depreciated plant. Their comfort was misplaced. Regardless of past depreciation policy, it paid to scrap first-generation equipment rather than keep it in production. Do not expect that numbers in your balance sheet can protect you from harsh economic reality.

11-4   SUMMARY

It helps to use present value when you are making investment decisions, but that is not the whole story. Good investment decisions depend both on a sensible criterion and on sensible forecasts. In this chapter we have looked at the problem of forecasting.

Projects may look attractive for two reasons: (1) There may be some errors in the sponsor's forecasts, and (2) the company can genuinely expect to earn excess profit from the project. Good managers, therefore, try to ensure that the odds are stacked in their favor by expanding in areas in which the company has a comparative advantage. We like to put this another way by saying that good managers try to identify projects which will generate "economic rents." Good managers carefully avoid expansion when competitive advantages are absent and economic rents unlikely. They do not project favorable current product prices into the future without checking whether entry or expansion by competitors will drive future prices down.

Our story of Marvin Enterprises illustrates the origin of rents and how they determine a project's cash flows and net present value.

Any present value calculation, including our calculation for Marvin Enterprises, is subject to error. That's life: There's no other sensible way to value most capital investment projects. But some assets, such as gold, real estate, crude oil, ships, and airplanes, and financial assets, such as stocks and bonds, are traded in reasonably competitive markets. When you have the market value of such an asset. *use it*, at least as a starting point for your analysis.

Further Reading

··

Most microeconomics texts contain a discussion of the determinants of economic rents. See, e.g.:
S. Fischer et al.: *Introduction to Microeconomics*, 2d ed., McGraw-Hill Book Company, New York, 1988.

For an interesting analysis of the likely effect of a new technology on the present value of existing assets, see:

S. P. Sobotka and C. Schnabel: "Linear Programming as a Device for Predicting Market Value: Prices of Used Commercial Aircraft, 1959–65," *Journal of Business,* **34**:10–30 (January 1961).

Quiz

1. Why is an M.B.A. student who has learned about DCF like a baby with a hammer? What was the point of our answer?

2. You have inherited 250 acres of prime Iowa farmland. There is an active market in land of this type, and similar properties are selling for $1000 per acre. Net cash returns per acre are $75 per year. These cash returns are expected to remain constant in real terms. How much is the land worth? A local banker has advised you to use a 12 percent discount rate.

3. True or false?
   (*a*) A firm that earns the opportunity cost of capital is earning economic rents.
   (*b*) A firm that invests in positive-NPV ventures expects to earn economic rents.
   (*c*) Financial managers should try to identify areas where their firms can earn economic rents, because it's there that positive-NPV projects are likely to be found.
   (*d*) Economic rent is the equivalent annual cost of operating capital equipment.

4. Demand for concave utility meters is expanding rapidly, but the industry is highly competitive. A utility meter plant costs $50 million to set up, and it has an annual capacity of 500,000 meters. The production cost is $5 per meter, and this cost is not expected to change. If the machines have an indefinite physical life and the cost of capital is 10 percent, what is the competitive price of a utility meter?
   (*a*) $5
   (*b*) $10
   (*c*) $15

5. The following comment appeared in *Aviation Week and Space Technology,* July 25, 1966: "Alitalia has decided against ordering an advanced-technology jet transport. The carrier's analysis, in common with some other airlines, indicates that it can operate fully depreciated Douglas DC-8's at fare levels competitive with a Boeing 747. This is because seat or ton-mile costs of a fully depreciated current generation subsonic jet may not differ greatly from the advanced-technology jet." (Here, "fully depreciated" means fully written off for *accounting* purposes.) Discuss whether the low depreciation charge on a DC-8 justifies the continued use of that plane. Under what circumstances would it pay to operate 747s?

6. If a capital equipment producer brings out a new, more efficient product, who is likely to get the benefits? In what circumstances would purchase of the new equipment be a positive-NPV investment?

7. Look back to the polyzone example at the end of Section 11-2. Explain why it was necessary to calculate the NPV of investment in polyzone capacity from the point of view of a potential European competitor.

8. Your brother-in-law wants you to join him in purchasing a building on the outskirts of town. You and he would then develop and run a Taco Palace restau-

rant. Both of you are extremely optimistic about future real estate prices in this area, and your brother-in-law has prepared a cash-flow forecast which implies a large positive NPV. This calculation assumes sale of the property after 10 years. What further calculations should you do before going ahead?

9. A new leaching process allows your company to recover some gold as a by-product of its aluminum mining operations. How would you calculate the present value of the future cash flows from gold sales?

Questions and Problems

1. Suppose that you are considering investing in an asset for which there is a reasonably good secondary market. Specifically, you're Delta Airlines, and the asset is a Boeing 757—a widely used airplane. How does the presence of a secondary market simplify your problem in principle? Do you think these simplifications could be realized in practice? Explain.

2. There is an active, competitive leasing (i.e., rental) market for most standard types of commercial jets. Many of the planes flown by the major domestic and international airlines are not owned by them but leased for periods ranging from a few months to several years.

    Gamma Airlines, however, owns two long-range DC-11s just withdrawn from Latin American service. Gamma is considering using these planes to develop the potentially lucrative new route from Akron to Yellowknife. A considerable investment in terminal facilities, training, and advertising will be required. Once committed, Gamma will have to operate the route for at least 3 years. One further complication: The manager of Gamma's international division is opposing commitment of the planes to the Akron-Yellowknife route because of anticipated future growth in traffic through Gamma's new hub in Ulan Bator.

    How would you evaluate the proposed Akron-Yellowknife project? Give a detailed list of the necessary steps in your analysis. Explain how the airplane leasing market would be taken into account. If the project is attractive, how would you respond to the manager of the international division?

3. New-model commercial airplanes are much more fuel-efficient than older models. How is it possible for an airline flying older models to make money when its direct competitors are flying newer planes? Explain.

4. Thanks to acquisition of a key patent, your company now has exclusive production rights for barkelgassers (BGs) in North America. Production facilities for 200,000 BGs per year will require a $25 million immediate capital expenditure. Production costs are estimated at $65 per BG. The BG marketing manager is confident that all 200,000 units can be sold for $100 per unit (in real terms) until the patent runs out 5 years hence. After that the marketing manager hasn't a clue about what the selling price will be.

    What is the NPV of the BG project? Assume the real cost of capital is 9 percent. To keep things simple, also make the following assumptions:

    ■ The technology for making BGs will not change. Capital and production costs will stay the same in real terms.

    ■ Competitors know the technology and can enter as soon as the patent expires, that is, in year 6.

- If your company invests immediately, full production begins after 12 months, that is, in year 1.
- There are no taxes.
- BG production facilities last 12 years. They have no salvage value at the end of their useful life.

5. How would your answer to question 4 change if:

- Technological improvements reduce the cost of new BG production facilities by 3 percent per year?

Thus a new plant built in year 1 would cost only 25 (1 − .03) = $24.25 million; a plant built in year 2 would cost $23.52 million; and so on. Assume that production costs per unit remain at $65.

6. Reevaluate the NPV of the proposed polyzone project under each of the following assumptions. Follow the format of Table 11-3. What's the right management decision in each case?
   (*a*) Competitive entry does not begin until year 5, when the spread falls to $1.10 per pound, and is complete in year 6, when the spread is $.95 per pound.
   (*b*) The U.S. chemical company can start up polyzone production at 40 million pounds in year 1 rather than year 2.
   (*c*) The U.S. company makes a technological advance which reduces its annual production costs to $25 million. Competitors' production costs do not change.

7. Photographic laboratories recover and recycle the silver used in photographic film. Stikine River Photo is considering purchase of improved equipment for their laboratory at Telegraph Creek. Here is the information they have:

- The equipment costs $100,000.
- It will cost $80,000 per year to run.
- It has an economic life of 10 years but can be depreciated over 5 years by the straight-line method (see Section 6-2).
- It will recover an additional 5000 ounces of silver per year.
- Silver is selling for $20 per ounce. Over the past 10 years, the price of silver has appreciated by 4.5 percent per year in real terms. Silver is traded in an active, competitive market.
- Stikine's marginal tax rate is 35 percent. Assume U.S. tax law.
- Stikine's company cost of capital is 8 percent in real terms.

   What is the NPV of the new equipment? Make additional assumptions as necessary.

8. The manufacture of polysyllabic acid is a competitive industry. Most plants have an annual output of 100,000 tons. Operating costs are 90 cents a ton, and the sales price is $1 a ton. A 100,000-ton plant costs $100,000 and has an indefinite life. Its current scrap value of $60,000 is expected to decline to $57,900 over the next 2 years.

   Phlogiston, Inc., proposes to invest $100,000 in a plant that employs a new low-cost process to manufacture polysyllabic acid. The plant has the same capacity as existing units, but operating costs are 85 cents a ton. Phlogiston estimates that it has 2 years' lead over each of its rivals in use of the process but is unable to build any more plants itself before year 2. Also it believes that demand over the next 2 years is likely to be sluggish and that its new plant will therefore cause temporary overcapacity.

You can assume that there are no taxes and that the cost of capital is 10 percent.

(a) By the end of year 2, the prospective increase in acid demand will require the construction of several new plants using the Phlogiston process. What is the likely NPV of such plants?

(b) What would be the present value of each of these new plants?

(c) What does that imply for the price of polysyllabic acid in year 3 and beyond?

(d) Would you expect existing plant to be scrapped in year 2? How would your answer differ if scrap value were $40,000 or $80,000?

(e) The acid plants of United Alchemists, Inc., have been fully depreciated. Can it operate them profitably after year 2?

(f) Acidosis, Inc., purchased a new plant last year for $100,000 and is writing it down by $10,000 a year. Should it scrap this plant in year 2?

(g) What would be the present value of Phlogiston's venture?

9. The Cambridge Opera Association has come up with a unique door prize for its December (1998) fund-raising ball: Twenty door prizes will be distributed, each one a ticket entitling the bearer to receive a cash award from the association on December 30, 1999. The cash award is to be determined by calculating the ratio of the level of the Standard and Poor's Composite Index of stock prices on December 30, 1999, to its level on June 30, 1999, and multiplying by $100. Thus, if the index turns out to be 250 on June 30, 1999, and 300 on December 30, 1999, the payoff will be $100 \times (300/250) = \$120$.

After the ball, a black market springs up in which the tickets are traded. What will the tickets sell for on January 1, 1999? On June 30, 1999? Assume the risk-free interest rate is 10 percent per year. Also assume the Cambridge Opera Association will be solvent at year-end 1999 and will, in fact, pay off on the tickets. Make other assumptions as necessary.

Would ticket values be different if the tickets' payoffs depended on the Dow Jones industrial index rather than the Standard and Poor's composite?

10. You are asked to value a large building in northern New Jersey. The valuation is needed for a bankruptcy settlement. Here are the facts:

■ The settlement *requires* that the building's value equal the present value of the *net cash proceeds* the railroad would receive if it cleared the building and sold it for its highest and best nonrailroad use, which is as a warehouse.

■ The building has been appraised at $1 million. This figure is based on actual recent selling prices of a sample of similar New Jersey buildings used as, or available for use as, warehouses.

■ If rented today as a warehouse, the building could generate $80,000 per year. This cash flow is calculated *after* out-of-pocket operating expenses and *after* real estate taxes of $50,000 per year:

Gross rents	$180,000
Operating expenses	50,000
Real estate taxes	50,000
Net	$80,000

Gross rents, operating expenses, and real estate taxes are uncertain but are expected to grow with inflation.

■ However, it would take 1 year and $200,000 to clear out the railroad equipment and prepare the building for use as a warehouse. This expenditure would be spread evenly over the next year.

■ The property will be put on the market when ready for use as a warehouse. Your real estate adviser says that properties of this type take, on average, 1 year to sell after they are put on the market. However, the railroad could rent the building as a warehouse while waiting for it to sell.

■ The opportunity cost of capital for investment in real estate is 8 percent in *real* terms.

■ Your real estate adviser notes that selling prices of comparable buildings in northern New Jersey have declined, in real terms, at an average rate of 2 percent per year over the last 10 years.

■ A 5 percent sales commission would be paid by the railroad at the time of the sale.

■ The railroad pays no income taxes. It would have to pay property taxes.

*11. The world airline system is composed of the routes X and Y, each of which requires 10 aircraft. These routes can be serviced by three types of aircraft—A, B, and C. There are 5 type A aircraft available, 10 type B, and 10 type C. These aircraft are identical except for their operating costs, which are as follows:

	ANNUAL OPERATING COST, THOUSANDS OF DOLLARS	
Aircraft Type	Route X	Route Y
A	15	15
B	25	20
C	45	35

The aircraft have a useful life of 5 years and a salvage value of $10,000.

The aircraft owners do not operate the aircraft themselves but rent them to the operators. Owners act competitively to maximize their rental income, and operators attempt to minimize their operating costs. Air fares are also competitively determined.

Assume the cost of capital is 10 percent.

(*a*) Which aircraft would be used on which route, and how much would each aircraft be worth?

(*b*) What would happen to usage and prices of each aircraft if the number of type A aircraft increased to 10?

(*c*) What would happen if the number of type A aircraft increased to 15?

(*d*) What would happen if the number of type A aircraft increased to 20? State any additional assumptions you need to make.

*12. Taxes are a cost, and, therefore, changes in tax rates can affect consumer prices, project lives, and the value of existing firms. The following (quite hard) problem illustrates this. It also illustrates that tax changes that appear to be "good for business" do not always increase the value of existing firms. Indeed, unless new investment incentives increase consumer demand, they can work only by rendering existing equipment obsolete.

The manufacture of bucolic acid is a competitive business. Demand is steadily expanding, and new plants are constantly being opened. Expected cash flows from an investment in plant are as follows:

	0	1	2	3
1. Initial investment	100			
2. Revenues		100	100	100
3. Cash operating costs		50	50	50
4. Tax depreciation		33.33	33.33	33.33
5. Income pretax		16.67	16.67	16.67
6. Tax at 40%		6.67	6.67	6.67
7. Net income		10	10	10
8. After-tax salvage				15
9. Cash flow (7 + 8 + 4 − 1)	−100	+43.33	+43.33	+58.33
NPV at 20% = 0				

Assumptions:
1. Tax depreciation is straight-line over 3 years.
2. Pretax salvage value is 25 in year 3 and 50 if the asset is scrapped in year 2.
3. Tax on salvage value is 40 percent of the difference between salvage value and depreciated investment.
4. The cost of capital is 20 percent.

(a) What is the value of a 1-year-old plant? Of a 2-year-old plant?

(b) Suppose that the government now changes tax depreciation to allow a 100 percent writeoff in year 1. How does this affect the value of existing 1- and 2-year-old plants? Existing plants must continue using the original tax depreciation schedule.

(c) Would it now make sense to scrap existing plants when they are 2 rather than 3 years old?

(d) How would your answers change if the corporate income tax were abolished entirely?

12

Organizing Capital Expenditure and Evaluating Performance

Up to this point we've considered how a firm *should* set its capital budget. In this chapter we discuss how it is done in practice. We pay particular attention to the organization of capital budgeting and to the administrative problems that inevitably crop up.

A good capital budgeting system does more than just make accept-reject decisions on individual projects. It must tie into the firm's long-range planning process—the process that chooses the direction of the firm's business and sets out plans for financing, production, marketing, research, and so on. It must also tie into a procedure for measurement of performance. Otherwise the firm has no way of knowing how its expenditure decisions finally turn out. Measurement of performance occupies a substantial part of this chapter. The pitfalls in measuring profitability are serious but not as widely recognized as they should be.

12-1 CAPITAL BUDGETS AND PROJECT AUTHORIZATIONS

For most sizable firms, the first step in the investment process is the preparation of an annual **capital budget,** which is a list of planned investments by plant and division. (In this chapter we will think of plants as building blocks for divisions and divisions as building blocks for firms. That is arbitrary: There may be more than two layers. Also, divisions are often organized by product line, region, or some other business unit.) In principle, the capital budget should be a list of all positive-NPV opportunities open to the firm.

Most firms let project proposals bubble up from plants for review by division management and from divisions for review by senior management. The administrative process typically works as follows.

Plant managers identify "interesting" opportunities, analyze them, and decide which ones are really worthwhile. Proposed expenditures for these projects are then submitted to division managers for further review. Some of the proposals by the plants do not "make the cut" at the divisional level. But divisional management may add its own ideas, usually new, larger ventures, such as manufacturing a new product, that plant managers could not be expected to initiate. The lists of the divisions are forwarded to the corporate controller, who prunes and consolidates them into a proposed company budget. For very large, diversified firms there may be several intermediate review stages.

The resulting budget is a list of proposed new projects for the coming year and any projects from former years that are incomplete. Supporting information is usually provided on standard forms, supplemented by descriptive memoranda for larger projects. Since approval of the budget does not give the final go-ahead to spend money, backup information is not as detailed at this stage as it is later. Projects below a specific size are typically not even listed separately, but are simply included under a blanket approval for a given division or plant. In many companies the budget also contains rough estimates of likely expenditures over a 5-year period.

The suggested budget is then reviewed by senior management and staff specializing in planning and financial analysis. Usually there are negotiations between the firm's senior management and its divisional management, and perhaps there will also be special analyses of major outlays or ventures into new areas, before the budget is submitted to the board for approval. Once approved, the budget generally remains the basis for planning over the ensuing year. In a few firms, however, it is updated each quarter.

Because each proposal in the budget needs to be authorized subsequently, the use of a budget involves some duplication of effort. But it allows information exchange up and down the management hierarchy before attitudes have hardened and personal commitments have been made. The danger with the whole procedure is loss of flexibility. There is a tendency for most projects to appear for the first time in the annual budget, and in some companies it is difficult to initiate project ideas at any other time of the year.

Project Authorizations

The approval of a capital budget rarely provides the go-ahead to make the expenditures listed in the budget. Most companies demand that formal **appropriation requests** be prepared for each proposal. These requests are accompanied by more or less elaborate backup, depending on the project's size, novelty, and strategic importance. Also, the type of backup information required depends on the project category. Some firms use a fourfold breakdown:

1. Safety or environmental outlays required by law or company policy, e.g., for pollution control equipment
2. Maintenance or cost reduction, e.g., machine replacement
3. Capacity expansion in existing businesses
4. Investment for new products or ventures

The information requirements for projects differ across these categories:

1. Pollution control does not have to pay its own way. The main issue is whether standards are met at minimum present value of cost. The decision is likely to hinge on engineering analyses of alternative technologies.
2. Engineering analysis is also important in machine replacement, but new machines have to pay their own way. In category 2, the firm faces the classic capital budgeting problems described in Chapter 6.

3. Projects in category 3 are less straightforward; these decisions may hinge on forecasts of demand, of possible shifts in technology, and of competitors' strategies. We looked at these issues in Chapter 11.

4. Projects in category 4 are most likely to depend on intangibles. The first projects in a new area may not have positive NPVs if they are considered in isolation, yet the firm may go ahead in order to establish a position in a market and to pave the way for profitable future projects. The first projects are not undertaken for their own sake, but because they generate valuable *options* to undertake follow-up projects.[1] Thus, for projects in category 4, cash-flow forecasts may be less important than the issue of whether the firm enjoys some technological or other advantage which promises to generate economic rents for the firm. That issue becomes the main focus of project analysis.

Most large firms have manuals providing checklists to make sure that all relevant costs and alternatives are considered. The manual may contain instructions showing how to forecast cash flows and how to compute NPV, internal rate of return, or other measures of project value. Usually the manual also specifies the opportunity cost of capital.[2]

Although appropriation requests may be prepared by the project originator, the plant manager is usually responsible for submitting them. These requests come up through the ranks of operating management for approval at each succeeding level. If the project is large, the request may be checked at some stage by staff accountants, engineers, and economists. The number of hurdles the proposal must pass depends on the expenditure involved.

Because the investment decision is central to the development of the firm, authorization tends to be reserved for senior management. Almost all companies set ceilings on the size of capital projects that divisional managers can authorize without specific approval from their superiors. Moreover, the ceilings are surprisingly low. Scapens and Sale surveyed 203 larger firms, with average capital budgets of $130 million per year, and found that the average ceiling for individual projects was only $136,000.[3] Ceilings have risen since this survey but are still small fractions of total capital expenditures. When you consider that a large company may generate thousands of appropriation requests each year, the limited extent of delegation is striking.

The Decision Criteria Firms Actually Use

These days almost all large companies use discounted cash flow in some form. But many companies also compute flawed measures such as payback. Why does payback survive even in successful and sophisticated companies?

---

[1] We discuss how to value these capital investment options in Chapter 21.

[2] As the following conversation with one finance director suggests, having a manual is not the same as using it:

> *Finance director:* I can give you a copy of our capital expenditure control manual.
> *Interviewer:* Did you have any hand in putting it together?
> *Finance director:* Absolutely not. I think they're extremely boring. I have no idea of my way around it.

Cited in P. R. Marsh, T. P. Barwise, K. Thomas, and J. R. C. Wensley, "Managing Strategic Investment Decisions in Large Diversified Companies," in A. M. Pettigrew (ed.), *Competitiveness and the Management Process,* Basil Blackwell, Oxford, 1988, p. 101.

[3] R. W. Scapens and J. T. Sale, "Performance Measurement and Formal Capital Expenditure Controls in Divisionalized Companies," *Journal of Business Finance and Accounting,* **8**:389–420 (Autumn 1981).

When pressed, managers usually concede that, if followed literally, the payback rule doesn't make sense. But they may point out that payback is the simplest way to *communicate* an idea of project profitability. Capital budgeting is a process of discussion and negotiation involving people from all parts of the firm, and therefore it is important to have a measure that everyone can understand. Insisting that everyone commenting on a project do so in terms of NPV may cut out those who don't understand NPV but who can still contribute useful information.

Other managers will check on the project's payback because they know that in a competitive world high profits do not last forever, and therefore they may distrust the more distant cash-flow forecasts. Looking at payback, which ignores the later cash flows completely, provides a rough-and-ready check on project profitability. Of course, it would be better to do a careful analysis of when competition will intensify and what effect that will have on cash flows.

The use of intelligent techniques does not guarantee intelligent decisions. You can have good technique and poor judgment, or vice versa. You can be conceptually perfect, by relying on NPV, and still fall down in execution. For example, many companies think they can ignore inflation in cash-flow forecasts because "on the average revenues increase to cover inflated costs." Others use nominal discount rates without fully reflecting future inflation in their cash-flow forecasts. We discussed these elementary mistakes in Chapter 6.

Before we get too smug, remember that businesspeople often act smarter than they talk. (For students and scholars it is the other way around.) They may make correct decisions, but they may not be able to explain them in the language of finance and economics. Many decisions are fundamentally intuitive. If *intuitive* sounds capricious, replace the word with *informed judgment*. As we argued in Chapter 11, if a firm enjoys an advantage that promises to generate economic rents, it should probably press on regardless of calculated payback or present value. Experience helps in identifying such opportunities.

Controlling Capital Investment Decisions

Most large companies have corporate capital budgeting staffs who help to enforce consistency, uncover unspecified assumptions, and undertake sophisticated analyses of major projects.

Their analyses may also have to ferret out local managers who are evading the controls in the capital investment process. For example, managers may be permitted to approve projects only up to a certain value. But this authority may become infinite if each project can be broken down into a large number of small parts. The following story illustrates this problem:

> *Our [top managers] like to make all the major capital decisions. They think they do, but I've just seen one case where a division beat them.*
>
> *I received for editing a capital request from the division for a large chimney. I couldn't see what anyone could do with just a chimney so I flew out for a visit. They've built and equipped a whole plant on plant expense orders. The chimney is the only indivisible item that exceeded the $50,000 limit we put on the expense orders. Apparently they learned informally that a new plant wouldn't be favorably received, and since they thought the business needed it, and the return would justify it, they built the damn thing.[4]*

---

[4]Cited in J. L. Bower, *Managing the Resource Allocation Process: A Study of Corporate Planning and Investment*, Division of Research, Graduate School of Business Administration, Harvard University, Boston, 1970, p. 15.

This embarrassment might have been avoided if the firm had imposed a limit on individual discretionary expenditures *and* on the total amount of such expenditures by each manager in any one year.

The boundaries of "capital expenditure" are often imprecise. Consider the investments in information technology, or IT (computers, software and systems, training, and telecommunications), made by large banks and securities firms. These investments soak up *hundreds* of millions of dollars annually, and some multiyear IT projects have cost well over $1 billion. Yet much of this expenditure goes to intangibles such as system design, testing, or training. Such outlays often bypass capital expenditure controls, particularly if they are made piecemeal rather than as large, discrete commitments. The problems here are obvious. Authorization procedures should be broadly construed and not encourage the inefficient substitution of one kind of investment for another.

Authorization requests should draw attention to all likely contingent expenditures. Too often, seemingly small and innocuous investments are the first step in a chain of economically dependent investments. Management should be aware of the full consequences of letting a plant or division get its foot in the door.

12-2 PROBLEMS AND SOME SOLUTIONS

Good investment decisions require good data. How can you organize the capital budgeting operation to get the kind of information that you need? We suggest five problems that you need to think about.

Ensuring That Forecasts Are Consistent

Inconsistent assumptions often creep into investment proposals. Suppose that the manager of your furniture division is bullish on housing starts but the manager of your appliance division is bearish. This inconsistency makes the furniture division's projects look better than the appliance division's. Senior management ought to negotiate a consensus estimate and make sure that all NPVs are recomputed using that joint estimate. Then a rational decision can be made.

This is why many firms begin the capital budgeting process by establishing forecasts of economic indicators, such as inflation and growth in gross national product, as well as forecasts of particular items that are important to the firm's business, such as housing starts or the price of raw materials. These forecasts can then be used as the basis for all project analyses.

Eliminating Conflicts of Interest

Plant and divisional managers are concerned about their own futures. Sometimes their interests conflict with stockholders', and that may lead to investment decisions that do not maximize shareholder wealth. For example, new plant managers naturally want to demonstrate good performance right away, in order to move up the corporate ladder. Perhaps they will propose quick-payback projects even if NPV is sacrificed. And if their performance is judged on book earnings, they will also be attracted by projects whose accounting results look good.

The problem lies in the way many firms measure performance and reward managers. Don't expect them to concentrate only on NPV if you always demand quick results or if you will reward them later on the basis of book return. More on this later in the chapter.

Another potential conflict of interest arises because some managers are less willing to take risks than others. They may let their attitude toward risk interfere with their business judgment. Managers of divisions that have assured good performance are more likely to propose high-risk projects than managers of faltering divisions with an uncertain future. Also, a large division is more likely than a small division to risk a $1 million loss. Such a loss might merely make a dent in the profits of the larger division, but it could put the manager of the small division out of work.

This problem ties back to how the manager's performance is measured and rewarded. A good measurement and reward system should have some tolerance for mistakes and should be able to discriminate between good decisions and lucky ones. Ideally, managers would be rewarded for good decisions thwarted by bad luck and penalized for bad decisions rescued by good luck.

Reducing Forecast Bias

Anyone who is keen to get a project proposal accepted is likely to look on the bright side when forecasting the project's cash flows. Such overoptimism seems to be a common feature in financial forecasts. (It afflicts governments too, probably more than private businesses. How often have you heard of a new missile, dam, or highway that actually cost *less* than was originally forecasted?)

You will probably never be able to eliminate bias completely, but if you are aware of why bias occurs, you are at least part of the way there. Project sponsors are likely to overstate their case deliberately only if you, the manager, encourage them to do so. For example, if they believe that success depends on having the largest division rather than the most profitable one, they will propose large expansion projects that they do not truly believe have positive NPVs. Or if they believe that you won't listen to them unless they paint a rosy picture, you will be presented with many rosy pictures. Or if you invite each division to compete for limited resources, you will find that each attempts to outbid the other for those resources. The fault in such cases is your own—if you hold up the hoop, others will try to jump through it.

Getting Senior Management the Information That It Needs

Valuing capital investment opportunities is hard enough when you can do the entire job yourself. In real life it is a cooperative effort. Although cooperation brings more knowledge to bear, it has its own problems. Some are unavoidable—just another cost of doing business. Others can be alleviated by adding checks and balances to the investment process.

Many of the problems stem from sponsors' eagerness to obtain approval for their favorite projects. As the proposal travels up the organization, alliances are formed. Preparation of the request inevitably involves discussions and compromises which limit subsequent freedom of action. Thus once a division has screened its plants' proposals, the plants unite in competing against "outsiders."

This competition among divisions can be put to good use if it forces division managers to develop a well-thought-out case for what they want to do. But the competition has its costs as well. Several thousand appropriation requests may reach the senior management level each year, all essentially sales documents presented by united fronts and designed to persuade. Alternative schemes have been filtered out at an earlier stage. The danger is that senior management cannot obtain (let alone absorb) the information to evaluate each project rationally.

The dangers are illustrated by the following practical question: Should we establish a definite opportunity cost of capital for computing the NPV of projects in our furniture division? The answer in theory is a clear yes, providing that the projects of the division are all in the same risk class. Remember that most project analysis is done at the plant or divisional level. Only a small proportion of project ideas analyzed survive for submission to top management. Plant and division managers cannot judge projects correctly unless they know the true opportunity cost of capital.

Suppose that senior management settles on 12 percent. That helps plant managers make rational decisions. But it also tells them exactly how optimistic they have to be to get their pet project accepted. Brealey and Myers's Second Law states that *the proportion of proposed projects having a positive NPV is independent of top management's estimate of the opportunity cost of capital.*[5]

This is not a facetious conjecture. The law was tested in a large oil company, whose capital budgeting staff kept careful statistics on forecasted profitability of proposed projects. One year top management announced a big push to conserve cash. It imposed discipline on capital expenditures by increasing the corporate hurdle rate by several percentage points. But staff statistics showed that the fraction of proposals with positive NPVs stayed rock-steady at about 85 percent of all proposals. Top management's tighter discipline was repaid with expanded optimism.

A firm that accepts poor information at the top faces two consequences. First, senior management cannot evaluate individual projects. In a study by Bower of a large multidivisional company, projects that had the approval of a division general manager were seldom turned down by his or her group of divisions, and those reaching top management were almost never rejected.[6] Second, since managers have limited control over project-by-project decisions, capital investment decisions are effectively decentralized regardless of what formal procedures specify.

Some senior managers try to impose discipline and offset optimism by setting rigid capital expenditure limits. This artificial capital rationing forces plant or division managers to set priorities. The firm ends up using capital rationing not because capital is truly unobtainable but as a way of decentralizing decisions.

There's a general point here. When we say that firms should accept all projects with positive NPVs, we implicitly assume that the forecasts on which those NPVs are based are unbiased. But if managers are fed optimistic forecasts, you may find that ad hoc procedures may actually lead to better decisions than the net present value rule. We should stress that we are not *recommending* the use of ad hoc criteria. The essential point is that improvements in one aspect of the decision-making process must take account of deficiencies in other areas.

Recognizing Strategic "Fit"

We have pictured the capital investment process as if all proposals bubbled up from the bottom of the organization. That is never the whole story. The managers of plants A and B cannot be expected to see the potential economies of scale of closing their plants and consolidating production at a new plant C. We expect divisional management to propose plant C. Similarly, divisions 1 and 2 may not be eager to give up their own data processing operations to a large, central computer. That proposal would come from senior management.

The final capital budget must also reflect strategic choices made by senior management. Strategic planning attempts to identify businesses in which the firm has a real competitive advantage. It also attempts to identify businesses to sell or liquidate as well as declining businesses that should be allowed to run down. Strategic planning is really capital budgeting on a grand scale.

The problem is that a firm's capital investment choices should reflect both "bottom-up" and "top-down" processes—capital budgeting and strategic planning, respectively. The two processes should complement each other. Plant and division managers, who do most of the work in bottom-up capital budgeting, may not see the

---

[5]There is no first law. We thought that "Second Law" sounded better. There *is* a third law, but that is for another chapter.

[6]See Bower, op. cit.

forest for the trees. Strategic planners may have a mistaken view of the forest because they do not look at the trees one by one.

12-3 EVALUATING PERFORMANCE

Managers are likely to act in shareholders' interest only if they have the right incentives. Therefore the way that managers are measured and rewarded must tie in with the capital investment process.

Most firms have formal procedures for evaluating the performance of their capital investments. There are three aspects to performance measurement. First, companies need to monitor projects under construction to ensure that there are no serious delays or cost overruns. Second, companies generally conduct **postaudits** on major projects shortly after they have begun to operate. These help to identify problems that need fixing, to check the accuracy of forecasts, and to suggest questions that should have been asked before the project was undertaken. Postaudits pay off mainly by helping managers do a better job when they come to analyze the next round of investment proposals. Finally, there is ongoing performance measurement, which is done through the firm's accounting and control system. We will explain how that system should work to support the capital investment process and why it sometimes fails.

Controlling Projects in Progress

A decision to authorize capital expenditure usually specifies how much money may be spent and when. Control is established by accounting procedures for recording expenditures as they occur. Typically, companies will permit up to 10 percent expenditure overruns, but beyond that the sponsor is required to submit a supplemental request for funds. To ensure that the money is not diverted to other uses, the sponsor is also required to submit a revised request if there is any significant change in the nature of the project.

To avoid delays, a few companies attempt to set limits on the length of time before construction begins. Almost all firms require the project sponsor to submit a formal notice of completion, so that the accumulated costs can be transferred to the permanent accounts and any unspent cash can be recovered rather than kept in a hidden kitty for miscellaneous uses.

These procedures are necessary aspects of control. More general information on progress is usually contained in monthly or quarterly status reports.

Postaudits

Postaudits of capital expenditures are now undertaken in most large firms. Not all projects are audited, and those that are are usually audited only once. A few firms require further audits for "problem" projects. The most common time for audits is 1 year after construction has been completed.

It makes sense to check on the progress of recent investments. Otherwise problems may go undetected and uncorrected. Postaudits can also provide useful insights to the next round of decision making on capital investments. After a postaudit the controller may say, "We should have anticipated the extra working capital needed to support the project." So the next time working capital will get the attention it deserves.

The postaudit is sometimes used to monitor the quality of forecasts made by project proposers. However, it is worth sounding a note of caution here. The audit is usually taken far too soon after installation to provide any clear assessment of the project's success. And since the forecasters rarely specify the economic assumptions underlying their forecasts, it is hard to tell whether they really got it right or whether they were bailed out by a buoyant economy. Finally, the number of audited projects is so small and their authorship so imprecise that it is difficult to associate forecasting ability with a particular type of project or proposer.

Of course, the mere threat of postaudit may spur the proposer to greater accuracy. But it can work the other way around. Many managers make conservative forecasts in the belief that what matters is to beat one's forecasts. This is illustrated in the following conversation:

First project team member: The other question we need to decide in a wider context is how much we want to declare we want to save.

Second project team member: Yes, we'll decide on the politics. . . . Don't want to be putting too much savings. . . . We can come back with another little bit later on.[7]

Problems in Measuring Incremental Cash Flows after the Fact

Often postaudits cannot measure all cash flows generated by a project. It may be impossible to split the project away from the rest of the business.

Suppose that you have just taken over a trucking firm which operates a package delivery service for local stores. You decide to try to revitalize the business by cutting costs and improving service. This requires three investment projects:

1. Buy five new trucks.
2. Construct two additional dispatching centers.
3. Buy a small computer to keep track of packages and schedule trucks.

A year later you try a postaudit of the computer. You verify that it is working properly and check actual costs of purchase, installation, and training against projections. But how do you identify the incremental *inflows* generated by the computer? No one has kept records of the extra gas that *would have* been used or the extra packages that *would have* been lost, had the computer not been installed. You may be able to verify that service is better, but how much of the improvement comes from the new trucks, how much from the dispatching centers, and how much from the new computer? It is impossible to say. The only meaningful way to judge success or failure of your revitalization program is to examine the delivery business as a whole.[8]

Evaluating Operating Performance

Think again of your package delivery business. We could measure its performance in two ways:

1. *Actual versus projected.* We could compare actual operating earnings or cash flow with what you predicted.
2. *Actual profitability versus an absolute standard of profitability.* We could also compare actual profitability with the cost of capital. In other words, we could look at whether with hindsight the project has provided the return that investors required.

The first measure is relatively easy to understand and implement, although it may be difficult to tell whether the deviations from forecast reflect poor analysis or bad luck. The second measure is full of pitfalls, as we will now see.

---

[7]Cited in P. R. Marsh, T. P. Barwise, K. Thomas, and J. R. C. Wensley, op. cit., p. 121.

[8]Even here you don't know the incremental cash flows that have resulted from your efforts unless you can establish what the business would have earned if you had not made the changes. It is often far from clear what is the appropriate base case from which to measure these incremental cash flows.

BIASES IN ACCOUNTING RATES OF RETURN.   Business periodicals regularly report book (accounting) rates of return on investment (ROIs) for companies and industries. ROI is just the ratio of after-tax operating income to the net (depreciated) book value of assets. We rejected book ROI as a capital investment criterion in Chapter 5, and in fact few companies now use it for that purpose. But they do use it to evaluate profitability of existing businesses, because there is usually no alternative.

Consider the pharmaceutical and chemical industries. According to Table 12-1, pharmaceutical companies have done much better than chemical companies. Are the pharmaceutical companies *really* that profitable? If so, lots of companies should be rushing

TABLE 12-1

Average after-tax accounting rates of return, as reported by *Fortune*, 1989–1993

Pharmaceutical	Average Book ROI	Chemical	Average Book ROI
Johnson & Johnson	12.8%	du Pont	1.6%
Bristol-Myers Squibb	16.8	Dow Chemical	4.4
Merck & Company	19.0	Monsanto	4.4
Abbot Laboratories	17.6	Hoechst Celanese	2.1
American Home Products	20.6	W. R. Grace	1.4
Pfizer	7.8	Union Carbide	1.6
Eli Lilly & Company	12.2		
Median	9.6%	Median	4.1%

Source: *Fortune* 500, various issues. Note that medians are calculated for a larger number of companies than listed in this table.

TABLE 12-2

Comparison of a pharmaceutical company and a chemical company, each in a no-growth steady state (figures in millions of dollars). Revenues, costs, total investment, and annual cash flow are identical. But the pharmaceutical company invests more in R&D.

	Pharmaceutical	Chemical
Revenues	1,000	1,000
Operating costs, out-of-pocket*	500	500
Net operating cash flow	500	500
Investment in:		
Plant and equipment	100	300
R&D	300	100
Total investment	400	400
Annual cash flow†	+100	+100

*Operating costs do *not* include any charge for depreciation.
†Cash flow = revenues − operating costs − total investment.

into the pharmaceutical business. Or is there something wrong with the ROI measure?

Pharmaceutical companies have done well, but they look more profitable than they really are. Book ROIs are biased upward for companies with intangible investments such as research and development (R&D), simply because accountants don't put these outlays on the balance sheet.

Table 12-2 shows cash inflows and outflows for two mature companies. Neither is growing. Each must plow back $400 million to maintain its existing business. The *only* difference is that the chemical company's plowback goes mostly to plant and equipment; the pharmaceutical company invests mostly in R&D. The chemical company invests only one-third as much in R&D ($100 versus $300 million) but triples the pharmaceutical company's investment in fixed assets.

Table 12-3 calculates the annual depreciation charges. Notice that the sum of R&D and total annual depreciation is identical for the two companies.

The companies' cash flows, true profitability, and true present values are also identical, but as Table 12-4 shows, the pharmaceutical company's book ROI is 18 percent, *triple* the chemical company's. The accountants would get annual income right (in this case it is identical to cash flow) but understate the value of the pharmaceutical company's assets relative to the chemical company's. Lower asset value creates the upward-biased pharmaceutical ROI.

TABLE 12-3

••

Book asset values and annual depreciation for the pharmaceutical and chemical companies described in Table 12-2 (figures in millions of dollars)

	PHARMACEUTICAL		CHEMICAL	
Age, Years	Original Cost of Investment	Net Book Value	Original Cost of Investment	Net Book Value
0 (new)	100	100	300	300
1	100	90	300	270
2	100	80	300	240
3	100	70	300	210
4	100	60	300	180
5	100	50	300	150
6	100	40	300	120
7	100	30	300	90
8	100	20	300	60
9	100	10	300	30
Total net book value		550		1,650

	Pharmaceutical	Chemical
Annual depreciation*	100	300
R&D expense	300	100
Total depreciation and R&D	400	400

*The pharmaceutical company has 10 vintages of assets, each depreciated by $10 per year. Total depreciation per year is 10 × 10 = $100 million. The chemical company's depreciation is 10 × 30 = $300 million.

TABLE 12-4
• •

Book ROIs for the companies described in Table 12-2 (figures in millions of dollars). The chemical and pharmaceutical companies' cash flows and values are identical. But the pharmaceutical's accounting rate of return is triple the chemical's. This bias occurs because accountants do not show the value of investment in R&D on the balance sheet.

	Pharmaceutical	Chemical
Revenues	1,000	1,000
Operating costs, out-of-pocket	500	500
R&D expense	300	100
Depreciation*	100	300
Net income	100	100
Net book value*	550	1,650
Book ROI	18%	6%

*Calculated in Table 12-3.

The first moral is this: Do not assume that businesses with high book ROIs are necessarily performing better. They may just have more "hidden" assets, that is, assets which accountants do not put on balance sheets.

This hidden-assets problem is only one of several reasons why accounting rates of return are biased. We take a closer look in the next section.

12-4 EXAMPLE—MEASURING THE PROFITABILITY OF THE NODHEAD SUPERMARKET

Supermarket chains invest heavily in building and equipping new stores. The regional manager of a chain is about to propose investing $1 million in a new store in Nodhead. Projected cash flows are:

	YEAR						
	1	2	3	4	5	6	After 6
Cash flow, thousands of dollars	100	200	250	298	298	298	0

Of course, real supermarkets last more than 6 years. But these numbers are realistic in one important sense: It may take 2 or 3 years for a new store to catch on—that is, to build up a substantial, habitual clientele. Thus cash flow is low for the first few years even in the best locations.

We will assume the opportunity cost of capital is 10 percent. The Nodhead store's NPV at 10 percent is zero. It is an acceptable project, but not an unusually good one:

TABLE 12-5

· ·

Forecasted book income and ROI for the proposed Nodhead store. Book ROI is lower than the true rate of return for the first 2 years and higher thereafter.

	YEAR					
	1	2	3	4	5	6
Cash flow	100	200	250	298	298	298
Book value at *start* of year, straight-line depreciation	1,000	833	667	500	333	167
Book value at *end* of year, straight-line depreciation	833	667	500	333	167	0
Change in book value during year	−167	−167	−167	−167	−167	−167
Book income	−67	+33	+83	+131	+131	+131
Book ROI	−.067	+.04	+.124	+.262	+.393	+.784
Book depreciation	167	167	167	167	167	167

$$\text{NPV} = -1000 + \frac{100}{1.10} + \frac{200}{(1.10)^2} + \frac{250}{(1.10)^3} + \frac{298}{(1.10)^4} + \frac{298}{(1.10)^5} + \frac{298}{(1.10)^6} = 0$$

With NPV = 0, the true (internal) rate of return of this cash-flow stream is also 10 percent.

Table 12-5 shows the store's forecasted *book* profitability, assuming straight-line depreciation over its 6-year life. The book ROI is lower than the true return for the first 2 years and higher afterward.[9]

Book Earnings versus True Earnings

At this point the regional manager steps up on stage for the following soliloquy:

"The Nodhead store's a decent investment. I really should propose it. But if we go ahead. I won't look very good at next year's performance review. And what if I also go ahead with the new stores in Russet, Gravenstein, and Sheepnose? Their cash-flow patterns are pretty much the same. I could actually appear to lose money next year. The stores I've got won't earn enough to cover the initial losses on four new ones.

"Of course, everyone knows new supermarkets lose money at first. The loss would be in the budget. My boss will understand—I think. But what about her

---

[9]The errors in book ROI always catch up with you in the end. If the firm chooses a depreciation schedule that overstates a project's return in some years, it must also understate the return in other years. In fact, you can think of a project's IRR as a kind of average of the book returns. It is not a simple average, however. The weights are the project's book values discounted at the IRR. See J. A. Kay, "Accountants, Too, Could Be Happy in a Golden Age: The Accountant's Rate of Profit and the Internal Rate of Return," *Oxford Economic Papers*, **28**:447–460 (1976).

*boss? What if the board of directors starts asking pointed questions about prof-
itability in my region? I'm under a lot of pressure to generate better earnings.
Pamela Quince, the upstate manager, got a bonus for generating a 40 percent
increase in book ROI. She didn't spend much on expansion. . . ."*

The regional manager is getting conflicting signals. On one hand, he is told to
find and propose good investment projects. *Good* is defined by discounted cash flow.
On the other hand, he is also urged to increase book earnings. But the two goals conflict because book earnings do not measure true earnings. The greater the pressure
for immediate book profits, the more the regional manager is tempted to forgo good
investments or to favor quick-payback projects over longer-lived projects, even if the
latter have higher NPVs.

<table>
<tr><td>

**Measur-
ing Eco-
nomic
Rates of
Return**

</td><td>

Let us think for a moment about how profitability should be measured in principle.
It is easy enough to compute the true, or "economic," rate of return for a common
stock that is continuously traded. We just record cash receipts (dividends) for the
year, add the change in price over the year, and divide by the beginning price:

</td></tr>
</table>

$$\text{Rate of return} = \frac{\text{cash receipts} + \text{change in price}}{\text{beginning price}}$$
$$= \frac{C_1 + (P_1 - P_0)}{P_0}$$

The numerator of the expression for rate of return (cash flow plus change in
value) is called **economic income:**

$$\text{Economic income} = \text{cash flow} + \text{change in present value}$$

Any reduction in present value represents **economic depreciation;** any increase in
present value represents *negative* economic depreciation. Therefore

$$\text{Economic depreciation} = \text{reduction in present value}$$

and

$$\text{Economic income} = \text{cash flow} - \text{economic depreciation}$$

The concept works for any asset. Rate of return equals cash flow plus change in
value divided by starting value:

$$\text{Rate of return} = \frac{C_1 + (PV_1 - PV_0)}{PV_0}$$

where PV_0 and PV_1 indicate the present values of the business at the ends of years 0
and 1.

The only hard part in measuring economic income and return is calculating present value. You can observe market value if shares in the asset are actively traded, but
few plants, divisions, or capital projects have *their own* shares traded in the stock market. You can observe the present market value of *all* the firm's assets but not of any
one of them taken separately.

Accountants rarely even attempt to measure present value. Instead they give us
net book value (BV), which is original cost less depreciation computed according to
some arbitrary schedule. Companies use the book value to calculate the book return
on investment (ROI):

$$\text{Book income} = \text{cash flow} - \text{book depreciation}$$
$$= C_1 + (BV_1 - BV_0)$$

TABLE 12-6

Forecasted economic income and rate of return for the proposed Nodhead store. Economic income equals cash flow plus change in present value. Rate of return equals economic income divided by value at start of year.

	YEAR					
	1	2	3	4	5	6
Cash flow	100	200	250	298	298	298
Present value, at *start* of year, 10 percent discount rate	1,000	1,000	901	741	517	271
Present value at *end* of year, 10 percent discount rate	1,000	901	741	517	271	0
Change in value during year	0	−99	−160	−224	−246	−271
Economic income	100	101	90	74	52	27
Rate of return	.10	.10	.10	.10	.10	.10
Economic depreciation	0	99	160	224	246	271

Note: There are minor rounding errors in some annual figures.

Therefore

$$\text{Book ROI} = \frac{C_1 + (BV_1 - BV_0)}{BV_0}$$

If book depreciation and economic depreciation are different (they are rarely the same), then the book profitability measures will be wrong; i.e., they will not measure true profitability. (In fact, it is not clear that accountants should even *try* to measure true profitability. They could not do so without heavy reliance on subjective estimates of value. Perhaps they should stick to supplying objective information and leave the estimation of value to managers and investors.)

It is not hard to forecast economic income and rate of return. Table 12-6 shows the calculations. From the cash-flow forecasts we can forecast present value at the start of periods 1 to 6. Cash flow plus *change* in present value equals economic income. Rate of return equals economic income divided by start-of-period value.

Of course, these are forecasts. Actual future cash flows and values will be higher or lower. Table 12-6 shows that investors *expect* to earn 10 percent in each year of the store's 6-year life. In other words, investors expect to earn the opportunity cost of capital each year from holding this asset.[10]

Does ROI Give the Right Answer in the Long Run?

Some people downplay the problem we have just described. Is a temporary dip in book profits a major problem? Don't the errors wash out in the long run, when the region settles down to a steady state with an even mix of old and new stores?

---

[10]This is a general result. Forecasted profitability always equals the discount rate used to calculate the estimated future present values.

TABLE 12-7
••

Book ROI for a group of stores like the Nodhead store. The steady-state book ROI overstates the 10 percent *economic* rate of return.

	YEAR					
	1	2	3	4	5	6
Book income for store*						
1	−67	+33	+83	+131	+131	+131
2		−67	+33	+83	+131	+131
3			−67	+33	+83	+131
4				−67	+33	+83
5					−67	+33
6						−67
Total book income	−67	−34	+49	+180	+311	+442
Book value for store						
1	1,000	833	667	500	333	167
2		1,000	833	667	500	333
3			1,000	833	667	500
4				1,000	833	667
5					1,000	833
6						1,000
Total book value	1,000	1,833	2,500	3,000	3,333	3,500
Book ROI for all stores = $\dfrac{\text{total book income}}{\text{total book value}}$	−.067	−.019	+.02	+.06	+.093	**+.126†**

*Book income = cash flow + change in book value during year.
†Steady-state book ROI.

It turns out that the errors diminish but do *not* exactly offset. The simplest steady-state condition occurs when the firm does not grow, but reinvests just enough each year to maintain earnings and asset values. Table 12-7 shows steady-state book ROIs for a regional division which opens one store a year. For simplicity we assume that the division starts from scratch and that each store's cash flows are carbon copies of the Nodhead store. The true rate of return on each store is, therefore, 10 percent. But as Table 12-7 demonstrates, steady-state book ROI, at 12.6 percent, overstates the true rate of return. Therefore, you cannot assume that the errors in book ROI will wash out in the long run.

Thus we still have a problem even in the long run. The extent of error depends on how fast the business grows. We have just considered one steady state with a zero growth rate. Think of another firm with a 5 percent steady-state growth rate. Such a firm would invest $1000 the first year, $1050 the second, $1102.50 the third, and so on. Clearly the faster growth means more new projects relative to old ones. The

Figure 12-1 The faster a firm grows, the lower its book rate of return, providing true profitability is constant and cash flows are constant or increasing over project life. This graph is drawn for a firm composed of identical projects, all like the Nodhead store (Table 12-5), but growing at a constant compound rate.

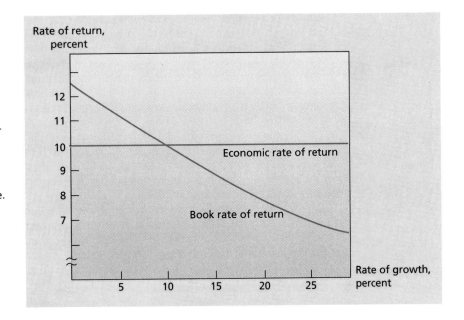

greater weight given to young projects, which have low book ROIs, the lower the business's apparent profitability. Figure 12-1 shows how this works out for a business composed of projects like the Nodhead store. Book ROI will either overestimate or underestimate the true rate of return unless the amount that the firm invests each year grows at the same rate as the true rate of return.[11]

12-5   WHAT CAN WE DO ABOUT BIASES IN ACCOUNTING PROFITABILITY MEASURES?

The dangers in judging profitability by accounting measures are clear from this chapter's discussion and examples. To be forewarned is to be forearmed. But we can say something beyond just "be careful."

It is natural for firms to set an absolute standard of profitability for plants or divisions. Ideally that standard should be the opportunity cost of capital for investment in the plant or division. But if performance is measured by book ROI, then the standard should be adjusted to reflect accounting biases.

This is easier said than done, because accounting biases are notoriously hard to measure in complex practical situations. Thus, many firms end up asking not "Did the widget division earn more than its cost of capital last year?" but "Was the widget division's book ROI typical of a successful firm in the widget industry?" The underlying assumptions are that (1) similar accounting procedures are used by other widget manufacturers and (2) successful widget companies earn their cost of capital.

---

[11]This also is a general result. Biases in steady-state book ROIs disappear when the growth rate equals the true rate of return. This was discovered by E. Solomon and J. Laya, "Measurement of Company Profitability: Some Systematic Errors in Accounting Rate of Return," in A. A. Robichek (ed.), *Financial Research and Management Decisions*, John Wiley & Sons, Inc., New York, 1967, pp. 152–183.

There are some simple accounting changes that could reduce biases in book ROI. Remember that the biases all stem from *not* using economic depreciation. Therefore why not switch to economic depreciation? The main reason is that each asset's present value would have to be reestimated every year. Imagine the confusion if this were attempted. You can understand why accountants set up a depreciation schedule when an investment is made and then stick to it apart from exceptional circumstances. But why restrict the choice of depreciation schedules to the old standbys such as straight-line depreciation? Why not specify a depreciation pattern that at least matches *expected* economic depreciation? For example, the Nodhead store could be depreciated according to the expected economic depreciation schedule shown in Table 12-6. This would avoid any systematic biases.[12] It would break no law or accounting standard. This step seems so simple and effective that we are at a loss to explain why firms have not adopted it.[13]

One final comment: Suppose that you *do* conclude that a project has earned less than its cost of capital. This indicates that you made a mistake in taking on the project and, if you could have your time over again, you would not accept it. But does that mean you should bail out now? Not necessarily. That depends on how much the assets would be worth if you sold them or put them to an alternative use. A plant that produces low profits may still be worth operating if it has few alternative uses. Conversely, on some occasions it may pay to sell or redeploy a highly profitable plant.

Do Managers Worry Too Much about Book Profitability?

Book measures of profitability can be wrong or misleading because:

1. Errors occur at different stages of project life. When true depreciation is decelerated, book measures are likely to understate true profitability for new projects and overstate it for old ones.

2. Errors also occur when firms or divisions have a balanced mix of old and new projects. Our "steady-state" analysis of Nodhead shows this.

3. Errors occur because of inflation, basically because inflation shows up in revenue faster than it shows up in costs. For example, a firm owning a plant built in 1970 will, under standard accounting procedures, calculate depreciation in terms of the plant's original cost in 1970 dollars. The plant's output is sold for current dollars. This is why the U.S. National Income and Product Accounts report corporate profits calculated under replacement cost accounting. This procedure bases depreciation not on the original cost of firms' assets, but on what it would cost to replace the assets at current prices.

4. Book measures are often confused by "creative accounting." Some firms pick and choose among available accounting procedures, or even invent new ones, in order to make their income statements and balance sheets look good. This was done with particular imagination in the "go-go years" of the mid-1960s.

Investors and financial managers, having been burned by inflation and creative accounting, have learned not to take accounting profitability at face value. Yet many people do not realize the depth of the problem. They think that if firms adopted in-

---

[12]Using expected economic depreciation will not generate book ROIs that are exactly right unless realized cash flows exactly match forecasted flows. But we expect forecasts to be right, on average.

[13]This procedure has been suggested by several authors, most recently by Zvi Bodie in "Compound Interest Depreciation in Capital Investment," *Harvard Business Review*, **60**:58–60 (May–June 1982).

flation accounting and eschewed creative accounting, everything would be all right except perhaps for temporary problems with very old or very young projects. In other words, they worry about reasons 3 and 4, and a little about reason 1, but not at all about 2. We think reason 2 deserves more attention.

Much of the pressure for good book earnings comes from top management. Chief executives have good reasons to shoot for good short-run earnings. Probably their bonuses depend on it. The market watches current earnings per share (partly because it isn't allowed to look over top management's shoulder at the 5-year plan). Is it surprising that top management does not always jump happily into high-NPV projects that will depress next year's earnings per share?

We do not mean to imply that chief executives typically sacrifice long-run value for immediate earnings. But they at least *worry* about earnings, and their worries affect attitudes and decisions down the line.

We think managers worry too much. They are uptight about book earnings. They often picture investors as mindless creatures who respond only to the latest earnings announcement. Investors are more sophisticated than that.

Financial managers can help investors do better by *not* playing the earnings game. That is, they should not hire creative accountants or emphasize book earnings while downplaying more fundamental information about their firm's performance. The firm that brags about only its book earnings will be judged on its book earnings.

12-6 SUMMARY

We began this chapter by describing how capital budgeting is organized and ended by exposing serious biases in accounting measures of financial performance. Inevitably such discussions stress the mechanics of organization, control, and accounting. It is harder to talk about the informal procedures that reinforce the formal ones. But remember that it takes informal communication and personal initiative to make capital budgeting work. Also, the accounting biases are partly or wholly alleviated because managers and stockholders are smart enough to look behind reported book earnings.

Formal capital budgeting systems usually have four stages:

1. Preparation of a *capital budget* for the firm. This is a plan for capital expenditure by plant, division, or other business unit.

2. *Project authorizations* give authority to go ahead with specific projects.

3. Procedures for *control of projects under construction* warn if projects are behind schedule or costing more than planned.

4. *Postaudits* check on the progress of recent investments.

The formal criteria used in project evaluation are a mixture of modern rules such as net present value and internal rate of return and old-fashioned rules such as payback. The old rules survive partly because everyone understands them; they provide a common language for discussing the project. They also survive because of the way performance is evaluated and rewarded. If managers are expected to generate quick results, then management is naturally interested in payback and book return.

Most specific project proposals originate at the plant or division level. If the project doesn't cost much, it may be approved by middle management. But the final say on major capital outlays belongs to top management. The desire of top management to retain control of capital budgeting is understandable. But the chief executive cannot undertake a detailed analysis of every project he or she approves. Information at the top is often limited; project proposals may be designed more to persuade than inform.

Top management copes by relying on staff financial analysts, by making capital budgeting part of a broader budgeting and planning process, and by keeping the capital budgeting process flexible and open to informal communication.

Capital budgeting is not entirely a bottom-up process. Strategic planners practice "capital budgeting on a grand scale" by attempting to identify those businesses in which the firm has a special advantage. Project proposals that support the firm's accepted overall strategy are much more likely to have clear sailing as they come up through the organization.

Usually the plant or division proposing a capital investment will be responsible for making the project work. A project's sponsors naturally want the project to perform well and to *appear* to perform well. Thus the way the firm evaluates operating performance can affect the kinds of project that middle management is willing to propose.

There are two approaches to performance measurement. The first and easier is to compare actual cash flow with forecasted cash flow. The second is to compare actual profitability with the opportunity cost of capital. Both approaches are needed.

The second approach is the difficult and dangerous one. Most firms measure performance in terms of accounting or book profitability. Unfortunately book income and ROI are often seriously biased measures of true profitability and thus should not be directly compared to the opportunity cost of capital.

In principle, true or economic income is easy to calculate: You just subtract economic depreciation from the asset's cash flow for the period you are interested in. Economic depreciation is simply the decrease in the asset's present value during the period. (If the asset's value increases, then economic depreciation is negative.)

Unfortunately we can't ask accountants to recalculate each asset's present value every time income is calculated. But it does seem fair to ask why they don't try at least to match book depreciation schedules to typical patterns of economic depreciation.

Further Reading

. . . .

The most extensive study of the capital budgeting process is:

J. L. Bower: *Managing the Resource Allocation Process*, Division of Research, Graduate School of Business Administration, Harvard University, Boston, 1970.

The articles by Scapens and Sale and by Pohlman, Santiago, and Markel are more up-to-date surveys of current practice:

R. W. Scapens and J. T. Sale: "Performance Measurement and Formal Capital Expenditure Controls in Divisionalized Companies," *Journal of Business Finance and Accounting*, **8**:389–420 (Autumn 1981).

R. A. Pohlman, E. S. Santiago, and F. L. Markel: "Cash Flow Estimation Practices of Large Firms," *Financial Management*, **17**:71–79 (Summer 1988).

Swalm and Weingartner discuss some of the incentive problems arising in corporations:

R. O. Swalm: "Utility Theory: Insights into Risk-Taking," *Harvard Business Review*, **44**:123–136 (November–December 1966).

H. M. Weingartner: "Some New Views on the Payback Period and Capital Budgeting," *Management Science*, **15**:B594–607 (August 1969).

Biases in book ROI and procedures for reducing the biases are discussed by:

E. Solomon and J. Laya: "Measurement of Company Profitability: Some Systematic Errors in the Accounting Rate of Return," in A. A. Robichek (ed.), *Financial Research and Management Decisions*, John Wiley & Sons, Inc., New York, 1967, pp. 152–183.

F. M. Fisher and J. I. McGowan: "On the Misuse of Accounting Rates of Return to Infer Monopoly Profits," *American Economic Review*, **73**:82–97 (March 1983).

J. A. Kay, "Accountants, Too, Could Be Happy in a Golden Age: The Accountant's Rate of Profit and the Internal Rate of Return," *Oxford Economic Papers*, **28**:447–460 (1976).

Z. Bodie, "Compound Interest Depreciation in Capital Investment," *Harvard Business Review*, **60**:58–60 (May–June 1982).

Quiz

1. True or false?
   (a) The approval of a capital budget allows managers to go ahead with any projects included in the budget.
   (b) In most companies the controller authorizes all appropriation requests for capital expenditures.
   (c) Typically, companies will permit up to 10 percent expenditure overruns, but beyond that the sponsor is required to submit a supplemental appropriation request.
   (d) Most firms use only NPV for project selection.
   (e) Postaudits are usually undertaken about 5 years after project completion.
   (f) Setting capital budgets and project authorizations is a bottom-up process. Strategic planning, insofar as it affects capital investment decisions, is a top-down process.

2. Explain how each of the following actions or problems can distort or disrupt the capital budgeting process:
   (a) Overoptimism by project sponsors
   (b) Inconsistent forecasts of industry and macroeconomic variables
   (c) Capital budgeting organized solely as a bottom-up process
   (d) A demand for quick results from operating managers, e.g., requiring new capital expenditures to meet a payback constraint
   (e) An increase in the hurdle rate for capital investment from 12 to 20 percent in response to top management's expectation of a fall in operating cash flow.

3. Fill in the blanks:
   "A project's economic income for a given year equals the project's _____ less its _____ depreciation. Book income is typically _____ than economic income early in the project's life and _____ than economic income later in its life."

4. Consider the following project:

	Period 0	Period 1	Period 2	Period 3
Net cash flow	−100	0	78.55	78.55

   The internal rate of return is 20 percent. The NPV, assuming a 20 percent opportunity cost of capital, is exactly zero. Calculate the expected *economic* income and economic depreciation in each year.

5. True or false? Explain briefly.
   (a) Book profitability measures are biased measures of true profitability for individual assets. However, these biases "wash out" when firms hold a balanced mix of old and new assets.

(*b*) Systematic biases in book profitability would be avoided if companies used depreciation schedules which matched expected economic depreciation. However, few, if any, firms have done this.

Questions and Problems

1. Discuss the value of postaudits. Who should conduct them? When? Should they consider solely financial performance? Should they be confined to the larger projects?

2. Draw up an outline or flowchart tracing the capital budgeting process from the initial idea for a new investment project to the completion of the project and its initial operations. Assume the idea for a new obfuscator machine comes from a plant manager in the Deconstruction Division of the Modern Language Corporation.

   Here are some questions your outline or flowchart should consider: Who will prepare the original proposal? What information will the proposal contain? Who will evaluate it? What approvals will be needed, and who will give them? What happens if the machine costs 40 percent more to purchase and install than originally forecast? What will happen when the machine is finally up and running?

3. Suppose that the cash flows from Nodhead's new supermarket are as follows:

	YEAR						
	0	1	2	3	4	5	6
Cash flows, thousands of dollars	−1,000	+298	+298	+298	+138	+138	+138

   (*a*) Recalculate economic depreciation. Is it accelerated or decelerated?
   (*b*) Rework Tables 12-5 and 12-6 to show the relationship between the "true" rate of return and book ROI in each year of the project's life.

4. Reconstruct Table 12-7 assuming a steady-state growth rate of 10 percent per year. Your answer will illustrate a fascinating theorem, namely, that book rate of return equals the economic rate of return when the economic rate of return and the steady-state growth rate are the same.

5. Consider an asset with the following cash flows:

	Year 0	Year 1	Year 2	Year 3
Cash flows, millions of dollars	−12	+5.20	+4.80	+4.40

   The firm uses straight-line book depreciation. Thus, for this project, it writes off $4 million per year in years 1, 2, and 3. The discount rate is 10 percent.
   (*a*) Show that economic depreciation equals book depreciation.
   (*b*) Show that the book rate of return is the same in each year.
   (*c*) Show that the project's book profitability is its true profitability.

Notice that you've just illustrated another interesting theorem: If the book rate of return is the same in each year of a project's life, the book rate of return equals the IRR.

6. Suppose operating managers' bonuses in the Modern Language Corporation are based on the book ROI of their plants or divisions. What kinds of capital investments will the managers tend to favor?

7. Some large companies' strategic (i.e., top-down) analyses emphasize accounting performance and tend to direct new investment toward businesses with high book ROIs. What kinds of problems would this create in a large, diversified company?

8. A project is expected to produce the following cash flows:

C_0	C_1	C_2	C_3
-900	$+300$	$+400$	$+500$

(a) Find the IRR of the project.

(b) Calculate the accounting return in each year, assuming straight-line depreciation.

(c) In footnote 9, we stated that the IRR is a weighted average of the accounting returns where the weights are equal to the book values (at start of year) discounted by the IRR. Show that this is true for the above project.

9. Here is a harder question: It is often said that book income is overstated when there is rapid inflation because book depreciation understates true depreciation. What definition of *true depreciation* is implicit in this statement? Does *true depreciation* equal *economic depreciation*, as we have defined the latter term?

10. Instead of looking at past market returns for a guide to the cost of capital, some financial managers look at past accounting returns. What do you think are the advantages and disadvantages of doing this?

11. Calculate the year-by-year book and economic profitability for investment in polyzone production, as described in Chapter 11. Use the cash flows and competitive spreads shown in Table 11-2.

What is the steady-state book rate of return (ROI) for a mature company producing polyzone? Assume no growth and competitive spreads.

12. The following are extracts from two newsletters sent to a stockbroker's clients:

Investment Letter—March 1995

Kipper Parlors was founded earlier this year by its president, Albert Herring. It plans to open a chain of kipper parlors where young people can get together over a kipper and a glass of wine in a pleasant, intimate atmosphere. In addition to the traditional grilled kipper, the parlors serve such delicacies as Kipper Schnitzel, Kipper Grandemere, and (for dessert) Kipper Sorbet.

The economics of the business are simple. Each new parlor requires an initial investment in fixtures and fittings of $200,000 (the property itself is rented). These fixtures and fittings have an estimated life of 5 years and are depreciated straight-line over that period. Each new parlor involves significant start-up costs and is not expected to reach full profitability until its fifth year. Profits per parlor are estimated as follows:

	YEAR AFTER OPENING				
	1	2	3	4	5
Profit	0	40	80	120	170
Depreciation	40	40	40	40	40
Profit after depreciation	−40	0	40	80	130
Book value at start of year	200	160	120	80	40
Return on investment, percent	−20	0	33	100	325

Kipper has just opened its first parlor and plans to open one new parlor each year. Despite the likely initial losses (which simply reflect start-up costs), our calculations show a dramatic profit growth and a long-term return on investment that is substantially higher than Kipper's 20 percent cost of capital.

The total market value of Kipper stock is currently only $250,000. In our opinion, this does not fully reflect the exciting growth prospects, and we strongly recommend clients to buy.

Investment Letter—April 1995

Albert Herring, president of Kipper Parlors, yesterday announced an ambitious new building plan. Kipper plans to open two new parlors next year, three the year after, and so on.

We have calculated the implications of this for Kipper's earnings per share and return on investment. The results are extremely disturbing, and under the

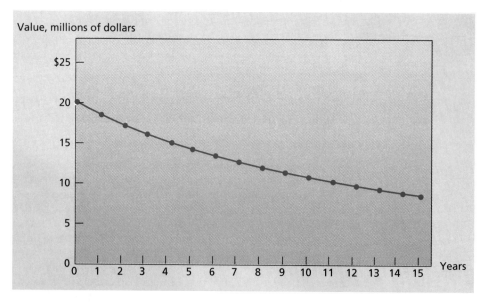

Figure 12-2 Estimated value of Boeing 737 in January 1987 as a function of age.

TABLE 12-8

Estimated market values of a Boeing 737 in January 1987 as a function of age, plus the cash flows needed to provide a 10 percent true rate of return (figures in millions of dollars except as noted)

Age, Years	Market Value	Cash Flow
1	19.69	
2	17.99	$3.67
3	16.79	3.00
4	15.78	2.69
5	14.89	2.47
6	14.09	2.29
7	13.36	2.14
8	12.68	2.02
9	12.05	1.90
10	11.46	1.80
11	10.91	1.70
12	10.39	1.61
13	9.91	1.52
14	9.44	1.46
15	9.01	1.37
	8.59	1.32

new plan, there seems to be no prospect of Kipper's *ever* earning a satisfactory return on capital.

Since March, the value of Kipper's stock has fallen by 40 percent. Any investor who did not heed our earlier warnings should take the opportunity to sell the stock now.

Compare Kipper's accounting and economic income under the two expansion plans. How does the change in plan affect the company's return on investment? What is the present value of Kipper stock? Ignore taxes in your calculations.

13. In our Nodhead example, true depreciation was decelerated. That is not always the case. For instance, Figure 12-2 shows how on average the value of a Boeing 737 has varied with its age.[14] Table 12-8 shows the market value at different points in the plane's life and the cash flow needed in each year to provide a 10 percent return. (For example, if you bought a 737 for $19.69 million at the start of year 1 and sold it a year later, your total profit would be 17.99 + 3.67 − 19.69 = $1.97 million, 10 percent of the purchase cost.)

Many airlines write off their aircraft straight-line over 15 years to a salvage value equal to 20 percent of the original cost.

(*a*) Calculate economic and book depreciation for each year of the plane's life.

(*b*) Compare the true and book rates of return in each year.

(*c*) Suppose an airline invested in a fixed number of Boeing 737s each year. Would steady-state book return overstate or understate true return?

---

[14]We are grateful to Mike Staunton for providing us with these estimates.

PART four

FINANCING DECISIONS AND MARKET EFFICIENCY

13

Corporate Financing and the Six Lessons of Market Efficiency

Up to this point we have concentrated almost exclusively on the left-hand side of the balance sheet—the firm's capital expenditure decision. Now we move to the right-hand side and to the problems involved in financing the capital expenditures. To put it crudely, you've learned how to spend money—now learn how to raise it.

Of course, we haven't totally ignored financing in our discussion of capital budgeting. But we made the simplest possible assumption: all-equity financing. That means we assumed the firm raises its money by selling stock and then invests the proceeds in real assets. Later, when those assets generate cash flows, the cash is either returned to stockholders or invested in a second generation of real assets. Stockholders supply all the firm's capital, bear all the business risks, and receive all the rewards.

Now we are turning the problem around. We take the firm's present portfolio of real assets and its future investment strategy as given, and then we determine what the best financing strategy is. We will analyze trade-offs between different financing alternatives. For example:

- Should the firm reinvest most of its earnings in the business, or should it pay them out as dividends?
- If the firm needs more money, should it issue more stock or should it borrow?
- Should it borrow short-term or long-term?
- Should it borrow by issuing a normal long-term bond or a convertible bond (i.e., a bond which can be exchanged by the bondholders for common stock of the firm)?

There are countless other financing trade-offs, as you will see.

The purpose of holding the firm's capital budgeting decision constant is to separate that decision from the financing decision. Strictly speaking, this assumes that capital budgeting and financing decisions are *independent*. In many circumstances this is a quite reasonable assumption. The firm is generally free to change its capital structure by repurchasing one security and issuing another. In that case there is no need to associate a particular investment project with a particular source of cash. The firm can think, first, about what projects to accept and, second, about how they should be financed.

Sometimes decisions about capital structure depend on project choice or vice versa, and in those cases the investment and financing decisions have to be considered jointly. However, we defer discussion of such interactions of financing and investment decisions until later in the book.

13-1 WE ALWAYS COME BACK TO NPV

Although it is helpful to separate investment and financing decisions, there are basic similarities in the criteria for making them. The decisions to purchase a machine tool and to sell a bond each involve valuation of a risky asset. The fact that one asset is real and the other financial doesn't matter. In both cases we end up computing net present value.

The phrase *net present value of borrowing* may seem odd to you. But the following example should help to explain what we mean: As part of its policy of encouraging small business, the government offers to lend your firm $100,000 for 10 years at an interest rate of 3 percent. This means that the firm is liable for interest payments of $3000 in each of the years 1 through 10 and that it is responsible for repaying the $100,000 in the final year. Should you accept the offer?

We can compute the NPV of the loan agreement in the usual way. The one difference is that the first cash flow is *positive* and the subsequent flows are *negative:*

$$\text{NPV} = \text{amount borrowed} - \text{present value of interest payments}$$
$$- \text{present value of loan repayment}$$

$$= +100,000 - \left[\sum_{t=1}^{10} \frac{3000}{(1+r)^t}\right] - \frac{100,000}{(1+r)^{10}}$$

The only missing variable is r, the opportunity cost of capital. You need that to value the liability created by the loan. We reason this way: The government's loan to you is a financial asset: a piece of paper representing your promise to pay $3000 per year plus the final repayment of $100,000. How much would that paper sell for if freely traded in capital markets? It would sell for the present value of those cash flows, discounted at r, the rate of return offered by other securities of equivalent risk. Now, the class of equivalent-risk securities includes other bonds issued by your firm, so all you have to do to determine r is to answer this question: "What interest rate would my firm have to pay to borrow money directly from the capital markets rather than from the government?"

Suppose that this rate is 10 percent. Then

$$\text{NPV} = +100,000 - \left[\sum_{t=1}^{10} \frac{3000}{(1.10)^t}\right] - \frac{100,000}{(1.10)^{10}}$$

$$= +100,000 - 56,988 = +\$43,012$$

Differences between Investment and Financing Decisions

Of course, you don't need any arithmetic to tell you that borrowing at 3 percent is a good deal when the fair rate is 10 percent. But the NPV calculation tells you just how much that opportunity is worth ($43,012).[1] It also brings out the essential similarity of investment and financing decisions.

In some ways investment decisions are simpler than financing decisions. The number of different financing instruments (i.e., securities) is continually expanding. You will have to learn the major families, genera, and species. You should also be aware of the major financial institutions which provide financing for business firms. Finally,

---

[1] We ignore here any tax consequences of borrowing. These are discussed in Chapter 19.

the vocabulary of financing has to be acquired. You will learn about *tombstones, red herrings, balloons, sinking funds,* and many other exotic beasts—behind each of these terms lies an interesting story.

There are also ways in which financing decisions are much easier than investment decisions. First, financing decisions do not have the same degree of finality as investment decisions. They are easier to reverse. In other words, their abandonment value is higher. Second, it's harder to make or lose money by smart or stupid financing strategies. In other words, it is difficult to find financing schemes with NPVs significantly different from zero. That reflects the nature of the competition.

When the firm looks at capital investment decisions, it does *not* assume that it is facing perfect, competitive markets. It may have only a few competitors that specialize in the same line of business in the same geographical area. And it may own some unique assets that give it an edge over its competitors. Often these assets are intangibles, such as patents, expertise, reputation, or market position. All this opens up the opportunity of making superior profits and of finding projects with positive NPVs. It also makes it difficult to tell whether any specific project truly has a positive NPV.

In financial markets your competition is all other corporations seeking funds, to say nothing of the state, local, and federal governments, financial institutions, individuals, and foreign firms and governments that also go to New York, London, or Tokyo for financing. The investors who supply financing are comparably numerous, and they are smart: Money attracts brains. The financial amateur often views capital markets as *segmented*, that is, broken down into distinct sectors. But money moves between those sectors, and it moves fast.

Remember that a good financing decision generates a positive NPV. It is one in which the amount of cash raised exceeds the value of the liability created. But turn that statement around. If selling a security generates a positive NPV for you, it must generate a negative NPV for the buyer. Thus, the loan we discussed was a good deal for your firm but a negative NPV investment from the government's point of view. By lending at 3 percent, it offered a $43,012 subsidy.

What are the chances that your firm could consistently trick or persuade investors into purchasing securities with negative NPVs to them? Pretty low. In general, firms should assume that the securities they issue are fairly priced.

....

Efficient Capital Markets

We are leading up to the fundamental financial concept of **efficient capital markets:** *If capital markets are efficient, then purchase or sale of any security at the prevailing market price is never a positive-NPV transaction.* Does that sound like a sweeping statement? It is. That is why we have devoted all the rest of this chapter to the history, logic, and tests of the efficient-market hypothesis.

You may ask why we start our discussion of financing issues with this conceptual point, before you have even the most basic knowledge about securities, issue procedures, and financial institutions. We do it this way because financing decisions seem overwhelmingly complex if you don't learn to ask the right questions. We are afraid you might flee from confusion to the myths that often dominate popular discussion of corporate financing. You need to understand the efficient-market hypothesis not because it is *universally* true but because it leads you to ask the right questions.

13-2   WHAT IS AN EFFICIENT MARKET?

When economists say that the security market is "efficient," they are not talking about whether the filing is up to date or whether desktops are tidy. They mean that information is widely and cheaply available to investors and that all relevant and ascertainable information is already reflected in security prices. That is why purchases or sales in an efficient market cannot be positive-NPV transactions.

A Startling Discovery: Price Changes Are Random

As is so often the case with important ideas, this concept of efficient markets was a by-product of a chance discovery. In 1953 the Royal Statistical Society met in London to discuss a rather unusual paper.[2] Its author, Maurice Kendall, was a distinguished statistician, and the subject was the behavior of stock and commodity prices. Kendall had been looking for regular price cycles, but to his surprise he could not find them. Each series appeared to be "a 'wandering' one, almost as if once a week the Demon of Chance drew a random number . . . and added it to the current price to determine the next week's price." In other words, prices seemed to follow a *random walk*.

If you are not sure what we mean by "random walk," you might like to think of the following example: You are given $100 to play a game. At the end of each week a coin is tossed. If it comes up heads, you win 3 percent of your investment; if it is tails, you lose 2.5 percent. Therefore, your capital at the end of the first week is either $103.00 or $97.50. At the end of the second week the coin is tossed again. Now the possible outcomes are:

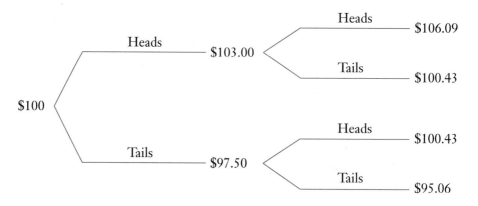

This process is a random walk with a positive drift of .25 percent per week.[3] It is a random walk because successive changes in value are independent. That is, the odds each week are 50 percent, regardless of the value at the start of the week or of the pattern of heads and tails in the previous weeks.

If you find it difficult to believe that there are no patterns in share price changes, look at the two charts in Figure 13-1. One of these charts shows the outcome from playing our game for 5 years; the other shows the actual performance of the Standard and Poor's index for a 5-year period. Can you tell which one is which?[4]

---

[2]See M. G. Kendall, "The Analysis of Economic Time-Series, Part I. Prices," *Journal of the Royal Statistical Society*, **96**:11–25 (1953).

[3]The drift is equal to the expected outcome: 1/2 (3) + 1/2 (−2.5) = .25%

[4]The top chart in Figure 13-1 shows the real Standard and Poor's index for the years 1980 through 1984; the bottom chart is a series of cumulated random numbers. Of course, 50 percent of you will have guessed right, but we bet it was just a guess. A similar comparison between cumulated random numbers and actual price series was first suggested by H. V. Roberts, "Stock Market 'Patterns' and Financial Analysis: Methodological Suggestions," *Journal of Finance*, **14**:1–10 (March 1959).

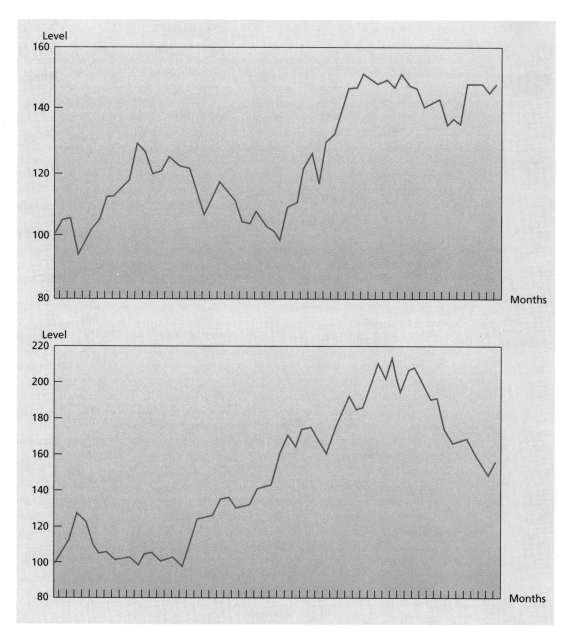

Figure 13-1 One of these charts shows the Standard and Poor's index for a 5-year period. The other shows the results of playing our coin-tossing game for 5 years. Can you tell which is which?

When Maurice Kendall suggested that stock prices follow a random walk, he was implying that the price changes are as independent of one another as the gains and losses in our game. To most economists this was a startling and bizarre idea. In fact, the idea was *not* completely novel. It had been proposed in an almost forgotten doctoral thesis written 53 years earlier by a Frenchman, Louis Bachelier.[5] Bachelier's suggestion was original enough, but his accompanying development of the mathematical theory of random processes anticipated by 5 years Einstein's famous work on the random Brownian motion of colliding gas molecules. Kendall's work did not suffer the neglect of Bachelier's. As computers and data became more readily available, economists and statisticians rapidly amassed a large volume of supporting evidence. Let us look very briefly at the kinds of tests that they have used.

Suppose that you wish to assess whether there is any tendency for price changes to persist from one day to the next. You might begin by drawing a scatter diagram of changes on successive days. Figure 13-2 is an example of such a diagram. Each dot shows the change in the price of Weyerhaeuser stock on successive days. The circled dot in the southeast quadrant refers to a pair of days in which a 1 percent increase was followed by a 2 percent decrease. If there had been a systematic tendency for increases to be followed by decreases, there would be many dots in the southeast quadrant and few in the northeast quadrant. It is obvious from a glance that there is very little pattern in these price movements, but we can test this more precisely by calculating the coefficient of correlation between each day's price change and the next. If price movements persisted, the correlation would be significantly positive; if there was no relationship, it would be 0. In our example, the correlation was +.07—there was a negligible tendency for price rises to be followed by further rises.[6]

Figure 13-2 shows the behavior of only one stock, but our finding is typical. Researchers have looked at many different stocks in many different countries and for many different periods; they have calculated the coefficient of correlation between the price changes; they have looked for runs of positive or negative price changes; they have examined the *technical rules* that have been used by some investors to exploit the "patterns" they claim to see in past stock prices. With remarkable unanimity researchers have concluded that there is no useful information in the sequence of past changes in stock price. As a result, many of the researchers have become famous. None has become rich.

A Theory to Fit the Facts

We have mentioned that the initial reaction to the random-walk finding was surprise. It was several years before economists appreciated that this price behavior is exactly what one should expect in any competitive market.

Suppose, for example, that you wish to sell an antique painting at an auction but you have no idea of its value. Can you be sure of receiving a fair price? The answer is that you can if the auction is sufficiently competitive. In other words, you need to

---

[5]See L. Bachelier, *Theorie de la Speculation*, Gauthier-Villars, Paris, 1900. Reprinted in English (A. J. Boness, trans.) in P. H. Cootner (ed.), *The Random Character of Stock Market Prices*, M.I.T. Press, Cambridge, Mass., 1964, pp. 17–78. During the 1930s the food economist Holbrook Working had also noticed the random behavior of commodity prices. See H. Working, "A Random Difference Series for Use in the Analysis of Time Series," *Journal of the American Statistical Association*, **29**:11–24 (March 1934).

[6]You may have noticed one unusual pattern in the Weyerhaeuser chart. The points on the chart resemble a starburst and cluster along a series of rays emanating from the center. The reason? The minimum amount by which prices can change on the New York Stock Exchange, or the *tick size*, is one-eighth of a dollar. For example, suppose the stock price is $50. Then we should observe a number of cases where a rise of .25 percent (.125/50) is followed by a rise of .249 percent (.125/50.125), but we would never observe a second-day rise that was between .249 and .499 percent (i.e., a rise of more than $.125 but less than $.25). This starburst pattern was discovered by Timothy Crack and Olivier Ledoit (see their paper "Robust Structure without Predictability: The 'Compass Rose' Pattern of the Stock Market," *Journal of Finance*, forthcoming).

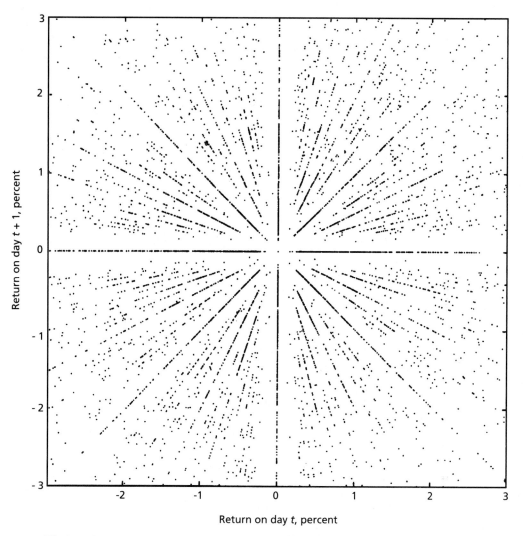

Figure 13-2 Each dot shows a pair of returns for Weyerhaeuser stock on two successive days between 1963 and 1993. (Some dots, such as those reflecting the stock market crash of October 19, 1987, are off-scale and thus not shown.) The circled dot records a daily return of +1 percent and then −2 percent on the next day. The scatter diagram shows no significant relationship between returns on successive days. (*Source:* T. Crack and O. Ledoit, "Robust Structure without Predictability: The 'Compass Rose' Pattern of the Stock Market," *Journal of Finance,* forthcoming.)

satisfy yourself that there is no collusion among the bidders, that there is no substantial cost involved in submitting a bid, and that the auction is attended by a reasonable number of skilled potential bidders, each of whom has access to the available information. In this case, no matter how ignorant *you* may be, competition among experts will ensure that the price you realize fully reflects the value of the painting.

In just the same way, competition among investment analysts will lead to a stock market in which prices at all times reflect true value. But what do we mean by *true value?* It is a potentially slippery phrase. True value does not mean ultimate *future*

Figure 13-3 Cycles self-destruct as soon as they are recognized by investors. The stock price instantaneously jumps to the present value of the expected future price.

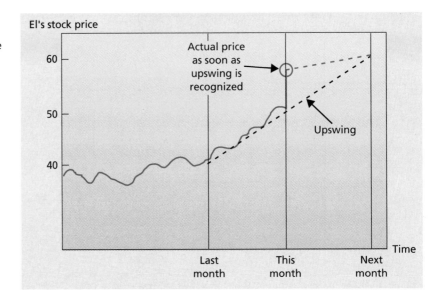

value—we do not expect investors to be fortune-tellers. It means an equilibrium price which incorporates *all* the information available to investors at that time. That was our definition of an efficient market.

Now you can begin to see why price changes in an efficient market are random. If prices always reflect all relevant information, then they will change only when new information arrives. But new information *by definition* cannot be predicted ahead of time (otherwise it would not be new information). Therefore, price changes cannot be predicted ahead of time. To put it another way, if stock prices already reflect all that is predictable, then stock price *changes* must reflect only the unpredictable. The series of price changes must be random.[7]

Suppose, however, that competition among research analysts was not so strong and that there were predictable cycles in stock prices. Investors could then make superior profits by trading on the basis of these cycles. Figure 13-3, for example, shows a 2-month upswing for Establishment Industries (EI). The upswing started last month, when EI's stock price was $40, and it is expected to carry the stock price to $60 next month. What will happen when investors perceive this bonanza? It will self-destruct. Since EI stock is a bargain at $50, investors will rush to buy. They will stop buying only when the stock offers a normal rate of return. Therefore, as soon as a cycle becomes apparent to investors, they immediately eliminate it by their trading.

Two types of investment analysts help to make price changes random. Many analysts study the company's business and try to uncover information about its profitability that will shed new light on the value of the stock. These analysts are often called *fundamental analysts*. Competition in fundamental research will tend to ensure that prices reflect *all* relevant information and that price changes are unpredictable. The other analysts study the past price record and look for cycles. These analysts are

---

[7]When economists speak of stock prices as following a random walk, they are being a little imprecise. A statistician reserves the term *random walk* to describe a series that has a constant expected change each period and a constant degree of variability. But market efficiency does not imply that risks and expected returns cannot shift over time.

called *technical analysts*. Competition in technical research will tend to ensure that current prices reflect all information in the past sequence of prices and that future price changes cannot be predicted from past prices.

Three Forms of the Efficient-Market Theory

Harry Roberts has defined three levels of market efficiency.[8] The first is the case in which prices reflect all information contained in the record of past prices. Roberts called this a *weak* form of efficiency. The random-walk research shows that the market is *at least* efficient in this weak sense.

The second level of efficiency is the case in which prices reflect not only past prices but all other published information. Roberts called this a *semistrong* form of efficiency. Researchers have tested this by looking at specific items of news such as announcements of earnings and dividends, forecasts of company earnings, changes in accounting practices, and mergers.[9] Most of this information was rapidly and accurately impounded in the price of the stock. For example, investors want to invest in companies with growing earnings and dividends, and therefore they always eagerly await the firm's earnings or dividend announcement. But the opportunity to take advantage of this information is very limited, for Patell and Wolfson found that most of the price adjustment occurs within 5 to 10 minutes of the announcement.[10]

Finally, Harry Roberts envisaged a *strong* form of efficiency in which prices reflect not just public information but all the information that can be acquired by painstaking analysis of the company and the economy. In such a market we would see lucky and unlucky investors, but we wouldn't find any superior investment managers who can consistently beat the market.

What is the evidence? Are professional investment managers able to earn above-average returns? Look, for example, at Figure 13-4, which is taken from a study by Mark Carhart of the average return on nearly 1500 U.S. mutual funds.[11] You can see that in some years the mutual funds beat the market, but as often as not it was the other way around. Figure 13-4 provides a fairly crude comparison, for mutual funds may have tended to specialize in particular sectors of the market, such as low-beta stocks or large-firm stocks, that have given below-average returns. To control for such differences, each fund should be compared to a benchmark portfolio of similar securities. The study by Mark Carhart did this, but the message was unchanged: The funds earned a lower return than the benchmark portfolios *after* expenses and roughly matched the benchmarks *before* expenses.

As in most other walks of life, some mutual fund managers are undoubtedly smarter than others. So it should be possible to distinguish managers whose perfor-

---

[8]See H. V. Roberts, "Statistical versus Clinical Prediction of the Stock Market," unpublished paper presented to the Seminar on the Analysis of Security Prices, University of Chicago, May 1967.

[9]See, for example, R. Ball and P. Brown, "An Empirical Evaluation of Accounting Income Numbers," *Journal of Accounting Research*, **6**:159–178 (Autumn 1968); R. R. Pettit, "Dividend Announcements, Security Performance, and Capital Market Efficiency," *Journal of Finance*, **27**:993–1007 (December 1972); G. Foster, "Stock Market Reaction to Estimates of Earnings per Share by Company Officials," *Journal of Accounting Research*, **11**:25–37 (Spring 1973); and G. Mandelker, "Risk and Return: The Case of Merging Firms," *Journal of Financial Economics*, **1**:303–335 (December 1974).

[10]See J. M. Patell and M. A. Wolfson, "The Intraday Speed of Adjustment of Stock Prices to Earnings and Dividend Announcements," *Journal of Financial Economics*, **13**:223–252 (June 1984). The price reaction to the sale of a large block of stock seems to be equally rapid. See L. Dann, D. Mayers, and R. Raab, "Trading Rules, Large Blocks, and the Speed of Adjustment," *Journal of Financial Economics*, **4**:3–22 (January 1977).

[11]See M. M. Carhart, "On Persistence in Mutual Fund Performance," unpublished paper, University of Chicago, December 1994.

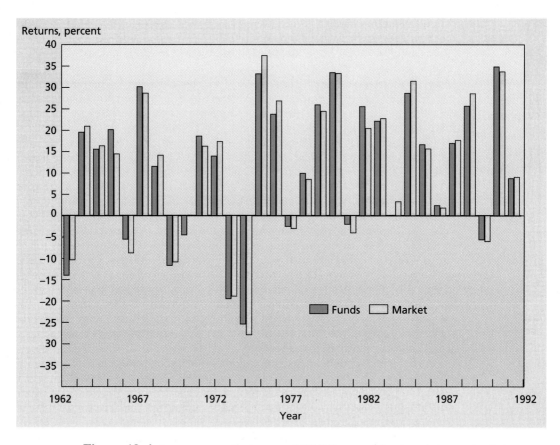

Returns, percent

Figure 13-4 Average annual returns on 1493 U.S. mutual funds and the market index, 1962–1992. Notice that mutual funds underperform the market in approximately half the years. (*Source:* M. M. Carhart, "On Persistence in Mutual Fund Performance," unpublished paper, University of Chicago, December 1994.)

mance was consistently above or below the average. It turns out that there were some predictably *bad* managers, whose performance was 2 to 3 percent a year worse than their colleagues'.[12] But among the remaining managers the differences in relative performance were far less significant.

It is difficult to measure precisely how well fund managers perform, but these findings are fairly typical.[13] The gains by professional fund managers appear to no

---

[12]Funds were classified into eight groups on the basis of their past performance. Group 8 incurred high expenses, traded heavily, and performed significantly worse than the average.

[13]The classic study was M. C. Jensen, "The Performance of Mutual Funds in the Period 1945–64," *Journal of Finance*, **23**:389–416 (May 1968). Recent studies include D. Hendricks, J. Patel, and R. Zeckhauser, "Hot Hands in Mutual Funds: Short-Run Persistence of Performance, 1974–1978," *Journal of Finance*, **48**:93–130 (March 1993); E. J. Elton, M. J. Gruber, S. Das, and M. Hlavka, "Efficiency with Costly Information: A Reinterpretation of Evidence from Managed Portfolios," *Review of Financial Studies*, **6**:1–21 (1993); M. Grinblatt and S. Titman, "The Persistence of Mutual Fund Performance," *Journal of Finance*, **47**:1977–1984 (December 1992); and R. A. Ippolito, "Efficiency with Costly Information: A Study of Mutual Fund Performance, 1965–84," *Quarterly Journal of Economics*, **104**:1–23 (February 1989).

more than cover the expenses of managing the portfolios. This finding has led many funds to give up the struggle; they strive only to match the market index by investing in a well-diversified portfolio. Corporate pension schemes now invest over a quarter of their United States equity holdings in index funds.[14]

If markets are efficient, then security prices reflect available information and investment in securities is simply a fair game. But, as we pointed out earlier, this does not imply that investors are clairvoyants. Nor does it mean that prices cannot fluctuate. Because the future is so uncertain and contains so many surprises, prices would not represent fair value *unless* they fluctuated. (Of course, when we look *back*, nothing seems quite so surprising: It is easy to convince ourselves that we really knew all along how prices were going to change.)

A rather different temptation is to believe that the inability of institutions to achieve superior portfolio performance is an indication that their portfolio managers are incompetent. This is not so. Market efficiency exists only because competition is keen and managers are doing their job.

The Crash of 1987

On Monday, October 19, 1987, the Dow Jones Industrial Average fell 23 percent in 1 day. Immediately after the crash, everybody started to ask two questions: "Who were the guilty parties?" and "Do prices really reflect fundamental values?"

As in most murder mysteries, the immediate suspects are not the ones "who done it." The first group of suspects included "index arbitrageurs," who trade back and forth between index futures[15] and the stocks comprising the market index, taking advantage of any price discrepancies. On Black Monday futures fell first and fastest because investors found it easier to bail out of the stock market by way of futures than by selling individual stocks. This pushed the futures price below the stock market index.[16] Then the arbitrageurs tried to make money by selling stocks and buying futures, but they found it difficult to get up-to-date quotes on the stocks they wished to trade. Thus the futures and stock markets were for a time disconnected. Arbitrageurs contributed to the trading volume that swamped the New York Stock Exchange, but they did not cause the crash—they were the messengers who tried to transmit the selling pressure in futures markets back to the exchange.

The second suspects were large institutional investors who were trying to implement portfolio insurance schemes. Portfolio insurance aims to put a floor on the value of an equity portfolio by progressively selling stocks and buying safe, short-term debt securities as stock prices fall. Thus the selling pressure that drove prices down on Black Monday led portfolio insurers to sell still more. One institutional investor on October 19 sold stocks and futures totaling $1.7 billion. The immediate cause of the price fall on Black Monday may have been a herd of elephants all trying to leave by the same exit.

Perhaps some large portfolio insurers can be convicted of disorderly conduct, but why did stock prices fall *worldwide*—see Table 13-1—when portfolio insurance is significant only in the United States? Moreover, if sales were triggered mainly by portfolio insurance or trading tactics, they should have conveyed little fundamental information, and prices should have bounced back after Black Monday's confusion had dissipated.

---

[14]Greenwich Associates, *Seismic Shift in Pension Planning*, 1994.

[15]An index future provides a way of trading in the stock market as a whole. It is a contract that pays investors the value of the stocks in the index at a specified future date. We discuss futures in Chapter 25.

[16]That is, sellers pushed the futures prices below their *proper relation* to the index—again, see Chapter 25. The "proper relation" is not exact equality.

TABLE 13-1

●●

Percentage changes in stock price indexes in October 1987. The column headed *U.S. Dollars* shows the return to a United States investor in these markets. This table shows that the crash of 1987 was worldwide. Therefore, it's hard to attribute the crash to index arbitrage, portfolio insurance, or other special customs of the New York market.

Country	Local Currency	U.S. Dollars
Australia	−41.8	−44.9
Austria	−11.4	−5.8
Belgium	−23.2	−18.9
Canada	−22.5	−22.9
Denmark	−12.5	−7.3
France	−22.9	−19.5
Germany	−22.3	−17.1
Hong Kong	−45.8	−45.8
Ireland	−29.1	−25.4
Italy	−16.3	−12.9
Japan	−12.8	−7.7
Malaysia	−39.8	−39.3
Mexico	−35.0	−37.6
Netherlands	−23.3	−18.1
New Zealand	−29.3	−36.0
Norway	−30.5	−28.8
Singapore	−42.2	−41.6
South Africa	−23.9	−29.0
Spain	−27.7	−23.1
Sweden	−21.8	−18.6
Switzerland	−26.1	−20.8
United Kingdom	−26.4	−22.1
United States	−21.6*	−21.6*

*Standard and Poor's 500 index.
Source: R. Roll, "The International Crash of October 1987," in R. Kamphis (ed.), *Black Monday and the Future of Financial Markets*, Richard D. Irwin, Inc., Homewood, Ill., 1989. See table 1, p. 37.

So why did prices fall so sharply? There was no obvious, new fundamental information to justify such a sharp decline in share values. For this reason, the idea that market price is the best estimate of intrinsic value seems less compelling than before. It appears that either prices were irrationally high before Black Monday or irrationally low afterward. Could the theory of efficient markets be another casualty of the crash?

The crash reminds us of how exceptionally difficult it is to value common stocks from scratch. For example, suppose that in May 1995 you wanted to check whether common stocks were fairly valued. At least as a first stab, you might have used the constant-growth formula that we introduced in Chapter 4. The annual dividend on the Standard and Poor's Composite Index was about 13.2. Suppose the dividend was expected to grow at a steady rate of 11 percent a year and investors required an annual return of 13.5 percent a year from common stocks. The constant-growth formula gives a value for the index of

$$PV(\text{index}) = \frac{DIV}{r - g} = \frac{13.2}{.135 - .11} = 528$$

which is close to the actual level of the index in May 1995. But how confident would you be about any of these figures? Perhaps the likely dividend growth was only 10.25 percent per year. This would produce a 23 percent downward revision in your estimate of the right level for the index, from 528 to 406!

$$PV(\text{index}) = \frac{13.2}{.135 - .1025} = 406$$

In other words, a price drop like Black Monday's could have occurred in May 1995 if investors had suddenly become .75 percentage point less optimistic about future dividend growth.

The extreme difficulty of valuing common stocks from scratch has two important consequences. First, investors almost always price a common stock relative to yesterday's price or relative to today's price of comparable securities. In other words, they generally take yesterday's price as correct, adjusting upward or downward on the basis of today's information. If information arrives smoothly, then as time passes, investors become more and more confident that today's market level is correct. However, when investors lose confidence in the benchmark of yesterday's price, there may be a period of confused trading and volatile prices before a new benchmark is established.

Second, the hypothesis that stock price *always* equals intrinsic value is nearly impossible to test, precisely because it's so difficult to calculate intrinsic value without referring to prices. Thus the crash didn't conclusively disprove the hypothesis, but many people now find it less *plausible*.[17]

However, the crash does not undermine the evidence for market efficiency with respect to *relative* prices. Take, for example, Alleghany Power, which sold for $22 per share in May 1995. Could we *prove* that true intrinsic value is $22? No, but we could be more confident that Alleghany's price should be close to Baltimore Gas & Electric's (also $22), since the two companies had identical earnings per share, paid a similar dividend, and had similar prospects. Moreover, if either company announced unexpectedly higher earnings, we could be quite confident that its share price would respond instantly and without bias. In other words, the subsequent price would be set correctly relative to the prior price.

No Theory Is Perfect

During the 1960s and 1970s financial journals were brimming with articles demonstrating market efficiency. The evidence was so overwhelming that any dissenting research was regarded with suspicion. But by the 1980s readers had become weary of hearing the same message. Puzzles and anomalies became the order of the day.

We have already referred to one such puzzle—the abnormally high returns on the stocks of small firms. For example, look back at Figure 7-1, which shows the results of investing $1 in 1926 in the stocks of either small or large firms. (Notice that the portfolio values in Figure 7-1 are plotted on a logarithmic scale.) By 1994 the $1

---

[17]Some economists believe that the market is prone to "bubbles"—situations in which price grows faster than fundamental value, but investors don't sell because they expect price to *keep* rising. Of course, all such bubbles pop eventually, but they can, in theory, be self-sustaining for a while. The *Journal of Economic Perspectives*, **4** (Spring 1990), contains several nontechnical articles on bubbles.

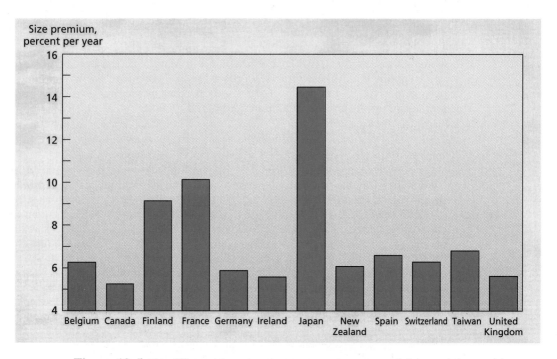

Figure 13-5 The difference between the average return on small firms and that on large firms has been positive in most countries. [*Source:* Data are drawn from a variety of studies and relate to a variety of periods since 1954. They are summarized in G. Hawawini and D. B. Keim, "On the Predictability of Common Stock Returns: World-Wide Evidence," in R. A. Jarrow, V. Maksimovic, and W. T. Ziemba (eds.), *Finance,* North Holland, Amsterdam, Netherlands, 1994.]

invested in small-firm stocks had appreciated to $2843, while the investment in large firms was worth only $811.[18] Although small firms had higher betas, the difference was not nearly large enough to explain the difference in returns.

Now, this may mean one of three things. First, it could be that investors have demanded a higher expected return from small firms to compensate for some extra risk factor that is not captured in the simple capital asset pricing model. That is why we asked in Chapter 8 whether the small-firm effect is evidence against the CAPM.

Second, the superior performance of small firms could simply be a coincidence, a finding that stems from the efforts of many researchers to find interesting patterns in the data. There is evidence for and against the coincidence theory. On the one hand, you can see from Figure 7-1 that the superior performance of small-firm stocks is limited to a relatively short period. Until the early 1960s small-firm and large-firm stocks were neck and neck. A wide gap then opened in the next two decades and narrowed again in the 1980s. On the other hand, if the small-firm effect is a coincidence, it is a fairly pervasive one, for you can see from Figure 13-5 that small-firm stocks have provided a higher return in many other countries.

The third possibility is that we have here an important exception to the efficient-market theory, one that provided investors with an opportunity to make predictably superior profits over a period of two decades.

---

[18]In each case the portfolio values assume that dividends are reinvested.

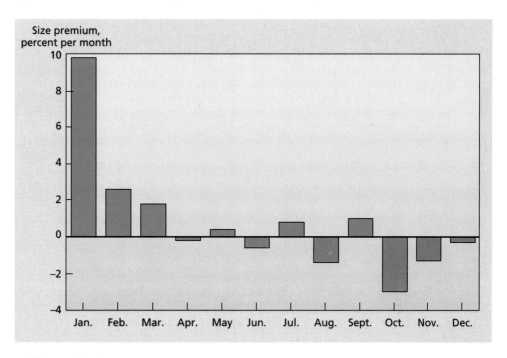

Figure 13-6 The size premium—difference between the average return on small firms and that on large firms—between April 1962 and December 1989, by month. Notice that the small-firm effect occurs entirely in January. [*Source:* G. Hawawini and D. B. Keim, "On the Predictability of Common Stock Returns: World-Wide Evidence," in R. A. Jarrow, V. Maksimovic, and W. T. Ziemba (eds.), *Finance,* North Holland, Amsterdam, Netherlands, 1994.]

But this is not the end of the puzzle, for look now at Figure 13-6, which shows the difference between the performance of small- and large-firm stocks in January and the remaining months. Notice that almost all the gains from investing in small firms came in the month of January. Indeed most of the gain came during the *first week* of January. What is the explanation? Another coincidence, or an example of an irrational and inefficient market?

One more puzzle! Fama and French have argued that there are long-term patterns in stock prices, with several years of upswing followed by more sluggish periods. Also, the periods of high return appear to be preceded by high dividend yields. For example, suppose that between 1927 and 1986 you had invested in the market whenever dividend yields were 1 percentage point higher than average. In this case over the following 4 years your annual return would have been 3 percent over the long-term average.[19]

---
[19]See E. F. Fama and K. R. French, "Dividend Yields and Expected Stock Returns, *Journal of Financial Economics,* **22**:3–26 (October 1988). It is difficult to be sure whether long-term relationships really exist, and there is some dispute about the reliability of these findings. See, for example, J. Boudoukh and M. Richardson, "The Statistics of Long-Horizon Regressions Revisited," *Mathematical Finance,* **4**:103–119 (April 1994); and M. Richardson and T. Smith, "Tests of Financial Models in the Presence of Overlapping Observations," *Review of Financial Studies,* **4**:227–254 (1991).

Once again it is difficult to know how to interpret such findings. Perhaps there are some years when investors rationally demand a higher reward for taking on the risk of stock market investment. Maybe Fama and French have just uncovered another coincidence. Or maybe markets are less efficient than they once seemed, and investors have ignored some simple profit opportunities.

While there is no lack of such puzzles, we believe that there is now widespread agreement that capital markets function well and that opportunities for easy profits are rare.[20] So nowadays when economists come across instances where market prices apparently don't make sense, they don't throw the efficient-market hypothesis onto the economic garbage heap. Instead, they think carefully about whether there is some missing ingredient that their theories ignore.

We suggest that financial managers should assume, at least as a starting point, that security prices are fair and that it is very difficult to outguess the market. This has some implications for the financial manager.

13-3   THE SIX LESSONS OF MARKET EFFICIENCY

Lesson 1: Markets Have No Memory

The weak form of the efficient-market hypothesis states that the sequence of past price changes contains no information about future changes. Economists express the same idea more concisely when they say that the market has no memory. Sometimes financial managers *seem* to act as if this were not the case. For example, studies by Taggart and others in the United States and by Marsh in the United Kingdom show that managers generally favor equity rather than debt financing after an abnormal price rise.[21] The idea is to "catch the market while it is high." Similarly, they are often reluctant to issue stock after a fall in price. They are inclined to wait for a rebound. But we know that the market has no memory and the cycles that financial managers seem to rely on do not exist.[22]

Sometimes a financial manager will have inside information indicating that the firm's stock is overpriced or underpriced. Suppose, for example, that there is some good news which the market does not know but you do. The stock price will rise sharply when the news is revealed. Therefore, if the company sold shares at the current price, it would be offering a bargain to new investors at the expense of present stockholders.

---

[20]Most people think they know a duck when they see one, but it is hard to come up with a satisfactory definition. It is rather like that with efficient markets. We have talked about "well-functioning" markets and "fair" markets without ever saying precisely what this means. Fama defined efficient markets in terms of the difference between the actual price and the price that investors expected given a particular set of information. An efficient market, Fama argues, is one in which the expected value of this difference is zero. See E. F. Fama, "Efficient Capital Markets: A Review of Theory and Empirical Work," *Journal of Finance*, **25**:383–417 (May 1970). Rubinstein defines an efficient market as one in which prices would not be altered if everyone revealed all that he or she knew. See M. Rubinstein, "Securities Market Efficiency in an Arrow-Debreu Economy," *American Economic Review*, **65**:812–824 (December 1975).

[21]R. A. Taggart, "A Model of Corporate Financing Decisions," *Journal of Finance*, **32**:1467–1484 (December 1977); P. Asquith and D. W. Mullins, Jr., "Equity Issues and Offering Dilution," *Journal of Financial Economics*, **15**:16–89 (January–February 1986); P. R. Marsh, "The Choice between Debt and Equity: An Empirical Study," *Journal of Finance*, **37**:121–144 (March 1982).

[22]If high stock prices signal expanded investment opportunities and the need to finance these new investments, we would expect to see firms raise more money *in total* when stock prices are historically high. But this does not explain why firms prefer to raise the extra cash at these times by an issue of equity rather than debt.

Naturally, managers are reluctant to sell new shares when they have favorable inside information. But such inside information has nothing to do with the history of the stock price. Your firm's stock could be selling now at half its price of a year ago, and yet you could have special information suggesting that it is *still* grossly overvalued. Or it may be undervalued at twice last year's price.

····················
Lesson 2:
Trust
Market
Prices

In an efficient market you can trust prices, for they impound all available information about the value of each security. This means that in an efficient market there is no way for most investors to achieve consistently superior rates of return. To do so, you not only need to know more than *anyone* else; you need to know more than *everyone* else. This message is important for the financial manager who is responsible for the firm's exchange-rate policy or for its purchases and sales of debt. If you operate on the basis that you are smarter than others at predicting currency changes or interest-rate moves, you will trade a consistent financial policy for an elusive will-o'-the-wisp.

The company's assets may also be directly affected by management's faith in its investment skills. For example, one company may purchase another simply because its management thinks that the stock is undervalued. On approximately half the occasions the stock of the acquired firm really will be undervalued. But on the other half it will be overvalued. On average the value will be correct, so the acquiring company is playing a fair game except for the costs of acquisition.

EXAMPLE—ORANGE COUNTY.   In December 1994 Orange County, one of the wealthiest counties in the United States, announced that it had lost $1.7 billion on its investment portfolio. The losses arose because the county treasurer, Robert Citron, had raised large short-term loans which he then used to bet on a rise in bond prices.[23] The bonds that the county bought were backed by government-guaranteed mortgage loans. However, many of them were of an unusual type known as *reverse floaters*, which means that as interest rates rise, the interest payment on each bond is reduced, and vice versa.

Reverse floaters are riskier than normal bonds. When interest rates rise, prices of all bonds fall, but prices of reverse floaters suffer a double whammy because the interest payments decline as the discount rate rises. Thus Robert Citron's policy of borrowing to invest in reverse floaters ensured that when, contrary to his forecast, interest rates subsequently rose, the fund suffered huge losses.

Like Robert Citron, financial managers sometimes take large bets because they believe that they can spot the direction of interest rates, stock prices, or exchange rates, and sometimes their employers may encourage them to speculate.[24] We do not mean to imply that such speculation always results in losses, as in Orange County's case, for in an efficient market speculators win as often as they lose. But corporate and municipal treasurers would do better to trust market prices rather than incur large risks in the quest for trading profits.

---

[23]Orange County borrowed money in the following way: Suppose it bought bond A and then sold it to a bank with a promise to buy it back at a slightly higher price. The cash from this sale was then invested in bond B. If bond prices fell, the county lost twice over: Its investment in bond B was worth less than the purchase price, and it was obliged to repurchase bond A for more than the bond was now worth. The sale and repurchase of bond A is known as a repurchase agreement, or "repo." We describe repos in Chapter 32.

[24]We don't know why Robert Citron gambled with Orange County's money, but he was under pressure to make up for a shortfall in tax revenues.

If the market is efficient, prices impound all available information. Therefore, if we can only learn to read the entrails, security prices can tell us a lot about the future. For example, in Chapter 27 we will show how information in the company's financial statements can help the financial manager to estimate the probability of bankruptcy. But the market's assessment of the company's securities can also provide important clues about the firm's prospects.[25] Thus, if the company's bonds are offering a much higher yield than the average, you can deduce that the firm is probably in trouble.

Here is another example: Suppose that investors are confident that interest rates are going to rise over the next year. In that case, they will prefer to wait before they make long-term loans, and any firm that wants to borrow long-term money today will have to offer the inducement of a higher rate of interest. In other words, the long-term rate of interest will have to be higher than the 1-year rate. Differences between the long-term interest rate and the short-term rate tell you something about what investors expect to happen to short-term rates in the future.[26]

ONE MORE EXAMPLE—VIACOM'S BID FOR PARAMOUNT. On September 12, 1993, the entertainment company Viacom announced an $8.2 billion friendly bid for Paramount. The following week QVC countered with its own bid for Paramount, worth $9.5 billion. These were the opening salvos in a bidding war that was to continue for 5 months before Viacom emerged the winner.

But what did investors think of the acquisition? When Viacom announced its bid, its shares fell by 6.8 percent, while the Standard and Poor's index fell by .4 percent. On past evidence a change in the market index affected Viacom's shares as follows:

$$\text{Expected return on Viacom} = \alpha + \beta \times \text{return on market}$$
$$= .01 + .78 \times \text{return on market}$$

The alpha (α) of .01 tells us that, when the market was unchanged, Viacom's shares rose on average by .01 percent a day.[27] The beta (β) of .78 indicates that each 1 percent rise in the market index added an additional .78 percent to Viacom's return. Since the market fell by .4 percent at the time of Viacom's bid, we would normally expect the share price to change by $.01 + .78 \times (-.4) = -.3$ percent.[28] So Viacom's shares provided an *abnormal* return of −6.5 percent:

$$\text{Abnormal return} = \text{actual return} - \text{expected return} = (-6.8) - (-.3) = -6.5\%$$

---

[25]See W. H. Beaver, "Market Prices, Financial Ratios and the Prediction of Failure," *Journal of Accounting Research*, **6**:179–192 (Autumn 1968).

[26]We will discuss the relationship between short-term and long-term interest rates in Chapter 23. Notice, however, that in an efficient market the difference between the prices of *any* short-term and long-term contracts always says something about how participants expect prices to move.

[27]It is important when estimating α and β that you choose a period in which you believe that the stock behaved normally. If its performance was abnormal, then estimates of α and β cannot be used to measure the returns that investors expected. As a precaution, ask yourself whether your estimates of expected returns *look* sensible.

[28]You will generally get a fairly similar answer if you use the capital asset pricing model to measure abnormal returns. This states that the expected return for Viacom stock is

Expected return = $r_f + \beta(r_m - r_f)$

The market return (r_m) was −.4 percent. The interest rate (r_f) was about 3 percent a year, or .01 percent a day. Therefore, the abnormal return for Viacom stock remains at −6.5 percent:

Expected return = $.01 + .78 (-.4 - .01) = -.3\%$

Abnormal return = actual return − expected return = $-6.8 - (-.3) = -6.5\%$

The total value of Viacom's shares just before the bid was about $7.9 billion. So the abnormal fall in the value of the firm's shares was .065 × 7.9 billion, or $.515 billion.

To see the performance of Viacom stock over a somewhat longer period, we can accumulate the daily abnormal returns. Thus, if Viacom stock offered an abnormal return of +5 percent on one day and +6 percent on the next, its *cumulative* abnormal return over the 2 days would be 1.05 × 1.06 − 1 = .113, or 11.3 percent. Figure 13-7 shows the cumulative abnormal performance of Viacom's stock both before and after its bid for Paramount. You can see that the abnormal return from just before the initial bid until the final acquisition was about −50 percent. This was equivalent to a $4 billion fall in the value of Viacom's stock.

Notice two things about our example. First, the market's unenthusiastic response to the bid should have suggested to management that investors regarded the proposed acquisition as a poor deal for Viacom. Figure 13-7 shows that during the next few months, as Viacom battled for control of Paramount, the stock price declined further and the message to management became correspondingly louder and clearer. Of course, Viacom's managers may have had other information which investors lacked and may have correctly decided to go ahead with the bid anyway. Our point is simply that Viacom's stock price provided a potentially valuable summary of investor opinion.

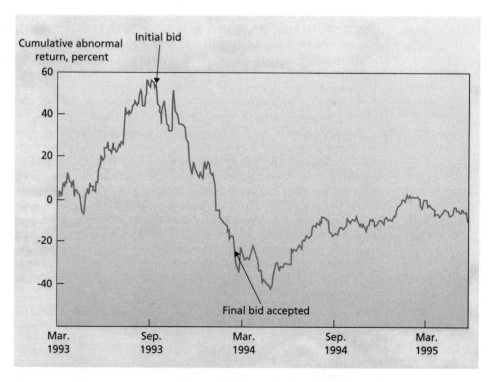

Figure 13-7 Cumulative abnormal returns from Viacom stock around the time of its takeover battle for Paramount. The negative abnormal return following Viacom's bid suggests that investors regarded the acquisition as a negative-NPV investment.

Second, our example illustrates a very handy way to calculate the abnormal return on a stock. You will come across many instances in the following chapters when we ask how a particular type of financing decision affects the value of the firm. To answer this question, we will focus on that part of the stock return that is not due to marketwide fluctuations. We refer to this as the *abnormal return* on the firm's stock. Remember:

- Abnormal return = actual return − expected return.
- To measure expected return, we can look at how the firm's stock has responded in the past to market fluctuations.[29]

**Lesson 4:
There
Are No
Financial
Illusions**

In an efficient market there are no financial illusions. Investors are unromantically concerned with the firm's cash flows and the portion of those cash flows to which they are entitled.

EXAMPLE—STOCK SPLITS AND DIVIDENDS.   We can illustrate our fourth lesson by looking at the effect of stock splits and stock dividends. Every year hundreds of companies increase the number of shares outstanding either by subdividing the existing shares or by distributing more shares of stock as dividends. For a large company, the administrative costs of such action may exceed $1 million. Yet it does not affect in any other way the company's cash flows or the proportion of these cash flows attributable to each shareholder. You may think that you are better off owning, say, 300 new shares in place of 100 old ones, but that is an illusion.

Suppose the stock of Chaste Manhattan Finance Company is selling for $210 per share. A 3-for-1 split would replace each outstanding share with three new shares.[30] Chaste would probably arrange this by printing two new shares for each original share and distributing the new shares to its stockholders as a "free gift." After the split we would expect each share to sell for 210/3 = $70. Dividends per share, earnings per share, and all other "per share" variables would be one-third their previous levels.

A variety of justifications have been proposed for splits and stock dividends. One endorsement came from the president of a large American corporation, who observed that stock dividends "give shareholders a reasonable hedge against inflation and let them participate in the increase in book value." "On the other hand," he warned, "it would be silly to declare [them] if not earned because that would just lower the book value." A further argument was proposed by the chairman of another company, who suggested that paying a stock dividend would provide investors with "a greater return while at the same time conserving cash to finance the company's anticipated growth."[31] A third and disarmingly simple explanation was offered by a textbook which observed that stockholders like stock splits because they expect them to be followed by more stock splits. Claims such as these contrast strongly with the efficient-market notion that investors are concerned solely with their share of the company's cash flows.

---

[29]A little knowledge is a dangerous thing: If you want a good estimate of the abnormal return, you need to know more about how to calculate it than the brief overview that we provide. We suggest that you consult S. J. Brown and J. B. Warner, "Measuring Security Price Performance," *Journal of Financial Economics,* **8**:205–258 (1980).

[30]There are some confusing transatlantic differences in terminology. In the United Kingdom such increases usually take the form of a "'scrip issue." A 2-for-1 scrip issue (i.e., two new shares in addition to one old) is equivalent to a 3-for-1 stock split.

[31]Cited in J. E. Walter, *Dividend Policy and Enterprise Valuation,* Wadsworth Publishing Company, Inc., Belmont, Calif., 1967.

Figure 13-8 Cumulative abnormal returns at the time of a stock split. (Returns are adjusted for the increase in the number of shares.) Notice the rise before the split and the absence of abnormal changes after the split. [*Source:* E. Fama, L. Fisher, M. Jensen, and R. Roll, "The Adjustment of Stock Prices to New Information," *International Economic Review,* **10:**1–21 (February 1969), fig. 2b, p. 13.]

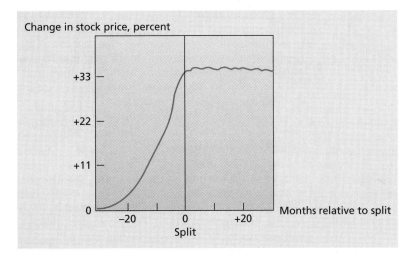

Of course, extremely high stock prices are inconvenient for small investors. In September 1994 shares in Japan Telecom Company (NTT) were issued at 4.7 million yen each, or about $48,000. That is a nuisance if you have only a few thousand dollars to invest. But this does not justify the many companies that split their shares when they are selling for less than $100.[32]

Figure 13-8 provides some evidence on whether investors were fooled by stock splits during the period from 1926 to 1960.[33] It shows the cumulative abnormal performance of stocks around the time of the split after adjustment for the increase in the number of shares.[34] Notice the rise in price before the split. The announcement of the split would have occurred in the last month or two of this period. That means the decision to split is both the consequence of a rise in price and the cause of a further rise. It looks as if shareholders are not as hardheaded as we have been making out: They do seem to care about form as well as substance. However, during the subsequent year two-thirds of the splitting companies announced above-average increases in cash dividends. Usually such an announcement would cause an unusual rise in the stock price, but in the case of the splitting companies there was no such occurrence at any time after the split. Indeed, the stocks of those companies that did *not* increase their dividends by an above-average amount declined in value to levels prevailing well before the split. The apparent explanation is that the split was ac-

---

[32]Lakonishok and Lev provide some evidence that many companies do split their stocks in order to keep the price in a desirable trading range. See J. Lakonishok and B. Lev, "Stock Splits and Stock Dividends: Why, Who and When," *Journal of Finance,* **42:**913–932 (September 1987).

[33]See E. F. Fama, L. Fisher, M. Jensen, and R. Roll, "The Adjustment of Stock Prices to New Information," *International Economic Review,* **10:**1–21 (February 1969). Later researchers have discovered that shareholders make abnormal gains both when the split or stock dividend is announced and when it takes place. Nobody has offered a convincing explanation for the latter phenomenon. See, for example, M. S. Grinblatt, R. W. Masulis, and S. Titman, "The Valuation Effects of Stock Splits and Stock Dividends," *Journal of Financial Economics,* **13:**461–490 (December 1984).

[34]By this we mean that the study looked at the change in the shareholders' wealth. A decline in the price of Chaste Manhattan stock from $210 to $70 at the time of the split would not affect shareholders' wealth. The authors used the same technique to calculate the abnormal returns that we used when looking at Viacom.

companied by an explicit or implicit promise of a subsequent dividend increase, and the rise in price at the time of the split had nothing to do with a predilection for splits as such but with the information that it was thought to convey.

This behavior does not imply that investors necessarily liked the dividend increases for their own sake, for companies that split their stocks appear to be unusually successful in other ways. For example, Asquith, Healy, and Palepu found that stock splits were frequently preceded by sharp increases in earnings.[35] Such earnings increases are very often transitory, and investors rightly regard them with suspicion. However, the stock split provided investors with an assurance that the rise in earnings was indeed permanent.

A SECOND EXAMPLE—ACCOUNTING CHANGES.   There are other occasions on which managers seem to assume that investors suffer from financial illusion. For example, some firms devote enormous ingenuity to the task of manipulating earnings reported to stockholders. This is done by "creative accounting"—that is, by choosing accounting methods which stabilize and increase reported earnings. Presumably firms go to this trouble because management believes that stockholders take the figures at face value. Some years ago a leading accountant echoed this belief in the following complaint:

> Let us assume that you sincerely want to report the profits in the way you feel fairly presents the true results of your company's business. This is an admirable and objective motive; but when you do this, you find that your competitor shows a relatively more favorable profit result than you do. This creates a demand for the competitor's stock, while yours lags behind. You put your analyst to work, and you find that if your competitor followed the same accounting practices you do, your results would be better than his. You show this analysis to your complaining stockholders. Naturally, they ask, "If this is true, and if your competitor's accounting practices are generally accepted, too, why not change your accounting practices and thus improve your profits?" At that point you try to explain why your accounting is much more factual and reliable than your competitor's. Your stockholders listen, but nothing you can say will convince them that they should give up a 20 percent, 50 percent, or 100 percent possible increase in the market value just because you like certain accounting practices better than others.[36]

Is this view right? Can the firm increase its market value by creative accounting? Or are the firm's shares traded in an efficient, well-functioning market, in which investors can see through such financial illusions?

A number of researchers have tried to resolve this question by looking at how the market reacts when companies change their accounting methods. For example, Robert Holthausen has studied what happens to stock prices when companies boost their reported profits by switching from accelerated depreciation to straight-line de-

[35]See P. Asquith, P. Healy, and K. Palepu, "Earnings and Stock Splits," *Accounting Review*, **64**:387–403 (July 1989).

[36]L. Spacek, "Business Success Requires an Understanding of Unsolved Problems of Accounting and Financial Reporting," address before the financial accounting class, Graduate School of Business Administration, Harvard University, September 25, 1959.

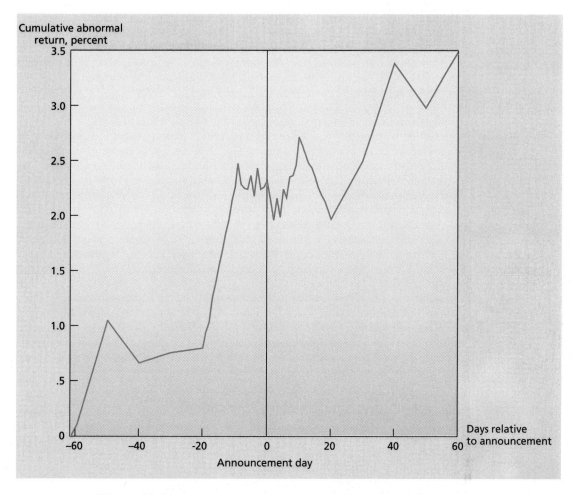

Figure 13-9 Cumulative abnormal return on stocks of firms switching from accelerated to straight-line depreciation, 1955–1978. Note: Returns are measured over 10-day periods, except during the 10 days on either side of the announcement, when they are measured daily. [*Source:* R. W. Holthausen, "Evidence on the Effect of Bond Covenants and Management Compensation Contracts on the Choice of Accounting Techniques: The Case of the Depreciation Switch-Back," *Journal of Accounting and Economics,* **3**:73–109 (1981).]

preciation.[37] This switch is purely cosmetic. It reduces the reported depreciation charge, but it does not affect the company's tax bill—the tax authorities allow firms to use accelerated depreciation for tax purposes and straight-line depreciation for reporting purposes.

Figure 13-9 shows the results of Holthausen's study. The average abnormal return over the 2 days following the announcement was a negligible −.1 percent. So it

---

[37]See R. W. Holthausen, "Evidence on the Effect of Bond Covenants and Management Compensation Contracts on the Choice of Accounting Techniques: The Case of the Depreciation Switch-Back," *Journal of Accounting and Economics,* **3**:73–109 (1981).

looks as if investors are not fooled by the accounting change, though we cannot be sure how the stock price would have reacted to the earnings announcement if the firms had *not* switched their depreciation method.[38]

This result not only suggests the futility of earnings manipulation. It also raises some more basic questions about the role of accounting conventions. Jack Treynor illustrates the problem with the fable of nail soup:

> There was once a band of itinerant soldiers who, when they had difficulty persuading townsmen to feed them, hit upon the following solution. They set a large pot of water to boiling and then, when all the townsmen were watching curiously, dropped in a nail and announced with much licking of lips that they were making nail soup. The townsmen were assured that there would be enough soup for everybody. When one of the soldiers allowed that a few carrots actually improved the flavor of nail soup, a townsman dashed off to fetch some carrots. When it was observed that tomatoes made a wonderful garnish for nail soup, another townsman quickly produced some tomatoes. Soon the nail soup contained beef stock, turnips and onions. Before the soup was served, the nail was removed. But the townsmen continued to regard the soup as nail soup.[39]

Nail soup was nourishing, but not because of the nail. Earnings have information content, but not because of the ingredients that have been the main concern of the Financial Accounting Standards Board (FASB). Accountants painstakingly put the nail into the soup; analysts painstakingly take it out, all the while believing that they are really supping on nail soup. The overall process may seem unnecessarily complicated since the same result could have been obtained without the nail.

Lesson 5: The Do-It-Yourself Alternative

In an efficient market investors will not pay others for what they can do equally well themselves. As we shall see, many of the controversies in corporate financing center on how well individuals can replicate corporate financial decisions. For example, companies often justify mergers on the grounds that they produce a more diversified and hence more stable firm. But if investors can hold the stocks of both companies, why should they thank the companies for diversifying? It is much easier and cheaper for them to diversify than it is for the firm.

The financial manager needs to ask the same question when considering whether it is better to issue debt or common stock. If the firm issues debt, it will create financial leverage. As a result, the stock will be more risky and it will offer a higher expected return. But stockholders can obtain financial leverage without the firm's issuing debt. They can borrow on their own accounts. The problem for the financial manager is, therefore, to decide whether the company can issue debt more cheaply than the individual shareholder.

---

[38]There may also have been other motives for the change in accounting method. For example, the switch to straight-line depreciation decreases the firm's book debt ratio. If there are restrictions on the firm's book leverage, it may be able to reduce their impact by the accounting change. Interestingly, the abnormal stock return was related to the degree of leverage.

[39]See J. L. Treynor, "Discussion: Changes in Accounting Techniques and Stock Prices," *Empirical Research in Accounting: Selected Studies, 1972.* Institute for Professional Accounting, Graduate School of Business, University of Chicago, 1972, p. 43.

**Lesson 6:
Seen
One
Stock,
Seen
Them All**

The elasticity of demand for any article measures the percentage change in the quantity demanded for each percentage addition to the price. If the article has close substitutes, the elasticity will be strongly negative; if not, it will be near zero. For example, coffee, which is a staple commodity, has a demand elasticity of about $-.2$. This means that a 5 percent increase in the price of coffee changes sales by $-.2 \times .05 = -.01$; in other words, it reduces demand by only 1 percent. Consumers are likely to regard different *brands* of coffee as much closer substitutes for each other. Therefore, the demand elasticity for a particular brand could be in the region of, say, -2.0. A 5 percent increase in the price of Maxwell House relative to that of Folgers would in this case reduce demand by 10 percent.

Investors don't buy a stock for its unique qualities; they buy it because it offers the prospect of a fair return for its risk. This means that stocks should be like *very* similar brands of coffee, almost perfect substitutes. Therefore, the demand for the company's stock should be very elastic. If its prospective return is too low relative to its risk, *nobody* will want to hold that stock. If it is higher, *everybody* will want to hold it.

Suppose that you want to sell a large block of stock. Since demand is elastic, you naturally conclude that you need only cut the offering price very slightly to sell your stock. Unfortunately, that doesn't necessarily follow. When you come to sell your stock, other investors may suspect that you want to get rid of it because you know something they don't. Therefore, they will revise their assessment of the stock's value downward. Demand is still elastic, but the whole demand curve moves down. Elastic demand does not imply that stock prices never change when a large sale or purchase occurs; it *does* imply that you can sell large blocks of stock at close to the market price *as long as you can convince other investors that you have no private information.*

Here is one case that supports this view: In June 1977 the Bank of England offered its holding of BP shares for sale at 845 pence each. The bank owned nearly 67 million shares of BP, so the total value of the holding was £564 million, or about $970 million. It was a huge sum to ask the public to find.

Anyone who wished to apply for BP stock had nearly 2 weeks within which to do so.[40] Just before the bank's announcement the price of BP stock was 912 pence. Over the next 2 weeks the price drifted down to 898 pence, largely in line with the British equity market. Therefore, by the final application date, the discount being offered by the bank was only 6 percent. In return for this discount, any applicant had to raise the necessary cash, taking the risk that the price of BP would decline before the result of the application was known, and had to pass over to the Bank of England the next dividend on BP.

If Maxwell House coffee is offered at a discount of 6 percent, the demand is unlikely to be overwhelming. But the discount on BP stock was enough to bring in applications for $4.6 billion worth of stock, 4.7 times the amount on offer.

We admit that this case was unusual in some respects, but an important study by Myron Scholes of a large sample of secondary offerings confirmed the ability of the market to absorb blocks of stock.[41] The average effect of the offerings was a slight

---

[40]However, applicants were required to put up only £3 per share on application and the remainder at a later date.

[41]See M. Scholes, "The Market for Securities: Substitution versus Price Pressure and the Effects of Information on Share Prices," *Journal of Business*, **45**:179–211 (April 1972). A secondary distribution is a large block of stock sold off the floor of the exchange.

reduction in the stock price, but the decline was almost independent of the amount offered. Scholes's estimate of the demand elasticity for a company's stock was -3000. Of course, this figure was not meant to be precise, and some researchers have argued that demand is not as elastic as Scholes's study suggests.[42] However, there seems to be widespread agreement with the general point that you can sell large quantities of stock at close to the market price as long as other investors do not deduce that you have some private information.

Here again we encounter an apparent contradiction with practice. Many corporations seem to believe not only that the demand elasticity is low but that it varies with the stock price, so that when the price is relatively low, new stock can be sold only at a substantial discount. State and federal regulatory commissions, which set the prices charged by local telephone companies, electric companies, and other utilities, have sometimes allowed significantly higher earnings to compensate the firm for price "pressure." This pressure is the decline in the firm's stock price that is supposed to occur when new shares are offered to investors. Yet Paul Asquith and David Mullins, who searched for evidence of pressure, found that new stock issues by utilities drove down their stock prices on average by only .9 percent.[43] We will come back to the subject of pressure when we discuss stock issues in Chapter 15.

13-4 SUMMARY

The patron saint of the Bolsa (stock exchange) in Barcelona, Spain, is Nuestra Senora de la Esperanza—Our Lady of Hope. She is the perfect patron, for we all hope for superior returns when we invest. But competition between investors will tend to produce an efficient market. In such a market, prices will rapidly impound any new information, and it will be very difficult to make consistently superior returns. We may indeed *hope*, but all we can rationally *expect* in an efficient market is that we shall obtain a return that is just sufficient to compensate us for the time value of money and for the risks we bear.

The efficient-market hypothesis comes in three different flavors. The weak form of the hypothesis states that prices efficiently reflect all the information contained in the past series of stock prices. In this case it is impossible to earn superior returns simply by looking for patterns in stock prices—in other words, price changes are random. The semistrong form of the hypothesis states that prices reflect all published information. That means it is impossible to make consistently superior returns just by reading the newspaper, looking at the company's annual accounts, and so on. The strong form of the hypothesis states that stock prices effectively impound all available information. It tells us that inside information is hard to find because in pursuing it you are in competition with thousands, perhaps millions, of active, intelligent, and greedy investors. The best you can do in this case is to assume that securities are fairly priced and to hope that one day Nuestra Senora will reward your humility.

The concept of an efficient market is simple and generally supported by the facts. Less than 30 years ago any suggestion that security investment is a fair game was gen-

---

[42]For example, see W. H. Mikkelson and M. M. Partch, "Stock Price Effects and Costs of Secondary Distributions," *Journal of Financial Economics*, **14**:165–194 (June 1985).

[43]See P. Asquith and D. W. Mullins, "Equity Issues and Offering Dilution," *Journal of Financial Economics*, **15**:61–89 (January–February 1986).

erally regarded as bizarre. Today it not only is widely discussed in business schools but also permeates investment practice and government policy toward the security markets.

For the corporate treasurer who is concerned with issuing or purchasing securities, the efficient-market theory has obvious implications. In one sense, however, it raises more questions than it answers. The existence of efficient markets does not mean that the financial manager can let financing "take care of itself." It provides only a starting point for analysis. It is time to get down to details about securities, issue procedures, and financial institutions. We start in Chapter 14.

Further Reading

The classic review articles on market efficiency are:
E. F. Fama: "Efficient Capital Markets: A Review of Theory and Empirical Work," *Journal of Finance,* **25**:383–417 (May 1970).
E. F. Fama: "Efficient Capital Markets: II," *Journal of Finance,* **46**:1575–1617 (December 1991).

The following book contains a selection of classic articles:
P. H. Cootner (ed.): *The Random Character of Stock Market Prices,* M.I.T. Press, Cambridge, Mass., 1964.

For evidence on possible exceptions to the efficient-market theory, we suggest:
G. Hawawini and D. B. Keim: "On the Predictability of Common Stock Returns: World-Wide Evidence," in R. A. Jarrow, V. Maksimovic, and W. T. Ziemba (eds.), *Finance,* North Holland, Amsterdam, Netherlands, 1994.
"Symposium on Some Anomalous Evidence on Capital Market Efficiency," a special issue of the *Journal of Financial Economics,* **6** (June 1977).

The following book contains an interesting collection of articles on the crash of 1987:
R. W. Kamphuis, Jr., et al. (eds.): *Black Monday and the Future of Financial Markets,* Dow Jones-Irwin, Inc., Homewood, Ill., 1989.

Quiz

1. Stock prices appear to behave as though successive values:
   (*a*) Are random numbers.
   (*b*) Follow regular cycles.
   (*c*) Differ by a random number.
   Which (if any) of these statements are true?

2. Supply the missing words:
   "There are three forms of the efficient-market hypothesis. Tests of randomness in stock prices provide evidence for the _____ form of the hypothesis. Tests of stock price reaction to well-publicized news provide evidence for the _____ form, and tests of the performance of professionally managed funds provide evidence for the _____ form. Market efficiency results from competition between investors. Many investors search for new information about the company's business that would help them to value the stock more accurately. This is known as _____ research. Such research helps to ensure that prices reflect all available informa-

tion: In other words, it helps to keep the market efficient in the _____ form. Other investors study past stock prices for recurrent patterns that would allow them to make superior profits. This is known as _____ research. Such research helps to ensure that prices reflect all the information contained in past stock prices: In other words, it helps to keep the market efficient in the _____ form."

3. Which of the following statements (if any) are true? The efficient-market hypothesis assumes:
    (*a*) That there are no taxes.
    (*b*) That there is perfect foresight.
    (*c*) That successive price changes are independent.
    (*d*) That investors are irrational.
    (*e*) That there are no transaction costs.
    (*f*) That forecasts are unbiased.

4. The stock of United Boot is priced at $400 and offers a dividend yield of 2 percent. The company has a 2-for-1 stock split.
    (*a*) Other things equal, what would you expect to happen to the stock price?
    (*b*) In practice would you expect the stock price to fall by more or less than this amount?
    (*c*) Suppose that a few months later United Boot announces a rise in dividends that is exactly in line with that of other companies. Would you expect the announcement to lead to a slight abnormal rise in the stock price, a slight abnormal fall, or no change?

5. True or false?
    (*a*) Financing decisions are less easily reversed than investment decisions.
    (*b*) Financing decisions don't affect the total size of the cash flows; they just affect who receives the flows.
    (*c*) Tests have shown that there is almost perfect negative correlation between successive price changes.
    (*d*) The semistrong form of the efficient-market hypothesis states that prices reflect all publicly available information.
    (*e*) In efficient markets the expected return on each stock is the same.
    (*f*) Myron Scholes's study of the effect of secondary distributions provided evidence that the demand schedule for a single company's shares is highly elastic.

6. Analysis of 60 monthly rates of return on United Futon common stock indicates $\beta = 1.45$ and $\alpha = -.2$ percent per month. A month later, the market is up by 5 percent, and United Futon is up by 6 percent. What is Futon's abnormal rate of return?

7. True or false?
    (*a*) Fundamental analysis by security analysts and investors helps keep markets efficient.
    (*b*) Technical analysis concentrates on the covariances among security returns. Technical trading rules attempt to make money by purchasing shares with low covariances.
    (*c*) If the efficient-market hypothesis is correct, managers will not be able to increase stock prices by "creative accounting," which boosts reported earnings.
    (*d*) Research on stock splits shows a strong tendency for the stock price to rise before the split is announced. This evidence supports the semistrong and strong forms of the efficient-market hypothesis.
    (*e*) Movements of the stock market are helpful in predicting future performance of the national economy.

8. Geothermal Corporation has just received good news: Its earnings increased by 20 percent from last year's value. Most investors are anticipating an increase of 25 percent. Will Geothermal's stock price increase or decrease when the announcement is made?

Questions and Problems

1. How would you respond to the following comments?
   (*a*) "Efficient market, my eye! I know of lots of investors who do crazy things."
   (*b*) "Efficient market? Balderdash! I know at least a dozen people who have made a bundle in the stock market."
   (*c*) "The trouble with the efficient-market theory is that it ignores investors' psychology."
   (*d*) "Despite all the limitations, the best guide to a company's value is its written-down book value. It is much more stable than market value, which depends on temporary fashions."

2. Respond to the following comments:
   (*a*) "The random-walk theory, with its implication that investing in stocks is like playing roulette, is a powerful indictment of our capital markets."
   (*b*) "If everyone believes you can make money by charting stock prices, then price changes won't be random."
   (*c*) "The random-walk theory implies that events are random, but many events are not random—if it rains today, there's a fair bet that it will rain again tomorrow."

3. Which of the following observations *appear* to indicate market inefficiency? Explain whether the inefficiency is weak, semistrong, or strong. (*Note:* If the market is not weak-form-efficient, it is said to be *weak-form-inefficient;* if it is not semistrong-form-efficient, it is *semistrong-form-inefficient;* and so on.)
   (*a*) Tax-exempt municipal bonds offer lower pretax returns than taxable government bonds.
   (*b*) Managers make superior returns on their purchases of their company's stock.
   (*c*) There is a positive relationship between the return on the market in one quarter and the change in aggregate corporate profits in the next quarter.
   (*d*) There is disputed evidence that stocks which have appreciated unusually in the recent past continue to do so in the future.
   (*e*) The stock of an acquired firm tends to appreciate in the period before the merger announcement.
   (*f*) Stocks of companies with unexpectedly high earnings *appear* to offer high returns for several months after the earnings announcement.
   (*g*) Very risky stocks on the average give higher returns than safe stocks.

4. Look again at Figure 13-8.
   (*a*) Is the steady rise in the stock price before the split evidence of market inefficiency?
   (*b*) How do you think those stocks performed that did *not* increase their dividends by an above-average amount?

5. Stock splits are important because they convey information. Can you suggest some other financial decisions that convey information?

6. Estimate the *abnormal* return in each of the past 3 months for one of the stocks shown in Table 9-1.

7. Between April 1985 and April 1990 Wang Laboratories' beta was $\beta = 1.02$. Wang's alpha was $\alpha = -1.52$, reflecting sharp declines in Wang's stock upon news of several serious business problems. Suppose that in a later month the stock market falls by 5 percent and Wang stock by 6 percent.

   (*a*) What is Wang's abnormal return for that month?

   (*b*) What is Wang's abnormal return compared to a predicted return based on the capital asset pricing model? The risk-free rate of interest is 8 percent per year.

   (*c*) Which measure of abnormal returns is more sensible in this case? (*Hint:* In an efficient market would you *forecast* $\alpha = -1.52$, looking forward from 1990?)

8. It is sometimes suggested that stocks with low price-earnings ratios are generally underpriced. Describe a possible test of this view. Be as precise as possible.

9. "If a project provides an unusually high rate of return in one year, it will probably do so again in the next year." Does this statement make sense if you use the definition of economic rate of return that we gave in Chapter 12?

10. "Long-term interest rates are at record highs. Most companies, therefore, find it cheaper to finance with common stock or relatively inexpensive short-term bank loans." Discuss.

11. "If the efficient-market hypothesis is true, then it makes no difference what securities a company issues. All are fairly priced." Does this follow?

12. "If the efficient-market hypothesis is true, the pension fund manager might as well select a portfolio with a pin." Explain why this is not so.

13. Bond dealers buy and sell bonds at very low spreads. In other words, they are willing to sell at a price only slightly higher than the price at which they buy. Used-car dealers buy and sell cars at very wide spreads. What has this got to do with the strong form of the efficient-market hypothesis?

14. In May 1987 Citicorp announced that it was bolstering its loan loss reserves by $3 billion in order to reflect its exposure to Third World borrowers. Consequently, second-quarter earnings were transformed from a $.5 billion profit to a $2.5 billion loss.

    In after-hours trading the price of Citicorp stock fell sharply from its closing level of $50, but the next day, when the market had had a chance to digest the news, the price recovered to $53. Other bank stocks fared less well, and *The Wall Street Journal* reported that Citicorp's decision "triggered a big sell-off of international banking stocks that roiled stock markets around the world."

    Comment on the Citicorp action varied. The bank's chairman claimed that "it significantly strengthens the institution," and analysts and bankers suggested that it was a notable step toward realism. For example, one argued that it was the recognition of the problem that made the difference, while another observed that the action "is merely recognizing what the stock market has been saying for several months: that the value of the sovereign debt of the big U.S. money center banks is between 25% and 50% less than is carried in their books." The London *Financial Times* made the more cautionary comment that Citicorp had "simply rearranged its balance sheet, not strengthened its capital base," and the Lex column described the move as an "outsize piece of cosmetic self-indulgence rather than a great stride towards the reconstruction of Third World debt." A lead article in the same paper stated that "even if all this means that Citicorp shareholders are $3 billion poorer today, the group as a whole is better placed to absorb whatever shocks lie ahead."

There was also considerable discussion of the implications for other banks. As one analyst summed up, "There's no question that the market will put higher confidence in those institutions that can reserve more fully."

Discuss the general reaction to the Citicorp announcement. It is not often that a company announces a $2.5 billion loss in one quarter and its stock price rises. Do you think that the share price reaction was consistent with an efficient market?

15. IBM announced its 1982 earnings per share (EPS) for the fourth quarter of 1982 on Friday, January 21, 1983. EPS was up 28 percent from the fourth quarter of 1981. Nevertheless, IBM's stock price dropped by $3.25 to $94.625. Security analysts explained the price drop by noting that an unexpectedly large part of the increase was due to an accounting restatement required by the Financial Accounting Standards Board's order FASB 52. The "true" increase in EPS was thought to be correspondingly less.

On Monday, January 24, IBM's stock price dropped by $.75 more, although overall market indexes were down sharply (−2.75 percent). Later in the day, IBM issued a statement clarifying the impact of FASB 52. IBM's EPS would have been just as high under prior accounting rules (FASB 8). "'The confusion on Friday was that we didn't have enough detail,' [said] Barry Tarasoff, an analyst at Goldman, Sachs & Co. 'Well, we got it today, and the fourth quarter looks fine.'"[44]

On Tuesday, IBM's stock price rose by $2.125. Is this an efficient market at work? Discuss carefully.

16. The top graph in Figure 13-1 shows the actual performance of the Standard and Poor's 500 index for a 5-year period. Two financial managers, Alpha and Beta, are contemplating this chart. Each manager's company needs to issue new shares of common stock sometime in the next year.

Alpha: My company's going to issue right away. The stock market cycle has obviously topped out, and the next move is almost surely down. Better to issue now and get a decent price for the shares.

Beta: You're too nervous—we're waiting. It's true that the market's been going nowhere for the past year or so, but the figure clearly shows a basic upward trend. The market's on the way up to a new plateau.

What would you say to Alpha and Beta?

17. (*a*) "I notice that short-term interest rates are about 1 percent below long-term rates. We should borrow short-term."

(*b*) "I notice that Swiss interest rates are about 1 percent less than rates in the United States. We would do better to borrow Swiss francs rather than dollars."

What does the efficient-market hypothesis have to say about these two statements?

18. We suggested that there are three possible interpretations of the small-firm effect—a required return for some unidentified risk factor, a coincidence, or a market inefficiency. Write three brief memos arguing each point of view.

---

[44]R. Foster Winans, "IBM's Second Set of 1982 Earnings Statistics Brings a Sigh of Relief from Puzzled Analysts," *The Wall Street Journal*, January 25, 1983, p. 55. We thank Paul Healy for suggesting this example.

TABLE 13-2
•••

See problem 20.

Month	(a) Market return	(b) Executive Cheese return	(c) Paddington Beer return
1993:			
January	0.7%	4.6%	4.4%
February	1.4	10.5	2.3
March	2.2	8.8	−5.6
April	−2.5	13.5	−12.5
May	2.7	15.3	−4.5
June	0.3	0.1	0.8
July	−0.5	−1.2	2.6
August	3.8	−2.4	7.7
September	−0.7	−12.7	5.4
October	2.0	3.5	12.9
November	−0.9	−14.5	10.1
December	1.2	−19.2	12.7
1994:			
January	3.4	12.0	9.8
February	−2.7	10.8	−8.1
March	−4.4	−15.9	−0.8
April	1.3	0.0	14.5
May	1.6	13.8	−0.4
June	−2.5	12.3	−9.2
July	3.3	−8.4	14.5
August	4.1	4.6	−0.1
September	−2.4	−4.9	−4.5
October	2.3	9.3	−5.5
November	−3.7	−4.1	−2.0
December	1.5	−10.7	8.9

19. "It may be true that in an efficient market there *should* be no patterns in stock prices, but, if everyone believes that they *do* exist, then this belief will be self-fulfilling." Discuss.

20. Column (*a*) in Table 13-2 shows the monthly returns on the Standard and Poor's index from January 1993 through December 1994. Columns (*b*) and (*c*) show the returns on the stocks of two firms. Both firms announced dividend increases during this period—Executive Cheese in April 1993 and Paddington Beer in July 1994. Calculate the average abnormal return of the two stocks during the month of the dividend announcement.

14

An Overview of Corporate Financing

This chapter begins our analysis of long-term financing decisions—a task we will not complete until Chapter 26. We will devote considerable space in these chapters to the classic finance problems of dividend policy and the use of debt versus equity financing. Yet to concentrate on these problems alone would miss the enormous *variety* of financing instruments that are used by companies today.

Look, for example, at Table 14-1. It shows the many debt securities issued by International Paper. One of these is a convertible issue. The company has also issued common stock to its shareholders, of course, and it has over $1 billion in short-term debt from banks and other lenders. The shareholders have also authorized two classes of preferred stock, but none of these securities was actually issued.

International Paper has a $1.5 billion standby line of credit: A group of banks has agreed to lend International Paper up to $1.5 billion on short notice if it needs the money. This line of credit was not in use at the end of 1993. The company has also executed interest-rate swaps converting the interest on $400 million of long-term debt from fixed payments to variable, or "floating," payments based on LIBOR, the London interbank offered rate. It has a small currency swap obligating it to pay British pounds in exchange for U.S. dollars.

You may not know what "swaps," "debentures," "convertibles," or "preferred stocks" are. Relax—we'll tell you in this chapter. Then we'll go on to discuss a series of questions chosen to put corporate financing in perspective. Do companies rely too heavily on internal financing rather than new issues of debt or equity? Are debt ratios of United States corporations dangerously high? How do patterns of financing differ across the major industrialized countries?

This chapter is an introductory survey of financing. It touches on many topics to be explored more carefully later. But later in this chapter we will come to an extremely important general issue, the problem of corporate control or governance, and the agency costs incurred when control is imperfect. We close the chapter by comparing the systems of corporate control in the United States, Germany, and Japan.

We begin, however, with a closer look at the common stock issued by United States corporations.

TABLE 14-1

Large firms typically issue many different securities. This table shows some of the debt securities on International Paper's balance sheet at the end of 1993 (figures in millions).

Debt Security	Amount
9.4 to 9.7% notes due 1995–2002	$400
7⅜% notes due 2004, 2023	398
6⅛% notes due 2003	199
6⅞% notes due 2023	197
Medium-term notes due 1994–2006	549
9¼% French franc note due 1994	95
5⅛% debentures due 2012	78
5¼% euro-convertible subordinated debentures due 2002	199
Environmental and industrial development bonds	747
Commercial paper	516
Other French franc borrowing	95
German mark borrowing	214

Source: International Paper, 1993 annual report.

14-1 COMMON STOCK

Defini-tions

Table 14-2 shows the common equity of International Paper as it was reported in the company's books at the end of 1993.

The maximum number of shares that can be issued is known as the *authorized share capital*—for International Paper, it is 400 million shares. This maximum is specified in the firm's articles of incorporation and can be increased only with the permission of the stockholders. International Paper has already issued 127 million shares, and so it can issue 273 million more without the stockholders' approval.

Most of the issued shares are held by investors. These shares are said to be *issued and outstanding*. But International Paper has also bought back 3.4 million shares from investors. These shares are held in the company's treasury until they are either canceled or resold. Treasury shares are said to be *issued but not outstanding*.

The issued shares are entered in the company's books at their par value. Each share has a par value of $1.00. Thus, the total book value of the issued shares is

$$127 \times \$1.00 = \$127 \text{ million}$$

Par value has little economic significance.[1] Some companies issue shares with no par value. In this case, the stock is listed in the accounts at an arbitrarily determined figure.

The price of new shares sold to the public almost always exceeds the par value. The difference is entered in the company's accounts as additional paid-in capital

---

[1]Because some states do not allow companies to sell shares below par value, par value is generally set at a low figure.

TABLE 14-2

Book value of common stockholders' equity of International Paper, December 31, 1993 (figures in millions)	
Common shares ($1.00 par value per share)	$ 127
Additional capital	1,704
Retained earnings	4,553
Treasury shares at cost	(159)
Net common equity	$6,225

Note:
Shares:
Authorized shares	400.0
Issued shares, of which:	127.3
Outstanding shares	123.9
Treasury shares	3.4

or capital surplus. Thus, if International Paper sold an additional 100,000 shares at $40 a share, the common stock account would be increased by $100,000 \times \$1.00 =$ $100,000 and the additional capital account by $100,000 \times (\$40 - \$1) = \$3,900,000$.

Usually International Paper pays out less than half of its earnings as dividends. The remainder is retained in the business and used to finance new investment. The cumulative amount of retained earnings is $4553 million.

Finally, the common stock account shows the amount that the company has spent on repurchasing its own stock. The repurchase has *reduced* the stockholders' equity by $159 million.

The net common equity has a book value of $6225 million. But in December 1993 International Paper shares were priced at $68 each. So the *market value* of the equity was $127 \times 68 = \$8636$ million, more than $2 billion higher than book.

Stockholders' Rights

The common stockholders are the owners of the corporation. They therefore have a general *preemptive right* to anything of value that the company may wish to distribute. They also have the ultimate control of the company's affairs. In practice this control is limited to a right to vote, either in person or by proxy, on appointments to the *board of directors* and a number of other matters. Mergers, for example, need to be submitted for shareholder approval.

If the corporation's articles specify a *majority voting* system, each director is voted upon separately and stockholders can cast one vote for each share that they own. If the articles permit *cumulative voting*, the directors are voted upon jointly and the stockholders can, if they want, allot all their votes to just one candidate.[2] Cumulative voting makes it easier for a minority group among the stockholders to elect directors representing the group's interests. That is why minority groups devote so much of their efforts to campaigning for cumulative voting.

---

[2]For example, suppose there are five directors to be elected and you own 100 shares. You therefore have a total of $5 \times 100 = 500$ votes. Under the majority voting system, you can cast a maximum of 100 votes for any one candidate. Under a cumulative voting system, you can cast all 500 votes for your favorite candidate.

On many issues a simple majority of votes cast are sufficient to carry the day, but the company charter will specify some decisions that require a supermajority of, say, 75 percent of those eligible to vote. For example, a supermajority vote is sometimes needed to approve a merger. This requirement makes it difficult for the firm to be taken over and therefore helps to protect the incumbent management.

The issues on which stockholders are asked to vote are rarely contested, particularly in the case of large, publicly traded firms. Occasionally there are *proxy contests* in which the firm's existing management and directors compete with outsiders for control of the corporation. But the odds are stacked against the outsiders, for the insiders can get the firm to pay all the costs of presenting their case and obtaining votes.

Most companies issue just one class of common stock. Occasionally, however, a firm may have two classes outstanding, which differ in their right to vote and receive dividends. Suppose that a firm needs fresh equity capital but its present stockholders do not want to relinquish their control of the firm. The existing shares could be labeled "class A," and "class B" shares issued to outside investors. The class B shares could have limited voting privileges, although they would probably sell for less as a result.[3]

Equity in Disguise

Common stockholders are the owners of the business. They hold the *equity interest* or *residual claim*, since they receive whatever assets or earnings are left over in the business after all its debts are paid. They have *limited liability:* The most shareholders can lose, if their company goes bust, is their investment in the stock. None of the shareholders' other assets is exposed to the company's troubles.

Common stocks are, of course, issued by corporations. But a few equity securities are issued not by corporations but by partnerships or trusts. We will give some brief examples.

PARTNERSHIPS.   Newhall Land and Farming is a *master limited partnership* which owns, farms, and is gradually developing large tracts of real estate, mostly in southern California. You can buy "units" in this partnership on the New York Stock Exchange, thus becoming a *limited* partner in Newhall. "Limited" means *limited liability:* The most the limited partners can lose is their investment in the company.[4] In this and most other respects, the Newhall partnership units are just like the shares of an ordinary corporation. The units share in the profits of the business and receive cash distributions (like dividends) from time to time.

Partnerships avoid corporate income tax; any profits or losses are passed straight through to the partners' tax returns. Offsetting this tax advantage are various limitations of partnerships. For example, the law regards a partnership merely as a voluntary association of individuals; like its partners, it is expected to have limited life. A corporation, on the other hand, is an independent legal "person" which can, and of-

---

[3]R. C. Lease, J. J. McConnell, and W. H. Mikkleson have studied companies with two classes of publicly traded shares. They found that the class with superior voting rights almost always traded at the higher price. Typical premiums were on the order of 2 to 4 percent. See "The Market Value of Control in Publicly Traded Corporations," *Journal of Financial Economics*, **11**:439–471 (April 1983), especially table 4, pp. 460–461.

[4]This may seem inconsistent with Chapter 1, where we said that partnerships do not have limited liability. But a partnership like Newhall can offer limited liability *only* to its limited partners. Such partnerships must also have one or more general partners, who have unlimited liability. However, general partners can be corporations. This puts the corporation's shield of limited liability between the partnership and the human beings who ultimately own the general partner.

ten does, outlive all its original shareholders, managers, and employees. The following description of a corporation was written in 1819 by Chief Justice John Marshall:

> A corporation is an artificial being, invisible, intangible, and existing only in contemplation of law. Being the mere creature of law, it possesses only those properties which the charter of its creation confers upon it. . . . Among the most important are immortality, and, if the expression may be allowed, individuality; properties, by which a perpetual succession of many persons are considered as the same, and may act as a single individual. They enable a corporation to manage its own affairs, and to hold property without the perplexing intricacies, the hazardous and endless necessity, of perpetual conveyances for the purpose of transmitting it from hand to hand. . . . By these means, a perpetual succession of individuals are capable of acting for the promotion of the particular object, like one immortal being.[5]

TRUSTS AND REITs.   Would you like to own a part of the oil in the Prudhoe Bay field on the north slope of Alaska? Just call your broker and buy a few units of the Prudhoe Bay Royalty Trust. British Petroleum (BP) set up this trust and gave it a royalty interest in production from BP's share of the Prudhoe Bay revenues. At the end of 1993 each trust unit represented about 2 barrels of "proved" oil in the ground. As the oil is produced, each trust unit gets its share of the revenues.

This trust is the passive owner of a single asset, the right to a share of the revenues from BP's Prudhoe Bay production. Operating businesses, which cannot be passive, are rarely organized as trusts, though there are exceptions, notably *real estate investment trusts*, or *REITs* (pronounced "reets").

REITs were created to facilitate public investment in commercial real estate; there are shopping center REITs, office building REITs, apartment REITs, and also REITs that specialize in lending to real estate developers and owners. REIT "shares" are traded just like common stocks.[6] The REITs themselves are not taxed, so long as they pay out at least 95 percent of earnings to the REITs' owners, who must pay whatever taxes are due on the dividends. However, REITs are tightly restricted to real estate investment. You cannot set up a widget factory and avoid corporate taxes by calling it a REIT.

14-2 A FIRST LOOK AT DEBT, PREFERREDS, AND CONVERTIBLES

When they borrow money, companies promise to make regular interest payments and to repay the principal (i.e., the original amount borrowed) according to an agreed schedule. However, this liability is limited. Stockholders have the right to default on any debt obligation if they are willing to hand over the corporation's assets to the lenders. Clearly they will choose to do this only if the value of the assets is less than the amount of the debt. In practice this handover of assets is far from straightforward. Sometimes there may be hundreds of lenders with different claims on the firm. Administration of the handover is usually left to the bankruptcy court.

Because lenders are not regarded as proprietors of the firm, they do not normally have any voting power. The company's payments of interest are regarded as a cost

---

[5]*Dartmouth College v. Woodward*, 4 Wheaton (U.S.) 518 (1819).

[6]There are also some private REITs, whose shares are not publicly traded.

and are deducted from taxable income. Thus interest is paid from *before-tax* income. In contrast, dividends on common stock are paid out of *after-tax* income. Therefore the government provides a tax subsidy on the use of debt which it does not provide on equity. We will cover debt and taxes in detail in Chapter 18.

Debt Comes in Many Forms

Some orderly scheme of classification is essential to cope with the almost infinite variety of corporate debt claims. We will spend several chapters in Part Seven examining the various features of corporate debt. But here is a preliminary guide to the major distinguishing characteristics.

MATURITY. **Funded** debt is any obligation repayable more than 1 year from the date of issue. Debt due in less than 1 year is termed **unfunded** and is carried on the balance sheet as a current liability.

Unfunded debt is often described as short-term debt and funded debt is described as long-term—although it is clearly artificial to call a 364-day note short-term and a 366-day note long-term (except on leap years).

There are corporate bonds of nearly every conceivable maturity. Walt Disney has issued a 100-year bond. Natwest and several other British banks have issued perpetuities, bonds with no specified maturity. They may survive forever. At the other extreme we find firms borrowing literally overnight. We describe how this is done in Chapter 32.

The most common short-term debt security is **commercial paper,**[7] which is issued by large, creditworthy companies. Usually industrial companies back up their commercial paper issues with a bank **line of credit**—that is, the bank agrees to lend money to repay the commercial paper if some crisis or setback prevents the company from repaying or refinancing the commercial paper directly. Of course, lines of credit are not used just for commercial paper. Financial managers arrange lines of credit to cover all kinds of seasonal or unexpected cash needs.

Smaller or less creditworthy companies, which do not have easy access to commercial paper, typically turn to banks for short-term debt financing.

REPAYMENT PROVISION. Long-term loans are commonly repaid in a steady, regular way, perhaps after an initial grace period. For publicly traded bonds this is done by means of a **sinking fund.** Each year the firm pays a sum of cash into a sinking fund which is then used to repurchase and retire the bonds.

Most firms issuing debt to the public reserve the right to **call** the debt—that is, to repay and retire all the bonds in a given issue before the final maturity date. Call prices are specified when the debt is originally issued. Usually lenders are given at least 5 years of call protection. During this period the firm cannot call the bonds.

SENIORITY. Some debt instruments are **subordinated.** In the event of default the subordinated lender gets in line behind the firm's general creditors. The subordinated lender holds a junior claim and is paid after all senior creditors are satisfied.

When you lend money to a firm, you can assume that you hold a senior claim unless the debt agreement says otherwise. However, this does not always put you at

---

[7]Commercial paper is normally shown on the balance sheet as short-term debt. International Paper showed it as long-term debt, because it had committed to "roll over" the paper and to use it as long-term financing.

the front of the line, for the firm may have set aside some of its assets specifically for the protection of other creditors. That brings us to our next classification.

SECURITY OR COLLATERAL.   We have used the word *bond* to refer to all kinds of corporate debt, but in some contexts it means **secured** debt; often *bonds* are secured by mortgages on plant and equipment, and unsecured long-term claims are called *debentures*.[8] In the event of default, the bondholders have first claim on the mortgaged assets; investors holding debentures have a general claim on the unmortgaged assets but only a junior claim on the mortgaged assets.

An asset pledged to ensure payment of a debt security or loan is called **collateral.** Thus a retailer might offer inventory or accounts receivable as collateral to obtain a short-term bank loan. If you start a small business and go to a bank for financing, the bank may ask you to put up your home as collateral until the business accumulates enough assets and earning power to support the loan on its own.

DEFAULT RISK.   Seniority and security do not guarantee payment. A bond can be senior and secured, but still be as risky as a vertiginous tightrope walker—it depends on the value and risk of the issuing firm's assets.

A debt security is **investment-grade** if it qualifies for one of the top four ratings from the Moody's or Standard and Poor's ratings services. (We describe the rating criteria in Chapter 23.) Below-investment-grade debt is traded in the so-called **junk bond** market.

Some junk debt issues are "fallen angels," securities issued as investment-grade which later fell from grace. But in the late 1970s, a *new-issue* junk bond market was created. Companies discovered a pool of investors willing to accept unusually high default risks in exchange for high promised yields. New issues of junk bonds were about $1 billion in 1977. By the peak in 1986 they totaled over $30 billion.[9] Many of these issues were made on short notice to finance mergers and so called *leveraged buy-outs* (described in Chapter 33).

Junk bond investors suffered greatly during the late 1980s and early 1990s, due to economic recession, a dry-up of acquisitions and buy-outs, and the collapse of Drexel Burnham Lambert. Drexel, led by the high-profile financier Michael Milken, had dominated issues and trading of junk bonds.

PUBLIC VERSUS PRIVATELY PLACED DEBT.   A **public issue** of bonds is offered to anyone who wants to buy, and once issued, it can be freely traded by United States and foreign investors. In a private placement the issue is sold directly to a small number of qualified lenders, including banks, insurance companies, and pension funds. The securities cannot be resold to individuals, only to qualified institutional investors. However, there is increasingly active trading *among* these investors.

The public debt market in the United States is more active than in most other countries. Large U.S. corporations look mostly to the public market for debt financing. Corporations in Germany, Japan, or France generally borrow directly from banks or other financial institutions. Bank debt is by definition privately placed.

---

[8] The terminology can be confusing. A *debenture* in the United States signifies unsecured debt; in Great Britain it usually refers to *secured* debt.

[9] See, for example, K. J. Perry and R. A. Taggart, "The Growing Role of Junk Bonds in Corporate Finance," *Journal of Applied Corporate Finance*, **1**:37–45 (Spring 1988), table 1.

FLOATING VERSUS FIXED RATES.   The interest payment or *coupon* on most long-term debt is fixed at the time of issue. If a $1000 bond is issued when long-term interest rates are 10 percent, the firm continues to pay $100 per year regardless of how interest rates fluctuate.

Loan agreements negotiated with banks usually incorporate a **floating rate.** For example, your firm may be offered a loan at "1 percent above prime." The **prime rate,** a benchmark interest rate charged by banks to creditworthy corporate customers, is adjusted up or down as interest rates on traded securities change.[10] Therefore when the prime rate changes the interest on your floating-rate loan also changes.

Floating interest rates are not necessarily tied to the prime rate. Another common base is **LIBOR** (London interbank offered rate), which is the interest rate at which major international banks in London lend dollars to each other. Yields on various Treasury securities are also frequently used.

COUNTRY AND CURRENCY.   Many large firms in the United States, particularly those having significant overseas operations, borrow abroad. If such a firm wants long-term debt, it will probably borrow by an issue of **eurobonds** sold simultaneously in several countries; if it wants unfunded debt, it will probably obtain a **eurodollar** loan from a bank.

Corporations in the United States sometimes issue bonds denominated in foreign currencies. International Paper, for example, issued $190 million in French franc debt—that means it has to generate or buy French francs for both interest and principal payments.

Often foreign subsidiaries of United States companies borrow directly from banks in the countries in which the subsidiaries are operating.[11] Cross-currency borrowing also occurs the other way around. That is, foreign corporations will offer debt denominated in dollars in the United States.

A Debt by Any Other Name

The word *debt* sounds straightforward, but companies enter into a number of financial arrangements that look suspiciously like debt but are treated differently in the accounts. Some of these obligations are easily identifiable. For example, accounts payable are simply obligations to pay for goods that have already been delivered. Other arrangements are not so easily detected. For example, instead of borrowing money to buy equipment, many companies **lease** or rent it on a long-term basis. As we will show in Chapter 26, such arrangements are economically equivalent to secured long-term debt.

Preferred Stock

In the chapters that follow we shall have much more to say about common stock and debt. **Preferred stock,** on the other hand, accounts for only a small part of new issues, and so it will occupy less time later on. However, we shall see that it is a useful method of financing in mergers and certain other special situations.

Preferred stock is legally an equity security. Despite the fact that it offers a fixed dividendlike debt, payment of the dividend is almost invariably within the complete

---

[10]"Prime" can be misleading, because the *most* creditworthy corporations—large, blue-chip companies—can negotiate bank loans at interest rates *below* prime.

[11]In these cases the parent company may get the added benefit of knowing that its foreign subsidiary is also being watched over by a bank which is familiar with local conditions.

discretion of the directors. The only stipulation is that no dividends be paid on the common until the preferred dividend has been paid. For some older issues the firm could pay common dividends *without* making up preferred dividends that had been skipped in previous years. This gave an opportunity for considerable abuse. Therefore, almost all new issues specifically provide that the obligation should be cumulative, so the firm must pay *all* past preferred dividends before common stockholders get a cent.

Like common stock, preferred stock does not have a final repayment date. However, roughly half the issues make some provision for periodic retirement, and in many cases companies have an option to repurchase or call preferred stock at a specified price. If the company goes out of business, the claim of the preferred stock is junior to any debt but senior to common stock.

Preferred stock rarely confers full voting privileges. However, almost always the consent of two-thirds of the preferred holders must be obtained on all matters affecting the seniority of their claim. Most issues also provide the holder with some voting power if the preferred dividend is skipped.

Unlike interest payments on debt, the preferred dividend is not an allowable deduction from taxable corporate income. Thus the dividend is paid from after-tax income. For most industrial firms this is a serious deterrent to issuing preferred. Regulated public utilities, which can take tax payments into account when negotiating the rates they charge customers, can effectively pass the tax disadvantage of preferred stock on to the consumer. As a result, a large fraction of the dollar value of new offerings of nonconvertible preferred stock consists of issues by utilities.

Preferred stock does have one important tax advantage, however. If one corporation buys another's stock, only 30 percent of the dividends received is treated as taxable income to the corporation. This rule applies to common as well as preferred dividends, but it is most important for preferred issues, because preferred stocks have higher dividend yields than most common stocks.

Suppose that your firm has surplus cash to invest. If it buys a bond, interest income will be taxed at the full marginal rate (35 percent). If it buys a preferred share, it owns an asset like a bond (the preferred dividends can be viewed as "interest"), but the effective tax rate is only 30 percent of 35 percent, $.35 \times .30 = .105$, or 10.5 percent. It is no surprise to find that most preferred shares are held by corporations.[12]

Convert-ible Securities	Corporations often issue securities with terms that can be altered subsequently at the option of the firm, the holder of the security, or both. We have already seen one example, the call option on corporate bonds, which allows the firm to retire a bond issue before its maturity date.

Options often have a substantial effect on value. The most dramatic example is provided by a **warrant,** which is *nothing but* an option. The owner of a warrant can purchase a set number of common shares at a set price on or before a set date. For example, in February 1990 you could have purchased a Navistar International "Series A" warrant for $3.50. That security gave the right to purchase one share of Navistar common stock for an *exercise price* of $5 per share at any time before December 15, 1993. Navistar had two other warrants outstanding—Series B and C—with different exercise prices and expiration dates.

---

[12]In Chapter 32, we will describe *floating-rate preferreds*, securities designed as temporary parking places for corporations' excess cash. These securities' dividends change with short-term interest rates, in the same way as coupon payments on floating-rate debt.

Warrants are often sold as part of a package of other securities. Thus, the firm might make a "combination offer" of bonds and warrants.[13]

A **convertible** bond gives its owner the option to exchange the bond for a predetermined number of common shares. The convertible bondholder hopes that the issuing company's share price will zoom up so that the bond can be converted for a big profit. But if the shares zoom down, there is no obligation to convert; the bondholder remains just that. A convertible is therefore like a package of a corporate bond and a warrant.[14] There is one principal difference. When the owners of a convertible wish to exercise their option to buy shares, they do not pay cash—they just give up the bond.

These examples do not exhaust the options encountered by the financial manager. Far from it: We will see in Chapter 20 that *all* corporate securities can be analyzed in terms of options. In fact, once you read that chapter and learn how to analyze options, you will find that they are all around you.

14-3 VARIETY'S THE VERY SPICE OF LIFE

We have indicated several dimensions along which corporate securities can be classified. The financial manager has at least that many alternatives in designing corporate securities. As long as you can convince investors of its attractions, you can issue a convertible, callable, subordinated, floating-rate bond denominated in deutschemarks. Rather than combining features of existing securities, you may create an entirely new one. We can imagine a coal mining company issuing preferred shares on which the dividend fluctuates with coal prices. We know of no such security, but it is perfectly legal to issue it and—who knows?—it might generate considerable interest among investors.[15]

Variety is intrinsically good. People have different tastes, levels of wealth, rates of tax, and so on. Why not offer them a choice? Of course the problem is the expense of designing and marketing new securities. But if you can think of a new security that will appeal to investors, you may be able to issue it on especially favorable terms and thus increase the value of your company.

Financial market innovation in recent years has been unusually fast and extensive. New varieties of debt seem to appear almost daily. In addition, there has been a remarkable growth in the use of **derivatives.** These are side bets on interest rates, exchange rates, commodity prices, and so on. Firms do not issue derivatives to raise money; they buy or sell them to protect against adverse changes in various external factors.

Here are four types of derivatives that have experienced rapid growth in the last decade.

TRADED OPTIONS.   An option gives the firm the right (but not the obligation) to buy or sell an asset in the future at a price that is agreed upon today. We have al-

---

[13]If the warrants are detachable, a portion of the proceeds from the sale would be shown separately on the balance sheet as the value of the warrants, and the remainder would be shown as a debt.

[14]Convertible preferred is also issued, usually to finance mergers.

[15]However, our coal bond seems humdrum compared with some bonds that have been issued. For example, in 1990 the Swedish company Electrolux issued a bond whose final payment is linked to the event of an earthquake in Japan.

ready seen that the firm sometimes issues options either on their own or tacked on to other securities. But, in addition, there is a huge volume of dealing in options that are created by specialized options exchanges. Trading in stock options took off in 1973 when the Chicago Board Options Exchange was established. Now you can deal in options to buy or sell common stocks, bonds, currencies, and commodities. We describe options and their applications in Chapters 20 and 21.

FUTURES. A futures contract is an order that you place in advance to buy or sell an asset or commodity. The price is fixed when you place the order, but you don't pay for the asset until the delivery date. Futures markets have existed for a long time in commodities such as wheat, soybeans, and copper. The major development of the 1970s occurred when the futures exchanges began to trade contracts on financial assets, such as bonds, currencies, and stock market indexes. Since then the worldwide daily volume of transactions in these financial futures has grown to more than $1 trillion.

FORWARDS. Futures contracts are standardized products bought and sold on organized exchanges. A forward contract is a tailor-made futures contract that is not traded on an organized exchange. For example, firms that need to protect themselves against a change in the exchange rate have usually bought or sold forward currency through a bank. Since 1983, banks have also been prepared to enter into forward contracts to borrow or lend money. If you buy one of these forward rate agreements (FRAs), you agree to borrow in the future at a rate that is fixed today; if you sell an FRA, you agree to lend in the future at a preset rate.

SWAPS. Suppose that you would like to swap your dollar debt for deutschemark debt. In this case, you can arrange for a bank to pay you each year the dollars that are needed to service your dollar debt, and in exchange you agree to pay the bank the cost of servicing a deutschemark loan. Such an arrangement is known as a *currency swap*. For example, International Paper swapped British pounds for dollars.

Companies also enter into *interest-rate swaps*. For example, the bank might agree to pay you each year the cost of servicing a fixed-rate loan, and in return you agree to pay the bank the cost of servicing a similar floating-rate loan.

We discuss swaps, as well as forward and futures contracts, in Chapter 25.

Financial Innovation

Developing a new financial instrument is like developing any other product. Initially, the emphasis is on creativity and experiment. Then, as the market develops, the focus switches to low-cost methods of volume production. Finally, it becomes economic to offer the customer optional extras.

For example, when swaps were invented, banks were unwilling to take one side of the swap for their own accounts. They acted solely as arrangers and looked about for another firm that was prepared to take on the other side of the bargain. No two swaps were alike, and they could take weeks to fix up. Within 5 years, banks were prepared to take on the risks of swaps themselves, documentation was standardized, and you could arrange a swap within hours. Banks were also beginning to work on the problem of making it easy for one party to resell its side of the swap to someone else. Perhaps by the time you read this chapter, there will be a regular market for trading swaps. As swaps have become more standardized and cheaper to arrange, banks have also been able to offer extra features. For example, you can now buy a forward swap and even an option on a swap (or "swaption").

What are the causes of financial innovation? One answer is taxes and regulation. In the following chapters, we shall come across a number of cases where taxes and government regulation have in effect subsidized innovation. But why do many new instruments survive long after the initial government stimulus has been removed? And why has so much innovation occurred in the last 20 years? Taxes and regulation have been around for much longer than that.

A second motive for innovation is to widen investor choice. In particular, the sharp recent fluctuations in exchange rates and interest rates have increased the demand by firms and investors for ways to hedge themselves against such hazards.

But this still cannot be the entire explanation. For example, firms have long been able to protect themselves against exchange-rate changes by buying or selling forward currency through a bank. So why are traded currency futures needed as well? The answer is that many of these new financial instruments are low-cost ways to mass-produce a particular service. These low production costs reflect improvements in telecommunications and computing which make it possible to disseminate prices and execute orders rapidly throughout the world.

14-4 PATTERNS OF CORPORATE FINANCING

That completes our tour of corporate securities and derivative instruments. You may feel like the tourist who has just seen 12 cathedrals in 5 days. But there will be plenty of time in later chapters for reflection and analysis.

Now turn to Table 14-3, which summarizes the relative importance of alternative sources of capital for corporations in the United States. The most striking aspect of this table is the dominance of internally generated cash (line 7), defined as cash flow from operations less cash dividends paid to stockholders.[16] Internally generated cash normally covers a majority of firms' capital requirements. During the 1980s it covered approximately three-quarters of the total requirements. The proportion not covered by internal sources is the financial deficit, shown in line 8.

....

Do Firms Rely Too Heavily on Internal Funds?

Gordon Donaldson, in a field survey of corporate debt policies, encountered several firms which acknowledged "that it was their long-term object to hold to a rate of growth which was consistent with their capacity to generate funds internally." A number of other firms appeared to apply more stringent criteria to expenditure proposals that might require outside finance.[17]

At first glance, this behavior doesn't make sense. As we have already noted, retained earnings are additional capital invested by shareholders, and represent, in effect, a compulsory issue of shares. A firm which retains $1 million could have paid out the cash as dividends and then sold new common shares to raise the same amount of additional capital. In the same way, any reinvestment of dollars labeled "depreciation" amounts to investing dollars that could have been paid to investors. The opportunity cost of capital ought not to depend on whether the project is financed by depreciation, retained earnings, or a new stock issue.

Why, then, do managers have an apparent preference for financing by retained earnings? Some believe that managers are simply taking the line of least resistance, dodging the "discipline of securities markets."

---

[16]In Table 14-3, internally generated cash was calculated by adding depreciation to retained earnings. Depreciation is a noncash expense. Thus, retained earnings understates the cash flow available for reinvestment.

[17]See G. Donaldson, *Corporate Debt Capacity*, Division of Research, Graduate School of Business Administration, Harvard University, Boston, 1961, chap. 3, especially pp. 51–56.

But there are other reasons for relying on internally generated funds. The issue costs of new securities are avoided, for example. Moreover, the announcement of a new equity issue is usually bad news to investors, who worry that the decision to issue signals lower future profits or higher risk.[18] A firm with a shortage of internally generated cash may have to issue shares, incurring the costs of issue and sending a bad-news signal to investors, in order to fund capital investment.

Issues and Retirements of Equity

Table 14-3 shows the remarkable year-to-year variation in aggregate stock issues. Compare 1983 and 1989:

Net Stock Issues	1983	1989
As percent of total sources	4.5	−21.9
As percent of financial deficit	13.1	−73.3
Amount, billions	$20.0	−$124.2

In 1983 issues of equity amounted to $20 billion. Just six years later stock issues were *negative* to the tune of $124.2 billion.

Some companies did raise new money by stock issues in 1989. But this new supply was overwhelmed by the unprecedented scale of stock repurchases made by companies which bought back their own shares or purchased and retired *other* companies' shares in the course of mergers and acquisitions.[19] This was all part of the takeover and leveraged buy-out boom of the late 1980s, which left many companies with uncomfortably high debt ratios. The early 1990s were spent paying down debt and replenishing equity. Note in Table 14-3 that debt issues were negative in 1991 (more debt was retired than issued). Net stock issues turned positive in the same year.

Has Capital Structure Changed?

In 1974 *Business Week* devoted a special edition to "The Debt Economy," which described a United States in which everybody appeared to be a borrower and there was not a lender in sight. Prominent among these borrowers were American corporations, which, it was pointed out, had tripled their debt in the previous 15 years. With typical understatement, *Business Week* concluded that this debt imposed "an ominously heavy burden with the world as it is today—ravaged by inflation, threatened with economic depression, torn apart by the massive redistribution. . . ." Twelve years later, *Business Week* found little consolation in the fall in inflation: "In a disinflationary environment, U.S. companies and individuals are finding it increasingly tough to manage the mountainous debt they've amassed."[20]

Is there really a trend to heavier reliance on debt financing? This is a hard question to answer in general, because financing policy varies so much from industry to industry and firm to firm. But a few statistics will do no harm as long as you keep these difficulties in mind.

Table 14-4 shows the aggregate balance sheet of all manufacturing corporations in the United States in 1994. If all manufacturing corporations were merged into one gigantic firm, Table 14-4 would be its balance sheet.

---

[18]Managers do have insiders' insights and naturally are tempted to issue when stock price looks good to them, i.e., when they are less optimistic than outside investors. The outside investors realize all this and will buy a new issue only at a discount from the preannouncement price. More on stock issues in Chapter 15.

[19]We discuss share repurchases in Chapter 16 and mergers and acquisitions in Chapter 33.

[20]Reprinted from the October 12, 1974, issue of *Business Week*, p. 45, and the August 4, 1986, issue, p. 24, by special permission; © 1974, 1986 by McGraw-Hill, Inc., New York, NY 10020. All rights reserved.

TABLE 14-3

Sources and uses of funds in nonfinancial corporations

	1981	1982	1983	1984	1985
Sources and Uses, Percent of Total*					
Uses:					
1. Capital expenditures	81	100	66	67	73
2. Investment in inventories	4	−7	2	12	4
3. Investment in liquid assets	6	15	12	9	10
4. Investment in accounts receivable	8	−4	13	11	10
5. Other	1	−4	7	2	4
6. Total expenditures	100	100	100	100	100
Sources:					
7. Internally generated cash‡	63	78	66	66	71
8. Financial deficit (6 − 7) = required external financing	37	22	34	34	29
Financial deficit covered by:					
9. Net stock issues	−4	1	4	−15	−17
10. Net increase in debt§	29	16	18	39	34
11. Increase in accounts payable	12	5	12	11	12
Expenditures and Deficit, Billions of Dollars					
Total expenditures	381.9	316.6	444.7	511.3	493.8
Financial deficit	143.0	69.1	152.4	175.0	141.9

*Columns may not add up to 100 percent because of rounding.
†Less than .5 percent.
‡Net income plus depreciation less cash dividend paid to stockholders.
§Includes increase in other liabilities.
Source: Board of Governors of the Federal Reserve System, Division of Research and Statistics, *Flow of Funds Accounts*, various issues.

The table shows that manufacturing corporations had total book assets of $3024 billion. On the right-hand side of the balance sheet, we find total long-term liabilities of $1137 billion and stockholders' equity of $1130 billion.

What was the debt ratio of manufacturing corporations in the United States in 1994? It depends on what you mean by *debt*. If all liabilities are counted as debt, the debt ratio is .63:

$$\frac{\text{Debt}}{\text{Total assets}} = \frac{757 + 1137}{3024} = .63$$

This measure of debt includes both current liabilities and long-term obligations. Sometimes financial analysts look at the proportions of debt and equity in long-term financing. The proportion of debt in long-term financing is

$$\frac{\text{Long-term liabilities}}{\text{Long-term liabilities} + \text{stockholders' equity}} = \frac{1137}{1137 + 1130} = .50$$

1986	1987	1988	1989	1990	1991	1992	1993	1994
64	62	58	69	80	87	75	84	76
2	6	4	5	1	0†	0†	3	6
15	8	5	10	7	4	2	0†	6
9	11	14	11	4	−1	7	6	13
10	13	18	5	8	10	15	6	−2
100	100	100	100	100	100	100	100	100
62	67	64	70	77	90	78	84	72
38	33	36	30	23	10	22	16	28
−16	−13	−20	−22	−12	4	5	4	−6
43	29	35	34	21	−2	7	7	17
10	18	21	18	14	8	10	5	16
538.8	564.7	634.2	567.7	535.5	471.7	560.5	552.7	689.6
202.1	188.8	229.9	168.1	123.9	45.7	122.1	90.4	189.8

Figure 14-1 plots these two ratios from 1954 to 1994. There is a clear upward shift from the 1950s to the 1990s. Recent events have dramatized the shift to debt financing. The rapid growth of the junk bond market means by definition that firms have levered up: Junk is junk *because* firms have borrowed beyond conventional targets. We also note the *minus* $480 billion in net equity issues for United States nonfinancial corporations between 1984 and 1989.

Let's try to put all this in perspective.

1990 VERSUS 1920. Debt ratios in the 1990s, though clearly higher than in the early postwar period, are not higher than in the 1920s and 1930s. You could argue that Figure 14-1 starts from an abnormally low point.

INFLATION. Some of the upward movement in Figure 14-1 may have reflected inflation, which was especially rapid—by United States standards—throughout the 1970s and early 1980s. Rapid inflation means that the *book* value of corporate assets falls behind the actual value of those assets. If corporations were borrowing against *actual* value, it would not be surprising to observe rising ratios of debt to book asset values.

To illustrate, suppose that you bought a house 10 years ago for $30,000. You financed the purchase in part with a $15,000 mortgage, 50 percent of the purchase price. Today the house is worth $60,000. Suppose that you repay the remaining bal-

TABLE 14-4

● ●

Aggregate balance sheet for manufacturing corporations in the United States, 1994 (figures in billions)*

Current assets[†]		$1,070	Current liabilities[†]		$ 757
Fixed assets[‡]	$1,913		Long-term debt	$649	
Less depreciation	948		Other long-term liabilities[§]	488	
Net fixed assets		964	Total long-term liabilities		1,137
Other long-term assets		990	Stockholders' equity		1,130
			Total liabilities and stockholders'		
Total assets		$3,024[¶]	equity		$3,024[¶]

*Excludes corporations with less than $250,000 in assets.
[†]See Table 29-1, Section 29-1, for a breakdown of current assets and liabilities.
[‡]Includes land, mineral rights, and construction in progress as well as plant and equipment.
[§]Includes deferred taxes and several miscellaneous categories.
[¶]Columns may not add because of rounding.
Source: U.S. Federal Trade Commission, *Quarterly Financial Report for Manufacturing, Mining and Trade Corporations,* Third Quarter, 1994, p. 4.

ance of your original mortgage and take out a new mortgage of $30,000, which is again 50 percent of current market value. Your *book* debt ratio would be 100 percent. The reason is that the book value of the house is its *original* cost of $30,000 (we assume no depreciation). An analyst having only book values to work with would conclude that you had decided to "use more debt"—10 years ago your book debt ratio was only 50 percent. But you have no more debt relative to the actual value of your house.

It would be better to measure debt as a fraction of the inflation-adjusted value of corporate assets—or better still as a fraction of the total market value of all debt and equity securities. Debt-to-market ratios fluctuate more than debt-to-book ratios, but they have still shown an upward trend since the 1940s and 1950s.[21]

INTERNATIONAL COMPARISONS. The United States is generally viewed as a low-debt country. That was surely true in the 1950s and 1960s. Now it is not so clear.

Rajan and Zingales examined the balance sheets of large samples of publicly traded firms in the seven largest industrialized countries. They calculated debt ratios using both book and market values of shareholders' equity. (The book value of debt was assumed to approximate market value.) A taste of their results is given in Table 14-5. Notice that the debt ratios for the United States sample fall in the middle of the pack.

International comparisons of this sort are always muddied by differences in accounting and financing methods. For example, German companies show pension liabilities as a debtlike obligation on their balance sheets, with no offsetting entry for pension assets.[22] They also report "reserves" separately from equity. These reserves

---

[21]See R. A. Taggart, Jr., "Secular Patterns in the Financing of U.S. Corporations," in B. F. Friedman (ed.), *Corporate Capital Structures in the United States,* University of Chicago Press, Chicago, 1985, p. 25. Inflation-adjusted values of debt and equity for United States corporations are also published in *OECD Financial Statistics.*

[22]United States companies show a net liability only if the pension plan is underfunded.

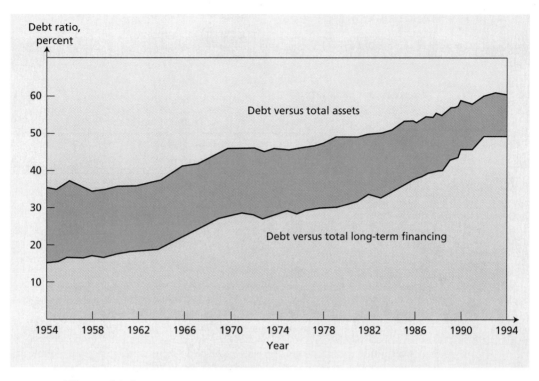

Figure 14-1 Average debt ratios for manufacturing corporations in the United States have increased in the postwar period. However, note that these ratios compare debt with the *book* value of total assets and total long-term financing. The actual value of corporate assets is higher as a result of inflation. (*Source:* U.S. Federal Trade Commission, *Quarterly Report for Manufacturing, Mining and Trade Corporations*, various issues.)

do not cover any specific future obligations but serve as "equity for a rainy day." Reserves might be drawn down to offset a future drop in operating earnings, for example. (This would be unacceptably creative accounting in the United States.) When Rajan and Zingales crossed out the pension liabilities and added back reserves to equity, the *adjusted* debt ratios for German companies dropped to the low levels reported in Table 14-5.

There were other adjustments. In Japan, for example, large companies borrow not only to fund their own operations but also to relend to suppliers or related companies. They may also hold large amounts of cash and marketable securities. Thus their *net* borrowing (debt minus cash, securities, and offsetting loans) is less than the right-hand sides of Japanese balance sheets suggest. The adjusted debt ratios in Table 14-5 are based on net borrowing. With this and other changes adjusted, market value debt ratios in Japan were lower than those in the United States in the early 1990s.

Despite all these qualifications, it's still the case that many United States corporations are carrying a lot more debt than they used to. Should we be worried? It's true that higher debt ratios mean that more companies will fall into financial distress if a serious recession hits the economy. But all companies live with this risk to some degree, and it does not follow that less risk is better. Finding the optimal debt ratio is like finding the optimal speed limit: We can agree that accidents at 30 miles per hour are less dangerous, other things being equal, than accidents at 60 miles per hour,

TABLE 14-5

· ·

Median debt-to-total-capital ratios in 1991 for samples of traded companies in major countries. Debt includes short- and long-term debt. Total capital is the sum of debt and equity. The adjusted figures correct for some international differences in accounting.

	DEBT TO TOTAL CAPITAL			
	Book	Book, Adjusted	Market	Market, Adjusted
Great Britain	28%	16%	19%	11%
Canada	39	37	35	32
France	48	34	41	28
Germany	38	18	23	15
Italy	47	39	46	36
Japan	53	37	29	17
United States	37	33	28	23

Source: R. G. Rajan and L. Zingales, "What Do We Know about Capital Structure? Some Evidence from International Data," *Journal of Finance*, forthcoming (1995), tables IIIa and IIIb.

but we do not therefore set the national speed limit at 30. Speed has benefits as well as risks. So does debt, as we will see in Chapter 18.

There is no God-given, correct debt ratio, and if there were, it would change. It may be that the recent wave of financial innovation, by giving firms easier access to financial markets and the ability to hedge operating risks, has made higher debt ratios possible without increasing the risks or costs of financial distress.

We hope these facts and commentary have provided an appreciation of real-world financing in the United States. We turn now to a deeper, conceptual issue, the problem of corporate governance.

14-5 CORPORATE GOVERNANCE IN THE UNITED STATES, GERMANY, AND JAPAN

At the end of 1993 about 124 million shares of International Paper common stock were outstanding, with a total market capitalization of over $8 billion. No single investor held more than a small fraction of these shares. The company's top management and board of directors together held only .41 percent.

In these respects International Paper is typical of large United States corporations.[23] Ownership is dispersed, and there is no controlling block of shares held by managers or any single outside investor. In 1988 the median percentage ownership by chief execu-

---

[23]There are plenty of exceptions, however, including large privately owned companies such as Cargill (food and agricultural commodities), United Parcel Service, Mars (candy), and Bechtel (construction and engineering). Some publicly traded companies are effectively controlled by families or by top management. For example, the CEOs of Microsoft (William Gates) and Berkshire Hathaway (Warren Buffett) own dominant blocks of their companies' shares.

tive officers (CEOs) of the largest public companies was only .037.[24] So there is separation of *ownership* (by many shareholders) and *control* (by professional managers).

Given this separation, it's natural to ask again[25] how managers are led to act in the owners' interests. Economists call this a *principal-agent problem*. Shareholders are the principals; managers, their agents. *Agency costs* are incurred when (1) agents depart from value-maximizing decisions and (2) principals incur costs to monitor agents and influence their actions. Of course, there are no costs if the shareholders are also the managers; but separation of ownership and control is inescapable in modern economies, and some agency costs naturally follow.

Laws, institutions, and practice have evolved to mitigate these costs, though in different ways in different countries. Each major industrialized country has its own system of *corporate control* or *corporate governance*.

Now, government is never perfect—do elected officials always do what their constituents want? A government that works reasonably well is something to be proud of. Does the United States' system of corporate governance work reasonably, or at least tolerably, well? Let us review how it operates.

A company's board of directors is elected by the shareholders and is supposed to represent them. The board appoints top management and approves major investment and financing decisions. But the responsiveness of directors to shareholders' interests has been questioned. The nomination of new directors is usually made by existing directors, who include top management. These candidates are almost always approved in routine shareholder votes. Dissatisfied shareholders can propose a competing slate of candidates and launch a proxy fight[26] in an attempt to vote them in, but this is expensive and usually not successful. Thus dissidents do not usually stand and fight but sell their shares instead.

Yet selling can send a powerful message. If enough shareholders bail out, the stock price tumbles. This damages top management's reputation and compensation. Part of the top managers' paychecks comes as bonuses tied to net earnings or from stock options, which pay off if the stock price rises but are worthless if the price falls below a stated threshold.[27] This should motivate managers to increase earnings and stock price and therefore to act for shareholders. Whether the motivation is adequate in practice is controversial.[28]

But managers and directors do watch stock price, and they listen to security analysts and major institutional investors. Moreover, directors do act when the long-run health of their company is threatened.

For managers and directors who forget to act, there is always the threat of a hostile takeover. The further a company's stock price falls, due to lax management or inappropriate financial policies, the easier it is for another company or group of investors to buy up a majority of the shares, take control, and make the changes needed to realize the company's potential value.

---

[24]This is the median ownership of CEOs of the 120 largest companies measured by market capitalization. See M. C. Jensen and K. J. Murphy, "CEO Incentives—It's Not How Much You Pay, But How," *Harvard Business Review*, **68**:138–153 (May–June 1990).

[25]Chapter 2 contains a preliminary discussion of corporate objectives and managers' interests.

[26]So called because the dissident group contacts other shareholders and asks for proxies to vote their shares for the alternate slate. If enough proxies are collected, the dissidents win and through their directors take control of the company.

[27]The threshold is called the *exercise price*. See Chapter 20.

[28]Jensen and Murphy, op. cit., argue that top managers of the largest corporations are "paid like bureaucrats"; that is, their total compensation is not sufficiently responsive to shareholder returns.

Thus in the United States the agency problems created by separation of ownership and control are offset by:

- The right incentives for top management, particularly compensation tied to changes in earnings and stock price
- The legal duty of managers and directors to act in shareholders' interests
- The threat of takeover

Ownership and Control in Germany

These principles of corporate governance do not apply worldwide. The United States, Canada, Britain, Australia, and other English-speaking countries all have broadly similar systems, but other countries do not. Germany is a good example.

Figure 14-2 summarizes the ownership in 1990 of Daimler-Benz, one of the largest German companies. The immediate owners were Deutsche Bank, the largest German bank, with 28 percent; Mercedes Automobil Holding, with 25 percent; and the Kuwait government, with 14 percent. The remaining 32 percent of the shares were widely held by about 300,000 individual and institutional investors.

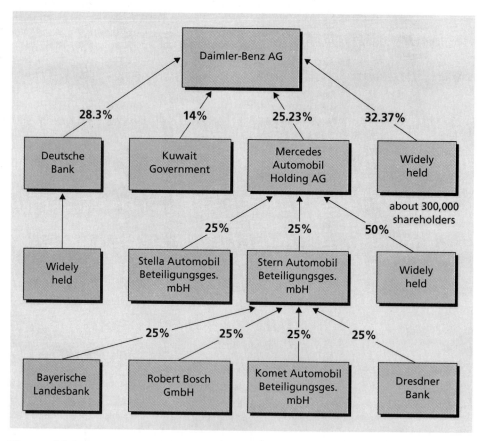

Figure 14-2 Ownership of Daimler-Benz. (*Source:* J. Franks and C. Mayer, "The Ownership and Control of German Corporations," working paper, London Business School, September 1994, figures 2 and 3a.)

But this was only the top layer. Mercedes Automobil Holding was half owned by two holding companies, "Stella" and "Stern" for short. The rest of its shares were widely held. Stern's shares were in turn split four ways: between two banks; Robert Bosch, an industrial company; and another holding company, "Komet." Stella's ownership was split four ways too, but we ran out of space.[29]

The differences between German and United States ownership patterns leap out from Figure 14-2. Note the concentration of ownership of Daimler-Benz shares in large blocks and the several layers of owners. A similar figure for General Motors would just say, "General Motors, 100 percent widely held."

In Germany these blocks are often held by other companies—a *cross-holding* of shares—or by holding companies for families. Franks and Mayer, who examined the ownership of 171 large German companies in 1990, found 47 with blocks of shares held by other companies and 35 with blocks owned by families. Only 26 of the companies did *not* have a substantial block of stock held by some company or institution. (A block was defined as at least 25 percent ownership.)[30]

Note also the bank ownership of Daimler-Benz. This would be impossible in the United States, where federal law prohibits equity investments by banks in nonfinancial corporations. Germany's *universal banking* system allows such investments. Moreover, German banks customarily hold shares for safekeeping on behalf of individual and institutional investors and often acquire proxies to vote these shares on the investors' behalf. For example, Deutsche Bank held 28 percent of Daimler-Benz for its own account and had proxies for 14 percent more. Therefore it *voted* 42 percent, which approaches a majority.[31]

Clearly the distance between ownership and control is much less in Germany than in the United States. The families, companies, and banks which hold blocks of shares in German companies can review top management's plans and decisions as "insiders." In most cases they have the power to force changes if necessary.

On the other hand, outside investors have much less influence in Germany than in the United States. Hostile takeovers, for example, are extremely rare. The "blocks" do not need them to exert control, and outside investors find takeovers nearly impossible. (Even if you could buy all of the publicly traded shares of Daimler-Benz, you would have less than one-third ownership and could not take control.) If the insiders acquiesce to empire-building or collude with managers in a too-comfortable life, there is not much that the ordinary German investor can do about it.

. . . .

. . . And in Japan

Japan's system of corporate governance is in some ways in between the systems of Germany and the United States and in other ways different from both.

Figure 14-3 shows the most important companies in one of the largest kiretsus, the Sumitomo group. A **kiretsu** is a network of companies, usually organized around a major bank. There are long-standing business relationships between the group companies; a manufacturing company might buy a substantial part of its raw materials from group suppliers and in turn sell much of its output to other group companies.

---

[29]A five-layer ownership tree for Daimler-Benz is given in S. Prowse, "Corporate Governance in an International Perspective: A Survey of Corporate Control Mechanisms among Large Firms in the U.S., U.K., Japan and Germany," *Financial Markets, Institutions, and Instruments,* **4** (February 1995), table 16.

[30]J. Franks and C. Mayer, "The Ownership and Control of German Corporations," working paper, London Business School, September 1994, table 1.

[31]Ibid., table 6.

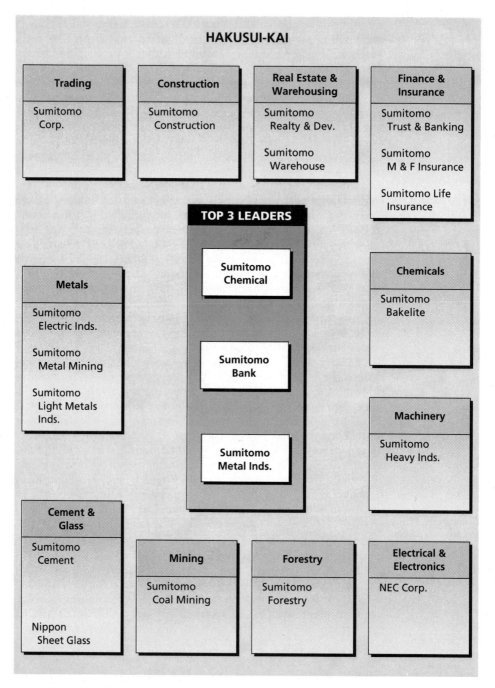

Figure 14-3 Some of the larger companies in the Sumitomo group. Over 40 smaller subsidiaries and affiliates are not shown. (*Source:* Dodwell Marketing Consultants, Industrial Groupings in Japan, 10th ed., Tokyo, 1992, p. 84.)

The bank and other financial institutions at the kiretsu's center own shares in most of the group companies (though a commercial bank in Japan is limited to 5 percent ownership of each company). Those companies may in turn hold the bank's shares or each others' shares. Here are the cross-holdings at the end of 1991 between Sumitomo Bank; the Sumitomo Corporation, a trading company; and Sumitomo Trust, which concentrates on investment management:

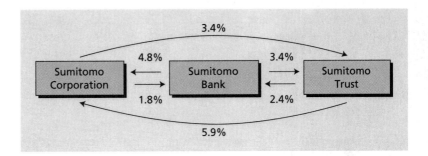

Thus the bank owns 4.8 percent of Sumitomo Corporation, which owns 1.8 percent of the bank. Both own shares in Sumitomo Trust . . . and so on. Table 14-6 is a matrix of cross-holdings between these three companies and three additional ones. Although these companies' stocks are publicly traded, because of the cross-holdings the supply of shares available for purchase by outside investors is much less than the total number outstanding.

The kiretsu is tied together in other ways. Most debt financing comes from the kiretsu's banks or from elsewhere in the group. (Until the mid-1980s, all but a handful of Japanese companies were forbidden access to public debt markets. By the mid-1990s, the fraction of debt provided by banks was still much greater than that in the United States.)[32] Managers may sit on the boards of directors of other group companies, and a "presidents' council" of the CEOs of the most important group companies meets regularly.

Think of the kiretsu as a system of corporate governance, where power is split between the main bank, the largest companies, and the group as a whole. This confers certain financial advantages. First, firms have access to additional "internal" financing—internal to the group, that is. Thus a company with capital budgets exceeding operating cash flows can turn to the main bank or other kiretsu companies for financing. This avoids the cost or possible bad-news signal of a public sale of securities. Second, when a kiretsu firm falls into financial distress, with insufficient cash to pay bills or fund necessary capital investments, a "workout" can usually be arranged. New management can be brought in from elsewhere in the group, and financing obtained, again "internally."

Hoshi, Kashyap, and Scharfstein tracked capital expenditure programs of a large sample of Japanese firms—many, but not all, members of kiretsus. The kiretsu companies' investments were more stable and less exposed to the ups and downs of op-

---

[32]German companies also rely heavily on bank debt, though public debt was never forbidden.

TABLE 14-6
• •

Cross-holdings of common stock between six companies in the Sumitomo group. Read *down* the columns to see holdings of each of the companies by the five others. Thus 4.6 percent of Sumitomo Chemical was owned by Sumitomo Bank, 4.4 percent by Sumitomo Trust, and 9.8 percent by other Sumitomo companies. These figures were compiled by examining the 10 largest shareholders of each company. Smaller cross-holdings are not reflected.

| | PERCENTAGE OF SHARES HELD IN: | | | | | |
Shareholder	Sumitomo Bank	Sumitomo Metal Industries	Sumitomo Chemical	Sumitomo Trust	Sumitomo Corporation	NEC
S. Bank	—	4.1	4.6	3.4	4.8	5.0
S. Metal Industries	*	—	*	2.5	2.8	*
S. Chemical	*	*	—	*	*	*
S. Trust	2.4	5.9	4.4	—	5.9	5.8
S. Corp. Trading	1.8	1.6	*	3.4	—	2.2
NEC	*	*	*	2.9	3.7	—
Other[†]	9.7	4.8	9.8	10.4	9.5	11.6
Total[†]	13.9	16.4	18.8	22.6	26.7	24.6

*Cross-holding does not appear in the 10 largest shareholdings.
[†]Based on the 10 largest shareholdings in 1991.
Source: Compiled from Dodwell Marketing Consultants, *Industrial Groupings in Japan*, 10th ed., Tokyo, 1992.

erating cash flows or to episodes of financial distress.[33] It seems that the financial support of the kiretsus enabled their members to invest "for the long run."

The Japanese system of corporate control has its disadvantages too, notably for outside investors, who have very little influence. Japanese managers' compensation is rarely tied to shareholder returns. Takeovers are unthinkable. Japanese companies have been particularly stingy with cash dividends—hardly a concern when growth was rapid and stock prices stratospheric, but a serious issue for the future.

14-6 SUMMARY

Financing is principally a marketing problem. The company tries to split the cash flows generated by its assets into different streams that will appeal to investors with different tastes, wealth, and tax rates. In this chapter we have introduced you to the principal sources of finance and outlined their relative importance.

The simplest and most important source of finance is shareholders' equity, raised by either stock issues or retained earnings.

The next most important source of finance is debt. Debtholders are entitled to a fixed regular payment of interest and the final repayment of principal. If the company cannot make these payments, it can file for bankruptcy. The usual result is that

---

[33]T. Hoshi, A. Kashyap, and D. Scharfstein, "Corporate Structure, Liquidity and Investment: Evidence from Japanese Industrial Groups," *Quarterly Journal of Economics*, **106**:33–60 (February 1991), and "The Role of Banks in Reducing the Costs of Financial Distress in Japan," *Journal of Financial Economics*, **27**:67–88 (September 1990).

the debtholders then take over and either sell off the company's assets or continue to operate them under new management.

Note that the tax authorities treat interest payments as a cost. That means the company can deduct interest when calculating its taxable income. Interest is paid from pretax income. Dividends and retained earnings come from after-tax income.

The variety of corporate debt instruments is almost endless. The instruments are classified by maturity, repayment provisions, seniority, security, default risk ("junk" bonds are riskiest), interest rates (floating or fixed), issue procedures (public or private placement), and currency of the debt.

The third source of finance is preferred stock. Preferred is like debt in that it promises a fixed dividend payment, but payment of this dividend is within the discretion of the directors. They must, however, pay the dividend on the preferred before they are allowed to pay a dividend on the common stock. Lawyers and tax experts treat preferred as part of the company's equity. That means preferred dividends are not tax-deductible. This is one reason that preferred is less popular than debt. Preferred shares play various specialized roles, however. For example, they are widely used by regulated utility companies, who can pass on the cost of preferred dividends to their customers.

The fourth source of finance consists of options. These may not be recorded separately in the company's balance sheet. The simplest option is the warrant which gives its holder the right to buy a share at a set price by a set date. Warrants are often sold in combination with other securities. Convertible bonds are securities that give their holder the right to convert the bond to shares. They are therefore like a mixture of straight debt and a warrant.

Corporations also trade in derivative securities to hedge their exposure to external risks, including fluctuations in commodity prices, interest rates, and foreign exchange rates. Derivative securities include traded options, futures and forward contracts, and swaps.

The large volume of trade in these derivative instruments reflects a wave of recent innovation in world financial markets. The innovation was stimulated by changes in taxes and government regulation; by demand from corporations and investors for new instruments to hedge against increasingly volatile interest and exchange rates; and by improvements in telecommunications and computing, which make it possible to execute transactions cheaply and quickly throughout the world.

Table 14-3 summarized the ways in which companies raise and spend money. Have another look at it and try to get some feel for the numbers. Notice that:

1. Internally generated cash is the principal source of funds. Some people worry about that; they think that if management does not have to go to the trouble of raising the money, it won't think so hard when it comes to spending it.

2. The mix of company financing changes from year to year. Sometimes companies prefer to issue debt, sometimes equity.

3. Net equity issues in the late 1980s were strongly *negative*; that is, much more equity was repurchased than issued. At the same time, the junk bond market grew enormously. Many billions of dollars of equity were retired and replaced with debt.

4. Equity issues recovered in the 1990s as financial managers worked to pay down debt accumulated during the previous decade.

Debt ratios of companies in the United States have generally increased over the postwar period. Some find this a cause for concern. However, debt ratios in the

United States are not appreciably higher than the ratios in the other major industri-alized countries.

We sketched the German and Japanese systems of corporate finance especially for readers in the United States, who may regard their system as natural. In some circum-stances the German or Japanese system can work better. Here are two key differences.

First, corporate finance in the United States, Britain, and the other English-speaking countries relies more on financial markets, and less on banks or other fi-nancial intermediaries, than is the case in most other countries. United States cor-porations routinely issue publicly traded debt in situations where Japanese or European companies borrow from banks.

Second, U.S.-style corporate finance puts fewer buffers between managers and the stock market. The block holdings and layered ownership structure of German companies are rare in the United States, and of course there is nothing remotely like a Japanese kiretsu. So CEOs and CFOs in the United States usually find their pay-checks tied to stockholder returns. Negative returns may bring insomnia or bad dreams about takeovers.

These international comparisons illustrate different approaches to the problem of corporate governance—the problem of ensuring that managers act in shareholders' in-terest. Agency costs are incurred when managers pursue other objectives or when share-holders have to spend time and money monitoring or controlling managers' actions.

Further Reading

Donaldson surveys corporate attitudes to different sources of finance in:
G. Donaldson: *Corporate Debt Capacity*, Division of Research, Graduate School of Business Administration, Harvard University, Boston, 1961.

Taggart describes long-term trends in corporate financing in:
R. A. Taggart: "Secular Patterns in the Financing of Corporations," in B. M. Friedman (ed.), *Corporate Capital Structures in the United States*, University of Chicago Press, 1985.

Here are two useful articles comparing financing in the United States, Japan, and other major indus-trialized countries:
W. C. Kester: "Capital and Ownership Structure: A Comparison of United States and Japanese Manufacturing Corporations," *Financial Management*, **15**:5–16 (Spring 1986).
R. G. Rajan and L. Zingales: "What Do We Know about Capital Structure? Some Evidence from International Data," *Journal of Finance*, forthcoming (1995).

The following, while not exciting reading, is a good, comprehensive survey of international differences in corporate governance:
S. Prowse: "Corporate Governance in an International Perspective: A Survey of Corporate Control Mechanisms among Large Firms in the U.S., U.K., Japan and Germany," *Financial Markets, Institutions, and Investments*, **4**:1–63 (1995).

The classic paper on agency issues is:
M. C. Jensen and W. C. Meckling: "Theory of the Firm: Managerial Behavior, Agency Costs and Capital Structure," *Journal of Financial Economics*, **3**:305–360 (1976).

Quiz

1. The authorized share capital of the Alfred Cake Company is 100,000 shares. The equity is currently shown in the company's books as follows:

Common stock ($.50 par value)	$40,000
Additional paid-in capital	10,000
Retained earnings	30,000
Common equity	80,000
Treasury stock (2,000 shares)	5,000
Net common equity	$75,000

(*a*) How many shares are issued?

(*b*) How many are outstanding?

(*c*) Explain the difference between your answers to (*a*) and (*b*).

(*d*) How many more shares can be issued without the approval of shareholders?

(*e*) Suppose that the company issues 10,000 shares at $2 a share. Which of the above figures would be changed?

2. If there are 10 directors to be elected and a shareholder owns 80 shares, indicate the maximum number of votes that he or she can cast for a favorite candidate under:

(*a*) Majority voting

(*b*) Cumulative voting

3. Fill in the blanks, using the terms listed at the end of this question.

(*a*) Debt maturing in more than 1 year is often called _____ debt.

(*b*) An issue of bonds that is sold simultaneously in several countries is called a(n) _____.

(*c*) If a lender ranks behind the firm's general creditors in the event of default, his or her loan is said to be _____.

(*d*) Unsecured bonds are usually termed _____.

(*e*) In many cases, a firm is obliged to make regular contributions to a(n) _____ which is then used to repurchase bonds.

(*f*) Most bonds give the firm the right to repurchase or _____ the bonds at specified prices.

(*g*) Interest on many bank loans is based on the _____ of interest.

(*h*) The interest rate on _____ loans is tied to short-term interest rates.

(*i*) Where there is a(n) _____, securities are sold directly to a small group of institutional investors. These securities cannot be resold to individual investors. In the case of a(n) _____, debt can be freely bought and sold by individual investors.

(*j*) A long-term, noncancelable rental agreement is called a(n) _____.

(*k*) A(n) _____ bond can be exchanged for shares of the issuing corporation.

(*l*) A(n) _____ gives its owner the right to buy shares in the issuing company at a predetermined _____.

Terms: *lease, funded, floating-rate, eurobond, exercise price, commercial paper, convertible, term loan, subordinated, call, sinking fund, prime rate, debentures, mortgage bond, private placement, public issue, senior, unfunded, eurodollar rate, warrant*

4. The figures in the following table are in the wrong order. Can you place them in their correct order?

	Percent of Total Sources, 1994
Internally generated cash	17
Financial deficit	−6
Net share issues	72
Debt issues	28

5. True or false?
    (a) Firms sell forward contracts primarily to raise money for new capital investment.
    (b) Firms trade in futures contracts to hedge their exposure to unexpected changes in interest rates, foreign exchange rates, or commodity prices.
    (c) Financial innovation is partly caused by deregulation of financial markets.
    (d) In several recent years, nonfinancial corporations in the United States have repurchased more stock than they have issued.
    (e) A new-issue junk debt market blossomed in the 1980s.
    (f) A corporation pays tax on only 30 percent of the common or preferred dividends it receives from other corporations.
    (g) Therefore, a large fraction of preferred shares is held by corporations.
    (h) In Japan one finds extensive cross-holdings of shares within kiretsus.
    (i) German universal banks may hold up to 5 percent of the shares of German industrial companies.
    (j) Investments in partnerships cannot be publicly traded.
    (k) Debt ratios of United States corporations have increased since the 1950s but fell sharply in the 1980s.
    (l) Hostile takeovers are extremely difficult, and therefore rare, in Japan.
    (m) Compared with companies in the United States, German companies are more likely to borrow from a bank than issue a debt security in public markets.

6. Agency costs are incurred when (a) _____ and (b) _____. Fill in the blanks.

7. What is meant by "separation of ownership and control"? Why does this separation concern investors and financial analysts?

8. What are the chief differences in the roles of banks in corporate finance in the United States, Germany, and Japan?

Questions and Problems

1. Inbox Software was founded in 1995. Its founder put up $2 million for 500,000 shares of common stock. Each share had a par value of $.10.
    (a) Construct an equity account (like the one in Table 14-2) for Inbox on the day after its founding. Ignore any legal or administrative costs of setting up the company.
    (b) After 2 years of operation, Inbox generated earnings of $120,000 and paid no dividends. What was the equity account at this point?
    (c) After 3 years the company sold 1 million additional shares for $5 per share. It earned $250,000 during the year and paid no dividends. What was the equity account?

2. It is sometimes suggested that since retained earnings provide the bulk of industry's capital needs, the securities markets are largely redundant. Do you agree?

3. Can you think of any new kinds of security that might appeal to investors? Why do you think they have not been issued?

4. Look back at Table 14-2.
    (a) Suppose that International Paper issues 15 million shares at $70 a share. Rework Table 14-2 to show the company's equity after the issue.

(*b*) Suppose that International Paper *subsequently* repurchases 10 million shares at $75 a share. Rework Table 14-2 to show the effect of the further change.

5. The shareholders of the Pickwick Paper Company need to elect five directors. There are 200,000 shares outstanding. How many shares do you need to own to *ensure* that you can elect at least one director if:
   (*a*) The company has majority voting?
   (*b*) It has cumulative voting?

6. Compare the yields on preferred stocks with those on corporate bonds. Can you explain the difference?

7. Who are the main holders and issuers of preferred stock? Explain why.

8. Michael Jensen has pointed to the dangers of excessive free cash flow. These dangers stem from a principal-agent problem. Explain why.

9. Work out the financing proportions given in Table 14-3 for a particular industrial company—General Mills, for example—for some recent year.

10. What is a kiretsu? What are the main financial and business linkages that hold a kiretsu together?

11. Some managers have argued that hostile takeovers are wasteful and that the United States economy would be more efficient and competitive if takeovers were made more difficult. Can you identify arguments for and against this view?

12. The German and Japanese financial systems have certain advantages when a company falls into financial difficulty. What are these advantages?

15

How Corporations Issue Securities

In Chapter 11 we encountered Marvin Enterprises, one of the most remarkable growth companies of the twenty-first century. It was founded by George and Mildred Marvin, two high school dropouts, together with their chum Charles P. (Chip) Norton. To get the company off the ground the three entrepreneurs relied on their own savings together with personal loans from a bank. However, the company's rapid growth meant that they had soon borrowed to the hilt and needed more equity capital. Equity investment in young private companies is generally known as **venture capital.** Such venture capital may be provided by specialist venture capital partnerships, by investment institutions, or by wealthy individuals who are prepared to back an untried company in exchange for a piece of the action. In the first part of this chapter we will explain how companies like Marvin go about raising venture capital.

Venture capital companies aim to help growing firms over that awkward adolescent period before they are large enough to "go public." For a successful firm such as Marvin there is likely to come a time when it needs to tap a wider source of capital and therefore decides to make its first public issue of common stock. The first public issue of a security by a company is known as an **unseasoned** issue. We will describe in the next section of the chapter what is involved in an unseasoned issue of stock.

A company's first public offering is rarely also its last. In Chapter 14 we saw that corporations face a persistent financial deficit which they meet by selling securities. We will look therefore at how established public corporations go about raising more capital.

If a stock or bond is sold publicly, it can then be traded on the securities markets. But sometimes investors intend to hold onto their securities and are not concerned about whether they can sell them. In these cases there is little advantage to a public issue, and the firm may prefer to place the securities directly with one or two financial institutions. At the end of this chapter we will discuss the choice between a public offer and a private placement.

15-1 VENTURE CAPITAL

On April 1, 2003, George and Mildred Marvin met with Chip Norton in their research lab (which also doubled as a bicycle shed) to celebrate the incorporation of Marvin Enterprises. The three entrepreneurs had raised $100,000 from savings and personal bank loans and had purchased 1 million shares in the new company. At this *zero-stage* investment, the company's assets were $90,000 in the bank ($10,000 had been spent for legal and other expenses of setting up the company), plus the *idea* for a new product, the household gargle blaster. George Marvin was the first to see that the gargle blaster, up to that point an expensive curiosity, could be commercially produced using microgenetic refenestrators.

Marvin Enterprises's bank account steadily drained away as design and testing proceeded. Local banks did not see Marvin's idea as adequate collateral, so a transfusion of equity capital was clearly needed. Preparation of a *business plan* was a necessary first step. The plan was a confidential document describing the proposed product, its potential market, the underlying technology, and the resources—time, money, employees, plant and equipment—needed for success.

Most entrepreneurs are able to spin a plausible yarn about their company. But it is as hard to convince a venture capitalist that your business plan is sound as it is to get a first novel published. Marvin's managers were able to point to the fact that they were prepared to put their money where their mouths were. Not only had they staked all their savings in the company but they were mortgaged to the hilt. This *signaled* their faith in the business.[1]

First Meriam Venture Partners was impressed with Marvin's presentation and agreed to buy 1 million new shares for $1 each. After this *first-stage* financing, the company's market value balance sheet looked like this:

Marvin Enterprises First-Stage Balance Sheet
(Market Values in Millions)

Cash from new equity	$1	$1	New equity from venture capital
Other assets, mostly intangible	1	1	Original equity held by entrepreneurs
Value	$2	$2	Value

By accepting a $2 million *after-the-money* valuation, First Meriam implicitly put a $1 million value on the entrepreneurs' idea and their commitment to the enterprise. It also handed the entrepreneurs a $900,000 paper gain over their original $100,000 investment. In exchange, the entrepreneurs gave up half their company and accepted First Meriam's representatives to the board of directors.[2]

The success of a new business depends critically on the effort put in by the managers. So venture capital firms try to structure a deal so that management has a strong incentive to work hard. For example, any entrepreneur who demands a watertight employment contract and a fat salary is not going to find it easy to raise venture capital. The Marvin team agreed to put up with modest salaries and, therefore, they

---

[1]For a formal analysis of how management's investment in the business can provide a reliable signal of the company's value, see H. E. Leland and D. H. Pyle, "Informational Asymmetries, Financial Structure, and Financial Intermediation," *Journal of Finance*, **32**:371–387 (May 1977).

[2]Venture capital investors do not necessarily demand a majority on the board of directors. Whether they do depends, for example, on how mature the business is and on what fraction of it they own. A common compromise gives an equal number of seats to the founders and to outside investors; the two parties then agree to one or more additional directors to serve as tie-breakers in case a conflict arises. Regardless of whether they have a majority of directors, venture capital companies are seldom silent partners; their judgment and contacts can often prove useful to a relatively inexperienced management team.

could cash in only from appreciation of their stock. If Marvin failed they would get nothing, because First Meriam actually bought *preferred* stock designed to convert automatically into common stock when and if Marvin Enterprises succeeded in an initial public offering or consistently generated more than a target level of earnings. This raised even further the stakes for the company's management.[3]

Venture capitalists rarely give a young company all the money it will need all at once. At each stage they give enough to reach the next major checkpoint. Thus in spring 2005, having designed and tested a prototype, Marvin Enterprises was back asking for more money for pilot production and test marketing. Its *second-stage* financing was $4 million, of which $1.5 million came from First Meriam, its original backers, and $2.5 million from two other venture capital partnerships and wealthy individual investors. The balance sheet just after the second stage was as follows:

Marvin Enterprises Second-Stage Balance Sheet
(Market Values in Millions)

Cash from new equity	$ 4	$ 4	New equity, second stage
Fixed assets	1	5	Equity from first stage
Other assets, mostly intangible	9	5	Original equity held by entrepreneurs
Value	$14	$14	Value

Now the after-the-money valuation was $14 million. First Meriam marked up its original investment to $5 million, and the founders noted an additional $4 million paper gain.

Does this begin to sound like a (paper) money machine? It was so only with hindsight. At stage one it wasn't clear whether Marvin would ever get to stage two: if the prototype hadn't worked, First Meriam could have refused to put up more funds and effectively closed the business down.[4] Or it could have advanced stage-two money in a smaller amount on less favorable terms. The board of directors could also have fired George, Mildred, and Chip and gotten someone else to try to develop the business.

For every 10 first-stage venture capital investments, only two or three may survive as successful, self-sufficient businesses, and one may pay off big as Marvin Enterprises did.[5] From these statistics come two rules for success in venture capital investment. First, don't shy away from uncertainty; accept a low probability of success. But don't buy into a business unless you can see the *chance* of a big, public company in a profitable market. There's no sense taking a long shot unless it pays off big

---

[3]Notice there is a trade-off here. Marvin's management is being asked to put all its eggs into one basket. That creates pressure for managers to work hard, but it also means that they take on risk that they could have diversified away.

[4]If First Meriam had refused to invest at stage two, it would have been an exceptionally hard sell convincing another investor to step in in its place. The other outside investors knew they had less information about Marvin than First Meriam and would have read its refusal as a bad omen for Marvin's prospects.

[5]One study of venture capital investments between 1960 and 1975 found that about one in six were total failures. On the other hand, thanks to a few outstanding successes the average return after costs was about 19 percent a year. See B. Huntsman and J. P. Hoban, Jr., "Investment in New Enterprise: Some Empirical Observations on Risk, Return, and Market Structure," *Financial Management*, **9**:44–51 (Summer 1980).

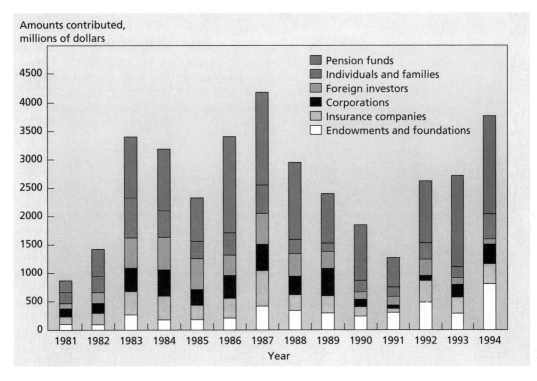

Figure 15-1 Venture capital commitments to independent private firms only. (*Source:* Venture Economics, Inc., Wellesley, Mass. Reproduced with permission.)

if you win. Second, cut your losses; identify losers early, and if you can't fix the problem—by replacing management, for example—throw no good money after bad.

For Marvin, fortunately, everything went like clockwork. Third-stage financing was arranged,[6] full-scale production began on schedule, and gargle blasters were acclaimed by music critics worldwide. Marvin Enterprises "went public" on February 3, 2009. Once its shares were traded, the paper gains earned by First Meriam and the company's founders turned into fungible wealth.

Before we go on to this initial public offering, let us look briefly at the venture capital market in the 1980s and 1990s.

Entrepreneurs have generated a continuous flow of successful new corporations for at least a century. Some of the new companies managed to grow by their own bootstraps, by borrowing and generating funds internally. Others sought out equity investment, often from wealthy families or established firms. So venture capital has been around for some time.

But today the United States has a well-developed venture capital *market*, in which specialists set up partnerships, pooling funds from a variety of investors; *seek out* fledgling companies to invest in, and then work with these companies as they try to grow into publicly traded firms. As Figure 15-1 shows, in recent years these part-

---

[6]Later-stage financing is often called *mezzanine financing*, in contrast to financing by those investors who get in on the "ground floor."

nerships have raised about $3 billion a year. Note the large amounts contributed by pension funds.

Governments around the world seem to believe that, unless they intervene, profitable new ventures are likely to fail for lack of finance. They therefore look for ways to provide subsidized finance for young companies. In the United States the government provides cheap loans to small-business investment companies (SBICs) that then relend the money to deserving entrepreneurs. SBICs occupy a small, specialized niche in the venture capital market.

15-2   THE INITIAL PUBLIC OFFERING

Very few new businesses make it big, but venture capitalists keep sane by forgetting about the many failures and reminding themselves of the success stories—the investors who got in on the ground floor of firms like DEC, Teledyne, Genentech, and Lotus Development Corporation.[7] When First Meriam invested in Marvin Enterprises, it was not looking for a high income stream from the investment; instead it was hoping for rapid growth that would allow Marvin to "go public" and give First Meriam an opportunity to cash in on some of its gains.

By 2009 Marvin had grown to the point at which it needed substantial new capital to implement its second-generation production technology. At this point it decided to make an initial public offering of stock. This was to be partly a **primary** offering—that is, new shares were to be sold to raise additional cash for the company. It was also to be partly a **secondary** offering—that is, the venture capitalists and the company's founders were looking to sell some of their existing shares.

Often when companies go public, the issue is solely intended to raise new capital for the company. But there are also occasions when no new capital is raised and all the shares on offer are being sold by existing shareholders. In fact some of the biggest initial public offerings occur when governments sell off their shareholdings in companies. For example, the United States government made a secondary issue of $1.6 billion when it divested Conrail.[8] But Sears Roebuck beat this when it sold an 18 percent stake in Allstate, its insurance subsidiary, for $2.1 billion in 1993.

Arranging a Public Issue[9]

Once Marvin had taken the decision to go public, the next task was to select the underwriters. Underwriters act as financial midwives to a new issue. Usually they play a triple role—first providing the company with procedural and financial advice, then buying the issue, and finally reselling it to the public. After some discussion Marvin settled on Klein Merrick as the lead underwriter. Klein Merrick would be responsible for forming and managing a syndicate of underwriters who would buy and resell the issue.

Together with Klein Merrick and firms of lawyers and accountants, Marvin prepared a **registration statement** for submission to the Securities and Exchange

---

[7]The founder of Lotus took a finance class from one of the authors. Within 5 years he had become a multimillionaire. Perhaps that will make you feel better about the cost of this book.

[8]Even the Conrail issue looks tiny compared with the secondary offering by the Japanese government of $12.6 billion of the stock of Nippon Telegraph and Telephone or the $9 billion offering by the British government of British Gas.

[9]For an excellent case study of how one company went public, see B. Uttal, "Inside the Deal That Made Bill Gates $350,000,000." *Fortune*, July 21, 1986.

Commission (SEC).[10] This statement is a detailed and sometimes cumbersome document which presents information about the proposed financing and the firm's history, existing business, and plans for the future.[11] The SEC studies this document and sends the company a "deficiency memorandum" requesting any changes. Finally an amended statement is filed with the SEC.[12]

Marvin was not allowed to sell securities during this waiting period, nor could it engage in any unusual publicity that might affect the sale. However, management did make a number of presentations to institutional investors, and the underwriters began to sound out the interest of potential buyers.

The first part of the registration statement was distributed by the company in the form of a preliminary **prospectus.** Such a prospectus is generally known as a *red herring* because of the statement printed in red ink, denying that the company is trying to sell securities before the registration is effective. In Appendix B to this chapter we have reproduced the prospectus for Marvin's first public issue of stock. Most prospectuses would go into much more detail on each topic, but this example should serve to give you a feel for the mixture of valuable information and redundant qualification that characterizes these documents. The Marvin prospectus also illustrates how the SEC takes care to ensure that investors' eyes are opened to the dangers of purchase (see "Certain Considerations" of the prospectus). Some investors have joked that if they read prospectuses carefully, they would never dare buy any new issue.

After registration, Marvin issued a final prospectus which differed from the preliminary one only by the addition of the final offering price and a few minor changes required by the SEC. Marvin was obliged to send this prospectus to all purchasers and to all those who were offered securities through the mail.

Marvin had other tasks before it was able to go public. It needed to appoint a **registrar** to record any issues of stock and to prevent any unauthorized issue. It appointed a **transfer agent** to look after the transfer of the newly issued securities. Finally it checked that the issue complied with the so-called blue-sky laws of each state that regulate sales of securities within the state.[13]

---

[10]The rules governing the sale of securities derive principally from the Securities Act of 1933. Some public issues are exempted from the registration requirement. The principal exemptions are *Regulation A* issues involving less than $1.5 million and loans maturing within 9 months.

[11]Fortunately, the amount of detail is considerably less than it used to be. (A registration statement filed by Republic Steel in 1934 comprised 19,897 pages!) Now a complete registration statement might run to 50 pages or so, and some are much shorter. For example, a solid public company may not be required to reprint the standard financial data published in its most recent annual report. These data are "incorporated by reference," i.e., by simply referring to them in the registration statement.

The example of the Republic Steel registration statement is cited in P. M. Van Arsdell, *Corporate Finance,* Ronald Press Co., New York, 1958.

[12]Occasionally the SEC will issue a "stop order" to prevent the sale until its requests have been complied with. Note incidentally that the SEC's concern is solely with disclosure and its has no power to prevent an issue as long as there has been proper disclosure.

[13]In 1980 when Apple Computer Inc. made its first public issue, the Massachusetts state government decided the offering was too risky for its residents and therefore barred sale of the shares to individual investors in the state. The state relented later, after the issue was out and the price had risen. Needless to say, this action was not acclaimed by Massachusetts investors.

States do not usually reject security issues by honest firms through established underwriters. We cite the example to illustrate the potential power of state securities laws, and to show why underwriters keep careful track of them.

**Pricing a
New
Issue**

During the registration period Marvin and its underwriters began to firm up the issue price. First they looked at the price-earnings ratios of the shares of Marvin's principal competitors. Then they worked through a number of discounted-cash-flow calculations like the ones we described in Chapter 4 and Chapter 11. Most of the evidence pointed to a market value of around $90 a share.

While Marvin's managers were anxious to secure the highest possible price for their stock, the underwriters were more cautious. Not only would they be left with any unsold stock if they overestimated investor demand; they also argued that some degree of underpricing was needed to tempt investors to buy the stock.

Immediately after the company received clearance from the SEC, Marvin and the underwriters agreed on an issue price of $80 a share. On February 3, 2009, Marvin finally went public and the underwriters began to telephone interested buyers of the stock. The issue proved popular with investors; the underwriters had no difficulty selling the stock at the issue price. By the end of the first week, the shares were trading at a price of $95. The issue brought the Marvin management team $16 million in cash before their share of the costs, and the 800,000 shares that they retained were worth $800,000 \times 95 = \$76$ million.

**Costs of
a Public
Issue**

Marvin's issue created substantial administrative costs. Preparation of the registration statement and prospectus involved management, legal counsel, and accountants, as well as the underwriters and their advisers. In addition, the firm had to pay fees for registering the new securities, printing and mailing costs, and so on. You can see from the first page of the Marvin prospectus (Appendix B) that these administrative and registration costs amounted in total to $820,000.

The second major cost of the Marvin issue was underwriting. Underwriters make their profit by buying the issue from the company at a discount from the price at which they resell it to the public. In Marvin's case this discount, or *spread*, amounted to $4.5 million, which was equivalent to 6.25 percent of the total amount of the issue.

Marvin's issue was costly in yet another way. Since the offering price was *less* than the true value of the issued securities, investors who bought the issue got a bargain at the expense of the firm's original stockholders.

These costs of *underpricing* are hidden but nevertheless real. For initial public offerings they generally exceed the other issue costs. Whenever any company goes public, it is very difficult for the underwriter to judge how much investors will be willing to pay for the stock. A number of researchers have tried to measure underwriters' success in gauging the value of such issues. With remarkable unanimity they have found that on average investors who buy at the issue price realize very high returns over the following weeks. For example, a study by Ibbotson, Sindelar, and Ritter of nearly 9000 new issues from 1960 to 1987 indicated average underpricing of 16 percent.[14]

This underpricing does not imply that any investor can expect to become wealthy by purchasing unseasoned stock from the underwriters, for if the issue is attractive, the underwriters will not have enough stock to go around. In order to get stock at the issue price, investors would probably have to be prepared to pay for it indirectly, for example, by allocating more brokerage business to the underwriter than they otherwise would. Therefore underpricing helps underwriters. It reduces the risk of underwriting and gains them the gratitude of investors who buy the issue. Does that mean the underwriter earns excessive profits? Possibly, but not necessarily. If the

---

[14]R. G. Ibbotson, J. L. Sindelar, and J. R. Ritter, "The Market's Problems with the Pricing of Initial Public Offerings," *Journal of Applied Corporate Finance,* **7**:66–74 (Spring 1994).

business is sufficiently competitive, underwriters will take all these hidden benefits into account when they negotiate the spread.

Suppose that you could always be sure of getting your fair share of any issue that you applied for without having to ingratiate yourself with the investment banker. Does that mean that you could make handsome profits on average by applying for an equal amount of each issue? Unfortunately, no. If an issue is cheap, it is also likely to be over-subscribed; if it is dear, it is likely to be undersubscribed. So you will receive a small proportion of the cheap issues and a large proportion of the dear ones. If you are smart, you will play the game only if there is substantial underpricing on the average.[15]

Many investment bankers and institutional investors argue that underpricing is in the interests of the issuing firm. They say that a low offering price on the initial offer raises the price of the stock when it is subsequently traded in the market and enhances the firm's ability to raise further capital.[16] At least one industrialist has accepted this argument, for writing some time after his company went public, the president described the pricing decision as follows:

> *Our underwriting group suggested a price of $15. The general market was strong . . . when our registration statement was filed and we felt that the public might well pay $17 or $18 for our stock rather than $15. Our underwriters were strong in their desire to have the stock sold at $15 a share on the basis that this was a proper price for the stock. They pointed out that the after-market was important and that the price could decline if the stock was overpriced. Having practiced law for many years . . . , it was always my opinion that clients should not second-guess their counselors. I had to follow the same rules in accepting the advice of our investment bankers. And how right our underwriting group was! Within six months our stock rose from $15 a share to $50. Would the stock have had this dramatic increase if the initial price had been $17 or $18? There may have been some who felt that it was overpriced initially and would not have been in the market for our stock. Suffice it to say that the overall result was extremely good. It points out the importance of working with competent investment bankers who guide you in these matters.[17]*

Contentment at selling an article for one-third of its subsequent value is a rare quality.

In these examples, the issue price was set by the underwriters. But an alternative is to hold an auction for the stock and let the market decide the price. The United States government regularly sells securities by public auction, and in many other countries it is common for companies to do so.[18] For example, in Singapore initial

---

[15]The problem faced by the new-issue investor is known as "the winner's curse." See K. Rock, "Why New Issues Are Underpriced," *Journal of Financial Economics.* **15**:187–212 (January–February 1986).

[16]For an analysis of how a firm could rationally underprice to facilitate subsequent stock issues, see I. Welch, "Seasoned Offerings, Imitation Costs and the Underpricing of Initial Public Offerings," *Journal of Finance*, **44**:421–449 (June 1989).

[17]From E. L. Winter, *A Complete Guide to Making a Public Offering*, ©1962, published by Prentice-Hall, Inc., Englewood Cliffs, N.J. Here's another example: In 1987 the British company Sock Shop International went public at 125p a share. First-day dealings were at a price of 205p. The company's chairman was reported to be "ecstatic" about the market's reaction. She dismissed suggestions that the issue was underpriced by saying that had the shares been more expensive, the company would "quite justifiably" have been accused of overpricing. See *Financial Times*, May 15, 1987.

[18]In the United States large issues of debt and common stock are often sold by the book-building method. In this case the underwriters solicit interest from investors and build up a book of orders before the price is established. The Wellcome sale, which we describe below, used the book-building method.

public offerings are often sold in two parts: one part is offered for sale at a fixed price, and the other is auctioned to the public.

15-3 GENERAL CASH OFFERS BY PUBLIC COMPANIES

After its initial public offering Marvin Enterprises continued to grow, and like most growing companies, it needed from time to time to make further issues of debt and equity. But at this point we will leave Marvin and review in general terms the procedures involved in these periodic security issues.

Any issue of securities needs to be formally approved by the firm's board of directors. If the stock issue requires an increase in the company's authorized capital, it also needs the consent of the stockholders.

Public companies can issue securities either by making a general cash offer to investors at large or by making a rights issue that is limited to existing stockholders. We will concentrate in this chapter on the mechanics of the general cash offer, which is used for virtually all debt and equity issues. However, although rights issues have become a rarity in the United States, they are widespread in other countries and you should know how they work. Therefore in Appendix A to this chapter we describe rights issues and we look at some interesting and controversial questions about their use.

General Cash Offers and Shelf Registration

When a public company makes a general cash offer of debt or equity, it goes through the same procedure as when it first went public. In other words, it registers the issue with the SEC and then sells it to an underwriter (or a syndicate of underwriters), which in turn offers the securities to the public.

In 1982 the SEC issued its Rule 415, which allows large companies to file a single registration statement covering financing plans for up to 2 years into the future. The actual issue, or issues, can be done with scant additional paperwork, whenever the firm needs the cash or thinks it can issue securities at an attractive price. This is called *shelf registration*—the registration statement is "put on the shelf," to be taken down and used as needed.

Think of how you as financial manager might use shelf registration. Suppose that your company is likely to need up to $200 million of new long-term debt over the next year or so. It can file a shelf registration for that amount. It then has prior approval to issue up to $200 million of debt, but it isn't obligated to issue a penny. Nor is it required to work through any *particular* underwriters—the registration statement may name one or more underwriters the firm thinks it may work with, but others can be substituted later.

Now you can sit back and issue debt as needed, in bits and pieces if you like. Suppose Merrill Lynch comes across an insurance company with $10 million ready to invest in corporate bonds. Your phone rings. It's Merrill Lynch offering to buy $10 million of your bonds, priced to yield, say, 10½ percent. If you think that's a good price, you say "OK" and the deal is done, subject to only a little additional paperwork. Merrill Lynch then resells the bonds to the insurance company, it hopes at a slightly higher price than it paid for them, thus earning an intermediary's profit.

Here is another possible deal: Suppose that you think you see a window of opportunity in which interest rates are "temporarily low." You invite bids for $100 million of bonds. Some bids may come from large investment bankers acting alone, others from ad hoc syndicates. But that's not your problem; if the price is right, you just take the best deal offered.

Thus shelf registration gives firms several different things that they did not have previously:

1. Securities can be issued in dribs and drabs without incurring excessive transaction costs.

2. Securities can be issued on short notice.

3. Security issues can be timed to take advantage of "market conditions" (although any financial manager who can *reliably* identify favorable market conditions could make a lot more money by quitting and becoming a bond or stock trader instead).

4. The issuing firm can make sure that underwriters compete for its business. It can in effect auction off securities.

Underwriters do compete. Although several large investment banking houses lobbied hard against Rule 415 when the SEC was considering it, once the rule was approved, they played the new game with gusto. As an attorney who works with them observed, "If the SEC passed a rule saying you had to do underwriting in Watertown, NY, in the snow stark naked, these guys would take the first plane up."[19]

Not all companies eligible for shelf registration actually use it for all their public issues. Sometimes they believe they can get a better deal by making one large issue through traditional channels, especially when the security to be issued has some unusual feature or when the firm believes it needs the investment banker's counsel or stamp of approval on the issue. Shelf registration is thus less often used for issues of common stock or convertible securities than for garden-variety corporate bonds.

International Security Issues

Well-established companies are not restricted to the capital market in the United States; they can also raise money in the international capital markets. We saw in Chapter 14 that this can mean one of two things. Either the company makes a foreign bond issue in another country's market (in which case it is subject to the laws and customs of that country), or it makes an issue of eurobonds which are offered internationally. The procedures for making a eurobond issue are broadly similar to the procedures for a domestic bond issue in the United States. Here are two points to note:

1. As long as the bond issue is not publicly offered in the United States, it does not have to be registered with the SEC. Therefore, the borrower saves the costs of registration. However, it must still provide a prospectus or offering circular.

2. Frequently a eurobond issue takes the form of a *bought deal*, in which case one or a few underwriters buy the entire issue. Bought deals allow companies to issue bonds at very short notice.

Large debt issues are now often split, with part sold in the euromarket and part registered and sold in the United States. Likewise with equity issues: in June 1995 the Westinghouse Air Brake Company simultaneously issued 6 million new shares in the United States and Canada and 1 million overseas. The price was identical, at $14 per share, worldwide. In 1992 Wellcome Trust, a British charitable foundation, de-

---

[19]Quoted in Tim Carrington, "New Ball Game: Investment Bankers Enter a New Era," *The Wall Street Journal*, June 21, 1982, p. 10.

cided to sell a substantial part of its holdings in the Wellcome Group. To handle the sale, it paid about $140 million to a group of 120 underwriters from around the world. Each day these underwriters collected bids from interested investors and forwarded them to Robert Fleming, a London merchant bank, which built up a book of the various bids. Particular classes of investors, such as existing shareholders or those who submitted their bids early, went to the front of the queue, while those who subsequently cut their bids or sold Wellcome stock were demoted.

By the end of the 3-week issue period Wellcome Trust was able to look at a demand curve showing how many shares investors were prepared to buy at each price. In the light of this information it decided to sell 270 million shares, with net proceeds of £2.1 billion, about $4 billion at contemporary exchange rates. About 1100 institutions and 30,000 individuals ended up buying the shares. Sixty percent of the issue was sold in the United Kingdom, 25 percent in the United States (over $1 billion), 5 percent in Japan, and most of the rest in France and Germany.

The shares of many companies are now listed and traded on major international exchanges. British Telecom trades on the New York Stock Exchange, as do British Steel, British Petroleum, Glaxo, ICI (Chemicals), National Westminster Bank, Shell (oil), and so on.[20] Several of these companies also trade in Tokyo. Citicorp, one of the largest United States banks, trades in New York, London, Amsterdam, Tokyo, Zurich, Toronto, and Frankfurt, as well as on several smaller exchanges.

Some companies' stocks do not trade at all in their home country. Elsag Bailey, a Netherlands company partly owned by Finmeccanica, an Italian engineering and manufacturing conglomerate, raised $134 million in a New York IPO. It was *not* traded in Amsterdam or in Italy. This was one of at least a dozen United States–only issues in 1993, 1994, and 1995. The issuers thought they could get a better price and more active follow-on trading in New York.[21]

The Costs of the General Cash Offer

Whenever a firm makes a cash offer, it incurs substantial administrative costs. Also the firm needs to compensate the underwriters by selling them securities below the price that they expect to receive from investors. Table 15-1 lists underwriting spreads for a few issues in late 1994. As the table shows, there are economies of scale in issuing securities—the underwriter's spread declines as the size of the issue increases. Stable, established companies also get a break: Nevada Power sold a relatively small, $34 million issue at a spread of only 3.28 percent. Spreads for debt securities are lower, less than 1 percent for large issues, but show the same economies of scale.

Figure 15-2 summarizes a study by Lee, Lochhead, Ritter, and Zhao of total issue costs (spreads plus other costs such as printing, legal fees, and auditing fees) for several thousand issues between 1990 and 1994.

Market Reaction to Stock Issues

Because stock issues usually throw a large additional supply of shares onto the market, it is widely believed that they must temporarily depress the stock price. If the proposed issue is very large, the price pressure may, it is thought, be so severe as to

---

[20]Rather than issuing their shares directly in the United States, foreign companies generally issue *American depository receipts* (ADRs). These are simply claims to the shares of the foreign company, held by a bank on behalf of the ADR owners.

[21]"High-tech firms are much better understood and valued in the U.S." "[The issuers] get a better price, a shareholder base that understands their business, and they can get publicity in a major market for their products." These are representative quotes from M. R. Sesit, "Foreign Firms Flock to U.S. for IPOs," *The Wall Street Journal*, June 23, 1995, p. C1.

TABLE 15-1
• •

Underwriting spreads of selected security issues, 1994. Costs are given as percentages of gross proceeds.

Type*	Company	Issue Amount, Millions of Dollars	Underwriter's Spread, Percent
IPO	American Bingo and Gaming	5	10.0
IPO	Chase Brass Industries	32	7.0
IPO	Young Broadcasting	84.4	6.74
IPO	Storage Trust Realty	100.8	6.97
IPO	British Sky Broadcasting Group	438.2†	4.0
Seasoned	Nevada Power	34.1	3.28
Seasoned	Keane, Inc.	48.7	5.0
Seasoned	Fusion Systems	56.1	4.98
Seasoned	Barnes & Noble	195.2	4.5
Seasoned	LTV	199.2	3.5
Seasoned	ASARCO (mining)	266	3.5
Debt:			
8-year notes‡	Florsheim Shoe	85	3.0
Notes	Penske Truck Leasing	150	.60
12-year notes	Columbia/HCA Health Care	150	.675
2-year floating-rate notes	Dean Witter Discover	350	.25
Bonds	China International Trust and Investment	200	.675
5-year notes	Ford Motor Credit	500	.45

*"IPO" refers to initial public offerings of common stock, "Seasoned" to issues of seasoned stock, "Debt" to long-term public debt issues.
†Domestic issue only. A further $791 million was offered outside the United States.
‡Below investment-grade credit rating; A so-called junk issue.
Source: Investment Dealers Digest, various issues, October through December 1994.

make it almost impossible to raise new money. If so, the firm effectively faces capital rationing.

Economists who have studied new issues of common stock have generally found that announcement of the issue *does* result in a decline in the stock price. For industrial issues in the United States this decline amounts to about 3 percent.[22] While this may not sound overwhelming, the fall in market value is equivalent, on average, to nearly a third of the new money raised by the issue.

---

[22]See, for example, P. Asquith and D. W. Mullins, "Equity Issues and Offering Dilution," *Journal of Financial Economics*, **15**:61–90 (January–February 1986); R. W. Masulis and A. N. Korwar, "Seasoned Equity Offerings: An Empirical Investigation," *Journal of Financial Economics*, **15**:91–118 (January–February 1986); W. H. Mikkelson and M. M. Partch, "Valuation Effects of Security Offerings and the Issuance Process," *Journal of Financial Economics*, **15**:31–60 (January–February 1986). There appears to be a smaller price decline for utility issues. Also Marsh observed a smaller decline for rights issues in the United Kingdom; see P. R. Marsh. "Equity Rights Issues and the Efficiency of the UK Stock Market," *Journal of Finance*, **34**:839–862 (September 1979).

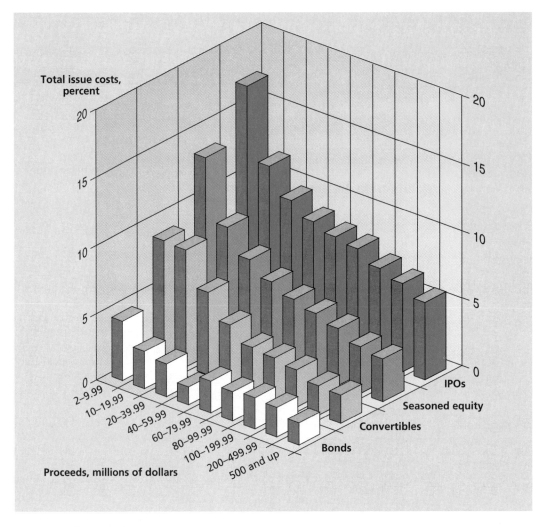

Figure 15-2 Issue costs as a percentage of gross proceeds, 1990–1994. (*Source:* I. Lee, S. Lochhead, J. Ritter, and Q. Zhao, "The Costs of Raising Capital," working paper, University of Illinois, Urbana-Champaign, July 1995. We thank the authors for allowing use of this chart prior to the paper's publication.)

What's going on here? Is the price of the stock simply depressed by the prospect of the additional supply? It is possible, but there is a better explanation.

Suppose that a restaurant chain's CFO is strongly optimistic about its prospects. From her point of view, the company's stock price is too low. Yet the company wants to issue shares to finance expansion into the new state of Northern California.[23] What is she to do? All the choices have drawbacks. If the chain sells stock, it will favor new investors at the expense of old shareholders. When investors come to share

---

[23]Northern California seceded from California and became the fifty-second state in 2007.

the CFO's optimism, the share price will rise, and the new investors' bargain price will be evident.

If the CFO could convince investors to accept her rosy view of the future, then new shares could be sold at a fair price. But this is not so easy. CEOs and CFOs always take care to *sound* upbeat, so just announcing "I'm optimistic" has little effect. But supplying sufficiently detailed information about business plans and profit forecasts is costly—and is also of great assistance to competitors.

The CFO could scale back or delay the expansion until the company's stock price recovers. That too is costly, but it may be rational if the stock price is severely undervalued and a stock issue is the only immediate source of financing.

If a CFO knows that the company's stock is *over*valued, the position is reversed. If the firm sells new shares at the high price, it will help its existing shareholders at the expense of the new ones. Managers might be prepared to issue stock even if the new cash was just put in the bank.

Of course, investors are not stupid. They can predict that managers are more likely to issue stock when they think it is overvalued and that optimistic managers may cancel or defer issues. Therefore, when an equity issue is announced, they mark the price of the stock down accordingly. Thus the decline in the price of the stock at the time of the new issue may have nothing to do with the increased supply but simply with the information that the issue provides.[24]

Cornett and Tehranian devised a natural experiment which pretty much proves this point.[25] They examined a sample of stock issues by commercial banks. Some of these issues were *involuntary*, that is mandated by banking authorities to meet regulatory capital standards. The rest were ordinary, voluntary stock issues designed to raise money for various corporate purposes. The involuntary issues caused a much smaller drop in stock prices than the voluntary ones—which makes perfect sense. If the issue is outside the manager's discretion, announcement of the issue conveys no information about the manager's view of the company's prospects.[26]

Most financial economists now interpret the stock price drop on equity issue announcements as an information effect, not a result of imperfect or inefficient markets.

There is, however, at least one big puzzle left. It appears that the long-run performance of companies which issue shares is substandard. Investors who bought these companies' shares *after* the stock issue announcements earned lower returns than they would have if they had bought into otherwise similar, nonissuing companies. This result holds for both IPOs and seasoned issues and does not appear to reflect differences in risk.[27] It seems that the investors who bought the issues were overly optimistic and failed to appreciate fully the issuing companies' information advantage. If so, we have an exception to the efficient-market theory laid out in Chapter 13. It will be interesting to see whether the poor relative long-term performance of

[24]This explanation was developed in S. C. Myers and N. S. Majluf, "Corporate Financing and Investment Decisions When Firms Have Information That Investors Do Not Have," *Journal of Financial Economics*, **13**:187–222 (1984).

[25]M. M. Cornett and H. Tehranian, "An Examination of Voluntary versus Involuntary Issuances by Commercial Banks," *Journal of Financial Economics*, **35**:99–122 (1994).

[26]The fact that regulators found it necessary to force a bank to raise additional capital is probably bad news too. Thus it's no surprise that Cornett and Tehranian found some drop in stock price even for the involuntary issues.

[27]T. Loughran and J. R. Ritter, "The New Issues Puzzle," *Journal of Finance*, **50**:23–51 (March 1995).

issuing companies' shares persists. We think the poor performance will disappear now that investors know about it.

The Dilution Fallacy

The popular price-earnings fallacies were amply described in Chapter 4. But we haven't yet dissected the dilution fallacy. We do so here because the fallacy sometimes confuses financial managers who are trying to decide whether to issue equity.

The imagined dangers of dilution are dramatized by the sad tale of Quangle Hats. Quangle's profitability is as follows:

- Book net worth $100,000
- Number of shares   1000
- Book value per share $100,000/1000 = $100
- Net earnings $8000
- Earnings per share $8000/1000 = $8
- Price-earnings ratio   10
- Stock price $10 \times \$8 = \$80$
- Total market value $80,000

The total amount of money that has been put up by Quangle's stockholders is $100,000—$100 per share. But that investment is earning only $8 per share—an 8 percent book return. Investors evidently regard this return as inadequate, for they are willing to pay only $80 per share for Quangle stock.

Now suppose that Quangle raises $10,000 by issuing 125 additional shares at the market price of $80 per share—suppose also that the $10,000 is invested to earn a return of 8 percent. In that case, we would expect investors to continue to pay $10 for each $1 of Quangle's earnings. Now we have:

	Before the Issue	After the Issue
Book net worth	$100,000	$110,000
Number of shares	1,000	1,125
Book value per share	$100,000/1,000 = $100	$110,000/1,125 = $97.78
Net earnings	$8,000	8% of book net worth = $8,800
Earnings per share	$8,000/1,000 = $8	$8,800/1,125 = $7.82
Price-earnings ratio	10	10
Stock price	10 × $8 = $80	10 × $7.82 = $78.20
Total market value	$80,000	$88,000

We note that selling stock below book *does* decrease book value per share and stock price as well.

But there are two things wrong with our example. First, we assumed investors could be tricked into paying $80 for shares shortly destined to be worth $78.20. Actually, if Quangle wishes to raise $10,000, it will have to offer shares *worth* $10,000. And since we know that aggregate market value after the stock issue is $88,000, the *original* 1000 shares must end up with an aggregate value of $78,000. The price per share will therefore be $78,000/1000 = $78, and the firm will have to issue $10,000/78 = 128 shares to raise the capital it requires.

Many financial analysts would stop at this point, satisfied that they had "proved" the folly of selling stock for less than book value. But there is a second thing wrong with our example: We never questioned Quangle's decision to expand. It is raising $10,000 and getting only $8000 in additional market value. In other words, the market's verdict is that expansion has an NPV of −$2,000. Note that this is exactly the loss suffered by the original shareholders.

What if the investment earned a *10* percent return? In that case the issue of shares would cause the firm's market value to increase by $10,000 to $90,000, and the earnings per share and stock price would be unchanged. Quangle could therefore raise $10,000 by selling only $10,000/80 = 125 new shares.

The point is simple: There is no harm whatsoever in selling stock at prices below book value per share, as long as investors know that you can earn an adequate rate of return on the new money. If the firm has good projects and needs equity capital to finance them, then "dilution" should not bar it from going to the market.

15-4 THE ROLE OF THE UNDERWRITER

We now look more carefully at the part played by the underwriters during a public offer. We have described them as playing a triple role—providing advice, buying a new issue from the company, and reselling it to the public. In return they receive a payment in the form of a *spread*—that is, they are allowed to buy the shares for less than the *offering price* at which the securities are sold on to investors. In the more risky cases the underwriter usually receives some extra noncash compensation, such as warrants to buy additional stock. Occasionally, where a new issue of common stock is regarded as particularly risky, the underwriter may be unwilling to enter into a fixed commitment and will handle the issue only on a "best-efforts" or an "all-or-none" basis. *Best efforts* means that the underwriter promises to sell as much of the issue as possible but does not guarantee the sale of the entire issue. *All or none* means that if the entire issue cannot be sold at the offering price, the deal is called off and the issuing company receives nothing.

If the issue is large, a group of underwriters will usually get together to form a syndicate to handle the sale. In this case one underwriter acts as syndicate manager and for this job keeps about 20 percent of the spread. A further 20 to 30 percent of the spread is used to pay those members of the group who buy the issue. The remaining 50 to 60 percent goes to the larger number of firms that provide the sales force for the issue.

The National Association of Security Dealers (NASD) requires that the underwriting syndicate sell the issue at the stated offering price. However, the underwriter is generally allowed to support the market by repurchasing shares at the market price.[28] (Look, for example, at the second page of the Marvin prospectus.) We have no information about the effects of such stabilizing transactions. But, if capital markets are efficient, then transactions affect prices only insofar as they are thought to convey information. In that case the underwriters' efforts at stabilization cannot have a lasting effect on prices.

In any case, if the issue obstinately remains unsold and the market price falls substantially below the offering price, the underwriters have no alternative but to break the syndicate. The members then dispose of their commitments individually as best they can.

---

[28]In such cases syndicate members could escape their obligation by selling their shares in the market to the principal underwriter. To prevent this, a record is kept so that syndicate members whose shares end up in the hands of the principal underwriter lose that part of their selling concession.

TABLE 15-2

The top managing underwriters in the first half of 1995. The total values include both debt and equity issues (figures in billions of dollars).

UNITED STATES		EUROMARKET	
Underwriter	Value of Issues	Underwriter	Value of Issues
Merrill Lynch	51.7	Deutsche Bank	8.5
Lehman Brothers	35.0	Goldman Sachs	8.0
CS First Boston	33.9	J.P. Morgan	7.8
Goldman Sachs	33.5	Merrill Lynch	7.6
Morgan Stanley	33.2	Swiss Bank Corp.	7.0
J.P. Morgan	23.2	ABN Amro	6.8
Salomon Brothers	22.1	CS First Boston	6.0
Bear Stearns	13.9	Banque Paribas	6.0
First Tennessee	11.6	Dresdner Bank	5.5
Donaldson Lufkin	10.6	UBS	4.8

Source: The Wall Street Journal, July 3, 1995, p. C16.

Most companies raise new capital only occasionally, but underwriters are in the business all the time. Established underwriters are, therefore, careful of their reputation and will not handle a new issue unless they believe the facts have been presented fairly to investors. Thus, in addition to handling the sale of an issue, the underwriters in effect give their seal of approval to it. This implied endorsement may be worth quite a bit to a company that is coming to the market for the first time.

Underwriting is not always fun. On October 15, 1987, the British government finalized arrangements to sell its holding of BP shares at £3.30 a share.[29] This huge issue involving more than $12 billion was the largest stock offering in history. It was underwritten by an international group of underwriters and simultaneously marketed in a number of countries. Four days after the underwriting was agreed, the October crash caused stock prices around the world to nose-dive. The underwriters unsuccessfully appealed to the British government to cancel the issue.[30] By the closing date of the offer, the price of BP stock had fallen to £2.96, and the underwriters had lost more than a billion dollars.

Who Are the Under-writers?

Since underwriters play such a crucial part in new issues, we should look at who they are. Several thousand investment banks, security dealers, and brokers are at least sporadically involved in underwriting. However, the market for the larger issues is dominated by the major investment banking firms, which enjoy great prestige, experience, and financial resources. Table 15-2 lists some of the largest underwriting firms, ranked by total volume of issues in the first half of 1995, an active period. Merrill

---

[29]The issue was partly a secondary issue (the sale of the British government's shares) and partly a primary issue (BP took the opportunity to raise additional capital by selling new shares).

[30]The government's only concession was to put a floor on the underwriters' losses by giving them the option to resell their stock to the government at £2.80 a share.

Lynch, the winner, was involved, either as lead underwriter or as participant, in issues which raised a total of $51.7 billion.

For each public issue a "tombstone" advertisement is published that lists the names of all the underwriters. In Figure 15-3 we reproduce the tombstone for the initial public offering by Orbital Sciences Corporation. The ordering of the names on the tombstone reflects a well-established hierarchy among underwriters. The most important underwriters are listed in alphabetical order at the top of the list. Then come the second-rankers, and so on.

Firms guard their ranking with remarkable possessiveness. Those that struggle to attain a particular ranking often have to consent to being listed "out of order." But the old regime does change. Firms with strong sales forces, such as Merrill Lynch, have over the years increased their participation and improved their ranking.

Since a eurobond issue is marketed internationally, a eurobond underwriting syndicate is not restricted to investment banks in the United States. As you can see from the right-hand side of Table 15-2, foreign banks are major players in this market. Also, the London branches of American commercial banks are involved in underwriting eurobond issues, whereas their parents in the United States are, for the most part, prohibited by the Glass-Steagall Act from underwriting domestic bond issues.[31]

15-5 THE PRIVATE PLACEMENT

Whenever a company makes a public offering, it is obliged to register the issue with the SEC. It could avoid this costly process by selling the security privately. There are no hard-and-fast definitions of a private placement, but the SEC has insisted that the security should be sold to no more than a dozen or so knowledgeable investors.

One of the disadvantages of a private placement is that the investor cannot easily resell the security. For the common stock investor this drawback looms large, so that *letter stock*, as it is called,[32] is rarely issued except by small, closely held companies. Liquidity is less important to institutions such as life insurance companies, which invest huge amounts of money in corporate debt for the long haul. Consequently, an active private placement mechanism has evolved for corporate debt. In 1980 private placements accounted for about one-fifth of all new corporate debt issues, but by 1989 this proportion had expanded to almost one-half.

Often the privately placed debt is negotiated directly between the company and the lender. If the issue is too large to be absorbed by one institution, the company generally employs an investment banker to draw up the prospectus and identify possible buyers.

As you would expect, it costs less to arrange a private placement than to make a public issue. This is a particular advantage for companies making smaller issues.

Another advantage of the private placement is that the debt contract can be custom-tailored for firms with special problems or opportunities. The relationship between borrower and lender is much more intimate. Imagine a $20 million debt issue privately placed with an insurance company, and compare it with an equivalent public issue held by 200 anonymous investors. The insurance company can justify a

---

[31]A few banks, including Bankers Trust and J.P. Morgan, have been allowed to set up underwriting subsidiaries. As we write this (in July 1995), Congress is considering various "banking reform" measures. The days of the Glass-Steagall barrier between commercial and investment banking seem to be numbered.

[32]So called because the SEC requires a letter from the buyer confirming that the stock is not bought for resale.

This advertisement is neither an offer to sell nor a solicitation of an offer to buy any of these securities.
The offering is made only by the Prospectus.

April 25, 1990

2,400,000 Shares

Orbital Sciences Corporation

Common Stock

Price $14 Per Share

Copies of the Prospectus may be obtained from such of the Underwriters as may legally offer these securities
in compliance with the securities laws of the respective states.

ALEX. BROWN & SONS
INCORPORATED

MERRILL LYNCH CAPITAL MARKETS

BEAR, STEARNS & CO. INC.   THE FIRST BOSTON CORPORATION   DILLON, READ & CO. INC.

DONALDSON, LUFKIN & JENRETTE   HAMBRECHT & QUIST   LAZARD FRERES & CO.
SECURITIES CORPORATION   INCORPORATED

MONTGOMERY SECURITIES   MORGAN STANLEY & CO.   PAINE WEBBER INCORPORATED
INCORPORATED

PRUDENTIAL-BACHE CAPITAL FUNDING   ROBERTSON, STEPHENS & COMPANY

SHEARSON LEHMAN HUTTON INC.   SMITH BARNEY, HARRIS UPHAM & CO.   WERTHEIM SCHRODER & CO.
INCORPORATED   INCORPORATED

DEAN WITTER REYNOLDS INC.   WHEAT FIRST BUTCHER & SINGER
CAPITAL MARKETS

WILLIAM BLAIR & COMPANY   DAIN BOSWORTH   A. G. EDWARDS & SONS, INC.
INCORPORATED

OPPENHEIMER & CO., INC.   PIPER, JAFFRAY & HOPWOOD   THE ROBINSON-HUMPHREY COMPANY, INC.
INCORPORATED

ADVEST, INC.   ROBERT W. BAIRD & CO.   BATEMAN EICHLER, HILL RICHARDS
INCORPORATED   INCORPORATED

SANFORD C. BERNSTEIN & CO., INC.   BLUNT ELLIS & LOEWI   COWEN & CO.   R. G. DICKINSON & CO.
INCORPORATED

INTERSTATE/JOHNSON LANE   JANNEY MONTGOMERY SCOTT INC.   JOHNSTON, LEMON & CO.
CORPORATION   INCORPORATED

LEGG MASON WOOD WALKER   McDONALD & COMPANY   MORGAN KEEGAN & COMPANY, INC.
INCORPORATED   SECURITIES, INC.

RAYMOND JAMES & ASSOCIATES INC.   SEIDLER AMDEC SECURITIES INC.

STEPHENS INC.   STIFEL, NICOLAUS & COMPANY   SUTRO & CO.
INCORPORATED   INCORPORATED

TUCKER ANTHONY   WEDBUSH MORGAN SECURITIES   WESSELS, ARNOLD & HENDERSON
INCORPORATED

Figure 15-3   "Tombstone" advertisements such as this list the underwriters to a new issue.

more thorough investigation of the company's prospects and therefore may be more willing to accept unusual terms or conditions.[33] Renegotiating the debt contract in response to unexpected developments is also extremely cumbersome for a public issue but relatively easy for a private placement.

Therefore, it is not surprising that private placements occupy a particular niche in the corporate debt market, namely loans to small and medium-size firms. These are the firms that face the highest issue costs in public issues, that require the most detailed investigation, and that may require specialized, flexible loan arrangements. However, many large companies use private placements as well.

Of course, these advantages are not free. Lenders in private placements have to be compensated for the risks they face and for the costs of research and negotiation. They also have to be compensated for holding an illiquid asset. All these factors are rolled into the interest rate paid by the firm. It is difficult to generalize about the differences in interest rates between private placements and public issues, but a typical differential is on the order of 50 basis points or .50 percentage point.

In 1990 the SEC relaxed its restrictions on who can buy and trade unregistered securities. The new rule, Rule 144A, allows large financial institutions (known as *qualified institutional buyers*) to trade unregistered securities among themselves. Rule 144A was intended to increase liquidity and reduce interest rates and issue costs for private placements. It was aimed largely at foreign corporations deterred by registration requirements in the United States. The SEC argued that such firms would welcome the opportunity to issue unregistered stocks and bonds which could then be freely traded by large U.S. financial institutions. The hope was that new-issue business would be brought to the United States at the expense of the euromarkets.

The Rule 144A market has been notably successful. By 1994 the volume of 144A issues reached $65 billion, larger than the traditional private placement market. About one-third of this amount was accounted for by foreign issuers.

15-6   SUMMARY

In this chapter we have summarized the various procedures for issuing corporate securities. We first looked at how infant companies raise venture capital to carry them through to the point at which they can make their first public issue of stock. We then looked at how companies can make further public issues of securities by a general cash offer. Finally, we reviewed the procedures for a private placement. It is always difficult to summarize a summary. Instead we will attempt to state the most important implications for the financial manager who must decide how to raise capital.

1. *Larger is cheaper.* There are always economies of scale in issuing securities. It is cheaper to go to the market once for $100 million than to make two trips for $50 million each. Consequently firms "bunch" security issues. That may often mean relying on short-term financing until a large issue is justified. Or it may mean issuing more than is needed at the moment in order to avoid another issue later.

---

[33]Of course debt with the same terms could be offered publicly, but then 200 separate investigations would be required—a much more expensive proposition.

2. *There are no issue costs for retained earnings.* There are significant costs associated with any stock issue. But stock issues can be avoided to the extent that the firm can plow back its earnings. Why then do we observe firms paying generous cash dividends *and* issuing stock from time to time? Why don't they cut the cash dividend, reduce new issues, and thereby avoid paying underwriters, lawyers, and accountants? This is a question to which we will return in Chapter 16.

3. *Private placements are well suited for the small, risky, and unusual.* We do not mean that large, safe, and conventional firms should rule out private placements. Enormous amounts of capital are sometimes raised by this method. For example, AT&T once borrowed $500 million in a single private placement. But the special advantages of private placement stem from avoiding registration expenses and having a more direct relationship with the lender. These are not worth as much to blue-chip borrowers.

4. *Watch out for underpricing.* Underpricing is a hidden cost to the existing shareholders. Fortunately, it is usually serious only for companies that are selling stock to the public for the first time.

5. *New stock issues may depress price.* The extent of this price pressure varies, but for industrial issues in the United States the fall in the value of the existing stock may amount to a significant proportion of the money raised. This pressure is due to the information the market reads into the company's decision to issue stock.

6. *Shelf registration often makes sense for debt issues by blue-chip firms.* Shelf registration reduces the time taken to arrange a new issue, it increases flexibility, and it may cut underwriting costs. It seems best suited for debt issues by large firms that are happy to switch between investment banks. It seems least suited for issues of unusually risky or complex securities or for issues by small companies that are likely to benefit from a close relationship with an investment bank.

APPENDIX A: THE PRIVILEGED SUBSCRIPTION OR RIGHTS ISSUE

In the United States most new issues of common stock are offered to investors at large. However, occasionally companies make a rights issue that is restricted to existing shareholders. In many other countries the rights issue is the most common or only method for issuing stock. In this appendix we look at how rights issues work and how much they cost.

Firms' articles of incorporation sometimes state that shareholders have a *preemptive right* to subscribe to new offerings. A strict interpretation of preemptive rights would place intolerable restrictions on management's freedom of action, and so it is not surprising that these rights have been interpreted in a limited way. First, they usually apply to issues of common stock, to convertible securities, and to voting preferred stock, but not to issues of debt. Second, they do not apply to issues of stock to employees or to stock which has been repurchased from shareholders and then held in the company treasury for subsequent resale. The last exemption will seem strange to those who believe that the life history of a particular share is an irrelevant bygone.

How Rights Issues Work

Here is an example of how rights issues work: In June 1977, American Electric Power Company issued $198 million of common stock by a rights issue. The preliminary stages of the issue, including registration requirements, were the same as those for any other public issue. The only difference lay in selling procedures. Shareholders were sent warrants showing that they owned one "right" for each share that they held. Eleven of these rights entitled a shareholder to buy one additional share at a subscription price of $22 at any time within 24 days of the offer date.[34]

Shareholders could sell, exercise, or throw away these rights. Those who didn't sell should have postponed any exercise decision until the end of the 24-day period. At that point, they should have taken advantage of the opportunity to buy stock at $22 if, and only if, the stock price was at least $22.

To guard against the danger that the price might end up below the subscription price, AEP arranged for the issue to be underwritten. Instead of actually buying the issue as in the cash offer, the underwriters were paid a *standby fee* of $900,000. In return, they stood ready to buy all unsubscribed shares at the subscription price less an additional *take-up fee* of $.287 per share purchased.[35] Most rights issues have standby underwriting, but occasionally companies save the underwriting fee by choosing a low subscription price and crossing their fingers that the market price won't fall below the subscription price.

As it turned out, AEP's stock price was $24⅛ at the end of the 24 days. Although this was above the $22 subscription price, holders of about 10 percent of the stock failed to exercise their rights. We must attribute this lapse to either ignorance or vacations.[36]

How a Rights Issue Affects the Stock Price

The left-hand portion of Table 15-4 shows the case of a stockholder who owned 11 shares of AEP stock just prior to the rights issue. The price of the stock at that time was about $24, and so this stockholder's total holding was worth $24 × 11, or $264. The AEP offer gave the opportunity to purchase one additional share for $22. Put yourself in the stockholder's shoes. If you buy the new share immediately, your holding increases to 12 shares and, other things being equal, the value of the 12 shares is $264 + $22 = $286. The price per share after the issue would no longer be $24, but $286/12 = $23.83.

The only difference between the old $24 shares and the new $23.83 shares is that the former carried rights to subscribe to the issue. Therefore the old shares are generally termed *rights-on* shares and the new shares are termed *ex-rights* shares. The 17-cent difference in price between the two shares represents the price of one right. We can confirm that this is the correct price of the right by imagining a second investor who has no stock in AEP but wishes to acquire some. One way to do this would be to buy 11 rights at 17 cents each and then exercise them at a further cost of $22. The total cost of this investor's share would be 11 × $.17 + $22 = $23.87, which, save for rounding error, is the same outlay required to buy one of the new shares directly.

Inside the back cover of this book we have listed the formulas for calculating the value of a right and the corresponding ex-rights price.

---

[34]A rights issue that gives the shareholder one right for each share held is known as a "New York right." In the United States, almost all issues are New York rights. But in some countries, such as the United Kingdom, you need one right to purchase one new share. This is known as a "Philadelphia right." If AEP were a company in the United Kingdom, the shareholder would need to own 11 shares in order to receive one right and this right would be correspondingly 11 times more valuable.

[35]You can think of standby underwriting as providing shareholders with an option. In return for paying the standby fee, they can sell their stock to the underwriters at the issue price. We will tell you how to value such options in Chapter 20.

[36]Despite this shortfall, AEP did not have to turn to its underwriters. AEP's shareholders had been given an oversubscription privilege, which allowed them to buy unsubscribed shares at the subscription price ($22). As it turned out, AEP had no trouble selling the unsubscribed shares to shareholders who applied for extra shares. Of course, these shareholders profited at the expense of the vacationers and *incognoscenti*.

TABLE 15-4

••

Issue price in a rights offering does not affect the shareholder's wealth.

	1-for-11 at $22	1-for-5½ at $11
Before issue:		
Number of shares held	11	11
Share price (rights on)	$24	$24
Value of holding	$264	$264
After issue:		
Number of new shares	1	2
Amount of new investment	$22	2 × $11 = $22
Total value of holding	$286	$286
Total number of shares	12	13
New share price (ex-rights)	$286/12 = $23.83	$286/13 = $22
Value of a right	$24 − 23.83 = $.17	$24 − 22 = $2

•••••••••••••••••••

Issue Price Is Irrelevant as Long as the Rights Are Exercised

It should be clear on reflection that AEP could have raised the same amount of money on a variety of terms. For example, instead of a 1-for-11 at $22, it could have made a 1-for-5½ at $11. In this case it would have sold twice as many shares at half the price. It we now work through the arithmetic again in the right-hand portion of Table 15-4, we can see that the issue price is irrelevant in a rights offering. After all, it cannot affect the real plant and equipment owned by the company or the proportion of these assets to which each shareholder is entitled. Therefore the only thing a firm ought to worry about in setting the terms of a rights issue is the possibility that the stock price will fall below the issue price. If that happens, shareholders will not take up their rights and the whole issue will be torpedoed. You can avoid this danger by arranging a standby agreement with the underwriter. But standby agreements tend to be expensive. It may be cheaper just to set the issue price low enough to foreclose the possibility of failure.

•••••••••••••••••••

The Choice between the Cash Offer and the Rights Issue

You now know about the two principal forms of public issue—the cash offer to all investors and the rights issue to existing shareholders. The former method is used for almost all debt issues and unseasoned stock issues and many seasoned stock issues. Rights issues are largely restricted to seasoned stock issues.

One essential difference between the two methods is that in a rights offering the issue price is largely irrelevant. Shareholders can sell their new stock or their rights in a free market. Therefore, they can expect to receive a fair price. In a cash offer, however, the issue price may be important. If the company sells stock for less than the market would bear, the buyer has made a profit at the expense of existing shareholders. Although this danger creates a natural presumption in favor of the rights issue, it can be argued that underpricing is a serious problem only in the case of the unseasoned issue of stock in which a rights issue is not a feasible alternative.

Not too long ago many companies, especially regulated utilities, were required to sell stock by rights issues. Almost all have now cajoled their stockholders to vote away this privilege. For example, consider the following appeal made in 1976 by Consolidated Edison to its stockholders:

Expenses involved in a pre-emptive Common Stock rights offering are significantly greater than expenses involved in a direct offering of Common Stock to the public due to additional printing and mailing costs, expenses associated with the handling of rights and the processing of subscriptions, higher underwriters' commissions and the longer time required for consummation of the financing. Thus, if the amendment is adopted, the Company will be able to obtain the amount of capital needed through the issuance of fewer shares. Over a period of time this will result in slightly less dilution, higher equity value per share, and better earnings per share.[37]

What are the major points in this argument?

1. *Higher expenses?* AEP certainly didn't think its offer was expensive.[38] The underwriting fees shown for rights issues are the sum of the standby fees and the take-up fees that would have been paid if the issues had failed. In practice, underwriters are rarely required to take up the issue, and therefore they usually receive only the standby fee. That can make an underwritten rights issue *less* expensive than a public issue.[39] Note also that rights issues don't have to be underwritten as long as the exercise price is set well below the stock price. Since they avoid the cost of underwriting, *nonunderwritten* rights issues might be significantly *cheaper* than general cash offers.[40]

2. *Longer time required?* Perhaps an extra month—rarely an important consideration.

3. *Fewer shares issued?* You should know the argument against that one by now.

In short, the arguments that firms make for avoiding rights issues don't make sense. We don't know why they use cash offers. Perhaps there are hidden reasons, but until they are uncovered we don't think you should rule out rights issues.

We should not end with the impression that the rights issue is dead in the United States. It continues to be used in special situations. Several closed-end mutual funds[41] raised capital via rights in the 1990s. For example, in August 1995 the Swiss Helvetia

---

[37]We are indebted to Clifford Smith for finding the quotation from Consolidated Edison.

[38]"Some financial executives dismiss rights offerings as expensive and cumbersome. American Electric, according to Gerald P. Maloney, senior vice-president for finance, has found them to be neither.

"'The underwriting costs on the utility's last offering totaled $1.1 million,' Mr. Maloney said in an interview the other day, 'only six-tenths of the total amount of money involved.'

"'We think that's very inexpensive,' he continued. He estimated that underwriting costs would have amounted to '3 or 4 percent' if the company had bypassed shareholders and gone directly to the public."

From Richard Phalon, "Personal Investing—American Electric's Rights Offering," *The New York Times*, July 9, 1977, p. 15.

[39]This difference between the underwriting costs of rights issues and cash offers was pointed out by Robert Hansen. But Hansen also argued that underwritten rights issues have been accompanied by a temporary drop in the share price during the offering period. That would not matter for shareholders who continued to hold the stock, but it would be a drawback for those who wished to sell. See R. S. Hansen, "The Demise of the Rights Issue," *The Review of Financial Studies*, 1:289–310 (Fall 1988).

[40]Clifford Smith calculated costs for a small sample of nonunderwritten rights issues and found average issue costs of only 2.5 percent. See C. W. Smith, "Alternative Methods for Raising Capital: Rights Issues versus Underwritten Offerings," *Journal of Financial Economics*, 5:273–307 (December 1977).

[41]Investors in an *open-end* mutual fund can buy more shares from the fund, or sell shares back to the fund, at any time. A *closed-end* fund issues a set number of shares which are then traded on one of the stock exchanges. Thus a closed-end fund must issue additional shares in order to expand.

Fund (an oddly redundant name) issued 3.1 million additional shares by a rights issue. Shareholders of the fund were given one right for every share they held; three rights gave the option to purchase one additional share at 95 percent of the market price at the end of the subscription period.[42]

The Swiss Helvetia rights were *nontransferable:* stockholders could not sell the rights but had to exercise them or lose their value. A rational, value-maximizing stockholder was therefore obliged to buy into the issue.

APPENDIX B: MARVIN'S NEW-ISSUE PROSPECTUS[43]

PROSPECTUS

900,000 Shares
Marvin Enterprises Inc.
Common Stock ($.10 par value)

Of the 900,000 shares of Common Stock offered hereby, 500,000 shares are being sold by the Company and 400,000 shares are being sold by the Selling Stockholders. See "Principal and Selling Stockholders." The Company will not receive any of the proceeds from the sale of shares by the Selling Stockholders.

Before this offering there has been no public market for the Common Stock. **These securities involve a high degree of risk. See "Certain Considerations."**

THESE SECURITIES HAVE NOT BEEN APPROVED OR DISAPPROVED BY THE SECURITIES AND EXCHANGE COMMISSION NOR HAS THE COMMISSION PASSED ON THE ACCURACY OR ADEQUACY OF THIS PROSPECTUS. ANY REPRESENTATION TO THE CONTRARY IS A CRIMINAL OFFENSE.

	Price to Public	Underwriting Discount	Proceeds to Company (1)	Proceeds to Selling Stockholders (1)
Per share	$80.00	$5.00	$75.00	$75.00
Total (2)	$72,000,000	$4,500,000	$37,500,000	$30,000,000

(1) Before deducting expenses payable by the Company estimated at $820,000, of which $455,555 will be paid by the Company and $364,445 by the Selling Stockholders.
(2) The Company has granted to the Underwriters an option to purchase up to an additional 50,000 shares at the initial public offering price, less the underwriting discount, solely to cover overallotment.

---

[42]An oversubscription privilege allowed exercising stockholders to buy any unsubscribed shares.

[43]Most prospectuses have content similar to that of the Marvin prospectus but go into considerably more detail. Also we have omitted Marvin's financial statements.

The Common Stock is offered subject to receipt and acceptance by the Underwriters, to prior sale, and to the Underwriters' right to reject any order in whole or in part and to withdraw, cancel, or modify the offer without notice.

Klein Merrick Inc.   **February 3, 2009**

No person has been authorized to give any information or to make any representations, other than as contained therein, in connection with the offer contained in this Prospectus, and, if given or made, such information or representations must not be relied upon. This Prospectus does not constitute an offer of any securities other than the registered securities to which it relates or an offer to any person in any jurisdiction where such an offer would be unlawful. The delivery of this Prospectus at any time does not imply that information herein is correct as of any time subsequent to its date.

IN CONNECTION WITH THIS OFFERING, THE UNDERWRITERS MAY OVERALLOT OR EFFECT TRANSACTIONS WHICH STABILIZE OR MAINTAIN THE MARKET PRICE OF THE COMMON STOCK OF THE COMPANY AT A LEVEL ABOVE THAT WHICH MIGHT OTHERWISE PREVAIL IN THE OPEN MARKET. SUCH STABILIZING, IF COMMENCED, MAY BE DISCONTINUED AT ANY TIME.

Prospectus Summary
The following summary information is qualified in its entirety by the detailed information and financial statements appearing elsewhere in this Prospectus.

The Offering
Common Stock offered by the Company . . . . .500,000 shares
Common Stock offered by the Selling Stockholders . . . . .400,000 shares
Common Stock to be outstanding after this offering . . . . .4,100,000 shares

Use of Proceeds
For the construction of new manufacturing facilities and to provide working capital.

The Company
Marvin Enterprises Inc. designs, manufactures, and markets gargle blasters for domestic use. Its manufacturing facilities employ integrated microcircuits to control the genetic engineering processes used to manufacture gargle blasters.

The Company was organized in Delaware in 2003.

Use of Proceeds
The net proceeds of this offering are expected to be $37,044,445. Of the net proceeds, approximately $27.0 million will be used to finance expansion of the Company's principal manufacturing facilities. The balance will be used for working capital.

Certain Considerations
Investment in the Common Stock involves a high degree of risk. The following factors should be carefully considered in evaluating the Company:
Substantial Capital Needs   The Company will require additional financing to continue its expansion policy. The Company believes that its relations with its lenders are good, but there can be no assurance that additional financing will be available in the future.

Licensing   The expanded manufacturing facilities are to be used for the production of a new imploding gargle blaster. An advisory panel to the U.S. Food and Drug Administration (FDA) has recommended approval of this product for the U.S. market but no decision has yet been reached by the full FDA committee.

Dividend Policy

The company has not paid cash dividends on its Common Stock and does not anticipate that dividends will be paid on the Common Stock in the foreseeable future.

Management

The following table sets forth information regarding the Company's directors, executive officers, and key employees.

Name	Age	Position
George Marvin	32	President, Chief Executive Officer, & Director
Mildred Marvin	28	Treasurer & Director
Chip Norton	30	General Manager

George Marvin—George Marvin established the Company in 2003 and has been its Chief Executive Officer since that date. He is a past president of the Institute of Gargle Blasters.

Mildred Marvin—Mildred Marvin has been employed by the Company since 2003.

Chip Norton—Mr. Norton has been General Manager of the Company since 2003. He is a former vice-president of Amalgamated Blasters, Inc.

Executive Compensation

The following table sets forth the cash compensation paid for services rendered for the year 2008 by the executive officers:

Name	Capacity	Cash Compensation
George Marvin	President and Chief Executive Officer	$300,000
Mildred Marvin	Treasurer	$220,000
Chip Norton	General Manager	$220,000

Certain Transactions

At various times between 2004 and 2007 First Meriam Venture Partners invested a total of $8.5 million in the Company. In connection with this investment, First Meriam Venture Partners was granted certain rights to registration under the Securities Act of 1933, including the right to have their shares of Common Stock registered at the Company's expense with the Securities and Exchange Commission.

Principal and Selling Stockholders

The following table sets forth certain information regarding the beneficial ownership of the Company's voting Common Stock as of the date of this prospectus by (i) each person known by the Company to be the beneficial owner of more than 5% of its voting Common Stock, and (ii) each director of the Company who beneficially owns voting Common Stock. Unless otherwise indicated, each owner has sole voting and dispositive power over his shares.

COMMON STOCK

Name of Beneficial Owner	SHARES BENEFICIALLY OWNED PRIOR TO OFFERING		Shares to Be Sold	SHARES BENEFICIALLY OWNED AFTER OFFER (1)	
	Number	Percent		Number	Percent
George Marvin	375,000	10.4	60,000	315,000	7.7
Mildred Marvin	375,000	10.4	60,000	315,000	7.7
Chip Norton	250,000	6.9	80,000	170,000	4.1
First Meriam Venture Partners	1,700,000	47.2	—	1,700,000	41.5
TFS Investors	260,000	7.2	—	260,000	6.3
Centri-Venture Partnership	260,000	7.2	—	260,000	6.3
Henry Pobble	180,000	5.0	—	180,000	4.4
Georgina Sloberg	200,000	5.6	200,000	—	—

(1) Assuming no exercise of the Underwriters' over-allotment option.

Description of Capital Stock

The Company's authorized capital stock consists of 10,000,000 shares of voting Common Stock.

As of the date of this Prospectus, there are 10 holders of record of the Common Stock.

Under the terms of one of the Company's loan agreements, the Company may not pay cash dividends on Common Stock except from net profits without the written consent of the lender.

Underwriting

Subject to the terms and conditions set forth in the Underwriting Agreement, the Company has agreed to sell to each of the Underwriters named below, and each of the Underwriters, for whom Klein Merrick Inc. are acting as Representatives, has severally agreed to purchase from the Company, the number of shares set forth opposite its name below.

Underwriters	Number of Shares to Be Purchased
Klein Merrick, Inc.	400,000
Salomon, Buffett & Co.	150,000
Goldman Stanley, Inc.	150,000
Orange County Securities	100,000
Bank of New England	100,000

In the Underwriting Agreement, the several Underwriters have agreed, subject to the terms and conditions set forth therein, to purchase all shares offered hereby if any such shares are purchased. In the event of a default by any Underwriter, the

Underwriting Agreement provides that, in certain circumstances, purchase commitments of the nondefaulting Underwriters may be increased or the Underwriting Agreement may be terminated.

There is no public market for the Common Stock. The price to the public for the Common Stock was determined by negotiation between the Company and the Underwriters and was based on, among other things, the Company's financial and operating history and condition, its prospects and the prospects for its industry in general, the management of the Company, and the market prices of securities for companies in businesses similar to that of the Company.

Legal Matters

The validity of the shares of Common Stock offered by the Prospectus is being passed on for the Company by Thatcher, Kohl, and Lubbers and for the Underwriters by Hawke and Mulroney.

Experts

The consolidated financial statements of the Company have been so included in reliance on the reports of Hooper Firebrand, independent accountants, given on the authority of that firm as experts in auditing and accounting.

Financial Statements

[Text and tables omitted.]

Further Reading

* *

A useful article on investment banking is:
C. W. Smith: "Investment Banking and the Capital Acquisition Process," *Journal of Financial Economics,* **15**:3–29 (January–February 1986).

The best sources of material on venture capital are the specialized journals. See, for example, recent issues of Venture Capital Journal. *A very readable analysis of how venture capital financing is structured to provide the right incentives is contained in:*
W. A. Sahlman: "Aspects of Financial Contracting in Venture Capital," *Journal of Applied Corporate Finance,* **1**:23–26 (Summer 1988).

There have been a number of studies of the market for unseasoned issues of common stock. Good articles to start with are:
R. G. Ibbotson, J. L. Sindelar, and J. R. Ritter: "The Market's Problem with Initial Public Offerings," *Journal of Applied Corporate Finance,* **7**:66–74 (Spring 1994).
K. Rock: "Why New Issues Are Underpriced," *Journal of Financial Economics,* **15**:187–212 (January–February 1986).
J. R. Ritter: "The 'Hot Issue' Market of 1980," *Journal of Business,* **57**:215–240 (1984).

The first two articles both find a significant and permanent fall in price after an industrial stock issue in the United States; the Marsh paper, using data from the United Kingdom, finds only a negligible fall in price:
P. Asquith and D. W. Mullins: "Equity Issues and Offering Dilution," *Journal of Financial Economics,* **15**:61–90 (January–February 1986).
R. W. Masulis and A. N. Korwar: "Seasoned Equity Offerings: An Empirical Investigation," *Journal of Financial Economics,* **15**:91–118 (January–February 1986).
P. R. Marsh: "Equity Rights Issues and the Efficiency of the UK Stock Market," *Journal of Finance,* **34**:839–862 (September 1979).

Myers and Majluf analyze the information problems associated with security issues:
S. C. Myers and N. S. Majluf: "Corporate Financing When Firms Have Information That Investors Do Not Have," *Journal of Financial Economics*, **13**:187–222 (June 1984).

The Federal Reserve system has published a useful survey of the private placement market:
M. Carey, S. Prowse, J. Rea, and G. Ledell: "The Economics of the Private Placement Market," Staff Study, Board of Governors of the Federal Reserve System, Washington, D.C., 1993.

Smith, in the following article, argues that the cheapest way to issue stock is to offer it by a rights issue to existing stockholders; Hansen and Pinkerton and Eckbo and Masulis disagree:
C. W. Smith: "Alternative Methods for Raising Capital: Rights versus Underwritten Offerings," *Journal of Financial Economics*, **5**:273–307 (December 1977).
R. S. Hansen and J. M. Pinkerton: "Direct Equity Financing: A Resolution of a Paradox," *Journal of Finance*, **37**:651–666 (June 1982).
B. E. Eckbo and R. W. Masulis: "Adverse Selection and the Rights Offer Paradox," *Journal of Financial Economics*, **32**:293–332 (December 1992).

Quiz

1. After each of the following issue methods we have listed two issues. Choose the one more likely to employ that method.
   (*a*) Rights issue *(issue of seasoned stock/issue of unseasoned stock)*
   (*b*) Rule 144A issue *(Eurobond issue/U.S. bond issue by a foreign corporation)*
   (*c*) Private placement *(issue of seasoned stock/bond issue by industrial company)*
   (*d*) Shelf registration *(issue of unseasoned stock/bond issue by a large industrial company)*
   (*e*) Sale of stock by auction *(issued in United States/issued outside United States)*

2. Each of the following terms is associated with one of the events beneath. Can you match them up?
   (*a*) Company registrar
   (*b*) Best efforts
   (*c*) Tombstone
   (*d*) Red herring
   (*e*) Shelf registration
   (*f*) Letter stock
   (*g*) Rule 144A

   Events:
   (**A**) The company issues a preliminary prospectus.
   (**B**) Some issues are privately placed and exempted from registration.
   (**C**) An advertisement is published in the financial press listing members of the underwriting syndicate.
   (**D**) A trust company is appointed to ensure that no unauthorized shares are issued.
   (**E**) The underwriter accepts responsibility only to *try* to sell the issue.
   (**F**) Some issues are not registered but can be traded freely among qualified institutional buyers.
   (**G**) Several tranches of the same security may be sold under the same registration. A "tranche" is a batch, a fraction of a larger issue.

3. For each of the following pairs of issues, state which issue is likely to involve the lower proportionate underwriting and administrative costs, other things equal:

(*a*) A large issue/a small issue

(*b*) A bond issue/a common stock issue

(*c*) Initial public offering of stock/seasoned issue of stock.

(*d*) A small private placement of bonds/a small general cash offer of bonds

4. True or false?

(*a*) Venture capitalists typically provide first-stage financing sufficient to cover all development expenses. Second-stage financing is provided by stock issued in an initial public offering.

(*b*) Large companies' stocks may be listed and traded on several different international exchanges.

(*c*) Stock issues should be avoided if the increased number of shares reduces earnings per share.

(*d*) Stock price generally falls when the company announces a new issue of shares. This is attributable to the information released by the decision to issue.

(*e*) Tombstones are published to announce the failure and withdrawal of an attempted security issue.

5. Look back at Marvin's initial public offering:

(*a*) If there is unexpectedly heavy demand for the issue, how many extra shares can the underwriters buy?

(*b*) How many shares are to be sold in the primary offering? How many will be sold in the secondary offering?

(*c*) What with the benefit of hindsight was the degree of underpricing? How does that compare with the average degree of underpricing for initial public offerings in the United States?

(*d*) There are three kinds of cost to Marvin's new issue—underwriting expense, administrative costs, and underpricing. What was the *total* dollar cost of the Marvin issue?

6. You need to choose between making a public offering and arranging a private placement. You have the following data for each:

■ *Offer A: A public issue of $10 million face value of 10-year debt.* The interest rate on the debt would be 8.5 percent, and the debt would be issued at face value. The underwriting spread would be 1.5 percent, and other expenses would be $80,000.

■ *Offer B: A private placement of $10 million face value of 10-year debt.* The interest rate on the private placement would be 9 percent, but the total issuing expenses would be only $30,000.

(*a*) What is the difference in the proceeds to the company net of expenses?

(*b*) Other things equal, which is the better deal?

(*c*) What other factors beyond the interest rate and issue costs would you wish to consider before deciding between the two offers?

7. Associated Breweries is planning to market unleaded beer. To finance the venture it proposes to make a rights issue at $10 of one new share for each two shares held. (The company currently has outstanding 100,000 shares priced at $40 a share.) Assuming that the new money is invested to earn a fair return, give values for the following:

(*a*) Number of rights needed to purchase one share

(*b*) Number of new shares

(c) Amount of new investment
(d) Total value of company after issue
(e) Total number of shares after issue
(f) Rights-on price
(g) Ex-rights price
(h) Price of a right

Questions and Problems

1. In some countries initial public offerings of common stock are sold by auction. Another procedure is for the underwriter to advertise the issue publicly and invite orders for shares at the issue price. If the applications exceed the number of shares on offer, then they are scaled down in proportion; if there are too few applications, any unsold shares are left with the underwriters. Compare these procedures with the initial public offering in the United States. Can you think of any better ways to sell new shares?

2. (a) Why do venture capital companies prefer to advance money in stages? If you were the management of Marvin Enterprises, would you have been happy with such an arrangement? With the benefit of hindsight did First Meriam gain or lose by advancing money in stages?
   (b) The price at which First Meriam would advance more money to Marvin was not fixed in advance. But Marvin could have given First Meriam an *option* to buy more shares at a preset price. Would this have been better?
   (c) At the second stage Marvin could have raised money from another venture capital company in preference to First Meriam. To protect themselves against this, venture capital firms sometimes demand first refusal on new capital issues. Would you recommend this arrangement?

3. "For small issues of common stock, the costs of flotation amount to about 10 percent of the proceeds. This means that the opportunity cost of external equity capital is about 10 percentage points higher than that of retained earnings." Does this follow?

4. Why are issue costs for debt issues generally less than those for equity issues? List the possible reasons.

5. In what circumstances is a private placement preferable to a public issue? Explain.

6. Do you think that there could be a shortage of finance for new ventures? Should the government help to provide such finance and, if so, how?

7. Get hold of a copy of the prospectus for a recent issue of securities. How do the issue costs compare with (a) those of the Marvin issue, (b) those shown in Table 15-1? Can you suggest reasons for the differences?

8. In 1991 Pandora, Inc., makes a rights issue at $5 a share of one new share for every four shares held. Before the issue there were 10 million shares outstanding and the share price was $6.
   (a) What is the total amount of new money raised?
   (b) How many rights are needed to buy one new share?
   (c) What is the value of one right?
   (d) What is the prospective ex-rights price?

(*e*) How far could the total value of the company fall before shareholders would be unwilling to take up their rights?

9. Problem 8 contains details of a rights offering by Pandora. Suppose that the company had decided to issue new stock at $4. How many new shares would it have needed to raise the same sum of money? Recalculate the answers to questions (*b*) to (*e*) in problem 8. Show that Pandora's shareholders are just as well off if it issues the shares at $4 a share rather than the $5 assumed in problem 8.

10. Construct a simple numerical example to show the following:
    (*a*) Existing shareholders are made worse off when a company makes a cash offer of new stock below the market price.
    (*b*) Existing shareholders are *not* made worse off when a company makes a rights issue of new stock below the market price even if the stockholders do not wish to take up their rights.

11. Here is recent financial data on Pisa Construction, Inc.

    ■ Stock price: $40   ■ Market value of firm: $400,000
    ■ Number shares: 10,000   ■ Earnings per share: $4
    ■ Book net worth: $500,000   ■ Return on investment: 8 percent

    Pisa has not performed spectacularly to date. However, it wishes to issue new shares to obtain $80,000 to finance expansion into a promising market. Pisa's financial advisers think a stock issue is a poor choice because, among other reasons, "sale of stock at a price below book value per share can only depress the stock price and decrease shareholders' wealth." To prove the point they construct the following example: "Suppose 2000 new shares are issued at $40 and the proceeds invested. (Neglect issue costs.) Suppose return on investment doesn't change. Then

    $$\text{Book net worth} = \$580,000$$
    $$\text{Total earnings} = .08\,(580,000) = \$46,400$$
    $$\text{Earnings per share} = \frac{46,400}{12,000} = \$3.87$$

    Thus, EPS declines, book value per share declines, and share price will decline proportionately to $38.70."
    Evaluate this argument with particular attention to the assumptions implicit in the numerical example.

12. There are three reasons that a common stock issue might cause a fall in price— (*a*) demand for the company's stock is inelastic, (*b*) the issue causes price pressure until it has been digested, and (*c*) management has information that stockholders do not have. Explain these reasons more fully. Which do you find most plausible? Is there any way that you could seek to test whether you are right?

13. (*a*) "A signal is credible only if a false signal is costly." Explain why management's willingness to invest in Marvin's equity rather than its debt was a credible signal. Was its willingness to accept only a part of the venture capital that would eventually be needed also a credible signal?
    (*b*) "When managers take their reward in the form of increased leisure or executive jets, the cost is borne by the shareholders." Explain how First Meriam's financing package avoided this problem.

PART five

DIVIDEND POLICY AND CAPITAL STRUCTURE

16

The Dividend Controversy

In this chapter we explain how companies set their dividend payments and we discuss the controversial question of how dividend policy affects value.

Why should you care about the answer to this question? Of course, if you are responsible for deciding on your company's dividend payment, you will want to know how it affects value. But there is a more general reason than that. We have up to this point assumed that the company's investment decision is independent of its financing policy. In that case a good project is a good project is a good project, no matter who undertakes it or how it is ultimately financed. If dividend policy does not affect value, that is still true. But perhaps it *does* affect value. In that case the attractiveness of a new project may depend on where the money is coming from. For example, if investors prefer companies with high payouts, companies might be reluctant to take on investments financed by retained earnings.

The first step toward understanding dividend policy is to recognize that the phrase means different things to different people. Therefore we must start by defining what *we* mean by it.

A firm's decisions about dividends are often mixed up with other financing and investment decisions. Some firms pay low dividends because management is optimistic about the firm's future and wishes to retain earnings for expansion. In this case the dividend is a by-product of the firm's capital budgeting decision. Suppose, however, that the future opportunities evaporate, that a dividend increase is announced, and that the stock price falls. How do we separate the impact of the dividend increase from the impact of investors' disappointment at the lost growth opportunities?

Another firm might finance capital expenditures largely by borrowing. This releases cash for dividends. In this case the firm's dividend is a by-product of the borrowing decision.

We must isolate dividend policy from other problems of financial management. The precise question we should ask is: "What is the effect of a change in cash dividends paid, *given the firm's capital budgeting and borrowing decisions?*" Of course the cash used to finance a dividend increase has to come from somewhere. If we fix the firm's investment outlays and borrowing, there is only one possible source—an issue of stock. Thus we define *dividend policy* as the trade-off between retaining earnings on the one hand and paying out cash and issuing new shares on the other.

This trade-off may seem artificial at first, for we do not observe firms scheduling a stock issue with every dividend payment. But there are many firms that pay dividends and also issue stock from time to time. They could avoid the stock issues by paying lower dividends. Many other firms restrict dividends so that they *do not* have to issue shares. They could issue stock occasionally and increase the dividend. Both groups of firms are facing the dividend policy trade-off.

16-1 HOW DIVIDENDS ARE PAID

The dividend is set by the firm's board of directors. The announcement states that the payment will be made to all those stockholders who are registered on a particular "record date." Then about 2 weeks later dividend checks are mailed to stockholders.

Shares are normally bought and sold "with dividend" until a few days before the record date. But investors who buy with dividend need not worry if their shares are not registered in time. The dividend must be paid over to them by the seller. Similarly, investors who buy a share "ex dividend" are obliged to return the dividend if they receive it.

Some Legal Limitations on Dividends

Suppose that an unscrupulous board decided to sell all the firm's assets and distribute the money as dividends. That would not leave anything in the kitty to pay the company's debts. Therefore, bondholders often guard against this danger by placing a limit on dividend payments.

State law also helps to protect the company's creditors against excessive dividend payments. Most states prohibit a company from paying dividends if doing so would make the company insolvent.[1] In addition, state law distinguishes between a company's "legal" (or "stated") capital and "surplus." *Legal capital* generally consists of the par value of all outstanding shares; where there is no par value, it consists of part or all the receipts from the issue of shares. *Surplus* is what remains after legal capital is subtracted from book net worth. Companies are allowed to pay a dividend out of surplus but they may not distribute legal capital.[2]

Par value and legal capital rarely have much economic significance. Par value is often arbitrarily set at $1 per share. The laws restricting payment of legal capital probably serve a purpose, however. They give most corporations a large degree of flexibility in deciding what to pay out, but they help prevent unscrupulous firms from escaping their creditors.

Dividends Come in Many Forms

Most dividends are paid in the form of cash. *Regular cash dividends* are usually paid quarterly, but a few companies declare them monthly, semiannually, or annually. The term *regular* merely indicates that the company expects that it will be able to maintain the payment in the future. If the company does not want to give that kind of assurance, it usually declares both a regular and an *extra dividend*. Investors understand that the extra dividend may not be repeated. Finally, the term *special dividend* tends to be reserved specifically for payments that are unlikely to be repeated.

---

[1] The statutes define insolvency in different ways. In some cases, it just means an inability to meet immediate obligations; in other cases, it means a deficiency of assets compared with all outstanding fixed liabilities.

[2] Companies with wasting assets, such as mining companies, may be an exception to this rule. They may be allowed to distribute legal capital to the extent of the depletion. Also, in some states companies may distribute current profits even though previous losses may have impaired legal capital.

Paying a dividend reduces the amount of retained earnings shown on the firm's balance sheet. However, if all retained earnings are "used up," and if funds are not needed for the protection of creditors, the company may be permitted to pay a *liquidating dividend*. Because such payments are regarded as a return of capital, they are not taxed as income.

Dividends are not always in the form of cash. Frequently companies declare *stock dividends*. For example, Archer Daniels Midland has paid a yearly stock dividend of 5 percent for nearly two decades. That means it sends each shareholder 5 extra shares for every 100 shares currently owned. You can see that a stock dividend is very much like a stock split. Both increase the number of shares, and both reduce value per share, other things equal. Neither makes anybody better off. The distinction between the two is a technical one. A stock dividend is shown in the accounts as a transfer from retained earnings to equity capital, whereas a split is shown as a reduction in the par value of each share.

There are also other types of noncash dividends. For example, companies sometimes send shareholders a sample of their product. The British company Dundee Crematorium once offered its more substantial shareholders a discount cremation. Needless to say, they were not *required* to receive this dividend.

Many companies have automatic dividend reinvestment plans ("DRIPs"). Often the new shares are issued at a 5 percent discount from the market price; the firm offers this sweetener because it saves the underwriting costs of a regular share issue. Sometimes 10 percent or more of total dividends will be reinvested under such plans.[3]

Share Repurchase

When a firm wants to pay cash to its shareholders, it usually declares a cash dividend. But an alternative and increasingly popular method is to repurchase its own stock. In the period 1973–1974 the government imposed a limit on dividends but it forgot to impose a limit on share repurchase. Many firms discovered share repurchase for the first time and the total value of repurchases swelled to about a fifth of the value of dividend payments.

Beginning in the 1980s repurchases seemed to become an everyday event. For example, in 1994 United States corporations authorized $69 billion of stock repurchases. Philip Morris and J.C. Penney each approved a $6 billion program, while Disney, Scott Paper, Chrysler, and Toys "R" Us were among those planning to spend more than $1 billion each on buying back shares. The biggest and most dramatic repurchases have been in the oil industry, where cash resources have generally outrun good capital investment opportunities. Exxon is in first place, having spent about $17 billion on repurchasing shares through year-end 1994.

Stock repurchase plans were big news in October 1987. On Monday, October 19, stock prices in the United States nose-dived more than 20 percent. The next day the board of Citicorp approved a plan to repurchase $250 million of the company's stock. Citicorp was joined by a number of other corporations whose managers were equally concerned about the market crash. Altogether, over a 2-day period these firms

---

[3]Sometimes companies do not restrict shareholders to reinvesting dividends but allow them to buy additional shares at a discount. In some cases substantial amounts of money have been raised through these plans. For example, in recent years AT&T has raised over $400 million a year through its shareowner plans. For an amusing and true rags-to-riches story about these stock purchase plans, see M. S. Scholes and M. A. Wolfson, "Decentralized Investment Banking: The Case of Dividend-Reinvestment and Stock-Purchase Plans," *Journal of Financial Economics,* **24**:7-36 (September 1989).

announced plans to buy back a total of $6.2 billion of stock. News of these huge buying programs helped to stem the slide in share prices.

These repurchases were like bumper dividends; they caused large amounts of cash to be paid to investors. But they did not *substitute* for dividends; none of the companies that we have mentioned reduced its dividend when it undertook a large repurchase program. If a company has accumulated large amounts of unwanted cash or if it wishes to change its capital structure by replacing equity with debt, it generally repurchases stock. Dividends are seldom used for these purposes.

There are three principal methods of repurchase: (1) Many repurchased shares are acquired in the open market. This activity is regulated by the SEC, which requires that the purchases not coincide with issues of stock or private negotiations to buy stock. The SEC also sets guidelines for how the repurchases are carried out. For example, repurchases cannot exceed a stated proportion of trading in the company's stock. (2) Shares may be repurchased by making a general tender offer either to all shareholders or just to small shareholders.[4] In this case the firm usually engages an investment banker to manage the tender and pays a special commission to brokers who persuade shareholders to accept the offer. (3) Finally, repurchase may take place by direct negotiation with a major shareholder. The most notorious instances are *greenmail* transactions, in which the target of a takeover attempt buys off the hostile bidder by repurchasing any shares that it has acquired. "Greenmail" means that these shares are repurchased by the target at a price which makes the bidder happy to agree to leave the target alone. This price does not always make the target's *shareholders* happy, as we point out in Chapter 33.

Reacquired shares are seldom deregistered and canceled. Instead, they are kept in the company's treasury and then resold when the company needs money. Stockholders are not required to authorize these resales of treasury stock, and they do not enjoy preemptive rights on such stock.

Stockholders who sell shares back to their firm pay tax only on capital gains realized in the sale, although the Internal Revenue Service has attempted to prevent firms from disguising dividends as repurchases; for example, proportional or regular repurchases may be taxed as dividend payments.

16-2 HOW DO COMPANIES DECIDE ON DIVIDEND PAYMENTS?

Lintner's Model

In the mid-1950s John Lintner conducted a classic series of interviews with corporate managers about their dividend policies.[5] His description of how dividends are determined can be summarized in four "stylized facts":[6]

1. Firms have long-run target dividend payout ratios. Mature companies with stable earnings generally pay out a high proportion of earnings; growth companies have low payouts.

---

[4]The costs of printing and mailing annual reports, dividend checks, etc., are the same for small stockholders as for large ones. Firms often try to reduce these costs by buying out small holdings.

[5]J. Lintner, "Distribution of Incomes of Corporations among Dividends, Retained Earnings, and Taxes," *American Economic Review*, **46**:97–113 (May 1956).

[6]The stylized facts are given by Terry A. Marsh and Robert C. Merton, "Dividend Behavior for the Aggregate Stock Market," *Journal of Business*, **60**:1–40 (January 1987). See pp. 5–6. We have paraphrased and embellished.

2. Managers focus more on dividend changes than on absolute levels. Thus, paying a $2.00 dividend is an important financial decision if last year's dividend was $1.00, but no big deal if last year's dividend was $2.00.

3. Dividend changes follow shifts in long-run, sustainable earnings. Managers "smooth" dividends. Transitory earnings changes are unlikely to affect dividend payouts.

4. Managers are reluctant to make dividend changes that might have to be reversed. They are particularly worried about having to rescind a dividend increase.

Lintner developed a simple model which is consistent with these facts and explains dividend payments well. Here it is: Suppose that a firm always stuck to its target payout ratio. Then the dividend payment in the coming year (DIV_1) would equal a constant proportion of earnings per share (EPS_1):

$$DIV_1 = \text{target dividend}$$
$$= \text{target ratio} \times EPS_1$$

The dividend *change* would equal

$$DIV_1 - DIV_0 = \text{target change}$$
$$= \text{target ratio} \times EPS_1 - DIV_0$$

A firm that always stuck to its payout ratio would have to change its dividend whenever earnings changed. But the managers in Lintner's survey were reluctant to do this. They believed that shareholders prefer a steady progression in dividends. Therefore, even if circumstances appeared to warrant a large increase in their company's dividend, they would move only partway toward their target payment. Their dividend changes therefore seemed to conform to the following model:

$$DIV_1 - DIV_0 = \text{adjustment rate} \times \text{target change}$$
$$= \text{adjustment rate} \times (\text{target ratio} \times EPS_1 - DIV_0)$$

The more conservative the company, the more slowly it would move toward its target and, therefore, the *lower* would be its adjustment rate.

Lintner's simple model suggests that the dividend depends in part on the firm's current earnings and in part on the dividend for the previous year, which in turn depends on that year's earnings and the dividend in the year before. Therefore, if Lintner is correct, we should be able to describe dividends in terms of a weighted average of current and past earnings.[7] The probability of an increase in the dividend rate should be greatest when *current* earnings have increased; it should be somewhat

---

[7]This can be demonstrated as follows: Dividends per share in time t are

$$DIV_t = aT(EPS_t) + (1 - a)DIV_{t-1} \qquad (1)$$

where a is the adjustment rate and T the target payout ratio. But the same relationship holds in $t - 1$:

$$DIV_{t-1} = aT(EPS_{t-1}) + (1 - a)DIV_{t-2} \qquad (2)$$

Substitute for DIV_{t-1} in (1):

$$DIV_t = aT(EPS_t) + aT(1 - a)(EPS_{t-1}) + (1 - a)^2 DIV_{t-2}$$

We can make similar substitutions for DIV_{t-2}, DIV_{t-3}, etc., thereby obtaining

$$DIV_t = aT(EPS_t) + aT(1 - a)(EPS_{t-1}) + aT(1 - a)^2(EPS_{t-2}) + \ldots + aT(1 - a)^n(EPS_{t-n})$$

less when only the earnings from the previous year have increased; and so on. An extensive study by Fama and Babiak confirmed this hypothesis.[8]

The Information Content of Dividends

We have suggested above that the dividend payment depends on both last year's dividend and this year's earnings. This simple model seems to provide a fairly good explanation of how companies decide on the dividend rate, but it is unlikely to be the whole story. We would also expect managers to take future prospects into account when setting the payment. And that is what we find.

For example, Healy and Palepu report that between 1970 and 1979 companies that made a dividend payment for the first time experienced relatively flat earnings growth until the year before the announcement.[9] In that year earnings grew by an average 43 percent. If managers thought that this was a temporary windfall, they might have been cautious about committing themselves to paying out cash. But it looks as if they had good reason to be confident about prospects, for over the next 4 years earnings grew by a further 164 percent.

Since dividends anticipate future earnings, it is no surprise to find that announcements of dividend cuts are usually taken as bad news (stock price typically falls) and that dividend increases are good news (stock price rises). In the case of the dividend initiations studied by Healy and Palepu, the announcement of the dividend resulted in an abnormal rise of 4 percent in the stock price.[10] It's important not to jump to the conclusion that this shows that investors like higher dividends for their own sake. The dividend may be welcomed only as a sign of the higher future earnings.

Do you remember from Chapter 13 that stock splits lead to stock price increases? That is not because splits create value but because they signal future prosperity, specifically increased dividends. Now we see that dividend increases in turn may be important mostly as signals of future earnings. (Finally, we could say that *earnings* are important because they tell investors something about the *true* measures of corporate prosperity: cash flow and the extent of positive-NPV capital investment opportunities.)

Market efficiency means that all information available to investors is quickly and accurately impounded in stock prices. It does not imply that fundamental information about a company's operations or prospects is always cheaply or easily obtained. Investors therefore seize on any clue. That is why stock prices respond to stock splits, dividend changes, and other actions or announcements which reveal managements' optimism or pessimism about their firms' futures.

16-3   CONTROVERSY ABOUT DIVIDEND POLICY

Now we turn to the controversial question of how dividend policy affects value. One endearing feature of economics is that it can always accommodate not just two but three opposing points of view. And so it is with the controversy about dividend policy. On the right there is a conservative group which believes that an increase in div-

---

[8]E. F. Fama and H. Babiak, "Dividend Policy: An Empirical Analysis," *Journal of the American Statistical Association,* **63**:1132–1161 (December 1968), p. 1134.

[9]See P. Healy and K. Palepu, "Earnings Information Conveyed by Dividend Initiations and Omissions," *Journal of Financial Economics,* **21**:149–175 (1988).

[10]Stock price changes were corrected for market movements by the methods explained in Chapter 13. Healy and Palepu also looked at companies that *stopped* paying a dividend. In this case the stock price on average declined by an abnormal 9.5 percent on the announcement, and earnings fell over the next four quarters.

idend payout increases firm value. On the left, there is a radical group which believes that an increase in payout reduces value. And in the center there is a middle-of-the-road party which claims that dividend policy makes no difference.

The middle-of-the-road party was founded in 1961 by Miller and Modigliani (always referred to as "MM" or "M and M"), when they published a theoretical paper showing the irrelevance of dividend policy in a world without taxes, transaction costs, or other market imperfections.[11] By the standards of 1961 MM were leftist radicals, because at that time most people believed that even under idealized assumptions increased dividends made shareholders better off.[12] But now MM's proof is generally accepted as correct, and the argument has shifted to whether taxes or other market imperfections alter the situation. In the process MM have been pushed toward the center by a new leftist party which argues for *low* dividends. The leftists' position is based on MM's argument modified to take account of taxes and costs of issuing securities. The conservatives are still with us, relying on essentially the same arguments as in 1961.

We begin our discussion of dividend policy with a presentation of MM's original argument. Then we will undertake a critical appraisal of the positions of the three parties. Perhaps we should warn you before we start that our own position has traditionally been marginally leftist. But now, after the 1986 Tax Reform Act, we have joined the middle-of-the-roaders.

Dividend Policy Is Irrelevant in Perfect Capital Markets

In their classic 1961 article MM argued as follows: Suppose your firm has settled on its investment program. You have worked out how much of this program can be financed from borrowing, and you plan to meet the remaining funds requirement from retained earnings. Any surplus money is to be paid out as dividends.

Now think what happens if you want to increase the dividend payment without changing the investment and borrowing policy. The extra money must come from somewhere. If the firm fixes its borrowing, the only way it can finance the extra dividend is to print some more shares and sell them. The new stockholders are going to part with their money only if you can offer them shares that are worth as much as they cost. But how can the firm do this when its assets, earnings, investment opportunities and, therefore, market value are all unchanged? The answer is that there must be a *transfer of value* from the old to the new stockholders. The new ones get the newly printed shares, each one worth less than before the dividend change was announced, and the old ones suffer a capital loss on their shares. The capital loss borne by the old shareholders just offsets the extra cash dividend they receive.

Figure 16-1 shows how this transfer of value occurs. Our hypothetical company pays out a third of its total value as a dividend and it raises the money to do so by selling new shares. The capital loss suffered by the old stockholders is represented by the reduction in the size of the shaded boxes. But that capital loss is exactly offset by the fact that the new money raised (the white boxes) is paid over to them as dividends.

Does it make any difference to the old stockholders that they receive an extra dividend payment plus an offsetting capital loss? It might if that were the only way

---

[11]M. H. Miller and F. Modigliani: "Dividend Policy, Growth and the Valuation of Shares," *Journal of Business*, **34**:411–433 (October 1961).

[12]Not *everybody* believed dividends make shareholders better off. MM's arguments were anticipated in 1938 in J. B. Williams, *The Theory of Investment Value.* Harvard University Press, Cambridge, Mass., 1938. Also, a proof very similar to MM's was developed by J. Lintner in "Dividends, Earnings, Leverage, Stock Prices and the Supply of Capital to Corporations," *Review of Economics and Statistics*, **44**:243–269 (August 1962).

Figure 16-1 This firm pays out a third of its worth as a dividend and raises the money by selling new shares. The transfer of value to the new stockholders is equal to the dividend payment. The total value of the firm is unaffected.

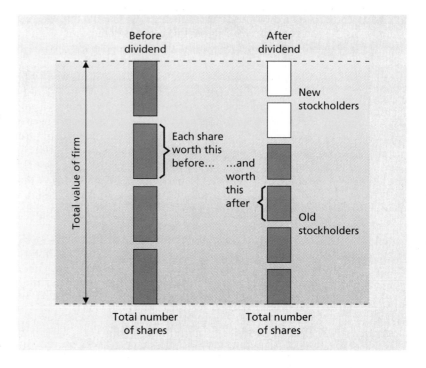

they could get their hands on cash. But as long as there are efficient capital markets, they can raise the cash by selling shares. Thus the old shareholders can "cash in" either by persuading the management to pay a higher dividend or by selling some of their shares. In either case there will be a transfer of value from old to new shareholders. The only difference is that in the former case this transfer is caused by a dilution in the value of each of the firm's shares, and in the latter case it is caused by a reduction in the number of shares held by the old shareholders. The two alternatives are compared in Figure 16-2.

Because investors do not need dividends to get their hands on cash, they will not pay higher prices for the shares of firms with high payouts. Therefore firms ought not to worry about dividend policy. They should let dividends fluctuate as a by-product of their investment and financing decisions.

Dividend Irrelevance— An Illustration

Consider the case of Rational Demiconductor, which at this moment has the following balance sheet:

Rational Demiconductor's Balance Sheet (Market Values)

Cash ($1,000 held for investment)	1,000	0	Debt
Fixed assets	9,000	10,000 + NPV	Equity
Investment opportunity ($1,000 investment required)	NPV		
Total asset value	$10,000 + NPV	$10,000 + NPV	Value of firm

Figure 16-2 Two ways of raising cash for the firm's original shareholders. In each case the cash received is offset by a decline in the value of the old stockholders' claim on the firm. If the firm pays a dividend, each share is worth less because more shares have to be issued against the firm's assets. If the old stockholders sell some of their shares, each share is worth the same but the old stockholders have fewer shares.

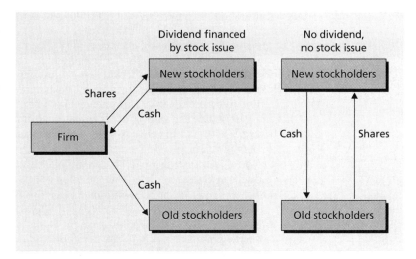

Rational Demiconductor has $1000 cash earmarked for a project requiring $1000 investment. We do not know how attractive the project is, and so we enter it at NPV; after the project is undertaken it will be worth $1000 + NPV. Note that the balance sheet is constructed with market values; equity equals the market value of the firm's outstanding shares (price per share times number of shares outstanding). It is not necessarily equal to book net worth.

Now Rational Demiconductor uses the cash to pay a $1000 dividend to its stockholders. The benefit to them is obvious: $1000 of spendable cash. It is also obvious that there must be a cost. The cash is not free.

Where does the money for the dividend come from? Of course, the immediate source of funds is Rational Demiconductor's cash account. But this cash was earmarked for the investment project. Since we want to isolate the effects of dividend policy on shareholders' wealth, we assume that the company *continues* with the investment project. That means that $1000 cash must be raised by new financing. This could consist of an issue of either debt or stock. Again, we just want to look at dividend policy for now, and we defer discussion of the debt-equity choice until Chapters 17 and 18. Thus Rational Demiconductor ends up financing the dividend with a $1000 stock issue.

Now we examine the balance sheet after the dividend is paid, the new stock sold, and the investment undertaken. Because Rational Demiconductor's investment and borrowing policies are unaffected by the dividend payment, its *overall* market value must be unchanged at $10,000 + NPV.[13] We know also that if the new stockholders pay a fair price, their stock is worth $1000. That leaves us with only one missing number—the value of the stock held by the original stockholders. It is easy to see that this must be

Value of original stockholders' shares = value of company − value of new shares

$$= (10,000 + \text{NPV}) - 1000$$
$$= \$9000 + \text{NPV}$$

---

[13]All other factors that might affect Rational Demiconductor's value are assumed constant. This is not a necessary assumption, but it simplifies the proof of MM's theory.

The old shareholders have received a $1000 cash dividend and incurred a $1000 capital loss. Dividend policy doesn't matter.

By paying out $1000 with one hand and taking it back with the other, Rational Demiconductor is recycling cash. To suggest that this makes shareholders better off is like advising a cook to cool the kitchen by leaving the refrigerator door open.

Of course, our proof ignores taxes, issue costs, and a variety of other complications. We will turn to those items in a moment. The really crucial assumption in our proof is that the new shares are sold at a fair price. The shares sold to raise $1000 must actually be *worth* $1000.[14] In other words, we have assumed efficient capital markets.

Calculating Share Price

We have assumed that Rational Demiconductor's new shares can be sold at a fair price, but what is that price and how many new shares are issued?

Suppose that before this dividend payout the company had 1000 shares outstanding and that the project had an NPV of $2000. Then the old stock was worth in total $10,000 + NPV = $12,000, which works out at $12,000/1000 = $12 per share. After the company has paid the dividend and completed the financing, this old stock is worth $9000 + NPV = $11,000. That works out at $11,000/1000 = $11 per share. In other words, the price of the old stock falls by the amount of the $1 per share dividend payment.

Now let us look at the new stock. Clearly, after the issue this must sell at the same price as the rest of the stock. In other words, it must be valued at $11. If the new stockholders get fair value, the company must issue $1000/$11 or 91 new shares in order to raise the $1000 that it needs.

Share Repurchase

We have seen that any increased cash dividend payment must be offset by a stock issue if the firm's investment and borrowing policies are held constant. In effect the stockholders finance the extra dividend by selling off part of their ownership of the firm. Consequently, the stock price falls by just enough to offset the extra dividend.

This process can also be run backward. With investment and borrowing policy given, any *reduction* in dividends must be balanced by a reduction in the number of shares issued or by repurchase of previously outstanding stock. But if the process has no effect on stockholders' wealth when run forward, it must likewise have no effect when run in reverse. We will confirm this by another numerical example.

Suppose that a technical discovery reveals that Rational Demiconductor's new project is not a positive-NPV venture but a sure loser. Management announces that the project is to be discarded, and that the $1000 earmarked for it will be paid out as an extra dividend of $1 per share. After the dividend payout, the balance sheet is:

Rational Demiconductor's Balance Sheet (Market Values)

Cash	$ 0	$ 0	Debt
Existing fixed assets	9,000	9,000	Equity
New project	0		
Total asset value	$9,000	$9,000	Total firm value

---

[14]The "old" shareholders get all the benefit of the positive NPV project. The "new" shareholders require only a fair rate of return. They are making a zero-NPV investment.

Since there are 1000 shares outstanding, the stock price is $10,000/1000 = $10 before the dividend payment and $9000/1000 = $9 *after* the payment.

What if Rational Demiconductor uses the $1000 to repurchase stock instead? As long as the company pays a fair price for the stock, the $1000 buys $1000/$10 = 100 shares. That leaves 900 shares worth 900 × $10 = $9000.

As expected, we find that switching from cash dividends to share repurchase has no effect on shareholders' wealth. They forgo a $1 cash dividend but end up holding shares worth $10 instead of $9.

Note that when shares are repurchased the transfer of value is in favor of those stockholders who do not sell. They forgo any cash dividend but end up owning a larger slice of the firm. In effect they are using their share of Rational Demiconductor's $1000 distribution to buy out some of their fellow shareholders.

16-4 THE RIGHTISTS

Much of traditional finance literature has advocated high payout ratios. Here, for example, is a statement of the rightist position made by Graham and Dodd in 1951:

> . . . the considered and continuous verdict of the stock market is overwhelmingly in favor of liberal dividends as against niggardly ones. The common stock investor must take this judgment into account in the valuation of stock for purchase. It is now becoming standard practice to evaluate common stock by applying one multiplier to that portion of the earnings paid out in dividends and a much smaller multiplier to the undistributed balance.[15]

Another author has written a book urging the government to enforce full distribution of earnings on the grounds that it "would almost certainly double or treble (within a short period) the market value of equities."[16]

This belief in the importance of dividend policy is common in the business and investment communities. Stockholders and investment advisers continually pressure corporate treasurers for increased dividends. When we had wage-price controls in the United States in 1974, it was deemed necessary to have dividend controls as well. As far as we know, no labor union objected that "dividend policy is irrelevant." After all, if wages are reduced, the employee is worse off. Dividends are the shareholders' wages, and so if the payout ratio is reduced the shareholder is worse off. Therefore fair play requires that wage controls be matched by dividend controls. Right?

Wrong! You should be able to see through that kind of argument by now. But let us turn to some of the more serious arguments for a high-payout policy.

Do MM Ignore Risk?

One of the most common and immediate objections to MM's argument about the irrelevance of dividends is that dividends are cash in hand while capital gains are at best in the bush. It may be true that the recipient of an extra cash dividend forgoes an

---

[15]These authors later qualified this statement, recognizing the willingness of investors to pay high price-earnings multiples for growth stocks. But otherwise they stuck to their position. We quoted their 1951 statement because of its historical importance. Compare B. Graham and D. L. Dodd, *Security Analysis: Principles and Techniques*, 3d ed., McGraw-Hill Book Company, New York, 1951, p. 432, with B. Graham, D. L. Dodd, and S. Cottle, *Security Analysis: Principles and Techniques*, 4th ed., McGraw-Hill Book Company, New York, 1962, p. 480.

[16]See A. Rubner, *The Ensnared Shareholder*, Macmillan International Ltd., London, 1965, p. 139.

equal capital gain, but if the dividend is safe and the capital gain is risky, isn't the stockholder ahead?

It's true that dividends are more predictable than capital gains. Managers can stabilize dividends but they cannot control stock price. From this it seems a small step to conclude that increased dividends make the firm less risky.[17] But the important point is, once again, that as long as investment policy and borrowing are held constant, a firm's *overall* cash flows are the same regardless of payout policy. The risks borne by *all* the firm's stockholders are likewise fixed by its investment and borrowing policies, and unaffected by dividend policy.[18]

A dividend increase creates a transfer of ownership between "old" and "new" stockholders. The old stockholders—those who receive the extra dividend and do not buy their part of the stock issue undertaken to finance the dividend—find their stake in the firm reduced. They have indeed traded a safe receipt for an uncertain future gain. But the reason their money is safe is not because it is special "dividend money" but because it is in the bank. If the dividend had not been increased, the stockholders could have achieved an equally safe position just by selling shares and putting the money in the bank.

If we really believed that old stockholders are better off by trading a risky asset for cash, then we would also have to argue that the new stockholders—those who trade cash for the newly issued shares—are worse off. But this doesn't make sense: The new stockholders are bearing risk, but they are getting paid for it. They are willing to buy because the new shares are priced to offer a return adequate to cover the risk.

MM's argument for the irrelevance of dividend policy does not assume a world of certainty: It assumes an efficient capital market. Market efficiency means that the transfers of value created by shifts in dividend policy are carried out on fair terms. And since the *overall* value of (old and new) stockholders' equity is unaffected, nobody gains or loses.

Market Imperfections

We believe—and it is widely believed—that MM's conclusions follow from their assumption of perfect and efficient capital markets. Nobody claims their model is an exact description of the so-called real world. Thus the dividend controversy finally boils down to arguments about imperfections, inefficiencies, or whether stockholders are fully rational.[19]

There is a natural clientele for high-payout stocks. For example, some financial institutions are legally restricted from holding stocks lacking established dividend records. Trusts and endowment funds may prefer high-dividend stocks because divi-

---

[17]By analogy one could presumably argue that interest payments are even more predictable, so that a company's risk would be diminished by increasing the proportion of receipts paid out as interest.

[18]There are a number of variations of the "bird-in-the-hand" argument. Perhaps the most persuasive is found in M. J. Gordon, "Dividends, Earnings and Stock Prices," *Review of Economics and Statistics*, **41**:99–105 (May 1959). He reasoned that investors run less risk if the firm pays them cash now rather than retaining and reinvesting it in the hope of paying higher future dividends. But careful analysis of Gordon's argument—see M. J. Brennan, "A Note on Dividend Irrelevance and the Gordon Valuation Model," *Journal of Finance*, **26**:1115–1122 (December 1971), for example—shows that he was really talking about changes in *investment* policy, not dividend policy.

[19]Psychologists' experiments show that human beings are not 100 percent–rational decision makers. Shefrin and Statman use some of the psychologists' results to argue that investors may have an irrational preference for cash dividends. See H. Shefrin and M. Statman, "Explaining Investor Preference for Cash Dividends," *Journal of Financial Economics*, **13**:253–282 (June 1984).

dends are regarded as spendable "income," whereas capital gains are "additions to principal," which cannot be spent.[20]

There is also a natural clientele of investors who look to their stock portfolios for a steady source of cash to live on. In principle this cash could be easily generated from stocks paying no dividends at all; the investor could just sell off a small fraction of his or her holdings from time to time. But it is simpler and cheaper for AT&T to send a quarterly check than for its stockholders to sell, say, one share every 3 months. AT&T's regular dividends relieve many of its shareholders of transaction costs and considerable inconvenience.

Those advocating generous dividends might go on to argue that a regular cash dividend relieves stockholders of the risk of having to sell shares at "temporarily depressed" prices. Of course, the firm will have to issue shares eventually to finance the dividend, but (the argument goes) the firm can pick the *right time* to sell. If firms really try to do this and if they are successful—two big *ifs*—then stockholders of high-payout firms do indeed get something for nothing.

There is another line of argument that you can use to justify high payouts. Think of a market in which investors receive very little reliable information about a firm's earnings. Such markets exist in some European countries where a passion for secrecy and a tendency to construct many-layered corporate organizations produce asset and earnings figures that are next to meaningless. Some people say that, thanks to creative accounting, the situation is little better in the United States. How does an investor in such a world separate marginally profitable firms from the real money makers? One clue is dividends. A firm which reports good earnings and pays a generous dividend is putting its money where its mouth is.[21] We can understand why investors would favor firms with established dividend records. We can also see how the information content of dividends would come about. Investors would refuse to believe a firm's reported earnings announcements unless they were backed up by an appropriate dividend policy.

MM regard the informational content of dividends as a temporary thing. A dividend increase signals management's optimism about future earnings, but investors will be able to *see for themselves* whether the optimism is justified. The jump in stock price that accompanies an unexpected dividend increase *would have happened anyway* as information about future earnings came out through other channels. Therefore, MM expect to find changes in dividends associated with stock price movements but no permanent relationship between stock price and the firm's long-run target payout ratio. MM believe management should be concerned with dividend *changes* but not with the average *level* of payout.

Dividends and Investment Policy

If it is true that nobody gains or loses from shifts in dividend policy, why do shareholders often clamor for higher dividends? One possible explanation is that they don't trust managers to spend retained earnings wisely and they fear that the money will be plowed back into building a larger empire rather than a more profitable one. In this case the dividend decision is mixed up with the firm's investment and operat-

---

[20]Most colleges and universities are legally free to spend capital gains from their endowments, but this is rarely done.

[21]Of course, firms can cheat in the short run by overstating earnings and scraping up cash to pay a generous dividend. But it is hard to cheat in the long run, for a firm that is not making money will not have the cash flow to pay out. Financing dividends by issuing stock is self-defeating, for it ultimately reduces dividends per share and thereby reveals that the initial dividend was not supported by earnings.

ing decisions. The dividend increase may lead to a rise in the stock price not because investors like dividends but because they want management to run a tighter ship.

16-5 TAXES AND THE RADICAL LEFT

The left-wing dividend creed is simple: Whenever dividends are taxed more heavily than capital gains, firms should pay the lowest cash dividend they can get away with. Available cash should be retained or used to repurchase shares.

By shifting their distribution policies in this way, corporations can transmute dividends into capital gains. If this financial alchemy results in lower taxes, it should be welcomed by any taxpaying investor. That is the basic point made by the leftist party when it argues for low-dividend payout.

If dividends are taxed more heavily than capital gains, investors should pay more for stocks with low dividend yields. In other words, they should accept a lower *pre-tax* rate of return from securities offering returns in the form of capital gains rather than dividends. Table 16-1 illustrates this. The stocks of firms A and B are equally risky. Investors expect A to be worth $112.50 per share next year. The share price of B is expected to be only $102.50, but a $10 dividend is also forecast, and so the total pretax payoff is the same, $112.50.

Yet we find B's stock selling for less than A's and therefore offering a higher pretax rate of return. The reason is obvious: Investors prefer A because its return comes in the form of capital gains. Table 16-1 shows that A and B are equally attractive to investors who pay a 50 percent tax on dividends and a 20 percent tax on capital gains (the maximum marginal rates before 1986). Each offers a 10 percent return after all

TABLE 16-1

Effects of a shift in dividend policy when dividends are taxed more heavily than capital gains. The high-payout stock (firm B) must sell at a lower price in order to provide the same after-tax return.

	Firm A (No Dividend)	Firm B (High Dividend)
Next year's price	$112.50	$102.50
Dividend	$0	$10.00
Total pretax payoff	$112.50	$112.50
Today's stock price	$100	$96.67
Capital gain	$12.50	$5.83
Before-tax rate of return, percent	$\frac{12.5}{100} \times 100 = 12.5$	$\frac{15.83}{96.67} \times 100 = 16.4$
Tax on dividend at 50 percent	$0	$.50 \times 10 = \$5.00$
Tax on capital gains at 20 percent	$.20 \times 12.50 = \$2.50$	$.20 \times 5.83 = \$1.17$
Total after-tax income (dividends plus capital gains less taxes)	$(0 + 12.50)$ $-2.50 = \$10.00$	$(10.00 + 5.83)$ $-(5.00 + 1.17) = \$9.66$
After-tax rate of return, percent	$\frac{10}{100} \times 100 = 10.0$	$\frac{9.66}{96.67} \times 100 = 10.0$

taxes. The difference between the stock prices of A and B is exactly the present value of the extra taxes the investors face if they buy B.[22]

The management of B could save these extra taxes by eliminating the $10 dividend and using the released funds to repurchase stock instead. Its stock price should rise to $100 as soon as the new policy is announced.

Why Pay Any Dividends at All?

It is true that when companies make very large one-off distributions of cash to shareholders, they generally choose to do so by share repurchase than by a large temporary hike in dividends. But if dividends attract more tax than capital gains, why should *any* firm *ever* pay a cash dividend? If cash is to be distributed to stockholders, isn't share repurchase always the best channel for doing so? The leftist position seems to call not just for low payouts but for *zero* payouts whenever capital gains have a tax advantage.

Few leftists would go quite that far. A firm which eliminates dividends and starts repurchasing stock on a regular basis may find that the Internal Revenue Service would recognize the repurchase program for what it really is and would tax the payments accordingly. That is why financial managers have never announced that they are repurchasing shares to save stockholders taxes; they give some other reason.[23]

The low-payout party has nevertheless maintained that the market rewards firms which have low-payout policies. They have claimed that firms which paid dividends and as a result had to issue shares from time to time were making a serious mistake. Any such firm was essentially financing its dividends by issuing stock; it should have cut its dividends at least to the point at which stock issues were unnecessary. This would not only have saved taxes for shareholders; it would also have avoided the transaction costs of the stock issues.[24]

Empirical Evidence on Dividends and Taxes

It is hard to deny that taxes are important to investors. You can see that in the bond market. Interest on municipal bonds is not taxed, and so municipals sell at low pretax yields. Interest on federal government bonds is taxed, and so these bonds sell at higher pretax yields. It does not seem likely that investors in bonds just forget about taxes when they enter the stock market. Thus, we would expect to find an historical tendency for high-dividend stocks to sell at lower prices and therefore to offer higher yields, just as in Table 16-1.

Unfortunately, there are difficulties in measuring this effect. For example, suppose that stock A is priced at $100 and is expected to pay a $5 dividend. The *expected* yield is, therefore, 5/100 = .05, or 5 percent. The company now announces bumper earnings and a $10 dividend. Thus with the benefit of hindsight, A's *actual* dividend yield is 10/100 = .10, or 10 percent. If the unexpected increase in earnings causes a rise in A's stock price, we will observe that a high actual yield is accompanied by a high actual return. But that would not tell us anything about whether a high *expected* yield was accompanied by a high *expected* return. In order to measure the effect of dividend policy, we need to estimate the dividends that investors expected.

---

[22]Michael Brennan has modeled what happens when you introduce taxes into an otherwise perfect market and found that the capital asset pricing model continues to hold, but on an *after-tax* basis. Thus, if A and B have the same beta, they should offer the same after-tax rate of return. The spread between pretax and posttax returns is determined by a weighted average of investors' tax rates. See M. J. Brennan, "Taxes, Market Valuation and Corporate Financial Policy," *National Tax Journal*, **23**:417–427 (December 1970).

[23]They might say, "Our stock is a good investment," or, "We want to have the shares available to finance acquisitions of other companies." What do you think of these rationales?

[24]These costs can be substantial. Refer back to Chapter 15, especially Table 15-1.

A second problem is that nobody is quite sure what is meant by high dividend yield. For example, utility stocks have generally offered high yields. But did they have a high yield all year, or only in months or on days that dividends are paid? Perhaps for most of the year, they had zero yields and were perfect holdings for the highly taxed individuals.[25] Of course, high-tax investors did not want to hold a stock on the days dividends were paid, but they could sell their stock temporarily to a security dealer. Dealers are taxed equally on dividends and capital gains and therefore should not have demanded any extra return for holding stocks over the dividend period.[26] If shareholders could pass stocks freely between each other at the time of the dividend payment, we should not observe any tax effects at all.

Given these difficulties in measuring the relationship between expected yield and return, it is not surprising that different researchers have come up with different results. Table 16-2 summarizes some of the findings. Notice that in each of these tests the estimated tax rate was positive. In other words, high-yielding stocks appeared to have lower prices and to offer higher returns. However, while the dividends-are-bad school could claim that the weight of evidence is on its side, the contest is by no means over. Many respected scholars, including Merton Miller and Myron Scholes, were unconvinced. They stressed the difficulty of measuring dividend yield properly and proving the link between dividend yield and expected return.[27]

The Taxation of Dividends and Capital Gains

But all this evidence has more historical than current interest, for it precedes the Tax Reform Act of 1986. Before reform there was a dramatic difference between the taxation of dividends and that of capital gains: Investors paid up to 50 percent tax on dividends versus a maximum 20 percent on capital gains. However, the 1986 Tax Reform Act equalized the tax rates on dividends and capital gains and so largely undercut the leftists' arguments and left the center party in the ascendancy. More recently, a gap has begun to open up again, though it is much smaller than it once was. As we write this chapter, the tax rate on capital gains for most shareholders is 28 percent, while for taxable incomes above $55,100 the tax rate on dividends ranges from 31 percent to 39.6 percent.[28]

---

[25]Suppose there are 250 trading days in a year. Think of a stock paying quarterly dividends. We could say that the stock offers a high dividend yield on 4 days but a zero dividend yield on the remaining 246 days.

[26]The stock could also be sold to a corporation, which could "capture" the dividend and then resell the shares. Corporations are natural buyers of dividends, because they pay tax only on 30 percent of dividends received from other corporations. (We say more on the taxation of intercorporate dividends later in this section.)

[27]Miller reviews several of the studies cited in Table 16-2 in "Behavioral Rationality in Finance: The Case of Dividends," *Journal of Business*, **59**:S451–S468 (October 1986).

[28]Here are two examples of 1994 marginal tax rates by income bracket:

	INCOME BRACKET	
Marginal Tax Rate	Single	Married, Joint Return
15%	$0–$22,750	$0–$38,000
28	$22,750–$55,100	$38,000–$91,850
31	$55,100–$115,000	$91,850–$140,000
36	$115,000–$250,000	$140,000–$250,000
39.6	Over $250,000	Over $250,000

There are different schedules for married taxpayers filing separately and for single taxpayers who are heads of households.

TABLE 16-2

. . . .

Some tests of the effect of yield on returns: A positive implied tax rate on dividends means that investors require a higher pretax return from high-dividend stocks.

Test	Test Period	Implied Tax Rate	Standard Error of Tax Rate
Brennan	1946–1965	34%	12
Black & Scholes (1974)	1936–1966	22	24
Litzenberger & Ramaswamy (1979)	1936–1977	24	3
Litzenberger & Ramaswamy (1982)	1940–1980	14–23	2–3
Rosenberg & Marathe (1979)	1931–1966	40	21
Bradford & Gordon (1980)	1926–1978	18	2
Blume (1980)	1936–1976	52	25
Miller & Scholes (1982)	1940–1978	4	3
Stone & Bartter (1979)	1947–1970	56	28
Morgan (1982)	1946–1977	21	2
Ang & Peterson (1985)	1973–1983	57	27

Sources: M. J. Brennan: "Dividends and Valuation in Imperfect Markets: Some Empirical Tests," unpublished paper, not dated.

F. Black and M. Scholes: "The Effects of Dividend Yield and Dividend Policy on Common Stock Prices and Returns," *Journal of Financial Economics*, **1**:1–22 (May 1974).

R. H. Litzenberger and K. Ramaswamy: "The Effect of Personal Taxes and Dividends on Capital Asset Prices: Theory and Empirical Evidence," *Journal of Financial Economics*, **7**:163–195 (June 1979).

R. H. Litzenberg and K. Ramaswamy: "The Effects of Dividends on Common Stock Prices: Tax Effects or Information Effects," *Journal of Finance*, **37**:429–443 (May 1982).

B. Rosenberg and V. Marathe: "Tests of Capital Asset Pricing Model Hypotheses," in H. Levy (ed.), *Research in Finance I*, JAI Press, Greenwich, Conn., 1979.

D. F. Bradford and R. H. Gordon: "Taxation and the Stock Market Valuation of Capital Gains and Dividends," *Journal of Public Economics*, **14**:109–136 (1980).

M. E. Blume: "Stock Returns and Dividend Yields: Some More Evidence," *Review of Economics and Statistics*, **62**:567–577 (November 1980).

M. H. Miller and M. Scholes: "Dividends and Taxes: Some Empirical Evidence," *Journal of Political Economy*, **90**:1118–1141 (1982).

B. K. Stone and B. J. Bartter: "The Effect of Dividend Yield on Stock Returns: Empirical Evidence on the Relevance of Dividends," W.P.E.-76–78, Georgia Institute of Technology, Atlanta, Ga., 1979.

I. G. Morgan: "Dividends and Capital Asset Prices," *Journal of Finance*, **37**:1071–1086 (September 1982).

J. S. Ang and D. R. Peterson: "Return, Risk and Yield: Evidence from Ex Ante Data," *Journal of Finance*, **40**:537–548 (June 1985).

Tax law favors capital gains in another way. Taxes on dividends have to be paid immediately, but taxes on capital gains can be deferred until shares are sold and capital gains are realized. Stockholders can choose when to sell their shares and thus when to pay the capital gains tax. The longer they wait, the less the present value of the capital gains tax liability.[29]

The distinction between capital gains and dividends is less important for financial institutions, many of which operate free of all taxes and therefore have no tax reason to prefer capital gains to dividends or vice vera. Pension funds are untaxed, for example. Only corporations have a tax reason to *prefer* dividends. They pay corporate income tax on only 30 percent of any dividends received. Thus the effective tax rate on dividends received by large corporations is 30 percent of 35 percent (the marginal corporate tax rate), or 10.5 percent. But they have to pay a 35 percent tax on the full amount of any realized capital gain.

Although the dividend affects the shareholder's tax liability, it does not in general alter the taxes that must be paid by the company itself. Corporate income tax has to be paid regardless of whether the company distributes or retains its profits. There is one exception: If the Internal Revenue Service (IRS) can prove that earnings are retained solely to avoid any taxes on dividends, it can levy an additional tax on the excess retentions. However, public companies are almost always able to justify their retentions to the IRS.

The implications of these tax rules for dividend policy are pretty simple. Capital gains have advantages to many investors, but they are far less advantageous than they were before the passage of the 1986 Tax Reform Act. Thus, the leftist case for minimizing cash dividends is weaker than it used to be. At the same time, the middle-of-the-road party has increased its share of the vote.

16-6   THE MIDDLE-OF-THE-ROADERS

The middle-of-the-road party, which is principally represented by Miller, Black, and Scholes, maintains that a company's value is not affected by its dividend policy.[30] We have already seen that this would be the case if there were no impediments such as transaction costs or taxes. The middle-of-the-roaders are aware of these phenomena but nevertheless raise the following disarming question: If companies could increase their share price by distributing more or less cash dividends, why have they not already done so? Perhaps dividends are where they are because no company believes that it could increase its stock price simply by changing its dividend policy.

---

[29]When securities are sold, capital gains tax is paid on the difference between the selling price and the initial purchase price or *basis*. Thus, shares purchased in 1993 for $20 (the basis) and sold for $30 in 1996, would generate $10 per share in capital gains and a tax of $2.80 at a 28 percent marginal rate.

Suppose the investor now decides to defer sale for 1 year. Then, if the interest rate is 8 percent, the present value of the tax, viewed from 1996, falls to 2.80/1.08 = $2.59. That is, the *effective* capital gains rate is 25.9 percent. The longer sale is deferred, the lower the effective rate.

The effective rate falls to zero if the investor dies before selling, because the investor's heirs get to "step up" the basis without recognizing any taxable gain. Suppose the price is still $30 when the investor dies. The heirs could sell for $30 and pay no tax, because they could claim a $30 basis. The $10 capital gain would escape tax entirely.

[30]F. Black and M. S. Scholes, "The Effects of Dividend Yield and Dividend Policy on Common Stock Prices and Returns," *Journal of Financial Economics*, **1**:1–22 (May 1974); M. H. Miller and M. S. Scholes, "Dividends and Taxes," *Journal of Financial Economics*, **6**:333–364 (December 1978); and M. H. Miller, "Behavioral Rationality in Finance: The Case of Dividends," *Journal of Business*, **59**:S451–S468 (October 1986).

This "supply effect" is not inconsistent with the existence of a clientele of investors who demand low-payout stocks. Firms recognized that clientele long ago. Enough firms may have switched to low-payout policies to satisfy fully the clientele's demand. If so, there is no incentive for *additional* firms to switch to low-payout policies.

Miller, Black, and Scholes similarly recognize possible "high-payout clienteles" but argue that they are satisfied also. If all clienteles are satisfied, their demands for high or low dividends have no effects on prices or returns. It doesn't matter which clientele a particular firm chooses to appeal to. If the middle-of-the-road party is right, we should not expect to observe any general association between dividend policy and market values, and the value of any individual company would be independent of its choice of dividend policy.

The middle-of-the-roaders stress that companies would not have generous payout policies unless they believed that this was what investors wanted. But this does not answer the question, "Why *should* so many investors want high payouts?"

Before the Tax Reform Act, this was the chink in the armor of the middle-of-the-roaders. If high dividends bring high taxes, it's difficult to believe that investors got what they wanted. The response of the middle-of-the-roaders was to argue that there were plenty of wrinkles in the tax system which determined stockholders could use to avoid paying taxes on dividends. For example, instead of investing directly in common stocks, they could do so through a pension fund or insurance company, which received more favorable tax treatment.

Since 1986, the tax disadvantage of dividends has diminished in the United States, so it is easier to suppose that there is a substantial clientele of investors who are content to receive high dividends. That is why there have been many new converts to the middle-of-the-road cause.

Has this Tax Reform Act led to a change in corporate and investor attitudes to dividends? Corporations *believe* that it has led to a pressure for higher payouts, but we still need to wait before we can be confident that there has been a shift in payouts or investors' required returns. Meanwhile, we may gain some clues from the experience of other countries that have changed tax rates on dividends relative to capital gains. In Canada, for example, dividend payouts increased after a capital gains tax was introduced and dividend tax rates were cut for many investors.[31]

Alternative Tax Systems

In the United States shareholders' returns are taxed twice. They are taxed at the corporate level (corporate tax) and in the hands of the shareholder (income tax or capital gains tax). These two tiers of tax are illustrated in Table 16-3, which shows the after-tax return to the shareholder if the company distributes all its income as dividends. We assume the company earns $100 a share before tax and therefore pays corporate tax of $.35 \times 100 = \$35$. This leaves $65 a share to be paid out as a dividend, which is then subject to a second layer of tax. For example, a shareholder who is taxed at the top marginal rate of 39.6 percent pays tax on this dividend of $.396 \times 65 = \$25.7$. Only a tax-exempt pension fund or charity would retain the full $65.

Of course, dividends are regularly paid by companies that operate under very different tax systems. In fact, the two-tier United States system is relatively rare. Some countries, such as Germany, tax investors at a higher rate on dividends than on capital gains, but they offset this by having a split-rate system of corporate taxes. Profits

---

[31]The Canadian experience is summarized in our Canadian edition, especially pp. 409–415. See R. Brealey, S. Myers, G. Sick, and R. Giammarino, *Principles of Corporate Finance*, 2d Canadian ed., McGraw-Hill Ryerson, Ltd., Toronto, 1992.

TABLE 16-3
• •

In the United States returns to shareholders are taxed twice (figures in dollars).

| | RATE OF INCOME TAX | |
Per share	0%	39.6%
Operating income	100	100
Corporate tax ($T_c = .35$)	35	35
After-tax income (paid out as dividends)	65	65
Income tax	0	25.7
Available to shareholder	65	39.3

that are retained in the business attract a higher rate of corporate tax than profits that are distributed. Under this split-rate system, tax-exempt investors prefer that the company pay high dividends, whereas millionaires might vote to retain profits.

In some other countries, shareholders' returns are not taxed twice. For example, in Australia shareholders are taxed on dividends, but they may deduct from this tax bill their share of the corporate tax that the company has paid. This is known as an *imputation tax system*. Table 16-4 shows how the imputation system works. Suppose that an Australian company earns pretax profits of $A100 a share. After it pays corporate tax at 33 percent, the profit is $A67 a share. The company now declares a net dividend of $A67 and sends each shareholder a check for this amount. This dividend is accompanied by a tax credit saying that the company has already paid $33 of tax on the shareholder's behalf. Thus shareholders are treated as if each received a total, or gross, dividend of 67 + 33 = $A100 and paid tax of $A33. If the shareholder's tax rate is 33 percent, there is no more tax to pay and the shareholder retains the net dividend of $A67. If the shareholder pays tax at the top personal rate of 47 percent, then he or she is required to pay an additional $14 of tax; if the tax rate is 15 percent (the rate at which Australian pension funds are taxed), then the shareholder receives a *refund* of 33 − 15 = $A18.[32]

Under an imputation tax system, millionaires have to cough up the extra personal tax on dividends. If this is more than the tax that they would pay on capital gains, then millionaires would prefer that the company does not distribute earnings. If it is the other way around, they would prefer dividends.[33] Investors with low tax rates have no doubts about the matter. If the company pays a dividend, these investors receive a check from the revenue service for the excess tax that the company has paid, and therefore they prefer high payout rates.

Look once again at Table 16-4 and think what would happen if the corporate tax rate was zero. The shareholder with a 15 percent tax rate would still end up with $A85, and the shareholder with the 47 percent rate would still receive $A53. Thus, under an imputation tax system, when a company pays out all its earnings, there is effectively only one layer of tax—the tax on the shareholder. The revenue service col-

---

[32] In Australia and New Zealand, shareholders receive a credit for the full amount of corporate tax that has been paid on their behalf. In other countries such as the United Kingdom and Spain, the tax credit is less than the corporate tax rate. You can think of the tax system in these countries as lying between the Australian and United States systems.

[33] In the case of Australia the tax rate on capital gains is the same as the tax rate on dividends. However, investors are taxed only on the real (i.e., inflation-adjusted) value of capital gains.

TABLE 16-4

Under imputation tax systems, such as that in Australia, shareholders receive a tax credit for the corporate tax that the firm has paid (figures in Australian dollars).

Per share	RATE OF INCOME TAX		
	15%	33%	47%
Operating income	100	100	100
Corporate tax ($T_c = .33$)	33	33	33
After-tax income	67	67	67
Grossed-up dividend	100	100	100
Income tax	15	33	47
Tax credit for corporate payment	−33	−33	−33
Tax due from shareholder	−18	0	14
Available to shareholder	85	67	53

lects this tax through the company and then sends a demand to the shareholder for any excess tax or makes a refund for any overpayment.[34]

16-7 SUMMARY

Dividends come in many forms. The most common is the regular cash dividend, but sometimes companies pay an extra or special cash dividend, and sometimes they pay a dividend in the form of stock. A firm is not free to pay whatever dividends it likes. It may have promised its bondholders not to declare large dividends, and it is also prevented by state law from paying dividends if it is insolvent or if it has insufficient surplus.

As an alternative to dividend payments, the company can repurchase its own stock. Although this has the same effect of distributing cash to shareholders, the Internal Revenue Service taxes shareholders only on the capital gains that they may realize as a result of the repurchase.

When managers decide on the dividend, their primary concern seems to be to give shareholders a "fair" level of dividends. Most managers have a conscious or subconscious long-term target payout rate. If firms simply applied the target payout rate to each year's earnings, dividends could fluctuate wildly. Managers therefore try to smooth dividend payments by moving only partway toward the target payout in each year. Also they don't just look at past earnings performance: They try to look into the future when they set the payment. Investors are aware of this and they know that a dividend increase is often a sign of optimism on the part of management.

If we hold the company's investment policy constant, then dividend policy is a trade-off between cash dividends and the issue or repurchase of common stock. Should firms retain whatever earnings are necessary to finance growth and pay out any residual as cash dividends? Or should they increase dividends and then (sooner

---

[34]This is only true for earnings that are paid out as dividends. Retained earnings are subject to corporate tax. Shareholders get the benefit of retained earnings in the form of capital gains.

or later) issue stock to make up the shortfall of equity capital? Or should they reduce dividends below the "residual" level and use the released cash to repurchase stock?

If we lived in an ideally simple and perfect world, there would be no problem, for the choice would have no effect on market value. The controversy centers on the effects of dividend policy in our flawed world. A common—though by no means universal—view in the investment community is that high payout enhances share price. There are natural clienteles for high-payout stocks. But we find it difficult to explain a *general* preference for dividends other than in terms of an irrational prejudice. The case for "liberal dividends" depends largely on a wealth of tradition.

The most obvious and serious market imperfection has been the different tax treatment of dividends and capital gains. Before the Tax Reform Act of 1986, dividends were taxed at rates up to 50 percent, but capital gains rates topped out at only 20 percent. Thus investors should have required a higher before-tax return on high-payout stocks to compensate for their tax disadvantage. High-income investors should have held mostly low-payout stocks.

This view has a respectable theoretical basis. It is supported by some evidence that gross returns have, on the average, reflected the tax differential. The weak link is the theory's silence on the question of why companies continued to distribute such large sums contrary to the preferences of investors.

The third view of dividend policy starts with the notion that the actions of companies *do* reflect investors' preferences; the fact that companies pay substantial dividends is the best evidence that investors want them. If the supply of dividends exactly meets the demand, no single company could improve its market value by changing its dividend policy. Although this explains corporate behavior, it is at a cost, for we cannot explain why dividends are what they are and not some other amount.

These theories are too incomplete and the evidence is too sensitive to minor changes in specification to warrant any dogmatism. Our sympathies, however, lie with the third, middle-of-the-road view. Our recommendations to companies would emphasize the following points: First, there is little doubt that sudden shifts in dividend policy can cause abrupt changes in stock price. The principal reason is the information that investors read into the company's actions, although some casual evidence suggests that there may be other less rational explanations.[35] Given such problems, there is a clear case for smoothing dividends, for example, by defining the firm's target payout and making relatively slow adjustments toward it. If it is necessary to make a sharp dividend change, the company should provide as much forewarning as possible and take care to ensure that the action is not misinterpreted.

Subject to these strictures, we believe that, at the very least, a company should adopt a target payout that is sufficiently low as to minimize its reliance on external equity. Why pay out cash to stockholders if that requires issuing new shares to get the cash back? It's better to hold on to the cash in the first place.

If dividend policy doesn't affect firm value, then you don't need to worry about it when estimating the cost of capital. But if (say) you believe that tax effects are important, then in principle you should recognize that investors demand higher returns from high-payout stocks. Some financial managers do take dividend policy into account, but most become de facto middle-of-the-roaders when estimating the cost of capital. It seems that the effects of dividend policy are too uncertain to justify fine-tuning such estimates.

---

[35]For example, in an article in *Fortune* Carol Loomis tells the story of General Public Utilities ("A Case for Dropping Dividends," *Fortune*, June 15, 1968, pp. 181 ff.). In 1968 its management decided to reduce its cash dividend to avoid a stock issue. Despite the company's assurances, it encountered considerable opposition. Individual shareholders advised the president to see a psychiatrist, institutional holders threatened to sell their stock, the share price fell nearly 10 percent, and eventually GPU capitulated.

Further Reading

Lintner's classic analysis of how companies set their dividend payments is provided in:
J. Lintner: "Distribution of Incomes of Corporations among Dividends, Retained Earnings, and Taxes," *American Economic Review*, **46**:97–113 (May 1956).

There have been a number of tests of how well Lintner's model describes dividend changes. One of the best known is:
E. F. Fama and H. Babiak: "Dividend Policy: An Empirical Analysis," *Journal of the American Statistical Association*, **63**:1132–1161 (December 1968).

Marsh and Merton have reinterpreted Lintner's findings and used them to explain the aggregate dividends paid by United States corporations:
T. A. Marsh and R. C. Merton: "Dividend Behavior for the Aggregate Stock Market," *Journal of Business*, **60**:1–40 (January 1987).

The pioneering article on dividend policy in the context of a perfect capital market is:
M. H. Miller and F. Modigliani: "Dividend Policy, Growth and the Valuation of Shares," *Journal of Business*, **34**:411–433 (October 1961).

There are several interesting models explaining the information content of dividends. Two influential examples are:
S. Bhattacharya: "Imperfect Information, Dividend Policy and the Bird in the Hand Fallacy," *Bell Journal of Economics and Management Science*, **10**:259–270 (Spring 1979).
M. H. Miller and K. Rock: "Dividend Policy Under Asymmetric Information," *Journal of Finance*, **40**:1031–1052 (September 1985).

The most powerful advocacy of the "dividends are good" case is Gordon's; Brennan discusses the source of the differences between Gordon and MM:
M. J. Gordon: "Dividends, Earnings and Stock Prices," *Review of Economics and Statistics*, **41**:99–105 (May 1959).
M. J. Brennan: "A Note on Dividend Irrelevance and the Gordon Valuation Model," *Journal of Finance*, **26**:1115–1122 (December 1971).

The effect of differential rates of tax on dividends and capital gains is analyzed rigorously in the context of the capital asset pricing model in:
M. J. Brennan: "Taxes, Market Valuation and Corporate Financial Policy," *National Tax Journal*, **23**:417–427 (December 1970).

The argument that dividend policy is irrelevant even in the presence of taxes is presented in:
F. Black and M. S. Scholes: "The Effects of Dividend Yield and Dividend Policy on Common Stock Prices and Returns," *Journal of Financial Economics*, **1**:1–22 (May 1974).
M. H. Miller and M. S. Scholes: "Dividends and Taxes," *Journal of Financial Economics*, **6**:333–364 (December 1978).

A brief review of some of the empirical evidence is contained in:
R. H. Litzenberger and K. Ramaswamy: "The Effects of Dividends on Common Stock Prices: Tax Effects or Information Effects," *Journal of Finance*, **37**:429–443 (May 1982).

Merton Miller reviews research on the dividend controversy in:
M. H. Miller: "Behavioral Rationality in Finance: The Case of Dividends," *Journal of Business*, **59**:S451–S468 (October 1986).

Quiz

1. In 1994 Nike paid a regular quarterly dividend of \$.20 a share.
   (*a*) Match each of the following sets of dates:

(A) August 22, 1994	(a) Record date
(B) Friday, September 2, 1994	(b) Payment date
(C) Monday, September 5, 1994	(c) Ex-dividend date
(D) September 14, 1994	(d) Last with-dividend date
(E) October 3, 1994	(e) Declaration date

   (*b*) One one of these dates the stock price is likely to fall by about the value of the dividend. Why?

   (*c*) The stock price at end-August was $65. What was the prospective dividend yield?

   (*d*) The earnings per share for 1994 were $3.96. What was the percentage payout rate?

   (*e*) Suppose that in 1994 the company paid a 10 percent stock dividend. What would be the expected fall in the stock price?

2. Which of the following statements are false?
   (*a*) A company may not generally pay a dividend out of legal capital.
   (*b*) A company may not generally pay a dividend if it is insolvent.
   (*c*) Realized long-term gains are taxed at the marginal rate of income tax.
   (*d*) Nevertheless, the *effective* tax rate on capital gains can be less than the tax rate on dividends.
   (*e*) Corporations are taxed on only 50 percent of dividends received from other corporations.

3. Here are several "facts" about typical corporate dividend policies. Which are true and which false? Explain.
   (*a*) Companies decide each year's dividend by looking at their capital expenditure requirements and then distributing whatever cash is left over.
   (*b*) Most companies have a target payout ratio.
   (*c*) They set each year's dividend equal to the target payout ratio times that year's earnings.
   (*d*) Managers and investors seem more concerned with dividend changes than with dividend levels.
   (*e*) Managers often increase dividends temporarily when earnings are unexpectedly high for a year or two.
   (*f*) Companies undertaking substantial share repurchases usually finance them with an offsetting reduction in cash dividends.

4. Between 1980 and 1993 GM's dividend changes were described by the following equation:

$$\text{DIV}_t - \text{DIV}_{t-1} = .23\,(.34\ \text{EPS}_t - \text{DIV}_{t-1})$$

   What do you think was:
   (*a*) GM's target payout ratio?
   (*b*) The rate at which dividends adjusted toward the target?

5. Stock price usually rises when there is an unexpected dividend increase, and falls when there is an unexpected dividend cut. Why?

6. How did the Tax Reform Act of 1986 affect the taxation of dividends and capital gains? Are there any investors left who could have a rational tax reason to prefer capital gains? Other things equal, how should the tax law changes affect prices and expected rates of return on high- versus low-payout stocks?

7. How does an imputation tax system differ from the two-tier tax system used in the United States? Other things equal, does an imputation system encourage generous dividend payouts?

8. Here are key financial data for House of Herring, Inc.:

 - Earnings per share for 2006: $5.50
 - Number of shares outstanding: 40 million
 - Target payout ratio: 50 percent
 - Planned dividend per share: $2.75
 - Stock price, year-end 2006: $130

House of Herring plans to pay the entire dividend early in January 2007. All corporate and personal income taxes were repealed in 2005.

(a) Other things equal, what will be House of Herring's stock price after the planned dividend payment?

(b) Suppose the company cancels the dividend and announces that it will use the money saved to repurchase shares. What happens to the stock price on the announcement date? Assume that investors learn nothing about the company's prospects from the announcement. How many shares will the company need to repurchase?

(c) Suppose the company increases dividends to $5.50 per share and then issues new shares to recoup the extra cash paid out as dividends. What happens to the with- and ex-dividend share prices? How many shares will need to be issued? Again, assume investors learn nothing from the announcement about House of Herring's prospects.

Questions and Problems

1. Look in a recent issue of *The Wall Street Journal* at "Dividend News" and choose a company reporting a regular dividend.
   (a) How frequently does the company pay a regular dividend?
   (b) What is the amount of the dividend?
   (c) By what date must your stock be registered for you to receive the dividend?
   (d) How many weeks later is the dividend paid?
   (e) Look up the stock price and calculate the annual yield on the stock.

2. Respond to the following comment: "It's all very well saying that I can sell shares to cover cash needs, but that may mean selling at the bottom of the market. If the company pays a regular dividend, investors avoid that risk."

3. "Dividends are the shareholder's wages. Therefore, if a government adopts an income policy which restricts increases in wages, it should in all logic restrict increases in dividends." Does this make sense?

4. Refer to the first balance sheet prepared for Rational Demiconductor in Section 16-3. Again it uses cash to pay a $1000 cash dividend, planning to issue stock to recover the cash required for investment. But this time catastrophe hits before the stock can be issued. A new pollution control regulation increases manufacturing costs to the extent that the value of Rational Demiconductor's existing business is cut in half, to $4500. The NPV of the new investment opportunity is unaffected, however. Show that dividend policy is still irrelevant.

5. "Risky companies tend to have lower target payout ratios and more gradual adjustment rates." Explain what is meant by this statement. Why do you think it is so?

6. Consider the following two statements: "Dividend policy is irrelevant." "Stock price is the present value of expected future dividends" (see Chapter 4). They *sound* contradictory. This question is designed to show that they are fully consistent.

   The current price of the shares of Charles River Mining Corporation is $50. Next year's earnings and dividends per share are $4 and $2, respectively. Investors expect perpetual growth at 8 percent per year. The expected rate of return demanded by investors is $r = 12$ percent.

   We can use the perpetual-growth model

   $$P_0 = \frac{DIV}{r - g} = \frac{2}{.12 - .08} = 50$$

   Suppose that Charles River Mining announces that it will switch to a 100 percent payout policy, issuing shares as necessary to finance growth. Use the perpetual-growth model to show that current stock price is unchanged.

7. The expected pretax return on three stocks is divided between dividends and capital gains in the following way:

Stock	Expected Dividend	Expected Capital Gain
A	$ 0	$10
B	5	5
C	10	0

   (*a*) If each stock is priced at $100, what are the expected net returns on each stock to (i) a pension fund, (ii) a corporation paying tax at 35 percent, (iii) an individual paying tax at 39.6 percent on investment income and 28 percent on capital gains, and (iv) a security dealer paying tax at 35 percent on investment income and capital gains?

   (*b*) Suppose that before the 1986 Tax Reform Act stocks A, B, and C were priced to yield an 8 percent *after-tax* return to individual investors paying 50 percent tax on dividends and 20 percent tax on capital gains. What would A, B, and C each sell for?

8. Answer the following question twice, once assuming current tax law and once assuming the same rate of tax on dividends and capital gains.

   Suppose all investments offered the same expected return *before* tax. Consider two equally risky shares, Hi and Lo. Hi shares pay a generous dividend and offer low expected capital gains. Lo shares pay low dividends and offer high expected capital gains. Which of the following investors would prefer the Lo shares? Which would prefer the Hi shares? Which wouldn't care? Explain.

   (*a*) A pension fund
   (*b*) An individual
   (*c*) A corporation
   (*d*) A charitable endowment
   (*e*) A security dealer
   Assume that any stock purchased will be sold after 1 year.

9. An article on stock repurchase in the *Los Angeles Times* noted: "An increasing number of companies are finding that the best investment they can make these

days is in themselves." Discuss this view. How is the desirability of repurchase affected by company prospects and the price of its stock?

10. Adherents of the "dividends-are-good" school sometimes point to the fact that stocks with high yields tend to have above-average price-earnings multiples. Is this evidence convincing? Discuss.

11. For each of the following four groups of companies, state whether you would expect them to distribute a relatively high or low proportion of current earnings and whether you would expect them to have a relatively high or low price-earnings ratio.
(*a*) High-risk companies
(*b*) Companies that have recently experienced an unexpected decline in profits
(*c*) Companies that expect to experience a decline in profits
(*d*) "Growth" companies with valuable future investment opportunities

12. "Many companies use stock repurchases to increase earnings per share. For example, suppose that a company is in the following position:

- Net profit: $10 million
- Number of shares before repurchase: 1 million
- Earnings per share: $10
- Price-earnings ratio: 20
- Share price: $200

The company now repurchases 200,000 shares at $200 a share. The number of shares declines to 800,000 shares and the earnings per share increase to $12.50. Assuming the price-earnings ratio stays at 20, the share price must rise to $250." Discuss.

13. (*a*) The Horner Pie Company pays a quarterly dividend of $1. Suppose that the stock price is expected to fall on the ex-dividend date by 90 cents. Would you prefer to buy on the with-dividend date or the ex-dividend date if you were (i) a tax-free investor, (ii) an investor with a marginal tax rate of 40 percent on income and 16 percent on capital gains?
(*b*) In a study of ex-dividend behavior Elton and Gruber estimated that the stock price fell on the average by 85 percent of the dividend. Assuming that the tax rate on capital gains was 40 percent of the rate on income tax, what did Elton and Gruber's result imply about investors' marginal rate of income tax?
(*c*) Elton and Gruber also observed that the ex-dividend price fall was different for high-payout stocks and for low-payout stocks. Which group would you expect to show the larger price fall?
(*d*) Would the fact that investors can trade stocks freely around the ex-dividend date alter your interpretation of Elton and Gruber's study?
(*e*) Suppose Elton and Gruber repeat their tests for the period 1988–1990, after the 1986 Tax Reform Act had equalized the tax on dividends and capital gains. How would you expect their results to change?

14. The middle-of-the-road party holds that dividend policy doesn't matter because the *supply* of high-, medium- and low-payout stocks has already adjusted to satisfy investors' demands. Investors who like generous dividends hold stocks which give them all they want. Investors who want capital gains see a

surfeit of low-payout stocks to choose from. Thus, high-payout firms cannot gain by transforming to low-payout firms or vice versa.

Suppose this was the way it was just before the Tax Reform Act of 1986. How would you expect the 1986 tax changes to affect the total cash dividends paid by United States corporations and the proportion of high- versus low-payout companies? Would dividend policy still be irrelevant after any dividend supply adjustments are completed? Explain.

15. How would you expect dividend policy to affect market value under *(a)* a split-rate tax system and *(b)* an imputation tax system? Construct simple examples to illustrate your arguments.

16. It is well documented that stock prices tend to rise when firms announce increases in their dividend payouts. How, then, can it be said that dividend policy is irrelevant?

17. Hors d'Age Cheeseworks has been paying a regular dividend of $4 per share each year for over a decade. The company is paying out all its earnings as dividends and is not expected to grow. There are 100,000 shares outstanding, selling for $80 per share. The company has sufficient cash on hand to pay the next annual dividend.

Suppose that Hors d'Age decides to cut its cash dividend to zero and announces that it will repurchase shares instead.

(a) What is the immediate stock price reaction? Ignore taxes, and assume that the repurchase program conveys no information about operating profitability or business risk.

(b) How many shares will Hors d'Age purchase?

(c) Project and compare future stock prices for the old and new policies. Do this for at least years 1, 2, and 3.

18. Formaggio Vecchio has just announced its regular quarterly dividend of $1 per share.

(a) When will the stock price fall to reflect this dividend payment—on the record date, the ex-dividend date, or the payment date?

(b) Assume that there are no taxes. By how much is the stock price likely to fall?

(c) Now assume that *all* investors pay tax of 30 percent on dividends and nothing on capital gains. What is the likely fall in the stock price?

(d) Suppose, finally, that everything is the same as in part *(c)* except that security dealers pay tax on *both* dividends and capital gains. How would your answer to *(c)* change? Explain.

19. Refer back to question 18. Assume no taxes and a stock price immediately after the dividend announcement of $100.

(a) If you own 100 shares, what is the value of your investment? How does the dividend payment affect your wealth?

(b) Now suppose that Formaggio Vecchio cancels the dividend payment and announces that it will repurchase 1 percent of its stock at $100. Do you rejoice or yawn? Explain.

20. Comment briefly on each of the following statements:

(a) "Unlike American firms, which are always being pressured by their shareholders to increase dividends, Japanese companies pay out a much smaller proportion of earnings and so enjoy a lower cost of capital."

(b) "Unlike new capital, which needs a stream of new dividends to service it, retained earnings are essentially free capital."

(c) "If a company repurchases stock instead of paying a dividend, the number of shares falls and earnings per share rise. Thus stock repurchase must always be preferred to paying dividends."

21. Little Oil has outstanding 1 million shares with a total market value of $20 million. The firm is expected to pay $1 million of dividends next year, and thereafter the amount paid out is expected to grow by 5 percent a year in perpetuity. Thus the expected dividend in year 2 is $1.05 million, and so on. However, the company has heard that the value of a share depends on the flow of dividends, and therefore it announces that next year's dividend will be increased to $2 million and that the extra cash will be raised immediately by an issue of shares. After that, the total amount paid out each year will be as previously forecast, i.e., $1.05 million in year 2 and increasing by 5 percent a year in each subsequent year.
    (a) At what price will the new shares be issued in year 1?
    (b) How many shares will the firm need to issue?
    (c) What will be the expected dividend payments on these new shares, and what therefore will be paid out to the *old* shareholders after year 1?
    (d) Show that the present value of the cash flows to current shareholders remains $20 million.

22. We stated in Section 16-4 that MM's dividend irrelevance proposition assumes that new shares are sold at a fair price. Look back at question 21. Assume that new shares are issued in year 1 at $10 a share. Show who gains and who loses. Is dividend policy still irrelevant? Why or why not?

23. Table 16-5 lists the dividends and earnings per share (EPS) for Merck and Westinghouse. Estimate the target payout rate for each company and the rate at which the dividend is adjusted toward the target. Suppose that in 1995

TABLE 16-5

See problem 23.

Year	MERCK EPS	MERCK Dividend	WESTINGHOUSE EPS	WESTINGHOUSE Dividend
1980	.31	.13	1.18	.35
1981	.30	.14	1.28	.45
1982	.31	.16	1.29	.45
1983	.34	.16	1.27	.45
1984	.37	.17	1.52	.49
1985	.42	.18	1.76	.58
1986	.54	.21	2.21	.70
1987	.74	.27	2.56	.82
1988	1.02	.43	2.83	.97
1989	1.26	.55	3.13	1.15
1990	1.52	.64	.91	1.35
1991	1.83	.77	(3.46)	1.40
1992	2.12	.92	.93	.72
1993	1.87	1.03	(.64)	.40
1994	2.38	1.14	.07	.20

Merck's earnings increase to $3 a share and Westinghouse's earnings increase to $.20 per share. How would you predict their dividends to change?

24. (a) "Merck, the biggest U.S. pharmaceuticals group, announced plans to buy back up to $2 billion of its shares. The repurchase programme would help repair some of the dilution to the company's earnings per share which stemmed from the acquisition of Medco Containment Services at the end of last year." (*Financial Times*, November 23, 1994, p. 36)

    (b) "Stock repurchase programmes tend to increase a company's share price because they reduce the amount of shares in issue, so increasing earnings per share." (*Financial Times*, September 1, p. 30, 1994)

    Are these valid reasons for stock repurchase?

25. The shares of firms A and B both sell for $100 and offer a pretax return of 10 percent. However, in the case of company A the return is entirely in the form of dividend yield (the company pays a regular annual dividend of $10 a share), while in the case of B the return comes entirely as capital gain (the shares appreciate by 10 percent a year). Suppose that dividends and realized capital gains are both taxed at 30 percent. What is the after-tax return on share A? What is the after-tax rate of return on share B to an investor who sells after 2 years? What about an investor who sells after 10 years?

26. In the United States, where there is a two-tier tax system, which investors are indifferent to the dividend payout ratio? How about investors in Australia, where there is an imputation tax system?

27. Suppose the Miller-Modigliani (MM) theory of dividend policy is correct. How would a government-imposed dividend freeze affect:

    (a) Stock prices?

    (b) Capital investment?

Does Debt Policy Matter?

A firm's basic resource is the stream of cash flows produced by its assets. When the firm is financed entirely by common stock, all those cash flows belong to the stockholders. When it issues both debt and equity securities, it undertakes to split up the cash flows into two streams, a relatively safe stream that goes to the debtholders and a more risky one that goes to the stockholders.

The firm's mix of different securities is known as its **capital structure.** The choice of capital structure is fundamentally a marketing problem. The firm can issue dozens of distinct securities in countless combinations, but it attempts to find the particular combination that maximizes its overall market value.

Are these attempts worthwhile? We must consider the possibility that *no* combination has any greater appeal than any other. Perhaps the really important decisions concern the company's assets, and decisions about capital structure are mere details— matters to be attended to but not worried about.

Modigliani and Miller (MM), who showed that dividend policy doesn't matter in perfect capital markets, also showed that financing decisions don't matter in perfect markets.[1] Their famous "proposition I" states that a firm cannot change the *total* value of its securities just by splitting its cash flows into different streams: the firm's value is determined by its real assets, not by the securities it issues. Thus capital structure is irrelevant as long as the firm's investment decisions are taken as given.

MM's proposition I allows complete separation of investment and financing decisions. It implies that any firm could use the capital budgeting procedures presented in Chapters 2 to 12 without worrying about where the money for capital expenditures comes from. In those chapters, we assumed all-equity financing without really thinking about it. If proposition I holds, that is exactly the right approach.

We believe that in practice capital structure *does* matter, but we nevertheless devote all of this chapter to MM's argument. If you don't fully understand the conditions under which MM's theory holds, you won't fully understand why one capital structure is better than another. The financial manager needs to know what kinds of market imperfection to look for.

---

[1] MM's paper [F. Modigliani and M. H. Miller, "The Cost of Capital, Corporation Finance and the Theory of Investment," *American Economic Review*, **48**:261–297 (June 1958)] was published in 1958, but their basic argument was anticipated in 1938 by J. B. Williams and to some extent by David Durand. See J. B. Williams, *The Theory of Investment Value*, Harvard University Press, Cambridge, Mass., 1938; and D. Durand, "Cost of Debt and Equity Funds for Business: Trends and Problems of Measurement," in *Conference on Research in Business Finance*, National Bureau of Economic Research, New York, 1952.

In Chapter 18 we will undertake a detailed analysis of the imperfections that are most likely to make a difference, including taxes, the costs of bankruptcy, and the costs of writing and enforcing complicated debt contracts. We will also argue that it is naive to suppose that investment and financing decisions can be completely separated.

But in this chapter we isolate the decision about capital structure by holding the decision about investment fixed. We also assume that dividend policy is irrelevant.

17-1   THE EFFECT OF LEVERAGE IN A COMPETITIVE TAX-FREE ECONOMY

We have referred to the firm's choice of capital structure as a *marketing problem.* The financial manager's problem is to find the combination of securities that has the greatest overall appeal to investors—the combination that maximizes the market value of the firm. Before tackling this problem, we ought to make sure that a policy which maximizes firm value also maximizes the wealth of the shareholders.

Let D and E denote the market values of the outstanding debt and equity of the Wapshot Mining Company. Wapshot's 1000 shares sell for $50 apiece. Thus

$$E = 1000 \times 50 = \$50,000$$

Wapshot has also borrowed $25,000, and so V, the aggregate market value of all Wapshot's outstanding securities, is

$$V = D + E = \$75,000$$

Wapshot's stock is known as *levered equity.* Its stockholders face the benefits and costs of *financial leverage,* or *gearing.* Suppose that Wapshot "levers up" still further by borrowing an additional $10,000 and paying the proceeds out to shareholders as a special dividend of $10 per share. This substitutes debt for equity capital with no impact on Wapshot's assets.

What will Wapshot's equity be worth after the special dividend is paid? We have two unknowns, E and V:

Old debt	$25,000 ⎫	$35,000 = D
New debt	$10,000 ⎭	
Equity		? = E
Firm value		? = V

If V is $75,000 as before, then E must be $V - D = 75,000 - 35,000 = \$40,000$. Stockholders have suffered a capital loss which exactly offsets the $10,000 special dividend. But if V *increases* to, say, $80,000 as a result of the change in capital structure, then $E = \$45,000$ and the stockholders are $5000 ahead. In general, any increase or decrease in V caused by a shift in capital structure accrues to the firm's stockholders. We conclude that a policy which maximizes the market value of the firm is also best for the firm's stockholders.

This conclusion rests on two important assumptions: first, that Wapshot can ignore dividend policy and, second, that after the change in capital structure the old and new debt is *worth* $35,000.

Dividend policy may or may not be relevant, but there is no need to repeat the discussion of Chapter 16. We need only note that shifts in capital structure sometimes force important decisions about dividend policy. Perhaps Wapshot's cash dividend has costs or benefits which should be considered in addition to any benefits achieved by its increased financial leverage.

Our second assumption that old and new debt ends up worth $35,000 seems innocuous. But it could be wrong. Perhaps the new borrowing has increased the risk of the old bonds. If the holders of old bonds cannot demand a higher rate of interest to compensate for the increased risk, the value of their investment is reduced. In this case Wapshot's stockholders gain at the expense of the holders of old bonds even though the overall value of the debt and equity is unchanged.

But this anticipates issues better left to Chapter 18. In this chapter we will assume that any issue of debt has no effect on the market value of existing debt.[2]

Enter Modigliani and Miller

Let us accept that the financial manager would like to find the combination of securities that maximizes the value of the firm. How is this done? MM's answer is that the financial manager should stop worrying: in a perfect market any combination of securities is as good as another. The value of the firm is unaffected by its choice of capital structure.

You can see this by imagining two firms that generate the same stream of operating income and differ only in their capital structure. Firm U is unlevered. Therefore the total value of its equity E_U is the same as the total value of the firm V_U. Firm, L, on the other hand, is levered. The value of its stock is, therefore, equal to the value of the firm less the value of the debt: $E_L = V_L - D_L$.

Now think which of these firms you would prefer to invest in. If you don't want to take much risk, you can buy common stock in the unlevered firm U. For example, if you buy 1 percent of firm U's shares, your investment is $.01V_U$ and you are entitled to 1 percent of the gross profits:

Dollar Investment	Dollar Return
$.01V_U$	.01 Profits

Now compare this with an alternative strategy. This is to purchase the same fraction of both the debt and the equity of firm L. Your investment and return would then be as follows:

	Dollar Investment	Dollar Return
Debt	$.01D_L$	.01 Interest
Equity	$.01E_L$	.01 (Profits − interest)
Total	$.01(D_L + E_L)$	.01 Profits
	$= .01V_L$	

---

[2] See E. F. Fama, "The Effects of a Firm's Investment and Financing Decisions," *American Economic Review*, **68**:272–284 (June 1978), for a rigorous analysis of the conditions under which a policy of maximizing the value of the firm is also best for the stockholders.

Both strategies offer the same payoff: 1 percent of the firm's profits. In well-functioning markets two investments that offer the same payoff must have the same cost. Therefore $.01V_U$ must equal $.01V_L$: the value of the unlevered firm must equal the value of the levered firm.

Suppose that you are willing to run a little more risk. You decide to buy 1 percent of the outstanding shares in the *levered* firm. Your investment and return are now as follows:

Dollar Investment	Dollar Return
$.01E_L$ $=.01(V_L - D_L)$	$.01$ (Profits − interest)

But there is an alternative strategy. This is to borrow $.01D_L$ on your own account and purchase 1 percent of the stock of the *unlevered* firm. In this case, your borrowing gives you an immediate cash *inflow* of $.01D_L$, but you have to pay interest on your loan equal to 1 percent of the interest that is paid by firm L. Your total investment and return are, therefore, as follows:

	Dollar Investment	Dollar Return
Borrowing	$-.01D_L$	$-.01$ Interest
Equity	$.01\ V_U$	$.01$ Profits
Total	$.01(V_U - D_L)$	$.01$ (Profits − interest)

Again both strategies offer the same payoff: 1 percent of profits after interest. Therefore, both investments must have the same cost. The quantity $.01(V_U - D_L)$ must equal $.01(V_L - D_L)$ and V_U must equal V_L.

It does not matter whether the world is full of risk-averse chickens or venturesome lions. All would agree that the value of the unlevered firm U must be equal to the value of the levered firm L. As long as investors can borrow or lend on their own account on the same terms as the firm, they can "undo" the effect of any changes in the firm's capital structure. This is the basis for MM's famous proposition I: "The market value of any firm is independent of its capital structure."

The Law of the Conservation of Value

MM's argument that debt policy is irrelevant is an application of an astonishingly simple idea. If we have two streams of cash flow, A and B, then the present value of $A + B$ is equal to the present value of A plus the present value of B. We met this principle of *value additivity* in our discussion of capital budgeting, where we saw that in perfect capital markets the present value of two assets combined is equal to the sum of their present values considered separately.

In the present context we are not combining assets but splitting them up. But value additivity works just as well in reverse. We can slice a cash flow into as many parts as we like; the values of the parts will always sum back to the value of the unsliced stream. (Of course, we have to make sure that none of the stream is lost in the slicing. We cannot say, "The value of a pie is independent of how it is sliced," if the slicer is also a nibbler.)

This is really a *law of conservation of value*. The value of an asset is preserved regardless of the nature of the claims against it. Thus proposition I: Firm value is determined on the *left-hand* side of the balance sheet by real assets—not by the proportions of debt and equity securities issued by the firm.

The simplest ideas often have the widest application. For example, we could apply the law of conservation of value to the choice between issuing preferred stock, common stock, or some combination. The law implies that the choice is irrelevant, assuming perfect capital markets and providing that the choice does not affect the firm's investment, borrowing, and operating policies. If the total value of the equity "pie" (preferred and common combined) is fixed, the firm's owners (its common stockholders) do not care how this pie is sliced.

The law also applies to the *mix* of debt securities issued by the firm. The choices of long-term versus short-term, secured versus unsecured, senior versus subordinated, and convertible versus nonconvertible debt all should have no effect on the overall value of the firm.

Combining assets and splitting them up will not affect values as long as they do not affect an investor's choice. When we showed that capital structure does not affect choice, we implicitly assumed that both companies and individuals can borrow and lend at the same risk-free rate of interest. As long as this is so, individuals can "undo" the effect of any changes in the firm's capital structure.

In practice corporate debt is not risk-free and firms cannot escape with rates of interest appropriate to a government security. Some people's initial reaction is that this alone invalidates MM's proposition. It is a natural mistake, but capital structure can be irrelevant even when debt is risky.

If a company borrows money, it does not *guarantee* repayment: It repays the debt in full only if its assets are worth more than the debt obligation. The shareholders in the company, therefore, have limited liability.

Many individuals would like to borrow with limited liability. They might, therefore, be prepared to pay a small premium for levered shares *if the supply of levered shares was insufficient to meet their needs.*[3] But there are literally thousands of common stocks of companies that borrow. Therefore it is unlikely that an issue of debt would induce them to pay a premium for *your* shares.[4]

An Example of Proposition I

Macbeth Spot Removers is reviewing its capital structure. Table 17-1 shows its current position. The company has no leverage and all the operating income is paid as dividends to the common stockholders (we assume still that there are no taxes). The expected earnings and dividends per share are $1.50, but this figure is by no means certain—it could turn out to be more or less than $1.50. The price of each share is $10. Since the firm expects to produce a level stream of earnings in perpetuity, the expected return on the share is equal to the earnings-price ratio, $1.50/10.00 = .15$, or 15 percent.[5]

Ms. Macbeth, the firm's president, has come to the conclusion that shareholders would be better off if the company had equal proportions of debt and equity. She therefore proposes to issue $5000 of debt at an interest rate of 10 percent and use the proceeds to repurchase 500 shares. To support her proposal, Ms. Macbeth has analyzed the situation under different assumptions about operating income. The results of her calculations are shown in Table 17-2.

---

[3]Of course, individuals could *create* limited liability if they chose. In other words, the lender could agree that borrowers need repay their debt in full only if the assets of company X are worth more than a certain amount. Presumably individuals don't enter into such arrangements because they can obtain limited liability more simply by investing in the stocks of levered companies.

[4]Capital structure is also irrelevant if each investor holds a fully diversified portfolio. In that case he or she owns all the risky securities offered by a company (both debt and equity). But anybody who owns *all* the risky securities doesn't care about how the cash flows are divided between different securities.

[5]See Chapter 4, Section 4.

TABLE 17-1
• •

> Macbeth Spot Removers is entirely equity-financed. Although it
> *expects* to have an income of $1500 a year in perpetuity, this income
> is not certain. This table shows the return to the stockholder under
> different assumptions about operating income. We assume no taxes.

	Data			
Number of shares	1,000			
Price per share	$10			
Market value of shares	$10,000			

	Outcomes			
Operating income, dollars	500	1,000	**1,500**	2,000
Earnings per share, dollars	.50	1.00	**1.50**	2.00
Return on shares, percent	5	10	**15**	20
			Expected outcome	

In order to see more clearly how leverage would affect earnings per share, Ms.
Macbeth has also produced Figure 17-1. The solid line shows how earnings per share
would vary with operating income under the firm's current all-equity financing. It is,
therefore, simply a plot of the data in Table 17-1. The dotted line shows how earn-

TABLE 17-2
• •

> Macbeth Spot Removers is wondering whether to issue $5000 of
> debt at an interest rate of 10 percent and repurchase 500 shares. This
> table shows the return to the shareholder under different
> assumptions about operating income.

	Data			
Number of shares	500			
Price per share	$10			
Market value of shares	$5,000			
Market value of debt	$5,000			
Interest at 10 percent	$500			

	Outcomes			
Operating income, dollars	500	1,000	**1,500**	2,000
Interest, dollars	500	500	**500**	500
Equity earnings, dollars	0	500	**1,000**	1,500
Earnings per share, dollars	0	1	**2**	3
Return on shares, percent	0	10	**20**	30
			Expected outcome	

Figure 17-1 Borrowing increases Macbeth's EPS (earnings per share) when operating income is greater than $1000 and reduces EPS when operating income is less than $1000. Expected EPS rises from $1.50 to $2.

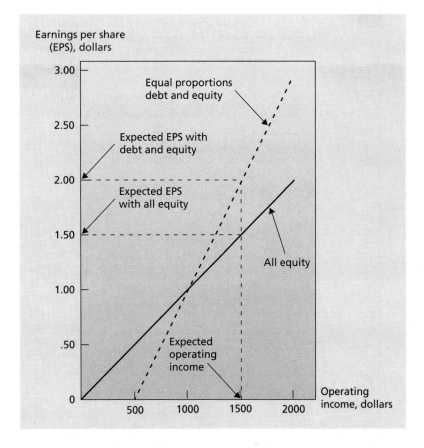

ings per share would vary given equal proportions of debt and equity. It is, therefore, a plot of the data in Table 17-2.

Ms. Macbeth reasons as follows: "It is clear that the effect of leverage depends on the company's income. If income is greater than $1000, the return to the equity holder is *increased* by leverage. If it is less than $1000, the return is *reduced* by leverage. The return is unaffected when operating income is exactly $1000. At this point the return on the market value of the assets is 10 percent, which is exactly equal to the interest rate on the debt. Our capital structure decision, therefore, boils down to what we think about income prospects. Since we expect operating income to be above the $1000 break-even point, I believe we can best help our shareholders by going ahead with the $5000 debt issue."

As financial manager of Macbeth Spot Removers, you reply as follows: "I agree that leverage will help the shareholder as long as our income is greater than $1000. But your argument ignores the fact that Macbeth's shareholders have the alternative of borrowing on their own account. For example, suppose that an investor borrows $10 and then invests $20 in two unlevered Macbeth shares. This person has to put up only $10 of his or her own money. The payoff on the investment varies with Macbeth's operating income, as shown in Table 17-3. This is exactly the same set of payoffs as the investor would get by buying one share in the levered company. (Compare the last two lines of Tables 17-2 and 17-3.) Therefore a share in the levered company must

TABLE 17-3

Individual investors can replicate Macbeth's leverage.

	OPERATING INCOME, DOLLARS			
	500	1,000	**1,500**	2,000
Earnings on two shares, dollars	1	2	**3**	4
Less interest at 10%, dollars	1	1	**1**	1
Net earnings on investment, dollars	0	1	**2**	3
Return on $10 investment, percent	0	10	**20**	30
			Expected outcome	

also sell for $10. If Macbeth goes ahead and borrows, it will not allow investors to do anything that they could not do already, and so it will not increase value."

The argument that you are using is exactly the same as the one MM used to prove proposition I.

17-2 HOW LEVERAGE AFFECTS RETURNS

Implications of Proposition I

Consider now the implications of proposition I for the expected returns on Macbeth stock:

	Current Structure: All Equity	Proposed Structure: Equal Debt and Equity
Expected earnings per share, dollars	1.50	2.00
Price per share, dollars	10	10
Expected return on share, percent	15	20

Leverage increases the expected stream of earnings per share but *not* the share price. The reason is that the change in the expected earnings stream is exactly offset by a change in the rate at which the earnings are capitalized. The expected return on the share (which for a perpetuity is equal to the earnings-price ratio) increases from 15 to 20 percent. We now show how this comes about.

The expected return on Macbeth's assets r_A is equal to the expected operating income divided by the total market value of the firm's securities:

$$\text{Expected return on assets} = r_A = \frac{\text{expected operating income}}{\text{market value of all securities}}$$

We have seen that in perfect capital markets the company's borrowing decision does not affect *either* the firm's operating income *or* the total market value of its securities. Therefore the borrowing decision also does not affect the expected return on the firm's assets r_A.

Suppose that an investor holds all of a company's debt and all its equity. This investor would be entitled to all the firm's operating income; therefore, the expected return on the portfolio would be equal to r_A.

The expected return on a portfolio is equal to a weighted average of the expected returns on the individual holdings. Therefore the expected return on a portfolio consisting of *all* the firm's securities is[6]

$$
\begin{pmatrix} \text{Expected return} \\ \text{on assets} \end{pmatrix} = \begin{pmatrix} \text{proportion} \\ \text{in debt} \end{pmatrix} \times \begin{pmatrix} \text{expected return} \\ \text{on debt} \end{pmatrix} + \begin{pmatrix} \text{proportion} \\ \text{in equity} \end{pmatrix} \times \begin{pmatrix} \text{expected return} \\ \text{on equity} \end{pmatrix}
$$

$$
r_A = \left(\frac{D}{D + E} \times r_D \right) + \left(\frac{E}{D + E} \times r_E \right)
$$

We can rearrange this equation to obtain an expression for r_E, the expected return on the equity of a levered firm:

$$
\begin{pmatrix} \text{Expected return} \\ \text{on equity} \end{pmatrix} = \begin{pmatrix} \text{expected return} \\ \text{on assets} \end{pmatrix} + \begin{pmatrix} \text{debt-equity} \\ \text{ratio} \end{pmatrix} \times \begin{pmatrix} \text{expected return} \\ \text{on assets} \end{pmatrix} - \begin{pmatrix} \text{expected return} \\ \text{on debt} \end{pmatrix}
$$

$$
r_E = r_A + \frac{D}{E} (r_A - r_D)
$$

....

Proposition II

This is MM's proposition II: The expected rate of return on the common stock of a levered firm increases in proportion to the debt-equity ratio (D/E), expressed in market values; the rate of increase depends on the spread between r_A, the expected rate of return on a portfolio of all the firm's securities, and r_D, the expected return on the debt. Note that $r_E = r_A$ if the firm has no debt.

We can check out this formula for Macbeth Spot Removers. Before the decision to borrow

$$
r_E = r_A = \frac{\text{expected operating income}}{\text{market value of all securities}}
$$

$$
= \frac{1500}{10,000} = .15, \text{ or } 15\%
$$

If the firm goes ahead with its plan to borrow, the expected return on assets r_A is still 15 percent. The expected return on equity is

$$
r_E = r_A + \frac{D}{E} (r_A - r_D)
$$

$$
= .15 + \frac{5000}{5000} (.15 - .10)
$$

$$
= .20, \text{ or } 20\%
$$

The general implications of MM's proposition II are shown in Figure 17-2. The figure assumes that the firm's bonds are essentially risk-free at low debt levels. Thus r_D is independent of D/E, and r_E increases linearly as D/E increases. As the firm borrows more, the risk of default increases and the firm is required to pay higher rates of interest. Proposition II predicts that when this occurs the rate of increase in r_E slows down. This is also shown in Figure 17-2. The more debt the firm has, the less sensitive r_E is to further borrowing.

---

[6]This equation should look familiar. We introduced it in Chapter 9 when we showed that the company cost of capital is a weighted average of the expected returns on the debt and equity. (*Company cost of capital* is simply another term for the expected return on assets, r_A.) We also stated in Chapter 9 that changing the capital structure does not change the company cost of capital. In other words, we implicitly assumed MM's proposition I.

Figure 17-2 MM's proposition II. The expected return on equity r_E increases linearly with the debt-equity ratio so long as debt is risk-free. But if leverage increases the risk of the debt, debtholders demand a higher return on the debt. This causes the rate of increase in r_E to slow down.

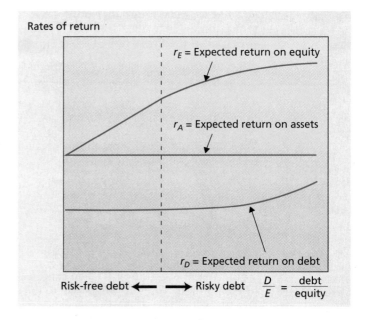

Why does the slope of the r_E line in Figure 17-2 taper off as D/E increases? Essentially because holders of risky debt bear some of the firm's business risk. As the firm borrows more, more of that risk is transferred from stockholders to bondholders.

The Risk-Return Trade-off

Proposition I says that financial leverage has no effect on shareholders' wealth. Proposition II says that the rate of return they can expect to receive on their shares increases as the firm's debt-equity ratio increases. How can shareholders be indifferent to increased leverage when it increases expected return? The answer is that any increase in expected return is exactly offset by an increase in risk and therefore in shareholders' *required* rate of return.

Look at what happens to the risk of Macbeth shares if it moves to equal debt-equity proportions. Table 17-4 shows how a shortfall in operating income affects the payoff to the shareholders.

The debt-equity proportion does not affect the *dollar* risk borne by equityholders. Suppose operating income drops from $1500 to $500. Under all-equity financing, eq-

TABLE 17-4

Leverage increases the risk of Macbeth shares.

		OPERATING INCOME	
		$500	$1,500
All equity:	Earnings per share, dollars	.50	1.50
	Return on shares, percent	5	15
50 percent debt:	Earnings per share, dollars	0	2
	Return on shares, percent	0	20

uity earnings drop by $1 per share. There are 1000 outstanding shares, and so *total* equity earnings fall by $1 × 1000 = $1000. With 50 percent debt, the same drop in operating income reduces earnings per share by $2. But there are only 500 shares outstanding, and so total equity income drops by $2 × 500 = $1000, just as in the all-equity case.

However, the debt-equity choice does amplify the spread of *percentage* returns. If the firm is all-equity-financed, a decline of $1000 in the operating income reduces the return on the shares by 10 percent. If the firm issues risk-free debt with a fixed interest payment of $500 a year, then a decline of $1000 in the operating income reduces the return on the shares by 20 percent. In other words, the effect of leverage is to double the amplitude of the swings in Macbeth's shares. Whatever the beta of the firm's shares before the refinancing, it would be twice as high afterward.

Just as the expected return on the firm's assets is a weighted average of the expected return on the individual securities, so likewise is the beta of the firm's assets a weighted average of the betas of the individual securities:[7]

$$\text{Beta of atoms} = \left(\begin{array}{c} \text{proportion} \\ \text{of debt} \end{array} \times \begin{array}{c} \text{beta of} \\ \text{debt} \end{array} \right) + \left(\begin{array}{c} \text{proportion} \\ \text{of equity} \end{array} \times \begin{array}{c} \text{beta of} \\ \text{equity} \end{array} \right)$$

$$\beta_A = \left(\frac{D}{D + E} \times \beta_D \right) + \left(\frac{E}{D + E} \times \beta_E \right)$$

We can rearrange this equation also to give an expression for β_E, the beta of the equity of a levered firm:

$$\text{Beta of equity} = \begin{array}{c} \text{beta of} \\ \text{assets} \end{array} + \begin{array}{c} \text{debt-equity} \\ \text{ratio} \end{array} \times \left(\begin{array}{c} \text{beta of} \\ \text{assets} \end{array} - \begin{array}{c} \text{beta of} \\ \text{debt} \end{array} \right)$$

$$\beta_E = \beta_A + \frac{D}{E} (\beta_A - \beta_D)$$

Now you can see why investors require higher returns on levered equity. The required return simply rises to match the increased risk.

In Figure 17-3, we have plotted the expected returns and the risk of Macbeth's securities, assuming that the interest on the debt is risk-free.[8]

17-3 THE TRADITIONAL POSITION

What did financial experts think about debt policy before MM? It is not easy to say because with hindsight we see that they did not think too clearly.[9] However, a "traditional" position has emerged in response to MM. In order to understand it, we have to discuss the **weighted-average cost of capital.**

The expected return on a portfolio of all the company's securities is often referred to as the weighted-average cost of capital:[10]

---

[7]This equation should also look old-hat. We used it in Section 9-2 when we stated that changes in the capital structure change the beta of stock but not the asset beta.

[8]In this case $\beta_D = 0$ and $\beta_E = \beta_A + (D/E)\beta_A$.

[9]Financial economists in 20 years may remark on Brealey and Myers's blind spots and clumsy reasoning. On the other hand, they may not remember us at all.

[10]Remember that in this chapter we ignore taxes. In Chapter 19, we shall see that the weighted-average cost of capital formula needs to be amended when debt interest can be deducted from taxable profits.

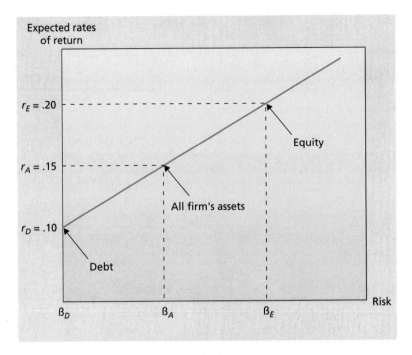

Figure 17-3 If Macbeth is unlevered, the expected return on its equity equals the expected return on its assets. Leverage increases both the expected return on equity (r_E) and the risk of equity (β_E).

$$\text{Weighted-average cost of capital} = r_A = \left(\frac{D}{V} \times r_D\right) + \left(\frac{E}{V} \times r_E\right)$$

The weighted-average cost of capital is used in capital budgeting decisions to find the net present value of projects that would not change the business risk of the firm.

For example, suppose that a firm has \$2 million of outstanding debt and 100,000 shares selling at \$30 per share. Its current borrowing rate is 8 percent, and the financial manager thinks that the stock is priced to offer a 15 percent return. Therefore $r_D = .08$ and $r_E = .15$. (The hard part is estimating r_E, of course.) This is all we need to calculate the weighted-average cost of capital:

$$D = \$2 \text{ million}$$
$$E = 100{,}000 \text{ shares} \times \$30 \text{ per share} = \$3 \text{ million}$$
$$V = D + E = 2 + 3 = \$5 \text{ million}$$

$$\text{Weighted-average cost of capital} = \left(\frac{D}{V} \times r_D\right) + \left(\frac{E}{V} \times r_E\right)$$
$$\left(\frac{2}{5} \times .08\right) + \left(\frac{3}{5} \times .15\right)$$
$$= .122, \text{ or } 12.2\%$$

Note that we are still assuming that proposition I holds. If it doesn't, we can't use this simple weighted average as the discount rate even for projects that do not change the firm's business "risk class." As we will see in Chapter 19, the weighted-average cost of capital is only a starting point for setting discount rates.

Two Warnings

Sometimes the objective in financing decisions is stated not as "maximize overall market value" but as "minimize the weighted-average cost of capital." If MM's proposition I holds, then these are equivalent objectives. If MM's proposition I does *not* hold, then the capital structure that maximizes the value of the firm also minimizes the weighted-average cost of capital, *provided* that operating income is independent of capital structure. Remember that the weighted-average cost of capital is the expected rate of return on the market value of all the firm's securities. Anything that increases the value of the firm reduces the weighted-average cost of capital if operating income is constant. But if operating income is varying too, all bets are off.

In Chapter 18 we will show that financial leverage can affect operating income in several ways. Therefore maximizing the value of the firm is *not* always equivalent to minimizing the weighted-average cost of capital.

WARNING 1.   Shareholders want management to increase the firm's value. They are more interested in being rich than in owning a firm with a low weighted-average cost of capital.

WARNING 2.   Trying to minimize the weighted-average cost of capital seems to encourage logical short circuits like the following: Suppose that someone says: "Shareholders demand—and deserve—higher expected rates of return than bondholders do. Therefore debt is the cheaper capital source. We can reduce the weighted-average cost of capital by borrowing more." But this doesn't follow if the extra borrowing leads stockholders to demand a still higher expected rate of return. According to MM's proposition II the "cost of equity capital" r_E increases by just enough to keep the weighted-average cost of capital constant.

This is not the only logical short circuit you are likely to encounter. We have cited two more in question 5 at the end of this chapter.

Rates of Return on Levered Equity— The Traditional Position

You may ask why we have even mentioned the aim of minimizing the weighted-average cost of capital if it is often wrong or confusing. We had to because the traditionalists accept this objective and argue their case in terms of it.

The logical short circuit we just described rested on the assumption that r_E, the expected rate of return demanded by stockholders, does not rise as the firm borrows more. Suppose, just for the sake of argument, that this is true. Then r_A, the weighted-average cost of capital, must decline as the debt-equity ratio rises.

Take Figure 17-4, for example, which is drawn on the assumption that shareholders demand 12 percent no matter how much debt the firm has and that bondholders always want 8 percent. The weighted-average cost of capital starts at 12 percent and ends up at 8. Suppose that this firm's operating income is a level, perpetual stream of $100,000 a year. Then firm value starts at

$$V = \frac{100,000}{.12} = \$833,333$$

and ends up at

$$V = \frac{100,000}{.08} = \$1,250,000$$

The gain of $416,667 falls into the stockholders' pockets.[11]

---

[11]Note that Figure 17-4 relates r_E and r_D to D/V, the ratio of debt to firm value, rather than to the debt-equity ratio D/E. In this figure we wanted to show what happens when the firm is 100 percent debt-financed. At that point $E = 0$ and D/E is infinite.

Figure 17-4 If the expected rate of return demanded by stockholders r_E is unaffected by financial leverage, then the weighted-average cost of capital r_A declines as the firm borrows more. At 100 percent debt r_A equals the borrowing rate r_D. Of course this is an absurd and totally unrealistic case.

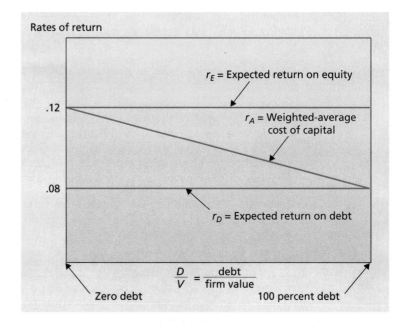

Of course this is absurd: A firm that reaches 100 percent debt *has to be bankrupt.* If there is *any* chance that the firm could remain solvent, then the equity retains some value, and the firm cannot be 100 percent debt-financed. (Remember that we are working with the *market* values of debt and equity.)

But if the firm is bankrupt and its original shares are worthless pieces of paper, than its *lenders are its new shareholders.* The firm is back to all-equity financing! We assumed that the original stockholders demanded 12 percent—why should the new ones demand any less? They have to bear all of the firm's business risk.[12]

The situation described in Figure 17-4 is just impossible.[13] However, it is possible to stake out a position somewhere *between* Figures 17-3 and 17-4. That is exactly what the traditionalists have done. Their hypothesis is shown in Figure 17-5. They hold that a moderate degree of financial leverage may increase the expected equity return r_E although not to the degree predicted by MM's proposition II. But irresponsible firms that borrow *excessively* find r_E shooting up faster than MM predict. Consequently, the weighted-average cost of capital r_A declines at first, then rises. Its minimum point is the point of optimal capital structure. Remember that minimizing r_A is equivalent to maximizing overall firm value if, as the traditionalists assume, operating income is unaffected by borrowing.

Two arguments might be advanced in support of the traditional position. First, it could be that investors don't notice or appreciate the financial risk created by

---

[12]We ignore the costs, delays, and other complications of bankruptcy. They are discussed in Chapter 18.

[13]This case is often termed the *net-income* (NI) approach because investors are assumed to capitalize income *after* interest at the same rate regardless of financial leverage. In contrast, MM's approach is a net-operating-income (NOI) approach because the value of the firm is fundamentally determined by operating income, the total dollar return to *both* bondholders and stockholders. This distinction was emphasized by Durand in his important, pre-MM paper (op. cit.).

Figure 17-5 The dashed lines show MM's view of the effect of leverage on the expected return on equity r_E and the weighted-average cost of capital r_A. (See Figure 17-2.) The solid lines show the traditional view. Traditionalists say that borrowing at first increases r_E more slowly than MM predict but that r_E shoots up with excessive borrowing. If so, the weighted-average cost of capital can be minimized if you use just the right amount of debt.

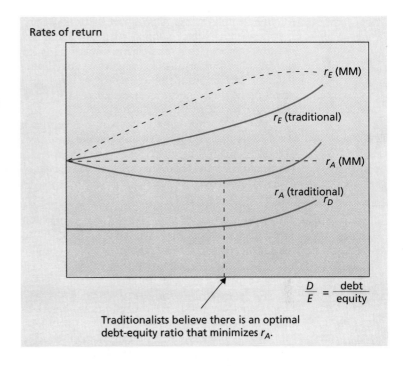

"moderate" borrowing, although they wake up when debt is "excessive." If so, investors in moderately leveraged firms may accept a lower rate of return than they really should.

That seems naive.[14] The second argument is better. It accepts MM's reasoning as applied to perfect capital markets but holds that actual markets are imperfect. Imperfections may allow firms that borrow to provide a valuable service for investors. If so, levered shares might trade at premium prices compared to their theoretical values in perfect markets.

Suppose that corporations can borrow more cheaply than individuals. Then it would pay investors who want to borrow to do so indirectly by holding the stock of levered firms. They would be willing to live with expected rates of return that do not fully compensate them for the business and financial risk they bear.

Is corporate borrowing really cheaper? It's hard to say. Interest rates on home mortgages are not too different from rates on high-grade corporate bonds.[15] Rates on margin debt (borrowing from a stockbroker with the investor's shares tendered as security) are not too different from the rates firms pay banks for short-term loans.

There are some individuals who face relatively high interest rates, largely because of the costs lenders incur in making and servicing small loans. There are economies

---

[14]This first argument may reflect a confusion between financial risk and the risk of default. Default is not a serious threat when borrowing is moderate; stockholders worry about it only when the firm goes "too far." But stockholders bear financial risk—in the form of increased volatility of rate of return and higher beta—even when the chance of default is nil. We demonstrated this in Figure 17-3.

[15]One of the authors once obtained a home mortgage at a rate ½ percentage point *less* than the contemporaneous yield on long-term AT&T bonds.

of scale in borrowing. A group of small investors could do better by borrowing via a corporation, in effect pooling their loans and saving transaction costs.[16]

But suppose that this class of investors is large, both in number and in the aggregate wealth it brings to capital markets. Shouldn't the investors' needs be fully satisfied by the thousands of levered firms already existing? Is there really an unsatisfied clientele of small investors standing ready to pay a premium for one more firm that borrows?

Maybe the market for corporate leverage is like the market for automobiles. Americans need millions of automobiles and are willing to pay thousands of dollars apiece for them. But that doesn't mean that you could strike it rich by going into the automobile business. You're at least 50 years too late.

Where to Look for Violations of MM's Propositions

MM's propositions depend on perfect capital markets. Here we are using the phrase *perfect capital markets* a bit loosely, for scholars have argued about the *degree* of perfection necessary for proposition I. (We remember an off-the-cuff comment made many years ago by Ezra Solomon: "A perfect capital market should be *defined* as one in which the MM theory holds.")

We believe capital markets are generally well-functioning, but they are not 100 percent perfect 100 percent of the time. Therefore, MM must be wrong some times in some places. The financial manager's problem is to figure out when and where.

That is not easy. Just finding market imperfections is insufficient.

Consider the traditionalists' claim that imperfections make borrowing costly and inconvenient for many individuals. That creates a clientele for whom corporate borrowing is better than personal borrowing. That clientele would, in principle, be willing to pay a premium for the shares of a levered firm.

But maybe it doesn't *have* to pay a premium. Perhaps smart financial managers long ago recognized this clientele and shifted the capital structures of their firms to meet its needs. The shifts would not have been difficult or costly to make. But if the clientele is now satisfied, it is no longer willing to pay a premium for levered shares. Only the financial managers who *first* recognized the clientele extracted any advantage from it.

Today's Unsatisfied Clienteles Are Probably Interested in Exotic Securities

So far we have made little progress in identifying cases where firm value might plausibly depend on financing. But our examples illustrate what smart financial managers look for. They look for an *unsatisfied* clientele, investors who want a particular kind of financial instrument but because of market imperfections can't get it or can't get it cheaply.

MM's proposition I is violated when the firm, by imaginative design of its capital structure, can offer some *financial service* that meets the needs of such a clientele. Either the service must be new and unique or the firm must find a way to provide some old service more cheaply than other firms or financial intermediaries can.

Now, is there an unsatisfied clientele for garden-variety debt or levered equity? We doubt it. But perhaps you can invent an exotic security and uncover a latent demand for it.

---

[16]Even here there are alternatives to borrowing on personal account. Investors can draw down their savings accounts or sell a portion of their investment in bonds. The impact of reductions in lending on the investor's balance sheet and risk position is exactly the same as increases in borrowing.

Inventing exotic securities is easy; finding investors who will rush to buy them is not. Here is an example of a recent, unsuccessful attempt to launch a new security: In 1988 Pfizer announced that it would replace part of its common stock with *unbundled stock units* (USUs).[17] Pfizer reasoned that when you buy a stock, you are effectively buying a package containing three components: (1) the current stream of dividend income, (2) possible *increases* in the dividend stream, and (3) any capital appreciation. The idea of USUs was to allow you to buy any combination of these three components.

The plan worked as follows. Each shareholder could exchange his or her stock for three new securities:

1. A 30-year *base yield bond* which would pay the investor the equivalent of the current dividend on the share

2. An *incremental dividend preferred share* which would give the holder any future increases in dividends on the share

After 30 years the first two securities would have been paid off by Pfizer for a total of $152.50. If Pfizer's stock price goes above $152.50, the third part of the USU package kicks in:

3. An *equity appreciation certificate* would give the holder the option at any time during the next 30 years to buy a share of common stock at a fixed price of $152.50. Thus the equity appreciation certificate would benefit from any appreciation in Pfizer's share price above $152.50.[18]

Unbundled stock units were the brainchild of the investment bank Shearson Lehman Hutton. Shearson hoped that investors would find the sum of the parts more attractive than a share of stock. As Shearson's managing director pointed out, "If you want to break up the parcel, you can. If you are interested in capital appreciation, you can get that. If you are after current yield, you can get that."[19]

Unbundled stock units provided a real-world test of MM. If shareholders had rushed to convert their stock to USUs, then you would have found a counterexample to MM's proposition I. Pfizer could have increased its overall market value by issuing a package of bonds, preferred stock, and options rather than garden-variety common stock.

But that was not the way things turned out. Shareholders were unimpressed. Two months later in an embarrassing and expensive U-turn Shearson announced that Pfizer had decided not to go ahead. MM's proposition I had survived intact.[20]

---

[17]Other companies announcing USUs at the same time were Dow Chemical, American Express, and Sara Lee. For an analysis of USUs, see J. D. Finnerty and V. M. Borun, "An Analysis of Unbundled Stock Units," *Global Finance Journal*, **1**:47–70 (Fall 1989).

[18]Suppose you hold the entire package for 30 years. You receive the current dividend on the share plus any increases in the dividend. Then at the end of 30 years you can buy the shares with the $152.50 that you receive from repayment of the bond and the preferred stock. But you are not *obliged* to do so. If the share price is below $152.50, you can just hold onto the cash.

[19]Quoted in "Eureka! A Capital Solution," *Corporate Finance*, **50**:5–6 (January 1989).

[20]There were a number of practical problems that Shearson had not ironed out. For example, the Securities and Exchange Commission objected to the loss of voting rights. There was also a tax wrinkle. Shareholders who exchanged their stock for USUs would be considered to have sold the stock and therefore would be taxed on any capital gains.

General Motors' Percs

The failure of USUs did not mark an end to the search for new ways to package equity returns. In 1991 Morgan Stanley announced that it was helping General Motors to raise over $600 million through the sale of *percs* (preferred equity redemption cumulative stock). If you bought a GM perc, you earned a fixed dividend yield of 8 percent for 3 years, well above the 4.9 percent yield on the common stock. At the end of the 3 years your percs were automatically converted into shares of common stock, but there was a limit on the value of the shares that you received. You participated fully in the appreciation of the common stock up to a maximum of 30 percent. Beyond that point, the more the shares rose in price, the fewer shares you obtained.

Percs had many of the features of USUs but proved to be more popular. Within a year nearly $5 billion had been issued. However, the demand was soon satisfied and issues of percs shrank to a trickle.

Imperfections and Opportunities

The most serious capital market imperfections are often those created by government. An imperfection which supports a violation of MM's proposition I *also* creates a money-making opportunity. Firms and financial intermediaries will find some way to reach the clientele of investors frustrated by the imperfection.

For many years the United States government imposed a limit on the rate of interest that could be paid on savings accounts. It did so in order to protect savings institutions by limiting competition for their depositors' money. The fear was that depositors would run off in search of higher yields, causing a cash drain that savings institutions would not be able to meet. This would cut off the supply of funds from those institutions for new real estate mortgages and knock the housing market for a loop. The savings institutions could not have afforded to offer higher interest rates on deposits—even if the government had allowed them to—because most of their past deposits had been locked up in fixed-rate mortgages issued when interest rates were much lower.

These regulations created an opportunity for firms and financial institutions to design new savings schemes that were not subject to the interest-rate ceilings. One invention was the *floating-rate note*, first issued on a large scale and with terms designed to appeal to individual investors by Citicorp in July 1974. Floating-rate notes are medium-term debt securities whose interest payments "float" with short-term interest rates. On the Citicorp issue, for example, the coupon rate used to calculate each semiannual interest payment was set at 1 percentage point above the contemporaneous yield on Treasury bills. The holder of the Citicorp note was therefore protected against fluctuating interest rates, because Citicorp sent a larger semiannual check when interest rates rose (and, of course, a smaller check when rates fell).

Citicorp evidently found an untapped clientele of investors, for it was able to raise $650 million in the first offering. The success of the issue suggests that Citicorp was able to add value by changing its capital structure. However, other companies were quick to jump on Citicorp's bandwagon, and within 5 months an additional $650 million of floating-rate notes was issued by other companies. By the mid-1980s about $43 billion of floating-rate securities was outstanding, though by that time the interest-rate ceiling was no longer a motive.[21]

Interest-rate regulation also provided financial institutions with an opportunity to create value by offering money-market funds. These are mutual funds invested in Treasury bills, commercial paper, and other high-grade, short-term debt instruments.

---

[21]A good review of the development of the floating-rate note market is by R. S. Wilson, "Domestic Floating-Rate and Adjustable Rate Debt Securities," in F. J. Fabozzi and T. D. Fabozzi (eds.), *Handbook of Fixed Income Securities*, 4th ed., Dow-Jones Irwin, Homewood, Ill., 1995.

Any saver with a few thousand dollars to invest can gain access to these instruments through a money-market fund and can withdraw money at any time by writing a check against his or her fund balance. Thus the fund resembles a checking or savings account which pays close to market interest rates.[22] These money-market funds have become enormously popular. By 1994, their assets had increased to $450 billion.

As floating-rate notes, money-market funds, and other instruments became more easily available, the protection given by government restrictions on savings account rates became less and less helpful. Finally the restrictions were lifted, and savings institutions met their competition head-on.

Long before interest-rate ceilings were finally removed, most of the gains had gone out of issuing new high-yield securities to individual investors. Once the clientele was finally satisfied, MM's proposition I was restored (until the government creates a new imperfection). The moral of the story is this: If you ever find an unsatisfied clientele, do something right away, or capital markets will evolve and steal it from you.

17-4   SUMMARY

At the start of this chapter we characterized the firm's financing decision as a marketing problem. Think of the financial manager as taking all the firm's real assets and selling them to investors as a package of securities. Some financial managers choose the simplest package possible: all-equity financing. Some end up issuing dozens of debt and equity securities. The problem is to find the particular combination that maximizes the market value of the firm.

Modigliani and Miller's (MM's) famous proposition I states that no combination is better than any other—that the firm's overall market value (the value of all its securities) is independent of capital structure. Firms that borrow do offer investors a more complex menu of securities, but investors yawn in response. The menu is redundant. Any shift in capital structure can be duplicated or "undone" by investors. Why should they pay extra for borrowing indirectly (by holding shares in a levered firm) when they can borrow just as easily and cheaply on their own accounts?

MM agree that borrowing increases the expected rate of return on shareholders' investment. But it also increases the risk of the firm's shares. MM show that the risk increase exactly offsets the increase in expected return, leaving stockholders no better or worse off.

Proposition I is an extremely general result. It applies not just to the debt-equity trade-off but to *any* choice of financing instruments. For example, MM would say that the choice between long-term and short-term debt has no effect on firm value.

The formal proofs of proposition I all depend on the assumption of perfect capital markets.[23] MM's opponents, the "traditionalists," argue that market imperfections make personal borrowing excessively costly, risky, and inconvenient for some investors. This creates a natural clientele willing to pay a premium for shares of levered firms. The traditionalists say that firms should borrow to realize the premium.

---

[22]Money-market funds offer rates slightly lower than those on the securities they invest in. This spread covers the fund's operating costs and profits.

[23]Proposition I can be proved umpteen different ways. The references at the end of this chapter include several more abstract and general proofs. Our formal proofs have been limited to MM's own arguments and (in the appendix to this chapter) a proof based on the capital asset pricing model.

But this argument is incomplete. There may be a clientele for levered equity, but that is not enough; the clientele has to be *unsatisfied*. There are already thousands of levered firms available for investment. Is there still an unsatiated clientele for garden-variety debt and equity? We doubt it.

Proposition I is violated when financial managers find an untapped demand and satisfy it by issuing something new and different. The argument between MM and the traditionalists finally boils down to whether this is difficult or easy. We lean toward MM's view: Finding unsatisfied clienteles and designing exotic securities to meet their needs is a game that's fun to play but hard to win.

APPENDIX: MM AND THE CAPITAL ASSET PRICING MODEL

We showed in Section 17-2 that, as the firm increases its leverage, the expected equity return goes up in lockstep with beta of the equity. Given this, it should be no surprise to find that we can use the capital asset pricing model to derive MM's proposition I. The following demonstration has been simplified by assuming that the firm can issue risk-free debt.

The firm is initially all-equity-financed. Its expected end-of-period value is V_1, which we take to include any operating income for the initial period. We now draw on the certainty-equivalent form of the capital asset pricing model which we derived in the appendix to Chapter 9. This states that the present value of the firm is

$$V = E = \frac{V_1 - \lambda \, \text{Cov}(\tilde{V}_1, \tilde{r}_m)}{1 + r_f}$$

where λ is the market price of risk $(r_m - r_f)/\sigma_m^2$.

Now suppose that the firm borrows D at the risk-free rate of interest and distributes the proceeds to stockholders. They get D dollars now but next year they will have to repay the debt with interest. Therefore instead of receiving V_1 at the end of the year, they can expect to receive only $V_1 - (1 + r_f)D$. The present value of their levered equity is

$$E = \frac{V_1 - (1 + r_f)D - \lambda \, \text{Cov}[\tilde{V}_1 - (1 + r_f)D, \ \tilde{r}_m]}{1 + r_f}$$

But since $(1 + r_f)D$ is known, it has no effect on the covariance. When debt is risk-free, stockholders have to bear *all* the risk associated with V_1. Therefore, we substitute $\text{Cov}(\tilde{V}_1, \tilde{r}_m)$ for $\text{Cov}[\tilde{V}_1 - (1 + r_f)D, \tilde{r}_m]$. This gives us

$$E = \frac{V_1 - (1 + r_f)D - \lambda \, \text{Cov}(\tilde{V}_1, \tilde{r}_m)}{1 + r_f}$$

$$= \frac{V_1 - \lambda \, \text{Cov}(\tilde{V}_1, \tilde{r}_m)}{1 + r_f} - D$$

To calculate the value of the *firm* we add the value of the debt D. This gives

$$V = \frac{V_1 - \lambda \, \text{Cov}(\tilde{V}_1, \tilde{r}_m)}{1 + r_f}$$

The value of the levered firm is identical to the value of the unlevered firm.

Further Reading

The pioneering work on the theory of capital structure is:
F. Modigliani and M. H. Miller: "The Cost of Capital, Corporation Finance and the Theory of Investment," *American Economic Review*, **48**:261–297 (June 1958).

However, Durand deserves credit for setting out the issues that MM later solved:
D. Durand: "Cost of Debt and Equity Funds for Business: Trends and Problems in Measurement," in *Conference on Research in Business Finance*, National Bureau of Economic Research, New York, 1952, pp. 215–247.

MM provided a shorter and clearer proof of capital structure irrelevance in:
F. Modigliani and M. H. Miller: "Reply to Heins and Sprenkle," *American Economic Review*, **59**:592–595 (September 1969).

A somewhat difficult article which analyzes capital structure in the context of capital asset pricing theory is:
R. S. Hamada: "Portfolio Analysis, Market Equilibrium and Corporation Finance," *Journal of Finance*, **24**:13–31 (March 1969).

More abstract and general theoretical treatments can be found in:
J. E. Stiglitz: "On the Irrelevance of Corporate Financial Policy," *American Economic Review*, **64**:851–866 (December 1974).
E. F. Fama: "The Effects of a Firm's Investment and Financing Decisions," *American Economic Review*, **68**:272–284 (June 1978).

The fall 1988 issue of the Journal of Economic Perspectives *contains an anniversary collection of articles, including one by Modigliani and Miller, which review and assess the MM propositions. The summer 1989 issue of* Financial Management *contains three more articles under the heading "Reflections on the MM Propositions 30 Years Later."*

Quiz

1. Assume a perfectly competitive market with no corporate or personal taxes. Companies A and B each earn gross profits of P and differ only in their capital structure—A is wholly equity-financed and B has debt outstanding on which it pays a certain $100 of interest each year. Investor X purchases 10 percent of the equity of A.
   (*a*) What profits does X obtain?
   (*b*) What alternative strategy would provide the same result?
   (*c*) Suppose investor Y purchases 10 percent of the equity of B. What profits does Y obtain?
   (*d*) What alternative strategy would provide the same result?

2. Ms. Kraft owns 50,000 shares of the common stock of Copperhead Corporation with a market value of $2 per share, or $100,000 overall. The company is currently financed as follows:

	Book Value
Common stock (8 million shares)	$2,000,000
Short-term loans	$2,000,000

Copperhead now announces that it is replacing $1 million of short-term debt with an issue of common stock. What action can Ms. Kraft take to ensure that she is entitled to exactly the same proportion of profits as before? (Ignore taxes.)

3. The common stock and debt of Northern Sludge are valued at $50 million and $30 million, respectively. Investors currently require a 16 percent return on the common stock and an 8 percent return on the debt. If Northern Sludge issues an additional $10 million of common stock and uses this money to retire debt, what happens to the expected return on the stock? Assume that the change in capital structure does not affect the risk of the debt and that there are no taxes. If the risk of the debt did change, would your answer underestimate or overestimate the expected return on the stock?

4. Company C is financed entirely by common stock and has a β of 1.0. The stock has a price-earnings multiple of 10 and is priced to offer a 10 percent expected return. The company decides to repurchase half the common stock and substitute an equal value of debt. Assume that the debt yields a risk-free 5 percent.
   (*a*) Give:
      (**i**) The beta of the common stock after the refinancing.
      (**ii**) The beta of the debt.
      (**iii**) The beta of the company (i.e., stock and debt combined).
   (*b*) Give:
      (**i**) The required return on the common stock before the refinancing.
      (**ii**) The required return on the common stock after the refinancing.
      (**iii**) The required return on the debt.
      (**iv**) The required return on the company (i.e., stock and debt combined) after the refinancing.
   (*c*) Assume that the operating profit of firm C is expected to remain constant. Give:
      (**i**) The percentage increase in earnings per share.
      (**ii**) The new price-earnings multiple.

5. Suppose that Macbeth Spot Removers issues $2500 of debt and uses the proceeds to repurchase 250 shares.
   (*a*) Rework Table 17-2 to show how earnings per share and share return now vary with operating income.
   (*b*) If the beta of Macbeth's assets is .8 and its debt is risk-free, what would be the beta of the equity after the increased borrowing?

6. True or false? Explain briefly.
   (*a*) Stockholders always benefit from an increase in company value.
   (*b*) MM's proposition I assumes that actions which maximize firm value also maximize shareholder wealth.
   (*c*) The reason that borrowing increases equity risk is because it increases the probability of bankruptcy.
   (*d*) If firms did not have limited liability, the risk of their assets would be increased.
   (*e*) If firms did not have limited liability, the risk of their equity would be increased.
   (*f*) Borrowing does not affect the return on equity if the return on the firm's assets is equal to the interest rate.
   (*g*) As long as the firm is certain that the return on assets will be higher than the interest rate, an issue of debt makes the shareholders better off.
   (*h*) MM's proposition I implies that an issue of debt increases expected earnings per share and leads to an offsetting fall in the price-earnings ratio.

(**i**) MM's proposition II assumes increased borrowing does not affect the interest rate on the firm's debt.

(**j**) Borrowing increases firm value if there is a clientele of investors with a reason to prefer debt.

7. Note the two blank graphs in Figure 17-6. On graph (**a**), assume MM are right, and plot the relationship between financial leverage and (i) the rates of return on debt and equity and (ii) the weighted-average cost of capital. Then fill in graph (**b**), assuming the traditionalists are right.

8. Look back to Section 17-1. Suppose that Ms. Macbeth's investment bankers have informed her that since the new issue of debt is risky, debtholders will demand a return of 12.5 percent, which is 2.5 percent above the risk-free interest rate.

(**a**) What are r_A and r_E?

(**b**) Suppose that the beta of the unlevered stock was .6. What will be β_A, β_E, and β_D *after* the change to the capital structure?

(**c**) Assuming that the capital asset pricing model is correct, what is the expected return on the market?

9. Capitale Netto s.a. is financed solely by common stock, which offers an expected return of 13 percent. Suppose now that the company issues debt and repurchases stock so that its debt ratio is .4. Investors note the extra risk and raise their required return on the stock to 15 percent.

(**a**) What is the interest rate on the debt?

(**b**) If the debt is risk-free and the beta of the equity after the refinancing is 1.5, what is the expected return on the market?

10. Executive Chalk is financed solely by common stock and has outstanding 25 million shares with a market price of $10 a share. It now announces that it intends to issue $160 million of debt and to use the proceeds to buy back common stock.

(**a**) How is the market price of the stock affected by the announcement?

(**b**) How many shares can the company buy back with the $160 million of new debt that it issues?

(**c**) What is the market value of the firm (equity plus debt) after the change in capital structure?

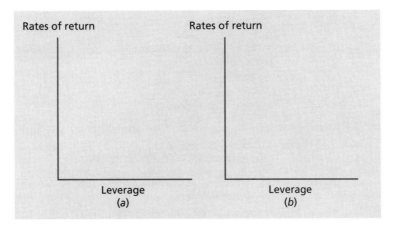

Figure 17-6 See Quiz question 7.

(**d**) What is the debt ratio after the change in structure?

(**e**) Who (if anyone) gains or loses?

Now try the next question.

11. Executive Cheese has issued debt with a market value of $100 million and has outstanding 15 million shares with a market price of $10 a share. It now announces that it intends to issue a further $60 million of debt and to use the proceeds to buy back common stock. Debtholders, seeing the extra risk, mark the value of the existing debt down to $70 million.

(**a**) How is the market price of the stock affected by the announcement?

(**b**) How many shares can the company buy back with the $50 million of new debt that it issues?

(**c**) What is the market value of the firm (equity plus debt) after the change in capital structure?

(**d**) What is the debt ratio after the change in structure?

(**e**) Who (if anyone) gains or loses?

Questions and Problems

1. Companies A and B differ only in their capital structure. A is financed 30 percent debt and 70 percent equity; B is financed 10 percent debt and 90 percent equity. The debt of both companies is risk-free.

(**a**) Mr. X owns 1 percent of the common stock of A. What other investment package would produce identical cash flows for Mr. X?

(**b**) Mrs. Y owns 2 percent of the common stock of B. What other investment package would produce identical cash flows for Mrs. Y?

(**c**) Show that neither Mr. X nor Mrs. Y would invest in the common stock of B if the *total* value of company A were less than that of B.

2. Hubbard's Pet Foods is financed 80 percent by common stock and 20 percent by bonds. The expected return on the common stock is 12 percent and the rate of interest on the bonds is 6 percent. Assuming that the bonds are default-free, draw a graph that shows the expected return of Hubbard's common stock r_E and the expected return on the package of common stock and bonds r_A for different debt-equity ratios.

3. Here is a limerick:

There once was a man named Carruthers,
Who kept cows with miraculous udders.
He said, "Isn't this neat?
They give cream from one teat,
And skim milk from each of the others!"

What is the analogy between Mr. Carruthers's cows and firms' financing decisions? What would MM's proposition I, suitably adapted, say about the value of Mr. Carruthers's cows? Explain.

4. "MM totally ignore the fact that as you borrow more, you have to pay higher rates of interest." Explain carefully whether this is a valid objection.

5. Indicate what's wrong with the following arguments:

(**a**) "As the firm borrows more and debt becomes risky, both stock- and bondholders demand higher rates of return. Thus by *reducing* the debt ratio we can reduce *both* the cost of debt and the cost of equity, making everybody better off."

(*b*) "Moderate borrowing doesn't significantly affect the probability of financial distress or bankruptcy. Consequently moderate borrowing won't increase the expected rate of return demanded by stockholders."

6. Each of the following statements is false or at least misleading. Explain why in each case.

(*a*) "A capital investment opportunity offering a 10 percent DCF rate of return is an attractive project if it can be 100 percent debt-financed at an 8 percent interest rate."

(*b*) "The more debt the firm issues, the higher the interest rate it must pay. That is one important reason why firms should operate at conservative debt levels."

7. Can you invent any new kinds of debt that might be attractive to investors? Why do you think they have not been issued?

8. It has been suggested that one disadvantage of common stock financing is that share prices tend to decline in recessions, thereby increasing the cost of capital and deterring investment. Discuss this view. Is it an argument for greater use of debt financing?

9. People often convey the idea behind MM's proposition I by various supermarket analogies, for example, "The value of a pie should not depend on how it is sliced," or, "The cost of a whole chicken should equal the cost of assembling one by buying two drumsticks, two wings, two breasts, and so on."

   Actually proposition I doesn't work in the supermarket. You'll pay less for an uncut whole pie than for a pie assembled from pieces purchased separately. Supermarkets charge more for chickens after they are cut up.

   Why? What costs or imperfections cause proposition I to fail in the supermarket? Are these costs or imperfections likely to be important for corporations issuing securities on the United States or world capital market? Explain.

10. Figure 17-5 shows that r_D increases as the debt-equity ratio increases. In MM's world r_E also increases but at a declining rate.

(*a*) Explain why.

(*b*) Redraw Figure 17-5, showing how r_D and r_E change for increasingly high debt-equity ratios. Can r_D ever be higher than r_A? Can r_E decline beyond a certain debt-equity ratio?

11. Imagine a firm that is expected to produce a level stream of operating profits. As leverage is increased, what happens to:

(*a*) The ratio of the market value of the equity to income after interest

(*b*) The ratio of the market value of the *firm* to income before interest if (i) MM are right and (ii) the traditionalists are right?

12. The proposed unbundled stock units of American Express would have allowed shareholders to exchange 25 percent of their shares for USUs. Each share exchanged would give the shareholder a package of three securities:

■ *Part 1:* There was a 30-year base yield bond with a face value of $75. The American Express share price was about $28. The base yield bond would receive the then-current dividend of $.84 per year.

■ *Part 2:* An incremental dividend depository preferred would receive any dividend increase over $.84.

■ *Part 3:* An equity appreciation certificate would allow its holder to purchase one American Express share for $75, the face value of the base yield bond. This was to be an opportunity, not an obligation. One preferred share (part 2 of the USU package) had to be turned in in order to buy the share of common stock.

The USUs would give no voting rights. However, they could be converted back to common shares in the event of a takeover of American Express.

Of course, the USUs were never issued. But suppose they had been.

(*a*) Would one USU be worth more or less than one share?

(*b*) Would you have accepted the exchange offer?

(*c*) Why do you think USUs failed to excite investors' interest?

13. Archimedes Levers is financed by a mixture of debt and equity. You have the following information about its cost of capital:

$$r_E = \underline{\hspace{1cm}} \qquad r_D = 12\% \qquad r_A = \underline{\hspace{1cm}}$$
$$\beta_E = 1.5 \qquad \beta_D = \underline{\hspace{1cm}} \qquad \beta_A = \underline{\hspace{1cm}}$$
$$r_f = 10\% \qquad r_m = 18\% \qquad D/V = .5$$

Can you fill in the blanks?

14. Look back at question 13. Suppose now that Archimedes repurchases debt and issues equity so that $D/V = .3$. The reduced borrowing causes r_D to fall to 11 percent. How do the other variables change?

15. Schuldenfrei a.g. pays no taxes and is financed entirely by common stock. The stock has a beta of .8 and a price-earnings ratio of 12.5 and is priced to offer an 8 percent expected return. Schuldenfrei now decides to repurchase half the common stock and substitute an equal value of debt. If the debt yields a *risk-free* 5 percent, calculate:

(*a*) The beta of the common stock after the refinancing.

(*b*) The required return and risk premium on the stock before the refinancing.

(*c*) The required return and risk premium on the stock after the refinancing.

(*d*) The required return on the debt.

(*e*) The required return on the company (i.e., stock and debt combined) after the refinancing.

Assume that the operating profit of the firm is expected to remain constant in perpetuity. Give:

(*f*) The percentage increase in expected earnings per share.

(*g*) The new price-earnings multiple.

16. Gamma Airlines is currently all-equity financed, and its shares offer an expected return of 18 percent. The risk-free interest rate is 10 percent. Draw a graph with return on the vertical axis and debt-equity ratio *(D/E)* on the horizontal axis, and plot for different levels of leverage the expected return on assets (r_A), the expected return on equity (r_E), and the return on debt (r_D). Assume that the debt is risk-free. Now draw a similar graph with the debt ratio *(D/V)* on the horizontal axis.

17. Consider the following three tickets: ticket A pays $10 if _____ is elected as president, ticket B pays $10 if _____ is elected, and ticket C pays $10 if neither is elected. (Fill in the blanks yourself.) Could the three tickets sell for less

than the present value of $10? Could they sell for more? Try auctioning off the tickets. What are the implications for MM's proposition I?

18. Two firms, U and L, are identical except for their capital structure. Both will earn $150 in a boom and $50 in a slump. There is a 50 percent chance of each event. U is entirely equity-financed, and therefore shareholders receive the entire income. Its shares are valued at $500. L has issued $400 of risk-free debt at an interest rate of 10 percent, and therefore $40 of L's income is paid out as interest. There are no taxes or other market imperfections. Investors can borrow and lend at the risk-free rate of interest.

   (*a*) What is the value of L's stock?

   (*b*) Suppose that you invest $20 in U's stock. Is there an alternative investment in L that would give identical payoffs in boom and slump? What is the expected payoff from such a strategy?

   (*c*) Now suppose that you invest $20 in L's stock. Design an alternative strategy with identical payoffs.

   (*d*) Now show that MM's proposition II holds.

18

How Much Should a Firm Borrow?

In Chapter 17 we found that debt policy rarely matters in well-functioning capital markets. Few financial managers would accept that conclusion as a practical guideline. If debt policy doesn't matter, then they shouldn't worry about it—financing decisions should be delegated to underlings. Yet financial managers do worry about debt policy. This chapter explains why.

If debt policy were *completely* irrelevant, then actual debt ratios should vary randomly from firm to firm and industry to industry. Yet almost all airlines, utilities, banks, and real estate development companies rely heavily on debt. And so do many firms in capital-intensive industries like steel, aluminum, chemicals, petroleum, and mining. On the other hand, it is rare to find a drug company or advertising agency that is not predominantly equity-financed. Glamorous "growth" companies like Genentech, Hewlett-Packard, and Merck rarely use much debt despite rapid expansion and often heavy requirements for capital.

The explanation of these patterns lies partly in the things we left out of the last chapter. We ignored taxes. We assumed bankruptcy was cheap, quick, and painless. It isn't, and there are costs associated with financial distress even if legal bankruptcy is ultimately avoided. We ignored potential conflicts of interest between the firm's security holders. For example, we did not consider what happens to the firm's "old" creditors when new debt is issued or when a shift in investment strategy takes the firm into a riskier business. We ignored the information problems that favor debt over equity when cash must be raised from new security issues. We ignored the incentive effects of financial leverage on management's investment and payout decisions.

Now we will put all these things back in: taxes first, then the costs of bankruptcy and financial distress. This will lead us to conflicts of interest and to information and incentive problems. In the end we will have to admit that debt policy *does* matter.

However, we will *not* throw away the MM theory we developed so carefully in Chapter 17. We're shooting for a theory combining MM's insights *plus* the effects of taxes, costs of bankruptcy and financial distress, and various other complications. We're not dropping back to the traditional view based on imperfections in the capital market. Instead, we want to see how well-functioning capital markets *respond* to taxes and the other things covered in this chapter.

TABLE 18-1

The tax deductibility of interest increases the total income that can be paid out to bondholders and stockholders.

	Income Statement of Firm U	Income Statement of Firm L
Earnings before interest and taxes	$1,000	$1,000
Interest paid to bondholders	0	80
Pretax income	1,000	920
Tax at 35%	350	322
Net income to stockholders	$ 650	$ 598
Total income to both bondholders and stockholders	$0 + 650 = $650	$80 + 598 = $678
Interest tax shield (.35 × interest)	$0	$28

18-1 CORPORATE TAXES

Debt financing has one important advantage under the corporate income tax system in the United States. The interest that the company pays is a tax-deductible expense. Dividends and retained earnings are not. Thus the return to bondholders escapes taxation at the corporate level.

Table 18-1 shows simple income statements for firm U, which has no debt, and firm L, which has borrowed $1000 at 8 percent. The tax bill of L is $28 less than that of U. This is the *tax shield* provided by the debt of L. In effect the government pays 35 percent of the interest expense of L. The total income that L can pay out to its bondholders and stockholders increases by that amount.

Tax shields can be valuable assets. Suppose that the debt of L is fixed and permanent. (That is, the company commits to refinance its present debt obligations when they mature and to keep "rolling over" its debt obligations indefinitely.) It looks forward to a permanent stream of cash flows of $28 per year. The risk of these flows is likely to be less than the risk of the operating assets of L. The tax shields depend only on the corporate tax rate[1] and on the ability of L to earn enough to cover interest payments. The corporate tax rate has been pretty stable. (It did fall from 46 to 34 percent after the Tax Reform Act of 1986, but that was the first material change since the 1950s.) And the ability of L to earn its interest payments must be reasonably sure—otherwise it could not have borrowed at 8 percent.[2] Therefore we should discount the interest tax shields at a relatively low rate.

---

[1]Always use the marginal corporate tax rate, not the average rate. For large corporations the marginal tax rate was 35 percent when this chapter was written (1995). Average rates were often much less than that because of accelerated depreciation and various other adjustments.

[2]If the income of L does not cover interest in some future year, the tax shield is not necessarily lost. L can "carry back" the loss and receive a tax refund up to the amount of taxes paid in the previous 3 years. If L has a string of losses, and thus no prior tax payments that can be refunded, then losses can be "carried forward" and used to shield income in subsequent years.

But what rate? The most common assumption is that the risk of the tax shields is the same as that of the interest payments generating them. Thus we discount at 8 percent, the expected rate of return demanded by investors who are holding the firm's debt:

$$PV(\text{tax shield}) = \frac{28}{.08} = \$350$$

In effect the government itself assumes 35 percent of the $1000 debt obligation of L.

Under these assumptions, the present value of the tax shield is independent of the return on the debt r_D. It equals the corporate tax rate T_c times the amount borrowed D:

$$\text{Interest payment} = \text{return on debt} \times \text{amount borrowed}$$

$$= r_D \times D$$

$$PV(\text{tax shield}) = \frac{\text{corporate tax rate} \times \text{expected interest payment}}{}$$

$$= \frac{T_c(r_D D)}{r_D} = T_c D$$

Of course, PV(tax shield) is less if the firm does not plan to borrow permanently, or if it may not be able to use the tax shields in the future.

How Do Interest Tax Shields Contribute to the Value of Stockholders' Equity?	MM's proposition I amounts to saying that "the value of a pie does not depend on how it is sliced." The pie is the firm's assets, and the slices are the debt and equity claims. If we hold the pie constant, then a dollar more of debt means a dollar less of equity value. But there is really a third slice, the government's. Look at Table 18-2. It shows an *expanded* balance sheet with *pretax* asset value on the left and the value of the government's tax claim recognized as a liability on the right. MM would still say that the value of the pie—in this case *pretax* asset value—is not changed by slicing. But anything the firm can do to reduce the size of the government's slice obviously makes stockholders better off. One thing it can do is borrow money, which reduces its tax bill and, as we saw in Table 18-1, increases the cash flows to debt and equity investors. The *after-tax* value of the firm (the sum of its debt and equity values as shown in a normal market value balance sheet) goes up by PV(tax shield).
Recasting Merck's Capital Structure	Merck & Company is a large, successful firm that uses essentially no long-term debt. Table 18-3a shows simplified book and market value balance sheets for Merck as of year-end 1994. Suppose that you were Merck's financial manager in 1994 with complete responsibility for its capital structure. You decide to borrow $1 billion on a permanent basis and use the proceeds to repurchase shares. Table 18-3b shows the new balance sheets. The book version simply has $1000 million more long-term debt and $1000 million less equity. But we know that Merck's assets must be worth more, for its tax bill has been reduced by 35 percent of the interest on the new debt. In other words, Merck has an increase in PV(tax shield), which is worth $T_c D = .35 \times 1000 = \$350$ million. If the MM theory holds *except* for taxes, firm value must increase by $350 million to $53,035 million. Merck's equity ends up worth $46,766 million.

TABLE 18-2
••

Normal and expanded market value balance sheets. In a normal balance sheet, assets are valued after tax. In the expanded balance sheet, assets are valued pretax, and the value of the government's tax claim is recognized on the right-hand side. Interest tax shields are valuable because they reduce the government's claim.

Normal Balance Sheet (Market Values)

Asset value (present value of after-tax cash flows)	Debt
	Equity
Total assets	Total liabilities

Expanded Balance Sheet (Market Values)

Pretax asset value (present value of *pretax* cash flows)	Debt
	Government's claim (present value of future taxes)
	Equity
Total pretax assets	Total liabilities

Now you have repurchased $1000 million worth of shares, but Merck's equity value has dropped by only $650 million. Therefore Merck's stockholders must be $350 million ahead. Not a bad day's work.[3]

MM and Taxes

We have just developed a version of MM's proposition I as "corrected" by them to reflect corporate income taxes.[4] The new proposition is

$$\text{Value of firm} = \text{value if all-equity-financed} + \text{PV(tax shield)}$$

In the special case of permanent debt,

$$\text{Value of firm} = \text{value if all-equity-financed} + T_c D$$

Our imaginary financial surgery on Merck provides the perfect illustration of the problems inherent in this "corrected" theory. That $350 million windfall came too easily; it seems to violate the law that "there is no such thing as a money machine." And if Merck's stockholders would be richer with $2146 million of corporate debt,

---

[3]Notice that as long as the bonds are sold at a fair price, all the benefits from the tax shield go to the shareholders.

[4]MM's original article [F. Modigliani and M. H. Miller, "The Cost of Capital, Corporation Finance and the Theory of Investment," *American Economic Review*, **48**:261–297 (June 1958)] recognized interest tax shields but did not value them properly. They put things right in their 1963 article "Corporate Income Taxes and the Cost of Capital: A Correction," *American Economic Review*, **53**:433–443 (June 1963).

TABLE 18-3a

• •

Simplified balance sheets for Merck & Co., December 31, 1994 (figures in millions)

Book Values

Net working capital	$ 1,473	$ 1,146	Long-term debt
Long-term assets	14,935	4,123	Other long-term liabilities
		11,139	Equity
Total assets	$16,408	$16,408	Total liabilities

Market Values

Net working capital	$ 1,473	$ 1,146	Long-term debt
Market value of long-term assets	51,212	4,123	Other long-term liabilities
		47,416	Equity
Total assets	$52,685	$52,685	Total liabilities

Notes:
1. Market value is assumed to equal book value for net working capital, long-term debt, and other long-term liabilities. Equity is entered at actual market value: number of shares times closing price on December 31, 1994. The difference between the market and book values of long-term assets is equal to the difference between the market and book values of equity.
2. The market value of the long-term assets includes the tax shield on the existing debt. This tax shield is worth $.35 \times 1146 = \$401$ million.

TABLE 18-3b

• •

Balance sheets for Merck & Co., with additional $1 billion of long-term debt substituted for stockholders' equity (figures in millions)

Book Values

Net working capital	$ 1,473	$ 2,146	Long-term debt
Long-term assets	14,935	4,123	Other long-term liabilities
		10,139	Equity
Total assets	$16,408	$16,408	Total liabilities

Market Values

Net working capital	$ 1,473	$ 2,146	Long-term debt
Market value of long-term assets	51,212	4,123	Other long-term liabilities
Present value of additional tax shields	350	46,766	Equity
Total assets	$53,035	$53,035	Total liabilities

Notes:
1. The figures in Table 18-3b for net working capital, long-term assets, and other long-term liabilities are identical to those in Table 18-3a.
2. Present value of tax shields assumed equal to corporate tax rate (35 percent) times amount of additional debt obligation.

why not $3146 or $12,285 million?[5] Our formula implies that firm value and stockholders' wealth continue to go up as D increases. The implied optimal debt policy is embarrassingly extreme: All firms should be 100 percent debt-financed.

MM were not that fanatical about it. No one would expect the formula to apply at extreme debt ratios. But that does not explain why firms like Merck not only exist but thrive with no debt at all. It is hard to believe that the management of Merck is simply missing the boat.

Therefore we have argued ourselves into a corner. There are just two ways out:

1. Perhaps a fuller examination of the United States system of corporate *and personal* taxation will uncover a tax disadvantage of corporate borrowing, offsetting the present value of the corporate tax shield.

2. Perhaps firms that borrow incur other costs—bankruptcy costs, for example—offsetting the present value of the tax shield.

We will now explore these two escape routes.

18-2 CORPORATE AND PERSONAL TAXES

When personal taxes are introduced, the firm's objective is no longer to minimize the *corporate* tax bill; the firm should try to minimize the present value of *all* taxes paid on corporate income. "All taxes" include *personal* taxes paid by bondholders and stockholders.

Figure 18-1 illustrates how corporate and personal taxes are affected by leverage. Depending on the firm's capital structure, a dollar of operating income will accrue to investors either as debt interest or equity income (dividends or capital gains). That is, the dollar can go down either branch of Figure 18-1.

Notice that Figure 18-1 distinguishes between T_p, the personal tax rate on interest, and T_{pE}, the effective personal rate on equity income. The two rates are equal if equity income comes entirely as dividends. But T_{pE} can be less than T_p if equity income comes as capital gains. By 1995, the top rate on ordinary income, including interest and dividends, was 39.6 percent. The rate on *realized* capital gains was 28 percent.[6] However, capital gains taxes can be deferred until shares are sold, so the top *effective* capital gains rate can be less than 28 percent.

The firm's objective should be to arrange its capital structure so as to maximize after-tax income. You can see from Figure 18-1 that corporate borrowing is better if $1 - T_p$ is more than $(1 - T_{pE}) \times (1 - T_c)$; otherwise, it is worse. The *relative* tax advantage of debt over equity is

$$\text{Relative tax advantage of debt} = \frac{1 - T_p}{(1 - T_{pE})(1 - T_c)}$$

This suggests two special cases. First, suppose all equity income comes as dividends. Then debt and equity income are taxed at the same effective personal rate. But with $T_{pE} = T_p$, the relative advantage depends only on the *corporate* rate:

---

[5]The last figure would correspond to a 100 percent book debt ratio. But Merck's *market* value would be $56,583 million according to our formula for firm value. Merck's common shares would have an aggregate value of $40,176 million.

[6]See Chapter 16, Section 16-5, for details. Note that we are simplifying by ignoring *corporate* investors, for example, banks, that pay top rates of 35 percent. Of course, banks shield their interest income by paying interest to lenders and depositors.

Figure 18–1 The firm's capital structure determines whether operating income is paid out as interest or equity income. Interest is taxed only at the personal level. Equity income is taxed at both the corporate and the personal levels. However, T_{pE}, the personal tax rate on equity income, can be less than T_p, the personal tax rate on interest income.

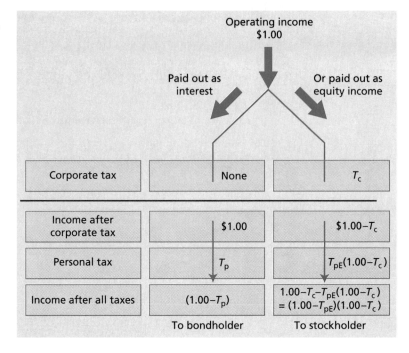

$$\text{Relative advantage} = \frac{1 - T_p}{(1 - T_{pE})(1 - T_c)} = \frac{1}{1 - T_c}$$

In this case, we can forget about personal taxes. The tax advantage of corporate borrowing is exactly as MM calculated it.[7] They do not have to assume away personal taxes. Their theory of debt and taxes requires only that debt and equity be taxed at the same rate.

The second special case occurs when corporate and personal taxes cancel, to make debt policy irrelevant. This requires

$$1 - T_p = (1 - T_{pE})(1 - T_c)$$

This case can happen only if T_c, the corporate rate, is less than the personal rate T_p *and* if T_{pE}, the effective rate on equity income, is small.

In any event we seem to have a simple, practical decision rule. Arrange the firm's capital structure to shunt operating income down that branch of Figure 18-1 where

---

[7]Of course, personal taxes reduce the dollar amount of corporate interest tax shields, but the appropriate discount rate for cash flows after personal tax is also lower. If investors are willing to lend at a prospective return *before* personal taxes of r_D, then they must also be willing to accept a return *after* personal taxes of $r_D(1 - T_p)$, where T_p is the marginal rate of personal tax. Thus we can compute the value after personal taxes of the tax shield on permanent debt:

$$\text{PV(tax shield)} = \frac{T_c \times (r_D D) \times (1 - T_p)}{r_D \times (1 - T_p)} = T_c D$$

This brings us back to our previous formula for firm value:

Value of firm = value if all-equity-financed + $T_c D$

the tax is least. We will now try a couple of back-of-the-envelope calculations to see what that rule could imply.

Before the 1986 Tax Reform Act, the corporate tax rules was 46 percent, and interest and dividends were taxed at rates up to 50 percent. The top capital gains rate was 20 percent. The *effective* rate was less than 20 percent because capital gains taxes can be deferred until shares are sold.

You can see the two opposing tax effects. Corporate tax rules subsidized debt—the government in effect paid 46 cents for every dollar of interest. But the personal tax rules favored equity because of the low tax rate on capital gains. For companies with low-dividend payouts, the two effects roughly canceled.

Consider a firm paying no dividends, and suppose that deferral of capital gains cuts the effective personal tax rate on equity income to half the pre-1986 statutory capital gains rate, that is, $T_{pE} = .10$. If T_p, the tax rate on interest, is .50, then:

	Interest	Equity Income
Income before tax	$1.00	$1.00
Less corporate tax		
at $T_c = .46$	0	.46
Income after corporate tax	1.00	.54
Personal tax at $T_p = .5$		
and $T_{pE} = .10$	.50	.054
Income after all taxes	$ .50	$ .496

Advantage to debt = $.004

For any practical purpose this is a dead heat. It's worth paying the 46 percent corporate tax on equity income to avoid the 50 percent personal tax on interest income.

The 1986 Tax Reform Act reduced the corporate tax rate to 34 percent, reduced the top personal rate on interest and dividends to 28 percent, and increased the tax on realized capital gains to 28 percent. By 1995, the corporate rate had edged up to 35 percent, and the top rate on interest and dividends had jumped to 39.6 percent. The capital gains rate remained at 28 percent.

Here is a second numerical example, using 1995 rates, and again assuming zero dividends and an effective capital gains rate of one-half the statutory rate on realized gains, that is, $28/2 = 14$ percent:

	Interest	Equity Income
Income before tax	$1.00	$1.00
Less corporate tax		
at $T_c = .35$	0	.35
Income after corporate tax	$1.00	.65
Personal tax at $T_p = .396$		
and $T_{pE} = .14$	.396	.091
Income after all taxes	$ .604	$ .559

Advantage to debt = $.045

Here debt takes the lead. Moreover, the lead lengthens when we consider companies that pay dividends. Suppose half of equity income comes as dividends and half as capital gains. Capital gains are deferred for long enough that their effective rate is half the statutory rate, i.e., one-half of 28, or 14 percent. Thus the effective rate on equity income is the average of the dividend and capital gains rates, or $(.396 + .14)/2 = .268$.

	Interest	Equity Income
Income before tax	$1.00	$1.00
Less corporate tax at $T_c = .35$	0	.35
Income after corporate tax	1.00	.65
Less personal tax at $T_p = .396$ and $T_{pE} = .268$	.396	.174
Income after all taxes	$ .604	$ .476

Advantage to debt = $.128

The advantage to debt financing is about 13 cents on the dollar.

As these back-of-the-envelope calculations show, the current (1995) United States tax system clearly favors debt over equity financing. But the magnitude of debt's tax advantage is not so clear. Which investors' tax rates should be used? What's T_{pE}, for example? The shareholder roster of a large corporation may include tax-exempt investors (such as pension funds or university endowments) as well as millionaires. All possible tax brackets will be mixed together. And it's the same with T_p, the personal tax rate on interest. The large corporation's "typical" bondholder might be a tax-exempt pension fund, but many taxpaying investors also hold corporate debt.

*Merton Miller's "Debt and Taxes"

How does capital structure affect firm value when investors have different tax rates? There is one model that may help us think through that question. It was put forward in "Debt and Taxes," Merton Miller's 1976 presidential address to the American Finance Association.[8]

Miller was considering debt policy before the 1986 Tax Reform Act. He started by assuming that all equity income comes as unrealized capital gains and nobody pays any tax on equity income; T_{pE} is zero for all investors. But the rate of tax on interest depends on the investor's tax bracket. Tax-exempt institutions do not pay any tax on interest; for them T_p is zero. At the other extreme, millionaires paid tax at a rate of 50 percent on bond interest; for them T_p was .50. Most investors fell somewhere between these two extremes.

Consider a simple world with these tax rates. Suppose that companies are initially financed entirely by equity. If financial managers are on their toes, this cannot represent a stable situation. Think of it in terms of Figure 18-1. If every dollar goes down the equity branch, there are no taxes paid at the personal level (remember $T_{pE} = 0$). Thus the financial manager need consider only corporate taxes, which we know create a strong incentive for corporate borrowing.

As companies begin to borrow, some investors have to be persuaded to hold corporate debt rather than common stock. There should be no problem in persuading tax-exempt investors to hold debt. They do not pay any personal taxes on bonds or

---

[8]M. H. Miller, "Debt and Taxes," *Journal of Finance*, **32**:261–276 (May 1977).

stocks. Thus, the initial impact of borrowing is to save corporate taxes and to leave personal taxes unchanged.

But as companies borrow more, they need to persuade taxpaying investors to migrate from stocks to bonds. Therefore they have to offer a bribe in the form of a higher interest rate on their bonds. Companies can afford to bribe investors to migrate as long as the corporate tax saving is greater than the personal tax loss. But there is no way that companies can bribe millionaires to hold their bonds. The corporate tax saving cannot compensate for the extra personal tax that those millionaires would need to pay. Thus the migrations stop when the corporate tax saving *equals* the personal tax loss. This point occurs when T_p, the personal tax rate of the migrating investor, equals the corporate tax rate T_c.

Let us put some numbers on this. The corporate tax rate T_c was 46 percent. We continue to assume that T_{pE}, the effective rate of tax on equity income, is zero for all investors. In this case, companies will bribe investors with tax rates below 46 percent to hold bonds. But there is nothing to be gained (or lost) by persuading investors with tax rates *equal* to 46 percent to hold bonds. In the case of these investors $1 of operating income will produce income after all taxes of $.54, regardless of whether the dollar is interest or equity income:

	Income Remaining after All Taxes
Income paid out as interest	$1 - T_p = 1 - .46 = \$.54$
Income paid out as equity income	$(1 - T_{pE})(1 - T_c) = (1 - 0)(1 - .46) = \$.54$

In this equilibrium taxes determine the aggregate amount of corporate debt but not the amount issued by any particular firm. The debt-equity ratio for corporations as a whole depends on the corporate tax rate and the funds available to individual investors in the various tax brackets. If the corporate tax rate is increased, migration starts again, leading to a higher debt-equity ratio for companies as a whole. If personal tax rates are increased, the migration reverses, leading to a lower debt-equity ratio. If *both* personal and corporate tax rates are increased by the same amount—10 percentage points, say—there is no migration and no change. That could explain why there was no substantial increase in the debt-equity ratio when the corporate income tax rose drastically at the start of World War II. Personal tax rates were simultaneously increased by about the same amount.

The companies in our example that first sold bonds to tax-exempt investors may have gained an advantage. But once the "low-tax" investors have bought bonds and the migrations have stopped, no single firm can gain an advantage by borrowing more or suffer any penalty by borrowing less. Therefore there is no such thing as an optimal debt-equity ratio *for any single firm*. The market is interested only in the *total* amount of debt. No single firm can influence that.

One final point about Miller's tax equilibrium: Because he assumes equity returns escape personal tax ($T_{pE} = 0$), investors are willing to accept lower rates of return on low-risk common stocks than on debt. Consider a safe (zero-beta) stock. The standard capital asset pricing model would give an expected return of $r = r_f$, the risk-free interest rate (see Chapter 7, Section 7-4). But the investor migrating from equity to debt gives up r and earns $r_f(1 - T_p)$, the *after-tax* interest rate. In equilibrium, the migrating investor is content with either debt or equity, so $r = r_f(1 - T_p)$. Moreover, that investor's T_p equals the corporate rate T_c. Therefore, $r = r_f(1 - T_c)$. If we accept Miller's argument lock, stock, and barrel, the security market line should pass through the after-tax risk-free interest rate.

Miller's model was intended not as a detailed description of the United States tax system but as a way of illustrating how corporate and personal taxes could cancel out and leave firm value independent of capital structure. Nevertheless, the model's predictions are plausible only if the effective tax rate on equity income is substantially lower than that on interest, enough lower to offset the corporate interest tax shield. Under today's tax system, it's hard to see how Miller's model could work out as he originally intended. Even if there were no tax advantage to borrowing before the 1986 tax law changes, there ought to be one now.

The majority of financial managers and economists believe our tax system favors corporate borrowing. But it's easy to overestimate the advantage. Analyses like Tables 18-2a and 18-2b, which calculate the present value of a safe, perpetual stream of corporate interest tax shields, must overestimate debt's net value added. As Miller's paper shows, the aggregate supplies of corporate debt and equity should adjust to minimize the sum of corporate and personal taxes; at the resulting equilibrium the higher personal tax rate on debt income should partially offset the tax deductibility of interest at the corporate level.

We should also reconsider the assumption that the corporate tax shield on debt is a constant 35 percent regardless of the amount borrowed. In practice few firms can be *sure* they will show a taxable profit in the future. If a firm shows a loss and cannot carry the loss back against past taxes, its interest tax shield must be carried forward with the hope of using it later. The firm loses the time value of money while it waits. If its difficulties are deep enough, the wait may be permanent and the interest tax shield lost forever.

Notice also that borrowing is not the only way to shield income against tax. Firms have accelerated write-offs for plant and equipment. Investment in many intangible assets can be expensed immediately. So can contributions to the firm's pension fund. The more that firms shield income in these other ways, the lower the expected tax shield from borrowing.[9]

Thus corporate tax shields are worth more to some firms than to others. Firms with plenty of noninterest tax shields and uncertain future prospects should borrow less than consistently profitable firms with lots of taxable profits to shield. Firms with large accumulated tax-loss carry-forwards shouldn't borrow at all. Why should such a firm "bribe" taxpaying investors to hold debt when it can't use interest tax shields?

We believe there is a moderate tax advantage to corporate borrowing, at least for companies that are reasonably sure they can use the corporate tax shields. For companies that do not expect to be able to use the corporate tax shields we believe there is a moderate tax disadvantage.

18-3 COSTS OF FINANCIAL DISTRESS

Financial distress occurs when promises to creditors are broken or honored with difficulty. Sometimes financial distress leads to bankruptcy. Sometimes it only means skating on thin ice.

---

[9]For a discussion of the effect of these other tax shields on company borrowing, see H. DeAngelo and R. Masulis, "Optimal Capital Structure under Corporate and Personal Taxation," *Journal of Financial Economics,* **8:**5–29 (March 1980). For some evidence on the average marginal tax rate of United States firms, see J. J. Cordes and S. M. Sheffrin, "Taxation and the Sectoral Allocation of Capital in the U.S.," *National Tax Journal,* **34:**419–432 (1981).

As we will see, financial distress is costly. Investors know that levered firms may fall into financial distress, and they worry about it. That worry is reflected in the current market value of the levered firm's securities. Thus, the value of the firm can be broken down into three parts:

$$\begin{matrix} \text{Value} \\ \text{of firm} \end{matrix} = \begin{matrix} \text{value if} \\ \text{all-equity-financed} \end{matrix} + \text{PV(tax shield)} - \begin{matrix} \text{PV(costs of} \\ \text{financial distress)} \end{matrix}$$

The costs of financial distress depend on the probability of distress and the magnitude of costs encountered if distress occurs.

Figure 18-2 shows how the trade-off between the tax benefits and the costs of distress determines optimal capital structure. PV(tax shield) initially increases as the firm borrows more. At moderate debt levels the probability of financial distress is trivial, and so PV(cost of financial distress) is small and tax advantages dominate. But at some point the probability of financial distress increases rapidly with additional borrowing; the costs of distress begin to take a substantial bite out of firm value. Also, if the firm can't be sure of profiting from the corporate tax shield, the tax advantage of debt is likely to dwindle and eventually disappear. The theoretical optimum is reached when the present value of tax savings due to additional borrowing is just offset by increases in the present value of costs of distress.

Costs of financial distress cover several specific items. Now we identify these costs and try to understand what causes them.

Bank-ruptcy Costs

You rarely hear anything nice said about corporate bankruptcy. But there is some good in almost everything. Corporate bankruptcies occur when stockholders exercise their *right to default*. That right is valuable; when a firm gets into trouble, limited liability allows stockholders simply to walk away from it, leaving all its troubles to its creditors. The former creditors become the new stockholders, and the old stockholders are left with nothing.

Figure 18–2 The value of the firm is equal to its value if all-equity-financed plus PV(tax shield) minus PV(costs of financial distress). The manager should choose the debt ratio that maximizes firm value.

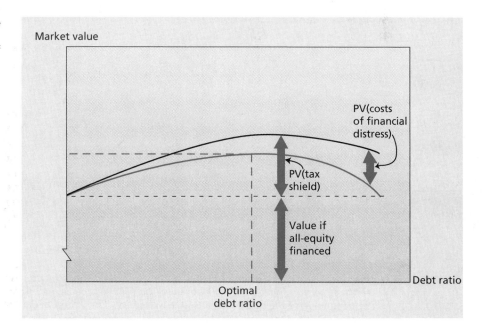

In our legal system all stockholders in corporations automatically enjoy limited liability. But suppose that this were not so. Suppose that there are two firms with identical assets and operations. Each firm has debt outstanding, and each has promised to repay $1000 (principal and interest) next year. But only one of the firms, Ace Limited, enjoys limited liability. The other firm, Ace Unlimited, does not; its stockholders are personally liable for its debt.

Figure 18-3 compares next year's possible payoffs to the creditors and stockholders of these two firms. The only differences occur when next year's asset value turns out to be less than $1000. Suppose that next year the assets of each company are worth only $500. In this case Ace Limited defaults. Its stockholders walk away;

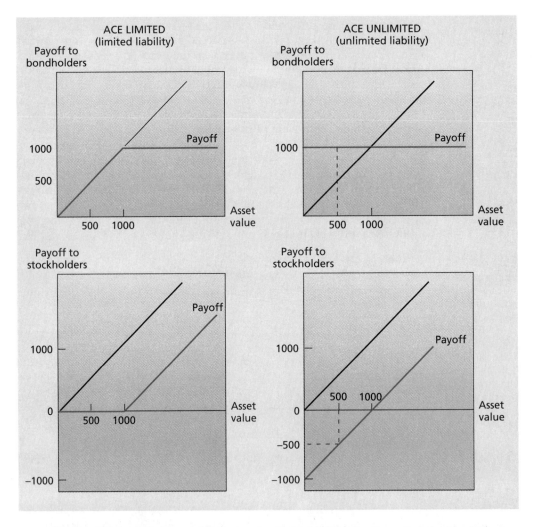

Figure 18–3 Comparison of limited and unlimited liability for two otherwise identical firms. If the two firms' asset values are less than $1000, Ace Limited stockholders default and its bondholders take over the assets. Ace Unlimited stockholders keep the assets, but they must reach into their own pockets to pay off its bondholders. The total payoff to both stockholders and bondholders is the same for the two firms.

their payoff is zero. Bondholders get the assets worth $500. But Ace Unlimited's stockholders can't walk away. They have to cough up $500, the difference between asset value and the bondholders' claim. The debt is paid whatever happens.

Suppose that Ace Limited does go bankrupt. Of course, its stockholders are disappointed that their firm is worth so little, but that is an operating problem having nothing to do with financing. Given poor operating performance, the right to go bankrupt—the right to default—is a valuable privilege. As Figure 18-3 shows, Ace Limited's stockholders are in better shape than Unlimited's are.

The example illuminates a mistake people often make in thinking about the costs of bankruptcy. Bankruptcies are thought of as corporate funerals. The mourners (creditors and especially shareholders) look at their firm's present sad state. They think of how valuable their securities used to be and how little is left. Moreover, they think of the lost value as a cost of bankruptcy. That is the mistake. The decline in the value of assets is what the mourning is really about. That has no necessary connection with financing. The bankruptcy is merely a legal mechanism for allowing creditors to take over when the decline in the value of assets triggers a default. Bankruptcy is not the *cause* of the decline in value. It is the result.

Be careful not to get cause and effect reversed. When a person dies, we do not cite the implementation of his or her will as the cause of death.

We said that bankruptcy is a legal mechanism allowing creditors to take over when a firm defaults. Bankruptcy costs are the costs of using this mechanism. There are no bankruptcy costs at all shown in Figure 18-3. Note that only Ace Limited can default and go bankrupt. But, regardless of what happens to asset value, the *combined* payoff to the bondholders and stockholders of Ace Limited is always the same as the *combined* payoff to the bondholders and stockholders of Ace Unlimited. Thus the overall market values of the two firms now (this year) must be identical. Of course, Ace Limited's *stock* is worth more than Ace Unlimited's stock because of Ace Limited's right to default. Ace Limited's *debt* is worth correspondingly less.

Our example was not intended to be strictly realistic. Anything involving courts and lawyers cannot be free. Suppose that court and legal fees are $200 if Ace Limited defaults. The fees are paid out of the remaining value of Ace's assets. Thus if asset value turns out to be $500, creditors end up with only $300. Figure 18-4 shows next year's *total* payoff to bondholders and stockholders net of this bankruptcy cost. Ace Limited, by issuing risky debt, has given lawyers and the court system a claim on the firm if it defaults. The market value of the firm is reduced by the present value of this claim.

It is easy to see how increased leverage affects the present value of the costs of financial distress. If Ace Limited borrows more, it must promise more to bondholders. This increases the probability of default and the value of the lawyers' claim. It increases PV (costs of financial distress) and reduces Ace's present market value.

The costs of bankruptcy come out of stockholders' pockets. Creditors foresee the costs and foresee that *they* will pay them if default occurs. For this they demand compensation in advance in the form of higher payoffs when the firm does *not* default. That is, they demand a higher promised interest rate. This reduces the possible payoffs to stockholders and reduces the present market value of their shares.

Evidence on Bankruptcy Costs

Bankruptcy costs can add up fast. *Aviation Week and Space Technology* reported in 1984 that legal and professional fees of the Braniff International Corporation bankruptcy were $12 million; legal fees in the Continental Airlines bankruptcy were running $2 million per month.[10] Daunting as these numbers may seem, they were not a large

---

[10]*Aviation Week and Space Technology*, April 23, 1984, p. 35.

Figure 18–4 Total payoff to Ace Limited security holders. There is a $200 bankruptcy cost in the event of default (shaded area).

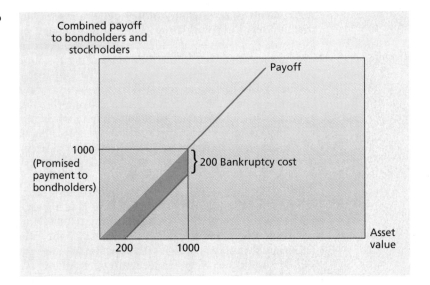

fraction of these airlines' *asset* values. For example, in 1984 it cost about $95 million to buy *one* airplane, a Boeing 747.

For Eastern Airlines, bankruptcy costs were much more serious. When it entered the "protection" of the bankruptcy court in 1989, it still had some valuable, profit-making routes and saleable assets such as planes and terminal facilities. A prompt liquidation probably would have generated enough cash to pay off all debt and preferred stockholders. Instead, the court allowed the company to operate for 2 more years. When Eastern finally closed down, it was *administratively* insolvent: there was almost nothing for creditors, and the company was running out of cash to pay legal expenses.

Of course this is an extreme example. What do we know about bankruptcy costs generally? Lawrence Weiss, who studied 31 firms that went bankrupt between 1980 and 1986, found average costs of about 3 percent of total book assets and 20 percent of the market value of equity in the year prior to bankruptcy. A study by Edward Altman found that costs were similar for retail companies but higher for industrial companies. Also, bankruptcy eats up a larger fraction of asset value for small companies than for large ones. There are significant economies of scale in going bankrupt.[11]

Direct versus Indirect Costs of Bank-ruptcy

So far we have discussed the *direct* (that is, legal and administrative) costs of bankruptcy. There are indirect costs too, which are nearly impossible to measure. But we have circumstantial evidence indicating their importance.

The indirect costs reflect the difficulties of running a railroad—or any company—while it is going through bankruptcy. Management's efforts to prevent further deterioration in the firm's business are often undermined by the delays and legal tangles that go with bankruptcy.

---

[11]The pioneering study of bankruptcy costs is J. B. Warner, "Bankruptcy Costs: Some Evidence," *Journal of Finance*, **26**:337–348 (May 1977). The Weiss and Altman papers are L. A. Weiss, "Bankruptcy Resolution: Direct Costs and Violation of Priority of Claims," *Journal of Financial Economics*, **27**:285–314 (October 1990); and E. I. Altman, "A Further Investigation of the Bankruptcy Cost Question," *Journal of Finance*, **39**:1067–1089 (September 1984).

The Penn Central Railroad went under in June 1970. Four years later, with bankruptcy proceedings nowhere near completion, *Business Week* published an article called "Why the Penn Central Is Falling Apart." Here are some excerpts.

> As its creditors hound it—some of them want to shut it down to get back their money—the railroad must continue operations at a time when it can barely keep running without pouring in huge sums to rebuild its facilities. Those sums, however, will not be available until the railroad shows that it can be reorganized.

Penn Central could have raised money by selling off some of its assets, but its creditors naturally opposed this:

> . . . Scores of other problems arise from a lack of money. Agonizingly for everyone on the Penn Central, there is a tremendous source of capital that cannot be touched. For example, just about every abandoned mine branch in the Allegheny Mountains is chock full of old Penn Central cars destined for scrap. With today's scrap prices, they are a potential gold mine. But the creditors will not allow this asset to be turned into cash that will be reinvested in the estate, since that estate is eroding day by day.

The creditors' interest also got in the way of sensible maintenance:

> And the creditors' problems do not stop there. Between Indianapolis and Terre Haute, the former Pennsylvania and New York Central RRs had double-track, high-speed main lines rarely more than three miles apart. After the merger, most traffic was routed over the old New York Central route and the Pennsy line's second track was picked up. There are still 11 mi. of double track on the old Pennsy, though, and the 132-lb. rail is in excellent shape. It is desperately needed on the old New York Central line where double traffic and deferred maintenance have left much of that stretch with 10 mph speed limits.

The obvious thing was to use the good rail on the Penn Central line. Unfortunately,

> . . . the rail belongs to a Pennsy subsidiary, itself in reorganization, and the creditors will not permit the asset to be moved to a subsidiary of the New York Central except for "cash on the barrel," which, of course, is unavailable.[12]

We do not know what the sum of direct and indirect costs of bankruptcy amounts to. We suspect it is a significant number, particularly for large firms for which proceedings would be lengthy and complex. Perhaps the best evidence is the reluctance of creditors to force bankruptcy. In principle, they would be better off to end the agony and seize the assets as soon as possible. Instead, creditors often overlook defaults in the hope of nursing the firm over a difficult period. They do this in part to avoid costs of bankruptcy.[13] There is an old financial saying, "Borrow $1000 and you've got a banker. Borrow $10,000,000 and you've got a partner."

---

[12]Reprinted from the October 12, 1974, issue of *Business Week* by special permission, © 1974 by McGraw-Hill, Inc., New York, NY 10020. All rights reserved.

[13]There is another reason. Creditors are not always given absolute priority in bankruptcy. *Absolute priority* means that creditors must be paid in full before stockholders receive a cent. Sometimes reorganizations are negotiated which provide "something for everyone," even though creditors are *not* paid in full. Thus creditors can never be sure how they will fare in bankruptcy.

TABLE 18-4

••

Texaco's stock price dropped by $3.375 when its bankruptcy filing was announced. Pennzoil was Texaco's largest creditor; its stock price dropped too, by $15.125. The combined market value of the two firms' stock fell $1445 million.

	SHARE PRICE			Number of Shares, Millions	Change in Value, Millions
	Friday April 10, 1987	Monday April 13, 1987	Change		
Texaco	$31.875	$28.50	−$ 3.375	242	−$ 817
Pennzoil	92.125	77.00	−15.125	41.5	−628
Total					−$1,445

Here is one final piece of evidence on the direct plus indirect costs of bankruptcy: On April 10, 1987, Texaco filed for bankruptcy, surprising most investors and financial analysts. Texaco's biggest creditor was Pennzoil, to whom it owed $10.5 billion in damages stemming from Texaco's 1984 takeover of Getty Oil.[14] Texaco had been negotiating with Pennzoil, trying to cut a deal in which Pennzoil would give up its claim—which Texaco was contesting—in exchange for an immediate cash settlement. When these negotiations broke down, Texaco turned to the bankruptcy court.

Table 18-4 reports that Texaco stock fell from $31.875 to 28.50 after the announcement, a fall of $817 million in Texaco's equity value. At the same time Pennzoil's equity value fell by $628 million. We do not know how Texaco's other creditors fared, but the value of their claims cannot have increased. Therefore, bankruptcy reduced the market value of (the claims on) Texaco's assets by at least $817 plus $628, or $1445 million, roughly $1.5 billion. We can take this loss as the stock market's estimate of the present value of the direct and indirect costs of the Texaco bankruptcy.

But how could bankruptcy cost $1.5 *billion?* Texaco's business operations were healthy and profitable, and thus unlikely to encounter the sort of problems that plagued Penn Central. We are at a loss to explain how a stock market could rationally forecast bankruptcy costs as large as those implied by Table 18-4.[15]

In all this discussion of bankruptcy costs we have said very little about bankruptcy *procedures*. These are described in the appendix at the end of this chapter.

Financial Distress without Bankruptcy

Not every firm which gets into trouble goes bankrupt. As long as the firm can scrape up enough cash to pay the interest on its debt, it may be able to postpone bankruptcy for many years. Eventually the firm may recover, pay off its debt, and escape bankruptcy altogether.

When a firm is in trouble, both bondholders and stockholders want it to recover, but in other respects their interests may be in conflict. In times of financial distress

---

[14]Pennzoil thought it had struck a deal to buy Getty when Texaco arrived with a higher bid. Texaco finally won, but Pennzoil sued, arguing that Texaco had broken up a valid contract between Pennzoil and Getty. The court agreed and ordered Texaco to pay over $11.1 billion. This amount was reduced on appeal, but *with interest* the damages still amounted to $10.5 billion by April 1987.

[15]The Texaco bankruptcy is discussed by L. Summers and D. M. Cutler, "The Costs of Conflict and Financial Distress: Evidence from the Texaco-Pennzoil Litigation," *RAND Journal of Economics*, **19**:157–172 (Summer 1988).

the security holders are like many political parties—united on generalities but threatened by squabbling on any specific issue.

Financial distress is costly when these conflicts of interest get in the way of proper operating, investment, and financing decisions. Stockholders are tempted to forsake the usual objective of maximizing the overall market value of the firm and to pursue narrower self-interest instead. They are tempted to play games at the expense of their creditors. We will now illustrate how such games can lead to costs of financial distress.

Here is the Circular File Company's book balance sheet:

Circular File Company (Book Values)

Net working capital	$ 20	$ 50	Bonds outstanding
Fixed assets	80	50	Common stock
Total assets	$100	$100	Total liabilities

We will assume there is only one share and one bond outstanding. The stockholder is also the manager. The bondholder is somebody else.

Here is its balance sheet in market values—a clear case of financial distress, since the face value of Circular's debt ($50) exceeds the firm's total market value ($30):

Circular File Company (Market Values)

Net working capital	$20	$25	Bonds outstanding
Fixed assets	10	5	Common stock
Total assets	$30	$30	Total liabilities

If the debt matured today, Circular's owner would default, leaving the firm bankrupt. But suppose that the bond actually matures 1 year hence, that there is enough cash for Circular to limp along for 1 year, and that the bondholder cannot "call the question" and force bankruptcy before then.

The 1-year grace period explains why the Circular share still has value. Its owner is betting on a stroke of luck that will rescue the firm, allowing it to pay off the debt with something left over. The bet is a long shot—the owner wins only if firm value increases from $30 to more than $50.[16] But the owner has a secret weapon: he controls investment and operating strategy.

Risk Shifting: The First Game

Suppose that Circular has $10 cash. The following investment opportunity comes up:

Now	Possible Payoffs Next Year
Invest $10	$120 (10% probability)
	$0 (90% probability)

---

[16]We are not concerned here with how to work out whether $5 is a fair price for stockholders to pay for the bet. We will come to that in Chapter 20 when we discuss the valuation of options.

This is a wild gamble and probably a lousy project. But you can see why the owner would be tempted to take it anyway. Why not go for broke? Circular will probably go under anyway, and so the owner is essentially betting with the bondholder's money. But the owner gets most of the loot if the project pays off.

Suppose that the project's NPV is −$2 but that it is undertaken anyway, thus depressing firm value by $2. Circular's new balance sheet might look like this:

Circular File Company (Market Values)

Net working capital	$10	$20	Bonds outstanding
Fixed assets	18	8	Common stock
Total assets	$28	$28	Total liabilities

Firm value falls by $2, but the owner is $3 ahead because the bond's value has fallen by $5.[17] The $10 cash that used to stand behind the bond has been replaced by a very risky asset worth only $8.

Thus a game has been played at the expense of Circular's bondholder. The game illustrates the following general point: Stockholders of levered firms gain when business risk increases. Financial managers who act strictly in their shareholders' interests (and *against* the interests of creditors) will favor risky projects over safe ones. They may even take risky projects with negative NPVs.

This warped strategy for capital budgeting clearly is costly to the firm and to the economy as a whole. Why do we associate the costs with financial distress? Because the temptation to play is strongest when the odds of default are high. Exxon would never invest in our negative-NPV gamble. Its creditors are not vulnerable to this type of game.

Refusing to Contribute Equity Capital: The Second Game

We have seen how stockholders, acting in their immediate, narrow self-interest, may take projects which reduce the overall market value of their firm. These are errors of commission. Conflicts of interest may also lead to errors of omission.

Assume that Circular cannot scrape up any cash, and therefore cannot take that wild gamble. Instead a *good* opportunity comes up: a relatively safe asset costing $10 with a present value of $15 and NPV = +$5.

This project will not in itself rescue Circular, but it is a step in the right direction. We might therefore expect Circular to issue $10 of new stock and to go ahead with the investment. Suppose that two new shares are issued to the original owner for $10 cash. The project is taken. The new balance sheet might look like this:

Circular File Company (Market Values)

Net working capital	$20	$33	Bonds outstanding
Fixed assets	25	12	Common stock
Total assets	$45	$45	Total liabilities

The total value of the firm goes up by $15 ($10 of new capital and $5 NPV). Notice that the Circular bond is no longer worth $25, but $33. The bondholder re-

---

[17]We are not calculating this $5 drop. We are simply using it as a plausible assumption. The tools necessary for a calculation come in Chapter 20.

ceives a capital gain of $8 because the firm's assets include a new, safe asset worth $15. The probability of default is less, and the payoff to the bondholder if default occurs is larger.

The stockholder loses what the bondholder gains. Equity value goes up not by $15 but by $15 − $8 = $7. The owner puts in $10 of fresh equity capital but gains only $7 in market value. Going ahead is in the firm's interest but not the owner's.

Again, our example illustrates a general point. If we hold business risk constant, any increase in firm value is shared among bondholders and stockholders. The value of any investment opportunity *to the firm's stockholders* is reduced because project benefits must be shared with bondholders. Thus it may not be in the stockholders' self-interest to contribute fresh equity capital even if that means forgoing positive-NPV investment opportunities.

This problem theoretically affects all levered firms, but it is most serious when firms land in financial distress. The greater the probability of default, the more bondholders have to gain from investments which increase firm value.

....

And Three More Games, Briefly

As with other games, the temptation to play the next three games is particularly strong in financial distress.

1. *Cash In and Run*: Stockholders may be reluctant to put money into a firm in financial distress, but they are happy to take the money out—in the form of a cash dividend, for example. The market value of the firm's stock goes down by less than the amount of the dividend paid, because the decline in *firm* value is shared with creditors. This game is just "refusing to contribute equity capital" run in reverse.

2. *Playing for Time*: When the firm is in financial distress, creditors would like to salvage what they can by forcing the firm to settle up. Naturally, stockholders want to delay this as long as they can. There are various devious ways of doing this, for example, through accounting changes designed to conceal the true extent of trouble, by encouraging false hopes of spontaneous recovery, or by cutting corners on maintenance, research and development, etc., in order to make this year's operating performance look better.

3. *Bait and Switch:* This game is not always played in financial distress, but it is a quick way to get *into* distress. You start with a conservative policy, issuing a limited amount of relatively safe debt. Then you suddenly switch and issue a lot more. That makes all your debt risky, imposing a capital loss on the "old" bondholders. Their capital loss is the stockholders' gain.

The most dramatic example of bait and switch occurred in October 1988, when the management of RJR Nabisco announced its intention to acquire the company in a *leveraged buy-out* (LBO). This put the company "in play" for a transaction in which existing shareholders would be bought out and the company "taken private." The cost of the buy-out would be almost entirely debt-financed. The new private company would start life with an extremely high debt ratio.

RJR Nabisco had debt outstanding with a market value of about $2.4 billion. The announcement of the coming LBO drove down this market value by $298 million.[18]

---

[18]We thank Paul Asquith for these figures. RJR Nabisco was finally taken private not by its management but by another LBO partnership.

Why should anyone object to these games so long as they are played by consenting adults? Because playing them means poor decisions about investments and operations. These poor decisions are *agency costs* of borrowing.

The more the firm borrows, the greater the temptation to play the games (assuming the financial manager acts in the stockholders' interest). The increased odds of poor decisions in the future prompt investors to mark down the present market value of the firm. The fall in value comes out of stockholders' pockets. Potential lenders, realizing that games may be played at their expense, protect themselves by demanding better terms.

Therefore it is ultimately in the stockholders' interest to avoid temptation. The easiest way to do this is to limit borrowing to levels at which the firm's debt is safe or close to it.

But suppose that the tax advantages of debt spur the firm on to a high debt ratio and a significant probability of default or financial distress. Is there any way to convince potential lenders that games will not be played? The obvious answer is to give lenders veto power over potentially dangerous decisions.

There we have the ultimate economic rationale for all that fine print backing up corporate debt. Debt contracts almost always limit dividends or equivalent transfers of wealth to stockholders; the firm may not be allowed to pay out more than it earns, for example. Additional borrowing is almost always limited. For example, many companies are prevented by existing bond indentures from issuing any additional long-term debt unless their ratio of earnings to interest charges exceeds 2.0.[19]

Sometimes firms are restricted from selling assets or making major investment outlays except with the lenders' consent. The risks of "playing for time" are reduced by specifying accounting procedures and by giving lenders access to the firm's books and its financial forecasts.

Of course, fine print cannot be a complete solution for firms that insist on issuing risky debt. The fine print has its own costs; you have to spend money to save money. Obviously a complex debt contract costs more to negotiate than a simple one. Afterward it costs the lender more to monitor the firm's performance. Lenders anticipate monitoring costs and demand compensation in the form of higher interest rates; thus the monitoring costs—another agency cost of debt—are ultimately paid by stockholders.

Perhaps the most severe costs of the fine print stem from the constraints it places on operating and investment decisions. For example, an attempt to prevent the "risk-shifting" game may also prevent the firm from pursuing *good* investment opportunities. At the minimum there are delays in clearing major investments with lenders. In some cases lenders may veto high-risk investments even if net present value is positive. Lenders can lose from risk shifting even when the firm's overall market value increases. In fact, the lenders may try to play a game of their own, forcing the firm to stay in cash or low-risk assets even if good projects are forgone.

Thus, debt contracts cannot cover every possible manifestation of the games we have just discussed. Any attempt to do so would be hopelessly expensive and doomed to failure in any event. Human imagination is insufficient to conceive of all the possible things that could go wrong. We will always find surprises coming at us on dimensions we never thought to think about.

---

[19]RJR Nabisco bondholders might have done better if they had effective covenants to protect them against drastic increases in financial leverage. We discuss covenants and the rest of the fine print in debt contracts in Section 24-5.

We hope we have not left the impression that managers and stockholders always succumb to temptation unless restrained. Usually they refrain voluntarily, not only from a sense of fair play but also on pragmatic grounds: A firm or individual that makes a killing today at the expense of a creditor will be coldly received when the time comes to borrow again. Aggressive game playing is done only by out-and-out crooks and by firms in extreme financial distress. Firms limit borrowing precisely because they don't wish to land in distress and be exposed to the temptation to play.

Costs of Distress Vary with Type of Asset

Suppose your firm's only asset is a large downtown hotel, mortgaged to the hilt. The recession hits, occupancy rates fall, and the mortgage payments cannot be met. The lender takes over and sells the hotel to a new owner and operator. You use your firm's stock certificates for wallpaper.

What is the cost of bankruptcy? In this example, probably very little. The value of the hotel is, of course, much less than you hoped, but that is due to the lack of guests, not to the bankruptcy. Bankruptcy doesn't damage the hotel itself. The direct bankruptcy costs are restricted to items such as legal and court fees, real estate commissions, and the time the lender spends sorting things out.[20]

Suppose we repeat the story of Heartbreak Hotel for Fledgling Electronics. Everything is the same, except for the underlying real assets—not real estate but a high-tech going concern, a growth company whose most valuable assets are technology, investment opportunities, and its employees' human capital.

If Fledgling gets into trouble, the stockholders may be reluctant to put up money to cash in on its growth opportunities. Failure to invest is likely to be much more serious for Fledgling than for a company like Heartbreak Hotel.

If Fledgling finally defaults on its debt, the lender would find it much more difficult to cash in by selling off the assets. Many of them are intangibles which have value only as a part of a going concern.

Could Fledgling be kept as a going concern through default and reorganization? It may not be as hopeless as putting a wedding cake through a car wash, but there are a number of serious difficulties. First, the odds of defections by key employees are higher than they would be if the firm had never gotten into financial trouble. Special guarantees may have to be given to customers who have doubts about whether the firm will be around to service its products. Aggressive investment in new products and technology will be difficult; each class of creditors will have to be convinced that it is in their interest for the firm to invest new money in risky ventures.

Some assets, like good commercial real estate, can pass through bankruptcy and reorganization largely unscathed; the values of other assets are likely to be considerably diminished. The losses are greatest for the intangible assets that are linked to the health of the firm as a going concern—for example, technology, human capital, and brand image. That may be why debt ratios are low in the pharmaceutical industry, where value depends on continued success in research and development, and in many service industries where value depends on human capital. We can also

---

[20]In 1989 the Rockefeller family sold 80 percent of Rockefeller Center—several acres of extremely valuable Manhattan real estate—to Mitsubishi Estate Company for $1.4 billion. A REIT, Rockefeller Center Properties, held a $1.3 billion mortgage loan (the REIT's only asset) secured by this real estate. But rents and occupancy rates did not meet forecasts, and by 1995 Mitsubishi had incurred losses of about $600 million. Then Mitsubishi quit, and Rockefeller Center was bankrupt. That triggered a complicated series of maneuvers and negotiations, still not complete as we finish this chapter in August 1995. But did this damage the value of the Rockefeller Center properties? Was Radio City Music Hall, one of the properties, any less valuable because of the bankruptcy? We doubt it.

understand why highly profitable growth companies, such as Microsoft or Hewlett Packard, use mostly equity finance.[21]

The moral of these examples is this: *Do not think only about the probability that borrowing will bring trouble. Think also of the value that may be lost if trouble comes.*

The Trade-off Theory of Capital Structure

Financial managers often think of the firm's debt-equity decision as a trade-off between interest tax shields and the costs of financial distress. Of course, there is controversy about how valuable interest tax shields are and what kinds of financial trouble are most threatening, but these disagreements are only variations on a theme. Thus, Figure 18-2 illustrates the debt-equity trade-off.

This *trade-off theory* of capital structure recognizes that target debt ratios may vary from firm to firm. Companies with safe, tangible assets and plenty of taxable income to shield ought to have high target ratios. Unprofitable companies with risky, intangible assets ought to rely primarily on equity financing.

If there were no costs of adjusting capital structure, then each firm should always be at its target debt ratio. However, there are costs, and therefore delays, in adjusting to the optimum. Firms cannot immediately offset the random events that bump them away from their capital structure targets, so we should see random differences in actual debt ratios among firms having the same target debt ratio.

All in all, this trade-off theory of capital structure choice tells a comforting story. Unlike MM's theory, which seemed to say that firms should take on as much debt as possible, it avoids extreme predictions and rationalizes moderate debt ratios.

But what are the facts? Can the trade-off theory of capital structure explain how companies actually behave?

The answer is "yes and no." On the "yes" side, the trade-off theory successfully explains many industry differences in capital structure. High-tech growth companies, for example, whose assets are risky and mostly intangible, normally use relatively little debt. Airlines can and do borrow heavily because their assets are tangible and relatively safe.[22]

The trade-off theory also helps explain what kinds of companies "go private" in leveraged buy-outs (LBOs). LBOs are acquisitions of public companies by private investors who finance a large fraction of the purchase price with debt. The target companies for LBO takeovers are usually mature "cash cow" businesses with established markets for their products but little in the way of high-NPV growth opportunities. That makes sense by the trade-off theory, because these are exactly the kind of companies that *ought* to have high debt ratios.

The trade-off theory also says that companies saddled with extra heavy debt—too much to pay down with a couple of years' internally generated cash—should issue stock, constrain dividends, or sell off assets to raise cash to rebalance capital structure. Here again, we can find plenty of confirming examples. When Texaco bought Getty Petroleum in January 1984, it borrowed $8 billion from a consortium of banks to help finance the acquisition. (The loan was arranged and paid

---

[21]Empirical research confirms that firms holding largely intangible assets borrow less. See M. Long and I. Malitz, "The Investment-Financing Nexus: Some Empirical Evidence," *Midland Corporate Finance Journal*, **3**:53–59 (Fall 1985).

[22]We are not suggesting that all airline *companies* are safe; many are not. But air*craft* can support debt where air*lines* cannot. If Fly-by-Night Airlines fails, its planes retain their value in another airline's operations. There's a good secondary market in used aircraft, so a loan secured by aircraft can be well protected even if made to an airline flying on thin ice (and in the dark).

over to Texaco within 2 weeks!) By the end of 1984, it had raised about $1.8 billion to pay down this debt, mostly by selling assets and forgoing dividend increases. Chrysler, when it emerged from near-bankruptcy in 1983, sold $432 million of new common stock to help regain a conservative capital structure.[23] In 1991, after a second brush with bankruptcy, it again sold shares to replenish equity, this time for $350 million.[24]

On the "no" side, there are a few things the trade-off theory cannot explain. It cannot explain why some of the most successful companies thrive with little debt, thereby giving up valuable interest tax shields. Think of Merck, which as Table 18-3a shows, is basically all-equity-financed. Granted, Merck's most valuable assets are intangible, the fruits of its pharmaceutical research and development. We know that intangible assets and conservative capital structures tend to go together. But Merck also has a very large corporate income tax bill ($1.4 billion in 1994) and the highest possible credit rating. It could borrow enough to save tens of millions of tax dollars without raising a whisker of concern about possible financial distress.[25]

Merck illustrates an odd fact about real-life capital structures: Within an industry, the most profitable companies generally borrow the least.[26] Here the trade-off theory fails, for it predicts exactly the reverse: Under the trade-off theory, high profits should mean more debt-servicing capacity and more taxable income to shield and should give a *higher* target debt ratio.[27]

A final point on the "no" side for the trade-off theory: Debt ratios in the early 1900s, when income tax rates were low (or zero), were just as high as those in the 1990s. Debt ratios in other industrialized countries are equal to or higher than those in the United States. Many of these countries have imputation tax systems, which should eliminate the value of the interest tax shields.[28]

---

[23]Note that Chrysler issued stock *after* it emerged from financial distress. It did not *prevent* financial distress by raising equity money when trouble loomed on its horizon. Why not? Refer back to "Refusing to Contribute Equity Capital: The Second Game" or forward to the analysis of asymmetric information in Section 18-4.

[24]Chrysler simultaneously contributed $300 million of newly issued shares to its underfunded pension plans.

[25]Research by Graham and Mackie-Mason has detected a tendency for taxpaying firms to prefer debt financing. See J. R. Graham, "Debt and the Marginal Tax Rate," *Journal of Financial Economics*, forthcoming; and J. Mackie-Mason, "Do Taxes Affect Corporate Financing Decisions?" *Journal of Finance*, **45**:1471–1493 (December 1990). However, it seems clear that public companies rarely make major shifts in debt ratios just because of taxes.

[26]For example, Carl Kester, in a study of the financing policies of firms in the United States and in Japan, found that in each country, high book profitability was the most statistically significant variable distinguishing low- from high-debt companies. See "Capital and Ownership Structure: A Comparison of United States and Japanese Manufacturing Corporations," *Financial Management*, **15**:5–16 (Spring 1986).

[27]Here we mean debt as a fraction of the book or replacement value of the company's assets. Profitable companies might not borrow a greater fraction of their market value. Higher profits imply higher market value as well as stronger incentives to borrow.

[28]We described the Australian imputation tax system in Section 16-6. Look again at Table 16-4, supposing that an Australian corporation pays $A10 of interest. This reduces the corporate tax by $A3.30; it also reduces the tax credit taken by the shareholders by $A3.30. The final tax does not depend on whether the corporation or the shareholder borrows.

You can check this by redrawing Figure 18-1 for the Australian system. The corporate tax rate T_c will cancel out. Since income after all taxes depends only on investors' tax rates, there is no special advantage to corporate borrowing.

None of this disproves the trade-off theory. As George Stigler emphasized, theories are not rejected by circumstantial evidence; it takes a theory to beat a theory. So we now turn to a completely different theory of financing.

18-4 THE PECKING ORDER OF FINANCING CHOICES

The pecking-order theory starts with *asymmetric information*—a fancy term indicating that managers know more about their companies' prospects, risks, and values than do outside investors.

Managers obviously know more than investors. We can prove that by observing stock price changes caused by announcements by managers. When a company announces an increased regular dividend, stock price typically rises, because investors interpret the increase as a sign of management's confidence in future earnings. In other words, the dividend increase transfers information from managers to investors. This can happen only if managers know more in the first place.

Asymmetric information affects the choice between internal and external financing and between new issues of debt and equity securities. This leads to a *pecking order*, in which investment is financed first with internal funds, reinvested earnings primarily; then by new issues of debt; and finally with new issues of equity. New equity issues are a last resort when the company runs out of debt capacity, that is, when the threat of costs of financial distress brings regular insomnia to existing creditors and to the financial manager.

We will take a closer look at the pecking order in a moment. First, you must appreciate how asymmetric information can force the financial manager to issue debt rather than common stock.

Debt and Equity Issues with Asymmetric Information

To the outside world Smith & Company and Jones, Inc., our two example companies, are identical. Each runs a successful business with good growth opportunities. The two businesses are risky, however, and investors have learned from experience that current expectations are frequently bettered or disappointed. Current expectations price each company's stock at $100 per share, but the true values could be higher or lower:

	Smith & Co.	Jones, Inc.
True value could be higher, say	$120	$120
Best current estimate	100	100
True value could be lower, say	80	80

Now suppose that both companies need to raise new money from investors to fund capital investment. They can do this either by issuing bonds or by issuing new shares of common stock. How would the choice be made? One financial manager—we will not tell you which one—might reason as follows:

Sell stock for $100 per share? Ridiculous! It's worth at least $120. A stock issue now would hand a free gift to new investors. I just wish those stupid, skeptical shareholders would appreciate the true value of this company. Our new factories will make us the world's lowest-cost producer. We've painted a rosy picture for the press and security analysts, but it just doesn't seem to be working. Oh well, the decision is obvious: we'll issue debt, not underpriced equity. A debt issue will save underwriting fees too.

The other financial manager is in a different mood:

Beefalo burgers were a hit for a while, but it looks like the fad is fading. The fast-food division's gotta find some good new products or it's all downhill from here. Export markets are OK for now, but how are we going to compete with those new Siberian ranches? Fortunately the stock price has held up pretty well—we've had some good short-run news for the press and security analysts. Now's the time to issue stock. We have major investments under way, and why add increased debt service to my other worries?

Of course, outside investors can't read the financial managers' minds. If they could, one stock might trade at $120 and the other at $80.

Why doesn't the optimistic financial manager simply educate investors? Then the company could sell stock on fair terms, and there would be no reason to favor debt over equity or vice versa.

This is not so easy. (Note that both companies are issuing upbeat press releases.) Investors can't be told what to think; they have to be convinced. That takes a detailed layout of the company's plans and prospects, including the inside scoop on new technology, product design, marketing plans, etc. Getting this across is expensive for the company and also valuable to its competitors. Why go to the trouble? Investors will learn soon enough, as revenues and earnings evolve. In the meantime the optimistic financial manager can finance growth by issuing debt.

Now suppose there are two press releases:

Jones, Inc., will issue $120 million of 5-year senior notes.

Smith & Co. announced plans today to issue 1.2 million new shares of common stock. The company expects to raise $120 million.

As a rational investor, you immediately learn two things. First, Jones's financial manager is optimistic and Smith's is pessimistic. Second, Smith's financial manager is also stupid to think that investors would pay $100 per share. The *attempt* to sell stock shows that it must be worth less. Smith might sell stock at $80 per share, but certainly not at $100.[29]

Smart financial managers think this through ahead of time. The end result? Both Smith and Jones end up issuing debt. Jones, Inc., issues debt because its financial manager is optimistic and doesn't want to issue undervalued equity. A smart, but pessimistic, financial manager at Smith issues debt because an attempt to issue equity would force the stock price down and eliminate any advantage from doing so. (Issuing equity also reveals the manager's pessimism immediately. Most managers prefer to wait. A debt issue lets bad news come out later through other channels.)

The story of Smith and Jones illustrates how asymmetric information favors debt issues over equity issues. If managers are better informed than investors and both groups are rational, then any company that can borrow will do so rather than issuing fresh equity. In other words, debt issues will be higher in the pecking order.

---

[29]A Smith stock issue might not succeed even at $80. Persistence in trying to sell at $80 could convince investors that the stock is worth even less!

Taken literally this reasoning seems to rule out any issue of equity. That's not right, because asymmetric information is not always important and there are other forces at work. For example, if Smith had already borrowed heavily, and would risk financial distress by borrowing more, then it would have a good reason to issue common stock. In this case announcement of a stock issue would not be entirely bad news. The announcement would still depress the stock price—it would highlight managers' concerns about financial distress—but the fall in price would not necessarily make the issue unwise or infeasible.

High-tech, high-growth companies can also be credible issuers of common stock. Such companies' assets are mostly intangible, and bankruptcy or financial distress would be especially costly. This calls for conservative financing. The only way to grow rapidly and keep a conservative debt ratio is to issue equity. If investors see equity issued for these reasons, problems of the sort encountered by Jones's financial manager become much less serious.

With such exceptions noted, asymmetric information can explain the dominance of debt financing over new equity issues in practice. Debt issues are frequent; equity issues, rare. The bulk of external financing comes from debt, even in the United States, where equity markets are highly information-efficient. Equity issues are even more difficult in countries with less well developed stock markets.

None of this says that firms ought to strive for high debt ratios—just that it's better to raise equity by plowing back earnings than issuing stock. In fact, a firm with ample internally generated funds doesn't have to sell any kind of security and thus avoids issue costs and information problems completely.[30]

Implica-tions of the Pecking Order	The pecking-order theory of corporate financing goes like this.[31]

1. Firms prefer internal finance.

2. They adapt their target dividend payout ratios to their investment opportunities, while trying to avoid sudden changes in dividends.

3. Sticky dividend policies, plus unpredictable fluctuations in profitability and investment opportunities, mean that internally generated cash flow is sometimes more than capital expenditures and other times less. If it is more, the firm pays off debt or invests in marketable securities. If it is less, the firm first draws down its cash balance or sells its marketable securities.

4. If external finance is required, firms issue the safest security first. That is, they start with debt, then possibly hybrid securities such as convertible bonds, then perhaps equity as a last resort.

In this theory, there is no well-defined target debt-equity mix, because there are two kinds of equity, internal and external, one at the top of the pecking order and one at the bottom. Each firm's observed debt ratio reflects its cumulative requirements for external finance.

---

[30]Even debt issues can create information problems if the odds of default are significant. A pessimistic manager may try to issue debt quickly, before bad news gets out. An optimistic manager will delay pending good news, perhaps arranging a short-term bank loan in the meantime. Rational investors will take this behavior into account in pricing the risky debt issue.

[31]The description is paraphrased from S. C. Myers, "The Capital Structure Puzzle," *Journal of Finance*, **39**:581–582 (July 1984). For the most part, this section follows Myers's arguments.

The pecking order explains why the most profitable firms generally borrow less—not because they have low target debt ratios but because they don't need outside money. Less profitable firms issue debt because they do not have internal funds sufficient for their capital investment program and because debt financing is first on the pecking order of *external* financing.

In the pecking-order theory, the attraction of interest tax shields is assumed to be a second-order effect. Debt ratios change when there is an imbalance of internal cash flow, net of dividends, and real investment opportunities. Highly profitable firms with limited investment opportunities work down to a low debt ratio. Firms whose investment opportunities outrun internally generated funds are driven to borrow more and more.

This theory explains the inverse intraindustry relationship between profitability and financial leverage. Suppose firms generally invest to keep up with the growth of their industries. Then rates of investment will be similar within an industry. Given sticky dividend payouts, the least profitable firms will have less internal funds and will end up borrowing more.

The pecking order seems to predict changes in many mature firms' debt ratios to a T. These companies' debt ratios increase when the firms have financial deficits and decline when they have surpluses. If asymmetric information makes major equity issues or retirements[32] rare, this behavior is nearly inevitable.

The pecking order is less successful in explaining *inter*industry differences in debt ratios. For example, debt ratios tend to be low in high-tech, high-growth industries, even when the need for external capital is great. There are also mature, stable industries—electric utilities, for example—in which ample cash flow is *not* used to pay down debt. High dividend payout ratios give the cash flow back to investors instead.

Financial Slack

Other things equal, it's better to be at the top of the pecking order than at the bottom. Firms that have worked down the pecking order and need external equity may end up living with excessive debt or passing by good investments because shares can't be sold at what managers consider a fair price.

In other words, *financial slack* is valuable. Having financial slack means having cash, marketable securities, readily saleable real assets, and ready access to the debt markets or to bank financing. Ready access basically requires conservative financing, so that potential lenders see the company's debt as a safe investment.

In the long run, a company's value rests more on its capital investment and operating decisions than on financing. Therefore, you want to make sure your firm has sufficient financial slack, so that financing is quickly available for good investments. Financial slack is most valuable to firms with plenty of positive-NPV growth opportunities. That is another reason why growth companies usually aspire to conservative capital structures.

Free Cash Flow and the Dark Side of Financial Slack[33]

There is also a dark side to financial slack. Too much of it may encourage managers to take it easy, expand their perks, or empire-build with cash that should be paid back to stockholders.

---

[32]Companies with low debt ratios and surplus cash often repurchase stock, but ordinary repurchases rarely cause material increases in debt ratios.

[33]Some of the following is drawn from S. C. Myers, "Still Searching for Optimal Capital Structure," *Journal of Applied Corporate Finance*, **6**:4–14 (Spring 1993).

Michael Jensen has stressed the tendency of managers with ample free cash flow (or unnecessary financial slack) to plow too much cash into mature businesses or ill-advised acquisitions. "The problem," Jensen says, "is how to motivate managers to disgorge the cash rather than investing it below the cost of capital or wasting it in organizational inefficiencies."[34]

If that's the problem, then maybe debt is an answer. Scheduled interest and principal payments are contractual obligations of the firm. Debt forces the firm to pay out cash. Perhaps the best debt level would leave just enough cash in the bank, after debt service, to finance all positive-NPV projects, with not a penny left over.

We do not recommend this degree of fine-tuning, but the idea is valid and important. Debt can discipline managers who are tempted to invest too much. It can also provide the pressure to force improvements in operating efficiency. Here is one very successful example.

SEALED AIR'S LEVERAGED RECAPITALIZATION.[35]   In 1989 Sealed Air Corporation undertook a *leveraged recapitalization*. It borrowed the money to pay a $328 million special cash dividend. In one stroke the company's debt increased 10 times. Its book equity (accounting net worth) went from $162 million to *minus* $161 million. Debt went from 13 percent of total book assets to 136 percent.

Sealed Air was a profitable company. The problem was that its profits were coming too easily, because its main products were protected by patents. When the patents expired, strong competition was inevitable, and the company was not ready for it. In the meantime, there was too much financial slack:

> . . . we didn't need to manufacture efficiently; we didn't need to worry about cash. At Sealed Air, capital tended to have limited value attached to it—cash was perceived as being free and abundant.[36]

So the leveraged recap was used to "disrupt the status quo, promote internal change," and simulate "the pressures of Sealed Air's more competitive future."[37] This shake-up was reinforced by new performance measures and incentives, including increases in stock ownership by employees.

It worked. Sales and operating profits increased steadily without major new capital investments, and net working capital *fell* by half, releasing cash to help service the company's debt. The company's stock price quadrupled in the 5 years after the recapitalization.

Sealed Air's recapitalization was not typical. It is an exemplar chosen with hindsight. It was also undertaken by a successful firm under no outside pressure. As we will see in Chapter 33, most leveraged recaps are responses to takeover threats or take the form of leveraged buy-outs (LBOs), in which management and/or private investors borrow to take over. But much of the value added in these cases has come from the same source as Sealed Air's. These are *diet deals* designed to force success-

---

[34]M. C. Jensen, "Agency Costs of Free Cash Flow, Corporate Finance and Takeovers," *American Economic Review*, **26**:323 (May 1986).

[35]See K. H. Wruck, "Financial Policy as a Catalyst for Organizational Change: Sealed Air's Leveraged Special Dividend," *Journal of Applied Corporate Finance*, **7**:20–37 (Winter 1995).

[36]Ibid, p. 21.

[37]Ibid.

ful but overweight organizations to shed financial fat, that is, to disgorge cash, reduce operating costs, and use assets more efficiently. The deals start with debt burdens that would be imprudent for normal firms. But the debt is used to make sure the diet is adhered to.

18-5   SUMMARY

Our task in this chapter was to show why capital structure matters. We did not throw away MM's proposition I, that capital structure is irrelevant; we added to it. However, we did not arrive at any simple, satisfactory theory of optimal capital structure.

The traditional trade-off theory emphasizes taxes and financial distress. The value of the firm is broken down as

Value if all-equity-financed + PV(tax shield) − PV(costs of financial distress)

According to this theory, the firm should increase debt until the value from PV(tax shield) is just offset, at the margin, by increases in PV(costs of financial distress).

The cost of financial distress can be broken down as follows:

1. Bankruptcy costs
   (*a*) Direct costs such as court fees
   (*b*) Indirect costs reflecting the difficulty of managing a company undergoing reorganization
2. Costs of financial distress short of bankruptcy
   (*a*) Conflicts of interest between bondholders and stockholders of firms in financial distress may lead to poor operating and investment decisions. Stockholders acting in their narrow self-interest can gain at the expense of creditors by playing "games" which reduce the overall value of the firm.
   (*b*) The fine print in debt contracts is designed to prevent these games. But fine print increases the costs of writing, monitoring, and enforcing the debt contract.

The value of the tax shield is more controversial. It would be easy to compute if we had only corporate taxes to worry about. In that case the net tax saving from borrowing would be just the marginal corporate tax rate T_c times $r_D D$, the interest payment. This tax shield is usually valued by discounting at the borrowing rate r_D. In the special case of fixed, permanent debt

$$\text{PV(tax shield)} = \frac{T_c(r_D D)}{r_D} = T_c D$$

Most economists have become accustomed to thinking only of the corporate tax advantages of debt. But many firms seem to thrive with no debt at all despite the strong tax inducement to borrow.

Miller has presented an alternative theory which may explain this. He argued that the net tax saving from corporate borrowing can be zero when personal taxes as well as corporate taxes are considered. Interest income is not taxed at the corporate level but is taxed at the personal level. Equity income is taxed at the corporate level but may largely escape personal taxes if it comes in the form of capital gains. Thus T_{pE}, the effective personal rate on equity income, is usually less than T_p, the regular personal rate which applies to interest income. This reduces the relative tax advantage of debt:

$$\text{Relative advantage} = \frac{1 - T_p}{(1 - T_{pE})(1 - T_c)}$$

Note that the relative advantage is $1/(1 - T_c)$ if interest and equity income are taxed at the same personal rates.

In Miller's theory, the supply of corporate debt expands as long as the corporate tax rate exceeds the personal tax rate of the investors absorbing the increased supply. The supply which equates these two tax rates establishes an optimal debt ratio for the aggregate of corporations. But, if the total supply of debt suits investors' needs, any single taxpaying firm must find that debt policy does not matter.

The Tax Reform Act of 1986 undercut Miller's argument by cutting back the extra personal taxes paid on interest income versus paid on equity income (dividends and capital gains). But there is probably still a personal tax disadvantage to debt which to some degree offsets its corporate tax advantage.

We suggest that borrowing may make sense for some firms but not for others. If a firm can be fairly sure of earning a profit, there is likely to be a net tax saving from borrowing. However, for firms that are unlikely to earn sufficient profits to benefit from the corporate tax shield, there is little, if any, net tax advantage to borrowing. For these firms the net tax saving could even be negative.

The trade-off theory balances the tax advantages of borrowing against the costs of financial distress. Corporations are supposed to pick a target capital structure that maximizes firm value. Firms with safe, tangible assets and plenty of taxable income to shield ought to have high targets. Unprofitable companies with risky, intangible assets ought to rely primarily on equity financing.

This theory of capital structure successfully explains many industry differences in capital structure, but it does not explain why the most profitable firms *within* an industry generally have the most conservative capital structures. (Under the trade-off theory, high profitability should mean high debt capacity *and* a strong corporate tax incentive to use that capacity.)

There is a competing, pecking-order theory, which states that firms use internal financing when available and choose debt over equity when external financing is required. This explains why the less profitable firms in an industry borrow more—not because they have higher target debt ratios but because they need more external financing and because debt is next on the pecking order when internal funds are exhausted.

The pecking order is a consequence of asymmetric information. Managers know more about their firms than outside investors do, and they are reluctant to issue stock when they believe the price is too low. They try to time issues when shares are fairly priced or overpriced. Investors understand this, and interpret a decision to issue shares as bad news. That explains why stock price usually falls when a stock issue is announced.

Debt is better than equity when these information problems are important. Optimistic managers will prefer debt to undervalued equity, and pessimistic managers will be pressed to follow suit. The pecking-order theory says that equity will be issued only when debt capacity is running out and financial distress threatens.

The pecking-order theory is clearly not 100 percent right. There are many examples of equity issued by companies that could easily have borrowed. But the theory does explain why most external financing comes from debt, and it explains why changes in debt ratios tend to follow requirements for external financing.

The pecking order theory stresses the value of financial slack. Without sufficient slack, the firm may be caught at the bottom of the pecking order and be forced to choose between issuing undervalued shares, borrowing and risking financial distress, or passing up positive-NPV investment opportunities.

There is, however, a dark side to financial slack. Surplus cash or credit tempts managers to overinvest or to indulge an easy and glamorous corporate lifestyle. When temptation wins, or threatens to win, a leveraged recapitalization may be in order. A recap drastically increases debt service, forcing the company to disgorge cash and prodding managers and organizations to try harder to be more efficient.

APPENDIX: BANKRUPTCY PROCEDURES

Each year nearly 100,000 businesses file for bankruptcy. Most are small private firms, but about 1 percent of listed firms also go under each year.

Occasionally bankruptcy proceedings are initiated by the creditors, but usually it is the firm itself that decides to file. It can choose one of two procedures, which are set out in Chapters 7 and 11 of the 1978 Bankruptcy Reform Act. The purpose of Chapter 7 is to oversee the firm's death and dismemberment, while Chapter 11 seeks to nurse the firm back to health.

Most small firms make use of Chapter 7. In this case the bankruptcy judge appoints a trustee, who then closes the firm down and auctions off the assets. The proceeds from the auction are used to pay off the creditors. There is a pecking order of unsecured creditors. The U.S. Treasury, court officers, and the trustee have first peck. Wages come next, followed by taxes and debts to some government agencies such as the Pension Benefit Guarantee Corporation. Frequently the trustee will need to prevent some creditors from trying to jump the gun and collect on their debts, and sometimes the trustee will retrieve property that a creditor has recently seized.

Instead of agreeing to a liquidation, large public companies generally attempt to rehabilitate the business. This is in the shareholders' interests—they have nothing to lose if things deteriorate further and everything to gain if the firm recovers.

The procedures for rehabilitation are set out in Chapter 11 of the 1978 act. Their purpose is to keep the firm alive and operating and to protect the value of its assets[38] while a plan of reorganization is worked out. During this period, other proceedings against the firm are halted, and the company usually continues to be run by its existing management.[39] The responsibility for developing the plan falls on the debtor firm. If it cannot devise an acceptable plan, the court may invite anyone to do so—for example, a committee of creditors.

The plan goes into effect if it is accepted by the creditors and confirmed by the court. Acceptance requires approval by at least one-half of the creditors voting, and the creditors voting "aye" must represent two-thirds of the value of the creditors' aggregate claim against the firm. The plan also needs to be approved by two-thirds of the shareholders. Once the creditors and shareholders have accepted the plan, the court normally approves it, provided that *each class* of creditors is in favor and that the creditors will be no worse off under the plan than they would be if the firm's assets were liquidated and distributed. Under certain conditions the court may confirm

---

[38]In order to keep the firm alive, it may be necessary to continue to use assets that were offered as collateral, but this denies secured creditors access to their collateral. In order to resolve this problem, the Bankruptcy Reform Act makes it possible for firms operating under Chapter 11 to keep such assets as long as the creditors who have a claim on those assets are compensated for any decline in their value. Thus, the firm might make cash payments to the secured creditors to cover economic depreciation of the assets.

[39]Occasionally the court will appoint a trustee to manage the firm.

a plan even if one or more classes of creditors vote against it,[40] but the rules for a "cram-down" are complicated, and we will not attempt to cover them here.

The reorganization plan is basically a statement of who gets what; each class of creditors gives up its claim in exchange for new securities or a mixture of securities and cash. The problem is to design a new capital structure for the firm that will (1) satisfy the creditors and (2) allow the firm to solve the *business* problems that got the firm into trouble in the first place.[41] Sometimes satisfying these two requirements requires a plan of baroque complexity. When the Penn Central Corporation was finally reorganized in 1978 (7 years after the largest railroad bankruptcy ever), more than a dozen new securities were created and parceled out among 15 classes of creditors.

The Securities and Exchange Commission (SEC) plays a role in many reorganizations, particularly for large, public companies. Its interest is to ensure that all relevant and material information is disclosed to the creditors before they vote on a proposed plan of reorganization. The SEC may take part in a hearing before court approval of a plan, for example.

Chapter 11 proceedings are often successful, and the patient emerges fit and healthy. But in other cases rehabilitation proves impossible, and the assets are liquidated. Sometimes the firm may emerge from Chapter 11 for a brief period before it is once again submerged by disaster and back in the bankruptcy court. For example, TWA came out of Chapter 11 bankruptcy at the end of 1993 and was back again less than 2 years later, prompting jokes about "Chapter 22."[42]

Is Chapter 11 Efficient?

Here is a simple view of the bankruptcy decision: Whenever a payment is due to creditors, management checks the value of the equity. If the value is positive, the firm pays the creditors (if necessary, raising the cash by an issue of shares). If the equity is valueless, the firm defaults on its debt and petitions for bankruptcy. If the assets of the bankrupt firm can be put to better use elsewhere, the firm is liquidated and the proceeds are used to pay off the creditors. Otherwise, the creditors simply become the new owners, and the firm continues to operate.[43]

In practice, matters are rarely so simple. For example, we observe that firms often petition for bankruptcy even when the equity has a positive value. And firms are often reorganized even when the assets could be used more efficiently elsewhere. The problems in Chapter 11 usually arise because the goal of paying off the creditors often conflicts with the goal of maintaining the business as a going concern. Take the case of Eastern Airlines. When Eastern filed for bankruptcy, it stated that it had sufficient funds ($3.7 billion) to repay its liabilities fully ($3.4 billion). One year later Eastern proposed to repay its creditors $1.6 billion. When it finally became clear that the airline was a terminal case, it was liquidated and the creditors received only about $300 million. The creditors would clearly have preferred Eastern to have been liquidated immediately; the unsuccessful attempt at resuscitation cost the creditors over $3 billion.

---

[40]But at least one class of creditors must vote for the plan—otherwise, the court cannot approve it.

[41]Although Chapter 11 is designed to keep the firm in business, the reorganization plan often involves the sale or closure of large parts of the business.

[42]One study found that after emerging from Chapter 11 bankruptcy about one in three firms again reentered bankruptcy or privately restructured their debt. See E. S. Hotchkiss, "Postbankruptcy Reform and Management Turnover," *Journal of Finance*, **50**:3–21 (March 1995).

[43]If there are several classes of creditors, the junior creditors initially become the owners of the company and are responsible for paying off the senior debt. They now face exactly the same decision as the original owners. If their equity is valueless, they will also default and turn over ownership of the company to the next class of creditors.

Here are some reasons that Chapter 11 proceedings do not always achieve an efficient solution:

1. Although the reorganized firm is legally a new entity, it is entitled to the tax-loss carry-forwards belonging to the old firm. If the firm is liquidated rather than reorganized, the tax-loss carry-forwards disappear. Thus there is a tax incentive to continue operating the firm even when its assets could be sold and put to better use elsewhere.

2. If the firm's assets are sold off, it is easy to determine what is available to pay the creditors. However, when the company is reorganized, it needs to conserve cash. Therefore, claimants are generally paid in a mixture of cash and securities. This makes it less easy to judge whether they receive a fair shake. For example, each bondholder may be offered $300 in cash and $700 in a new bond which pays no interest for the first 2 years and a low rate of interest thereafter. A bond of this kind in a company that is struggling to survive may not be worth much, but the bankruptcy court usually looks at the face value of the new bonds and may therefore regard the bondholders as paid off in full.

   Senior creditors who know they are likely to get a raw deal in a reorganization are likely to press for a liquidation. Shareholders and junior creditors prefer a reorganization. They hope that the court will not interpret the pecking order too strictly and that they will receive some crumbs when the firm's remaining value is sliced up. In the majority of cases their hopes are realized; often they receive a substantial portion of the equity of the reorganized company even though the unsecured creditors receive less than they are owed.[44]

3. Although shareholders and junior creditors are at the bottom of the pecking order, they have a secret weapon—they can play for time. On average it takes 2 to 3 years before a plan is presented to the court and agreed to by each class of creditor. (The bankruptcy proceedings of the Missouri Pacific Railroad took a total of 22 years.) When they use delaying tactics, the junior claimants are betting on a stroke of luck that will rescue their investment. On the other hand, the senior claimants know that time is working against them, so they may be prepared to accept a smaller payoff as part of the price for getting a plan accepted. Also, prolonged bankruptcy cases are costly (the bankruptcy proceedings of Wickes Corporation involved about $250 million in legal and administrative costs). Senior claimants may see their money seeping into lawyers' pockets and therefore decide to settle quickly.

4. While a reorganization plan is being drawn up, the company is likely to need additional working capital. It is therefore allowed to buy goods on credit and borrow money. The new creditors have priority over the old creditors, and their debt may even be secured by assets that are already mortgaged to existing debtholders. This also gives the old creditors an incentive to settle quickly, before their claims are diluted by the new debt.

5. While the firm is in Chapter 11, secured debt receives interest but unsecured debt does not. For unsecured debtholders that is another reason for a fast settlement.

---

[44]Franks and Torous found that stockholders received some payoff—usually securities—in two-thirds of Chapter 11 reorganizations. See J. R. Franks and W. N. Torous, "An Empirical Investigation of U.S. Firms in Reorganization," *Journal of Finance*, **44**:747–770 (July 1989). A similar study concluded that in a third of the cases shareholders received more than 25 percent of the equity in the new firm. See L. A. Weiss, "Bankruptcy Resolution: Direct Costs and Violation of Priority of Claims," *Journal of Financial Economics*, **27**:285–314 (October 1990).

6. Sometimes profitable companies have filed for Chapter 11 bankruptcy to protect themselves against "burdensome" suits.[45] For example, Continental Airlines, which was bedeviled by a costly labor contract, filed for Chapter 11 in 1982 and immediately cut pay by up to 50 percent.[46] In 1995 Dow Corning was threatened with costly litigation for damage allegedly caused by its silicone-gel breast implants. Dow filed for bankruptcy under Chapter 11, and the bankruptcy judge agreed to stay the damage suits. Needless to say, lawyers and legislators worry that these actions were contrary to the original intent of the bankruptcy acts.

Workouts

If Chapter 11 reorganizations are not efficient, why don't firms bypass the bankruptcy courts and get together with their creditors to work out a solution?

Many firms that are in distress *do* first seek a negotiated settlement. For example, they can seek to delay repayment of the debt or negotiate an interest-rate holiday. However, shareholders and junior creditors know that senior creditors are anxious to avoid formal bankruptcy proceedings. So they are likely to be tough negotiators, and senior creditors generally need to make concessions to reach agreement.[47] The larger the firm, and the more complicated its capital structure, the less likely it is that everyone will agree to any proposal. For example, Wickes Corporation tried—and failed—to reach a negotiated settlement with its 250,000 creditors.

Sometimes the firm does agree to an informal workout with its creditors and then files under Chapter 11 to obtain the approval of the bankruptcy court.[48] Such *prepackaged bankruptcies* reduce the likelihood of subsequent litigation and allow the firm to gain the special tax advantages of Chapter 11.

Alternative Bankruptcy Procedures

The United States bankruptcy system is often described as a debtor-oriented system: its principal focus is on rescuing firms in distress. But this comes at a cost, for there are many instances in which the firm's assets would be better redeployed in other uses. One critic of Chapter 11, Michael Jensen, has argued that "the U.S. bankruptcy system is fundamentally flawed. It is expensive, it exacerbates conflicts of interest among different classes of creditors, and it often takes years to resolve individual cases."[49] Jensen's proposed solution is to require that any bankrupt company be put immediately on the auction block and the proceeds be distributed to claimants in accordance with the priority of their claims.[50]

In other countries the main purpose of bankruptcy law is not to rehabilitate the business but to recover as much as possible for the lenders and to ensure that the senior claimants get first peck. For example, in the United Kingdom creditors can ap-

---

[45]See, for example, A. Cifelli, "Management by Bankruptcy," *Fortune*, October 1983, pp. 69–73.

[46]The pay cut enabled Continental to reduce fares aggressively and improve its load factors, but it did not solve Continental's problems. Shortly after emerging from bankruptcy, it was back in the bankruptcy court.

[47]Franks and Torous show that creditors make even greater concessions to junior claimholders in informal workouts than in Chapter 11 reorganizations. See J. R. Franks and W. N. Torous, "How Shareholders and Creditors Fare in Workouts and Chapter 11 Reorganizations," *Journal of Financial Economics*, **35**:349–370 (May 1994).

[48]For example, when TWA reentered Chapter 11 in 1995, it had already agreed to a *prepack* with its creditors.

[49]M. C. Jensen, "Corporate Control and the Politics of Finance," *Journal of Applied Corporate Finance*, **4**:13–33 (Summer 1991).

[50]An ingenious alternative set of bankruptcy procedures is proposed in P. Aghion, O. Hart, and J. Moore, "The Economics of Bankruptcy Reform," *Journal of Law, Economics and Organization*, **8**:523–546 (1992).

ply for the appointment of a *liquidator* or a *receiver*, whose principal responsibility is to sell enough of the firm's assets to pay off its debts. Similarly, in Germany an administrator (called a *konkursverwalter*) is appointed to sell the firm for cash, though he or she may decide that it is preferable not to do so immediately.[51] In principle these procedures should help to ensure that assets are quickly and efficiently transferred to their best use. However, the arguments are not one-sided. Many observers worry that assets are sold off at fire-sale prices just to satisfy the senior creditors.

Further Reading

Modigliani and Miller's analysis of the present value of interest tax shields at the corporate level is in:
F. Modigliani and M. H. Miller: "Corporate Income Taxes and the Cost of Capital: A Correction," *American Economic Review*, **53**:433–443 (June 1963).
F. Modigliani and M. H. Miller: "Some Estimates of the Cost of Capital to the Electric Utility Industry, 1954–57," *American Economic Review*, **56**:333–391 (June 1966).

Miller extends the MM model to personal as well as corporate taxes; DeAngelo and Masulis argue that firms with plenty of noninterest tax shields, e.g., shields from depreciation, should borrow less:
M. H. Miller: "Debt and Taxes," *Journal of Finance*, **32**:261–276 (May 1977).
H. DeAngelo and R. Masulis: "Optimal Capital Structure under Corporate Taxation," *Journal of Financial Economics*, **8**:5–29 (March 1980).

The following articles analyze the conflicts of interest between bondholders and stockholders and their implications for financing policy (do not read the last article until you have read Chapter 20):
M. C. Jensen and W. H. Meckling: "Theory of the Firm: Managerial Behavior, Agency Costs and Ownership Structure," *Journal of Financial Economics*, **3**:305–360 (October 1976).
S. C. Myers: "Determinants of Corporate Borrowing," *Journal of Financial Economics*, **5**:146–175 (1977).
D. Galai and R. W. Masulis: "The Option Pricing Model and the Risk Factor of Stock," *Journal of Financial Economics*, **3**:53–82 (January–March 1976).

Myers describes the pecking-order theory, which is in turn based on work by Myers and Majluf; Baskin surveys some of the evidence for that theory:
S. C. Myers: "The Capital Structure Puzzle," *Journal of Finance*, **39**:575–592 (July 1984).
S. C. Myers and N. S. Majluf: "Corporate Financing and Investment Decisions When Firms Have Information Investors Do Not Have," *Journal of Financial Economics*, **13**:187–222 (June 1984).
J. Baskin: "An Empirical Investigation of the Pecking Order Hypothesis," *Financial Management*, **18**:26–35 (Spring 1989).

Three useful reviews of theory and evidence on optimal capital structure are:
M. J. Barclay, C. W. Smith, and R. L. Watts: "The Determinants of Corporate Leverage and Dividend Policies," *Journal of Applied Corporate Finance*, **7**:4–19 (Winter 1995).
M. Harris and A. Raviv: "The Theory of Optimal Capital Structure," *Journal of Finance*, **48**:297–356 (March 1991).
S. C. Myers: "Still Searching for Optimal Capital Structure," *Journal of Applied Corporate Finance*, **6**:4–14 (Spring 1993).

---

[51]A *receiver* is appointed by secured creditors and a *liquidator* by unsecured creditors. For more information on the UK and German systems, see J. R. Franks, K. Nyborg, and W. N. Torous, "A Comparison of US, UK and German Insolvency Codes," unpublished working paper, London Business School, May 1995.

The Spring 1993 and Winter 1995 issues of the Journal of Applied Corporate Finance *contain several articles on the incentive effects of capital structure, including:*

K. H. Wruck: "Financial Policy as a Catalyst for Organizational Change: Sealed Air's Leveraged Special Dividend," *Journal of Applied Corporate Finance*, **7**:20–37 (Winter 1995).

Altman's book is a general survey of the bankruptcy decision; also listed below are several good studies of the conflicting interests of different security holders and the costs and consequences of reorganization:

E. A. Altman: *Corporate Financial Distress: A Complete Guide to Predicting, Avoiding and Dealing with Bankruptcy*, John Wiley & Sons, New York, 1983.

M. White: "The Corporate Bankruptcy Decision," *Journal of Economic Perspectives*, **3**:129–152 (Spring 1989).

J. R. Franks and W. N. Torous: "An Empirical Analysis of U.S. Firms in Reorganization," *Journal of Finance*, **44**:747–770 (July 1989).

J. R. Franks and W. N. Torous: "How Shareholders and Creditors Fare in Workouts and Chapter 11 Reorganizations," *Journal of Financial Economics*, **35**:349–370 (May 1994).

L. A. Weiss, "Bankruptcy Resolution: Direct Costs and Violation of Priority of Claims," *Journal of Financial Economics*, **27**:285–314 (October 1990).

The Summer 1991 issue of the Journal of Applied Corporate Finance *contains several articles on bankruptcy and reorganizations.*

The January–February 1986 issue of the Journal of Financial Economics *(vol. 15, no. 1/2) collects a series of empirical studies on the stock price impacts of debt and equity issues and capital structure changes.*

Quiz

1. Compute the present value of interest tax shields generated by these three debt issues. Consider corporate taxes only. The marginal tax rate is $T_c = .35$.
   (*a*) A $1000, 1-year loan at 8 percent.
   (*b*) A 5-year loan of $1000 at 8 percent. Assume no principal is repaid until maturity.
   (*c*) A $1000 perpetuity at 7 percent.

2. Here are book and market value balance sheets of the United Frypan Company:

Book				Market			
Net working capital	$ 20	Debt	$ 40	Net working capital	$ 20	Debt	$ 40
Long-term assets	80	Equity	60	Long-term assets	140	Equity	120
	$100		$100		$160		$160

Assume that MM's theory holds with taxes. There is no growth, and the $40 of debt is expected to be permanent. Assume a 40 percent corporate tax rate.
(*a*) How much of the firm's value is accounted for by the debt-generated tax shield?
(*b*) How much better off will UF's shareholders be if the firm borrows $20 more and uses it to repurchase stock?
(*c*) Now suppose that Congress passes a law which eliminates the deductibility of interest for tax purposes after a grace period of 5 years. What will be the new value of the firm, other things equal? (Assume an 8 percent borrowing rate.)

3. What is the relative tax advantage of corporate debt if the corporate tax rate is $T_c = .35$, the personal tax rate is $T_p = .31$, but all equity income is received as capital gains and escapes tax entirely ($T_{pE} = 0$)? How does the relative tax advantage change if the company decides to pay out all equity income as cash dividends?

4. This question tests your understanding of "financial distress."
   (a) What are the costs of going bankrupt? Define these costs carefully.
   (b) "A company can incur costs of financial distress without ever going bankrupt." Explain how this can happen.
   (c) Explain how conflicts of interest between bondholders and stockholders can lead to costs of financial distress.

5. On February 29, 2003, when PDQ Computers announced bankruptcy, its share price fell from $3.00 to $.50 per share. There were 10 million shares outstanding. Does that imply bankruptcy costs of $10 \times (3.00 - .50) = \$25$ million? Explain.

6. "The firm can't use interest tax shields unless it has (taxable) income to shield." What does this statement imply for the debt policy? Explain briefly.

7. Let us go back to Circular File's market value balance sheet:

Net working capital	$20	$25	Bonds outstanding
Fixed assets	10	5	Common stock
Total assets	$30	$30	Total liabilities

   Who gains and who loses from the following maneuvers?
   (a) Circular scrapes up $5 in cash and pays a cash dividend.
   (b) Circular halts operations, sells its fixed assets, and converts net working capital into $20 cash. Unfortunately the fixed assets fetch only $6 on the secondhand market. The $26 cash is invested in Treasury bills.
   (c) Circular encounters an acceptable investment opportunity, NPV = 0, requiring an investment of $10. The firm borrows to finance the project. The new debt has the same security, seniority, etc., as the old.
   (d) Suppose that the new project has NPV = +$2 and is financed by an issue of preferred stock.
   (e) The lenders agree to extend the maturity of their loan from 1 year to 2 in order to give Circular a chance to recover.

8. What types of firms would be likely to incur heavy costs in the event of bankruptcy or financial distress? What types would incur relatively light costs? Give a few examples of each type.

9. The conventional theory of optimal capital structure states that firms trade off corporate interest tax shields against the possible costs of financial distress due to borrowing. What does this theory predict about the relationship between book profitability and target book debt ratios? Is the theory's prediction consistent with the facts?

10. What is meant by the "pecking-order" theory of capital structure? Could this theory explain the observed relationship between profitability and debt ratios? Explain briefly.

11. Why does asymmetric information push companies to raise external funds by borrowing rather than issuing common stock?

12. "A high debt ratio forces the company to pay out cash, thereby increasing value to investors." Explain why, or in what circumstances, this is true.

13. For what kinds of companies is financial slack most valuable? Are there situations in which financial slack should be reduced by borrowing and paying out the proceeds to the stockholders? Explain.

14. What is the difference between Chapter 7 bankruptcy and Chapter 11 bankruptcy?

15. True or false?
    (*a*) When a company becomes bankrupt, it is usually in the interests of the equityholders to seek a liquidation rather than a reorganization.
    (*b*) A reorganization plan must be presented for approval by each class of creditor.
    (*c*) The Internal Revenue Service has first claim on the company's assets in the event of bankruptcy.
    (*d*) In a reorganization, creditors may be paid off with a mixture of cash and securities.
    (*e*) When a company is liquidated, one of the most valuable assets to be sold is often the tax-loss carry-forward.

16. Explain why equity can sometimes have a positive value even when companies petition for bankruptcy.

Questions and Problems

1. Suppose that, in an effort to reduce the federal deficit, Congress increases the top personal tax rate on interest and dividends to 44 percent but retains a 28 percent tax rate on realized capital gains. The corporate tax rate stays at 35 percent. Compute the total corporate plus personal taxes paid on debt versus equity income if (*a*) all capital gains are realized immediately and (*b*) capital gains are deferred forever. Assume capital gains are half of equity income.

2. "The trouble with MM's argument is that it ignores the fact that individuals can deduct interest for personal income tax." Show why this is not an objection. What difference would it make if individuals were not allowed to deduct interest for personal tax?

3. Look back at the Merck example in Section 18-1. Suppose that Merck moves to a 40 percent book debt ratio by issuing debt and using the proceeds to repurchase shares. Consider only corporate taxes. Now reconstruct Table 18-3*b* to reflect the new capital structure. Before it changes its capital structure, Merck has 1248 million shares outstanding. What is the stock price before and after the change?

4. Calculate the tax shield for an actual United States company assuming:
    (*a*) Debt is permanent.
    (*b*) Personal tax rates on debt and equity income are the same.
    How would the stock price change if the company announced tomorrow that it intended to replace all its debt with equity?

*5. Explain the implications of Miller's capital structure theory for the debt policy of:

(*a*) A company that pays corporate income tax.

(*b*) A company that is not in a taxpaying position.

(*c*) A company that is paying taxes now but is unsure that it will have taxable income in the future.

Assume 1985 tax rates for the United States: 46 percent for corporations, personal rates of up to 50 percent for dividends and interest, and effective personal rates of, say, 10 percent on capital gains.

*6. Imagine a very simple world. There are three groups of investors with the following tax rates:

Group	Tax Rate
A	60%
B	40
C	0

They can choose from perpetual municipal bonds, perpetual corporate bonds, and common stock. Municipals and common stock attract no personal tax. Interest from corporate bonds attracts personal tax but is deductible for corporate tax. The corporate tax rate is 50 percent. Interest payments on municipals total $20 million. Cash flow (before interest and taxes) from corporations totals $300 million. Each group starts with the same amount of money. Regardless of what changes are made in capital structure, the three groups always invest the same amount, and they require a minimum return of 10 percent after taxes on any security.

(*a*) Suppose that companies are financed initially by common stock. Company X now decides to allocate $1 million of its pretax cash flows to interest payments on debt. Which group or groups of investors will buy this debt? What will be the rate of interest? What will be the effect on the value of Company X?

(*b*) Other companies have followed the example of X and interest payments now total $150 million. At this point company Y decides to allocate $1 million to interest payments on debt. Which group or groups will buy this debt? What will be the rate of interest? What will be the effect on the value of company Y?

(*c*) Total interest payments have somehow risen to $250 million. Now company Z substitutes common stock for debt, thereby *reducing* interest payments by $1 million. Which group or groups will sell their debt to Z? At what rate of interest can Z repurchase the debt? What will be the effect on Z's value?

(*d*) What is the equilibrium capital structure? Which groups will hold which securities? What is the rate of interest? What is the total value of all companies? Show that in equilibrium even an unlevered company has no incentive to issue debt. Similarly show that even a company with above-average leverage has no incentive to reduce its debt.

*7. Here is a difficult problem: What difference does the deduction for depreciation make to Miller's equilibrium? Try recalculating the equilibrium in problem 6, assuming that companies can deduct depreciation of:

(*a*) $100 million.

(*b*) $50 million.

*8. The expected return on (risk-free) equity is 14 percent, and the risk-free inter-
est rate is 20 percent.
   (*a*) What is the implied personal tax rate of the marginal lender? (Assume that
        equity income is free of personal tax.)
   (*b*) Company A has large depreciation tax shields and uncertain income. As a
        result, A's expected marginal rate of corporate tax is 40 percent if it fi-
        nances solely with equity. For every 5 percent increase in A's debt ratio, A's
        marginal tax rate is expected to decline by 2 percent. How much should A
        borrow?

9. Look at some real companies with different types of assets. What operating
   problems would each encounter in the event of financial distress? How well
   would the assets keep their value?

10. The Salad Oil Storage (SOS) Company has financed a large part of its facili-
    ties with long-term debt. There is a significant risk of default, but the com-
    pany is not on the ropes yet. Explain:
   (*a*) Why SOS stockholders could lose by investing in a positive-NPV project
        financed by an equity issue.
   (*b*) Why SOS stockholders could gain by investing in a negative-NPV project
        financed by cash.
   (*c*) Why SOS stockholders could gain from paying out a large cash dividend.
   How might the firm's adherence to a target debt ratio mitigate some or all of
   the problems noted above?

11. (*a*) Who benefits from the "fine print" in bond contracts when the firm gets
        into financial trouble? Give a one-sentence answer.
   (*b*) Who benefits from the fine print when the bonds are issued? Suppose the
        firm is offered the choice of issuing (i) a bond with standard restrictions on
        dividend payout, additional borrowing, etc., and (ii) a bond with minimal
        restrictions but a much higher interest rate? Suppose the interest rates on
        both (i) and (ii) are fair from the viewpoint of lenders. Which bond would
        you expect the firm to issue? Why?

12. Caldor, the retailing chain, filed for bankruptcy in September 1995. Shortly af-
    ter the bankruptcy its stock traded at $5.25 per share, down from about $20
    earlier in the year. How much of this drop should be attributed to bankruptcy
    costs—all, part, or none? Explain.

13. "I was amazed to find that the announcement of a stock issue drives down the
    value of the issuing firm by *30 percent*, on average, of the proceeds of the issue.
    That issue cost dwarfs the underwriter's spread and the administrative costs of
    the issue. It makes common stock issues prohibitively expensive."
   (*a*) You are contemplating a $100 million stock issue. On past evidence,
        you anticipate that announcement of this issue will drive down stock
        price by 3 percent and that the market value of your firm will fall by 30
        percent of the amount to be raised. On the other hand, additional eq-
        uity funds are necessary to fund an investment project which you be-
        lieve has a positive NPV of $40 million. Should you proceed with the
        issue?
   (*b*) Is the fall in market value on announcement of a stock issue an *issue cost* in
        the same sense as an underwriter's spread? Respond to the quote which be-
        gins this question.
   Use your answer to (*a*) as a numerical example to explain your response to (*b*).

14. Ronald Masulis[52] has analyzed the stock price impact of *exchange offers* of debt for equity or vice versa. In an exchange offer, the firm offers to trade freshly issued securities for seasoned securities in the hands of investors. Thus, a firm that wanted to move to a higher debt ratio could offer to trade new debt for outstanding shares. A firm that wanted to move to a more conservative capital structure could offer to trade new shares for outstanding debt securities.

    Masulis found that debt for equity exchanges were good news (stock price increased on announcement) and equity for debt exchanges were bad news.

    (*a*) Are these results consistent with the "trade-off" theory of capital structure?

    (*b*) Are the results consistent with the evidence that investors regard announcements of (i) stock issues as bad news, (ii) stock repurchases as good news, and (iii) debt issues as no news, or at most trifling disappointments?

    (*c*) How could Masulis's results be explained?

15. Suppose the trade-off theory of capital structure is true. Can you predict how companies' debt ratios should change over time? How do these predictions differ from the pecking-order theory's?

16. Leveraged recapitalizations usually increase the market value of the firm. In other words, the aggregate value of all the firm's debt and equity securities is higher after the recap than before. Is this inconsistent with MM's proposition I? Explain carefully.

17. In what circumstances is the British system of bankruptcy (which encourages prompt liquidation) more efficient than the United States system (which under Chapter 11 tries to rehabilitate the firm)? In what situations is the United States system more efficient than the British system?

18. The appendix summarizes several problems with Chapter 11 bankruptcy. Which of these problems could be mitigated by negotiating a prepackaged bankruptcy?

---

[52]R. W. Masulis, "The Effects of Capital Structure Change on Security Prices: A Study of Exchange Offers," *Journal of Financial Economics*, **8**:139–177 (June 1980), and "The Impact of Capital Structure Change on Firm Value," *Journal of Finance*, **38**:107–126 (March 1983).

Interactions of Investment and Financing Decisions

We first addressed problems of capital budgeting in Chapter 2. At that point we said hardly a word about financing decisions; we proceeded under the simplest possible assumption about financing, namely, all-equity financing. We were really assuming an idealized Modigliani-Miller (MM) world in which all financing decisions are irrelevant. In a strict MM world, firms can analyze real investments as if they are to be all-equity-financed; the actual financing plan is a mere detail to be worked out later.

Under MM assumptions, decisions to spend money can be separated from decisions to raise money. In this chapter we reconsider the capital budgeting decision when investment and financing decisions *interact* and cannot be wholly separated.

In the early chapters you learned how to value a capital investment opportunity by a four-step procedure:

1. Forecast the project's incremental after-tax cash flow, assuming the project is entirely equity-financed.

2. Assess the project's risk.

3. Estimate the opportunity cost of capital, that is, the expected rate of return offered to investors by the equivalent-risk investments traded in capital markets.

4. Calculate NPV, using the discounted-cash-flow formula.

In effect, we were thinking of each project as a mini-firm, and asking, "How much would that mini-firm be worth if we spun it off as a separate, all-equity-financed enterprise? How much would investors be willing to pay for shares in the project?"

Of course, this procedure rests on the concept of *value additivity*. In well-functioning capital markets the market value of the firm is the sum of the present value of all the assets held by the firm[1]—the whole equals the sum of the parts. If value additivity did *not* hold, then the value of the firm with the project could be more or less than the sum of the separate value of the project and the value of the firm without

---

[1] *All assets* means intangible as well as tangible assets. For example, a going concern is usually worth more than a haphazard pile of tangible assets. Thus, the aggregate value of a firm's tangible assets often falls short of its market value. The difference is accounted for by going-concern value or by other intangible assets such as accumulated technical expertise, an experienced sales force, or valuable growth opportunities.

the project. We could not determine the project's contribution to firm value by evaluating it as a separate mini-firm.

In this chapter we stick with the value-additivity principle but extend it to include value contributed by financing decisions. There are two ways of doing this:

1. *Adjust the discount rate.* The adjustment is typically downward, to account for the value of interest tax shields. This is the most common approach. It is usually implemented via the after-tax weighted-average cost of capital.

2. *Adjust the present value.* That is, start by estimating the project's "base-case" value as an all-equity-financed mini-firm, and then adjust this base-case NPV to account for the project's impact on the firm's capital structure. Thus

Adjusted NPV (ANPV, or just APV for short) = base-case NPV

+ NPV of financing decisions caused by project acceptance

Once you identify and value the side effects of financing a project, calculating its APV (adjusted net present value) is no more than addition or subtraction.

We conclude the chapter by reexamining a basic and apparently simple issue: What should the discount rate be for a risk-free project? Once we recognize the tax deductibility of debt interest, we will find that all risk-free, or *debt-equivalent*, cash flows can be evaluated by discounting at the *after-tax* interest rate.

19-1 THE AFTER-TAX WEIGHTED-AVERAGE COST OF CAPITAL

Think back to Chapter 17 and Modigliani and Miller's (MM's) proposition I. MM showed that, without taxes or financial market imperfections, the cost of capital does not depend on financing. In other words, the weighted average of the expected returns to debt and equity investors equals the opportunity cost of capital, regardless of the debt ratio:

$$\text{Weighted-average return to debt and equity} = r_D \frac{D}{V} + r_E \frac{E}{V}$$

$$= r, \text{ a constant, independent of } D/V$$

Here r is the opportunity cost of capital, the expected rate of return investors would demand if the firm had no debt at all; r_D and r_E are the expected rates of return on debt and equity, the "cost of debt" and "cost of equity." The weights D/V and E/V are the fractions of debt and equity, based on market values; V, the total market value of the firm, is the sum of D and E.

But you can't look up r, the opportunity cost of capital, in *The Wall Street Journal* or find it on the Internet. So financial managers turn the problem around: they start with the estimates of r_D and r_E and then infer r. Under MM's assumptions,

$$r = r_D \frac{D}{V} + r_E \frac{E}{V}$$

We have discussed this weighted-average cost of capital formula in Chapters 9 and 17. However, the formula misses a crucial difference between debt and equity: interest payments are tax-deductible. Therefore we move on to the *after-tax* weighted-average cost of capital, nicknamed WACC:

$$r^* = r_D(1 - T_c)\frac{D}{V} + r_E\frac{E}{V} = \text{WACC}$$

Here T_c is the marginal corporate tax rate.

Notice that the after-tax WACC (r^*) is less than the opportunity cost of capital (r), because the "cost of debt" is calculated after tax as $r_D(1 - T_c)$. Thus the tax advantages of debt financing are reflected in a lower discount rate. Notice too that all the variables in the weighted-average formula refer to the firm as a whole. As a result, the formula gives the right discount rate only for projects that are just like the firm undertaking them. The formula works for the "average" project. It is incorrect for projects that are safer or riskier than the average of the firm's existing assets. It is incorrect for projects whose acceptance would lead to an increase or decrease in the firm's debt ratio.

The idea behind the weighted-average formula is simple and intuitively appealing. If the new project is profitable enough to pay the (after-tax) interest on the debt used to finance it, and also to generate a superior expected rate of return on the equity invested in it, then it must be a good project. What is a "superior" equity return? One that exceeds r_E, the expected rate of return required by investors in the firm's shares. Let us see how this idea leads to the weighted-average formula.

Suppose that the firm invests in a new project which is expected to produce the same yearly income in perpetuity. If the firm maintains its debt ratio, the amount of debt used to finance the project is

$$\text{Firm's debt ratio} \times \text{investment} = \frac{D}{V} \times \text{investment}$$

Similarly, the equity used to finance the project is

$$\text{Firm's equity ratio} \times \text{investment} = \frac{E}{V} \times \text{investment}$$

If the project is worthwhile, the income must cover after-tax interest charges and provide an acceptable return to equityholders. The after-tax interest costs on the additional debt are equal to

$$\frac{\text{After-tax}}{\text{interest rate}} \times \frac{\text{value of}}{\text{debt}} = r_D(1 - T_c) \times \frac{D}{V} \times \text{investment}$$

The minimum acceptable income to equityholders is

$$\frac{\text{Expected return}}{\text{on equity}} \times \frac{\text{value of}}{\text{equity}} = r_E \times \frac{E}{V} \times \text{investment}$$

Therefore, for the project to be acceptable, its income *must exceed*

$$r_D(1 - T_c) \times \frac{D}{V} \times \text{investment} + r_E \times \frac{E}{V} \times \text{investment}$$

This brings us back to the weighted-average formula. Just divide through by the initial investment:

$$\frac{\text{Income}}{\text{Investment}} \text{ must exceed } r_D(1 - T_c)\frac{D}{V} + r_E\frac{E}{V}$$

Note that the ratio of the project's annual income to investment is just the project's return. Therefore our formula gives the minimum acceptable rate of return from the project.

We have derived the textbook formula only for firms and projects offering perpetual cash flows. But Miles and Ezzell have shown that the formula works for any cash-flow pattern if the firm adjusts its borrowing to maintain a constant debt ratio D/V, regardless of whether things turn out well or poorly. When the firm departs from this policy, the weighted-average formula is only approximately correct.[2]

....

Example: The Geothermal Project

Geothermal, Inc., has only one asset, a brand-new well and pumping station which extracts geothermal energy to supply heat and air conditioning for a shopping center. The company has $5 million of debt outstanding, yielding 8 percent. Equity investors put up the rest of the $10 million required to build the geothermal project.

The project has turned out well. It is generating $2.085 million in profits before interest and taxes, 25 percent higher than originally forecast. The company's 1 million shares of stock are now trading at $7.50, a 50 percent capital gain on the shareholders' original outlay of $5 per share. The shares offer an expected future rate of return of 14.6 percent. The marginal corporate rate is 35 percent.

Geothermal's book and market value balance sheets are as follows:

Geothermal, Inc. (Book Values, Millions)

Project value	$10	$ 5	Debt
		5	Equity
	$10	$10	

Geothermal, Inc. (Market Values, Millions)

Project value	$12.5	$ 5	Debt (D)
		7.5	Equity (E)
	$12.5	$12.5	Firm value (V)

Of course we can't observe the market value of Geothermal's project directly, but we know what it is worth to debt and equity investors ($5 + 7.5 = $12.5 million). This value is entered on the left of the market value balance sheet. The project's NPV is +$2.5 million, the difference between its market value and the $10 million investment.

Why did we show the book balance sheet? Only so you could draw a big X through it. Do so now.

When estimating the weighted-average cost of capital, you are not interested in past investments but in current values and expectations for the future. Geothermal's true debt ratio is not 50 percent, the book ratio, but 40 percent, because its project is worth $12.5 million. The cost of equity, $r_E = .146$, is the expected rate of return from purchase of stock at $7.50 per share, the current market price. It is not the return on book value per share. You can't buy shares in Geothermal for $5 anymore.

So we have the following inputs for Geothermal:

- Cost of debt (r_D):   .08
- Cost of equity (r_E):   .146
- Marginal tax rate (T_c):   .35

---

[2]J. Miles and R. Ezzell, "The Weighted Average Cost of Capital, Perfect Capital Markets, and Project Life: A Clarification," *Journal of Financial and Quantitative Analysis*, **15**:719–730 (September 1980).

- Debt ratio (D/V):   .4
- Equity ratio (E/V):   .6

The company's WACC is

$$r^* = .08(1 - .35)(.4) + .146(.6) = .1084, \text{ or } 10.84\%$$

That's how you calculate the weighted-average cost of capital.[3]
    Let's now use it to value Geothermal's project. We undertake a standard discounted-cash-flow analysis, exactly as in Chapter 6. Since the project does not depreciate, after-tax earnings and cash flow are the same.

Pretax earnings	$2.085
Tax at 35%	.73
After-tax earnings	$1.355 million

This is a perpetual cash flow, $C = 1.355$, so

$$PV = \frac{C}{r^*} = \frac{1.355}{.1084} = \$12.5 \text{ million}$$

which confirms that the Geothermal project is accurately valued by discounting its after-tax cash flows at the weighted-average cost of capital.
    Note that the interest tax shield on Geothermal's debt is not reflected in the $1.355 million annual cash flow. Standard capital budgeting practice calculates taxes *as if* all financing comes from equity. The value added by the tax shield is not lost, however: it is picked up in the discount rate r^*.[4] The WACC formula subtracts the annual interest tax shield, $T_c r_D$, times the debt ratio D/V.
    Finally, we confirm that Geothermal's stockholders can actually expect to earn 14.6 percent:

$$\text{After-tax interest} = r_D(1 - T_c)D$$
$$= .08(1 - .35)(5) = .26$$
$$\text{Expected equity income} = C - (1 - T_c)r_D D$$
$$= 1.355 - .26 = 1.095$$

Geothermal's earnings are level and perpetual, so the expected rate of return on equity is equal to the expected equity income divided by the equity value:

$$\text{Expected equity return} = r_E = \frac{\text{expected equity income}}{\text{equity value}}$$
$$= \frac{1.095}{7.5} = .146, \text{ or } 14.6\%$$

Because this project is Geothermal's only asset, its PV equals the market value of Geothermal's debt and equity securities. But if Geothermal wants to expand the proj-

---

[3]In practice it's pointless to calculate discount rates to four decimal places. We do so here to avoid confusion from rounding errors. Earnings and cash flows are carried to three decimal places for the same reason.

[4]In this example it would be easy to add the interest tax shield back to the project cash flow. This "adjusted" cash flow could be discounted at a weighted-average cost of capital calculated using the *pretax* cost of debt. But for most projects (not perpetuities) it is much easier to capture the value of interest tax shields in the discount rate.

ect, or undertake another one, it could use the same 10.84 percent discount rate. Of course, this requires that:

1. The new investment has the same risk and opportunity cost of capital as the existing project.
2. Geothermal will stick to a 40 percent market value debt ratio.

Some Tricks of the Trade

Geothermal had just one asset and two sources of financing. A real company's market value balance sheet has many more elements, for example:[5]

Current assets,	Current liabilities,
including cash, inventory,	including accounts payable
and accounts receivable	and short-term debt
Plant and equipment	Long-term debt (D)
	Preferred stock (P)
Growth opportunities	Equity (E)
	Firm value (V)

Several questions immediately arise:

1. *How does the formula change when there are more than two sources of financing?* Easy: There is one cost for each element. The weight for each element is proportional to its market value. For example,

$$r^* = r_D(1 - T_c)\frac{D}{V} + r_P\frac{P}{V} + r_E\frac{E}{V}$$

where r_p is investors' expected rate of return on preferred stocks.

2. *What about short-term debt?* Many companies consider only long-term financing when calculating WACC. They leave out the cost of short-term debt. In principle this is incorrect. The lenders who hold short-term debt are investors who can claim their share of operating earnings. A company that ignores this claim will misstate the required return on capital investments.

But "zeroing out" short-term debt is not a serious error if the debt is only temporary, seasonal, or incidental financing or if it is offset by holdings of cash and

---

[5]This balance sheet is for exposition and should not be confused with a real company's books. It includes the value of growth opportunities, which accountants do not recognize, though investors do. It excludes certain accounting entries, for example, deferred taxes.

Deferred taxes arise when a company uses faster depreciation for tax purposes than it uses in reports to investors. That means the company reports more taxes than it pays. The difference is accumulated as a liability for deferred taxes. In a sense there is liability, because the Internal Revenue Service "catches up," collecting extra taxes, as assets age. But this is irrelevant in capital investment analysis, which focuses on actual after-tax cash flows and uses accelerated tax depreciation.

Deferred taxes should not be regarded as a source of financing or an element of the weighted-average cost of capital formula. The liability for deferred taxes is not a security held by investors. It is a balance sheet entry created to serve the needs of accounting.

Deferred taxes can be important in regulated industries, however. Regulators take deferred taxes into account in calculating allowed rates of return and the time patterns of revenues and consumer prices.

marketable securities.[6] Suppose, for example, that your company's Italian subsidiary takes out a 6-month loan from an Italian bank to finance its inventory and accounts receivable. The dollar equivalent of this loan will show up as a short-term debt on the parent's balance sheet. At the same time headquarters may be lending money by investing surplus dollars in short-term securities. If lending and borrowing offset, there is no point in including the cost of short-term debt in the weighted-average cost of capital, because the company is not a *net* short-term borrower.

3. *What about other current liabilites?* Current liabilities are usually "netted out" by subtracting them from current assets. The difference is entered as net working capital on the left-hand side of the balance sheet. The sum of long-term financing on the right is called *total capitalization.*

Net working capital
  = current assets
  − current liabilities
Plant and equipment
Growth opportunities
	Long-term debt (D)
	Preferred stock (P)
	Equity (E)

	Total capitalization (V)

When net working capital is treated as an asset, forecasts of cash flows for capital investment projects must treat increases in net working capital as a cash outflow and decreases as an inflow. This is standard practice, which we followed in Section 6-2.

Since current liabilities include short-term debt, netting them out against current assets excludes the cost of short-term debt from the weighted-average cost of capital. We have just explained why this can be an acceptable approximation. But when short-term debt is an important source of financing—as is common for small firms and firms outside the United States—it should be shown explicitly on the right side of the balance sheet, not netted out against current assets. The interest cost of short-term debt is then one element of the weighted-average cost of capital.

4. *How are the costs of the financing elements calculated?* You can often use stock market data to get an estimate of r_E, the expected rate of return demanded by investors in the company's stock. With that estimate, WACC is not too hard to calculate, because the borrowing rate r_D and the debt and equity ratios D/V and E/V can be directly observed or estimated without too much trouble.[7] Estimating the value and required return for preferred shares is likewise usually not too complicated.

---

[6]Financial practitioners have rules of thumb for deciding whether short-term debt is worth including in the weighted-average cost of capital. Suppose, for example, that short-term debt is 10 percent of total assets and net working capital is negative. Then short-term debt is almost surely being used to finance long-term assets and should be explicitly included in WACC.

[7]Most corporate debt is not actively traded, so its market value cannot be observed directly. But you can usually value a nontraded debt security by looking to securities which *are* traded and which have approximately the same default risk and maturity. See Chapter 23.

For healthy firms the market value of debt is usually not too far from book value, so many managers and analysts use book value for D in the weighted-average cost of capital formula. However, be sure to use *market*, not book, values for E.

Estimating the required return on other security types can be troublesome. Convertible debt, where the investors' return comes partly from an option to exchange the debt for the company's stock, is one example. We will leave convertibles to Chapter 22.

Junk debt, where the risk of default is high, is likewise difficult. The higher the odds of default, the lower the market price of the debt and the higher the *promised* rate of interest. But the weighted-average cost of capital is an *expected*, that is, average, rate of return, not a promised one. For example, in mid-1995 USAir's senior debentures maturing in the year 2000 offered a 12.8 percent promised return, about 6 percentage points above yields on the highest-grade debt maturing at the same time. The company's business had deteriorated, and cumulative losses exceeded $1 billion from 1990 to 1994. Investors were concerned that the company might have to default and therefore demanded 12.8 percent to hold the issue. But this was not an expected return, because it did not average in the losses to be incurred if USAir is Buffeted by financial turbulence and defaults. Including 12.8 percent as a "cost of debt" would therefore overstate USAir's true weighted-average cost of capital.

This is bad news: There is no easy or tractable way of estimating the expected rate of return on most junk debt issues.[8] Good news: For most debt the odds of default are small. That means the promised and expected rates of return are close, and the promised rate can be used as an approximation in the weighted-average cost of capital.

Industry Costs of Capital

The WACC is a *company* cost of capital. Strictly speaking, it works only for projects that are carbon copies of the firm's existing assets, in both business risk and financing. Often it is used as a companywide benchmark discount rate; the benchmark is adjusted upward for unusually risky projects and downward for unusually safe ones.

You can also calculate WACC for *industries*. Suppose that a pharmaceutical company has a subsidiary which produces specialty chemicals. What discount rate is better for the subsidiary's projects—the company WACC or a weighted-average cost of capital for a portfolio of "pure-play" specialty chemical companies? The latter rate is better in principle, and also in practice if good data are available for firms with operations and markets similar to the subsidiary's.

AN APPLICATION TO THE RAILROAD INDUSTRY. In mid-1974 the assets of the Penn Central Railroad were taken over by Conrail, a new, federally sponsored corporation. Since Penn Central had declared bankruptcy in 1971, the assets taken by Conrail really belonged to the railroad's creditors. Congress set up a special court to determine fair compensation.

Although the Penn Central system was generating hair-curling losses overall, some of its freight lines were potentially profitable. In 1978 one of the authors was asked to estimate a discount rate for valuing the cash flows these lines would have produced had Conrail not taken them over. He was asked to assume that these freight lines had the same business risk and financing as the railroad industry generally. That sounded like a job for the weighted-average formula. An extensive investigation boiled down to the following calculation:

---

[8]When betas can be estimated for the junk issue or for a sample of similar issues, the expected return can be calculated from the capital asset pricing model. Otherwise, an estimate of the annual probability of default should be subtracted from the promised yield. Evidence on historical default rates on junk bonds is described in Chapter 24.

$$r^*(\text{in mid-1974}) = r_D(1 - T_c)\frac{D}{V} + r_E\frac{E}{V}$$

$$= .087(1 - .5)(.45) + .16(.55)$$

$$= .1076, \text{ or about } 10\tfrac{3}{4}\%$$

The formula's components were derived as follows:

r_D = .087, a weighted average of bond yields for 10 major railroads in mid-1974

T_c = .50. The corporate income tax rate in mid-1974 was 48 percent. Two percentage points were added to cover state income taxes.

D/V = .45. The estimated average market debt-to-value ratio for 10 major railroads. Thus E/V = .55.

r_E = .16. Railroad stocks on average appeared to have about the same risk as the market portfolio. Their betas averaged out close to 1.0. Thus $r_E = r_m$. The 16 percent market return equals the sum of the Treasury bill yield in mid-1974 plus the historical risk premium on the market portfolio.

Of course each of these numbers was to some extent controversial. Other expert witnesses used the same weighted-average formula to arrive at substantially different answers. Anyone brave enough to estimate a discount rate in public can expect controversy.

AND TO THE OIL INDUSTRY. Figure 19-1 shows the weighted-average cost of capital for the oil industry, defined as the 10 largest integrated United States producers. The long-term interest rate on Treasury bonds is plotted as a reference point. The top line is the expected rate of return on oil company stocks (r_E). (A time series of betas for these companies was shown in Figure 9-4.)

These are nominal rates of return, so naturally the weighted-average cost of capital is highest around 1980, when interest and inflation rates peaked. The dramatic upward spike in WACC in 1981 may be just statistical noise, however.

Mistakes People Make in Using the Weighted-Average Formula

The weighted-average formula is very useful but also dangerous. It tempts people to make logical errors. For example, manager Q, who is campaigning for a pet project, might look at the formula

$$r^* = r_D(1 - T_c)\frac{D}{V} + r_E\frac{E}{V}$$

and think, "Aha! My firm has a good credit rating. It could borrow, say, 90 percent of the project's cost if it likes. That means D/V = .9 and E/V = .1. My firm's borrowing rate r_D is 8 percent, and the required return on equity, r_E, is 15 percent. Therefore

$$r^* = .08(1 - .35)(.9) + .15(.1) = .062$$

or 6.2 percent. When I discount at that rate, my project looks great."

Manager Q is wrong on several counts. First, the weighted-average formula works only for projects that are carbon copies of the firm. The firm isn't 90 percent debt-financed.

Second, the immediate source of funds for a project has no necessary connection with the hurdle rate for the project. What matters is the project's overall contribution to the firm's borrowing power. A dollar invested in Q's pet project will not increase the firm's debt capacity by 90 cents. If the firm borrows 90 percent of the

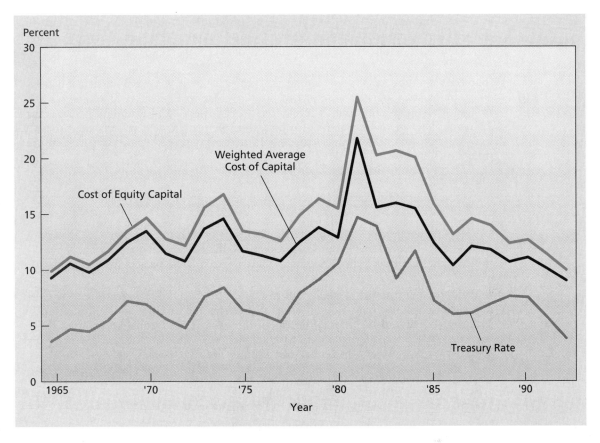

Figure 19-1 Estimates of the weighted-average cost of capital for the United States oil industry, 1965–1992. (Source: Brattle/IRI, Inc.)

project's cost, it is really borrowing in part against its *existing* assets. Any advantage from financing the new project with more debt than normal should be attributed to the old projects, not to the new one.

Third, even if the firm were willing and able to lever up to 90 percent debt, its cost of capital would not decline to 6.2 percent (as Q's naive calculation predicts). You cannot increase the debt ratio without creating financial risk for stockholders and thereby increasing r_E, the expected rate of return they demand from the firm's common stock. Going to 90 percent debt would certainly increase the borrowing rate, too.

19-2   ADJUSTED PRESENT VALUE

The weighted-average cost of capital is a bit of a black box—when it works, it's great; when it doesn't, most managers don't know how to adjust it. Too much is rolled into a (deceptively simple) tax adjustment to the "cost of debt."

We now take a different tack. Instead of messing around with the discount rate, we explicitly adjust cash flows and present values for costs or benefits of financing. This approach is called **adjusted present value**, or **APV.**

The adjusted-present-value rule is easiest to understand in the context of simple numerical examples. We start by analyzing a project under base-case assumptions and then consider possible financing side effects of accepting the project.

The Base Case

The APV method begins by valuing the project as if it were a mini-firm financed solely by equity. Consider a project to produce solar water heaters. It requires a $10 million investment and offers a level after-tax cash flow of $1.8 million per year for 10 years. The opportunity cost of capital is 12 percent, which reflects the project's business risk. Investors would demand a 12 percent expected return to invest in the mini-firm's shares.

Thus the mini-firm's base-case NPV is

$$NPV = -10 + \sum_{t=1}^{10} \frac{1.8}{(1.12)^t} = + \$.17 \text{ million, or } \$170,000$$

Considering the project's size, this figure is not significantly greater than zero. In a pure MM world where no financing decision matters, the financial manager would lean toward taking the project but would not be heartbroken if the project were discarded.

Issue Costs

But suppose that the firm actually has to finance the $10 million investment by issuing stock (it will not have to issue stock if it rejects the project) and that issue costs soak up 5 percent of the gross proceeds of the issue. That means the firm has to issue $10,526,000 in order to obtain $10,000,000 cash. The $526,000 difference goes to underwriters, lawyers, and others involved in the issue process.

The project's APV is calculated by subtracting the issue cost from base-case NPV:

$$APV = \text{base-case NPV} - \text{issue cost}$$
$$= +170,000 - 526,000 = -\$356,000$$

The firm would reject the project because APV is negative.

Additions to the Firm's Debt Capacity

Consider a different financing scenario. Suppose that the firm has a 50 percent target debt ratio. Its policy is to limit debt to 50 percent of its assets. Thus, if it invests more, it borrows more; in this sense investment adds to the firm's debt capacity.[9]

Is debt capacity worth anything? The most widely accepted answer is "yes" because of the tax shields generated by interest payments on corporate borrowing. (Look back to our discussion of debt and taxes in Chapter 18.) For example, MM's theory states that the value of the firm is independent of its capital structure *except* for the present value of interest tax shields:

$$\text{Firm value} = \text{value with all-equity financing} + \text{PV(tax shield)}$$

This theory tells us to compute the value of the firm in two steps: First compute its base-case value under all-equity financing, and then add the present value of taxes saved due to a departure from all-equity financing. This procedure is like an APV calculation for the firm as a whole.

We can repeat the calculation for a particular project. For example, suppose that the solar heater project increases the firm's assets by $10 million and therefore prompts

---

[9]*Debt capacity* is potentially misleading because it seems to imply an absolute limit to the amount the firm is *able* to borrow. That is not what we mean. The firm limits borrowing to 50 percent of assets as a rule of thumb for optimal capital structure. It could borrow more if it wanted to.

TABLE 19-1

• •

Calculating the present value of interest tax shields on debt supported by the solar heater project (dollar figures in thousands)

Year	Debt Outstanding at Start of Year	Interest	Interest Tax Shield	Present Value of Tax Shield
1	$5,000	$400	$140	$129.6
2	4,500	360	126	108.0
3	4,000	320	112	88.9
4	3,500	280	98	72.0
5	3,000	240	84	57.2
6	2,500	200	70	44.1
7	2,000	160	56	32.6
8	1,500	120	42	22.7
9	1,000	80	28	14.0
10	500	40	14	6.5
				Total $576

Assumptions:
1. Marginal tax rate = T_c = .35; tax shield = .35 × interest.
2. Debt principal repaid at end of year in ten $500,000 installments.
3. Interest rate on debt is 8 percent.
4. Present value calculated at the 8 percent borrowing rate. The assumption here is that the tax shields are just as risky as the interest payments generating them.

it to borrow $5 million more. To keep things simple, we assume that this $5 million loan is repaid in equal installments, so that the amount borrowed declines with the depreciating book value of the solar heater project. We also assume that the loan carries an interest rate of 8 percent. Table 19-1 shows how the value of the interest tax shields is calculated. This is the value of the additional debt capacity contributed to the firm by the project. We obtain APV by adding this amount to the project's NPV:

$$APV = \text{base-case NPV} + \text{PV(tax shield)}$$
$$= +170,000 + 576,000 = \$746,000$$

• • • • • • • • • • • • • • • •

The Value of Interest Tax Shields

In Table 19-1, we boldly assume that the firm can fully capture interest tax shields of 35 cents on every dollar of interest. We also treat the interest tax shields as safe cash inflows and discount them at a low 8 percent rate.

The true present value of the tax shields is almost surely less than $576,000:

1. You can't use tax shields unless you pay taxes, and you don't pay taxes unless you make money. Few firms can be *sure* that future profitability will be sufficient to use up the interest tax shields.

2. The government takes two bites out of corporate income: the corporate tax and the tax on bondholders' and stockholders' personal income. The corporate tax favors debt; the personal tax favors equity.

3. A project's debt capacity depends on how well it does. When profits exceed expectations, the firm can borrow more; if the project fails, it won't support any

debt. If the future amount of debt is tied to project value, then the interest tax shields given in Table 19-1 are estimates, not fixed amounts.

In Chapter 18, we argued that the effective tax shield on interest was probably not 35 percent ($T_c = .35$) but some lower figure, call it T^*. We were unable to pin down an exact figure for T^*.

Suppose, for example, that we believe $T^* = .25$. We can easily recalculate the APV of the solar heater project. Just multiply the present value of the interest tax shields by 25/35. The bottom line of Table 19-1 drops from \$576,000 to $576,000(25/35) = \$411,000$. APV drops to

$$\text{APV} = \text{base-case NPV} + \text{PV(tax shield)}$$
$$= +170,000 + 411,000 = \$581,000$$

PV(tax shield) drops still further if the tax shields are treated as forecasts and discounted at a higher rate. Suppose the firm ties the amount of debt to actual future project cash flows. Then the interest tax shields become just as risky as the project and should be discounted at the 12 percent opportunity cost of capital.[10] PV(tax shield) drops to \$362,000 at $T^* = .25$.

<table>
<tr><td>

Review of the Adjusted-Present-Value Approach

</td><td>

If the decision to invest in a capital project has important side effects on other financial decisions made by the firm, those side effects should be taken into account when the project is evaluated. They include interest tax shields on debt supported by the project (a plus), any issue costs of raising financing for the project (a minus), or perhaps other side effects such as the value of a government-subsidized loan tied to the project.

The idea behind APV is "divide and conquer." The approach does not attempt to capture all the side effects in a single calculation. A series of present value calculations is made instead. The first establishes a base-case value for the project: its value as a separate, all-equity-financed mini-firm. Then each side effect is traced out, and the present value of its cost or benefit to the firm is calculated. Finally, all the present values are added together to estimate the project's total contribution to the value of the firm. Thus, in general,

</td></tr>
</table>

$$\text{Project APV} = \text{base-case NPV} + \frac{\text{sum of the present values of the side}}{\text{effects of accepting the project}}$$

The wise financial manager will want to see not only the adjusted present value but also where that value is coming from. For example, suppose that base-case NPV is positive but the benefits are outweighed by the costs of issuing stock to finance the project. That should prompt the manager to look around to see if the project can be rescued by an alternative financing plan.

19-3 ADJUSTED DISCOUNT RATES AND ADJUSTED PRESENT VALUE

Calculating APV is not mathematically difficult, but tracing out and evaluating a project's financing side effects take financial sophistication. It is usually simpler to adjust the discount rate than to adjust the present value. The after-tax weighted-average

---

[10]This is not quite right. Note, for example, that the first interest tax shield depends on the original debt amount of \$5 million, which is not uncertain. The second tax shield is in turn known in period 1. The exact discounting procedure is covered later.

cost of capital is one example of an adjusted discount rate, but there are other formulas. Let us take a closer look.

APV for the Geo-thermal Project

We start by calculating the APV of the Geothermal project covered in Section 19-1. We ignore any issue costs and concentrate on the value of interest tax shields supported by the project. To keep things simple, we assume throughout this section that the only financing side effect is the interest tax shields on debt supported by the project, and we consider corporate taxes only. (In other words, $T^* = T_c$.)

Base-case NPV is found by first discounting after-tax project cash flows of $1.355 million at the opportunity cost of capital (r) of 12 percent and then subtracting the $10 million outlay. (We will explain later how we know that Geothermal's opportunity cost of capital is 12 percent.) The cash flows are perpetual, so

$$\text{Base-case NPV} = -10 + \frac{1.355}{.12} = +\$1.29 \text{ million}$$

Thus the project would be worthwhile even with all-equity financing. But it actually supports debt of $5 million. At an 8 percent borrowing rate ($r_D = .08$) and a 35 percent tax rate ($T_c = .35$), annual interest tax shields are $.35 \times .08 \times 5 = .14$, or $140,000.

What are those tax shields worth? It depends on the *financing rule* the company follows. There are two common rules:

■ Financing rule 1: *Debt fixed.* Borrow a fraction of *initial* project value and make any debt repayments on a predetermined schedule. (We followed this rule in Table 19-1.)

■ Financing rule 2: *Debt rebalanced.* Adjust the debt in each future period to keep it at a constant fraction of *future* project value.

What do these rules mean for the Geothermal project? Under financing rule 1, debt stays at $5 million come hell or high water, and interest tax shields stay at $140,000 per year. The tax shields are tied to fixed interest payments, so the 8 percent cost of debt is a reasonable discount rate:

$$\text{PV(tax shields, debt fixed)} = \frac{140,000}{.08} = \$1,750,000, \text{ or } \$1.75 \text{ million}$$

$$\begin{aligned}\text{APV} &= \text{base-case NPV} + \text{PV(tax shield)} \\ &= +1.29 + 1.75 = +3.04, \text{ or about } \$3 \text{ million}\end{aligned}$$

If Geothermal were financed solely by equity, firm value would be $11.29 million. With fixed debt of $5 million, firm value increases by PV(tax shield) to $11.29 + 1.75 = $13.04 million.

Under financing rule 2, debt is rebalanced to 40 percent of actual project value. That means future debt levels are not known at the start of the project; they depend on the project's actual performance. It also means that future interest payments track changes in actual project cash flows and pick up the business risk of the project.

Figure 19-2 shows how the debt supported by the Geothermal project changes for three possible cash flows in year 1. If cash flows are below the $1.355 million forecast, project value falls, debt is reduced, and interest tax shields in year 2 fall proportionately. You can see that interest tax shields are perfectly correlated with the surprises in project cash flows and have basically the same risk characteristics. The next period's interest tax shields are, however, known once this period's debt is determined.

Start: YEAR 0	Actual Cash Flow	Updated Cash Flow	YEAR 1 Project Value	Rebalanced Debt	Interest Tax Shield in Year 1 (Based on Debt at Year 0)
	1.49	1.49	13.75	5.5	.14
Cash flow forecast = 1.355 → 1.355	1.355	1.355	12.5	5.0	.14
	1.23	1.23	11.36	4.55	.14

Project value = 12.5

Debt = 5.0

Continue: YEAR 1	Actual Cash Flow	Updated Cash Flow	YEAR 2 Project Value	Rebalanced Debt	Interest Tax Shield in Year 2 (Based on Debt at Year 1)
	1.355	1.355	12.5	5.0	.127
(Assuming cash flows drop to 1.23) → 1.23	1.23	1.23	11.36	4.55	.127
	1.12	1.12	10.33	4.13	.127

Project value = 11.36

Debt = 4.55

Figure 19-2 Interest tax shields assuming debt is rebalanced to 40 percent of the value of the Geothermal project (figures in millions of dollars). Cash flows may rise, fall, or remain the same. Project value and debt adjust proportionally, so that debt is always 40 percent of project value. The top decision tree starts at year 0, the bottom at year 1, assuming cash flows fall below forecasts in year 1. Note that interest tax shields are based on the previous year's debt.

Valuing these forecasted interest tax shields exactly is a bit of work, but it's worth it to demonstrate that everything comes out right. The first tax shield is not uncertain (it depends on the initial debt of $5 million), so we discount at the borrowing rate of 8 percent:

$$PV = \frac{.14}{1.08} = .13, \text{ or } \$130,000$$

The second tax shield is also forecasted at $.14 million but depends on the first year's cash flow and project value (as in Figure 19-2). It is uncertain for 1 year and *then* known when debt is rebalanced in year 1. Therefore we discount for the first year at the opportunity cost of capital (12 percent) and for the second year at 8 percent:

$$PV = \frac{.14}{(1.12)(1.08)} = .116, \text{ or } \$116,000$$

The third tax shield is not known for 2 years, so we discount for 2 years at 12 percent and for 1 year at 8 percent:

$$PV = \frac{.14}{(1.12)^2(1.08)} = .103, \text{ or } \$103,000$$

and so on.

This may look complicated, but it's actually easy to remember. You can always *approximate* the value of interest tax shields generated under financing rule 2 just by discounting at the opportunity cost of capital. For the third shield, this would give

$$\text{Approximate PV} = \frac{.14}{(1.12)^3} \times .100, \text{ or } \$100,000$$

For practical purposes you can usually stop here. But to correct the approximation, just multiply the approximate PV by 1.12/1.08, that is $(1 + r)/(1 + r_D)$. This cancels out 1 year's discounting at r and adds 1 year at r_D, for the third tax shield,

$$PV = \frac{1.12}{1.08} \times .100 = .103, \text{ as before}$$

So the general procedure for valuing interest tax shields under financing rule 2 is:

1. Discount at the opportunity cost of capital, because future tax shields are tied to actual cash flows.

2. Multiply the resulting PV by $(1 + r)/(1 + r_D)$, because the tax shields are fixed one period before receipt.

For the Geothermal project, the forecasted interest tax shields are $.14 million in perpetuity, and the opportunity cost of capital is 12 percent:

$$\text{Approximate PV} = \frac{.14}{.12} = 1.17$$

$$\text{PV(tax shield)} = \frac{1.12}{1.08} \times 1.17 = \$1.21 \text{ million}$$

The APV of the project, given these assumptions about future debt capacity, is

$$\begin{aligned} \text{APV} &= \text{base-case NPV} + \text{PV(tax shield)} \\ &= 1.29 + 1.21 = \$2.5 \text{ million} \end{aligned}$$

Firm value with debt rebalancing is

	Firm value with all-equity financing	+	PV (tax shield)	
=	11.29	+	1.21	= $12.50 million

Notice that value is less with financing rule 2 than with rule 1 because the tax shields are uncertain.

APV and the Weighted-Average Cost of Capital

We have now valued the Geothermal project three different ways:

1. APV (debt fixed) = +$3.1 million

2. APV (debt rebalanced) = +$2.5 million

3. NPV (discounting at WACC) = +$2.5 million

The second and third calculations are identical because the underlying assumptions about financing are the same. Though we didn't stress the point in Section 19-1, *discounting at WACC assumes that debt is rebalanced every period to maintain a constant ratio of debt to the market value of the firm.*

This is certainly a more reasonable assumption than financing rule 1, which says that debt is paid off on an absolutely fixed schedule. Any capital budgeting procedure that assumes debt levels are fixed when a project is undertaken is grossly oversimplified. Should we assume that the Geothermal project contributes $5 million to the firm's debt capacity not just when the project is undertaken but "from here to eternity"? That amounts to saying that the future value of the project will not change—a strong assumption indeed. Suppose the price of oil shoots up unexpectedly a year after the project is undertaken; since the Geothermal project *saves* oil, its cash flow and value shoot up too. Suppose the project's value doubles. In that case, won't its contribution to debt capacity also double, to $10 million? It works the other way too: if the oil price falls out of bed, the contribution to debt capacity tumbles.

The better rule is not "Always borrow $5 million," but "Always borrow 40 percent of the Geothermal project's value." Then if project value increases, the firm borrows more. If it decreases, the firm borrows less. Under this policy you can no longer discount future interest tax shields at the borrowing rate, because the shields are no longer certain. Their size depends on the amount actually borrowed and, therefore, on the actual future value of the project.

·················

APV and Hurdle Rates

APV tells you whether a project makes a net contribution to the value of the firm. It can also tell you a project's *break-even* cash flow or internal rate of return. Let's check this for the Geothermal project. We first calculate the income at which APV = 0. We will then determine the project's minimum acceptable internal rate of return (IRR).

$$\text{APV} = \frac{\text{annual income}}{r} - \text{investment} + \text{PV(tax shield)}$$

$$= \frac{\text{annual income}}{.12} - 10 + \text{PV(tax shield)} = 0$$

This equation sets APV = 0, but what is PV(tax shield)? It will be less than the values calculated above, because if APV = 0 the project is worth only $10 million, not $12.5 million, and will support only $4, not $5, million in debt. In other words, debt drops by 20 percent, and so must PV(tax shield).

Therefore we reduce PV(tax shield) by 20 percent, from $1.21 million, under financing rule 2, to $.97 million. Then

$$\text{APV} = \frac{\text{annual income}}{.12} - 10 + .97 = 0$$

Annual income = $1.084 million

or 10.84 percent of the $10 million outlay. In other words, the minimum acceptable IRR for the project is 10.84 percent. At this IRR project APV is zero.

Suppose that we encounter another project with perpetual cash flows. Its opportunity cost of capital is also $r = .12$, and it also expands the firm's borrowing power by 40 percent of project value. We know that if such a project offers an IRR greater than 10.84 percent, it will have a positive APV. Therefore, we could shorten the analysis by just discounting the project's cash inflows at 10.84 percent.[11] This dis-

---

[11]Remember that forecasted project cash flows do *not* reflect the tax shields generated by any debt the project may support. Project taxes are calculated assuming all-equity financing.

count rate is the *adjusted cost of capital.* It reflects both the project's business risk and its contribution to the firm's debt capacity.

We labeled the adjusted cost of capital as r^*. To calculate r^* we find the minimum acceptable internal rate of return—the IRR at which APV = 0. The rule is this: *Accept projects which have a positive NPV at the adjusted cost of capital r^*.*

The 10.84 percent adjusted cost of capital for the Geothermal project is (no surprise) identical to Geothermal's weighted-average cost of capital, or WACC, calculated in Section 19-1.

A General Definition of the Adjusted Cost of Capital

We recapitulate the two concepts of cost of capital:

■ Concept 1: *The opportunity cost of capital (r).* This is the expected rate of return offered in capital markets by equivalent-risk assets. This depends on the risk of the project's cash flows. The opportunity cost of capital is the correct discount rate for the project if it is all-equity-financed.

■ Concept 2: *The adjusted cost of capital (r^*).* This is an adjusted opportunity cost or hurdle rate that reflects the financing side effects of an investment project.

Some people just say "cost of capital." Sometimes their meaning is clear in context. At other times, they don't know which concept they are referring to, and that can sow widespread confusion.

When financing side effects are important, you should accept projects with positive APVs. But if you know the adjusted discount rate, you don't have to calculate APV; you just calculate NPV at the adjusted rate. If we could find a simple, universally correct method for calculating r^*, we would be all set.

The weighted-average cost of capital formula is one way to calculate the adjusted cost of capital, but it isn't universally correct. Remember, WACC works when the project being valued has the same business risk and financing as the firm as a whole. The WACC formula does not tell you what to do if a project is safer or riskier than the company average or if it is financed in a different way.

So when all projects are "average," WACC works fine. When projects differ, their adjusted costs of capital differ, too. To understand these differences, we need a formula showing how WACC depends on financial leverage and the opportunity cost of capital. We will give two formulas which rest on somewhat different assumptions.

THE MILES-EZZELL FORMULA. James Miles and Russell Ezzell came up with the following useful formula for adjusting WACC:[12]

$$r^* = \text{WACC} = r - Lr_D T^* \left[\frac{1 + r}{1 + r_D} \right]$$

where L is the debt-to-value ratio and T^* is the net tax saving per dollar of interest paid. In practice T^* is very hard to pin down, and the marginal corporate tax rate T_c is used instead.

The formula assumes financing rule 2, that the firm adjusts its future borrowing to keep debt proportions constant. Therefore it is consistent with the weighted-average cost of capital formula and can be used to adjust WACC if, say, a new project has a different debt capacity than the firm's other assets.

---

[12]J. Miles and R. Ezzell, op. cit.

This is a common problem. Financial managers can usually get reasonable estimates of WACC, and for "average" projects WACC is the only discount rate needed. But when financing or business risks change, the WACC formula does not tell the manager what to do.

Suppose, for example, that Geothermal's financial manager does not know r, the opportunity cost of capital. However, the manager observes that Geothermal has $5 million of debt and that firm value with financing rule 2 is $12.5 million. Thus the debt-to-value ratio, L, is $5/12.5 = .4$. The manager also calculates that WACC is 10.84 percent. Since the Miles-Ezzell r^* equals WACC and all variables but r are known (including $T^* = T_c = .35$),

$$r^* = r - Lr_D T_c \left[\frac{1 + r}{1 + r_D} \right] = \text{WACC}$$

$$= r - .4(.08)(.35) \left(\frac{1 + r}{1.08} \right) = .1084$$

You can check that $r = .12$, which is the same figure that we used to calculate APV.

Now that you know the return investors would demand if Geothermal were all-equity-financed, you can use the Miles-Ezzell formula to find the adjusted cost of capital at any debt level. If a new project's debt capacity is only, say, 30 percent of project value, the financial manager could substitute in the formula to get the correct hurdle rate. With $L = .30$,

$$r^* = .12 - .3(.08)(.35) \left(\frac{1.12}{1.08} \right) = .111, \text{ or } 11.1\%$$

The adjusted cost of capital (equal to WACC in this case) is the downward-sloping line in Figure 19-3.[13]

The financial manager can also calculate the cost of equity (r_E) at 30 percent debt. (It will be lower than at Geothermal's 40 percent ratio because financial risk is reduced.) If WACC $= .111$ at $L = .3$ and the cost of debt stays at $r_D = .08$,

$$\text{WACC} = r_D(1 - T_c) \frac{D}{V} + r_E \frac{E}{V} = r^*$$

$$= .08(1 - .35)(.3) + r_E(.7) = .111$$

$$r_E = .136, \text{ or } 13.6\%$$

We have plotted r_E as the upward-sloping line in Figure 19-3.

The general formula for r_E as a function of the opportunity cost of capital and financial leverage is a bit elaborate, but the following formula (familiar from Chapters 9 and 17) is an excellent approximation:

$$r_E = r + (r - r_D) \frac{D}{E}$$

For Geothermal, $D/V = .4$, so $D/E = .4/.6 = .667$. That implies

$$r_E = .12 + (.12 - .08)(.667) = .147, \text{ or } 14.7\%$$

a trifle higher than the true cost of equity of 14.6 percent. The true cost of equity is the upward-sloping line in Figure 19-3.

---

[13]Note that the horizontal axis in Figures 19-3 and 19-4 is the debt-equity ratio, D/E. This is the format used in Figure 17-2. Debt-to-value ratios of .3 and .4 correspond to debt-equity ratios of $.3/.7 = .43$ and $.4/.6 = .67$.

Figure 19-3 Miles and
Ezzell's formula shows how
the weighted-average cost
of capital (WACC) declines
as a function of the debt
ratio. The example shown
here applies to the
Geothermal project, with an
opportunity cost of capital
of 12 percent and WACC of
10.84 percent at a 40 percent debt-to-value ratio.

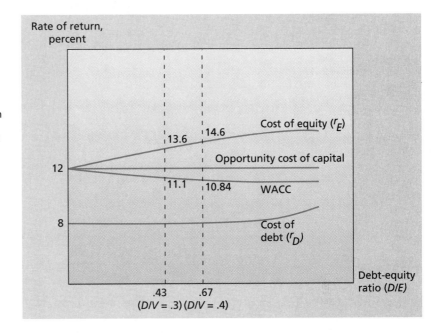

In drawing this figure, we have assumed that the cost of debt is 8 percent regardless of whether the debt ratio is 30 or 40 percent. This assumption is not too bad
if the risk of default is small, and it simplifies the figure because r_E plots as a straight
line as long as r_D is constant. But at higher debt ratios life is more complicated. The
cost of debt increases as the debt ratio increases, and the rate of increase in the cost
of equity declines (compare Figure 17-1). Moreover, the firm becomes less and less
sure that it will generate enough future income to use all interest tax shields. Therefore
the curve for WACC "bottoms out," as shown in Figure 19-3 for high debt ratios.

MM's FORMULA.　Another formula for adjusting WACC was suggested by
Modigliani and Miller (MM).[14] MM's formula is

$$r^* = \text{WACC} = r\,(1 - T^*L)$$

The MM formula assumes that debt is fixed at the start of the project, not rebalanced. In practice, T^* is usually replaced with T_c, the marginal corporate tax rate.

　The MM formula works for the Geothermal project or for any other project that
is expected to (1) generate a level, perpetual cash flow and (2) support fixed permanent
debt. The formula is exactly right only if these two assumptions are met. Assets offering perpetual cash-flow streams are like abominable snowmen: often referred to but
seldom seen. But MM's formula still works reasonably well for projects with limited
lives or irregular cash-flow streams if the fixed-debt assumption (financing rule 1)
holds. Using the formula to calculate the present value of these projects typically re-

---

[14]The formula first appeared in F. Modigliani and M. H. Miller, "Corporate Income Taxes and the Cost
of Capital: A Correction," *American Economic Review,* **53**:433–443 (June 1963). It is explained more fully
in M. H. Miller and F. Modigliani, "Some Estimates of the Cost of Capital to the Electric Utility Industry:
1954–1957," *American Economic Review,* **56**:333–391 (June 1966). In these articles, MM assumed that T^*
equals the corporate tax rate T_c.

Figure 19-4 MM's formula assumes that debt is fixed and interest tax shields are safe. The implied present value of interest tax shields is higher than that in the Miles-Ezzell formula, so the weighted-average cost of capital declines faster as financial leverage increases. Compare Figure 19-3.

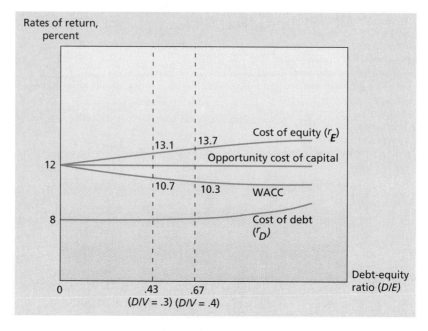

sults in an error of 2 to 6 percent.[15] This is not too bad when you consider that a biased cash-flow forecast could easily put project value off the mark by 20 to 60 percent.

When MM's fixed-debt assumption is appropriate, their formula can be used to calculate the opportunity cost of capital, given an estimate for WACC, or to see how WACC or r_E, the cost of equity, changes at different debt ratios. WACC and r_E for this case are plotted in Figure 19-4. By the way, MM's formula for r_E is

$$r_E = r + (1 - T_c)(r - r_D)\frac{D}{E}$$

Example: We illustrate the differences between the MM and Miles-Ezzell formulas with one last look at the Geothermal project. If debt financing is fixed, firm value is $13.04 million. Therefore, if the firm borrows $5 million, the debt-to-value ratio is $L = 5/13.04 = .383$. The project's opportunity cost of capital is $r = .12$, and we continue to assume that $T^* = T_c = .35$. So the MM formula gives

$$\begin{aligned} r^* &= r(1 - T^*L) \\ &= .12[1 - .35(.383)] = .1039, \text{ or } 10.39\% \end{aligned}$$

The project's NPV at this discount rate is

$$\text{NPV} = \frac{1.355}{.1039} - 10 = \$3.04 \text{ million}$$

Thus the MM formula for the adjusted cost of capital gives the same answer as APV calculated under the "debt-fixed" financing rule.

---

[15]See S. C. Myers, "Interactions of Corporate Financing and Investment Decisions—Implications for Capital Budgeting," *Journal of Finance,* **29**:1–25 (March 1974).

19-4 DISCOUNTING SAFE, NOMINAL CASH FLOWS

Suppose you're considering purchase of a $100,000 machine. The manufacturer sweetens the deal by offering to finance the purchase by lending you $100,000 for 5 years, with annual interest payments of 5 percent. You would have to pay 13 percent to borrow from a bank. Your marginal tax rate is 35 percent ($T_c = .35$).

How much is this loan worth? If you take it, the cash flows, in thousands of dollars, are:

			PERIOD			
	0	1	2	3	4	5
Cash flow	100	-5	-5	-5	-5	-105
Tax shield		$+1.75$	$+1.75$	$+1.75$	$+1.75$	$+1.75$
After-tax cash flow	100	-3.25	-3.25	-3.25	-3.25	-103.25

What is the right discount rate?

Here you are discounting *safe, nominal* cash flows—safe because your company must commit to pay if it takes the loan,[16] and nominal because the payments would be fixed regardless of future inflation. Now, the correct discount rate for safe, nominal cash flows is your company's *after-tax, un*subsidized borrowing rate.[17] In this case $r^* = r_D(1 - T_c) = .13(1 - .35) = .0845$. Therefore:

$$\text{NPV} = +100 - \frac{3.25}{1.0845} - \frac{3.25}{(1.0845)^2} - \frac{3.25}{(1.0845)^3} - \frac{3.25}{(1.0845)^4} - \frac{103.25}{(1.0845)^5}$$

$$= +20.52, \text{ or } \$20,520$$

The manufacturer has effectively cut the machine's purchase price from $100,000 to $100,000 - $21,520 = $78,480. You can now go back and recalculate the machine's NPV using this fire-sale price, or you can use the NPV of the subsidized loan as one element of the machine's adjusted present value.

A General Rule

Clearly, we owe an explanation of why $r^* = r_D(1 - T_c)$ for safe, nominal cash flows. It's no surprise that r^* depends on r_D, the unsubsidized borrowing rate, for that is investors' opportunity cost of capital, the rate they would demand from your company's debt. But why should r_D be converted to an *after-tax* figure?

Let's simplify by taking a *1-year* subsidized loan of $100,000 at 5 percent. The cash flows, in thousands of dollars, are:

---

[16]In theory, *safe* means literally "risk-free," like the cash returns on a Treasury bond. In practice, it means that the risk of not paying or receiving a cash flow is small.

[17]In Section 13-1, we calculated the NPV of subsidized financing using the *pretax* borrowing rate. Now you can see that was a mistake. Using the pretax rate implicitly defines the loan in terms of its pretax cash flows, violating a rule promulgated way back in Section 6-1: *Always* estimate cash flows on an after-tax basis.

	Period 0	Period 1
Cash flow	100	−105
Tax shield		+1.75
After-tax		
cash flow	100	−103.25

Now ask, "What is the maximum amount X that could be borrowed for 1 year through regular channels if $103,250 is set aside to service the loan?"

"Regular channels" means borrowing at 13 percent pretax and 8.45 percent after tax. Therefore you will need 108.45 percent of the amount borrowed to pay back principal plus after-tax interest charges. If $1.0845X = 103,250$, $X = 95,205$. Now if you can borrow $100,000 by a subsidized loan, but only $95,205 through normal channels, the difference ($4795) is money in the bank. Therefore, it must also be the NPV of this one-period subsidized loan.

When you discount a safe, nominal cash flow at an after-tax borrowing rate, you are implicitly calculating the *equivalent loan*, the amount you could borrow through normal channels, using the cash flow as debt service. Note that

$$\frac{\text{Equivalent}}{\text{loan}} = PV\left(\frac{\text{cash flow available}}{\text{for debt service}}\right) = \frac{103,250}{1.0845} = 95,205$$

In some cases, it may be easier to think of taking the lender's side of the equivalent loan rather than the borrower's. For example, you could ask, "How much would my company have to invest today in order to cover next year's debt service on the subsidized loan?" The answer is $95,205: If you lend that amount at 13 percent, you will earn 8.45 percent after tax, and therefore have $95,205(1.0845) = 103,250$. By this transaction, you can in effect cancel, or "zero out," the future obligation. If you can borrow $100,000 and then set aside only $95,205 to cover all the required debt service, you clearly have $4795 to spend as you please. That amount is the NPV of the subsidized loan.

Therefore, regardless of whether it's easier to think of borrowing or lending, the correct discount rate for safe, nominal cash flows is an after-tax interest rate.[18]

In some ways, this is an obvious result once you think about it. Companies are free to borrow or lend money. If they *lend*, they receive the after-tax interest rate on their investment; if they *borrow* in the capital market, they pay the after-tax interest rate. Thus, the opportunity cost to companies of investing in debt-equivalent cash flows is the after-tax interest rate. This is the adjusted cost of capital for debt-equivalent cash flows.

Some Further Examples

Here are some further examples of debt-equivalent cash flows.

PAYOUT FIXED BY CONTRACT.   Suppose you sign a maintenance contract with a truck leasing firm, which agrees to keep your leased trucks in good working order for

---

[18]Borrowing and lending rates should not differ by much if the cash flows are truly safe—that is, if the chance of default is small. Usually your decision will not hinge on the rate used. If it does, ask which offsetting transaction—borrowing or lending—seems most natural and reasonable for the problem at hand. Then use the corresponding interest rate.

the next 2 years in exchange for 24 fixed monthly payments. These payments are debt-equivalent flows.[19]

DEPRECIATION TAX SHIELDS.   Capital projects are normally valued by discounting the total after-tax cash flows they are expected to generate. Depreciation tax shields contribute to project cash flow, but they are not valued separately; they are just folded into project cash flows along with dozens, or hundreds, of other specific inflows and outflows. The project's opportunity cost of capital reflects the average risk of the resulting aggregate.

However, suppose we ask what depreciation tax shields are worth *by themselves*. For a firm that's sure to pay taxes, depreciation tax shields are a safe, nominal flow. Therefore, they should be discounted at the firm's after-tax borrowing rate.[20]

Suppose we buy an asset with a depreciable basis of $200,000, which can be depreciated by the 5-year tax depreciation schedule (see Table 6-5). The resulting tax shields are:

	PERIOD					
	1	2	3	4	5	6
Percentage deductions	20	32	19	11.5	11.5	6
Dollar deductions, thousands	$40	$64	$38	$23	$23	$12
Tax shields at $T_c = .35$, thousands	$14	$22.4	$13.3	$8.1	$8.1	$4.2

The after-tax discount rate is $r_D(1 - T_c) = .13(1 - .35) = .0845$. (We continue to assume a 13 percent pretax borrowing rate and a 35 percent marginal tax rate.) The present value of these shields is

$$PV = \frac{14}{1.0845} + \frac{22.4}{(1.0845)^2} + \frac{13.3}{(1.0845)^3} + \frac{8.1}{(1.0845)^4} + \frac{8.1}{(1.0845)^5} + \frac{4.2}{(1.0845)^6}$$
$$= +56.2, \text{ or } \$56,200$$

*Adjusted Discount Rates for Debt-Equivalent Cash Flows

You may have wondered whether our procedure for valuing debt-equivalent cash flows is consistent with the adjusted-discount-rate approaches presented earlier in this chapter. Yes, it is consistent, as we will now illustrate.

Remember from Section 18-2 that the value of corporate interest tax shields depends on the personal tax rates paid by debt and equity investors. No one knows for sure what the relevant personal rates actually are. The polar views are those of Modigliani and Miller (MM), on one hand, and Miller, on the other. MM assume that investors face the same tax rate on debt and equity income, so that only corporate taxes need be considered; in that case, $T^* = T_c$. But Miller argues that debt

---

[19]We assume you are locked into the contract. If it can be canceled without penalty, you may have a valuable option.

[20]The depreciation tax shields are cash inflows, not outflows as for the contractual payout or the subsidized loan. For safe, nominal inflows, the relevant question is, "How much could the firm borrow today if it uses the inflow for debt service?" You could also ask, "How much would the firm have to lend today to generate the same future inflow?"

investors pay higher effective tax rates than equity investors, so much so that any advantage of the corporate interest tax shield is entirely offset, and $T^* = 0$.

Let's look at a very simple numerical example from each viewpoint. Our problem is to value a \$1 million payment to be received from a blue-chip company 1 year hence. After taxes at 35 percent, the cash inflow is \$650,000. The payment is fixed by contract.

Since the contract generates a debt-equivalent flow, the opportunity cost of capital is the rate investors would demand on a 1-year note issued by the blue-chip company, which happens to be 8 percent. For simplicity, we'll assume this is your company's borrowing rate too. Our valuation rule for debt-equivalent flows is therefore to discount at $r^* = r_D(1 - T_c) = .08(1 - .35) = .052$:

$$PV = \frac{650,000}{1.052} = \$617,900$$

VALUING DEBT-EQUIVALENT CASH FLOWS UNDER MM ASSUMPTIONS.   Now let's see how MM would address this same problem. The opportunity cost of capital is still $r_D = .08$, or 8 percent. With $T^* = T_c$, the MM adjusted-cost-of-capital formula is $r^* = r_D(1 - T_c L)$.

What is L? In Section 19-2, we defined it as a project's "marginal contribution to the firm's debt capacity," expressed as a fraction of project value, which is normally well below 1. But the debt capacity of a safe cash flow is 100 percent of its value, because the firm could "zero out" the cash flow by taking out an equivalent loan with the same after-tax debt service. Thus, we can think of "debt capacity" as the offsetting equivalent loan. Since the equivalent loan has exactly the same present value as the debt-equivalent flow, $L = 1$.

The MM adjusted-cost-of-capital formula for debt-equivalent cash flows therefore boils down to the same after-tax borrowing rate we used to discount the \$650,000 inflow:

$$r^* = r(1 - T_c L) = r_D(1 - T_c) = .08(1 - .35) = .052$$

We get the same result from the Miles-Ezzell formula. With $r = r_D$ and $L = 1$,

$$r^* = r]- L r_D T_c \left(\frac{1 + r}{1 + r_D} \right)$$

$$= r_D - 1 \times r_D T_c \left(\frac{1 + r_D}{1 + r_D} \right)$$

$$= r_D - r_D T_c = r_D(1 - T_c)$$

Let's also try an APV calculation under MM assumptions. This is a two-part calculation. First, the \$650,000 inflow is discounted at the opportunity cost of capital, 8 percent. Second, we add the present value of interest tax shields on debt supported by the project. Since the firm can borrow 100 percent of the cash flow's value, the tax shield is $r_D T_c$ APV, and APV is

$$APV = \frac{650,000}{1.08} + \frac{.08(.35)APV}{1.08}$$

Solving for APV, we get \$617,900, the same answer we obtained by discounting at the after-tax borrowing rate.

Thus our valuation rule for debt-equivalent flows is a special case of the APV rule once we adopt MM's assumptions about debt and taxes.

VALUING DEBT-EQUIVALENT CASH FLOWS UNDER MILLER'S ASSUMPTIONS. But suppose that you share Miller's view that there is no tax advantage to debt, so that $T^* = 0$. That would seem to imply that debt-equivalent cash flows should be discounted at the *pretax* borrowing rate. For example, if we set $T^* = 0$ in the MM adjusted-cost-of-capital formula, $r^* = r(1 - T^*L) = r(1 - 0 \times L) = r$, the opportunity cost of capital, which we would normally set at $r = r_D$ for debt-equivalent flows.

However, the reason why $T^* = 0$ in Miller's theory is that debt investors' personal tax rate equals the corporate rate ($T_p = T_c$), while the effective tax rate on equity income is zero ($T_{pE} = 0$). (See Section 18-2.) Thus debt investors demand a higher pretax rate of return on safe investments than equity investors do. For example, if the after-personal-tax return on debt is $.08(1 - .35) = .052$, or 5.2 percent, then investors will also be content with a 5.2 percent rate of return on a safe, *untaxed* equity investment.

Therefore, equity investors' opportunity cost of capital for a safe cash flow is the *after-tax* interest rate: $r = r_D(1 - T_p) = r_D(1 - T_c)$.

Thus, although $T^* = 0$ in Miller's world, we nevertheless end up discounting debt-equivalent flows at $r_D(1 - T_c)$, because that is the rate the firm's stockholders demand.

19-5 YOUR QUESTIONS ANSWERED

Question: All these cost of capital formulas—which ones do financial managers actually use?

Answer: The after-tax weighted-average cost of capital, most of the time. WACC is estimated for the company, or sometimes for an industry. We recommend industry WACCs when data are available for several comparable firms. The firms should have similar assets, operations, business risks, and growth opportunities.

Of course, conglomerate companies, with divisions operating in two or more unrelated industries, should not use a single company or industry WACC. Such firms should try to estimate a different industry WACC for each operating division.

Question: But WACC is the correct discount rate only for "average" projects. What if the project's financing differs from the company's or industry's?

Answer: Remember, investment projects are usually not separately financed. Even when they are, you should focus on the project's contribution to the firm's overall debt capacity, not on its immediate financing. (Suppose it's convenient to raise all the money for a particular project with a bank loan. That doesn't mean the project itself supports 100 percent debt financing. The company is borrowing against its existing assets as well as the project.)

But if the project's debt capacity is materially different from the company's existing assets, or if the company's overall debt policy changes, WACC should be adjusted. Brealey and Myers recommend two nearly equivalent approaches. First, you can adjust WACC using the Miles-Ezzell formula. Second, you can estimate new costs of debt and equity and recalculate WACC at the new debt ratio.

Question: Could we do one more numerical example?

Answer: Sure. Suppose that WACC has been estimated as follows at a 30 percent debt ratio:

$$\text{WACC} = r_D(1 - T_c)\frac{D}{V} + r_E\frac{E}{V}$$

$$= .09(1 - .35)(.3) + .15(.7) = .1226, \text{ or } 12.26\%$$

What is the correct discount rate at a 50 percent debt ratio?

First, let's use the Miles-Ezzell formula:

$$r^* = \text{WACC} = r - Lr_DT^*\left(\frac{1+r}{1+r_D}\right)$$

where r is the opportunity cost of capital, that is, investors' required rate of return under all-equity financing. At a 30 percent debt ratio ($L = .3$), the formula is

$$r^* = \text{WACC} = r - .3(.09)(.35)\left(\frac{1+r}{1.09}\right) = .1226$$

which implies an opportunity cost of capital of $r = .1325$, or 13.25 percent.

The opportunity cost of capital will not change at a 50 percent debt ratio, but the cost of debt, r_D, will probably be higher. Say it is 9.5 percent. Now recalculate r^* with $L = D/V = .50$. (We assume for simplicity that T^*, the net tax advantage of corporate borrowing, is the same as the marginal corporate rate, $T_c = .35$.)

$$r^* = .1325 - .5(.095)(.35)\left(\frac{1.1325}{1.095}\right) = .1153, \text{ or about } 11.5\%$$

Question: Do we have to use Miles-Ezzell? Why not just calculate a new WACC?

Answer: That's the second approach. It may look easier, but you must change the cost of equity, because r_E, stockholders' required rate of return, increases with financial risk. The formula for r_E is MM's proposition II:

$$r_E = r + (r - r_D)\frac{D}{E}$$

Note that r_E depends on the debt-equity ratio D/E, not on the ratio of debt to firm value. At 50 percent debt, $D/E = .50/.50 = 1.0$. The new cost of equity at this debt policy is

$$r_E = .1325 + (.1325 - .095)(1.0) = .17$$

Now recalculate WACC:

$$\text{WACC} = .095(1 - .35)(.5) + .17(.5) = 11.59, \text{ or again about } 11.5\%$$

This is a very close approximation to the r^* obtained from the Miles-Ezzell formula.[21]

Question: How do I use the capital asset pricing model to calculate the after-tax weighted-average cost of capital?

Answer: First plug the equity beta into the capital asset pricing formula to calculate r_E, the expected return to equity. Then use this figure, along with the after-tax cost of debt and the debt-to-value and equity-to-value ratios, in the WACC formula. We covered this in Chapter 9. The only change here is use of the after-tax cost of debt, $r_D(1 - T_c)$.

Question: What if I have to recalculate the equity beta for a different debt ratio?

Answer: The formula for beta is

$$\beta_E = \beta_A + (\beta_A - \beta_D)\frac{D}{E}$$

where β_E is the equity beta, β_A the asset beta, and β_D the beta of the company's debt.

---

[21] The Miles-Ezzell formula implies a very similar, but more complicated, expression for r_E.

Question: Can I use the capital asset pricing model to calculate the asset beta and the opportunity cost of capital?

Answer: Sure. We covered this in Chapter 9. The asset beta is a weighted average of the debt and equity betas:[22]

$$\beta_A = \beta_D \frac{D}{V} + \beta_E \frac{E}{V}$$

Suppose you needed the opportunity cost of capital as an input to the Miles-Ezzell formula. You could calculate β_A, and then r from the capital asset pricing model.

Question: I think I understand how to adjust for differences in debt capacity or debt policy. How about differences in business risk?

Answer: If business risk is different, then r, the opportunity cost of capital, is different.

Figuring out the right r for an unusually safe or risky project is never easy. Sometimes the financial manager can use estimates of risk and expected return for companies similar to the project. Suppose, for example, that a traditional pharmaceutical company is considering a major commitment to biotech research. The financial manager could pick a sample of biotech companies, estimate their average beta and cost of capital, and use these estimates as benchmarks for the biotech investment.

But in many cases it's difficult to find a good sample of matching companies for an unusually safe or risky project. Then the financial manager has to adjust the opportunity cost of capital by judgment.[23] Section 9-4 may be helpful in such cases.

Question: Let's go back to the cost of capital formulas. The tax rates are confusing. When should I use T_c and when T^*?

Answer: Always use T_c, the marginal corporate tax rate, (1) when calculating WACC as a weighted average of the costs of debt and equity and (2) when discounting safe, nominal cash flows. In each case the discount rate is adjusted *only* for corporate taxes.[24]

The Miles-Ezzell and MM formulas, which show how the cost of capital depends on financing, in principle call for T^*, the net tax saving per dollar of interest paid by the firm. This depends on the effective personal tax rates on debt and equity income. T^* is almost surely less than T_c, but it is very difficult to pin down the numerical difference. Therefore in practice T_c is almost always used as an approximation.

Question: When do I need adjusted present value (APV)?

Answer: The WACC and Miles-Ezzell formulas pick up only one financing "side effect": the value of interest tax shields on debt supported by a project. If there are other side effects—subsidized financing tied to a project, for example—you should use APV. You can also use APV to show the value of interest tax shields:

$$APV = \text{base-case NPV} + \text{PV(tax shield)}$$

---

[22]This formula assumes financing rule 2. If debt is fixed, taxes complicate the formulas. For example, if debt is fixed and permanent, and only corporate taxes are considered, the formula for β_E changes to
$\beta_E = \beta_A + (\beta_A - \beta_D)(1 - T_c)D/E$

[23]The judgment is usually implicit. That is, the manager will not explicitly announce that the discount rate for a high-risk project is, say, 2.5 percentage points above the standard rate. But the project will not be approved unless it offers a higher-than-standard rate of return.

[24]Any effects of personal income taxes are reflected in r_D and r_E, the rates of return demanded by debt and equity investors.

where base-case NPV assumes all-equity financing. But it's usually easier to do this calculation in one step, by discounting project cash flows at an adjusted cost of capital (WACC or r^*). Remember, though, that discounting by WACC or the Miles-Ezzell r^* assumes financing rule 2, that is, debt rebalanced to a constant fraction of future project value. If this financing rule is not right, you may need APV to calculate PV(tax shield), as we did for the solar heater project in Table 19-1.[25]

Suppose, for example, that you are analyzing a company just after a leveraged recapitalization. The company has a very high initial debt level but plans to pay down the debt as rapidly as possible. This would not match either financing rule 1 or rule 2. However, APV could be used to obtain an accurate valuation.

19-6 SUMMARY

Investment decisions always have side effects on financing: every dollar spent has to be raised somehow. Sometimes the side effects are irrelevant or at least unimportant. In an ideal world with no taxes, transaction costs, or other market imperfections, only investment decisions would affect firm value. In such a world firms could analyze all investment opportunities as if they were all-equity-financed. Firms would decide which assets to buy and then worry about getting the money to pay for them. No one would worry about where the money might come from because debt policy, dividend policy, and all other financing choices would have no impact on stockholders' wealth.

Side effects cannot be ignored in practice. There are two ways to take them into account. You can calculate NPV by discounting at an adjusted discount rate, or you can discount at the opportunity cost of capital and then add or subtract the present value of financing side effects. The second approach is called adjusted present value, or APV.

The most commonly used adjusted discount rate is the after-tax weighted-average cost of capital, or WACC:

$$r^* = r_D(1 - T_c)\frac{D}{V} + r_E\frac{E}{V}$$

Here r_D and r_E are the expected rates of return demanded by investors in the firm's debt and equity securities, respectively; D and E are the current *market values* of debt and equity; and V is the total market value of the firm ($V = D + E$).

Strictly speaking, this formula works only for projects that are carbon copies of the existing firm—projects with the same business risk that will be financed to maintain the firm's current, market-debt ratio. But firms can use WACC as a benchmark rate, to be adjusted for differences in business risk or financing.

Miles and Ezzell have developed a formula relating WACC to financial leverage:

$$r^* = r - Lr_D T^*\left[\frac{1 + r}{1 + r_D}\right]$$

---

[25]Having read Section 19-4, you may be wondering why we did not discount at the *after-tax* borrowing rate in Table 19-1. The answer is that we wanted to simplify and take one thing at a time. If debt is fixed and the odds of financial distress are low, interest tax shields are safe, nominal flows, and there is a case for using the after-tax rate. Doing so assumes that the firm will, or can, take out an additional loan with debt service exactly covered by the interest tax shields.

Here r is the opportunity cost of capital, which depends on business risk; T^* is the net tax saving per dollar of interest paid; and L is the ratio of debt supported by the project to project value. For the firm as a whole, $L = D/V$.

The exact value of T^* is extremely elusive, so most financial managers set it to T_c, the marginal corporate tax rate. Then they can use the Miles-Ezzell formula to calculate how WACC varies with the debt ratio D/V. They can also calculate how r_E, the "cost of equity," changes with financial leverage. The following formula is a very close approximation:

$$r_E = r + (r - r_D)\frac{D}{E}$$

Miles and Ezzell assumed the firm adjusts its borrowing to keep a constant debt-to-market value ratio. This assumption also underlies WACC. In cases where debt is paid off on a fixed schedule, MM's adjusted-discount-rate formula applies.

$$r^* = r(1 - T^*L)$$

Again, in practice T^* is usually replaced with T_c.

Remember that all these formulas rest on special assumptions. For example, they assume financing matters *only* because of interest tax shields. When this or other assumptions are violated, only APV will give an absolutely correct answer.

APV is, in concept at least, simple. First calculate the present value of the project as if there are no important side effects. Then adjust present value to calculate the project's total impact on firm value. The rule is to accept the project if adjusted net present value (APV) is positive:

$$\text{Accept project if APV} = \text{base-case NPV} + \begin{matrix}\text{present value}\\\text{of financing}\\\text{side effects}\end{matrix} > 0$$

The base-case NPV is the project's NPV computed assuming all-equity financing and perfect capital markets. Think of it as the project's value if it were set up as a separate mini-firm. You would compute the mini-firm's value by forecasting its cash flows and discounting at the opportunity cost of capital for the project. The cash flows should be net of the taxes that an all-equity-financed mini-firm would pay.

Financing side effects are evaluated one by one and their present values added to or subtracted from base-case NPV. We looked at several cases:

1. *Issue costs.* If accepting the project forces the firm to issue securities, then the present value of issue costs should be subtracted from base-case NPV.

2. *Interest tax shields.* Debt interest is a tax-deductible expense. Most people believe that interest tax shields contribute to firm value. Thus a project that prompts the firm to borrow more generates additional value. The project's APV is increased by the present value of interest tax shields on debt the project supports.

3. *Special financing.* Sometimes special financing opportunities are tied to project acceptance. For example, the government might offer subsidized financing for socially desirable projects. You simply compute the present value of the financing opportunity and add it to base-case NPV.

Remember not to confuse *contribution to corporate debt capacity* with the immediate source of funds for investment. For example, a firm might, as a matter of convenience, borrow $1 million for a $1 million research program. But the research would be unlikely to contribute $1 million in debt capacity; a large part of the $1 million new debt would be supported by the firm's other assets.

Also remember that *debt capacity* is not meant to imply an absolute limit on how much the firm *can* borrow. The phrase refers to how much it *chooses* to borrow. Normally the firm's optimal debt level increases as its assets expand; that is why we say that a new project contributes to corporate debt capacity.

Calculating APV may require several steps: one step for base-case NPV, and one for each financing side effect. Many firms try to calculate APV in a single calculation. They do so by the following procedure: After-tax cash flows are forecast in the usual way—that is, as if the project is all-equity-financed. But the discount rate is adjusted to reflect the financing side effects. If the discount rate is adjusted correctly, the result is APV:

$$\begin{array}{c}\text{NPV at adjusted} \\ \text{discount rate}\end{array} = \text{APV} = \begin{array}{c}\text{NPV at opportunity} \\ \text{cost of capital}\end{array} + \begin{array}{c}\text{present value of} \\ \text{financing side effects}\end{array}$$

WACC and the Miles-Ezzell and MM formulas are, of course, examples of adjusted discount rates.

This chapter is almost 100 percent theory. The theory is difficult. If you think you understand all the formulas, assumptions, and relationships on the first reading, we suggest psychiatric assistance. We can, however, offer one simple, bulletproof, easy-to-remember rule: Discount safe, nominal cash flows at the after-tax borrowing rate.

Further Reading

The adjusted-present-value rule was developed in:
S. C. Myers: "Interactions of Corporate Financing and Investment Decisions—Implications for Capital Budgeting," *Journal of Finance,* **29**:1–25 (March 1974).

Formulas for the adjusted discount rate are explained in:
F. Modigliani and M. H. Miller: "Corporate Income Taxes and the Cost of Capital: A Correction," *American Economic Review,* **53**:433–443 (June 1963).
M. H. Miller and F. Modigliani: "Some Estimates of the Cost of Capital to the Electric Utility Industry: 1954–1957," *American Economic Review,* **56**:333–391 (June 1966).
J. Miles and R. Ezzell: "The Weighted Average Cost of Capital, Perfect Capital Markets and Project Life: A Clarification," *Journal of Financial and Quantitative Analysis,* **15**:719–730 (September 1980).

There have been dozens of articles on the weighted-average cost of capital and other issues discussed in this chapter. Here are three representative ones:
M. J. Brennan: "A New Look at the Weighted-Average Cost of Capital," *Journal of Business Finance,* **5**:24–30 (1973).
D. R. Chambers, R. S. Harris, and J. J. Pringle: "Treatment of Financing Mix in Analyzing Investment Opportunities," *Financial Management,* **11**:24–41 (Summer 1982).
R. A. Taggart, Jr.: "Consistent Valuation and Cost of Capital Expressions with Corporate and Personal Taxes," *Financial Management,* **20**:8–20 (Autumn 1991).

The valuation rule for safe, nominal cash flows is developed in:
R. S. Ruback: "Calculating the Market Value of Risk-Free Cash Flows," *Journal of Financial Economics,* **15**:323–339 (March 1986).

Quiz

1. Calculate the weighted-average cost of capital (WACC) for Federated Junkyards of America, using the following information.

   ▪ Debt: $75,000,000 book value outstanding. The debt is trading at 90 percent of par. The yield to maturity is 9 percent.
   ▪ Equity: 2,500,000 shares selling at $42 per share. Assume the expected rate of return on Federated's stock is 18 percent.
   ▪ Taxes: Federated's marginal tax rate is $T_c = .35$.

   What are the key assumptions underlying your calculation? For what type of project would Federated's weighted-average cost of capital be the right discount rate?

2. Refer again to question 1. Using the Miles-Ezzell formula, calculate Federated's average opportunity cost of capital. Then calculate Federated's WACC at 25 percent debt-to-value ratio. What would the expected rate of return on Federated stock be at this ratio? Assume that Federated's borrowing rate stays at 9 percent, and that $T_c = T^* = .35$.

3. Table 19-2 shows a *book* balance sheet for the Wishing Well Motel chain. The company's long-term debt is secured by its real estate assets, but it also uses short-term bank financing. It pays 10 percent interest on the bank debt and 9 percent interest on the secured debt. Wishing Well has 10 million shares of stock outstanding, trading at $90 per share. The expected return on Wishing Well's common stock is 18 percent.
   Calculate Wishing Well's WACC. Assume that the book and market values of Wishing Well's debt are the same. The marginal tax rate is 35 percent.

4. Suppose Wishing Well is evaluating a new motel and resort on a romantic site in Madison County, Wisconsin. Explain how you would forecast the after-tax cash flows for this project. (*Hints:* How would you treat taxes? Interest expense? Changes in working capital?)

5. In order to finance the Madison County project, Wishing Well will have to arrange an additional $80 million of long-term debt and make a $20 million equity issue. Underwriting fees, spreads, and other costs of this financing will

TABLE 19-2

Balance sheet for Wishing Well, Inc. (figures in millions of dollars)

Cash, marketable securities	100	Accounts payable	120
Inventory	50	Bank loan	280
Accounts receivable	200	Current liabilities	400
Current assets	350		
Real estate	2,100	Long-term debt	1,800
Other assets	150	Equity	400
Total	2,600	Total	2,600

total $4 million. How would you take this into account in valuing the proposed investment?

6. A project costs $1 million and has a base-case NPV of exactly zero (NPV = 0). What is the project's APV in the following cases?
   (a) If the firm invests, it has to raise $500,000 by stock issue. Issue costs are 15 percent of *net* proceeds.
   (b) The firm has ample cash on hand. But if it invests, it will have access to $500,000 of debt financing at a subsidized interest rate. The present value of the subsidy is $175,000.
   (c) If the firm invests, its debt capacity increases by $500,000. The present value of interest tax shields on this debt is $76,000.
   (d) If the firm invests, it issues equity, as in (a), and borrows, as in (c).

7. Use the Miles-Ezzell and MM adjusted-discount-rate formulas to value the solar heater project analyzed in Section 19-2. Assume 50 percent debt financing (L = .50). Explain why the two formulas give different NPVs.

8. Whispering Pines, Inc., is all-equity-financed. The expected rate of return on the company's shares is 12 percent.
   (a) What is the opportunity cost of capital for an average-risk Whispering Pines investment?
   (b) Suppose the company issues debt, repurchases shares, and moves to a 30 percent debt-to-value ratio ($D/V = .30$). What will the company's weighted-average cost of capital and expected return on equity be at the new capital structure? The borrowing rate is 7.5 percent and the tax rate 35 percent. Use the Miles-Ezzell formula with $T^* = T_c$.

9. Consider the APV of the solar heater project, as calculated in Table 19-2. How would the APV change if the net tax shield per dollar of interest were not $T_c = .35$, but $T^* = .10$?

10. Consider a project lasting 1 year only. The initial outlay is $1000 and the expected inflow is $1200. The opportunity cost of capital is $r = .20$. The borrowing rate is $r_D = .10$, and the net tax shield per dollar of interest is $T^* = T_c = .35$.
    (a) What is the project's base-case NPV?
    (b) What is its APV if the firm borrows 30 percent of the project's required investment?

11. The WACC formula seems to imply that debt is "cheaper" than equity—i.e., that a firm with more debt could use a lower discount rate r^*. Does this make sense? Explain briefly.

12. What discount rate should be used to value safe, nominal cash flows? Explain briefly.

13. You are considering a 5-year lease of office space for R&D personnel. Once signed, the lease cannot be canceled. It would commit your firm to six annual $100,000 payments, with the first payment due immediately. What is the present value of the lease if your company's borrowing rate is 9 percent and its tax rate is 35 percent? *Note:* The lease payments would be tax-deductible.

14. Figure 19-1 shows estimates of WACC and r_E, the cost of equity, for major oil companies. Suppose you estimated the opportunity cost of capital (r) and plotted it in the figure. Would it be below both lines? Above? In the middle? Explain.

Questions and Problems

1. Consider another perpetual project like the Geothermal venture described in this chapter. Its initial investment is $1,000,000, and the expected cash inflow is $85,000 a year in perpetuity. The opportunity cost of capital with all-equity financing is 10 percent, and the project allows the firm to borrow an additional 40 percent of project value at 7 percent. Assume the net tax advantage to borrowing is 35 cents per dollar of interest paid ($T^* = T_c = .35$).
   (a) What is the project's value if debt is adjusted each period to maintain the 40 percent debt-to-value ratio? Use an adjusted discount rate for your calculation.
   (b) Show that your answer to (a) is also the project's APV. (*Hint:* How much debt will the project support at the start?)
   (c) What is the project's value if debt is *not* increased if the project does well or reduced if it does poorly? Otherwise use the same assumptions as in (a). Use an adjusted discount rate for your calculation.
   (d) Show that your answer to (c) is the project's APV assuming fixed borrowing.

2. Suppose the project described in problem 1 is to be undertaken by a university. Funds for the project will be withdrawn from the university's endowment, which is invested in a widely diversified portfolio of stocks and bonds. However, the university can also borrow at 7 percent.

   Suppose the university treasurer proposes to finance the project by issuing $400,000 of perpetual bonds at 7 percent and by selling $600,000 worth of common stocks from the endowment. The expected return on the common stocks is 10 percent. He therefore proposes to evaluate the project by discounting at a weighted-average cost of capital, calculated as

   $$r^* = r_D \frac{D}{V} + r_E \frac{E}{V}$$
   $$= .07 \left(\frac{400,000}{1,000,000} \right) + .10 \left(\frac{600,000}{1,000,000} \right)$$
   $$= .088, \text{ or } 8.8\%$$

   What's right or wrong with the treasurer's approach? Should the university invest? Should it borrow?

3. Table 19-3 shows a simplified balance sheet for Rensselaer Felt. Calculate this company's weighted-average cost of capital. The debt has just been refinanced at an interest rate of 6 percent (short term) and 8 percent (long term). The expected rate of return on the company's shares is 15 percent. There are 7.46 million shares outstanding, and the shares are trading at $46. The tax rate is 35 percent.

4. How will Rensselaer Felt's WACC and cost of equity change if it issues $50 million in new equity and uses the proceeds to retire long-term debt? Assume the company's borrowing rates are unchanged.

5. Short-term interest rates are frequently below long-term rates. Tax effects aside, does that mean that using more short-term debt reduces the overall cost of capital? (*Hint:* Think back to Chapter 17.)

6. Rapidly growing companies may have to issue shares to finance capital expenditures. In doing so, they incur underwriting and other issue costs. Some analysts have tried to adjust WACC to account for these costs. For example, if is-

TABLE 19-3

· ·

Simplified book balance sheet for Rensselaer Felt (figures in thousands of dollars)			
Cash and marketable securities	1,500	Short-term debt	75,600
Accounts receivable	120,000	Accounts payable	62,000
Inventories	125,000	Current liabilities	137,600
Current assets	246,500	Long-term debt	208,600
Property, plant, and equipment	302,000	Deferred taxes	45,000
Other assets	89,000	Shareholders' equity	246,300
Total	637,500	Total	637,500

sue costs are 8 percent of equity issue proceeds, and equity issues account for all of equity financing, the cost of equity might be divided by $1 - .08 = .92$. This would increase a 15 percent cost of equity to $15/.92 = 16.3$ percent.

Explain why this sort of adjustment is *not* a smart idea. What is the correct way to take issue costs into account in project valuation?

7. Digital Organics (DO) has the opportunity to invest $1 million now ($t = 0$) and expects after-tax returns of $600,000 in $t = 1$ and $700,000 in $t = 2$. The project will last for 2 years only. The appropriate cost of capital is 12 percent with all-equity financing, the borrowing rate is 8 percent, and DO will borrow $300,000 against the project. This debt is to be repaid in two equal installments. Assume debt tax shields have a net value of 30 cents per dollar of interest paid. Calculate the project's APV, using the procedure followed in Table 19-1.

8. Refer again to Quiz question 10 for this chapter. Suppose the firm borrows 30 percent of the project's *value*.
   (*a*) What is the project's APV?
   (*b*) What is the minimum acceptable rate of return for projects of this type?
   (*c*) Show that your answer to (*b*) is consistent with the Miles-Ezzell formula.

9. List the assumptions underlying the MM adjusted-discount-rate formula. Derive the formula algebraically for a perpetual project. Then try to derive it for a one-period project like the one described in Quiz question 10. Keep MM's other assumptions intact. (*Hint:* You will end up with the Miles-Ezzell formula. In other words, their formula works for one-period projects; MM's does not.)

10. The Bunsen Chemical Company is currently at its target debt ratio of 40 percent. It is contemplating a $1 million expansion of its existing business. This expansion is expected to produce a cash inflow of $130,000 a year in perpetuity.

   The company is uncertain whether to undertake this expansion and how to finance it. The two options are a $1 million issue of common stock or a $1 million issue of 20-year debt. The flotation costs of a stock issue would be around 5 percent of the amount raised, and the flotation costs of a debt issue would be around 1½ percent.

   Bunsen's financial manager, Miss Polly Ethylene, estimates that the required return on the company's equity is 14 percent, but she argues that the flotation costs increase the cost of new equity to 19 percent. On this basis, the project does not appear viable.

On the other hand, she points out that the company can raise new debt on a 7 percent yield which would make the cost of new debt 8½ percent. She therefore recommends that Bunsen should go ahead with the project and finance it with an issue of long-term debt.

Is Miss Ethylene right? How would you evaluate the project?

11. Curtis Bog, chief financial officer of Sphagnum Paper Corporation, is reviewing a consultant's analysis of Sphagnum's weighted-average cost of capital. The consultant proposes

$$r^* = (1 - T_c) \, r_D \frac{D}{V} + r_E \frac{E}{V} = \text{WACC}$$

$$= (1 - .35)(.103)(.55) + .183(.45)$$

$$= .1192, \text{ or about } 12\%$$

Mr. Bog wants to check that this calculation is consistent with the capital asset pricing model. He has observed or estimated the following numbers:

- Betas: $\beta_{\text{debt}} = .15, \beta_{\text{equity}} = 1.09$
- Expected market risk premium $(r_m - r_f)$:   .085
- Risk-free rate of interest (r_f):   9 percent

Show Mr. Bog how to calculate β_{assets}, the opportunity cost of capital for Sphagnum's assets, and the adjusted hurdle rate r^*. Does your r^* match the consultant's weighted-average cost of capital? (Expect some rounding errors.)

Note: We suggest you simplify by ignoring personal income taxes and assuming that the promised and expected rates of returns on Sphagnum debt are equal.

12. Nevada Hydro is 40 percent debt-financed and has a weighted-average cost of capital of 9.7 percent:

$$r^* = (1 - T_c) \, r_D \frac{D}{V} + r_E \frac{E}{V} = \text{WACC}$$

$$= (1 - .35)(.085)(.40) + .125(.60) = .097$$

Banker's Tryst Company is advising Nevada Hydro to issue $75 million of preferred stock at a dividend yield of 9 percent. The proceeds would be used to repurchase and retire common stock. The preferred issue would account for 10 percent of the preissue market value of the firm.

Banker's Tryst argues that these transactions would reduce Nevada Hydro's WACC to 9.4 percent:

$$\text{WACC} = r^* = (1 - .35)(.085)(.40) + .09(.10) + .125(.50)$$

$$= .094, \text{ or } 9.4\%$$

Do you agree with this calculation? Explain.

13. Suppose you wanted to figure out the *opportunity* cost of capital (r) for the railroad industry in mid-1974. You have an estimate of r^*, the adjusted discount rate: 10¾ percent as reported in Section 19-1. (*Hint:* We presented two formulas linking r and r^*.)

14. Consider a different financing scenario for the solar water heater project discussed in Section 19-2. The project requires $10 million and has a base-case

NPV of $170,000. Suppose the firm happens to have $5 million in the bank which could be used for the project.

The government, eager to encourage solar energy, offers to help finance the project by lending $5 million at a subsidized rate of 5 percent. The loan calls for the firm to pay the government $647,500 annually for 10 years (this amount includes both principal and interest).

(a) What is the value of being able to borrow from the government at 5 percent? Assume the company's normal borrowing rate is 8 percent and the corporate tax rate is 35 percent.

(b) Suppose the company's normal debt policy is to borrow 50 percent of the book value of its assets. It calculates the present value of interest tax shields by the procedure shown in Table 19-1 and includes this present value in APV. Should it do so here, given the government's offer of cheap financing?

(c) Suppose instead that the firm normally borrows 30 percent of the *market* value of its assets. Does this change your answer to part (*b*)? (*Hint:* The Miles-Ezzell formula can be used to calculate project APV in this case; that formula does not capture the value of the subsidized loan, however.)

15. Table 19-4 is a simplified book balance sheet for Phillips Petroleum at year-end 1994. Other information:

- Number of outstanding shares (N):   261.6 million
- Price per share (P), end of year: $33
- Beta based on 60 monthly returns, against the S&P Composite: $\beta = .87$; Standard error of $\beta = .20$
- Historical average market risk premium, 1926–1994:   8.4 percent
- Interest rates, start of year 1995:
    Treasury bills: 6.5 percent
    20-year Treasury bonds: 7.9 percent
    New issue rate for Phillips assuming straight long-term debt: 9.5 percent

TABLE 19-4

Simplified book balance sheet for Phillips Petroleum, 1994 (figures in millions of dollars)

Current assets	2,465	Current liabilities	2,441
Net property, plant, and equipment	8,042	Long-term debt	3,106
Investments and other assets	929	Deferred taxes	944
		Other liabilities	1,992
		Shareholders' equity	2,953
Total	11,436	Total	11,436

- Excess return of Treasury bonds over
  bills, 1926–1994:   1.4 percent
- Marginal tax rate: 35 percent

(*a*) Calculate Phillips's weighted-average cost of capital. Use the capital asset pricing model and the data given above. Make additional assumptions and approximations as necessary.

(*b*) What would Phillips's weighted-average cost of capital be if it moved to *and maintained* a debt–market value ratio (*D/V*) of 25 percent? Consider corporate income taxes only.

16. In question 15 you calculated a WACC for Phillips Petroleum. Phillips could also use an industry WACC as shown in Figure 19-1. Under what conditions would the industry WACC be the better choice? Explain (*Hint:* See Section 9-2.)

PART six

OPTIONS

Corporate Liabilities and the Valuation of Options

The Chicago Board Options Exchange (CBOE) was founded in 1973. It was an almost instant success. Within 5 years investors were trading daily options to buy or sell more than 10 million shares.

Options trading now takes place on a number of exchanges. In addition to options on individual common stocks, there are also options on stock indexes, bonds, foreign exchange, and commodities. And if you can't find a traded option to suit your needs, there is no shortage of large banks that will be prepared to tailor-make options of the most byzantine complexity.

Why should the financial manager of an industrial company be interested in such esoteric issues? Because companies routinely use commodity, currency, and interest-rate options to reduce risk. For example, a meatpacking company that wishes to put a ceiling on the cost of beef might take out an option to buy live cattle. A company that wishes to limit its future borrowing costs might take out an option to sell long-term bonds. And so on. In Chapter 25 we will explain how firms employ options to insure or hedge against risk.

But there are two additional important reasons why financial managers need to know how options work. First, many capital investments include an embedded option to expand in the future. For instance, the company may invest in a patent that allows it to exploit a new technology, or it may purchase adjoining land that gives it the option in the future to increase capacity. In each case the company is paying money today for the opportunity to make a further investment. To put it another way, the company is acquiring *growth opportunities*.

Here is another disguised option to invest: You are considering the purchase of a tract of desert land that is known to contain gold deposits. Unfortunately, the cost of extraction is higher than the current price of gold. Does this mean the land is almost worthless? Not at all. You are not obliged to mine the gold, but ownership of the land gives you the option to do so. Of course, if you know that the gold price will remain below the extraction cost, then the option is worthless. But if there is uncertainty about future gold prices, you could be lucky and make a killing.[1]

---

[1]In Chapter 11 we valued Kingsley Solomon's gold mine by calculating the value of the gold in the ground and then subtracting the value of the extraction costs. That is correct only if we *know* that the gold will be mined. Otherwise, the value of the mine is increased by the value of the option to leave the gold in the ground if its price is less than the extraction cost.

If the option to expand has value, what about the option to bail out? Projects don't usually go on until the equipment disintegrates. The decision to terminate a project is usually taken by management, not by nature. Once the project is no longer profitable, the company will cut its losses and exercise its option to abandon the project. Some projects have higher abandonment value than others. Those that use standardized equipment may offer a valuable abandonment option. Others may actually cost money to discontinue. For example, it is very costly to decommission nuclear power plants or to reclaim land that has been strip-mined.

We took a peek at these investment options in Chapter 10, and we showed there how to use decision trees to analyze Magna Charter's options to expand its airline operation or abandon it. We will return to Magna Charter in the next chapter, which is devoted principally to an analysis of capital investment options.

The other important reason why financial managers need to understand options is that they are often tacked on to an issue of corporate securities and so provide the investor or the company with the flexibility to change the terms of the issue. For example, in Chapter 22 we will show how warrants and convertibles give their holders an option to buy common stock in exchange for cash or bonds. Then in Chapter 24 we will see how corporate bonds may give the issuer or the investor the option of early repayment.

In fact, we shall see that whenever a company borrows, it creates an option. The reason is that the borrower is not *compelled* to repay the debt at maturity. If the value of the company's assets is less than the amount of the debt, the company will choose to default on the payment and the bondholders will get to keep the company's assets. Thus, when the firm borrows, the lender effectively acquires the company and the shareholders obtain the option to buy it back by paying off the debt. This is an extremely important insight. It means that anything that we can learn about traded call options applies equally to corporate liabilities.[2]

In this chapter we use traded stock options to explain how options work and how they are valued. But we hope that our brief survey has convinced you that the interest of financial managers in options goes far beyond traded stock options. That is why we are asking you here to invest to acquire several important ideas. The return to this investment comes primarily in later chapters.

20-1 CALLS, PUTS, AND SHARES

Table 20-1 is an extract from the table of option prices in a daily newspaper for July 1995. It shows the prices for two types of options on Intel stock—calls and puts. We will explain each in turn.

A **call option** gives its owner the right to buy stock at a specified *exercise* or *striking* price on or before a specified exercise date. In some cases, the option can be exercised only on one particular day, and it is then conventionally known as a *European call*; in other cases (such as the Intel options shown in Table 20-1), the option can be exercised on or at any time before that day, and it is then known as an *American call*.

The third column of Table 20-1 sets out the prices of Intel call options with different exercise prices and exercise dates. The first entry shows that for $6.25 you could acquire an option to buy a share of Intel stock for $65 on or before October 1995. Moving down to the boldfaced row, you can see that for a price of $8 you could

---

[2]This relationship was first recognized by Fischer Black and Myron Scholes, in "The Pricing of Options and Corporate Liabilities," *Journal of Political Economy*, **81**:637–654 (May–June 1973).

TABLE 20-1

The prices of call and put options on Intel stock in July 1995. Intel stock was trading around $65 per share.

Exercise Date	Exercise Price	Price of Call Option	Price of Put Option
October 1995	$65	$6.25	$4.625
January 1996	**65**	**8**	**5.875**
January 1996	70	5.875	8.5

extend your option to buy Intel stock until January 1996. The third row also shows the price of a January call option, but this one has an exercise price of $70.

In Chapter 13 we met Louis Bachelier, who in 1900 first suggested that security prices follow a random walk. Bachelier also devised a very convenient shorthand to illustrate the effects of investing in different options.[3] We will use this shorthand to compare three possible investments in Intel—a call option, a put option, and the stock itself.

The *position diagram* in Figure 20-1a shows the possible consequences of investing in Intel January call options with an exercise price of $65 (boldfaced in row 2 of Table 20-1). The outcome from investing in Intel calls depends on what happens to the stock price. If the stock price at the end of this 6-month period turns out to be less than the $65 exercise price, nobody will pay $65 to obtain the share via the call option. Your call will in that case be valueless, and you will throw it away. On the other hand, if the stock price turns out to be greater than $65, it will pay to exercise your option to buy the share. In this case the call will be worth the market price of the share minus the $65 that you must pay to acquire it.

Now let us look at the Intel **put options** in the right-hand column of Table 20-1. Whereas the call option gives you the right to *buy* a share for a specified exercise price, the comparable put gives you the right to *sell* the share. For example, the boldfaced entry in the right-hand column of Table 20-1 shows that for $5.875 you could acquire an option to sell Intel stock for a price of $65 anytime within the next 6 months. The circumstances in which the put turns out to be profitable are just the opposite of those in which the call is profitable. You can see this from the position diagram in Figure 20-1b. If Intel's share price immediately before expiration turns out to be *greater* than $65, you won't want to sell stock at that price. You would do better to sell the share in the market, and your put option will be worthless. Conversely, if the share price turns out to be *less* than $65, it will pay to buy stock at the low price and then take advantage of the option to sell it for $65. In this case, the value of the put option on the exercise date is the difference between the $65 proceeds of the sale and the market price of the share. For example, if the share is worth $45, the put is worth $20:

$$\text{Value of put option at expiration} = \text{exercise price} - \text{market price of the share}$$
$$= \$65 - \$45$$
$$= \$20$$

---

[3]L. Bachelier, *Théorie de la Speculation*, Gauthier-Villars, Paris, 1900. Reprinted in English in P. H. Cootner (ed.), *The Random Character of Stock Market Prices*, M.I.T. Press, Cambridge, Mass., 1964.

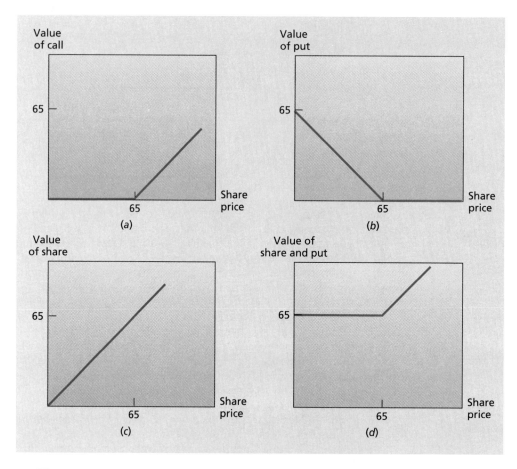

Figure 20-1 Payoffs to owners of Intel calls, puts, and shares (shown by the colored lines) depend on the share price. (a) Result of buying Intel call exercisable at $65. (b) Result of buying Intel put exercisable at $65. (c) Result of buying Intel share. (d) Result of buying Intel share *and* put option exercisable at $65; this is equivalent to owning an Intel call and having $65 in the bank.

Our third investment consists of Intel stock itself. Figure 20-1*c* betrays few secrets when it shows that the value of this investment is always exactly equal to the market value of the share.

**Selling
Calls,
Puts, and
Shares**

Let us now look at the position of an investor who *sells* these investments. If you sell, or "write," a call, you promise to deliver shares if asked to do so by the call buyer. In other words, the buyer's asset is the seller's liability. If by the exercise date the share price is below the exercise price, the buyer will not exercise the call and the seller's liability will be zero. If it rises above the exercise price, the buyer will exercise and the seller will give up the shares. The seller loses the difference between the share price and the exercise price received from the buyer. Notice that it is the buyer who always has the option to exercise; the seller simply does as he or she is told.

Suppose that the price of Intel stock turns out to be $100, which is above the option's exercise price of $65. In this case the buyer will exercise the call. The seller is

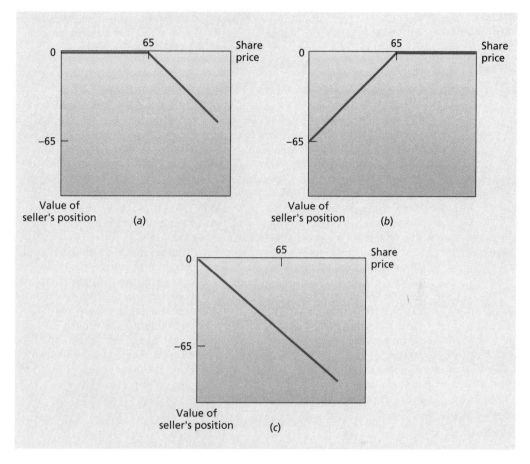

Figure 20-2 Payoffs to sellers of Intel calls, puts, and shares (shown by the colored lines) depend on the share price. (*a*) Result of selling Intel call exercisable at $65. (*b*) Result of selling Intel put exercisable at $65. (*c*) Result of selling Intel share short.

forced to sell stock worth $100 for only $65 and so loses $35. Of course, that $35 loss is the buyer's gain. Figure 20-2*a* shows how the payoffs to the seller of the Intel call option vary with the stock price. Note that Figure 20-2*a* is just Figure 20-1*a* drawn upside down.

In just the same way we can depict the position of an investor who sells, or "writes," a put by standing Figure 20-1*b* on its head. The seller of the put has agreed to pay the exercise price of $65 for the share if the buyer of the put should request it. Clearly the seller will be safe as long as the share price remains above $65 but will lose money if the share price falls below this figure. The worst thing that can happen is that the stock becomes worthless. The seller would then be obliged to pay $65 for a stock worth $0. The "value" of the option position would be −$65.

Finally, Figure 20-2*c* shows the position of someone who sells Intel stock short. Short sellers sell stock which they do not yet own. As they say on Wall Street:

He who sells what isn't his'n
Buys it back or goes to prison.

Eventually, therefore, the short seller will have to buy the stock back. The short seller will make a profit if it has fallen in price and a loss if it has risen.[4] You can see that Figure 20-2*c* is simply an upside-down Figure 20-1*c*.

HOLDING CALLS, PUTS, AND SHARES IN COMBINATION

We now return to the option buyer and see what happens when we add two investments together. Suppose, for example, that your portfolio contains *both* a share of Intel stock and an option to sell (put) it for $65. You can read off the value of each of these holdings from panels *b* and *c* in Figure 20-1. Notice that if Intel's stock price is higher than $65 when the option expires at the end of 6 months, the put option will be worthless and the value of your portfolio will be equal to the share price. Conversely, if the stock price falls below $65, the decline in the value of the share will be exactly offset by the rise in that of the put. In Figure 20-1*d* we have plotted the total value of these two holdings.[5]

This diagram tells us something about the relationship between a call option and a put option. You can see why if you compare it with Figure 20-1*a*. Regardless of the share price, the final value of your combined investment in the share and the put is exactly $65 greater than that of a simple investment in the call. In other words, if you (1) buy the share and (2) retain a put option to sell it after 6 months for $65, you have the same payoff as you would get by (1) buying a 6-month call option and (2) setting aside enough money to pay the $65 exercise price. At the expiration date both strategies give the investor the choice between having $65 cash or owning the share. Therefore, if you are committed to holding the two packages until the end of 6 months, the two packages should sell for the same price. This gives us a fundamental relationship for European options:[6]

Value of call + present value of exercise price = value of put + share price

To repeat, this relationship holds because the payoff of

[Buy call, invest present value of exercise price in safe asset[7]]

is identical to the payoff of

[Buy put, buy share]

---

[4]Selling short is not as simple as we have described it. For example, a short seller usually has to put up margin, that is, deposit cash or securities with the broker. This assures the broker that the short seller will be able to repurchase the stock when the time comes to do so.

[5]You may find it helpful to check that Figure 20-1*d* is the sum of Figure 20-1*b* and Figure 20-1*c*. For example, for a stock price of zero, the value of the package is
    Value of share + value of put = 0 + 65 = $65.
For a stock price of $10, the value of the package is
    Value of share + value of put = 10 + 55 = $65.
And so on.

[6]This relationship holds only if you are committed to holding the options until the final exercise date. It therefore does not hold for American options, which you can exercise *before* the final date. We discuss possible reasons for early exercise in Chapter 21. In the case of the Intel options the probability that you would want to exercise early is very small, so our formula provides a close approximation for the relationship between the value of the Intel call and put options.

[7]This present value is calculated at the *risk-free* rate of interest. It is the amount you would have to invest today in Treasury bills to realize the exercise price on the option's expiration date.

Figure 20-3 Result of buying an Intel call *and* selling a put, each exercisable at $65. Whatever happens to the share price, you end up paying $65 and acquiring the share at the expiration date of the option. You could achieve the same outcome by buying an Intel share and borrowing the present value of $65, to be repaid on the expiration date.

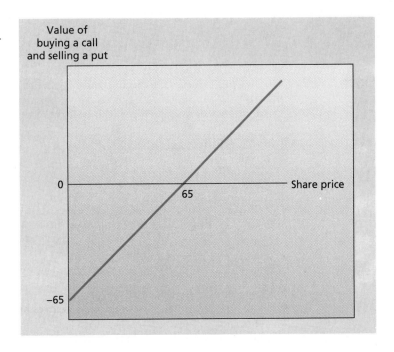

Here is a slightly different example: Suppose that in July 1995 you want to invest in Intel stock but do not have enough cash on hand. However, you know you will receive $65 6 months hence. Therefore you borrow the present value of $65 from your bank and use it to help buy an Intel share. At the end of 6 months your payoff is the share price less the $65 owed to the bank.

Now compare this with an alternative strategy in which you *buy* a 6-month call option with an exercise price of $65 and *sell* a 6-month put option with an exercise price of $65. The final value of such a package would be equal to the sum of Figures 20-1*a* and 20-2*b*. Figure 20-3 shows that this sum is always equal to the market price of the share less $65. It is not difficult to see why. If the share price rises, you would exercise your call and pay $65 to obtain the share; if it goes down, the other person would exercise his or her put option and sell you a share for $65. In either case, you would pay $65 and acquire the share. Since our two investment strategies have exactly the same consequences, they should have exactly the same value.[8] In other words, we have the following rearrangement of our earlier equation:

$$\text{Value of call} - \text{value of put} = \text{share price} - \text{present value of exercise price}$$

which holds because

[Buy call, sell put]

---

[8]*Reminder:* This relationship is strictly true only for European options, which you are committed to hold until the final exercise date. Since the Intel options are American options, the relationship is only an approximation.

is identical to

[Buy share, borrow present value of exercise price[9]]

Of course, there are many ways to express the basic relationship between share price, call and put values, and the present value of the exercise price. Each expression implies two investment strategies that give identical results.

One more example: Solve the basic relationship for the value of a put:

Value of put = value of call − value of share + present value of exercise price

From this expression you can deduce that

[Buy put]

is identical to

[Buy call, sell share, invest present value of exercise price]

In other words, if puts were not available, you could create them by buying calls, selling shares, and lending.

·················

***The
Difference
between
Safe and
Risky
Bonds**

In Chapter 18 we discussed the plight of Circular File Company, which borrowed $50 per share. Unfortunately the firm fell on hard times and the market value of its assets fell to $30. Circular's bond and stock prices fell to $25 and $5, respectively. Circular's *market* value balance sheet is now:

Circular File Company (Market Values)

Asset value	$30	$25	Bonds
		5	Stock
	$30	$30	Firm value

If Circular's debt were due and payable now, the firm could not repay the $50 it originally borrowed. It would default, bondholders receiving assets worth $30 and shareholders receiving nothing. The reason Circular stock is worth $5 is that the debt is *not* due now but rather is due a year from now. A stroke of good fortune could increase firm value enough to pay off the bondholders in full, with something left over for the stockholders.

Let us go back to a statement that we made at the start of the chapter. Whenever a firm borrows, the lender effectively acquires the company and the shareholders obtain the option to buy it back by paying off the debt. The stockholders have in effect purchased a call option on the assets of the firm. The bondholders have sold them this call option. Thus the balance sheet of Circular File can be expressed as follows:

Circular File Company (Market Values)

Asset value	$30	$25	Bond value = asset value − value of call
		5	Stock value = value of call
	$30	$30	Firm value = asset value

---

[9]Again, present value is computed at the risk-free rate of interest. In other words, the comparison assumes that you are certain to pay off the loan.

Figure 20-4 The value of Circular's common stock is the same as the value of a call option on the firm's assets with an exercise price of $50.

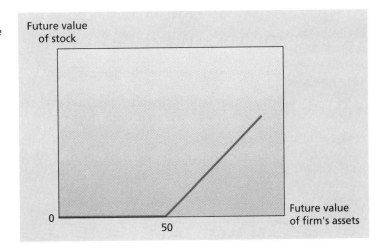

If this still sounds like a strange idea to you, try drawing one of M. Bachelier's position diagrams for Circular File. It should look like Figure 20-4. If the future value of the assets is less than $50, Circular will default and the stock will be worthless. If the value of the assets exceeds $50, the stockholders will receive asset value *less* the $50 paid over to the bondholders. The payoffs in Figure 20-4 are identical to a call option on the firm's assets, with an exercise price of $50.

Now look again at the basic relationship between calls and puts:

Value of call + present value of exercise price = value of put + value of share

To apply this to Circular File, we have to interpret "value of share" as "asset value," because the common stock is a call option on the firm's assets. Also, "present value of exercise price" is the present value of receiving the promised payment of $50 to bondholders *for sure* next year. Thus

> Value of call + present value of promised payment to bondholders
> = value of put + asset value

Now we can solve for the value of Circular bonds. This is equal to the firm's asset value less the value of the shareholders' call option on these assets:

Bond value = asset value − value of call

> = present value of promised payment to bondholders − value of put

Circular's bondholders have in effect (1) bought a safe bond and (2) given the shareholders the option to sell them the firm's assets for the amount of the debt. You can think of the bondholders as receiving the $50 promised payment, but they have given the shareholders the option to take the $50 back in exchange for the assets of the company. If firm value turns out to be less than the $50 that is promised to bondholders, the shareholders will exercise their put option.

Circular's risky bond is equal to a safe bond less the value of the shareholders' option to default. To value this risky bond we need to value a safe bond and then subtract the value of the default option. The default option is equal to a put option on the firm's assets.

In the case of Circular File the option to default is extremely valuable because default is likely to occur. At the other extreme, the value of AT&T's option to default is trivial compared to the value of AT&T's assets. Default on AT&T bonds is possible but extremely unlikely. Option traders would say that for Circular File the put option is "deep in the money" because today's asset value ($30) is well below the exercise price ($50). For AT&T the put option is well "out of the money" because the value of AT&T's assets substantially exceeds the value of AT&T's debt.

We know that Circular's stock is equivalent to a call option on the firm's assets. It is also equal to (1) owning the firm's assets, (2) borrowing the present value of $50 with the obligation to repay regardless of what happens, but also (3) buying a put on the firm's assets with an exercise price of $50.

We can sum up by presenting Circular's balance sheet in terms of asset value, put value, and the present value of a sure $50 payment:

Circular File Company (Market Values)

Asset value	$30	$25	Bond value = present value of promised payment − value of put
		5	Stock value = asset value − present value of promised payment + value of put
	$30	$30	Firm value = asset value

Again you can check this with a position diagram. The colored line in Figure 20-5 shows the payoffs to Circular's bondholders. If the firm's assets are worth more than $50, the bondholders are paid off in full; if the assets are worth less than $50, the firm defaults and the bondholders receive the value of the assets. You could get an identical payoff pattern by buying a safe bond (the upper black line) and selling a put option on the firm's assets (the lower black line).

Figure 20-5 You can also think of Circular's bond (the colored line) as equivalent to a risk-free bond (the upper black line) *less* a put option on the firm's assets with an exercise price of $50 (the lower black line).

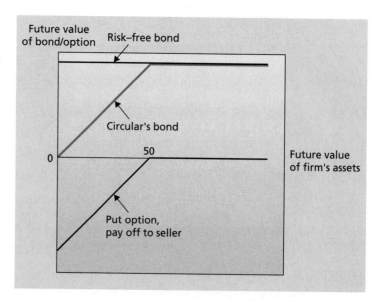

*Spotting the Option

Options rarely come with a large label attached. Often the trickiest part of the problem is to identify the option. For example, we suspect that until it was pointed out, you did not realize that every risky bond contains a hidden option. When you are not sure whether you are dealing with a put or a call or a complicated blend of the two, it is a good precaution to draw a position diagram. Here is an example.

The Flatiron and Mangle Corporation has offered its president, Ms. Higden, the following incentive scheme: At the end of the year Ms. Higden will be paid a bonus of $50,000 for every dollar that the price of Flatiron stock exceeds its current figure of $120. However, the maximum bonus that she can receive is set at $1 million.

You can think of Ms. Higden as owning 50,000 tickets, each of which pays nothing if the stock price fails to beat $120. The value of each ticket then rises by $1 for each dollar rise in the stock price up to the maximum of $1,000,000/50,000 = $40. Figure 20-6 shows the payoffs from just one of these tickets. The payoffs are not the same as those of the simple put and call options that we drew in Figure 20-1, but it is possible to find a combination of options that exactly replicates Figure 20-6. Before going on to read the answer, see if you can spot it yourself. (If you are someone who enjoys puzzles of the make-a-triangle-from-just-two-matchsticks type, this one should be a walkover.)

The answer is in Figure 20-7. The solid black line represents the purchase of a call option with an exercise price of $120, and the dotted line shows the sale of another call option with an exercise price of $160. The colored line shows the payoffs from a combination of the purchase and the sale—exactly the same as the payoffs from one of Ms. Higden's tickets.

Thus, if we wish to know how much the incentive scheme is costing the company, we need to calculate the difference between the value of 50,000 call options with an exercise price of $120 and the value of 50,000 calls with an exercise price of $160.

We could have made the incentive scheme depend in a much more complicated way on the stock price. For example, the bonus could peak at $1 million and then fall steadily back to zero as the stock price climbs above $160. (Don't ask why anyone would want to offer such an arrangement—perhaps there's some tax angle.) You could

Figure 20-6 The payoff from one of Ms. Higden's "tickets" depends on Flatiron's stock price.

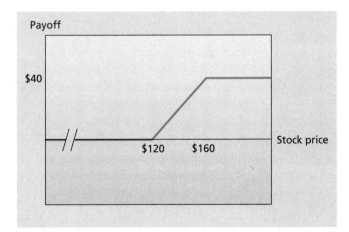

Figure 20-7 The solid black line shows the payoff from buying a call with an exercise price of $120. The dotted line shows the *sale* of a call with an exercise price of $160. The combined purchase and sale (shown by the colored line) is identical to one of Ms. Higden's "tickets."

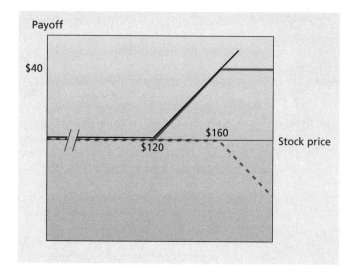

still have represented this scheme as a combination of options. In fact, we can state a general theorem:

> *Any set of contingent payoffs—that is, payoffs which depend on the value of some other asset—can be valued as a mixture of simple options on that asset.*

For instance, if you needed to value a capital project that would pay off $2 million if the price of copper was less than $1500 per ton but only $1 million if the price was greater than $1500, you could use option theory to do so.

20-3   WHAT DETERMINES OPTION VALUES?

So far we have said nothing about how the market value of an option is determined. We do know what an option is worth when it matures, however. Consider, for instance, our earlier example of an option to buy Intel stock at $65. If Intel's stock price is below $65 on the exercise date, the call will be worthless; if the stock price is above $65, the call will be worth $65 less than the value of the stock. In terms of Bachelier's position diagram, the relationship is depicted by the heavy line in Figure 20-8.

Even before maturity the price of the option can never remain *below* the heavy line in Figure 20-8. For example, if our option were priced at $5 and the stock at $100, it would pay any investor to sell the stock and then buy it back by purchasing the option and exercising it for an additional $65. That would give a money machine with a profit of $30. The demand for options from investors using the money machine would quickly force the option price up at least to the heavy line in the figure. For options that still have some time to run, the heavy line is therefore a *lower* limit on the market price of the option.

The diagonal line in Figure 20-8 is the *upper* limit to the option price. Why? Because the stock gives a higher ultimate payoff, whatever happens. If at the option's expiration the stock price ends up above the exercise price, the option is worth the stock price *less* the exercise price. If the stock price ends up below the exercise price, the option is worthless, but the stock's owner still has a valuable security. Let *P* be

Figure 20-8 Value of a call before its expiration date (dashed line). The value depends on the stock price. It is always worth more than its value if exercised now (heavy line). It is never worth more than the stock price itself.

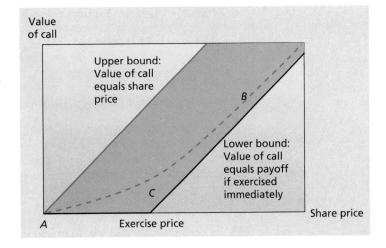

the stock price at the option's expiration date, and assume the option's exercise price is $100. Then the extra dollar returns realized by stockholders are:

	Stock Payoff	Option Payoff	Extra Payoff from Holding Stock Instead of Option
Option exercised (*P* greater than $100)	*P*	*P* − 100	$100
Option expires unexercised (*P* less than or equal to $100)	*P*	0	*P*

If the stock and the option have the same price, everyone will rush to sell the option and buy the stock. Therefore, the option price must be somewhere in the shaded region of Figure 20-8. In fact, it will lie on a curved, upward-sloping line like the dashed curve shown in the figure. This line begins its travels where the upper and lower bounds meet (at zero). Then it rises, gradually becoming parallel to the upward-sloping part of the lower bound. This line tells us an important fact about option values: *The value of an option increases as stock price increases,* if the exercise price is held constant.

That should be no surprise. Owners of call options clearly hope for the stock price to rise, and are happy when it does. But let us look more carefully at the shape and location of the dashed line. Three points, *A*, *B*, and *C*, are marked on the dashed line. As we explain each point you will see why the option price has to behave as the dashed line predicts.

Point A. *When the stock is worthless, the option is worthless:* A stock price of zero means that there is no possibility the stock will ever have any future value.[10] If so, the option is sure to expire unexercised and worthless, and it is worthless today.

---

[10]If a stock *can* be worth something in the future, then investors will pay *something* for it today, although possibly a very small amount.

Point B. When the stock price becomes large, the option price approaches the stock price less the present value of the exercise price: Notice that the dashed line representing the option price in Figure 20-8 eventually becomes parallel to the ascending heavy line representing the lower bound on the option price. The reason is as follows: The higher the stock price, the higher the probability that the option will eventually be exercised. If the stock price is high enough, exercise becomes a virtual certainty; the probability that the stock price will fall below the exercise price before the option expires becomes trivially small.

If you own an option which you *know* will be exchanged for a share of stock, you effectively own the stock now. The only difference is that you don't have to pay for the stock (by handing over the exercise price) until later, when formal exercise occurs. In these circumstances, buying the call is equivalent to buying the stock but financing part of the purchase by borrowing. The amount implicitly borrowed is the present value of the exercise price. The value of the call is therefore equal to the stock price less the present value of the exercise price.

This brings us to another important point about options. Investors who acquire stock by way of a call option are buying on credit. They pay the purchase price of the option today, but they do not pay the exercise price until they actually take up the option. The delay in payment is particularly valuable if interest rates are high and the option has a long maturity. With an interest rate r_f and the time to maturity t, then we would expect the value of the option to depend on the product[11] of r_f and t: *The value of an option increases with both the rate of interest and the time to maturity.*

Point C. The option price always exceeds its minimum value (except when stock price is zero): We have seen that the dashed and heavy lines in Figure 20-8 coincide when stock price is zero (point A), but elsewhere the lines diverge; that is, the option price must exceed the minimum value given by the heavy line. The reason for this can be understood by examining point C.

At point C, the stock price exactly equals the exercise price. The option is therefore worthless if exercised today. However, suppose that the option will not expire until 3 months hence. Of course we do not know what the stock price will be at the expiration date. There is roughly a 50 percent chance that it will be higher than the exercise price, and a 50 percent chance that it will be lower. The possible payoffs to the option are therefore:

Outcome	Payoff
Stock price rises (50 percent probability)	Stock price less exercise price (option is exercised)
Stock price falls (50 percent probability)	Zero (option expires worthless)

If there is a positive probability of a positive payoff, and if the worst payoff is zero, then the option must be valuable. That means the option price at point C exceeds its lower bound, which at point C is zero. In general, the option prices will exceed their lower-bound values as long as there is time left before expiration.

---

[11]Using continuous compounding, the present value of the exercise price is (exercise price $\times e^{-r_f t}$). The discount factor $e^{-r_f t}$ depends on the product of r_f and t.

One of the most important determinants of the *height* of the dashed curve (i.e., of the difference between actual and lower-bound value) is the likelihood of substantial movements in the stock price. An option on a stock whose price is unlikely to change by more than 1 or 2 percent is not worth much; an option on a stock whose price may halve or double is very valuable.

Panels *a* and *b* in Figure 20-9 illustrate this point. The panels compare the payoffs at expiration of two options with the same exercise price and the same stock price. The panels assume that stock price equals exercise price (like point *C* in Figure 20-8), although this is not a necessary assumption. The only difference is that the price of stock Y at its option's expiration date (Figure 20-9*b*) is much harder to predict than the price of stock X at its option's expiration date. You can see this from the probability distributions superimposed on the figures.

Figure 20-9 Call options are written against the shares of (*a*) firm X and (*b*) firm Y. In each case, the current share price equals the exercise price, so each option has a 50 percent chance of ending up worthless (if the share price falls) and a 50 percent chance of ending up "in the money" (if the share price rises). However, the chance of a *large* payoff is *greater* for the option on firm Y's share, because Y's stock price is more volatile and therefore has more "upside potential."

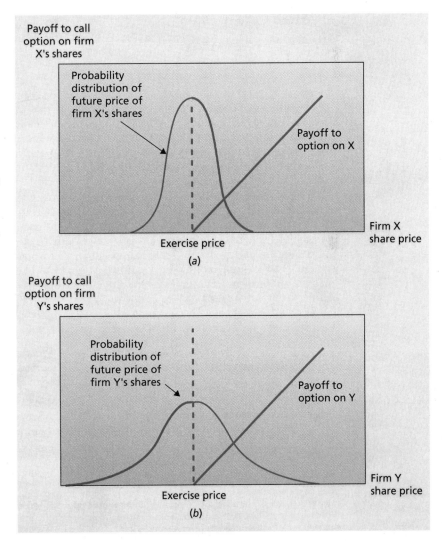

Figure 20-10 Values of calls on shares of firm X and shares of firm Y. The call on Y's shares is worth more because Y's shares are more volatile (see Figure 20-9). The higher curved line describes the value of a call on Y's shares; the lower curved line describes the value of a call on X's shares.

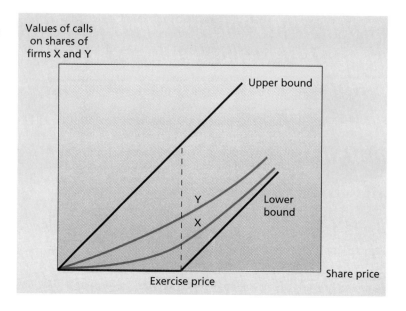

In both cases there is roughly a 50 percent chance that the stock price will decline and make the options worthless, but if the prices of stocks X and Y rise, the odds are that Y will rise more than X. Thus there is a larger chance of a big payoff from the option on Y. Since the chance of a zero payoff is the same, the option on Y is worth more than the option on X. Figure 20-10 illustrates this: The higher curved line belongs to the option on Y.

The probability of large stock price changes during the remaining life of an option depends on two things: (1) the variance (i.e., volatility) of the stock price *per period* and (2) the number of periods until the option expires. If there are t remaining periods, and the variance per period is σ^2, the value of the option should depend on cumulative variability $\sigma^2 t$.[12] Other things equal, you would like to hold an option on a volatile stock (high σ^2). Given volatility, you would like to hold an option with a long life ahead of it (large t). Thus the value of an option increases *with both the variability of the share and the time to maturity.*

It's a rare person who can keep all these properties straight at first reading. Therefore, we have summed them up in Table 20-2.

20-4   AN OPTION-VALUATION MODEL

We would now like to replace the qualitative statements of Table 20-2 with an exact option-valuation model—a formula we can plug numbers into and get a definite answer. The search for that formula went on for years before Fischer Black and Myron

---

[12]Here is an intuitive explanation: If the stock price follows a random walk (see Section 13-2), successive price changes are statistically independent. The cumulative price change before expiration is the sum of t random variables. The variance of a sum of independent random variables is the sum of the variances of those variables. Thus, if σ^2 is the variance of the daily price change, and there are t days until expiration, the variance of the cumulative price change is $\sigma^2 t$.

TABLE 20-2

··

What the price of a call option depends on

1. Increases in variables:

If there is an *increase* in:	The changes in the call option price are:
Stock price (P)	Positive
Exercise price (EX)	Negative
Interest rate (r_f)	Positive*
Time to expiration (t)	Positive
Volatility of stock price (σ)	Positive*

2. Other properties:
   a. Upper bound. The option price is always less than the stock price.
   b. <u>Lower bound.</u> The option price never falls below the payoff to immediate exercise ($P - EX$ or zero, whichever is larger).
   c. If the stock is worthless, the option is worthless.
   d. As the stock price becomes very large, the option price approaches the stock price less the present value of the exercise price.

---

*The *direct* effects of increases in r_f or σ on option price are positive. There may also be *indirect* effects. For example, an increase in r_f could reduce stock price P. This in turn could reduce option price.

Scholes finally found it. Before we show you what they found, we should say a few words to explain why the search was so difficult.

Why Discounted Cash Flow Won't Work for Options

Our standard operating procedure of (1) forecasting expected cash flow and (2) discounting at the opportunity cost of capital is not helpful for options. The first step is messy but feasible. Finding *the* opportunity cost of capital is impossible, because the risk of an option changes every time the stock price moves,[13] and we know it *will* move along a random walk through the option's lifetime.

When you buy a call, you are *taking a position* in the stock but putting up less of your own money than if you had bought the stock directly. Thus an option is always riskier than the underlying stock. It has a higher beta and a higher standard deviation of return.

How much riskier the option is depends on the stock price relative to the exercise price. An option that is in the money (stock price greater than exercise price) is safer than one that is out of the money (stock price less than exercise price). Thus a stock price increase raises the option's price *and* reduces its risk. When the stock price falls, the option's price falls *and* its risk increases. That is why the expected rate of return investors demand from an option changes day by day, or hour by hour, every time the stock price moves.

We repeat the general rule: The higher the stock price relative to the exercise price, the safer the option, although the option is always riskier than the stock. The option's risk changes every time the stock price changes.

---

[13] It also changes over time even with the stock price constant.

Construct-ing Option Equiva-lents from Common Stocks and Borrow-ing

If you've digested what we've said so far, you can appreciate why options are hard to value by standard discounted-cash-flow formulas and why a rigorous option-valuation technique eluded economists for many years. The breakthrough came when Black and Scholes exclaimed, "Eureka! We have found it![14] The trick is to set up an *option equivalent* by combining common stock investment and borrowing. The net cost of buying the option equivalent must equal the value of the option."

We will show you how this works with a simple numerical example. In Table 20-1 we saw that in July 1995 you could have bought 6-month call options on Intel stock with an exercise price of $65. Intel's stock price at that time was also $65, so the options were *at the money*.[15] The interest rate was 2.5 percent for 6 months, or just over 5 percent a year. To keep matters simple, we will assume that Intel stock can do only two things over the 6 months—either the price will fall by 20 percent to $52 or it will rise by 25 percent to $81.25.

If Intel's stock price falls to $52, the call option will be worthless, but if the price rises to $81.25, the option will be worth $81.25 − 65 = \$16.25$. The possible payoffs to the option are therefore:

	Stock Price = $52	Stock Price = $81.25
1 call option	$0	$16.25

Now compare these payoffs with what you would get if you bought % of a share and borrowed $28.18 from the bank:[16]

	Stock Price = $52	Stock Price = $81.25
% of a share	$28.89	$45.14
Repayment of loan + interest	−28.89	−28.89
Total payoff	$ 0	$16.25

Notice that the payoffs from the levered investment in the stock are identical to the payoffs from the call option. Therefore, both investments must have the same value:

$$\text{Value of call} = \text{value of \% of a share} - \$28.18 \text{ bank loan}$$
$$= (65 \times \%) - 28.18 = \$7.93$$

Presto! You've valued a call option.

To value the Intel option, we borrowed money and bought stock in such a way that we exactly replicated the payoff from a call option. The number of shares that are needed to replicate one call is often called the **hedge ratio** or **option delta.** In our Intel example one call is replicated by a levered position in % of a share. The option delta is, therefore, %, or about .56.

How did we know that Intel's call option was equivalent to a levered position in % of a share? We used a simple formula that says

---

[14]We do not know whether Black and Scholes, like Archimedes, were sitting in bathtubs at the time.

[15]We ignore here the fact that Intel stockholders receive a small quarterly dividend of $.04 a share, while the option holders do not. We discuss how to handle dividends in the next chapter.

[16]The amount that you need to borrow from the bank is simply the present value of the difference between the payoffs from the option and the payoffs from the % share.

$$\text{Option delta} = \frac{\text{Spread of possible option prices}}{\text{Spread of possible share prices}} = \frac{16.25 - 0}{81.25 - 52} = \frac{5}{9}$$

You have learned not only to value a simple option. You have also learned that you can replicate an investment in the option by a levered investment in the underlying asset. Thus, if you can't buy or sell an option on an asset, you can create a homemade option by a replicating strategy or buying or selling delta shares and borrowing or lending the balance.

*THE RISK-NEUTRAL METHOD. Notice why the Intel call option has to sell for $7.93. If the option price is higher than $7.93, you could make a certain profit by buying ⅝ of a share of stock, selling a call option, and borrowing $28.18. Similarly, if the option price is less than $7.93, you could make an equally certain profit by selling ⅝ of a share, buying a call, and lending the balance. In either case there would be a money machine.[17]

If there's a money machine, everyone scurries to take advantage of it. So when we said that the option price must be $7.93 or there would be a money machine, we did not have to know anything about investor attitudes to risk. The price cannot depend on whether investors detest risk or could not care a jot.

This suggests an alternative way to calculate the value of the Intel option. We can *pretend* that all investors are *indifferent* about risk, work out the expected future value of the option in such a world, and discount it back at the risk-free interest rate to give the current value. Let us check that this method gives the same answer.

If investors are indifferent to risk, the expected return on the stock must be equal to the rate of interest:

Expected return on Intel stock = 2.5% per 6 months

We know that Intel stock can either rise by 25 percent to $81.25 or fall by 20 percent to $52. We can, therefore, calculate the probability of a price rise in our hypothetical risk-neutral world:

Expected return = [probability of rise × 25]
                  + [(1 − probability of rise) × (−20)]
                = 2.5 percent

Therefore,

Probability of rise = .50, or 50%[18]

We know that if the stock price rises, the call option will be worth $16.25; if it falls, the call will be worth nothing. Therefore, if investors are risk-neutral, the expected value of the call option is

[Probability of rise × 16.25] + [(1 − probability of rise) × 0]
  = (.5 × 16.25) + (.5 × 0)
  = $8.125

---

[17]Of course, you don't get seriously rich by dealing in ⅝ of a share. But if you multiply each of our transactions by a million, it begins to look like real money.

[18]Notice that this is not the *true* probability that Intel stock will rise. Since investors dislike risk, they will almost surely require a higher expected return than the interest rate from Intel stock. Therefore the true probability is greater than .5.

And the current value of the call is

$$\frac{\text{Expected future value}}{1 + \text{interest rate}} = \frac{8.125}{1.025} = \$7.93$$

Exactly the same answer that we got earlier!

We now have two ways to calculate the value of an option:

1. Find the combination of stock and loan that replicates an investment in the option. Since the two strategies give identical payoffs in the future, they must sell for the same price today.

2. Pretend that investors do not care about risk, so that the expected return on the stock is equal to the interest rate. Calculate the expected future value of the option in this hypothetical *risk-neutral* world and discount it at the interest rate.

Valuing the Intel Put Option

Valuing the Intel call option may well have seemed like pulling a rabbit out of a hat. To give you a second chance to watch how it is done, we will use the same method to value another option—this time, the 6-month Intel put option with a $65 exercise price.[19] We continue to assume that the stock price will either rise to $81.25 or fall to $52.

If Intel's stock price rises to $81.25, the option to sell for $65 will be worthless. If the price falls to $52, the put option will be worth $65 - 52 = \$13$. Thus the payoffs to the put are:

	Stock Price = $52	Stock Price = $81.25
1 put option	$13	$0

We start by calculating the option delta using the formula that we presented above:[20]

$$\text{Option delta} = \frac{\text{Spread of possible option prices}}{\text{Spread of possible stock prices}} = \frac{0 - 13}{81.25 - 52} = -\frac{4}{9}$$

Notice that the delta of a put option is always negative—that is, you need to *sell* delta shares of stock to replicate the put. In the case of the Intel put you can replicate the option payoffs by *selling* ⁴⁄₉ of an Intel share and *lending* $35.23. Since you have sold the share short, you will need to lay out money at the end of 6 months to buy it back, but you will have money coming in from the loan. Your net payoffs are exactly the same as the payoffs you would get if you bought the put option:

	Stock Price = $52	Stock Price = $81.25
Sale of ⁴⁄₉ of a share	-$23.11	-$36.11
Repayment of loan + interest	+36.11	+36.11
Total payoff	$13	$ 0

---

[19]When valuing *American* put options, you need to recognize the possibility that it will pay to exercise early. We discuss this complication in the next chapter, but it is not important for valuing the Intel put and we ignore it here.

[20]The delta of a put option is always equal to the delta of a call option with the same exercise price minus one. In our example, delta of put = ⁵⁄₉ - 1 = -⁴⁄₉.

Since the two investments have the same payoffs, they must have the same value:

Value of put $= -\frac{4}{5}$ of a share $+ \$35.23$ bank loan
$= \$6.34$

Valuing the Put Option by the Risk-Neutral Method. Valuing the Intel put option with the risk-neutral method is a cinch. We already know that the probability of a rise in the stock price is .5. Therefore the expected value of the put option in a risk-neutral world is

[Probability of rise $\times$ 0] $+$ [(1 $-$ probability of rise) $\times$ 13]
$= (.5 \times 0) + (.5 \times 13)$
$= \$6.5$

And therefore the current value of the put is

$$\frac{\text{Expected future value}}{1 + \text{interest rate}} = \frac{6.5}{1.025} = \$6.34$$

The Relationship between Call and Put Prices. We pointed out earlier that for European options there is a simple relationship between the value of the call and that of the put:[21]

Value of put $=$ value of call $-$ share price $+$ present value of exercise price

Since we had already calculated the value of the Intel call, we could also have used this relationship to find the value of the put:

$$\text{Value of put} = 7.93 - 65 + \frac{65}{1.025} = \$6.34$$

Everything checks.

20-5 THE BLACK-SCHOLES FORMULA

The essential trick in pricing any option is to set up a package of investment in the stock and a loan that will exactly replicate the payoffs from the option. If we can price the stock and the loan, then we can also price the option.

This *concept* is completely general. But so far all our *examples* use a simplified version of a special approach, called the **binomial method**. This method starts by reducing the possible changes in next period's stock price to two, an "up" move and a "down" move. This simplification is OK if the time period is very short, so that a large number of small moves is accumulated over the life of the option. But it was fanciful to assume just two possible prices for Intel stock at the end of six months.

We could make the problem slightly more realistic by assuming that there were two possible changes in the stock price in each 3-month period. That would give a wider range of 6-month prices. It would still be possible to construct a series of levered investments in the stock that would give exactly the same prospects as the option.[22]

---

[21]*Reminder:* This formula applies only when the two options have the same exercise price and exercise date.

[22]We will work through a two-period example in the next chapter.

There is no reason to stop at 3-month periods. We could go on to take shorter and shorter intervals, with each interval showing two possible changes in Intel's stock price. Eventually we would reach a situation in which the stock price was changing continuously and generating a continuum of possible year-end prices. We could still replicate the call option by a levered investment in the stock, but we would need to adjust the degree of leverage continuously as the year went by.

Calculating the value of this levered investment may sound like a hopelessly tedious business, but Black and Scholes derived a formula that does the trick. It is an unpleasant-looking formula, but on closer acquaintance you will find it exceptionally elegant and useful. The formula is

$$\text{Value of call option} = \underset{\substack{\uparrow \\ [N(d_1)\ \times\ P]}}{[\text{delta} \times \text{share price}]} - \underset{\substack{\uparrow \\ -N(d_2) \times \text{PV(EX)}]}}{\underset{\uparrow}{[\text{bank loan}]}}$$

where

$$d_1 = \frac{\log\,[P/\text{PV(EX)}]}{\sigma\sqrt{t}} + \frac{\sigma\sqrt{t}}{2}$$

$$d_2 = d_1 - \sigma\sqrt{t}$$

$N(d)$ = cumulative normal probability density function[23]

EX = exercise price of option; PV(EX) is calculated by discounting at the continuously compounded risk-free interest rate r_f

t = number of periods to exercise date

P = price of stock now

σ = standard deviation per period of (continuously compounded) rate of return on stock

Notice that the value of the call in the Black-Scholes formula has the same properties that we identified earlier. It increases with the level of the stock price P and decreases with the present value of the exercise price PV(EX), which in turn depends on the interest rate and time to maturity. It also increases with the time to maturity and the stock's variability ($\sigma\sqrt{t}$).

To derive their formula Black and Scholes assumed that there is a continuum of stock prices, and therefore to replicate an option investors must continuously adjust their holding in the stock. Of course this is not literally possible, but even so the formula performs remarkably well in the real world, where stocks trade only intermittently and prices jump from one level to another. The Black-Scholes model has also proved very flexible; it can be adapted to value options on a variety of assets with special features, such as foreign currency, bonds, and futures. It is not surprising therefore that it has been extremely influential and has become the standard model for valuing options. Every day dealers on the options exchanges use this formula to make huge trades. These dealers are not for the most part trained in the formula's mathematical derivation; they just use a computer or a specially programmed calculator to find the value of the option.

---

[23]That is, $N(d)$ is the probability that a normally distributed random variable $\tilde{x}$ will be less than or equal to d. $N(d_1)$ in the Black-Scholes formula is the option delta. Thus the formula tells us that the value of a call is equal to an investment of $N(d_1)$ in the common stock less borrowing of $N(d_2) \times$ PV(EX).

Using the Black-Scholes Formula

Appendix Tables 6 and 7 provide data that allow you to use the Black-Scholes formula to value a variety of simple options. In order to use the tables, follow these four steps:

STEP 1.   Multiply the standard deviation of the proportionate changes in the asset's value by the square root of time to the option's expiration. For example, suppose that you wish to value the 6-month call option on Intel stock and that the standard deviation of the continuously compounded stock price changes is 32 percent per year:

$$\text{Standard deviation} \times \sqrt{\text{time}} = .32 \times \sqrt{.5} = .226$$

STEP 2.   Calculate the ratio of the stock price to the present value of the option's exercise price. For example, if Intel's stock price and the exercise price are both $65 and the interest rate is 2.5 percent for 6 months, then

$$\text{Share price} \div \text{PV(exercise price)} = 65 \div \frac{65}{1.025} = 1.025$$

STEP 3.   Now turn to Table 6. There is no entry corresponding exactly to the figures that we have just calculated—that's always the problem with tables. But we have highlighted the four entries that bracket the value of the Intel option. Interpolating about halfway between the two rows and a quarter of the way between the two columns tells us that the value of the Intel call is about 10.2 percent of the stock price, or $6.63. This is lower than the price of the Intel option shown in Table 20-1. It looks as if we are using a lower estimate of the variability of Intel stock than the market. The *implied volatility*—that is, the standard deviation that would produce the market price of $8—is 40 percent.[24]

If you want to know the value of a put option with the same exercise price, then you can use the simple relationship that we derived in Section 20-2:

$$\text{Value of put} = \text{value of call} + \text{PV(exercise price)} - \text{stock price}$$

$$= 6.63 + \frac{65}{1.025} - 65 = \$5.04$$

Step 4.   Table 7 tells you the option delta. For example, if you look up the equivalent entry in Table 7, you see that the Intel call option has a delta of about .59. This means that instead of buying a call for $6.63, you could achieve the same result by buying .59 share of stock (at a cost of .59 × 65 = $38.35) and borrowing the balance (38.35 − 6.63 = $31.72).

To find the option delta for the put, you simply subtract 1 from the entry in Table 7. In our example

$$\text{Put option delta} = \text{call option delta} - 1$$

$$= .59 - 1 = -.41$$

In other words, instead of *paying* out $5.04 to buy an Intel put option, you could *sell* .41 share of stock (for a cash inflow of .41 × 65 = $26.65) and buy a Treasury bill with the available cash (5.04 + 26.65 = $31.69).

---

[24]The Black-Scholes formula is often used not to calculate the option value but to forecast volatility. That is, investors assume that the formula and the quoted call price are correct, and then back out the implied volatility.

20-6   SUMMARY

If you have managed to reach this point, you are probably in need of a rest and a stiff gin and tonic. So we will summarize what we have learned so far and take up the subject of options again in the next chapter when you are rested (or drunk).

There are two basic types of option. An American call is an option to buy an asset at a specified exercise price on or before a specified exercise date. Similarly, an American put is an option to sell the asset at a specified price on or before a specified date. European calls and puts are exactly the same except that they cannot be exercised before the specified exercise date. Calls and puts are the basic building blocks that can be combined to give any pattern of payoffs.

What determines the value of a call option? Common sense tells us that it ought to depend on three things:

1. In order to exercise an option you have to pay the exercise price. Other things being equal, the less you are obliged to pay, the better. Therefore, the value of an option increases with the ratio of the asset price to the exercise price.

2. You do not have to pay the exercise price until you decide to exercise the option. Therefore, an option gives you a free loan. The higher the rate of interest and the longer the time to maturity, the more this free loan is worth. Therefore the value of an option increases with the interest rate multiplied by the time to maturity.

3. If the price of the asset falls short of the exercise price, you won't exercise the option. You will, therefore, lose 100 percent of your investment in the option no matter how far the asset depreciates below the exercise price. On the other hand, the more the price rises *above* the exercise price, the more profit you will make. Therefore the option holder does not lose from increased variability if things go wrong, but gains if they go right. The value of an option increases with the variance per period of the stock return multiplied by the number of periods to maturity.

We showed you how to value an option on a stock when there are only two possible changes in the stock price in each subperiod. Black and Scholes have also derived a formula that gives the value of an option when there is a continuum of possible future stock prices. Tables in the Appendix should allow you to apply this formula to a number of simple option problems.

Unfortunately, not all option problems are simple. Therefore, in the next chapter we will look at some of the complications and work through several examples of moderate complexity.

Further Reading

····································

The classic articles on option valuation are:
F. Black and M. Scholes: "The Pricing of Options and Corporate Liabilities," *Journal of Political Economy*, **81**:637–654 (May–June 1973).
R. C. Merton: "Theory of Rational Option Pricing," *Bell Journal of Economics and Management Science*, **4**:141–183 (Spring 1973).

There are also a number of good texts on option valuation. They include:
J. Cox and M. Rubinstein: *Options Markets*, Prentice-Hall, Inc., Englewood Cliffs, N.J., 1985.
J. Hull: *Options, Futures and Other Derivative Securities*, Prentice-Hall, Inc., Englewood Cliffs, N.J., 2d ed., 1993.
R. Jarrow and A. Rudd: *Option Pricing*, Dow Jones-Irwin, Inc., Homewood, Ill., 1983.

The magazine Risk *contains regular articles on the valuation of more complex options. For example, in 1991 it published a series of articles by Mark Rubinstein on exotic options.*

Quiz

1. Complete the following passage:
   A _____ option gives its owner the opportunity to buy a stock at a specified price which is generally called the _____ price. A _____ option gives its owner the opportunity to sell stock at a specified price. Options that can be exercised only at maturity are called _____ options.
   The common stock of firms that borrow is a _____ option. Stockholders effectively sell the firm's _____ to _____, but retain the option to buy the _____ back. The exercise price is the _____.

2. Fill in the blanks:
   (*a*) A firm that issues warrants is selling a _____ option.
   (*b*) A firm that enters a standby agreement, whereby the underwriter to a rights issue guarantees to take up any unwanted stock, acquires a _____ option.
   (*c*) Rights are _____ options on the issuing firm's stock.
   (*d*) An oil company acquires mining rights to a silver deposit. It is not obligated to mine the silver, however. The company has effectively acquired a _____ option, where the exercise price is the cost of opening the mine.
   (*e*) Some preferred shareholders have the right to redeem their shares at par value after a specified date. (If they hand over their shares, the firm sends them a check equal to the shares' par value.) These shareholders have a _____ option.
   (*f*) An executive who qualifies for a stock option plan acquires _____ options.
   (*g*) An investor who buys stock in a levered firm acquires a _____ option on the firm's assets.
   (*h*) A firm buys a standard machine with a ready secondhand market. The secondhand market gives the firm a _____ option.

3. Note Figure 20-11. Match each diagram (*a* and *b*) with one of the following positions:
   (*a*) Call buyer
   (*b*) Call seller
   (*c*) Put buyer
   (*d*) Put seller

4. Suppose that you hold a share of stock and a put option on that share. What is the payoff when the option expires if:
   (*a*) The stock price is below the exercise price?
   (*b*) The stock price is above the exercise price?

5. There is another strategy involving calls and borrowing and lending which gives the same payoffs as the strategy described in question 4. What is the alternative strategy?

6. What is the lower bound to the price of a call option? What is the upper bound?

7. What is a call option worth if:
   (*a*) The stock price is zero?
   (*b*) The stock price is extremely high relative to the exercise price?

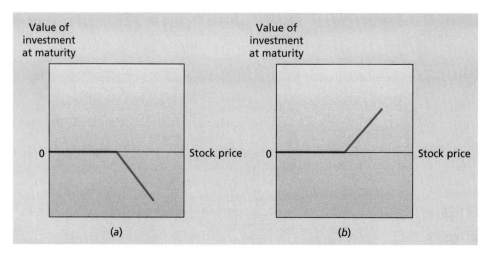

Figure 20-11 See Quiz question 3.

8. How does the price of a call option respond to the following changes, other things equal? Does the call price go up or down?
   (*a*) Stock price increases.
   (*b*) Exercise price is increased.
   (*c*) Risk-free interest rate increases.
   (*d*) Expiration date of the option is extended.
   (*e*) Volatility of the stock price falls.
   (*f*) Time passes, so the option's expiration date comes closer.

9. "An option is always riskier than the stock it is written on." True or false? How does the risk of an option change when the stock price changes?

10. Why can't you value options using a standard discounted-cash-flow formula?

11. Use Appendix Table 6 to value the following options:
    (*a*) A call option written on a stock selling for $60 per share with a $60 exercise price. The stock's standard deviation is 6 percent per month. The option matures in 3 months. The risk-free interest rate is 1 percent per month.
    (*b*) A put option written on the same stock at the same time, with the same exercise price and expiration date.
    Now for each of these options use Appendix Table 7 to calculate the combination of stock and risk-free asset that would replicate the option.

12. Imagine that the range of 6-month prices for Intel stock widens to $48.75 to $86.67 (see Section 20-4). Recalculate the value of the call option using (*a*) the replicating-portfolio method and (*b*) the risk-neutral method. Explain intuitively why the option value increases.

13. As manager of United Bedstead you own substantial executive stock options. These entitle you to buy the firm's shares during the next 5 years at a price of $100 a share. The plant manager has just outlined two alternative proposals to reequip the plant. Both proposals have the same net present value, but one is substantially riskier than the other. At first you are undecided about which to choose, but then you remember your stock options. How might these influence your choice?

14. Suppose you buy a 1-year European call option on Wombat stock with an exercise price of $110 and sell a 1-year European put option with the same exercise price. The current stock price is $100, and the interest rate is 10 percent.
    (*a*) Draw a position diagram showing the payoffs from your investments.
    (*b*) How much will the combined position cost you? Explain.

15. Over the coming year Ragwort's stock price will halve to $50 from its current level of $100, or it will rise to $200. The 1-year interest rate is 10 percent.
    (*a*) What is the delta of a 1-year call option on Ragwort stock with an exercise price of $100?
    (*b*) Use the replicating-portfolio method to value this call.
    (*c*) In a risk-neutral world what is the probability that Ragwort stock will rise in price?
    (*d*) Use the risk-neutral method to check your valuation of the Ragwort option.
    (*e*) If someone told you that in reality there is a 60 percent chance that Ragwort's stock price will rise to $200, would you change your view about the value of the option? Explain.

16. Pintail's stock price is currently $200. A 1-year European call option has an exercise price of $50 and is priced at $75. How would you take advantage of this great opportunity?

Questions and Problems

1. Look up the terms of actual call and put options on stocks, currencies, etc. Plot their payoffs at maturity using diagrams like those in Figures 20-1 and 20-2.

2. Explain why the value of a call depends on each of the following:
    (*a*) The *product* of volatility per period and time to maturity
    (*b*) The *product* of the (continuously compounded) risk-free interest rate and time to maturity.

3. Look at actual trading prices of call options on stocks to check whether they behave as the theory presented in this chapter predicts. For example:
    (*a*) Follow several options as they approach maturity. How would you expect their prices to behave? Do they actually behave that way?
    (*b*) Compare two call options written on the same stock with the same maturity but different exercise prices.
    (*c*) Compare two call options written on the same stock with the same exercise price but different maturities.

* 4. How would the value of Circular File common stock (see Section 20-2) change if:
    (*a*) The value of the firm's assets increased?
    (*b*) The maturity of its debt were extended?
    (*c*) The assets became safer (less volatile)?
    (*d*) The risk-free rate of interest increased (hold the value of the firm's assets constant)?

5. The Rank and File Company is considering a rights issue to raise $50 million. An underwriter offers to "stand by" (i.e., to guarantee the success of the issue by buying any unwanted stock at the issue price). The underwriter's fee is $2 million.
    (*a*) What kind of option does Rank and File acquire if it accepts the underwriter's offer?

   (*b*) What determines the value of the option?

   (*c*) How would you calculate whether the underwriter's offer is a fair deal?

6. Which *one* of the following statements is correct?

   (*a*) Value of put + present value of exercise price = value of call + share price

   (*b*) Value of put + share price = value of call + present value of exercise price

   (*c*) Value of put − share price = present value of exercise price − value of call

   (*d*) Value of put + value of call = share price − present value of exercise price

   The correct statement equates the value of two investment strategies. Plot the payoffs to each strategy as a function of the stock price. Show that the two strategies give identical payoffs.

7. The price of Backwoods Chemical Company stock on January 20 is $90 per share. Three call options are trading on the stock, one maturing on April 20, one on July 20, and one on October 20. All three options have the same $100 exercise price. The standard deviation of Backwoods stock is 42 percent per year. The risk-free interest rate is 11 percent per year. What are the three call options worth?

8. The common stock of Triangular File Company is selling at $90. A 26-week call option written on Triangular File's stock is selling for $8. The call's exercise price is $100. The risk-free interest rate is 10 percent per year.

   (*a*) Suppose that puts on Triangular stock are not traded, but you want to buy one. How would you do it?

   (*b*) Suppose that puts *are* traded. What should a 26-week put with an exercise price of $100 sell for?

9. Test the formula linking put and call prices that you used to answer problem 8 by using it to explain the relative prices of traded puts and calls. (Note that the formula is exact only for European options. Most traded puts and calls are American.)

* 10. Refer again to the Circular File balance sheet given in Section 20-2. Suppose that the United States government suddenly offers to guarantee the $50 principal payment due bondholders next year and also to guarantee the interest payment due next year. (In other words, if firm value falls short of the promised interest and principal payment, the government will make up the difference.) This offer is a complete surprise to everyone. The government asks nothing in return, and so its offer is cheerfully accepted.

   (*a*) Suppose that the promised interest rate on Circular's debt is 10 percent. The rate on 1-year United States government notes is 8 percent. How will the guarantee affect bond value?

   (*b*) The guarantee does *not* affect the value of Circular stock. Why? (*Note:* There could be some effect if the guarantee allows Circular to avoid costs of financial distress or bankruptcy. See Section 18-3.)

   (*c*) How will the value of the firm (debt plus equity) change?

   Now suppose that the government offers the same guarantee for *new* debt issued by *Rectangular* File Company. Rectangular's assets are identical to Circular's, but Rectangular has no existing debt. Rectangular accepts the offer and uses the proceeds of a $50 debt issue to repurchase or retire stock.

   Will Rectangular stockholders gain from the opportunity to issue the guaranteed debt? By how much, approximately? (Ignore taxes.)

11. How would you use Appendix Table 6 to estimate the volatility of a common stock on which call options are written and actively traded? Use the price of the Intel 3-month calls to estimate the implied volatility.

12. Show how the option delta changes as the stock price rises relative to the exercise price. Explain intuitively why this is the case. (What would happen to the option delta if the exercise price of an option were zero? What would happen if the exercise price became indefinitely large?)

13. Use either the replicating-portfolio method or the risk-neutral method to value the 6-month call and put options on Intel stock with an exercise price of $70 (see Table 20-1). Use the formula relating put and call prices that we derived in Section 20-2 to check your answer.

14. Is it more valuable to own an option to buy a portfolio of stocks or to own a portfolio of options to buy each of the individual stocks? Say briefly why.

15. Discuss briefly the relative risk of the following positions:
    (*a*) Buy stock and a put option on the stock.
    (*b*) Buy stock.
    (*c*) Buy call.
    (*d*) Buy stock and sell call option on the stock.
    (*e*) Buy bond.
    (*f*) Buy stock, buy put, and sell call.
    (*g*) Sell put.

16. "The buyer of a call and the seller of a put both hope that the stock price will rise. Therefore the two positions are identical." Is the speaker correct? Illustrate with a simple example.

17. A difficult question: Use the formula that relates the values of the call and the put (see Section 20-2) and the one-period binomial model to show that the option delta for a put option is equal to the option delta for a call option minus 1.

* 18. Option traders often refer to "straddles" and "butterflies." Here is an example of each:

    ■ *Straddle:* Buy call with exercise price of $100 and simultaneously buy put with exercise price of $100.

    ■ *Butterfly:* Simultaneously buy one call with exercise price of $100, sell two calls with exercise price of $110, and buy one call with exercise price of $120.

    (*a*) Draw position diagrams for the straddle and butterfly, showing the payoffs from the investor's net position. Each strategy is a bet on variability. Explain briefly the nature of each bet.
    (*b*) The profitability of a straddle or a butterfly depends on how much the stock price has changed by the time the option matures, and not on how the stock price varies *before* maturity. If you believe that volatility *during* the option's life will be higher than expected, how can you construct a hedged position to take advantage of your belief? What if you believe that volatility will be lower than expected?

19. In 1988 the Australian firm Bond Corporation sold a share in some land that it owned near Rome for $110 million and as a result boosted its 1988 earnings by $74 million. In 1989 a television program revealed that the buyer was given a put option to sell its share in the land back to Bond for $110 million and that Bond had paid $20 million for a call option to repurchase the share in the land for the same price.[25]

---

[25]See *Sydney Morning Herald*, March 14, 1989, p. 27. The options were subsequently renegotiated.

(*a*) What happens if the land is worth more than $110 million when the options expire? What if it is worth less than $110 million?

(*b*) Use position diagrams to show the net effect of the land sale and the option transactions.

(*c*) Assume a 1-year maturity on the options. Can you deduce the interest rate?

(*d*) The television program argued that it was misleading to record a profit on the sale of land. What do you think?

20. (*a*) The Chase Manhattan Bank has offered its more wealthy customers an unusual type of time deposit known as the *guaranteed market investment account*. The account does not pay a fixed rate of interest; instead, the depositor receives a proportion of any rise in the Standard and Poor's index. How should the bank invest the money in order to minimize its risk?

(*b*) Suppose that the interest rate is 10 percent, the standard deviation of returns on the Standard and Poor's index is 20 percent per year, and the deposit has a maturity of 3 months. What proportion of any appreciation in the index could the bank afford to offer depositors?

(*c*) You can also make a deposit with Chase Manhattan which does not pay interest if the market index rises but which makes an increasingly large payment as the market index falls. How should the bank protect itself against the risk of offering this deposit?

 21. Figure 20-12 shows some complicated position diagrams. Work out the combination of stocks, bonds, and options that produces each of these positions.

22. (*a*) If you can't sell a share short, you can achieve exactly the same final payoff by a combination of bonds and options. What is this combination?

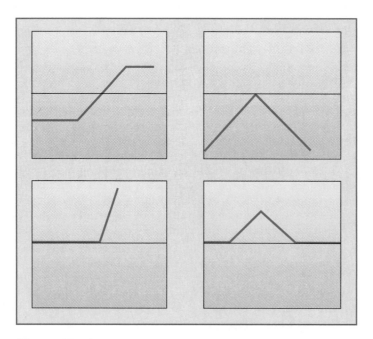

Figure 20-12 Some complicated position diagrams. See problem 21.

(b) Now work out the mixture of stock and options that gives the same final payoff as a bond.

23. A difficult question: Three 6-month call options are traded on Hogswill stock:

Exercise Price	Call Option Price
$ 90	$ 5
100	11
110	15

How could you make money by trading in Hogswill options? (*Hint:* Draw a graph with the option price on the vertical axis and the ratio of stock price to exercise price on the horizontal axis. Plot the three Hogswill call options on your graph. Does this fit with what you know about how option prices should vary with the ratio of stock price to exercise price?) Now look in the newspaper at options with the same maturity date but different exercise prices. Can you find any money-making possibilities?

24. Table 20-3 lists some prices of options on common stocks (prices are quoted to the nearest dollar). The interest rate is 10 percent a year. Can you spot any mispricing? What would you do to take advantage of it?

25. Construct a table similar to Table 20-2 showing what the price of a *put* option depends on. In each case construct a simple example to illustrate your point.

26. The exchange rate for sterling is currently $1.5 = £1. Suppose you need to buy pounds at the end of the year. You want to be sure that, regardless of the future market price, you will not pay more than $1.6 = £1. In return you are prepared to guarantee a minimum price of $1.4 = £1. What option positions would provide you with this ceiling and floor?

27. Suppose that you borrow the present value of $100, buy a put option on stock X with an exercise price of $150, and sell a put option on X with an exercise price of $50 and the same exercise date.
    (a) Draw a position diagram showing the payoffs when the options expire.
    (b) Suggest two other combinations of loans, options, and the underlying stock that would give the same set of payoffs.

TABLE 20-3

Prices of options on common stocks (in dollars). See problem 24.

Stock	Time to Exercise	Exercise Price	Stock Price	Put Price	Call Price
Drongo Corp.	6 months	50	80	20	52
Ragwort, Inc.	6 months	100	80	10	15
Wombat Corp.	3 months	40	50	7	18
	6 months	40	50	5	17
	6 months	50	50	8	10

28. In everyday speech the term *option* sometimes just means "choice," whereas in finance it refers specifically to the right to buy or sell an asset in the future on terms that are fixed today. Which of the following are the odd statements out? Are the options involved in the other statements puts or calls?
    (*a*) "The preferred stockholders in Chrysalis Motors have the option to redeem their shares at par value after a specified date."
    (*b*) "What I like about Toit à Porcs is its large wine list. You have the option to choose from over 100 wines."
    (*c*) "I don't have to buy IBM stock now. I have the option to wait and see if the stock price goes lower over the next month or two."
    (*d*) "By constructing an assembly plant in Mexico, Chrysalis Motors gave itself the option to switch a substantial proportion of its production to that country if the dollar should appreciate in the future."

29. We will discuss early exercise of American options in the next chapter, but here are two extreme examples. The first illustrates that you would never want to exercise early a call option on a stock which does not pay dividends; the second, that there may be occasions when you may want to exercise a put option early. Over the coming year the price of Wombat stock may double from its current level of $100 or it may halve. The interest rate is 10 percent a year.
    (*a*) What is the value of a 1-year call option with an exercise price of $40? What would be the value if you were obliged to exercise now?
    (*b*) What is the value of a 1-year put option with an exercise price of $250? What would be the value of the put if you were obliged to exercise now?

30. In Section 20-2 we suggested a more complicated incentive scheme for Ms. Higden.
    (*a*) Draw a position diagram showing the payoffs from such a scheme.
    (*b*) Show that this scheme is a combination of simple options.
    (*c*) Assume that the stock price after announcement of the scheme is $100, the standard deviation of the stock price is 30 percent a year, and the rate of interest is 10 percent. What is the value of this incentive scheme?

31. A very difficult question: Ms. Higden has been offered yet another incentive scheme (see Section 20-2). She will receive a bonus of $500,000 if the stock price at the end of the year is $120 or more; otherwise, she will receive nothing.
    (*a*) Draw a position diagram illustrating the payoffs from such a scheme.
    (*b*) What combination of options would provide these payoffs? (*Hint:* You need to buy a large number of options with one exercise price and sell a similar number with a different exercise price.)

32. Draw a diagram similar to Figure 20-8 for a put option. What would you do if a put option was priced below your lower bound? What if the price was above the upper bound?

33. In Section 17-3 we described how Morgan Stanley invented a new security, percs. Show how you could replicate the payoffs from percs using a combination of the underlying share, options, and bonds.

21

Applications of Option Pricing Theory

This chapter brings the first reward to your investment in learning about options. We describe four common and important *real options* found in capital investment projects:

- The option to make follow-on investments if the immediate investment project succeeds
- The option to abandon a project
- The option to wait (and learn) before investing
- The option to vary the firm's output or its production methods

Real options such as these allow managers to add value to their firms by acting to amplify good fortune or to mitigate loss. Managers do not often use the term *option* to describe these opportunities; for example, they may refer to "intangibles" rather than to puts or calls. But when they review major investment proposals, these option "intangibles" are often the key to their decisions.

 We will also work through some simple numerical examples to show how real options can be valued. These examples ignore many complexities that are encountered in practice; think of them as back-of-the-envelope estimates of the value of more realistic but complex real options.

 The examples will also provide an opportunity to learn more about the *technique* of option valuation. In the last chapter we introduced you to the binomial method, which we used to value options on an asset whose price can make a single step up or down. By the time you have worked through this chapter, you should know how to use the same method to value options on assets whose prices can take on a number of future values. You will also learn how to pick sensible figures for the upside and downside price changes and how to value an option on an asset that pays dividends.

 Since the only feasible way to solve most practical option problems is to use a computer, why do we ask you to work through a number of option problems by hand? The reason is that unless you understand the basics of option valuation, you are likely to make mistakes in setting up an option problem, and you won't know how to interpret the computer's answers and explain them to others.

21-1   THE VALUE OF FOLLOW-ON INVESTMENT OPPORTUNITIES

It is 1982. You are assistant to the chief financial officer (CFO) of Blitzen Computers, an established computer manufacturer casting a profit-hungry eye on the rapidly developing personal computer market. You are helping the CFO evaluate the proposed introduction of the Blitzen Mark I Micro.

The Mark I's forecasted cash flows and NPV are shown in Table 21-1. Unfortunately the Mark I can't meet Blitzen's customary 20 percent hurdle rate and has a $46 million negative NPV, contrary to top management's strong gut feeling that Blitzen ought to be in the personal computer market.

The CFO has called you in to discuss the project:

"The Mark I just can't make it on financial grounds," the CFO says, "But we've got to do it for strategic reasons. I'm recommending we go ahead."

"But you're missing the all-important financial advantage, Chief," you reply.

"Don't call me 'Chief.' What financial advantage?"

"If we don't launch the Mark I, it will probably be too expensive to enter the micro market later, when Apple, IBM, and others are firmly established. If we go ahead, we have the opportunity to make follow-on investments which could be extremely profitable. The Mark I gives not only its own cash flows but also a call option to go on with a Mark II micro. That call option is the real source of strategic value."

"So it's strategic value by another name. That doesn't tell me what the Mark II investment's worth. The Mark II could be a great investment or a lousy one—we haven't got a clue."

"That's exactly when a call option is worth the most," you point out perceptively. "The call lets us invest in the Mark II if it's great and walk away from it if it's lousy."

"So what's it worth?"

"Hard to say precisely, but I've done a back-of-the-envelope calculation which suggests that the value of the option to invest in the Mark II could more than offset the Mark I's $46 million negative NPV. [The calculations are shown in Table 21-2.] If the option to invest is worth $55 million, the total value of the Mark I is its own NPV, −$46 million, plus the $55 million option attached to it, or +$9 million."

TABLE 21-1
....

Summary of cash flows and financial analysis of the Mark I microcomputer (figures in millions of dollars)

	YEAR					
	1982	1983	1984	1985	1986	1987
After-tax operating cash flow (1)*	−200	+110	+159	+295	+185	0
Capital investment (2)	250	0	0	0	0	0
Increase in working capital (3)	0	50	100	100	−125	−125
Net cash flow (1) − (2) − (3)	−450	+60	+59	+195	+310	+125
NPV at 20% = −$46.45, or about −$46 million						

*After-tax operating cash flow is negative in 1982 because of R&D costs.

TABLE 21-2
••

Valuing the option to invest in the Mark II microcomputer

Assumptions
1. The decision to invest in the Mark II must be made after 3 years, in 1985.
2. The Mark II investment is double the scale of the Mark I (note the expected rapid growth of the industry). Investment required is $900 million (the exercise price), which is taken as fixed.
3. Forecasted cash inflows of the Mark II are also double those of the Mark I, with present value of about $800 million in 1985 and $800/(1.2)^3 = \$463$ million in 1982.
4. The future value of the Mark II cash flows is highly uncertain. This value evolves as a stock price does with a standard deviation of 35 percent per year. (Many high-technology stocks have standard deviations higher than 35 percent.)
5. The annual interest rate is 5 percent.

Interpretation
The opportunity to invest in the Mark II is a 3-year call option on an asset worth $463 million with a $900 million exercise price.

Valuation
See Appendix Table 6:

$$\text{Standard deviation} \times \sqrt{\text{time}} = .35\sqrt{3} = .61$$

$$\frac{\text{Asset value}}{\text{PV(exercise price)}} = \frac{463}{900/(1.1)^3} = .68$$

$$\frac{\text{Call value}}{\text{Asset value}} = .119 \text{ (closest figure from Appendix Table 6)}$$

$$\text{Call value} = .119 \times 463 = 55.1, \text{ or about } \$55 \text{ million}$$

"You're just overestimating the Mark II," the CFO says gruffly. "It's easy to be optimistic when an investment is 3 years away."

"No, no," you reply patiently. "The Mark II is expected to be no more profitable than the Mark I—just twice as big and therefore twice as bad in terms of discounted cash flow. I'm forecasting it to have a negative NPV of about $100 million. But there's a chance the Mark II could be extremely valuable. The call option allows Blitzen to cash in on those upside outcomes. The chance to cash in could be worth $55 million.

"Of course, the $55 million is only a trial calculation, but it illustrates how valuable follow-on investment opportunities can be, especially when uncertainty is high and the product market is growing rapidly. Moreover, the Mark II will give us a call on the Mark III, the Mark III on the Mark IV, and so on. My calculations don't take subsequent calls into account."

"I think I'm beginning to understand a little bit of corporate strategy," mumbles the CFO.

Real Options and the Value of Management

Discounted cash flow (DCF) implicitly assumes that firms hold real assets passively. It ignores the options found in real assets—options that sophisticated managers can act to take advantage of. You could say that DCF does not reflect the value of management.

Remember that the DCF valuation method was first developed for bonds and stocks. Investors in these securities are necessarily passive: with rare exceptions, there is nothing investors can do to improve the interest rate they are paid or the dividends they receive. A bond or common stock can be sold, of course, but that merely substitutes one passive investor for another.

Options and securities which contain options, such as convertible bonds, are fundamentally different. Investors who hold options do not have to be passive. They are given a right to make a decision, which they can exercise to capitalize on good fortune or to mitigate loss. This right clearly has value whenever there is uncertainty. However, calculating that value is not a simple matter of discounting. Option pricing theory tells us what the value is, but the necessary formulas do not look like DCF.

Now consider the firm as an investor in *real* assets. Management can *add value* to those assets by responding to changing circumstances—by taking advantage of good fortune or mitigating loss. Management has the opportunity to act because many investment opportunities have real options embedded in them, options which management can exercise when it is in the firm's interest to do so. DCF misses this extra value because it implicitly treats the firm as a passive investor. Thus the true value of the Blitzen project was the DCF value *plus* the value of the option to expand.

21-2 THE OPTION TO ABANDON

In the case of Blitzen Computers, we needed to value an option to expand. Sometimes we face the opposite problem and need to value an option to abandon a business. For example, suppose you must choose between two technologies for production of a new product, a Wankel-engine outboard motor.

1. Technology A uses computer-controlled machinery custom-designed to produce the complex shapes required for Wankel engines in high volumes and at low cost. But if the Wankel engine doesn't sell, this equipment will be worthless.

2. Technology B uses standard machine tools. Labor costs are much higher, but the tools can be sold or shifted to another use if the engine doesn't sell.

Technology A looks better in a discounted-cash-flow analysis of the new product, because it was designed to have the lowest possible cost at the planned production volume. Yet you can sense the advantage of technology B's flexibility if you are unsure about whether the new outboard will sink or swim in the marketplace. In such cases managers may ignore technology A's better DCF value and choose technology B instead for its "intangible" flexibility advantage. But we can make the value of this flexibility more concrete by modeling it as a put option.

Just for simplicity, assume that the initial capital outlays for technologies A and B are the same. Technology A, with its low-cost customized machinery, will provide a payoff of $20 million if the outboard is popular with boat owners and $5 million if it is not. Think of these payoffs as the project's cash flow in its first year of production plus the present value of all subsequent cash flows. The corresponding payoffs to technology B are $18 million and $3 million.

	PAYOFFS FROM PRODUCING OUTBOARD, MILLIONS	
	Technology A	Technology B
Buoyant demand	$20	$18
Sluggish demand	5	3

If you are obliged to continue in production regardless of how unprofitable the project turns out to be, then technology A is clearly the superior choice. But suppose that you can bail out of technology B for $8 million.[1] If the outboard is not a success in the market, you would do better to sell off the plant and equipment for $8 million rather than continue with a project that has a present value of only $3 million. Thus, once you recognize the option to sell the assets, the payoffs to technology B change as follows:

Buoyant demand $\longrightarrow$ continue production $\longrightarrow$ own business worth $18 million

Sluggish demand $\longrightarrow$ exercise option to sell assets $\longrightarrow$ receive $8 million

A put option on a stock is an insurance policy that pays off when the stock ends up below the put's exercise price. Technology B provides the same kind of insurance policy: if the outboard's sales are disappointing, you can abandon the machinery and realize its $8 million value. This abandonment option is a put option with an exercise price equal to the sale value of the machinery. The total value of the project using technology B is its DCF value, assuming that the company does not abandon, *plus* the value of the abandonment put.[2] When you value this put option, you are placing a value on flexibility.

Valuing the Abandonment Put—An Example

In Chapter 10 we introduced you to that airborne pioneer Agnes Magna, who was pondering the purchase of a turboprop for her new airline, Magna Charter. Figure 21-1 summarizes the possible payoffs from the turbo. If the airline gets off to a good start and demand is high, Ms. Magna calculates she will have a business worth $738,000 by the end of the first year. If things don't work out, it will be worth only $415,000. Ms. Magna estimates that there is a 60 percent chance that the business will succeed and therefore calculates the expected value in year 1 as $(.6 \times 738) + (.4 \times 415) = 609$, or $609,000. She discounts this at a 10 percent cost of capital,

---

[1]In practice the abandonment value of technology B is unlikely to be certain. For example, suppose that it could be either $2 million or $14 million. In the former case you would do better to continue with the project even if demand is sluggish; in the latter case you are better off by $11 million if you abandon when demand is sluggish.

[2]Imagine a stock which pays either $3 or $18. If you own both the stock and a put option on the stock with an exercise price of $8, the possible payoffs on your investment are

Stock price $18 $\longrightarrow$ keep stock $\longrightarrow$ own stock worth $18
Stock price $3 $\longrightarrow$ exercise put option $\longrightarrow$ receive $8 exercise price

Investing in technology B is exactly like owning both the stock and the put option.

Figure 21-1 The possible payoffs to Magna Charter from investing in a turboprop. (The payoffs assume that the company continues to operate the plane.)

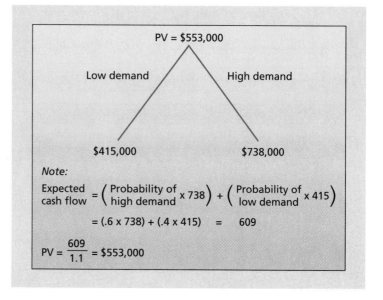

PV = $553,000

Low demand | High demand

$415,000 | $738,000

Note:

$$\text{Expected cash flow} = \left(\begin{array}{c}\text{Probability of}\\\text{high demand}\end{array} \times 738\right) + \left(\begin{array}{c}\text{Probability of}\\\text{low demand}\end{array} \times 415\right)$$

$$= (.6 \times 738) + (.4 \times 415) = 609$$

$$PV = \frac{609}{1.1} = \$553,000$$

which gives a present value of 609/1.1 = 553, or $553,000.[3] Note that these calculations do not allow for the possibility of abandonment. If the business does not take off[4] in the first year, Ms. Magna would do better to sell the turboprop for $500,000 rather than retain a business that is worth only $415,000.

What is the value of this option to bail out? In Chapter 10 we tried to answer that question by using standard discounted-cash-flow techniques. We know now that you cannot use standard DCF when there is an option involved, because the discount rate changes as the value of the underlying asset changes. To value Ms. Magna's option to abandon, you need to value a 1-year option to sell the turboprop for $500,000. You require the following information to value the put (dollar figures in thousands):

- Present value of business without option to abandon: $553
- Exercise price: $500
- Maturity: 1 year
- Interest rate: 5 percent
- Future value of business with high demand: $738
- Future value with low demand: $415

Since Ms. Magna can foresee only two outcomes, this problem is tailor-made for the binomial method that we used in Chapter 20 to value the Intel option. Here is a chance to show that you haven't forgotten it. Remember that there are two ways to use the binomial method:

---

[3]If you look back at Chapter 10, you will see that this is not the *total* value of the business to Ms. Magna, since she also expects to earn some income during the first year. This income does not affect the value of the option to abandon at the end of the first year, and so we ignore it here.

[4]The pun was unintentional.

1. Construct a package of the underlying asset and a loan that would provide the same payoffs as the option.

2. Pretend that individuals are risk-neutral, and then value the expected payoffs from the option in this risk-neutral world.

We will use the risk-neutral approach.

If Ms. Magna was indifferent to risk, she would be content if the business just offered the 5 percent risk-free rate of interest. We know that either the value of the business will go from $553,000 to $738,000, a rise of 33 percent, or it will go to $415,000, a fall of 25 percent. We can therefore calculate the probability that the value will rise in our hypothetical risk-neutral world:

$$\text{Expected} \atop \text{return} = \left(\text{probability} \atop \text{of rise} \times 33 \right) + \left(1 - \text{probability} \atop \text{of rise} \right) \times (-25) = 5\%$$

Therefore the probability of rise equals 52 percent.[5]

We know that if the business is successful, the option to abandon will be worthless. If it is unsuccessful, Ms. Magna will sell the turboprop and save herself 500 − 415 = 85, or $85,000. Therefore the expected future value of the option to abandon is

$$\left(\text{Probability} \atop \text{of rise} \times 0 \right) + \left(1 - \text{probability} \atop \text{of rise} \right) \times 85 = (.52 \times 0) + (.48 \times 85)$$
$$= 41, \text{ or } \$41,000$$

And the current value of the option to abandon is[6]

$$\frac{\text{Expected future value}}{1 + \text{interest rate}} = \frac{41}{1.05} = 39, \text{ or } \$39,000$$

Thus recognizing the option to abandon increases the value of Ms. Magna's business by $39,000:

$$\text{Value of business} \atop \text{with abandonment} \atop \text{option} = \text{value of business} \atop \text{without abandonment} \atop \text{option} + \text{value} \atop \text{of} \atop \text{option}$$

$$= 553 + 39 = 592, \text{ or } \$592,000$$

What Happens to Ms. Magna's Option If There Are More Than Two Possible Outcomes?

Ms. Magna's option provides a good opportunity to extend our understanding of the binomial model. Notice that Ms. Magna considered only two possible changes to the value of her business—a rise of 33 percent if demand is high or a fall of 25 percent if demand is low. As an alternative, suppose that in each 6-month period the value of Ms. Magna's firm could either rise by 22.6 percent or fall by 18.4 percent (we'll tell you shortly how we picked these figures). Figure 21-2 shows the possible firm values by the year's end. You can see that there are now three possible outcomes: Firm value could rise to $832,000, remain unchanged, or decline to $368,000. That might be somewhat more realistic than Ms. Magna's initial "boom or bust" scenario.

---

[5]Notice that the *true* probability of a rise in value is 60 percent. However, we don't need to know this in order to value the option (though we needed the true probability to calculate the present value of the business *without* the abandonment option).

[6]In Section 10-3 we valued the option at $31,000.

Figure 21-2 The possible future values of Magna Charter airline. Figures in parentheses show the values of an option to sell the airline's assets for $500,000.

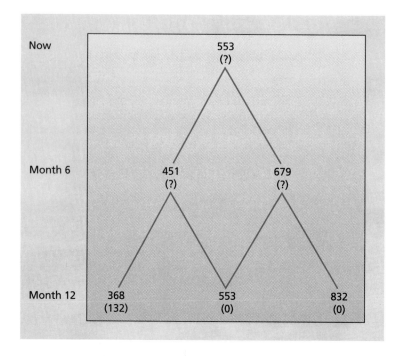

We continue to assume that Ms. Magna has the option to sell the plane at the end of the year for $500,000. In Figure 21-2, we show the associated value of this option in parentheses below each possible year-end value.[7] For example, if the value of the firm turns out to be $832,000, the abandonment option will be worthless; at the other extreme, if firm value is $368,000, the option will be worth

$$\text{Exercise price} - \text{firm value} = 500 - 368 = 132, \text{ or } \$132,000$$

Option Values after 6 Months

We first use the risk-neutral trick to work out option values at the end of 6 months. If investors are risk-neutral, the expected return on the firm must be equal to the interest rate, which is 5 percent a year, or 2.5 percent for 6 months. So[8]

$$\left(\begin{array}{c}\text{Probability} \times 22.6 \\ \text{of rise}\end{array}\right) \times \left(\begin{array}{c}1 - \text{probability} \\ \text{of rise}\end{array}\right) \times (-18.4) = 2.5$$

Probability of rise = .51, or 51%

---

[7]We assume that the plane cannot be sold at the end of 6 months. In other words, we assume that the abandonment option is European.

[8]The general formula for calculating the probability of a rise is

$$p = \frac{\text{interest rate} - \text{downside change}}{\text{upside change} - \text{downside change}}$$

Thus in the case of Magna Charter

$$p = \frac{2.5 - (-18.4)}{22.6 - (-18.4)} = .51$$

Suppose that we are in month 6 and the firm value is 451. In that case there is a .51 chance that at the end of the year the option will be worthless and a .49 chance that it will be worth 132. Thus

Expected value of option at end of year = $(.51 \times 0) + (.49 \times 132) = 65$

And with an interest rate of 2.5 percent every 6 months,

$$\text{Value at month 6} = \frac{65}{1.025} = 63$$

If firm value at month 6 is 679, the option is certain to be worthless at year-end, and therefore its value at month 6 is zero.

Option Value Now

We can now get rid of two of the question marks in Figure 21-2. Figure 21-3 shows that if firm value in month 6 is 451, the option value is 63 and if firm value is 679, the option value is zero. It now remains to work back to the value of the option today.

The expected value of the option in month 6 is

$$\binom{\text{Probability}}{\text{of rise}} \times 0 + \binom{1 - \text{probability}}{\text{of rise}} \times 63 = (.51 \times 0) + (.49 \times 63) = 31$$

Therefore, the value today is

$$\frac{\text{Expected value of option at month 6}}{1 + \text{interest rate}} = \frac{31}{1.025} = 30, \text{ or } \$30,000$$

In the one-step example we assumed that demand could be only high or low, and that gave us an option value of \$39,000. The two-step calculation allowed us to rec-

Figure 21-3 We have worked back from the month-12 values to calculate the value of the Magna Charter abandonment option in month 6.

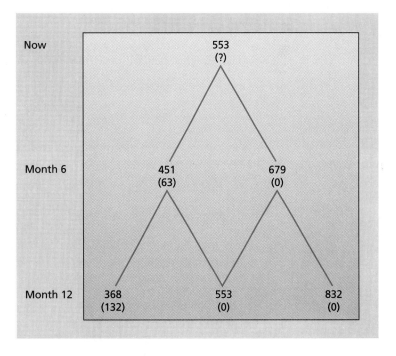

Now		553 (?)	
Month 6	451 (63)		679 (0)
Month 12	368 (132)	553 (0)	832 (0)

ognize that demand could take on three possible values, and that changed our estimate of the option value to \$30,000. It took us longer to value the option in the two-step case, but the principle was exactly the same and it didn't require any mathematics more advanced than multiplication and division.

The General Binomial Method

Moving to two steps when valuing the Magna Charter option probably added extra realism. But there is no reason to stop there. We could go on to take shorter and shorter intervals in each of which there are only two possible changes in the value of the enterprise. For example, we could divide the year into 12 subintervals of 1 month each. That would give 13 possible year-end values. We could still use the binomial method to work back from the final date to the present. Of course, it would be tedious to do such a calculation by hand, but with a computer you can whisk through options with hundreds of periods to run.

Since an asset can usually take on an almost limitless number of future values, the binomial method is likely to give a more realistic and accurate measure of the option's value if we work with a large number of subperiods. But that raises an important question: How do we pick sensible figures for the up and down changes in value? For example, why did we pick figures of 22.6 percent and -18.4 percent when we revalued the Magna Charter option by using two subperiods? Fortunately there is a neat little formula that relates the up and down changes to the standard deviation of the returns on the asset:

$$1 + \text{upside change} = u = e^{\sigma\sqrt{h}}$$

$$1 + \text{downside change} = d = \frac{1}{u}$$

where e = base for natural logarithms = 2.718
σ = standard deviation of (continuously compounded) annual returns on asset
h = interval as a fraction of a year

When Ms. Magna said that the value of her business could either rise by 33 percent or fall by 25 percent over 1 year, her figures were consistent with a figure of 28.8 percent for the standard deviation of the annual returns on her business:

$$1 + \text{upside change (1-year interval)} = u = e^{.288\sqrt{1}} = 1.33$$

$$1 + \text{downside change} = d = \frac{1}{u} = \frac{1}{1.33} = .75$$

To work out the equivalent upside and downside changes when we chop the year into two 6-month intervals, we use the same formula:

$$1 + \text{upside change (6-month interval)} = u = e^{.288\sqrt{.5}} = 1.226$$

$$1 + \text{downside change} = d = \frac{1}{u} = \frac{1}{1.226} = .816$$

The center columns in Table 21-3 show the equivalent up and down moves in the value of the firm if we chop the year into monthly or weekly subperiods.

As the number of intervals is increased, the values that you obtain from the binomial method should get closer and closer to the Black-Scholes value. In fact, you can think of the Black-Scholes formula as a shortcut alternative to the binomial method as the number of intervals gets very large. For the Magna Charter option the Black-Scholes formula gives a value of \$28,200. The right-hand column of

TABLE 21-3

As the number of intervals is increased, you must adjust the range of possible stock price changes to keep the same standard deviation. But you will get increasingly close to the Black-Scholes value of the Magna Charter option. (Note that sometimes you may temporarily move away from the Black-Scholes value. For example, this happens when the number of intervals is increased from three to four.)

Intervals in a Year (1/h)	CHANGE IN INTERVAL, PERCENT		Estimated Option Value, Thousands
	Upside	Downside	
1	+33.3	−25.0	$39.4
2	+22.6	−18.4	30.2
3	+18.2	−15.3	29.8
4	+15.5	−13.4	30.4
12	+8.7	−8.0	29.1
52	+4.1	−3.9	28.3
		Black-Scholes value = 28.2	

Note: The standard deviation is $\sigma = .288$.

Table 21-3 shows that if you divide the year into 52 weekly subperiods, the binomial method gives a good approximation to the Black-Scholes formula.

Why do the option values change as we chop time into ever smaller pieces? Figure 21-4 shows the answer. A one-step binomial assumes that only two things can happen—a very good outcome or a very bad one. The Black-Scholes formula is more realistic: it recognizes a continuum of outcomes.

If the Black-Scholes formula is more accurate and quicker to use than the binomial method, why bother with the binomial method at all? The answer is that there are circumstances in which you cannot use the Black-Scholes formula but the binomial method will still give you a good measure of the option's value. We will come across one such case in the next section.

21-3 THE TIMING OPTION

Optimal investment timing is easy when there is no uncertainty. You just calculate project NPV at various future investment dates and pick the date that gives the highest current value.[9] Unfortunately, this simple rule breaks down in the face of uncertainty.

Suppose that you have a project which could be a big winner or a big loser. The project's upside outweighs its downside, and it has a positive NPV if undertaken today. However, the project is not "now or never." Should you invest right away or wait? It's hard to say: If the project is truly a winner, waiting means loss or deferral

---

[9]See Section 6-3.

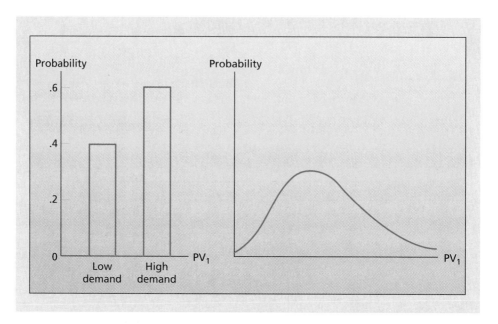

Figure 21-4 In the left-hand histogram, we assume that only two things can happen to Ms. Magna's venture—high demand or low demand. The histogram shows present values at year 1, assuming no abandonment. The lognormal distribution on the right is more realistic because it recognizes a continuum of possible present values and does not ignore intermediate outcomes. The Black-Scholes model is based on the lognormal distribution.

of its early cash flows. But if it turns out to be a loser, waiting could prevent a bad mistake.

In Chapter 6 we sidestepped this problem of optimal investment timing under uncertainty. Now we have the tools to confront it head-on, because the opportunity to invest in a positive-NPV project is equivalent to an in-the-money call option. Optimal investment timing means exercising that call at the best time.

<table>
<tr><td>

Example of the Timing Option

</td><td>

We'll suppose that the positive-NPV project involves construction of a malted herring factory for $180 million. As most of our readers probably know, the demand for malted herring fluctuates widely, depending on the price of competing fertilizers.

Assume first that construction of the plant is a now-or-never opportunity. That's the same as having an about-to-expire call option on the factory with an exercise price equal to the $180 million investment required to build it. If the present value of the plant's forecasted cash flows exceeds $180 million, the call option's payoff is the project's NPV. But if project NPV is negative, the call option's payoff is zero, because in that case the firm will not make the investment. We've plotted these payoffs as the solid colored line in Figure 21-5.

Now suppose that you can choose to delay construction of the plant for a year. Even though the project may have a zero or negative NPV if undertaken today, your call option has value because the year's delay gives room for hope that the volatile malted herring market will take off. We have shown a possible range of option values as the dashed line in Figure 21-5.

</td></tr>
</table>

Figure 21-5 The opportunity to invest in the malted herring factory amounts to a call option. If investment is now or never, the call's payoffs are shown by the solid line. If investment can be postponed, the call option is valuable even if project NPV is zero or negative. Compare Figure 20-8.

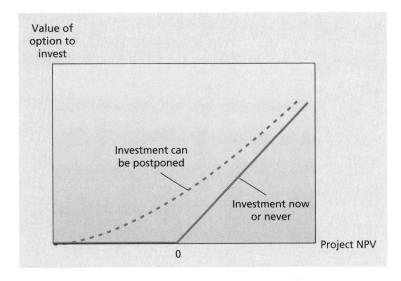

The decision to launch or defer investment in the malted herring factory amounts to deciding whether to exercise the call option immediately or to wait and possibly exercise later.[10] Naturally this involves a trade-off. You are reluctant to exercise, because despite today's rosy forecasts, investment in the malted herring plant may still turn out to be a mistake. When you give up your option to wait, you can no longer take advantage of the volatility of the project's future value. Remember, option holders like volatility because it generates upside potential and the option contract limits loss. On the other hand, as long as the project has a positive NPV, you are eager to exercise in order to get your hands on the cash inflows. If the cash flows (and NPV) are high enough, you will gladly exercise your call before its time is up.

The cash flows from an investment project play the same role as dividend payments on a stock. When a stock does not pay dividends, an American call option is always worth more alive than dead and should never be exercised early. But payment of a dividend before the option matures reduces the ex-dividend price and the possible payoffs to the call option at maturity. Think of the extreme case: If a company pays out all its assets in one bumper dividend, then afterward the stock price must be zero and the call is worthless. Therefore, any in-the-money call would be exercised just before this liquidating dividend.

Dividends do not always prompt early exercise, but if they are sufficiently large, call option holders capture them by exercising just before the ex-dividend date. We see managers acting in the same way: when a project's forecasted cash flows are sufficiently large, managers "capture" the cash flows by investing right away.[11] But when forecasted cash flows are small, managers are inclined to hold on to their call rather

---

[10]We are thinking here of American options. European options cannot be exercised immediately.

[11]In this case the call's value equals its lower-bound value because it is exercised immediately. The two lines in Figure 21-5 touch where project PV is high enough to trigger immediate investment. At this and higher PVs, the value of a European call option, which could not be exercised immediately, would lie below the value of a now-or-never investment.

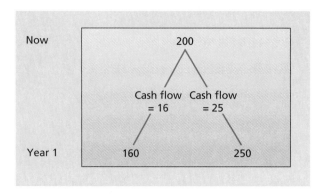

Figure 21-6 The possible cash flows and end-of-period values for the first year of the malted herring project.

than investing, even when project NPV is positive.[12] This explains why managers are sometimes reluctant to commit to positive-NPV projects. This caution is rational as long as the option to wait is open and sufficiently valuable.

Valuing the Malted Herring Option

We will put some numbers on the malted herring project and then show how to calculate option values when there are cash flows on the asset. Figure 21-6 shows the possible cash flows and end-of-year values for the malted herring project. You can see that the current value of the project is $200 million. If demand turns out to be low in year 1, the cash flow is only $16 million and the value of the project falls to $160 million. But if demand is high in year 1, the cash flow is $25 million and value rises to $250 million. Although the project lasts indefinitely, we assume that investment cannot be postponed beyond the end of the first year, and therefore we show only the cash flows for the first year and the possible values at the end of the year. Notice that if you undertake the investment right away, you capture the first year's cash flow ($16 million or $25 million); if you delay, you miss out on this cash flow, but you will have more information on how the project is likely to work out.

If demand is high in the first year, the malted herring plant has a cash flow of $25 million and a year-end value of $250 million. The total return is $(25 + 250)/200 - 1 = .375$, or 37.5 percent. If demand is low, the plant has a cash flow of $16 million and a year-end value of $160 million. Total return is $(16 + 160)/200 - 1 = -.12$, or -12 percent. In a *risk-neutral* world, the expected return would be equal to the interest rate, which we assume is 5 percent:

$$\begin{matrix} \text{Expected} \\ \text{return} \end{matrix} = \left(\begin{matrix} \text{Probability of} \\ \text{high demand} \end{matrix} \right) \times 37.5 + \left(\begin{matrix} 1 - \text{probability of} \\ \text{high demand} \end{matrix} \right) \times (-12) = 5\%$$

Therefore the (pretend) probability of high demand is 34.3 percent.

---

[12]We have been a bit vague about "forecasted project cash flows." If competitors can enter and take away cash that you could have earned, the meaning is clear. But what about the decision to, say, develop an oil well? Here delay doesn't waste barrels of oil in the ground; it simply postpones production and the associated cash flow. The cost of waiting is the decline in today's *present value* of revenues from production. Present value declines if the future rate of increase in oil prices is not sufficiently high, that is, if the discounted price of oil is less than the current price. See Chapters 11 and 25.

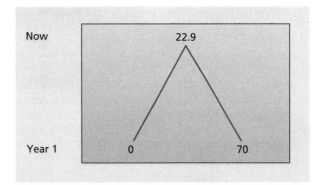

Figure 21-7 The values of the option to build a malted herring factory. The option to build the factory in the future is worth more than the NPV of the factory if built today.

We want to value a call option on the malted herring project with an exercise price of $180 million. We begin as usual at the end and work backward. The bottom row of Figure 21-7 shows the possible values of this option at the end of the year. If project value is $160 million, the option to invest is worthless. At the other extreme, if project value is $250 million, option value is $250 - 180 = \$70$ million.

To calculate the value of the option today, we work out the expected payoffs in a risk-neutral world and discount at the interest rate of 5 percent. Thus, the value of your option to invest in the malted herring plant is

$$\frac{(.343 \times 70) + (.657 \times 0)}{1.05} = \$22.9 \text{ million}$$

But here is where we need to recognize the opportunity to exercise the option immediately. The option is worth $22.9 million if you keep it open, and it is worth $200 - 180 = \$20$ million if exercised now. Thus the fact that the malted herring project has a positive NPV is not sufficient reason for investing. There is a still better strategy: Wait and see.

Notice how we worked this out. We worked backward from year 1 to today, but then we checked whether the option was worth more dead than alive and we used the higher of the two values. Suppose that construction of the malted herring plant could be delayed until the end of the second year. In this case we would have two steps to the binomial tree. Again we would start from the final exercise date and work back through the tree. However, at each step we should remember to check whether the option is worth more dead than alive and use the higher of the two values as we work back to today. The same technique can be used whenever you need to value an American option on a dividend-paying stock.

Option Valuation and Decision Trees

Calculating option values by the binomial method is basically a process of solving decision trees. You start at some future date and work back through the tree to the present, checking at each decision point to determine the best future action. Eventually the possible cash flows generated by future events and actions are folded back to a present value.

Is the binomial method *merely* another application of decision trees, a tool of analysis that you learned about in Chapter 10? The answer is no, for at least two reasons. First, option theory gives us a simple, powerful framework for describing complex decision trees. If you could postpone construction of the malted herring factory for many years, the complete decision tree would overflow the largest classroom chalkboard. Now that you know about options, you can just refer to the opportunity to invest in malted herring production as "an American call on a perpetuity with a constant dividend yield." Of course, not all real problems have such easy option analogues, but we can often approximate complex decision trees by some simple package of assets and options. A custom decision tree may get closer to "reality," but the time and expense may not be worth it. Most men buy their suits off the rack even though a custom-made suit from Saville Row would fit better and look nicer.

Second, and more important, option pricing theory is absolutely essential for discounting within decision trees. Standard discounted cash flow doesn't work within decision trees for the same reason that it doesn't work for puts and calls. As we pointed out in Section 20-4, there is no single, constant discount rate for options because the risk of the option changes as time and the price of the underlying asset change. There is no single discount rate inside a decision tree, because if the tree contains meaningful future decisions, it also contains options. The market value of the future cash flows described by the decision tree has to be calculated by option pricing methods.

21-4   FLEXIBLE PRODUCTION FACILITIES

A sheep is not a flexible production facility. It produces mutton and wool in roughly fixed proportions. If the price of mutton suddenly rises and that of wool falls, there is little that the farmer with a flock of sheep can do about it. Many manufacturing operations are different, for they have built-in flexibility to vary their output mix as demand changes. Since we have mentioned sheep, we might point to the knitwear industry as a case in which manufacturing flexibility has become particularly important in recent years. Fashion changes have made the pattern of demand in the knitwear industry notoriously difficult to predict, and firms have increasingly invested in computer-controlled knitting machines, which provide an option to vary the product mix as demand changes.[13]

Companies also try to avoid becoming dependent on a single source of raw materials. Consider, for example, the problem faced by electric utilities. Utilities are allotted emission allowances which permit them to emit a specified tonnage of sulfur dioxide. These allowances can be bought and sold, so a utility may face the choice between reducing emissions or buying the needed allowances in the market. There are several ways to reduce emissions. One is to burn expensive low-sulfur coal; a second is to invest in cofiring equipment, which allows the utility to burn a mixture of natural gas and coal. For one midwestern utility the cost of installing cofiring equipment at two of its coal-fired plants was nearly $5 million. If everything works out as expected, the utility will continue just to burn coal and its investment in cofiring will be wasted. But you can see the flexibility that having the cofiring equipment has added. If the cost of emission allowances rises or the price of natural gas falls relative to the price of low-sulfur coal, cofiring could prove to be a cheaper means of production.[14] In effect, the company spent $5 million to acquire the option to switch between a pure coal-fired unit and a cofired unit.

---

[13]J. M. Stopford and C. Baden-Fuller, "Flexible Strategies—The Key to Success in Knitwear," *Long Range Planning,* **23**:56–62 (December 1990).

[14]The value of flexibility in electricity generating plants is discussed in B. F. Hobbs, J. C. Honious, and J. Bluestein, "Estimating the Flexibility of Utility Resource Plans: An Application to Natural Gas Cofiring for SO_2 Control," *IEEE Transactions on Power Systems* (February 1994).

Auto manufacturers also have discovered the importance of flexibility in their production facilities. For example, Toyota has manufacturing operations in Japan, the United States, and a variety of other countries. This has enabled Toyota to balance production between different countries as relative costs changed. Thus, as the yen appreciated against the dollar, Toyota increased its exports of the Camry from the United States to Japan.[15]

In each of these three examples the firm was acquiring an option to exchange one risky asset for another. We are not going to value these options here, but you should be aware that the option pricing methods we have described in this chapter can be adapted to valuing an option to exchange assets.

21-5 OPTION VALUE AT A GLANCE

When we introduced option valuation in the previous chapter, we focused on the valuation of European calls. In the course of this chapter we have encountered European and American options, calls and puts, and options on assets that pay dividends and on those that don't. You may find it useful to have the following summary of how different combinations of features affect option value.

AMERICAN CALLS—NO DIVIDENDS.   We know that in the absence of dividends the value of a call option increases with time to maturity. So if you exercised an American call option early, you would needlessly reduce its value. Since an American call should not be exercised before maturity, its value is the same as that of a European call, and the Black-Scholes formula applies to both options.

EUROPEAN PUTS—NO DIVIDENDS.   If we wish to value a European put, we can use a formula that we developed in Chapter 20:

$$\text{Value of put} = \text{value of call} - \text{value of stock} + \text{PV(exercise price)}$$

AMERICAN PUTS—NO DIVIDENDS.   It can sometimes pay to exercise an American put before maturity in order to reinvest the exercise price. For example, suppose that immediately after you buy an American put, the stock price falls to zero. In this case there is no advantage to holding on to the option since it *cannot* become more valuable. It is better to exercise the put and invest the exercise money. Thus an American put is always more valuable than a European put. In our extreme example, the difference is equal to the present value of the interest that you could earn on the exercise price. In all other cases the difference is less.

Because the Black-Scholes formula does not allow for early exercise, it cannot be used to value an American put exactly. But you can use the step-by-step binomial method as long as you check at each point whether the option is worth more dead than alive and then use the higher of the two values.

EUROPEAN CALLS ON DIVIDEND-PAYING STOCKS.   Part of the share value is composed of the present value of dividends, to which the option holder is not entitled.

---

[15]See J. Perlez, "Japanese Mix and Match Auto Plans and Markets," *The New York Times*, March 26, 1993.

Therefore, when using the Black-Scholes model to value a European call on a dividend-paying stock, you should reduce the price of the stock by the present value of dividends paid before the option's maturity.[16]

Example: Dividends don't always come with a label attached, so look out for instances where the asset holder gets a benefit and the option holder does not. For example, when you buy foreign currency, you can invest it to earn interest; but if you own an option to buy foreign currency, you miss out on this income.

Suppose that in fall 1995 you are offered a 1-year option to buy sterling at the current exchange rate of $1.58; that is, $1.58 = £1. You have the following information:

- Maturity of option (t):   1 year
- Exercise price (E): $1.58
- Current price of sterling (P): $1.58
- Standard deviation of exchange-rate changes (σ)   .10
- Dollar interest rate ($r_\$$):   .055
- Sterling interest rate ($r_£$):   .0675

If you buy sterling, you can invest it to earn interest at 6.75 percent. By buying the option rather than sterling itself, you miss out on this "dividend." Therefore, to value the call option, you must first reduce the current price of sterling by the amount of the lost interest:[17]

$$\text{Adjusted price of sterling} = P^* = \frac{\text{current price}}{1 + r_£} = \frac{1.58}{1.0675} = \$1.48$$

Now you can apply the Black-Scholes formula:

$$\text{Standard deviation} \times \text{square root of time} = .10\sqrt{1} = .10$$

$$\frac{\text{Price}}{\text{PV(exercise price)}} = \frac{P^*}{E/(1 + r_\$)} = \frac{1.48}{1.58/1.055} = .99$$

Using the call option data in Appendix Table 6 gives

$$\text{Value of call} = .035 \times P^* = .035 \times 1.48 = .051$$

that is, 5.1 cents per pound. An option to purchase £1 million on these terms would be worth $51,000.

AMERICAN CALLS ON DIVIDEND-PAYING STOCKS. We have seen that when the stock does not pay dividends, an American call option is *always* worth more alive than dead. By holding on to the option, you not only keep your option open but also earn

---

[16]For real options the "dividends" are cash flows generated by some real asset. The present value of these cash flows would be excluded from the asset's present value when you value an option on the asset. For example, our valuation of the abandonment option for Magna Charter's turboprop ignored (correctly) the income that the plane would generate in year 1, before the option to sell the plane could be exercised.

[17]Note that

$$\text{Current price} - \text{PV(interest)} = P - \frac{r_£P}{1 + r_£} = \frac{P}{1 + r_£}$$

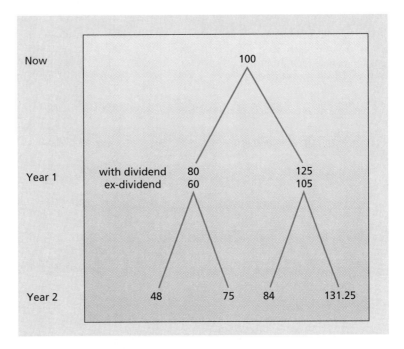

Figure 21-8 Possible values of Consolidated Pork Bellies stock.

interest on the exercise money. Even when there are dividends, you should never exercise early if the dividend you gain is less than the interest you lose by having to pay the exercise price early. However, if the dividend is sufficiently large, you might want to capture it by exercising the option just before the ex-dividend date.

The only general method for valuing an American call on a dividend-paying stock is to use the step-by-step binomial method. In this case you must check at each stage to see whether the option is more valuable if exercised just before the ex-dividend date than if held for at least one more period.

Example: Here is a last chance to practice your option valuation skills by valuing an American call on a dividend-paying stock. Figure 21-8 summarizes the possible price movements in Consolidated Pork Bellies stock. The stock price is currently $100, but over the next year it could either fall by 20 percent to $80 or rise by 25 percent to $125. In either case the company will then pay its regular dividend of $20. Immediately after payment of this dividend the stock price will fall to $80 − 20 = $60, or $125 − 20 = $105. Over the second year the price will again either fall by 20 percent from the ex-dividend price or rise by 25 percent.[18]

Suppose that you wish to value a 2-year American call option on Consolidated stock. Figure 21-9 shows the possible option values at each point, assuming an exercise price of $70 and an interest rate of 12 percent. We won't go through all the cal-

[18]Notice that the payment of a fixed dividend in year 1 results in four possible stock prices at the end of year 2. In other words, 60×1.25 does not equal $105 \times .8$. Don't let that put you off. You still start from the end and work back one step at a time to find the possible option values at each date.

Figure 21-9 Values of a 2-year call option on Consolidated Pork Bellies stock. Exercise price is $70. Although we show option values for year 2, the option will not be alive then. It will be exercised in year 1.

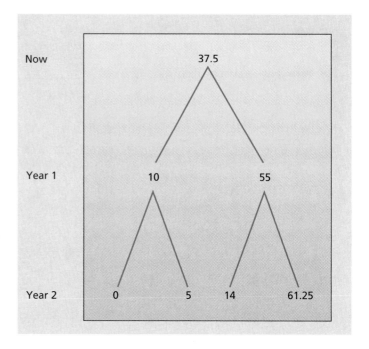

culations behind these figures, but we will focus on the option values at the end of year 1.

Suppose that the stock price has fallen in the first year. What is the option worth if you hold on to it for a further period? You should be used to this problem by now. First pretend that investors are risk-neutral and calculate the probability that the stock will rise in price. This probability turns out to be 71 percent.[19] Now calculate the expected payoff on the option and discount at 12 percent:

$$\text{Option value if not exercised in year 1} = \frac{(.71 \times 5) + (.29 \times 0)}{1.12} = \$3.18$$

Thus, if you hold on to the option, it is worth $3.18. However, if you exercise the option just before the ex-dividend date, you pay an exercise price of $70 for a stock worth $80. This $10 value from exercising is greater than the $3.18 from holding on to the option. Therefore in Figure 21-9 we put in an option value of $10 if the stock price falls in year 1.

You will also want to exercise if the stock price *rises* in year 1. The option is worth $42.45 if you hold on to it but $55 if you exercise. Therefore in Figure 21-9 we put in a value of $55 if the stock price rises.

The rest of the calculation is routine. Calculate the expected option payoff in year 1 and discount by 12 percent to give the option value today:

$$\text{Option value today} = \frac{(.71 \times 55) + (.29 \times 10)}{1.12} = \$37.5$$

---

[19]Using the formula in footnote 8 gives

$$p = \frac{r - d}{u - d} = \frac{12 - (-20)}{25 - (-20)} = .71$$

······

A Conceptual Problem?

The explanations above obviously apply to traded puts and calls. But do the valuation techniques developed for these financial options always work for *real* options?

When we introduced option pricing models in Chapter 20, we suggested that the trick is to construct a package of the underlying asset and a loan that would give exactly the same payoffs as the option. If the two investments do not sell for the same price, then there are arbitrage possibilities. But many assets are not freely traded. This means that we can no longer rely on arbitrage arguments to justify the use of option models.

The risk-neutral method still makes practical sense, however. It's really just an application of the *certainty-equivalent* method introduced in Chapter 9. The key assumption—implicit till now—is that the company's *shareholders* have access to assets with the same risk characteristics, e.g., the same beta, as the capital investments being evaluated by the firm.

Think of each real investment opportunity as having a "double," a security or portfolio with identical risk. Then the expected rate of return offered by the double is also the cost of capital for the real investment and the discount rate for a DCF valuation of the investment project. Now what would investors pay for a real *option* based on the project? The same as for an identical traded option written on the double. This traded option does not have to exist; it is enough to know how it would be valued by investors, who could employ either the arbitrage or the risk-neutral method. The two methods give the same answer, of course.

When we value a real option by the risk-neutral method, we are calculating the option's value if it could be traded. This exactly parallels standard capital budgeting. As we stressed way back in Chapters 2 and 5, a DCF calculation of project NPV is an estimate of the project's market value if the project could be set up as a mini-firm with shares traded on the stock market. The certainty-equivalent (i.e., risk-neutral) value of a real option is likewise an estimate of the option's market value if it were traded.

21-6 SUMMARY

In Chapter 20 you learned the basics of option valuation. In this chapter we described four important real options:

1. *The option to make follow-on investments.* Companies often cite "strategic" value when taking on negative-NPV projects. A close look at the projects' payoffs reveals call options on follow-on projects in addition to the immediate projects' cash flows. Today's investments can generate tomorrow's opportunities.

2. *The option to abandon.* The option to abandon a project provides partial insurance against failure. This is a put option; the put's exercise price is the value of the project's assets if sold or shifted to a more valuable use.

3. *The option to wait (and learn) before investing.* This is equivalent to owning a call option on the investment project. The call is exercised when the firm commits to the project. But often it's better to defer a positive-NPV project in order to keep the call alive. Deferral is most attractive when uncertainty is great and immediate project cash flows—which are lost or postponed by waiting—are small.

4. *The option to vary the firm's output or its production methods.* Firms often build flexibility into their production facilities so that they can use the cheapest raw materials or produce the most valuable set of outputs. In this case they effectively acquire the option to exchange one asset for another.

We should offer here a healthy warning: The real options encountered in practice are usually considerably more complex than the simple examples that we examined in this chapter. For instance, you may be able to bail out from a project at any time rather than simply on the single occasion that we assumed for Magna Charter. The price at which you can bail out is likely to change over time and will rarely be known in advance. Also, once you have abandoned, you may be able to reinstate the project if business improves. Handling such complexities typically requires a number-crunching computer.

Modeling the problem also requires informed judgment. For example, when we discussed the option to postpone investment, we assumed that postponement causes you to miss out on the first year's cash flow but that you learn what this flow would have been if you had undertaken the project. That may not always be the case. Sometimes you may learn nothing by waiting, so that at the end of the year you are at exactly the same position as you were at when you started. Obviously, how much you learn by waiting makes a considerable difference to your estimate of option value.

Our examples of real options provided an opportunity to review and extend the option-valuation methods introduced in Chapter 20.

The binomial method assumes that the time to the option's maturity can be divided into a number of subintervals in each of which there are only two possible price changes. In the previous chapter we valued an option with only one period to expiration. Here we showed you how to value an option with many periods to expiration. The advantage of chopping the life of the option into many subperiods is that doing so allows you to recognize that the asset may take on many future values. You can think of the Black-Scholes formula as a shortcut solution when there is an infinite number of these subperiods and therefore an infinite number of possible future asset prices.

Regardless of the number of subperiods, the basic idea behind the binomial method is the same. You start at the option's maturity and work back one step at a time to find the option's initial value. But that raises a question: How do we pick sensible numbers for the up and down moves in the asset values? We introduced a formula that allows you to derive the up and down moves consistent with a given standard deviation of asset returns.

One of the advantages of holding the asset is that you may receive dividends; the option holder generally doesn't get these dividends. If there are no dividends, you would never want to exercise a call option before maturity. (Even if you *knew* that you were going to exercise it, you would prefer to pay the exercise money later rather than sooner.) But when the asset does pay a dividend, it may pay to exercise a call option early in order to capture the dividend. You can still use the binomial method to value the option, but at each point you need to check whether the option is worth more dead than alive.

Further Reading

· ·

The spring 1987 issue of the Midland Corporate Finance Journal *contains articles on real options. See also the following article for a review of the role of options in capital investment decisions:*
A. K. Dixit and R. S. Pindyck: "The Options Approach to Capital Investment," *Harvard Business Review*, **73**:105–115 (May–June 1995).

The standard text on the valuation of real options is:
A. K. Dixit and R. S. Pindyck: *Investment under Uncertainty*, Princeton University Press, Princeton, N.J., 1994.

Mason and Merton review a range of option applications to corporate finance:
S. P. Mason and R. C. Merton: "The Role of Contingent Claims Analysis in Corporate Finance," in E. I. Altman and M. G. Subrahmanyan (eds.), *Recent Advances in Corporate Finance*, Richard D. Irwin, Inc., Homewood, Ill., 1985.

Brennan and Schwartz have worked out an interesting application to natural resource investments:
M. J. Brennan and E. S. Schwartz: "Evaluating Natural Resource Investments," *Journal of Business*, **58**:135–157 (April 1985).

The texts listed under "Further Reading" in Chapter 20 can be referred to for additional discussion of the binomial method and the practical complications of applying option pricing theory.

Quiz

1. Describe the real option in each of the following cases:
    (*a*) Backwoods Chemical postpones a major plant expansion. The expansion has positive NPV on a discounted-cash-flow basis, but top management wants to get a better fix on product demand before proceeding.
    (*b*) Western Telecom commits to production of digital switching equipment specially designed for the European market. The project has a negative DCF NPV, but it is justified on strategic grounds by the need for a strong market position in the rapidly growing, and potentially very profitable, market.
    (*c*) Western Telecom vetoes a fully integrated, automated production line for the new digital switches. It relies on standard, less-expensive equipment. The automated production line is more efficient overall, according to a discounted-cash-flow calculation.
    (*d*) Phoenix Airways buys a jumbo jet with special equipment that allows the plane to be switched quickly from freight to passenger use or vice versa.

 2. Backwoods Chemical's stock price changes only once a month: either it goes up by 20 percent, or it falls by 16.7 percent. Its price now is $40. The interest rate is 12.7 percent per year, or about 1 percent per month.
    (*a*) What is the value of a 1-month call option with an exercise price of $40?
    (*b*) What is the option delta?
    (*c*) Show how the payoffs of this call option can be replicated by buying Backwoods stock and borrowing.
    (*d*) What is the value of a 2-month call option with an exercise price of $40?
    (*e*) What is the option delta of the 2-month call over the first 1-month period?

3. "The Black-Scholes formula gives the same answer as the binomial method when _____." Complete the sentence and briefly explain.

4. For which of the following options *might* it be rational to exercise before maturity? Explain briefly why or why not.
    (*a*) American put on a non-dividend-paying stock.
    (*b*) American call—the dividend payment is $5 per annum, the exercise price is $100, and the interest rate is 10 percent.
    (*c*) American call—the interest rate is 10 percent, and the dividend payment is 5 percent of future stock price. (*Hint:* The dividend depends on the stock price, which could either rise or fall.)

 5. Suppose a stock price can go up by 15 percent or down by 13 percent over the next period. You own a 1-period put on the stock. The interest rate is 10 percent, and the current stock price is $60.

(*a*) What exercise price leaves you indifferent between holding the put or exercising it now?

(*b*) How does this "break-even" exercise price change if the interest rate is increased?

6. After a good night's sleep, your boss, the CFO in Section 21-1, still hasn't got it. Try again. Explain why the Mark I microcomputer has a positive NPV even though DCF analyses of both the Mark I and the Mark II seem to show *negative* NPVs.

7. Dr. Livingstone I. Presume holds £600,000 in East African gold stocks. Bullish as he is on gold mining, he requires absolute assurance that at least £500,000 will be available in 6 months to fund an expedition. Describe two ways for Dr. Presume to achieve this goal. There is an active market for puts and calls on East African gold stocks, and the sterling rate of interest is 12.4 percent per year.

Questions and Problems

1. Describe each of the following situations in the language of options:

(*a*) Drilling rights to undeveloped heavy crude oil in southern California. Development and production of the oil now is a negative-NPV endeavor. (The break-even oil price is $32 per barrel, versus a spot price of $20.) However, the decision to develop can be put off for up to 5 years. Development costs are expected to increase by 5 percent per year.

(*b*) A restaurant is producing net cash flows, after all out-of-pocket expenses, of $700,000 per year. There is no upward or downward trend in the cash flows, but they fluctuate, with an annual standard deviation of 15 percent. The real estate occupied by the restaurant is owned, not leased, and could be sold for $5 million. Ignore taxes.

(*c*) A variation on part (*b*): Assume the restaurant faces known fixed costs of $300,000 per year, incurred as long as the restaurant is operating. Thus

$$\text{Net cash flow} = \text{revenue less variable costs} - \text{fixed costs}$$
$$\$700,000 = 1,000,000 - 300,000$$

The annual standard deviation of the forecast error of revenue less variable costs is 10.5 percent. The interest rate is 10 percent. Ignore taxes.

(*d*) The British-French treaty giving a concession to build a railroad link under the English Channel also requires the concessionaire to propose by the year 2000 to build a "drive-through link" if "technical and economic conditions permit . . . and the increase in traffic shall justify it without undermining the expected return on the first [rail] link." Other companies will not be permitted to build a link before the year 2020.

2. Perform a sensitivity analysis on Table 21-1. The CFO would like to know how the present value of the option on the Mark II depends on:

(*a*) The degree of uncertainty (standard deviation)

(*b*) The forecasted NPV of the Mark II

(*c*) The rate of growth of the micro market (which determines the possible *scale* of the Mark II project)

3. You own a 1-year call option on 1 acre of Los Angeles real estate. The exercise price is $2 million, and the current, appraised market value of the land is

$1.7 million. The land is currently used as a parking lot, generating just enough money to cover real estate taxes. Over the last 5 years, similar properties have appreciated by 20 percent per year. The annual standard deviation is 15 percent and the interest rate 12 percent. How much is your call worth? Use the Black-Scholes formula and Appendix Table 6.

4. A variation on question 3: Suppose the land is occupied by a warehouse, generating rents of $150,000 after real estate taxes and all other out-of-pocket costs. The value of the land plus warehouse is again $1.7 million. Other facts are as in question 3. You have a *European* call option. What is it worth?

5. The price of Wigeon Corporation stock is $100. During each of the next two 6-month periods the price may either rise by 25 percent or fall by 20 percent (equivalent to a standard deviation of 31.5 percent a year). At month 6 the company will pay a dividend of $20. The interest rate is 10 percent per 6-month period. What is the value of a 1-year American call option with an exercise price of $80? Now recalculate the option value, assuming that the dividend is equal to 20 percent of the with-dividend stock price.

6. Buffelhead's stock price is $220 and could halve or double in each 6-month period (equivalent to an annual standard deviation of 98 percent). A 1-year call option on Buffelhead has an exercise price of $165. The interest rate is 21 percent a year.
   (*a*) What is the value of the Buffelhead call?
   (*b*) Now calculate the option delta for the second 6 months if (i) the stock price rises to $440 and (ii) the stock price falls to $110.
   (*c*) How does the call option delta vary with the level of the stock price? Explain, intuitively, why.
   (*d*) Suppose that in month 6 the Buffelhead stock price is $110. How at that point could you replicate an investment in the stock by a combination of call options and risk-free lending? Show that your strategy does indeed produce the same returns as those from an investment in the stock.

7. Suppose that you own an American put option on Buffelhead stock (see question 6) with an exercise price of $220.
   (*a*) Would you ever want to exercise the put early?
   (*b*) Calculate the value of the put.
   (*c*) Now compare the value with that of an equivalent European put option.

8. Recalculate the value of the Buffelhead call option (see question 6), assuming that the option is American and that at the end of the first 6 months the company pays a dividend of $25. (Thus the price at the end of the year is either double or half the *ex*-dividend price in month 6.) How would your answer change if the option were European?

9. Suppose that you have an option which allows you to sell Buffelhead stock (see question 6) in month 6 for $165 *or* to buy it in month 12 for $165. What is the value of this unusual option?

10. The current price of Northern Airlines stock is $100. During each 6-month period it will either rise by 11.1 percent or fall by 10 percent (equivalent to an annual standard deviation of 14.9 percent). The interest rate is 5 percent per 6-month period.
    (*a*) Calculate the value of a 1-year European put option on Northern stock with an exercise price of $102.
    (*b*) Recalculate the value of the Northern put option, assuming that it is an American option.

11. The current price of United Carbon (UC) stock is $200. The standard deviation is 22.3 percent a year, and the interest rate is 21 percent a year. A 1-year call option on UC has an exercise price of $180.
    (*a*) Use the Black-Scholes model to value the call option on UC.
    (*b*) Use the formula given in Section 21-2 to calculate the up and down moves that you would use if you valued the UC option with the one-period binomial method. Now value the option by using that method.
    (*c*) Recalculate the up and down moves and revalue the option by using the two-period binomial method.
    (*d*) Use your answer to part (*c*) to calculate the option delta (i) today, (ii) next period if the stock price rises, and (iii) next period if the stock price falls. Show at each point how you would replicate a call option with a levered investment in the company's stock.

12. Options have many uses. They allow you (*a*) to take a levered position in the asset, (*b*) to sell the asset short, (*c*) to ensure against a fall in the value of the asset, (*d*) to hedge against any changes in the asset value, and (*e*) to bet on the asset's variability. Explain *how* you can use options in each of these ways. Are there other means to achieve the same ends?

13. Suppose you construct an option hedge by buying a levered position in delta shares of stock and selling one call option. As the share price changes, the option delta changes, and you will need to adjust your hedge. You can minimize the cost of adjustments if changes in the stock price have only a small effect on the option delta. Construct an example to show whether the option delta is likely to vary more if you hedge with an in-the-money option, an at-the-money option, or an out-of-the-money option.

14. Suppose you expect to need a new plant that will be ready to produce turbo-encabulators in 36 months. If design A is chosen, construction must begin immediately. Design B is more expensive, but you can wait 12 months before breaking ground. Figure 21-10 shows the cumulative present value of construction costs for the two designs up to the 36-month deadline. Assume that the designs, once built, will be equally efficient and have equal production capacity.
    A standard discounted-cash-flow analysis ranks design A ahead of design B. But suppose the demand for turbo-encabulators falls and the new factory is not needed; then, as Figure 21-10 shows, the firm is better off with design B, provided the project is abandoned before month 24.
    Describe this situation as the choice between two (complex) call options. Then describe the same situation in terms of (complex) abandonment put options. The two descriptions should imply identical payoffs to each design, given optimal exercise strategies.

15. In August 1986 Salomon Brothers issued 4-year Standard and Poor's 500 Index Subordinated Notes (SPINS). The notes paid no interest, but at maturity the investor received the face value plus a possible bonus. The bonus was equal to $1000 times the proportionate appreciation in the market index.
    (*a*) What would be the value of SPINS if issued today?
    (*b*) If Salomon Brothers wished to hedge itself against a rise in the market index, how should it have done so?

16. Other things equal, which of these American options are you most likely to want to exercise early?

Figure 21-10 Cumulative construction cost of the two plant designs. Plant A takes 36 months to build, plant B only 24. But plant B costs more.

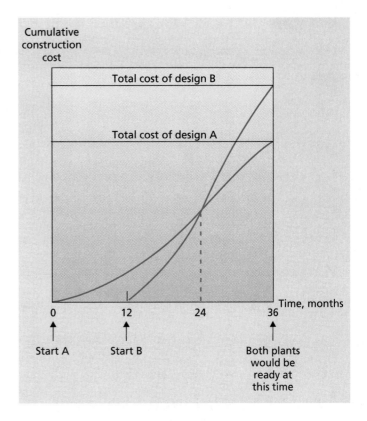

(*a*) A put option on a stock with a large dividend or a call on the same stock

(*b*) A put option on a stock that is selling well below exercise price or a call on the same stock

(*c*) A put option when the interest rate is high or the same put option when the interest rate is low

Illustrate your answer with examples, using the two-step binomial.

17. Is it better to exercise a call option on the with-dividend date or on the ex-dividend date? How about a put option? Explain.

18. Reconcile the following statements:

(*a*) "The option pricing model assumes that price depends on variance rather than beta. It is therefore inconsistent with the CAPM."

(*b*) "DCF models of company value state that higher dividends increase stock values. This is inconsistent with the option pricing model, which states that higher dividends reduce option values."

(*c*) "An increase in interest rates leads investors to demand a higher return and therefore leads to a fall in stock prices. This is inconsistent with the option pricing model, which states that higher interest rates lead to a rise in option values."

(*d*) "It's crazy to say that the value of a call option does not depend on the probability that the stock price will rise. It is clear that the greater the likelihood of a rise in the stock price, the more it makes sense to buy the call."

19. You can buy each of the following items of information about an American call option for $10 apiece: stock price; PV(exercise price); exercise price; standard deviation × square root of time to maturity; interest rate (per annum); time to maturity; value of European put; expected return on stock.
How much would you need to spend to value the option? Explain.

20. Suppose investment in the malted herring project (see Section 21-3) can be postponed to the end of 2 years.
    (*a*) Show under what circumstances you would want to delay construction for 2 years.
    (*b*) How does this additional choice affect project NPV?
    (*c*) Would NPV change if you could undertake the project *only* in years 0 or 2?

21. In Section 21-4 we described the problem faced by a utility that was contemplating an investment in equipment that would allow it to cofire coal and gas. How would the value of the option to cofire be affected if (*a*) the prices of both coal and gas were very variable, (*b*) the prices of coal and gas were highly correlated?

22. Consumers appear to require returns of 25 percent or more before they are prepared to make energy-efficient investments, even though a more reasonable estimate of the cost of capital might be around 15 percent. Here is a highly simplified problem which illustrates that such behavior *could* be rational.[20]

Suppose you have the opportunity to invest $1000 in new space-heating equipment that would generate fuel savings of $250 a year forever given current fuel prices. What is the present value of this investment if the cost of capital is 15 percent? What is the net present value?

Now recognize that fuel prices are uncertain and that the savings could equally well turn out to be $50 a year or $450 a year. If the risk-free interest rate is 10 percent, would you invest in the new equipment now or wait and see how fuel prices change? Explain.

---

[20]See, for example, A. H. Sanstad, C. Blumstein, and S. E. Stoft, "How High Are Option Values in Energy-Efficiency Investments," *Energy Policy*, **9**:739–743 (1995). However, the authors argue that in practice the option to delay investment is not sufficiently valuable to explain consumer behavior.

22

Warrants and Convertibles

Many debt issues are either packages of bonds and warrants or convertibles. The warrant gives its owner the right to buy other company securities. A convertible bond gives its owner the right to exchange the bond for other securities.

There is also convertible preferred stock—it is often used to finance mergers, for example. Convertible preferred gives its owner the right to exchange the preferred share for other securities.

What are these strange hybrids, and how should you value them? Why are they issued? We will answer each of these questions in turn.

22-1   WHAT IS A WARRANT?

A significant proportion of private placement bonds and a smaller proportion of public issues are sold with warrants. In addition, warrants are sometimes sold with issues of common or preferred stock; they are also often given to investment bankers as compensation for underwriting services or used to compensate creditors in the case of bankruptcy.[1]

In April 1994 Centennial Technologies, a small firm producing font cartridges for laser printers, raised $6.2 million by selling 1 million shares at $6 each and 1 million warrants at $.20 each. Each of these warrants allowed the holder to buy one share for $7.20 at any time before April 1997. This meant that the share price needed to rise by at least 20 percent over the 3-year period to make it worthwhile to exercise the warrants. As we write this chapter, 1 year after the issue, the share price of Centennial stock has nearly doubled to $11½ and the price of the warrants has multiplied over 20 times to $4¼.

The warrant holders are not entitled to vote or to receive dividends. But the exercise price of the warrant is automatically adjusted for any stock dividends or stock splits. For example, if Centennial splits its stock 2 for 1, it must also split the warrants 2 for 1 and reduce the exercise price per warrant to 7.20/2 = $3.60.[2]

---

[1] The term *warrant* usually refers to a long-term option issued by a company on its own stock or bonds, but investment banks and other financial institutions also issue "warrants" to buy the stock of another firm. For example, in October 1994 the French bank Credit Lyonnais sold 1 million warrants that entitled their holders to buy shares in three German automobile firms.

[2] The Centennial warrant is fairly standard, but you do occasionally encounter "funnies." For example, Emerson Electric has issued a warrant in which the owner gets some money back if the warrant is *not* exercised. There are also "income warrants" that make a regular interest payment.

Figure 22-1 Relationship between warrant value and stock price. The heavy line is the lower limit for warrant value. Warrant value falls to the lower limit just before the option expires. Before expiration, warrant value lies on a curve like the one shown here.

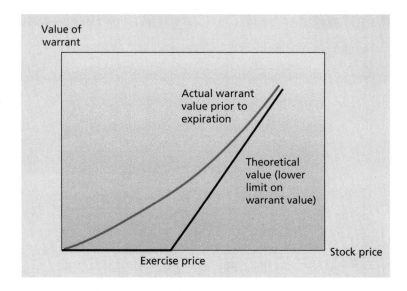

Valuing Warrants

As a trained option spotter (having read Chapter 20), you have probably already classified the Centennial warrant as a 3-year American call option exercisable at $7.20. You can depict the relationship between the value of the warrant and the value of the common stock with our standard option shorthand, as in Figure 22-1. The lower limit on the value of the warrant is the heavy line in the figure.[3] If the price of Centennial stock is less than $7.20, the lower limit on the warrant price is zero; if the price of the stock is greater than $7.20, the lower limit is equal to the stock price minus $7.20. Investors in warrants sometimes refer to this lower limit as the *theoretical* value of the warrant. It is a misleading term because both theory and practice tell us that before the final exercise date the value of the warrant should lie *above* the lower limit, on a curve like the one shown in Figure 22-1.

The height of this curve depends on two things. As we explained in Section 20-3, it depends on the variance of the stock returns per period (σ^2) times the number of periods before the option expires ($\sigma^2 t$). It also depends on the rate of interest times the length of the option period ($r_f t$). Of course as time runs out on a warrant, its price snuggles closer and closer to the lower bound. On the final day of its life, its price hits the lower bound.

Two Complications: Dividends and Dilution

If the warrant has no unusual features and the stock pays no dividends, then the value of the option can be estimated from the Black-Scholes formula described in Section 20-4.

But there is a problem when warrants are issued against dividend-paying stocks. The warrant holder is not entitled to dividends. In fact the warrant holder loses every time a cash dividend is paid, because the dividend reduces stock price and thus reduces the value of the warrant. It may pay to exercise the warrant before maturity in order to capture the extra income.[4]

---

[3]Do you remember why this is a lower limit? What would happen if, by some accident, the warrant price was *less* than the stock price minus $7.20? (See Section 20-3.)

[4]This cannot make sense unless the dividend payment is larger than the interest that could be earned on the exercise price. By *not* exercising, the warrant holder keeps the exercise price and can put this money to work.

Remember that the Black-Scholes option-valuation formula assumes that the stock pays no dividends. Thus it will not give the theoretically correct value for a warrant issued by a dividend-paying firm. However, we showed in Chapter 21 how you can use the one-step-at-a-time binomial method to value options on dividend-paying stocks.

Another complication is that exercising the warrants increases the number of shares. Therefore, exercise means that the firm's assets and profits are spread over a larger number of shares. For example, Centennial's net income in the first quarter of 1995 was $141,000, and the company had 3.1 million shares outstanding. So earnings per share were $141/3100 = \$.05$. If the warrants are exercised, there will be $3.1 + 1 = 4.1$ million shares outstanding. Unless net income is increased by the influx of cash from exercise, earnings per share will fall to $141/4100 = \$.03$. Firms with significant amounts of warrants or convertible issues outstanding are required to report earnings on a "fully diluted" basis.

This problem of *dilution* never arises with call options. If you buy or sell an option on the Chicago Board Options Exchange, you have no effect on the number of shares outstanding.

Example: Valuing United Glue's Warrants

United Glue has just issued a $2 million package of debt and warrants. Here are some basic data that we can use to value the warrants:

- Number of shares outstanding (N):   1 million
- Current stock price (P): $12
- Number of warrants issued per share outstanding (q):   .10
- Total number of warrants issued (Nq):   100,000
- Exercise price of warrants (EX): $10
- Time to expiration of warrants (t):   4 years
- Annual standard deviation of stock price changes (σ):   .40
- Rate of interest (r):   10 percent

Suppose that without the warrants the debt is worth $1.5 million. Then investors must be paying $.5 million for the warrants:

$$\begin{matrix} \text{Cost of} \\ \text{warrants} \end{matrix} = \begin{matrix} \text{total amount} \\ \text{of financing} \end{matrix} - \begin{matrix} \text{value of loan} \\ \text{without warrants} \end{matrix}$$

$$500,000 = 2,000,000 \quad - 1,500,000$$

$$\text{Each warrant costs investors } \frac{500,000}{100,000} = \$5$$

Table 22-1 shows the market value of United's assets and liabilities both before and after the issue.

Now let us take a stab at checking whether the warrants are really worth the $500,000 that investors are paying for them. Remember that the warrant is a call option to buy United stock. The stock does not pay a dividend. Therefore we can use the call option data in Appendix Table 6 to value the warrants. First we need two inputs:

$$\begin{matrix} \text{Standard} \\ \text{deviation} \end{matrix} \times \begin{matrix} \text{square root} \\ \text{of time} \end{matrix} = \sigma\sqrt{t} = .40\sqrt{4} = .80$$

$$\begin{matrix} \text{Share price divided by} \\ \text{PV(exercise money)} \end{matrix} = \frac{P}{\text{PV(EX)}} = \frac{12}{10/(1.1)^4} = 1.75$$

TABLE 22-1

• •

United Glue's market value balance sheet (in millions)

Before the Issue

Existing assets	$16	$ 4	Existing loans
		12	Common stock
			(1 million shares
			at $12 a share)
Total	$16	$16	Total

After the Issue

Existing assets	$16	$ 4	Existing loans
New assets financed		1.5	New loan without warrants
by debt and warrants	2	5.5	Total debt
		.5	Warrants
		12	Common stock
		12.5	Total equity
Total	$18	$18.0	Total

From Appendix Table 6, we find

$$\frac{\text{Call option value}}{\text{Share price}} = \frac{C}{P} = .511$$

Therefore,

$$\frac{\text{Call option}}{\text{value}} = .511 \times \frac{\text{share}}{\text{price}} = .511 \times 12 = \$6.13$$

Thus the warrant issue looks like a good deal for investors and a bad deal for United. Investors are paying $5 a share for warrants that are worth $6.13.

• • • • • • • • • • • • • • • •

*How the Value of United Warrants Is Affected by Dilution

Unfortunately, our calculations for United warrants do not tell the whole story. Remember that when investors exercise a traded call or put option, there is no change in either the company's assets or the number of shares outstanding. But, if United's warrants are exercised, the number of shares outstanding will increase by $Nq = 100,000$. Also the assets will increase by the amount of the exercise money ($Nq \times EX = 100,000 \times \$10 = \$1$ million). In other words, there will be dilution. We need to allow for this dilution when we value the warrants.

Let us call the value of United's equity V:

$$\frac{\text{Value of}}{\text{equity}} = V = \frac{\text{value of United's}}{\text{total assets}} - \frac{\text{value of}}{\text{debt}}$$

If the warrants are exercised, equity value will increase by the amount of the exercise money to $V + NqEX$. At the same time the number of shares will increase to $N + Nq$. So the share price after the warrants are exercised will be

$$\text{Share price after exercise} = \frac{V + NqEX}{N + Nq}$$

At maturity the warrant holder can choose to let the warrants lapse or to exercise them and receive the share price less the exercise price. Thus the value of the warrants will be the share price minus the exercise price or zero, whichever is the higher. Another way to write this is

$$\text{Warrant value at maturity} = \text{maximum}\left(\frac{\text{share}}{\text{price}} - \frac{\text{exercise}}{\text{price}}, \text{zero}\right)$$

$$= \text{maximum}\left(\frac{V + NqEX}{N + Nq} - EX, 0\right)$$

$$= \text{maximum}\left(\frac{V/N - EX}{1 + q}, 0\right)$$

$$= \frac{1}{1 + q}\,\text{maximum}\left(\frac{V}{N} - EX, 0\right)$$

This tells us the effect of dilution on the value of United's warrants. The warrant value is the value of $1/(1 + q)$ call options written on the stock of an alternative firm with the same total equity value V, *but with no outstanding warrants.* The alternative firm's stock price would be equal to V/N—that is, the total value of United's equity (V) divided by the number of shares outstanding (N).[5] The stock price of this alternative firm is more variable than United's stock price. So when we value the call option on the alternative firm, we must remember to use the standard deviation of the changes in V/N.

Now we can recalculate the value of United's warrants allowing for dilution. First we find the value of one call option on the stock of an alternative firm with a stock price of V/N.

$$\text{Current equity value of alternative firm} = V = \frac{\text{value of United's}}{\text{total assets}} - \frac{\text{value of}}{\text{loans}}$$

$$= 18 - 5.5 = \$12.5\text{ million}$$

$$\text{Current share price of alternative firm} = \frac{V}{N} = \frac{12.5\text{ million}}{1\text{ million}} = \$12.50$$

To use the option table we calculate

$$\text{Share price divided by PV(exercise price)} = 12.50 \div \frac{10}{(1.1)^4} = 1.83$$

Also, suppose the standard deviation of the share price changes of the alternative firm

---

[5]The modifications to allow for dilution when valuing warrants were originally proposed in F. Black and M. Scholes, "The Pricing of Options and Corporate Liabilities," *Journal of Political Economy,* **81**:637–654 (May–June 1973). Our exposition follows a discussion in D. Galai and M. I. Schneller, "Pricing of Warrants and the Valuation of the Firm," *Journal of Finance,* **33**:1333–1342 (December 1978).

is $\sigma^* = .41.$[6] Then

$$\text{Standard deviation} \times \text{square root of time} = \sigma^* \times \sqrt{t} = .41 \times \sqrt{4} = .82$$

Using a little interpolation in Appendix Table 6, we find

$$\frac{\text{Call option value}}{\text{share price}} = \frac{C}{P} = .53 \text{ (approximately)}$$

Therefore,

$$\text{Value of call on alternative firm} = \frac{C}{P} \times \frac{V}{N} = .53 \times 12.50 = \$6.63$$

The value of United warrants is equal to

$$\frac{1}{1 + q} \times \text{value of call on alternative firm} = \frac{1}{1.1} \times 6.63 = \$6.02$$

This is a somewhat lower value than the one we computed when we ignored dilution, but still a bad deal for United.

It may sound from all this as if you need to know the value of United warrants to compute their value. This is not so. The formula does not call for warrant value but for V, the value of United's equity (that is, the shares *plus* warrants). Given equity value, the formula calculates how the overall value of equity should be split up between stock and warrants. Thus, suppose that United's underwriter advises that $500,000 extra can be raised by issuing a package of bonds and warrants rather than bonds alone. Is this a fair price? You can check using the Black-Scholes formula with the adjustment for dilution.

Finally, notice that these modifications are necessary to apply the Black-Scholes formula to value a warrant. They are not needed by the warrant holder, who must decide whether to exercise at maturity. If at maturity the price of the stock exceeds the exercise price of the warrant, the warrant holder will of course exercise.

---

[6]How in practice could we compute σ^*? It would be easy if we could wait until the warrants had been trading for some time. In that case σ^* could be computed from the returns on a package of *all* the company's shares and warrants. In the present case we need to value the warrants *before* they start trading. We argue as follows: The standard deviation of the *assets* before the issue is equal to the standard deviation of a package of the common stock and the existing loans. For example, suppose that the company's debt is risk-free and that the standard deviation of stock returns *before* the bond-warrant issue is 38 percent. Then we calculate the standard deviation of the initial assets as follows:

$$\text{Standard deviation of initial assets} = \text{proportion in common stock} \times \text{standard deviation of common stock}$$

$$= \frac{12}{16} \times 38 = 28.5\%$$

Now suppose that the assets after the issue are equally risky. Then

$$\text{Standard deviation of assets after issue} = \text{proportion of equity after issue} \times \text{standard deviation of equity } (\sigma^*)$$

$$28.5 = \frac{12.5}{18} \times \text{standard deviation of equity } (\sigma^*)$$

Standard deviation of equity $(\sigma^*) = 41\%$

Notice that in our example the standard deviation of the stock returns *before* the warrant issue was slightly lower than the standard deviation of the package of stock and warrants. However, the warrant holders bear proportionately more of this risk than do the stockholders; so the bond/warrant package could either increase or reduce the risk of the stock.

22-2 WHAT IS A CONVERTIBLE BOND?

The convertible bond is a close relative of the bond-warrant package. Also, many companies choose to issue convertible preferred as an alternative to issuing packages of preferred stock and warrants. We will concentrate on convertible bonds. But almost all our comments apply to convertible preferred issues.

In 1991 Wendy's International issued $100 million of 7 percent convertible bonds due in 2006.[7] These could be converted at any time to 81.3 shares of common stock. In other words, the owner had a 15-year option to return the bond to the company and receive 81.3 shares of stock in exchange. The number of shares into which each bond can be converted is called the bond's *conversion ratio*. The conversion ratio of the Wendy's bond was 81.3.

In order to receive 81.3 shares of Wendy's stock, the owner had to surrender bonds with a face value of $1000. Therefore in order to receive one share, the owner had to surrender a face amount of 1000/81.3 = $12.30. This figure is called the *conversion price*. Anybody who bought the bond at $1000 in order to convert it into 81.3 shares paid the equivalent of $12.30 per share.

At the time of issue the price of Wendy's stock was $11. Therefore the conversion price was 12 percent higher than the stock price.

Convertibles are usually protected against stock splits or stock dividends. If Wendy's split its stock 2 for 1, the conversion ratio would be increased to 162.6 and the conversion price would drop to 1000/162.6 = $6.15.

The Convertible Menagerie

The Wendy's convertible issue is fairly typical, but you may come across more complicated cases. One of the most unusual types of convertible is the *LYON* (liquid yield option note). This is a callable and putable, convertible zero coupon bond (and you can't get much more complicated than that). LYONs have been issued by a number of large firms, including Eastman Kodak, American Airlines, and Motorola. Eurodisney once raised almost $1 billion through an issue of LYONs.

Let us look at an example. In 1990 Chemical Waste Management issued a LYON at a price of 30.7 percent. It was a 20-year zero coupon bond that was convertible at any time into a fixed number of shares, although the company could instead pay out the cash equivalent of these shares. Notice that if investors converted immediately, they would be giving up a bond worth $307. If they waited 20 years to convert, they would be relinquishing a bond worth $1000. So the cost of buying stock through the convertible increases each year.

The Chemical Waste LYON contained two other options. The company had the option to *call* the bond for cash, and the bondholders had an annual option to *put* the bond back to the company for cash. The exercise price of each of these options increased each year.[8] The put option on the LYON provided a more solid floor for investors. Even if interest rates rose and prices of other bonds fell, LYON holders had

---

[7]The Wendy's issue was a convertible subordinated debenture. The term *subordinated* indicates that the bond is a junior debt—its holders will be at the bottom of the heap of creditors in the event of default. A *debenture* is simply an unsecured bond. Therefore there are no specific assets that have been reserved to pay off the holders in the event of default. There is more about these terms in Section 24-3.

[8]To further confuse matters, the company could exercise its call option immediately, but investors could not exercise their put option until 1993. Thereafter both options had the same exercise price. However, in the first 2 years the company could not call the bond if the price of the common stock was below a specified minimum. If the bond is called, investors have a final chance to convert to common stock.

a guaranteed price at which they could sell their bonds.[9] Obviously investors who exercised the put would be giving up the opportunity to convert their bonds into stock: it would be worth taking advantage of the guarantee only if the conversion price of the bond was well below the exercise price of the put.[10]

Valuing Convertible Bonds

The owner of a convertible owns a bond and a call option on the firm's stock. So does the owner of a bond-warrant package. There are differences, of course, the most important being the requirement that a convertible owner give up the bond in order to exercise the call option. The owner of a bond-warrant package can (generally) exercise the warrant for cash and keep the bond. Nevertheless, understanding convertibles is easier if you analyze them first as bonds and then as call options.

Imagine that Eastman Kojak has issued convertible bonds with a total face value of $1 million and that these can be converted at any stage to 1 million shares of common stock. The price of Kojak's convertible bond depends on its *bond value* and its *conversion value*. The bond value is what each bond would sell for if it could *not* be converted. The conversion value is what the bond would sell for if it had to be converted immediately.

VALUE AT MATURITY.   Figure 22-2a shows the possible *bond values* when the Kojak convertible matures. As long as the value of the firm's assets does not fall below $1 million, the bond will pay off in full. But if the firm value is *less* than $1 million, there will not be enough to pay off the bondholders. In the extreme case that the assets are worthless, the bondholders will receive nothing. Thus the horizontal line in Figure 22-2a shows the payoff if the bond is repaid in full, and the sloping line shows the payoffs if the firm defaults.[11]

You can think of the bond value as a lower bound, or "floor," to the price of the convertible. But remember, if the firm falls on hard times, the bonds may not be worth very much. So the "floor" has a nasty slope.

Figure 22-2b shows the possible *conversion values* at maturity. We assume that Kojak already has 1 million shares of common stock outstanding, so the convertible holders will be entitled to half the value of the firm. For example, if the firm is worth $2 million,[12] the 1 million shares obtained by conversion would be worth $1 each. Each convertible bond can be exchanged for 1000 shares of stock and therefore would have a conversion value of $1000 \times 1 = \$1000$.

Kojak's convertible also cannot sell for less than its conversion value. If it did, smart investors would buy the convertible, exchange it rapidly for stock, and sell the stock. Their profit would be equal to the difference between the conversion value and the price of the convertible.

Therefore, there are *two* lower bounds to the price of the convertible: its bond value and its conversion value. Investors will not convert if bond value exceeds conversion value; they will do so if conversion value exceeds bond value. In other words,

---

[9]Of course, this guarantee would not be worth much if the company was in financial distress and *couldn't* buy the bonds back.

[10]The reasons for issuing LYONs are discussed in J. J. McConnell and E. S. Schwartz, "The Origin of LYONs: A Case Study in Financial Innovation," *Journal of Applied Corporate Finance*, 4:40–47 (Winter 1992). For a discussion of how to value an earlier LYON issue by Chemical Waste Management's parent company, see J. McConnell and E. S. Schwartz, "Taming LYONs," *Journal of Finance*, 41:561–576 (July 1986).

[11]You may recognize this as the position diagram for a default-free bond *minus* a put option on the assets with an exercise price equal to the face value of the bonds. See Section 20-1.

[12]Firm value is equal to the value of Kojak's common stock *plus* the value of its convertible bonds.

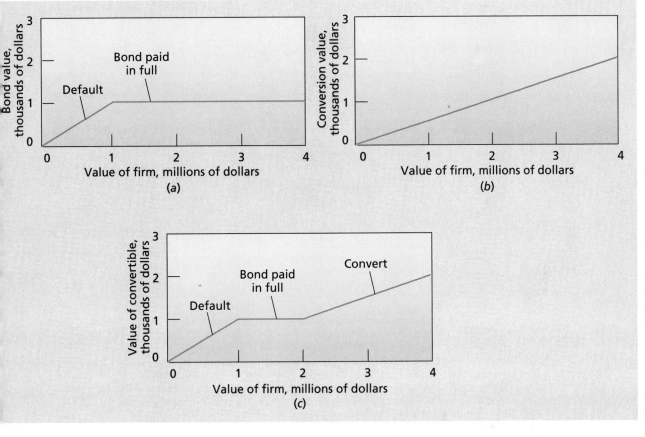

Figure 22-2 *(a)* The bond value when Eastman Kojak's convertible bond matures. If firm value is at least $1 million, the bond is paid off in full; if it is less than $1 million, the bondholders receive the value of the firm's assets. *(b)* The conversion value at maturity. If converted, the value of the convertible bond rises in proportion to firm value. *(c)* At maturity the convertible bondholder can choose to receive the principal repayment on the bond or convert to common stock. The value of the convertible bond is therefore the higher of its bond value and its conversion value.

the price of the convertible at maturity is represented by the higher of the two lines in Figure 22-2*a* and *b*. This is shown in Figure 22-2*c*.

VALUE BEFORE MATURITY.   We can also draw a similar picture to Figure 22-2 when the convertible is *not* about to mature. Because even healthy companies may subsequently fall sick and default on their bonds, other things equal, the bond value will be lower when the bond has some time to run. Thus bond value before maturity is represented by the curved line in Figure 22-3*a*.[13]

Figure 22-3*c* shows that the lower bound to the price of a convertible before maturity is again the lower of the bond value and conversion value. However, before maturity the convertible bondholders *do not have to make a now-or-never choice for or*

_____

[13]Remember, the value of a risky bond is the value of a safe bond *less* the value of a put option on the firm's assets. The value of this option increases with maturity.

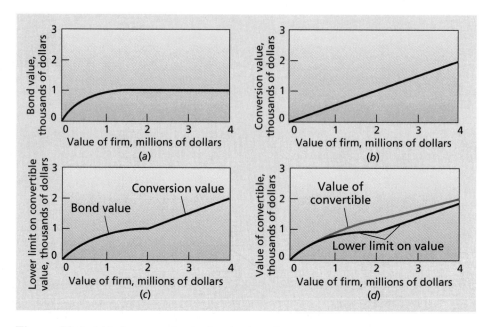

Figure 22-3 (a) Before maturity the bond value of Eastman Kojak's convertible bond is close to that of a similar default-free bond when firm value is high, but it falls sharply if firm value falls to a very low level. (b) The conversion value at maturity. If converted, the value of the convertible bond rises in proportion to firm value. (c) If investors were obliged to make an immediate decision for or against conversion, the value of the convertible would be equal to the higher of bond value or conversion value. (d) Since convertible bondholders do not have to make a decision until maturity, (c) represents a lower limit. The value of the convertible bond is worth *more* than either bond value or conversion value.

against conversion. They can wait and then, with the benefit of hindsight, take whatever course turns out to give them the highest payoff. Thus before maturity a convertible is always worth more than its lower-bound value. Its actual selling price will behave as shown by the top line in Figure 22-3*d*. The difference between the top line and the lower bound is the value of a call option on the firm. Remember, however, that this option can be exercised only by giving up the bond. In other words, the option to convert is a call option with an exercise price equal to the bond value.

Dilution and Dividends Revisited

If you want to value a convertible, it is easiest to break the problem down into two parts. First estimate bond value; then add the value of the conversion option.

When you value the conversion option, you need to look out for the same things that make warrants more tricky to value than traded options. For example, dilution may be important. If the bonds are converted, the company saves on its interest payments and is relieved of having to eventually repay the loan; on the other hand, net profits have to be divided among a larger number of shares.[14]

---

[14]In practice investors often ignore dilution and calculate conversion value as the share price times the number of shares into which the bonds can be converted. A convertible bond actually gives an option to acquire a fraction of the "new equity"—the equity *after* conversion. When we calculated the conversion value of Kojak's convertible, we recognized this by multiplying the proportion of common stock that the convertible bondholders would receive by the total value of the firm's assets (i.e., the value of the common stock plus the value of the convertible).

Companies are obliged to show in their financial statements how earnings would be affected by conversion.[15]

Also, you must remember that the convertible owner is missing out on the dividends on the common stock. If these dividends are higher than the interest on the bonds, it may pay to convert before the final exercise date in order to pick up the extra cash income.

Forcing Conversion

Companies usually retain an option to buy back or "call" the convertible bond at a preset price. If the company calls the bond, the owner has a brief period, usually about 30 days, within which to convert the bond or surrender it.[16] If a bond is surrendered, the investor receives the call price in cash. But if the share price is higher than the call price, the investor will convert the bond instead of surrendering it. Thus a call can *force conversion* if the stock price is high enough.

Most convertible bonds provide for 2 or more years of *call protection.* During this period the company is not permitted to call the bonds. However, many convertibles can be called "early," before the end of the call protection, if the stock price has risen enough to provide a nice conversion profit. For example, a convertible with a call price of $40 might be callable early if the stock price trades above $65 for at least 2 weeks.

Calling the bond obviously does not affect the total size of the company pie, but it can affect the size of the individual slices. In other words, conversion has no effect on the total value of the firm's assets, but it does affect how asset value is *distributed* among the different classes of security holders. Therefore, if you want to maximize your shareholders' slice of the pie, you must minimize the convertible bondholders' slice. That means you must not call the bonds if they are worth *less* than the call price, for that would be giving the bondholders an unnecessary present. Similarly, you must not allow the bonds to remain uncalled if their value is *above* the call price, for that would not be minimizing the value of the bonds.

Let's apply this reasoning to specific cases. Refer to Figure 22-4, which matches Figure 22-3d but has the call price drawn in as a horizontal line. Consider the firm values corresponding to three stock prices, marked A, B, and C:

- At price A, the convertible is "out of the money." Calling the bond leads to redemption for cash and hands bondholders a "free gift" equal to the difference between the call price and the convertible value. Therefore the company should not call.

- Suppose call protection ends with price at level C. Then the financial manager should call immediately, forcing the convertible value down to the call price.[17]

- What if call protection ends with price at level B, barely above the call price? In this case the financial manager will probably wait. Remember, if a call is an-

---

[15]These "diluted" earnings take into account the extra shares but not the savings in interest payments.

[16]Companies may also reserve the right to force conversion of warrants. For example, Centennial Technologies has the right to redeem its warrants for $.20 each provided that the market price of the stock is at least $9 for 10 consecutive days. Obviously, in these circumstances holders will exercise their warrants if Centennial announces its intention to redeem.

[17]The financial manager might delay calling for a time at price C if interest payments on the convertible debt are less than the extra dividends that would be paid after conversion. This delay would reduce cash payments to bondholders. Nothing is lost if the financial manager always calls "on the way down" if stock price subsequently falls toward level B. Note that investors may convert voluntarily if dividends after conversion exceed interest on the convertible bond.

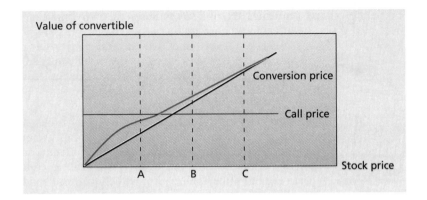

Figure 22-4 The decision to call a convertible. The financial manager should call at price C but wait at prices A and B. (*Note:* The conversion price is the straight upward-sloping line.)

nounced, bondholders have a 30-day period in which to decide whether to convert or redeem. The stock price could easily fall below the call price during this period, forcing the company to redeem for cash. Usually calls are not announced until the stock price is about 20 percent above the call price. This provides a safety margin to ensure conversion.[18]

Do companies follow these simple guidelines? On the surface they don't, for there are many instances of convertible bonds selling well above the call price. But the explanation seems to lie in the call-protection period, during which companies are not allowed to call their bonds. Paul Asquith found that most convertible bonds that are worth calling are called as soon as possible after this period ends.[19] The typical delay for bonds that can be called is slightly less than 4 months after the conversion value first exceeds the call price.

22-3 THE DIFFERENCE BETWEEN WARRANTS AND CONVERTIBLES

We have dwelt on the basic similarity between warrants and convertibles. Now let us look at some of the differences:

1. *Warrants are usually issued privately.* Packages of bonds with warrants or preferred stock with warrants tend to be more common in private placements. By contrast most convertible bonds are issued publicly.

2. *Warrants can be detached.* When you buy a convertible, the bond and the option are bundled up together. You cannot sell them separately. This may be inconvenient. If your tax position or attitude to risk inclines you to bonds, you may not want to hold options as well. Sometimes warrants are also "nondetachable," but usually you can keep the bond and sell the warrant.

3. *Warrants may be issued on their own.* Warrants do not have to be issued in conjunction with other securities. Often they are used to compensate investment

---

[18]See P. Asquith and D. Mullins, "Convertible Debt: Corporate Call Policy," *Journal of Finance*, **46**: 1273–1290 (September 1991).

[19]See P. Asquith, "Convertible Bonds Are Not Called Late," *Journal of Finance*, **50**:1275–1289 (September 1995).

bankers for underwriting services. Many companies also give their executives long-term options to buy stock. These executive stock options are not usually called warrants, but that is exactly what they are. Companies can also sell warrants on their own directly to investors, though they rarely do so.

4. *Warrants are exercised for cash.* When you convert a bond, you simply exchange your bond for common stock. When you exercise warrants, you generally put up extra cash, though occasionally you have to surrender the bond or can choose to do so. This means that bond-warrant packages and convertible bonds usually have different effects on the company's cash flow and on its capital structure.

5. *A package of bonds and warrants may be taxed differently.* There are some tax differences between warrants and convertibles. Suppose that you are wondering whether to issue a convertible bond at 100. You can think of this convertible as a package of a straight bond worth, say, 90 and an option worth 10. If you issue the bond and option separately, the IRS will note that the bond is issued at a discount and that its price will rise by 10 points over its life. The IRS will allow you, the issuer, to spread this prospective price appreciation over the life of the bond and deduct it from your taxable profits. The IRS will also allocate the prospective price appreciation to the taxable income of the bondholder. Thus, by issuing a package of bonds and warrants rather than a convertible, you may reduce the tax paid by the issuing company and increase the tax paid by the investor.[20]

22-4   WHY DO COMPANIES ISSUE WARRANTS AND CONVERTIBLES?

You hear many arguments for issuing warrants and convertibles, but most of them have a "Heads I win, tails you lose" flavor. For example, here is one such argument:[21]

> *A company that wishes to sell common stock must usually offer the new stock at 10 percent to 20 percent below the market price for the flotation to be a success.[22] However, if warrants are sold for cash, exercisable at 20 percent to 50 percent above the market price of the common, the result will be equivalent to selling common stock at a premium rather than a discount; and if the warrants are never exercised, the proceeds from their sale will become a clear profit to the company.*

There is something immediately suspicious about an argument like this. If the shareholder inevitably wins, the warrant holder must inevitably lose. But that doesn't make sense. Surely there must be some price at which it pays to buy warrants.

Suppose that your company's stock is priced at $100 and that you are considering an issue of warrants exercisable at $120. You believe that you can sell these warrants at $10. If the stock price subsequently fails to reach $120, the warrants will not

---

[20]See J. D. Finnerty, "The Case for Issuing Synthetic Convertible Bonds," *Midland Corporate Finance Journal*, 4:73–82 (Fall 1986).

[21]See S. T. Kassouf: *Evaluation of Convertible Securities*, Analytical Investors, New York, 1966, p. 6. We hasten to add that Kassouf's lapse is *not* characteristic of him. He is a respected scholar who has made important contributions to finance.

[22]This is an overestimate of the discount associated with seasoned issues. See Section 15-3.

be exercised. You will have sold warrants for $10 each, which with the benefit of hind-sight proved to be worthless to the buyer. If the stock price reaches $130, say, the warrants will be exercised. Your firm will have received the initial payment of $10 *plus* the exercise price of $120. On the other hand, it will have issued to the warrant hold-ers stock worth $130 per share. The net result is a standoff. You have received a pay-ment of $130 in exchange for a liability worth $130.

Think now what happens if the stock price rises above $130. Perhaps it goes to $200. In this case the warrant issue will end up producing a loss of $70. This is not a cash outflow but an opportunity loss. The firm receives $130, but in this case it could have sold stock for $200. On the other hand, the warrant holders gain $70: they invest $130 in cash to acquire stock that they can sell, if they like, for $200.

Our example is oversimplified—for instance, we have kept quiet about the time value of money and risk—but we hope it has made the basic point. When you sell warrants, you are selling options and getting cash in exchange. Options are valuable securities. If they are properly priced, this is a fair trade—in other words, it is a zero-NPV transaction.

You can see why the quotation is misleading. When it refers to "selling stock at a premium," the implicit comparison is with the market value of the stock today. The relevant comparison is with what it may be worth tomorrow.

Managers often use similar arguments to justify the sale of convertibles. For ex-ample, several surveys have revealed two main motives for their use. A large number of managers look on convertibles as "cheap debt." A somewhat higher proportion re-gard them as a deferred sale of stock at an attractive price.[23]

We have seen that a convertible is like a package of a straight bond and an op-tion. The difference between the market value of the convertible and that of the straight bond is therefore the price investors place on the call option. The convert-ible is "cheap" only if this price overvalues the option.

What then of the other managers—those who regard the issue as a deferred sale of common stock? A convertible bond gives you the right to buy stock by giving up a bond.[24] Bondholders may decide to do this, but then again they may not. Thus is-sue of a convertible bond *may* amount to a deferred stock issue. But if the firm *needs* equity capital, a convertible issue is an unreliable way of getting it.

Taken at their face value the motives of these managers are irrational. Convertibles are not just cheap debt, nor are they a deferred sale of stock. But we suspect that these simple phrases encapsulate some more complex and rational motives.

Notice that convertibles tend to be issued by the smaller and more speculative firms. They are almost invariably unsecured and generally subordinated.[25] Now put yourself in the position of a potential investor. You are approached by a small firm

---

[23]See, for example, E. F. Brigham, "An Analysis of Convertible Debentures: Theory and Some Empirical Evidence," *Journal of Finance*, **21**:35–54 (March 1966).

[24]That is much the same as already having the stock together with the right to sell it for the convertible's bond value. In other words, instead of thinking of a convertible as a bond plus a call option, you could think of it as the stock plus a put option. Now you see why it is wrong to think of a convertible as equiv-alent to the sale of stock; it is equivalent to the sale of both stock *and* a put option. If there is any possi-bility that investors will want to hold onto their bond, the put option will have some value.

[25]The Wendy's convertible was a subordinated debenture. See footnote 7.

with an untried product line that wants to issue some junior unsecured debt. You know that if things go well, you will get your money back, but if they do not, you could easily be left with nothing. Since the firm is in a new line of business, it is difficult to assess the chances of trouble. Therefore you don't know what the fair rate of interest is. Also, you may be worried that once you have made the loan, management will be tempted to run extra risks. It may take on additional senior debt, or it may decide to expand its operations and go for broke on your money. In fact, if you charge a very high rate of interest, you could be encouraging this to happen.

What can management do to protect you against a wrong estimate of the risk and to assure you that its intentions are honorable? In crude terms, it can give you a piece of the action. You don't mind the company running unanticipated risks as long as you share in the gains as well as the losses.[26]

Convertible securities and warrants make sense whenever it is unusually costly to assess the risk of debt or whenever investors are worried that management may not act in the bondholders' interest.[27]

You can also think of a convertible issue as a *contingent* issue of equity. If a company's investment opportunities expand, its stock price is likely to increase, allowing the financial manager to call and force conversion of a convertible bond into equity. Thus the company gets fresh equity when it is most needed for expansion. Of course, it is also stuck with debt if the company does not prosper.[28]

The relatively low coupon rate on convertible bonds may also be a convenience for rapidly growing firms facing heavy capital expenditures. They may be willing to give up the conversion option to reduce immediate cash requirements for debt service. Without the conversion option, lenders might demand extremely high (promised) interest rates to compensate for the probability of default. This would not only force the firm to raise still more capital for debt service but also increase the risk of financial distress. Paradoxically, lenders' attempts to protect themselves against default may actually increase the probability of financial distress by increasing the burden of debt service on the firm.[29]

---

[26]See M. J. Brennan and E. S. Schwartz, "The Case for Convertibles," *Journal of Applied Corporate Finance,* **1**:55–64 (Summer 1988).

[27]Changes in risk ought to be more likely when the firm is small and its debt is low-grade. If so, we should find that the convertible bonds of such firms offer their owners a larger potential ownership share. This is indeed the case. See C. M. Lewis, R. J. Rogalski, and J. K. Seward, "An Empirical Analysis of Convertible Debt Financing by NYSE/AMEX and NASDAQ Firms," unpublished paper, Amos Tuck School of Business Administration, Dartmouth College, August 1994.

[28]Jeremy Stein points out that an issue of a convertible sends a better signal to investors than a straight equity issue. As we explained in Chapter 15, announcement of a common stock issue prompts worries of overvaluation and usually depresses stock price. Convertibles are hybrids of debt and equity and send a less negative signal. Also, if the company is likely to need equity, its willingness to issue a convertible, and to take the chance that stock price will rise enough to allow forced conversion, also signals management's confidence. See J. Stein, "Convertible Bonds as Backdoor Equity Financing," *Journal of Financial Economics,* **32**:3–21 (1992).

[29]This fact led to an extensive body of literature on "credit rationing." A lender rations credit if it is irrational to lend more to a firm regardless of the interest rate the firm is willing to *promise* to pay. Whether this can happen in efficient, competitive capital markets is controversial. We give an example of credit rationing in Chapter 32. For a review of this literature, see E. Baltensperger, "Credit Rationing: Issues and Questions," *Journal of Money, Credit and Banking,* **10**:170–183 (May 1978).

22-5 SUMMARY

Instead of issuing straight bonds, companies may sell either packages of bonds and warrants or convertible bonds.

A warrant is just a long-term call option issued by the company. You already know a good deal about valuing call options. You know from Chapter 20 that call options must be worth at least as much as the stock price less the exercise price. You know that their value is greatest when they have a long time to expiration, when the underlying stock is risky, and when the interest rate is high.

Warrants are somewhat trickier to value than call options traded on the options exchanges. First, because they are long-term options, it is important to recognize that the warrant holder does not receive any dividends. Second, dilution must be allowed for.

A convertible bond gives its holder the right to swap the bond for common stock. The rate of exchange is usually measured by the *conversion ratio*—that is, the number of shares that the investor gets for each bond. Sometimes the rate of exchange is expressed in terms of the *conversion price*—that is, the face value of the bond that must be given up in order to receive one share.

Convertibles are like a package of a bond and a call option. When you evaluate the conversion option, you must again remember that the convertible holder does not receive dividends and that conversion results in dilution of the common stock. There are two other things to watch out for. One is the problem of default risk. If the company runs into trouble, you may have not only a worthless conversion option but also a worthless bond. Second, the company may be able to force conversion by calling the bond. It should do this when the market price of the convertible exceeds the call price.

You hear a variety of arguments for issuing warrants or convertibles. Convertible bonds and bonds with warrants are almost always junior bonds and are frequently issued by risky companies. We think that this says something about the reasons for their issue. Suppose that you are lending to an untried company. You are worried that the company may turn out to be riskier than you thought or that it may issue additional senior bonds. You can try to protect yourself against such eventualities by imposing very restrictive conditions on the debt, but it is often simpler to allow some extra risk as long as you get a piece of the action. The convertible and bond-warrant package give you a chance to participate in the firm's successes as well as its failures. They diminish the possible conflicts of interest between bondholder and stockholder.

Further Reading

The items listed in Chapter 20 under "Further Reading" are also relevant to this chapter, in particular Black and Scholes's discussion of warrant valuation.

Ingersoll's work represents the "state of the art" in valuing convertibles:
J. E. Ingersoll: "A Contingent Claims Valuation of Convertible Securities," *Journal of Financial Economics*, **4**:289–322 (May 1977).

Ingersoll also examines corporate call policies on convertible bonds in:
J. E. Ingersoll: "An Examination of Corporate Call Policies on Convertible Securities," *Journal of Finance*, **32**:463–478 (May 1977).

Brennan and Schwartz's paper was written about the same time as Ingersoll's and reaches essentially the same conclusions; they also present a general procedure for valuing convertibles:

M. J. Brennan and E. S. Schwartz: "Convertible Bonds: Valuation and Optimal Strategies for Call and Conversion," *Journal of Finance*, **32**:1699–1715 (December 1977).

Two useful articles on warrants are:

E. S. Schwartz: "The Valuation of Warrants: Implementing a New Approach," *Journal of Financial Economics*, **4**:79–93 (January 1977).

D. Galai and M. A. Schneller: "Pricing of Warrants and the Value of the Firm," *Journal of Finance*, **33**:1333–1342 (December 1978).

Asquith's analysis of the effect of call protection provides evidence that firms' decisions on calling convertibles are more efficient than was previously believed:

P. Asquith: "Convertible Bonds Are Not Called Late," *Journal of Finance*, **50**:1275–1289 (September 1995).

For a nontechnical discussion of the pricing of convertibles and the reasons for their use, see:

M. J. Brennan and E. S. Schwartz: "The Case for Convertibles," *Journal of Applied Corporate Finance*, **1**:55–64 (Summer 1988).

Quiz

1. Associated Elk warrants entitle the owner to buy one share at $40.
   (*a*) What is the "theoretical" value of the warrant if the stock price is:
      (i) $20?
      (ii) $30?
      (iii) $40?
      (iv) $50?
      (v) $60?
   (*b*) Plot the theoretical value of the warrant against the stock price.
   (*c*) Suppose the stock price is $60 and the warrant price is $5. What would you do?

2. In 1994 Viacom issued warrants. Each warrant can be exercised before 1999 at a price of $70 per share. The stock price is currently $46.
   (*a*) Does the warrant holder have a vote?
   (*b*) Does the warrant holder receive dividends?
   (*c*) If the stock were split 3 for 1, how would the exercise price be adjusted?
   (*d*) Suppose that, instead of reducing the exercise price after a 3-for-1 split, the company gives each warrant holder the right to buy *three* shares at $70 apiece. Would this have the same effect?
   (*e*) What is the "theoretical" value of the warrant?
   (*f*) Prior to maturity, is the warrant worth more or less than the "theoretical" value?
   (*g*) *Other things being equal,* would the warrant be more or less valuable if:
      (i) The company increased its rate of dividend payout?
      (ii) The interest rate declined?
      (iii) The stock became riskier?
      (iv) The company extended the exercise period?
      (v) The company reduced the exercise price?

(*b*) A few companies issue perpetual warrants (that is, warrants with no final exercise date). Suppose that the Viacom warrants were perpetual. In what circumstances might it make sense for investors to exercise their warrants?

3. Amalgamated Sludge has outstanding 10 million warrants, each of which may be converted into one share of common stock. Assume that net income is $40 million and that there are 20 million shares outstanding.
   (*a*) Calculate earnings per share.
   (*b*) Calculate earnings per share on a fully diluted basis.

4. Suppose that Maple Aircraft has issued a 4¾ percent convertible subordinated debenture due 2002. The conversion price is $47.00 and the debenture is callable at 102.75. The market price of the convertible is 91 percent of face value, and the price of the common is $41.50. Assume the value of the bond in the absence of a conversion feature is about 65 percent of face value.
   (*a*) What is the conversion ratio of the debenture?
   (*b*) If the conversion ratio were 50, what would be the conversion price?
   (*c*) What is the conversion value?
   (*d*) At what stock price is the conversion value equal to the bond value?
   (*e*) Can the market price be less than the conversion value?
   (*f*) How much is the convertible holder paying for the option to buy one share of common stock?
   (*g*) By how much does the common have to rise by 2002 to justify conversion?
   (*h*) When should Maple call the debenture?

5. Financing with convertible debt is especially appropriate for small, rapidly growing, or risky companies. Briefly explain why.

Questions and Problems

1. Refer again to the Centennial Technologies warrant discussed in Section 22-1. Immediately after the issue Centennial had 3 million shares and 1 million warrants outstanding. Suppose Centennial splits its stock 3 for 1 (i.e., each share of stock is split into three shares).
   (*a*) After the stock split how many shares and warrants are outstanding?
   (*b*) What would be the exercise price of the warrants after the split? Would this also be adjusted?
   (*c*) Suppose that when the warrants expire, the stock price is $10. What is the value of the warrants?
   (*d*) Suppose that 1 year *before* expiration the stock price is $10. Would the warrants sell for more or less than your answer to (*c*)? Would they have sold for their theoretical value? Explain.
   (*e*) In 1994 Centennial's net income was $464,000, and at year-end there were 3 million shares outstanding. Calculate its undiluted and diluted earnings per share.

*2. How would you use the Black-Scholes formula to compute the value of the Centennial Technologies warrant immediately after its issue, assuming a stock price of $6 and a warrant price of $.20? Begin by ignoring the problem of dilution. Then go on to describe how dilution would affect your calculations.

3. Occasionally firms extend the life of warrants that would otherwise expire unexercised. What is the cost of doing this?

*4. Here's a question on dilution: The Electric Bassoon Company has outstanding 2000 shares with a total market value of $20,000 *plus* 1000 warrants with a total market value of $5000. Each warrant gives its holder the option to buy one share at $20.

(*a*) To value the warrants, you first need to value a call option on an alternative share. What is the current price of this alternative share? How might you calculate its standard deviation?

(*b*) Suppose that the value of a call option on this alternative share were $6. Calculate whether the Electric Bassoon warrants were undervalued or overvalued.

5. The Surplus Value Company had $10 million (face value) of convertible bonds outstanding in 1990. Each bond has the following features:

- Conversion price: $25
- Current call price: 105 (percent of face value)
- Current trading price: 130 (percent of face value)
- Maturity: 2000
- Current stock price: $30 (per share)
- Interest rate: 10 (coupon as percent of face value)

(*a*) What is the bond's conversion value?
(*b*) Can you explain why the bond is selling above conversion value?
(*c*) Should Surplus call? What will happen if it does so?

6. Growth-Tech has issued $10 million of a 10 percent subordinated convertible debenture. Assume:

- Net income: $50 million
- Number of shares outstanding: 2.5 million
- Conversion ratio: 50
- Tax rate: 50 percent

(*a*) Calculate earnings per share.
(*b*) Calculate earnings per share on a fully diluted basis.

7. Associated Elk warrants have an exercise price of $40. The share price is $50. The dividend on the stock is $3, and the interest rate is 10 percent.

(*a*) Would you exercise your warrants now or later? State why.
(*b*) If the dividend increased to $5, it could pay to exercise now if the stock price had low variability and it could be better to exercise later if the stock price had high variability. Explain why.

8. "The company's decision to issue warrants should depend on the management's forecast of likely returns on the stock." Do you agree?

9. In each case, state which of the two securities is likely to provide the higher return:

(*a*) When the stock price rises (stock *or* convertible bond?)
(*b*) When interest rates fall (straight bond *or* convertible bond?)

(*c*) When the specific risk of the stock decreases (straight bond *or* convertible bond?)

(*d*) When the dividend on the stock increases (stock *or* convertible bond?)

10. Towncorp has issued 3-year warrants to buy 12 percent perpetual debentures at a price of 120 percent. The current interest rate is 12 percent, and the standard deviation of returns on the bond is 20 percent. Use the Black-Scholes model to obtain a rough estimate of the value of Towncorp warrants.

11. Moose Stores has outstanding 1 million shares of common stock with a total market value of $40 million. It now announces an issue of 1 million warrants at $5 each. Each warrant entitles the owner to buy one Moose share for a price of $30 at any time within the next 5 years. Moose Stores has stated that it will not pay a dividend within this period.

   The standard deviation of the returns on Moose's equity is 20 percent a year, and the interest rate is 8 percent.

   (*a*) What is the market value of each warrant?

   (*b*) What is the market value of each share after the warrant issue? (*Hint:* The value of the shares is equal to the total value of the equity less the value of the warrants.)

12. Look again at question 11. Suppose that Moose now forecasts the following dividend payments:

End of Year:	Dividend
1	$2
2	3
3	4
4	5
5	6

   Reestimate the market values of the warrant and stock.

13. Occasionally it is said that issuing convertible bonds is better than issuing stock when the firm's shares are undervalued. Suppose that the financial manager of the Butternut Furniture Company does in fact have inside information indicating that the Butternut stock price is too low. Butternut's future earnings will in fact be higher than investors expect. Suppose further that the inside information cannot be released without giving away a valuable competitive secret. Clearly, selling shares at the present low price would harm Butternut's existing shareholders. Will they also lose if convertible bonds are issued? If they do lose in this case, is the loss more or less than it would be if common stock is issued?

   Now suppose that investors forecast earnings accurately, but still undervalue the stock because they overestimate Butternut's actual business risk. Does this change your answers to the questions posed in the preceding paragraph? Explain.

14. Banks or insurance companies sometimes negotiate "equity kickers" when lending money. The firm pays interest and also gives warrants to the lender.

Thus the lender has an equity interest in the firm (via the warrants) and shares in the rewards if the firm is successful. Of course, in negotiating the loan, the lender always has the alternative of forgoing the warrants and demanding a higher interest rate instead. What are the advantages of the equity-kicker arrangement compared to this alternative? In what circumstances would use of the equity kicker be most sensible?

15. This question illustrates that when there is scope for the firm to vary its risk, lenders may be more prepared to lend if they are offered a piece of the action through the issue of a convertible bond.

    Ms. Blavatsky is proposing to form a new start-up firm with initial assets of $10 million. She can invest this money in one of two projects. Each has the same expected payoff, but one has more risk than the other. The relatively safe project offers a 40 percent chance of a $12.5 million payoff and a 60 percent chance of an $8 million payoff. The risky project offers a 40 percent chance of a $20 million payoff and a 60 percent chance of a $5 million payoff.

    Ms. Blavatsky initially proposes to finance the firm by an issue of straight debt with a promised payoff of $7 million. Ms. Blavatsky will receive any remaining payoff. Show the possible payoffs to the lender and to Ms. Blavatsky (*a*) if she chooses to invest in the safe project and (*b*) if she chooses to invest in the risky project. Which project is Ms. Blavatsky likely to choose? Which will the lender want her to choose?

    Suppose now that Ms. Blavatsky offers to make the debt convertible into 50 percent of the value of the firm. Show that in this case the lender receives the same expected payoff from the two projects.

16. Piglet Pies has issued a zero coupon 10-year bond, which can be converted into 10 Piglet shares. Comparable straight bonds are yielding 8 percent. Piglet stock is priced at $50 a share.
    (*a*) Suppose that you had to make a now-or-never decision on whether to convert or to stay with the bond. Which would you do?
    (*b*) If the convertible bond is priced at $550, how much are investors paying for the option to buy Piglet shares?

17. Rupert Thorndike, the autocratic CEO of Thorndike Oil, was found dead this morning in a pool of blood on his office floor. He had been shot through the head. Yesterday Thorndike had flatly rejected an offer by T. Spoone Dickens to buy all Thorndike Oil's assets for $1 billion cash, effective January 1, 1998. With Thorndike out of the way, Dickens's offer will be immediately accepted.

    The immediate suspects are Thorndike's two nieces, Doris and Patsy, and his nephew John.

    Thorndike Oil's capital structure is as follows:

    ■ *Debt:* $250 million face value, issued in 1985 at a coupon rate of 6 percent, with market value of 60 percent of face value. This debt will be paid off at par if Dickens's offer goes through.

    ■ *Stock:* 30 million shares closing yesterday at $10 per share.

    ■ *Warrants:* Warrants to buy an additional 20 million shares at $10 per share, expiring December 31, 1997. The last trade of the warrants was at $1 per warrant.

Here are Doris, John, and Patsy's stakes in Thorndike Oil:

	Debt (Market Value)	Stock (Number of Shares)	Warrants (Number)
Doris	$6 million	1.0 million	0
John	0	.5 million	2 million
Patsy	0	1.5 million	1 million

Which niece or nephew stands to gain most (in portfolio value) by eliminating old Thorndike and allowing Dickens's offer to succeed? Explain. Make additional assumptions if you find them necessary.

PART seven

DEBT
FINANCING

23

Valuing Risky Debt

How do you estimate the present value of a company's bonds? The answer is simple. You take the cash flows and discount them at the opportunity cost of capital. Therefore, if a bond produces cash flows of C dollars per year for N periods and is then repaid at its face value ($1000), the present value is

$$PV = \frac{C}{1 + r_1} + \frac{C}{(1 + r_2)^2} + \cdots + \frac{C}{(1 + r_N)^N} + \frac{\$1000}{(1 + r_N)^N}$$

where $r_1, r_2, \ldots, r_N$ are the appropriate discount rates for the cash flows to be received by the bond's owner in periods $1, 2, \ldots, N$.

That is correct as far as it goes but it does not tell us anything about what *determines* the discount rates. For example:

1. In 1945, U.S. Treasury bills offered a return of .4 percent: At their 1981 peak they offered a return of over 17 percent. Why does the same security offer radically different yields at different times?

2. In May 1995 the U.S. Treasury could borrow for 1 year at an interest rate of 5 percent, but it had to pay a rate of about 7 percent for 20-year loans. Why do bonds maturing at different dates offer different rates of interest? In other words, why is there a *term structure* of interest rates?

3. In May 1995 the United States government could issue long-term bonds at a rate of about 7 percent. You could not have borrowed at that rate. Why not? What explains the premium you have to pay?

These questions lead to deep issues which will keep economists simmering for years. But we can give general answers and at the same time present some fundamental ideas.

Why should the financial manager care about these ideas? Who needs to know how bonds are priced as long as the bond market is active and efficient? Efficient markets protect the ignorant trader. If it is necessary to check whether the price is right for a proposed bond issue, you can check the prices of similar bonds. There is no need to worry about the historical behavior of interest rates, about the term structure, or about the other issues discussed in this chapter.

We do not believe that ignorance is desirable even when it is harmless. At least you ought to be able to read *The Wall Street Journal* and talk to investment bankers. More important, you will encounter many problems of bond pricing where there are no similar instruments already traded. How do you evaluate a private placement with a custom-tailored repayment schedule? How about financial leases? In Chapter 26 we will see that they are essentially debt contracts, but often extremely complicated ones, for which traded bonds are not close substitutes. You will find that the terms, concepts, and facts presented in this chapter are essential to the analysis of these and other practical problems in financing covered in later chapters.

We start, therefore, with our first question: "Why does the general level of interest rates change over time?"

23-1 THE CLASSICAL THEORY OF INTEREST

Real Interest Rates

Suppose that everyone knows that there is not going to be any inflation. If so, all interest rates are *real* rates—they include no premium for anticipated inflation. What are the essential determinants of the rate of interest in such a world? The classical economist's answer to this question is summed up in the title of Irving Fisher's great book: *The Theory of Interest: As Determined by Impatience to Spend Income and Opportunity to Invest It.*[1] The real interest rate, according to Fisher, is the price which equates the supply and demand for capital. The supply depends on people's willingness to save—that is, to postpone consumption.[2] The demand depends on the opportunities for productive investment.

For example, suppose that investment opportunities generally improve. Firms have more good projects, and so are willing to invest more at any interest rate. Therefore, the rate has to rise to induce individuals to save the additional amount that firms want to invest.[3] Conversely, if investment opportunities deteriorate, there will be a fall in the real interest rate.

Fisher's theory emphasizes that the real rate of interest depends on real phenomena. A high aggregate willingness to save may be associated with such factors as high aggregate wealth (because wealthy people usually save more), an uneven distribution of wealth (an even distribution would mean few rich people, who do most of the saving), and a high proportion of middle-aged people (the young don't need to save and the old don't want to—"You can't take it with you"). Correspondingly, a high propensity to invest may be associated with a high level of industrial activity or major technological advances.

Inflation and Interest Rates

Now let us see what Irving Fisher had to say about the effect of inflation on interest rates. Suppose that consumers are equally happy with 100 apples today or 105 apples in a year's time. The real, or "apple," rate of interest is 5 percent. Suppose also that I know the price of apples will increase over the year by 10 percent. Then I will part with $100 today if I am repaid $115 at the end of the year. That $115 is needed to buy me 5 percent more apples than I can get for my $100 today. In other words, the

---

[1] Augustus M. Kelley, Publishers, New York, 1965; originally published in 1930.

[2] Some of this saving is done indirectly. For example, if you hold 100 shares of GM stock, and GM retains earnings of $1 per share, GM is saving $100 on your behalf.

[3] We assume that investors save more as interest rates rise. It doesn't *have* to be that way; here is an example of how a higher interest rate could mean *less* saving: Suppose that 20 years hence you will need $50,000 for your children's college expenses. How much will you have to set aside today to cover this obligation? The answer is the present value of $50,000 after 20 years, or $50,000/(1 + r)^{20}$. The higher the r, the lower the present value and the less you have to set aside.

nominal, or "money," rate of interest must equal the real, or "apple," rate plus the prospective rate of inflation. A change of 1 percentage point in the expected inflation rate produces a change of 1 percentage point in the nominal interest rate. That is Fisher's theory: A change in the expected inflation rate will cause the same change in the nominal interest rate.[4]

In principle, there is no upper limit to the real rate of interest. But is there any lower limit? For example, is it possible for the money rate of interest to be 5 percent and the expected rate of inflation to be 10 percent, thus giving a negative real interest rate? If this happens, you may be able to make money in the following way: You borrow $100 at an interest rate of 5 percent and you use the money to buy apples. You store the apples and sell them at the end of the year for $110, which leaves you enough to pay off your loan plus $5 for yourself.

Since easy ways to make money are rare, we can conclude that, if it doesn't cost anything to store goods, the money rate of interest is unlikely to be less than the expected rise in prices. But many goods are even more expensive to store than apples, and others cannot be stored at all (you can't store haircuts, for example). For these goods, the money interest rate can be less than the expected price rise.

COMMENT. If you look back to our discussion of inflation and discount rates in Chapter 3, you will see that our apple example is a bit oversimplified. If apples cost $1.00 apiece today and $1.10 next year, you need $1.10 \times 105 = \$115.50$ next year to buy 105 apples. The money interest rate is 15.5 percent, not 15.

The exact formula relating real and money rates is

$$1 + r_{money} = (1 + r_{real})(1 + i)$$

where i is the expected inflation rate. Thus

$$r_{money} = r_{real} + i + i(r_{real})$$

In our example, the money rate should be

$$r_{money} = .05 + .10 + .10(.05) = .155$$

When we said the money rate should be 15 percent, we ignored the "cross-product" term $i(r_{real})$. This is a common rule of thumb, because the cross-product is usually small. But there are countries where i is large (sometimes 100 percent per year or more). In such cases it pays to use the full formula.

BACK TO FISHER'S THEORY. Not all economists would agree with Fisher that the real rate of interest is unaffected by the inflation rate. For example, if changes in prices are associated with changes in the level of industrial activity, then in inflationary conditions I might want more or less than 105 apples in a year's time to compensate me for the loss of 100 today.

We wish we could show you the past behavior of interest rates and *expected* inflation. Instead, we have done the next best thing and plotted in Figure 23-1 the return on U.S. Treasury bills against the *actual* inflation. Notice that between 1926 and 1994 the return on Treasury bills has been below the inflation rate about as often as it has been above. The average real interest rate during this period was .6 percent. Since 1981 the return on bills has been significantly higher than inflation.

---

[4]The apple example was taken from R. Roll, "Interest Rates on Monetary Assets and Commodity Price Index Changes," *Journal of Finance*, 27:251–278 (May 1972).

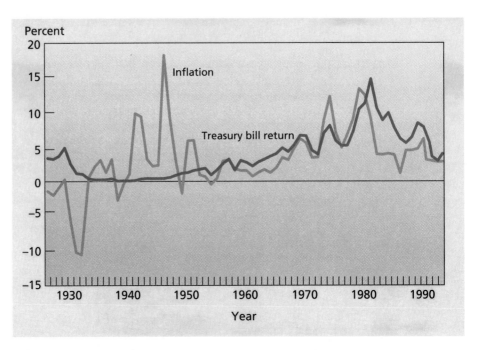

Figure 23-1 The return on U.S. Treasury bills and the rate of inflation 1926–1994. (*Source:* Ibbotson Associates, *Stocks, Bonds, Bills, and Inflation: 1995 Yearbook,* Ibbotson Associates, Inc., Chicago, 1995.)

Fisher's theory states that changes in anticipated inflation produce corresponding changes in the rate of interest. But there is little evidence of this in the 1930s and 1940s. During this period, the return on Treasury bills scarcely changed even though inflation fluctuated sharply. Either these changes in inflation were unanticipated or Fisher's theory was wrong. Since the early 1950s, there appears to have been a closer relationship between interest rates and inflation in the United States.[5] Therefore, it is worth looking more carefully at how well Fisher's theory has worked in these recent years.

Eugene Fama has suggested that one way to test Fisher's theory is to twist it around and measure whether the inflation rate can be forecasted by subtracting a constant real rate from the observed nominal rate. That is, if Fisher's theory is right,

$$\frac{\text{Nominal}}{\text{interest rate}} = \frac{\text{real}}{\text{interest rate}} + \frac{\text{inflation rate}}{\text{forecasted by investors}}$$

or

$$\frac{\text{Inflation rate}}{\text{forecasted by investors}} = \frac{\text{nominal}}{\text{interest rate}} - \frac{\text{real}}{\text{interest rate}}$$

Of course, investors cannot predict the actual inflation rate perfectly—there will be a random forecast error. But in an efficient market, we expect them to be right on the average. Thus, the forecast error should be zero on the average.

---

[5]This probably reflects government policy, which before 1951 stabilized nominal interest rates. The 1951 "accord" between the Treasury and the Federal Reserve System permitted more flexible nominal interest rates after 1951.

Suppose that we observe the nominal returns on Treasury bills and the *actual* rates of inflation. We fit the following equation to these data:

Actual
inflation = $a + b$ (nominal interest rate) + random forecasting error
rate

If Fisher is correct, the coefficient b should be close to 1.0 and the constant term a should be equal to minus the real interest rate.

We estimated b for 1953 to 1994 as .80, which is a little less than we should expect if Fisher is right *and* if the real interest rate is constant.[6]

Before leaving this topic, we must add two qualifications. First, the real interest rate is really an *expected* rate. When you buy a Treasury bill and hold it to maturity, you know what the dollar payoff will be, but the *real* payoff is uncertain because future inflation is not wholly predictable. Thus, to be perfectly precise, we should define the real interest rate as follows:

Real interest rate = *expected* real rate of return from
U.S. Treasury bills

= nominal rate of return on Treasury bills
− *expected* rate of inflation

Second, Nelson and Schwert, and Hess and Bicksler, have pointed out that the (expected) real interest rate *does* vary over time. Indeed we have seen that the real rate appears to have been unusually high since 1981. If that is so, Fama's test may be inappropriate.[7]

Until these problems have been resolved, we recommend that you look on Fisher's theory simply as a useful rule of thumb. Thus, if the expected inflation rate changes, your best bet is that there will be a corresponding change in the interest rate.

23-2   TERM STRUCTURE AND YIELDS TO MATURITY

We turn now to the relationship between short-term and long-term rates of interest. Suppose that we have a simple loan which pays $1 at time 1. The present value of this loan is

$$PV = \frac{1}{1 + r_1}$$

Thus we discount the cash flow at r_1, the rate appropriate for a one-period loan. This rate is fixed today; it is often called today's one-period **spot rate.**

If we have a loan which pays $1 at both time 1 and time 2, present value is

$$PV = \frac{1}{1 + r_1} + \frac{1}{(1 + r_2)^2}$$

---

[6]Fama fitted his equation to quarterly data for the period 1953 to 1971. His estimate of b was .98, which is almost identical to the figure that Fisher would predict. See E. F. Fama, "Short-Term Interest Rates as Predictors of Inflation," *American Economic Review,* **65**:269–282 (June 1975).

[7]C. R. Nelson and G. Schwert, "Short-Term Interest Rates as Predictors of Inflation: On Testing the Hypothesis that the Real Rate of Interest Is Constant," *American Economic Review,* **67**:478–486 (June 1977); P. Hess and J. Bicksler, "Capital Asset Prices versus Time Series Models as Predictors of Inflation," *Journal of Financial Economics,* **2**:341–360 (December 1975).

Thus the first period's cash flow is discounted at today's one-period spot rate and the second period's flow is discounted at today's two-period spot rate. The series of spot rates r_1, r_2, etc., is one way of expressing the **term structure** of interest rates.

Yield to Maturity

Rather than discounting each of the payments at a different rate of interest, we could find a single rate of discount that would produce the same present value. Such a rate is known as the **yield to maturity**, though it is in fact no more than our old acquaintance, the internal rate of return (IRR), masquerading under another name. If we call the yield to maturity y, we can write the present value as

$$PV = \frac{1}{1 + y} + \frac{1}{(1 + y)^2}$$

All you need to calculate y is the price of a bond, its annual payment, and its maturity. You can then rapidly work out the yield with the aid of a preprogrammed calculator, or you can find it in a set of bond tables.

Look at Table 23-1, which contains two pages from a mini-book of bond tables. Each page shows yields for bonds with a particular coupon. For example, suppose that you have an 8 percent bond maturing in 10 years and priced at 85. (Bond prices are quoted as percentages of the bond's face value.) Look at the second page of our mini–bond tables. This shows yields for bonds with an 8 percent coupon. If you run your eye down the column for 10 years, you will see that a bond priced at 87.54 yields 10 percent and a bond priced at 82.07 yields 11 percent. Obviously the yield on your bond lies somewhere in between, about 10.5 percent.

Real books of bond tables contain several hundred pages, each crammed with bond prices for different combinations of coupon, yield, and maturity, but in all other respects, they are the same as our mini-book of Table 23-1.

An Example: The yield to maturity is unambiguous and easy to calculate. It is the stock-in-trade of any bond dealer. By now, however, you should have learned to treat any internal rate of return with suspicion.[8] The more closely we examine the yield to maturity, the less informative it is seen to be. Here is an example.

It is 1996. You are contemplating an investment in U.S. Treasury bonds and come across the following quotations for two bonds:

Bond	Price	Yield to Maturity (IRR)
5s of '01	85.21%	8.78%
10s of '01	105.43	8.62

The phrase "5s of '01" refers to a bond maturing in 2001 paying annual interest amounting to 5 percent of the bond's face value. The interest payment is called the *coupon* payment. Bond investors would say that such bonds have a 5 percent coupon. Face value plus interest is paid back at maturity, 2001. The price of each bond is quoted as a percent of face value. Therefore, if face value is $1000, you would have to pay $852.11 to buy the bond and your yield would be 8.78 percent. Letting 1996

---

[8]See Section 5-5.

TABLE 23-1
• • • • • • • •

Each page of this mini-book of bond tables shows bond prices for a different coupon level.

COUPON = 7%   PAGE 1

| | | | YEARS | | |
Yield	6	8	10	12	14
6.00%	104.98	106.28	107.44	108.47	109.38
7.00	100.00	100.00	100.00	100.00	100.00
8.00	95.31	94.17	93.20	92.38	91.67
9.00	90.88	88.77	86.99	85.50	84.26
10.00	86.71	83.74	81.31	79.30	77.65
11.00	82.76	79.08	76.10	73.70	71.76
12.00	79.04	74.74	71.33	68.62	66.48
13.00	75.52	70.70	66.94	64.03	61.76
14.00	72.20	66.94	62.92	59.86	57.52

COUPON = 8%   PAGE 2

| | | | YEARS | | |
Yield	6	8	10	12	14
6.00%	109.95	112.56	114.88	116.94	118.76
7.00	104.83	106.05	107.11	108.03	108.83
8.00	100.00	100.00	100.00	100.00	100.00
9.00	95.44	94.38	93.50	92.75	92.13
10.00	91.14	89.16	87.54	86.20	85.10
11.00	87.07	84.31	82.07	80.27	78.82
12.00	83.23	79.79	77.06	74.90	73.19
13.00	79.60	75.58	72.45	70.02	68.13
14.00	76.17	71.66	68.22	65.59	63.59

be $t = 0$, 1997 be $t = 1$, etc., we have the following discounted-cash-flow calculation:[9]

CASH FLOWS
• •

Bond	C_0	C_1	C_2	C_3	C_4	C_5	Yield
5s of '01	−852.11	+50	+50	+50	+50	+1,050	8.78%
10s of '01	−1,054.29	+100	+100	+100	+100	+1,100	8.62

Although the two bonds mature at the same date, they presumably were issued at different times, the 5s when interest rates were low and the 10s when interest rates were high.

---

[9]Coupon payments are actually made semiannually—the owners of the 5s of '01 would receive $25 every 6 months. Thus our calculations are a little bit off what you would get from using bond tables like Table 23-1. Also, the yields are rounded, not exact.

TABLE 23-2

· ·

Calculating present value of two bonds when long-term interest rates are higher
than short-term rates

		PRESENT VALUE CALCULATIONS			
		5s OF '01		10s OF '01	
Period	Interest Rate	C_t	PV at r_t	C_t	PV at r_t
$t = 1$	$r_1 = .05$	$ 50	$ 47.62	$ 100	$ 95.24
$t = 2$	$r_2 = .06$	50	44.50	100	89.00
$t = 3$	$r_3 = .07$	50	40.81	100	81.63
$t = 4$	$r_4 = .08$	50	36.75	100	73.50
$t = 5$	$r_5 = .09$	1,050	682.43	1,100	714.92
	Totals	$1,250	$852.11	$1,500	$1,054.29

Are the 5s of '01 a better buy? Is the market making a mistake by pricing these
two issues at different yields? The only way you will know for sure is to calculate the
bonds' present values by using spot rates of interest: r_1 for 1997, r_2 for 1998, etc.
This is done in Table 23-2.

The important assumption in Table 23-2 is that long-term interest rates are
higher than short-term interest rates. We have assumed that the 1-year interest rate
is $r_1 = .05$, the 2-year rate is $r_2 = .06$, and so on. When each year's cash flow is discounted at the rate appropriate to that year, we see that each bond's present value is
exactly equal to the quoted price. Thus each bond is *fairly priced.*

Why do the 5s have a higher yield? Because for each dollar that you invest in the
5s you receive relatively little cash inflow in the first 4 years and a relatively high cash
inflow in the final year. Therefore, although the two bonds have identical maturity
dates, the 5s provide a greater proportion of their cash flows in 2001. In this sense
the 5s are a longer-term investment than the 10s. Their higher yield to maturity just
reflects the fact that long-term interest rates are higher than short-term rates.

· · · · · · · · · · · · · · · · · · ·

**Problems
with
Yield to
Maturity**

With this in mind, we can sum up the problems with the yield to maturity.

First, when a bond's yield to maturity is calculated, the *same* rate is used to discount *all* payments to the bondholder. The bondholder may actually demand different rates of return (r_1, r_2, etc.) for different periods. Unless two bonds offer exactly
the same pattern of cash flows, they are likely to have different yields to maturity.
Therefore the yield to maturity on one bond can offer only a rough guide to the appropriate yield on another.

Second, yields to maturity do not determine bond prices. It is the other way
around. The demand by companies for capital and the supply of savings by individuals combine to determine the spot rates r_1, r_2, etc. These rates then determine the
value of any package of future cash flows. Finally, *given* the value, we can compute
the yield to maturity. We cannot, however, derive the appropriate yield to maturity
without first knowing the value. We cannot, for example, assume that the yield
should be the same for two bonds with the same maturity unless they also happen to
have the same coupon.

The yield to maturity is a complicated average of spot rates of interest. Suppose that r_2 is greater than r_1. Then the yield on a 2-year coupon bond must lie between r_1 and r_2. In this case, the yield on the 2-year bond provides an underestimate of the 2-year spot rate. Of course, if r_2 is less than r_1, it would be the other way around—the yield on the 2-year bond would overestimate the 2-year spot rate. Sometimes these differences can be dramatic. For example, in Britain in 1977 the 20-year spot rate of interest r_{20} was nearly 20 percent. But the *yield* on high-coupon bonds maturing in 20 years was only about 13 percent. The reason was that short-term spot rates of interest were much lower than 20 percent. The yield on 20-year bonds was an average of short-term and long-term rates.[10]

In Chapter 5 we asserted that one problem with internal rates of return is that they don't add up. In other words, even if you know the return on A and the return on B, you cannot generally work out the return on A + B. Let us illustrate: Suppose your portfolio is evenly divided between two bonds both priced at 100. Bond A is a 1-year bond with a 10 percent coupon and therefore yields 10 percent. Bond B is a 2-year bond with an 8 percent coupon and therefore yields 8 percent. You might think that the yield on your portfolio would be halfway between at 9 percent. You would be wrong. The yield is 8.68 percent. In other words

$$200 = \frac{110 + 8}{1.0868} + \frac{108}{(1.0868)^2}$$

Thus it is dangerous to rely on yield to maturity—like most averages, it hides much of the interesting information.

....

Measuring the Term Structure

Financial managers who want just a quick, summary measure of interest rates look in the financial press at the yields to maturity on government bonds. Thus managers will make broad generalizations such as "If we borrow money today, we will have to pay an interest rate of 8 percent." But if you wish to understand why different bonds sell at different prices, you must dig deeper and look at the separate rates of interest for 1-year cash flows, for 2-year cash flows, and so on. In other words, you must look at the spot rates of interest.

To find the spot interest rate, you need the price of a bond that simply makes one future payment. Fortunately, such bonds do exist. They are known as *stripped bonds* or *strips*. Strips originated in 1982 when several investment bankers came up with a novel idea. They bought U.S. Treasury bonds and reissued their own separate mini-bonds, each of which made only one payment.[11] The idea proved to be popular with investors, who welcomed the opportunity to buy the mini-bonds rather than the complete package.

If you've got a smart idea, you can be sure that others will soon clamber onto your bandwagon. It was therefore not long before the Treasury issued its own mini-bonds.[12] The prices of these bonds are shown each day in the daily press. For

---

[10]For a good analysis of the relationship between the yield to maturity and spot interest rates, see S. M. Schaefer, "The Problem with Redemption Yields," *Financial Analysts Journal*, **33**:59–67 (July–August 1977).

[11]These mini-bonds had a variety of exotic names. The Merrill Lynch issues were known as TIGRs (Treasury Investment Growth Receipts). Those issued by Salomon Brothers were known as CATS (Certificates of Accrual on Treasury Securities).

[12]The Treasury continued to auction coupon bonds in the normal way, but investors could exchange them at the Federal Reserve Bank for stripped bonds.

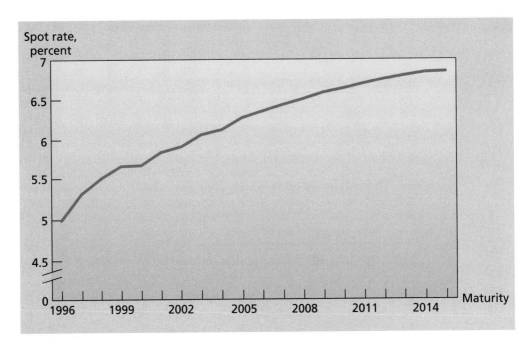

Figure 23-2 Spot rates on U.S. Treasury strips, May 1995.

example, in May 1995, a 20-year strip cost $265.25 and in return gave the investor a single payment of $1000 in May 2015. Thus the 20-year spot rate was $(1000/265.25)^{1/20} - 1 = .0686$, or 6.86 percent.[13]

In Figure 23-2 we have used the prices of strips with different maturities to plot the term structure of spot rates from 1 to 20 years. You can see that investors required an interest rate of about 5 percent from a bond that made a payment only at the end of year 1 and a rate of nearly 7 percent from a bond that paid off only in year 20.

23-3 DURATION AND VOLATILITY

In Chapter 7 we reviewed the historical performance of different security classes. We showed that since 1926 long-term government bonds have provided a higher average return than short-term bills but have also been more variable. The standard deviation of annual returns on a portfolio of long-term bonds was 8.7 percent compared with a standard deviation of 3.3 percent for bills.

We now need to look more carefully at the variability of long-term and short-term bonds. But what do we mean by these phrases? For example, a bond that matures in year 6 also makes interest payments in each of years 1 through 5. Therefore, it is somewhat misleading to describe the bond as a 6-year bond; the average time to each cash flow is less than 6 years.

[13]This is an annually compounded rate. The yields quoted by investment dealers are semiannually compounded rates.

TABLE 23-3

••

The first four columns show that the cash flow in year 6 accounts for only 58.7 percent of the present value of the 13⅛s of 2001. The final column shows how to calculate a weighted average of the time to each cash flow. This average is the bond's duration.

Year	C_t	PV(C_t) at 6.5%	Proportion of Total Value [PV(C_t)/V_t]	Proportion of Total Value × Time
1	131.25	123.24	.093	.093
2	131.25	115.72	.088	.175
3	131.25	108.66	.082	.247
4	131.25	102.02	.077	.309
5	131.25	95.80	.073	.362
6	1,131.25	775.28	.587	3.522
		$V = 1,320.72$	1.000	Duration = 4.708 years

In May 1995 Treasury 13⅛s of 2001 had a present value of 132.07 and yielded 6.5 percent. Table 23-3 shows where this present value comes from. Notice that the cash flow in year 6 accounts for only 58.7 percent of value. About 40 percent of the value comes from earlier cash flows.

Bond analysts often use the term **duration** to describe the average time to each payment. If we call the total value of the bond V, then duration is calculated as follows:[14]

$$\text{Duration} = \left[\frac{1 \times \text{PV}(C_1)}{V}\right] + \left[\frac{2 \times \text{PV}(C_2)}{V}\right] + \left[\frac{3 \times \text{PV}(C_3)}{V}\right] + \cdots$$

For the 13⅛s of 2001,

$$\text{Duration} = (1 \times .093) + (2 \times .088) + (3 \times .082) + \cdots = 4.708 \text{ years}$$

The Treasury 8s of 2001 have the same maturity as the 13⅛s, but the first 5 years' coupon payments account for a smaller fraction of the bonds' value. In this sense the 8s are longer bonds than the 13⅛s. The duration of the 8s is 5.031 years.

Consider now what happens to the prices of our two bonds as interest rates change:

	13⅛s OF 2001		8s OF 2001	
	New Price	Change	New Price	Change
Yield falls .5%	135.04	+2.25%	109.83	+2.40%
Yield rises .5%	129.20	−2.17	104.77	−2.32
Difference	5.84	4.42%	5.06	4.72%

Thus a 1 percent variation in yield causes the price of the 13⅛s to change by 4.42 percent. We can say that the 13⅛s have a **volatility** of 4.42 percent.

---

[14]We assume annual interest payments. Actual payments are semiannual.

Notice that the 8 percent bonds have the greater volatility and that they also have the longer duration. In fact, a bond's volatility is directly related to its duration:

$$\text{Volatility (percent)} = \frac{\text{duration}}{1 + \text{yield}}$$

In the case of the 13⅛s,

$$\text{Volatility (percent)} = \frac{4.708}{1.065} = 4.42$$

Volatility is a useful summary measure of the likely effect of a change in interest rates on the value of a bond. The longer a bond's duration, the greater its volatility. In Chapter 25 we will make use of this relationship between duration and volatility to describe how firms can protect themselves against interest-rate changes. Here is an example that should give you a flavor of things to come.

Suppose your firm has promised to make pension payments to retired employees. The discounted value of these pension payments is $1 million, and therefore the firm puts aside $1 million in the pension fund and invests that money in government bonds. So the firm has a liability of $1 million and (through the pension fund) an off-setting asset of $1 million. But, as interest rates fluctuate, the value of the pension liability will change and so will the value of the bonds in the pension fund. How can the firm ensure that the value of the bonds is always sufficient to meet the liabilities? Answer: By making sure that the duration of the bonds is the same as the duration of the pension liability.

23-4 EXPLAINING THE TERM STRUCTURE

The term structure in Figure 23-2 is upward-sloping. In other words, long rates of interest are higher than short rates. This is the more common pattern but sometimes it is the other way around, with short rates higher than long rates. Why do we get these shifts in term structure?

Ms. Long's Problem

Let us look at a simple example. Ms. Long wants to invest $1000 for 2 years. Two strategies open to her are described in Table 23-4. Strategy L1 is to put the money in a 1-year bond at an interest rate of r_1. At the end of the year she must then take her money and find another 1-year bond. Let us call the rate of interest on this second bond $_1r_2$—that is, the spot rate of interest at time 1 on a loan maturing at time 2.[15] As Table 23-4 shows, the final payoff to this strategy is $1000(1 + r_1)(1 + {_1r_2})$.

Of course Ms. Long cannot know for sure what the one-period spot rate of interest $_1r_2$ will be next year. Suppose that she *expects* it to be 11 percent. That is, $E(_1r_2) = .11$. The current one-period spot rate is 10 percent. The expected final payoff is

$$1000(1 + r_1)[1 + E(_1r_2)] = 1000(1.10)(1.11) = \$1221$$

Instead of making two separate investments of 1 year each, Ms. Long could invest her money today in a bond that pays off in year 2 (strategy L2 in Table 23-4). That is, she would invest at the *2-year* spot rate r_2 and receive a final payoff of $1000(1 + r_2)^2$. If $r_2 = .105$, the payoff is $1000(1.105)^2 = \$1221$.

---

[15]Be careful to distinguish $_1r_2$ from r_2, the spot interest rate on a 2-year bond held from time 0 to time 2. The quantity $_1r_2$ is a *1-year* spot rate established at time 1.

TABLE 23-4
....

Two investment strategies for Ms. Long, who wants to invest $1,000 for 2 years

Strategy	Now		Year 1		Year 2 (Final Payoff)
L1: Invest in two 1-year bonds	$1,000	→ Invest in first bond yielding r_1	$1,000(1 + r_1)$	→ Invest in second bond yielding $_1r_2$	$1,000(1 + r_1)(1 + {_1r_2})$
L2: Invest in one 2-year bond	$1,000	→ Invest in bond yielding r_2		→	$1,000(1 + r_2)^2$
Strategy L2 can be expressed as	$1,000	→ Invest for 1 year at r_1	$1,000(1 + r_1)$	→ Invest for second year at implicit forward rate f_2	$1,000(1 + r_1)(1 + f_2)$

Now look below the dashed line in Table 23-4. The table shows that strategy L2 can be reinterpreted as investing for 1 year at the spot rate r_1 and for the second year at a **forward rate** f_2. The forward rate is the extra return that Ms. Long gets by lending for 2 years rather than 1. This forward rate is *implicit* in the 2-year spot rate r_2. It is also *guaranteed*: By buying the 2-year bond, Ms. Long can "lock in" an interest rate of f_2 for the second year.

Suppose that the 2-year spot rate is 10.5 percent as before. Then the forward rate f_2 must be 11 percent. By definition, this forward rate is the implicit interest rate in the second year of the 2-year loan:

$$(1 + r_2)^2 = (1 + r_1)(1 + f_2)$$
$$(1.105)^2 = (1.10)(1 + f_2)$$
$$f_2 = \frac{(1.105)^2}{1.10} - 1 = .11$$

or 11 percent.[16] The 2-year spot rate of 10.5 percent is an average of the 10 percent 1-year spot rate and the 11 percent forward rate.

What should Ms. Long do? One possible answer is that she should follow the strategy that gives the highest *expected* payoff. That is, she should compare:

Expected Payoff to Strategy L1	To	(Certain) Payoff to Strategy L2
$1,000(1 + r_1)[1 + E({_1r_2})]$	to or to	$1,000(1 + r_2)^2$ $1,000(1 + r_1)(1 + f_2)$

----

[16]Actually 11.002 percent. We rounded.

Strategy L1 gives the higher expected return if $E(_1r_2)$, the expected future spot rate, exceeds the forward rate f_2 implicit in the 2-year spot rate r_2. In our numerical example, with $r_1 = .10$, $r_2 = .105$, and $E(_1r_2) = .11$, the two strategies give the same expected return:

Strategy	Payoff
L1	$1,000(1.10)(1.11) = \$1,221$ (expected)
L2	$1,000(1.105)^2 = \$1,221$ (certain)

Mr. Short's Problem

Now let us look at the decision faced by Mr. Short. He also has $1000 to invest, but he wants it back in 1 year. An obvious strategy is to invest in a 1-year bond. In this case his payoff is $1000(1 + r_1)$. This is strategy S1 in Table 23-5. A second strategy (S2 in the table) is to buy a 2-year bond and sell it after 1 year. The sale price will be the bond's present value in year 1. At that time, the bond will have 1 year to maturity. Its present value will be equal to its year-2 payoff $1000(1 + r_2)^2$ discounted at $_1r_2$, the one-period spot rate prevailing in year 1:

$$\text{PV of 2-year bond at year 1} = \frac{1000(1 + r_2)^2}{1 + {}_1r_2}$$

We know from Ms. Long's problem that the two-period rate r_2 can be expressed in terms of the one-period spot rate r_1 and the forward rate f_2. Thus

$$\text{PV of 2-year bond at year 1} = \frac{1000(1 + r_1)(1 + f_2)}{1 + {}_1r_2}$$

Of course Mr. Short cannot predict the future spot rate, and therefore he cannot predict the price at year 1 of the 2-year bond. But if $r_2 = .105$, and he expects the spot rate to be $_1r_2 = .11$, then the expected price is[17]

$$\frac{1000(1.105)^2}{1.11} = \frac{1221}{1.11} = \$1100$$

---

[17]Here we are making an approximation because the expected payoff of S2 in $t = 1$ is not exactly equal to $[1000(1 + r_2)^2]/[1 + E(_1r_2)]$. We should calculate the expected price of the 2-year bond at $t = 1$. Call this P. By definition

$$\tilde{P} = \frac{1000(1 + r_2)^2}{1 + {}_1\tilde{r}_2}$$

and

$$E(\tilde{P}) = E\left[\frac{1000(1 + r_2)^2}{1 + {}_1\tilde{r}_2}\right]$$

But

$$E\left[\frac{1000(1 + r_2)^2}{1 + {}_1\tilde{r}_2}\right]$$

is only approximately equal to

$$\frac{1000(1 + r_2)^2}{1 + E(_1\tilde{r}_2)}$$

In general, for any positive random variable $\tilde{x}$, $E(1/\tilde{x})$ is greater than $1/E(\tilde{x})$. This is called *Jensen's inequality*. Ignoring Jensen's inequality can be dangerous if the variance of $\tilde{x}$ is large.

TABLE 23-5
....

Two investment strategies for Mr. Short, who wants to invest $1,000 for 1 year

Strategy	Now		Year 1 (Final Payoff)
S1: Invest in 1-year bond	$1,000	$\xrightarrow{\text{Invest at } r_1}$	$1,000(1 + r_1)$
S2: Invest in 2-year bond, but sell in year 1	$1,000	$\xrightarrow[\substack{\text{Invest, sell} \\ \text{for PV at} \\ \text{year 1}}]{}$	$\dfrac{1,000(1 + r_2)^2}{1 + {}_1r_2}$

What should Mr. Short do? Suppose that he prefers the strategy that gives the highest expected payoff. Then he should compare:

(Certain) Payoff to Strategy S1	To	Expected Payoff to Strategy S2
$1000(1 + r_1)$	to	$\dfrac{1,000(1 + r_2)^2}{1 + E({}_1r_2)}$
	or to	$\dfrac{1,000(1 + r_1)(1 + f_2)}{1 + E({}_1r_2)}$

Strategy S2 is better if the forward rate f_2 exceeds the expected future spot rate $E({}_1r_2)$ If Mr. Short faces the same interest rates as Ms. Long [$r_1 = .10$, $r_2 = .105$, $E({}_1r_2) = .11$, $f_2 = .11$], the two strategies give the same expected return:

Strategy	Payoff
S1	$1,000(1.10) = \$1,100$ (certain)
S2	$\dfrac{1,000(1.105)^2}{1.11} = \dfrac{1,000(1.10)(1.11)}{1.11} = \$1,100$ (expected)

The Expectations Hypothesis

If the world is made up of people like Ms. Long and Mr. Short, all trying to maximize their expected return, then 1-year and 2-year bonds can exist side by side only if

$$f_2 = E({}_1r_2)$$

This condition was satisfied in our numerical example—both f_2 and $E({}_1r_2)$ equaled 11 percent. But what happens if the forward rate exceeds the expected future spot rate? Then both Long and Short prefer investing in 2-year bonds. If the world were entirely made up of expected-return maximizers, and f_2 exceeds $E({}_1r_2)$, no one would be willing to hold 1-year bonds. On the other hand, if the forward rate were *less* than the expected future spot rate, no one would be willing to hold 2-year bonds. Since investors *do* hold both 1-year and 2-year bonds, it follows that forward rates of interest must equal expected future spot rates (providing that investors are interested only in expected return).

This is the **expectations hypothesis** of the term structure.[18] It says that the *only* reason for an upward-sloping term structure is that investors expect future spot rates to be higher than current spot rates; the *only* reason for a declining term structure is that investors expect spot rates to fall below current levels. The expectations hypothesis also implies that investing in short-term bonds (as in strategies L1 and S1) gives exactly the same expected return as investing in long-term bonds (as in strategies L2 and S2).

The Liquidity-Preference Theory

Unfortunately the expectations theory says nothing about risk. Look back for a moment at our two simple cases. Ms. Long wants to invest for 2 years. If she buys a 2-year bond, she can nail down her final payoff today. If she buys a 1-year bond, she knows her return for the first year but she does not know at what rate she will be able to reinvest her money. If she does not like this uncertainty, she will tend to prefer the 2-year bond, and she will hold the 1-year bond only if

$$E(_1r_2) \text{ is greater than } f_2$$

What about Mr. Short? He wants to invest for 1 year. If he invests in a 1-year bond, he can nail down his payoff today. If he buys the 2-year bond, he will have to sell it next year at an unknown price. If he does not like this uncertainty, he will prefer the 1-year investment, and he will hold the 2-year bond only if

$$E(_1r_2) \text{ is less than } f_2$$

Here we have the basis for the **liquidity-preference** theory of term structure.[19] Other things equal, Ms. Long will prefer to invest in 2-year bonds and Mr. Short in 1-year bonds. If more companies want to issue 2-year bonds than there are Ms. Longs to hold them, they will need to offer a bonus to tempt some of the Mr. Shorts to hold them. Conversely, if more companies want to issue 1-year bonds than there are Mr. Shorts to hold them, they will need to offer a bonus to tempt some of the Ms. Longs to hold them.

Any bonus shows up as a difference between forward rates and expected future spot rates. This difference is usually called the **liquidity premium.**

The liquidity-preference theory assumes that there is a shortage of lenders like Ms. Long. In this case the liquidity premium is positive and the forward rate will exceed the expected spot rate. A positive liquidity premium rewards investors for lending long by offering them higher long-term rates of interest. Thus, if this view is right, the term structure should be upward-sloping more often than not. Of course, if future spot rates are expected to fall, the term structure could be downward-sloping and *still* reward investors for lending long. But the liquidity-preference hypothesis would predict a less dramatic downward slope than the expectations hypothesis.

Introducing Inflation

We argued above that Ms. Long could nail down her return by investing in 2-year bonds. What do we mean by that? If the bonds are issued by the U.S. Treasury, she can be virtually certain that she will be paid the promised number of dollars. But she cannot be certain what that money will buy. The expectations theory and the liquidity-preference theory of term structure implicitly assume that future inflation rates

---

[18]The expectations hypothesis is usually attributed to Lutz and Lutz. See F. A. Lutz and V. C. Lutz, *The Theory of Investment in the Firm*, Princeton University Press, Princeton, N.J., 1951.

[19]The liquidity-preference hypothesis is usually attributed to Hicks. See J. R. Hicks, *Value and Capital: An Inquiry into Some Fundamental Principles of Economic Theory*, 2d ed., Oxford University Press, Oxford, 1946. For a theoretical development, see R. Roll, *The Behavior of Interest Rates: An Application of the Efficient Market Model to U.S. Treasury Bills*, Basic Books, Inc., New York, 1970.

are known. Let us consider the opposite case in which the *only* uncertainty about interest rates stems from uncertainty about inflation.[20]

Suppose that Irving Fisher is right and short rates of interest always incorporate fully the market's latest views about inflation. Suppose also that the market learns more as time passes about the likely inflation rate in a particular year. Perhaps today it has only a very hazy idea about inflation in year 2, but in a year's time it expects to be able to make a much better prediction.

Because future inflation rates are never known with certainty, neither Ms. Long nor Mr. Short can make a completely risk-free investment. But since they expect to learn a good deal about the inflation rate in year 2 from experience in year 1, next year they will be in a much better position to judge the appropriate interest rate in year 2. It is therefore more risky for either of them to make a forward commitment to lend in year 2. Even Ms. Long, who wants to invest for 2 years, would be incurring unnecessary risk by buying a 2-year bond. Her least risky strategy is to invest in successive 1-year bonds. She does not know what her reinvestment rate will be, but at least she knows that it will incorporate the latest information about inflation in year 2.

Of course this means that borrowers must offer some incentive if they want investors to lend long. Therefore the forward rate of interest f_2 must be greater than the expected spot rate $E({}_1r_2)$ by an amount that compensates investors for the extra inflation risk.

Example: Suppose that the real interest rate is always 2 percent. Nominal interest rates therefore equal 2 percent plus the expected rate of inflation. Suppose that the *expected* inflation rate is 8 percent for both year 1 and year 2. However, inflation may accelerate to 10 percent in year 1, or it may decrease to 6 percent. To keep things simple, assume that the actual inflation rate for year 1 continues for year 2:

	Actual Inflation in Year 1		Actual Inflation in Year 2
Expected inflation rate = .08	→ .10	———	→ .10
	→ .08	———	→ .08
	→ .06	———	→ .06

Each outcome has a probability of 1/3.

Now reconsider Ms. Long's problem. Suppose that she can lend for either 1 or 2 years at 10 percent (the 2 percent real rate plus the 8 percent expected inflation rate). If she invests in a 1-year bond, she will get $1000(1.1) = \$1100$ in year 1. This amount is reinvested, but at what rate? The answer is that the future spot rate ${}_1r_2$ will be 2 percent plus the inflation rate experienced in year 1 and projected for year 2:

Actual Inflation Rate	Spot Interest Rate in Year 1
.10	.12
.08	.10
.06	.08

---

[20]The following is based on R. A. Brealey and S. M. Schaefer, "Term Structure and Uncertain Inflation," *Journal of Finance,* **32**:277–290 (May 1977).

Thus the final payoffs to lending short are:

	Year 1	Reinvest at	Final Payoff in Year 2
Invest for first year at $r_1 = .10$	$1,100	$_1r_2 = .12$	$1,232
	1,100	$_1r_2 = .10$	1,210
	1,100	$_1r_2 = .08$	1,188

Note that this strategy gives high payoffs when inflation turns out high.

Now Ms. Long could lock in a $1210 payoff in year 2 by purchasing a 2-year bond at 10 percent $[1000(1 + r_2)^2 = 1000(1.1)^2 = \$1210]$. But this would not lock in her *real* return. In fact, lending short is the *safer* strategy when the final payoffs are converted back to current dollars:

Strategy	Final Payoffs	Inflation Rate	Inflation-Adjusted Payoffs*
Buy 2-year bond	$1,210	.10	$1,000
	1,210	.08	1,037
	1,210	.06	1,077
Buy 1-year bond	1,232	.10	1,018
	1,210	.08	1,037
	1,188	.06	1,057

*The inflation-adjusted payoffs are calculated by dividing by $(1 + i)^2$. In this case i is the actual inflation rate.

A Comparison of Theories of Term Structure

We have described three views about why long and short interest rates differ. The first view, the expectations theory, is somewhat extreme and not fully supported by the facts. For example, if we look back over the period 1926-1994, we find that the return on long-term U.S. Treasury bonds has been on average 1½ percent higher than the return on short-term Treasury bills.[21] Perhaps short-term interest rates did not go up as much as investors expected, but it seems more likely that investors wanted a higher expected return for holding long bonds and that on the average they got it. If so, the expectations theory is wrong.

The expectations theory states that if the forward rate of interest is 1 percent above the spot rate of interest, then your best estimate is that the spot rate of interest will rise by 1 percent. In a study of the U.S. Treasury bill market between 1959 and 1982, Eugene Fama found that a forward premium *does* on average precede a rise in the spot rate but the rise is less than the expectations theory would predict.[22]

The expectations theory has few strict adherents, but Fama's study confirms that long-term interest rates do reflect, in part, investors' expectations about future short-term rates.

---

[21]See Ibbotson Associates, *Stocks, Bonds, Bills, and Inflation: 1995 Yearbook*, Ibbotson Associates, Inc., Chicago, 1995.

[22]See E. F. Fama, "The Information in the Term Structure," *Journal of Financial Economics*, **13**:509–528 (December 1984).

Our other two theories both suggest that long-term bonds ought to offer some additional return to compensate for their additional risk. The liquidity-preference theory supposes that risk comes solely from uncertainty about the underlying real rates. This may be a fair approximation in periods of price stability such as the early 1990s. The inflation-premium theory supposes that the risk comes solely from uncertainty about the inflation rate, which may be a fair approximation in periods of fluctuating inflation such as the 1970s and 1980s.

If short-term rates of interest are significantly lower than long-term rates, it is often tempting to borrow short-term rather than long-term. Our discussion of term structure theories should serve to warn against such naive strategies. One reason for higher long rates could be that short rates are expected to rise in the future. Also, investors who buy long bonds may be accepting liquidity or inflation risks for which they correctly want compensation. You should borrow short when the term structure is upward-sloping only if you feel that investors are *overestimating* future increases in interest rates or *overestimating* the risks of lending long.

If the risk of bond investment comes primarily from uncertainty about the real rate, then the safest strategy for investors is to hold bonds that match their liabilities. For example, the firm's pension fund generally has long-term liabilities. The liquidity-preference theory, therefore, implies that the pension fund should favor long-term bonds. If the risk comes from uncertainty about the inflation rate, then the safest strategy is to hold short bonds. For example, most pension funds have real liabilities that depend on the level of wage inflation. The inflation-premium theory implies that, if a pension fund wants to minimize risk, it should favor short-term bonds.

*Some New Theories of Term Structure

These term structure theories tell us how bond prices may be determined at a point in time. More recently, financial economists have proposed some important theories of how price *movements* are related.

The basic idea underlying these new theories is that the returns on bonds with different maturities tend to move together. For example, if short-term interest rates are high, it is a good bet that long-term rates will also be high. If short-term rates fall, long-term rates usually keep them company. These linkages between interest-rate movements can tell us something about relationships between bond prices. Let us illustrate.[23]

Each branch in Figure 23-3 shows what could happen to the short-term rate of interest. The rate is currently 8 percent, but next year it is equally likely to halve to 4 percent or rise to 12 percent. Then in year 2 with equal probability it could again either halve or rise 1.5 times, giving possible interest rates of 2, 6, or 18 percent.

Figure 23-4 shows the prices of two zero coupon bonds, which we have called "Short" and "Medium." (For the moment ignore the third bond, "Long.") Each branch in the diagram shows how the prices of the two bonds and their yields to maturity will vary, depending on what happens to the short-term interest rate:

1. Short is a 1-year bond that pays off 100 in period 1. It offers the 1-year interest rate of 8 percent and is therefore priced at $100/1.08 = 92.59$.

2. Medium is a 2-year bond. We know that next year the 1-year interest rate is equally likely to be 4 percent or 12 percent. So in year 1 there is a 50 percent chance that Medium will be priced at $100/1.04 = 96.15$ or $100/1.12 = 89.29$. The expected price is $(.5 \times 96.15) + (.5 \times 89.29) = 92.72$.

---

[23]We are grateful to John Cox, from whom we have borrowed and adapted the following example.

Figure 23-3 The current 1-year interest rate is 8 percent. We assume that in each future year the rate will either halve or increase 1.5 times.

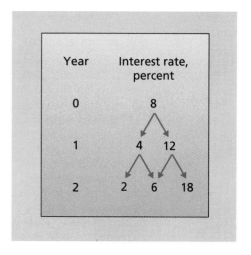

Year	Interest rate, percent
0	8
1	4 12
2	2 6 18

The return from Short is a surefire 8 percent. But the return from Medium is uncertain. Since investors don't like this uncertainty, they will require a higher expected return to compensate. Suppose that they demand a premium to invest in Medium of 2 percent over the 8 percent risk-free rate and therefore price it at 92.72/1.10 = 84.29. At this price they stand to make a return of 14.07 percent if interest rates fall

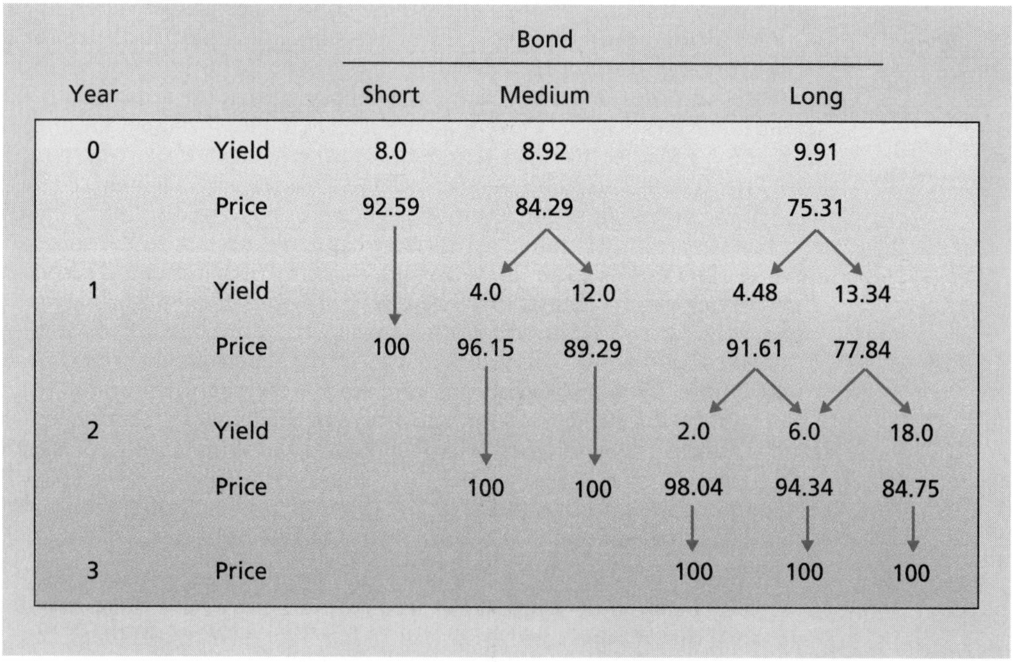

			Bond			
Year		Short	Medium		Long	
0	Yield	8.0	8.92		9.91	
	Price	92.59	84.29		75.31	
1	Yield		4.0	12.0	4.48	13.34
	Price	100	96.15	89.29	91.61	77.84
2	Yield				2.0	6.0	18.0
	Price		100	100	98.04	94.34	84.75
3	Price				100	100	100

Figure 23-4 We show above how the yield to maturity and the price of three bonds might vary with the short-term rate of interest (shown in Figure 23-3). These bonds offer the same expected reward per unit of risk.

and 5.93 percent if they rise. The spread of possible returns is $14.07 - 5.93 = 8.14$ percent. So we can say that the ratio of reward to risk on Medium is

$$\frac{\text{Expected risk premium}}{\text{Spread of possible returns}} = \frac{2}{8.14} = .246[24]$$

In a well-functioning market all bonds must be priced to offer the same ratio of expected reward to risk. So we can now use this information about the price of the Medium bond to value any other bond. The third bond shown in Figure 23-4 is a 3-year bond, Long. At each point in the diagram we have added the price at which Long would offer the same ratio of reward to risk as Medium offers. For example, look at what happens if the short-term interest rate falls to 4 percent in year 1 and the price of Long is 91.61. We know that at the end of the following year its price will be either 98.04 (a return of 7.01 percent) or 94.34 (a return of 2.97 percent). Since the two outcomes are equally likely, Long offers an expected return of $(.5 \times 7.01) + (.5 \times 2.97) = 4.99$ percent, 0.99 percent above the 4 percent risk-free interest rate. The spread of possible returns is $7.01 - 2.97 = 4.04$ percent and the ratio of reward to risk is $.99/4.04 = .246$, exactly the same as the ratio for Medium.

In Figure 23-4 all three bonds offer the same expected risk premium per unit of risk. However, the 3-year bond is the most risky and therefore offers the highest expected return.[25]

Why do we say that the three bonds have to offer the same risk premium per unit of risk? Because if they didn't do so, there would be arbitrage opportunities. To see why this is the case, consider the following two strategies:

| | | CASH FLOW, YEAR 1 | |
Strategy	Cash Flow Today	Interest Rate = 4%	Interest Rate = 12%
1: Buy 1 Medium bond	−84.29	+96.15	+89.29
2: Buy .5047 Short bond	−46.73	+50.47	+50.47
Buy .4987 Long bond	−37.56	+45.68	+38.82
Total	−84.29	+96.15	+89.29

Notice that, regardless of whether interest rates rise or fall, Medium provides exactly the same payoff as a mixture of Short and Long. Since the two investments provide the same payoffs, they must cost the same today—that is, they must cost 84.29.

Suppose that the price of Medium is greater than 84.29 and all other prices are unchanged. Then Medium would offer a lower reward for risk than the other two bonds and you could make an arbitrage profit by selling one Medium bond and buying a package of the other two.

If you read about options in Chapter 20, you may remember that we were able to price an option by designing a package of a risk-free asset and a common stock that would give the same payoffs as the option. We are using the same idea here. To

---

[24]Where there are only two possible outcomes, it is acceptable to measure risk by the range of outcomes. If there were many possible outcomes, this would not be the case.

[25]Notice that Long has the longest duration and therefore the greatest volatility.

value the Medium bond, we constructed a package of a risk-free short-term bond and a long-term bond that provided identical payoffs.

We can also borrow another idea from Chapter 20. We have seen that if the Medium bond does not sell for the same price as the equivalent package of Short and Long bonds, then there are arbitrage opportunities. Regardless of investors' attitude to risk, such arbitrage opportunities cannot exist if securities are fairly priced. So, even if investors are totally indifferent to risk, the two equivalent packages must sell for the same price. This suggests an alternative way to value the Medium bond. We can *pretend* that investors are indifferent to risk, work out the expected bond payoffs in such a world, and discount at the risk-free interest rate. Let's check that this gives the same set of bond values.

Look, for example, at the returns that are offered by the Long bond in year 1. If interest rates fall, the bond provides a return of $(91.61/75.31) - 1 = 21.64$ percent; if rates rise, it provides a return of $(77.84/75.31) - 1 = 3.36$ percent. If investors are indifferent to risk and the expected return on Long is equal to the 8 percent risk-free interest rate, then

$$\text{(Probability of interest-rate fall} \times 21.64)$$
$$+ [(1 - \text{probability of interest-rate fall)} \times 3.36] = 8\%$$

Therefore,

$$\text{Probability of interest rate fall} = .254$$

Now we can use this (pretend) probability to price the Medium bond. We know that if interest rates fall, Medium will be worth 96.15 and that if they rise it will be worth 89.29. So, if investors are indifferent to risk, the expected value of Medium in year 1 is

$$(.254 \times 96.15) + (.746 \times 89.29) = 91.03$$

The current value of Medium is therefore

$$\frac{\text{Expected future value}}{1 + \text{interest rate}} = \frac{91.03}{1.08} = 84.29$$

the same value that we obtained by constructing a replicating portfolio.

Our simple example should give you a flavor for these modern theories of term structure, but you can probably think of a number of improvements that would make the example more realistic. First, short-term interest rates have more built-in stability than we implied. If they rise this year, they are more likely to fall back to a "normal" level next year. If they fall next year, they are more likely to bounce back later. Second, short-term interest rates fluctuate more than long-term rates. Third, short-term and long-term rates do not move in perfect lockstep, as our example implied. Sometimes, for example, short-term rates rise, but the spread between short- and long-term rates falls. In this case it might be more realistic to assume that the return on each bond depends on both the change in the short-term interest rate and the change in the spread between the long and short rates. Making the model more realistic also makes it more complex, but if we know how interest rates can change and how the returns on different bonds are linked, we can still say something about consistent patterns of bond prices.

23-5   ALLOWING FOR THE RISK OF DEFAULT

You should by now be familiar with some of the basic ideas about why interest rates change and why short rates may differ from long rates. It only remains to consider our third question: "Why do some borrowers have to pay a higher rate of interest than others?"

The answer is obvious: "Bond prices go down, and interest rates go up, when the probability of default increases." But when we say "interest rates go up," we mean *promised* interest rates. If the borrower defaults, the *actual* interest rate paid to the lender is less than the promised rate. The *expected* interest rate may go up with increasing probability of default, but this is not a logical necessity.

These points can be illustrated by a simple numerical example. Suppose that the interest rate on 1-year, *risk-free* bonds is 9 percent. Backwoods Chemical Company has issued 9 percent notes with face values of $1000, maturing in 1 year. What will the Backwoods notes sell for?

The answer is easy—if the notes are risk-free, just discount principal ($1000) and interest ($90) at 9 percent:

$$\text{PV of notes} = \frac{\$1000 + 90}{1.09} = \$1000$$

Suppose instead that there is a 20 percent chance that Backwoods will default. If default does occur, holders of its notes receive nothing. In this case, the possible payoffs to the noteholder are:

	Payoff	Probability
Full payment	$1,090	.8
No payment	0	.2

The expected payment is .8($1090) + .2($0) = $872.

We can value the Backwoods notes like any other risky asset, by discounting their expected payoff ($872) at the appropriate opportunity cost of capital. We might discount at the risk-free interest rate (9 percent) if Backwoods's possible default is totally unrelated to other events in the economy. In this case the default risk is wholly diversifiable, and the beta of the notes is zero. The notes would sell for

$$\text{PV of notes} = \frac{\$872}{1.09} = \$800$$

An investor who purchased these notes for $800 would receive a *promised* yield of about 36 percent:

$$\text{Promised yield} = \frac{\$1090}{\$800} - 1 = .363$$

That is, an investor who purchased the notes for $800 would earn a 36.3 percent rate of return *if* Backwoods does not default. Bond traders therefore might say that the Backwoods notes "yield 36 percent." But the smart investor would realize that the notes' *expected* yield is only 9 percent, the same as on risk-free bonds.

This of course assumes that risk of default with these notes is wholly diversifiable, so that they have no market risk. In general, risky bonds do have market risk (that is, positive betas) because default is more likely to occur in recessions when all businesses are doing poorly. Suppose that investors demand a 2 percent risk premium and an 11 percent expected rate of return. Then the Backwoods notes will sell for 872/1.11 = $785.59 and offer a promised yield of (1090/785.59) − 1 = .388, or about 39 percent.

You rarely see traded bonds offering 39 percent yields, although we will soon encounter an example of one company's bonds that had a promised yield of 50 percent.

**Bond
Ratings**

The relative quality of most traded bonds can be judged from bond ratings given by Moody's and Standard and Poor's. For example, Moody's classifies several thousand bond issues into the categories described in Table 23-6.

Bonds rated Baa or above are known as *investment-grade* bonds. Commercial banks and many pension funds and other financial institutions are not allowed to invest in bonds unless they are investment-grade.[26]

Bond ratings are judgments about firms' financial and business prospects. If there is insufficient information to permit a judgment, the bond will not be rated. There is no fixed formula by which ratings are calculated. Nevertheless, investment bankers, bond portfolio managers, and others who follow the bond market closely can get a fairly good idea of how a bond will be rated by looking at a few key numbers such as the firm's debt-equity ratio, the ratio of earnings to interest, and the return on assets.[27]

Since bond ratings reflect the probability of default, it is not surprising that there is also a close correspondence between a bond's rating and its promised yield. For example, in the postwar period the promised yield on Aaa corporate bonds has been on average about 1.3 percent less than on Baa's.

Once Moody's or Standard and Poor's rates a bond, the rating is not changed unless there is a significant shift in the company's financing or prospects. But the rating agencies do change their minds when conditions warrant it.

In July 1965 the issue of an additional $175 million of New York City bonds led Moody's to down-rate the city's debt from A to Baa. As a result a city official complained that the rating services were "causing leading cities to be shortchanged out of hundreds of millions of dollars in unwarranted interest charges." Suggested remedies included the idea that a federal agency be established that could rate municipal bonds "more objectively." Ten years later, after New York had nearly defaulted, Moody's was again the subject of criticism—this time for overoptimistic ratings. "Moody's," complained one senator, "continued to signal 'All is well,' " even while the city "was floundering on the financial rocks and was being abandoned by its crew of bankers and money men." A bond rater's lot is not a happy one.

**Junk
Bonds**

Bonds rated below Baa are known as **junk bonds.** Until recently most junk bonds were "fallen angels," i.e., they were bonds of companies that had fallen on hard times. But during the 1980s new issues of junk bonds multiplied tenfold as more and more companies issued large quantities of low-grade debt to finance takeovers or to defend themselves against being taken over.

The development of this market for low-grade corporate bonds was largely the brainchild of the investment banking firm Drexel Burnham Lambert. The result was that for the first time corporate midgets were able to take control of corporate giants, and they could finance this activity by issues of debt. However, issuers of junk bonds often had debt ratios of 90 or 95 percent. Many worried that these high levels of leverage resulted in undue risk and pressed for legislation to ban junk bonds.

Between 1986 and 1988 Campeau Corporation amassed a huge retailing empire by acquiring major department store chains such as Federated Department Stores and Allied Stores. Unfortunately, it also amassed $10.9 billion in debt, which was supported by just $.9 billion of book equity. So when in September 1989 Campeau announced that it was having difficulties meeting the interest payments on its debt, the

---

[26]Investment-grade bonds can usually be entered at face value on the books of banks and life insurance companies.

[27]See, for example, R. S. Kaplan, and G. Urwitz, "Statistical Models of Bond Ratings: A Methodological Inquiry," *Journal of Business*, **52**:231–261 (April 1979).

TABLE 23-6

● ●

Key to Moody's bond ratings

Aaa
Bonds which are rated **Aaa** are judged to be of the best quality. They carry the
smallest degree of investment risk and are generally referred to as "gilt edge."
Interest payments are protected by a large or by an exceptionally stable margin,
and principal is secure. While the various protective elements are likely to change,
such changes as can be visualized are most unlikely to impair the fundamentally
strong position of such issues.

Aa
Bonds which are rated **Aa** are judged to be of high quality by all standards.
Together with the **Aaa** group they comprise what are generally known as high-
grade bonds. They are rated lower than the best bonds because margins of
protection may not be as large as in **Aaa** securities, or fluctuation of protective
elements may be of greater amplitude, or there may be other elements present
which make the long-term risks appear somewhat larger than in **Aaa** securities.

A
Bonds which are rated **A** possess many favorable investment attributes and are to
be considered as upper-medium-grade obligations. Factors giving security to
principal and interest are considered adequate but elements may be present which
suggest a susceptibility to impairment sometime in the future.

Baa
Bonds which are rated **Baa** are considered as medium-grade obligations; i.e., they
are neither highly protected nor poorly secured. Interest payments and principal
security appear adequate for the present but certain protective elements may be
lacking or may be characteristically unreliable over any great length of time. Such
bonds lack outstanding investment characteristics and in fact have speculative
characteristics as well.

Ba
Bonds which are rated **Ba** are judged to have speculative elements; their future
cannot be considered as well assured. Often the protection of interest and principal
payments may be very moderate and thereby not well safeguarded during both
good and bad times over the future. Uncertainty of position characterizes bonds in
this class.

B
Bonds which are rated **B** generally lack characteristics of the desirable investment.
Assurance of interest and principal payments or of maintenance of other terms of
the contract over any long period of time may be small.

Caa
Bonds which are rated **Caa** are of poor standing. Such issues may be in default or
there may be present elements of danger with respect to principal or interest.

Ca
Bonds which are rated **Ca** represent obligations which are speculative in a high
degree. Such issues are often in default or have other marked shortcomings.

C
Bonds which are rated **C** are the lowest-rated class of bonds, and issues so rated
can be regarded as having extremely poor prospects of ever attaining any real
investment standing.

Note: Moody's further divides each class into three ranges, marked 1, 2, and 3. Thus an A1 rating is better than A2, which is in turn better than A3.
Source: Moody's Investor Services.

junk bond market took a nosedive and worries about the riskiness of junk bonds intensified. Campeau's own bonds fell to the point at which they offered a promised yield of nearly 50 percent. Campeau eventually filed for bankruptcy, and investors with large holdings of junk bonds took large losses. The originator of junks, Drexel Burnham Lambert, was also driven into bankruptcy.

Defaults by some major junk bond issuers, such as Campeau, caused new issues of junk bonds to fall sharply. But in more recent years there has been an increasing number of new issues. Many of the early bonds matured and were replaced with new ones.

Table 23-7 shows the results of a study by Edward Altman and Vellore Kishore of default rates of junk bonds. On average the annual default rates for these bonds has been about 3 percent, but at the peak in 1990 and 1991 it was over 10 percent.

Junk bonds promise a higher yield than U.S. Treasuries, but of course companies can't always keep their promises. Many junk bonds have defaulted, while some of the more successful issuers have called their bonds, thus depriving their holders of

TABLE 23-7

Historical default rates for straight junk bonds, 1971–1994

Year	Principal outstanding, Billions	Principal defaulting, Billions	Default rate, Percent
1971	$ 6.6	$ .08	1.2
1972	6.9	.19	2.8
1973	7.8	.05	.7
1974	10.9	.12	1.1
1975	7.5	.20	2.7
1976	7.7	.03	.4
1977	8.2	.38	4.7
1978	8.9	.12	1.3
1979	10.4	.02	.2
1980	14.9	.22	1.5
1981	17.1	.03	.2
1982	18.1	.58	3.2
1983	27.5	.30	1.1
1984	40.9	.34	.8
1985	58.1	.99	1.7
1986	90.2	3.16	3.5
1987	129.6	7.49	5.8
1988	148.2	3.94	2.7
1989	189.3	8.11	4.3
1990	181.0	18.35	10.1
1991	183.6	18.86	10.3
1992	163.0	5.55	3.4
1993	206.9	2.29	1.1
1994	235.0	3.42	1.5

Source: E. I. Altman and V. Kishore, "Defaults and Returns on High Yields Bonds: Analysis through 1994," New York University Salomon Center, Leonard N. Stern School of Business.

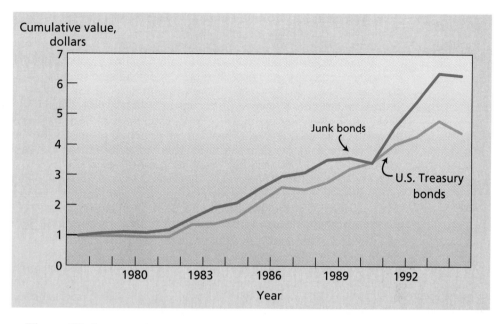

Figure 23-5 Cumulative value of investments in junk and Treasury bonds, 1978–1994. The plot assumes investment of $1 in 1977. (*Source:* E. I. Altman and V. Kishore, "Defaults and Returns on High Yields Bonds: Analysis through 1994," New York University Salomon Center, Leonard N. Stern School of Business.)

the prospect of a continuing stream of high coupon payments. Figure 23-5 shows the performance since 1978 of a portfolio of junk bonds and of 10-year Treasury bonds. On average the *promised yield* on junk bonds was 4.5 percent higher than that on Treasuries, but the annual *realized return* was only 2.1 percent higher.

*Option Pricing and Risky Debt

In Section 20-2 we showed that holding a corporate bond is equivalent to lending money with no chance of default *but* at the same time giving stockholders a put option on the firm's assets. When a firm defaults, its stockholders are in effect exercising their put. The put's value is the value of limited liability—of stockholders' right to walk away from their firm's debts in exchange for handing over the firm's assets to its creditors. To summarize,

$$\text{Bond value} = \begin{array}{c}\text{bond value}\\\text{assuming no chance}\\\text{of default}\end{array} - \text{value of put}$$

Thus, valuing bonds should be a two-step process. The first step is easy: Calculate the bond's value assuming no default risk. (Discount promised interest and principal payments at the rates offered by Treasury issues.) Second, calculate the value of a put written on the firm's assets, where the maturity of the put equals the maturity of the bond and the exercise price of the put equals the promised payments to bondholders.

Owning a corporate bond is *also* equivalent to owning the firm's assets *but* giving a call option on these assets to the firm's stockholders:

$$\text{Bond value} = \text{asset value} - \text{value of call on assets}$$

Thus you can also calculate a bond's value, given the value of the firm's assets, by valuing a call on these assets and subtracting the call value from the asset value. (The call value is just the value of the firm's common stock.)

Therefore, if you can value puts and calls on a firm's assets, you can value its debt.[28]

In practice, this is a good bit more difficult than it sounds. The put or call you have to value is usually not the simple option described in Chapter 20 but a much more complex one. Suppose, for example, that Backwoods Chemical issues a 10-year bond which pays interest annually. We can still think of Backwoods stock as a call option which can be exercised by making the promised payments. But in this case there are 10 payments rather than just 1. To value Backwoods stock, we would have to value 10 sequential call options. The first option can be exercised by making the first interest payment when it comes due. By exercise the stockholders obtain a second call option, which can be exercised by making the second interest payment. The reward to exercising is that the stockholders get a third call option, and so on. Finally, in year 10 the stockholders can exercise the tenth option. By paying off both the principal and the last year's interest, the stockholders regain unencumbered ownership of Backwoods's assets.

Of course if the firm does not make any of these payments when due, bondholders take over and stockholders are left with nothing. In other words, by not exercising one call option, stockholders give up all subsequent call options.

Valuing Backwoods stock when the 10-year bond is issued is equivalent to valuing the first of the 10 call options. But you cannot value the first option without valuing the nine following ones.[29] Even this example understates the practical difficulties, because large firms may have dozens of outstanding debt issues with different interest rates and maturities, and before the current debt matures they may make further issues. But do not lose heart. Computers can solve these problems, more or less by brute force, even in the absence of simple, exact valuation formulas.

Figure 23-6 shows a simple application. The figure is designed to give you some feel for the effect of default risk on (promised) bond yields. It takes a company with average operating risk and shows how the interest rate should increase with the amount of bonds that are issued and their maturity. You can see, for example, that, if the company raises 20 percent of its capital in the form of 20-year bonds, it should pay about one-half of a percentage point above the government borrowing rate to compensate for the default risk. Companies with more leverage or with longer-maturity bonds ought to pay higher premiums.[30]

In practice, interest-rate differentials tend to be greater than those shown in Figure 23-6. High-grade corporate bonds typically offer promised yields about 1 percentage point greater than U.S. Treasury bonds. Does this mean that these companies are paying too much for their debt?

Probably not; there are a number of other possible explanations. For example, notice that Figure 23-6 makes several artificial assumptions. One assumption is that the company does not pay dividends. If it does regularly pay out part of its assets to

---

[28]However, option valuation procedures cannot value the *assets* of the firm. Puts and calls must be valued as a proportion of asset value. For example, note that the Black-Scholes formula (Section 20-5) requires stock price in order to compute the value of a call option.

[29]The other approach to valuing Backwoods's debt (subtracting put value from risk-free bond value) is no easier. The analyst would be confronted by not one simple put but a package of 10 sequential puts.

[30]But beyond a certain point (not shown in Figure 23-6), the yield premiums begin to decline with increasing maturity.

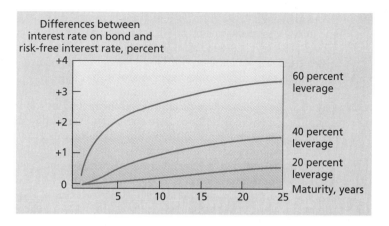

Figure 23-6 How the interest rate on risky corporate debt changes with leverage and maturity. These curves are calculated using option pricing theory under the following simplifying assumptions: (1) The risk-free interest rate is constant for all maturities. (2) The standard deviation of the return on the company's assets is 25 percent per annum. (3) No dividends are paid. (4) Debt is in the form of discount bonds (i.e., only one payment is made, at maturity). (5) Leverage is the ratio of the *market* value of the debt to the *market* value of the debt plus equity.

stockholders, there may be substantially fewer assets to protect the bondholder in the event of trouble. In this case, the market may be quite justified in requiring a higher yield on the company's bonds.

*Valuing Government Loan Guarantees

In the summer of 1971 Lockheed Corporation was in trouble. It was nearly out of cash after absorbing heavy cost overruns on military contracts and, at the same time, committing more than $800 million[31] to the development of the L1011 TriStar airliner. Introduction of the TriStar had been delayed by unexpected problems with its Rolls-Royce engines, and it would be many years before the company could recoup its investment in the plane. Lockheed was on the brink of bankruptcy. (Rolls-Royce was itself driven to the brink by the costs of fixing the engine problems. It was taken over by the British government.)

After months of suspense and controversy, the United States government rescued Lockheed by agreeing to guarantee up to $250 million of new bank loans. If Lockheed had defaulted on these loans, the banks could have gotten their money back directly from the government.

From the banks' point of view, these loans were as safe as Treasury notes. Thus, Lockheed was assured of being able to borrow up to $250 million at a favorable rate.[32] This assurance in turn gave Lockheed's banks the confidence to advance the rest of the money the firm needed.

The loan guarantee was a helping hand—a subsidy—to bring Lockheed through a difficult period. What was it worth? What did it cost the government?

This loan guarantee did not turn out to cost the government anything, because Lockheed survived, recovered, and paid off the loans the government guaranteed.

---

[31]See U. Reinhardt, "Break-Even Analysis for Lockheed's TriStar: An Application of Financial Theory," *Journal of Finance*, **28**:821–838 (September 1973).

[32]Lockheed paid the current Treasury bill rate plus a fee of roughly 2 percent to the government.

Does that mean that the value of the guarantee to Lockheed was also zero? Does it mean the government absorbed no risks when it gave the guarantee in 1971, when Lockheed's survival was still uncertain? Of course not. The government absorbed the risk of default. Obviously the banks' loans to Lockheed were worth more with the guarantee than they would have been without it.

The present value of a loan guarantee is the amount lenders would be willing to pay to relieve themselves of all risk of default on an otherwise equivalent unguaranteed loan. It is the difference between the present value of the loan with the guarantee and its present value without the guarantee. A guarantee can clearly have substantial value on a large loan when the chance of default by the firm is high.

It turns out that a loan guarantee can be valued as a put on the firm's assets, where the put's maturity equals the loan's maturity and its exercise price equals the interest and principal payments promised to lenders. We can easily show the equivalence by starting with the definition of the value of the guarantee.

$$\text{Value of guarantee} = \text{value of guaranteed loan} - \text{loan value without the guarantee}$$

Without a guarantee, the loan becomes an ordinary debt obligation of the firm. We know from Section 20-2 that

$$\text{Value of ordinary loan} = \text{value assuming no chance of default} - \text{value of put}$$

The loan's value, assuming no chance of default, is exactly its guaranteed value. Thus the put value equals the difference between the values of a guaranteed and an ordinary loan. This is exactly the value of the loan guarantee.

Thus option pricing theory should lead to a way of calculating the actual cost of the government's many loan guarantee programs. This will be a healthy thing. The government's possible liability under existing guarantee programs has been enormous. In 1987, for example, $4 billion in loans to shipowners had been guaranteed under the so-called Title IX program to support shipyards in the United States.[33] This program is one of dozens. Yet the true cost of these programs is not widely recognized. Because loan guarantees involve no immediate outlay, they do not appear in the federal budget. Members of Congress sponsoring loan guarantee programs do not, as far as we know, present careful estimates of the value of the programs to business and the present value of the programs' cost to the public.

23-6 SUMMARY

Efficient debt management presupposes that you understand how bonds are valued. That means you need to consider three problems:

1. What determines the general level of interest rates?
2. What determines the difference between long-term and short-term rates?
3. What determines the difference between the interest rates on company and government debt?

---

[33]The actual figure on March 31, 1987, was $4,497,365,297.98. Since 1987 these government guarantees to shipowners have been substantially reduced.

Here are some things to remember.

The rate of interest depends on the demand for savings and the supply. The *demand* comes from firms who wish to invest in new plant and equipment. The *supply* of savings comes from individuals who are willing to consume tomorrow rather than today. The equilibrium interest rate is the rate which produces a *balance* between the demand and supply.

The best-known theory about the effect of inflation on interest rates is that suggested by Irving Fisher. He argued that the nominal, or money, rate of interest is equal to the expected real rate plus the expected inflation rate. If the expected inflation rate increases by 1 percent, so too will the money rate of interest. During the past 30 years Fisher's simple theory has not done a bad job of explaining changes in short-term interest rates in the United States.

The value of any bond is equal to the cash payments discounted at the spot rates of interest. For example, the value of a 10-year bond with a 5 percent coupon equals

$$\text{PV(percent of face value)} = \frac{5}{1 + r_1} + \frac{5}{(1 + r_2)^2} + \cdots + \frac{105}{(1 + r_{10})^{10}}$$

Bond dealers generally look at the yield to maturity on a bond. This is simply the internal rate of return y, the discount rate at which

$$\text{Bond price} = \frac{5}{1 + y} + \frac{5}{(1 + y)^2} + \cdots + \frac{105}{(1 + y)^{10}}$$

The yield to maturity y is a complex average of the spot interest rates r_1, r_2, etc. Like most averages it can be a useful summary measure, but it can also hide a lot of interesting information. We suggest you refer to yields on stripped bonds as measures of the spot rates of interest.

When you invest in a bond you usually receive a regular interest payment and then the final principal payment. Duration measures the *average* time to each payment. It is a useful summary measure of the length of a loan. It is also important because there is a direct relationship between the duration of a bond and its volatility. A change in interest rates has a greater effect on the price of a bond with a long duration.

The one-period spot rate r_1 may be very different from the two-period spot rate r_2. In other words, investors often want a different annual rate of interest for lending for 1 year than for 2 years. Why is this? The *expectations theory* says that bonds are priced so that the expected rate of return from investing in bonds over any period is independent of the maturity of the bonds held by the investor. The expectations theory predicts that r_2 will exceed r_1 *only* if *next* year's one-period interest rate is expected to rise.

The *liquidity-preference* theory points out that you are not exposed to risks of changing interest rates and changing bond prices if you buy a bond that matures exactly when you need the money. However, if you buy a bond that matures *before* you need the money, you face the risk that you may have to reinvest your savings at a low rate of interest. And if you buy a bond that matures *after* you need the money, you face the risk that the price will be low when you come to sell it. Investors don't like risk and they need some compensation for taking it. Therefore when we find that r_2 is generally higher than r_1, it may mean that investors have relatively short horizons and have to be offered an inducement to hold long bonds.

No bonds are risk-free in real terms. If inflation rates are uncertain, the safest strategy for an investor is to keep investing in short bonds and to trust that the rate of interest on the bonds will vary as inflation varies. Therefore another reason why

r_2 may be higher than r_1 is that investors have to be offered an inducement to accept additional inflation risk.

Finally, we come to our third question: "What determines the difference between interest rates on company and government debt?" Company debt sells at a lower price than government debt. This discount represents the value of the company's option to default. We showed you how the value of this option varies with the degree of leverage and the time to maturity. Moody's and Standard and Poor's rate company bonds according to their default risk, and the price of the bonds is closely related to these ratings.

Further Reading

The classic work on interest rates is:
Irving Fisher: *The Theory of Interest: As Determined by Impatience to Spend Income and Opportunity to Invest It*, Augustus M. Kelley, Publishers, New York, 1965. Originally published in 1930.

Fisher's work also anticipated Lutz and Lutz's expectations hypothesis of the term structure of interest rates:
F. A. Lutz and V. C. Lutz: *The Theory of Investment of the Firm*, Princeton University Press, Princeton, N.J., 1951.

The liquidity-premium hypothesis is due to Hicks, and our description of the effect of inflation on term structure is taken from Brealey and Schaefer:
J. R. Hicks: *Value and Capital: An Inquiry into Some Fundamental Principles of Economic Theory*, 2d ed., Oxford University Press, Oxford, 1946.
R. A. Brealey and S. M. Schaefer: "Term Structure and Uncertain Inflation," *Journal of Finance*, **32**:277–290 (May 1977).

Good reviews of the term structure literature may be found in Nelson and Roll:
C. R. Nelson: "The Term Structure of Interest Rates: Theories and Evidence," in J. L. Bicksler (ed.), *Handbook of Financial Economics*, North-Holland Publishing Company, Amsterdam, 1980.
R. Roll: *The Behavior of Interest Rates: An Application of the Efficient Market Model to U.S. Treasury Bills*, Basic Books, Inc., Publishers, New York, 1970.

Dobson, Sutch, and Vanderford review empirical tests of term structure theories; two more recent tests of term structure theories are provided by Fama:
S. Dobson, R. Sutch, and D. Vanderford: "An Evaluation of Alternative Empirical Models of the Term Structure of Interest Rates," *Journal of Finance*, **31**:1035–1066 (September 1976).
E. F. Fama: "The Information in the Term Structure," *Journal of Financial Economics*, **13**:509–528 (December 1984).
E. F. Fama: "Term Premiums in Bond Returns," *Journal of Financial Economics*, **13**:529–546 (December 1984).

When there are no zero coupon bonds or strips, measuring term structure is more complicated. See, for example:
S. M. Schaefer: "Measuring a Tax Specific Term Structure of Interest Rates in the Market for British Government Securities," *Economic Journal*, **91**:415–438 (June 1981).

The following paper by Schaefer is a good review of the concept of duration and of how it is used to hedge fixed liabilities:
S. M. Schaefer: "Immunisation and Duration: A Review of Theory, Performance and Applications," *Midland Corporate Finance Journal*, **3**:41–58 (Autumn 1984).

The Cox, Ingersoll, and Ross paper uses no-arbitrage conditions to derive a rigorous model of the term structure; the Brennan and Schwartz paper is a readable description of a model that links each bond's return to both the short-term and long-term interest rates and then derives consistent bond prices; Ho provides an up-to-date survey of interest rate models:

J. C. Cox, J. E. Ingersoll, and S. A. Ross: "A Theory of the Term Structure of Interest Rates," *Econometrica*, **53**:385–407 (May 1985).

M. J. Brennan and E. S. Schwartz: "Bond Pricing and Market Efficiency," *Financial Analysts Journal*, **38**:49–56 (September–October 1982).

T. S. Y. Ho, "Evolution of Interest Rate Models: A Comparison," *Journal of Derivatives*, **2**:9–20 (Summer 1995).

Fama's tests indicate that the expected real rate of interest was essentially constant between 1953 and 1971; however, if you read Fama's paper, you should also read the replies by Hess and Bicksler and by Nelson and Schwert:

E. F. Fama: "Short-Term Interest Rates as Predictors of Inflation," *American Economic Review*, **65**:269–282 (June 1975).

P. Hess and J. Bicksler: "Capital Asset Prices versus Time Series Models as Predictors of Inflation," *Journal of Financial Economics*, **2**:341–360 (December 1975).

C. R. Nelson and G. Schwert: "Short-Term Interest Rates as Predictors of Inflation: On Testing the Hypothesis That the Real Rate of Interest Is Constant," *American Economic Review*, **67**:478–486 (June 1977).

The following papers take a detailed look at the default experience of junk debt in the 1980s:

P. Asquith, D. W. Mullins, and E. D. Wolff: "Original Issue High Yield Bonds: Aging Analyses of Defaults, Exchanges, and Calls," *Journal of Finance*, **44**:923–952 (September 1989).

E. Altman: "Measuring Corporate Bond Mortality and Performance," *Journal of Finance*, **44**:909–922 (September 1989).

R. Merton: "On the Pricing of Corporate Debt: The Risk Structure of Interest Rates," *Journal of Finance*, **29**:449–470 (May 1974).

Evidence on long-run average bond returns may be found in:

Ibbotson Associates: *Stocks, Bonds, Bills, and Inflation: 1995 Yearbook*, Ibbotson Associates, Inc., Chicago, 1995.

Quiz

1. The real interest rate is determined by the demand and supply for capital. Draw a diagram showing how the demand by companies for capital and the supply of capital by investors vary with the interest rate. Use this diagram to show the following:
   (*a*) What will happen to the amount of investment and saving if firms' investment prospects improve? How will the equilibrium interest rate change?
   (*b*) What will happen to the amount of investment and saving if individuals' willingness to save increases at each possible interest rate? How will the equilibrium interest rate change? Assume firms' investment opportunities do not change.

2. (*a*) What is the formula for the value of a 2-year, 5 percent bond in terms of spot rates?
   (*b*) What is the formula for its value in terms of yield to maturity?
   (*c*) If the 2-year spot rate is higher than the 1-year rate, is the yield to maturity greater or less than the 2-year spot rate?
   (*d*) In each of the following sentences choose the correct term from within the parentheses:

"The (yield-to-maturity/spot-rate) formula discounts all cash flows from one bond at the same rate even though they occur at different points in time." "The (yield-to-maturity/spot-rate) formula discounts all cash flows received at the same point in time at the same rate even though the cash flows may come from different bonds."

3. Use Table 23-1 to check your answers to the following:
   (a) If interest rates rise, do bond prices rise or fall?
   (b) If the bond yield is greater than the coupon, is the price of the bond greater or less than 100?
   (c) If the price of a bond exceeds 100, is the yield greater or less than the coupon?
   (d) Do high-coupon bonds sell at higher or lower prices than low-coupon bonds?

4. Use Table 23-1 to answer the following questions:
   (a) What is the yield to maturity on a 7 percent, 8-year bond selling at 74¼?
   (b) What is the approximate price of a 7 percent, 9-year bond yielding 10 percent?
   (c) An 8 percent, 12-year bond yields 14 percent. If the yield remains unchanged, what will be its price 2 years hence? What will the price be if the yield falls to 10 percent?

5. (a) Suppose that the 1-year spot rate of interest at time 0 is 1 percent and the 2-year spot rate is 3 percent. What is the forward rate of interest for year 2?
   (b) What does the expectations theory of term structure say about the relationship between this forward rate and the 1-year spot rate at time 1?
   (c) Over a very long period of time, the term structure in the United States has been, on average, upward-sloping. Is this evidence for or against the expectations theory?
   (d) What does the liquidity-preference theory say about the relationship between the forward rate and the 1-year spot rate at time 1?
   (e) If the liquidity-preference theory is a good approximation and you have to meet long-term liabilities (college tuition for your children, for example), is it safer to invest in long-term or short-term bonds? Assume inflation is predictable.
   (f) If the inflation-premium theory is a good approximation and you have to meet long-term real liabilities, is it safer to invest in long-term or short-term bonds?
   (g) What does the inflation-premium theory say about the relationship between the forward rate and the 1-year spot rate at time 1?

6. (a) State the four Moody's ratings which are generally known as "investment-grade" ratings.
   (b) Other things equal, would you expect the yield to maturity on a corporate bond to increase or decrease with:
      (i) The company's business risk?
      (ii) The expected rate of inflation?
      (iii) The risk-free rate of interest?
      (iv) The degree of leverage?

*7. (a) How in principle would you calculate the value of a government loan guarantee?
   (b) The difference between the price of a government bond and a simple corporate bond is equal to the value of an option. What is this option and what is its exercise price?

8. True or false? Explain.
   (*a*) Longer-maturity bonds necessarily have longer durations.
   (*b*) The longer a bond's duration, the lower is its volatility.
   (*c*) Other things equal, the lower the bond coupon, the higher its volatility.
   (*d*) If interest rates rise, bond durations rise also.

9. Calculate the durations and volatilities of securities A, B, and C. Their cash flows are shown below. The interest rate is 8 percent.

	Period 1	Period 2	Period 3
A	40	40	40
B	20	20	120
C	10	110	

10. In May 1995 the 10¾s of May 2003 offered a semiannually compounded yield of 6.65 percent. Recognizing that coupons are paid semiannually, calculate the bond's price.

Questions and Problems

1. Why might Fisher's theory about inflation and interest rates *not* be true?

2. You have estimated spot interest rates as follows:

Year	Spot rate
1	$r_1 = 5.00\%$
2	$r_2 = 5.40$
3	$r_3 = 5.70$
4	$r_4 = 5.90$
5	$r_5 = 6.00$

   (*a*) What are the discount factors for each date (that is, the present value of $1 paid in year *t*)?
   (*b*) What are the forward rates for each period?
   (*c*) Calculate the PV of the following Treasury notes:
      (i) 5 percent, 2-year note
      (ii) 5 percent, 5-year note
      (iii) 10 percent, 5-year note
   (*d*) Explain intuitively why the yield to maturity on the 10 percent bond is less than that on the 5 percent bond.
   (*e*) What should be the yield to maturity on a 5-year zero coupon bond?
   (*f*) Show that the correct yield to maturity on a 5-year annuity is 5.75 percent.
   (*g*) Here is a harder question: Explain intuitively why the yield on the 5-year Treasury notes described in part (*c*) must lie between the yield on a 5-year zero coupon bond and a 5-year annuity.

3. Look at the spot interest rates shown in problem 2. Suppose that someone told you that the 6-year spot interest rate was 4.80 percent. Why would you not

believe him? How could you make money if he was right? What is the minimum sensible value for the 6-year spot rate?

4. Look just one more time at the spot interest rates shown in problem 2. What can you deduce about the 1-year spot interest rate in 4 years if:
   (a) The expectations theory of term structure is right?
   (b) The liquidity-preference theory of term structure is right?
   (c) The term structure contains an inflation uncertainty premium?

5. Assume the term structure of interest rates is upward-sloping. How would you respond to the following comment? "The present term structure of interest rates makes short-term debt more attractive to corporate treasurers. Firms should avoid new long-term debt issues."

6. It has been suggested that the Fisher theory is a tautology. If the real rate of interest is defined as the difference between the nominal rate and the expected inflation rate, then the nominal rate *must* equal the real rate plus the expected inflation rate. In what sense is Fisher's theory *not* a tautology?

7. Look up prices of 10 U.S. Treasury bonds with different coupons and different maturities. Calculate how their prices would change if their yields to maturity increased by one percentage point. Are long-term bonds or short-term bonds most affected by the change in yields? Are high-coupon bonds or low-coupon bonds most affected?

*8. Look up prices of 10 corporate bonds with different coupons and maturities. Be sure to include some low-rated bonds on your list. Now estimate what these bonds would sell for if the United States government had guaranteed them. Calculate the value of the guarantee for each bond. Can you explain the differences between the 10 guarantee values?

9. Look in a recent issue of *The Wall Street Journal* at New York Stock Exchange bonds.
   (a) The yield shown in *The Wall Street Journal* is the current yield—that is, the coupon divided by price. Calculate the yield to maturity for a long-dated AT&T issue (assume annual interest payments).
   (b) How much higher is the yield on the AT&T bond than the yield on a Treasury bond with a similar maturity?
   (c) Glance quickly through the list of bonds and find one with a very high current yield. Calculate the yield to maturity on this bond.
   (d) Why is the yield to maturity on this bond so high?
   (e) Would the expected return be more or less than the yield to maturity?

10. Under what conditions can the expected real interest rate be negative?

11. Bond-rating services usually charge corporations for rating their bonds.
   (a) Why do they do this, rather than charge those investors who use the information?
   (b) Why will a company pay to have its bonds rated even when it knows that the service is likely to assign a below-average rating?
   (c) A few companies are not willing to pay for their bonds to be rated. What can investors deduce about the quality of these bonds?

*12. A 6 percent, 6-year bond yields 12 percent and a 10 percent, 6-year bond yields 8 percent. Calculate the 6-year spot rate. (Assume annual coupon payments.)

*13. In July 1989, stripped U.S. Treasury bonds were priced as follows:

Maturity	Price
1990	92.8%
1991	86.4
1992	80.3
1993	74.6
1994	69.2
1995	64.1
1996	59.3

Stripped bonds are "zero coupon" securities which make only one payment at maturity.
(*a*) Estimate the spot rates of interest.
(*b*) Estimate the forward rates of interest.
(*c*) If the expectations theory of term structure is correct, what was the expected 1-year rate of interest in 1995?

14. Are high-coupon bonds more likely to yield more than low-coupon bonds when the term structure is upward-sloping or when it is downward-sloping?

*15. Look back to the first Backwoods Chemical example at the start of Section 23-5. Suppose that the firm's book balance sheet is:

Backwoods Chemical Company (Book Values)

Net working capital	$ 400	$1,000	Debt
Net fixed assets	1,600	1,000	Equity (net worth)
Total assets	$2,000	$2,000	Total liabilities and net worth

The debt has a 1-year maturity and a promised interest rate of 9 percent. Thus, the promised payment to Backwoods's creditors is $1090. The market value of the assets is $1200, and the standard deviation of asset value is 45 percent per year. The risk-free interest rate is 9 percent. Use Appendix Table 6 to value the Backwoods debt and equity.

*16. Assume that Figure 23-3 correctly describes the path of short-term interest rates. The prices and yields of the three bonds that we described in Section 23-4 have changed. The yield to maturity of Medium is 8.18 percent. The yield to maturity on Long is currently 7.80 percent. Next period it will fall to 3.98 percent if the short-term interest rate falls and rise to 11.84 percent if the short-term rate rises.
(*a*) Are these yields consistent, or are there arbitrage profits to be made?
(*b*) How would your answer change if the yield of Medium were currently 7.93 percent and all other yields were unchanged?

17. In Section 23-3, we stated that the duration of the 8s of 2001 was 5.031 years. Construct a table like Table 23-3 to show that this is so.

*18. Look back at the example of the Short, Medium, and Long bonds in Section 23-4. Assume that to invest in Medium, investors require an expected return of 11 percent in year 1 (i.e., a risk premium of 3 percent).

(a) Recalculate the value of Medium and the ratio of its expected reward to risk.

(b) Now find the value of Long at each point in time. Remember that Long must offer the same expected reward per unit of risk as Medium.

(c) Show now how you could replicate the Medium bond with a package of the Short and Long bonds. (*Hint:* If the spread of possible returns on Medium is x percent of the spread on Long, then your investment in Long should be x percent of your investment in Medium.)

(d) Finally, pretend that investors are risk-neutral and show that the prices you have estimated for each bond are equal to the expected future price in a risk-neutral world discounted at the risk-free interest rate.

19. The formula for the duration of a perpetual bond which makes an equal payment each year in perpetuity is $(1 + \text{yield})/\text{yield}$. If bonds yield 5 percent, which has the longer duration—a perpetual bond or a 15-year zero coupon bond? What if the yield is 10 percent?

20. Here is a difficult question: We stated in question 19 that the duration of a perpetual bond which makes an equal payment each year in perpetuity is $(1 + \text{yield})/\text{yield}$. Can you prove this result?

21. You have just been fired as CEO. As consolation the board of directors gives you a 5-year consulting contract at $150,000 per year. What is the duration of this contract if your personal borrowing rate is 9 percent? Use duration to calculate the change in the contract's present value for a .5 percent increase in your borrowing rate.

22. The 1-year spot rate is $r_1 = 6$ percent, and the forward rate for a 1-year loan maturing in year 2 is $f_2 = 6.4$ percent. Similarly, $f_3 = 7.1$ percent, $f_4 = 7.3$ percent, and $f_5 = 8.2$ percent. What are the spot rates r_2, r_3, r_4, and r_5? If the expectations hypothesis holds, what can you say about expected future interest rates?

23. Suppose your company will receive $100 million at $t = 4$ but must make a $107 million payment at $t = 5$. Assume the spot and forward rates from problem 22. Show how the company can lock in the interest rate at which it can invest at $t = 4$. Will the $100 million, invested at this locked-in rate, be sufficient to cover the $107 million liability?

24. Use the rates from problem 22 one more time. Consider the following bonds, each with a 5-year maturity. Calculate the yield to maturity for each. Which is the better investment (or are they equally attractive)? Each has $1000 face value and pays coupons annually.

Coupon	Price
5	92.07%
7	100.31
12	120.92

25. Find the arbitrage opportunity (opportunities?).

Bond	Maturity (years)	Coupon ($)	Price ($)
A	3	zero	751.30
B	4	50	842.30
C	4	120	1065.28
D	4	100	980.57
E	3	140	1120.12
F	3	70	1001.62
G	2	zero	834.00

Assume for simplicity that coupons are paid annually. In each case the face value of the bond is $1000.

26. (**a**) What spot and forward rates are embedded in the following Treasury bonds? The price of 1-year Treasury bills is 93.46 percent. Assume for simplicity that bonds make only annual payments.

Coupon (percent)	Maturity (years)	Price (percent)
4	2	94.92
8	3	103.64

(*Hint:* Can you devise a mixture of long and short positions in these bonds that give a cash payoff only in year 2? In year 3?)

(**b**) A 3-year bond with a 4 percent coupon is selling at 95.00 percent. Is there a profit opportunity here? If so, how would you take advantage of it?

27. In Figure 23-6 we defined leverage as the ratio of the *market value* of debt to the market value of assets. An alternative would be to define it as the *face value* of debt to the market value of assets. Using this definition and assuming a zero risk-free rate of interest, use the Black-Scholes model to calculate the value of a zero-coupon bond for different maturities for (*a*) a firm with 40 percent leverage and (*b*) one with 60 percent leverage. In all other respects make the same assumptions that were used to produce Figure 23-6. Now plot draw two graphs. In the first, show bond value on the vertical axis and maturity on the horizontal axis. In the second, show the bond yield on the vertical axis.

24

The Many Different Kinds of Debt

In Chapters 17 and 18 we discussed how much a company should borrow. But companies also need to think about what *type* of debt to issue. They must decide whether to issue short-term or long-term debt, whether to issue straight bonds or convertible bonds, whether to issue in the United States or in the euromarkets, and whether to sell the debt publicly or place it privately with a few large investors.

Large companies are almost continuously facing these decisions. Take, for example, Grand Metropolitan Company, a British multinational, whose brands include Pillsbury, Burger King, and Häagen Dazs. During 1994 GrandMet raised over $2 billion by selling a variety of different debt and preferred securities.[1] Until then, a high proportion of GrandMet's dollar funding had come from selling commercial paper in the United States—that is, a very short term debt sold directly by the company to investors. Early in 1994 GrandMet became concerned about the possible effect of rising interest rates on the cost of this short-term borrowing. Therefore, its first step was to issue a $400 million 5-year eurobond at a fixed interest rate of 7 percent, which was just over half a percent more than yields on U.S. Treasury bonds. The issue proved so popular with investors that GrandMet was later able to issue an additional $200 million of the same bond.

Less than 1 week after the first tranche of this eurobond issue, GrandMet raised a further $600 million by a second bond offering, this time in the United States. The bond was a 10-year zero coupon issue. This means that it did not pay any interest, but since each bond was sold at only 46.54 percent of its face value, investors could look forward to more than doubling their money over the 10 years.

Later in the same year, GrandMet was again raising money in the United States, this time by a $500 million issue of *MIPs (monthly income preferred securities)*. MIPs work as follows: A firm sets up a special-purpose subsidiary in a tax haven, which issues the preferred stock and then lends the money to the parent company. Since the parent company can deduct the interest on the loan from taxable income, it is able to capture the tax advantage of debt even though it issues (through the subsidiary) preferred stock.

---

[1] GrandMet's debt issues in 1994 are described in C. Olivier, "Sidestepping the Bear Market," *Corporate Finance*, 28–30 (December 1994).

Each of these issues was sold through underwriters and publicly traded, but in addition GrandMet made arrangements to sell up to $1.2 billion of medium-term notes directly to investors. During the year it made about a dozen issues of these medium-term notes, raising a total of $250 million.

GrandMet also did not wholly do away with short-term borrowing in 1994. Indeed, it set up a program that enabled it to sell up to $1 billion of commercial paper in the eurocurrency markets as well as in the United States. In addition, it took advantage of intense competition in the eurocurrency markets to make arrangements to borrow up to $3 billion from a syndicate of international banks.

Like GrandMet's financial manager, you need to choose the type of debt that makes sense for your company. For example, short-term debt may be more appropriate if the firm has mainly short-term assets such as working capital. Secured debt is generally best suited for firms with readily saleable assets such as commercial real estate. Sometimes, also like GrandMet's financial manager, you may be able to take advantage of competition between lenders that opens a temporary window of opportunity in a particular sector of the debt market. The effect may be only a few basis-points reduction in yield, but on a large issue that can translate into a saving of several million dollars. Remember the saying, "A million dollars here and a million there—pretty soon it begins to add up to real money."[2]

Our focus in this chapter is on straight long-term debt.[3] We begin our discussion by looking at the different types of bonds. We examine the differences between senior and junior bonds and between secured and unsecured bonds. Then we describe how bonds may be repaid by means of a sinking fund and how the borrower or the lender may have an option for early repayment. We also look at some of the restrictive provisions that seek to prevent the company from taking actions that would damage the bonds' value. We not only describe the different features of corporate debt but also try to explain *why* sinking funds, repayment options, and the like exist. They are not simply matters of custom; there are generally good economic reasons for their use.

Debt may be sold to the public or placed privately with large financial institutions. Because privately placed bonds are broadly similar to public issues, we will not discuss them at length. However, we will discuss another form of private debt, known as project finance. This is the glamorous part of the debt market. The words *project finance* conjure up images of multimillion-dollar loans to finance mining ventures in exotic parts of the world. You'll find there's something to the popular image, but it's not the whole story.

We conclude the chapter by looking at a few unusual bonds and considering the reasons for innovation in the debt markets.

24-1 DOMESTIC BONDS, FOREIGN BONDS, AND EUROBONDS

A firm can issue a bond either in its home country or in another country. For example, we saw earlier how the British firm GrandMet raised $600 million by an offering of bonds in the United States. Of course, any firm that raises money abroad is subject to the rules of the country in which it does so. For example, any issue in the United States of publicly traded bonds needs to be registered with the SEC. Since

---

[2]The remark was made by the late Senator Everett Dirksen. However, he was talking billions.

[3]We describe short- and medium-term debt in Chapter 32.

the cost of registration can be particularly large for foreign firms, these firms often avoid registration by complying with the SEC's Rule 144A for bond issues in the United States. Rule 144A bonds can be bought and sold only by large financial institutions.[4]

Bonds that are sold in another country's bond market are known as *foreign bonds*. The United States is by far the largest market for foreign bonds, but Japan and Switzerland are also important. These bonds have a variety of nicknames: a bond sold by a foreign company in the United States is known as a *yankee bond;* one sold by a foreign firm in Japan is a *samurai;* and so on.

There is also an international market for long-term debt known as the eurobond market. A **eurobond** is a bond that is sold simultaneously in a number of foreign countries by an international syndicate of underwriters. Although eurobonds may be sold throughout the world, eurobond underwriters and dealers are mainly located in London. They include the London branches of United States, European, and Japanese commercial and investment banks. As barriers to the movement of capital have come down, the distinction between eurobonds and domestic bonds has become less clear-cut. For example, a U.S. firm may offer its bonds simultaneously in the United States and internationally.

Eurobond issues are generally made in currencies that are actively traded, fully convertible, and relatively stable. The United States dollar has been the most popular choice, followed by the yen, the deutschemark, the British pound, and the French franc. There is also a sizeable market in ECU bonds. An *ECU*, or European currency unit, is simply a basket of European currencies.[5] Occasionally, companies issue dual-currency bonds that pay interest in one currency and principal in another.

The eurobond market arose during the 1960s because the United States government imposed an interest-equalization tax on the purchase of foreign securities and discouraged American corporations from exporting capital. Therefore both European and American multinationals were forced to tap an international market for capital. The interest-equalization tax was removed in 1974, and there are no longer any controls on capital exports.[6] Since firms in the United States can now choose whether to borrow in New York or London, the interest rates in the two markets are usually similar. However, the eurobond market is not directly subject to regulation by the United States authorities, and therefore the financial manager needs to be alert to small differences in the costs of borrowing in one market rather than another.

24-2 THE BOND CONTRACT

To give you some feel for the bond contract (and for some of the language in which it is couched), we have summarized in Table 24-1 the terms of an issue of thirty-year bonds by Ralston Purina Company. We will look at each of the principal items in turn.

---

[4]We described Rule 144A in Section 15-3.

[5]When an ECU bond matures, lenders don't receive a mixture of currencies. They take payment in the currency of their choice at the current exchange rate for ECUs.

[6]Also, until 1984 the United States imposed a withholding tax on interest payments to foreign investors. Investors could avoid this tax by buying a eurobond issued in London rather than a similar bond issued in New York.

TABLE 24-1

Summary of terms of 9½ percent sinking fund debenture 2016 issued by Ralston Purina Company

Listed	New York Stock Exchange
Trustee	Continental Bank, Chicago
Rights on default	The trustee or 25% of the debentures outstanding may declare interest due and payable.
Indenture modification	Indenture may be modified except as provided with the consent of two-thirds of the debentures outstanding.
Registered	Fully registered
Denomination	$1000
To be issued	$86.4 million
Issue date	June 4, 1986
Offered	Issued at a price of 97.60% plus accrued interest (proceeds to Company 96.725%) through First Boston Corporation, Goldman Sachs and Company, Shearson Lehman Brothers, Stifel Nicolaus and Company, and associates.
Interest	At a rate of 9½% per annum, payable June 1 and December 1 to holders registered on May 15 and November 15.
Security	Not secured. Company will not permit to have any lien on its property or assets without equally and ratably securing the debt securities.
Sale and lease-back	Company will not enter into any sale and lease-back transaction unless the Company within 120 days after the transfer of title to such principal property applies to the redemption of the debt securities at the then-applicable option redemption price an amount equal to the net proceeds received by the Company upon such sale.
Maturity	June 1, 2016
Sinking fund	Annually between June 2, 1996, and June 2, 2015, sufficient to redeem not less than $13.5 million principal amount, plus similar optional payments. Sinking fund is designed to redeem 90% of the debentures prior to maturity.
Callable	At whole or in part at any time at the option of the Company on at least 30, but not more than 60, days' notice to each May 31 as follows:

1989	106.390	1990	106.035	1991	105.680
1992	105.325	1993	104.970	1994	104.615
1995	104.260	1996	103.905	1997	103.550
1998	103.195	1999	102.840	2000	102.485
2001	102.130	2002	101.775	2003	101.420
2004	101.065	2005	100.710	2006	100.355

and thereafter at 100 plus accrued interest; provided, however, that prior to June 1, 1996, the Company may not redeem the bonds from, or in anticipation of, moneys borrowed having an effective interest cost of less than 9.748%.

....

**Inden-
ture, or
Trust
Deed**

The Ralston Purina offering was a public issue of bonds which was registered with the SEC and listed on the New York Stock Exchange. In the case of a public issue, the bond agreement is in the form of an **indenture,** or **trust deed,** between the borrower and a trust company.[7] Continental Bank, which is the trust company for the Ralston-Purina bond, represents the bondholders. It must see that the terms of the indenture are observed, administer any sinking fund, and look after the bondholders' interests in the event of default. A copy of the bond indenture is included in the registration statement. It is a turgid legal document,[8] and its main provisions are summarized in the prospectus to the issue.[9]

In the case of a private issue of debt, where there may often be only a single lender, there is usually no need for a separate trustee and the contract may just be a simple promissory note or IOU.

Moving down Table 24-1, you will see that the Ralston Purina bonds are registered. This means that the company's registrar records the ownership of each bond and the company pays the interest and the final principal amount directly to each owner.[10]

Almost all bond issues in the United States are issued in *registered* form, but in many countries bonds may be issued in *bearer* form. In this case, the certificate constitutes the primary evidence of ownership, so the bondholder must send in coupons to claim interest and must send the certificate itself to claim the final repayment of principal. Eurobonds almost invariably allow the owner to hold them in bearer form. However, since the ownership of such bonds cannot be traced, the IRS has tried to deter United States residents from holding them.[11]

....

**The
Bond
Terms**

Like most dollar bonds, the Ralston Purina bonds have a face value of $1000. Notice, however, that the bond price is shown as a percentage of face value. Also, the price is stated net of *accrued interest*. This means that the bond buyer must pay not only the quoted price but also the amount of any future interest that may have accrued. For example, an investor who bought bonds for delivery on (say) June 11, 1986, would be receiving them 10 days into the first interest period. Therefore, accrued interest would be $10/360 \times 9.5 = .26$ percent, and the investor would pay a price of 97.60 percent plus .26 percent of accrued interest.[12]

---

[7]In the case of a eurobond, there is a *fiscal agent* who carries out broadly similar functions to a bond trustee.

[8]For example, the indenture for one J. C. Penney bond states: "In any case where several matters are required to be certified by, or covered by an opinion of, any specified Person, it is not necessary that all such matters be certified by, or covered by the opinion of, only one such Person, or that they be certified or covered by only one document, but one such Person may certify or give an opinion with respect to some matters and one or more other such Persons as to other matters, and any such Person may certify or give an opinion as to such matters in one or several documents." Try saying that three times fast.

[9]Eurobonds and many private placements are accompanied by an *offering memorandum,* which is similar to a prospectus.

[10]Often, investors do not physically hold the security; instead, their ownership is represented by a book entry. (The "book" is in practice a computer.)

[11]United States residents cannot generally deduct capital losses on bearer bonds. Also, payments on such bonds cannot be made to a bank account in the United States.

[12]In the U.S. corporate bond market accrued interest is calculated on the assumption that a year is composed of twelve 30-day months; in some other markets (such as the U.S. Treasury bond market) calculations recognize the actual number of days in each calendar month.

The Ralston Purina bonds were offered to the public at a price of 97.60 percent, but the company received only 96.725 percent. The difference represents the underwriters' spread. Of the $86.4 million raised, about $85.6 million went to the company and $.8 million to the underwriters.

Since the bonds were issued at a price of 97.60 percent, investors who hold the bonds to maturity receive a capital gain over the 30 years of 2.40 percent.[13] However, the bulk of their return is provided by the regular interest payment. The annual interest or *coupon* payment on each bond is 9.50 percent of $1000, or $95. This interest is payable semiannually, so every 6 months investors receive interest of 95/2 = $47.50. Most United States bonds pay interest semiannually, but a comparable eurobond would generally pay interest annually.[14]

The regular interest payment on a bond is a hurdle that the company must keep jumping.[15] If the company ever fails to pay the interest, lenders can demand their money back instead of waiting until matters may have deteriorated further. Thus interest payments provide added protection for lenders.[16]

Sometimes bonds are sold with a lower interest payment but at a larger discount on their face value, so investors receive a significant part of their return in the form of capital appreciation.[17] The ultimate is the zero coupon bond, which pays no interest at all; in this case the entire return consists of price appreciation.[18]

The Ralston Purina interest payment is fixed for the life of the bond, but in some issues the payment varies with the general level of interest rates. For example, the payment may be tied to the U.S. Treasury bill rate or to the London interbank offered rate (LIBOR), which is the rate at which banks lend eurodollars to one another. Often, floating-rate notes specify a minimum (or "floor") interest rate, or they may specify a maximum (or "cap") on the rate.[19] You may also come across "collars," which stipulate both a maximum and a minimum payment, or "drop-locks," which provide that if the rate falls to a specified trigger point, the payment is then fixed for the remainder of the bond's life.

Floating-rate notes (FRNs) are particularly common in the eurobond market. Until 1974 they were rare in the United States, but in that year Citicorp made an

---

[13]This gain is not taxed as income as long as it amounts to less than .25 percent a year. We discuss later the taxation of bonds that are sold at a deep discount on their face value.

[14]In Table 23-1 we showed you an extract from a book of yields to maturity. These yields were semiannually compounded; in other words, they are equal to twice the 6-month yield. Because eurobonds pay interest annually, it is conventional to quote yields to maturity on eurobonds on an *annually* compounded basis. Remember this when comparing yields.

[15]There is one type of bond on which the borrower is obliged to pay interest only if it is covered by the year's earnings. Such so-called *income bonds* are rare and have largely been issued as part of railroad reorganizations. For a discussion of the attractions of income bonds, see J. J. McConnell and G. G. Schlarbaum, "Returns, Risks, and Pricing of Income Bonds, 1956–1976 (Does Money Have an Odor?)," *Journal of Business*, **54**:33–64 (January 1981).

[16]See F. Black and J. C. Cox, "Valuing Corporate Securities: Some Effects of Bond Indenture Provisions," *Journal of Finance*, **31**:351–367 (May 1976). Black and Cox point out that the interest payment would be a trivial hurdle if the company could sell assets to make the payment. Such sales are, therefore, restricted.

[17]A zero coupon is often called a "pure discount bond." Any bond that is issued at a discount is known as an *original issue discount (OID)* bond.

[18]The ultimate of ultimates was an issue on behalf of a charity of a perpetual zero coupon bond.

[19]Instead of issuing a straight (uncapped) FRN, a company will sometimes issue a capped FRN and at the same time sell the cap to another investor. The first investor receives a coupon payment up to the specified maximum, and the second investor receives any interest in excess of this maximum.

$850 million issue, which prompted a small boom in FRNs. The reason? Floating-rate notes allowed banks to sidestep the limits on the interest rate that they could pay for time deposits.[20] Although the ceilings on interest rates have now been removed, floating-rate notes continue to be popular with banks and finance companies. Since the interest that these companies earn on their assets varies with the level of interest rates, they can offset some of these fluctuations by simultaneously issuing floating-rate notes. If short-term interest rates fall, then banks *receive* lower interest on their loans to customers, but they also *pay* less interest on their floating-rate debt.

24-3 SECURITY AND SENIORITY

Almost all debt issues by industrial and financial companies are general unsecured obligations. Longer-term unsecured issues like the Ralston Purina bond are usually called **debentures;** shorter-term issues are usually called **notes.** Occasionally, unsecured issues may be guaranteed by another company, and private placements by smaller companies are guaranteed by the company's management. It does not necessarily matter in these cases that the manager is not personally wealthy—the guarantee serves as an important signal of the manager's confidence and is a fine incentive.

Utility company bonds are commonly secured. This means that if the company defaults on the debt, the trustee or lender may take possession of the relevant assets. If these are insufficient to satisfy the claim, the remaining debt will have a general claim alongside any unsecured debt against the other assets of the firm.

The vast majority of secured debt consists of **mortgage bonds.** Some of these mortgages are *closed*, which means that no more bonds may be issued against the mortgage. However, usually there is no specific limit to the amount of bonds that may be secured (in which case the mortgage is said to be *open*). Mortgage bonds sometimes provide a claim against a specific building, but they are more often secured on almost all the company's property.[21] The issuer undertakes to insure this property and to keep it in good repair. Frequently the indenture will provide for a fixed annual contribution for such maintenance, with any unspent balance being used to redeem bonds. Of course, the value of any mortgage depends not only on how well the property is maintained but also on whether it has value in alternative uses. A custom-built machine for producing buggy whips will not be worth much when the market for buggy whips dries up.

Collateral trust bonds closely resemble mortgage bonds except that with a collateral trust bond the claim is against securities held by the corporation. Generally these bonds are issued by holding companies—that is, firms whose main assets con-

---

[20]See Section 17-3. In 1985 a change in government regulation again led Citicorp to make an issue of floating-rate notes. The SEC required that investments made by money-market funds must have an average maturity of no more than 120 days, where *maturity* was defined as "the period until the next readjustment of the interest rate." Citicorp therefore reset the interest rate on the notes each *week*. SEC regulations also required that money-market funds should buy only debt due within 1 year. The Citicorp notes had a maturity of 364 days, but each quarter the notes were automatically extended unless the investor requested otherwise. Therefore the notes could be held by money-market funds even though the final repayment could be extended indefinitely.

[21]Many mortgage bonds are secured not only by existing property but also by "after-acquired" property. However, if the company buys only property that is already mortgaged, the bondholder would have only a junior claim on the new property. Therefore, mortgage bonds with after-acquired-property clauses also restrict the extent to which the company can purchase additional mortgaged property.

sist of common stock in a number of subsidiaries. The problem for the lender is that this stock is junior to *all* other claims on the assets of the subsidiaries, and so the collateral trust bond will usually include detailed restrictions on the freedom of the subsidiaries to issue debt or preferred stock.

The third principal form of secured debt is the **equipment trust certificate.** This is most frequently used to finance new railroad rolling stock but may also be used to finance trucks, aircraft, and ships. Under this arrangement a trustee obtains formal ownership of the equipment. The company makes a down payment of 10 to 25 percent of the cost of the equipment, and the balance is provided by a package of trust certificates with different maturities that might typically run from 1 to 15 years. Only when all these debts have finally been paid off does the company become the formal owner of the equipment. Because the trustee holds the title to the pledged equipment and can immediately repossess it in the event of default, equipment trust certificates offer good security to their holders. Bond rating agencies such as Moody's or Standard and Poor's usually rate equipment trust certificates one grade higher than the railroad's regular debt.

Bonds may be senior claims, or they may be subordinated to the senior bonds or to *all* other creditors.[22] If the firm defaults, the senior bonds come first in the pecking order. For example, a company may issue first and second mortgage bonds. The first mortgage bonds have first claim against the assets, then come the second mortgage bonds.

24-4 REPAYMENT PROVISIONS

Sinking Funds

The maturity date of the Ralston Purina bond is June 1, 2016, but part of the issue is repaid on a regular basis before maturity. To do this, the company makes a regular payment into a *sinking fund.* If it pays cash into the sinking fund, then the trustee selects bonds by lottery and uses the cash to redeem them at par.[23] As an alternative to paying cash, the company can buy bonds in the marketplace and pay these into the fund.[24] This is a valuable option for the company. If the price of the bond is low, the firm will satisfy the sinking fund requirement by buying bonds in the market; if the price is high, it will call the bonds by lottery.

Generally, there is a mandatory fund which *must* be satisfied and an optional fund which can be satisfied if the borrower chooses. For example, Ralston Purina *must* contribute at least $13.5 million each year to the sinking fund but has the option to contribute a further $13.5 million. A number of private placements (particularly those in extractive industries) require a payment only when net income exceeds some specified level.

---

[22]If a bond does not specifically state that it is junior, you can assume that it is senior.

[23]Every investor dreams of buying up the entire supply of a sinking fund bond that is selling way below face value and then forcing the company to buy the bonds back at face value. "Cornering the market" in this way is fun to dream about but difficult to do. For a discussion, see K. B. Dunn and C. S. Spatt, "A Strategic Analysis of Sinking Fund Bonds," *Journal of Financial Economics,* **13**:399–424 (September 1984).

[24]If the bonds are privately placed, the company obviously cannot repurchase them in the marketplace—it must call them at par. Similarly, equipment trust certificates consist of a package of bonds that mature in successive years. Such bonds are usually called *serial bonds.* A package of serial bonds is rather like a sinking fund bond. Both provide regular repayments of the debt. But the serial bond does not give the borrower the option to buy the bonds in the marketplace—the borrower *must* redeem the bonds at par.

As in the case of Ralston Purina, most "sinkers" begin to operate after about 10 years. For lower-quality issues the payments are usually sufficient to redeem the entire issue in equal installments over the life of the bond. In contrast, high-quality bonds often have light sinking fund requirements with large "balloon" payments at maturity. Generally, bonds may be redeemed for the sinking fund at par, but some issues provide for a gently declining schedule of repayment prices.[25]

We saw earlier that interest payments provide a regular test of the company's solvency. Sinking funds provide an additional hurdle that the firm must keep jumping. If it cannot pay the cash into the sinking fund, the lenders can demand their money back. That is why long-dated, low-quality issues usually involve larger sinking funds.

Unfortunately, a sinking fund is a weak test of solvency *if the firm is allowed to repurchase bonds in the market.* Since the *market* value of the debt must always be less than the value of the firm, financial distress reduces the cost of repurchasing debt in the market. So the sinking fund is a hurdle that gets progressively lower as the hurdler gets weaker.

Call Provisions

Corporate bond issues often include a call option that allows the company to pay back the debt early. Occasionally, you come across bonds that give the *investor* the repayment option. Retractable (or putable) bonds give investors the option to demand early repayment, and extendible bonds give them the option to extend the bond's life.

Ralston Purina has an option to buy back, or "call," the entire bond issue. If it does so, it is required to pay a premium which declines from 6.390 percent in the first year to zero in the year 2007. The company is subject to two limitations on the use of this call option: Until 1989 the company is prohibited from calling the bond in any circumstances, and from 1989 to 1996 it cannot call the bond in order to replace it with new debt yielding less than the 9.748 percent yield on the original bond.

These repayment provisions are fairly typical of long-term bonds. Most such issues mature in 25 or 30 years, are callable at a premium that is initially roughly equal to the coupon, and are "nonrefundable" (NR) "below interest cost" for 10 to 15 years. Medium-term loans either are wholly noncallable (NC) or are nonrefundable below interest cost for most of their lives.

The option to call the bond is obviously attractive to the issuer. If interest rates decline and bond prices rise, the issuer has the opportunity to repurchase the bonds below their potential value. For example, suppose that by 2000 yields on investment-equality bonds have fallen to 7 percent. A 9.5 percent bond with 16 years to run would be worth 123.8 percent, or $1238. The call provision allows Ralston Purina to repurchase bonds that are worth $1238 for only $1024.85. Or the company can, if it chooses, hold on and hope to do even better by calling the bonds in 2001.

How does Ralston Purina know when to call its bonds? The answer is simple: Other things equal, if it wishes to maximize the value of its stock, it must minimize the value of its bond. Therefore, the company should never call the bond if its market value is less than the call price, for that would just be giving a present to the bondholders. Equally, Ralston Purina *should* call the bond if it is worth *more* than the call price.

Of course, investors take the call option into account when they buy or sell the bond. They know that the company will call the bond as soon as it is worth more

---

[25]Some bonds have a *purchase fund.* In this case the company agrees to put aside money which is to be used to repurchase bonds in the market only if the price is below par.

Figure 24-1 Relationship between the value of a callable bond and that of a straight (non-callable) bond. Assumptions: (1) Both bonds have an 8 percent coupon and a 5-year maturity. (2) The callable bond may be called at any time before maturity. (3) The short-term interest rate follows a random walk, and the expected returns on bonds of all maturities are equal. [*Source:* M. J. Brennan and E. S. Schwartz, "Savings Bonds, Retractable Bonds, and Callable Bonds," *Journal of Financial Economics,* **5**:67–88 (1977).]

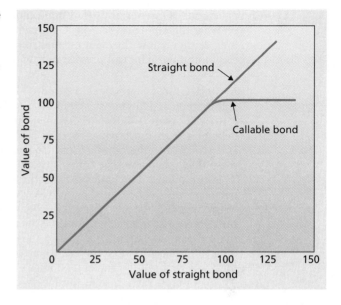

than the call price, so no investor will be willing to pay more than the call price for the bond. The market price of the bond may, therefore, reach the call price, but it will not rise above it. This gives the company the following rule for calling its bonds: *Call the bond when, and only when, the market price reaches the call price.*[26]

If we know how bond prices behave over time, we can modify our basic option-valuation model of Chapter 20 to get the value of the callable bond, *given* that investors know the company will call the issue as soon as the market price reaches the call price. For example, look at Figure 24-1. It illustrates the relationship between the value of a straight 8 percent 5-year bond and the value of a callable 8 percent 5-year bond. Suppose that the value of the straight bond is very low. In this case there is little likelihood that the company will ever wish to call its bonds. (Remember that it will call the bonds only if they are worth more than the call price.) Therefore the value of the callable bond will be almost identical to the value of the straight bond. Now suppose that the straight bond is worth exactly 100. In this case there is a good chance that the company will wish at some time to call its bonds. Therefore the value of our callable bond will be slightly less than that of the straight bond. If interest rates decline further, the price of the straight will move above 100. But nobody will ever pay *more* than 100 for the callable bond.

A call provision is not a free lunch. It provides the issuer with a valuable option, but that is recognized in a lower issue price. So why do companies bother with call

---

[26]See M. J. Brennan and E. S. Schwartz, "Savings Bonds, Retractable Bonds, and Callable Bonds," *Journal of Financial Economics,* **5**:67–88 (1977). Of course, this assumes that the bond is correctly priced, that investors are acting rationally, and that investors expect the *firm* to act rationally. Also, we ignore some complications. First, you may not wish to call a bond if you are prevented by a nonrefunding clause from issuing new debt. Second, the call premium is a tax-deductible expense for the company but is taxed as a capital gain to the bondholder. Third, there are other possible tax consequences to both the company and the investor from replacing a low-coupon bond with a higher-coupon bond. Fourth, there are costs to calling and reissuing debt.

provisions? One reason is that bond indentures often place a number of restrictions on what the company can do. Companies are happy to agree to these restrictions as long as they know they can escape from them if the restrictions subsequently prove too inhibiting. The call provision provides the escape route.

<table>
<tr><td>

**Defeas-
ance**
</td><td>

In 1985 United States Steel retired its issue of 4⅝ percent subordinated debentures and thereby added almost $70 million to pretax income. The method that it used to retire the bonds is known as *defeasance*. This works as follows: The firm transfers the debt to a trust fund, which is then responsible for making all payments of interest and principal to the bondholders. To provide the trust fund with the wherewithall to make these payments, the firm also contributes to the trust a package of United States Treasury bonds. The cash flows on these Treasury bonds are designed to match the payments on the firm's debt.
</td></tr>
</table>

When U.S. Steel retired its debentures, interest rates were relatively high and the debentures were selling well below their face value of $168 million. Thus it cost the company less than $168 million to buy the matching portfolio of Treasury bonds. This difference between the face value of the debt and the cost of the matching portfolio was reported by the company as extraordinary income.

As interest rates rose in the 1980s, the prices of many company bonds fell below their face values, and this led to a flurry of interest in defeasance. Firms found that defeasance increased their reported income and removed debt from the balance sheet.[27] But how did investors respond? The bondholders were understandably delighted, since they now had a bond that was backed by United States treasuries. Despite the higher reported earnings, shareholders were *less* pleased. The Treasury bonds that the firms bought were risk-free and therefore cost more than the risky bonds that the firm retired. So an announcement of bond defeasance usually led to a rise in the price of the defeased bonds but a fall in the price of the stock.[28]

24-5 RESTRICTIVE COVENANTS

The difference between a corporate bond and a comparable Treasury bond is that the company has an option to default whereas the government supposedly doesn't. That is a valuable option. If you don't believe us, think about whether (other things equal) you would prefer to be a shareholder in a company with limited liability or in a company with unlimited liability. Of course you would prefer to have the option to walk away from your debts. Unfortunately, every silver lining has its cloud, and the drawback to having a default option is that corporate bondholders expect to be compensated for giving it to you. That is why corporate bonds sell at lower prices and therefore higher yields than government bonds.[29]

Investors know there is a risk of default when they buy a corporate bond. But they still want to make sure that the company plays fair. They don't want it to gam-

---

[27]There are two forms of defeasance. With *in-substance defeasance* the debt is no longer shown on the balance sheet but the firm is still obliged to observe the terms of the indenture. With *legal defeasance* (or *novation*) all the firm's obligations are extinguished.

[28]See, for example, J. R. Hand, P. J. Hughes, and S. E. Sefcik, "In-Substance Defeasances: Security Price Reactions and Motivations," *Journal of Accounting and Economics*, **13**:47–89 (May 1990).

[29]In Chapters 20 and 23 we showed that this option to default is equivalent to a put option on the assets of the firm.

ble with their money or to take unreasonable risks. Therefore, the bond indenture may include a number of restrictive covenants to prevent the company from purposely increasing the value of its default option.[30]

After Ralston Purina had issued its bonds, the company had a total market value of $7.6 billion and total long-term debt of $2.1 billion. The debt-to-value ratio was .28. This meant that the value of the company could fall by about 72 percent before Ralston Purina would want to default. But suppose that after issuing the 9.5 percent bonds, Ralston Purina announces a further $1 billion bond issue. The company now has a market value of $8.6 billion and long-term debt of $3.1 billion. The debt ratio has increased from 28 to 36 percent of the value of the assets. The original bondholders are slightly worse off. If they had known about the new issue, they would not have been willing to pay such a high price for their bonds.

The new issue hurts the original bondholders by increasing the *ratio* of senior debt to company value. The bondholders would not object to the issue if the company kept the ratio the same by simultaneously issuing common stock. Therefore, the bond agreement often states that the company may issue more senior debt only if the ratio of senior debt to the net asset value is within a specified limit.

Why don't senior lenders demand limits on *subordinated* debt? The answer is that the subordinated lender does not get *any* money until the senior bondholders have been paid in full.[31] The senior bondholders, therefore, view subordinated bonds in much the same way that they view equity: they would be happy to see an issue of either. Of course, the converse is not true. Holders of subordinated debt *do* care both about the total amount of debt and about the proportion that is senior to their claim. As a result, the indenture for an issue of subordinated debt generally includes a restriction on both total debt and senior debt.

All bondholders worry that the company may issue more secured debt. An issue of mortgage bonds usually imposes a limit on the amount of secured debt. This is not necessary when you are issuing unsecured debentures. As long as the debenture holders are given equal protection, they do not care how much you mortgage your assets. Therefore the bond agreement for the Ralston Purina debenture includes a so-called **negative pledge clause,** in which the debenture holders simply say, "Me, too."[32]

During the 1950s and 1960s many companies found that they could circumvent some of these restrictions if, instead of borrowing money to buy an asset, they entered into a long-term agreement to rent or lease it. For the debtholder this arrangement is very similar to secured borrowing. Therefore indentures began to include limitations on leasing.

Leases are an example of hidden debt. After their fingers had been burned, bondholders began to impose restrictions on leases. But you want to shut the stable door *before* your fingers have been burned. Perhaps, therefore, lenders should be placing restrictions on other kinds of hidden debt, such as some of the project financings that we describe in Section 24-6.

---

[30]We described in Section 18-3 some of the games that managers can play at the expense of bondholders.

[31]In practice the courts do not always observe the strict rules of precedence (see the appendix to Chapter 18). Therefore the subordinated debtholder may receive *some* payment even when the senior debtholder is not fully paid off.

[32]"Me too" is not acceptable legal jargon. Instead, the Ralston Purina bond agreement states that the company will not consent to any lien on its assets without securing the debentures "equally and ratably." If the firm *does* subsequently issue secured debt, this negative pledge clause allows the debenture holders to demand repayment. But it does not invalidate the security given to the other debtholders.

We have talked about how an unscrupulous borrower can try to increase the value of the default option by issuing more debt. But that is not the only way that such a company can exploit its existing bondholders. For example, we know that the value of an option is affected by dividend payments. If the company pays out large dividends to its shareholders and doesn't replace the cash by an issue of stock, there is less asset value available to cover the debt. Therefore many bond issues restrict the amount of dividends that the company may pay.[33]

Changes in Covenant Protection

Before 1980 most bonds had covenants limiting further issues of debt and payments of dividends. But then large institutions relaxed their requirements for large public companies and accepted bonds with no such restrictions. This was the case with RJR Nabisco, the food and tobacco giant, which in 1988 had $5 billion of A-rated debt outstanding. In that year the company was taken over, and $19 billion of additional debt was substituted for equity. As soon as the first plans for the takeover were announced, the value of the existing debt fell by about 12 percent, and it was downrated to BB. For one of the bondholders, Metropolitan Life Insurance, this meant a $40 million loss. Metropolitan sued the company, arguing that the bonds contained an *implied* covenant preventing major financing changes that would undercut existing bondholders.[34] However, Metropolitan lost: the courts held that only the written covenants count.

Restrictions on debt issues and dividend payments quietly returned to fashion. Bond analysts and lawyers began to look more closely at *event risks* like the debt-financed takeover that socked Metropolitan. Some companies offered *poison put* clauses that oblige the borrower to repay the bonds if a large quantity of stock is bought by a single investor and the firm's bonds are down-rated. Would covenants have protected Metropolitan Life and the other bondholders against loss? A study by Paul Asquith and Thierry Wizman suggests that they would have.[35] On average, the announcement of a leveraged buy-out led to a fall of 5.2 percent in the value of the bond if there were no restrictions on further debt issues, dividend payments, or mergers. However, if the bond was protected by strong covenants, announcement of a leveraged buy-out led to a *rise* in the bond price of 2.6 percent.[36]

Affirmative Covenants

The restrictions on new debt issues or dividend payments prevent the company from doing things that would benefit the shareholders at the expense of the bondholders, but they don't make the bonds safe. Therefore lenders also seek to protect themselves by arrangements that give them the chance to demand repayment at the first sign of trouble. For example, bank loans sometimes specify that the bank can demand re-

---

[33]For example, these restrictions might prohibit the company from paying dividends if their cumulative amount would exceed the sum of (1) cumulative net income, (2) the proceeds from the sale of stock or conversion of debt, and (3) a dollar amount equal to about 1 year's dividend.

[34]*Metropolitan Life Insurance Company* (plaintiff) *v. RJR Nabisco, Inc., and F. Ross Johnson* (defendants), Supreme Court of the State of New York, County of New York, Complaint, Nov. 16, 1988.

[35]P. Asquith and T. A. Wizman, "Event Risk, Bond Covenants, and the Return to Existing Bondholders in Corporate Buyouts," *Journal of Financial Economics,* **27**:195–213 (September 1990).

[36]One reason for the price rise is that bonds with strong covenant protection were often called or repurchased following the buy-out.

payment if there is a "material adverse change" which impairs the borrower's ability to repay the loan.[37]

We have already seen that lenders impose a number of hurdles which the company must keep jumping. The most obvious of these hurdles are the regular interest payments and sinking fund contributions. If these obligations are not met, the loan becomes repayable immediately. That is why the company will always try to make the payment if it possibly can. Another, rather different hurdle is the repayment of other outstanding debt. Many issues contain a *cross-default* clause. This says that the company is in default if it fails to meet its obligations on *any* of its debt issues. Thus a cross-default clause may enable the lender to get out from under before the firm has missed a payment on the particular loan covered by the clause.

Most indentures also include so-called *affirmative* covenants, which impose certain duties on the borrower. In the case of public bond issues affirmative covenants are usually innocuous. For example, the company may be obliged to furnish bondholders with a copy of its annual accounts. If it doesn't do so, it is in default on the bonds. Many privately placed issues impose much more onerous affirmative covenants. The most common of these are covenants to maintain at all times some minimum level of working capital or of net worth. If the amount of working capital or net worth is a good guide to the value of the company, the lenders are putting a ceiling on the amount they can lose.

We do not want to give the impression that lenders are constantly seeking an opportunity to cry "default" and then demand their money back. If the company does default, the lenders have the *right* to claim repayment but generally will not do so. The more usual result is that the lenders or the trustee will seek a detailed explanation from the company and discuss possible changes in its operating policy. It is only as a last resort that lenders demand early repayment and force the company into bankruptcy.

24-6 PRIVATE PLACEMENTS AND PROJECT FINANCE

The Ralston Purina debenture was registered with the SEC and sold to the public. However, debt is often placed privately with a small number of financial institutions. Whether you decide to make a public issue or a private placement will depend partly on the relative issue costs, for a public issue involves higher issue costs but a lower rate of interest.[38] But your choice should not depend solely on these costs: there are three other ways in which the private placement bond may differ from its public counterpart.

First, if you place an issue privately with one or two financial institutions, it may be necessary to sign only a simple promissory note. This is just an IOU which lays down certain conditions that the borrower must observe. However, when you make a public issue of debt, you must worry about who is to represent the bondholders in

---

[37]"Material adverse change" is usually not specifically defined—the clause protects the lender in scenarios where the borrower falls into default without triggering specific covenants. Of course, this clause might be a dangerous weapon in the hands of a shortsighted and unscrupulous lender, who could pretend to see an adverse change and try to extort a higher interest rate by threatening to demand immediate repayment. Fortunately, few if any financial institutions play this game. They would be sued for trying it, and their reputation for *not* taking unfair advantage of their customers is a valuable business asset.

[38]See Section 15-5.

any subsequent negotiations and what procedures are needed for paying interest and principal. Therefore the contractual arrangement has to be that much more complicated.

The second characteristic of publicly issued bonds is that they are highly standardized products. They *have* to be—investors are constantly buying and selling them without checking the fine print in the agreement. This is not so necessary in private placements. They are not regularly traded; they are bought and held by large institutions that are well equipped to evaluate any unusual features. Furthermore, because private placements involve lower fixed issue costs, they tend to be issued by smaller companies. These are just the companies that most need custom-tailored debt.

All bond agreements seek to protect the lender by imposing a number of conditions on the borrower. In the case of private placements these restrictions may be severe. For example, if the borrower wishes to issue any more bonds, the firm may need the permission of the existing bondholders. Because there are only a few lenders involved, this permission is usually easily obtained. That outcome would not be possible with publicly issued debt. Therefore the limitations tend to be less stringent in the case of public issues. This is the third difference between public and most private debt.

We are not going to dwell on the topic of private placement bonds, because the greater part of what we've said about public issues is also true of private placements. However, we do need to discuss briefly a rather different form of private loan, one that is tied as far as possible to the fortunes of a particular project and that minimizes the exposure of the parent. Such a loan is usually referred to as *project finance* and is a specialty of large international banks.

An Example of Project Finance

Let us look at how British Petroleum (BP) used project financing in 1972 to pay for development of its huge Forties Field in the North Sea. Since BP needed to finance very large expenditures elsewhere in the world, management wanted to segregate the financing of the Forties Field project as far as possible from BP's other fund-raising activities. Ideally it would have liked to isolate its other business completely from the fate of the North Sea, but no bank could be expected to take the risk of lending solely on the security of a field that was not yet producing.

BP's solution is illustrated in Figure 24-2. A syndicate of 66 major banks agreed to lend a total of $945 million—at that time the largest industrial bank loan in history. Instead of lending the money directly to BP, the banks lent it to a company called Norex, which they controlled. Norex in turn paid the money to BP Development, the subsidiary of BP that was responsible for developing the Forties Field. But Norex's payment to BP Development was not in the form of a loan; it was an advance payment for future deliveries of oil. In other words, in return for the money, BP Development promised to deliver to Norex an agreed quantity of oil. Of course, the last thing the banks wanted was a load of oil on their doorsteps. Therefore, they also arranged to have another BP subsidiary, BP Trading, repurchase the oil from Norex at a prescribed price.

Payments to Norex had to be completed within 10 years. But, because a number of unpredictable factors could affect the development of the Forties Field, the speed with which Norex was to be paid off was tied to the production rate of the field.

The banks consented to bear the ultimate risk that the oil reserves were insufficient to service their loan. However, they were protected against three other hazards. The first was the possible failure of BP Development to construct the necessary facilities. The agreement, therefore, specified in considerable detail the manner in which the field should be developed, and BP guaranteed that its subsidiary would carry out this plan.

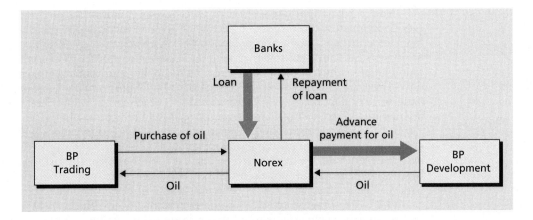

Figure 24-2 Financing for the Forties Field project. The banks made a loan to Norex, which then made an advance payment to BP Development for future deliveries of oil. This oil was resold to BP Trading at an agreed-on price. The payments by BP Trading allowed Norex to repay the banks. The heavy arrows show how the banks provided financing; the lighter arrows show how BP repaid the banks.

The second danger was that the field might be depleted more rapidly than was envisaged. To protect the banks against this possibility, BP guaranteed that each year the difference between the market value of the oil produced and the amount needed to service the loan would be paid into a "reclaim account," which could be drawn upon by Norex if the oil flow was subsequently reduced. The third risk was that of force majeure. If it proved impossible to produce any oil before the end of 6 years and if the assessed reserves would have been adequate to service the loan, then Norex could claim repayment from a restitution account that was guaranteed by BP.

One effect of this complicated financing arrangement was that the banks accepted some of the risk associated with the Forties Field. For example, if the oil reserves were inadequate to service the banks' loan to Norex, the banks had no claim against BP's other assets. A second difference between the Forties project financing and a straight bank loan was that the project financing did not show up on BP's balance sheet as a debt. Instead, BP Trading's promise to repurchase the oil from Norex was recorded as a deferred liability against future oil delivery.

Who Uses Project Finance?

The basic requirement of any project financing is that the project be physically isolated from the parent and that it offer the lender tangible security. The additional research and legal costs also mean that project financing makes sense only when the sums involved are large. Traditionally, project finance has been widely used for major mineral extraction and processing developments, often involving joint ventures with overseas firms. More recently in the United States the most common use of project finance has been for electric power plants.[39]

---

[39]Kensinger and Martin estimate that between January 1987 and August 1988 almost 50 percent of the funds raised in the United States by project finance were used for power generation—about $5.7 billion. See J. W. Kensinger and J. D. Martin, "Project Finance: Raising Money the Old-Fashioned Way," *Journal of Applied Corporate Finance*, **1**:69–81 (Fall 1988).

Project finance for production of electric power was stimulated by the Public Utility Regulatory Power Act (PURPA) of 1978, which requires that utilities buy from independent producers under long-term contracts. For example, an electric utility company may get together with an industrial company to construct a cogeneration plant, which provides electricity to the utility and waste heat to a nearby industrial plant. The utility either contracts to buy from the cogeneration plant at a fixed price or agrees to a *fuel adjustment clause*, which requires that the utility absorb fluctuations in the cost of the oil, gas, or coal required to run the plant.

Such a contract is excellent security for a loan. The utility stands behind the cogeneration project and guarantees its revenue stream. Once the plant is up and running, the cash flow for debt service is insulated from most of the risks facing normal businesses. Thus some power projects have been more than 90 percent debt-financed.[40]

There are some interesting regulatory implications, however. When a utility builds a power plant, it is entitled to a fair return on its investment: regulators are supposed to set customer charges that will allow the utility to earn its cost of capital. Unfortunately, the cost of capital is not easily measured and is a natural focus for argument in regulatory hearings. But when a utility buys electric power, the cost of capital is rolled into the contract price and treated as an operating cost. In this case the pass-through to consumers may be less controversial.

Project Finance —Some Common Features	We can classify project financings according to the contractual obligations of the projects' owners. The purest, but least common, method of financing offers the lender *no recourse* against the owners at any stage. This notion of no recourse is somewhat imprecise, for the banks may well require a general assurance from the parent that it will do its best to ensure the success of the project. Although these "comfort letters" are not cast-iron guarantees, they do represent a potentially embarrassing commitment on the part of the parent.

One of the most common threats to a successful project loan is a serious delay in completion. Occasionally the project may even turn out to be technically infeasible. Our second class of loans, therefore, consists of those that are supported by a *completion guarantee*. Such a guarantee may be provided by the parent company or by an insurance company in the form of completion bonding.

Most project loans provide lenders with more recourse against the parent. For instance, we saw that BP promised to repurchase oil from Norex at a prescribed price. Here are three other examples of limited guarantees that parent companies may provide:

1. *The throughput and deficiency agreement.* Many oil pipeline loans involve a throughput agreement. This states that if other companies do not make sufficient use of the pipeline, the owners themselves will ship enough oil through it to provide the pipeline company with the cash that it needs to service the loan and if *that* is insufficient, the owners will advance the cash to cover the deficiency.

---

[40]Such extremely high debt ratios must rest on the utility's creditworthiness. In a sense, the utility has borrowed money "off balance sheet," since the contract to purchase power is a fixed, debtlike, long-term commitment. This fixed commitment should act as financial leverage and increase the volatility of utility earnings and shareholder returns.

2. *The cost company arrangement.* Under a cost company arrangement, the project's owners receive all the project's output free of charge. In exchange they agree to pay all operating costs including loan service. Thus the project has no net income, and each parent firm simply deducts from its own profits its share of the project's expenses.

3. *The cash deficiency arrangement.* Under this arrangement, the project's owners agree to provide the operating company with enough funds to maintain a certain level of working capital. In other words, if debt service depletes working capital, the owners are obliged to replenish it.

In any project financing the payments on the loan are designed to match as closely as possible the ability of the project to generate cash. For example, if the project's completion date is uncertain, the first payment date may simply be set at a specified number of months after completion. If the loan involves a large final payment, it is common to include an *earnings recapture* clause, under which a proportion of any surplus earnings is applied to reduce the final payment. A lender who bears the risk of inadequate reserves will wish to ensure that the reserves are not depleted too rapidly; in this case, therefore, it is common to assign a *proportion* of revenues, rather than a fixed sum, to loan repayments.

The Benefits of Project Finance

Various motives have been suggested for the use of project finance rather than direct borrowing by the parent company. It is tempting to believe that the value of a project to the parent is enhanced if the project can be made to stand alone as a self-financing entity, so that the parent benefits from its success and is isolated from its failure. That is unrealistic. When we look at actual project loans, we find that not only is the parent rarely isolated from the vicissitudes of the project but the rate of interest on the project loan is directly related to the degree of support that the parent provides. However, project finance does allow the parent to transfer specific risks to the lenders. For example, if BP had borrowed on its general credit, it would have borne the risk of inadequate North Sea reserves, whereas the Forties financing effectively provided insurance against this contingency. Correspondingly, with many loans for projects in politically unstable countries the lenders are taking on the risk of adverse government action. Many companies believe that expropriation by a foreign government is less likely when they raise money by project financing.

Project financing may not be recorded as debt on the company's balance sheet. For example, we have already seen how BP's financing of the Forties Field showed up as a deferred liability against future deliveries. Sometimes the owner's guarantees may not appear on the balance sheet at all. In this case, the financing is said to be "off balance sheet." This attracts some financial managers—but lenders or shareholders usually recognize these hidden liabilities.

Project financing can be costly to arrange, but sometimes the arrangement is simpler than a direct loan. Projects are often jointly owned, and it may be easier to negotiate one project loan than separate financing for each of several parents. Also, security for project lenders commonly derives as much from contractual arrangements as from tangible assets. For example, a bank's security for a pipeline loan depends on throughput agreements, and its security for a tanker loan depends on charter agreements. In such instances it may be simplest to tie the loan directly to these contracts.

24-7 INNOVATION IN THE BOND MARKET

Domestic bonds and eurobonds; fixed-rate and floating-rate bonds; coupon bonds and zeros; callable, extendible, and retractable bonds; secured and unsecured bonds; senior and junior bonds; privately placed bonds and project finance—you might think that all this would give you as much choice as you need. Yet almost every day some new type of bond seems to be issued.

If we had to award a prize for the most unusual bond, it would probably go to a eurobond issued in 1990 by the Swedish company Electrolux. The principal repayment on this bond depends on whether an earthquake occurs in Japan. But there are many other bonds that are only a little less exotic. For example, in 1989 the Norwegian Christiania Bank issued a 3-year bond that came in two tranches. Tranche A paid interest equal to the long-term prime rate but subject to a maximum (or "cap") of 12.8 percent. Tranche B paid interest of 12.8 percent *less* the long-term prime rate. Thus, if the general level of interest rates rose, the interest payment on tranche B fell.[41] However, it was not allowed to fall below zero. You may like to check for yourself that if you invested an equal amount in each tranche, the average interest rate on your two holdings was 6.4 percent, which was well above the going interest rate for Japanese bonds.

That was not the end of the complications of tranche B, since the principal repayment was not fixed at 100 percent. Instead, it declined if the Japanese stock market index fell. If the index fell by about 50 percent, the bondholder did not receive any principal repayment at all. Thus investing tranche B was like buying an unusual variable-rate note and also selling a put option on the Japanese stock market. The high yield on the bonds was therefore offset by the possible capital loss.

For several years the majority of public euroyen issues involved some option such as this. Why? One reason is that life insurance companies in Japan cannot distribute capital gains to policy holders and therefore have a powerful appetite for high-yielding bonds even if such investments involve the risk of a capital loss. Christiania Bank paid a high interest rate on the package, but it got a put option in exchange. If it did not want to hold on to this put option, it could easily sell it to foreign investors who were worried that the Japanese equity market may have been overpriced and wanted to protect themselves against a fall in that market.

Here is one more example of an unusual bond: *Pay-in-kind* bonds (PIKs) make regular interest payments, but in the early years of the bond's life the issuer can choose to pay interest in the form of either cash or more bonds with an equivalent face value.[42] That can be a valuable option. If the company falls on hard times and bond prices drop, it can hand over low-priced bonds instead of hard cash.[43] Many of the companies that have issued PIKs had been taken over in a leveraged buy-out. Such firms are often very short of cash in the initial years and therefore find the option to pay interest in the

---

[41]Bonds whose interest payments move in the opposite direction to the general level are called *reverse floaters* or *yield-curve notes*. Our favorite example of a reverse floater is an issue in 1986 by Hong Kong Mass Transit Railway which offered a 5-year United States dollar floater with warrants. The warrants had a maturity of 1 year and gave the holder the right to buy a 5-year, Hong Kong dollar reverse floater paying 15.15 percent *less* than the short-term Hong Kong interest rate (HIBOR).

[42]For a discussion of PIKs, see L. S. Goodman and A. H. Cohen, "Pay-in-Kind Debentures: An Innovation," *Journal of Portfolio Management*, **15**:9–16 (Winter 1989).

[43]To complicate matters, most PIKs are callable. So if interest rates fall and bond prices rise, the firm may buy the bonds back at the call price.

form of bonds particularly attractive. For example, when Kohlberg, Kravis and Roberts took over RJR Nabisco, the shareholders were partly paid off in PIKs.[44]

The Causes of Innova- tion

It is often difficult to foresee which new securities will become popular and which will never get off the ground. However, Merton Miller believes that government often plays a crucial role in fostering innovation. He compares government regulation and tax with the grain of sand that irritates the oyster and produces the pearl.[45] This would suggest that the wave of innovation that has swept capital markets in recent decades may be prompted by the increasing strains of a tax and regulatory system that dates back to the 1930s and 1940s.

We have seen how one unusual bond, the option-linked euroyen bond, is a consequence of Japanese insurance regulation. Let us also look at how a quirk in the tax rules brought about a new type of bond in the United States.

Example: In June 1981 General Motors Acceptance Corporation issued $750 million of 10-year zero coupon notes. The issue price was $252.50 for each note. Thus the investor faced a prospective fourfold increase in value over 10 years, which is equivalent to a compound return of about 14.8 percent a year.

Table 24-2 shows the expected yearly change in the value of the GMAC notes. In year 1, the prospective appreciation is .148 × 252.5 = $37.3. At the start of year 2, the expected value of the notes is 252.5 + 37.3 = $289.8. Thus the appreciation in year 2 is .148 × 289.8 = $42.8. And so on. Of course, the total appreciation over the 10 years is 1000 − 252.5 = $747.5.

The attraction to GMAC of zero coupon debt arose from an IRS mistake. The IRS correctly recognized that even if debt does not pay interest, it is still costly to the issuer. Therefore, it allowed the company to deduct a portion of the original issue discount from taxable income. But in calculating this deduction, the IRS employed simple, rather than compound, interest. Thus GMAC was permitted to deduct the same amount in each year, 747.5/10 = $74.75.

If you compare columns 2 and 3 of Table 24-2, you will see that in the early years of the loan's life, GMAC could deduct more than the cost of the loan from its taxable income. For example, in year 1 each note *cost* GMAC $37.3, or 14.8 percent of the amount of the loan. However, when calculating taxable profits, GMAC was allowed to deduct $74.75, or 29.6 percent of the amount of the loan. From year 7 onward, the deduction is less than the cost of the loan, but, other things equal, GMAC benefited from having the extra tax shield in the early years.

Of course, this is not the whole story. Just as the IRS pretended that GMAC paid interest of $74.75 a year, so it pretended that the noteholders received interest of $74.75 a year. But as long as GMAC notes were bought by tax-exempt investors, this was no disadvantage.[46]

---

[44]The use of PIKs to finance highly leveraged buy-outs earned them a bad reputation. Ross Johnson, the president of RJR Nabisco, was reported to have marveled at the potential for PIKs. " 'I mean,' Johnson went on, 'we have found something better than the U.S. printing press. And they've got it all down here on Wall Street. And nobody knows it's going on. I wonder if the World Bank knows about it. You could solve the third world debt crisis with this stuff. It's a brand new currency.' " (Quoted in B. Burrough and J. Helyar, *Barbarians at the Gate: The Fall of RJR Nabisco*, Harper & Row, N.Y., 1990, p. 489.)

[45]See M. H. Miller, "Financial Innovation: The Last Twenty Years and the Next," *Journal of Financial and Quantitative Analysis*, **21**:459–471 (December 1986).

[46]Zero coupon bonds were popular with the Japanese, since the Japanese tax authorities treated the price appreciation as a capital gain. This ruling was changed in 1985.

TABLE 24-2
....

GMAC's original issue discount bonds were expected to appreciate by an increasing percentage amount each year, but the IRS allowed GMAC to deduct the same *dollar* amount each year from taxable income.

Year	(1) PV at Start of Year	(2) Change in PV During Year	(3) Allowable Tax Write-Off
1	$252.5	$ 37.3	$74.75
2	289.8	42.8	74.75
3	332.5	49.1	74.75
4	381.6	56.3	74.75
5	437.9	64.6	74.75
6	502.5	74.1	74.75
7	576.6	85.1	74.75
8	661.7	97.6	74.75
9	759.4	112.0	74.75
10	871.4	128.6	74.75
		$747.5	$747.50

The tax advantage of zero coupon bonds led to a flurry of issues in 1981. By 1982, the IRS had become sufficiently concerned about the loss of revenue that it began to use compound interest to calculate the tax deduction. From that point on, the tax incentive to issue zero coupon debt disappeared. Yet zeros survived. Companies continued to issue them, though at a much slower rate than before.[47]

....

The Gains from Innovation

Initially the benefits of zero coupon debt went to those investment banks that were smart enough to devise and market the idea and to issuers such as GMAC.[48] But, remember, there was an advantage to zero coupon debt only if the marginal investor had a lower tax rate than the borrower had. This takes us back to the capital structure controversy of Chapter 18. As long as only a few companies issued zero coupons, there were enough tax-exempt investors who were happy to hold them. But as more such debt was issued, those companies that came late on the scene faced a higher rate of interest. Thus, as soon as everyone had cottoned on to the idea, all the benefits went to the tax-exempt investors in the form of this higher interest rate.

The lesson is a simple one: Investment banks and companies can be sure of benefiting from an innovation only if they are early in the field. Once the market is in equilibrium, all the benefits go to the players that are in short supply (in our example, the tax-exempt investors).

---

[47]For a further analysis of the tax incentives for OID debt, see D. Pyle, "Is Deep Discount Debt Financing a Bargain?" *Chase Financial Quarterly*, **1**:39–61 (1981).

[48]We may oversimplify: If investors foresee that further issues are going to force up the interest rate on zero coupon bonds, they may be reluctant to buy the early issues at the lower interest rate.

Lasting Innovations

In effect, the IRS subsidized the development of zero coupon bonds. But the important and worthwhile innovations are those like zero coupon bonds that survive once such subsidies have been removed. Some endure because they reduce costs. Often an idea starts as a one-off deal between a bank and its customer. As demand grows, the tailor-made product is replaced by tradeable securities that perform a similar function.

There are economies of scale in the securities markets just as there are in other businesses, and this creates a continuing pressure for standardization. In the next chapter we shall see how the increased volatility of interest rates and exchange rates brought about a demand for low-cost ways to hedge these risks. The huge volume of potential business made it possible to offer standardized futures contracts at very low cost.[49]

Innovations also survive because they widen investor choice. When economists smile in their sleep, they are probably dreaming of a complete capital market in which there are as many different securities as there are possible future states of the world. Such a market would give investors the widest possible choice and allow them to select portfolios that would protect them against any combination of hazards.

Of course complete markets are just make-believe, but we do observe a constant demand for new securities to protect against new dangers. For example, in countries such as Israel and Brazil that suffer from persistent inflation, investors don't want bonds that offer a fixed money return; they want ones that give a fixed *real* return. Therefore, in these countries debt payments are usually indexed to the rate of inflation. Indexed bonds were almost unknown in the United States until 1988, when Franklin Savings Association made history by issuing a 20-year bond whose interest (but not principal) was tied to the rate of inflation. Since then, several other companies have followed suit.[50]

Instead of being tied to the general rate of inflation, payments are sometimes indexed to the price of a particular commodity. French Rail, for example, once issued a bond which was linked to the price of rail travel and which therefore resembled a long-term transferable season ticket. A few companies in the United States have also sought to limit shareholders' risk by tying bond payments to the price of a particular commodity. For instance, in June 1986 Standard Oil issued a zero coupon note maturing in 1992. At maturity the lenders were repaid at least the $1000 face value. In addition, they were entitled to a bonus equal to 200 times the amount by which the oil price exceeded $25 a barrel.[51] The Standard Oil bond gave the firm protection against the vagaries of oil prices. As it turned out, oil prices in 1992 were low, which adversely affected the company's income. However, this was partly mitigated by the fact that the cost of its debt was also low.[52]

---

[49]For a general discussion of the way that market innovations have stemmed from a drive for more efficient ways to provide a financial service, see I. A. Cooper, "Innovations: New Market Instruments," *Oxford Review of Economic Policy*, **2**:1–17 (1986).

[50]Franklin Savings was not quite the first United States company to issue an indexed bond. In 1925 the Rand Kardex Company issued a bond that was linked to the wholesale price index, but the experiment was short-lived and the bond was converted soon after issue.

[51]However, the bonus could not be greater than $200 \times \$15 = \$3000$ per bond. In the same month Standard Oil also issued a 4½-year note. The bonus on this note was equal to 170 times the amount by which the oil price exceeded $25 a barrel.

[52]Of course, companies that are heavy *users* of oil are adversely affected by a *high* oil price. Thus, Shin Etsu, a Japanese chemical company, reduced risk by issuing a bond whose coupon payments declined as the oil price went up.

24-8 SUMMARY

Now that you have read this chapter, you should have a fair idea of what you are letting yourself in for when you make a public issue of bonds. You can make an issue of bonds in the domestic United States market, or you can do so in a foreign bond market or in the eurobond market. Eurobonds are bonds that are marketed simultaneously in a number of foreign countries, usually by the London branches of international banks and security dealers.

The detailed bond agreement is set out in the indenture between your company and a trustee, but the main provisions are summarized in the prospectus to the issue.

The indenture states whether the bonds are senior or subordinated and whether they are secured or unsecured. Most bonds are unsecured debentures or notes. This means that they are general claims on the corporation. The principal exceptions are utility first mortgage bonds, collateral trust bonds, and equipment trust certificates. In the event of a default, the trustee to these issues can repossess the company's assets in order to pay off the debt.

Most long-term bond issues have a *sinking fund*. This means that the company must set aside enough money each year to retire a specified number of bonds. A sinking fund reduces the average life of the bond, and it provides a yearly test of the company's ability to service its debt. It therefore protects the bondholders against the risk of default.

Long-dated bonds are often callable before maturity. The company usually has to pay a call premium which is initially equal to the coupon and which declines progressively to zero. There is one common limitation to this right—companies are generally prohibited from calling the bond in the first few years if they intend to replace it with another bond at a lower rate of interest. Nevertheless, the option to call the bond may be very valuable: if interest rates decline and bond values rise, you may be able to call a bond that would be worth substantially more than the call price. Of course, if investors know that you may call the bond, the call price will act as a ceiling on the market price. Your best strategy, therefore, is to call the bond as soon as the market price hits the call price. You are unlikely to do better than that.

The bond indenture also imposes certain conditions on the borrower. Here are some examples of *negative covenants:*

1. Issues of senior bonds prohibit the company from issuing further senior or junior debt if the ratio of senior debt to net tangible assets is too high.

2. Issues of subordinated bonds may also prohibit the company from issuing further senior or junior debt if the ratio of *all* debt to net tangible assets is too high.

3. Unsecured bonds incorporate a *negative pledge* clause, which prohibits the company from securing additional debt without giving equal treatment to the existing unsecured bonds.

4. Many bonds place a limit on the company's dividend payments.

Conditions which require that the company take positive steps to protect the bondholders are known as *affirmative covenants*. The really important affirmative covenants are those that give the bondholder the chance to claim a default and get money out while the company still has substantial value. For example, some privately placed bond issues require that the company maintain a minimum level of working capital or net worth. Since a deficiency in either is a good indication of financial weakness, this condition is tantamount to giving the bondholders the right to demand their money back as soon as life appears hazardous.

Private placements are less standardized than public issues, and they impose more stringent covenants. Otherwise, they are generally close counterparts of publicly issued bonds. Sometimes private debt takes the form of project finance. In this case the loan is tied to the fortunes of a particular project.

There is an enormous variety of bond issues, and new forms of bonds are spawned almost daily. By a principle of natural selection some of these new instruments become popular and may even replace existing species. Others are ephemeral curiosities. We don't know all the reasons for the success of some innovations, but we suggest that many new securities owe their origin to tax rules and government regulation. The lasting innovations are those that reduce costs or widen investor choice.

Further Reading

Two useful general works on debt securities are:

F. J. Fabozzi and T. D. Fabozzi (eds.): *Handbook of Fixed Income Securities*, 4th ed., Dow Jones–Irwin, Inc., Homewood, Ill., 1995.

R. S. Wilson and F. J. Fabozzi: *The New Corporate Bond Market*, Probus Publishing Company, Chicago, 1990.

The articles by Brennan and Schwartz and by Kraus are general discussions of call provisions:

M. J. Brennan and E. S. Schwartz: "Savings Bonds, Retractable Bonds and Callable Bonds," *Journal of Financial Economics*, **5**:67–88 (1977).

A. Kraus: "An Analysis of Call Provisions and the Corporate Refunding Decision," *Midland Corporate Finance Journal*, **1**:46–60 (Spring 1983).

Smith and Warner provide an extensive survey and analysis of covenants:

C. W. Smith and J. B. Warner: "On Financial Contracting: An Analysis of Bond Covenants," *Journal of Financial Economics*, **7**:117–161 (June 1979).

For developments in project finance, see:

J. W. Kensinger and J. D. Martin: "Project Finance: Raising Money the Old-Fashioned Way," *Journal of Applied Corporate Finance*, **1**:69–81 (Fall 1988).

Quiz

1. Select the most appropriate term from within the parentheses:
   (*a*) (High-grade utility bonds/Low-grade industrial bonds) generally have only light sinking fund requirements.
   (*b*) (Short-dated notes/Long-dated debentures) are often noncallable.
   (*c*) Collateral trust bonds are often issued by (utilities/industrial holding companies).
   (*d*) (Utility bonds/Industrial bonds) are usually unsecured.
   (*e*) Equipment trust certificates are usually issued by (railroads/financial companies).

2. *Vocabulary check.* Define the following terms: indenture or trust deed, notes (vs. debentures), mortgage bonds, call provision, sinking fund, foreign bond, eurobond, defeasance, negative pledge clause, affirmative covenant, negative covenant.

3. For each of the following sinking funds, state whether the fund increases or decreases the value of a bond at the time of issue (or whether it is impossible to say):
   (*a*) An optional sinking fund operating by drawings at par
   (*b*) A mandatory sinking fund operating by drawings at par *or* by purchases in the market
   (*c*) A mandatory sinking fund operating by drawings at par

4. (*a*) As a senior debtholder, would you like the company to issue more junior debt, would you prefer it not to do so, or would you not care?
   (*b*) You hold debt secured on the company's existing property. Would you like the company to issue more unsecured debt, would you prefer it not to do so, or would you not care?

5. Use Table 24-1 (but not the text) to answer the following questions:
   (*a*) Who are the principal underwriters for the Ralston Purina bond issue?
   (*b*) Who is the trustee for the issue?
   (*c*) How many dollars does the company receive for each debenture after deduction of the underwriters' spread?
   (*d*) Is the debenture "bearer" or "registered"?
   (*e*) At what price is the issue callable in 1995?
   (*f*) Can the company call the bond in 1990 and replace it with a debenture yielding 5 percent?

6. Look at Table 24-1:
   (*a*) Suppose the debenture was issued on July 1, 1986, at 97.60%. How much would you have to pay to buy one bond delivered on July 1? Don't forget to include accrued interest.
   (*b*) When is the first interest payment on the bond, and what is the total amount of that payment?
   (*c*) On what date do the bonds finally mature, and what is the principal amount of the bonds that is due to be repaid on that date?
   (*d*) Suppose that the market price of the bonds rises to 102 and thereafter does not change. When should the company call the issue?

7. True or false? Briefly explain in each case.
   (*a*) Lenders in project financings rarely have recourse against the project's owners if the project fails.
   (*b*) Most new and exotic debt securities are triggered by governments' tax policies or regulations. When these are changed, the new securities disappear.
   (*c*) Call provisions give a valuable option to debt investors.
   (*d*) Restrictive covenants have been shown to protect debt investors when takeovers are financed with large amounts of debt.
   (*e*) Privately placed debt issues often include stricter covenants than public debt. However, public debt covenants are more difficult and expensive to renegotiate.

Questions and Problems

1. After a sharp change in interest rates, newly issued bonds generally sell at yields different from those of outstanding bonds of the same quality. One suggested explanation is that there is a difference in the value of the call provision. Explain how this could arise.

2. Obtain a prospectus for a recent bond issue and compare the terms and conditions with those of the Ralston Purina issue.

3. What restrictions are imposed on a company's freedom to issue further debt? Be as precise as possible. Explain carefully the reasons for such restrictions.

4. Explain carefully why senior and subordinated bond indentures place different restrictions on a company's freedom to issue additional debt.

5. A retractable bond is a bond which may be repaid before maturity at the investor's option. Sketch a diagram similar to Figure 24-1 showing the relationship between the value of a straight bond and that of a retractable bond.

6. What determines the value of an indexed bond? Should the rate of interest on an indexed bond be higher or lower than the expected real rate on a nominal bond?

7. Explain carefully why bond indentures place limitations on the following actions:
   (*a*) Sale of the company's assets
   (*b*) Payment of dividends to shareholders
   (*c*) Issue of additional senior debt

8. Look up the terms of a commodity-linked bond issue (e.g., the Standard Oil "oil bond" or the gold bond issued by International Refining). Find out what has happened to the bonds as the commodity price changed. Did the bonds increase shareholders' risk or reduce it?

9. Suppose that instead of issuing the original issue discount bonds, GMAC has raised the same amount of money by an issue of 14.8 percent 10-year notes at a price of $100.
   (*a*) What face amount of notes would GMAC have needed to issue?
   (*b*) Value the gain to GMAC from the issue of OID debt rather than the 14.8 percent notes. (Assume the MM theory of debt and taxes. See Section 18-1.)
   (*c*) Show that the gain to GMAC disappears if the annual tax deduction is calculated using compound interest rather than simple interest.

10. Does the issue of additional junior debt harm senior bondholders? Would your answer be the same if the junior debt matured *before* the senior debt? Explain.

11. Estimate the value of the Standard Oil "oil bond" (see Section 24-7).

12. In Section 24-7 we referred to Christiania Bank's exotic bond. Explain how you would value tranche B. Assume that the principal repayment is fixed at 100 percent of par. (*Hint:* Find a package of other securities that would produce identical cash flows.) What does this tell you about the riskiness of Hong Kong Mass Transit Railway's warrants?

13. Dorlcote Milling has outstanding a $1 million 3 percent mortgage bond maturing in 10 years. The coupon on any new debt issued by the company is 10 percent. The finance director, Mr. Tulliver, cannot decide whether there is a tax benefit to repurchasing the existing bonds in the marketplace and replacing them with new 10 percent bonds. What do you think? Start by assuming that all bondholders are tax-exempt. Then introduce Miller's idea that higher-rate taxpayers will gravitate to tax-efficient securities and force up their prices. (See Section 18-3.)

14. Look up a recent issue of an unusual bond in, say, a recent issue of the periodical *Euromoney*. Why do you think this bond was issued? What investors do you think it would appeal to? How would you value the unusual features?

15. In a number of countries such as France it is not uncommon for firms to band together to make a debt issue. A portion of the receipts is put aside in a safe government bond, and the remainder is parceled out among the different issuers. Each firm is responsible for its portion of the total debt, but in the event of default by any one firm the lenders can draw on the money invested in the government bond. Do you think this is a good idea? How would you value this debt?

16. Some eurobonds involve payments in more than one currency. For example, in 1985 Anheuser-Busch issued a 10-year yen bond at a price of 101. The coupon payment is made in yen, but the final repayment of principal is in dollars at an exchange rate of 208 yen to the dollar. How would you value such a bond? When the bond matured in 1995, the exchange rate was approximately 99 yen to the dollar. Would Anheuser-Busch have done better to have issued a straight yen bond?

17. Bond prices can fall either because of a change in the general level of interest rates or because of an increased risk of default. To what extent do floating-rate bonds and putable bonds protect the investor against each of these risks?

18. Residential mortgages may stipulate either a fixed interest rate or a variable rate. As a borrower, what considerations might cause you to prefer one rather than the other?

19. Suppose that the Ralston Purina bond was issued at face value and that investors continue to demand a yield of 9.5 percent. Sketch what you think would happen to the bond price as the first interest payment date approaches and then passes? What about the price of the bond plus accrued interest?

20. Suppose that a company simultaneously issues a zero coupon bond and a coupon bond with identical maturities. Both are callable at any time at their face values. Other things equal, which is likely to offer the higher yield? Why?

21. In 1981 J.C. Penney issued a 25-year zero coupon bond at a price of 42.06 percent. Construct a table similar to Table 24-2 showing the annual change in the value of the bonds and the allowable tax write-off.

22. Explain when it may make sense to use project finance rather than a direct debt issue by the parent company.

23. (*a*) If interest rates rise, will callable or noncallable bonds fall more in price?
    (*b*) The Belgian government once issued bonds that could have been repaid at face value after a specified date at the option of *either* the government or the bondholder. If each side acted rationally, what should have happened on that date?

25

Hedging Financial Risk

Most of the time we take risk as God-given. An asset or business has its beta, and that's that. Its cash flow is exposed to unpredictable changes in raw material costs, tax rates, technology, and a long list of other variables. There's nothing the manager can do about it.

That's not wholly true. To some extent managers can choose the risks that the business takes. We have already come across one way that they can do so. In our discussion of real options in Chapter 21 we described how companies reduce risk by building flexibility into their operations. A company that uses standardized machine tools rather than specialized equipment lowers the cost of bailing out if things go wrong. A petrochemical plant that is designed to use either oil or natural gas as a feedstock reduces the impact of an unfavorable shift in relative fuel prices. And so on.

In this chapter we shall explain how companies also enter into financial contracts that insure against or hedge (i.e., offset) a variety of business hazards. But first we should give some reasons *why* they do so.

Insurance and hedging are seldom free: At best they are zero-NPV transactions.[1] Most businesses insure or hedge to reduce risk, not to make money. Why, then, bother to reduce risk in this way? For one thing, it makes financial planning easier and reduces the odds of an embarrassing cash shortfall. A shortfall might mean only an unexpected trip to the bank, but if financing is hard to obtain on short notice, the company might need to cut back its capital expenditure program. In extreme cases an unhedged setback could trigger financial distress or even bankruptcy. Banks and bondholders are aware of this possibility, and, before lending to your firm, they will often insist that it is properly insured.

In some cases hedging also makes it easier to decide whether an operating manager deserves a stern lecture or a pat on the back. Suppose your confectionery division shows a 60 percent profit increase in a period when cocoa prices decline by 12 percent. How much of the increase is due to the change in cocoa prices and how much to good management? If cocoa prices were hedged, it's probably good management. If they were not, things have to be sorted out with hindsight by asking, "What would profits have been *if* cocoa prices had been hedged?"[2]

---

[1]Hedging transactions are zero-NPV when trading is costless and markets are completely efficient. In practice the firm has to pay small trading costs at least.

[2]Many large firms insure or hedge away operating divisions' risk exposures by setting up internal, make-believe markets between each division and the treasurer's office. Trades in the internal markets are at real (external) market prices. The object is to relieve the operating managers of risks outside their control. The treasurer makes a separate decision on whether to offset the *firm's* exposure.

Finally, hedging extraneous events can help focus the operating manager's attention. It's naive to expect the manager of the confectionery division *not* to worry about cocoa prices if her bottom line and bonus depend on them. That worrying time would be better spent if the prices were hedged.[3]

Of course, managers are not paid to avoid all risks, but if they can reduce their exposure to risks for which there are no compensating rewards, they can afford to place larger bets when the odds are in their favor. Many financial decisions involve a package of bets. For example, when Porsche decides to launch a new model aimed at the American market—a 10- or 15-year commitment—it is betting on, among other things, the exchange rate between dollars and deutschemarks (since Porsche's costs are in deutschemarks and its revenues are in dollars). It is also betting on the exchange rate between dollars and pounds (since this affects the competitive position of Jaguar). Perhaps Porsche is optimistic about everything except the short-run dollar-deutschemark exchange rate—it fears that the deutschemark will appreciate, making German cars expensive in the United States. Should that pessimism stop Porsche from going ahead with the new model? It might if there were no way to hedge out the exchange-rate bet. But Porsche can use the currency forward markets to eliminate the bet on the exchange rate.[4] Therefore, management should ask two questions:

1. Should we go ahead with the new model, assuming that the company hedges the currency risk?

2. What bets, if any, should be placed on the currency?[5]

We start the chapter by looking briefly at how firms use insurance to reduce risk. We then turn to hedging: We first introduce you to some of the basic tools of hedging, including forward and futures contracts and swaps. Finally, we explain how to set up a hedge.

25-1 INSURANCE

Most businesses buy insurance against a variety of hazards—the risk that their plant will be damaged by fire; that their ships, planes, or vehicles will be involved in accidents; that the firm will be held liable for environmental damage; and so on.

When a firm takes out insurance, it is simply transferring the risk to the insurance company. Insurance companies have some advantages in bearing risk. First, they may have considerable experience in insuring similar risks, so they are well placed to

---

[3]A Texas oilman who lost hundreds of millions in ill-fated deals protested, "Why should I worry? Worry is for strong minds and weak characters." If there are any financial managers with weak minds and strong characters, we especially advise them to hedge whenever they can.

[4]We explain later how currency forward markets work.

[5]One final point: If Porsche's worries about the exchange rate are confirmed, is the company in a stronger competitive position if it has hedged against a change in the exchange rate? It is certainly true that Porsche will make more money if it has hedged. But there is a general maxim that you should not let the profits in one part of your business (currency hedging) cross-subsidize losses in another part (making cars). If, for example, the deutschemark should appreciate to the point where Porsche would do better to stop exporting to the United States, it should do just that. It should *not* go on selling cars at a loss just because it is making large profits on its currency position.

estimate the probability of loss and price the risk accurately. Second, they may be skilled at providing advice on measures that the firm can take to reduce the risk, and they may offer lower premiums to firms that take this advice. Third, an insurance company can *pool* risks by holding a large diversified portfolio of policies. The claims on any individual policy can be highly uncertain, yet the claims on a portfolio of policies may be very stable. Of course, insurance companies cannot diversify away macroeconomic risks; firms use insurance policies to reduce their specific risk, and they find other ways to avoid macro risks.

Insurance companies also suffer some *disadvantages* in bearing risk, and these are reflected in the prices they charge. Suppose your firm owns a $1 billion offshore oil platform. A meteorologist has advised you that there is a 1-in-10,000 chance that in any year the platform will be destroyed as a result of a storm. Thus the *expected* loss from storm damage is $1 billion/10,000 = $100,000.

The risk of storm damage is almost certainly not a macroeconomic risk and can potentially be diversified away.[6] So you might expect that an insurance company would be prepared to insure the platform against such destruction as long as the premium was sufficient to cover the expected loss. In other words, a fair premium for insuring the platform should be $100,000 a year.[7] Such a premium would make insurance a zero-NPV deal for your company. Unfortunately, no insurance company would offer a policy for only $100,000. Why not?

- *Reason 1: Administrative costs.* An insurance company, like any other business, incurs a variety of costs in arranging the insurance and handling any claims. For example, disputes about the liability for environmental damage can eat up millions of dollars in legal fees. Insurance companies need to recognize these costs when they set their premiums.

- *Reason 2: Adverse selection.* Suppose that an insurer offers life insurance policies with "no medical needed, no questions asked." There are no prizes for guessing who will be most tempted to buy this insurance. Our example is an extreme case of the problem of *adverse selection*. Unless the insurance company can distinguish between good and bad risks, the latter will always be most eager to take out insurance. The premium to insure your oil platform will need to recognize this fact.

- *Reason 3: Moral hazard.* Two Russian farmers met on the road to town. "Ivan," said one, "I was sorry to hear about your barn burning down"; "Shh," replied the other, "that's tomorrow night." The story is an example of another problem for insurers, known as *moral hazard*. Once a risk has been insured, the owner may be less careful to take proper precautions against damage. Insurance companies are aware of this and factor it into their pricing.

When these extra costs are small, insurance may be close to a zero-NPV transaction. When they are large, insurance may be a costly way to protect against risk.

---

[6]If the potential liability is large, insurance companies often spread the risk among themselves. But the consequences of major catastrophes, such as earthquakes, hurricanes, and other environmental disasters, can be so huge that it is difficult for even a group of insurers to diversify the risk. For example, claims for asbestosis against members of Lloyd's of London alone have already amounted to over $5 billion and could eventually reach several times that figure.

[7]This is imprecise. If the premium is paid at the beginning of the year and the claim is not settled until the end, then the zero-NPV premium equals the discounted value of the expected claim or $100,000/(1 + r)$.

How
British
Petrol-
eum (BP)
Changed
Its
Insurance
Strategy[8]

Major public companies typically buy insurance against large potential losses and self-insure against routine ones. The idea is that large losses can trigger financial distress. On the other hand, routine losses for a corporation are predictable, so there is little point paying premiums to an insurance company and receiving back a fairly constant proportion as claims.

BP has challenged this conventional wisdom. Like all oil companies, BP is exposed to a variety of potential losses. Some arise from routine events such as vehicle accidents and industrial injuries. At the other extreme, they may result from catastrophes such as a major oil spill or the loss of an offshore oil rig. In the past BP purchased considerable external insurance.[9] During the 1980s it paid out an average of $115 million a year in insurance premiums and recovered $25 million a year in claims.

Recently BP took a hard look at its insurance strategy. It reasoned that it made sense to allow local managers to insure against relatively routine risks, for in those cases insurance companies have an advantage in assessing and pricing risk and compete vigorously against one another. However, it decided that for the most part it would no longer insure externally against losses above $10 million. For these larger, more specialized risks BP felt that insurance companies had less ability to assess the risk and were less well placed to advise on safety measures. As a result, BP concluded, insurance against large risks was not competitively priced.

How much extra risk does BP assume by its decision not to insure against major losses? BP estimated that large losses of above $500 million could be expected to occur once in 30 years. But BP is a huge company with equity worth about $35 billion. So even a $500 million loss, which could throw most companies into bankruptcy, would translate after tax into a fall of only 1 percent in the value of BP's equity. BP concluded that this was a risk worth taking. In other words, it concluded that for large, low-probability risks the stock market was a more efficient risk-absorber than the insurance industry.

The insurance policies that we have been discussing are offered by specialist insurance companies. But sometimes you may be able to construct your own policies using traded options. For example, suppose that an investment dealer has a large inventory of IBM stock worth $90 a share. The dealer can insure this holding against loss by acquiring an option to sell IBM at $90. If the price of the stock falls, the dealer exercises the option and receives the $90.

Here is another example: Imagine that you have just bid on a large construction project in France. Payment will be in French francs, but many of the costs will be in United States dollars. By the time that you will find out whether you have been awarded the contract, the value of the franc may have declined and the project may no longer be profitable. In that case you can insure yourself against currency loss by taking out an option to sell francs. If you get the contract and the franc depreciates, the value of the option should offset the reduction in the dollar value of the contract. If you *don't* get the contract, you simply have an option which will be profitable if the franc depreciates and valueless otherwise.

---

[8]Our description of BP's insurance strategy draws heavily on N. A. Doherty and C. W. Smith, Jr., "Corporate Insurance Strategy: The Case of British Petroleum," *Journal of Applied Corporate Finance*, **6**:4–15 (Fall 1993).

[9]However, with one or two exceptions insurance has not been available for the very largest losses of $500 million or more.

Of course, such insurance doesn't come free; the price you pay for the option is the insurance premium. If the franc appreciates, you have with hindsight bought unnecessary insurance.

25-2 HEDGING WITH FUTURES

Hedging involves taking on one risk to offset another. We will explain shortly how to set up a hedge, but first we will give some examples and describe some tools that are specially designed for hedging. These are futures, forwards, and swaps. Together with options, they are known as **derivative instruments** or **derivatives** because their value depends on the value of another asset. You can think of them as side bets on the value of the underlying asset.[10]

We start with the oldest actively traded derivative instruments, **futures contracts.** Futures were originally developed for agricultural and other commodities. For example, suppose that a wheat farmer expects to have 100,000 bushels of wheat to sell next September. If he is worried that the price may decline in the interim, he can hedge by selling 100,000 bushels of September wheat futures. In this case he agrees to deliver 100,000 bushels of wheat in September at a price that is set today. Do not confuse this futures contract with an option, in which the holder has a choice whether or not to make delivery; the farmer's futures contract is a firm promise to deliver wheat.

A miller is in the opposite position. She needs to *buy* wheat after the harvest. If she would like to fix the price of this wheat ahead of time, she can do so by *buying* wheat futures. In other words, she agrees to take delivery of wheat in the future at a price that is fixed today. The miller also does not have an option; if she holds the contract to maturity, she is obliged to take delivery.

Both the farmer and the miller have less risk than before.[11] The farmer has hedged risk by *selling* wheat futures; this is termed a *short hedge*. The miller has hedged risk by *buying* wheat futures; this is known as a *long hedge*.

The price of wheat for immediate delivery is known as the *spot price*. When the farmer sells wheat futures, the price that he agrees to take for his wheat may be very different from the spot price. But as the date for delivery approaches, a futures contract becomes more and more like a spot contract and the price of the future snuggles up to the spot price.

The farmer may decide to wait until his futures contract matures and then deliver wheat to the buyer. In practice such delivery is very rare, for it is more convenient for the farmer to buy back the wheat futures just before maturity.[12] If he is properly hedged, any loss on his wheat crop will be exactly offset by the profit on his sale and subsequent repurchase of wheat futures.

---

[10]"Side bet" conjures up an image of wicked speculators. Derivatives attract their share of speculators, some of whom may be wicked, but they are also used by sober and prudent businesspeople to reduce risk.

[11]We oversimplify. For example, the miller won't reduce risk if bread prices vary in proportion to the postharvest wheat price. In this case the miller is in the hazardous position of having fixed her cost but not her selling price. This point is discussed in A. C. Shapiro and S. Titman, "An Integrated Approach to Corporate Risk Management," *Midland Corporate Finance Journal*, **3**:41–56 (Summer 1985).

[12]In the case of some of the financial futures described below, you *cannot* deliver the asset. At maturity the buyer simply receives (or pays) the difference between the spot price and the price at which he or she agreed to purchase the asset.

TABLE 25-1

··

The most active commodity futures and the principal exchanges on which they are traded			
Future	Exchange	Future	Exchange
Barley	WPG	Orange juice	CTN
Canola	WPG	Sugar	CSCE
Corn	CBT, MCE		
Oats	CBT, WPG	Aluminum	LME
Rice	CBT	Copper	COMEX, LME, MCE
Wheat	CBT, KC, MCE, MPLS	Gold	COMEX
		Lead	LME
Flaxseed	WPG	Nickel	LME
Soybeans	CBT	Palladium	NYMEX
Soybean meal	CBT	Platinum	NYMEX
Soybean oil	CBT, MCE	Silver	COMEX, CBT, MCE
		Zinc	LME
Cattle	CME		
Live hogs	CME	Crude oil	IPE, NYMEX
Pork bellies	CME	Gas oil	IPE
		Heating oil	NYMEX
Cocoa	CSCE, LCE	Natural gas	NYMEX
Coffee	CSCE, LCE	Unleaded gasoline	NYMEX
Cotton	CTN		
Lumber	CME	Freight rates	LCE

Key to abbreviations:

CBT	Chicago Board of Trade	LCE	London Commodity Exchange
CME	Chicago Mercantile Exchange	LME	London Metal Exchange
COMEX	Commodity Exchange, New York	MCE	MidAmerica Commodity Exchange
CSCE	Coffee, Sugar and Cocoa Exchange, New York	MPLS	Minneapolis Grain Exchange
CTN	New York Cotton Exchange	NYMEX	New York Mercantile Exchange
IPE	International Petroleum Exchange of London	WPG	Winnipeg Commodity Exchange
KC	Kansas City Board of Trade		

················

Commodity and Financial Futures

Futures contracts are bought and sold on organized futures exchanges. Table 25-1 lists the principal commodity futures contracts and the exchanges on which they are traded. Notice that our farmer and miller are not the only businesses that can hedge risk with commodity futures. The lumber company and the builder can hedge against changes in lumber prices, the copper producer and the cable manufacturer against changes in copper prices, the oil producer and the trucker against changes in gasoline prices, and so on.[13]

For many firms the wide fluctuations in interest rates and exchange rates have become at least as important a source of risk as changes in commodity prices. Financial futures are similar to commodity futures, but instead of placing an order to buy or sell a commodity at a future date, you place an order to buy or sell a financial asset at a future date. Table 25-2 lists some of the most important U.S. financial futures.

---

[13]By the time you read this, the list of futures contracts will almost certainly be out of date. Unsuccessful contracts are regularly dropped, and at any time the exchanges may be seeking approval for literally dozens of new contracts.

TABLE 25-2

Active U.S. financial futures contracts and the principal exchanges on which they are traded

Future	Exchange
U.S. Treasury bonds	CBT
U.S. Treasury notes	CBT
U.S. Treasury bills	CME
U.S. municipal bond index	CBT
Eurodollar deposits	CME
LIBOR	CME
Standard and Poor's index	CME
Australian dollar	CME
British pound	CME
Canadian dollar	CME
German mark	CME
Japanese yen	CME
Mexican peso	CME
Swiss franc	CME

Key to abbreviations:

CBT   Chicago Board of Trade
CME   Chicago Mercantile Exchange

In addition, futures on a variety of other bonds and stock market indexes are actively traded on overseas futures exchanges.

Financial futures have been a remarkably successful innovation. They were invented in 1972; within a few years, trading in financial futures significantly exceeded trading in commodity futures.

The Mechanics of Futures Trading

When you buy or sell a futures contract, the price is fixed today but payment is not made until later. You will, however, be asked to put up margin in the form of either cash or Treasury bills to demonstrate that you have the money to honor your side of the bargain. As long as you earn interest on the margined securities, there is no cost to you.

In addition, futures contracts are *marked to market*. This means that each day any profits or losses on the contract are calculated; you pay the exchange any losses and receive any profits. For example, suppose that our farmer agreed to deliver 100,000 bushels of wheat at $2.50 a bushel. The next day the price of wheat futures declines to $2.45 a bushel. The farmer now has a profit on his sale of $100,000 \times \$.05 = \$5000$. The exchange's clearinghouse therefore pays this $5000 to the farmer. You can think of the farmer as closing out his position every day and then opening up a new position. Thus after the first day the farmer has realized a profit of $5000 on his trade and now has an obligation to deliver wheat for $2.45 a bushel. The 5 cents that the farmer has already been paid *plus* the $2.45 that remains to be paid equals the $2.50 selling price at which the farmer originally agreed to deliver wheat.

Of course, our miller is in the opposite position. The fall in the futures price leaves her with a *loss* of 5 cents a bushel. She must, therefore, pay over this loss to the exchange's clearinghouse. In effect the miller closes out her initial purchase at a 5-cent loss and opens a new contract to take delivery at $2.45 a bushel.[14]

Spot and Futures Prices— Financial Futures

If you want to buy a security, you have a choice. You can buy it for immediate delivery at the spot price. Alternatively, you can place an order for later delivery; in this case you buy at the futures price. When you buy a financial future, you end up with exactly the same security that you would have if you bought in the spot market. However, there are two differences. First, you don't pay for the security up front, and so you can earn interest on its purchase price. Second, you miss out on any dividend or interest that is paid in the interim. This tells us something about the relationship between the spot and futures prices:[15]

$$\frac{\text{Futures price}}{(1 + r_f)^t} = \frac{\text{spot}}{\text{price}} - PV\left(\begin{array}{l}\text{dividends or}\\\text{interest payments}\\\text{forgone}\end{array}\right)$$

Here r_f is the t-period risk-free interest rate.

An example will show how and why this formula works.

Example—Stock Index Futures: Suppose 6-month stock index futures trade at 473.98 when the index is 464. The 6-month interest rate is 7 percent, and the average dividend yield of stocks in the index is 2.7 percent per year. Are these numbers consistent?

Suppose you buy the futures contract and set aside the money to exercise it. At a 7 percent annual rate, you'll earn about 3.5 percent interest over the next 6 months. Thus you invest

$$\frac{\text{Futures price}}{(1 + r_f)^t} = \frac{473.98}{1.035} = 457.95$$

What do you get in return? Everything you would have gotten by buying the index now at the spot price, except for the dividends paid over the next 6 months. If we assume, for simplicity, that a half-year's dividends are paid in month 6 (rather than evenly over 6 months), your payoff is

$$\text{Spot price} - PV(\text{dividends}) = 464 - \frac{464(.0135)}{1.035} = 457.95$$

You get what you pay for.

Spot and Futures Prices— Commodities

The difference between buying *commodities* today and buying commodity futures is more complicated. First, because payment is again delayed, the buyer of the future earns interest on her money. Second, she does not need to store the commodities and, therefore, saves warehouse costs, wastage, and so on. On the other hand, the futures

---

[14]Notice that neither the farmer nor the miller need be concerned about whether the other party will honor his or her side of the bargain. The futures exchange guarantees the contract and protects itself by settling up profits and losses each day.

[15]This relationship is strictly true only if the contract is not marked to market. Otherwise, the value of the future depends on the path of interest rates up to the delivery date. In practice this qualification is usually unimportant. See J. C. Cox, J. E. Ingersoll, and S. A. Ross, "The Relationship between Forward and Futures Prices," *Journal of Financial Economics,* **9**:321–346 (1981).

contract gives no *convenience yield*, which is the value of being able to get your hands on the real thing. The manager of a supermarket can't burn heating oil futures if there's a sudden cold snap, and he can't stock the shelves with orange juice futures if he runs out of inventory at 1 P.M. on a Saturday. All this means that for commodities,

$$\frac{\text{Futures price}}{(1 + r_f)^t} = \text{spot price} + \text{PV}\left(\begin{array}{c}\text{storage}\\\text{costs}\end{array}\right) - \text{PV}\left(\begin{array}{c}\text{convenience}\\\text{yield}\end{array}\right)$$

No one would be willing to hold the futures contract at a higher futures price or to hold the commodity at a lower futures price.[16]

It's interesting to compare the formulas for futures prices of commodities to the formulas for securities. PV(convenience yield) plays the same role as PV(dividends or interest payments forgone). But financial assets cost nothing to store, so PV(storage costs) does not appear in the formula for financial futures.

You can't observe PV(convenience yield) or PV(storage) separately, but you can infer the difference between them by comparing the spot price to the discounted futures price. This difference—that is, convenience yield less storage cost—is called *net convenience yield.*

Here is an example using quotes for late June 1995: At that time the spot price of heating oil (delivered in New York harbor) was about $.47 per gallon. The futures price for June 1996 was $.475. Of course, if you bought and held the futures, you would pay after 1 year. The present value of this outlay in June 1995 was .475/(1.057) = .45, using the 1-year risk-free rate of 5.7 percent. So PV(net convenience yield) is positive, about 2 cents per gallon:

$$\text{PV(net convenience yield)} = \text{spot prices} - \frac{\text{futures price}}{1 + r_f}$$

$$= .47 - .45 = \$.02$$

Sometimes the net convenience yield is expressed as a percentage of the spot price, or in this case as .02/.47 = .043, or 4.3 percent. Figure 25-1 plots percentage net convenience yields for gold, copper, and heating oil. Notice that the convenience of holding gold rather than a future entitlement to gold is very small. However, the spread between the spot and futures prices of oil bounces around and can rise to very high levels when troubles in the Middle East revive fears of an interruption of supply.[17]

25-3   FORWARD CONTRACTS

Each day billions of dollars of futures contracts are bought and sold. This liquidity is possible only because futures contracts are standardized and mature on a limited number of dates each year.

Fortunately there is usually more than one way to skin a financial cat. If the terms of futures contracts do not suit your particular needs, you may be able to buy or sell a **forward contract.** Forward contracts are simply tailor-made futures contracts. The

---

[16]Our formula could overstate the futures price if no one is willing to hold the commodity, that is, if inventories fall to zero or some absolute minimum.

[17]For evidence that the net convenience yield is related to the level of inventories, see M. J. Brennan, "The Price of Convenience and the Valuation of Commodity Contingent Claims," in D. Lund and B. Øksendal (eds.), *Stochastic Models and Option Values*, North-Holland Publishing Company, Amsterdam, 1991.

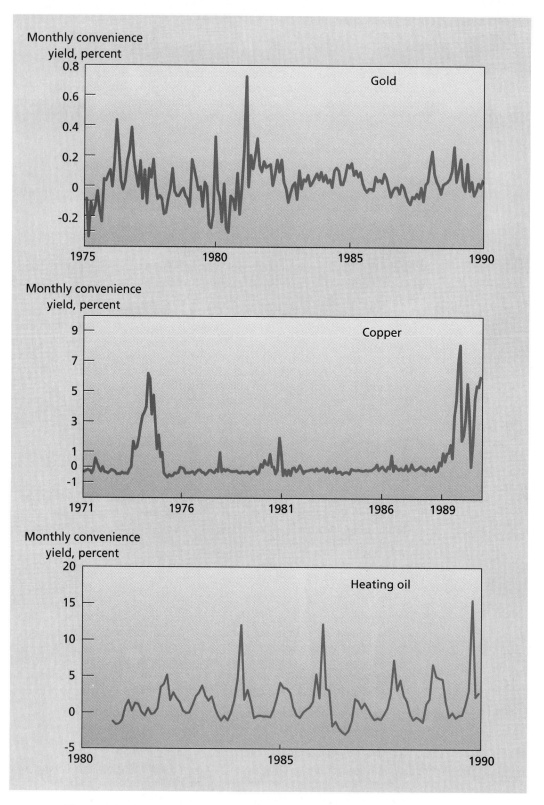

Figure 25-1 *Monthly* percentage net convenience yields (convenience yield *less* storage costs) for three commodities. Note the different vertical scales. [*Source:* R. S. Pindyck, "The Present Value Model of Rational Commodity Pricing," *Economic Journal,* **103**:511–530 (May 1993).]

main forward market is in foreign currency. Banks quote prices at which they will buy and sell forward currency for periods up to 1 year ahead, and in the case of the major currencies they are prepared to fix a price for 5 years or more. There is a huge volume of business in forward currency. In 1992 the total value of outstanding forward contracts was $5.5 trillion ($5,500,000,000,000), and the annual turnover was more than 10 times this figure.

It is also possible to enter into a forward interest-rate contract. For example, suppose that you know that at the end of 6 months you are going to need a 3-month loan. You can lock in the interest rate on that loan by buying a forward rate agreement (FRA) from a bank.[18] For example, the bank might offer to sell you a 6-month forward rate agreement on 3-month LIBOR at 7 percent.[19] If at the end of 6 months the 3-month LIBOR rate is greater than 7 percent, the bank will pay you the difference; if 3-month LIBOR is less than 7 percent, you pay the bank the difference.[20] At the end of 1992 the total principal amount of FRAs outstanding was $2 trillion.

Home-made Forward Contracts

Suppose that you borrow $90.91 for 1 year at 10 percent and lend $90.91 for 2 years at 12 percent. These interest rates are for loans made today; therefore, they are spot interest rates.

The cash flows on your transactions are as follows:

	Year 0	Year 1	Year 2
Borrow for 1 year at 10%	+90.91	−100	
Lend for 2 years at 12%	−90.91		+114.04
Net cash flow	0	−100	+114.04

Notice that you do not have any net cash outflow today but you have contracted to pay out money in year 1. The interest rate on this forward commitment is 14.04 percent. To calculate this forward interest rate, we simply worked out the extra return for lending for 2 years rather than 1:

$$\text{Forward interest rate} = \frac{(1 + 2\text{-year spot rate})^2}{1 + 1\text{-year spot rate}} - 1$$

$$= \frac{(1.12)^2}{1.10} - 1 = .1404, \text{ or } 14.04\%$$

In our example you manufactured a forward loan by borrowing short-term and lending long. But you can also run the process in reverse. If you wish to fix today the rate at which you borrow next year, you borrow long and lend the money until you need it next year.

You can also construct a do-it-yourself forward contract to buy or sell foreign exchange. For example, suppose that you want to place an order today to buy Swiss

---

[18]Note that the party which profits from a rise in rates is described as the "buyer." In our example you would be said to "buy 6 against 9 months" money, meaning that the forward rate agreement is for a 3-month loan in 6 months' time.

[19]LIBOR (London interbank offered rate) is the interest rate at which major international banks in London lend each other dollars.

[20]Unlike futures contracts, forwards are not marked to market. Thus all profits or losses are settled when the contract matures.

francs in 1 year. The current (or spot) exchange rate is $1 = 2$ francs, the 1-year dollar interest rate is 6 percent, and the 1-year franc interest rate is 4 percent. You now borrow $50 for 1 year, exchange these dollars into francs, and lend your francs for a year. Your cash flows are as follows:

	NOW		AFTER 1 YEAR	
	Dollars	Francs	Dollars	Francs
Borrow dollars at 6%	+50		−53	
Change dollars into francs	−50	+100		
Lend francs at 4%		−100		+104
Net cash flow	0	0	−53	+104

Your net cash flow today is zero, but you have committed to pay out $53 at the end of the year and receive 104 francs. Thus you have constructed a homemade forward contract to buy Swiss francs at an exchange rate of $1 = 104/53 = 1.96$ francs.

This homemade forward contract tells us the fair price for a forward (or futures) contract to buy Swiss francs:

$$\text{Forward price} = \text{Spot price} \times \frac{1 + \text{franc interest rate}}{1 + \text{dollar interest rate}}$$

$$= (100/50) \times \frac{104}{106} = 1.96 \text{ francs}$$

What would happen if the price of futures was higher than this figure, say 2.0 francs per dollar? Then everyone would rush to buy forward, thereby generating extra francs at year 1. The forward commitment could be covered by borrowing francs, changing to dollars at the spot rate, and lending dollars. If the futures price was lower, everyone would do the reverse. Sharp-eyed arbitrageurs with families to support (or expensive extrafamilial relationships) are constantly on the lookout for such discrepancies.

If you can make your own forward contracts for interest rates or currencies, why does anyone bother to trade on the financial futures exchanges? The answer is, "Convenience and cost." Some of the most popular futures contracts are the interest-rate and currency futures contracts that are closest to maturity. In principle these are the easiest to replicate, but the huge volume of business in financial futures makes them a very low cost tool for hedging (or speculation).

25-4 SWAPS

Suppose that the Possum Company wishes to borrow deutschemarks to help finance its European operations. Since Possum is better known in the United States, the financial manager believes that the company can obtain more attractive terms on a dollar loan than on a deutschemark loan. Therefore, the company issues $10 million of 5-year 12 percent notes in the United States. At the same time Possum arranges with a bank to **swap** its future dollar liability for deutschemarks. Under this arrangement the bank agrees to pay Possum sufficient dollars to service its dollar loan; in exchange Possum agrees to make a series of annual payments in deutschemarks to the bank. Possum and the bank are referred to as *counterparties*.

Here are Possum's cash flows (in millions):

	YEAR 0		YEARS 1–4		YEAR 5	
	Dollars	Deutsche-marks	Dollars	Deutsche-marks	Dollars	Deutsche-marks
1. Issue dollar loan	+10		−1.2		−11.2	
2. Swap dollars for deutschemarks	−10	+20	+1.2	−1.6	+11.2	−21.6
3. Net cash flow	0	+20	0	−1.6	0	−21.6

The combined effect of Possum's two steps (line 3) is to convert a 12 percent dollar loan into an 8 percent deutschemark loan. The device that makes this possible is the *currency swap*. You can think of the cash flows for the swap (line 2) as a series of forward currency contracts. In each of years 1 through 4 Possum agrees to purchase $1.2 million at a cost of 1.6 million deutschemarks; in year 5 it agrees to buy $11.2 million at a cost of 21.6 million deutschemarks.[21]

The bank's cash flows from the swap are the reverse of Possum's. It has undertaken to pay out dollars in the future and receive deutschemarks. Since the bank is now exposed to the risk that the deutschemark will weaken unexpectedly against the dollar, it will try to hedge this risk by engaging in a series of futures or forward contracts or by swapping deutschemarks for dollars with another counterparty. As long as Possum and the other counterparty honor their promises, the bank is fully protected against risk. The recurring nightmare for swap managers is that one party will default, leaving the bank with a large unmatched position.

Swaps are not new. For many years the British government limited purchases of foreign currency to invest abroad. These restrictions led many British firms to arrange so-called back-to-back loans. The firm would lend sterling to a company in the United States and simultaneously borrow dollars, which could then be used for foreign investment. In taking out the back-to-back loan, the British firm agreed to make a series of future dollar payments in exchange for receiving a flow of sterling income.

In 1979 these limits on overseas investment were removed, and British firms no longer needed to take out back-to-back loans. However, during the 1980s the banks did a respray job on the back-to-back loan and relaunched it as a swap. Swaps turned out to be very popular with corporate customers; in recent years some two-thirds of dollar eurobond issues have been accompanied by a swap.

Swaps are not limited to future exchanges of currency. The most common form of swap is actually an *interest-rate swap*, in which counterparties swap fixed-interest-rate loans for floating-rate loans. In this case one party promises to make a series of fixed annual payments in return for receiving a series of payments that are linked to the level of short-term interest rates. Sometimes swaps are used to convert between floating-rate loans that are tied to different base rates. For example, a firm might wish to swap a series of payments that are linked to the prime rate for a series of payments that are linked to the Treasury bill rate.

---

[21]Usually in a currency swap the two parties make an initial payment to each other (i.e., Possum pays the bank $10 million and receives 20 million deutschemarks). However, this is not necessary, and in the case of interest-rate swaps that are in the *same* currency, no initial payments occur and there are no final principal repayments. Interest-rate swaps are explained below.

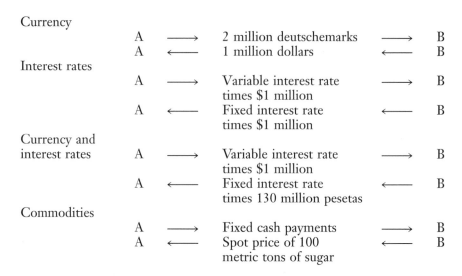

Figure 25-2 Some examples of swaps. A swap is an agreement by two counterparties (A and B) to exchange currencies, interest payments, or commodities on a series of future dates.

Cadbury Schweppes is an example of a company that uses both currency swaps and interest-rate swaps. It has access to an active dollar commercial paper program, which it estimates reduces its interest costs by 30 basis points (i.e., .30 percentage points). But Cadbury does not want all its funding to be variable-rate and denominated in U.S. dollars. So it swaps the dollars raised from its commercial paper program for fixed-rate pesetas, Australian dollars, and so on.

It is also possible to *swap commodities*. In this case you don't need to deliver the commodities; you just settle up any differences in their value. For example, Cadbury Schweppes could lock in the price at which it buys sugar by agreeing to pay an amount that goes up and down with sugar prices; the counterparty pays Cadbury a fixed stream of payments. In contrast, a sugar producer could lock in the price at which it *sells* sugar by paying a fixed cash amount, while its counterparty pays an amount that is linked to sugar prices.

Figure 25-2 provides a summary of the different kinds of swaps.

·················

*Do-It-Yourself Interest-Rate Swaps

Before we leave swaps, one more example may be helpful. We begin with a home-made fixed-to-floating interest-rate swap.

Friendly Bancorp has made a 5-year, $50 million loan to fund part of the construction cost of a large cogeneration project. The loan carries a fixed interest rate of 8 percent. Annual interest payments are therefore $4 million. Interest payments are made annually, and all the principal will be repaid at year 5. The bank wants to swap the $4 million, 5-year annuity (the fixed interest payments) into a floating-rate annuity.

The bank could borrow at a 6 percent fixed rate for 5 years.[22] Therefore, the $4 million interest it receives could support a fixed-rate loan of 4/.06 = $66.67 million. This will be the *notional principal* amount of the swap.

The bank can construct the homemade swap as follows: It borrows $66.67 million at a fixed interest rate of 6 percent for 5 years and simultaneously lends the same amount

---

[22]The spread between the bank's 6 percent borrowing rate and the 8 percent lending rate is the bank's profit on the project financing.

TABLE 25-3

The top part shows the cash flows to a homemade fixed-to-floating interest-rate swap. The bottom part shows the cash flows to a standard swap transaction.

	YEAR					
	0	1	2	3	4	5
			Homemade Swap			
1. Borrow $66.67 at 6% fixed rate	+66.67	−4	−4	−4	−4	−(4+66.67)
2. Lend $66.67 at LIBOR floating rate (initially 5%)	−66.67	+.05 ×66.67	+LIBOR$_1$ ×66.67	+LIBOR$_2$ ×66.67	+LIBOR$_3$ ×66.67	+LIBOR$_4$ ×66.67 +66.67
Net cash flow	0	−4 +.05 ×66.67	−4 +LIBOR$_1$ ×66.67	−4 +LIBOR$_2$ ×66.67	−4 +LIBOR$_3$ ×66.67	−4 +LIBOR$_4$ ×66.67
			Standard Fixed-to-Floating Swap			
Net cash flow	0	−4 +.05 ×66.67	−4 +LIBOR$_1$ ×66.67	−4 +LIBOR$_2$ ×66.67	−4 +LIBOR$_3$ ×66.67	−4 +LIBOR$_4$ ×66.67

at LIBOR. We assume that LIBOR is now 5 percent.[23] LIBOR is a short-term interest rate, so future interest receipts will fluctuate as the bank's investment is rolled over.

The net cash flows to this strategy are shown in the top panel of Table 25-3. Notice that there is no net cash flow in year 0 and that in year 5 the principal amount of the short-term investment is used to pay off the $66.67 million loan. What's left? A cash flow equal to the *difference* between the interest earned (LIBOR × 66.67) and the $4 million outlay on the fixed loan. The bank also has $4 million per year coming in from the project financing, so it has transformed that fixed payment into a floating payment keyed to LIBOR.

Of course, there's an easier way to do this, shown in the bottom panel of Table 25-3. The bank can just call a swap dealer and agree to a 5-year, fixed-to-LIBOR swap on a notional principal of $66.67 million.[24] Naturally, Friendly Bancorp takes the easier route and enters the swap. Let's see what happens.

The starting payment is based on the starting LIBOR rate of 5 percent:

Bank	$\longrightarrow$	$4	$\longrightarrow$	Counterparty
Bank	$\longleftarrow$	.05 × $66.67 = $3.33	$\longleftarrow$	Counterparty
Bank	$\longrightarrow$	Net = $.67	$\longrightarrow$	Counterparty

[23]Maybe the short-term interest rate is below the 5-year interest rate because investors expect interest rates to rise.

[24]Both strategies are equivalent to a series of forward contracts on LIBOR. The forward prices are $4 million each for LIBOR$_1$ × 66.67, LIBOR$_2$ × 66.67, and so on. Separately negotiated forward prices would not be $4 million for any one year, but the PVs of the "annuities" of forward prices would be identical.

The second payment is based on LIBOR at year 1. Suppose it increases to 6 percent:

| Bank | $\longrightarrow$ | $4 | $\longrightarrow$ | Counterparty |
| Bank | $\longleftarrow$ | .06 × $66.67 = $4 | $\longleftarrow$ | Counterparty |

| Bank | | Net = 0 | | Counterparty |

What about the *value* of the swap at year 2? That depends on long-term interest rates. First, suppose that they do not move, so a 6 percent note issued by the bank would still trade at par. In this case the swap still has zero value. (You can confirm this by checking that the NPV of a new 3-year homemade swap is zero.) But if long rates increase, say, to 7 percent, the value of a 3-year note falls to

$$PV = \frac{4}{1.07} + \frac{4}{(1.07)^2} + \frac{4 + 66.67}{(1.07)^3} = \$64.92 \text{ million}$$

Now the swap is worth $66.67 - 64.92 = \$1.75$ million.

How do we know the swap is worth $1.75 million? Consider the following strategy:

1. The bank can enter a new 3-year swap deal in which it agrees to *pay* LIBOR on the same notional principal of $66.67 million.

2. In return it receives fixed payments at the new 7 percent interest rate, that is, .07 × 66.67 = $4.67 per year.

The new swap cancels the cash flows of the old one, but it generates an extra $.67 million for 3 years. This extra cash flow is worth

$$PV = \sum_1^3 \frac{.67}{(1.07)^t} = \$1.75 \text{ million}$$

Remember, ordinary interest-rate swaps have no initial cost or value (PV = 0), but their value drifts away from zero as time passes and long-term interest rates change. One counterparty wins as the other loses.

25-5 HOW TO SET UP A HEDGE

In each of our examples of hedging the firm has offset the risk by buying one asset and selling an equal amount of another asset. For example, our farmer owned 100,000 bushels of wheat and sold 100,000 bushels of wheat futures. As long as the wheat that the farmer owns is identical to the wheat that he has promised to deliver, this strategy minimizes risk.

In practice the wheat that the farmer owns and the wheat that he sells in the futures markets are unlikely to be identical. For example, if he sells wheat futures on the Kansas City exchange, he agrees to deliver hard, red winter wheat in Kansas City in September. But perhaps he is growing northern spring wheat many miles from Kansas City; in this case the prices of the two wheats will not move exactly together.

Figure 25-3 shows how changes in the prices of the two types of wheat may have been related in the past. Notice two things about this figure: First, the scatter of points suggests that the price changes are imperfectly related. If so, it is not possible to con-

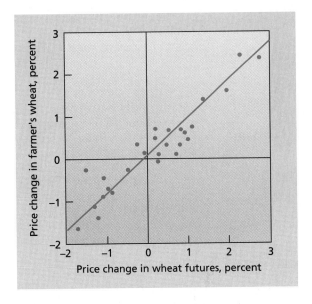

Figure 25-3 Hypothetical plot of past changes in the price of the farmer's wheat against changes in the price of Kansas City wheat futures.

struct a hedge that eliminates all risk. Some residual, or *basis*, risk will remain. Second, the slope of the fitted line shows that a 1 percent change in the price of Kansas wheat was on average associated with an .8 percent change in the price of the farmer's wheat. Because the price of the farmer's wheat is relatively insensitive to changes in Kansas prices, he needs to sell .8 × 100,000 bushels of wheat futures to minimize risk.

Let us generalize. Suppose that you already own an asset, A (e.g., wheat), and that you wish to hedge against changes in the value of A by making an offsetting sale of another asset, B (e.g., wheat futures). Suppose also that percentage changes in the value of A are related in the following way to percentage changes in the value of B:

$$\text{Expected change in value of A} = a + \delta \left(\text{change in value of B} \right)$$

Delta (δ) measures the sensitivity of A to changes in the value of B. It is also equal to the *hedge ratio*—that is, the number of units of B which should be sold to hedge the purchase of A. You minimize risk if you offset your position in A by the sale of delta units of B.[25]

The trick in setting up a hedge is to estimate the delta or hedge ratio. This sometimes calls for a strong dose of judgment. For example, we referred above to the fact that Porsche is exposed to fluctuations in the exchange rate between dollars and deutschemarks. But how much would the value of the company fall if the deutschemark appreciated? The answer depends on how demand for Porsche cars in the United States would be affected by a rise in price, on whether Porsche could shift production to lower-cost countries, on how competitors would react, and so on.

Sometimes, as in our example of the wheat farmer, a little past history may help to estimate the sensitivity of the value of asset A to fluctuations in the value of B. It may also be possible to call on a little theory to set up the hedge.

[25]Notice that A, the item that you wish to hedge, is the dependent variable. Delta measures the sensitivity of A to changes in B.

Using
Theory
to Set
Up the
Hedge:
An
Example

Potterton Leasing has just purchased some equipment and arranged to rent it out for $2 million a year over 8 years. At an interest rate of 12 percent, Potterton's rental income has a present value of $9.94 million:[26]

$$PV = \frac{2}{1.12} + \frac{2}{(1.12)^2} + \cdots + \frac{2}{(1.12)^8} = \$9.94 \text{ million}$$

Potterton proposes to finance the deal by issuing a package of $1.91 million of 1-year debt and $8.03 million of 6-year debt, each with a 12 percent coupon. Think of its new asset (the stream of rental income) and the new liability (the issue of debt) as a package. Does Potterton stand to gain or lose on this package if interest rates change?

To answer this question, it is helpful to go back to the concept of duration that we introduced in Chapter 23. Duration, you may remember, is the weighted-average time to each cash flow. Duration is important because it is directly related to volatility. If two assets have the same duration, their prices will be equally affected by any change in interest rates. If we call the total value of Potterton's rental income V, then the duration of Potterton's rental income is calculated as follows:

$$\text{Duration} = \frac{1}{V}[PV(C_1) \times 1] + [PV(C_2) \times 2] + [PV(C_3) \times 3] + \cdots$$

$$= \frac{1}{9.94}\left\{\left[\frac{2}{1.12} \times 1\right] + \left[\frac{2}{(1.12)^2} \times 2\right] + \cdots + \left[\frac{2}{(1.12)^8} \times 8\right]\right\}$$

$$= 3.9 \text{ years}$$

We can also calculate the duration of Potterton's new liabilities. The duration of the 1-year debt is 1 year, and the duration of the 6-year debt is 4.6 years. The duration of the package of 1- and 6-year debt is a weighted average of the durations of the individual issues:

$$\text{Duration of liability} = (1.91/9.94) \times \text{duration of 1-year debt}$$
$$+ (8.03/9.94) \times \text{duration of 6-year debt}$$
$$= (.192 \times 1) + (.808 \times 4.6) = 3.9 \text{ years}$$

Thus, both the asset (the lease) and the liability (the debt package) have a duration of 3.9 years. Therefore, both are affected equally by a change in interest rates. If rates rise, the present value of Potterton's rental income will decline, but the value of its debt obligation will also decline by the same amount. By equalizing the duration of the asset and that of the liability, Potterton has *immunized* itself against any change in interest rates. It looks as if Potterton's financial manager knows a thing or two about hedging.

When Potterton set up the hedge, it needed to find a package of loans that had a present value of $9.94 million and a duration of 3.9 years. Call the proportion of the proceeds raised by the 6-year loan x and the proportion raised by the 1-year loan $(1 - x)$. Then

$$\text{Duration of package} = (x \times \text{duration of 6-year loan}) + [(1 - x) \times \text{duration of 1-year loan}]$$
$$3.9 \text{ years} = (x \times 4.6 \text{ years}) + [(1 - x) \times 1 \text{ year}]$$
$$x = .808$$

---

[26]We ignore tax in this example.

TABLE 25-4

· ·

Potterton can hedge by issuing this sinking fund bond that pays out $2 million each year.

Cash Flows, Millions of Dollars

	YEAR							
	1	2	3	4	5	6	7	8
Balance at start of year	9.94	9.13	8.23	7.22	6.08	4.81	3.39	1.79
Interest at 12%	1.19	1.10	.99	.87	.73	.58	.40	.21
Sinking fund payment	.81	.90	1.01	1.13	1.27	1.42	1.60	1.79
Interest plus sinking fund payment	2.00	2.00	2.00	2.00	2.00	2.00	2.00	2.00

Since the package of loans must raise $9.94 million, Potterton needs to issue .808 × 9.94 = $8.03 million of the 6-year loan.

An important feature of this hedge is that it is dynamic. As interest rates change and time passes, the duration of Potterton's asset may no longer be the same as that of its liability. Thus, to remain hedged against interest-rate changes, Potterton must be prepared to keep adjusting the duration of its debt.

If Potterton is not disposed to follow this dynamic hedging strategy, it has an alternative. It can devise a debt issue whose cash flows exactly match the rental income from the lease. For example, suppose that it issues an 8-year sinking fund bond; the amount of the sinking fund is $810,000 in year 1, and the payment increases by 12 percent annually. Table 25-4 shows that the bond payments (interest plus sinking fund) are $2 million in each year.

Since the cash flows on the asset exactly match those on the liability, Potterton's financial manager can now relax. Each year the manager simply collects the $2 million rental income and hands it to the bondholders. Whatever happens to interest rates, the firm is always perfectly hedged.

Why wouldn't Potterton's financial manager *always* prefer to construct matching assets and liabilities? One reason is that it may be relatively costly to devise a bond with a specially tailored pattern of cash flows. Another may be that Potterton is continually entering into new lease agreements and issuing new debt. In this case the manager can never relax; it may be simpler to keep the durations of the assets and liabilities equal than to maintain an exact match between the cash flows.

· · · · · · · · · · · · · · · ·

Options, Deltas, and Betas

Here's another case where some theory can help you set up a hedge. In Chapter 20 we came across options. These give you the right, but not the obligation, to buy or sell an asset. Options are derivatives; their value depends only on what happens to the price of the underlying asset.

The *option delta* summarizes the link between the option and the asset. For example, if you own an option to buy a share of Walt Disney stock, the change in the value of your investment will be the same as it would be if you held delta shares of Disney.

Since the option price is tied to the asset price, options can be used for hedging. Thus, if you own an option to buy a share of Disney and at the same time you sell delta shares of Disney, any change in the value of your position in the stock will be exactly offset by the change in the value of your option position.[27] In other words, you will be perfectly hedged—hedged, that is, for the next short period of time. Option deltas change as the stock price changes and time passes. Therefore, option-based hedges need to be adjusted frequently.

Options can be used to hedge commodities too. The miller could offset changes in the cost of future wheat purchases by buying call options on wheat (or on wheat futures). But this is not the simplest strategy if the miller is trying to lock in the future cost of wheat. She would have to check the option delta to determine how many options to buy, and she would have to keep track of changes in the option delta and reset the hedge as necessary.[28]

It's the same for financial assets. Suppose you hold a well-diversified portfolio of stocks with a beta of 1.0 and near-perfect correlation with the market return. You want to lock in the portfolio's value at year-end. You could accomplish this by selling call options on the index, but to maintain the hedge, the option position would have to be adjusted frequently. It's simpler just to sell index futures maturing at year-end. But if you wish to lock in the price of an individual stock, you will probably hedge with options, since futures contracts trade only on market indexes.

Speaking of betas . . . what if your portfolio has a beta of .60, not 1.0? Then your hedge will require 40 percent fewer index futures contracts. And since your low-beta portfolio is probably not perfectly correlated with the market, there will be some basis risk as well. In this context our old friend beta (β) and the hedge ratio (δ) are one and the same. Remember, to hedge A with B, you need to know δ because

$$\text{Expected change in value of A} = a + \delta(\text{change in value of B})$$

When A is a stock or portfolio, and B the market, we estimate beta from the same relationship:

$$\text{Expected change in stock or portfolio value} = a + \beta(\text{change in market index})$$

25-6 IS "DERIVATIVE" A FOUR-LETTER WORD?

Our earlier example of the farmer and miller showed how futures may be used to reduce business risk. However, if you were to copy the farmer and sell wheat futures without an offsetting holding of wheat, you would not be *reducing* risk: You would be *speculating*.

Speculators in search of large profits (and prepared to tolerate large losses) are attracted by the leverage that derivatives provide. By this we mean that it is not necessary to lay out much money up front and the profits or losses may be many times the initial outlay.[29] "Speculation" has an ugly ring, but a successful derivatives market needs speculators who are prepared to take on risk and provide more cautious people like our farmer and miller with the protection they need. For example, if an excess of farmers wish to sell wheat futures, the price of futures will be forced down until enough speculators are tempted to buy in the hope of a profit. If there is a sur-

---

[27]We are assuming that you hold one option and hedge by selling δ shares. If you owned one share and wanted to hedge by selling options, you would need to sell $1/\delta$ options.

[28]*Quiz:* What is the miller's position if she buys call options on wheat and simply holds them to maturity?

[29]For example, if you buy or sell forward, no money changes hands until the contract matures, though you may be required to put up margin to show that you can honor your commitment. This margin does not need to be cash; it may be in the form of safe securities.

plus of millers wishing to buy wheat futures, the reverse will happen. The price of wheat futures will be forced *up* until speculators are drawn in to sell.

Speculation may be necessary to a thriving derivatives market, but it can get companies into serious trouble. For example, the Japanese company Showa Shell reported a loss of $1.5 billion on positions in foreign exchange futures. The German metals and oil trading company Metallgesellschaft took a loss of about $1.3 billion from oil futures and Procter & Gamble lost $157 million on swap positions.[30] Banks also have had their share of derivative losses. In 1995 Baring Brothers, a blue-chip British merchant bank with a 200-year history, became insolvent. The reason: A trader in its Singapore office had placed very large bets on the Japanese stock market index resulting in losses of $1.4 billion.

These tales of woe have some cautionary messages for corporations. During the 1970s and 1980s many firms turned their treasury operations into profit centers and proudly announced their profits from trading in financial instruments. But it is not possible to make large profits in financial markets without also taking large risks, so these profits should have served as a warning rather than a matter of congratulation.

A Boeing 747 weighs 400 tons, flies at nearly 600 miles per hour, and is inherently very dangerous. But we don't ground 747s; we just take precautions to ensure that they are flown with care. Similarly, it is foolish to suggest that firms should ban the use of derivatives, but it makes obvious sense to take precautions against their misuse. Here are two bits of horse sense:

■ *Precaution 1.* Don't be taken by surprise. By this we mean that senior management needs to monitor regularly the value of the firm's derivatives positions and to know what bets the firm has placed. At its simplest, this might involve asking what would happen if interest rates or exchange rates were to change by 1 percent. But large banks and consultants have also developed sophisticated models for measuring the risk of derivatives positions. J.P. Morgan, for example, offers corporate clients its *RiskMetrics* software to keep track of their risk.

■ *Precaution 2.* Place bets only when you have some comparative advantage that ensures the odds are in your favor. If a bank were to announce that it was drilling for oil or launching a new soap powder, you would rightly be suspicious about whether it had what it takes to succeed. Conversely, when an industrial corporation places large bets on interest rates or exchange rates, it is competing against some highly paid pros in banks and other financial institutions. Unless it is better informed than they are about future interest rates or exchange rates, it should use derivatives for hedging, not for speculation.

---

[30]We should be cautious, however, not to fall into the trap of assuming that losses on derivatives positions always indicate speculation. If those derivatives form part of a hedge, there should be offsetting profits from other assets. For example, it is not clear how far Metallgesellschaft (MG) was hedging or speculating. The company had agreed to deliver oil to customers in the future at a fixed price, and, since it stood to take a large loss if oil prices rose, the firm's policy was to hedge this risk by buying oil futures. Culp and Miller argue that the company was following a reasonable hedging strategy and would not have incurred serious losses had it stuck to its policy. But MG's top management bailed out when oil prices fell and large losses were recorded on its futures contracts. (MG's management may have been misled by its accounting system, which recorded the losses on the futures positions but not the profits on the contracts to deliver oil.) Unfortunately, the managers bailed out at the worst possible time, since they had to renegotiate delivery contracts in a period of *rising* oil prices. See C. Culp and M. H. Miller, "Metallgesellschaft and the Economics of Synthetic Storage," *Journal of Applied Corporate Finance*, **7**:62–76 (Winter 1995).

Imprudent speculation in derivatives is undoubtedly an issue of concern for the company's shareholders, but is it a matter for more general concern? Some people believe so. They point to the huge volume of trading in derivatives and argue that speculative losses could lead to major defaults that might threaten the whole financial system. These worries have led to calls for increased regulation of derivatives markets.

Now, this is not the place for a discussion of regulation, but we should warn you about careless measures of the size of the derivatives markets and the possible losses. In 1992 the total principal amount of derivatives outstanding in the world was estimated as $17.6 trillion (i.e., $17.6 thousand billion).[31] This is a very large sum, but it tells you *nothing* about the amount of money at risk. For example, suppose that a bank enters into a $10 million interest-rate swap and the other party goes bankrupt the next day. How much has the bank lost? Nothing. It hasn't paid anything up front; the two parties simply promised to pay sums to each other in the future. Now the deal is off.

Suppose that the other party does not go bankrupt until a year after the bank entered into the swap. In the meantime interest rates have moved in the bank's favor, so it should be receiving more money from the swap than it is paying out. When the other side defaults on the deal, the bank loses the difference between the interest that it is due to receive and the interest that it should pay. But it doesn't lose $10 million.[32]

The only meaningful measure of the potential loss from default is the amount that it would cost firms showing a profit to replace their swap positions. In 1992 this figure was only about 1 percent of the $4.7 trillion principal amount of swaps outstanding.[33]

25-7 SUMMARY

As a manager, you are paid to take risks, but you are not paid to take *any* risks. Some are simply bad bets, and others could jeopardize the success of the firm. In these cases you should look for ways to insure or hedge.

Most businesses take out insurance against a variety of risks. Insurance companies have considerable expertise in assessing risk and may be able to pool risks by holding a diversified portfolio. Insurance works less well when the insurance policy attracts only the worst risks (*adverse selection*) or when the insured firm is tempted to skip on maintenance and safety procedures (*moral hazard*).

Insurance is generally purchased from specialist insurance companies, but there are also occasions when the firm can use financial options to insure against a decline in an asset's value.

The idea behind hedging is straightforward. You find two closely related assets. You then buy one and sell the other in proportions that minimize the risk of your net position. If the assets are *perfectly* correlated, you can make the net position risk-free.

The trick is to find the hedge ratio or delta—that is, the number of units of one asset that is needed to offset changes in the value of the other asset. Sometimes the best solution is to look at how the prices of the two assets have moved together in the

---

[31]United States General Accounting Office, "Financial Derivatives: Actions Needed to Protect the Financial System," report to congressional requesters, May 1994.

[32]This does not mean that firms don't worry about the possibility of default, and there are a variety of ways that they try to protect themselves. In the case of swaps firms are reluctant to deal with banks that do not have the highest credit rating.

[33]United States General Accounting Office, op. cit. This does not mean that swaps have *increased* risk. If counterparties use swaps to hedge risk, they are *less likely* to default.

past. For example, suppose you observe that a 1 percent change in the value of B has been accompanied on average by a 2 percent change in the value of A. Then delta equals 2.0; to hedge each dollar invested in A, you need to sell two dollars of B.

On other occasions a little theory can help to set up the hedge. For example, the effect of a change in interest rates on an asset's value depends on the asset's duration. If two assets have the same duration, they will be equally affected by fluctuations in interest rates.

Many of the hedges described in this chapter are static. Once you have set up the hedge, you can take a long vacation, confident that the firm is well protected. However, some hedges, such as those that match durations, are dynamic. As time passes and prices change, you may need to rebalance your position to maintain the hedge.

Firms use a number of tools to hedge:

1. Futures contracts are advance orders to buy or sell an asset. The price is fixed today, but the final payment does not occur until the delivery date. The futures markets allow firms to place advance orders for dozens of different commodities, securities, and currencies.

2. Futures contracts are highly standardized and are traded in huge volume on the futures exchanges. Instead of buying or selling a standardized futures contract, you may be able to arrange a tailor-made contract with a bank. These tailor-made futures contracts are called forward contracts. Firms regularly protect themselves against exchange-rate changes by buying or selling forward currency contracts.

3. It is also sometimes possible to construct homemade forward contracts. For example, as an alternative to buying forward currency, you could borrow dollars, exchange them for foreign currency, and then lend the foreign currency until it is needed. This has exactly the same cash-flow consequences as a purchase of forward currency.

4. In recent years firms have entered into a variety of swap arrangements. For example, a firm may arrange for the bank to make all the future payments on its dollar debt in exchange for paying the bank the cost of servicing a deutschemark loan.

Instead of using derivatives for hedging, some companies have decided that speculation is more fun, and this has sometimes got them into serious trouble. We do not believe that such speculation makes sense for an industrial company, but we caution against the view that derivatives are a threat to the financial system.

Further Reading

Two general articles on corporate risk management are:

C. W. Smith and R. M. Stultz: "The Determinants of Firms' Hedging Policies," *Journal of Financial and Quantitative Analysis,* **20**:391–405 (December 1985).

K. A. Froot, D. Scharfstein, and J. C. Stein: "A Framework for Risk Management," *Journal of Applied Corporate Finance,* **7**:22–32 (Fall 1994).

Useful material on the ways that companies use derivatives and on regulation of derivatives is provided by:

Global Derivatives Study Group, *Derivatives: Practices and Principles,* July 1993, The Group of Thirty, Washington, D.C.

United States General Accounting Office: "Financial Derivatives: Actions Needed to Protect the Financial System," report to congressional requesters, May 1994.

Schaefer's paper is a useful review of how duration measures are used to immunize fixed liabilities:

S. M. Schaefer: "Immunisation and Duration: A Review of Theory, Performance and Applications," *Midland Corporate Finance Journal*, 3:41–58 (Autumn 1984).

For material on futures and swaps, see:

S. Figlewski, K. John, and J. Merrick: *Hedging with Financial Futures for Institutional Investors: From Theory to Practice*, Ballinger Publishing Company, Cambridge, Mass., 1986.

D. Duffie: *Futures Markets*, Prentice-Hall, Inc., Englewood Cliffs, N.J., 1989.

J. C. Hull: *Options, Futures and Other Derivative Securities*, 2d ed., Prentice-Hall, Inc., Englewood Cliffs, N.J., 1993.

D. R. Siegel and D. F. Siegel: *Futures Markets*, Dryden Press, Chicago, 1989.

C. W. Smith, C. H. Smithson, and D. S. Wilford: *Managing Financial Risk*, Harper & Row, Inc., New York, 1990.

The Metallgesellschaft debacle makes fascinating reading. The following three papers cover all sides of the ensuing debate:

C. Culp and M. H. Miller: "Metallgesellschaft and the Economics of Synthetic Storage," *Journal of Applied Corporate Finance*, 7:62–76 (Winter 1995).

F. Edwards: "The Collapse of Metallgesellschaft: Unhedgeable Risks, Poor Hedging Strategy, or Just Bad Luck?" *Journal of Futures Markets*, 15 (May 1995).

A. Mello and J. Parsons: "Maturity Structure of a Hedge Matters: Lessons from the Metallgesellschaft Debacle," *Journal of Applied Corporate Finance*, 7 (Spring 1995).

Quiz

1. True or false?
   (a) A perfect hedge of asset A requires an asset B that's perfectly correlated with A.
   (b) Hedging transactions in an active futures market have zero or slightly negative NPVs.
   (c) Longer maturity bonds necessarily have longer durations.
   (d) The longer a bond's duration, the lower is its volatility.
   (e) When you buy a futures contract, you pay now for delivery at a future date.
   (f) The holder of a futures contract receives the convenience yield on the underlying commodity.
   (g) The holder of a financial futures contract misses out on any dividend or interest payments made on the underlying security.

2. You own a $1 million portfolio of aerospace stocks with a beta of 1.2. You are enthusiastic about aerospace but uncertain about the prospects for the overall stock market. Explain how you could "hedge out" your market exposure by selling the market short. How much would you sell? How in practice would you go about "selling the market"?

3. Securities A, B, and C have the following cash flows:

	Period 1	Period 2	Period 3
A	40	40	40
B	120	—	—
C	10	10	110

(*a*) Calculate their durations if the interest rate is 8 percent.

(*b*) Suppose that you have an investment of $10 million in A. What combination of B and C would immunize this investment against interest-rate changes?

(*c*) Now suppose that you have a $10 million investment in B. How would you immunize? (*Hint:* Try selling A *or* B and borrowing short-term.)

4. Calculate the value of a 6-month futures contract on a Treasury bond. You have the following information:

   ■ 6-month interest rate: 10 percent per year, or 4.9 percent for 6 months

   ■ Spot price of bond: 95

   ■ Coupon payments on the
      bond over the next 6 months: Present value of 4

5. Calculate PV(convenience yield) for magnoosium scrap from the following information:

   ■ Spot price: $2550 per ton
   ■ Futures price: $2408 for a 1-year contract
   ■ Interest rate: 12 percent
   ■ PV(storage costs): $100 per year

6. What is a currency swap? An interest-rate swap? Give an example of how swaps might be used.

7. Residents of the northeastern United States suffered record-setting low temperatures throughout November and December 2005. Spot prices of heating oil rose 25 percent, to over $2 a gallon.

   (*a*) What effect did this have on the net convenience yield and on the relationship between futures and spot prices?

   (*b*) In late 2006 refiners and distributors were surprised by record-setting high temperatures. What was the effect on net convenience yield and spot and futures prices for heating oil?

8. What is basis risk? In which of the following cases would you expect basis risk to be most serious?

   (*a*) A broker owning a large block of Walt Disney common stock hedges by selling index futures.

   (*b*) An Iowa corn farmer hedges the selling price of her crop by selling Chicago corn futures.

   (*c*) An importer must pay 900 million Italian lira in 6 months. He hedges by buying lira forward.

9. Why might a large, multinational company choose to insure against common events, such as vehicle accidents, but not against rare events which could cause large losses? Explain briefly.

10. What is meant by "moral hazard" and "adverse selection"? Explain why these effects tend to increase insurance premiums.

Questions and Problems
· ·

1. Legs Diamond owns shares in Vanguard Index 500 mutual fund worth $1 million on July 15. (This is an index fund that tracks the Standard and Poor's 500.) He wants to cash in now, but his accountant advises him to wait 6 months so as to defer a large capital gains tax. Explain to Legs how he can use stock index futures to hedge out his exposure to market movements over the next 6 months. Could Legs "cash in" without actually selling his shares?

2. Refer back to question 1. Suppose that the nearest index futures contract matures in 7 months rather than 6. Show how Legs Diamond can still use index futures to hedge his position. How would the maturity date affect the hedge ratio?

3. Price changes on two gold mining stocks have shown strong positive correlation. Their historical relationship is

$$\begin{pmatrix} \text{Average} \\ \text{percentage} \\ \text{change in A} \end{pmatrix} = .001 + .75 \begin{pmatrix} \text{percentage} \\ \text{change} \\ \text{in B} \end{pmatrix}$$

Changes in B explain 60 percent of the variation of the changes in A ($R^2 = .6$).
   (a) Suppose you own $100,000 of A. How much of B should you sell to minimize the risk of your net position?
   (b) What is the hedge ratio?
   (c) How would you construct a zero-value hedge?
   (d) Here is the historical relationship between A and gold prices:

$$\begin{pmatrix} \text{Average} \\ \text{percentage} \\ \text{change in A} \end{pmatrix} = -.002 + 1.2 \begin{pmatrix} \text{percentage} \\ \text{change in} \\ \text{gold price} \end{pmatrix}$$

If $R^2 = .5$, can you lower the risk of your net position by hedging with gold (or gold futures) rather than with stock B? Explain.

4. What is meant by "delta" in the context of hedging? Give examples of how delta can be estimated or calculated.

5. In Section 25-5, we stated that the duration of Potterton's lease equals the duration of its debt.
   (a) Show that this is so.
   (b) Now suppose that the interest rate falls to 3 percent. Show how the value of the lease and the debt package are now affected by a .5 percent rise or fall in the interest rate. What would Potterton need to do to reestablish the interest-rate hedge?

6. Line 1 of the following table shows cash outflows that your company has just promised to make. Below that are the cash flows on a blue-chip corporate note. The interest rate is 10 percent. Your company can borrow at this rate if it wishes.

	Year 1	Year 2	Year 3	Year 4
Liability, millions	0	0	−$20	−$20
Note's cash payments as percent of face value	12	12	12	112

   (*a*) What is the present value of your liability?

   (*b*) Calculate the durations of the liability and the note.

   (*c*) Suppose you wish to hedge the liability by investing in a combination of the note and a short-term bank deposit with a duration of zero. How much must you invest in each?

   (*d*) Would this hedge continue to protect your company

     (**i**) If interest rates dropped by 3 percent?

     (**ii**) If short-term interest rates fluctuate while longer-term rates remain basically constant?

     (**iii**) If interest rates remain the same but 2 years pass?

   (*e*) Can you set up a hedge portfolio that relieves the financial manager of all the worries mentioned in (*d*)? Describe that portfolio.

7. Explain the chief differences between futures and forward contracts, e.g., for foreign exchange.

8. In May 1995, 8-month futures on the Standard and Poor's Composite Index traded at 525. Spot was 515. Assume an interest rate of 6.25 percent. What was the PV of the average dividend yield on the stocks in this index?

9. Table 25-5 contains spot and 6-month futures prices for several commodities and financial instruments. There may be some money-making opportunities. See if you can find them, and explain how you would trade to take advantage of them. The interest rate is 14.5 percent, or 7 percent over the 6-month life of the contracts.

10. The following table shows gold futures prices for varying contract lengths. Gold is predominantly an investment good, not an industrial commodity. Investors hold gold because it diversifies their portfolios and because they hope its price will rise. They do not hold it for its convenience yield.

   Calculate the interest rate faced by traders in gold futures for each of the contract lengths shown below. The spot price is $456.90 per ounce.

	CONTRACT LENGTH, MONTHS				
	1	3	9	15	21
Futures price	$458.90	$464.50	$483.30	$503.90	$525.70

11. The Commodities and Futures Trading Commission needs to be assured that new futures contracts serve the public interest. One of the tests that it applies is that the contract should provide price discovery—that is, the futures price should provide the public with new information on investors' forecasts of changes in spot prices. In justifying their proposals to trade index futures, the exchanges have argued that index futures provide information about investor views on future prices. Evaluate this claim.

12. Firms A and B face the following borrowing rates for making a 5-year fixed-rate debt issue in U.S. dollars or Swiss francs:

	U.S. Dollars	Swiss Francs
Firm A	10%	7%
Firm B	8	6

TABLE 25-5

Spot and 6-month futures prices for selected commodities and securities. See problem 9.

Commodity	Spot Price	Futures Price	Comments
Magnoosium	$2,550 per ton	$2,728.50 per ton	PV(storage costs) = PV(convenience yield).
Frozen quiche	$.50 per pound	$.514 per pound	PV(storage costs) = $.10 per pound; PV(convenience yield) = $.05 per pound.
Nevada Hydro 8s of 2002	77	78.39	4% semiannual coupon payment is due just before futures contract expires.
Costaguanan pulgas (currency)	9,300 pulgas = $1	6,900 pulgas = $1	Costaguanan interest rate is 95% per year.
Establishment Industries common stock	$95	$97.54	Establishment pays dividends of $2 per quarter. Next dividend is paid 2 months from now.
Cheap white wine	$12,500 per 10,000-gal. tank	$14,200 per 10,000-gal. tank	PV(convenience yield) = $250 per tank. Your company unexpectedly has surplus storage and can store 50,000 gallons at no cost.

Suppose that A wishes to borrow U.S. dollars and B wishes to borrow Swiss francs. Show how a swap could be used to reduce the borrowing costs of each company. Assume a spot exchange rate of 2 Swiss francs per dollar.

13. "Last year we had a substantial income in sterling, which we hedged by selling sterling forward. In the event sterling rose, and our decision to sell forward cost us a lot of money. I think that in future we should either stop hedging our currency exposure or just hedge when we think sterling is overvalued." As financial manager, how would you respond to this chief executive's comment?

14. "Speculators want futures contracts to be incorrectly priced; hedgers want them to be correctly priced." Why?

15. Hoopoe Corporation wants to borrow 100 million U.S. dollars at a fixed rate with a maturity of 5 years. It calculates that it can make a eurobond issue with the following terms:

- Interest: 10⅝ percent payable annually
- Maturity: 5 years
- Commissions: 1⅞ percent
- Agency fees: .15 percent on coupon
                   .075 percent on principal
- Issue expenses: .2 percent

A bank has presented Hoopoe with a proposal for a Swiss franc issue combined with a currency swap in U.S. dollars. The proposed terms for the Swiss franc issue are:

- Amount: 200 million Swiss francs
- Interest: 5⅜ percent annually
- Maturity: 5 years
- Commissions: 2.8 percent
- Agency fees: .75 percent on coupon
                    .30 percent on principal
- Issue expenses: .2 percent

The counterparty of the swap would raise fixed dollars on the following terms:

- Amount: 100 million U.S. dollars (equivalent to 200 million
                    Swiss francs)
- Interest: 10⅜ percent annually
- Maturity: 5 years
- Commissions: 1.8 percent
- Agency expenses: .15 percent on coupon
                    .075 percent on principal
- Issue expenses: .2 percent

The counterparty would be happy with an all-in cost in Swiss francs of 6.4 percent.

(*a*) Which alternative should Hoopoe undertake? (Ignore credit risk in your analysis.)

(*b*) Suppose that you are the corporate finance manager of Hoopoe. Discuss the credit risk issues involved in the alternatives.

16. If you buy a 9-month Treasury bill future, you undertake to buy a 3-month bill in 9 months' time. Suppose that Treasury bills currently offer the following yields:

Months to Maturity	Annual Yield
3	6 %
6	6.5
9	7
12	8

What is the value of a 9-month bill future?

17. In 1985 a German corporation bought $250 million forward to cover a future purchase of goods from the United States. However, the dollar subsequently depreciated, and the company found that if it had waited and then bought spot dollars, it would have paid 225 million deutschemarks (DM) less. One financial manager pointed out that the company could have waited to buy the dollars and meanwhile covered its exposure by using options. In that case it would have saved itself 225 million DM and would have lost only the cost of the options—around 20 million DM.[34] Evaluate the company's decision and the financial manager's criticism.

---

[34]Example cited in *Managing Risks and Costs through Financial Innovation*, Business International Corporation, New York, 1987.

18. Large businesses spend millions of dollars annually on insurance. Why? Should they insure against all risks or does insurance make more sense for some risks than others?

19. (a) An investor currently holding $1 million in long-term Treasury bonds becomes concerned about increasing volatility in interest rates. She decides to hedge her risk using Treasury-bond futures contracts. Should she buy or sell such contracts?

    (b) The Treasurer of a corporation that will be issuing bonds in three months also is concerned about interest-rate volatility and wants to lock in the price at which he could sell 8 percent coupon bonds. How would he use Treasury-bond futures contracts to hedge his firm's position?

20. A gold-mining firm is concerned about short-term volatility in its revenues. Gold currently sells for $300 an ounce, but the price is extremely volatile and could fall as low as $280 or rise as high as $320 in the next month. The company will bring 1000 ounces to the market next month.

    (a) What will be total revenues if the firm remains unhedged for gold prices of $280, $300, and $320 an ounce?

    (b) The futures price of gold for 1-month-ahead delivery is $301. What will be the firm's total revenues at each gold price if the firm enters a 1-month futures contract to deliver 1000 ounces of gold?

    (c) What will total revenues be if the firm buys a 1-month put option to sell gold for $300 an ounce? The put option costs $2 per ounce.

21. Your firm has just tendered for a contract in Japan. You won't know for 3 months whether you get the contract, but if you do, you will receive a payment of 10 million yen 1 year from now. You are worried that if the yen declines in value, the dollar value of this payment will be less than you expect and the project could even show a loss. Discuss the possible ways that you could protect the firm against a decline in the value of the yen. Illustrate the possible outcomes if you do get the contract and if you don't.

22. Petrochemical Parfum (PP) is concerned about possible increases in the price of heavy fuel oil, which is one of its major inputs. Show how PP can use either options or futures contracts to protect itself against a rise in the price of crude oil. Show how the payoffs in each case would vary if the oil price is $18, $20, or $22 a barrel. What are the advantages and disadvantages for PP of using futures rather than options to reduce risk?

23. What other commodity futures are traded on futures exchanges? Who do you think could usefully reduce risk by buying each of these contracts? Who do you think might wish to sell each contract?

24. "The farmer does not avoid risk by selling wheat futures. If wheat prices stay about $2.80 a bushel, then he will actually have lost by selling wheat futures at $2.50." Is this a fair comment?

25. Explain the difference between insurance and hedging. Give an example of how options can be used for each.

26. Your investment bank has an investment of $100 million in the stock of the Swiss Roll Corporation and a short position in the stock of the Frankfurter Sausage Company. Here is the recent price history of the two stocks:

PERCENTAGE PRICE CHANGE

Month	Frankfurter Sausage	Swiss Roll
January	−10	−10
February	−10	− 5
March	−10	0
April	+10	0
May	+10	+ 5
June	+10	+10

On the evidence of these six months, how large would your short position in Frankfurter Sausage need to be to hedge you as far as possible against movements in the price of Swiss Roll?

27. A year ago your bank entered into a $50 million 5-year interest-rate swap. It agreed to pay company A each year a fixed rate of 6 percent and to receive in return LIBOR plus 1 percent. When the bank entered into this swap, LIBOR was 5 percent, but now interest rates have risen, so on a 4-year interest-rate swap the bank could expect to pay 6½ percent and receive LIBOR plus 1 percent.
    (*a*) Is the swap showing a profit or a loss to the bank?
    (*b*) Suppose that at this point company A approaches your bank and asks to terminate the swap. If there are four annual payments still remaining, how much should the bank charge A to terminate?

28. At the time of the 1992 sterling crisis the London *Financial Times* commented, "Many treasurers said yesterday that the direction of exchange rates was still too uncertain to justify [hedging by] locking in now." Does this make sense?

29. Phillip's Screwdriver Company has borrowed $20 million from a bank at a floating interest rate of 2 percentage points above 3-month Treasury bills, which now yield 5 percent. Assume that interest payments are made quarterly and that the entire principal of the loan is repaid after 5 years.
    Phillip's wants to convert the bank loan to fixed-rate debt. It could have issued a 5-year note at a fixed yield to maturity of 9 percent. Such a note would now trade at par. The 5-year Treasury note's yield to maturity is 7 percent.
    (*a*) Is Phillip's stupid to want long-term debt at an interest rate of 9 percent? It is borrowing from the bank at 7 percent.
    (*b*) Explain how the conversion could be carried out by an interest-rate swap. What will be the initial terms of the swap? (Ignore transaction costs and the swap dealer's profit.)
    One year from now medium- and long-term Treasury yields have *decreased* to 6 percent. Treasury bill rates have *increased* to 6 percent, so the term structure is now flat. (The changes actually occurred in month 5.) Phillip's credit standing is unchanged; it could still borrow at 2 percentage points over Treasury rates.
    (*c*) What net swap payment will Phillip's make or receive?
    (*d*) Suppose that Phillip's now wants to cancel the swap. How much would it need to pay the swap dealer? Or would the dealer pay Phillip's? Explain.

30. Consider the commodities and financial assets listed in Table 25-6. The risk-free interest rate is 6 percent a year, and the term structure is flat.

TABLE 25-6
••

Spot prices for selected commodities and financial assets. See problem 30.

Asset	Spot price	Comments
Magnoosium	$2,800 per ton	Net convenience yield = 4% per year
Oat bran	$.44 per bushel	Net convenience yield = .5% per month
Biotech stock index	140.2	Dividend yield = 0
Allen Wrench Co. common stock	$58.00	Cash dividend = $2.4 per year
5-year Treasury note	108.93	8% coupon
Westonian ruple	3.1 ruples = $1	12% interest rate in ruples

(a) Calculate the 6-month futures price for each case.

(b) Explain how a magnoosium producer would use a futures market to "lock in" the selling price of a planned shipment of 1000 tons of magnoosium 6 months from now.

(c) Suppose the producer takes the actions recommended in your answer to (b), but after 1 month magnoosium prices have fallen to $2200. What happens? Will the producer have to undertake additional futures market trades to restore its hedged position?

(d) Does the biotech index futures price provide useful information about the expected future performance of biotech stocks?

(e) Suppose Allen Wrench stock falls suddenly by $10 per share. Investors are confident that the cash dividend will not be reduced. What happens to the futures price?

(f) Suppose interest rates suddenly fall. The spot rate for cash flows 6 months from now is 4 percent (per year); it is 4.5 percent for cash flows 12 months from now, 4.8 percent for cash flows 18 months from now, and 5 percent for all subsequent cash flows. What happens to the 6-month futures price on the 5-year Treasury note? What happens to a trader who shorted 100 notes at the futures price calculated in part (a).

(g) An importer must make a payment of 1 million ruples 3 months from now. Explain *two* strategies the importer could use to hedge against unfavorable shifts in the ruple-dollar exchange rate.

26

Leasing

Most of us occasionally rent a car, bicycle, or boat. Usually such personal rentals are short-lived—we may rent a car for a day or week. But in corporate finance longer-term rentals are common. A rental agreement that extends for a year or more and involves a series of fixed payments is called a **lease.**

Firms lease as an alternative to buying capital equipment. Computers are often leased; so are trucks, railroad cars, aircraft, and ships. Just about every kind of asset has been leased sometime by somebody, including electric power plants, nuclear fuel, handball courts, and zoo animals.

Every lease involves two parties. The *user* of the asset is called the *lessee*. The lessee makes periodic payments to the *owner* of the asset, who is called the *lessor*. For example, if you sign an agreement to rent an apartment for a year, you are the lessee and the owner is the lessor.

You often see references to the *leasing industry*. This refers to lessors. (Almost all firms are lessees to at least a minor extent.) Who are the lessors?

Some of the largest lessors are equipment manufacturers. For example, GATX is the largest lessor of railcars (it leased about 51,000 cars at the end of 1994); IBM is the largest lessor of computers, and Xerox is the largest lessor of copiers.

The other two major groups of lessors are banks and independent leasing companies. The latter offer a variety of services. Some act as lease brokers (arranging lease deals) as well as lessors. Others specialize in leasing automobiles, trucks, and standardized industrial equipment; they succeed because they can buy equipment in quantity, service it efficiently, and if necessary resell it at a good price.

We began this chapter by cataloging the different kinds of leases and some of the reasons for their use. Then we show how short-term, or cancelable, lease payments can be interpreted as equivalent annual costs. The remainder of the chapter analyzes long-term leases used as alternatives to debt financing.

26-1 WHAT IS A LEASE?

Leases come in many forms, but in all cases the lessee (user) promises to make a series of payments to the lessor (owner). The lease contract specifies the monthly or semiannual payments, with the first payment usually due as soon as the contract is signed. The payments are usually level, but their time pattern can be tailored to the user's needs. For example, suppose that a manufacturer leases a machine to produce a complex new product. There will be a year's "shakedown" period before volume production starts. In this case, it might be possible to arrange for lower payments during the first year of the lease.

When a lease is terminated, the leased equipment reverts to the lessor. However, the lease agreement often gives the user the option to purchase the equipment or take out a new lease.

Some leases are short-term and cancelable during the contract period at the option of the lessee. These are generally known as *operating leases*. Others extend over most of the estimated economic life of the asset and cannot be canceled or can be canceled only if the lessor is reimbursed for any losses. These are called *capital, financial,* or *full-payout leases.*[1]

Financial leases are a *source of financing.* Signing a financial lease contract is like borrowing money. There is an immediate cash inflow because the lessee is relieved of having to pay for the asset. But the lessee also assumes a binding obligation to make the payments specified in the lease contract. The user could have borrowed the full purchase price of the asset by accepting a binding obligation to make interest and principal payments to the lender. Thus the cash-flow consequences of leasing and borrowing are similar. In either case, the firm raises cash now and pays it back later. A large part of this chapter will be devoted to comparing leasing and borrowing as financing alternatives.

Leases also differ in the services provided by the lessor. Under a *full-service,* or *rental,* lease, the lessor promises to maintain and insure the equipment and to pay any property taxes due on it. In a *net* lease, the lessee agrees to maintain the asset, insure it, and pay any property taxes. Financial leases are usually net leases.

Most financial leases are arranged for brand new assets. The lessee identifies the equipment, arranges for the leasing company to buy it from the manufacturer, and signs a contract with the leasing company. This is called a *direct* lease. In other cases, the firm sells an asset it already owns and leases it back from the buyer. These *sale and lease-back* arrangements are common in real estate. For example, firm X may wish to raise cash by selling a factory but still retain use of the factory. It could do this by selling the factory for cash to a leasing company and simultaneously signing a long-term lease contract for the factory. Legal ownership of the factory passes to the leasing company, but the right to use it stays with firm X.

You may also encounter *leveraged* leases. These are financial leases in which the lessor borrows part of the purchase price of the leased asset, using the lease contract as security for the loan. This does not change the lessee's obligations, but it can complicate the lessor's analysis considerably. We have more to say about leveraged leases later in this chapter.

26-2 WHY LEASE?

You hear many suggestions about why companies should lease equipment rather than buy it. Let us look at some sensible reasons and then at four that are more dubious.

Sensible Reasons for Leasing

SHORT-TERM LEASES ARE CONVENIENT. Suppose you want the use of a car for a week. You could buy one and sell it 7 days later, but that would be silly. Quite apart from the fact that registering ownership is a nuisance, you would spend some time selecting a car, negotiating purchase, and arranging insurance. Then at the end of the week you would negotiate resale and cancel the registration and insurance. When you need a car only for a short time, it clearly makes sense to rent it. You save the trouble of register-

---

[1]In the shipping industry, a financial lease is called a *bareboat charter* or a *demise hire.*

ing ownership, and you know the effective cost. In the same way, it pays a company to lease equipment that it needs for only a year or two. Of course, this kind of lease is always an operating lease.

Sometimes the cost of short-term rentals may seem prohibitively high, or you may find it difficult to rent at any price. This can happen for equipment that is easily damaged by careless use. The owner knows that short-term users are unlikely to take the same care they would with their own equipment. When the danger of abuse becomes too high, short-term rental markets do not survive. Thus, it is easy enough to buy a Lamborgini Diablo, provided your pockets are deep enough, but nearly impossible to rent one.

CANCELLATION OPTIONS ARE VALUABLE. Some leases that *appear* expensive really are fairly priced once the option to cancel is recognized. We return to this point in the next section.

MAINTENANCE IS PROVIDED. Under a full-service lease, the user receives maintenance and other services. Many lessors are well equipped to provide efficient maintenance. However, bear in mind that these benefits will be reflected in higher lease payments.

STANDARDIZATION LEADS TO LOW ADMINISTRATIVE AND TRANSACTION COSTS. Suppose that you operate a leasing company which specializes in financial leases for trucks. You are effectively lending money to a large number of firms (the lessees) which may differ considerably in size and risk. But, because the underlying asset is in each case the same saleable item (a truck), you can safely "lend" the money (lease the truck) without conducting a detailed analysis of each firm's business. You can also use a simple, standard lease contract. This standardization makes it possible to "lend" small sums of money without incurring large investigative, administrative, or legal costs.

For these reasons leasing is often a relatively cheap source of cash for the small company. It offers financing on a flexible, piecemeal basis, with lower transaction costs than in a private placement or a public bond or stock issue.

TAX SHIELDS CAN BE USED. The lessor owns the leased asset and deducts its depreciation from taxable income. If the lessor can make better use of depreciation tax shields than an asset's user can, it may make sense for the leasing company to own the equipment and pass on some of the tax benefits to the lessee in the form of low lease payments.

AVOIDING THE ALTERNATIVE MINIMUM TAX. Red-blooded financial managers want to earn lots of money for their shareholders but *report* low profits to the tax authorities. Tax law allows this. A firm may use straight-line depreciation in its annual report but choose accelerated depreciation (and the shortest possible asset life) for its tax books. By this and other perfectly legal and ethical devices, profitable companies have occasionally managed to escape tax entirely. Almost all companies pay less tax than their public income statements suggest.[2]

---

[2]Year-by-year differences between reported tax expense and taxes actually paid are explained in footnotes to the financial statements. The cumulative difference is shown on the balance sheet as a deferred tax liability. (Note that accelerated depreciation *postpones* taxes; it does not eliminate taxes.)

But the 1986 Tax Reform Act has a trap for companies that shield too much income: the alternative minimum tax (AMT). Corporations must pay the AMT whenever it is higher than their tax computed in the regular way.

Here is how the AMT works: It requires a second calculation of taxable income, in which part of the benefit of accelerated depreciation and other tax-reducing items[3] is added back. The AMT is 20 percent of the result.

Suppose Yuppytech Services would have $10 million in taxable income but for the AMT, which forces it to add back $9 million of tax privileges:

	Regular Tax	Alternative Minimum Tax
Income	$10	10 + 9 = 19
Tax rate	.35	.20
Tax	$ 3.5	$3.8

Yuppytech must pay $3.8 million, not $3.5.[4]

How can this painful payment be avoided? How about leasing? Lease payments are *not* on the list of items added back in calculating the AMT. If you lease rather than buy, tax depreciation is less and the AMT is less. There is a net gain if the *lessor* is not subject to the AMT and can pass back depreciation tax shields in the form of lower lease payments.

Some Dubious Reasons for Leasing

LEASING AVOIDS CAPITAL EXPENDITURE CONTROLS. In many companies lease proposals are scrutinized as carefully as capital expenditure proposals, but in others leasing may enable an operating manager to avoid the elaborate approval procedures needed to buy an asset. Although this is a dubious reason for leasing, it may be influential, particularly in the public sector. For example, city hospitals have sometimes found it politically more convenient to lease their medical equipment than to ask the city government to provide funds for purchase. Another example is provided by the United States Navy, which leased a fleet of new tankers and supply ships instead of asking Congress for the money to buy them.

LEASING PRESERVES CAPITAL. Leasing companies provide "100 percent financing"; they advance the full cost of the leased asset. Consequently, they often claim that leasing preserves capital, allowing the firm to save its cash for other things.

But the firm can also "preserve capital" by borrowing money. If Greymare Bus Lines leases a $100,000 bus rather than buying it, it does conserve $100,000 cash. It could also (1) buy the bus for cash and (2) borrow $100,000, using the bus as security. Its bank balance ends up the same whether it leases or buys and borrows. It has the bus in either case, and it incurs a $100,000 liability in either case. What's so special about leasing?

---

[3]Other items include some interest receipts from tax-exempt municipal securities and taxes deferred by use of completed contract accounting. (The completed contract method allows a manufacturer to postpone reporting taxable profits until a production contract is completed. Since contracts may span several years, this deferral can have a substantial positive NPV.)

[4]But Yuppytech can carry forward the $.3 million difference. If later years' AMTs are *lower* than regular taxes, the difference can be used as a tax credit. Suppose the AMT next year is $4 million and the regular tax is $5 million. Then Yuppytech pays only 5 − .3 = $4.7 million.

LEASES MAY BE OFF-BALANCE-SHEET FINANCING. Until the end of 1976, financial leases were *off-balance-sheet financing.* That is, a firm could acquire an asset, finance it through a financial lease, and show neither the asset nor the lease contract on its balance sheet. The firm was required only to add a brief footnote to its accounts describing its lease obligation. Accounting standards now require that all *capital* (financial) leases be *capitalized.*[5] That is, the present value of the lease payments must be calculated and shown alongside debt on the right-hand side of the balance sheet. The same amount must be shown as an asset on the left-hand side of the balance sheet.[6]

In order to implement this new requirement, the Financial Accounting Standards Board (FASB) had to come up with objective rules for distinguishing between operating and capital (financial) leases. The board defined capital leases as leases which meet *any one* of the following requirements:

1. The lease agreement transfers ownership to the lessee before the lease expires.

2. The lessee can purchase the asset for a bargain price when the lease expires.

3. The lease lasts for at least 75 percent of the asset's estimated economic life.

4. The present value of the lease payments is at least 90 percent of the asset's value.

All other leases are operating leases as far as the accountants are concerned.

Many financial managers have tried to take advantage of this arbitrary boundary between operating and financial leases. Suppose that you wanted to finance a computer-controlled machine tool costing $1 million. The machine tool's life is expected to be 12 years. You could sign a lease contract for 8 years, 11 months (just missing requirement 3) with lease payments having a present value of $899,000 (just missing requirement 4). You would also make sure the lease contract avoids requirements 1 and 2. Result? You have off-balance-sheet financing. This lease would not have to be capitalized, although it is clearly a long-term, fixed obligation.

Now we come to the $64,000 question: "Why should anyone *care* whether financing is off balance sheet or on balance sheet?" Shouldn't the financial manager worry about substance rather than appearance?

When a firm obtains off-balance-sheet financing, the conventional measures of financial leverage, such as the debt-equity ratio, understate the true degree of financial leverage. Some believe that financial analysts do not always notice off-balance-sheet lease obligations (which are still referred to in footnotes) or the greater volatility of earnings that results from the fixed lease payments. They may be right, but we would not expect such an imperfection to be widespread.

When a company borrows money, it must usually consent to certain restrictions on future borrowing. Early bond indentures did not include any restrictions on financial leases. Therefore leasing was seen as a way to circumvent restrictive covenants. Loopholes such as these are easily stopped, and most bond indentures now include limits on leasing.

Long-term lease obligations ought to be regarded as debt whether or not they appear on the balance sheet. Financial analysts may overlook moderate leasing activity, just as they overlook minor debts. But major lease obligations are generally recognized and taken into account.

---

[5]See "Accounting for Leases," *Statement of Financial Accounting Standards No. 13*, Financial Accounting Standards Board, Stamford, Conn., 1976.

[6]This "asset" is then amortized over the life of the lease. The amortization is deducted from book income, just as depreciation is deducted for a purchased asset.

In May 1979, *Business Week* described the financial problems facing San Diego Gas and Electric Company (SDG&E). A "cash squeeze" on the company led to the following sale and lease-back deal:

> In March [the company] sold a new generating unit for $132 million to a group of banks headed by Bank of America and then took a lease on the plant. . . . Its near-term profit picture has not been affected. But ultimately, the desperate measure will remove a huge asset from the utility's rate [i.e., asset] base, thus lowering potential profits and further weakening SDG&E's bond rating. "The rating agencies look at the $132 million obligation as if it were long-term debt," explains [Robert E. Morris, the company's president].[7]

LEASING AFFECTS BOOK INCOME.   Leasing can make the firm's balance sheet and income statement *look* better by increasing book income or decreasing book asset value, or both.

A lease which qualifies as off-balance-sheet financing affects book income in only one way: The lease payments are an expense. If the firm buys the asset instead and borrows to finance it, both depreciation and interest expense are deducted. Leases are usually set up so that payments in the early years are less than depreciation plus interest under the buy-and-borrow alternative. Consequently, leasing increases book income in the early years of an asset's life. The book rate of return can increase even more dramatically, because the book value of assets (the denominator in the book-rate-of-return calculation) is understated if the leased asset never appears on the firm's balance sheet.

Leasing's impact on book income should in itself have no effect on firm value. In efficient capital markets investors will look through the firm's accounting results to the true value of the asset and the liability incurred to finance it.

26-3   OPERATING LEASES

Remember our discussion of *equivalent annual costs* in Chapter 6? We defined the equivalent annual cost of, say, a machine as the annual rental payment sufficient to cover the present value of all the costs of owning and operating it.

In Chapter 6's examples, the rental payments were hypothetical—just a way of converting a present value to an annual cost. But in the leasing business the payments are real. Suppose you decide to lease a machine tool for 1 year. What will the rental payment be in a competitive leasing industry? The lessor's equivalent annual cost, of course.

••••••••••••••••••

Example of an Operating Lease

The boyfriend of the daughter of the CEO of Establishment Industries takes her to the senior prom in a pearly white stretch limo. The CEO is impressed. He decides Establishment Industries ought to have one for VIP transportation. Establishment's CFO prudently suggests a 1-year operating lease instead and approaches Acme Limolease for a quote.

Table 26-1 shows Acme's analysis. Suppose it buys a new limo for $75,000 which it plans to lease out for 7 years (years 0 through 6). The table gives Acme's forecasts of operating, maintenance, and administrative costs, the latter including the costs of negotiating the lease, keeping track of payments and paperwork, and finding a replacement

---

[7]*Business Week*, May 28, 1979, p. 110. Reprinted by special permission; © 1979 by McGraw-Hill, Inc., New York, NY 10020. All rights reserved.

TABLE 26-1

Calculating the zero-NPV rental rate (or equivalent annual cost) for Establishment Industries' pearly white stretch limo (figures in thousands of dollars)

	YEAR						
	0	1	2	3	4	5	6
Initial cost	−75						
Maintenance, insurance, selling, and administrative costs	−12	−12	−12	−12	−12	−12	−12
Tax shield on costs	+4.2	+4.2	+4.2	+4.2	+4.2	+4.2	+4.2
Depreciation tax shield*		+5.25	+8.40	+5.04	+3.02	+3.02	+1.51
Total	−82.80	−2.55	.60	−2.76	−4.78	−4.78	−6.29
NPV at 7% = −$98.15[†]							
Break-even rent (level)	26.18	26.18	26.18	26.18	26.18	26.18	26.18
Tax	−9.16	−9.16	−9.16	−9.16	−9.16	−9.16	−9.16
Break-even rent after tax	17.02	17.02	17.02	17.02	17.02	17.02	17.02
NPV at 7% = $98.15[†]							

Note: We assume no inflation and a 7 percent real cost of capital. The tax rate is 35 percent.
[*]Depreciation tax shields are calculated using the 5-year schedule from Table 6-5.
[†]Note that the first payment of these annuities comes immediately. The standard annuity formula must be multiplied by $1 + r = 1.07$.

lessee when Establishment's year is up. For simplicity we assume zero inflation and use a 7 percent real cost of capital. We also assume that the limo will have zero salvage value at the end of year 6. The present value of all costs, partially offset by the value of depreciation tax shields,[8] is $98,150. Now, how much does Acme have to charge in order to break even?

Acme can afford to buy and lease out the limo only if the rental payments forecasted over 6 years have a present value of at least $98,150. The problem, then, is to calculate a 6-year annuity with a present value of $98,150. We will follow common leasing practice and assume rental payments in advance.[9]

As Table 26-1 shows, the required annuity is $26,180, that is, about $26,000.[10] This annuity's present value (after taxes) exactly equals the present value of the after-tax costs of owning and operating the limo. The annuity provides Acme with a competitive expected rate of return (7 percent) on its investment. Acme could try to charge

[8]The depreciation tax shields are safe cash flows if the tax rate does not change and Acme is sure to pay taxes. If 7 percent is the right discount rate for the other flows in Table 26-1, the depreciation tax shields deserve a lower rate. A more refined analysis would discount safe depreciation tax shields at an after-tax borrowing or lending rate. See Section 19-4 or the next section of this chapter.

[9]In Section 6-3 the hypothetical rentals were paid *in arrears*.

[10]This is a level annuity because we are assuming that (1) there is no inflation and (2) the services of a 6-year-old limo are no different than a brand-new limo's. If users of aging limos see them as obsolete or unfashionable, or if new limos are cheaper, then lease rates for older limos would have to be cut. This would give a *declining* annuity: initial users would pay more than the amount shown in Table 26-1, later users less.

Establishment Industries more than $26,000, but if the CFO is smart enough to ask for bids from Acme's competitors, the winning lessor will end up receiving this amount.

Remember that Establishment Industries is not obligated to continue using the limo for more than 1 year. Acme may have to find several new lessees over the limo's economic life. Even if Establishment continues, it can renegotiate a new lease at whatever rates prevail in the future. Thus Acme does not know what it can charge in year 1 or afterward. If pearly white falls out of favor with teenagers and CEOs, Acme is probably out of luck.

In real life Acme would have several further things to worry about. For example, how long will the limo stand idle when it is returned at year 1? If idle time is likely before a new lessee is found, then lease rates have to be higher to compensate.[11]

In an operating lease, the *lessor* absorbs these risks, not the lessee. The discount rate used by the lessor must include a premium sufficient to compensate its shareholders for the risks of buying and holding the leased asset. In other words, Acme's 7 percent real discount rate must cover the risks of investing in stretch limos. (As we will see in the next section, risk bearing in *financial* leases is fundamentally different.)

Lease or Buy?

If you need a car or limo for only a day or a week you will surely rent it; if you need one for 5 years you will probably buy it. In between there is a gray region in which the choice of lease or buy is not obvious. The decision rule should be clear in concept, however: If you need an asset for your business, *buy it if the equivalent annual cost of ownership and operation is less than the best lease rate you can get from an outsider.* In other words, buy if you can "rent to yourself" cheaper than you can rent from others. (Again we stress that this rule applies to *operating* leases.)

If you plan to use the asset for an extended period, your equivalent annual cost of owning the asset will usually be less than the operating lease rate. The lessor has to mark up the lease rate to cover the costs of negotiating and administering the lease, the foregone revenues when the asset is off lease and idle, and so on. These costs are avoided when the company buys and rents to itself.

There are two cases in which operating leases may make sense even when the company plans to use an asset for an extended period. First, the lessor may be able to buy and manage the asset at less expense than the lessee. For example, the major truck leasing companies buy thousands of new vehicles every year. That puts them in an excellent bargaining position with truck manufacturers. These companies also run very efficient service operations, and they know how to extract the most salvage value when trucks wear out and it is time to sell them. A small business, or a small division of a larger one, cannot achieve these economies and often finds it cheaper to lease trucks than to buy them.

Second, operating leases often contain useful options. Suppose Acme offers Establishment Industries the following two leases:

1. A 1-year lease for $26,000

2. A 6-year lease for $28,000, *with the option to cancel the lease* at any time from year 1 on.[12]

---

[11]If, say, limos were off lease and idle 20 percent of the time, lease rates would have to be 25 percent above those shown in Table 26-1.

[12]Acme might also offer a 1-year lease for $28,000 but give the lessee an option to *extend* the lease on the same terms for up to 5 additional years. This is, of course, identical to lease 2. It doesn't matter whether the lessee has the (put) option to cancel or the (call) option to continue.

The second lease has obvious attractions. Suppose Establishment's CEO becomes fond of the limo and wants to use it for a second year. If rates increase, lease 2 allows Establishment to continue at the old rate. If rates decrease, Establishment can cancel lease 2 and negotiate a lower rate with Acme or one of its competitors.

Of course, lease 2 is a more costly proposition for Acme: in effect it gives Establishment an insurance policy protecting it from increases in future lease rates. The difference between the costs of leases 1 and 2 is the annual insurance premium. But lessees may happily pay for insurance if they have no special knowledge of future asset values or lease rates. A leasing company acquires such knowledge in the course of its business and can generally sell such insurance at a profit.

Computers are frequently leased on a short-term cancelable basis. It is difficult to estimate how soon such equipment will become obsolete, because the technology of computers is advancing rapidly and somewhat unpredictably. Leasing with an option to cancel passes the risk of premature obsolescence from the user to the lessor. Usually the lessor is a computer manufacturer or a computer leasing specialist and therefore knows more about the risks of obsolescence than the user does. Thus the lessor is better equipped than the user to bear these risks. It makes sense for the user to pay the lessor for the option to cancel.

Be sure to check out the options before you sign (or reject) an operating lease.[13]

26-4 VALUING FINANCIAL LEASES

For operating leases the decision centers on "lease versus buy." For *financial* leases the decision amounts to "lease versus borrow." Financial leases extend over most of the economic life of the leased equipment. They are *not* cancelable. The lease payments are fixed obligations equivalent to debt service.

Financial leases make sense when the company is prepared to take on the business risks of owning and operating the leased asset. If Establishment Industries signs a *financial* lease for the stretch limo, it is stuck with that asset. The financial lease is just another way of borrowing money to pay for the limo.

Financial leases do offer special advantages to some firms in some circumstances. However, there is no point in further discussion of these advantages until you know how to value financial lease contracts.

Example of a Financial Lease

Imagine yourself in the position of Thomas Pierce III, president of Greymare Bus Lines. Your firm was established by your grandfather, who was quick to capitalize on the growing demand for transportation between Widdicombe and nearby townships. The company has owned all its vehicles from the time the company was formed; you are now reconsidering that policy. Your operating manager wants to buy a new bus costing $100,000. The bus will last only 8 years before going to the scrap yard. You are convinced that investment in the additional equipment is worthwhile. However, the representative of the bus manufacturer has pointed out that her firm would also be willing to lease the bus to you for eight annual payments of $16,900 each. Greymare would remain responsible for all maintenance, insurance, and operating expenses.

Table 26-2 shows the direct cash-flow consequences of signing the lease contract. (An important indirect effect is considered later.) The consequences are:

---

[13]McConnell and Schallheim calculate the value of options in operating leases under various assumptions about asset risk, depreciation rates, etc. See J. J. McConnell and J. S. Schallheim, "Valuation of Asset Leasing Contracts," *Journal of Financial Economics*, **12**:237–261 (August 1983).

TABLE 26-2

Cash-flow consequences of the lease contract offered to Greymare Bus Lines (figures in thousands of dollars; some columns do not add due to rounding)

| | YEAR | | | | | | | |
	0	1	2	3	4	5	6	7
Cost of new bus	+100							
Lost depreciation tax shield		−7.00	−11.20	−6.72	−4.03	−4.03	−2.02	0
Lease payment	−16.9	−16.9	−16.9	−16.9	−16.9	−16.9	−16.9	−16.9
Tax shield of lease payment	+5.92	+5.92	+5.92	+5.92	+5.92	+5.92	+5.92	+5.92
Cash flow of lease	+89.02	−17.99	−22.19	−17.71	−15.02	−15.02	−13.00	−10.98

1. Greymare does not have to pay for the bus. This is equivalent to a cash inflow of $100,000.

2. Greymare no longer owns the bus, and so it cannot depreciate it. Therefore it gives up a valuable depreciation tax shield. In Table 26-2, we have assumed depreciation would be calculated using 5-year tax depreciation schedules. (See Table 6-5.)

3. Greymare must pay $16,900 per year for 8 years to the lessor. The first payment is due immediately.

4. However, these lease payments are fully tax-deductible. At a 35 percent marginal tax rate, the lease payments generate tax shields of $5920 per year. You could say that the after-tax cost of the lease payment is $16,900 − $5920 = $10,980.

We must emphasize that Table 26-2 assumes that Greymare will pay taxes at the full 35 percent marginal rate. If the firm were sure to lose money, and therefore pay no taxes, lines 2 and 4 would be left blank. The depreciation tax shields are worth nothing to a firm that pays no taxes, for example.

Table 26-2 also assumes the bus will be worthless when it goes to the scrap yard at the end of year 7. Otherwise there would be an entry for salvage value lost.

Who Really Owns the Leased Asset?

To a lawyer or a tax accountant, that would be a silly question: the lessor is clearly the *legal* owner of the leased asset. That is why the lessor is allowed to deduct depreciation from taxable income.

From an *economic* point of view, you might say that the *user* is the real owner, because in a *financial* lease, the user faces the risks and receives the rewards of ownership. Greymare cannot cancel a financial lease. If the new bus turns out to be hopelessly costly and unsuited for Greymare's routes, that is Greymare's problem, not the lessor's. If it turns out to be a great success, the profit goes to Greymare, not the lessor. The success or failure of the firm's business operations does not depend on whether the buses are financed by leasing or some other financial instrument.

In many respects, a financial lease is equivalent to a secured loan. The lessee must make a series of fixed payments; if the lessee fails to do so, the lessor can repossess the asset. Thus we can think of a balance sheet like this:

Greymare Bus Lines (Figures in Thousands of Dollars)

Bus	100	100	Loan secured by bus
All other assets	1,000	450	Other loans
		550	Equity
Total assets	1,100	1,100	Total liabilities

as being economically equivalent to a balance sheet like this:

Greymare Bus Lines (Figures in Thousands of Dollars)

Bus	100	100	Financial lease
All other assets	1,000	450	Other loans
		550	Equity
Total assets	1,100	1,100	Total liabilities

Having said this, we must immediately add two qualifications. First, legal ownership can make a big difference when a financial lease expires, because the lessor gets the salvage value of the asset. Once a secured loan is paid off, the user owns the asset free and clear.

Second, lessors and secured creditors may be treated differently in bankruptcy. If a company defaults on a lease payment, you might think that the lessor could pick up the leased asset and take it home. But if the bankruptcy court decides the asset is "essential" to the lessee's business, it "affirms" the lease. Then the bankrupt firm can continue to use the asset, *but* it must also continue to make the lease payments. This can be *good* news for the lessor: it is paid cash while other creditors cool their heels. Even secured creditors are not paid until the bankruptcy process works itself out.

If the lease is not affirmed but "rejected," the lessor can of course recover the leased asset. If it is worth less than the future payments the lessee had promised, the lessor can try to recoup this loss. But in this case the lender must get in line with the unsecured creditors.

Of course, neither the lessor nor the secured lender can be sure it will come out whole. Our point is that lessors and secured creditors have different rights when the asset user gets into trouble.

Leasing and the Internal Revenue Service

We have already noted that the lessee loses the tax depreciation of the leased asset but can deduct the lease payment in full. The *lessor*, as legal owner, uses the depreciation tax shield but must report the lease payments as taxable rental income.

However, the Internal Revenue Service is suspicious by nature and will not allow the lessee to deduct the entire lease payment unless it is satisfied that the arrangement is a genuine lease and not a disguised installment purchase or secured loan agreement. Here are examples of lease provisions that will arouse its suspicion:

1. Designating any part of the lease payment as "interest."

2. Giving the lessee the option to acquire the asset for, say, $1 when the lease expires. Such a provision would effectively give the asset's salvage value to the lessee.

3. Adopting a schedule of payments such that the lessee pays a large proportion of the cost over a short period and thereafter is able to use the asset for a nominal rent.

4. Including a so-called hell-or-high-water clause that obliges the lessee to make payments regardless of what subsequently happens to the lessor or the equipment.

5. Limiting the lessee's right to issue debt or pay dividends while the lease is in force.

6. Leasing "limited use" property—for example, leasing a machine or production facility which is custom-designed for the lessee's operations and which therefore will have scant secondhand value.

Some leases are designed *not* to qualify as a true lease for tax purposes. Suppose a manufacturer finds it convenient to lease a new computer but wants to keep the depreciation tax shields. This is easily accomplished by giving the manufacturer the option to purchase the computer for $1 at the end of the lease. Then the Internal Revenue Service treats the lease as an installment sale, and the manufacturer can deduct depreciation and the interest component of the lease payment for tax purposes. But the lease is still a lease for all other purposes.

A First Pass at Valuing a Lease Contract

When we left Thomas Pierce III, president of Greymare Bus Lines, he had just set down in Table 26-2 the cash flows of the financial lease proposed by the bus manufacturer.

These cash flows are typically assumed to be about as safe as the interest and principal payments on a secured loan issued by the lessee. This assumption is reasonable for the lease payments because the lessor is effectively lending money to the lessee. But the various tax shields might carry enough risk to deserve a higher discount rate. For example, Greymare might be confident that it could make the lease payments but not confident that it could earn enough taxable income to use these tax shields. In that case the cash flows generated by the tax shields would probably deserve a higher discount rate than the borrowing rate used for the lease payments.

A lessee might, in principle, end up using a separate discount rate for each line of Table 26-2, each rate chosen to fit the risk of that line's cash flow. But established, profitable firms usually find it reasonable to simplify by discounting the types of flows shown in Table 26-2 at a single rate based on the rate of interest the firm would pay if it borrowed rather than leased. We will assume Greymare's borrowing rate is 10 percent.

At this point we must go back to our discussion in Chapter 19 of debt-equivalent flows. When a company lends money, it pays tax on the interest it receives. Its net return is the after-tax interest rate. When a company borrows money, it can *deduct* interest payments from its taxable income. The net cost of borrowing is the after-tax interest rate. Thus the after-tax interest rate is the effective rate at which a company can transfer debt-equivalent flows from one time period to another. Therefore, to value the incremental cash flows stemming from the lease, we need to discount them at the after-tax interest rate.

Since Greymare can borrow at 10 percent, we should discount the lease cash flows at $r^* = .10(1 - .35) = .065$, or 6.5 percent. This gives

$$\text{NPV lease} = + 89.02 - \frac{17.99}{1.065} - \frac{22.19}{(1.065)^2} - \frac{17.71}{(1.065)^3} - \frac{15.02}{(1.065)^4}$$

$$- \frac{15.02}{(1.065)^5} - \frac{13.00}{(1.065)^6} - \frac{10.98}{(1.065)^7}$$

$$= -.70, \text{ or } -\$700$$

Since the lease has a negative NPV, Greymare is better off buying the bus.

A positive or negative NPV is not an abstract concept; in this case Greymare's shareholders really are $700 poorer if the company leases. Let us now check how this situation comes about.

Look once more at Table 26-2. The lease cash flows are:

	YEAR							
	0	1	2	3	4	5	6	7
Lease cash flows, thousands	+89.02	−17.99	−22.19	−17.71	−15.02	−15.02	−13.00	−10.98

The lease payments are contractual obligations like the principal and interest payments on secured debt. Thus you can think of the incremental lease cash flows in years 1 through 7 as the "debt service" of the lease. Table 26-3 shows a loan with *exactly* the same debt service as the lease. The initial amount of the loan is 89.72 thousand dollars. If Greymare borrowed this sum, it would need to pay interest in the first year of .10 × 89.72 = 8.97 and would *receive* a tax shield on this interest of .35 × 8.97 = 3.14. Greymare could then repay 12.15 of the loan, leaving a net cash outflow of 17.99 (exactly the same as for the lease) in year 1 and an outstanding debt at the start of year 2 of 60.42.

As you walk through the calculations in Table 26-3, you see that it costs exactly the same to service a loan that brings an immediate inflow of 89.72 as it does to service the lease, which brings in only 89.02. That is why we say that the lease has a net present value of 89.02 − 89.72 = −.7, or −$700. If Greymare leases the bus rather than raising an equivalent loan,[14] there will be $700 less in Greymare's bank account.

Our example illustrates two general points about leases and equivalent loans. First, if you can devise a borrowing plan that gives the same cash flow as the lease in every future period but a higher immediate cash flow, then you should not lease. If, however, the equivalent loan provides the same future cash outflows as the lease but a lower immediate inflow, then leasing is the better choice.

TABLE 26-3

. . . .

Details of the equivalent loan to the lease offered to Greymare Bus Lines (figures in thousands of dollars; cash outflows shown with negative sign)

	YEAR							
	0	1	2	3	4	5	6	7
Amount borrowed at year-end	89.72	77.56	60.42	46.64	34.66	21.89	10.31	0
Interest paid at 10%		−8.97	−7.76	−6.04	−4.66	−3.47	−2.19	−1.03
Interest tax shield at 35%		+3.14	+2.71	+2.11	+1.63	+1.21	+.77	+.36
Interest paid after tax		−5.83	−5.04	−3.93	−3.03	−2.25	−1.42	−.67
Principal repaid		−12.15	−17.14	−13.78	−11.99	−12.76	−11.58	−10.31
Net cash flow of equivalent loan	89.72	−17.99	−22.19	−17.71	−15.02	−15.02	−13.00	−10.98

---

[14]When we compare the lease to its equivalent loan, we do not mean to imply that the bus alone could support all of that loan. Some part of the loan would be supported by Greymare's other assets. Some part of the lease would likewise be supported by the other assets.

Second, our example suggests two ways to value a lease:

1. *Hard way.* Construct a table like Table 26-3 showing the equivalent loan.
2. *Easy way.* Discount the lease cash flows at the *after-tax* interest rate that the firm would pay on an equivalent loan. Both methods give the same answer—in our case an NPV of −$700.

The Story So Far

We concluded that the lease contract offered to Greymare Bus Lines was *not* attractive because the lease provided $700 less financing than the equivalent loan. The underlying principle is as follows: A financial lease is superior to buying and borrowing if the financing provided by the lease exceeds the financing generated by the equivalent loan.

The principle implies this formula:

$$\text{Net value of lease} = \text{initial financing provided} - \sum_{t=1}^{N} \frac{\text{LCF}_t}{[1 + r(1 - T_c)]^t}$$

where LCF_t is the cash outflow attributable to the lease in period t and N is the length of the lease. Initial financing provided equals the cost of the leased asset minus any immediate lease payment or other cash outflow attributable to the lease.

Notice that the value of the lease is its incremental value relative to borrowing via an equivalent loan. A positive lease value means that *if* you acquire the asset, lease financing is advantageous. It does not prove you should acquire the asset.

However, sometimes favorable lease terms rescue a capital investment project. Suppose that Greymare had decided *against* buying a new bus because the NPV of the $100,000 investment was −$5000 assuming normal financing. The bus manufacturer could rescue the deal by offering a lease with a value of, say, +$8000. By offering such a lease, the manufacturer would in effect cut the price of the bus to $92,000, giving the bus-lease package a positive value to Greymare. We could express this more formally by treating the lease's NPV as a favorable financing side effect which adds to project adjusted present value (APV):[15]

$$\text{APV} = \text{NPV of project} + \text{NPV of lease}$$
$$= -5000 + 8000 = +\$3000$$

Notice also that our formula applies to net financial leases. Any insurance, maintenance, and other operating costs picked up by the lessor have to be evaluated separately and added to the value of the lease. If the asset has salvage value at the end of the lease, that value should be taken into account also.

Suppose, for example, that the bus manufacturer offers to provide routine maintenance that would otherwise cost $2000 per year after tax. However, Mr. Pierce reconsiders and decides that the bus will probably be worth $10,000 after 8 years. (Previously he assumed the bus would be worthless at the end of the lease.) Then the value of the lease increases by the present value of the maintenance savings and decreases by the present value of the lost salvage value.

Maintenance and salvage value are harder to predict than the cash flows shown in Table 26-2, and so they normally deserve a higher discount rate. Suppose that Mr. Pierce uses 12 percent. Then the maintenance savings are worth

---

[15]See Chapter 19 for the general definition and discussion of APV.

$$\sum_{t=0}^{7} \frac{2000}{(1.12)^t} = \$11,100$$

The lost salvage value is worth $\$10,000/(1.12)^8 = \$4000$.[16] Remember that we previously calculated the value of the lease as $-\$700$. The revised value is therefore $-700 + 11,100 - 4000 = \$6400$. Now the lease looks like a good deal.

26-5 WHEN DO FINANCIAL LEASES PAY?

We have examined the value of a lease from the viewpoint of the lessee. However, the lessor's criterion is simply the reverse. As long as lessor and lessee are in the same tax bracket, every cash outflow to the lessee is an inflow to the lessor, and vice versa. In our numerical example, the bus manufacturer would project cash flows in a table like Table 26-2, but with the signs reversed. The value of the lease to the bus manufacturer would be

$$\begin{aligned}
\text{Value of} \\
\text{lease to} \\
\text{lessor}
\end{aligned} = -89.02 + \frac{17.99}{1.065} + \frac{22.19}{(1.065)^2} + \frac{17.71}{(1.065)^3} + \frac{15.02}{(1.065)^4} + \frac{15.02}{(1.065)^5}$$

$$+ \frac{13.00}{(1.065)^6} + \frac{10.98}{(1.065)^7}$$

$$= +.70, \text{ or } \$700$$

In this case, the values to lessee and lessor exactly offset ($-\$700 + \$700 = 0$). The lessor can win only at the lessee's expense.

But both lessee and lessor can win if their tax rates differ. Suppose that Greymare paid no tax ($T_c = 0$). Then the only cash flows of the bus lease would be:

	YEAR							
	0	1	2	3	4	5	6	7
Cost of new bus	+100							
Lease payment		−16.9	−16.9	−16.9	−16.9	−16.9	−16.9	−16.9	−16.9

These flows would be discounted at 10 percent, because $r_D(1 - T_c) = r_D$ when $T_c = 0$. The value of the lease is

$$\text{Value of lease} = +100 - \sum_{t=0}^{7} \frac{16.9}{(1.10)^t}$$

$$= +100 - 99.18 = +.82, \text{ or } \$820$$

In this case there is a net gain of $700 to the lessor (who has the 35 percent tax rate) *and* a net gain of $820 to the lessee (who pays zero tax). This mutual gain is at the expense of the government. On one hand, the government gains from the lease contract

---

[16]For simplicity, we have assumed that maintenance expenses are paid at the start of the year and that salvage value is measured at the *end* of year 8.

because it can tax the lease payments. On the other hand, the contract allows the lessor to take advantage of depreciation and interest tax shields which are of no use to the lessee. However, because the depreciation is accelerated and the interest rate is positive, the government suffers a net loss in the present value of its tax receipts as a result of the lease.

Now you should begin to understand the circumstances in which the government incurs a loss on the lease and the other two parties gain. Other things being equal, the potential gains to lessor and lessee are highest when:

- The lessor's tax rate is substantially higher than the lessee's.

- The depreciation tax shield is received early in the lease period.

- The lease period is long and the lease payments are concentrated toward the end of the period.

- The interest rate r_D is high—if it were zero, there would be no advantage in present value terms to postponing tax.

26-6 EVALUATING A LARGE, LEVERAGED LEASE

Now let us try using our newfound knowledge to evaluate a large leasing deal. In 1971 Anaconda began to build a $138 million aluminum reduction mill at Sebree, Kentucky. The company's original intention was to finance the project largely by a private placement of debt, but before it could do so, the Allende government expropriated Anaconda's Chilean copper mines and so provided the company with a $356 million tax-deductible loss.

Anaconda clearly was unlikely to pay taxes for a number of years. If it went ahead and bought the mill, it could not make immediate use of depreciation tax shields or of the 7 percent investment tax credit which was then available. By leasing the mill, however, Anaconda could pass on these benefits to someone who could use them.[17] It therefore decided to purchase only the real estate at Sebree and to pay $1.1 million to a leasing broker, U.S. Leasing International, to put together a *leveraged* lease for the $110.7 million of plant and equipment. Figure 26-1 shows how this was arranged. First Kentucky Trust Company issued $39 million of equity to a group of banks and finance companies and $72 million of debt to a group of insurance companies. It then used this money to purchase the mill and lease it to Anaconda. Anaconda agreed to make 40 lease payments, prepaid semiannually, over a 20-year period. The first 21 payments were set at $3.99 million each and the last 19 at $5.46 million each.

The $72 million loan was secured by a first claim on Anaconda's lease payments and by a mortgage on the plant. It was *not* guaranteed by First Kentucky or the equity investors. It was a *nonrecourse* loan: if Anaconda had defaulted on the lease payments, the insurance companies' only protection would have been the value of the mill and a general claim against Anaconda.

This is called a *leveraged* lease because part of the cost of the plant was raised by a loan secured by the asset and the lease payments. The lessor, First Kentucky Trust, really acted as an intermediary, receiving the lease payments from Anaconda, paying the debt service, and distributing what was left over to the equity investors. First Kentucky in effect financed the lease contract by selling off debt and equity claims against it.

---

[17]The Anaconda lease was described in P. Vanderwicken, "Powerful Logic of the Leasing Boom," *Fortune*, **87**:132–161 (November 1973). Our analysis of its present value is taken from S. C. Myers, D. A. Dill, and A. J. Bautista, "Valuation of Financial Lease Contracts," *Journal of Finance*, **31**:799–819 (June 1976), and J. R. Franks and S. D. Hodges, "Valuation of Financial Lease Contracts: A Note," *Journal of Finance*, **33**:647–669 (May 1978).

Figure 26-1 How Anaconda arranged a lease on its aluminum reduction mill. This is a leveraged lease because part of the cost of the plant was raised by borrowing.

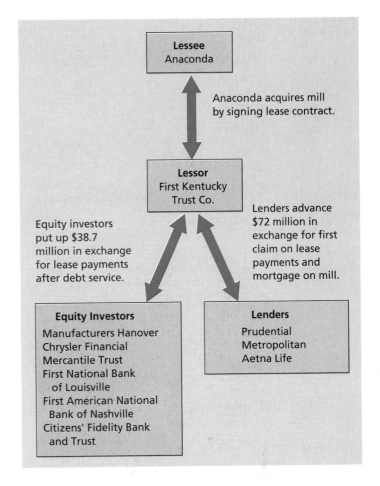

Anaconda acquires mill by signing lease contract.

Lessee
Anaconda

Lessor
First Kentucky Trust Co.

Equity investors put up $38.7 million in exchange for lease payments after debt service.

Lenders advance $72 million in exchange for first claim on lease payments and mortgage on mill.

Equity Investors
Manufacturers Hanover
Chrysler Financial
Mercantile Trust
First National Bank
  of Louisville
First American National
  Bank of Nashville
Citizens' Fidelity Bank
  and Trust

Lenders
Prudential
Metropolitan
Aetna Life

But let's look at the lease contract itself from the lessor's viewpoint. The initial outlay was $110.7 million less the investment tax credit of $7.75 million[18] and the initial prepaid lease payment. The major subsequent cash inflows were the 39 semiannual lease payments, the depreciation tax shields, and the salvage value in 1993.

As frequently happens in financial analysis, the hardest problem is to choose the right discount rate. Here is one way to look at it: The interest rate on the insurance companies' loan was 9.125 percent. Because this debt is also protected by the lessor's equity, the lease payments must be *riskier* than the debt. On the other hand, the depreciation tax shield must be *safer* than the lease payments, for once the contract is signed, the size of the shields is independent of Anaconda's fortunes. Since our formula calls for a single rate of discount for both the after-tax lease payments and the depreciation tax shield, we will compromise on a discount rate of 9.125 percent. The adjusted discount rate is 4.5625 percent. (The marginal tax rate at the time was approximately 50 percent.)

The present value calculations are set out in Table 26-4 along with a list of the other assumptions we have made. You can see that for the lessor the lease was moderately profitable: its net value was roughly 3 percent of the plant's cost.

---

[18] The investment tax credit (ITC) no longer exists. United States companies used to be able to deduct 7 percent of capital investment outlays directly from their corporate income taxes. Note that the ITC was not a deduction from taxable income but a *credit* against taxes.

TABLE 26-4

Value of Anaconda lease to lessor (figures in millions of dollars)

Item	Present Value
1. Price	−110.7
2. Investment tax credit	+7.7
3. Depreciation tax shield	+44.3
4. After-tax lease payments	+60.8
5. Salvage value	+.9
Total value to *lessor*	+3.0

Notes:
1. Assumed tax rate is $T_c = .5$.
2. The adjusted discount rate for items 3 and 4 is 4.5625 percent. (The present values were actually calculated assuming semiannual cash flows and an equivalent semiannual rate.)
3. The discount rate for item 5 is 15 percent, our guesstimate of the average cost of capital for Anaconda's assets.
4. The depreciation schedule was based on an 11-year depreciable life and a 5 percent book salvage value. The double-declining-balance method was used for the first 2 years and then a switch was made to sum-of-the-years' digits. This appears to be the fastest write-off available under 1973 regulations.
5. The lessor's estimate of the plant's after-tax salvage value appears to be $10.9 million. This is not from the horse's mouth; it is inferred from other information.
6. In principle, ownership of the salvage value also creates debt capacity. We have not included an estimate of the NPV of this capacity to the lessors. It is in any event a small number.
Source: S. C. Myers, D. A. Dill, and A. J. Bautista, "Valuation of Financial Lease Contracts," *Journal of Finance,* **31**:799–819 (June 1976), table 1, p. 809.

Table 26-4 is a practical application of the procedures we worked out in the previous section of this chapter. As such it takes no notice of the $72 million partial debt financing for the purchase of the Anaconda mill. The calculation doesn't look to the sources of the up-front money required of the lessors. It looks at the alternative *uses* of this money: it compares the lease to an equivalent loan to Anaconda.[19]

Did the availability of the $72 million loan add anything to the $3 million NPV calculated in Table 26-4? Not if the loan was issued at a fair rate of interest. If it was, the present value of the loan immediately after issue was $72 million, and the balance sheet for the Anaconda lease looked like this:

Present value of lease cash flows[20]	113.7	72	Present value of loan
		41.7	Present value of equity investment
	113.7	113.7	

---

[19]For lessors the equivalent-loan method compares leasing and lending. Suppose we add all the after-tax cash flows of the proposed lease, including lease payments, depreciation tax shields, investment tax credit, and salvage value. How much debt would these cash flows support? Table 26-4 tells us the answer: about $3 million more than the $110.7 million cost of the mill. That is why we say the lease has an NPV of $3 million to the lessors.

[20]This is the sum of lines 2 through 5 in Table 26-4.

The equity lessors put up $38.7 million, so their NPV was $41.7 - 38.7 = +\$3$ million. (If the loan had been issued at an especially favorable rate, its present value would have been less than $72 million, and the lessors' value would have been correspondingly higher.)

All this analysis is from the lessors' point of view. It is not so easy to evaluate the lease from Anaconda's side because we do not know when the company expected to resume paying taxes. If the "tax holiday" extended for 15 years, the lease was worth about $36 million to Anaconda.[21]

26-7   SUMMARY

A lease is just an extended rental agreement. The owner of the equipment (the *lessor*) allows the user (the *lessee*) to operate the equipment in exchange for regular lease payments.

There are a wide variety of possible arrangements. Short-term, cancelable leases are known as *operating leases*. In these leases the lessor bears the risks of ownership. Long-term, noncancelable leases are called *full-payout, financial,* or *capital* leases. In these leases the lessee bears the risks. Financial leases are *sources of financing* for assets the firm wishes to acquire and use for an extended period.

Many vehicle or office equipment leases include insurance and maintenance. They are *full-service* leases. If the lessee is responsible for insurance and maintenance, the lease is a *net* lease.

Frequently the lessor acquires the asset directly from the manufacturer. This is a *direct* lease. Sometimes the lessor acquires the asset from the user and then leases it back to the user. This is a *sale and lease-back*.

Most leases involve only the lessee and the lessor. But if the asset is very costly, it may be convenient to arrange a *leveraged* lease, in which the cost of the leased asset is financed by issuing debt and equity claims against the asset and the future lease payments.

The key to understanding operating leases is equivalent annual cost. In a competitive leasing market, the annual operating lease payment will be forced down to the lessor's equivalent annual cost. Operating leases are attractive to equipment users if the lease payment is less than the *user's* equivalent annual cost of buying the equipment. Operating leases make sense when the user needs the equipment only for a short time, when the lessor is better able to bear the risks of obsolescence, or when the lessor can offer a good deal on maintenance. Remember too that operating leases often have valuable options attached.

A financial lease extends over most of the economic life of the leased asset and cannot be canceled by the lessee. Signing a financial lease is like signing a secured loan to finance purchase of the leased asset. With financial leases, the choice is not "lease versus buy" but "lease versus borrow."

Many companies have sound reasons for financing via leases. For example, companies that are not paying taxes can usually strike a favorable deal with a taxpaying lessor. Also, it may be less costly and time-consuming to sign a standardized lease contract than to negotiate a long-term secured loan.

---

[21]See J. R. Franks and S. Hodges, "Valuation of Financial Lease Contracts: A Note," *Journal of Finance*, **33** (May 1983), table 3, p. 667.

When a firm borrows money, it pays the after-tax rate of interest on its debt. Therefore, the opportunity cost of lease financing is the after-tax rate of interest on the firm's bonds. To value a financial lease, we need to discount the incremental cash flows from leasing by the after-tax interest rate.

An equivalent loan to a lease is one that commits the firm to exactly the same future cash flows. When we calculate the net present value of the lease, we are measuring the difference between the amount of financing provided by the lease and the financing provided by the equivalent loan:

$$\begin{matrix} \text{Value} \\ \text{of lease} \end{matrix} = \begin{matrix} \text{financing provided} \\ \text{by lease} \end{matrix} - \begin{matrix} \text{value of} \\ \text{equivalent loan} \end{matrix}$$

We can also analyze leases from the lessor's side of the transaction, using the same approaches we developed for the lessee. If lessee and lessor are in the same tax bracket, they will receive exactly the same cash flows but with signs reversed. Thus, the lessee can gain only at the lessor's expense, and vice versa. However, if the lessee's tax rate is lower than the lessor's, then both can gain at the federal government's expense.

Further Reading

The approach to valuing financial leases presented in this chapter is based on:

S. C. Myers, D. A. Dill, and A. J. Bautista: "Valuation of Financial Lease Contracts," *Journal of Finance*, **31**:799–819 (June 1976).

J. R. Franks and S. D. Hodges: "Valuation of Financial Lease Contracts: A Note," *Journal of Finance*, **33**:647–669 (May 1978).

Other useful works include Nevitt and Fabozzi's book and the theoretical discussions of Miller and Upton and of Lewellen, Long, and McConnell:

P. K. Nevitt and F. J. Fabozzi: *Equipment Leasing*, 3d ed., Dow Jones–Irwin, Inc., Homewood, Ill., 1988.

M. H. Miller and C. W. Upton: "Leasing, Buying and the Cost of Capital Services," *Journal of Finance*, **31**:761–786 (June 1976).

W. G. Lewellen, M. S. Long, and J. J. McConnell: "Asset Leasing in Competitive Capital Markets," *Journal of Finance*, **31**:787–798 (June 1976).

Harold Bierman gives a detailed account of leasing and the AMT in:

H. Bierman: "Buy versus Lease with an Alternative Minimum Tax," *Financial Management*, **17**:87–92 (Winter 1988).

The options embedded in many operating leases are discussed in:

T. E. Copeland and J. F. Weston: "A Note on the Evaluation of Cancellable Operating Leases," *Financial Management*, **11**:68–72 (Summer 1982).

J. J. McConnell and J. S. Schallheim: "Valuation of Asset Leasing Contracts," *Journal of Financial Economics*, **12**:237–261 (August 1983).

Quiz

1. The following terms are often used to describe leases:
   (*a*) Direct
   (*b*) Full-service
   (*c*) Operating
   (*d*) Financial

(*e*) Rental
(*f*) Net
(*g*) Leveraged
(*h*) Sale and lease-back
(*i*) Full-payout
Match each of these terms with one of the following statements:
(*A*) The initial lease period is shorter than the economic life of the asset.
(*B*) The initial lease period is long enough for the lessor to recover the cost of the asset.
(*C*) The lessor provides maintenance and insurance.
(*D*) The lessee provides maintenance and insurance.
(*E*) The lessor buys the equipment from the manufacturer.
(*F*) The lessor buys the equipment from the prospective lessee.
(*G*) The lessor finances the lease contract by issuing debt and equity claims against it.

2. Some of the following reasons for leasing are rational. Others are irrational or assume imperfect or inefficient capital markets. Which of the following reasons are the rational ones?
(*a*) The lessee's need for the leased asset is only temporary.
(*b*) Specialized lessors are better able to bear the risk of obsolescence.
(*c*) Leasing provides 100 percent financing and thus preserves capital.
(*d*) Leasing allows firms with low marginal tax rates to "sell" depreciation tax shields.
(*e*) Leasing increases earnings per share.
(*f*) Leasing reduces the transaction cost of obtaining external financing.
(*g*) Leasing avoids restrictions on capital expenditures.
(*h*) Leasing can reduce the alternative minimum tax.

3. Explain why the following statements are true:
(*a*) In a competitive leasing market, the annual operating lease payment equals the lessor's equivalent annual cost.
(*b*) Operating leases are attractive to equipment users if the lease payment is less than the *user's* equivalent annual cost.

4. True or false?
(*a*) Lease payments are usually made at the start of each period. Thus the first payment is usually made as soon as the lease contract is signed.
(*b*) Financial leases can still provide off-balance-sheet financing.
(*c*) The cost of capital for a financial lease is the interest rate the company would pay on a bank loan.
(*d*) An equivalent loan's principal plus after-tax interest payments exactly matches the after-tax cash flows of the lease.
(*e*) A financial lease should not be undertaken unless it provides more financing than the equivalent loan.
(*f*) It makes sense for firms that pay no taxes to lease from firms that do.
(*g*) Other things equal, the net tax advantage of leasing increases as nominal interest rates increase.

5. Acme has branched out to rentals of office furniture to start-up companies. Consider a $3000 desk. Desks last for 6 years and can be depreciated on a 5-year ACRS schedule (see Table 6-5). What is the break-even operating lease rate for a new desk? Assume that lease rates for old and new desks are the same and that Acme's pretax administrative costs are $400 per desk per year. The cost of capital is

9 percent and the tax rate 35 percent. Lease payments are made in advance, that is, at the start of each year. The inflation rate is zero.

6. Refer again to Quiz question 5. Suppose a blue-chip company requests a 6-year *financial* lease for a $3000 desk. The company has just issued 5-year notes at an interest rate of 6 percent per year. What is the break-even lease rate in this case? Assume administrative costs drop to $200 per year. Explain why your answers to question 5 and this question differ.

7. Suppose that National Waferonics has before it a proposal for a 4-year financial lease. The firm constructs a table like Table 26-2. The bottom line of its table shows the lease cash flows:

	Year 0	Year 1	Year 2	Year 3
Lease cash flow	+62,000	−26,800	−22,200	−17,600

These flows reflect the cost of the machine, depreciation tax shields, and the after-tax lease payments. Ignore salvage value. Assume the firm could borrow at 10 percent and faces a 35 percent marginal tax rate.
(*a*) What is the value of the equivalent loan?
(*b*) What is the value of the lease?
(*c*) Suppose the machine's NPV under normal financing is −$5000. Should National Waferonics invest? Should it sign the lease?

Questions and Problems

1. A lessee does not have to pay to buy the leased asset. Thus it's said that "leases provide 100 percent financing." Explain why this is *not* a true advantage to the lessee.

2. In Quiz question 5 we assumed identical lease rates for old and new desks.
   (*a*) How does the initial break-even lease rate change if the expected inflation rate is 5 percent per year? Assume that the *real* cost of capital does not change. (*Hint:* Look at the discussion of equivalent annual costs in Chapter 6.)
   (*b*) How does your answer to part (*a*) change if wear and tear force Acme to cut lease rates by 10 percent in real terms for every year of a desk's age?

3. Why do you think that leasing of trucks, airplanes, and computers is such big business? What efficiencies offset the costs of running these leasing operations?

4. Look at Table 26-1. How would the initial break-even operating lease rate change if rapid technological change in limo manufacturing reduces the costs of new limos by 5 percent per year? (*Hint:* We discussed technological change and equivalent annual costs in Chapter 6.)

5. Financial leases make sense when the lessee faces a lower marginal tax rate than the lessor. Does this tax advantage carry over to *operating* leases?

6. Magna Charter has been asked to operate a Beaver bush plane for a mining company exploring north and west of Fort Liard. Magna will have a firm 1-year contract with the mining company and expects that the contract will be renewed for the 5-year duration of the exploration program. If the mining company renews at year 1, it will commit to use the plane for 4 more years.

Magna Charter has the following choices.

- Buy the plane for $500,000.
- Take a 1-year operating lease for the plane. The lease rate is $118,000, paid in advance.
- Arrange a 5-year, noncancelable financial lease at a rate of $75,000 per year, paid in advance.

These are net leases: all operating costs are absorbed by Magna Charter.

How would you advise Agnes Magna, the charter company's CEO? For simplicity assume 5-year, straight-line depreciation for tax purposes. The company's tax rate is 35 percent. The weighted-average cost of capital for the bush-plane business is 14 percent, but Magna can borrow at 9 percent. The expected inflation rate is 4 percent.

Ms. Magna thinks the plane will be worth $300,000 after 5 years. But if the contract with the mining company is not renewed (there is a 20 percent probability of this outcome at year 1), the plane will have to be sold on short notice for $400,000.

If Magna Charter takes the 5-year financial lease and the mining company cancels at year 1, Magna can sublet the plane, that is, rent it out to another user.

Make additional assumptions as necessary.

7. Here is a variation on question 6. Suppose Magna Charter is offered a 5-year *cancelable* lease at an annual rate of $125,000, paid in advance. How would you go about analyzing this lease? You do not have enough information to do a full option pricing analysis, but you can calculate costs and present values for different scenarios.

The following questions all apply to financial leases.

8. Look again at the bus lease described in Table 26-2.
   (*a*) What is the value of the lease if Greymare's marginal tax rate is $T_c = .20$?
   (*b*) What would the lease value be if Greymare had to use straight-line depreciation for tax purposes?

9. In Section 26-4 we showed that the lease offered to Greymare Bus Lines had a positive NPV of $820 if Greymare paid no tax *and* a +$700 NPV to a lessor paying 35 percent tax. What is the minimum lease payment the lessor could accept under these assumptions? What is the maximum amount that Greymare could pay?

10. Recalculate the value of the lease to Greymare Bus Lines if the company pays no taxes until year 3. Calculate the lease cash flows by modifying Table 26-2. Remember that the after-tax borrowing rate for periods 1 and 2 differs from the rate for periods 3 through 7.

 11. Nodhead College needs a new computer. It can either buy it for $250,000 or lease it from Compulease. The lease terms require Nodhead to make six annual payments (prepaid) of $62,000. Nodhead pays no tax. Compulease pays tax at 35 percent. Compulease can depreciate the computer for tax purposes over 5 years. The computer will have no residual value at the end of year 5. The interest rate is 8 percent.
   (*a*) What is the NPV of the lease for Nodhead College?
   (*b*) What is the NPV for Compulease?
   (*c*) What is the overall gain from leasing?

12. Many companies calculate the internal rate of return of the incremental after-tax cash flows from financial leases. What problems do you think this may give rise to? To what rate should the IRR be compared?

13. The overall gain from leasing is the sum of the lease's value to the lessee and its value to the lessor. Construct simple numerical examples showing how this gain is affected by:
    (*a*) The rate of interest
    (*b*) The choice of depreciation schedule
    (*c*) The difference between the tax rates of the lessor and lessee
    (*d*) The length of the lease

14. Discuss the following two opposite statements. Which do you think makes more sense?
    (*a*) "Leasing is tax avoidance and should be legislated against."
    (*b*) "Leasing ensures that the government's investment incentives work. It does so by allowing companies in nontaxpaying positions to take advantage of depreciation allowances."

15. The Safety Razor Company has a large tax-loss carry-forward and does not expect to pay taxes for another 10 years. The company is therefore proposing to lease $100,000 of new machinery. The lease terms consist of eight equal lease payments prepaid annually. The lessor can write the machinery off over 7 years using the tax depreciation schedules given in Table 6-5. There is no salvage value at the end of the machinery's economic life. The tax rate is 35 percent, and the rate of interest is 10 percent. Wilbur Occam, the president of Safety Razor, wants to know the maximum lease payment that his company should be willing to make and the minimum payment that the lessor is likely to accept. Can you help him? How would your answer differ if the lessor was obliged to use straight-line depreciation?

16. In Section 26-5 we listed four circumstances in which there are potential gains from leasing. Check them out by conducting a sensitivity analysis on the Greymare Bus Lines lease, assuming that Greymare does not pay tax. Try, in turn, (*a*) a lessor tax rate of 50 percent (rather than 35 percent), (*b*) immediate 100 percent depreciation in year 0 (rather than 5-year ACRS), (*c*) a 3-year lease with four annual rentals (rather than an 8-year lease), and (*d*) an interest rate of 20 percent (rather than 10 percent). In each case, find the minimum rental that would satisfy the lessor and calculate the NPV to the lessee.

17. In Section 26-5 we stated that if the interest rate were zero, there would be no advantage in postponing tax and therefore no advantage in leasing. Value the Greymare Bus Lines lease with an interest rate of zero. Assume that Greymare does not pay tax. Can you devise any lease terms that would make both a lessee and a lessor happy? (If you can, we would like to hear from you.)

18. A lease with a varying rental schedule is known as a *structured lease*. Try structuring the Greymare Bus Lines lease to increase value to the lessee while preserving the value to the lessor. Assume that Greymare does not pay tax. (*Note:* In practice the tax authorities will allow some structuring of rental payments but might be unhappy with some of the schemes you devise.)

PART eight

FINANCIAL PLANNING

27

Analyzing Financial Performance

"Divide and conquer" is the only practical strategy for presenting a complex field like financial management. We have broken down the financial manager's job into a series of clearly defined topics, such as capital budgeting, dividend policy, stock issue procedures, debt policy, and leasing. But in the end the financial manager has to consider the combined effects of these decisions on the firm as a whole.

In this chapter we look at how you can use financial data to analyze a firm's overall performance and assess its current financial standing. For example, you may need to check whether your own firm's financial performance is in the ballpark of standard practice. Or you may wish to understand the policies of a competitor or to check on the financial health of a customer.

Understanding the past is a necessary prelude to contemplating the future. Therefore the other chapters in Part Eight are devoted to financial planning. Chapter 28 shows how managers use long-term financial plans to establish concrete goals and to anticipate surprises. Chapter 29 then discusses short-term planning, in which the emphasis is on ensuring that the firm has enough cash to pay its bills and puts any spare cash to good use. Chapter 29 also serves as an introduction to Part Nine, which covers the management of the firm's short-term assets and liabilities.

But all that comes later. The business at hand is to analyze financial performance. We start with the time-honored method of financial ratio analysis. We discuss how ratios are used, and we note the limitations of the accounting data which most of the ratios are based on. We also take the opportunity to refer back to earlier chapters in which we discussed the firm's long-term financial decisions, and we look ahead to the later chapters on short-term financial decisions.

27-1 FINANCIAL RATIOS

We have all heard stories of financial whizzes who in minutes can take a company's accounts apart and find its innermost secrets in financial ratios. The truth, however, is that financial ratios are no substitute for a crystal ball. They are just a convenient way to summarize large quantities of financial data and to compare firms' performances. Ratios help you to ask the right questions; they seldom answer them.

We will describe and calculate four types of financial ratios:

- *Leverage ratios* show how heavily the company is in debt.
- *Liquidity ratios* measure how easily the firm can lay its hands on cash.
- *Profitability ratios* are used to judge how efficiently the firm is using its assets.
- *Market value ratios* show how the firm is valued by investors.

Table 27-1 contains the basic information that you need to calculate these financial ratios for International Paper. The income statement shows the amount that the company earned during 1994. After deducting the cost of goods sold and other expenses, International Paper had total earnings before interest and taxes (EBIT) of $1013 million. Of this sum, $349 million was used to pay debt interest (remember, interest is paid out of pretax income), and $232 million was set aside for taxes. The balance of $432 million belonged to the common stockholders.[1] However, International Paper did not pay out all its earnings to the stockholders; $222 million was plowed back into the business.[2]

The balance sheet in Table 27-1 shows a snapshot of International Paper's assets and liabilities at the end of 1994. Both the assets and liabilities are listed in declining order of liquidity. For example, you can see that the accountant lists first the assets most likely to be turned into cash in the near future. They include cash itself, short-term securities, receivables (that is, bills to be paid by the firm's customers), and inventories of raw materials, work in process, and finished goods. These assets are all known as *current assets*. Then the accountant lists long-term, usually illiquid, assets such as pulp and paper mills, office buildings, and timberlands. The balance sheet does not show the up-to-date market values of long-term assets. Instead, the accountant records the amount that each asset originally cost and then, in the case of plant and equipment, deducts a fixed annual amount for depreciation.

International Paper's liabilities are also classified as current or long term. *Current liabilities* are bills that the company expects to pay in the near future. They include debts that are due to be repaid within the next year and payables (that is, amounts owed by the company to its suppliers). In addition to having these short-term obligations, International Paper has issued bonds and leases that will not be repaid for many years. These are shown as long-term liabilities. After all these liabilities have been paid off, the remaining assets belong to the common stockholders. The common stockholders' equity is simply the total value of the assets less the current and long-term liabilities and any preferred stock. It is also equal to common stock plus retained earnings, that is, the net amount that the firm has received from stockholders or reinvested on their behalf.

Table 27-1 provides some other financial information about International Paper. For example, it shows the market value of the common stock. It is often helpful to compare the *book value* of the equity (shown in the company's accounts) with the *market value* established in the capital markets.

---

[1]If International Paper had issued any preferred stock, the dividend on this preferred would be deducted before calculating the earnings available for common stockholders.

[2]This is in addition to $885 million of cash flow earmarked as depreciation and $42 million of deferred income taxes. The figure for deferred tax arises because companies can take advantage of a variety of ways to postpone tax payments. The 1994 provision for deferred tax is the difference between the tax that the company shows as due in its income statement and the amount that it actually paid to the tax authorities.

TABLE 27-1

• •

Summary financial statements for International Paper (figures in millions of dollars except as noted)

	1994	1993
Income Statement*		
Net sales	14,966	13,685
Cost of goods sold	11,143	10,191
Other expenses	1,925	1,786
Depreciation	885	898
Earnings before interest and tax (EBIT)	1,013	810
Net interest	349	310
Tax	232	211
Earnings available for common stock	432	289
Balance Sheet		
Cash and short-term securities	270	242
Receivables	2,241	1,856
Inventories	2,075	2,024
Other current assets	244	279
Total current assets	4,830	4,401
Timberland, plant, and equipment	9,941	9,658
Other long-term assets	3,065	2,572
Total assets	17,836	16,631
Short-term debt	2,083	2,089
Payables	1,204	1,089
Other current liabilities	747	751
Total current liabilities	4,034	3,929
Long-term debt and capital leases	4,464	3,601
Other long-term liabilities	2,824	2,876
Common shareholders' equity	6,514	6,225
Total liabilities	17,836	16,631
Other Financial Information		
Market value of equity	9,414	8,347
Average number of shares, millions	124.9	123.2
Earnings per share, dollars†	3.46	2.34
Dividend per share, dollars	1.68	1.68
Share price, dollars	75.375	67.75

*Columns may not add because of rounding.
†Based on average number of shares outstanding during the year.
Source: International Paper Company 1994 annual report.

When a firm borrows money, it promises to make a series of fixed payments. Because the shareholders get only what is left after the debtholders have been paid, debt is said to create *financial leverage*. Our first set of ratios measures this leverage.

DEBT RATIO.   Financial leverage is usually measured by the ratio of long-term debt to total long-term capital. Since long-term lease agreements also commit the firm to a series of fixed payments, it makes sense to include the value of lease obligations with the long-term debt. Thus for International Paper,

$$\text{Debt ratio} = \frac{\text{long-term debt} + \text{value of leases}}{\text{long-term debt} + \text{value of leases} + \text{equity}}$$

$$= \frac{4464}{4464 + 6514} = .41$$

Another way to express leverage is in terms of the company's debt-equity ratio:

$$\text{Debt-equity ratio} = \frac{\text{long-term debt} + \text{value of leases}}{\text{equity}}$$

$$= \frac{4464}{6514} = .69$$

Notice that both these measures make use of book (i.e., accounting) values rather than market values.[3] The market value of the company finally determines whether debtholders get their money back, so you would expect analysts to look at the face amount of the debt as a proportion of the total market value of debt and equity. The main reason that they don't do this is that the market values are often not readily available. Does it matter much? Perhaps not; after all, the market value includes the value of intangible assets generated by research and development, advertising, staff training, and so on. These assets are not readily saleable, and if the company falls on hard times, the value of these assets may disappear altogether. For some purposes, it may be just as good to follow the accountant and ignore these intangible assets. As we saw in Section 24-5, this is just what lenders do when they insist that the borrower should not allow the book debt ratio to exceed a specified limit.

Debt ratios can be calculated in several ways. There is another common method. Suppose the financial analyst "nets out" current liabilities against current assets, leaving only long-term financing on the right-hand side of the balance sheet. The sum of long-term debt, other liabilities, and equity is called total capitalization. For International Paper:

Net working capital		4,464	Long-term debt
(current assets − current liabilities)	796	2,824	Other liabilities
Long-term assets	13,006	6,514	Equity
	13,802	13,802	Total capitalization

---

[3]In the case of leased assets accountants try to estimate the present value of the lease commitments. In the case of long-term debt they simply show face value. This can sometimes be very different from present value. For example, the present value of low-coupon debt may be only a fraction of its face value. The difference between the book value of equity and its market value can be even more dramatic.

The ratio of debt to total capitalization is

$$\frac{\text{Long-term debt}}{\text{Total capitalization}} = \frac{4464}{13,802} = .32$$

If other liabilities are treated as debt-equivalent, the ratio increases to

$$\frac{\text{Long-term debt + other liabilities}}{\text{Total capitalization}} = \frac{4464 + 2824}{13,802} = .53$$

TIMES INTEREST EARNED (OR INTEREST COVER). Another measure of financial leverage is the extent to which interest is covered by earnings before interest and taxes (EBIT) plus depreciation. For International Paper,[4]

$$\text{Times interest earned} = \frac{\text{EBIT + depreciation}}{\text{interest}} = \frac{1013 + 885}{349} = 5.44$$

The regular interest payment is a hurdle that companies must keep jumping if they are to avoid default. The times-interest-earned ratio measures how much clear air there is between hurdle and hurdler. However, always bear in mind that such summary measures tell only part of the story. For example, it might make sense to measure whether the firm is generating enough cash to cover other fixed charges such as regular repayments of existing debt or long-term lease payments.[5]

Liquidity Ratios

If you are extending credit or lending to a company for a short period, you are not interested only in the amount of the company's debts. You also want to know whether the company will be able to lay its hands on the cash to repay you. That is why credit managers and bankers look at several measures of *liquidity*. Another reason that managers focus on liquid assets is that the figures are more reliable. The book value of a catalytic cracker may be a poor guide to its true value, but at least you know what cash in the bank is worth.

Liquidity ratios also have some *less* desirable characteristics. Because short-term assets and liabilities are easily changed, measures of liquidity can rapidly become out of date. You might not know what that catalytic cracker is worth, but you can be fairly sure that it won't disappear overnight. Also, companies often choose a slack period for the end of their financial year. For example, retailers may end their financial year in January, after the Christmas boom. At such times the companies are likely to have more cash and less short-term debt than is the case during the busier seasons.

NET WORKING CAPITAL TO TOTAL ASSETS. Current assets are those assets which the company expects to turn into cash in the near future. The difference between current assets and current liabilities is known as *net working capital*. It roughly mea-

---

[4]The numerator of times interest earned can be defined in several ways. Sometimes depreciation is excluded. Sometimes it is just earnings plus interest—that is, earnings before interest *but after tax*. This last definition seems nutty to us, because the point of times interest earned is to assess the risk that the firm won't have enough money to pay interest. If EBIT falls below interest obligations, the firm won't have enough money to worry about taxes. Interest is paid before the firm pays taxes.

[5]In 1994 International Paper repaid $275 million of long-term debt. That gives

$$\frac{\text{EBIT + depreciation}}{\text{Interest + repayments of long-term debt}} = \frac{1013 + 885}{349 + 275} = 3.04$$

sures the company's potential reservoir of cash. Managers often express net working capital as a proportion of total assets:

$$\frac{\text{Net working capital}}{\text{Total assets}} = \frac{4830 - 4034}{17,836} = .04$$

CURRENT RATIO. Another measure which serves a similar purpose is the current ratio:

$$\text{Current ratio} = \frac{\text{current assets}}{\text{current liabilities}} = \frac{4830}{4034} = 1.20$$

Changes in the current ratio can sometimes mislead. For example, suppose that a company borrows a large sum from the bank and invests it in short-term securities. If nothing else changes, net working capital is unaffected, but the current ratio changes. For this reason it might be preferable to net off the short-term investments and the short-term debt when calculating the current ratio.

QUICK (OR ACID-TEST) RATIO. Some assets are closer to cash than others. If trouble comes, inventories may not sell at anything above fire-sale prices. (Trouble typically comes *because* customers are not buying and the firm's warehouse is stuffed full of unwanted goods.) Thus, managers often focus only on cash, short-term securities, and bills that customers have not yet paid:

$$\text{Quick ratio} = \frac{\text{cash} + \text{short-term securities} + \text{receivables}}{\text{current liabilities}}$$

$$= \frac{270 + 2241}{4034} = .62$$

CASH RATIO. Of course, a company's most liquid assets are its holdings of cash and marketable securities. That is why financial analysts also look at the cash ratio:

$$\text{Cash ratio} = \frac{\text{cash} + \text{short-term securities}}{\text{current liabilities}} = \frac{270}{4034} = .07$$

INTERVAL MEASURE. Instead of looking at a firm's liquid assets relative to its current liabilities, it may be useful to measure whether the liquid assets are large relative to the firm's regular cash outgoings. One suggestion is the so-called interval measure:

$$\text{Interval measure} = \frac{\text{cash} + \text{short-term securities} + \text{receivables}}{\text{average daily expenditure from operations}}$$

$$= \frac{270 + 2241}{(11,143 + 1925) \div 365} = 70 \text{ days}$$

Thus International Paper has sufficient liquid assets to finance operations for 70 days, even if it receives no further cash.

Profitability, or Efficiency, Ratios

Financial analysts employ a different set of ratios to judge how efficiently companies are using their assets. As we will see, there is a much greater degree of ambiguity in these ratios. For example, we can be fairly sure that it is safer to lend to a company that has relatively little leverage and a predominance of liquid assets. But how should the lender interpret the fact that a firm has a high ratio of profits to sales? Perhaps it is in a low-volume, high-markup business. (Jewelers operate on higher profit margins than food wholesalers, but they are not necessarily safer.) Or perhaps the firm has acquired its component supplier and is therefore more vertically integrated than its rivals. Again, that is not necessarily safer or better. Perhaps the firm charges higher prices, which may be a bad sign if it is trying to expand sales volume. Or perhaps it has lower costs, which is a good sign. We think that you should use the following profitability ratios to help you *ask* the important questions and *perhaps* to help answer them.

SALES TO TOTAL ASSETS. The sales-to-assets ratio shows how hard the firm's assets are being put to use:

$$\frac{\text{Sales}}{\text{Average total assets}} = \frac{14,966}{(17,836 + 16,631) \div 2} = .87$$

A high ratio could indicate that the firm is working close to capacity. It may prove difficult to generate further business without an increase in invested capital.

Notice that since the assets are likely to change over the course of a year, we use the *average* of the assets at the beginning and the end of the year. Averages are usually used whenever a *flow* figure (in this case, sales) is compared with a *stock* or snapshot figure (total assets).

SALES TO NET WORKING CAPITAL. Net working capital can be measured more accurately than other assets. Also, the level of net working capital can be adjusted more rapidly to reflect temporary fluctuations in sales. Thus managers sometimes focus on how hard working capital has been put to use:

$$\frac{\text{Sales}}{\text{Average net working capital}} = \frac{14,966}{(796 + 472) \div 2} = 23.6$$

NET PROFIT MARGIN. If you want to know the proportion of sales that finds its way into profits, you look at the profit margin. Thus,[6]

$$\text{Net profit margin} = \frac{\text{EBIT} - \text{tax}}{\text{sales}} = \frac{1013 - 232}{14,966} = .052, \text{ or } 5.2\%$$

INVENTORY TURNOVER. Managers sometimes look at the rate at which companies turn over their inventories. In International Paper's case,

$$\text{Inventory turnover} = \frac{\text{cost of goods sold}}{\text{average inventory}} = \frac{11,143}{(2075 + 2024) \div 2} = 5.4$$

---

[6]Net profit margin is sometimes measured as net income/sales. This ignores the profits that are paid out to debtholders as interest and therefore should not be used to compare firms with different capital structures.

When making comparisons between firms, it makes sense to recognize that firms which pay more interest pay less taxes. We suggest that you calculate the taxes that the firm would pay if it were all-equity-financed. To do this you need to adjust taxes by adding back interest tax shields (interest payments $\times$ marginal tax rate). Using the 1994 tax rate of 35 percent,

$$\text{Net profit margin} = \frac{\text{EBIT} - (\text{tax} + \text{interest tax shields})}{\text{sales}}$$

$$= \frac{1013 - (232 + .35 \times 349)}{14,966} = .044, \text{ or } 4.4\%$$

A high inventory turnover is often regarded as a sign of efficiency. But don't jump to conclusions—it may simply indicate that the firm is living from hand to mouth. We will touch on these issues in Chapter 31, where we show that there is an optimal rate of inventory turnover. Inventories may be *too low* as well as too high.

AVERAGE COLLECTION PERIOD.   The average collection period measures how quickly customers pay their bills:

$$\text{Average collection period} = \frac{\text{average receivables}}{\text{average daily sales}}$$

$$= \frac{(2241 + 1856) \div 2}{14{,}966 \div 365} = 50 \text{ days}$$

A low ratio is again believed to indicate an efficient collection department, but it sometimes results from an unduly restrictive credit policy.[7]

RETURN ON TOTAL ASSETS.   Managers often measure the performance of a firm by the ratio of income to total assets (income is usually defined as earnings before interest but after taxes):[8]

$$\text{Return on total assets} = \frac{\text{EBIT} - \text{tax}}{\text{average total assets}}$$

$$= \frac{1013 - 232}{(17{,}836 + 16{,}631) \div 2} = .045, \text{ or } 4.5\%$$

Another measure focuses on the return on the firm's equity:

$$\text{Return on equity} = \frac{\text{earnings available for common}}{\text{average equity}}$$

$$= \frac{432}{(6514 + 6225) \div 2} = .068, \text{ or } 6.8\%$$

---

[7]We discuss credit policy in Chapter 30.

[8]When comparing the returns on total assets of firms with different capital structures, it makes sense to add back interest tax shields (see footnote 6). This adjusted ratio then measures the return that the company would have earned if it were all-equity-financed.

One other point about return on assets: Since profits are a flow figure and assets are a snapshot figure, analysts commonly divide profits by the average of assets at the start and end of the year. The reason they do this is that the firm may raise large amounts of new capital during the year and then put it to work. Therefore part of the year's earnings is a return on the new capital.

However, this measure is potentially misleading; be careful not to compare it with the cost of capital. After all, when we defined the return that shareholders require from investing in the capital market, we divided expected profit by the initial outlay, not by an average of starting and ending values.

It's better to recognize explicitly when and how much new capital is raised. For example, in 1994 International Paper raised only $291 million by new financing. If this capital was on average invested for 6 months, then we can calculate return on assets by adding one-half of $291 million to assets at the start of the year:

$$\text{Return on assets} = \frac{\text{EBIT} - \text{tax}}{\text{assets at start of year} + (\text{new capital raised} \div 2)}$$

$$= \frac{1013 - 232}{16{,}631 + (291 \div 2)} = .047, \text{ or } 4.7\%$$

It is natural for firms to compare the return that they are earning with the opportunity cost of capital. Since short-term interest rates in 1994 were 5 to 6 percent, International Paper's return on assets appears to be well short of its cost of capital. Of course, the assets in International Paper's books are shown at *net book value*, that is, original cost (less any depreciation).[9] The assets' actual values may be less, so the low return on assets does not necessarily imply that those assets could be better employed elsewhere. Nor would a high return mean that you could buy the same assets today and get a high return.

Some profitability or efficiency ratios can be linked in useful ways. For example, the return on assets depends on the firm's sales-to-assets ratio and profit margin:

$$\frac{\text{Income}}{\text{Assets}} = \frac{\text{sales}}{\text{assets}} \times \frac{\text{income}}{\text{sales}}$$

All firms would like to earn a higher return on assets, but their ability to do so is limited by competition. If the expected return on assets is fixed by competition, firms face a trade-off between the sales-to-assets ratio and the profit margin. Thus we find that fast-food chains, which turn over their capital frequently, also tend to operate on low profit margins. Classy hotels have relatively high margins, but this is offset by lower sales-to-assets ratios.

Firms often seek to increase their profit margins by becoming more vertically integrated—for example, they may acquire a supplier or one of their sales outlets. Unfortunately, unless they have some special skill in running these new businesses, they are likely to find that any gain in profit margin is offset by a decline in the sales-to-assets ratio.

PAYOUT RATIO.   The payout ratio measures the proportion of earnings that is paid out as dividends. Thus,

$$\text{Payout ratio} = \frac{\text{dividend per share}}{\text{earnings per share}} = \frac{1.68}{3.46} = .49$$

We saw in Section 16-2 that managers don't like to cut dividends and that they try to maintain them despite temporary shortfalls in earnings. Therefore, if a company's earnings are particularly variable, management is likely to play it safe by setting a low average payout ratio. When earnings fall unexpectedly, the payout ratio is likely to rise temporarily. Likewise, if earnings are expected to rise next year, management may feel that it can pay slightly more generous dividends, and this year's payout ratio will be higher.

Earnings not paid out as dividends are plowed back into the business:

$$\text{Proportion of earnings plowed back} = 1 - \text{payout ratio}$$
$$= \frac{\text{earnings} - \text{dividend}}{\text{earnings}}$$

If you multiply this figure by the return on equity, you can see roughly how rapidly the shareholders' investment is growing as a result of plowback. Thus for International Paper,

---

[9]More careful comparisons between the return on assets and the cost of capital need to recognize the biases in accounting numbers. We discussed these biases in Chapter 12.

$$\text{Growth in equity from plowback} = \frac{\text{earnings} - \text{dividend}}{\text{earnings}} \times \frac{\text{earnings}}{\text{equity}}$$

$$= .51 \times .068 = .035, \text{ or } 3.5\%$$

If International Paper continues to plow back 51 percent of earnings and earn 6.8 percent on its book equity, then earnings, dividends, and equity will all grow at 3.5 percent a year.[10] However, in 1994 International Paper was still recovering from recession, and investors were forecasting that in 1995 the company would earn 12 percent on book equity. If it can hold that return and plow back 51 percent of earnings, the growth rate would increase to $.51 \times .12 = .061$, or 6.1 percent.

Market Value Ratios

There is no law that prohibits the financial manager from introducing data which are not in the company accounts. For example, in the case of a steel company, you might want to look at the cost per ton of steel produced; for an airline, you might calculate revenues per passenger mile; and so on. Managers find it helpful to look at ratios that combine accounting and stock market data. Here are four of these market-based ratios.

PRICE-EARNINGS RATIO.   The price-earnings, or P/E, ratio measures the price that investors are prepared to pay for each dollar of earnings. In the case of International Paper,[11]

$$\text{P/E ratio} = \frac{\text{stock price}}{\text{earnings per share}} = \frac{75.375}{3.46} = 21.8$$

Thus it costs $21.8 to buy one dollar of International Paper's earnings. In Section 4-4 we explained that a high P/E ratio may indicate that investors think the firm has good growth opportunities or that its earnings are relatively safe and therefore more valuable. Of course, it may also mean temporarily depressed earnings. If a company just breaks even, reporting zero earnings, its P/E ratio is infinite.

DIVIDEND YIELD.   The stock's dividend yield is simply the expected dividend as a proportion of the stock price. Thus for International Paper,

$$\text{Dividend yield} = \frac{\text{dividend per share}}{\text{stock price}} = \frac{1.68}{75.375} = .022, \text{ or } 2.2\%$$

Remember that the return to an investor comes in two forms, dividend yield and capital appreciation. If a stock has a low dividend yield, it may indicate that investors are content with a relatively low rate of return or that they are looking for the compensation of a rapid growth in dividends and consequent capital gains.

MARKET-TO-BOOK RATIO.   The market-to-book ratio is the ratio of the stock price to book value per share. For International Paper,

---

[10]Analysts sometimes refer to this figure as the *sustainable rate of growth*. In Section 4-3 we used this measure to help estimate the market capitalization rate for Duke Power stock. (Note that our measure of return on equity leads to a slight underestimate of sustainable growth. See footnote 8.)

[11]We use 1994 earnings per share and the stock price at the end of 1994. Since stockholders always look forward, not back, it would be better to use earnings that were forecasted for 1995. See Section 4-4.

$$\text{Market-to-book ratio} = \frac{\text{stock price}}{\text{book value per share}} = \frac{75.375}{6514 \div 124.9} = 1.45$$

Book value per share is just stockholders' book equity (net worth) divided by the number of shares outstanding. Book equity equals common stock plus retained earnings—the net amount that the firm has received from stockholders or reinvested on their behalf.[12] Thus International Paper's market-to-book ratio of 1.45 means that the firm is worth 45 percent more than past and present shareholders have put into it.

TOBIN'S q. The ratio of the market value of a company's debt and equity to the current replacement cost of its assets is often known as *Tobin's q*, after the economist James Tobin:[13]

$$q = \frac{\text{market value of assets}}{\text{estimated replacement cost}}$$

This ratio is like the market-to-book ratio, but there are several important differences. The numerator of q includes all the firm's debt and equity securities, not just its common stock. The denominator includes all assets, not just the firm's net worth. Also, these assets are not entered at original cost, as shown in the firm's books, but at what it would cost to replace them. Since inflation has driven the replacement cost of many assets well above their original cost, the Financial Accounting Standards Board (FASB) recommended procedures that would take into account the impact of inflation. Until 1985 large companies were obliged to report these "current-cost" adjustments. Since inflation subsided in the mid-1980s, it has become a voluntary inclusion in the firm's financial statements. In common with most firms, International Paper no longer reports the current cost of its assets, and therefore you would need to adjust historic asset costs for inflation before you could calculate q.

Tobin argued that firms have an incentive to invest when q is greater than 1 (i.e., when capital equipment is worth more than the cost of replacing it) and that they will stop investing only when q is less than 1 (i.e., when equipment is worth less than its replacement cost). When q is less than 1, it may be cheaper to acquire assets through merger than to buy new assets.

Of course, it is possible to think of cases where the existing assets are worth much more than they cost but there is no scope for further profitable investment. Nevertheless, a high value for q is usually a sign of valuable growth opportunities. The reverse is also true. Just because an asset is worth *less* than what it would cost if bought today, do not conclude that it can be better employed elsewhere. But companies whose assets are valued below replacement cost ought to look over their shoulders to see whether predators are threatening to take them over and redeploy the assets.

We should also expect q to be higher for firms with a strong competitive advantage, and so it turns out. The companies with the highest values for q tend to be those

---

[12]Retained earnings are measured net of depreciation. They represent stockholders' new investment in the business over and above the amount needed to maintain the firm's existing stock of assets.

[13]J. Tobin, "A General Equilibrium Approach to Monetary Theory," *Journal of Money, Credit, and Banking*, **1**:15–29 (February 1969). For estimates of q, see G. von Furstenberg, "Corporate Investment: Does Market Valuation Really Matter?" *Brookings Papers on Economic Activity*, **2**:347–397 (1977); and E. B. Lindberg and S. A. Ross, "Tobin's q Ratio and Industrial Organization," *Journal of Business*, **54**:1–33 (January 1981).

with very strong brand images or know-how. Those with the lowest values have generally been in highly competitive and shrinking industries.[14]

Many years ago a British bank chairman observed that not only did the bank's accounts show its true position but the actual situation was a little better still.[15] Since that time accounting standards have been much more carefully defined, but companies still have considerable discretion in calculating profits and deciding what to show on the balance sheet. Thus, when you calculate financial ratios, you need to look below the surface and understand some of the decisions taken by the firm's accountants.

Here are some examples of things to think about when interpreting a firm's financial ratios.

DEPRECIATION. Firms have considerable leeway on how they depreciate their assets. The choice of depreciation method and the length of the period over which the firm depreciates its assets can have a major impact on earnings and return on assets. For example, IBM added $375 million to reported earnings in 1984 by switching from accelerated to straight-line depreciation. In 1987 GM added $1.2 billion to its earnings when it increased the assumed life of its plant and equipment.[16]

DEFERRED TAX. As we pointed out in Section 6-2, most firms use straight-line depreciation in their financial statements and accelerated depreciation in their tax returns. For example, only part of International Paper's reported taxes of $232 million was owed immediately. The Internal Revenue Service got $190 million, and $42 million was set aside in a deferred tax reserve. (Since accelerated depreciation simply postpones the payment of tax, this $42 million will have to be paid eventually—hence the reserve account.) International Paper's provision for deferred tax reduced net income and common stockholders' equity.

INTANGIBLE ASSETS. Many firms spend large sums on research and development, advertising, staff training, and so on. These expenditures create valuable assets— know-how, brand loyalty, and a skilled workforce—that may generate cash flows for many years. However, the investment expenditures are deducted immediately from earnings, and therefore the assets *never* show up on the balance sheet.[17] Book rates of return, which are ratios of income to assets, end up overstated because assets are understated. We gave an example in Section 12-3.

GOODWILL. "Other long-term assets" shown on International Paper's balance sheet include a figure of $763 million for "goodwill." This is the difference between the amount that International Paper paid when it acquired several companies and the book value of their assets. International Paper writes off 2½ percent of this goodwill from each year's profits. We don't want to get into a discussion as to whether good-

---

[14]See E. B. Lindberg and S. A. Ross, op. cit.

[15]Speech by the chairman of the London and County Bank at its annual meeting, February 1901. Reported in *The Economist*, 1901, p. 204, and cited in C. A. E. Goodhart, *The Business of Banking 1891–1914*, Weidenfeld and Nicholson, Ltd., London, 1972, p. 15.

[16]See *Letter from Howard P. Hodges to General Motors Corporation*, reprinted in S. A. Zeff and B. G. Dharan (eds.), *Readings and Notes on Financial Accounting*, 4th ed., McGraw-Hill, Inc., New York, 1994.

[17]Accountants prefer assets you can kick. Since you can't see or touch intangible assets, how can you be *sure* they are there?

will is really an asset, but we should warn you about the dangers of comparing ratios of firms that include a substantial goodwill element on their balance sheets with ratios of firms that do not.

OFF-BALANCE-SHEET DEBT. Firms don't usually own all their plant and equipment; some of it may be leased. If the lease is long-term, the plant and equipment is shown on the balance sheet as an asset, and the value of the lease payments is shown as a liability. But assets that are leased on a short-term basis don't show up on the balance sheet at all.[18] As a result, some airlines at times have not had any aircraft on their balance sheets. In contrast, General Electric owns the world's largest private air-fleet through its leasing business.[19]

PENSIONS. The pensions that firms promise to employees are like a debt. To pay these future pensions, companies make contributions to a pension fund. The pension fund's portfolio is one of the firm's most important assets, though it is not shown on the balance sheet.

In International Paper's case, the pension scheme was $648 million in surplus; that is, the assets in the fund were worth $648 million more than the pension promises. If International Paper's pension scheme had been in deficit, the deficiency would show up on the balance sheet as a liability. But the company is not permitted to record the surplus on the balance sheet.

To provide for future pensions, International Paper makes a regular payment into the pension fund, but this payment is not deducted from the company's income. Instead, the company calculates the difference between the return earned on the pension fund's investments and the annual cost of the pension plan. In 1994 the return on the pension fund was $77 million *more* than the pension cost, so the company was considered to have made a profit on the pension scheme, and this profit was added into the company's income.

DERIVATIVES. In Chapter 25 we looked at how companies use derivatives, such as futures, options, and swaps, to protect themselves against fluctuations in interest rates, exchange rates, and commodity prices. These contracts do not show up on the balance sheet. In 1994 International Paper had on average over $2 billion of foreign exchange contracts outstanding and $600 million of interest-rate swaps. Changes in the value of derivatives can make a large difference to the bottom line. For example, in 1994 Procter and Gamble shocked investors by announcing losses of $157 million on several complicated derivatives positions.

FOREIGN ACCOUNTING PRACTICES. Accounting practices can vary greatly from one country to another, and therefore the need to understand how accounts are constructed is even more crucial when comparing the financial statements of firms in different countries. For example, German firms can tuck money away in hidden reserve accounts. When Daimler-Benz a.g., producer of Mercedes-Benz automobiles, decided to list its shares on the New York Stock Exchange in 1993, it was required to revise its accounting practices to conform to United States standards. While it reported a modest profit using German accounting rules in the first half of 1993, it

---

[18]We explained the distinction between on-balance-sheet and off-balance-sheet leases in Section 26-2.

[19]Other forms of debt that do not show up on the balance sheet include many forms of project finance. See Section 24-7.

TABLE 27-2

Financial ratios for International Paper and a sample of 25 other paper and forest product companies

	INTERNATIONAL PAPER		OTHER COMPANIES IN THE PAPER AND FOREST PRODUCT INDUSTRIES
	1994	1993	Latest Year
Leverage Ratios			
Debt ratio	.41	.35	.43
Times interest earned	5.4	6.7	3.7
Liquidity Ratios			
Net working capital to total assets	.04	.03	.06
Current ratio	1.2	1.1	1.5
Quick ratio	.62	.56	.67
Cash ratio	.07	.06	.05
Interval measure, days	70	66	54
Profitability (or Efficiency) Ratios			
Sales to total assets	.87	.94	.71
Sales to net working capital	23.6	53.3	8.3
Net profit margin, percent	5.2	5.8	4.8
Inventory turnover	5.4	5.8	6.2
Average collection period, days	50	48	36
Return on total assets, percent	4.5	5.6	3.7
Return on equity, percent	6.8	8.4	3.6
Market Value Ratios			
Price-earnings ratio	21.8	13.3	15.5
Dividend yield, percent	2.2	2.7	2.2
Market-to-book ratio	1.45	1.3	1.8

reported a *loss* of $592 million under the much more revealing United States rules, primarily because of differences in the treatment of reserves.

Choosing a Bench-mark

We have shown you how to calculate the principal financial ratios for International Paper. But you still need some way of judging whether a ratio is high or low.

A good starting point is to compare the current year's ratios with equivalent figures for earlier years. For example, you can see from the first two columns of Table 27-2 that in 1994 International Paper was somewhat more liquid than in the earlier year but was earning a lower return on assets. The market, however, was valuing International Paper's earnings and assets more highly than in the past. Presumably investors were looking for more rapid earnings growth.

When making comparisons of this kind, remember our earlier warning about the need to dig behind the figures. For example, notice that the decline in return on as-

TABLE 27-3

Financial ratios for major industry groups, first quarter 1995

	All Manufacturing Corporations	Food and Kindred Products	Printing and Publishing	Chemical and Allied Products	Petroleum and Coal Products	Machinery except Electrical	Electrical and Electronic Equipment	Retail Trade
Debt ratio*	.39	.46	.41	.38	.34	.29	.21	.46
Net working capital to total assets	.10	.04	.10	.04	.01	.19	.15	.15
Current ratio	1.40	1.19	1.49	1.16	1.05	1.66	1.49	1.51
Quick ratio	.73	.53	.97	.56	.61	.93	.73	.47
Sales to total assets	1.09	1.19	.96	.80	.87	1.15	1.07	1.92
Net profit margin, percent[†]	5.2	5.3	5.7	7.3	3.7	3.2	6.5	2.5
Inventory turnover	7.4	8.3	13.7	7.2	15.1	6.7	5.6	6.4
Return on total assets, percent	5.7	9.4	8.2	9.0	4.3	6.0	10.7	6.5
Return on equity, percent [‡]	17.4	18.4	22.1	21.2	10.2	14.5	17.9	9.2
Dividend payout ratio	.35	.47	.23	.43	.98	.24	.27	.39

*Long-term debt includes capitalized leases and deferred income taxes.
[†]Reflects operating income only.
[‡]Reflects nonoperating as well as operating income.
Source: United States Department of Commerce, *Quarterly Financial Report for Manufacturing, Mining and Trade Corporations,* Second Quarter, 1995.

sets is partly due to a lower ratio of sales to assets and partly to a fall in the profit margin. Was this due to a change in the product mix or to the effect of a recession? You can obtain some clues by comparing the segment accounts, which break down profitability according to product and area of operation. Are there any indications that the reduction in margins may be temporary? A closer examination of the cost of goods sold may help you decide.

It is also helpful to compare International Paper's financial position with that of other firms in the same industry. The third column of Table 27-2 shows the average financial ratios for other paper and forest product companies. You can see that International Paper is somewhat more profitable than its competitors, but in other respects the two sets of financial ratios are remarkably similar.[20]

Financial ratios for industries are published by the U.S. Department of Commerce, Dun and Bradstreet, Robert Morris Associates, and others. Table 27-3 gives the principal ratios for major industry groups. The data should give you a feel for some of the differences between industries.

---

[20]Averages of ratios are dangerous animals. For example, you wouldn't want to take an average of P/E ratios if one company had negligible earnings and a P/E of 500 or 1000.

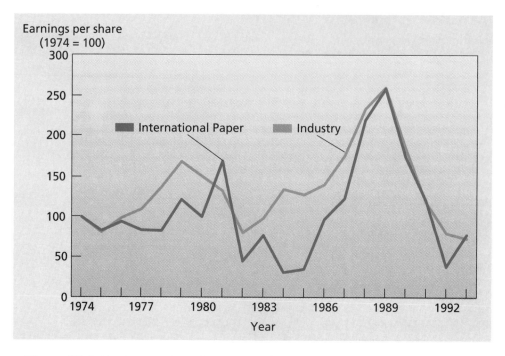

Figure 27-1 Earnings per share of International Paper and other paper and forest product companies. Industry data are calculated from the yearly median change in earnings of a sample of companies.

Which Financial Ratios?

Be selective in your choice of financial ratios, because many ratios tell you similar things. For example, as sure as pigs have tails, a firm with a high debt ratio will also have a high debt-equity ratio. So it is pointless to calculate both these measures. Conversely, there is almost no relationship between changes in a firm's current ratio and its return on equity. You can get additional information by looking at both figures.[21]

27-2 THE EARNINGS RECORD

Figure 27-1 summarizes International Paper's earnings record over the past 10 years. To interpret this record, you need to take into account what was happening to other companies. The reason for this is that International Paper is affected by the state of the economy as a whole and by the prosperity of its particular industry. The importance of these external influences on a company's income is shown in Table 27-4. On average an estimated 17 percent of the yearly variation in income is due to changes in the aggregate income of all corporations. A further 26 percent is explained by changes in the industry's income.

Figure 27-1 also shows the average earnings performance of other paper and forest product companies. Notice that International Paper's earnings record closely mir-

---

[21]For evidence on the correlations between financial ratios, see G. Foster, *Financial Statement Analysis*, 2d ed., Prentice-Hall, Inc., Englewood Cliffs, N.J., 1986.

TABLE 27-4

. . . .

Percentage of changes in net income due to economywide influences and
industry influences (measured for 315 firms, 1964–1983)

	Economywide Influence	Industry Influence
Crude petroleum and natural gas	14%	23%
Paper and allied products	49	12
Drugs	14	26
Petroleum refining	37	23
Steel and blast furnaces	35	23
General industrial machinery	23	21
Radio and TV transmitting equipment	14	15
Electronic components	32	12
Trucking	21	27
Air transportation	12	13
Electric services	8	39
Natural gas distribution	13	8
Electric and other service combinations	6	45
Retail, grocery stores	9	17
State banks, Federal Reserve System	5	25
Average	17	26

Source: G. Foster, *Financial Statement Analysis,* 2d ed., Prentice-Hall, Inc., Englewood Cliffs, N.J., 1986.

rors that of its competitors. If we want to understand the reasons for International Paper's recent growth in profits, we probably need to look at events affecting the whole industry.

Does this growth in earnings bode well for the future? Not necessarily. Statisticians who have studied the time path of firms' reported earnings conclude that earnings behave much like stock prices—that is, they follow a random walk.[22] There is very little relationship between a company's earnings growth in one period and that in the next. Therefore do not extrapolate growth mechanically. A firm with above-average earnings growth may sustain it, but such growth is equally likely to be followed by below-average growth.[23]

Since earnings changes are unrelated from one year to the next, your best measure of past growth is the simple average of past annual percentage growth rates. There is little point in fitting a trend line to past earnings, and such a trend line tells you little about likely future earnings.

Of course, there are many sources of information that may help you forecast earnings. For example, when a firm enjoys a high P/E ratio despite disappointing

---

[22]See, for example, R. Ball and R. Watts, "Some Time Series Properties of Accounting Income," *Journal of Finance,* **27**:663–682 (June 1972).

[23]In fact, it is slightly *more* likely to be followed by below-average growth. This is particularly true when there has been a sharp jump in earnings. See, for example, L. D. Brooks and D. A. Buckmaster, "First-Difference Signals and Accounting Income Time-Series Properties," *Journal of Business Finance and Accounting,* **7**:437–454 (Autumn 1980).

earnings, this suggests that investors expect an earnings rebound. Or suppose a firm announces a significant technological jump ahead of its competitors; you don't need a Ph.D. to figure out the likely impact on earnings.

*The
Meaning
of
Account-
ing
Earnings

In Chapter 12 we discussed the distinction between economic earnings and accounting earnings. Economists often define *earnings* as cash flow plus the change in value of the company's assets. But we know from the behavior of stock prices that changes in asset values are fundamentally unpredictable and very volatile. A company's published earnings follow a much smoother path than economic earnings.

Accountants don't really try to track year-to-year economic income. They seem to be more interested in showing the long-run average profitability of the firm's assets.[24] For example, they do not try to record actual yearly changes in the value of the firm's plant and equipment. Instead, they set up a depreciation schedule ahead of time and, except in abnormal circumstances, they stick to it. Thus the company's income statement reflects partly what actually happened (the operating cash flow) and partly what was forecasted to happen (the depreciation in asset value).

*How
Inflation
Affects
Book
Returns

We will steer clear of "inflation accounting" because the subject is so complex when one gets down to practical proposals. We will simply remind you of how inflation bears on standard book earnings.

First, inflation increases the nominal value of work in process and finished inventory. Suppose you are a clothing manufacturer. In January you make up 1000 men's suits worth $300 apiece, but you do not sell the suits until June. During this time your competitors have raised their prices by 6 percent, and you have quite literally followed suit. Thus the goods are finally sold for $300 \times 1.06 = \$318$. Part of your profit on this batch of suits can be attributed to inflation while the suits sat in inventory. You receive an *inventory profit* of $18 per suit.

Inventory profits are indeed profits. You are better off with them than without. They are properly included in nominal income. However, they are not part of real income, except to the extent that the inventories appreciate faster than the general price level.

There is a second problem. As inflation progresses, the net book value of fixed assets becomes more and more out of date—that is, book value understates current value or replacement cost. Reported income is also affected in two ways. First, income is overstated because depreciation is understated. Second, nominal income is understated because appreciation of asset values due to inflation is ignored. (A calculation of real, that is, inflation-adjusted, economic income would not include the second effect.)

Inflation has a third effect on book profits of firms that borrow. Lenders are paid back in inflated future dollars, so they demand a higher interest rate to compensate for the declining real value of their loan. The part of the interest rate which compensates for expected inflation is called the *inflation premium*. The full interest payment, including the inflation premium, is deducted from the firm's net book income. But book income does not recognize the compensating gain that the stockholders make at the expense of lenders. Remember, lenders gain from the inflation premium but lose as inflation drives down the real value of their asset. Stockholders lose by paying the inflation premium but gain because inflation drives down the real value

---

[24]Fischer Black has made this point in an extreme and very interesting way in his article "The Magic in Earnings: Economic Earnings versus Accounting Earnings," *Financial Analysts Journal*, **36**:3–8 (November–December 1980).

of their obligation. Book income recognizes stockholders' loss but not the offsetting gain.[25]

27-3 APPLICATIONS OF FINANCIAL ANALYSIS

We have discussed how to calculate and interpret summary measures of a company's financial position. We conclude this chapter with a glimpse at some of the ways that these measures can help the financial manager.

Suppose that you are a credit analyst or bank lending officer with the job of deciding whether a particular company is likely to repay its debts. What can you learn from the company's financial statements?

To answer this question, William Beaver compared the financial ratios of 79 firms that subsequently failed with the ratios of 79 that remained solvent.[26] Beaver's sample of failed firms behaved much as you would expect. They had more debt than the surviving firms, and they had a lower return on sales and assets. They had less cash but more receivables. As a result, they had somewhat lower current ratios and dramatically lower cash ratios. Contrary to popular belief, the failed firms had less, rather than more, inventory.

Figure 27-2 provides some idea of the predictive power of these financial ratios. You can see that 5 years before failure the group of failed firms appeared to be consistently less healthy. As we move progressively closer to the date of collapse, the difference between the two groups becomes even more marked.

Instead of looking at a number of separate clues, it may be more useful to combine the different bits of information into a single measure of the likelihood of bankruptcy. We will describe in Chapter 30 how companies construct such a measure.

Using Financial Ratios to Estimate Market Risk

Chapter 9 described how the return that investors require from a company's stock depends on its market risk, or beta. If you have sufficient history of stock price data, you can estimate beta by looking at the extent to which the price was affected by fluctuations in the market. But stock price data are not always available, so economists have examined whether accounting data can be used to estimate beta. For example, we know that as the firm issues more debt, the market risk of the equity increases. So it is no surprise that there is a strong relationship between a firm's debt ratio and its equity beta.

In addition to looking at these standard ratios, financial managers sometimes calculate an "accounting beta." In other words, they estimate the sensitivity of each company's earnings changes to changes in the aggregate earnings of all companies. An accounting beta of less than 1.0 means that on average the company's earnings changed by less than 1 percent for each 1 percent change in aggregate earnings. Conversely, an accounting beta of more than 1.0 implies that the firm's earnings changed by more than 1 percent for each 1 percent change in aggregate earnings.

Instead of looking at these measures one by one, it makes sense to combine them into a single measure of risk. Hochman found that the debt ratio, dividend yield, and

---

[25]For a provocative discussion of inflationary biases in book income, see F. Modigliani and R. A. Cohn, "Inflation, Rational Valuation and the Market," *Financial Analysts Journal*, **35**:24–44 (March–April 1979).

[26]See W. H. Beaver, "Financial Ratios and Predictors of Failure," *Empirical Research in Accounting: Selected Studies*, supplement to *Journal of Accounting Research*, 1966, pp. 77–111. Several later studies have come up with similar (but pictorially less eye-catching) findings. For a review of these studies, see G. Foster, *Financial Statement Analysis*, 2d ed., Prentice-Hall, Inc., Englewood Cliffs, N.J., 1986.

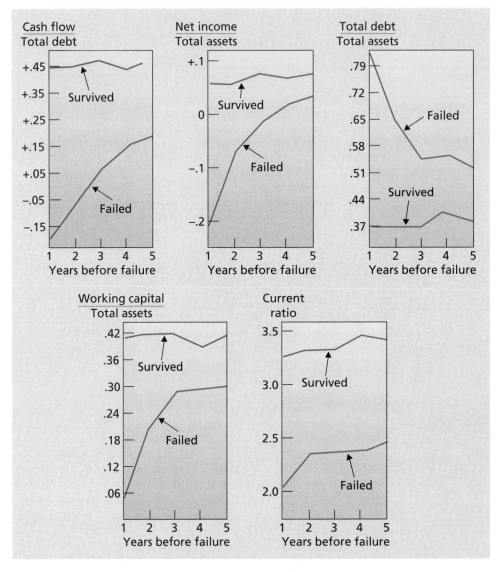

Figure 27-2 Beaver's study showed that the financial ratios of firms which subsequently fail are different from those of firms which survive. Note that the horizontal axis measures the number of years *before* failure; thus moving from right to left brings the failed firms *closer* to failure. (*Source:* W. H. Beaver, "Financial Ratios and Predictors of Failure," *Empirical Research in Accounting: Selected Studies,* supplement to *Journal of Accounting Research,* 1966, pp. 77-111, fig. 1, p. 82.)

TABLE 27-5

....

Moody's bond ratings for a sample of new issues were similar to the predicted ratings (For example, a total of 31 bonds were predicted to have A ratings, and of these, 18 actually received an A rating)

| | PREDICTED RATINGS | | | | | |
Actual Ratings	Aa	A	Baa	Ba	B	Total
Aa	7	8				15
A	4	18	2		1	25
Baa		4	4			8
Ba		1	2	1	1	5
B			2	1	5	8
Total	11	31	10	2	7	61

Source: J. A. Gentry, D. T. Whitford, and P. Newbold, "Predicting Industrial Bond Ratings with a Probit Model and Fund Flow Components," *Financial Review*, **23**:269–286 (August 1988).

accounting beta could together provide about as good a prediction of a stock's beta as an estimate based on past stock price data.[27]

....

Using Financial Ratios to Predict Bond Ratings

Moody's bond ratings are widely used as a yardstick of bond quality. Therefore, they indicate which investors are likely to buy your company's bonds and what interest rate they will require. Financial managers pay considerable attention to their company's bond ratings and would like to know in advance how a new issue of bonds would be rated or how a change in circumstances would affect the ratings on existing debt.

Financial ratios can help to predict bond ratings. For example, one study found that issuers of the more highly rated bonds generally had lower debt ratios, a higher ratio of earnings to interest, a higher return on assets, and a long history of dividend payments.[28] The bond issues were also more likely to be senior and to be large in value. The study also combined these variables into a single measure of bond quality and looked at how well it could forecast Moody's ratings for a sample of newly issued bonds in 1984. Table 27-5 shows that the forecast was spot on almost 60 percent of the time and was out by more than one category on only four occasions.

Of course, lenders also are interested in bond quality; they don't want to lend to a triple-A borrower only to find a few years later that they now own a junk bond. That is why lenders will often specify key financial ratios that the borrower must maintain. For example, firms are often obliged to observe a maximum debt ratio or a minimum current ratio. We discussed these restrictions in Section 24-5.

----

[27]S. Hochman, "The Beta Coefficient: An Instrumental Variables Approach," in *Research in Finance*, vol. 4, JAI Press, Greenwich, Conn., 1983. The pioneering study in the use of accounting data to measure risk was W. H. Beaver, P. Kettler, and M. Scholes, "The Association between Market-Determined and Accounting-Determined Risk Measures," *Accounting Review*, **45**:654–682 (October 1970).

[28]J. A. Gentry, D. T. Whitford, and P. Newbold, "Predicting Industrial Bond Ratings with a Probit Model and Fund Flow Components," *Financial Review*, **23**:269–286 (August 1988).

27-4　SUMMARY

If you are analyzing a company's financial statements, there is a danger of being over-whelmed by the sheer volume of data. That is why managers use a few salient ratios to summarize the firm's leverage, liquidity, profitability, and market valuation. We have described some of the more popular financial ratios.

We offer the following general advice to users of these ratios:

1. Financial ratios seldom provide answers, but they do help you ask the right questions.

2. There is no international standard for financial ratios. A little thought and common sense are worth far more than blind application of formulas.

3. Be selective in your choice of ratios. Different ratios often tell you similar things.

4. You need a benchmark for assessing a company's financial position. Compare financial ratios with the company's ratios in earlier years and with the ratios of other firms in the same business.

5. Be careful not to extrapolate past rates of earnings growth—earnings follow approximately a random walk.

6. Accounting earnings don't incorporate the year-by-year fluctuations in the true values of the company's assets. Instead, accountants try to provide a picture of long-run sustainable earnings.

Financial statement analysis helps you understand what makes the firm tick. We looked briefly at three particular applications. First, healthy firms have different financial ratios than firms that are heading for insolvency. Second, financial ratios provide valuable clues about a firm's market risk. Finally, we saw that a company's financial ratios can be used to predict the rating on a new issue of bonds.

Further Reading

There are some good general texts on financial statement analysis. See, for example:
G. Foster: *Financial Statement Analysis*, 2d ed., Prentice-Hall, Inc., Englewood Cliffs, N.J., 1986.

Fischer Black's provocative paper argues that the true object of accounting rules is to produce earnings proportional to value, not changes in value:
F. Black: "The Magic in Earnings: Economic Earnings versus Accounting Earnings," *Financial Analysts Journal*, **36**:3–8 (November–December 1980).

Three classic articles on the application of financial ratios to specific problems are:
W. H. Beaver: "Financial Ratios and Predictors of Failure," *Empirical Research in Accounting: Selected Studies*, supplement to *Journal of Accounting Research*, 1966, pp. 77–111.
W. H. Beaver, P. Kettler, and M. Scholes: "The Association between Market-Determined and Accounting-Determined Risk Measures," *Accounting Review*, **45**:654–682 (October 1970).
J. O. Horrigan: "The Determination of Long Term Credit Standing with Financial Ratios," *Empirical Research in Accounting: Selected Studies*, supplement to *Journal of Accounting Research*, 1966, pp. 44–62.

Quiz

1. Table 27-6 gives abbreviated balance sheets and income statements for Georgia-Pacific Corporation. Calculate the following financial ratios:
   (*a*) Debt ratio
   (*b*) Times interest earned
   (*c*) Current ratio
   (*d*) Quick ratio
   (*e*) Net profit margin
   (*f*) Inventory turnover
   (*g*) Return on equity
   (*h*) Payout ratio

TABLE 27-6

Income statement and balance sheet for Georgia-Pacific Corporation, 1994 (figures in millions)

Income Statement

Net sales	$12,738
Cost of goods sold	9,881
Other expenses	1,086
Depreciation	746
Earnings before interest and tax (EBIT)	1,025
Net interest	453
Tax	246
Earnings	$ 326
Dividends	145

Balance Sheet

	End of Year	Start of Year
Cash and short-term securities	$ 53	$ 41
Receivables	566	377
Inventories	1,209	1,202
Other current assets	34	26
Total current assets	1,862	1,646
Timberland, plant, and equipment	6,851	6,829
Other long-term assets	2,015	2,070
Total assets	$10,728	$10,545
Short-term debt	$ 1,117	$ 880
Payables	603	582
Other current liabilities	605	602
Total current liabilities	2,325	2,064
Long-term debt and capital leases	3,904	4,157
Other long-term liabilities	1,879	1,922
Common shareholders' equity	2,620	2,402
Total liabilities	$10,728	$10,545

Source: Georgia-Pacific Corporation, 1994 annual report.

2. There are no universally accepted definitions of financial ratios, but five of the following ratios make no sense at all. Substitute the correct definitions.

(a) Debt-equity ratio $= \dfrac{\text{long-term debt} + \text{values of leases}}{\text{long-term debt} + \text{value of leases} + \text{equity}}$

(b) Return on equity $= \dfrac{\text{EBIT} - \text{tax}}{\text{average equity}}$

(c) Payout ratio $= \dfrac{\text{dividend}}{\text{stock price}}$

(d) Profit margin $= \dfrac{\text{EBIT} - \text{tax}}{\text{sales}}$

(e) Inventory turnover $= \dfrac{\text{sales}}{\text{average inventory}}$

(f) Current ratio $= \dfrac{\text{current liabilities}}{\text{current assets}}$

(g) Sales to net working capital $= \dfrac{\text{average sales}}{\text{net working capital}}$

(h) Interval measure $= \dfrac{\text{current assets} - \text{inventories}}{\text{average daily expenditure from operations}}$

(i) Average collection period $= \dfrac{\text{sales}}{\text{average receivables} \div 365}$

(j) Quick ratio $= \dfrac{\text{current assets} - \text{inventories}}{\text{current liabilities}}$

(k) Tobin's $q = \dfrac{\text{market value of assets}}{\text{replacement cost of assets}}$

3. True or false?
   (a) A company's debt-equity ratio is always less than 1.
   (b) The quick ratio is always less than the current ratio.
   (c) The return on equity is always less than the return on assets.
   (d) Successive earnings levels are unrelated to each other.
   (e) Successive earnings changes are unrelated to each other.
   (f) Earnings follow roughly a random walk. This means that if earnings turn out to be higher than expected, you should revise upward your forecast of future earnings by a similar proportion.
   (g) Accounting earnings follow a less smooth path than economic earnings.
   (h) If a project is slow to reach full profitability, straight-line depreciation is likely to produce an overstatement of profits in the early years.
   (i) A substantial new advertising campaign by a cosmetics company will tend to depress earnings and cause the stock to sell at a low price-earnings multiple.

4. In each of the following cases, explain briefly which of the two companies is likely to be characterized by the higher ratio:
   (a) Debt-equity ratio: a shipping company or a computer software company
   (b) Payout ratio: United Foods Inc. or Computer Graphics Inc.
   (c) Ratio of sales to assets: an integrated pulp and paper manufacturer or a paper mill

(**d**) Average collection period: a supermarket chain or a mail order company

(**e**) Price-earnings multiple: Basic Sludge Company or Fledgling Electronics

(**f**) Tobin's q: an iron foundry or a pharmaceutical company with strong patent protection

5. A firm has $30,000 of inventories. If this represents 30 days' sales, what is the annual cost of goods sold? What is the inventory turnover ratio?

6. Keller Cosmetics maintains a profit margin of 4 percent and a sales-to-assets ratio of 3.

(**a**) What is its return on assets?

(**b**) If its debt-equity ratio is 1.0, its interest payments and taxes are each $10,000, and EBIT is $40,000, what is the return on equity?

7. A firm has a long-term debt-equity ratio of .4. Shareholders' equity is $1 million. Current assets are $200,000, and the current ratio is 2.0. Long-term assets total $1.5 million. What is the ratio of debt to total capitalization?

8. Magic Flutes has total receivables of $3000, which represents 20 days' sales. Average total assets are $75,000. The firm's profit margin is 5 percent. Find the firm's return on assets and sales-to-assets ratio.

9. Consider this simplified balance sheet for Geomorph Trading:

Current assets	100	60	Current liabilities
		280	Long-term debt
Long-term assets	500	70	Other liabilities
		190	Equity
	600	600	

(**a**) Calculate the ratio of debt to equity.

(**b**) What are Geomorph's net working capital and total capitalization? Calculate the ratio of debt to total capitalization.

10. Airlux Antarctica has current liabilities of $200 million and a crash—sorry, *cash* ratio of .05. How much cash and marketable securities does it hold?

11. On average, it takes Microlimp's customers 60 days to pay their bills. If Microlimp has annual sales of $500 million, what is the average value of unpaid bills?

12. This question reviews some of the difficulties encountered in interpreting accounting numbers.

(**a**) Give four examples of important assets, liabilities, or transactions which may not be shown on the company's books.

(**b**) How does investment in intangible assets, such as research and development, distort accounting ratios? Give at least two examples.

*(**c**) Explain the three ways in which accelerating inflation affects earnings and profitability ratios based on historical-cost accounting.

Questions and Problems

1. Discuss alternative measures of financial leverage. Should the market value of equity be used or the book value? Is it better to use the market value of debt, the book value, or the book value discounted at the risk-free interest rate?

How should you treat off-balance-sheet obligations such as pension liabilities? How would you treat preferred stock, deferred tax reserves, and minority interest?

2. As you can see, someone has spilt ink over some of the entries in the balance sheet and income statement of Transylvania Railroad (Table 27-7). Can you use the following information to work out the missing entries?

- Financial leverage: .4
- Times interest earned: 8
- Current ratio: 1.4
- Quick ratio: 1.0
- Cash ratio: .2
- Return on total assets: .18

TABLE 27-7

Balance sheet and income statement of Transylvania Railroad (figures in millions of dollars)

	December 1996	December 1995
Balance Sheet		
Cash	■■■	30
Accounts receivable	■■■	34
Inventory	■■■	26
Total current assets	■■■	80
Fixed assets, net	■■■	25
Total	■■■	105
Notes payable	30	35
Accounts payable	25	20
Total current liabilities	■■■	55
Long-term debt	■■■	20
Equity	■■■	30
Total	115	105
Income Statement		
Sales	■■■	
Cost of goods sold	■■■	
Selling, general and administrative expenses	10	
Depreciation	20	
EBIT	■■■	
Interest	■■■	
Earnings before tax	■■■	
Tax	■■■	
Earnings available for common stock	■■■	

- Return on equity: .41
- Inventory turnover: 5.0
- Receivables' collection period: 71.2 days

3. Use financial ratio analysis to compare two companies chosen from the same industry.

*4. Read and discuss Fischer Black's paper "The Magic in Earnings."

5. Describe some of the ways that the choice of accounting technique can temporarily depress or inflate earnings.

6. Suppose that at year-end 1994 International Paper had unused lines of credit which would have allowed it to borrow a further $300 million. Suppose also that it used this line of credit to raise short-term loans of $300 million and invested the proceeds in marketable securities. Would the company have appeared to be (*a*) more or less liquid, (*b*) more or less highly levered? Calculate the appropriate ratios.

7. Recalculate International Paper's financial ratios at the end of 1995. What problems arise in ensuring figures comparable with those of 1994?

8. Here are some data for five companies in the saucepan industry:

	COMPANY CODE				
	A	B	C	D	E
Net income, millions	$ 10	$ .5	$ 6.67	−$ 1	$ 6.67
Total book assets, millions	$300	$30	$120	$50	$120
Shares outstanding, millions	3	4	2	5	10
Share price	$100	$ 5	$ 50	$ 8	$ 10

You have been asked to calculate a measure of the industry price-earnings ratio. Discuss the possible ways that you might calculate such a measure. Does changing the method of calculation make a significant difference in the end result?

9. (*a*) "When calculating times interest earned, we average earnings over the past 5 years. This gives a better measure of the company's typical earnings."

(*b*) "For simplicity we just divide current earnings by interest payments."

(*c*) "We fit a trend line to earnings and then measure times interest earned using the current trend value."

(*d*) "We also fit a trend line to earnings and then use that trend to forecast earnings. We then measure times interest earned using forecasted earnings. After all, it is the future, not the past, that any credit analyst is concerned with."

What assumption is each of these speakers making? If you wished to measure the creditworthiness of a business, what would be the best way to compute times interest earned? (Perhaps there are alternatives that none of the speakers has considered.)

10. Look at the segment accounts of International Paper for 1995. For the different segments, calculate three profitability measures: sales to assets, profit mar-

gin, and return on assets. Which appear to be the most profitable parts of the business? Do segments with a high sales-to-assets ratio tend to have a high or low profit margin? Why?

11. Suppose you wish to use financial ratios to estimate the risk of a company's stock. Which of those that we have described in this chapter are likely to be helpful? Can you think of other accounting measures of risk?

12. In 1970 United Airlines bought four new jumbos for $21.8 million each. These planes were written down straight-line over 16 years to a residual value of $0.2 million each. However, they could have been sold in 1986 for about $20 million each.[29] How would the company's financial ratios have changed if it had used a depreciation schedule that more nearly reflected the actual decline in aircraft values?

13. The British food company Ranks Hovis McDougall (RHM) believes that some of its most valuable assets are its brand names. Yet these assets have usually not been shown on the balance sheet. In 1988 RHM changed its accounting policy to include the value of brand names and thereby added £678 million (nearly $1.2 billion) to the balance sheet.[30] Do you think this change would facilitate comparisons between firms?

14. How would the following actions affect a firm's current ratio?
    (*a*) Inventory is sold.
    (*b*) The firm takes out a bank loan to pay its suppliers.
    (*c*) A customer pays its accounts receivable.
    (*d*) The firm uses cash to purchase additional inventories.

15. Sara Togas sells all its output to Federal Stores. The following table shows selected financial data, in millions, for the two firms:

	Sales	Profits	Assets
Federal Stores	$100	$10	$50
Sara Togas	20	4	20

    Calculate the sales-to-assets ratio, the profit margin, and the return on assets for the two firms. Now assume that the two companies merge. If Federal continues to sell goods worth $100 million, how will the three financial ratios change?

16. Take another look at Geomorph Trading's balance sheet in Quiz question 9, and consider the following additional information:

Current Assets		Current Liabilities		Other Liabilities	
Cash	15	Payables	35	Deferred tax	32
Inventories	35	Taxes due	10	Unfunded pensions	22
Receivables	50	Bank loan	15	R&R reserve	16
	100		60		70

---

[29]See M. D. Staunton, *Pricing of Airline Assets and Their Valuation by Securities Markets*, unpublished Ph.D. dissertation, London Business School, 1992.

[30]RHM reasoned that the omission of these assets could lead investors to undervalue the firm and could attract predators.

The "R&R reserve" covers the future costs of removal of an oil pipeline and environmental restoration of the pipeline route.

There are many ways to calculate a debt ratio for Geomorph. Suppose you are evaluating the safety of Geomorph's debt and want a debt ratio for comparison with the ratios of other companies in the same industry. Would you calculate the ratio in terms of total liabilities or total capitalization? What would you include in debt—the bank loan, the deferred tax account, the R&R reserve, the unfunded pension liability? Explain the pros and cons of these choices.

17. How would rapid inflation affect the accuracy and relevance of a manufacturing company's balance sheet and income statement? Does your answer depend on how much debt the company has issued?

18. United Ratios common stock has a dividend yield of 4 percent. Its dividend per share is $2, and it has 10 million shares outstanding. If the market-to-book ratio is 1.5, what is the total book value of the equity?

19. Look up some firms that have been in trouble. Plot the changes over the preceding years in the principal financial ratios. Are there any patterns?

20. International Paper's return on equity is higher than its return on assets. Is this always the case? Explain.

28

Approaches to Financial Planning

A camel looks like an animal designed by a committee. If a firm made all its financial decisions piecemeal, it would end up with a financial camel. Therefore, smart financial managers consider the overall effect of financing and investment decisions. This process is called *financial planning*, and the end result is a *financial plan*.

Financial planning is necessary because investment and financing decisions interact and should not be made independently. In other words, the whole may be more or less than the sum of the parts.

Planning also helps financial managers avoid surprises and think ahead about how they should react to those surprises that *cannot* be avoided. In Chapter 10 we stressed that financial managers are unwilling to treat capital investment proposals as "black boxes." They insist on understanding what makes projects work and what could go wrong with them. They attempt to trace out the possible impact of today's decisions on tomorrow's opportunities. The same approach is, or should be, taken when financing and investment decisions are considered in the aggregate. Without financial planning, the firm itself becomes a black box.

Finally, financial planning helps establish concrete goals to motivate managers and provide standards for measuring performance.

Planning should never be the exclusive preserve of the planners. Unless management is widely involved in the process, it will lack faith in the output. Also, financial plans should be tied in closely to the firm's business plans. A series of financial forecasts has little operational value unless management has thought about the production and marketing decisions which are needed to make those forecasts come about.

Financial planning is not easy to write about—it is the sort of topic that attracts empty generalities or ponderous detail. A full, formal treatment is beyond the scope of this book and probably beyond the capability of its authors. But there are a few specific helpful points we can make. We will first summarize what financial planning involves. Then we will describe the contents of a typical completed financial plan. Finally, we will discuss the use of *financial models* in the planning process.

28-1 WHAT IS FINANCIAL PLANNING?

Financial planning is a *process* of:

1. Analyzing the financing and investment choices open to the firm.

2. Projecting the future consequences of present decisions, in order to avoid surprises and understand the link between present and future decisions.

3. Deciding which alternatives to undertake. (These decisions are embodied in the final financial plan.)

4. Measuring subsequent performance against the goals set in the financial plan.

Of course, there are different kinds of planning. Short-term financial planning is discussed in the next chapter. In short-term planning the *planning horizon* is rarely longer than the next 12 months. The firm wants to make sure that it has enough cash to pay its bills and that short-term borrowing and lending are arranged to the best advantage.

Here we are more concerned with long-term planning, in which a typical horizon is 5 years, although some firms look ahead 10 years or more. For example, it can take at least 10 years for an electric utility to design, obtain approval for, build, and test a major generating plant.

Financial Planning Focuses on the Big Picture

Many of the firm's capital expenditures are proposed by plant managers. But the expenditure decisions must also reflect strategic plans made by senior management. These strategic plans attempt to identify the businesses in which the firm has a real competitive advantage and which should be expanded. They also seek to identify businesses to sell or liquidate as well as those that should be allowed to run down.

Strategic planning involves capital budgeting on a grand scale. Financial planners try to look at the aggregate investment by each line of business and avoid getting bogged down in details. Of course, some projects are large enough to have significant individual impact. For example, Ford committed $6 billion to the development of its self-proclaimed "world car," the Mondeo, and you can safely bet that this project was explicitly analyzed as part of Ford's long-range financial plan.

At the beginning of the planning process the corporate staff might ask each division to submit three alternative business plans covering the next 5 years:

1. A *best-case* or aggressive growth plan calling for heavy capital investment and new products, increased share of existing markets, or entry into new markets.

2. A *normal growth* plan in which the division grows with its markets but not significantly at the expense of its competitors.

3. A plan of *retrenchment* and specialization designed to minimize required capital outlays. This is planning for lean economic times.

Of course, the planners might also look at the opportunities and costs of moving into a wholly new area where the company may be able to exploit its existing strengths. Often they may recommend entering a market for "strategic" reasons—that is, not because the *immediate* investment has positive net present value but because it establishes the firm in the market and creates *options* for possibly valuable follow-up investments. In other words, there is a two-stage decision. At the second stage (the follow-up project) the financial manager faces a standard capital budgeting problem. But at the first stage projects may be valuable primarily for the options they bring with them. A financial manager could value a first-stage project's "strategic value" by using option pricing theory.[1]

Sometimes there are three or more stages. Think of the progress of a technological innovation from its inception in basic research to product development to pilot production and market testing and finally to full-scale commercial production. The decision to produce at commercial scale is a standard capital budgeting problem. The decision to proceed with pilot production and test marketing is like purchasing an option to produce at commercial scale. The commitment of funds to development is like purchasing an option for pilot production and test marketing: the firm acquires an option to purchase an option. The investment in research at the very first stage is like acquiring an option to purchase an option to purchase an option.

Here we will stick our necks out by predicting the increasing use of option pricing theory for formal analysis of these sequential investment decisions. Financial planning eventually will be thought of not as a search for a single investment plan but rather as the management of the portfolio of options held by the firm. This portfolio consists not of traded puts and calls but of *real* options (options to purchase real assets on possibly favorable terms) or options to purchase other real options.[2] Because the firm's long-term future is likely to depend on the options that it acquires today, we would expect planners to take a particular interest in these options.

Planned Financing

Most plans contain a summary of planned financing. This part of the plan should logically include a discussion of dividend policy, because the more the firm pays out, the more capital it will need to find from sources other than retained earnings.

Growing firms will need to pay for investments in plant, equipment, and working capital. A commitment to pay interest on debt may also absorb large amounts of cash. For example, in 1995 Eurotunnel needed to lay its hands on more than $3 million a day simply to pay debt interest. If cash flows from operations do not cover these outflows, the firm will have to raise additional funds.

Some firms need to worry much more than others about raising money. A firm with limited investment opportunities, ample operating cash flow, and a moderate dividend payout accumulates considerable "financial slack" in the form of liquid assets and unused borrowing power. Life is relatively easy for the managers of such firms, and their financing plans are routine. Whether that easy life is in the interests of their stockholders is another matter.

Other firms have to raise capital by selling securities. Naturally, they give careful attention to planning what kinds of securities are to be sold and when. Such firms may also find their financing plans complicated by covenants on their existing debt. For example, electric utility bonds often prohibit the firm from issuing more bonds if interest coverage drops below a certain level. Typically, the minimum level is two times earnings.

---

[1]See the Blitzen Computers example in Section 21-1.

[2]The importance of real options to strategic decisions is emphasized in S. C. Myers, "Finance Theory and Financial Strategy," *Interfaces*, **14**:126–137 (January–February 1984).

> #### Financial Planning Is Not Just Forecasting

Forecasting concentrates on the most likely future outcome. But financial planners are not concerned solely with forecasting. They need to worry about unlikely events as well as likely ones. If you think ahead about what could go wrong, then you may be able to build flexibility into the plan and react faster to trouble if it occurs. Also, financial planning does not attempt to *minimize* risk. Instead, it is a process of deciding which risks to take and which are unnecessary or not worth taking.

Companies have developed a number of ways of looking at these "what if" questions. Some work through the consequences of the plan under the most likely set of circumstances and then use *sensitivity analysis* to vary the assumptions one at a time. For example, they might look at how badly the company would be hit if a policy of aggressive growth coincided with a recession. Other companies might look at the consequences of each business plan under several plausible scenarios.[3] For example, one scenario might envisage high interest rates leading to a slowdown in world economic growth and lower commodity prices. The second scenario might involve a buoyant domestic economy, high inflation, and a weak currency.

> #### The Contents of a Completed Financial Plan

A completed financial plan for a large company is a substantial document. A smaller corporation's plan would have the same elements but less detail and documentation. For the smallest, youngest businesses, the financial plan may be entirely in the financial manager's head. The basic elements of the plans will be similar, however, for firms of any size.

The plan will present pro forma (that is, forecasted) balance sheets, income statements, and statements describing sources and uses of cash. Because these statements embody the firm's financial goals, they may not be strictly unbiased forecasts. The earnings figure in the plan may be somewhere between an honest forecast and the earnings that management *hopes* to achieve.

The plan will also describe planned capital expenditures, usually broken down by category (for example, investment for replacement, for expansion, for new products, for mandated expenditures such as pollution control equipment) and by division or line of business. There will be a narrative description of why these amounts are needed for investment and of the business strategies to be used to reach these financial goals. The descriptions might cover areas such as research and development efforts, steps to improve productivity, design and marketing of new products, pricing strategy, and so on.

These written descriptions record the end result of discussions and negotiations between operating managers, corporate staff, and top management. They ensure that everyone involved in implementing the plan understands what is to be done.[4]

28-2 THREE REQUIREMENTS FOR EFFECTIVE PLANNING

The requirements for effective planning follow from the purposes of planning and the desired end result. Three points deserve emphasis.

---

[3]For a description of the use of different planning scenarios in the Royal Dutch/Shell group, see P. Wack, "Scenarios: Uncharted Waters Ahead," *Harvard Business Review*, **63** (September–October 1985), and "Scenarios: Shooting the Rapids," *Harvard Business Review*, **63** (November–December 1985).

[4]Managers come up with better strategies when they are forced to present them formally and expose them to criticism. Haven't you often found that you didn't *really* understand an issue until you were forced to explain it to someone else?

The firm will never have perfectly accurate forecasts. If it did, there would be less need for planning. Still, the firm must do the best it can.

Forecasting should not be reduced to a mechanical exercise. For example, as we pointed out in Chapter 27, earnings follow roughly a random walk, so naive extrapolation of past earnings growth won't work.

To supplement their judgment, forecasters rely on a variety of data sources and forecasting methods. For example, forecasts of the economic and industry environment may involve use of econometric models which take account of interactions between economic variables. Forecasts of demand will partly reflect these projections of the economic environment, but they may also be based on formal models that marketing specialists have developed for predicting buyer behavior or on recent consumer surveys to which the firm has access.[5]

Because information and expertise may be inconveniently scattered throughout the firm, effective planning requires administrative procedures to ensure that this information is not passed by. Also, many planners reach outside for help. There is a thriving industry of firms that specialize in preparing macroeconomic and industry forecasts for use by corporations.

Inconsistency of forecasts is a potential problem because planners draw on information from many sources. Forecasted sales may be the sum of separate forecasts made by managers of several business units. Left to their own devices, these managers may make different assumptions about inflation, growth of the national economy, availability of raw materials, and so on. Achieving consistency is particularly hard for vertically integrated firms, where the raw material for one business unit is the output of another. For example, an oil company's refining division might plan to produce more gasoline than the marketing division plans to sell. The oil company's planners would be expected to uncover this inconsistency and align the plans of the two divisions.

It is tempting to conduct planning in a vacuum and to ignore the fact that the firm's competitors are developing their own plans. For example, your ability to implement an aggressive growth plan and increase market share depends on what the competition is likely to do. In fact, we can generalize by rephrasing a recommendation from Chapter 11: *When you are presented with a set of corporate forecasts, do not accept them at face value. Probe behind the forecasts and try to identify the economic model on which they are based.*

In the end the financial manager has to judge which plan is best. We would like to tell you exactly how to make this choice, but we can't. There is no model or procedure that encompasses all the complexity and intangibles encountered in financial planning.

As a matter of fact, there never will be one. This bold statement is based on Brealey and Myers's third law:[6]

- *Axiom:* The supply of unsolved problems is infinite.

- *Axiom:* The number of unsolved problems that humans can hold in their minds is at any time limited to 10.

- *Law:* Therefore, in any field there will always be 10 problems which can be addressed but which have no formal solution.

---

[5]For an interesting example of how forecasting is organized in one company, see R. N. Dino, R. E. Riley, and P. G. Yatrakis, "The Role of Forecasting in Corporate Strategy: The Xerox Experience," *Journal of Forecasting,* **1**:335–348 (October–December 1982).

[6]The second law is presented in Section 12-2.

You will note that the last chapter of this book discusses 10 unsolved problems in finance.

Financial planners have to face the unsolved issues and cope as best they can by judgment. Take dividend policy, for example. At the end of Chapter 16 we were unable to say for sure whether a generous dividend policy was a good or bad thing, though we were able to identify some of the issues that managers need to consider. Nevertheless, financial planners have to *decide* on the dividend policy.

You sometimes hear managers stating corporate goals in terms of accounting numbers. They might say, "Our objective is to achieve an annual sales growth of 20 percent," or "We want a 25 percent return on book equity and a profit margin of 10 percent." On the surface such objectives don't make sense. Shareholders want to be richer, not to have the satisfaction of a 10 percent profit margin. Also, a goal that is stated in terms of accounting ratios is nonoperational unless it is translated back into what the statement means for business decisions. For example, what does a 10 percent profit margin imply—higher prices, lower costs, a move into new, high-margin products, or increased vertical integration?

So why do managers define objectives in this way? In part such goals may be a mutual exhortation to try harder, like singing the company song before work. But we suspect that managers are often using a code to communicate real concerns. For example, the goal to increase sales rapidly may reflect managers' belief that increased market share is needed to achieve scale economies, or a target profit margin may be a way of saying that the firm has been pursuing sales growth at the expense of margins.

The danger is that everyone may forget the code and the accounting targets may be seen as goals in themselves.

Watching the Financial Plan Unfold

Long-term plans have an annoying habit of falling out of date almost as soon as they are made. They are then left to gather dust. Of course, you can always restart the planning process from scratch, but it may help if you can think ahead of time about how to revise your forecasts in the light of unexpected events. For example, suppose that profits in the first 6 months turn out to be 10 percent below forecast. Since profits follow roughly a random walk, they don't generally bounce back after a fall. Unless you know that there were some temporary influences at work, you should revise your profit forecasts for later years by reducing them 10 percent.

We have mentioned that long-term plans are also used as a benchmark to judge subsequent performance. But performance appraisals have little value unless you also take into account the business background against which they were achieved. If you know how a downturn in the economy is likely to throw you off plan, then you have a standard against which to judge your performance during such a downturn.

28-3 FINANCIAL PLANNING MODELS

Financial planners often use a financial planning model to help them explore the consequences of alternative financial strategies. These models range from general-purpose ones, not much more complicated than the illustration presented later in this section, to models containing literally hundreds of equations and interacting variables.

Most large firms have a financial model or have access to one. Sometimes they may use more than one—perhaps a detailed model integrating capital budgeting and operational planning, a simpler model focusing on the aggregate impacts of financing strategy, and a special model for evaluating mergers.

The reason for the popularity of such models is a simple and practical one. They support the financial planning process by making it easier and cheaper to construct pro forma financial statements. The models automate an important part of planning that used to be boring, time-consuming, and labor-intensive.

Programming these financial planning models used to consume large amounts of computer time and high-priced talent. These days standard spreadsheet programs are regularly used to solve quite complex financial planning problems.

Executive Fruit's Financial Model

Table 28-1 shows year-end 1995 financial statements for Executive Fruit Company. Earnings before interest and taxes were 10 percent of sales revenue. Net earnings were $90,000 after payment of taxes and 9 percent interest on $400,000 outstanding debt. The company paid out 60 percent of its earnings as dividends. Executive Fruit's operating cash flow was not sufficient to pay the dividend and also to provide the cash needed for investment and expand net working capital. Therefore $64,000 of common stock was issued. The firm ended the year with debt equal to 40 percent of total capitalization.

Now suppose that you are asked to prepare pro forma statements for Executive Fruit Company for 1996. You are told to assume business as usual *except* that (1) sales and operating costs are expected to be up 30 percent over 1995, and (2) common stock is not to be issued again. You interpret "business as usual" to mean that (3) interest rates will remain at 9 percent, (4) the firm will stick to its traditional 60 percent dividend payout, and (5) net working capital and fixed assets will increase by 30 percent to support the larger sales volume.

These assumptions lead to the pro forma statements shown in Table 28-2. Note that projected net income is up by 23 percent, to $111,000, which is heartening. But a glance at the sources and uses of funds statement shows that $404,000 has to be raised for additional working capital and for replacement and expansion of fixed capital.[7] Executive Fruit's generous dividend payout and its decision against another stock issue mean that $255,600 has to be raised by additional borrowing. The result is an increase in the book debt ratio to over 50 percent and a reduction in the pretax interest coverage ratio to 4.8. (Earnings before interest and taxes divided by interest is 281/59 = 4.8.)

To produce Table 28-2, you forecasted sales, costs, and the capital needed to generate the increased sales. Given the payout ratio, these forecasts determined the amount of external finance that the firm needs. Finally, the decision not to issue new equity ensured that the need for funds had to be satisfied by an issue of debt. Thus debt was the *balancing item*. This did not have to be the case. For example, we could have limited the amount of external financing and asked how much Executive Fruit needed to retain in order to finance its growth plan. In this case the dividend payment would have been the balancing item. Or we could have specified the amount of external financing and the dividend policy and then looked at how rapidly Executive Fruit could grow.

We have spared you the trouble of actually calculating the figures necessary for Table 28-2. The calculations do not take more than a few minutes for this simple ex-

---

[7]Executive Fruit's existing fixed capital is assumed to depreciate by $104,000 in 1996. Thus it has to invest $104,000 simply to maintain the net book value of its fixed assets. Total investment is $104,000 plus the growth in net fixed assets required by the increased sales volume. Incidentally, we realize that requiring the net book value of fixed assets to grow in lockstep with sales volume is an arbitrary and probably unrealistic assumption. We adopt it only to keep things simple.

TABLE 28-1

• •

1995 financial statements for Executive Fruit Company (figures in thousands of dollars)

Income Statement

Revenue (REV)	2,160
Cost of goods sold (CGS)	1,944
Earnings before interest and taxes	216
Interest (INT)*	36
Earnings before taxes	180
Tax at 50% (TAX)	90
Net income (NET)	90

Sources and Uses of Funds

Sources:	
Net income (NET)	90
Depreciation (DEP)†	80
Operating cash flow	170
Borrowing (ΔD)	0
Stock issues (SI)	64
Total sources	234
Uses:	
Increase in net working capital (ΔNWC)	40
Investment (INV)	140
Dividends (DIV)	54
Total uses	234

Balance Sheet

	1995	1994	Change
Assets:			
Net working capital (NWC)‡	200	160	+ 40
Fixed assets (FA)	800	740	+ 60§
Total assets	1,000	900	+100
Liabilities:			
Debt (D)	400	400	0
Book equity (E)	600	500	+100¶
Total liabilities	1,000	900	+100

*Interest is 9 percent of the $400 in outstanding debt.
†Depreciation is a noncash expense. Therefore we add it back to net income to find operating cash flow.
‡Net working capital is defined as current assets less current liabilities.
§The increase in the book value of fixed assets equals investment less depreciation. Change in FA = ΔFA = INV − DEP = 140 − 80 = 60.
¶Book equity increases by retained earnings less dividends plus stock issues. Change in E = ΔE = NET − DIV + SI = 90 − 54 + 64 = 100.

TABLE 28-2

1996 pro forma financial statements for Executive Fruit Company (figures in thousands of dollars)

Income Statement

Revenue (REV)	2,808	(+30%)
Cost of goods sold (CGS)	2,527	
Earnings before interest and taxes	281	
Interest (INT)	59	
Earnings before tax	222	
Tax (TAX)	111	
Net income (NET)	111	(+23%)

Sources and Uses of Funds

Sources:	
Net income (NET)	111
Depreciation (DEP)	104
Operating cash flow	215
Borrowing (ΔD)	255.6
Stock issues (SI)	0
Total sources	470.6

Uses:		
Increase in net working capital (ΔNWC)	60	(+30%)
Investment (INV)	344	
Dividends (DIV)	66.6	
Total uses	470.6	

Balance Sheet

	1996	1995	Change
Assets:			
Net working capital (NWC)	260	200	+ 60
Fixed assets (FA)	1,040	800	+240
Total assets	1,300	1,000	+300
Liabilities:			
Debt (D)	655.6	400	+255.6
Book equity (E)	644.4	600	+ 44.4
Total liabilities	1,300.0	1,000	+300.0

Assumptions:

CGS	Assumed to remain at 90 percent of REV.
INT	Nine percent of debt (D). This assumes all new debt is taken out early in 1996 so that a full year's interest must be paid.
TAX	Tax rate remains at 50 percent.
DEP	Remains at 10 percent of FA. This assumes all new investment is made early in 1996 so that a full year's depreciation is taken.
ΔD	Balancing item. Executive Fruit must borrow $255.6 to cover planned expenditures.
SI	Executive Fruit's management has decided not to issue stock in 1996, therefore SI = 0.
ΔNWC	Net working capital expands in proportion to the increase in REV.
INV, FA	Required fixed assets FA are assumed to expand in proportion to the growth in sales. Investment must therefore cover depreciation plus the increase in FA.
DIV	Payout stays at 60 percent of NET.
E	The increase in equity equals retained earnings (NET − DIV) plus stock issues (SI). NET − DIV + SI = 111 − 66.6 + 0 = 44.4

ample, *provided* you set up the calculations correctly and make no arithmetic mistakes. If that time requirement seems trivial, remember that in reality you probably would be asked for four similar sets of statements covering each year from 1996 to 1999. Probably you would be asked for alternative projections under different assumptions (e.g., a 25 instead of 30 percent growth rate of revenue) or different financial strategies (e.g., freezing dividends at their 1995 level of $54,000). This would require lots of work. Building a model and letting the computer toil in your place have obvious attractions.

Table 28-3 shows a 15-equation model for Executive Fruit. There is one equation for each variable needed to construct pro forma statements like Tables 28-1 and 28-2. Of the equations, six are accounting identities ensuring that the income statement adds up, the balance sheet balances, and sources of funds match uses. The functions of the equations are as follows: (1) and (8) set revenues and stock issues equal to values specified by the model user. Equations (2), (12), and (13) specify cost of goods sold, net working capital, and fixed assets as constant proportions of sales. The remaining equations relate interest to debt outstanding (3), taxes to income (4), depreciation to fixed assets (6), and dividends to net income (11).

The *input* for our model comprises nine items: a sales forecast (REV); a decision on the amount of stock to be issued (SI); and seven coefficients, a_1 through a_7, tying cost of goods sold to revenue, interest payments to borrowing, and so on. Take the coefficient a_5, for example. In developing Table 28-2, we assumed dividends to be 60 percent of net income. In the model this would be expressed as $a_5 = .6$.

TABLE 28-3

Financial model for Executive Fruit Company

Income Statement Equations

(1)	REV = forecast by model user	
(2)	$CGS = a_1 REV$	
(3)	$INT = a_2 D$	(a_2 = interest rate)
(4)	$TAX = a_3(REV - CGS - INT)$	(a_3 = tax rate)
(5)	$NET = REV - CGS - INT - TAX$	(accounting identity)

Sources and Uses Statement Equations

(6)	$DEP = a_4 FA$	
(7)	$\Delta D = \Delta NWC + INV + DIV -$ $\quad NET - DEP - SI$	(accounting identity)
(8)	SI = value specified by model user	
(9)	$\Delta NWC = NWC - NWC(-1)$	(accounting identity)
(10)	$INV = DEP + FA - FA(-1)$	(accounting identity)
(11)	$DIV = a_5 NET$	(a_5 = dividend payout ratio)

Balance Sheet Equations

(12)	$NWC = a_6 REV$	
(13)	$FA = a_7 REV$	
(14)	$D = \Delta D + D(-1)$	(accounting identity)
(15)	$E = E(-1) + NET - DIV + SI$	(accounting identity)

Note: "(-1)" means a number taken from the previous year's balance sheet. These numbers are constants, not variables.

Table 28-4 shows that our model works. In the table we insert the values for REV, SI, and a_1 through a_7 that correspond to the assumptions underlying Table 28-2. And we get the right answers, confirming that the model can be used to forecast Executive Fruit's financial results. All we would have to do is give the computer the 9 input items, tell it to solve the 15 simultaneous equations, and instruct it to print out the results in the format of Table 28-2.

····················
Pitfalls in Model Design

The Executive Fruit Model is too simple for practical application. You probably have already thought of several ways to improve it—by keeping track of the number of outstanding shares, for example, and printing out earnings and dividends per share.

TABLE 28-4
··

Model forecast for Table 28-2

Income Statement

(1) REV = forecast = 2,808
(2) CGS = .9 REV   (a_1 = .9)
     = .9(2,808) = 2,527
(3) INT = .09D   (a_2 = .09)
     = .09(655.6) = 59
(4) TAX = .5(REV − CGS − INT)   (a_3 = .5)
     = .5(2,808 − 2,527 − 59) = 111
(5) NET = REV − CGS − INT − TAX
     = 2,808 − 2,527 − 59 − 111 = 111

Sources and Uses of Funds Statement

(6) DEP = .1FA   (a_4 = .1)
     = .1(1,040) = 104
(7) ΔD = ΔNWC + INV + DIV − NET − DEP − SI
     = 60 + 344 + 66.6 − 111 − 104 − 0 = 255.6
(8) SI = specified as 0
(9) ΔNWC = NWC − NWC(−1)
     = 260 − 200 = 60
(10) INV = DEP + FA − FA(−1)
     = 104 + 1,040 − 800 = 344
(11) DIV = .6NET   (a_5 = .6)
     = .6(111) = 66.6

Balance Sheet

(12) NWC = .093REV   (a_6 = .093)
     = .093(2,808) = 260
(13) FA = .37REV   (a_7 = .37)
     = .37(2,808) = 1,040
(14) D = ΔD + D(−1)
     = 255.6 + 400 = 655.6
(15) E = E(−1) + NET − DIV + SI
     = 600 + 111 − 66.6 − 0 = 644.4

Or you might want to distinguish short-term lending and borrowing opportunities, now buried in net working capital.

But beware: There is always the temptation to make a model bigger and more detailed. You may end up with an exhaustive model that is too cumbersome for routine use. Exhaustive detail gets in the way of the intended use of corporate planning models, namely, to project the financial consequences of a variety of strategies and assumptions. The fascination of detail, if you give in to it, distracts attention from crucial decisions like stock issues and dividend policy and allocation of capital by business area. Sometimes decisions like these end up being "wired into" the model, just as the Executive Fruit model arbitrarily sets dividends equal to a constant proportion of net income.

....

There Is No Finance in Corporate Financial Models

Why do we say that there is no finance in corporate financial models? The first reason is that most such models incorporate an accountant's view of the world. They are designed to forecast accounting statements, and their equations naturally embody the accounting conventions employed by the firm. Consequently, the models do not emphasize the tools of financial analysis: incremental cash flow, present value, market risk, and so on.[8]

Second, corporate financial models produce no signposts pointing toward optimal financial decisions. They do not even tell which alternatives are worth examining. All this is left to their users.

Brealey and Myers's third law implies that no model can find the best of all financial strategies. However, it is possible to build linear programming models that help search for the best financial strategy subject to specified assumptions and constraints. These "intelligent" financial planning models should prove more flexible for sensitivity analysis and more effective in screening alternative financial strategies. Ideally they will suggest strategies that would never occur to the unaided financial manager.

The appendix to this chapter sketches a linear programming model based on the modern finance theory presented in this book.

28-4 EXTERNAL FINANCING AND GROWTH

We started this chapter by noting that financial plans force managers to be consistent in their goals for growth, investment, and financing. Before leaving the topic of financial planning, therefore, we should look at the relationship between a firm's growth objectives and its requirements for external financing.

Recall that Executive Fruit starts with $1,000,000 of fixed assets and working capital. It forecasts sales growth of 30 percent, which will result in retentions of

$$\text{Net income} - \text{dividends} = \$111,000 - \$66,600 = \$44,000$$

However, the higher sales volume also requires a 30 percent addition to assets. Thus

$$\text{New investment} = \text{growth rate} \times \text{initial assets}$$
$$\$300,000 = .30 \times \$1,000,000$$

Part of the funds needed to pay for the new assets is provided by the retained earnings. The remainder must come from external financing. Therefore,

---

[8] Of course, there is no reason that the manager can't use the output to calculate the present value of the firm (given some assumptions about growth beyond the planning period), and this is sometimes done.

$$\text{Required external financing} = \text{new investment} - \text{retained earnings}$$
$$= \$300,000 - \$44,400 = \$255,600$$

The amount of external financing that Executive Fruit requires depends on the projected growth. Each $100 of additional sales increases retained earnings by $6.85 but requires an additional $46.30 of new investment. The faster the firm grows, the more it needs to invest and therefore the more it needs to raise new capital. This is illustrated by the sloping line in Figure 28-1. At low growth rates, Executive Fruit generates more funds than necessary for expansion. In this sense, its requirement for further external funds is negative. It may choose to use its surplus to pay off some of its debt or buy back its stock. In fact the vertical intercept in Figure 28-1, at zero growth, is the negative of retained earnings. When growth is zero, no funds are needed for expansion, so all retained earnings are surplus.

As the projected growth rate increases, more funds are needed to pay for the necessary investments. Therefore, the plot in Figure 28-1 is upward-sloping. For high rates of growth Executive Fruit must issue new securities to pay for the investments. The sloping line crosses the horizontal axis at a growth rate of 3.8 percent. At this point external financing is zero; Executive Fruit is growing as fast as possible without raising new capital. This is called the *internal growth rate*. The growth rate is internal in the sense that it can be maintained without resort to additional sources of capital.

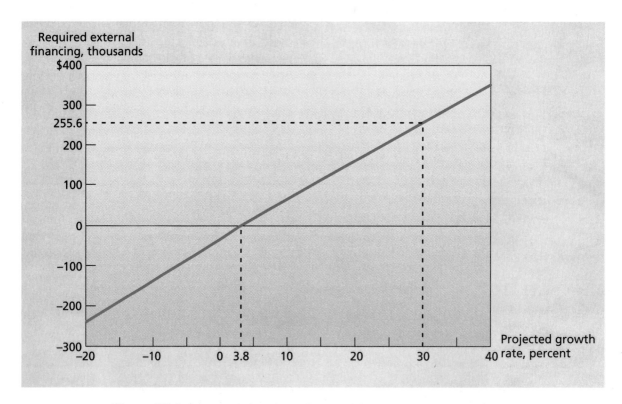

Figure 28-1 Executive Fruit's required external financing increases with the projected growth rate. Forecast growth of 30 percent requires external financing of $255,600. With no external financing Executive can grow by only 3.8 percent. This is the internal growth rate.

Notice that if we set required external financing to zero, we can solve for the internal growth rate as

$$\text{Internal growth rate} = \frac{\text{retained earnings}}{\text{assets}}$$

Thus the firm's rate of growth without additional sources of capital will equal the ratio of retained earnings to assets.

We can gain more insight into what determines the internal growth rate by multiplying the top and bottom of the expression for internal growth by *net income* and *equity*, as follows:

$$\text{Internal growth rate} = \frac{\text{retained earnings}}{\text{net income}} \times \frac{\text{net income}}{\text{equity}} \times \frac{\text{equity}}{\text{assets}}$$

$$= \text{plowback ratio} \times \text{return on equity} \times \frac{\text{equity}}{\text{assets}}$$

A firm can achieve a higher growth rate without raising external capital if (1) it plows back a high proportion of its earnings, (2) it has a high return on equity (ROE), and (3) it has a low debt-to-asset ratio.[9]

Instead of focusing on the maximum growth rate that can be supported without *any* external financing, firms may be interested in the growth rate that can be sustained without additional *equity* issues. Of course, if the firm is able to issue enough debt, virtually any growth rate can be financed. It makes more sense to assume that the firm has settled on an optimal capital structure which it will maintain even as equity is augmented by retained earnings. The firm issues only enough debt to keep its debt ratio constant. The *sustainable growth rate* is the highest growth rate the firm can maintain without increasing its financial leverage. It turns out that the sustainable growth rate depends only on the plowback rate and return on equity:[10]

---

[9]Notice that the internal growth rate does not stay constant over time. If the proportion of debt in the balance sheet declines, retained earnings make proportionately larger additions to the firm's assets and the internal growth rate increases.

[10]Here is a proof:

$$\text{Required equity issues} = \text{growth rate} \times \text{assets} - \text{retained earnings} - \text{new debt issues}$$

We find the sustainable growth rate by setting required new equity issues to zero and solving for growth:

$$\text{Sustainable growth rate} = \frac{\text{retained earnings} + \text{new debt issues}}{\text{assets}}$$

$$= \frac{\text{retained earnings} + \text{new debt issues}}{\text{debt} + \text{equity}}$$

However, because both debt and equity are growing at the same rate, new debt issues must equal retained earnings multiplied by the ratio of debt to equity, *D/E*. Therefore, we can write the sustainable growth as

$$\text{Sustainable growth rate} = \frac{\text{retained earnings} \times (1 + D/E)}{\text{debt} + \text{equity}}$$

$$= \frac{\text{retained earnings} \times (1 + D/E)}{\text{equity} \times (1 + D/E)} = \frac{\text{retained earnings}}{\text{equity}}$$

$$= \frac{\text{retained earnings}}{\text{net income}} \times \frac{\text{net income}}{\text{equity}} = \text{plowback} \times \text{ROE}$$

Sustainable growth rate = plowback ratio × return on equity

We first encountered this formula in Chapter 4, where we used it to help value the firm's equity.

These simple formulas remind us that financial plans need to be consistent. Firms may grow rapidly in the short term by relying on debt finance, but such growth cannot be maintained without incurring excessive debt levels.

28-5   SUMMARY

Most firms take financial planning seriously and devote considerable resources to it. What do they get for this effort?

The tangible product of the planning process is a financial plan describing the firm's financial strategy and projecting its future consequences by means of pro forma balance sheets, income statements, and statements of sources and uses of funds. The plan establishes financial goals and is a benchmark for evaluating subsequent performance. Usually it also describes why that strategy was chosen and how the plan's financial goals are to be achieved.

The plan is the end result. The process that produces the plan is valuable in its own right. First, planning forces the financial manager to consider the combined effects of all the firm's investment and financing decisions. This is important because these decisions interact and should not be made independently.

Second, planning, if it is done right, forces the financial manager to think about events that could upset the firm's progress and to devise strategies to be held in reserve for counterattack when unhappy surprises occur. Planning is more than forecasting, because forecasting deals with the most likely outcome. Planners also have to think about events that may occur even though they are unlikely.

To repeat, financial planning is a *process* of:

1. Analyzing the interactions of the financing and investment choices open to the firm.

2. Projecting the future consequences of present decisions, in order to avoid surprises and understand the links between present and future decisions.

3. Deciding which alternatives to undertake. (These decisions are embodied in the final financial plan.)

4. Measuring subsequent performance against the goals set in the financial plan.

In this chapter we discussed long-range or "strategic" planning, in which the *planning horizon* is usually 5 years or more. This kind of planning deals with aggregate decisions; for example, the planner would worry about whether the broadax division should go for heavy capital investment and rapid growth, but not whether the division should choose machine tool A versus tool B. In fact, planners must be constantly on guard against the fascination of detail, because giving in to it means slighting crucial issues like investment strategy, debt policy, and the choice of a target dividend payout ratio.

There is no theory or model that leads straight to *the* optimal financial strategy. Consequently, financial planning proceeds by trial and error. Many different strategies may be projected under a range of assumptions about the future before one strategy is finally chosen.

The dozens of separate projections that may be made during this trial-and-error process generate a heavy load of arithmetic and paperwork. Firms have responded by developing corporate planning models to forecast the financial consequences of specified strategies and assumptions about the future. These models are efficient and widely used. But remember that there is no finance in them. Their primary purpose is to produce accounting statements. The models do not search for the best financial strategy but only trace out the consequences of a strategy specified by the model user.

One of the most difficult aspects of deciding which strategies to examine closely is that the best strategy may not be an obvious one. In the appendix to this chapter we describe a linear programming model which is based on the concepts of finance rather than accounting and which does help the financial manager search for the best financial plan.

APPENDIX: LONGER

This appendix is a brief introduction to LONGER, a linear programming model devised by Myers and Pogue to support financial planners.[11] Other applications of linear programming to financial planning are described in the articles listed in "Further Reading" below.

LONGER differs from the typical corporate financial model described in this chapter in two important respects. First, it *optimizes:* it calculates the *best* financial plan, given specified assumptions and constraints. The typical planning model merely *projects* the consequences of a financial strategy chosen by the model user. Second, the model is based on finance theory rather than accounting. It assumes well-functioning capital markets. Consequently, its objective is to maximize the firm's net present value. It relies on value additivity and the Modigliani-Miller theory that the chief advantage of debt is the tax shields created by debt interest payments.

LONGER will be introduced by a simple numerical example. Then extensions of the model are briefly described. The final part of this appendix shows how the shadow prices generated as part of LONGER's solution are interpreted. The shadow prices are an easy way to understand *adjusted present value* (APV), which measures the value of capital projects which have important financing side effects. APV and its practical implications were covered more fully in Chapter 19. This appendix should give a deeper appreciation of the APV method and the assumptions underlying it.

....
Example[12]

Consider a firm which has to decide how much to invest or borrow in the coming year. Let:

x = new investment, in millions of dollars (We assume for simplicity that the firm has only one project.)
y = new borrowing, in millions of dollars

Also, assume that:

---

[11]S. C. Myers and G. A. Pogue, "A Programming Approach to Corporate Financial Management," *Journal of Finance*, **29**:579–599 (May 1974).

[12]This example is based on one presented by Myers and Pogue, op. cit.

1. Available investment opportunities can absorb $1 million at most. The investments generate a perpetual stream of after-tax cash flows. Let the expected average value of these flows be C. In this case $C = .09x$; thus the project offers a 9 percent internal rate of return.

2. Assume that the market will capitalize the returns at the rate $r = .10$. Thus, if all-equity financing is used, these assets generate a net present value of $-\$.10$ per dollar invested $(-x + .09x/.10 = -.1x)$.

3. The firm's policy is to limit new debt to 40 percent of new investment.

4. The firm has $800,000 in cash available.

5. Any excess cash is paid out in dividends.

6. The additions to debt and equity are expected to be permanent.

For simplicity we begin with the Modigliani-Miller valuation formula for the firm.[13] If the firm does nothing (x and $y = 0$), then V will be given by

$$V = V_0 + T_c D$$

where V_0 = market value of firm's *existing* assets if they were all-equity-financed
T_c = marginal corporate income tax rate (.5 in this example)
D = amount of debt *already* outstanding, excluding any borrowing for new investments

The amount $T_c D$ is the present value of the tax shields generated by the outstanding debt, assuming the debt is fixed and permanent.

For our example,

$$V = V_0 + .5D - .1x + .5y$$

Now V_0 and D are fixed and therefore not relevant to the choice of x and y. Therefore we can just maximize the quantity $-.1x + .5y$, subject to constraints on the amount invested ($x \leq 1$), the amount of debt issued ($y \leq .4x$), and the balance of sources and uses of funds ($x \leq y + .8$).

THE SOLUTION.   This is the linear programming problem depicted in Figure 28-2. First look at the shaded area representing the set of feasible solutions. The feasible region is below the line $x = 1$ because the firm's investment opportunity will absorb $1 million at most. It is below the line $x = .8 + y$ because the amount invested is limited to cash on hand ($.8 million) plus additional borrowing. It is above and to the left of the line $y = .4x$ because new debt is limited to 40 percent of new investment.

Now look at the dashed line in Figure 28-2. It shows different combinations of x and y that would produce the same increase in firm value (i.e., they give the same value for $-.1x + .5y$). We could also have drawn a series of parallel dashed lines. Those to the left would represent lower increases in firm value (i.e., lower values of $-.1x + .5y$). Those to the right would represent higher increases in firm value. The dashed line in Figure 28-2 shows the greatest feasible increase in firm value, given the constraints.

The firm does not want to invest (because NPV $= -\$.10$ per dollar invested), but it does want to borrow, and in order to borrow it has to invest. Thus, firm value is maximized when $x = 1$, $y = .4$. The firm invests and borrows as much as it can.

[13]See Section 18-1.

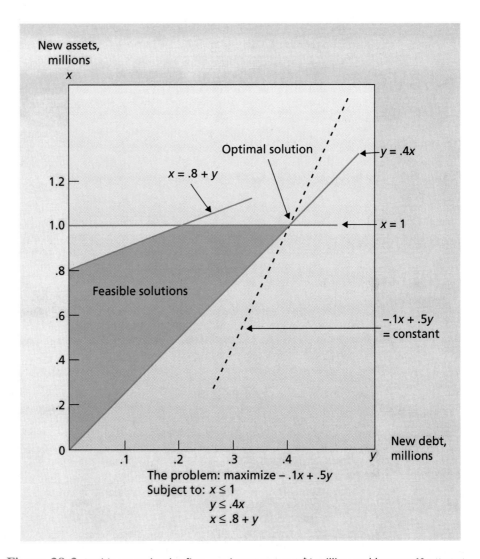

Figure 28-2 In this example, the firm can invest at most $1 million and borrow 40 percent of new investment. Funds for the new investment must come from existing cash ($.8 million) or new borrowing. The investment is not attractive in its own right (NPV = −$.1x), but the firm is willing to invest in order to borrow because the tax shields created by borrowing outweigh the net loss in value attributable to the new investment.

However, note that the constraint $x \le .8 + y$ is not binding at the optimal solution. The firm borrows $200,000 more than it needs for investment. Thus it has $200,000 available for dividends.

Why does the optimal solution call for investing in a project with a negative net present value? The reason is that the project allows the firm to issue more debt, and the value of tax savings generated by the debt more than offsets the investment's inadequate return. (In fact, the optimal solution remains $x = 1.0$, $y = .4$ so long as the investment generates more than −$.20 per dollar invested. If it generates less than that, $-\$.30$, for example, the solution becomes $x = y = 0$.) The debt capacity constraint thus makes financing and investment decisions interdependent.

EFFECTS OF DIVIDEND POLICY.   The sources-uses constraint is not binding in the example, and therefore does not create an interaction of financing and investment decisions. However, what if it is binding? What if the firm has, say, only $500,000 cash on hand?

At first glance the effect is to change the sources-uses constraint to $x \le .5 + y$, which changes the optimal solution to $x = \frac{5}{6}$, $y = \frac{1}{3}$. However, if we consider dividend policy, then we should also allow new issues of equity. The constraint should really be

$$x + \text{DIV} \le .5 + y + \text{SI}$$

where DIV and SI are dividends paid and equity issued in millions. If dividend policy is irrelevant, then DIV and SI have no effect in the objective function, and the constraint itself is irrelevant. Thus, the optimal solution remains at $x = 1$, $y = .4$. The firm must make a $100,000 stock issue, but this is a mere detail once the investment and borrowing decisions are made.

However, in practice there would be transaction costs associated with the stock issue. These costs would have to be subtracted from the objective function, and the sources-uses constraint would become relevant and binding. The solution values for x and y will clearly be affected if the transaction cost is large enough.

Thus, the sources-uses constraint becomes important only if there are transaction costs to security issues or if dividend policy matters for other reasons.

Extending the Model

The example we have just examined was limited to two variables by our goal of presenting it graphically on the two dimensions of the printed page. But the computer does not need a picture like Figure 28-2 to solve a linear program. We can extend LONGER to a practical level of detail by adding variables and constraints.

We have already referred to one extension. Suppose that the firm can pay dividends or issue common stock but that cash available is cut to $.5 million. The linear program becomes

■ Maximize: $-.1x + .5y + a\text{DIV} + b\text{SI}$
■ Subject to: $x \le 1$
                       $y \le .4x$
                       $x + \text{DIV} \le .5 + y + \text{SI}$

If dividend policy is irrelevant, then both a and b are set at zero. But in practice b would have to be negative to reflect the transaction costs of a stock issue. And a might be positive, negative, or zero depending on your position on the dividend controversy (see Chapter 16).

Now suppose that there is a second investment opportunity to invest up to $2 million in a project offering $.12 of NPV per dollar invested. However, the performance of project 2 is less predictable than project 1's performance, and so the firm is willing to borrow only 20 percent of the amount invested in project 2. Our model now becomes

■ Maximize: $-.1x_1 + .12x_2 + .5y + a\text{DIV} + b\text{SI}$

■ Subject to: $x_1 \le 1$
$x_2 \le 2$
$y \le .4x_1 + .2x_2$
$x_1 + x_2 + \text{DIV} \le .5 + y + \text{SI}$

Because present values add, we can include as many projects as we like without upsetting the linear form of the objective. Moreover, there is no need for included projects to have the same risk or time pattern of cash flows. There is nothing wrong with setting an office building alongside a wildcat oil well, so long as you can come up with a net present value for each.

If we introduce projects with irregular patterns of cash flow over time, we would naturally want to allow borrowing to vary period by period. Suppose that the firm has a 5-year planning horizon. Then we could replace the debt variable y with five new variables $y_1, y_2, \ldots, y_5$, where y_t is planned total borrowing for year t. This naturally suggests that dividends and stock issues should be allowed to vary over time also. Our objective function becomes:

■ Maximize: $-.1x_1 + .12x_2$
$+ c_1y_1 + c_2y_2 + \cdots + c_5y_5$
$+ a_1\text{DIV}_1 + a_2\text{DIV}_2 + \cdots + a_5\text{DIV}_5$
$+ b_1\text{SI}_1 + b_2\text{SI}_2 + \cdots + b_5\text{SI}_5$

Also, we will now need twelve constraints: two limiting the amount that can be invested in each project, five limiting the amount that can be borrowed in each of the 5 years covered by the financial plan, and five constraints ensuring that planned uses of funds do not exceed planned sources in any year.

Still more constraints might be added. The financial manager might wish to try to avoid any planned cut in dividends, for example. This would call for five more constraints:

■ $\text{DIV}_1 \ge$ dividends in period 0
■ $\text{DIV}_2 \ge \text{DIV}_1$
■ $\text{DIV}_3 \ge \text{DIV}_2$
■ $\text{DIV}_4 \ge \text{DIV}_3$
■ $\text{DIV}_5 \ge \text{DIV}_4$

Some firms might require that their financial plan generate a steady growth in reported (book) earnings. Suppose that the target growth rate is g. Then we would need five more constraints of the form $Z_t \ge (1 + g)Z_{t-1}$, where Z_t represents forecasted earnings in year t. The variable Z_t would be determined by the other decision variables in the programming model.

But we must immediately add a caveat: Any constraint on acceptable *book* earnings, as opposed to economic earnings, raises difficult issues. Should the firm be willing to sacrifice present value just to achieve regular growth in reported earnings? If capital markets are efficient, investors ought to be able to look through any fluctuations of short-run earnings to the true, underlying value of the firm. If so, any constraint on earnings is superfluous at best.

Constraints on the growth of book earnings might perhaps be useful for keeping track of how pursuit of present value affects reported earnings. It may be that the financial plan can be changed to generate a pretty earnings pattern. If there is real conflict between value and book earnings, comparing solutions with and without this constraint will at least awaken financial managers to the cost of that pretty pattern.[14]

There are several other items of optional equipment that most might wish to add to LONGER, but we will stop at this point. You may wish to refer to Myers and Pogue's paper and the other suggested readings for the full story.

Comparison of LONGER with the Typical Corporate Planning Model

A full-scale linear programming model for financial planning would become formidably complex, but no more so than a typical simulation model.[15] The two models applied to the same firm would have approximately the same number of variables, and the number of constraints included in LONGER would about match the number of equations in the simulation model. But the input requirements for LONGER would be greater because an objective function must be specified. In return, LONGER allows the planner to screen all feasible financial strategies, to reject the inferior ones automatically, and to identify the best strategy consistent with the assumptions and constraints embodied in the model.

However, linear programming models do not automate the *decisions* required by the financial plan. No model can capture all the issues that the financial manager must face. Nor would access to an optimization model change the trial-and-error process of developing a financial plan; it only promises to make the process somewhat more efficient. The optimum plan generated by any run of LONGER does no more than reflect the assumptions and constraints specified by the model user, who will naturally explore a variety of assumptions and constraints before reaching a final decision.[16]

Shadow Prices, or Marginal Costs

The solution to any linear program includes a shadow price, or marginal cost, for each constraint. There are three constraints in the simple numerical example introduced at the start of this appendix, and therefore three shadow prices:

Constraint	Shadow Price	Explanation
Limit on investment $(x \leq 1)$	.1	Project NPV is $-.1x$. But investment supports $.4x$ in debt worth $\$.50$ per dollar borrowed: $-.1x + .4(.5x) = +.1x$.
Limit on debt $(y \leq .4x)$	.5	$\$1$ of additional debt generates tax shields worth $\$.50$.
Limit on available cash $(x \leq .8 + y)$	0	Firm has surplus cash at optimal solution. Additional cash has NPV of zero.

---

[14]Eugene Lerner and Arnold Rappaport demonstrate the conflicts between pursuit of value and short-run earnings in "Limit DCF in Capital Budgeting," *Harvard Business Review*, **46**:133–139 (September–October 1968).

[15]Note our warning on the temptation to go into excessive detail. See Section 28-3.

[16]Willard T. Carleton, Charles L. Dick, Jr., and David H. Downes give a comprehensive and insightful discussion of the differences in design and use of the two model types, and argue that optimization models are potentially more useful, in "Financial Policy Models: Theory and Practice," *Journal of Financial and Quantitative Analysis*, **8**:691–709 (December 1973).

A *shadow price* is defined as the change in the objective per unit change in the constraint.[17] In our example the objective is to increase net present value. Therefore the shadow price of .1 on the investment limit means that if the firm were allowed to invest $1,000,001 instead of $1 million, net present value would increase by 10 cents. The shadow price of .5 on the debt limit means that if the firm were allowed to borrow $400,001 instead of $400,000, holding investment fixed at $1 million, value would increase by 50 cents.

The limit on available cash is not binding at the optimal solution. The firm borrows $200,000 more than it needs, and so the shadow price on that constraint is zero. That is, extra cash would have a *net* present value of zero.

Consider a slightly more complex example. Cash on hand is reduced to $500,000. Equity issues and dividend payments are allowed, but transactions costs absorb 10 percent of the net proceeds of any issue. The linear programming problem changes to:

- Maximize: $-.1x + .5y + (0)\text{DIV} - .1\text{SI}$
- Subject to: $x \le 1$
  $y \le .4x$
  $x + \text{DIV} \le .5 + y + \text{SI}$

The solution is $x = 1$, $y = .4$, $\text{DIV} = 0$, and $\text{SI} = .1$. The firm invests and borrows as before but has to issue $100,000 of equity to raise the necessary cash for investment.

The shadow prices for this problem are as follows:

Constraint	Shadow Price	Explanation
Limit on investment $(x \le 1)$	.04	(See below.)
Limit on debt $(y \le .4x)$	.6	$1 of additional debt generates tax shields worth $.50 *and* reduces equity issued by $1, saving $.10 in issue costs.
Limit on available cash $(x + \text{DIV} \le .5 + y + \text{SI})$	.1	Extra cash reduces equity issued and saves $.10 per $1.

The shadow price on project investment goes down by .06, from $.10 to $.04 per dollar invested. This occurs because additional investment can be only 40 percent debt-financed. The remainder must come from issuing new equity. Therefore, the value of the opportunity to invest an additional dollar decreases by $.6 \times .1 = .06$.

The shadow prices on the investment limits are particularly interesting because they show the project's net marginal contribution to firm value, when all of the project's financing side effects are accounted for. In this example the project's marginal contribution is 4 cents per dollar invested. Remember that the project has negative NPV separately considered. But it has one favorable side effect (investment allows the firm to borrow) and one unfavorable side effect (investment requires equity issues and generates issue costs).

The shadow price for the project can be calculated by starting with its base-case NPV of $-.1$, adding the value of its marginal contribution to corporate borrowing, and subtracting the marginal cost of the equity issue needed to finance it:

[17]Shadow prices are valid only for marginal shifts in the constraints. The range over which shifts qualify as marginal varies from problem to problem.

$$\begin{array}{ccccc}\text{Net contribution} \\ \text{to firm value}\end{array} = \begin{array}{c}\text{base-case} \\ \text{NPV}\end{array} + \begin{array}{c}\text{value of project's} \\ \text{marginal contribution} \\ \text{to borrowing power}\end{array} - \begin{array}{c}\text{marginal cost} \\ \text{of equity issue} \\ \text{needed to finance} \\ \text{project}\end{array}$$

Investing $1 more effectively loosens the debt constraint by $.40 and tightens the cash constraint by $1. Therefore we can "price out" the project's financing side effects by noting the shadow prices on these two constraints. Extra borrowing power is worth 60 cents per dollar, and cash used up costs 10 cents per dollar. Therefore

$$\text{Net contribution to firm value} = -.1 + .40(.6) - (1.00)(.1) = .04$$

"Net contribution to firm value" is no more or less than *adjusted present value*, or APV. APV is calculated automatically as a by-product of LONGER. But, as you saw in Chapter 19, for simple problems you can calculate APV by hand. You need APV because it is the only generally reliable approach to capital budgeting when investment decisions have important financing side effects.

Further Reading

Corporate planning has an extensive literature of its own. Good books and articles include:
G. Donaldson: "Financial Goals and Strategic Consequences," *Harvard Business Review,* **63**:57–66 (May–June 1985).
G. Donaldson: *Strategy for Financial Mobility,* Harvard Business School Press, Boston, 1986.
A. C. Hax and N. S. Majluf: *The Strategy Concept and Process—A Pragmatic Approach,* 2d. ed., Prentice-Hall, Inc., Englewood Cliffs, N.J., 1984.
P. Lorange and R. F. Vancil: *Strategic Planning Systems,* Prentice-Hall, Inc., Englewood Cliffs, N.J., 1977.

Our description of what planning is and is not was influenced by:
P. Drucker: "Long-Range Planning: Challenge to Management Science," *Management Science,* **5**:238–249 (April 1959).

The links between capital budgeting, strategy, and financial planning are discussed in:
S. C. Myers: "Finance Theory and Financial Strategy," *Interfaces,* **14**:126–137 (January–February 1984).

Here are two references on corporate planning models:
W. T. Carleton, C. L. Dick, Jr., and D. H. Downes: "Financial Policy Models: Theory and Practice," *Journal of Financial and Quantitative Analysis,* **8**:691–709 (December 1973).
W. T. Carleton and J. M. McInnes: "Theory, Models and Implementation in Financial Management," *Management Science,* **28**:957–978 (September 1982).

LONGER is presented in:
S. C. Myers and G. A. Pogue: "A Programming Approach to Corporate Financial Management," *Journal of Finance,* **29**:579–599 (May 1974).

Quiz

1. True or false?
   (*a*) Financial planning should attempt to minimize risk.

TABLE 28-5
••

1996 financial statements for Drake's Bowling Alleys (figures in thousands)

Income Statement

Sales	$1,000 (40% of *average* assets)*
Costs	750 (75% of sales)
Interest	25 (5% of debt at start of year)†
Pretax profit	225
Tax	90 (40% of pretax profit)
Net income	$ 135

Balance Sheet

Assets	$2,600	Debt	$ 500
		Equity	2,100
Total	$2,600	Total	$2,600

*Assets at end-1995 were $2,400,000.
†Debt at end-1995 was $500,000.

(b) The primary aim of financial planning is to obtain better forecasts of future cash flows and earnings.
(c) Financial planning is necessary because financing and investment decisions interact and should not be made independently.
(d) Firms' planning horizons rarely exceed 3 years.
(e) Individual capital investment projects are not considered in a financial plan unless they are very large.
(f) Financial planning requires accurate and consistent forecasting.
(g) Financial planning models should include as much detail as possible.

2. List the major elements of a completed financial plan.

3. "There is no finance in financial planning models." Explain.

4. Table 28-5 summarizes the 1996 income statement and end-year balance sheet of Drake's Bowling Alleys. Drake's financial manager forecasts a 10 percent increase in sales and costs in 1997. The ratio of sales to *average* assets is expected to remain at .40. Interest is forecast at 5 percent of debt at start of year.
(a) What is the implied level of assets at the end of 1997?
(b) If the company pays out 50 percent of net income as dividends, how much cash will Drake's need to raise in the capital markets in 1997?
(c) If Drake's is unwilling to make an equity issue, what will be the debt ratio at the end of 1997?

5. Abbreviated financial statements for Archimedes Levers are shown in Table 28-6. If sales increase by 10 percent in 1997 and all other items, including debt, increase correspondingly, what must be the balancing item? What will be its value?

6. What is the maximum possible growth rate for Archimedes (see question 5) if the payout ratio is set at 50 percent and:
(a) No external debt or equity is to be issued?
(b) The firm maintains a fixed debt ratio but issues no equity?

TABLE 28-6
· ·

1996 financial statements for Archimedes Lever

Income Statement

Sales	$4,000
Costs, including interest	3,500
Net income	$ 500

Balance Sheet, Year-End

	1995	1996		1995	1996
Assets	$2,700	$3,200	Debt	$1,033	$1,200
			Equity	1,667	2,000
Total	$2,700	$3,200	Total	$2,700	$3,200

Questions and Problems
· ·

1. What are the dangers and disadvantages of using a financial model? Discuss.

2. Should a financial plan be considered an unbiased forecast of future cash flows, earnings, and other financial variables? Why or why not?

3. How would Executive Fruit's financial model change if dividends were cut to zero in 1996? Use the revised model to generate a new financial plan for 1996. Show how the financial statements given in Table 28-2 would change. Do you think the new plan is an improvement on the old one? Discuss.

4. The balancing item in the Executive Fruit model is borrowing. What is meant by *balancing item?* How would the model change if dividends were made the balancing item instead? In that case how would you suggest that planned borrowing be determined?

5. Construct a new model for Executive Fruit based on your answer to question 4. Does your model generate a feasible financial plan for 1996? (*Hint:* If it doesn't, you may have to allow the firm to issue stock.)

6. Executive Fruit's financial manager believes that revenues in 1996 could rise by as much as 50 percent or by as little as 10 percent. Recalculate the pro forma financial statements under these two assumptions. How does the rate of growth in revenues affect the firm's borrowing requirement?

7. (*a*) Use the Executive Fruit model (Table 28-3) to produce pro forma income statements, balance sheets, and sources and uses of funds statements for 1997 and 1998. Assume "business as usual" except that sales and costs expand by 30 percent per year, as do fixed assets and net working capital. The interest rate is forecasted to remain at 9 percent, and stock issues are ruled out. Executive Fruit also plans to stick to its 60 percent dividend payout ratio. (*Hint:* Interest expense depends on additional borrowing, which in turn depends on profit after interest and taxes. You may find it helpful to rearrange the equations so that you can calculate interest first.)

(*b*) What are the firm's debt ratio and interest coverage under this plan?

(*c*) Can the company continue to finance expansion by borrowing?

TABLE 28-7

1996 financial statements for Executive Cheese Company (figures in thousands)

Income Statement

Revenue	$1,785
Fixed costs	53
Variable costs (80% of revenue)	1,428
Depreciation	80
Interest (at 8%)	24
Taxes (at 40%)	80
Net income	$ 120

Sources and Uses of Funds

Sources:	
Operating cash flow	$ 200
Borrowing	36
Stock issues	104
Total sources	$ 340
Uses:	
Increase in net working capital	$ 60
Investment	200
Dividends	80
Total uses	$ 340

Balance Sheet, Year-End

	1996	1995
Assets:		
Net working capital	$ 400	$ 340
Fixed assets	800	680
Total assets	$1,200	$1,020
Liabilities:		
Debt	$ 240	$ 204
Book equity	960	816
Total liabilities	$1,200	$1,020

8. Discuss the relative merits of descriptive financial models, such as the Executive Fruit model, and optimizing models such as LONGER. Descriptive models are much more commonly used in practice. Why do you think this is so?

9. Table 28-7 shows the 1996 financial statements for the Executive Cheese Company. Annual depreciation is 10 percent of fixed assets at the beginning of this year, plus 10 percent of new investment. The company plans to invest a further $200 per year in fixed assets for the next 5 years and forecasts that the ratio of revenues to total assets at the start of each year will remain at 1.75. Fixed costs are expected to remain at $53 and variable costs at 80 percent of revenue. The company's policy is to pay out two-thirds of net income as dividends and to maintain a book debt ratio of 20 percent.

(a) Construct a model like the one in Table 28-3 for Executive Cheese.

(b) Use your model to produce a set of financial statements for 1997.

10. Our model for Executive Fruit is an example of a "top-down" planning model. Some firms use a "bottom-up" financial planning model, which incorporates forecasts of revenues and costs for particular products, advertising plans, major investment projects, and so on. What are the advantages and disadvantages of the two model types? What sort of firms would you expect to use each type, and what would they use them for?

11. Corporate financial plans are often used as a basis for judging subsequent performance. What do you think can be learned from such comparisons? What problems are likely to arise, and how might you cope with these problems?

12. What problems are likely to be encountered in keeping the corporate financial plan up to date?

13. The financial statements of Eagle Sport Supply are shown in Table 28-8. For simplicity, "Costs" includes interest. Assume that Eagle's assets are proportional to its sales.

(a) Find Eagle's required external funds if it maintains a dividend payout ratio of 60 percent and plans a growth rate of 15 percent in 1997.

(b) If Eagle chooses not to issue new shares of stock, what variable must be the balancing item? What will its value be?

(c) Now suppose that the firm plans instead to increase long-term debt only to $1100 and does not wish to issue any new shares of stock. Why must the dividend payment now be the balancing item? What will its value be?

14. (a) What is the internal growth rate of Eagle Sports (see problem 13) if the dividend payout ratio is fixed at 60 percent and the equity-to-asset ratio is fixed at $\frac{2}{3}$?

(b) What is the sustainable growth rate?

15. Table 28-9 contains financial statements for Dynastatics Corporation. Although the company has not been growing, it now plans to expand and will increase net fixed assets (that is, assets net of depreciation) by $200 per year for the next

TABLE 28-8
. . . .

1996 financial statements for Eagle Sport Supply

Income Statement

Sales	$950
Costs	250
EBIT	700
Taxes	200
Net income	$500

Balance Sheet, Year-End

	1995	1996		1995	1996
Assets	$2,700	$3,000	Debt	$ 900	$1,000
			Equity	1,800	2,000
Total	$2,700	$3,000	Total	$2,700	$3,000

TABLE 28-9

● ●

1995 financial statements for Dynastatics Corporation (figures in thousands)

Income Statement

Revenue	$1,800
Fixed costs	56
Variable costs (80% of revenue)	1,440
Depreciation	80
Interest (8% of beginning-of-year debt)	24
Taxable income	200
Taxes (at 40%)	80
Net income	$ 120

Dividends	$80
Retained earnings	$40

Balance Sheet, Year-End

	1994	1995
Assets:		
Net working capital	$ 400	$ 400
Fixed assets	800	800
Total assets	$1,200	$1,200
Liabilities and shareholders' equity:		
Debt	$ 300	$ 300
Equity	900	900
Total liabilities and shareholders' equity	$1,200	$1,200

5 years. It forecasts that the ratio of revenues to total assets will remain at 1.50. Annual depreciation is 10 percent of fixed assets at the start of the year. Fixed costs are expected to remain at $56 and variable costs at 80 percent of revenue. The company's policy is to pay out two-thirds of net income as dividends and to maintain a book debt ratio of 25 percent of total capital.

(*a*) Produce a set of financial statements for 1996. Assume that net working capital will equal 50 percent of fixed assets.

(*b*) Now assume that the balancing item is debt and that no equity is to be issued. Prepare a completed pro forma balance sheet for 1996. What is the projected debt ratio for 1996?

16. Go Go Industries is growing at 30 percent per year. It is all-equity-financed and has total assets of $1 million. Its return on equity is 20 percent. Its plowback ratio is 40 percent.

(*a*) What is the internal growth rate?

(*b*) What is the firm's need for external financing this year?

(*c*) By how much would the firm increase its internal growth rate if it reduced its payout ratio to zero?

(*d*) By how much would such a move reduce the need for external financing? What do you conclude about the relationship between dividend policy and requirements for external financing?

29

Short-Term Financial Planning

Most of this book is devoted to long-term financial decisions such as capital budgeting and the choice of capital structure. Such decisions are called *long-term* for two reasons. First, they usually involve long-lived assets or liabilities. Second, they are not easily reversed and therefore may commit the firm to a particular course of action for several years.

Short-term financial decisions generally involve short-lived assets and liabilities, and usually they *are* easily reversed. Compare, for example, a 60-day bank loan for $50 million with a $50 million issue of 20-year bonds. The bank loan is clearly a short-term decision. The firm can repay it 2 months later and be right back where it started. A firm might conceivably issue a 20-year bond in January and retire it in March, but it would be extremely inconvenient and expensive to do so. In practice, such a bond issue is a long-term decision, not only because of the bond's 20-year maturity but because the decision to issue it cannot be reversed on short notice.

A financial manager responsible for short-term financial decisions does not have to look far into the future. The decision to take the 60-day bank loan could properly be based on cash-flow forecasts for the next few months only. The bond issue decision will normally reflect forecasted cash requirements 5, 10, or more years into the future.

Managers concerned with short-term financial decisions can avoid many of the difficult conceptual issues encountered elsewhere in this book. In a sense, short-term decisions are easier than long-term decisions—but they are not less important. A firm can identify extremely valuable capital investment opportunities, find the precise optimal debt ratio, follow the perfect dividend policy, and yet founder because no one bothers to raise the cash to pay this year's bills. Hence the need for short-term planning.

In this chapter, we will review the major classes of short-term assets and liabilities, show how long-term financing decisions affect the firm's short-term financial planning problem, and describe how financial managers trace changes in cash and working capital. We will also describe how managers forecast month-by-month cash requirements or surpluses and how they develop short-term investment and financing strategies.

Part Nine of the book takes a more detailed look at working-capital management. Chapter 30 examines the decision to extend credit to the firm's customers. Chapter 31 describes the decision to hold cash (instead of investing cash to earn interest) and the relationship between firms and commercial banks. Chapter 32 describes the many channels firms can use to invest or raise funds for short periods.

TABLE 29-1

· ·

Current assets and liabilities for U.S. manufacturing corporations, third quarter 1994 (figures in billions of dollars)

Current Assets*		Current Liabilities*	
Cash	76.9	Short-term loans	121.1
Marketable securities	79.1	Accounts payable	232.8
Accounts receivable	403.9	Accrued income taxes	29.7
Inventories	389.4	Current payments due on long-term debt	46.2
Other current assets	120.5	Other current liabilities	327.5
Total	1,069.8	Total	757.3

*Net working capital (current assets − current liabilities) is $1,069.8 − $757.3 = $312.5 billion. *Source:* U.S. Department of Commerce, *Quarterly Financial Report for Manufacturing, Mining and Trade Corporations*, Third Quarter, 1994, p. 4.

29-1 THE COMPONENTS OF WORKING CAPITAL

Short-term or *current* assets and liabilities are collectively known as **working capital**. Table 29-1 gives a breakdown of current assets and liabilities for all manufacturing corporations in the United States in 1994. Note that total current assets were $1069.8 billion and current liabilities $757.3 billion. **Net working capital** (current assets less current liabilities) was $312.5 billion.

One important current asset is *accounts receivable*. When one company sells goods to another company or a government agency, it does not usually expect to be paid immediately. These unpaid bills, or *trade credit*, make up the bulk of accounts receivable. Companies also sell goods on credit to the final consumer. This *consumer credit* makes up the remainder of accounts receivable. We will discuss the management of receivables in Chapter 30. You will learn how companies decide which customers are good or bad credit risks and when it makes sense to offer credit.

Another important current asset is *inventory*. Inventories may consist of raw materials, work in process, or finished goods awaiting sale and shipment. Firms *invest* in inventory. The cost of holding inventory includes not only storage cost and the risk of spoilage or obsolescence but also the opportunity cost of capital—that is, the rate of return offered by other, equivalent-risk investment opportunities.[1] The benefits of holding inventory are often indirect. For example, a large inventory of finished goods (large relative to expected sales) reduces the chance of a "stockout" if demand is unexpectedly high. A producer holding a small finished-goods inventory is more likely to be caught short, unable to fill orders promptly. Similarly, large inventories of raw materials reduce the chance that an unexpected shortage would force the firm to shut down production or use a more costly substitute material.

---

[1]How risky are inventories? It is hard to generalize. Many firms just assume inventories have the same risk as typical capital investments and therefore calculate the cost of holding inventories using the firm's average opportunity cost of capital. You can think of many exceptions to this rule of thumb, however. For example, some electronics components are made with gold connections. Should an electronics firm apply its average cost of capital to its inventory of gold? (See Section 11-1.)

Bulk orders for raw materials lead to large average inventories but may be worthwhile if the firm can obtain lower prices from suppliers. (That is, bulk orders may yield quantity discounts.) Firms are often willing to hold large inventories of finished goods for similar reasons. A large inventory of finished goods allows longer, more economical production runs. In effect, the production manager gives the firm a quantity discount.

The task of inventory management is to assess these benefits and costs and to strike a sensible balance. In manufacturing companies the production manager is best placed to make this judgment. Since the financial manager is not usually directly involved in inventory management, we will not discuss the inventory problem in detail.

The remaining current assets are cash and marketable securities. The cash consists of currency, demand deposits (funds in checking accounts), and time deposits (funds in savings accounts). The principal marketable security is commercial paper (short-term, unsecured notes sold by other firms). Other securities include U.S. Treasury bills and state and local government securities.

In choosing between cash and marketable securities, the financial manager faces a task like that of the production manager. There are always advantages to holding large "inventories" of cash—they reduce the risk of running out of cash and having to raise more on short notice. On the other hand, there is a cost to holding idle cash balances rather than putting the money to work in marketable securities. In Chapter 31 we will tell you how the financial manager collects and pays out cash and decides on an optimal cash balance.

We have seen that a company's principal current asset consists of unpaid bills from other companies. One firm's credit must be another's debit. Therefore it is not surprising that a company's principal current liability consists of *accounts payable*—that is, outstanding payments to other companies.

To finance its investment in current assets, a company may rely on a variety of short-term loans. Commercial banks are by far the largest source of such loans, but an industrial firm may also borrow from other sources. Another way of borrowing is to sell commercial paper.

Many short-term loans are unsecured, but sometimes the company may offer its inventory or receivables as security. For example, a firm may decide to borrow short-term money secured by its accounts receivable. When its customers have paid their bills, it can use the cash to repay the loan. An alternative procedure is to *sell* the receivables to a financial institution and let it collect the money. In other words, some companies solve their financing problem by borrowing on the strength of their current assets; others solve it by selling their current assets. In Chapter 32 we will look at the varied and ingenious methods of financing current assets.

29-2 LINKS BETWEEN LONG-TERM AND SHORT-TERM FINANCING DECISIONS

All businesses require capital—that is, money invested in plant, machinery, inventories, accounts receivable, and all the other assets it takes to run a business efficiently. Typically, these assets are not purchased all at once but obtained gradually over time. Let us call the total cost of these assets the firm's *cumulative capital requirement*.

Most firms' cumulative capital requirement grows irregularly, like the wavy line in Figure 29-1. This line shows a clear upward trend as the firm's business grows. But there is also seasonal variation around the trend: in the figure the capital requirements

Figure 29-1 The firm's cumulative capital requirement (heavy line) is the cumulative investment in plant, equipment, inventory and all other assets needed for the business. In this case the requirement grows year by year, but there is seasonal fluctuation within each year. The requirement for short-term financing is the difference between long-term financing (lines A^+, A, B, and C) and the cumulative capital requirement. If long-term financing follows line C, the firm *always* needs short-term financing. At line B, the need is seasonal. At lines A and A^+, the firm never needs short-term financing. There is always extra cash to invest.

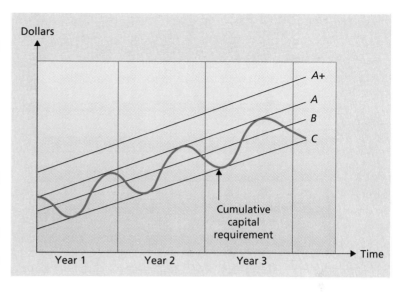

peak late in each year. Finally, there would be unpredictable week-to-week and month-to-month fluctuations, but we have not attempted to show these in Figure 29-1.

The cumulative capital requirement can be met from either long-term or short-term financing. When long-term financing does not cover the cumulative capital requirement, the firm must raise short-term capital to make up the difference. When long-term financing *more* than covers the cumulative capital requirement, the firm has surplus cash available for short-term investment. Thus the amount of long-term financing raised, given the cumulative capital requirement, determines whether the firm is a short-term borrower or lender.

Lines A, B, and C in Figure 29-1 illustrate this, Each depicts a different long-term financing strategy. Strategy A always implies a short-term cash surplus. Strategy C implies a permanent need for short-term borrowing. Under B, which is probably the most common strategy, the firm is a short-term lender during part of the year and a borrower during the rest.

What is the *best* level of long-term financing relative to the cumulative capital requirement? It is hard to say. There is no convincing theoretical analysis of this question. We can make practical observations, however. First, most financial managers attempt to "match maturities" of assets and liabilities. That is, they finance long-lived assets like plant and machinery with long-term borrowing and equity. Second, most firms make a permanent investment in net working capital (current assets less current liabilities). They finance this investment from long-term sources.[2]

The Comforts of Surplus Cash

Many financial managers would feel more comfortable under strategy A than strategy C. Strategy A^+ (the highest line) would be still more relaxing. A firm with a surplus of long-term financing never has to worry about borrowing to pay next month's bills. But is the financial manager paid to be comfortable? Firms usually put surplus

[2] In a sense this statement is true by definition. If net working capital (current assets less current liabilities) is positive, it must be financed by long-term debt or equity. Our point is that firms *plan* it that way.

TABLE 29-2
••

Year-end balance sheets for 1994 and 1995 for Dynamic
Mattress Company (figures in millions of dollars)

	1994	1995
Current assets:		
Cash	4	5
Marketable securities	0	5
Inventory	26	25
Accounts receivable	25	30
Total current assets	55	65
Fixed assets:		
Gross investment	56	70
Less depreciation	−16	−20
Net fixed assets	40	50
Total assets	95	115
Current liabilities:		
Bank loans	5	0
Accounts payable	20	27
Total current liabilities	25	27
Long-term debt	5	12
Net worth (equity and retained earnings)	65	76
Total liabilities and net worth	95	115

cash to work in Treasury bills or other marketable securities. This is at best a zero-NPV investment for a taxpaying firm.[3] Thus we think that firms with a *permanent* cash surplus ought to go on a diet, retiring long-term securities to reduce long-term financing to a level at or below the firm's cumulative capital requirement. That is, if the firm is on line A^+, it ought to move down to line A, or perhaps even lower.

29-3 TRACING CHANGES IN CASH AND WORKING CAPITAL

Table 29-2 compares 1994 and 1995 year-end balance sheets for Dynamic Mattress Company. Table 29-3 shows the firm's income statement for 1995. Note that Dynamic's cash balance increased by $1 million during 1995. What caused this increase? Did the extra cash come from Dynamic Mattress Company's additional long-term borrowing, from reinvested earnings, from cash released by reducing inventory, or from extra credit extended by Dynamic's suppliers? (Note the increase in accounts payable.)

The correct answer is "all the above," as well as many other activities and actions taken by the firm during the year. All we can say is that *sources* of cash exceeded *uses* by $1 million.

---

[3]If there is a tax advantage to borrowing, as most people believe, there must be a corresponding tax *dis*advantage to lending, and investment in Treasury bills has a negative NPV. See Section 18-2.

TABLE 29-3

Income statement for 1995 for Dynamic Mattress Company (figures in millions of dollars)	
Sales	350
Operating costs	−321
	29
Depreciation	−4
	25
Interest	−1
Pretax income	24
Tax at 50 percent	−12
Net income	12

Note: Dividend = $1 million; retained earnings = $11 million.

Financial analysts often summarize sources and uses of cash in a statement like the one shown in Table 29-4. The statement shows that Dynamic *generated* cash from the following sources:

1. It issued $7 million of long-term debt.
2. It reduced inventory, releasing $1 million.
3. It increased its accounts payable, in effect borrowing an additional $7 million from its suppliers.

TABLE 29-4

Sources and uses of cash for 1995 for Dynamic Mattress Company (figures in millions of dollars)	
Sources:	
Issued long-term debt	7
Reduced inventories	1
Increased accounts payable	7
Cash from operations:	
Net income	12
Depreciation	4
Total sources	31
Uses:	
Repaid short-term bank loan	5
Invested in fixed assets	14
Purchased marketable securities	5
Increased accounts receivable	5
Dividend	1
Total uses	30
Increase in cash balance	1

4. By far the largest source of cash was Dynamic's operations, which generated $16 million. See Table 29-3, and note: Income ($12 million) understates cash flow because depreciation is deducted in calculating income. Depreciation is *not* a cash outlay. Thus, it must be added back in order to obtain operating cash flow.

Dynamic *used* cash for the following purposes:

1. It paid a $1 million dividend. (*Note:* The $11 million increase in Dynamic's equity is due to retained earnings: $12 million of equity income, less the $1 million dividend.)

2. It repaid a $5 million short-term bank loan.[4]

3. It invested $14 million. This shows up as the increase in gross fixed assets in Table 29-2.

4. It purchased $5 million of marketable securities.

5. It allowed accounts receivable to expand by $5 million. In effect, it lent this additional amount to its customers.

Tracing Changes in Net Working Capital

Financial analysts often find it useful to collapse all current assets and liabilities into a single figure for net working capital. Dynamic's net-working-capital balances were (in millions):

	Current Assets	Less	Current Liabilities	Equals	Net Working Capital
Year-end 1994	$55	–	$25	=	$30
Year-end 1995	$65	–	$27	=	$38

Table 29-5 gives balance sheets which report only net working capital, not individual current asset or liability items.

"Sources and uses" statements can likewise be simplified by defining *sources* as activities which contribute to net working capital and *uses* as activities which use up working capital. In this context working capital is usually referred to as *funds*, and a *sources and uses of funds statement* is presented.

In 1994, Dynamic contributed to net working capital by:

1. Issuing $7 million of long-term debt

2. Generating $16 million from operations

It used up net working capital by:

1. Investing $14 million

2. Paying a $1 million dividend

---

[4]This is principal repayment, not interest. Sometimes interest payments are explicitly recognized as a use of funds. If so, operating cash flow would be defined *before* interest, that is, as net income plus interest plus depreciation.

TABLE 29-5
. . . .

Condensed year-end balance sheets for 1994 and 1995 for Dynamic Mattress Company (figures in millions of dollars)

	1994	1995
Net working capital	30	38
Fixed assets:		
Gross investment	56	70
Less depreciation	−16	−20
Net fixed assets	40	50
Total assets	70	88
Long-term debt	5	12
Net worth	65	76
Long-term liabilities and net worth*	70	88

*When only *net* working capital appears on a firm's balance sheet, this figure (the sum of long-term liabilities and net worth) is often referred to as *total capitalization.*

The year's changes in net working capital are thus summarized by Dynamic Mattress Company's sources and uses of funds statement, given in Table 29-6.

Profits and Cash Flow

Now look back to Table 29-4, which shows sources and uses of *cash*. We want to register two warnings about the entry called *cash from operations*. It may not actually represent real dollars—dollars you can buy beer with.

First, depreciation may not be the only noncash expense deducted in calculating income. For example, most firms use different accounting procedures in their tax books than in their reports to shareholders. The point of special tax accounts is to minimize

TABLE 29-6
. . . .

Sources and uses of funds (net working capital) for 1995 for Dynamic Mattress Company (figures in millions of dollars)

Sources:	
Issued long-term debt	7
Cash from operations:	
Net income	12
Depreciation	4
	23
Uses:	
Invested in fixed assets	14
Dividend	1
	15
Increase in net working capital	8

current taxable income. The effect is that the shareholder books overstate the firm's current cash tax liability,[5] and after-tax cash flow from operations is therefore understated.

Second, income statements record sales when made, not when the customer's payment is received. Think of what happens when Dynamic sells goods on credit. The company records a profit at the time of sale, but there is no cash inflow until the bills are paid. Since there is no cash inflow, there is no change in the company's cash balance, although there is an increase in working capital in the form of an increase in accounts receivable. No net addition to cash would be shown in a sources and uses statement like Table 29-4. The increase in cash from operations would be offset by an increase in accounts receivable.

Later, when the bills are paid, there is an increase in the cash balance. However, there is no further profit at this point and no increase in working capital. The increase in the cash balance is exactly matched by a decrease in accounts receivable.

That brings up interesting characteristics of working capital. Imagine a company that conducts a very simple business. It buys raw materials for cash, processes them into finished goods, and then sells these goods on credit. The whole cycle of operations looks like this:

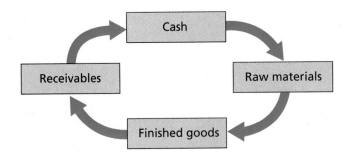

If you draw up a balance sheet at the beginning of the process, you see cash. If you delay a little, you find the cash replaced by inventories of raw materials and, still later, by inventories of finished goods. When the goods are sold, the inventories give way to accounts receivable, and finally, when the customers pay their bills, the firm draws out its profit and replenishes the cash balance.

There is only one constant in this process—namely, working capital. The components of working capital are constantly changing. That is one reason why (net) working capital is a useful summary measure of current assets or liabilities.

The strength of the working-capital measure is that it is unaffected by seasonal or other temporary movements between different current assets or liabilities. But the strength is also its weakness, for the working-capital figure hides a lot of interesting information. In our example cash was transformed into inventory, then into receivables, and back into cash again. But these assets have different degrees of risk and liquidity. You can't pay bills with inventory or with receivables—you must pay with cash.

---

[5]The difference between taxes reported and paid to the Internal Revenue Service shows up on the balance sheet as an increased deferred tax liability. The reason why a liability is recognized is that accelerated depreciation and other devices used to reduce current taxable income do not eliminate taxes; they only delay them. Of course, this reduces the present value of the firm's tax liability, but still the ultimate liability has to be recognized. In the sources and uses statements an increase in deferred taxes would be treated as a source of funds. In the Dynamic Mattress example we ignore deferred taxes.

TABLE 29-7
. . . .

To forecast Dynamic Mattress's collections on accounts receivable, you have to forecast sales and collection rates (figures in millions of dollars)

	First Quarter	Second Quarter	Third Quarter	Fourth Quarter
1. Receivables at start of period	30	32.5	30.7	38.2
2. Sales	87.5	78.5	116	131
3. Collections:				
Sales in current period (80%)	70	62.8	92.8	104.8
Sales in last period (20%)	15*	17.5	15.7	23.2
Total collections	85	80.3	108.5	128.0
4. Receivables at end of period				
4 = 1 + 2 − 3	32.5	30.7	38.2	41.2

*Sales in the fourth quarter of the previous year were $75 million.

29-4 CASH BUDGETING

The past is interesting only for what one can learn from it. The financial manager's problem is to forecast *future* sources and uses of cash. These forecasts serve two purposes. First, they alert the financial manager to future cash needs. Second, the cash-flow forecasts provide a standard, or budget, against which subsequent performance can be judged.

. . . .

Preparing the Cash Budget: Inflow

There are at least as many ways to produce a quarterly cash budget as there are to skin a cat. Many large firms have developed elaborate "corporate models"; others use a spreadsheet program to plan their cash needs. The procedures of smaller firms may be less formal. But there are common issues that all firms must face when they forecast. We will illustrate these issues by continuing the example of Dynamic Mattress.

Most of Dynamic's cash inflow comes from the sale of mattresses. We therefore start with a sales forecast by quarter[6] for 1996:

	First Quarter	Second Quarter	Third Quarter	Fourth Quarter
Sales, millions of dollars	87.5	78.5	116	131

But sales become accounts receivable before they become cash. Cash flow comes from *collections* on accounts receivable.

Most firms keep track of the average time it takes customers to pay their bills. From this they can forecast what proportion of a quarter's sales is likely to be converted into cash in that quarter and what proportion is likely to be carried over to the next quarter as accounts receivable. Suppose that 80 percent of sales are "cashed in" in the immediate quarter and 20 percent in the next. Table 29-7 shows forecasted collections under this assumption.

---

[6]Most firms would forecast by month instead of by quarter. Sometimes weekly or even daily forecasts are made. But presenting a monthly forecast would triple the number of entries in Table 29-7 and subsequent tables. We wanted to keep the examples as simple as possible.

In the first quarter, for example, collections from current sales are 80 percent of $87.5, or $70 million. But the firm also collects 20 percent of the previous quarter's sales, or .2(75) = $15 million. Therefore total collections are $70 + $15 = $85 million.

Dynamic started the first quarter with $30 million of accounts receivable. The quarter's sales of $87.5 million were *added* to accounts receivable, but collections of $85 million were *subtracted.* Therefore, as Table 29-7 shows, Dynamic ended the quarter with accounts receivable of $30 + 87.5 − 85 = $32.5 million. The general formula is

$$\text{Ending accounts receivable} = \text{beginning accounts receivable}$$

$$+ \text{ sales} - \text{collections}$$

The top section of Table 29-8 shows forecasted sources of cash for Dynamic Mattress. Collection of receivables is the main source, but it is not the only one. Perhaps the firm plans to dispose of some land or expects a tax refund or payment of an insurance claim. All such items are included as "other" sources. It is also possible that you may raise additional capital by borrowing or selling stock, but we don't want to prejudge that question. Therefore, for the moment we just assume that Dynamic will not raise further long-term finance.

TABLE 29-8

Dynamic Mattress's cash budget for 1996 (figures in millions of dollars)

	First Quarter	Second Quarter	Third Quarter	Fourth Quarter
Sources of cash:				
Collections on accounts receivable	85	80.3	108.5	128
Other	0	0	12.5	0
Total sources	85	80.3	121	128
Uses of cash:				
Payments on accounts payable	65	60	55	50
Labor, administrative, and other expenses	30	30	30	30
Capital expenditures	32.5	1.3	5.5	8
Taxes, interest, and dividends	4	4	4.5	5
Total uses	131.5	95.3	95	93
Sources minus uses	−46.5	−15.0	+26	+35
Calculation of short-term financing requirement:				
1. Cash at start of period	5	−41.5	−56.5	−30.5
2. Change in cash balance (sources less uses)	−46.5	−15.0	+26	+35
3. Cash at end of period*				
1 + 2 = 3	−41.5	−56.5	−30.5	+4.5
4. Minimum operating cash balance	5	5	5	5
5. Cumulative short-term financing required[†]				
5 = 4 − 3	46.5	61.5	35.5	.5

*Of course, firms cannot literally hold a negative amount of cash. This is the amount the firm will have to raise to pay its bills.
[†]A negative sign would indicate a cash *surplus.* But in this example the firm must raise cash for all quarters.

Preparing the Cash Budget: Outflow

So much for the incoming cash. Now for the outgoing cash. There always seem to be many more uses for cash than there are sources. For simplicity, we have condensed the uses into four categories in Table 29-8.

1. *Payments on accounts payable.* You have to pay your bills for raw materials, parts, electricity, etc. The cash-flow forecast assumes all these bills are paid on time, although Dynamic could probably delay payment to some extent. Delayed payment is sometimes called *stretching your payables*. Stretching is one source of short-term financing, but for most firms it is an expensive source, because by stretching they lose discounts given to firms that pay promptly. This is discussed in more detail in Section 30-1.

2. *Labor, administrative, and other expenses.* This category includes all other regular business expenses.

3. *Capital expenditures.* Note that Dynamic Mattress plans a major capital outlay in the first quarter.

4. *Taxes, interest, and dividend payments.* This includes interest on presently outstanding long-term debt but does not include interest on any additional borrowing to meet cash requirements in 1996. At this stage in the analysis, Dynamic does not know how much it will have to borrow, or whether it will have to borrow at all.

The forecasted net inflow of cash (sources minus uses) is shown in the box in Table 29-8. Note the large negative figure for the first quarter: a $46.5 million forecasted *outflow*. There is a smaller forecasted outflow in the second quarter, and then substantial cash inflows in the second half of the year.

The bottom part of Table 29-8 (below the box) calculates how much financing Dynamic will have to raise if its cash-flow forecasts are right. It starts the year with $5 million in cash. There is a $46.5 million cash outflow in the first quarter, and so Dynamic will have to obtain at least $46.5 − 5 = $41.5 million of additional financing. This would leave the firm with a forecasted cash balance of exactly zero at the start of the second quarter.

Most financial managers regard a planned cash balance of zero as driving too close to the edge of the cliff. They establish a *minimum operating cash balance* to absorb unexpected cash inflows and outflows. Also, banks usually require firms to maintain a minimum average cash balance as partial compensation for services the bank provides to the firm—this is described in more detail in Chapter 31. We will assume that Dynamic's minimum operating cash balance is $5 million. That means it will have to raise the full $46.5 million cash outflow in the first quarter and $15 million more in the second quarter. Thus its cumulative financing requirement is $61.5 million in the second quarter. This is the peak, fortunately: the cumulative requirement declines in the third quarter by $26 million to $35.5 million. In the final quarter Dynamic is almost out of the woods: its cash balance is $4.5 million, just $.5 million shy of its minimum operating balance.

The next step is to develop a *short-term financing plan* that covers the forecasted requirements in the most economical way possible. We will move on to that topic after two general observations:

1. The large cash outflows in the first two quarters do not necessarily spell trouble for Dynamic Mattress. In part, they reflect the capital investment made in the first quarter: Dynamic is spending $32.5 million, but it should be acquiring an asset worth that much or more. In part, the cash outflows reflect low sales in the first half

of the year; sales recover in the second half.[7] If this is a predictable seasonal pattern, the firm should have no trouble borrowing to tide it over the slow months.

2. Table 29-8 is only a best guess about future cash flows. It is a good idea to think about the *uncertainty* in your estimates. For example, you could undertake a sensitivity analysis, in which you inspect how Dynamic's cash requirements would be affected by a shortfall in sales or by a delay in collections. The trouble with such sensitivity analyses is that you are changing only one item at a time, whereas in practice a downturn in the economy might affect, say, sales levels *and* collection rates. An alternative but more complicated solution is to build a model of the cash budget and then to simulate to determine the probability of cash requirements significantly above or below the forecasts shown in Table 29-8.[8] If cash requirements are difficult to predict, you may wish to hold additional cash or marketable securities to cover a possible unexpected cash outflow.

29-5 THE SHORT-TERM FINANCING PLAN

Dynamic's cash budget defines its problem: Its financial manager must find short-term financing to cover the firm's forecasted cash requirements. There are dozens of sources of short-term financing, but for simplicity we start by assuming that there are just two options.

Options for Short-Term Financing

1. *Unsecured bank borrowing:* Dynamic has an existing arrangement with its bank allowing it to borrow up to $41 million at an interest cost of 11.5 percent per year or 2.875 percent per quarter. The firm can borrow and repay whenever it wants so long as it does not exceed the credit limit. Dynamic does not have to pledge any specific assets as security for the loan. This kind of arrangement is called a *line of credit*.[9]

   When a company borrows on an unsecured line of credit, it is generally obliged to maintain a *compensating balance* on deposit at the bank. In our example, Dynamic has to maintain a balance of 20 percent of the amount of the loan. In other words, if the firm wants to raise $100, it must actually borrow $125, because $25 (20 percent of $125) must be left on deposit in the bank.

2. *Stretching payables:* Dynamic can also raise capital by putting off paying its bills. The financial manager believes that Dynamic can defer the following amounts in each quarter:

	Quarter 1	Quarter 2	Quarter 3	Quarter 4
Amount deferrable, millions of dollars	52	48	44	40

That is, $52 million can be saved in the first quarter by *not* paying bills in that quarter. (Table 29-8 assumes these bills *are* paid in the first quarter.) If deferred, these payments *must* be made in the second quarter. Similarly, $48 million of quarter 2's bills can be deferred to quarter 3, and so on.

---

[7]Maybe people buy more mattresses late in the year when the nights are longer.

[8]In other words, you could use Monte Carlo simulation. See Section 10-2.

[9]Lines of credit are discussed in more detail in Chapter 32.

Stretching payables is often costly, however, even if no ill will is incurred. The reason is that suppliers often offer discounts for prompt payment. Dynamic loses this discount if it pays late. In this example we assume the lost discount is 5 percent of the amount deferred. In other words, if a $100 payment is delayed, the firm must pay $105 in the next quarter.

The First Financing Plan

With these two options, the short-term financing strategy is obvious: Use the line of credit first, if necessary up to the $41 million credit limit. If cash requirements exceed the credit limit, stretch payables.

Table 29-9 shows the resulting financing plan. In the first quarter the plan calls for borrowing the full amount available under the line of credit ($41 million) and stretching $3.6 million of payables (see lines 1 and 2 in the table). In addition, the

TABLE 29-9

Dynamic Mattress's first financing plan (figures in millions of dollars)

	First Quarter	Second Quarter	Third Quarter	Fourth Quarter
New borrowing:				
1. Line of credit	41	0	0	0
2. Stretching payables	3.6	20	0	0
3. Total	44.6	20	0	0
Repayments:				
4. Line of credit	0	0	4.8	36.2
5. Stretched payables	0	3.6	20	0
6. Total	0	3.6	24.8	36.2
7. Net new borrowing	44.6	16.4	−24.8	−36.2
8. Plus securities sold	5*	0	0	0
9. Less securities bought	0	0	0	0
10. Total cash raised	49.6	16.4	−24.8	−36.2
Interest payments:				
11. Line of credit	0	1.2	1.2	1.0
12. Stretching payables	0	.2	1.0	0
13. Less interest on marketable securities	−.1*	0	0	0
14. Net interest paid	−.1	1.4	2.2	1.0
15. Additional funds for compensating balance†	3.2	0	−1.0	−2.2
16. Cash required for operations‡	46.5	15	−26	−35
17. Total cash required	49.6	16.4	−24.8	−36.2

*Dynamic held $5 million in marketable securities at the end of 1995. The yield is assumed to be 2.4 percent per quarter.
†Twenty percent of the amount borrowed on the line of credit in excess of $25 million. Dynamic's $5 million minimum operating cash balance serves as compensating balance for loans up to $25 million.
‡From Table 29-8.

firm sells the $5 million of marketable securities it held at the end of 1995 (line 8). Thus, under this plan it raises $49.6 million in the first quarter (line 10).

Why raise $49.6 million when Table 29-8 shows a cash requirement of only $46.5 million? The major reason is that the $41 million borrowed under the line of credit requires a compensating balance of 20 percent of $41 million, or $8.2 million. Dynamic can cover part of this with its $5 million minimum balance, but $3.2 million still has to be raised (line 15).

In the second quarter, the plan calls for Dynamic to maintain line-of-credit borrowing at the upper limit and stretch $20 million in payables. This raises $16.4 million after payment of the $3.6 million of payables stretched in the first quarter.

Again, the amount of cash raised exceeds the amount required for operations ($16.4 versus $15 million). In this case, the difference is the interest cost of the first quarter's borrowing: $1.2 million for the line of credit and $.2 million for the stretched payables (lines 11 and 12.)[10]

In the third and fourth quarters the plan calls for Dynamic to pay off its debt. In turn, this releases cash tied up by the compensating balance requirement of the line of credit.

EVALUATING THE FIRST PLAN.   Does the plan shown in Table 29-9 solve Dynamic's short-term financing problem? No: the plan is feasible, but Dynamic can probably do better. The most glaring weakness of this first plan is its reliance on stretching payables, an extremely expensive financing device. Remember that it costs Dynamic 5 percent *per quarter* to delay paying bills—20 percent per year at simple interest. The first plan would merely stimulate the financial manager to search for cheaper sources of short-term borrowing. Perhaps the $41 million limit on the line of credit could be increased, for example.

The financial manager would ask several other questions as well. For example:

1. Does the plan yield satisfactory current and quick ratios?[11] Its bankers may be worried if these ratios deteriorate.[12]

2. Are there intangible costs of stretching payables? Will suppliers begin to doubt Dynamic's creditworthiness?

3. Does the plan for 1996 leave Dynamic in good financial shape for 1997? (Here the answer is yes, since Dynamic will have paid off all short-term borrowing by the end of the year.)

4. Should Dynamic try to arrange long-term financing for the major capital expenditure in the first quarter? This seems sensible, following the rule of thumb that long-term assets deserve long-term financing. It would also reduce the need for short-term borrowing dramatically. A counterargument is that Dynamic is financing the capital investment *only temporarily* by short-term borrowing. By year-end, the investment is paid for by cash from operations. Thus Dynamic's initial decision not to seek immediate long-term financing may reflect a preference for ultimately financing the investment with retained earnings.

---

[10]The interest rate on the line of credit is 11.5 percent per year, or 11.5/4 = 2.875 percent per quarter. Thus the interest due is .02875(41) = 1.2, or $1.2 million. The "interest" cost of the stretched payables is actually the 5 percent discount lost by delaying payment. Five percent of $3.6 million is $180,000, or about $.2 million.

[11]These ratios are discussed in Chapter 27.

[12]We have not worked out these ratios explicitly, but you can infer from Table 29-9 that they would be fine at the end of the year but relatively low in midyear, when Dynamic's borrowing is high.

5. Perhaps the firm's operating and investment plans can be adjusted to make the short-term financing problem easier. Is there any easy way of deferring the first quarter's large cash outflow? For example, suppose that the large capital investment in the first quarter is for new mattress-stuffing machines to be delivered and installed in the first half of the year. The new machines are not scheduled to be ready for full-scale use until August. Perhaps the machine manufacturer could be persuaded to accept 60 percent of the purchase price on delivery and 40 percent when the machines are installed and operating satisfactorily.

6. Dynamic may also be able to release cash by reducing the level of other current assets. For example, it could reduce receivables by getting tough with customers who are late paying their bills. (The cost is that in future these customers may take their business elsewhere.) Or it may be able to get by with lower inventories of mattresses. (The cost is that it may lose business if there is a rush of orders that it cannot supply.)

Short-term financing plans are developed by trial and error. You lay out one plan, think about it, and then try again with different assumptions on financing and investment alternatives. You continue until you can think of no further improvements.

Trial and error is important because it helps you understand the real nature of the problem the firm faces. Here we can draw a useful analogy between the *process* of planning and Chapter 10, A Project Is Not a Black Box. In Chapter 10 we described sensitivity analysis and other tools used by firms to find out what makes capital investment projects tick and what can go wrong with them. Dynamic's financial manager faces the same kind of task: not just to choose a plan but to understand what can go wrong with it and what will be done if conditions change unexpectedly.[13]

We cannot trace through each trial and error in Dynamic Mattress's search for the best short-term financing plan. The reader may be buried in numbers already. Instead we will wrap up this chapter by looking at Dynamic's second try.

The Second Financing Plan

The second financing plan, shown in Table 29-10, reflects two significant new assumptions.

1. A commercial finance company[14] has offered to lend Dynamic up to 80 percent of its accounts receivable at an interest rate of 15 percent per year, or 3.75 percent per quarter. In return, Dynamic is to pledge accounts receivable as security for the loan. This is clearly cheaper than stretching payables. It appears much more expensive than the bank line of credit—but remember that the line of credit requires a 20 percent compensating balance, whereas every dollar borrowed against receivables can be spent.

2. The financial manager is uncomfortable with the first plan, which includes no cushion of marketable securities. The second plan calls for a $2.5 million marketable securities portfolio held throughout the year.

A comparison of Tables 29-9 and 29-10 shows that the second plan is broadly similar to the first, except that borrowing against receivables replaces stretching payables and the firm holds $2.5 million of marketable securities. The second plan is also cheaper than the first. This can be seen by comparing net interest paid (line 14) under the two plans.

---

[13]This point is even more important in *long-term* financial planning. See Chapter 28.

[14]Commercial finance companies are nonbank financial institutions that specialize in lending to businesses.

	Quarter 1	Quarter 2	Quarter 3	Quarter 4	Total
First plan	−.1	1.4	2.2	1.0	4.5
Second plan	−.1	1.3	2.0	1.0	4.2

Over the year the second plan saves $4.5 − 4.2 = $.3 million, or about $300,000 of interest.[15]

. . . .

A Note on Short-Term Financial Planning Models

Working out a consistent short-term plan requires burdensome calculations.[16] Fortunately much of the arithmetic can be delegated to a computer. Many large firms have built *short-term financial planning models* to do this. Smaller companies like Dynamic Mattress do not face so much detail and complexity and find it easier to work with a spreadsheet program on a personal computer. In either case the financial manager specifies forecasted cash requirements or surpluses, interest rates, credit limits, etc., and the model grinds out a plan like those shown in Tables 29-9 and 29-10. The computer also produces balance sheets, income statements, and whatever special reports the financial manager may require.

Smaller firms that do not want custom-built models can rent general-purpose models offered by banks, accounting firms, management consultants, or specialized computer software firms.

Most of these models are *simulation* programs.[17] They simply work out the consequences of the assumptions and policies specified by the financial manager. *Optimization* models for short-term financial planning are also available. These models are usually linear programming models. They search for the *best* plan from a range of alternative policies identified by the financial manager.

As a matter of fact, we used a linear programming model developed by Pogue and Bussard[18] to generate Dynamic Mattress's financial plans. Of course, in that simple example we hardly needed a linear programming model to identify the best strategy. It was obvious that Dynamic should always use the line of credit first, turning to the second-best alternative (stretching payables or borrowing against receivables) only when the limit on the line of credit was reached. The Pogue-Bussard model nevertheless did the arithmetic quickly and easily.

Optimization helps when the firm faces complex problems with many interdependent alternatives and restrictions for which trial and error might never identify the *best* combination of alternatives.

Of course the best plan for one set of assumptions may prove disastrous if the assumptions are wrong. Thus the financial manager has to explore the implications of alternative assumptions about future cash flows, interest rates, and so on. Linear programming can help identify good strategies, but even with an optimization model the financial plan is still sought by trial and error.

---

[15]These are pretax figures. We simplified this example by forgetting that each dollar of interest paid is a tax-deductible expense.

[16]If you doubt that, look again at Table 29-9 or 29-10. Notice that the cash requirements in each quarter depend on borrowing in the previous quarter, because borrowing creates an obligation to pay interest. Also, borrowing under a line of credit may require additional cash to meet compensating balance requirements; if so, that means still more borrowing and still higher interest charges in the next quarter. Moreover, the problem's complexity would have been tripled had we not simplified by forecasting per quarter rather than by month.

[17]Like the simulation models described in Section 10-2, except that the short-term planning models rarely include uncertainty explicitly. The models referred to here are built and used in the same way as the long-term financial planning models described in Section 28-3.

[18]G. A. Pogue and R. N. Bussard, "A Linear Programming Model for Short-Term Financial Planning under Uncertainty," *Sloan Management Review*, **13**:69–99 (Spring 1972).

TABLE 29-10

. . . .

Dynamic Mattress's second financing plan (figures in millions of dollars)

	First Quarter	Second Quarter	Third Quarter	Fourth Quarter
New borrowing:				
1. Line of credit	41	0	0	0
2. Secured borrowing (receivables pledged)	6.1	16.4	0	0
3. Total	47.1	16.4	0	0
Repayments:				
4. Line of credit	0	0	2.0	36.7
5. Secured borrowing	0	0	22.4	0
6. Total	0	0	24.4	36.7
7. Net new borrowing	47.1	16.4	−24.4	−36.7
8. Plus securities sold	2.5*	0	0	0
9. Less securities bought	0	0	0	0
10. Total cash raised	49.6	16.4	−24.4	−36.7
Interest payments:				
11. Line of credit	0	1.2	1.2	1.1
12. Secured borrowing	0	.2	.8	0
13. Less interest on marketable securities	−.1*	−.1	−.1	−.1
14. Net interest paid	−.1	1.3	2.0	1.0
15. Additional funds for compensating balance[†]	3.2	0	−.4	−2.8
16. Cash required for operations[‡]	46.5	15	−26	−35
17. Total cash required	49.6	16.4	−24.4	−36.7

Note: There are minor inconsistencies in this table because of rounding.
*Dynamic held $5 million in marketable securities at the end of 1995.
[†]Twenty percent of the amount borrowed on the line of credit in excess of $25 million. Dynamic's $5 million minimum operating cash balance serves as compensating balance for loans up to $25 million.
[‡]From Table 29-8.

29-6 SUMMARY

Short-term financial planning is concerned with the management of the firm's short-term, or *current*, assets and liabilities. The most important current assets are cash, marketable securities, inventory, and accounts receivable. The most important current liabilities are bank loans and accounts payable. The difference between current assets and current liabilities is called *(net) working capital.*

Current assets and liabilities are turned over much more rapidly than the other items on the balance sheet. Short-term financing and investment decisions are more quickly and easily reversed than long-term decisions. Consequently, the financial manager does not need to look so far into the future when making them.

The nature of the firm's short-term financial planning problem is determined by the amount of long-term capital it raises. A firm that issues large amounts of long-term debt or common stock, or which retains a large part of its earnings, may find that it has permanent excess cash. In such cases there is never any problem paying bills, and short-term financial planning consists of managing the firm's portfolio of marketable securities. We think that firms with permanent cash surpluses ought to return the excess cash to their stockholders.

Other firms raise relatively little long-term capital and end up as permanent short-term debtors. Most firms attempt to find a golden mean by financing all fixed assets and part of current assets with equity and long-term debt. Such firms may invest cash surpluses during part of the year and borrow during the rest of the year.

The starting point for short-term financial planning is an understanding of sources and uses of cash.[19] Firms forecast their net cash requirements by forecasting collections on accounts receivable, adding other cash inflows, and subtracting all forecasted cash outlays.

If the forecasted cash balance is insufficient to cover day-to-day operations and to provide a buffer against contingencies, you will need to find additional finance. It may make sense to raise long-term finance if the deficiency is permanent and large. Otherwise, you may choose from a variety of sources of short-term finance. For example, you may be able to borrow from a bank on an unsecured line of credit, you may borrow on the security of your receivables or inventory, or you may be able to finance the deficit by not paying your bills for a while. In addition to the explicit interest costs of short-term financing, there are often implicit costs. For example, the firm may be required to maintain a compensating balance at the bank, or it may lose its reputation as a prompt payer if it raises cash by delaying payment on its bills. The financial manager must choose the financing package that has lowest total cost (explicit and implicit costs combined) and yet leaves the firm with sufficient flexibility to cover contingencies.

The search for the best short-term financial plan inevitably proceeds by trial and error. The financial manager must explore the consequences of different assumptions about cash requirements, interest rates, limits on financing from particular sources, and so on. Firms are increasingly using computerized financial models to help in this process. The models range from simple spreadsheet programs that merely help with the arithmetic to linear programming models that help find the best financial plan.

Further Reading

Here are some general textbooks on working-capital management:
G. W. Gallinger and P. B. Healey: *Liquidity Analysis and Management*, 2d. ed., Addison-Wesley Publishing Company, Inc., Reading, Mass., 1991.
K. V. Smith and G. W. Gallinger: *Readings on the Management of Working Capital*, 3d ed., West Publishing Company, New York, 1988.

---

[19]We pointed out in Section 29-3 that sources and uses of *funds* are often analyzed rather than sources and uses of cash. Anything that contributes to working capital is called a *source of funds;* anything that diminishes working capital is called a *use of funds.* Sources and uses of funds statements are relatively simple because many sources and uses of cash are buried in changes in working capital. However, in forecasting, the emphasis is on cash flow: You pay bills with cash, not working capital.

J. H. Vander Weide and S. F. Maier: *Managing Corporate Liquidity: An Introduction to Working Capital Management*, John Wiley & Sons, Inc., New York, 1985.

J. D. Wilson and J. F. Duston: *Financial Information Systems Manual*, Warren, Gorham and Lamont, Inc., Boston, 1986.

F. C. Scherr: *Modern Working Capital Management—Text and Cases*, Prentice-Hall, Inc., Englewood Cliffs, N.J., 1989.

Pogue and Bussard present a linear programming model for short-term financial planning:

G. A. Pogue and R. N. Bussard: "A Linear Programming Model for Short-Term Financial Planning under Uncertainty," *Sloan Management Review*, **13**:69–99 (Spring 1972).

Quiz

....

1. Listed below are six transactions that Dynamic Mattress might make. Indicate how each transaction would affect each of the following:
   (*a*) Cash
   (*b*) Working capital

   The transactions are:
   1. Pay out $2 million cash dividend.
   2. Receive $2500 from a customer who pays a bill resulting from a previous sale.
   3. Pay $5000 previously owed to one of its suppliers.
   4. Borrow $1 million long term and invest the proceeds in inventory.
   5. Borrow $1 million short term and invest the proceeds in inventory.
   6. Sell $5 million of marketable securities for cash.

2. Here is a forecast of sales by National Bromide for the first 4 months of 1997 (figures in thousands of dollars):

	Month 1	Month 2	Month 3	Month 4
Cash sales	15	24	18	14
Sales on credit	100	120	90	70

   On the average 50 percent of credit sales are paid for in the current month, 30 percent in the next month, and the remainder in the month after that. What is the expected cash inflow from operations in months 3 and 4?

3. Fill in the blanks in the following statements:
   (*a*) A firm has a cash surplus when its _____ exceeds its _____ . The surplus is normally invested in _____ .
   (*b*) In developing the short-term financial plan, the financial manager starts with a _____ budget for the next year. This budget shows the _____ generated or absorbed by the firm's operations and also the minimum _____ needed to support these operations. The financial manager may also wish to invest in _____ as a reserve for unexpected cash requirements.
   (*c*) Short-term financing plans are developed by _____ and _____, often aided by computerized _____.

4. State how each of the following events would affect the firm's balance sheet. State whether each change is a source or use of cash and whether it is a source or use of funds.

(a) An automobile manufacturer increases production in response to a forecasted increase in demand. Unfortunately, the demand does not increase.

(b) Competition forces the firm to give customers more time to pay for their
purchases.

(c) Inflation increases the value of raw material inventories by 20 percent.

(d) The firm sells a parcel of land for $100,000. The land was purchased 5
years earlier for $200,000.

(e) The firm repurchases its own common stock.

(f) The firm doubles its quarterly dividend.

(g) The firm issues $1 million of long-term debt and uses the proceeds to re-
pay a short-term bank loan.

5. Each of the following events affects one or more tables in the chapter. Show the
effects of each event by adjusting the tables listed in parentheses:

(a) Dynamic repays only $2 million of short-term debt in 1995. (Tables 29-2,
29-4, 29-5, and 29-6)

(b) Dynamic issues an additional $10 million of long-term debt in 1995 and in-
vests $12 million in a new warehouse. (Tables 29-2, 29-4, 29-5, and 29-6)

(c) In 1995 Dynamic reduces the quantity of stuffing in each mattress.
Customers don't notice, but operating costs fall by 10 percent. (Tables 29-
2, 29-3, 29-4, 29-5, and 29-6)

(d) Starting in the third quarter of 1996, Dynamic employs new staff members
who will prove very effective in persuading customers to pay more
promptly. As a result, 90 percent of sales are paid for immediately, and 10
percent are paid in the following quarter. (Tables 29-7 and 29-8)

(e) Starting in the first quarter of 1996, Dynamic cuts wages by $4 million a
quarter. (Table 29-8)

(f) In the second quarter of 1996 a disused warehouse mysteriously catches
fire. Dynamic receives a $10 million check from the insurance company.
(Table 29-8)

(g) Dynamic's treasurer decides he can scrape by on a $2 million operating
cash balance. (Table 29-8)

6. Dynamic Futon forecasts the following purchases from suppliers:

	Jan.	Feb.	Mar.	Apr.	May	Jun.
Value of goods, millions of dollars	32	28	25	22	20	20

(a) Forty percent of goods are supplied cash on delivery. The remainder are paid
with an average delay of 1 month. If Dynamic Futon starts the year with
payables of $22 million, what is the forecast level of payables for each month?

(b) Suppose that from the start of the year the company stretches payables by
paying 40 percent after 1 month and 20 percent after 2 months. (The remainder continue to be paid cash on delivery.) Recalculate payables for
each month assuming that there are no cash penalties for late payment.

Questions and Problems

1. Table 29-11 shows Dynamic Mattress's year-end 1993 balance sheet, and Table
29-12 shows its income statement for 1994. Work out statements of sources
and uses of cash and sources and uses of funds for 1994.

TABLE 29-11
• •

Year-end balance sheet for 1993 (figures in millions of dollars)

Current assets:		Current liabilities:	
Cash	4	Bank loans	4
Marketable securities	2	Accounts payable	15
Inventory	20	Total current liabilities	19
Accounts receivable	22		
Total current assets	48	Long-term debt	5
		Net worth (equity and	
Fixed assets:		retained earnings)	60
Gross investment	50		
Less depreciation	−14	Total liabilities	
Net fixed assets	36	and net worth	84
Total assets	84		

TABLE 29-12
• •

Income statement for 1994
(figures in millions of dollars)

Sales	300
Operating costs	−285
	15
Depreciation	−2
	13
Interest	−1
Pretax income	12
Tax at 50 percent	−6
Net income	6

Note: Dividend = $1 million; retained earnings = $5 million.

2. Work out a short-term financing plan for Dynamic Mattress Company, assuming the limit on the line of credit is raised from $41 to $50 million. Otherwise adhere to the assumptions used in developing Table 29-10.

3. Look again at Dynamic Mattress's second plan in Table 29-10. Note that the line of credit is cheaper than borrowing against accounts receivable. Would you expect this to be true in practice? Why or why not?

4. Suppose that Dynamic's bank offers to forget about the compensating balance requirement if the firm pays interest at a rate of 3.375 percent per quarter. Should the firm accept this offer? Why or why not? (Except for this change, follow the assumptions underlying Table 29-10.) Would your answer change if Dynamic's cash requirements in quarters 1 and 2 were much smaller—say, only $20 million and $10 million, respectively?

5. In some countries the market for long-term corporate debt is limited, and firms turn to short-term bank loans to finance long-term investments in plant

TABLE 29-13

Selected budget data for Ritewell Publishers

	February	March	April
Total sales	200	220	180
Purchases of materials			
For cash	70	80	60
For credit	40	30	40
Other expenses	30	30	30
Taxes, interest, and dividends	10	10	10
Capital investment	100	0	0

TABLE 29-14

Cash budget for Ritewell Publishers

	February	March	April
Sources of cash:			
Collections on cash sales			
Collections on accounts receivable	—	—	—
Total sources of cash			
Uses of cash:			
Payments of accounts payable			
Cash purchases of materials			
Other expenses			
Capital expenditures			
Taxes, interest, and dividends	—	—	—
Total uses of cash			
Net cash inflow			
Cash at start of period	100		
+ Net cash inflow			
= Cash at end of period			
+ Minimum operating cash balance	100	100	100
= Cumulative short-term financing required			

and machinery. When a short-term loan comes due, it is replaced by another one, so that the firm is always a short-term debtor. What are the disadvantages of such an arrangement? Does it have any advantages? (*Hint:* See Section 23-4, especially "Introducing Inflation.")

6. Suppose a firm has surplus cash but is *not* paying taxes. Would you advise it to invest in Treasury bills or other safe, marketable securities? How about investment in the preferred or common stock of other companies? (*Hint:* Your an-

swer will reflect your stand on the "debt and taxes" controversy. See Section 18-2.)

7. Dynamic Mattress decides to lease its new mattress-stuffing machines rather than buy them. As a result, capital expenditure in the first quarter is reduced by $30 million, but the company must make lease payments of $1.5 million for each of the four quarters. Assume that the lease has no effect on tax payments until after the fourth quarter.

    Construct two tables like Tables 29-8 and 29-10 showing Dynamic's cumulative financing requirement and a new financing plan.

8. Table 29-13 lists data from the budget of Ritewell Publishers. Half the company sales are for cash on the nail; the other half are paid for with a 1-month delay. The company pays all its credit purchases with a 1-month delay. Credit purchases in January were $30, and total sales in January were $180. Complete the cash budget in Table 29-14.

9. If a firm pays its bills with a 30-day delay, what fraction of its purchases will be paid in the current quarter? In the following quarter? What if the delay is 60 days?

10. Which items in Table 29-9 would be affected by the following events?
    (*a*) There is a rise in interest rates.
    (*b*) The bank eliminates the compensating balance requirement.
    (*c*) Suppliers demand interest for late payment.
    (*d*) Dynamic receives an unexpected bill in the third quarter from the Internal Revenue Service for underpayment of taxes in previous years.

PART nine

SHORT-TERM FINANCIAL DECISIONS

30

Credit Management

Chapter 29 provided an overall idea of what is involved in short-term financial management. Now it is time to get down to detail.

When companies sell their products, they sometimes demand cash on or before delivery, but in most cases they allow some delay in payment. If you turn back to the balance sheet in Table 29-1, you can see that for the average manufacturing company, *accounts receivable* constitute on the average about one-third of its current assets. Receivables include both trade credit and consumer credit. The former is by far the larger and will, therefore, be the main focus of this chapter.

Companies that do not pay for their purchases immediately are effectively borrowing money from their suppliers. Such "debts" show up as *accounts payable* in the purchasing companies' balance sheets. Table 29-1 shows that payables are the most important source of short-term finance, almost twice as large as short-term loans from banks and other institutions.

Management of trade credit requires answers to five sets of questions:

1. On what terms do you propose to sell your goods or services? How long are you going to give customers to pay their bills? Are you prepared to offer a cash discount for prompt payment?
2. What evidence do you need of indebtedness? Do you just ask the buyer to sign a receipt, or do you insist on some more formal IOU?
3. Which customers are likely to pay their bills? To find out, do you examine customers' past records or past financial statements? Or do you rely on bank references?
4. How much credit are you prepared to extend to each customer? Do you play safe by turning down any doubtful prospects? Or do you accept the risk of a few bad debts as part of the cost of building up a large regular clientele?
5. How do you collect the money when it becomes due? How do you keep track of payments? What do you do about reluctant payers or deadbeats?

We will discuss each set of questions in turn.

30-1 TERMS OF SALE

Not all sales involve credit. For example, if you are producing goods to the customer's specification or incurring substantial delivery costs, then it may be sensible to ask for cash before delivery (CBD). If you are supplying goods to a wide variety of irregular customers, you may prefer cash on delivery (COD).[1] If your product is expensive and custom-designed, you may require **progress payments** as work is carried out. For example, a large, extended consulting contract might call for 30 percent payment after completion of field research, 30 percent more on submission of a draft report, and the remaining 40 percent when the project is finally completed.

When we look at transactions that do involve credit, we find that each industry seems to have its own particular usage with regard to payment terms.[2] These norms have a rough logic. For example, firms selling consumer durables may allow the buyer a month to pay, while those selling perishable goods, such as cheese or fresh fruit, typically demand payment in a week. Similarly, a seller will generally allow more extended payment if its customers are in low-risk businesses, if their accounts are large, if the customers need time to ascertain the quality of the goods, and if the goods are not quickly resold.

In order to induce customers to pay before the final date, it is common to offer a cash discount for prompt settlement. For example, shoe manufacturers commonly require payment within 30 days but offer a 5 percent discount to customers who pay within 10 days. These terms are referred to as "5/10, net 30." Toy manufacturers generally sell goods on terms of 2/30, net 50; their customers receive a 2 percent discount for payment within 30 days and must pay in full within 50 days.

Cash discounts are often very large. For example, a customer who buys on terms of 5/10, net 30 may decide to forgo the cash discount and pay on the thirtieth day. This means that the customer obtains an extra 20 days' credit but pays about 5 percent more for the goods. This is equivalent to borrowing money at a rate of 155 percent per annum.[3] Of course, any firm that delays payment beyond the due date gains a cheaper loan but damages its reputation for creditworthiness.

You can think of the terms of sale as fixing both the price for the cash buyer and the rate of interest charged for credit. For example, suppose that a firm reduces the cash discount from 5 to 4 percent. That would represent an *increase* in the price for the cash buyer of 1 percent but a *reduction* in the implicit rate of interest charged the credit buyer from just over 5 percent per 20 days to just over 4 percent per 20 days.

For many items that are bought on a recurrent basis, it is inconvenient to require separate payment for each delivery. A common solution is to pretend that all sales during the month in fact occur at the end of the month (EOM). Thus goods may be sold on terms of 8/10, EOM, net 60. This arrangement allows the customer a cash discount of 8 percent if the bill is paid within 10 days of the end of the month; otherwise, the full payment is due within 60 days of the invoice date.[4] When purchases are subject to seasonal fluctuations, manufacturers often encourage customers to take

---

[1]Some goods *can't* be sold on credit—a glass of beer, for example.

[2]Standard credit terms in different industries are reported in *Handbook of Credit Terms*, Dun and Bradstreet, New York, 1970. They are analyzed in B. Wilner, "Paying Your Bills: An Empirical Study of Trade Credit," unpublished working paper, University of Michigan, Ann Arbor, November 1995.

[3]The cash discount allows you to pay $95 rather than $100. If you do not take the discount, you get a 20-day loan, but you pay $5/95 = 5.26$ percent more for your goods. The number of 20-day periods in a year is $365/20 = 18.25$. A dollar invested for 18.25 periods at 5.26 percent per period grows to $(1.0526)^{18.25} = \$2.55$, a 155 percent return on the original investment. If a customer is happy to borrow at this rate, it's a good bet that he or she is desperate for cash (or can't work out compound interest). For a discussion of this issue, see J. K. Smith, "Trade Credit and Information Asymmetry," *Journal of Finance*, **42**:863–872 (September 1987).

[4]Terms of 8/10, prox., net 60 would entitle the customer to a discount if the bill is paid within 10 days of the end of the following (or "proximo") month.

early delivery by allowing them to delay payment until the usual order season. This practice is known as "season dating."

30-2 COMMERCIAL CREDIT INSTRUMENTS

The terms of sale define when payment is due but not the nature of the contract. Repetitive sales to domestic customers are almost always made on **open account** and involve only an implicit contract. There is simply a record in the seller's books and a receipt signed by the buyer.

If an order is very large and there is no complicating cash discount, the customer may be asked to sign a **promissory note.** This is just a straightforward IOU, worded along the following lines:

New York
April 1, 1996

Sixty days after date I promise to pay to the order of the XYZ Company one thousand dollars ($1000.00) for value received.

Signature

Such an arrangement is not common,[5] but it has two advantages. First, as long as the note is payable to "order" or to "bearer," the holder may sell it or use it as a security for a loan. Second, the note prevents any argument about the existence of the debt.

If you want a clear commitment from the buyer, it is more useful to have it *before* you deliver the goods. In this case the simplest procedure is to arrange a **commercial draft.**[6] It works as follows: The seller draws a draft ordering payment by the customer and sends this draft to the customer's bank together with the shipping documents. If immediate payment is required, the draft is termed a **sight draft;** otherwise, it is known as a **time draft.** Depending on whether it is a sight or a time draft, the customer either pays up or acknowledges the debt by adding the word *accepted* and his or her signature. The bank then hands the shipping documents to the customer and forwards the money or the **trade acceptance** to the seller.[7] The latter may hold the trade acceptance to maturity or use it as security for a loan.

If the customer's credit is for any reason suspect, the seller may ask the customer to arrange for his or her bank to accept the time draft. In this case, the bank guarantees the customer's debt. These **bank acceptances** are often used in overseas trade; they have a higher standing and greater negotiability than trade acceptances.

The exporter who requires greater certainty of payment can ask the customer to arrange for an **irrevocable letter of credit.** In this case the customer's bank sends the exporter a letter stating that it has established a credit in his or her favor at a bank in the United States. The exporter then draws a draft on the customer's bank and presents it to the bank in the United States together with the letter of credit and the

---

[5]In some countries, such as Japan, sales on open account are rare, and promissory notes tend to be the rule.

[6]Commercial drafts are sometimes known by the more general term *bills of exchange.*

[7]You often see the terms of sale defined as "SD-BL." This means that the bank will hand over the bill of lading in return for payment on a sight draft.

shipping documents. The bank in the United States arranges for this draft to be accepted or paid and forwards the documents to the customer's bank.

If you sell goods to a customer who proves unable to pay, you cannot get your goods back. You simply become a general creditor of the company, in common with other unfortunates. You can avoid this situation by making a *conditional sale*, whereby title to the goods remains with the seller until full payment is made. The conditional sale is common practice in Europe. In the United States it is used only for goods that are bought on an installment basis. In this case, if the customer fails to make the agreed number of payments, then the goods can be immediately repossessed by the seller.

30-3 CREDIT ANALYSIS

Firms are not allowed to discriminate between customers by charging them different prices. Neither may they discriminate by offering the same prices but different credit terms.[8] You *can* offer different terms of sale to different *classes* of buyers. You can offer volume discounts, for example, or discounts to customers willing to accept long-term purchase contracts. But as a rule, if you have a customer of doubtful standing, you should keep to your regular terms of sale and protect yourself by restricting the volume of goods that the customer may buy on credit.

There are a number of ways by which you can find out whether customers are likely to pay their debts. The most obvious indication is whether they have paid promptly in the past. However, beware of the customer who establishes a high credit limit on the basis of a series of small payments and then disappears, leaving you with a large unpaid bill.

If you are dealing with a new customer, you will probably arrange for a credit agency to undertake a credit check. Dun and Bradstreet is by far the largest of such agencies: its database contains information on more than 9 million companies. Credit agencies usually report the experience that other firms have had with the customer; you may also be able to get this information by checking with a credit bureau or by contacting the firms directly.

Your bank can also do a credit check. It will contact the customer's bank and ask for information on the customer's average bank balance, access to bank credit, and general reputation.

In addition to checking with your customer's bank, it might make sense to check what everybody else in the financial community thinks about your customer's credit standing. Does that sound expensive? It isn't if your customer is a public company. You just look at the Moody's or Standard and Poor's rating for the customer's outstanding bonds.[9] You can also compare prices of these bonds to prices of other firms' bonds. (Of course, the comparisons should be between bonds of similar maturity, coupon, etc.) Finally, you can look at how the customer's stock price has been behaving recently. A sharp fall in price doesn't mean that the company is in trouble, but it does suggest that prospects are less bright than they formerly were.

Financial Ratio Analysis

We have suggested a number of ways to check whether your customer is a good risk. You can ask your collection manager, a specialized credit agency, a credit bureau, a banker, or the financial community at large. But if you don't like relying on the judg-

---

[8]Price discrimination, and by implication credit discrimination, is prohibited by the Robinson-Patman Act.
[9]See Section 23-5.

ment of others, you can do your own homework. Ideally this would involve a detailed analysis of the company's business prospects and financing, but this approach is usually too expensive. Therefore credit analysts concentrate on the company's financial statements, using rough rules of thumb to judge whether the firm is a good credit risk. The rules of thumb are based on *financial ratios*. Chapter 27 described how these ratios are calculated and interpreted.

Numerical Credit Scoring

When the firm has a small, regular clientele, the credit manager can easily handle the investigation process informally. But when the company is dealing directly with consumers or with a large number of small-trade accounts, some streamlining is essential. In these cases it may make sense to use a mechanical scoring system to prescreen credit applications.

If you apply for a credit card or bank loan, you will be asked various questions about your job, home, and financial position. One medium-size bank required each loan applicant to answer a standard questionnaire, of which a condensed version is shown in Table 30-1.[10] It found that in total only 1.2 percent of the borrowers subsequently defaulted. Some categories of borrower, however, proved to be much worse credit risks than others. We have added the actual default rates for each category on the right side of Table 30-1. For example, you can see that 7 percent of the borrowers who had no telephone subsequently defaulted. Similarly, borrowers who lived in rented rooms, had no bank account, needed the loan to pay medical bills, and so on, were much worse credit risks than the average.

Given this experience, it might make sense for the bank to calculate an overall risk index for each applicant.[11] For example, it could construct a rough-and-ready index by adding up all the probabilities in Table 30-1. The wretch who gave the most unfavorable response to each question would have a risk index of

$$7.0 + 7.3 + 2.6 + \cdots + 2.6 = 51.8$$

As if he or she didn't have enough troubles!

The questionnaire in Table 30-1 is of course dated—not many loan applicants have a monthly income below $200! We wish we could give a current version, but they are all top secret: a bank with a superior method for identifying good and bad borrowers has a significant leg up on the competition. In fact, when a British bank recently laid off a number of employees, one unhappy staff member decided that the best way to get his own back was to leak details of the bank's credit scoring system to the press.[12]

Banks and the credit departments of industrial firms have also found that similar mechanical scoring systems can help them cut the costs of assessing credit applications from small businesses. For example, one bank claimed that credit scoring reduced the cost of loan appraisal by two-thirds. It cited the case of an application for a $5000 credit line from an accounting firm. A clerk entered information from the loan application into a computer and checked the firm's deposit balances with the bank, as well as the owner's personal and business credit files. Immediately the loan

---

[10]See P. F. Smith, "Measuring Risk on Consumer Installment Credit," *Management Science*, **11**:327–340 (November 1964).

[11]There are some measures you *cannot* use now in calculating a risk index or in any other credit evaluation: the applicant's sex, race, or age, for example.

[12]See V. Orvice, "Would You Get a Loan?" *Daily Mail*, March 16, 1994, p. 29.

TABLE 30-1

· ·

A condensed version of a questionnaire used by a bank for personal loan applicants. We have added in parentheses the percentage of borrowers in each category who subsequently defaulted.

1. Do you have:
   1 or more telephones? (.7)
   No telephone? (7.0)
2. Do you:
   Own your home? (.7)
   Rent a house? (2.2)
   Rent an apartment? (3.3)
   Rent a room? (7.3)
3. Do you:
   Have 1 or more bank accounts? (.8)
   No bank account? (2.6)
4. Is the purpose of the loan:
   To buy an automobile? (.8)
   To buy household goods? (.6)
   To pay medical expenses? (2.5)
   Other? (1.3)
5. How long did you spend in your last residence:
   6 months or less? (3.1)
   7 to 60 months? (1.4)
   More than 60 months? (.8)
6. How long did you spend in your last job:
   6 months? (3.2)
   7 to 60 months? (1.5)
   More than 60 months? (.9)
7. What is your marital status:
   Single? (1.6)
   Married? (1.0)
   Divorced? (2.9)
8. What is your postal zone? (.1 to 11.4)
9. For how long do you require the loan:
   12 months or less? (1.6)
   More than 12 months? (1.0)
10. What is your occupation? (.4 to 3.5)
11. What is your monthly income:
    $200 or less? (2.3)
    $200 to $1000? (1.1)
    More than $1000? (.7)
12. What is your age:
    25 or under? (1.5)
    26 to 30? (1.8)
    More than 30? (1.0)
13. How many are there in your family:
    One? (1.6)
    Two to seven? (1.1)
    Eight or more? (2.6)

Source: Reprinted by permission from P. F. Smith, "Measuring Risk on Consumer Installment Credit," *Management Science*, **11**:327–340 (November 1964). Copyright 1964 The Institute of Management Science.

Figure 30-1 The x's represent a hypothetical group of bank borrowers who subsequently repaid their loans; the o's represent those who defaulted. The sloping line discriminates between the two groups on the basis of time spent in last home and time spent in last job. The line represents the equation

$Z = 2$ (months in last residence)
$+ 1$ (months in last job) $= 60$

Borrowers who plot above the line have Z scores greater than 60.

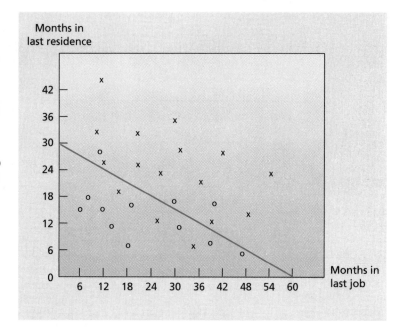

officer could see the applicant's score: 240 on a scale of 100 to 300, well above the bank's cutoff figure. All that remained for the bank to do was to check that there was nothing obviously suspicious about the application. "We don't want to lend to set up an alligator farm in the desert," said one bank official.[13]

Constructing Better Risk Indexes

Many lenders that use credit scoring systems employ ad hoc formulas. You should be able to do better than that.

Just adding up the separate probabilities, as in our earlier bank example, isn't the answer, for it ignores the interactions between the different factors. It may be much more alarming when a single applicant has a family of eight than when a married one does. On the other hand, you may not be so concerned when a single applicant lives in a rented room (unless, of course, the person also has a family of eight).

Suppose that you take just two factors—time spent in last residence and time spent in last job. You then plot a scatter diagram like the one in Figure 30-1. The x's represent customers who subsequently paid their debts; the o's represent customers who defaulted. Now try to draw a straight dividing line between the two groups. You can't completely separate them, but the line in our diagram keeps the two groups as far apart as possible. (Note that there are only three x's below the line and three o's above it.) This line tells us that if we wish to *discriminate* between the good and the bad risks, we should give only half as much weight to job stability as we give to home stability. The index of creditworthiness is

$$\text{Index of creditworthiness} = Z = 2 \text{ (months in last residence)}$$
$$+ 1 \text{ (months in last job)}$$

---

[13]Quoted in S. Hansell, "Need a Loan? Ask the Computer; 'Credit Scoring' Changes Small-Business Lending," *New York Times*, April 18, 1995, sec. D, p. 1.

TABLE 30-2
· ·

Recent *Z* scores for a sample of large firms. Firms with a high *Z* score have lower default risk.

Company	Z Score	Company	Z Score
Bethlehem Steel	0.7	Merck	4.3
Coca-Cola	7.3	Occidental Petroleum	0.7
Exxon	3.2	USAir	0.6
Hewlett-Packard	3.8	Wal-Mart	6.2
IBM	1.1	Westinghouse	1.3

Source: Standard and Poor's Compustat Services, Inc., 1995.

You minimize the degree of misclassification if you predict that applicants with *Z* scores over 60 will pay their bills and that those with *Z* scores below 60 will not pay.[14]

In practice we do not need to consider only two variables, nor do we need to estimate the equation by eye. *Multiple-discriminant analysis* (MDA) is a straightforward statistical technique for calculating how much weight to put on each variable in order to separate the creditworthy sheep from the impecunious goats.[15]

Edward Altman has used MDA to predict bad business risks. Altman's object was to see how well financial ratios could be used to determine which firms would go bankrupt during the period 1946–1965. MDA gave him the following index of creditworthiness:[16]

$$Z = 3.3 \left(\frac{\text{EBIT}}{\text{total assets}} \right) + 1.0 \left(\frac{\text{sales}}{\text{total assets}} \right) + .6 \left(\frac{\text{market value equity}}{\text{book value of debt}} \right)$$
$$+ 1.4 \left(\frac{\text{retained earning}}{\text{total assets}} \right) + 1.2 \left(\frac{\text{working capital}}{\text{total assets}} \right)$$

This equation did a good job at distinguishing the bankrupt and nonbankrupt firms. Of the former, 94 percent had *Z* scores of *less* than the cutoff score the year before they went bankrupt. In contrast, 97 percent of the nonbankrupt firms had *Z* scores *above* the cutoff.[17]

Although updated, refined (and secret) versions of Altman's original Z-score model are used by a number of institutions, the original model continues to be very much alive and used. Table 30-2, for example, lists recent *Z* scores for a small sample of large companies. Of course, the probability of most large firms' entering bankruptcy is fairly remote.

---

[14]The quantity 60 is an arbitrary constant. We could just as well have used 6, in which case the *Z* score is
   Z = .2 (months in last residence) + .1 (months in last job)

[15]MDA is not the only statistical technique that you can use for this purpose. Probit and logit are two other potentially useful techniques. These estimate the probability of some event (e.g., default) as a function of observable attributes.

[16]EBIT is earnings before interest and taxes. E. I. Altman, "Financial Ratios, Discriminant Analysis and the Prediction of Corporate Bankruptcy," *Journal of Finance*, **23**:589–609 (September 1968).

[17]This equation was fitted with hindsight. The equation did slightly less well when used to *predict* bankruptcies after 1965.

Credit scoring systems should carry a health warning. When you construct a risk index, it is tempting to experiment with many different combinations of variables until you find the equation that would have worked best in the past. Unfortunately, if you "mine" the data in this way, you are likely to find that the system works less well in the future than it did previously. If you are misled by the past successes into placing too much faith in your model, you may refuse credit to a number of potentially good customers. The profits that you lose by turning away customers could more than offset the gains that you make from avoiding a few bad eggs. As a result, you could be worse off than if you had pretended that you could tell one customer from another and extended credit to all of them.

Does this mean that you should not use credit scoring systems? Not a bit. It simply implies that it is not sufficient to have a good credit scoring system; you also need to know how much to rely on it. That is the topic of the next section.

30-4 THE CREDIT DECISION

Let us suppose that you have taken the first three steps toward an effective credit operation. In other words, you have fixed your terms of sale; you have decided whether to sell on open account or to ask your customers to sign IOUs; and you have established a procedure for estimating the probability that each customer will pay up. Your next step is to work out which of your customers should be offered credit.

If there is no possibility of repeat orders, the decision is relatively simple. Figure 30-2 summarizes your choice. On one hand, you can refuse credit. In this case you make neither a profit nor a loss. The alternative is to offer credit. Suppose that the probability that the customer will pay up is p. If the customer does pay, you receive additional revenues (REV) and you incur additional costs; your net gain is the present value of REV − COST. Unfortunately, you can't be certain that the customer will pay; there is a probability $(1 - p)$ of default. Default means you receive nothing and incur the additional costs. The *expected* profit from each course of action is therefore as follows:

Figure 30-2 If you refuse credit, you make neither profit nor loss. If you offer credit, there is a probability p that the customer will pay and you will make REV − COST; there is a probability $(1 - p)$ that the customer will default and you will lose COST.

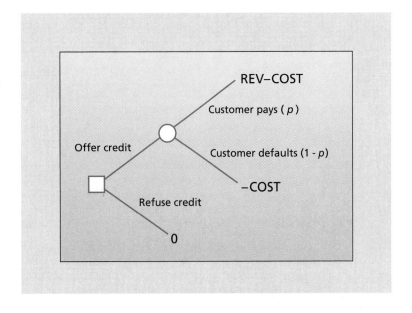

	Expected Profit
Refuse credit	0
Grant credit	$p\text{PV(REV} - \text{COST}) - (1 - p)\text{PV(COST)}$

You should grant credit if the expected profit from doing so is greater than the expected profit from refusing.

Consider, for example, the case of the Cast Iron Company. On each nondelinquent sale Cast Iron receives revenues with a present value of $1200 and incurs costs with a value of $1000. Therefore the company's expected profit if it offers credit is

$$p\text{PV(REV} - \text{COST}) - (1 - p)\text{PV(COST)} = p \times 200 - (1 - p) \times 1000$$

If the probability of collection is 5/6, Cast Iron can expect to break even:

$$\text{Expected profit} = \frac{5}{6} \times 200 - \left(1 - \frac{5}{6}\right) \times 1000 = 0$$

Therefore Cast Iron's policy should be to grant credit whenever the chances of collection are better than 5 out of 6.

When to Stop Looking for Clues

We told you earlier where to *start* looking for clues about a customer's creditworthiness, but we never said anything about when to *stop*. Now we can work out how your profits would be affected by more detailed credit analysis.

Suppose that Cast Iron Company's credit department undertakes a study to determine which customers are most likely to default. It appears that 95 percent of its customers have been prompt payers and 5 percent have been slow payers. However, customers with a record of slow payment are much more likely to default on the next order than those with a record of prompt payment. On the average 20 percent of the slow payers subsequently default, but only 2 percent of the prompt payers do so.

In other words, consider a sample of 1000 customers, none of whom has defaulted yet. Of these, 950 have a record of prompt payment, and 50 have a record of slow payment. On the basis of past experience Cast Iron should expect 19 of the prompt payers to default in the future and 10 of the slow payers to do so:

Category	Number of Customers	Probability of Default	Expected Number of Defaults
Prompt payers	950	.02	19
Slow payers	50	.20	10
All customers	1,000	.029	29

Now the credit manager must make a decision: Should the company refuse to give any more credit to customers that have been slow payers in the past?

If you are aware that a customer has been a slow payer, the answer is clearly "yes." Every sale to a slow payer has only an 80 percent chance of payment ($p = .8$). Selling to a *slow* payer, therefore, gives an expected *loss* of $40:

$$\text{Expected profit} = p\text{PV(REV} - \text{COST}) - (1 - p)\text{PV(COST)}$$
$$= .8(200) - .2(1000) = -\$40$$

But suppose that it costs $10 to search through Cast Iron's records to determine whether a customer has been a prompt or slow payer. Is it worth doing so? The expected payoff to such a check is

$$\begin{array}{ll} \text{Expected payoff} \\ \text{to credit check} \end{array} = \begin{array}{l} \text{(probability of identifying a slow payer} \times \text{gain from} \\ \text{not extending credit)} - \text{cost of credit check} \end{array}$$
$$= (.05 \times 40) - 10 = -\$8$$

In this case checking isn't worth it. You are paying $10 to avoid a $40 loss 5 percent of the time. But suppose that a customer orders 10 units at once. Then checking is worthwhile because you are paying $10 to avoid a *$400* loss 5 percent of the time:

$$\text{Expected payoff to credit check} = (.05 \times 400) - 10 = \$10$$

The credit manager therefore decides to check customer's past payment records only on orders of more than five units. You can verify that a credit check on a five-unit order just pays for itself.

Our illustration is simplistic, but you have probably grasped the message: You don't want to subject each order to the same credit analysis. You want to concentrate your efforts on the large and doubtful orders.

....

Credit Decisions with Repeat Orders

So far we have ignored the possibility of repeat orders. But one of the reasons for offering credit today is that you may get yourself a good, regular customer by doing so.

Figure 30-3 illustrates the problem.[18] Cast Iron has been asked to extend credit to a new customer. You can find little information on the firm, and you believe that the probability of payment is no better than .8. If you grant credit, the expected profit on this customer's order is

$$\begin{array}{ll} \text{Expected profit on} \\ \text{initial order} \end{array} = p_1 \times \text{PV(REV} - \text{COST)} - (1 - p_1) \times \text{PV(COST)}$$
$$= (.8 \times 200) - (.2 \times 1000) = -\$40$$

You decide to refuse credit.

This is the correct decision if there is no chance of a repeat order. But look again at the decision tree in Figure 30-3. If the customer does pay up, there will be a reorder next year. Because the customer has paid once, you can be 95 percent sure that he or she will pay again. For this reason any repeat order is very profitable.

$$\begin{array}{ll} \text{Next year's} \\ \text{expected profit} \\ \text{on repeat order} \end{array} = p_2 \text{PV(REV}_2 - \text{COST}_2) - (1 - p_2)\, \text{PV(COST}_2)$$
$$= (.95 \times 200) - (.05 \times 1000) = \$140$$

Now you can reexamine today's credit decision. If you grant credit today, you receive the expected profit on the initial order *plus* the possible opportunity to extend credit next year:

$$\begin{array}{ll} \text{Total expected} \\ \text{profit} \end{array} = \begin{array}{l} \text{expected profit on initial order} + \text{probability of} \\ \text{payment and repeat order} \\ \times \text{PV(next year's expected profit on repeat order)} \end{array}$$
$$= -40 + .80 \times \text{PV(140)}$$

At any reasonable discount rate, you ought to extend credit. For example, if the discount rate is 20 percent,

---

[18]Our example is adapted from H. Bierman, Jr., and W. H. Hausman, "The Credit Granting Decision," *Management Science*, **16**: B519–B532 (April 1970).

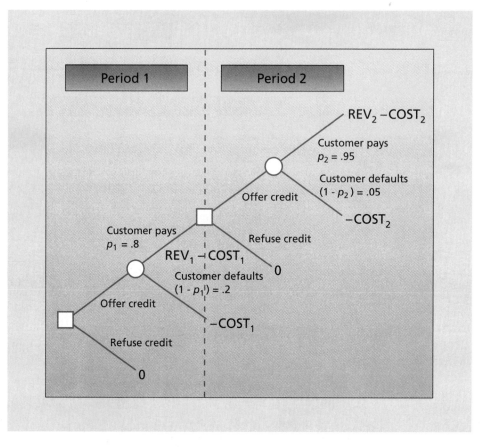

Figure 30-3 In this example there is only a .8 probability that your customer will pay in period 1; but if payment is made, there will be another order in period 2. The probability that the customer will pay for the second order is .95. The possibility of this good repeat order more than compensates for the expected loss in period 1.

$$\text{Total expected profit (present value)} = -40 + \frac{.8(140)}{1.2} = \$53.33$$

In this example you should grant credit even though you expect to take a loss on the order. The expected loss is more than outweighed by the possibility that you will secure a reliable and regular customer.

Some General Principles

Sometimes the credit manager faces clear-cut choices. In such circumstances it may be possible to estimate fairly precisely the consequences of a more liberal or a more stringent credit policy. But real-life situations are generally far more complex than our simple examples. Customers are not all good or all bad. Many of them pay consistently late; you get your money, but it costs more to collect and you lose a few months' interest. Then there is the question of risk: You may be able to measure the revenues and costs, but at what rate do you discount them?

Like almost all financial decisions, credit allocation involves a strong dose of judgment. Our examples are intended as reminders of the issues involved rather than as cookbook formulas. Here are the basic things to remember.

1. *Maximize Profit:* As credit manager, you should not focus on minimizing the number of bad accounts; your job is to maximize expected profit. You must face up to the following facts: The best that can happen is that the customer pays promptly; the worst is default. In the best case, the firm receives the full additional revenues from the sale less the additional costs; in the worst, it receives nothing and loses the costs. You must weigh the chances of these alternative outcomes. If the margin of profit is high, you are justified in a liberal credit policy; if it is low, you cannot afford many bad debts.

2. *Concentrate on the Dangerous Accounts:* You should not expend the same effort on analyzing all credit applications. If an application is small or clear-cut, your decision should be largely routine; if it is large or doubtful, you may do better to move straight to a detailed credit appraisal. Most credit managers don't make credit decisions on an order-by-order basis. Instead, they set a credit limit for each customer. The sales representative is required to refer the order for approval only if the customer exceeds this limit.

3. *Look beyond the Immediate Order:* The credit decision is a dynamic problem. You cannot look only at the present. Sometimes it may be worth accepting a relatively poor risk as long as there is a likelihood that the customer will become a regular and reliable buyer. New businesses must, therefore, be prepared to incur more bad debts than established businesses. This is part of the cost of building up a good customer list.

30-5 COLLECTION POLICY

It would be nice if all customers paid their bills by the due date. But they don't—and since you may also occasionally "stretch" your payables, you can't altogether blame them.

The credit manager keeps a record of payment experiences with each customer. Thus the manager knows that company Alpha always takes the discount and that company Omega generally takes 90 days to pay. In addition, the manager monitors overdue payments by drawing up a schedule of the aging of receivables. This may look roughly like Table 30-3.

When a customer is in arrears, the usual procedure is to send a statement of account and to follow this at intervals with increasingly insistent letters or telephone calls. If none of these has any effect, most companies turn the debt over to a collec-

TABLE 30-3

. . . .

Schedule of the aging of receivables (figures in dollars)				
Customer's Name	Amount Not Yet Due	1 Month Overdue	More than 1 Month Overdue	Total Owed
Alpha	10,000	0	0	10,000
Beta	0	0	5,000	5,000
⋮	⋮	⋮	⋮	⋮
Omega	5,000	4,000	21,000	30,000
Total	200,000	40,000	58,000	298,000

tion agency or an attorney. The fee for such services is usually between 15 and 40 percent of the amount collected.

There is always a potential conflict of interest between the collection department and the sales department. Sales representatives commonly complain that they no sooner win new customers than the collection department frightens them off with threatening letters. The collection manager, on the other hand, bemoans the fact that the sales force is concerned only with winning orders and does not care whether the goods are subsequently paid for.

There are also many instances of cooperation between sales managers and the financial managers who worry about collections. For example, the specialty chemicals division of a major pharmaceutical company actually made a business loan to an important customer that had been suddenly cut off by its bank. The pharmaceutical company bet that it knew its customer better than the customer's bank did. The bet paid off. The customer arranged alternative bank financing, paid back the pharmaceutical company, and became an even more loyal customer. It was a nice example of financial management supporting sales.

It is not common for suppliers to make business loans to customers in this way, but they lend money indirectly whenever they allow a delay in payment. Trade credit can be an important source of short-term funds for indigent customers that cannot obtain a bank loan. But that raises an important question: If the bank is unwilling to lend, does it make sense for you, the supplier, to continue to extend trade credit? Here are two possible reasons why it may make sense: First, as in the case of our pharmaceutical company, you may have more information than the bank does about the customer's business. Second, you need to look beyond the immediate transaction and recognize that your firm may stand to lose some profitable future sales if the customer goes out of business.[19]

Factoring and Credit Insurance

A large firm has some advantages in managing its accounts receivable. First, it may be possible for divisions to pool information on the creditworthiness of their customers. Second, there are potential economies of scale in record keeping, billing, and so on. Third, debt collection is a specialized business that calls for experience and judgment. The small firm may not be able to hire or train a specialized credit manager. However, it may be able to obtain some of these economies by farming part of the job out to a **factor.**

Factoring works as follows: The factor and the client agree on credit limits for each customer and on the average collection period. The client then notifies each customer that the factor has purchased the debt. Thereafter, for any sale, the client sends a copy of the invoice to the factor, the customer makes payment directly to the factor, and the factor pays the client on the basis of the agreed average collection period regardless of whether the customer has paid. There are, of course, costs to such an operation, and the factor typically charges a fee of 1 to 2 percent of the value of the invoice.[20]

---

[19]Of course, banks also need to recognize future opportunities to make profitable loans to the firm. The question therefore is whether suppliers have a *greater* stake in the continued prosperity of the firm. For some evidence on the determinants of the supply and demand for trade credit, see M. A. Petersen and R. G. Rajan, "Trade Credit: Theories and Evidence," unpublished working paper, Kellogg Graduate School of Management, Northwestern University, Evanston, Ill., 1995.

[20]Many factors are subsidiaries of commercial banks. Their typical client is a relatively small manufacturing company selling on a repetitive basis to a large number of industrial or retail customers. Factoring is particularly common in the clothing industry.

This factoring arrangement, known as *maturity factoring*, provides assistance with collection and insurance against bad debts. Generally, the factor is also willing to advance 70 to 80 percent of the value of the accounts at an interest cost of 2 or 3 percent above the prime rate. Factoring that provides collection, insurance, and finance is generally termed *old-line factoring*.[21]

If you don't want help with collection but do want protection against bad debts, you can obtain credit insurance. The credit insurance company obviously wants to be certain that you do not throw caution to the winds by extending boundless credit to the most speculative accounts. It therefore generally imposes a maximum amount that it will cover for accounts with a particular credit rating. Thus it may agree to insure up to a total of $100,000 of sales to customers with the highest Dun and Bradstreet rating, up to $50,000 to those with the next-highest rating, and so on. You may claim not only if the customer actually becomes insolvent but also if an account is overdue. Such a delinquent account is then turned over to the insurance company, which makes vigorous efforts to collect.

In 1962 the United States government encouraged a group of insurance companies to form a consortium known as the *Foreign Credit Insurance Association (FCIA)*. The FCIA now accounts for the bulk of short-term and medium-term insurance of export credits. You will find that banks are much more willing to lend against receivables that are insured with the FCIA.

30-6 SUMMARY

Credit management involves five steps. The first is to establish normal terms of sale. This means that you must decide the length of the payment period and the size of any cash discounts. In most industries these conditions are standardized.

The second step is to decide the form of the contract with your customer. Most domestic sales are made on open account. In this case the only evidence that the customer owes you money is the entry in your ledger and a receipt signed by the customer. Particularly if the customer is located in a foreign country, you may require a more formal contract. We looked at three such devices—the promissory note, the trade acceptance, and the letter of credit.

The third step is to assess each customer's creditworthiness. There are a variety of sources of information—your own experience with the customer, the experience of other creditors, the assessment of a credit agency, a check with the customer's bank, the market value of the customer's securities, and an analysis of the customer's financial statements. Firms that handle a large volume of credit information often use a formal system for combining the data from various sources into an overall credit score. Such numerical scoring systems help separate the borderline cases from the obvious sheep or goats. We showed how you can use statistical techniques such as multiple-discriminant analysis to give an efficient measure of default risk.

When you have made an assessment of the customer's credit standing, you can move to the fourth step in credit management, which is to establish sensible credit limits. The job of the credit manager is not to minimize the number of bad debts; it is to maximize profits. This means that you should increase the customer's credit limit as long as the probability of payment times the expected profit is greater than the probability of default times the cost of the goods. Remember not to be too short-

---

[21]Under an arrangement known as *with-recourse factoring*, the company is liable for any delinquent accounts. In this case the factor provides collection, but not insurance.

sighted in reckoning the expected profit. It is often worth accepting the marginal applicant if there is a chance that the applicant may become a regular and reliable customer.

The fifth, and final, step is to *collect*. Doing so requires tact and judgment. You want to be firm with the truly delinquent customer, but you don't want to offend the good one by writing demanding letters just because a check has been delayed in the mail. You will find it easier to spot troublesome accounts if you keep a careful record of the aging of receivables.

These five steps are interrelated. For example, you can afford more liberal terms of sale if you are very careful about whom you grant credit to. You can accept higher-risk customers if you are very active in pursuing any late payers. A good credit policy is one that adds up to a sensible whole.

Further Reading

A standard text on the practice and institutional background of credit management is:
R. H. Cole: *Consumer and Commercial Credit Management*, 9th ed., Richard D. Irwin, Inc., Homewood, Ill., 1992.

For a more analytical discussion of credit policy, see:
S. Mian and C. W. Smith: "Extending Trade Credit and Financing," *Journal of Applied Corporate Finance*, **7**:75–84 (Spring 1994).

Altman's paper is the classic on numerical credit scoring:
E. I. Altman: "Financial Ratios, Discriminant Analysis and the Prediction of Corporate Bankruptcy," *Journal of Finance*, **23**:589–609 (September 1968).

Quiz

1. Company X sells on a 1/30, net 60 basis. Customer Y buys goods invoiced at $1000.
   (*a*) How much can Y deduct from the bill if Y pays on day 30?
   (*b*) What is the effective annual rate of interest if Y pays on the due date rather than on day 30?
   (*c*) How would you expect payment terms to change if:
      (**i**) The goods are perishable.
      (**ii**) The goods are not rapidly resold.
      (**iii**) The goods are sold to high-risk firms.

2. The lag between the purchase date and the date on which payment is due is known as the *terms lag*. The lag between the due date and the date on which the buyer actually pays is the *due lag*, and the lag between the purchase and actual payment dates is the *pay lag*. Thus,

$$\text{Pay lag} = \text{terms lag} + \text{due lag}$$

   State how you would expect the following events to affect each type of lag:
   (*a*) The company imposes a service charge on late payers.
   (*b*) A recession causes customers to be short of cash.
   (*c*) The company changes its terms from net 10 to net 20.

3. Complete the passage below by selecting the appropriate terms for each blank from the following list (some terms may be used more than once): *acceptance,*

open, commercial, trade, the United States, his or her own, note, draft, account, promissory, bank, the customer's, letter of credit, shipping documents.

Most goods are sold on ＿＿ ＿＿. In this case the only evidence of the debt is a record in the seller's books and a signed receipt. When the order is very large, the customer may be asked to sign a(n) ＿＿ ＿＿, which is just a simple IOU. Alternatively, the seller can arrange a(n) ＿＿ ＿＿ ordering payment by the customer. In order to obtain the ＿＿ ＿＿, the customer must acknowledge this order and sign the document. The signed acknowledgment is known as a(n) ＿＿ ＿＿. Sometimes the seller may ask ＿＿ ＿＿ bank to sign the document. In this case it is known as a(n) ＿＿ ＿＿. The fourth form of contract is used principally in overseas trade. The customer's bank sends the exporter a(n) ＿＿ ＿＿ ＿＿ stating that it has established a credit in his or her favor at a bank in the United States. The exporter than draws a draft on ＿＿ bank and presents it to ＿＿ ＿＿ bank together with the ＿＿ ＿＿ and ＿＿ ＿＿. The bank then arranges for this draft to be accepted and forwards the ＿＿ ＿＿ to the customer's bank.

4. The Branding Iron Company sells its irons for $50 apiece wholesale. Production cost is $40 per iron. There is a 25 percent chance that wholesaler Q will go bankrupt within the next year. Q orders 1000 irons and asks for 6 months' credit. Should you accept the order? Assume that the discount rate is 10 percent per year, there is no chance of a repeat order, and Q will pay either in full or not at all.

5. Look back at Section 30-4. Cast Iron's costs have increased from $1000 to $1050. Assuming there is no possibility of repeat orders, answer the following:
   (*a*) When should Cast Iron grant or refuse credit?
   (*b*) If it costs $12 to determine whether a customer has been a prompt or slow payer in the past, when should Cast Iron undertake such a check?

6. Look back at the discussion in Section 30-4 of credit decisions with repeat orders. If $p_1 = .8$, what is the minimum level of p_2 at which Cast Iron is justified in extending credit?

7. True or False?
   (*a*) Exporters who require greater certainty of payment arrange for the customers to sign a bill of lading in exchange for a sight draft.
   (*b*) Multiple-discriminant analysis is often used to construct an index of creditworthiness. This index is generally called a Z score.
   (*c*) It makes sense to monitor the credit manager's performance by looking at the proportion of bad debts.
   (*d*) If a customer refuses to pay despite repeated reminders, the company will usually turn the debt over to a factor or an attorney.
   (*e*) The Foreign Credit Insurance Association insures export credits.

Questions and Problems

1. Listed below are some common terms of sale. Can you explain what each means?
   (*a*) 2/30, net 60
   (*b*) net 10
   (*c*) 2/5, EOM, net 30
   (*d*) 2/10, prox., net 60

2. Some of the items in question 1 involve a cash discount. For each of these, calculate the rate of interest paid by customers who pay on the due date instead of taking the cash discount.

3. As treasurer of the Universal Bed Corporation, Aristotle Procrustes is worried about his bad-debt ratio, which is currently running at 6 percent. He believes that imposing a more stringent credit policy might reduce sales by 5 percent and reduce the bad-debt ratio to 4 percent. If the cost of goods sold is 80 percent of the selling price, should Mr. Procrustes adopt the more stringent policy?

4. Jim Khana, the credit manager of Velcro Saddles, is reappraising the company's credit policy. Velcro sells on terms of net 30. Cost of goods sold is 85 percent of sales, and fixed costs are a further 5 percent of sales. Velcro classifies customers on a scale of 1 to 4. During the past 5 years, the collection experience was as follows:

Classification	Defaults as Percent of Sales	Average Collection Period in Days for Nondefaulting Accounts
1	.0	45
2	2.0	42
3	10.0	40
4	20.0	80

The average interest rate was 15 percent.

What conclusions (if any) can you draw about Velcro's credit policy? What other factors should be taken into account before changing this policy?

5. Look again at question 4. Suppose (*a*) that it costs $95 to classify each new credit applicant and (*b*) that an almost-equal proportion of new applicants falls into each of the four categories. In what circumstances should Mr. Khana not bother to undertake a credit check?

6. Until recently, Augean Cleaning Products sold its products on terms of net 60, with an average collection period of 75 days. In an attempt to induce customers to pay more promptly, it has changed its terms to 2/10, EOM, net 60. The initial effect of the changed terms is as follows:

| Percent of Sales with Cash Discount | AVERAGE COLLECTION PERIODS, DAYS | |
	Cash Discount	Net
60	30*	80

*Some customers deduct the cash discount even though they pay after the specified date.

Calculate the effect of the changed terms. Assume:
(*a*) Sales volume is unchanged.
(*b*) The interest rate is 12 percent.
(*c*) There are no defaults.
(*d*) Cost of goods sold is 80 percent of sales.

7. Look back at question 6. Assume that the change in credit terms results in a 2 percent increase in sales. Recalculate the effect of the changed credit terms.

8. Financial ratios were described in Chapter 27. If you are a credit manager, to which financial ratios would you pay most attention? Which do you think would be the least informative?

9. Discuss ways in which real-life decisions are more complex than the decision illustrated in Figure 30-3. How do you think these differences ought to affect the credit decision?

10. Discuss the problems with developing a numerical credit scoring system for evaluating personal loans.

11. If a company experiences a sudden decrease in sales, the aging schedule in Table 30-3 will indicate that an abnormally high proportion of payments is overdue. Show why this happens. Can you suggest an alternative form of presentation that would make it easier to recognize a change in customer payment patterns?

12. Why do firms grant "free" credit? Would it be more efficient if all sales were for cash and late payers were charged interest?

13. Sometimes a firm sells its receivables at a discount to a wholly owned captive finance company. This captive finance company is partly financed by the parent, but it also issues substantial amounts of debt. What are the possible advantages of such an arrangement?

14. Reliant Umbrellas has been approached by Plumpton Variety Stores of Nevada. Plumpton has expressed interest in an initial purchase of 5000 umbrellas at $10 each on Reliant's standard terms of 2/30, net 60. Plumpton estimates that if the umbrellas prove popular with customers, its purchases could be in the region of 30,000 umbrellas a year. After deductions for variable costs, this account would add $47,000 per year to Reliant's profits.

Reliant has been anxious for some time to break into the lucrative Nevada market, but its credit manager has some doubts about Plumpton. In the past 5 years, Plumpton had embarked on an aggressive program of store openings. In 1996, however, it went into reverse. The recession, combined with aggressive price competition, caused a cash shortage. Plumpton laid off employees, closed one store, and deferred store openings. The company's Dun and Bradstreet rating is only fair, and a check with Plumpton's other suppliers reveals that, although Plumpton traditionally took cash discounts, it has recently been paying 30 days slow. A check through Reliant's bank indicates that Plumpton has unused credit lines of $350,000 but has entered into discussions with the banks for a renewal of a $1,500,000 term loan due at the end of the year. Table 30-4 summarizes Plumpton's latest financial statements.

As credit manager of Reliant, how do you feel about extending credit to Plumpton?

15. Galenic, Inc., is a wholesaler for a range of pharmaceutical products. Before deducting any losses from bad debts, Galenic operates on a profit margin of 5 percent. For a long time the firm has employed a numerical credit scoring system based on a small number of key ratios. This has resulted in a bad-debt ratio of 1 percent.

Galenic has recently commissioned a detailed statistical study of the payment record of its customers over the past 8 years and, after considerable experimentation, has identified five variables that could form the basis of a new credit scoring system. On the evidence of the past 8 years, Galenic calculates

TABLE 30-4

···

Plumpton Variety Stores: summary financial statements (figures in millions)

	1996	1995		1996	1995
Cash	$ 1.0	$ 1.2	Payables	$ 2.3	$ 2.5
Receivables	1.5	1.6	Short-term loans	3.9	1.9
Inventory	10.9	11.6	Long-term debt	1.8	2.6
Fixed assets	5.1	4.3	Equity	10.5	11.7
Total assets	$18.5	$18.7	Total liabilities	$18.5	$18.7

	1996	1995
Sales	$55.0	$59.0
Cost of goods sold	32.6	35.9
Selling, general and administrative expenses	20.8	20.2
Interest	.5	.3
Tax	.5	.3
Net income	$ .6	$ 1.3

that for every 10,000 accounts it would have experienced the following default rates:

Credit Score under Proposed System	NUMBER OF ACCOUNTS		
	Defaulting	Paying	Total
Greater than 80	60	9,100	9,160
Less than 80	40	800	840
Total	100	9,900	10,000

By refusing credit to firms with a low credit score (less than 80), Galenic calculates that it would reduce its bad-debt ratio to 60/9160, or just under .7 percent. While this may not seem like a big deal, Galenic's credit manager reasons that this is equivalent to a decrease of one-third in the bad-debt ratio and would result in a significant improvement in the profit margin.

(*a*) What is Galenic's current profit margin, allowing for bad debts?

(*b*) Assuming that the firm's estimates of default rates are right, how would the new credit scoring system affect profits?

(*c*) Why might you suspect that Galenic's estimates of default rates will not be realized in practice? What are the likely consequences of overestimating the accuracy of such a credit scoring scheme?

(*d*) Suppose that one of the variables in the proposed scoring system is whether the customer has an existing account with Galenic (new customers are more likely to default). How would this affect your assessment of the proposal?

31

Cash Management

In 1995 citizens and corporations in the United States held approximately $1.15 trillion in cash. This included about $370 billion of currency and $780 billion of demand deposits with commercial banks. Cash pays no interest. Why, then, do sensible people hold it? Why, for example, don't you take all your cash and invest it in interest-bearing securities? The answer of course is that cash gives you more *liquidity* than securities. You can use it to buy things. It is hard enough getting New York cab drivers to give you change for a $20 bill, but try asking them to split a Treasury bill.

In equilibrium all assets in the same risk class are priced to give the same expected marginal benefit. The benefit from holding Treasury bills is the interest that you receive; the benefit from holding cash is that it gives you a convenient store of liquidity. In equilibrium the marginal value of this liquidity is equal to the marginal value of the interest on an equivalent investment in Treasury bills. This is just another way of saying that Treasury bills are investments with zero net present value—they are fair value relative to cash.

Does this mean that it does not matter how much cash you hold? Of course not. The marginal value of liquidity declines as you hold increasing amounts of cash. When you have only a small proportion of your assets in cash, a little extra can be extremely useful; when you have a substantial holding, any additional liquidity is not worth much. Therefore, as financial manager you want to hold cash balances up to the point where the marginal value of the liquidity is equal to the value of the interest forgone.

If that seems more easily said than done, you may be comforted to know that production managers must make a similar trade-off. Ask yourself why they carry inventories of raw materials. They are not obliged to do so; they could simply buy materials day by day, as needed. But then they would pay higher prices for ordering in small lots, and they would risk production delays if the materials were not delivered on time. That is why they order more than the firm's immediate needs.[1]

But there is a cost to holding inventories. Interest is lost on the money that is tied up in inventories, storage must be paid for, and often there is spoilage and deterioration. Therefore production managers try to strike a sensible balance between the costs of holding too little inventory and those of holding too much.

---

[1]Not much more, in many manufacturing operations. "Just-in-time" assembly systems provide for a continuous stream of parts deliveries, with no more than 2 or 3 hours' worth of parts inventory on hand. Financial managers likewise strive for just-in-time cash management systems, in which no cash lies idle anywhere in the company's business. This ideal is never quite reached because of the costs and delays discussed in this chapter. Large corporations get close, however.

That is all we are saying you need to do with cash. Cash is just another raw material that you require to carry on production. If you keep too small a proportion of your funds in the bank, you will need to make repeated small sales of securities every time you want to pay your bills. On the other hand, if you keep excessive cash in the bank, you are losing interest. The trick is to hit a sensible balance.

The trade-off between the benefits and costs of liquidity is one essential part of cash management. The other part is making sure that the collection and disbursement of cash are as efficient as possible. To understand this, we will have to look closely at the relationships between firms and their banks. Most of the latter part of this chapter is devoted to the mechanics of cash collection and disbursement and the services offered by banks to assist firms in cash management.

31-1 INVENTORIES AND CASH BALANCES

Let us take a look at what economists have had to say about managing inventories and then see whether some of these ideas may help us to manage cash balances. Here is a simple inventory problem.

Everyman's Bookstore experiences a steady demand for *Principles of Corporate Finance* from customers who find that it makes a serviceable bookend. Suppose that the bookstore sells 100 copies of the book a year and that it orders Q books at a time from the publishers. Then it will need to place $100/Q$ orders per year:

$$\text{Number of orders per year} = \frac{\text{sales}}{Q} = \frac{100}{Q}$$

Just before each delivery, the bookstore has effectively no inventory of *Principles of Corporate Finance*. Just *after* each delivery it has an inventory of Q books. Therefore its *average* inventory is midway between 0 books and Q books:

$$\text{Average inventory} = \frac{Q}{2} \text{ books}$$

For example, if the store increases its regular order by one book, the average inventory increases by ½ book.

There are two costs to holding this inventory. First, there is the carrying cost. This includes the cost of the capital that is tied up in inventory, the cost of shelf space, and so on. Let us suppose that these costs work out to a dollar per book per

TABLE 31-1
. . . .

How order cost varies with order size		
Order Size, Number of Books	Number of Orders per Year	Total Order Costs, Dollars
1	100	200
2	50	100
3	33	66
4	25	50
10	10	20
100	1	2

year. Adding one more book to each order therefore increases the average inventory by ½ book and the carrying cost by ½ × $1.00 = $.50. Thus the marginal carrying cost is a constant $.50:

$$\text{Marginal carrying cost} = \frac{\text{carrying cost per book}}{2} = \$.50$$

The second type of cost is the order cost. Imagine that each order placed with the publisher involves a fixed clerical and handling expense of $2. Table 31-1 illustrates what happens to order costs as you increase the size of each order. You can see that the bookstore gets a large reduction in costs when it orders two books at a time rather than one, but thereafter the savings from increases in order size steadily diminish. In fact, the *marginal* reduction in order cost depends on the *square* of the order size:[2]

$$\text{Marginal reduction in order cost} = \frac{\text{sales} \times \text{cost per order}}{Q^2} = \frac{\$200}{Q^2}$$

Here, then, is the kernel of the inventory problem: As the bookstore increases its order size, the number of orders falls but the average inventory rises. Costs that are related to the number of orders decline; those that are related to inventory size increase. It is worth increasing order size as long as the decline in order cost outweighs the increase in carrying cost. The optimal order size is the point at which these two effects exactly offset each other. In our example this occurs when $Q = 20$:

$$\text{Marginal reduction in order cost} = \frac{\text{sales} \times \text{cost per order}}{Q^2} = \frac{\$200}{20^2} = \$.50$$

$$\text{Marginal carrying cost} = \frac{\text{carrying cost per book}}{2} = \$.50$$

The optimal order size is 20 books. Five times a year the bookstore should place an order for 20 books, and it should work off this inventory over the following 10 weeks. Its inventory of *Principles of Corporate Finance* will therefore follow the sawtoothed pattern in Figure 31-1.

The general formula for optimum order size is found by setting marginal reduction in order cost equal to marginal carrying cost and solving for Q:

$$\text{Marginal reduction in order cost} = \text{marginal carrying cost}$$

$$\frac{\text{Sales} \times \text{cost per order}}{Q^2} = \frac{\text{carrying cost}}{2}$$

$$Q^2 = \frac{2 \times \text{sales} \times \text{cost per order}}{\text{carrying cost}}$$

$$Q = \sqrt{\frac{2 \times \text{sales} \times \text{cost per order}}{\text{carrying cost}}}$$

---

[2]Let T = total order cost, S = sales per year, and C = cost per order. Then

$$T = \frac{SC}{Q}$$

Differentiate with respect to Q:

$$\frac{dT}{dQ} = -\frac{SC}{Q^2}$$

Thus, an *increase* of dQ reduces T by SC/Q^2.

Figure 31-1 Everyman's Bookstore minimizes inventory costs by placing 5 orders per year for 20 books per order. That is, it places orders at about 10-week intervals.

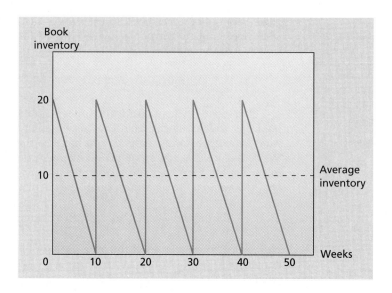

In our example,

$$Q = \sqrt{\frac{2 \times 100 \times 2}{1}} = \sqrt{400} = 20$$

The Extension to Cash Balances

William Baumol was the first to notice that this simple inventory model can tell us something about the management of cash balances.[3] Suppose that you keep a reservoir of cash that is steadily drawn down to pay bills. When it runs out, you replenish the cash balance by selling Treasury bills. The main carrying cost of holding this cash is the interest that you are losing. The order cost is the fixed administrative expense of each sale of Treasury bills. In these circumstances your inventory of cash also follows a sawtoothed pattern as in Figure 31-1.

In other words, your cash management problem is exactly analogous to the problem of optimum order size faced by Everyman's Bookstore. You just have to redefine variables. Instead of books per order, Q becomes the amount of Treasury bills sold each time the cash balance is replenished. Cost per order becomes cost per sale of Treasury bills. Carrying cost is just the interest rate. Total cash disbursements take the place of books sold. The optimum Q is

$$Q = \sqrt{\frac{2 \times \text{annual cash disbursements} \times \text{cost per sale of Treasury bills}}{\text{interest rate}}}$$

Suppose that the interest rate on Treasury bills is 8 percent, but every sale of bills costs you $20. Your firm pays out cash at a rate of $105,000 per month or $1,260,000 per year. Therefore the optimum Q is

$$Q = \sqrt{\frac{2 \times 1,260,000 \times 20}{.08}}$$

$$= \$25,100, \text{ or about } \$25,000$$

---

[3]W. J. Baumol, "The Transactions Demand for Cash: An Inventory Theoretic Approach," *Quarterly Journal of Economics,* **66**:545–556 (November 1952).

Figure 31-2 In Miller and Orr's model the cash balance is allowed to meander until it hits an upper or lower limit. At this point the firm buys or sells securities to restore the balance to the return point, which is the lower limit plus one-third of the spread between the upper and lower limits.

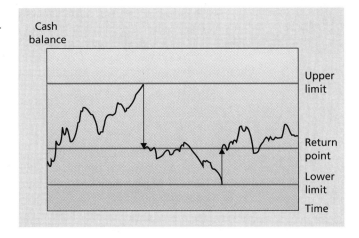

Thus your firm would sell approximately $25,000 of Treasury bills four times a month—about once a week. Its average cash balance will be $25,000/2, or $12,500.

In Baumol's model a higher interest rate implies a lower Q.[4] In general, when interest rates are high, you want to hold small average cash balances. On the other hand, if you use up cash at a high rate or if there are high costs to selling securities, you want to hold large average cash balances. Think about that for a moment. *You can hold too little cash.* Many financial managers point with pride to the tight control that they exercise over cash and to the extra interest that they have earned. These benefits are highly visible. The costs are less visible, but they can be very large. When you allow for the time that the manager spends in monitoring his or her cash balance, it may make sense to forgo some of that extra interest.

The Miller-Orr Model

Baumol's model works well as long as the firm is steadily using up its cash inventory. But that is not what usually happens. In some weeks the firm may collect some large unpaid bills and therefore receive a net *inflow* of cash. In other weeks it may pay its suppliers and so incur a net *outflow* of cash.

Economists and management scientists have developed a variety of more elaborate and realistic models that allow for the possibility of both cash inflows and outflows. Let us look briefly at a model developed by Miller and Orr.[5] It represents a nice compromise between simplicity and realism.

Miller and Orr consider how the firm should manage its cash balance if it cannot predict day-to-day cash inflows and outflows. Their answer is shown in Figure 31-2. You can see that the cash balance meanders unpredictably until it reaches an upper limit. At this point the firm buys enough securities to return the cash balance to a more normal level. Once again the cash balance is allowed to meander until this time it hits a lower limit. When it does, the firm *sells* enough securities to restore the balance to its normal level. Thus the rule is to allow the cash holding to wander freely until it hits an upper or lower limit. When this happens, the firm buys or sells securities to regain the desired balance.

---

[4]Note that the interest rate is in the denominator of the expression for optimal Q. Thus, increasing the interest rate reduces the optimal Q.

[5]M. H. Miller and D. Orr, "A Model of the Demand for Money by Firms," *Quarterly Journal of Economics*, **80**:413–435 (August 1966).

How far should the firm allow its cash balance to wander? Miller and Orr show that the answer depends on three factors. If the day-to-day variability in cash flows is large or if the fixed cost of buying and selling securities is high, then the firm should set the control limits far apart. Conversely, if the rate of interest is high, it should set the limits close together. The formula for the distance between barriers is[6]

$$\text{Spread between upper and lower cash balance limits} = 3\left(\frac{3}{4} \times \frac{\text{transaction cost} \times \text{variance of cash flows}}{\text{interest rate}}\right)^{1/3}$$

Have you noticed one odd feature about Figure 31-2? The firm does not return to a point halfway between the lower and upper limits. The firm always returns to a point one-third of the distance from the lower limit to the upper limit. In other words, the return point is

$$\text{Return point} = \text{lower limit} + \frac{\text{spread}}{3}$$

Always starting at this return point means the firm hits the lower limit more often than the upper limit. This does not minimize the number of transactions—that would require always starting exactly in the middle of the spread. However, always starting in the middle would mean a larger average cash balance and larger interest costs. The Miller-Orr return point minimizes the sum of transaction costs and interest costs.

....

Using the Miller-Orr Model

The Miller-Orr model is easy to use. The first step is to set the lower limit for the cash balance. This may be zero, some minimum safety margin above zero, or a balance necessary to keep the bank happy—more on bank requirements later in the chapter. The second step is to estimate the variance of cash flows. For example, you might record net cash inflows or outflows for each of the last 100 days and compute the variance of those 100 sample observations. More sophisticated measurement techniques could be applied if there were, say, seasonal fluctuations in the volatility of cash flows. The third step is to observe the interest rate and the transaction cost of each purchase or sale of securities. The final step is to compute the upper limit and the return point and to give this information to a clerk with instructions to follow the "control limit" strategy built into the Miller-Orr model. Table 31-2 gives a numerical example.

This model's practical usefulness is limited by the assumptions it rests on. For example, few managers would agree that cash inflows and outflows are entirely unpredictable, as Miller and Orr assume. The manager of a toy store knows that there will be substantial cash inflows around Christmastime. Financial managers know when dividends will be paid and when income taxes will be due. In Chapter 29 we described how firms forecast cash inflows and outflows and how they arrange short-term investment and financing decisions to supply cash when needed and put cash to work earning interest when it is not needed.

This kind of short-term financial plan is usually designed to produce a cash balance that is stable at some lower limit. But there are always fluctuations that finan-

---

[6]This formula assumes that the expected daily change in the cash balance is zero. Thus it assumes that there are no systematic upward or downward trends in the cash balance. If the Miller-Orr model is applicable, you need know only the variance of the daily cash flows, that is, the variance of the daily *changes* in the cash balance.

TABLE 31-2

· ·

Numerical example of the Miller-Orr model

A. Assumptions:
   1. Minimum cash balance = $10,000
   2. Variance of daily cash flows = 6,250,000 (equivalent to a standard deviation of $2,500 per day)
   3. Interest rate = .025 percent per day
   4. Transaction cost for each sale of purchase of securities = $20
B. Calculation of spread between upper and lower cash balance limits:

$$\text{Spread} = 3\left(\frac{\text{¾} \times \text{transaction cost} \times \text{variance of cash flows}}{\text{interest rate}}\right)^{\frac{1}{3}}$$

$$= 3\left(\frac{\text{¾} \times 20 \times 6{,}250{,}000}{.00025}\right)^{\frac{1}{3}}$$

$$= 21{,}634, \text{ or about } \$21{,}600$$

C. Calculate upper limit and return point:

$$\text{Upper limit} = \text{lower limit} + 21{,}600 = \$31{,}600$$

$$\text{Return point} = \text{lower limit} + \frac{\text{spread}}{3} = 10{,}000 + \frac{21{,}600}{3} = \$17{,}200$$

D. Decision rule:
   If cash balance rises to $31,600, invest $31,600 − 17,200 = $14,400 in marketable securities; if cash balance falls to $10,000, sell $7,200 of marketable securities and replenish cash.

cial managers cannot plan for, certainly not on a day-to-day basis. You can think of the Miller-Orr policies as responding to the cash inflows and outflows which cannot be predicted or which are not *worth* predicting. Trying to predict *all* cash flows would chew up enormous amounts of management time.

The Miller-Orr model has been tested on daily cash-flow data for several firms. It performed as well as or better than the intuitive policies followed by these firms' cash managers. However, the model was not an unqualified success; in particular, simple rules of thumb seem to perform just as well.[7] The Miller-Orr model may improve our *understanding* of the problem of cash management, but it probably will not yield substantial savings compared with policies based on a manager's judgment, providing of course that the manager understands the trade-offs we have discussed.

· · · · · · · · · · · · · · · ·

Raising Cash by Borrowing

So far we have assumed that surplus cash is invested in securities such as Treasury bills and that cash is replenished when necessary by selling these securities. The alternative may be to replenish cash by borrowing—for example, by drawing on a bank line of credit.

---

[7]For a review of tests of the Miller-Orr model, see D. Mullins and R. Homonoff, "Applications of Inventory Cash Management Models," in S. C. Myers (ed.), *Modern Developments in Financial Management*, Frederick A. Praeger, Inc., New York, 1976.

Borrowing raises another problem. The interest rate that you pay to the bank is likely to be higher than the rate that you receive on securities. As financial manager, you therefore face a trade-off. To earn the maximum interest on your funds, you want to hold low cash balances, but this means that you are more likely to have to borrow to cover an unexpected cash outflow. For example, suppose you can either hold cash that pays no interest or invest in securities that pay interest at 10 percent. The cost of keeping cash balances is the interest forgone by not investing the money in securities:

$$\text{Cost of cash balances} = 10\%$$

If you need more cash at short notice, it may be difficult or costly to sell securities, but you can borrow from the bank at 12 percent. In this case, there is a simple rule for maximizing expected return. You should adjust the cash balances until the probability that you will need to borrow from the bank equals[8]

$$\frac{\text{Cost of cash balances}}{\text{Cost of borrowing}} = \frac{10}{12} = .83$$

When we look at the problem this way, the best cash balance depends on the cost of borrowing and the extent of uncertainty about future cash flow. If the cost of borrowing is high relative to the interest rate on securities, you should make sure that there is only a low probability that you will be obliged to borrow. If you are very uncertain about the future cash flow, you may need to keep a large cash balance in order to be confident that you will not have to borrow. If you are fairly sure about cash flow, you can keep a lower cash balance.

Cash Management in the Largest Corporations

For very large firms, the transaction costs of buying and selling securities become trivial compared with the opportunity cost of holding idle cash balances. Suppose that the interest rate is 8 percent per year, or roughly $\frac{8}{365} = .022$ percent per day. Then the daily interest earned by $1 million is $.00022 \times 1,000,000 = \$220$. Even at a cost of $50 per transaction, which is generously high, it pays to buy Treasury bills today and sell them tomorrow rather than to leave $1 million idle overnight.

A corporation with $1 billion of annual sales has an average daily cash flow of $1,000,000,000/365$, about $2.7 million. Firms of this size end up buying or selling securities once a day, every day, unless by chance they have only a small positive cash balance at the end of the day.

---

[8]See, for example, J. H. W. Gosling, "One-Period Optimal Cash Balances," unpublished paper presented to the European Finance Association, Scheviningen, Holland, 1981. Instead of keeping the money in cash, you may be able to keep it in very liquid securities that are therefore easily sold but pay only a low rate of interest. The model works in this case also. For example, suppose that the interest rate on these liquid balances is 4 percent. Then the cost of investing in liquid balances is the interest that you forgo by not investing in the less marketable securities:

Cost of liquid balances = $10 - 4 = 6\%$

The cost of borrowing is the difference between the interest that you pay on the borrowing and the rate that you earn on liquid balances:

Cost of borrowing = $12 - 4 = 8\%$

Our rule states that you should adjust the liquid balances until the probability that you will need to borrow equals

$$\frac{\text{Cost of liquid balances}}{\text{Cost of borrowing}} = \frac{6}{8} = .75$$

Why do such firms hold any significant amounts of cash? There are basically two reasons. First, cash may be left in non-interest-bearing accounts to compensate banks for the services they provide. Second, large corporations may have literally hundreds of accounts with dozens of different banks. It is often better to leave idle cash in some of these accounts than to monitor each account daily and make daily transfers between them.

One major reason for the proliferation of bank accounts is decentralized management. You cannot give a subsidiary operating autonomy without giving its managers the right to spend and receive cash.

Good cash management nevertheless implies some degree of centralization. You cannot maintain your desired inventory of cash if all the subsidiaries in the group are responsible for their own private pools of cash. And you certainly want to avoid situations in which one subsidiary is investing its spare cash at 8 percent while another is borrowing at 10 percent. It is not surprising, therefore, that even in highly decentralized companies there is generally central control over cash balances and bank relations.

31-2 CASH COLLECTION AND DISBURSEMENT SYSTEMS

We have talked loosely about a firm's cash balance; it is now time to be more precise about how cash enters and exits the corporation and how the available cash balance is computed. The first necessary step is understanding *float*.

. . . .

Float

Suppose that the United Carbon Company has $1 million on demand deposit with its bank. It now pays one of its suppliers by writing and mailing a check for $200,000. The company's ledgers are immediately adjusted to show a cash balance of $800,000. But the company's bank won't learn anything about this check until it has been received by the supplier, deposited at the supplier's bank, and finally presented to United Carbon's bank for payment.[9] During this time United Carbon's bank continues to show in its ledger that the company has a balance of $1 million. The company obtains the benefit of an extra $200,000 in the bank while the check is clearing. This sum is often called *payment*, or *disbursement*, *float*.

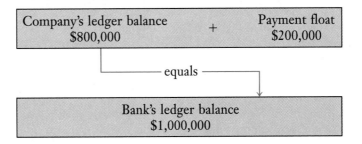

Float sounds like a marvelous invention, but unfortunately it can also work in reverse. Suppose that in addition to paying its supplier, United Carbon *receives* a check for $100,000 from a customer. It deposits the check, and both the company and the bank increase the ledger balance by $100,000:

---

[9]Checks deposited with a bank are cleared through the Federal Reserve clearing system, through a correspondent bank, or through a clearinghouse of local banks.

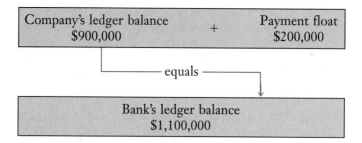

But this money isn't available to the company immediately. The bank doesn't actually have the money in hand until it has sent the check to, and received payment from, the customer's bank. Since the bank has to wait, it makes United Carbon wait too—usually 1 or 2 business days. In the meantime, the bank will show that United Carbon has an *available balance* of $1 million and an *availability float* of $100,000:

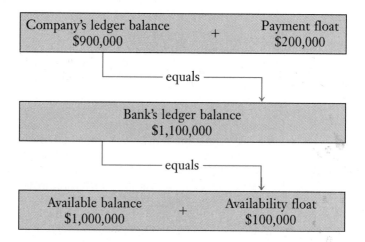

Notice that the company gains as a result of the payment float and loses as a result of the availability float. The difference is often termed the *net float*. In our example, the net float is $100,000. The company's available balance is therefore $100,000 greater than the balance shown in its ledger.

As financial manager you are concerned with the available balance, not with the company's ledger balance. If you know that it is going to be a week or two before some of your checks are presented for payment, you may be able to get by on a smaller cash balance. This game is often called *playing the float*.

You can increase your available cash balance by increasing your net float. This means that you want to ensure that checks paid in by customers are cleared rapidly and those paid to suppliers are cleared slowly. Perhaps this may sound like rather small beer, but think what it can mean to a company like Ford. Ford's daily sales average about $350 million. Therefore if it can speed up the collection process by 1 day, it frees $350 million, which is available for investment or payment to Ford's stockholders.

Some financial managers have become overenthusiastic in managing the float. In 1985 E. F. Hutton pleaded guilty to 2000 separate counts of mail and wire fraud. Hutton admitted that it had created nearly $1 billion of float by shuffling funds between its branches, and through various accounts at different banks. These activities cost the company a $2 million fine and its agreement to repay the banks any losses they may have incurred.

Managing Float

Float is the child of delay. Actually there are several kinds of delay, and so people in the cash management business refer to several kinds of float. Figure 31-3 summarizes.

Of course the delays that help the payer hurt the recipient. Recipients try to speed up collections. Payers try to slow down disbursements.

Speeding Up Collections

Many companies use **concentration banking** to speed up collections. In this case customers in a particular area make payment to a local branch office rather than to company headquarters. The local branch office then deposits the checks into a local bank account. Surplus funds are periodically transferred to a *concentration account* at one of the company's principal banks.

This can be done by using a *depository transfer check (DTC)*, which is a preprinted check made out directly by the local bank to a particular company account at the concentration bank. It takes 2 days to transfer funds by DTC. If you want faster service,

Figure 31-3 Delays create float. Each heavy arrow represents a source of delay. Recipients try to reduce delay to get available cash sooner. Payers prefer delay because they can use their cash longer. (*Note:* The delays causing availability float and presentation float are equal on average but can differ from case to case.)

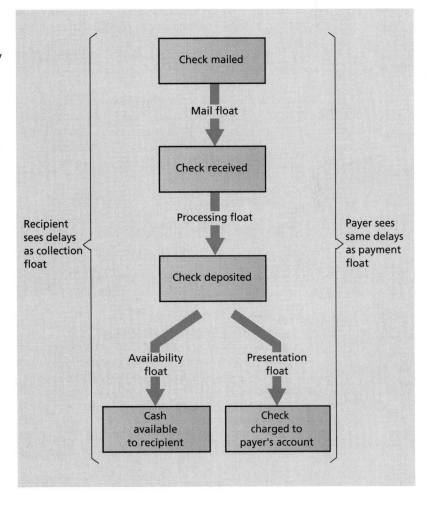

you must abandon paper and send money electronically. High-volume, low-value payments generally travel through the Automated Clearinghouse (ACH) system, which gives next-day delivery. Larger transfers are made through more expensive wire transfer systems, such as the Federal Reserve System's Fedwire or a private, international network known as CHIPS. Wire transfers give same-day service.

Concentration banking brings many small balances together in one large, central balance, which then can be invested in interest-paying assets through a single transaction. Concentration banking also reduces float in two ways. First, because the branch office is nearer to the customer, mailing time is reduced. Second, since the customer's check is likely to be drawn on a local bank, the time taken to clear the check is also reduced.

Often concentration banking is combined with a **lock-box system.** In a lock-box system, you pay the local bank to take on the administrative chores. The system works as follows: The company rents a locked post office box in each principal region. All customers within a region are instructed to send their payments to the post office box. The local bank, as agent for the company, empties the box at regular intervals and deposits the checks in the company's local account. Surplus funds are transferred periodically to one of the company's principal banks.

How many collection points do you need if you use a lock-box system or concentration banking? The answer depends on where your customers are and on the speed of the United States mail. For example, suppose that you are thinking of opening a lock box. The local bank shows you a map of mail delivery times. From that and knowledge of your customers' locations, you come up with the following data:

- Average number of daily payments to lock box: 150
- Average size of payment: $1200
- Rate of interest *per day*:   .02 percent
- Saving in mailing time: 1.2 days
- Saving in processing time: .8 day

On this basis, the lock box would increase your collected balance by

150 items per day × $1200 per item × (1.2 + .8) days saved = $360,000

Invested at .02 percent per day, $360,000 gives a daily return of

.0002 × $360,000 = $72

The bank's charge for operating the lock-box system depends on the number of checks processed. Suppose that the bank charges $.26 per check. That works out to 150 × .26 = $39 per day. You are ahead by $72 − 39 = $33 per day, plus whatever your firm saves from not having to process the checks itself.

Our example assumes that the company has only two choices. It can do nothing, or it can operate the lock box. But maybe there is some other lock-box location, or some mixture of locations, that would be still more effective. Of course, you can always find this out by working through all possible combinations, but it may be simpler to solve the problem by linear programming. Many banks offer linear programming models to solve the problem of locating lock boxes.[10]

---

[10] See, for example, A. Kraus, C. Janssen, and A. McAdams, "The Lock-Box Location Problem," *Journal of Bank Research*, **1**:50–58 (Autumn 1970).

Controlling Disbursements

Speeding up collections is not the only way to increase the net float. You can also do so by slowing down disbursements. One tempting strategy is to increase mail time. For example, United Carbon could pay its New York suppliers with checks mailed from Nome, Alaska, and its Los Angeles suppliers with checks mailed from Vienna, Maine.

But on second thought you will realize that such post office tricks are unlikely to give more than a short-run payoff. Suppose you have promised to pay a New York supplier on February 29. Does it matter whether you mail the check from Alaska on the 26th or from New York on the 28th? Of course, you could use a remote mailing address as an excuse for paying late, but that's a trick easily seen through. If you have to pay late, you may as well mail late.[11]

There are effective ways of increasing presentation float, however. For example, suppose that United Carbon pays its suppliers with checks written on a New York City bank. From the time that the check has been deposited by the supplier, there will be an average lapse of little more than a day before it is presented to United Carbon's bank for payment. The alternative is that United Carbon pays its suppliers with checks mailed to *arrive* on time but written on a bank in Helena, Montana; Midland, Texas; or Wilmington, Delaware. In these cases, it may take 3 or 4 days before each check is presented for payment. United Carbon, therefore, gains several days of additional float.[12]

Some firms even maintain disbursement accounts in different parts of the country. The computer looks up each supplier's zip code and automatically produces a check on the most distant bank.

The suppliers won't object to these machinations because the Federal Reserve guarantees a maximum clearing time of 2 days on all checks cleared through the Federal Reserve system. The Federal Reserve does object and has been trying to prevent remote disbursement.

A New York City bank receives several check deliveries each day from the Federal Reserve System as well as checks that come directly from other banks or through the local clearinghouse. Thus, if United Carbon uses a New York City bank for paying its suppliers, it will not know at the beginning of the day how many checks will be presented for payment. It must either keep a large cash balance to cover contingencies or be prepared to borrow. However, instead of having a disbursement account with, say, Morgan Guaranty Trust in New York, United Carbon could open a *zero-balance* account with Morgan's affiliated bank in Wilmington, Delaware. Because it is not in a major banking center, this affiliated bank receives almost all check deliveries in the form of a single, early-morning delivery from the Federal Reserve. Therefore, it can let the cash manager at United Carbon know early in the day exactly how much money will be paid out that day. The cash manager then arranges for this sum to be transferred from the company's concentration account to the disbursement account. Thus by the end of the day (and at the start of the next day), United Carbon has a zero balance in the disbursement account.

United Carbon's Wilmington account has two advantages. First, by choosing a remote location, the company has gained several days of float. Second, because the bank can forecast early in the day how much money will be paid out, United Carbon does not need to keep extra cash in the account to cover contingencies.

---

[11]Since the tax authorities look at the date of the postmark rather than the date of receipt, companies have been tempted to use a remote mailing address to pay their tax bills. But the tax authorities have reacted by demanding that large tax bills be paid by electronic transfer.

[12]Remote disbursement accounts are described in I. Ross, "The Race Is to the Slow Payer," *Fortune*, April 18, 1983, pp. 75–80.

Information Technology and Cash Management

Cash collection and disbursement have traditionally involved the creating, transporting, recording, and filing of checks and other paper documents. Sooner or later these activities will most often be done electronically.

The chief barrier to paperless cash management systems is that most consumers and small- and medium-size businesses are not set up to use them. But for companies that are "wired" to their banks, customers, and suppliers, such a system has at least three advantages:

- The marginal cost of transactions is very low. For example, in 1992 Campbell Soup estimated costs of $7 per wire transfer and 8 cents per ACH transfer.[13]
- Float is drastically reduced. Wire transfers generate no float at all.
- Record keeping and routine transactions are easy to automate when money moves electronically.[14]

We do not mean to imply that cash management will ever require supercomputers or rocket scientists. Substantial savings often come from plain common sense. For example, cash managers at Occidental Petroleum found that one plant was paying out about $8 million per month 3 to 5 days early to avoid any risk of late fees if checks were delayed in the mail. The solution was obvious: the plant's managers switched to paying large bills exactly on time by means of wire or ACH transfers.[15]

International Cash Management

Cash management in domestic firms is child's play compared with that in large multinational corporations operating in dozens of countries, each with its own currency, banking system, and legal structure. A single, centralized cash management system is an unattainable ideal for these companies, although they are edging toward it. A multinational typically sets up regional systems to prevent each of its operations from accumulating a little hoard of cash. For example, EDS, a computer services company, has centralized its European cash management by setting up local concentration accounts with a bank in each country. EDS sweeps any surplus cash into multicurrency accounts in London, and then draws on these accounts to invest in marketable securities or to finance any subsidiaries that have a cash shortage.[16]

There are many possible ways of pooling funds. For example, a multinational can open several accounts with the same bank but in different countries or currencies. In return, the bank agrees to lump all the accounts together when it calculates the interest that it pays on overall positive balances or charges on shortfalls.

Electronic transfers and computer-based cash management systems are especially valuable in international business. The costs and delays involved in paper transactions can be very significant. (Try clearing a check made out in Tugriks and drawn on the First National Bank of Ulan Bator.)

---

[13]James D. Moss, "Campbell Soup's Cutting-Edge Cash Management," *Financial Executive*, **8**:39–42 (September–October 1992).

[14]Campbell Soup's Treasury Management Department handles cash management, short-term borrowing and lending, and bank relationships with a total staff of seven. The company's domestic cash flow was about $5 billion. See ibid.

[15]Robert J. Pisapia, "The Cash Manager's Expanding Role: Working Capital," *Journal of Cash Management*, **10**:11–14 (November–December 1990).

[16]A. Querée, "What Do Treasurers Want from Banks?" *Corporate Finance*, 12–13 (January 1994).

31-3 BANK RELATIONS

Much of the work of cash management—processing checks, transferring funds, running lock boxes, helping keep track of the company's accounts—is done by banks. And banks provide many other services not so directly linked to cash management, e.g., handling payments and receipts in foreign currency, executing the purchase or sale of Treasury securities, or acting as a custodian for securities. Of course, banks also lend money or give firms the *option* to borrow under a *line of credit.*[17]

All these services have to be paid for. Banks demand fees for processing checks, operating lock boxes, or standing by ready to lend. These fees can be paid directly—by paying a monthly charge based on services provided—or indirectly, by letting money sit in non-interest-bearing bank accounts.

Banks like demand deposits. After setting aside a portion of the deposits in a reserve account with the Federal Reserve Bank, they can relend these deposits and earn interest on them. Banks would, therefore, be prepared to pay interest to attract demand deposits, but the government prohibits them from doing so.

One thing that governments never learn is that it is very difficult to legislate prices. Although they stop banks from offering money in payment for demand deposits, they do not stop them from offering services to attract deposits. Therefore, if a firm keeps a sufficiently large balance with the bank, the bank will process the firm's checks without charge, it will operate a lock-box system—it will provide all kinds of advice and services.

Thus firms can pay for bank services by maintaining interest-free demand deposits. These deposits generate *earnings credits*, which are used to pay for bank services. The earnings credits are interest by another name.[18]

Demand deposits earmarked to pay for bank services are termed *compensating balances*. There has been a steady trend toward direct fees for bank services and away from compensating balances. But some banks still request them, e.g., in exchange for a line of credit. In some cases *you* may request them. Suppose you had other reasons for keeping a working balance in a certain bank, perhaps to support local operations. This money may also serve as a compensating balance. In other words, it may be more efficient to let the money sit in the bank and generate earnings credits than to pay the costs of frequent transfers into or out of interest-bearing securities.

What Happens If Money Pays Interest?

The prohibition on paying interest on demand deposits is breaking down. The United States is closing in on other countries in which interest is paid routinely on corporate checking accounts.[19] But even where explicit interest-bearing checking accounts are the norm, firms and individuals still face a trade-off between liquidity and forgone interest, because checking accounts offer lower interest rates than direct investment in securities. (Otherwise, banks lose money; and in the long run they cannot offer a money-losing service.) Thus, the less money kept in a checking account, the more interest earned. Yet low balances in checking accounts mean frequent sales or purchases of securities and thus frequent transaction costs. This is the same problem we started the chapter with.

---

[17]See Section 32-4.

[18]Under this system of indirect rewards the bank will insist that you maintain a specified average level of balances over the month. Therefore you don't want to allow your cash inventory to run down to zero before replenishing it.

[19]In these countries, bank services are almost always paid by fee rather than indirectly by compensating balances.

31-4 SUMMARY

Cash provides liquidity, but it doesn't pay interest. Securities pay interest, but you can't use them to buy things. As financial manager you want to hold cash up to the point where the marginal value of liquidity is equal to the interest that you could earn on securities.

Cash is just one of the raw materials that you need to do business. It is expensive keeping your capital tied up in large inventories of raw materials when it could be earning interest. Why do you hold inventories at all? Why not order materials as and when you need them? The answer is that it is also expensive to keep placing many small orders. You need to strike a balance between holding too large an inventory of cash (and losing interest on the money) and making too many small adjustments to your inventory (and incurring additional administrative costs). If interest rates are high, you want to hold relatively small inventories of cash. If your cash needs are variable and your administrative costs are high, you want to hold relatively large inventories.

If the securities are not easily sold, you have the alternative of borrowing to cover a cash deficiency. Again, you face a trade-off. Since banks charge a high interest rate on borrowing, you want to keep sufficiently large liquid funds so that you don't need to keep borrowing. On the other hand, by having large liquid balances, you are also not earning the maximum return on your cash.

The cash shown in the company ledger is not the same as the available balance in your bank account. The difference is the net float. When you have written a large number of checks awaiting clearance, the available balance will be larger than the ledger balance. When you have just deposited a large number of checks which have not yet been collected by the bank, the available balance will be smaller. If you can predict how long it will take checks to clear, you may be able to *play the float* and get by on a smaller cash balance.

You can also *manage* the float by speeding up collections and slowing down payments. One way to speed collections is to use *concentration banking*. Customers make payments to a regional office which then pays the checks into a local bank account. Surplus funds are transferred from the local account to a concentration bank. An alternative technique is *lock-box banking*. In this case customers send their payments to a local post office box. A local bank empties the box at regular intervals and clears the checks. Concentration banking and lock-box banking reduce mailing time and the time required to clear checks.

Banks provide many services. They handle checks, manage lock boxes, provide advice, obtain references, and so on. Firms either pay cash for these services or pay by maintaining sufficient cash balances with the bank.

In many cases you will want to keep somewhat larger balances than are needed to pay for the tangible services. One reason is that the bank may be a valuable source of ideas and business connections. Another reason is that you may use the bank as a source of short-term funds. Leaving idle cash at your bank may be implicit compensation for the willingness of the bank to stand ready to advance credit when needed. A large cash balance may, therefore, be good insurance against a rainy day.

Further Reading

· ·

Baumol and Miller and Orr were the pioneers in applying inventory models to cash management:
W. J. Baumol: "The Transactions Demand for Cash: An Inventory Theoretic Approach," *Quarterly Journal of Economics,* **66**:545–556 (November 1952).

M. H. Miller and D. Orr: "A Model of the Demand for Money by Firms," *Quarterly Journal of Economics,* **80**:413–435 (August 1966).

Mullins and Homonoff review tests of inventory models for cash management:
D. Mullins and R. Homonoff: "Applications of Inventory Cash Management Models," in S. C. Myers (ed.), *Modern Developments in Financial Management,* Frederick A. Praeger, Inc., New York, 1976.

The next three articles analyze the design of lock-box and concentration banking systems:
A. Kraus, C. Janssen, and A. McAdams: "The Lock-Box Location Problem," *Journal of Bank Research,* **1**:50–58 (Autumn 1970).
G. Cornuejols, M. L. Fisher, and G. L. Nemhauser: "Location of Bank Accounts to Optimize Float: An Analytic Study of Exact and Approximate Algorithms," *Management Science,* **23**:789–810 (April 1977).
S. F. Maier and J. H. Van der Weide: "What Lock-Box and Disbursement Models Really Do," *Journal of Finance,* **37**:361–371 (May 1983).

The Journal of Cash Management, *published by the National Corporate Cash Management Association, is a good reference for recent developments. Specialized texts include:*
J. C. Kallberg, K. L. Parkinson, and J. R. Ochs (eds.): *Essentials of Cash Management,* National Corporate Cash Management Association, Newtown, Conn., 1989.
N. C. Hill and W. L. Sartoris: *Short-Term Financial Management,* Macmillan Publishing Company, New York, 1988.
J. Van der Weide and S. F Maier: *Managing Corporate Liquidity: An Introduction to Working Capital Management,* John Wiley & Sons, Inc., New York, 1985.
J. E. Finnerty: *How to Manage Corporate Cash Effectively,* American Management Association, New York, 1991.

Quiz

1. Everyman's Bookstore has experienced an increase in demand for *Principles of Corporate Finance.* It now expects to sell 200 books a year. Unfortunately, inventory carrying costs have increased to $2 per book per year, whereas order costs have remained steady at $2 per order.
   (*a*) What is the marginal carrying cost (for a unit increase in order size)?
   (*b*) At what point does the marginal carrying cost equal the marginal reduction in order cost?
   (*c*) How many orders should the store place per year?
   (*d*) What is its average inventory?

2. Now assume that Everyman's Bookstore uses up cash at a steady rate of $20,000 a year. The interest rate is 2 percent, and each sale of securities costs $2.
   (*a*) What is the marginal carrying cost of the cash (for a $1 increase in order size)?
   (*b*) At what point does the marginal carrying cost equal the marginal reduction in order costs?
   (*c*) How many times a year should the store sell securities?
   (*d*) What is its average cash balance?

3. In the Miller and Orr cash balance model the firm should allow the cash balance to move within limits.
   (*a*) What three factors determine how far apart these limits are?
   (*b*) How far should the firm adjust its cash balance when it reaches the upper or lower limit?
   (*c*) Why does it not restore the cash balance to the halfway point?

4. Suppose that you can hold cash that pays no interest or invest in securities paying interest of 8 percent. The securities are not easily sold on short notice; therefore, you must make up any cash deficiency by drawing on a bank line of credit which charges interest at 10 percent. Should you invest more or less in securities under each of the following circumstances?
   (*a*) You are unusually uncertain about future cash flows.
   (*b*) The interest rate on bank loans rises to 11 percent.
   (*c*) The interest rates on securities and on bank loans both rise by the same proportion.
   (*d*) You revise downward your forecast of future cash needs.

5. A company has the following cash balances:

   - Company's ledger balance: $600,000
   - Bank's ledger balance: $625,000
   - Available balance: $550,000

   (*a*) Calculate the payment float and availability float.
   (*b*) Why does the company gain from the payment float?
   (*c*) Suppose the company adopts a policy of writing checks on a remote bank. How is this likely to affect the three measures of cash balance?

6. Anne Teak, the financial manager of a furniture manufacturer, is considering operating a lock-box system. She forecasts that 300 payments a day will be made to lock boxes, with an average payment size of $1500. The bank's charge for operating the lock boxes is *either* $.40 a check *or* compensating balances of $800,000.
   (*a*) If the interest rate is 9 percent, which method of payment is cheaper?
   (*b*) What reduction in the time to collect and process each check is needed to justify use of the lock-box system?

7. Explain why companies use zero-balance accounts to make disbursements.

8. Complete the passage below by choosing the appropriate term from the following list: *lock-box banking, wire transfer, payment float, concentration banking, availability float, net float, depository transfer check.*
   The firm's available balance is equal to its ledger balance plus the _____ and minus the _____. The difference between the available balance and the ledger balance is often called the _____. Firms can increase their cash resources by speeding up collections. One way to do this is to arrange for payments to be made to regional offices which pay the checks into local banks. This is known as _____. Surplus funds are then transferred from the local bank to one of the company's main banks. Transfer may be by the quick but expensive _____ or by the slightly slower but cheaper _____. Another technique is to arrange for a local bank to collect the checks directly from a post office box. This is known as _____.

Questions and Problems
....

1. How would you expect a firm's cash balance to respond to the following changes?
   (*a*) Interest rates increase.
   (*b*) The volatility of daily cash flow decreases.
   (*c*) The transaction cost of buying or selling marketable securities goes up.

2. A firm maintains a separate account for cash disbursements. Total disbursements are $100,000 per month, spread evenly over the month. Administrative and transaction costs of transferring cash to the disbursement account are $10 per transfer. Marketable securities yield 1 percent per month. Determine the size and number of transfers that will minimize the cost of maintaining the special account.

3. Refer to Table 31-2. Calculate the optimal strategy under the following alternative assumptions:

   - Minimum cash balance: $20,000
   - Standard deviation of daily cash flows: $5000
   - Interest rate: .03 percent per day
   - Transaction cost of each purchase or sale of securities: $25

4. Suppose that the rate of inflation accelerates from 5 to 10 percent per year. Would firms' cash balances go up or down relative to sales? Explain.

5. A parent company settles the collection account balances of its subsidiaries once a week. (That is, each week it transfers any balances in the accounts to a central account.) The cost of a wire transfer is $10. A depository transfer check costs $.80. Cash transferred by wire is available the same day, but the parent must wait 3 days for depository transfer checks to clear. Cash can be invested at 12 percent per year. How much money must be in a collection account before it pays to use a wire transfer?

6. The financial manager of JAC Cosmetics is considering opening a lock box in Pittsburgh. Checks cleared through the lock box will amount to $300,000 per month. The lock box will make cash available to the company 3 days earlier than is currently the case.
   (a) Suppose that the bank offers to run the lock box for a $20,000 compensating balance. Is the lock box worthwhile?
   (b) Suppose that the bank offers to run the lock box for a fee of $.10 per check cleared instead of a compensating balance. What must the average check size be for the fee alternative to be less costly? Assume an interest rate of 6 percent per year.
   (c) Why did you need to know the interest rate to answer (b) but not to answer (a)?

7. On January 25, Coot Company has $250,000 deposited with a local bank. On January 27, the company writes and mails checks of $20,000 and $60,000 to suppliers. At the end of the month, Coot's financial manager deposits a $45,000 check received from a customer in the morning mail and picks up the end-of-month account summary from the bank. The manager notes that only the $20,000 payment of the 27th has cleared the bank. What are the company's ledger balance and payment float? What is the company's net float?

8. Knob, Inc., is a nationwide distributor of furniture hardware. The company now uses a central billing system for credit sales of $180 million annually. First National, Knob's principal bank, offers to establish a new concentration banking system for a flat fee of $100,000 per year. The bank estimates that mailing and collection time can be reduced by 3 days. By how much will Knob's avail-

ability float be reduced under the new system? How much extra interest income will the new system generate if the extra funds are used to reduce borrowing under Knob's line of credit with First National? Assume that the borrowing rate is 12 percent. Finally, should Knob accept First National's offer if collection costs under the old system are $40,000 per year?

9. A few years ago, Merrill Lynch increased its float by mailing checks drawn on west coast banks to customers in the east and checks drawn on east coast banks to customers in the west. A subsequent class action suit against Merrill Lynch revealed that in 28 months, from September 1976, Merrill Lynch disbursed $1.25 billion in 365,000 checks to New York State customers alone. The plaintiff's lawyer calculated that by using a remote bank Merrill Lynch had increased its average float by 1½ days.[20]
   (*a*) How much did Merrill Lynch disburse per day to New York State customers?
   (*b*) What was the total gain to Merrill Lynch over the 28 months, assuming an interest rate of 8 percent?
   (*c*) What was the present value of the increase in float if the benefits were expected to be permanent?
   (*d*) Suppose that the use of remote banks had involved Merrill Lynch in extra expenses. What was the maximum extra cost per check that Merrill Lynch would have been prepared to pay?

10. The processing cost of making a payment through the Automated Clearinghouse (ACH) system is roughly half the cost of making the same payment by check. Why, therefore, do firms often rationally choose to make payments by check?

11. Suppose that interest rates double.
   (*a*) What, according to the Baumol model, would happen to the firm's average cash balances?
   (*b*) Recalculate the gain from operating the lock-box system described in Section 31-2 given the new level of interest rates.

12. Every day, General Blancmange writes checks worth $100,000. These checks take an average of 5 days to clear. The company also receives payments of $150,000 every day. These take 3 days to clear.
   (*a*) Calculate payment float, availability float, and net float.
   (*b*) What would be the company's annual savings if it could reduce float availability to 1 day? The interest rate is 6 percent a year. What would be the present value of these savings?

---

[20]See, for example, I. Ross, op. cit.

32

Short-Term Lending and Borrowing

If a company has a temporary cash surplus, it can invest in short-term securities. If it has a temporary deficiency, it can replenish cash by selling securities or by borrowing on a short-term basis. Chapter 31 discussed when to make such changes. But you need to know more than that. There is an elaborate menu of short-term securities; you should be familiar with the most popular entrées. Similarly there are many kinds of short-term debts, and you should know their distinguishing characteristics. That is why we have included the present chapter on short-term lending and borrowing. You will encounter little in the way of new theory, but there is a good deal of interesting institutional material.

32-1 SHORT-TERM LENDING

The Money Market

The market for short-term investments is generally known as the **money market.** The money market has no physical marketplace. It consists of a loose agglomeration of banks and dealers linked together by telex, telephones, and computers. But a huge volume of securities is regularly traded on the money market, and competition is vigorous.

Most large corporations manage their own money-market investments, buying and selling through banks or dealers. Small companies sometimes find it more convenient to hire a professional investment-management firm or to put their cash into a money-market fund. This is a mutual fund that invests only in short-term securities. In return for a fee, money-market funds provide professional management and a diversified portfolio of high-quality, short-term securities. We discussed money-market funds in Section 17-3.

In Chapter 24 we pointed out that there are two main markets for long-term dollar bonds. There is the domestic market in the United States, and there is an international market for eurobonds. Similarly in this chapter we shall see that in addition to the domestic money market, there is also an international market for short-term eurodollar investments.

A *eurodollar* is not some strange bank note—it is simply a dollar deposit in a bank outside the United States. For example, suppose that an American oil company buys crude from an Arab sheik and pays for it with a $1 million check drawn on Morgan

Guaranty Bank. The sheik then deposits the check into his account at Barclays Bank in London.[1] As a result, Barclays has an asset in the form of a $1 million credit in its account with Morgan Guaranty. It also has an offsetting liability in the form of a dollar deposit. The dollar deposit is placed in Europe; it is, therefore, a eurodollar deposit.

We will describe the principal domestic and eurodollar investments shortly, but bear in mind that there is also a market for investments in other eurocurrencies. For example, if a United States corporation wishes to make a short-term investment in deutschemarks, it can do so in the Frankfurt money market or it can make a euromark deposit with a bank in London.

If we lived in a world without regulation and taxes, the interest rate on a eurodollar loan would have to be the same as that on an equivalent domestic dollar loan, the rate on a eurosterling loan would have to be the same as that on a domestic sterling loan, and so on. However, the eurocurrency markets exist largely because individual governments attempt to regulate domestic bank lending. For example, between 1963 and 1974 the United States government controlled the export of funds for corporate investment. Therefore, companies that wished to expand abroad were forced to turn to the eurodollar market. This demand for eurodollar loans tended to push the eurodollar interest rate above the domestic rate. At the same time the government limited the rate of interest that banks in the United States could pay on domestic deposits; this also tended to keep the eurodollar rate of interest above the domestic rate. By early 1974 the restrictions on the export of funds had been removed, and for large deposits the interest-rate ceiling had also been abolished. In consequence, the difference between the interest rate on eurodollars and the rate on domestic deposits narrowed. But it did not disappear: Banks are not subject to Federal Reserve requirements on eurodollar deposits and are not obliged to insure these deposits with the Federal Deposit Insurance Corporation. On the other hand, depositors are exposed to the (very low) risk that a foreign government could prohibit banks from repaying eurodollar deposits. For these reasons eurodollar investments continue to offer slightly higher rates of interest than domestic dollar deposits.

The term *eurodollar* indicates that most of the business is conducted in Europe and principally in London, but there is also a growing market for dollar deposits in Singapore and other Asian centers.[2]

The United States government has become increasingly concerned that its regulations are driving banking business overseas to foreign banks and the overseas branches of American banks. In an attempt to attract some of this business back to the States, the government in 1981 allowed United States and foreign banks to establish so-called *international banking facilities* (IBFs). An IBF is the financial equivalent of a free-trade zone; it is physically situated in the United States, but it is not required to maintain reserves with the Federal Reserve and depositors are not subject to any United States tax.[3] However, there are tight restrictions on what business an IBF can conduct. In particular, it cannot accept deposits from domestic United States corporations or make loans to them.

Banks in London lend dollars to one another at the *London interbank offered rate* (LIBOR). LIBOR is a benchmark for pricing many types of short-term loans in the United States and overseas. For example, a corporation in the United States may issue a floating-rate note with interest payments tied to LIBOR.

---

[1]The sheik could equally well deposit the check with the London branch of a United States bank or a Japanese bank. He would still have made a eurodollar deposit.

[2]These are often known as *Asian dollars* or *Asian currency units* (ACUs).

[3]For these reasons dollars held on deposit in an IBF are also classed as eurodollars.

Valuing Money-Market Invest-ments

When we value long-term debt, it is important to take default risk into account. Almost anything may happen in 30 years; even today's most respectable company may get into trouble eventually. This is the basic reason why corporate bonds offer higher yields than Treasury bonds.

Short-term debt is not risk-free either. When Penn Central failed, it had $82 million of short-term commercial paper outstanding. After that shock, investors became much more discriminating in their purchases of commercial paper, and the spread between interest rates on high- and low-quality paper widened dramatically.

Such examples of failure are exceptions that prove the rule; in general, the danger of default is less for money-market securities issued by corporations than for corporate bonds. There are two reasons for this. First, the range of possible outcomes is smaller for short-term investments. Even though the distant future may be clouded, you can usually be confident that a particular company will survive for at least the next month. Second, for the most part only well-established companies can borrow in the money market. If you are going to lend money for only 1 day, you can't afford to spend too much time in evaluating the loan. Thus you will consider only blue-chip borrowers.

Despite the high quality of money-market investments, there are often significant differences in yield between corporate and United States government securities. For example, in August 1995 the rate of interest on 3-month commercial paper was about .4 percentage points higher than the rate on Treasury bills. Why is this? One answer is the risk of default on commercial paper. Another is that the investments have different degrees of liquidity or "moneyness." Investors prefer Treasury bills because they are easier to turn into cash on short notice. Securities that can be converted quickly and cheaply into cash offer relatively low yields.

Calculat-ing the Yield on Money-Market Invest-ments

Many money-market investments are pure discount securities. This means that they don't pay interest: the return consists of the difference between the amount you pay and the amount you receive at maturity. Unfortunately, it is no good trying to persuade the Internal Revenue Service that this difference represents a capital gain. The IRS is wise to that one and will tax your return as ordinary income.

Two features make it difficult to work out the yield on money-market securities. One is the fact that they are often quoted on a discount basis; the other is that they are usually quoted on a 360-day year. For example, in August 1995, 91-day Treasury bills were issued at a discount of 5.43 percent. This is a rather complicated way of saying that the price of a 91-day bill was $100 - 91/360 \times 5.43 = \$98.63$. For each $98.63 that you invested in August, the government agreed to pay $100 to you 91 days later. The yield over the 91 days was therefore $(100 - 98.63)/98.63 = 1.392$ percent, equivalent over a 365-day year to 5.58 percent simple interest and 5.70 percent if interest is compounded annually.[4] Notice that the yield is higher than the discount. When you read that Treasury bills are at a discount of 5.43 percent, it is very easy to slip into the mistake of thinking that this is their yield.[5]

---

[4]Money-market dealers calculate yields on bills of 6 months or less on the basis of simple interest, using either a 360-day year (the so-called *money-market yield*) or a 365-day year (the *equivalent bond yield*). In other words, they multiply the 91-day yield by either 360/91 or 365/91. This is often confusing and not, in principle, the right way to do it. The compound rate is better:
$(1.01392)^{365/91} - 1 = .0570$, or 5.70%

[5]For more detail on how to calculate yields on money-market investments, see M. Stigum, *Fixed Income Calculations, Vol. 1: Money Market Paper and Bonds*, Dow Jones-Irwin, Inc., Homewood, Ill., 1994.

32-2 MONEY MARKET INVESTMENTS

Table 32-1 summarizes the principal money-market investments. We will describe each in turn, but you should note that in the United States the volume of business in three of these investments is much larger than in the others. These three are Treasury bills, commercial paper, and repurchase agreements.

U.S. Treasury Bills

The first item in Table 32-1 is U.S. Treasury bills. These mature in 3 months, 6 months, or 1 year.[6] Both 3-month and 6-month bills are issued every week and 1-year bills are generally issued every month. Sales are by auction. You can enter a competitive bid and take your chance of receiving an allotment at your bid price. Alternatively, if you want to be sure of getting your bills, you can enter a noncompetitive bid. Noncompetitive bids are filled at the *average* price of the successful competitive bids. You don't have to participate in the auction in order to invest in Treasury bills. There is also an excellent secondary market in which billions of dollars of bills are bought and sold every day.

Federal Agency Securities

Agencies of the federal government such as the Federal Home Loan Bank (FHLB) and the Federal National Mortgage Association ("Fannie Mae") borrow both short and long term. The short-term debt consists of discount notes, which are similar to Treasury bills. They are very actively traded and are often held by corporations. Their yields are slightly above those on comparable Treasury securities. One reason for the slightly higher yields is that agency debt is not quite as marketable as Treasury issues. Another is that most agency debt is backed not by the "full faith and credit" of the United States government but only by the agency itself. It is possible that the government would allow one of its agencies to default on its debt, but most investors regard this risk as exceedingly remote.

Short-Term Tax-Exempts

Short-term notes are also issued by municipalities, states, and agencies such as state universities and school districts.[7] These are slightly more risky than Treasury bills and not as easy to buy or sell.[8] Nevertheless they have one particular attraction—the interest is not subject to federal income tax.[9]

Pretax yields on tax-exempts are substantially lower than those on comparable taxed securities. But if your company pays tax at the standard 35 percent corporate rate, the lower gross yield of the municipals may be more than offset by the savings in tax.

Tax-exempt issues also include variable-rate demand bonds (VRDBs). These are long-term securities, whose interest payments are linked to the level of short-term interest rates. Whenever the interest rate is reset, investors have the right to sell the bonds back to the issuer for their face value. This ensures that on these reset dates

---

[6]So-called 3-month bills actually mature 91 days after issue, and 6-month bills mature 182 days after issue.

[7]Some of these notes are *general obligations* of the issuer; others are *revenue securities*, and in these cases payments are made from rent receipts or other user charges.

[8]Defaults on tax-exempts are rare but not unknown. For example, in 1983 the municipal utility Washington Public Power Supply System (unfortunately known as WPPSS) defaulted on $2.25 billion of bonds. The 1994 default of Orange County is described in Section 13-3.

[9]This advantage is partly offset by the fact that Treasury securities are free of state and local taxes.

TABLE 32-1

. . . .

Money-market investments in the United States

Investment	Borrower	Maturities when Issued	Marketability	Basis for Calculating Interest	Comments
Treasury bills	United States government	3-month, 6-month, and 1-year	Excellent secondary market	Discount	3-month and 6-month bills auctioned weekly; 1-year bills auctioned monthly
Federal agency discount notes	FHLB, "Fannie Mae," "Sallie Mae," "Freddie Mac," etc.	Typically 3 to 6 months	Very good secondary market	Discount	Sold through dealers
Tax-exempt municipal notes	Municipalities, states, school districts, etc.	1 month to 1 year	Good secondary market	Usually interest-bearing; interest at maturity	Tax anticipation notes (TANs), revenue anticipation notes (RANs), bond anticipation notes (BANs), etc.
Tax-exempt variable-rate demand bonds (VRDBs)	Municipalities, states, state universities, etc.	20 to 40 years	Good secondary market	Variable interest rate	Long-term bonds but with put options to demand repayment
Negotiable certificates of deposit (CDs)	Commercial banks, savings and loans	Usually 1 to 3 months; also longer-maturity variable-rate CDs	Poor secondary market	Interest-bearing with interest at maturity	Receipt for time deposit
Commercial paper (CP)	Industrial firms, finance companies, and bank holding companies; also municipalities	Maximum 270 days; usually 60 days or less	Dealers or issuer will repurchase paper	Discount	Unsecured promissory note; may be placed through dealer or directly with investor
Medium-term notes (MTNs)	Largely finance companies and banks; also industrial firms	Minimum 270 days; usually less than 10 years	Dealers will repurchase notes	Interest-bearing; usually fixed rate	Unsecured promissory note; usually placed through dealer
Bankers' acceptances (BSs)	Major commercial banks	1 to 6 months	Fair secondary market	Discount	Demands to pay that have been accepted by a bank
Repurchase agreements (repos)	Dealers in U.S. government securities	Overnight to about 3 months; also open repos (continuing contracts)	No secondary market	Repurchase price set higher than selling price; difference quoted as repo interest rate	Sales of government securities by dealer with simultaneous agreement to repurchase

the price of the bonds cannot be less than their face value. Therefore, although VRDBs are long-term bonds, their prices are very stable and they compete with short-term tax-exempt notes as a home for spare cash.

Bank Time Deposits and Certificates of Deposit

When you make a time deposit with a bank, you are lending money to the bank for a fixed period. If you need the money before maturity, the bank will usually allow you to withdraw it but will exact a penalty in the form of a reduced rate of interest.

Wouldn't it be nice if you could avoid that penalty by selling your loan to another would-be lender? You can if you have $1 million or more to invest.[10] In this case, when the bank borrows, it issues a **negotiable certificate of deposit (CD)**. A CD is simply evidence of a time deposit with a bank. However, if you decide that you need the money before maturity, you don't have to ask the bank: you just sell your CD to another investor. When the loan matures, the new owner of the CD presents it to the bank and receives payment.

CDs typically have a maturity of between 30 days and 3 months, but banks also issue longer-term CDs with a variable interest rate. The supply of CDs in the United States expanded rapidly until the mid-1980s, but since then it has fallen away as banks found more attractive ways to raise funds.[11]

We pointed our earlier that, instead of depositing dollars with a bank in the United States, a corporation can deposit them overseas with a foreign bank or the foreign branch of a United States bank. Unlike domestic banking, such eurocurrency banking is a wholesale rather than a retail business. The customers are corporations and governments—not individuals. They don't want checking accounts; they want to earn interest on their money. Therefore, eurodollar bank deposits pay a fixed rate of interest, and either they are for a fixed term that may vary from 1 day to several years or they are for an undefined term but may be called at 1 or more days' notice. Since a time deposit is an illiquid investment, the London branches of the major banks also issue negotiable eurodollar CDs. The eurodollar CD market has not suffered the dramatic decline seen in the United States CD market, but it is less active than it once was.

Commercial Paper

A bank is an intermediary which borrows short-term funds from one group of firms or individuals and relends the money to another group. It makes its profit by charging the borrower a higher rate of interest than it offers the lender.

Sometimes it is convenient to have a bank in the middle. It saves lenders the trouble of looking for borrowers and assessing their creditworthiness, and it saves borrowers the trouble of looking for lenders. Depositors do not care whom the bank lends to: they need only satisfy themselves that the bank as a whole is safe.

There are also occasions on which it is *not* worth paying an intermediary to perform these functions. Large, safe, and well-known companies can bypass the banking system by issuing their own short-term unsecured notes. These notes are known as **commercial paper.**

---

[10]Banks also sell nonegotiable CDs to individuals. Most of these pay a fixed rate of interest, but there are also some quirky CDs. Peterson Bank sold a World Soccer CD which paid double interest if the United States won the World Cup, and Bank of Boulder sold CDs that paid interest in the form of sporting rifles and shotguns.

[11]One disadvantage with any time deposit is that the bank has to set aside part of the money as a reserve with the Federal Reserve Bank. This cash does not earn interest. The reserve is therefore equivalent to a tax on the deposit.

Financial institutions, such as bank holding companies and finance companies,[12] also issue commercial paper, sometimes in very large quantities. For example, GE Capital Corporation has almost $50 billion of commercial paper in issue. Often such firms set up their own marketing department and sell their issues directly to investors. Other companies sell through dealers who receive a fee for marketing the issue.

Commercial paper has a maximum maturity of 9 months, though most paper is for 60 days or less. Most buyers of commercial paper hold it to maturity, but the company or dealer that sells the paper is usually prepared to repurchase it earlier.

Only nationally known companies can find a market for their commercial paper, and even then dealers are reluctant to handle a company's paper if there is any uncertainty about its financial position.[13] Companies generally support their issue of commercial paper by arranging a backup line of credit with a bank, which guarantees that they can find the money to repay the paper. The risk of default is, therefore, small.[14]

Commercial paper is very popular with major companies. By cutting out the intermediary, they are able to borrow at rates that may be 1 to 1½ percent below the prime rate charged by banks. Even after allowing for a dealer's commission and the cost of any backup line of credit, this is still a substantial saving. Banks have felt the competition from commercial paper and have been prepared to reduce their rates to blue-chip customers. As a result, "prime rate" doesn't mean what it used to. It once meant the rate banks charged their most creditworthy customers. Now the prime customers often pay less than the prime rate.

As an alternative to issuing commercial paper in the United States, companies can also sell euro–commercial paper (ECP). For example, AT&T has a $1 billion ECP program in addition to selling its commercial paper in the United States. The market for ECP is broadly similar to the domestic market.[15]

Medium-Term Notes

New Issues of securities do not need to be registered with the SEC as long as they mature within 270 days. So by limiting the maturity of commercial paper issues, companies can avoid the delays and expenses of registration. However, in 1982 the SEC introduced shelf registration, which permits companies to file a single registration statement for a series of similar issues.[16] This encouraged large blue-chip companies to make regular issues of unsecured **medium-term notes (MTNs).**

---

[12]A *bank holding company* is a firm that owns a bank and also nonbanking subsidiaries. Thus a bank holding company might hold a bank (the major part of its business) and also a leasing company, a management consulting company, etc. *Finance companies* are firms that specialize in lending to businesses or individuals. They include independent firms such as Household Finance as well as subsidiaries of nonfinancial corporations, such as General Motors Acceptance Corporation (GMAC). In their lending finance companies compete with banks. However, they raise funds not by attracting deposits, as banks do, but by issuing commercial paper and other, longer-term securities.

[13]Moody's and Standard and Poor's publish quality ratings for commercial paper. For example, Moody's provides three ratings, from P-1 (denoting Prime 1, the highest-grade paper) to P-3. Investors rely on these ratings, along with other information, when they compare the quality of different firms' paper. Most are reluctant to buy low-rated paper.

[14]Firms may also issue *asset-backed paper*. For example, General Motors Acceptance Corporation (GMAC) has set up a special-purpose company which buys up to $5 billion of GMAC's receivables at a discount and finances the purchase by selling commercial paper. The cash flows from the receivables are then used to repay the paper. This form of arrangement removes both the receivables and the debt from the firm's balance sheet. See I. Picker, "GM's Monster Loan," *Institutional Investor,* **27:**37–39 (May 1993).

[15]For a general discussion of commercial paper, see M. A. Post, "The Evolution of the U.S. Commercial Paper Market since 1980," *Federal Reserve Bulletin,* **78:**879–891 (December 1992); and T. K. Hahn, "Commercial Paper," *Economic Quarterly* (Federal Reserve Bank of Richmond), **79:**45–67 (Spring 1993).

[16]We described shelf registration in Section 15-3.

You can think of MTNs as a hybrid between corporate bonds and commercial paper. Like bonds, they are relatively long-term instruments; their maturity is never less than 270 days and may be as long as 30 years.[17] On the other hand, like commercial paper, MTNs are not underwritten but are sold on a regular basis either through dealers or, occasionally, directly to investors. Borrowers, such as finance companies that are always needing cash, welcome the flexibility of MTNs. For example, a company may tell its dealers the amount of money that it needs to raise that week, the range of maturities that it can offer, and the maximum interest rate that it is prepared to pay. It is them up to the dealers to find the buyers.

Just as there is both a domestic and an international market for commercial paper, so there are two parallel markets for medium-term notes. The euro-MTN market is younger than that in the United States, but it has grown rapidly.

We have described MTNs in this chapter because they are an important part of the money market. However, buyers of MTNs tend to be long-term investors who want to nail down a fixed rate of interest for a number of years. Unlike most other money-market investments, MTNs are not commonly used as a temporary home for spare cash.[18]

Bankers' Acceptances

A **banker's acceptance (BA)** begins life as a written demand for the bank to pay a given sum at a future date. The bank then agrees to this demand by writing "accepted" on it. Once accepted, the draft becomes the bank's IOU and is a negotiable security, which can be bought and sold through money-market dealers.

A banker's acceptance may arise in one of two ways. We have already seen in Chapter 30 that an acceptance may be arranged to finance exports or imports. Later in this chapter we shall see that acceptances are also occasionally used in connection with inventory financing.

Acceptances by the large U.S. banks generally mature in 1 to 6 months and involve very low credit risk.[19]

Repurchase Agreements

Repurchase agreements, or *repos*, are effectively secured loans to a government security dealer. They work as follows: The investor buys part of the dealer's holding of Treasury securities and simultaneously arranges to sell them back again at a later date at a specified higher price.

Repos sometimes run for several months, but more frequently they are just overnight (24-hour) agreements. No other domestic money-market investment offers such liquidity. Corporations can treat overnight repos almost as if they were interest-bearing demand deposits.

Suppose that you decide to invest cash in repos for several days or weeks. You don't want to keep renegotiating agreements every day. One solution is to enter into an *open repo* with a security dealer. In this case there is no fixed maturity to the agree-

---

[17]Walt Disney Company has even used its MTN shelf registration to issue a 100-year bond. See L. E. Crabbe, "Medium Term Notes," In F. J. Fabozzi and T. D. Fabozzi (eds.), *Handbook of Fixed Income Securities*, 4th ed., Dow Jones-Irwin, Inc., Homewood, Ill., 1995.

[18]A few MTNs have floating interest rates and offer investors the right to demand early repayment. These are used as a parking lot for short-term cash.

[19]For further information, see "Recent Developments in the Bankers' Acceptance Market," *Federal Reserve Bulletin*, **72:**1–12 (January 1986); and R. K. LaRoche, "Bankers' Acceptances," *Economic Quarterly* (Federal Reserve Bank of Richmond), **79:**75–85 (Winter 1993).

ment; either side is free to withdraw at 1 day's notice. Alternatively, you may arrange with your bank to transfer any excess cash automatically into repos.[20]

For many years repos appeared to be not only very liquid instruments but also very safe. This reputation took a knock in 1982 when two money-market dealers went bankrupt. Each case involved heavy use of repos. One dealer, Drysdale Securities, had been in existence for only 3 months and had total capital of $20 million. However, it went bankrupt, owing Chase Bank $250 million. It's not easy to run up debts that fast, but Drysdale did it.

Ever since the Drysdale collapse lawyers have been trying to sort out the legal status of the repo. Is it, as the name implies, a promise to repurchase the bond at an agreed price, or is it, as some lawyers argue, a loan secured by a bond?[21]

32-3 FLOATING-RATE PREFERRED STOCK—AN ALTERNATIVE TO MONEY-MARKET INVESTMENTS

There is no law preventing firms from making short-term investments in long-term securities. If a firm has $1 million set aside for an income tax payment, it could buy a long-term bond on January 1 and sell it on April 15, when the taxes must be paid. However, the danger in this strategy is obvious: What happens if bond prices fall by 10 percent between January and April? There you are, with a $1 million liability to the Internal Revenue Service, bonds worth only $900,000, and a very red face. Of course, bond prices could also go up, but why take the chance? Corporate treasurers entrusted with excess funds for short-term investment are naturally averse to the price volatility of long-term bonds.

We saw earlier how municipalities devised variable-rate demand bonds, which investors could periodically sell back to the issuer. The prices of these bonds are largely immune to fluctuations in interest rates. In addition, the interest on municipal loans has the attraction of being tax-exempt. So a municipal variable-rate demand bond offers a safe, tax-free, short-term haven for your $1 million of cash.

Common stock and preferred stock also have an interesting tax advantage for corporations, since firms pay tax on only 30 percent of dividends received from other corporations. For each $1 of dividends received, the firm gets to keep $1 - .30 \times .35 = \$.895$. Thus the effective tax rate is only 10.5 percent. This is higher than the zero tax rate on the interest from municipal debt but much lower than the rate that the company pays on other debt interest.

Suppose you consider putting that $1 million in some other corporation's preferred shares.[22] The 10.5 percent tax rate is very tempting. On the other hand, since preferred dividends are fixed, the prices of preferred shares change when long-term interest rates change. A $1 million investment in preferred shares could be worth

---

[20]See "Federal Funds and Repurchase Agreements," *Federal Reserve Bank of New York Quarterly Review,* **2:**33–48 (Summer 1977).

[21]To reduce the risk of repos, it is common to value the security at less than its market value. This difference is known as a *haircut.*

[22]Preferred shares are usually better short-term investments for a corporation than common shares. The preferred shares' expected return is virtually all dividends; most common shares are expected to generate capital gains, too. The corporate tax on capital gains is usually 35 percent. Corporations therefore have a strong incentive to like dividends and dislike capital gains.

only $900,000 on April 15, when taxes are due. Wouldn't it be nice if someone invented a preferred share that was insulated from fluctuating interest rates?

Well, there are such securities, and you can probably guess how they work: Specify a dividend payment which goes up and down with the general level of interest rates.[23] The prices of these securities are less volatile than those of fixed-dividend preferreds.

Varying the dividend payment on preferred stock doesn't quite do the trick. For example, if investors become more concerned about the risk of preferred stock, they might demand a higher relative return and the price of the stock could fall. So investment bankers added another wrinkle to floating-rate preferred. Instead of being tied rigidly to interest rates, the dividend can be reset periodically by means of a Dutch auction which is open to all investors. Existing shareholders can enter the auction by stating the minimum dividend they are prepared to accept; if this turns out to be higher than the rate that is needed to sell the issue, the shareholders sell the stock to the new investors at its face value. Alternatively, shareholders can simply enter a noncompetitive bid, keeping their shares and receiving whatever dividend is set by the other bidders. The result is similar to the variable-rate demand note: because auction-rate preferred stock can be resold at regular intervals for its face value, its price cannot wander far in the interim.[24]

Why would any firm want to *issue* floating-rate preferreds? Dividends must be paid out of *after-tax* income, whereas interest comes out of before-tax income. Thus, if a taxpaying firm wants to issue a floating-rate security, it would normally choose to issue floating-rate debt in order to generate interest tax shields.

However, there are plenty of firms that are not paying taxes. These firms cannot make use of the interest tax shield. Moreover, they have been able to issue floating-rate preferreds at yields *lower* than what they would have to pay on a floating-rate debt issue. (The corporations buying the preferreds are happy with these lower yields because 70 percent of the dividends they receive escape tax.)

Floating-rate preferreds were invented in Canada in the mid-1970s, when several billion dollars' worth were issued before the Canadian tax authorities cooled off the market by limiting the dividend tax exclusion on some types of floating-rate issues. They were reinvented in the United States in May 1982, when Chemical New York Corporation, the holding company for the Chemical Bank, raised $200 million. The securities proved so popular that over $4 billion of floating-rate preferreds were issued by the following spring. Then the novelty wore off, and the frequency of new issues slowed down. It was back to business as usual, with one important exception: There was one more item on the menu of investment opportunities open to corporate money managers.

32-4   SHORT-TERM BORROWING

You now know where to invest your surplus cash. But suppose that you have the opposite problem and face a temporary cash deficit. Where can you find the short-term funds?

---

[23]Usually there are limits on the maximum and minimum dividends that can be paid. Thus if interest rates leap to 100 percent, the preferred dividend would hit a ceiling of, say, 15 percent. If interest rates fall to 1 percent, the preferred dividend would hit a floor at, say, 5 percent.

[24]See M. J. Alderson, K. C. Brown, and S. L. Lummer, "Dutch Auction Rate Preferred Stock," *Financial Management*, **16**:68–73 (Summer 1987).

We have in part already answered that question. Remember that all those money-market investments that we discussed above must be *issued* by someone. So your firm may be able to raise short-term money by issuing commercial paper or discounting a banker's acceptance or (in the case of a bank) issuing CDs. But there are also other possible sources of cash that we have not yet discussed. In particular, you may take out a loan from a bank or finance company.

Obviously, if you approach a bank for a loan, the bank's lending officer is likely to ask searching questions about your firm's financial position and its plans for the future. Also, the bank will want to monitor the firm's subsequent progress. There is a good side to this. Other investors know that banks are hard to convince, and, there-fore, when a company announces that it has arranged a large bank facility, the share price tends to rise.[25]

*Credit Rationing

Before we discuss the different types of bank loans, we should notice an interesting general point. The more that you borrow from the bank, the higher the rate of in-terest that you will be required to pay. However, there may come a stage at which the bank will refuse to lend you more, no matter how high an interest rate you are prepared to pay.

This takes us back to our discussion in Chapter 18 of the games that borrowers can play with lenders. Suppose that Henrietta Ketchup is a budding entrepreneur with two possible investment projects offering the following payoffs:

	Investment	Payoff	Probability of Payoff
Project 1	−12	+15	1.0
Project 2	−12	$\begin{cases} +24 \\ 0 \end{cases}$	.5 .5

Project 1 is surefire and very profitable; project 2 is risky and a rotten project. Ms. Ketchup now approaches her bank and asks to borrow the present value of $10 (the remaining money she will find out of her own purse). The bank calculates that the payoff will be split as follows:

	Expected Payoff to Bank	Expected Payoff to Ms. Ketchup
Project 1	110	15
Project 2	$(.5 \times 10) + (.5 \times 0) = +5$	$.5 \times (24 - 10) = +7$

If Ms. Ketchup accepts project 1, the bank's debt is certain to be paid in full; if she ac-cepts project 2, there is only a 50 percent chance of payment and the expected payoff to the bank is only $5. Unfortunately, Ms. Ketchup will prefer to take project 2, for if things go well, she gets most of the profit, and if they go badly, the bank bears most of the loss. Unless the bank can specify in the fine print which project must be un-

---

[25]See C. James, "Some Evidence on the Uniqueness of Bank Loans," *Journal of Financial Economics,* **19**:217–235 (1987).

dertaken, it will not lend to Ms. Ketchup the present value of $10. Suppose, however, that the bank agrees to lend the present value of $5. Then the payoffs would be:

	Expected Payoff to Bank	Expected Payoff to Ms. Ketchup
Project 1	+5	+10
Project 2	$(.5 \times 5) + (.5 \times 0) = +2.5$	$.5 \times (24 - 5) = +9.5$

By rationing Ms. Ketchup to a smaller loan, the bank has now made sure that she will not be tempted to speculate with its money.[26]

Unsecured Loans

We have so far referred to bank loans as if they were a standard product, but in practice they come in a variety of flavors. The simplest and most common solution is to arrange an unsecured loan from your bank. For example, many companies rely on unsecured bank loans to finance a temporary increase in inventories. Such loans are described as *self-liquidating*—in other words, the sale of the goods provides the cash to repay the loan. Another popular use of bank loans is for construction or "bridging" finance. In this case the loan serves as interim financing until a project is completed and long-term financing is arranged.

Companies that frequently require short-term bank loans often ask their banks for a line of credit. This allows them to borrow at any time up to an established limit. A line of credit usually extends for a year and is then subject to review by the bank's loan committee. Banks are anxious that companies do not use a line of credit to cover their need for long-term finance. Thus, they often require the company to "clean up" its short-term bank loans for at least 1 month during the year.

The interest rate on a line of credit is usually tied either to the bank's prime rate of interest or to the CD rate—that is, the rate at which the bank can raise additional funds. In addition to the interest charge, banks often insist that in return for the line of credit the firm must maintain an interest-free demand deposit at the bank. For example, the firm might be asked to maintain a minimum average compensating balance equal to 10 percent of funds potentially available under the line of credit plus 10 percent of the amount actually borrowed. If as a result the firm maintains a higher cash balance than it otherwise would, the interest forgone on the additional deposit represents an extra cost to the loan.

Earlier in the chapter we noted that large companies often bypass the banking system and issue their own short-term unsecured debt, i.e., commercial paper. Even after allowing for the issue expenses and the cost of backup lines of credit, commercial paper is generally substantially cheaper than a bank loan. Remember, however, that when times are hard and money is tight, the bank will give priority to its regular customers. Thus few firms bypass the banking system entirely, even in good times when commercial paper is cheap and easy to sell.

---

[26]You might think that if the bank suspects Ms. Ketchup will undertake project 2, it should raise the interest rate on its loan. In this case Ms. Ketchup will not want to take on project 2 (they can't *both* be happy with a lousy project). But Ms. Ketchup also would not want to pay a high rate of interest if she is going to take on project 1 (she would do better to borrow less money at the risk-free rate). So, simply raising the interest rate is not the answer. If you find this surprising, imagine that you offered to lend someone a large sum at 100 percent. Would you be happier if he accepted or declined?

Loans Secured by Receivables

Banks often ask firms to provide security for loans. Since the bank is lending on a short-term basis, the security generally consists of liquid assets such as receivables, inventories, or securities. Sometimes the bank will accept a "floating lien" against receivables and inventory. This gives it a general claim against these assets, but it does not specify them in detail, and it sets few restrictions on what the company can do with the assets. More commonly, banks will require specific collateral.

If the bank is satisfied with the credit standing of your customers and the soundness of your product, it may be willing to lend you as much as 80 percent of accounts receivable. In return, you pledge your receivables as collateral for the loan. If you fail to repay your debt, the bank can collect the receivables and apply the proceeds to repaying the debt. If the proceeds are insufficient, you are liable for any deficiency. The loan is therefore said to be *with recourse*.

When you pledge receivables, you must keep the bank up to date on credit sales and collections. When you deliver goods to your customers, you send the bank a copy of the invoice, together with a form of assignment which gives the bank the right to the money your customers owe you. Then the firm can borrow up to the agreed proportion of this collateral.

Each day, as you make new sales, your collateral increases and you can borrow more money. Each day customers pay their bills. This money is placed in a special collateral account under the bank's control and is periodically used to reduce the size of the loan. Therefore, as the firm's business fluctuates, so does the amount of collateral and the size of the loan.

A few receivables loans are on a notification basis. In this case the bank informs your customer of the lending arrangement and asks that the money be paid directly to the bank. Firms generally do not like their customers to know they are in debt, and therefore such loans are made more frequently without notification.

Receivables loans can be obtained not only from commercial banks but also from finance companies which specialize in lending to businesses.

Loans against receivables are flexible, and they provide a continuous source of funds. Also, banks are willing to lend the firm more with collateral than without it. However, it can be costly for borrower and lender alike to supervise and record changes in the collateral. Therefore the rate of interest on receivables financing is usually high, and there may be an additional service charge on the loan.

We discussed factoring in Chapter 30. Don't confuse factoring with lending against receivables. Factors *buy* your receivables and, if you wish, advance a portion of the money. They are, therefore, responsible for collecting the debt and suffer any losses if the customers don't pay. When you pledge your receivables as collateral for a loan, *you* remain responsible for collecting the debt and *you* suffer if a customer is delinquent.

If it moves, as investment banker will try to turn it into a security. In recent years receivables have sometimes been repackaged into securities. For instance, in 1986 First Boston Corporation set up a special-purpose subsidiary, which bought 367,000 vehicle loans from General Motors Acceptance Corporation (GMAC). It then bundled these loans into three packages, each with a different maturity, and resold the packages to investors in the form of notes with the huge total value of $4 billion. GMAC provided a limited guarantee on these notes, but if a large number of car buyers defaulted on their payments, the noteholders would suffer a loss.[27]

---

[27]In footnote 14, we pointed out that GMAC has also used receivables to back issues of commercial paper.

The GAMC notes are known as *CARs (certificates for automobile receivables)*. Other companies have bundled together a large number of credit card loans and sold these packages to investors. As you might guess, these packages are called *CARDs (certificates for amortizing revolving debts)*.

Banks and finance companies also lend on the security of inventory, but they are choosy about the collateral they will accept. They want to make sure that they can identify and sell the inventory if you default. Automobiles and other standardized, nonperishable commodities are good collateral for a loan; work in process and ripe Camemberts are poor collateral.

The procedure for lending against inventories depends on where the goods are stored. If you place goods in a public warehouse, the warehouse company gives you a **warehouse receipt** and will then release the goods only on the instructions of the holder of the receipt. Because the holder of the receipt controls the inventory, the receipt can be used as collateral for a loan. Notice, however, that the warehouse receipt only identifies the goods and where they are stored. It doesn't guarantee the grade of the goods, nor does it guarantee your claim to the goods, nor does it provide insurance against fire, theft, and other hazards. Therefore the lender will also need to be satisfied on all these matters.

Lenders want to make sure that goods are not released without their permission. Therefore the law states that a warehouse receipt can be issued only by a bona fide warehouse company independent of the company that owns the goods. That is fine if you want to store your goods in a large public warehouse—but what do you do if you want to keep them on your own premises? The answer is that you establish a **field warehouse.** In other words, you arrange for a warehouse company to lease your warehouse or storage area. The warehouse company puts up signs stating that a field warehouse is being operated. It them remains responsible for storing your pledged goods and releases them only on the instructions of the holder of the warehouse receipt.

When you borrow from a bank, generally you sign an IOU and the bank hands you the money. Sometimes warehouse loans involve a somewhat more complicated arrangement. In exchange for your IOU the bank signs a banker's acceptance that matures on the same date. In other words, in exchange for your IOU the bank gives you not cash but *its* IOU. The advantage of this strange procedure is that the banker's acceptance is marketable whereas your promissory note is not. Therefore, you can sell your acceptance to the bank whenever you want the cash, and the bank can, if it chooses, resell the acceptance to another institution.

The important feature of warehouse loans is that goods are physically segregated and under the control of an independent warehouse company. Suppose, however, that you are an automobile dealer who needs to finance an inventory of new cars. You can't put the cars in a warehouse; you need to keep them in the showroom under your control. The common solution is to enter into a **floor-planning** arrangement. Under this arrangement the finance company buys the cars from the manufacturer and you hold them in trust for the finance company. As evidence of this, you sign a *trust receipt* that identifies the cars involved. You are free to sell the cars, but when you do so, the proceeds are used to redeem the trust receipt. To make sure that the collateral is properly maintained, the finance company will make periodic inspections of the inventory.

The fact that liquid assets are easily saleable does not always make them good collateral. It also means the lender has to make sure that the borrower doesn't suddenly sell the assets and run off with the money. If you want to make your hair stand on end, read the story of the great salad oil swindle. Fifty-one banks and companies made loans of nearly $200 million to the Allied Crude Vegetable Oil Refining Corporation. Warehouse receipts issued by a field warehousing company were taken as security. Unfortunately, the cursory inspections by the employees of the field warehousing company failed to uncover the fact that, instead of containing salad oil, Allied's storage tanks were mainly filled with soap stock, seawater, and unidentifiable sludge. When the fraud was discovered, the president of Allied went to jail, the field warehousing company went into bankruptcy, and the 51 lenders were left out in the cold, looking for their $200 million. Lenders have been more careful since then, but no doubt they'll be caught by some new scam sooner or later.

32-5   TERM LOANS

When firms need medium-term financing, they can raise it directly from investors by selling medium-term notes (MTNs) or short-dated bonds. Alternatively, they can take out a **term loan** from a bank or insurance company. Banks typically make term loans of 1 to 8 years. Insurance companies make longer-maturity term loans.

Instead of arranging a term loan with a bank in the United States, you may take out a eurodollar term loan. If the sums involved are very large, these eurodollar loans may be arranged by a lead bank and then syndicated among a group of banks.[28] For example, when Eurotunnel needed to arrange over $10 billion of borrowing to construct the tunnel between Britain and France, it used a syndicate of more than 200 major banks.

Term loans are usually repaid in level amounts over the period of the loan, although often there may be a large final "balloon" payment or just a single "bullet" payment at maturity. Banks can accommodate repayment patterns to the anticipated cash flows of the borrowing firm. For example, the first principal repayment might be delayed for a year pending completion of a new factory. Often terms loans are renegotiated in midstream—that is, before maturity. Banks are usually willing to do this if the borrowing firm is an established customer, remains creditworthy, and has a sound business reason for making the change.

The rate of interest on the term loan is sometimes fixed for the life of the loan. But usually it is linked to the prime rate or to the London interbank offered rate (LIBOR). Thus, if the rate is set at "1 percent over prime," the borrower may pay 5 percent in the first year when prime is 4 percent, 6 percent in the second year when prime is 5 percent, and so on. Occasionally these variable-rate loans include a "collar," which sets upper and lower limits on the interest that can be charged, or a "cap," which sets an upper limit only.

In addition to bearing the interest cost, the borrower is often obliged to maintain a minimum interest-free demand deposit with the bank. This compensating balance is commonly set at 10 to 20 percent of the amount of the loan, so the true interest rate, calculated on the money the firm can actually use, may be significantly higher than the quoted interest rate.

Term loans are for the most part unsecured debt. The conditions of a term loan are like those of most unsecured bonds. They generally do not include the very re-

---

[28]Occasionally banks would like to sell their share in a syndicated loan. They could do this by arranging for another bank to "participate" in their portion, but, as we shall see, there are dangers to this approach. Therefore loan agreements sometimes make it possible for each bank to transfer its portion of the loan. Transferable syndicated loans are a response by the banks to the trend away from bank lending and toward marketable securities.

strictive negative conditions of private placement bonds, but they do stipulate minimum levels of net worth and working capital. Term loans that are made to small companies often impose conditions on senior management. For example, the bank may require the company to insure the lives of senior managers, may place limits on management's remuneration, and may require personal guarantees for the loan.

A variant on the straight loan is the *revolving credit.* This is a legally assured line of credit with a maturity of up to 3 years. The borrower may be allowed to convert the credit at the end of the period into a straight term loan. Rather less common is the *evergreen credit,* which is a revolving credit without maturity that the *bank* may in any year convert into a straight loan. For both revolving credit and evergreen credit the company pays interest on any borrowings plus an "insurance premium" on the unused amount, and it may also be required to maintain a compensating balance with the bank.

Revolving credit agreements are relatively expensive compared to straight lines of credit or short-term bank loans. But in exchange for the extra cost, the firm receives a valuable option: It has guaranteed access to the bank's money at a fixed spread above the prime rate. This amounts to a put option, because the firm can sell its debt to the bank on fixed terms even if its own creditworthiness deteriorates.

Loan Participations and Assignments

The large money-center banks have more demand for loans than they can satisfy; for smaller banks it is the other way around. As a result, a lead bank may arrange a loan and then sell a large portion of it to other institutions. This has led to an increasingly active secondary market in bank loans.

These loan sales generally take one of two forms, *assignments* or *participations.* In the first case a portion of the loan is transferred with the agreement of the borrower to the new lenders. In the second case the lead bank provides a "certificate of participation" which states that it will pay over a proportion of the cash flows from the loan. In such cases cases the borrower may not be aware that the sale has occurred. These loan participations differ from the syndicated loans that we described earlier; with a syndicated loan each bank has a separate loan agreement with the borrower.

Participation loans hit the headlines in 1982 when Penn Square National Bank went belly up. One reason for consternation was that Penn Square had sold more than $200 million of its loan portfolio to Chase Bank. To make matters worse, the borrowers had deposited money with Penn Square, and the receiver claimed that the losses on these deposits should be deducted from the amount of the borrowers' debt. This reduced the cash flows to be paid over the Chase. Since the Penn Square collapse, banks and their lawyers have been more careful about the fine print in loan participations.

32-6   SUMMARY

If you have more cash then you currently need, you can invest the surplus in the money market. The principal money-market investments in the United States are:

- U.S. Treasury bills
- Short-term tax-exempts
- Certificates of deposit
- Commercial paper

■ Bankers' acceptances

■ Repurchase agreements

If none of these catches your fancy, you can make a short-term eurocurrency investment. For example, you can make a dollar deposit with a bank in London.

No two of these securities are exactly the same. If you want to make effective use of your cash, you need to be aware of the differences in their liquidity, risk, and yield. Table 32-1 summarizes the main features of money-market instruments. Figure 32-1 shows money-market rates for August 22, 1995, as reported in *The Wall Street Journal.*

Most corporations making short-term investments of excess cash buy one or more of the instruments described in Table 32-1. But there are many alternatives, including floating-rate preferreds. The securities are attractive for two reasons. First, corporations pay tax on only 30 percent of the dividends received. Second, the dividend moves up and down with changes in interest rates, so the preferred shares' prices are more or less stabilized.

For many companies surplus cash is not a worry; their problem is how to finance a temporary cash deficiency. One of the main sources of short-term funds is the unsecured bank loan. This is often taken out under a bank line of credit, which entitles the firm to borrow up to an agreed limit. The interest rate that banks charge on unsecured loans must be sufficient to cover not only the opportunity cost of capital for the loans but also the costs of running a loan department. As a result, large regular borrowers have found it cheaper to bypass the banking system and issue their own short-term unsecured debt. This debt is known as *commercial paper.*

Bank loans with maturities exceeding 1 year are called *term loans.* These may be arranged with a bank in the United States, or the firm take out a eurodollar term loan with a bank overseas. Large eurodollar term loans may be syndicated among a group of banks.

Another form of medium-term bank finance is the *revolving credit,* which guarantees the firm access to a line of credit. Revolving credits can often be converted into regular term loans.

If you ask to borrow more and more from a bank, you will eventually be asked to provide security for the loan. Sometimes this security consists of a floating lien on receivables and inventories, but usually you will be asked to pledge specific assets. The bank or finance company will take precautions to make sure that the collateral is properly identified and within its control. For example, when you borrow against receivables, the bank must be informed of all sales of goods and the resulting accounts receivable must be pledged to the bank. As customers pay their bills, the money is paid into a special collateral account under the bank's control. Similarly, when you borrow against stocks of raw materials, the bank may insist that the goods be held by an independent warehouse company. As long as the bank holds the warehouse receipt for these goods, they cannot be released without the bank's permission. Loans secured on finished goods are usually made under a floor-planning arrangement. In this case you will be required to sign a trust receipt promising that you are merely holding the specified goods in trust for the lender, and the lender will make periodic inspections to see that you are keeping your promise.

You may also find that there comes a point at which the bank will not increase its lending no matter how high a rate of interest you are prepared to pay. Banks know that the more they lend, the more they are encouraging you to gamble with their money. Your aims and the bank's are more likely to coincide if your borrowing is kept to a responsible level.

Figure 32-1 Short-term interest rates on August 22, 1995. (*Source:* Reprinted by permission if *The Wall Street Journal.* © 1995 Dow Jones & Company, Inc. All Rights Reserved Worldwide.)

INTEREST RATES

Tuesday, August 22, 1995

MONEY RATES

The key U.S. and foreign annual interest rates shown are a guide to general levels but don't always represent actual transactions.

PRIME RATE: 8.75%. The base rate on corporate loans posted by at least 75% of the nation's 30 largest banks.

DISCOUNT RATE: 5 1/4%. The charge on loans to depository institutions by the Federal Reserve Banks.

CALL MONEY: 7 1/2%. The charge on loans to brokers on stock exchange collateral. Source: Dow Jones Telerate Inc.

COMMERCIAL PAPER placed directly by General Electric Capital Corp.: 5.72% 30 to 59 days; 5.68% 60 to 119 days; 5.65% 120 to 179 days; 5.62% 180 to 224 days; 5.59% 225 to 270 days.

COMMERCIAL PAPER: High-grade unsecured notes sold through dealers by major corporations: 5.84% 30 days; 5.83% 60 days; 5.83% 90 days.

CERTIFICATES OF DEPOSIT: 5.19% one month; 5.20% two months; 5.25% three months; 5.29% six months; 5.32% one year. Average of top rates paid by major New York banks on primary new issues of negotiable C.D.s, usually on amounts of $1 million and more. The minimum unit is $100,000. Typical rates in the secondary market: 5.78% one month; 5.78% three months; 5.80% six months.

BANKERS ACCEPTANCES: 5.72% 30 days; 5.69% 60 days; 5.66% 90 days; 5.64% 120 days; 5.63% 150 days; 5.64% 180 days. Offered rates of negotiable, bank-backed business credit instruments typically financing an import order.

LONDON LATE EURODOLLARS: 5 15/16% - 5 13/16% one month; 5 15/16% - 5 13/16% two months; 5 15/16% - 5 13/16% three months; 5 15/16% - 5 13/16% four months; 6% - 5 7/8% five months; 6% - 5 7/8% six months;

LONDON INTERBANK OFFERED RATES (LIBOR): 5 15/16% one month; 5 15/16% three months; 6% six months; 6 1/16% one year. The average of interbank offered rates for dollar deposits in the London market based on quotations at five major banks. Effective rate for contracts entered into two days from date appearing at top of this column.

OTHER PRIME RATES: Canada 8.25%; Germany 4.46%; Japan 2.00%; Switzerland 5.00%; Britain 6.75%. These rate indications aren't directly comparable; lending practices vary widely by location.

TREASURY BILLS: Results of the Monday, August 21, 1995 auction of short-term U.S. government bills, sold at discount from face value in units of $10,000 to $1 million: 5.43% 13 weeks; 5.43% 26 weeks.

FEDERAL HOME LOAN MORTGAGE CORP. (Freddie Mac): Posted yields on 30-year mortgage commitments. Delivery within 30 days 8.04%, 60 days 8.09%, standard conventional fixed-rate mortgages; 5.875%, 2% rate capped one-year adjustable rate mortgages. Source: Dow Jones Telerate Inc.

FEDERAL NATIONAL MORTGAGE ASSOCIATION (Fannie Mae): Posted yields on 30 year mortgage commitments (priced at par) for delivery within 30 days 8.05%, 60 days 8.11%, standard conventional fixed rate-mortgages; 6.90%, 6/2 rate capped one-year adjustable rate mortgages. Source: Dow Jones Telerate Inc.

MERRILL LYNCH READY ASSETS TRUST: 5.37%. Annualized average rate of return after expenses for the past 30 days; not a forecast of future returns.

Further Reading

For a detailed description of the money market and short-term lending opportunities, see:
M. Stigum: *The Money Market: Myth, Reality and Practice*, 3d ed., Richard D. Irwin, Inc., Homewood, Ill., 1990.
F. J. Fabozzi (ed.): *The Handbook of Treasury and Agency Securities*, Probus Publishing, Chicago, 1990.

Here is a practically oriented book on sources of short- and medium-term financing:
W. J. Korvuik and C. O. Maiburg: *The Loan Officer's Handbook*, Dow Jones-Irwin, Homewood, Ill., 1986.

Quiz

1. For each item below, choose the investment that best fits the accompanying description:
   (*a*) Maturity often overnight (repurchase agreements *or* bankers' acceptances)
   (*b*) Maturity never more than 270 days (tax-exempts *or* commercial paper)
   (*c*) Maturity never less than 30 days (eurodollar deposits *or* U.S. certificates of deposit)
   (*d*) Often directly placed (finance company commercial paper *or* industrial commercial paper)
   (*e*) Registered with the SEC (commercial paper *or* medium-term notes)
   (*f*) Issued by the U.S. Treasury (tax-exempts *or* 360-day bills)
   (*g*) Quoted on a discount basis (certificates of deposit *or* Treasury bills)
   (*h*) Sold by auction (tax-exempts *or* Treasury bills)

2. On August 21, 1995, 6-month Treasury bills were issued at a discount of 5.43 percent. (See Figure 32-1.) What is the annual yield?

3. Complete the passage below by selecting the most appropriate terms from the following list: *floating lien, field warehouse, cleanup provision, commercial paper, floor planning, line of credit, prime rate, public warehouse, compensating balance, trust receipt, warehouse receipt, collateral, medium-term notes, with recourse.*

   Companies with fluctuating capital needs often arrange a _____ with their bank. To make sure that this facility is not used to provide permanent funds, the bank usually incorporates a _____. The interest on any borrowing is tied to the bank's _____. In addition the bank generally requires that the company keep a _____ on deposit at the bank.

   Secured short-term loans are sometimes covered by a _____ on all receivables and inventory. Generally, however, the borrower pledges specific assets as _____. If these assets are insufficient to repay the debt, the borrower is liable for the deficiency. Therefore such loans are said to be _____. Warehouse loans are examples of secured short-term loans. The goods may be stored in a _____ or in a _____ that is established by the warehouse company on the borrower's premises. The warehouse company issues a _____ to the lender and releases the goods only on instructions. Loans to automobile dealers are usually made on a different basis. The dealer holds the inventory on behalf of the lender and issues a _____. This arrangement is known as _____.

   Banks are not the only source of short-term debt. Many large companies issue their own unsecured debt directly to investors, often on a regular basis. If the maturity is less than 270 days, it is known as _____ and does not need to be registered with the SEC. Companies also sell debt to investors with maturities over 270 days. This is called _____.

4. Consider three securities:
   (a) A floating-rate bond
   (b) A preferred share paying a fixed dividend
   (c) A floating-rate preferred
       A financial manager responsible for short-term investment of excess cash would probably choose the floating-rate preferred over *either* of the other two securities. Why? Explain briefly.

5. Here are six questions about term loans:
   (a) What is the usual minimum maturity of a term loan?
   (b) Are compensating balances required?
   (c) Are term loans usually secured loans? That is, are they usually backed up by specific collateral?
   (d) How is the interest rate usually determined?
   (e) What is a balloon payment?
   (f) What is a revolving credit?

Questions and Problems

1. Look up current interest rates offered by short-term investment alternatives. Suppose that your firm has $1 million excess cash to invest for the next 2 months. How would you invest this excess cash? How would your answer change if the excess cash were $5000, $20,000, $100,000, or $100 million?

2. In August 1995 Treasury bonds sold at a 7 percent yield, while tax-exempts of comparable maturity offered 6.2 percent annually. If an investor receives the same *after-tax* return from Treasury bonds and tax-exempts, what is that investor's marginal rate of tax? What other factors might affect an investor's choice between the two types of securities?

3. Interest rates on bank loans exceed rates on commercial paper. Why don't all firms issue commercial paper rather than borrow from banks?

4. Do you think you could make money by setting up a firm which would (a) issue commercial paper and (b) relend money to businesses at a rate slightly higher than the commercial paper rate but still less than the rate charged by banks?

5. Roy's Toys needs an extra $1 million in October to build up inventory for the Christmas season. First National has offered to lend at 9 percent subject to a 20 percent compensating balance. Hometown Trust will lend at 11 percent with no strings attached. Which bank is offering the better deal? Why? Would your answer change if Roy's Toys already had a $100,000 normal working balance at First National? (Assume in this case that the working balance can be used to cover part of the compensating balance.)

6. Axle Chemical Corporation's treasurer has forecast a $1 million cash deficit for the next quarter. However, there is only a 50 percent chance this deficit will actually occur. The treasurer estimates that there is a 20 percent probability the company will have no deficit at all and a 30 percent probability that it will actually need $2 million in short-term financing. The company can either take

out a 90-day unsecured loan at 1 percent per month or establish a line of credit, costing 1 percent per month on the amount borrowed plus a commitment fee of $20,000. Both alternatives also required a 20 percent compensating balance for outstanding loans. If excess cash can be reinvested at 9 percent, which source of financing gives the lower expected cost?

7. Suppose that you are a banker responsible for approving corporate loans. Nine firms are seeking secured loans. They offer the following assets as collateral:
   (*a*) Firm A, a heating oil distributor, offers a tanker load of fuel oil in transit from the Middle East.
   (*b*) Firm B, a wine wholesaler, offers 1000 cases of Beaujolais Nouveau, located in a field warehouse.
   (*c*) Firm C, a stationer, offers an account receivable for office supplies sold to the city of New York.
   (*d*) Firm D, a bookstore, offers its entire inventory of 15,000 used books.
   (*e*) Firm E, a wholesale grocer, offers a boxcar full of bananas.
   (*f*) Firm F, an appliance dealer, offers its inventory of electric typewriters.
   (*g*) Firm G offers 100 ounces of gold.
   (*h*) Firm H, a government securities dealer, offers its portfolio of Treasury bills.
   (*i*) Firm I, a boat builder, offers a half-completed luxury yacht. The yacht will take 4 months more to complete.
   Which of these assets are most likely to be good collateral? Which are likely to be poor collateral? Explain.

8. Any one of the assets mentioned in the preceding question *could* be acceptable collateral under certain circumstances if appropriate safeguards were taken. What circumstances? What safeguards? Explain.

9. The first floating-rate preferreds were successfully issued at initial dividend yields *below* yields on Treasury bills. How was this possible? The preferreds were clearly riskier than the bills. What would you predict for the *long-run* relationship between yields on bills and on floating-rate preferreds? (We say "long-run" to give time for all firms that will want to issue floating-rate preferreds to get around to doing so.)

10. Most floating-rate preferreds have both a "floor" and a "ceiling" on their dividend rate. (See Section 32-3, footnote 23.) How do these limits affect the behavior of the *prices* of these securities as interest rates change? Why do you think the issuing companies included the limits in the first place?

11. Term loans usually require firms to pay a fluctuating interest rate. For example, the interest rate may be set at "1 percent above prime." The prime rate sometimes varies by several percentage points within a single year.
   Suppose that your firm has decided to borrow $40 million for 5 years. It has three alternatives:
   (*a*) Borrow from a bank at the prime rate, currently 10 percent. The proposed loan agreement requires no principal repayments until the loan matures in 5 years.
   (*b*) Issue 26-week commercial paper, currently yielding 9 percent. Since funds are required for 5 years, the commercial paper will have to be "rolled over" semiannually. That is, financing the $40 million requirement for 5 years will require 10 successive commercial paper sales.
   (*c*) Borrow from an insurance company at a fixed rate of 11 percent. As in the bank loan, no principal has to be repaid until the end of the 5-year period.

What factors would you consider in analyzing these alternatives? Under what circumstances would you choose (*a*)? Under what circumstances would you choose (*b*) or (*c*)? (*Hint:* Don't forget Chapter 23.)

12. The IRS prohibits companies from borrowing money to buy tax-exempts and also deducting the interest payments on the borrowing from taxable income. Should the IRS prohibit such activity? If it didn't, would you advise the company to borrow to buy tax-exempts?

13. In Section 32-1 we described a 3-month Treasury bill that was issued on an annually compounded yield of 5.70 percent. Suppose that 1 month (30 days) has passed and the bill still offers the same annually compounded return. What is the percentage discount? What was your return over the month?

14. Look again at question 13. Suppose another month has passed, so the bill has only 31 days left to run. It is now selling at a discount of 5 percent. What is the yield calculated on a simple interest basis over a 365-day year? What was your realized return over the 2 months?

15. Suppose you are a wealthy individual paying 39.6 percent tax on income. What is the expected after-tax yield on each of the following investments?
    (*a*) A municipal note yielding 6.5 percent pretax
    (*b*) A Treasury bill yielding 10 percent pretax
    (*c*) A floating-rate preferred stock yielding 7.5 percent pretax
    How would your answer change if the investor is a corporation paying tax at 35 percent? What other factors would you need to take into account when deciding where to invest the corporation's spare cash?

* 16. The possible payoffs from Ms. Ketchup's projects (see Section 32-4) have not changed, but there is now a 40 percent chance that project 2 will pay off $24 and a 60 percent chance that it will pay off $0.
    (*a*) Recalculate the expected payoffs to the bank and Ms. Ketchup if the bank lends the present value of $10. Which project would Ms. Ketchup undertake?
    (*b*) What is the maximum sum the bank could lend that would induce Ms. Ketchup to take project 1?

17. A 3-month Treasury bill and a 6-month bill both sell at a discount of 10 percent. Which offers the higher annual yield?

18. Look at the rates quoted in Figure 32-1 for CDs, commercial paper, bankers' acceptances, and Treasury bills. Why do you think the rates are different? (*Note:* Yields on CDs are quoted on a simple interest basis; the rates for the other three investments are rates of discount.)

PART ten

Mergers and International Finance

33

Mergers

The scale and pace of merger activity in the United States are remarkable. Table 33-1 lists just a few of the more important mergers in the mid-1990s. You can see that they involved big money. During periods of intense merger activity, the financial manager spends significant amounts of time either searching for firms to acquire or worrying about whether some other firm will acquire his or her company.

TABLE 33-1

Some important mergers in 1994 and 1995

Year	Selling Company	Acquiring Company	Payment, Billions of Dollars
1994	McCaw Cellular Communications	AT&T	18.9
1994	Paramount	Viacom	9.6
1994	Blockbuster Entertainment	Viacom	8.0
1994	American Cyanamid	American Home Products	9.6
1994	Syntex	Roche Holding a.g.	5.3
1995	Capital Cities/ABC	Disney	19.0
1995	Chase Manhattan	Chemical Banking	10.0
1995	CBS	Westinghouse Electric	5.4
1995	Scott Paper	Kimberly-Clark	7.4
1995	Marion Merrell Dow	Hoechst a.g.	7.1
1995	HCA-Hospital Corp.	Columbia Healthcare	5.6
1995	Health Trust-The Hospital Co.	Columbia Healthcare	5.2
1995	Martin Marietta	Lockheed Martin	10.0
1995	Lotus	IBM	3.5
1995	80% of MCA unit of Matsushita Electrical Industrial	Seagram	5.7
1995	Pharmacia a.b.	Upjohn	6.0
1995	First Fidelity Bancorp	First Union	5.4
1995	NBD Bancorp	First Chicago	5.1

Source: Mergers and Acquisitions, various issues.

When you buy another company, you are making an investment, and the basic principles of capital investment decisions apply. You should go ahead with the purchase if it makes a net contribution to shareholders' wealth. But mergers are often awkward transactions to evaluate. First, you have to be careful to define benefits and costs properly. Second, buying a company is more complicated than buying a new machine; special tax, legal, and accounting issues must often be addressed. Third, you must be aware of the offensive and defensive tactics used in hostile takeovers, just in case a friendly deal cannot be consummated. Finally, you need to have a general understanding of why mergers occur and who typically gains or loses as a result.

We start by reviewing the possible benefits and costs of a merger. We also comment on the legal, tax, and accounting problems encountered in putting two firms together.

Many mergers are arranged amicably, but sometimes one firm will make a hostile takeover bid for the other. We describe the principal techniques of modern merger warfare, and since the threat of hostile takeovers has stimulated corporate restructurings and leveraged buy-outs (LBOs), we describe them, too, and attempt to explain why these deals have generated such enormous rewards for investors.

We close with a look at the public policy issues raised by leveraged buy-outs and the aggressive use of debt in corporate restructurings.

33-1 ESTIMATING THE ECONOMIC GAINS AND COSTS FROM MERGERS[1]

Suppose that you are the financial manager of firm A and you want to analyze the possible purchase of firm B. The first thing to think about is whether there is an *economic gain* from the merger. There is an economic gain *only if the two firms are worth more together than apart*. For example, if you think that the combined firm would be worth PV_{AB} and that the separate firms are worth PV_A and PV_B, then

$$\text{Gain} = PV_{AB} - (PV_A + PV_B)$$

If this gain is positive, there is an economic justification for merger. But you also have to think about the *cost* of acquiring firm B. Take the easy case in which payment is made in cash. Then the cost of acquiring B is equal to the cash payment minus B's value as a separate entity. Thus

$$\text{Cost} = \text{cash} - PV_B$$

The net present value to A of a merger with B is measured by the difference between the gain and the cost. Therefore, you should go ahead with the merger if its net present value, defined as

$$\begin{aligned} \text{NPV} &= \text{gain} - \text{cost} \\ &= PV_{AB} - (PV_A + PV_B) - (\text{cash} - PV_B) \end{aligned}$$

is positive.

We like to write the merger criterion in this way because it focuses attention on two distinct questions. When you estimate the benefit, you concentrate on whether there are any gains to be made from the merger. When you estimate cost, you are concerned with the division of these gains between the two companies.

---

[1] This chapter's definitions and interpretations of the gains and costs of merger follow those set out in S. C. Myers, "A Framework for Evaluating Mergers," in S. C. Myers (ed.), *Modern Developments in Financial Management*, Frederick A. Praeger, Inc., New York, 1976.

An example may help make this clear. Firm A has a value of $200 million, and B has a value of $50 million. Merging the two would allow cost savings with a present value of $25 million. This is the gain from the merger. Thus,

$$PV_A = \$200$$
$$PV_B = \$50$$
$$Gain = +\$25$$
$$PV_{AB} = \$275 \text{ million}$$

Suppose that B is bought for cash, say, for $65 million. The cost of the merger is

$$Cost = cash - PV_B$$
$$= 65 - 50 = \$15 \text{ million}$$

Note that the stockholders of firm B—the people on the other side of the transaction—are ahead by $15 million. *Their* gain is *your* cost.[2] They have captured $15 million of the $25 million merger gain. Thus when we write down the NPV of the merger from A's viewpoint, we are really calculating that part of the gain which A's stockholders get to keep. The NPV to A's stockholders equals the overall gain from the merger less that part of the gain captured by B's stockholders:

$$NPV = 25 - 15 = +\$10 \text{ million}$$

Just as a check, let's confirm that A's stockholders really come out $10 million ahead. They start with a firm worth $PV_A = \$200$ million. They pay out $65 million in cash to B's stockholders and end up with a firm worth $275 million. Thus their net gain is

$$NPV = \text{wealth with merger} - \text{wealth without merger}$$
$$= (PV_{AB} - cash) - PV_A$$
$$= (\$275 - \$65) - \$200 = +\$10 \text{ million}$$

Suppose investors do not anticipate the merger between A and B. The announcement will cause the value of B's stock to rise from $50 million to $65 million, a 30 percent increase. If investors share management's assessment of the merger gains, the market value of A's stock will increase by $10 million, only a 5 percent increase.

It makes sense to keep an eye on what investors think the gains from merging are. If A's stock price falls when the deal is announced, then investors are sending the message that the merger benefits are doubtful or that A is paying too much for them.[3]

Some companies begin their merger analyses with a forecast of the target firm's future cash flows. Any revenue increases or cost reductions attributable to the merger are included in the forecasts, which are then discounted back to the present and compared with the purchase price:

$$\begin{matrix} \text{Estimated} \\ \text{net gain} \end{matrix} = \begin{matrix} \text{DCF valuation} \\ \text{of target, including} \\ \text{merger benefits} \end{matrix} - \begin{matrix} \text{cash required} \\ \text{for acquisition} \end{matrix}$$

---

[2]In practice, B's gain may be *less than* A's cost because money leaks out in fees for investment bankers, lawyers, and accountants.

[3]Think back to Section 13-3, where we saw how Viacom's stock price fell as Viacom battled for control of Paramount.

This is a dangerous procedure. Even the brightest and best-trained analyst can make large errors in valuing a business. The estimated net gain may come up positive not because the merger makes sense but simply because the analyst's cash-flow forecasts are too optimistic. On the other hand, a good merger may not be pursued if the analyst fails to recognize the target's potential as a stand-alone business.

Our procedure *starts* with the target's stand-alone market value (PV_B) and concentrates on the *changes* in cash flow that would result from the merger. *Ask yourself why the two firms should be worth more together than apart.*

The same advice holds when you are contemplating the *sale* of part of your business. There is no point in saying to yourself, "This is an unprofitable business and should be sold." Unless the buyer can run the business better than you can, the price you receive will reflect the poor prospects.

Sometimes you may come across managers who believe that there are simple rules for identifying good acquisitions. They may say, for example, that they always try to buy into growth industries or that they have a policy of acquiring companies that are selling below book value. But our comments in Chapter 11 about the characteristics of a good investment decision also hold true when you are buying a whole company. *You add value only if you can generate additional economic rents*—some competitive edge that other firms can't match and the target firm's managers can't achieve on their own.

One final piece of horse sense: Often two companies bid against each other to acquire the same target firm. In effect, the target firm puts itself up for auction. In such cases, ask yourself whether the target is worth more to you than to the other bidder. If the answer is no, you should be cautious about getting into a bidding contest. Winning such a contest may be more expensive than losing it. If you lose, you have simply wasted your time; if you win, you have probably paid too much.

33-2 SENSIBLE MOTIVES FOR MERGERS

Mergers are often categorized as horizontal, vertical, or conglomerate. A *horizontal merger* is one that takes place between two firms in the same line of business; most of the mergers around the turn of the century were of this type. Recent examples include bank mergers, such as Chemical Bank's merger with Chase, and pharmaceutical mergers, such as Roche Holding's purchase of Syntex.

During the 1920s vertical mergers were predominant. A *vertical merger* involves companies in related lines of business. The buyer expands backward toward the source of raw materials or forward in the direction of the ultimate consumer.

A *conglomerate merger* involves companies in unrelated lines of business. Conglomerate mergers became common in the 1960s and 1970s. The Federal Trade Commission estimated that between 1965 and 1975, 80 percent of mergers were conglomerate.[4] (However, the percentage of conglomerate mergers declined in the 1980s. In fact, much of the action since the 1980s has come from breaking up the conglomerates that had been formed 10 to 20 years earlier.)

With these distinctions in mind, we are about to consider motives for mergers, that is, reasons why two firms may be worth more together than apart. We proceed with some trepidation. The motives, though they often lead the way to real benefits, are sometimes just mirages that tempt unwary or overconfident managers into takeover disasters. This was the case for AT&T, which spent $7.5 billion to buy

---

[4]*Statistical Report on Mergers and Acquisitions,* Federal Trade Commission, 1977, p. 106, table 19.

NCR. The aim was to shore up AT&T's computer business and to "link people, organizations and their information into a seamless, global computer network."[5] It didn't work. Even more embarrassing (on a smaller scale) was the acquisition of Apex One, a sporting apparel company, by Converse Inc. The purchase was made on May 18, 1995. Apex One was closed down on August 11, after Converse failed to produce new designs quickly enough to satisfy retailers. Converse lost an investment of over $40 million in 85 days.[6]

Many mergers that seem to make economic sense fail because managers cannot handle the complex task of integrating two firms with different production processes, accounting methods, and corporate cultures. This was one of the problems in the AT&T-NCR merger. It also bedeviled Novell's acquisition of Wordperfect. That merger at first seemed a perfect fit between Novell's strengths in networks for personal computers and Wordperfect's applications software. But Wordperfect's postacquisition sales were horrible, partly because of competition from other word processing systems but also because of a series of battles over turf and strategy:

> Wordperfect executives came to view Novell executives as rude invaders of the corporate equivalent of Camelot. They repeatedly fought with . . . Novell's staff over everything from expenses and management assignments to Christmas bonuses. [This led to] a strategic mistake: dismantling a Wordperfect sales team . . . needed to push a long-awaited set of office software products.[7]

The value of most businesses depends on *human* assets—managers, skilled workers, scientists, and engineers. If these people are not happy in their new roles in the acquiring firm, the best of them will leave. One Portuguese bank (BCP) learned this lesson the hard way when it bought an investment management firm against the wishes of the firm's employees. The entire workforce immediately quit and set up a rival investment management firm with a similar name. Beware of paying too much for assets that go down the elevator and out to the parking lot at the close of each business day. They may drive into the sunset and never return.

There are also occasions when the merger does achieve gains but the buyer nevertheless loses because it pays too much. For example, the buyer may overestimate the value of stale inventory or underestimate the costs of renovating old plant and equipment, or it may overlook the warranties on a defective product. Buyers need to be particularly careful about environmental liabilities. If there is pollution from the seller's operations or toxic waste on its property, the costs of cleaning up will probably fall on the buyer.

Economies of Scale

Just as most of us believe that we would be happier if only we were a little richer, so every manager seems to believe that his or her firm would be more competitive if only it were just a little bigger. Achieving *economies of scale* is the natural goal of horizontal mergers.[8] But such economies have been claimed in conglomerate mergers,

---

[5]Robert E. Allen, AT&T chairman, quoted in J. J. Keller, "Disconnected Line: Why AT&T Takeover of NCR Hasn't Been a Real Bell Ringer," *Wall Street Journal*, September 9, 1995, p. A1.

[6]Mark Maremount, "How Converse Got Its Laces All Tangled," *Business Week*, September 4, 1995, p. 37.

[7]D. Clark, "Software Firm Fights to Remake Business after Ill-Fated Merger," *Wall Street Journal*, January 12, 1996, p. A1.

[8]Economies of scale are enjoyed when the average unit cost of production goes down as production increases. One way to achieve economies of scale is to spread fixed costs over a larger volume of production.

too. The architects of these mergers have pointed to the economies that come from sharing central services such as office management and accounting, financial control, executive development, and top-level management.

The most prominent recent examples of mergers in pursuit of economies of scale come from the banking industry. The United States entered the 1990s with far too many banks, largely as a result of outdated regulations on interstate banking. As these regulations eroded and communications and technology improved, hundreds of small banks were bought out and merged into regional or "supra-regional" firms. Merger gains came from closing redundant branches, consolidating systems and back offices, and marketing products such as credit cards to broader customer bases. Even Chase and Chemical, two of the largest money-center banks, found it possible to merge, combine operations, and lay off thousands of employees with no material loss of revenue.

Optimistic financial managers can see potential economies of scale in almost any industry. But it is easier to buy another business than to integrate it with yours afterward. Some companies that have gotten together in pursuit of scale economies still function as a collection of separate and sometimes competing operations with different production facilities, research efforts, and marketing forces. Even economies in central services may be elusive. The complicated structure of conglomerate companies may actually increase the administrative staff. And top-level managers of conglomerates sometimes find that their general skills are not easily applied to the specialized problems of individual subsidiaries.

Economies of Vertical Integration

Vertical mergers seek economies in vertical integration. Large industrial companies commonly like to gain as much control as possible over the production process by expanding back toward the output of the raw material and forward to the ultimate consumer. One way to achieve this is to merge with a supplier or a customer.

One reason for vertical integration is that it facilitates coordination and administration. We illustrate via an extreme example. Think of an airline that does not own any planes. If it schedules a flight from Boston to San Francisco, it sells tickets and then rents a plane for that flight from a separate company. This strategy might work on a small scale, but it would be an administrative nightmare for a major carrier, which would have to coordinate hundreds of rental agreements daily. In view of these difficulties, it is not surprising that all major airlines have integrated backward, away from the consumer, by buying and flying airplanes rather than patronizing "rent-a-plane" companies.[9]

Do not assume that more vertical integration is better than less. Carried to extremes, it is absurdly inefficient, as in the case of LOT, the Polish state airline, which in the late 1980s found itself raising pigs to make sure that its employees had fresh meat on their tables. (Of course, in a centrally managed economy it may be necessary to raise your own cattle or pigs, since you can't be sure you'll be able to buy meat.)

Complementary Resources

Many small firms are acquired by large ones that can provide the missing ingredients necessary for the small firms' success. The small firm may have a unique product but lack the engineering and sales organization required to produce and market it on a

---

[9]However, some companies known as *network organizations* outsource a very high proportion of their activity. For example, Lewis Galoob Toys has only about 100 employees. It makes use of independent designers, contracts out its production, and then sells its products through a variety of retail firms. See "And Now, the Post-Industrial Corporation," *Business Week*, March 3, 1986, and J. W. Kensinger and J. D. Martin, "Financing Network Organizations," *Journal of Applied Corporate Finance*, 4:66–76 (Spring 1991).

large scale. The firm could develop engineering and sales talent from scratch, but it may be quicker and cheaper to merge with a firm that already has ample talent. The two firms have *complementary resources*—each has what the other needs—and so it may make sense for them to merge. The two firms are worth more together than apart because each acquires something it does not have and gets it cheaper than it would by acting on its own. Also, the merger may open up opportunities that neither firm would pursue otherwise.

Of course, two large firms may also merge because they have complementary resources. Consider the 1989 merger between two electric utilities, Utah Power & Light and PacifiCorp, which serves customers in California. Utah Power's peak demand comes in the summer, for air conditioning. PacifiCorp's peak comes in the winter, for heating. The savings from combining the two firms' generating systems were estimated at $45 million annually in 1990.

Unused Tax Shields

Sometimes a firm may have potential tax shields but not have the profits to take advantage of them. For example, after its bankruptcy and reorganization, Penn Central had billions of dollars of unused tax-loss carry-forwards. It subsequently purchased Buckeye Pipeline and several other mature, taxpaying companies so that these carry-forwards could be used.[10]

Surplus Funds

Here's another argument for mergers: Suppose that your firm is in a mature industry. It is generating a substantial amount of cash, but it has few profitable investment opportunities. Ideally such a firm should distribute the surplus cash to shareholders by increasing its dividend payment or repurchasing stock. Unfortunately, energetic managers are often reluctant to adopt a policy of shrinking their firm in this way. If the firm is not willing to purchase its own shares, it can instead purchase another company's shares. Firms with a surplus of cash and a shortage of good investment opportunities often turn to mergers *financed by cash* as a way of redeploying their capital.

Some firms have excess cash and do not pay it out to stockholders or redeploy it by wise acquisitions. Such firms often find themselves targeted for takeover by other firms that propose to redeploy the cash for them.[11] During the oil price slump of the early 1980s, many cash-rich oil companies found themselves threatened by takeover. This was not because their cash was a unique asset. The acquirers wanted to capture the companies' cash flow to make sure it was not frittered away on negative-NPV oil exploration projects. We return to this *free-cash-flow* motive for takeovers later in this chapter.

Eliminating Inefficiencies

Cash is not the only asset that can be wasted by poor management. There are always firms with unexploited opportunities to cut costs and increase sales and earnings. Such firms are natural candidates for acquisition by other firms with better management. In some instances "better management" may simply mean the determination to force painful cuts or realign the company's operations. Notice that the motive for such acquisitions has nothing to do with benefits from combining two firms.

---

[10]Mergers undertaken *just* to use tax-loss carry-forwards will be challenged by the Internal Revenue Service, and the use of the carry-forwards may be denied. Suppose that you own a profitable firm. You find another company on the ropes, with large cumulative losses. If you bought that company and then liquidated its assets, the IRS would regard the tax-loss carry-forwards as liquidated also and not allow you to use them to reduce your taxable income.

[11]Takeovers in this case often take the form of leveraged buy-outs.

Acquisition is simply the mechanism by which a new management team replaces the old one.

A merger is not the only way to improve management, but sometimes it is the only simple and practical way. Managers are naturally reluctant to fire or demote themselves, and stockholders of large public firms do not usually have much *direct* influence on how the firm is run or who runs it.[12]

If this motive for merger is important, one would expect to observe that acquisitions often precede a change in the management of the target firm. This seems to be the case. For example, Martin and McConnell found that the chief executive is four times more likely to be replaced in the year after a takeover than during earlier years.[13] The firms they studied had generally been poor performers; in the 4 years before acquisition their stock prices had lagged behind those of other firms in the same industry by 15 percent. Apparently many of these firms fell on bad times and were rescued, or reformed, by merger.

Of course, it is easy to criticize another firm's management but not so easy to improve it. Some of the self-appointed scourges of poor management turn out to be less competent than those they replace. Here is how Warren Buffet, the chairman of Berkshire Hathaway, summarizes the matter:[14]

> Many managers were apparently over-exposed in impressionable childhood years to the story in which the imprisoned, handsome prince is released from the toad's body by a kiss from the beautiful princess. Consequently, they are certain that the managerial kiss will do wonders for the profitability of the target company. Such optimism is essential. Absent that rosy view, why else should the shareholders of company A want to own an interest in B at a takeover cost that is two times the market price they'd pay if they made direct purchases on their own? In other words investors can always buy toads at the going price for toads. If investors instead bankroll princesses who wish to pay double for the right to kiss the toad, those kisses better pack some real dynamite. We've observed many kisses, but very few miracles. Nevertheless, many managerial princesses remain serenely confident about the future potency of their kisses, even after their corporate backyards are knee-deep in unresponsive toads.

33-3 SOME DUBIOUS REASONS FOR MERGER

The benefits that we have described so far all make economic sense. Other arguments that are sometimes given for mergers are dubious. Here are a few of the dubious ones.

To Diversify

We have suggested that the managers of a cash-rich company may prefer to see it use that cash for acquisitions rather than distribute it as extra dividends. That is why we often see cash-rich firms in stagnant industries merging their way into fresh woods and pastures new.

---

[12]It is difficult to assemble a large-enough block of stockholders to effectively challenge management and the incumbent board of directors. Stockholders can have enormous indirect influence, however. Their displeasure shows up in the firm's stock price. A low stock price may encourage a takeover bid by another firm.

[13]K. J. Martin and J. J. McConnell, "Corporate Performance, Corporate Takeovers, and Management Turnover," *Journal of Finance*, **46**:671–687 (June 1991).

[14]Berkshire Hathaway 1981 annual report, cited in G. Foster, "Comments on M&A Analysis and the Role of Investment Bankers," *Midland Corporate Finance Journal*, **1**:36–38 (Winter 1983).

What about diversification as an end in itself? It is obvious that diversification reduces risk. Isn't that a gain from merging?

The trouble with this argument is that diversification is easier and cheaper for the stockholder than for the corporation. No one has shown that investors pay a premium for diversified firms—in fact, discounts are common. For example, Kaiser Industries was dissolved as a holding company in 1977 because its diversification apparently *subtracted* from its value. Kaiser Industries' main assets were shares of Kaiser Steel, Kaiser Aluminum, and Kaiser Cement. These were independent companies, and the stock of each was publicly traded. Thus you could value Kaiser Industries by looking at the stock prices of Kaiser Steel, Kaiser Aluminum, and Kaiser Cement. But Kaiser Industries' stock was selling at a price reflecting a significant *discount* from the value of its investment in these companies. The discount vanished when Kaiser Industries revealed its plan to sell its holdings and distribute the proceeds to its stockholders.

Why the discount existed in the first place is a puzzle. But the example at least shows that diversification does not *increase* value. The appendix to this chapter provides a simple proof that corporate diversification does not affect value in perfect markets as long as investors' diversification opportunities are unrestricted. This is the *value-additivity* principle introduced in Chapter 7.

There are exceptional cases in which personal diversification may be more expensive than corporate diversification. Suppose you are the president and majority owner of a closely held corporation. You may be wealthy, but you have all your eggs in one corporate basket. You could sell off a substantial part of your shares in order to diversify, but this could result in a large capital gains tax. It may be better to merge with a firm in another line of business and hold on to the shares of that firm. If the deal is properly structured, you can defer the capital gains tax, and you will have your eggs in two baskets rather than one.

Increasing Earnings per Share: The Bootstrap Game[15]

During the 1960s some conglomerate companies made acquisitions that offered no evident economic gains. Nevertheless the conglomerates' aggressive strategy produced several years of rising earnings per share. To see how this can happen, let us look at the acquisition of Muck and Slurry by the well-known conglomerate World Enterprises.

The position before the merger is set out in the first two columns of Table 33-2. Notice that because Muck and Slurry has relatively poor growth prospects, its stock sells at a lower price-earnings ratio than does World Enterprises' stock (line 3). The merger, we assume, produces no economic benefits, and so the firms should be worth exactly the same together as they are apart. The market value of World Enterprises after the merger should be equal to the sum of the separate values of the two firms (line 6).

Since World Enterprises stock is selling for double the price of Muck and Slurry stock (line 2), World Enterprises can acquire the 100,000 Muck and Slurry shares for 50,000 of its own shares. Thus World will have 150,000 shares outstanding after the merger.

Total earnings double as a result of the merger (line 5), but the number of shares increases by only 50 percent. Earnings *per share* rise from $2.00 to $2.67. We call this the *bootstrap effect* because there is no real gain created by the merger and no increase

---

[15]The discussion of the bootstrap game follows S. C. Myers, "A Framework for Evaluating Mergers," op. cit.

TABLE 33-2
• •

Impact of merger on market value and earnings per share of World Enterprises			
	World Enterprises before Merger	Muck and Slurry	World Enterprises after Merger
1. Earnings per share	$2.00	$2.00	$2.67
2. Price per share	$40	$20	$40
3. Price-earnings ratio	20	10	15
4. Number of shares	100,000	100,000	150,000
5. Total earnings	$200,000	$200,000	$400,000
6. Total market value	$4,000,000	$2,000,000	$6,000,000
7. Current earnings per dollar invested in stock (line 1 ÷ line 2)	$.05	$.10	$.067

Note: When World Enterprises purchases Muck and Slurry, there are no gains. Therefore, total earnings and total market value should be unaffected by the merger. But earnings *per share* increase. World Enterprises issues only 50,000 of its shares (priced at $40) to acquire the 100,000 Muck and Slurry shares (priced at $20).

in the two firms' combined value. Since the stock price is unchanged, the price-earnings ratio falls (line 3).

Figure 33-1 illustrates what is going on here. Before the merger $1 invested in World Enterprises bought 5 cents of current earnings and rapid growth prospects. On the other hand, $1 invested in Muck and Slurry bought 10 cents of current earnings but slower growth prospects. If the *total* market value is not altered by the merger, then $1 invested in the merged firm gives 6.7 cents of immediate earnings but slower growth than World Enterprises offered alone. Muck and Slurry shareholders get lower immediate earnings but faster growth. Neither side gains or loses provided everybody understands the deal.

Financial manipulators sometimes try to ensure that the market does *not* understand the deal. Suppose that investors are fooled by the exuberance of the president of World Enterprises and by plans to introduce modern management techniques into its new Earth Sciences Division (formerly known as Muck and Slurry). They could easily mistake the 33 percent postmerger increase in earnings per share for real growth. If they do, the price of World Enterprises stock rises and the shareholders of both companies receive something for nothing.

You should now see how to play the bootstrap, or "chain letter," game. Suppose that you manage a company enjoying a high price-earnings ratio. The reason why it is high is that investors anticipate rapid growth in future earnings. You achieve this growth not by capital investment, product improvement, or increased operating efficiency but by the purchase of slow-growing firms with low price-earnings ratios. The long-run result will be slower growth and a depressed price-earnings ratio, but in the short run earnings per share can increase dramatically. If this fools investors, you may be able to achieve higher earnings per share without suffering a decline in your price-earnings ratio. But in order to *keep* fooling investors, you must continue to expand by merger *at the same compound rate.* Obviously you cannot do this forever; one day expansion must slow down or stop. Then earnings growth will cease, and your house of cards will fall.

Figure 33-1 Effects of merger on earnings growth. By merging with Muck and Slurry, World Enterprises increases current earnings but accepts a slower rate of future growth. Its stockholders should be no better or worse off unless investors are fooled by the bootstrap effect. [*Source:* S. C. Myers, "A Framework for Evaluating Mergers," in S. C. Myers (ed.), *Modern Developments in Financial Management,* Frederick A. Praeger, Inc., New York, 1976, fig. 1, p. 639.]

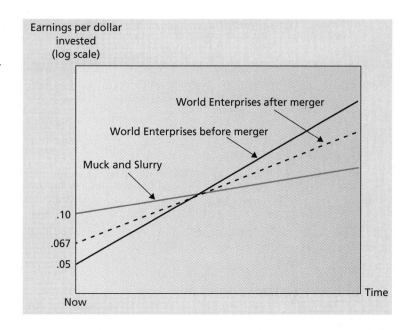

This kind of game is not played so often now, after investors' bitter experience with it in the 1960s. But there is still a widespread belief that a firm should not acquire companies with higher price-earnings ratios than its own. Of course you know better than to believe that low-P/E stocks are cheap and high-P/E stocks are dear. If life were as simple as that, we should all be wealthy by now. Beware of false prophets who suggest that you can appraise mergers on the basis of their immediate impact on earnings per share.

Lower Financing Costs

You often hear it said that a merged firm is able to borrow more cheaply than its separate units could. In part this is true. We have already seen (in Section 15-3) that there are significant economies of scale in making new issues. Therefore, if firms can make fewer, larger security issues by merging, there is a genuine saving.

But when people say that borrowing costs are lower for the merged firm, they usually mean something more than lower issue costs. They mean that when two firms merge, the combined company can borrow at lower interest rates than either firm could separately. This, of course, is exactly what we should expect in a well-functioning bond market. While the two firms are separate, they do not guarantee each other's debt—if one fails, the bondholder cannot ask the other for money. But after the merger each enterprise effectively does guarantee the other's debt—if one part of the business fails, the bondholders can still take their money out of the other part. Because these mutual guarantees make the debt less risky, lenders demand a lower interest rate.

Does the lower interest rate mean a net gain to the merger? Not necessarily. Compare the following two situations:

■ *Separate issues.* Firm A and firm B each make a $50 million bond issue.

■ *Single issue.* Firms A and B merge, and the new firm AB makes a single $100 million issue.

Of course AB would pay a lower interest rate, other things equal. But it does not make sense for A and B to merge just to get that lower rate. Although AB's shareholders do gain from the lower rate, they lose by having to guarantee each other's debt. In other words, they get the lower interest rate only by giving bondholders better protection. There is no *net* gain.

In Sections 20-2 and 23-5 we showed that

$$\text{Bond value} = \begin{array}{c} \text{bond value} \\ \text{(assuming no} \\ \text{chance of default)} \end{array} - \begin{array}{c} \text{value of} \\ \text{shareholders' (put)} \\ \text{option to default} \end{array}$$

Merger increases bond value (or reduces the interest payments necessary to support a *given* bond value) only by reducing the value of stockholders' options to default. In other words, the value of the default option for AB's $100 million issue is less than the combined value of the two default options on A's and B's separate $50 million issues.

Now suppose that A and B each borrow $50 million and *then* merge. If the merger is a surprise, it is likely to be a happy one for the bondholders. The bonds they thought were guaranteed by one of the two firms end up guaranteed by both. The stockholders lose, other things equal, because they have given bondholders better protection but have received nothing for it.

There is one situation in which mergers can create value by making debt safer. In Section 18-3 we described the choice of an optimal debt ratio as a trade-off of the value of tax shields on interest payments made by the firm against the present value of possible costs of financial distress due to borrowing too much. Merging decreases the probability of financial distress, other things being equal. If it allows increased borrowing, and increased value from the interest tax shields, there will be a net gain to the merger.[16]

33-4   ESTIMATING THE COST OF A MERGER

To recapitulate: You should go ahead with a merger if the gain exceeds the cost. The gain is the difference between the value of the merged firm and the value of the separate entities:

$$\text{Gain} = \text{PV}_{AB} - (\text{PV}_A + \text{PV}_B)$$

We have looked at where these gains may come from and how to estimate them. It is now time to focus on the costs.

Estimating Cost When the Merger Is Financed by Cash

The cost of a merger is the premium that the buyer pays for the selling firm over the seller's value as a separate entity. It is a straightforward problem to estimate cost as long as the merger is financed by cash. However, it is important to bear in mind that if investors *expect* A to acquire B, the market value of B may be a poor measure of its value as a separate entity. Thus it may help to rewrite our formula for cost as

---

[16]This merger rationale was first suggested by W. G. Lewellen, "A Pure Financial Rationale for the Conglomerate Merger," *Journal of Finance*, **26**:521–537 (May 1971). If you want to see some of the controversy and discussion that this idea led to, look at R. C. Higgins and L. D. Schall, "Corporate Bankruptcy and Conglomerate Merger," *Journal of Finance*, **30**:93–114 (March 1975), and D. Galai and R. W. Masulis, "The Option Pricing Model and the Risk Factor of Stock," *Journal of Financial Economics*, **3**:53–81, (January–March 1976), especially pp. 66–69.

$$\text{Cost} = (\text{cash} - MV_B) + (MV_B - PV_B)$$

= premium paid over market value of B
  + difference between market value of B and B's value as a separate entity

This is one of the few places in this book where we draw an important distinction between market value (MV) and the true, or "intrinsic," value (PV) of the firm as a separate entity. The problem here is not that the market value of B is wrong but that it may not be the value of firm B as a separate entity. Potential investors in B's stock will see two possible outcomes and two possible values:

Outcome	Value of B's Stock
1. No merger	PV_B: Value of B as a separate firm
2. Merger occurs	PV_B *plus* some part of the benefits of the merger

If the second outcome is possible, MV_B, the stock market value we observe for B, will overstate PV_B. This is exactly what *should* happen in a competitive capital market. Unfortunately, it complicates the task of a financial manager who is evaluating a merger.

Here is an example: Suppose that just before the merger announcement we observe the following:

	Firm A	Firm B
Market price per share	$75	$15
Number of shares	1,000,000	600,000
Market value of firm	$75 million	$9 million

Firm A intends to pay $12 million cash for B. If B's market price reflects only its value as a separate entity, then

$$\text{Cost} = (\text{cash} - MV_B) + (MV_B - PV_B)$$
$$= (12 - 9) + (9 - 9) = \$3 \text{ million}$$

However, suppose that B's share price has already risen $2 because of rumors of a favorable merger offer. That means MV_B overstates PV_B by $2 \times 600{,}000 = 1{,}200{,}000$, or $1.2 million. The true value, PV_B, is only $7.8 million. Then

$$\text{Cost} = (\text{cash} - MV_B) + (MV_B - PV_B)$$
$$= (12 - 9) + (9 - 7.8) = \$4.2 \text{ million}$$

Notice that if the market made a mistake and the market value of B was *less* than B's true value as a separate entity, the cost could be negative. In other words, B would be a *bargain* and the merger would be worthwhile from A's point of view, even if the two firms were worth no more together than apart. Of course, A's stockholders' gain would be B's stockholders' loss because B would be sold for less than its true value.

Firms have made acquisitions just because their managers believed they had spotted a company whose intrinsic value was not fully appreciated by the stock market. However, we know from the evidence on market efficiency that "cheap" stocks often turn out to be expensive. It is not easy for outsiders, whether investors or managers, to find firms that are truly undervalued by the market. Moreover, if the shares are bargain-priced, A doesn't need a merger to profit by its special knowledge. It can just buy up B's shares on the open market and hold them passively, waiting for other investors to wake up to B's true value.

If firm A is wise, it will not go ahead with a merger if the cost exceeds the gain. Conversely, firm B will not consent to a merger if it thinks the cost to A is negative, for a negative cost to A means a negative gain to B. This gives us a range of possible cash payments that would allow the merger to take place. Whether the payment is at the top or the bottom of this range depends on the relative bargaining power of the two participants. For example, if A makes an acquisition solely to use a tax-loss carry-forward, then it could equally well merge with B, C, or D; firm B has nothing special to offer, and its management is in no position to demand a large fraction of the gains. In this case, the cost of the merger to A is likely to be relatively low.

Estimating Cost When the Merger Is Financed by Stock

Estimating cost is more complicated when a merger is financed by an exchange of shares. Suppose that firm A offers 160,000 shares instead of $12 million in cash. Since A's share price before the announcement is $75 and B's market value is $9 million,[17] the cost *appears* to be

$$\text{Apparent cost} = 160,000 \times \$75 - \$9,000,000 = \$3,000,000$$

However, the apparent cost may not equal the true cost. Are A's shares really worth $75 each?

These shares may be worth $75 before the merger is announced but not afterward. Suppose the merger is expected to generate cost savings worth $4.75 million:

$$\text{Gain} = PV_{AB} - (PV_A + PV_B)$$
$$= 88.75 - (75 + 9) = \$4.75 \text{ million}$$

Given the gain and the terms of the deal, we can calculate share prices and market values *after* the merger is negotiated and announced. Note that the new firm will have 1,160,000 shares outstanding. Therefore,

$$\text{New share price} = \frac{88,750,000}{1,160,000} = \$76.50$$

The true cost is

$$\text{Cost} = (160,000 \times \$76.50) - \$9,000,000 = \$3,240,000$$

The true cost can also be calculated by figuring out the gain to B's shareholders. They end up with 160,000 shares, or 13.8 percent of the new firm AB. Their gain is

$$.138(88,750,000) - 9,000,000 = \$3,240,000$$

In general, if B's shareholders are given the fraction x of the combined firms,

$$\text{Cost} = xPV_{AB} - PV_B$$

We can now understand the first key distinction between cash and stock as financing instruments. If cash is offered, the cost of the merger is unaffected by the merger gains. If stock is offered, the cost depends on the gains because the gains show up in the postmerger share price.

---

[17]In this case we assume that B's market value reflects only its value as a separate firm.

Stock financing also mitigates the effect of overvaluation or undervaluation of either firm. Suppose, for example, that A overestimates B's value as a separate entity, perhaps because it has overlooked some hidden liability. Thus A makes too generous an offer. Other things being equal, A's stockholders are better off if it is a stock offer rather than a cash offer. With a stock offer, the inevitable bad news about B's value will fall partly on the shoulders of B's stockholders.

Asymmetric Information

There is a second key difference between cash and stock financing for mergers. A's managers will usually have access to information about A's prospects that is not available to outsiders. Economists call this *asymmetric information.*

Suppose A's managers are more optimistic than outside investors. They may think that A's shares will really be worth $80 after the merger, rather than the $76.50 market price we just calculated. If they are right, the true cost of a stock-financed merger with B is

$$\text{Cost} = 160{,}000 \times \$80 - \$9{,}000{,}000 = \$3{,}800{,}000$$

B's shareholders would get a "free gift" of $3.50 for every A share they receive—an extra gain of $3.50 \times 160,000, or $560,000 in all.

Of course, if A's managers were really this optimistic, they would strongly prefer to finance the merger with cash. Financing with stock would be favored by *pessimistic* managers who think their company's shares are *over*valued.

Does this sound like "win-win" for A—just issue shares when overvalued, cash otherwise? No, it's not that easy, because B's shareholders, and outside investors generally, understand what's going on. Suppose you are negotiating on behalf of B. You find that A's managers keep suggesting stock rather than cash financing. You quickly infer A's managers' pessimism, mark down your own opinion of what the shares are worth, and drive a harder bargain. Investors who would pay $76.50 for A's shares after a cash deal might value the shares at, say, only $74 if A insists on stock financing. A would have to hand over more than 160,000 shares to get the deal done.

This asymmetric-information story explains why buying-firms' share prices generally fall when stock-financed mergers are announced.[18] Franks, Harris, and Titman found an average market-adjusted fall of 3.2 percent on the announcement of stock-financed mergers between 1975 and 1984. There was a small *gain* (.8 percent) for a sample of cash-financed deals.[19]

33-5   THE MECHANICS OF A MERGER

Buying a company is a much more complicated affair than buying a piece of machinery. Thus we should look at some of the problems encountered in arranging mergers. In practice, these problems are often *extremely* complex, and specialists must be consulted. We are not trying to replace those specialists; we simply want to alert you to the kinds of legal, tax, and accounting issues they deal with.

---

[18]The same reasoning applies to stock issues. See Sections 15-3 and 18-4.

[19]See J. R. Franks, R. S. Harris, and S. Titman, "The Postmerger Share-Price Performance of Acquiring Firms," *Journal of Financial Economics,* **29**:81–96 (March 1991). This article confirms the results of earlier research by Nickolaos Travlos. See "Corporate Takeover Bids, Methods of Payment, and Bidding Firms' Stock Returns," *Journal of Finance,* **42**:943–963 (September 1987).

Mergers and Antitrust Law

Mergers can get bogged down in the federal antitrust law. This law is enshrined in three principal statutes. The first is the Sherman Act of 1890, which declared that "every contract, combination . . . or conspiracy, in restraint of trade" is illegal. The second is the Federal Trade Commission Act of 1914, which prohibits "unfair methods of competition" and (by amendment) "unfair or deceptive acts or practices." The third and most important statute is the Clayton Act of 1914. Section 7 of the Clayton Act, together with the amending Celler-Kefauver Act of 1950, forbids the acquisition of assets or stock whenever "in any line of commerce or in any section of the country" the effect of doing so "*may be* substantially to lessen competition, or to *tend* to create a monopoly." Notice that under the Sherman Act a contract must not be in constraint of trade. The Clayton Act goes beyond that to prohibit *potential* restraints. As a result, prosecutions under the Sherman Act are now rare, and the Clayton Act has become the principal weapon in the crusade against the ogre of monopoly.

Antitrust law can be enforced by the federal government in either of two ways: by a civil suit brought by the Justice Department or by a proceeding initiated by the Federal Trade Commission (FTC).[20] The Hart-Scott-Rodino Antitrust Act of 1976 requires that these agencies be informed of all acquisitions of stock amounting to $15 million or 15 percent of the target's stock, whichever is less. Thus almost all large mergers are reviewed at an early stage.[21] Both the Justice Department and the FTC then have the right to seek injunctions delaying a merger.

Relatively few mergers are challenged on antitrust grounds, but the threat is always there. For example, the Justice Department and FTC have been concerned about ensuring that the spate of mergers between hospital groups does not reduce competition. Thus, when Columbia Healthcare acquired Health Trust for $5.4 billion in 1995, Columbia agreed to sell some of its hospitals to head off antitrust proceedings.

The Form of Acquisition

Suppose you have been advised that the purchase of company B will not be challenged on antitrust grounds. Next you will want to consider the form of the acquisition.

One possibility is literally to *merge* the two companies, in which case one company automatically assumes *all* the assets and *all* the liabilities of the other. Such a merger must have the approval of at least 50 percent of the stockholders of each firm.[22]

An alternative is simply to buy the seller's stock in exchange for cash, shares, or other securities. In this case the buyer can deal individually with the shareholders of the selling company. The seller's managers may not be involved at all. Their approval and cooperation are generally sought, but if they resist, the buyer will attempt to acquire an effective majority of the outstanding shares. If successful, the buyer has control and can, if necessary, complete the merger and toss out the incumbent management.

The third approach is to buy some or all of the seller's assets. In this case ownership of the assets needs to be transferred, and payment is made to the selling firm rather than directly to its stockholders.

Merger Accounting

Mergers sometimes raise complex accounting issues. One such issue is whether a merger should be treated as a *purchase of assets* or as a *pooling of interests*. In efficient capital markets, the choice between purchase accounting and pooling should make

---

[20]Competitors or third parties who think they will be injured by the merger can also bring antitrust suits.

[21]The target has to be notified also, and it in turn informs investors. Thus the Hart-Scott-Rodino Act effectively forces an acquiring company to "go public" with its bid.

[22]Corporate charters and state laws sometimes specify a higher percentage.

TABLE 33-3

· ·

Purchasing versus pooling in the merger of A Corporation and B Corporation
(figures in millions of dollars)

Initial Balance Sheets

A CORPORATION				B CORPORATION			
NWC	2.0	3.0	D	NWC	.1	0	D
FA	8.0	7.0	E	FA	.9	1.0	E
	10.0	10.0			1.0	1.0	

Balance Sheets of AB Corporation

		AB CORPORATION			
Under pooling of interests	{	NWC	2.1	3.0	D
		FA	8.9	8.0	E
			11.0	11.0	

		AB CORPORATION			
Under purchase accounting, assuming that A Corporation pays $1.8 million for B corporation	{	NWC	2.1	3.0	D
		FA	8.9	8.8	E
		Goodwill	.8		
			11.8	11.8	

Key:
  NWC = Net working capital
  FA   = Net book value of fixed assets
  D   = Debt
  E   = Book value of equity

no difference whatsoever, but managers and accountants agonize over it anyway.

The essential differences between the two methods are illustrated in Table 33-3. The table shows what happens when A Corporation buys B Corporation, leading to the new AB Corporation. The two firms' initial (book) balance sheets are shown at the top of the table. The next balance sheet is for AB Corporation under pooling of interest. It is nothing more than the two firms' separate balance sheets added together. The final balance sheet shows what happens when purchase accounting is used. We assume that B Corporation has been purchased for $1.8 million, 180 percent of book value.

Why did A Corporation pay an $800,000 premium over book value? There are two possible reasons. First, the true values of B's *tangible* assets—its working capital, plant, and equipment—may be greater than $1 million. We will assume that this is *not* the reason; that is, we assume that the assets listed on its balance sheet are valued there correctly.[23] Second, A Corporation may be paying for an *intangible* asset

---

[23]If purchase accounting is used and if B's tangible assets are worth more than their previous book values, they would be reappraised and their current values entered on AB Corporation's balance sheet. Goodwill would be decreased by an amount equal to the write-up of tangible assets.

that is not listed on B Corporation's balance sheet. The intangible asset may be a promising product or technology developed by B Corporation, for example. Or it may be no more than B Corporation's share of the economic gains from the merger.

Under the purchase method of accounting, A Corporation is viewed as buying an asset worth $1.8 million—as indeed it is. The problem is how to show that asset on the left-hand side of AB Corporation's balance sheet. B Corporation's tangible assets are worth only $1 million. This leaves $.8 million. The accountant takes care of this by creating a new asset category called *goodwill* and assigning $.8 million to it.

All this is somewhat arbitrary, but reasonable enough. Intangible assets do have value, and so there is no reason why such assets shouldn't be shown on the balance sheet when a firm buys them. Nevertheless, most managers prefer to pool when they can. The reason is that goodwill has to be amortized over a period not exceeding 40 years, and the regular amortization charges have to be deducted from reported income. Thus AB Corporation's reported income will be reduced by at least $800,000/40 = $20,000 each year. Under pooling, goodwill never appears, and so reported income is at least $20,000 higher.

Now all this has absolutely no cash consequences. The amortization charges are *not* cash outflows, and they are not tax-deductible expenses. Thus the choice between purchase accounting and pooling should have no effect on the value of the merged firms.[24]

Some
Tax
Consider-
ations

An acquisition may be either taxable or tax-free. In a taxable acquisition, the selling stockholders are treated, for tax purposes, as having *sold* their shares, and they must pay tax on any capital gains or losses. In a tax-free acquisition, the selling shareholders are viewed as *exchanging* their old shares for essentially similar new ones; no capital gains or losses are recognized.

The tax status of the acquisition also affects the taxes paid by the merged firm afterward. After a tax-free acquisition, the merged firm is taxed as if the two firms had always been together. In a taxable acquisition, the assets of the selling firm are revalued, the resulting write-up or write-down is treated as a taxable gain or loss, and tax depreciation is recalculated on the basis of the restated asset values.

A very simple example will illustrate these distinctions. In 1985 Captain B forms Seacorp, which purchases a fishing boat for $300,000. Assume, for simplicity, that the boat is depreciated for tax purposes over 20 years on a straight-line basis (no salvage value). Thus annual depreciation is $300,000/20 = $15,000, and in 1995 the boat has a net book value of $150,000. But in 1995, Captain B finds that, owing to careful maintenance, inflation, and good times in the local fishing industry, the boat is really worth $280,000. In addition, Seacorp holds $50,000 of marketable securities.

Now suppose that Captain B sells the firm to Baycorp for $330,000. The possible tax consequences of the acquisition are shown in Table 33-4. In this case, Captain B is better off with a tax-free deal because capital gains taxes can be deferred. Baycorp will probably go along; it covets the $13,000-per-year extra depreciation tax shield that a taxable merger would generate, but the increased annual tax shields do not justify paying taxes on a $130,000 write-up.[25]

---

[24]Hong, Mandelker, and Kaplan tested this proposition by looking at a sample of 159 acquisitions made between 1954 and 1964, a period in which there were fewer restrictions on pooling than there are now. They found no evidence showing that shareholders of acquiring firms did better under pooling than under purchase accounting. See H. Hong, G. Mandelker, and R. S. Kaplan: "Pooling vs. Purchase: The Effects of Accounting for Mergers on Stock Prices," *Accounting Review*, **53**:31–47 (January 1978).

[25]Before the 1986 Tax Reform Act, assets of the acquired company could be revalued *without* recognizing the write-up or write-down as taxable corporate income. This old rule would make a taxable merger much more attractive to Baycorp, which might pay Captain B a premium to accept a taxable deal.

TABLE 33-4

Possible tax consequences when Baycorp buys Seacorp for $330,000. Captain B's original investment in Seacorp was $300,000. Just before the merger Seacorp's assets were $50,000 of marketable securities and one boat with a book value of $150,000 but a market value of $280,000.

	Taxable Merger	Tax-Free Merger
Impact on Captain B	Captain B must recognize a $30,000 capital gain.	Capital gain can be deferred until Captain B sells the Baycorp shares.
Impact on Baycorp	Boat is revalued at $280,000. Baycorp must pay tax on the $130,000 write-up, but tax depreciation increases to $280,000/10 = $28,000 per year (assuming 10 years of remaining life).	Boat's value remains at $150,000, and tax depreciation continues at $15,000 per year.

33-6 MERGER TACTICS

Many mergers are agreed upon by both parties, but sometimes the acquirer will go over the heads of the target firm's management and appeal directly to its stockholders. There are two ways of doing this. First, the acquirer can seek the support of the target firm's stockholders at the next annual meeting. This is called a *proxy fight* because the right to vote someone else's share is called a *proxy*.[26]

Proxy fights are expensive and difficult to win. The alternative for the would-be acquirer is to make a *tender offer* directly to the shareholders. The management of the target firm may advise its shareholders to accept the tender, or it may attempt to fight the bid.

Tender battles resemble a complex game of poker. The rules are set mostly by the Williams Act of 1968, by state law, and by the courts. The problem in setting the rules is deciding who requires protection. Should the management of the target firm be given more weapons to defend itself against unwelcome predators? Or should it simply be encouraged to sit the game out? Or should it be obliged to conduct an auction to obtain the highest price for its shareholders? And what about would-be acquirers? Should they be forced to reveal their intentions at an early stage, or would that allow other firms to piggy-back on their good ideas and enter competing bids?[27] We will return to the game and its rules after looking at one classic contest.

The Fight for Cities Service[28]

The battle for Cities Service began in May 1982 when Boone Pickens, the chairman of Mesa Petroleum, began buying Cities shares as preparation for a takeover bid.

---

[26]Peter Dodd and Jerrold Warner have written a detailed description and analysis of proxy fights. See "On Corporate Governance: A Study of Proxy Contests," *Journal of Financial Economics*, 2:401–438 (April 1985).

[27]The Williams Act obliges firms who own 5 percent or more of another company's shares to tip their hand by reporting their holding in a Schedule 13(d) filing with the SEC.

[28]The Cities Service takeover is described in R. S. Ruback, "The Cities Service Takeover: A Case Study," *Journal of Finance*, **38**:319–330 (May 1983).

Foreseeing the bid, Cities made an issue of equity that diluted Mesa's holding, and it followed this up with a retaliatory offer for Mesa.[29] Over the following month Mesa's bid was revised once and Cities' bid was revised twice before both companies agreed to drop their bids for each other. Cities repurchased Mesa's holdings—at an $80 million profit to Mesa—and in exchange Mesa agreed not to attempt a hostile takeover of Cities for 5 years.

The principal reason for the cessation of hostilities between Mesa and Cities was the announcement that Cities had found a more congenial partner in Gulf Oil. Also, Gulf was prepared to pay substantially more than Mesa for Cities stock. Unfortunately, this proposal fell afoul of the Federal Trade Commission (FTC), which issued a temporary restraining order. Shortly thereafter Gulf withdrew its offer.

In response, Cities charged Gulf with not attempting to resolve the FTC's objections, and it filed a $3 billion lawsuit against Gulf. At the same time it began to look for another "white knight" that would take it over. The only interested suitor was Occidental Petroleum. Occidental's initial offer for Cities was revised twice and finally accepted. The battle for Cities Service had lasted 3 months and involved a total of nine bids from four separate companies.

Many of these bids were *two-tier offers*. For example, Occidental's final offer for Cities consisted of a tender offer of $55 a share for 45 percent of the stock, followed by a package of fixed-income securities worth about $40 a share for the remaining stock. In effect, Occidental was saying, "Last one through the door does the washing up," since there was a big advantage in selling for cash rather than waiting for the securities. The plan worked, for almost all Cities' stockholders rushed to take advantage of the cash offer, and Occidental gained control.

In several instances the bidders employed both carrot and stick. For example, Occidental followed up its initial friendly offer for Cities with a hostile tender offer before finally reaching a friendly agreement.

The generous Gulf offer would have provided Cities' shareholders with a cumulative profit of almost 80 percent, but the collapse of that offer and the shortage of other suitors caused Cities' stock price to lose all its earlier gains. From then on Cities was in a relatively weak bargaining position, and the Occidental offer resulted in a profit of only 12 percent for Cities' stockholders. The merger scarcely affected Occidental's stock price, which suggests that investors believed the merger to be a zero-NPV investment. Gulf's stockholders fared the worst. Its high-priced offer led to a 14 percent fall in the price of Gulf stock. Even though this offer was subsequently withdrawn, the prospect of a costly lawsuit left Gulf's stock price depressed.

One year after losing its battle for Cities, Gulf itself became a takeover target, when Mesa Petroleum proposed to buy Gulf stock in order to break the company up and sell it in pieces. At this point Chevron came to the rescue and acquired Gulf for $13.2 billion, more than double its value 6 months earlier. Chevron's bid gave Mesa a profit of $760 million on the Gulf shares that it had bought. Asked for his views, Pickens commented, "Shucks, I guess we lost another one."

Is It Better to Sell than to Buy?

Although Cities' stockholders gained "only" 12 percent, they still did better than Occidental's or Gulf's stockholders. In mergers, is it better for stockholders to sell than to buy?

In general, yes. Franks, Harris, and Titman, who studied 399 acquisitions by large U.S. firms between 1975 and 1984, found that following the announcement of

---

[29]This practice of defending yourself against merger by making a counterbid for the predator's stock is sometimes known as the "Pacman defense."

the bid selling shareholders received a healthy gain averaging 28 percent.[30] On the other hand, it appears that investors expected acquiring companies to just about break even. The prices of their shares fell by 1 percent.[31] The value of the *total* package—buyer plus seller—increased by 4 percent. Of course, these are averages; selling shareholders sometimes obtain much higher returns. When IBM took over Lotus Corporation, it paid a premium of 100 percent, or about $1.7 billion, for Lotus stock.

Why do sellers earn higher returns? There are two reasons. First, buying firms are typically larger than selling firms. In many mergers the buyer is so much larger that even substantial net benefits would not show up clearly in the buyer's share price. Suppose, for example, that company A buys company B, which is only one-tenth A's size. Suppose the dollar value of the net gain from the merger is split equally between A and B.[32] Each company's shareholders receive the same *dollar* profit, but B's receive ten times A's *percentage* return.

The second, and more important, reason is the competition among potential bidders. Once the first bidder puts the target company "in play," one or more additional suitors often jump in, sometimes as white knights at the invitation of the target firm's management. Every time one suitor tops another's bid, more of the merger gain slides toward the target. At the same time, the target firm's management may mount various legal and financial counterattacks, ensuring that capitulation, if and when it comes, is at the highest attainable price.

Of course, bidders and targets are not the only possible winners. Unsuccessful bidders often win, too, by selling off their holdings in target companies at substantial profits. Such shares may be sold on the open market or sold back to the target company in a *greenmail* transaction. Sometimes they are sold to the successful suitor. We saw how Mesa Petroleum earned $80 million by selling its Cities Service shares back to Cities Service and $760 million by selling its Gulf stock to Chevron, the winning bidder.

Other winners include investment bankers, lawyers, accountants, and in some cases arbitrageurs, or "arbs," who speculate on the likely success of takeover bids.[33] *Speculate* has a negative ring, but it can be a useful social service. A tender offer may present shareholders with a difficult decision. Should they accept, should they wait to see if someone else produces a better offer, or should they sell their stock in the market? This dilemma presents an opportunity for the arbitrageurs, who specialize in answering such questions. In other words, they buy from the target's shareholders and take on the risk that the deal will not go through.

As Ivan Boesky demonstrated, arbitrageurs can make even more money if they learn about the offer *before* it is publicly announced. Because arbitrageurs may accumulate large amounts of stock, they can have an important effect on whether a deal goes through, and the bidding company or its investment bankers may be tempted to take the arbitrageurs into their confidence. This is the point at which a legitimate and useful activity becomes an illegal and harmful one.

---

[30]See J. R. Franks, R. S. Harris, and S. Titman, "The Postmerger Share-Price Performance of Acquiring Firms," *Journal of Financial Economics,* **29**:81–96 (March 1991).

[31]The small loss to the shareholders of acquiring firms is not statistically significant. Other studies using different samples have observed a small positive return.

[32]In other words, the *cost* of the merger to A is one-half the gain ΔPV_{AB}.

[33]Strictly speaking, an arbitrageur is an investor who takes a fully hedged, that is, riskless, position. But arbitrageurs in merger battles often take very large risks indeed. Their activities are oxymoronically known as "risk arbitrage."

TABLE 33-5

• •

A summary of takeover defenses

Type of Defense	Description
Preoffer Defenses	
Shark-repellent charter amendments:	
Staggered board	The board is classified into three equal groups. Only one group is elected each year. Therefore the bidder cannot gain control of the target immediately.
Supermajority	A high percentage of shares is needed to approve a merger, typically 80%.
Fair price	Mergers are restricted unless a fair price (determined by formula or appraisal) is paid.
Restricted voting rights	Shareholders who own more than a specified proportion of the target have no voting rights unless approved by the target's board.
Waiting period	Unwelcome acquirers must wait for a specified number of years before they can complete the merger.
Other:	
Poison pill	Existing shareholders are issued rights which, if there is a significant purchase of shares by a bidder, can be used to purchase additional stock in the company at a bargain price.
Poison put	Existing bondholders can demand repayment if there is a change of control as a result of a hostile takeover.
Postoffer Defenses	
Litigation	File suit against bidder for violating antitrust or securities laws.
Asset restructuring	Buy assets that bidder does not want or that will create an antitrust problem.
Liability restructuring	Issue shares to a friendly third party or increase the number of shareholders. Repurchase shares from existing shareholders at a premium.

Source: This table is loosely adapted from R. S. Ruback, "An Overview of Takeover Defenses," Working Paper No. 1836-86, Sloan School of Management, M.I.T., September 1986, tables 1 and 2. See also L. Herzel and R. W. Shepro, *Bidders and Targets: Mergers and Acquisitions in the U.S.*, Basil Blackwell, Inc., Cambridge, Mass., 1990, chap. 8.

• • • • • • • • • • • • • • •

Takeover Defenses

The Cities Service case illustrates several tactics managers use to fight takeover bids. Frequently they don't wait for a bid before taking defensive action. Instead, they deter potential bidders by devising *poison pills* that make their companies unappetizing, or they persuade shareholders to agree to "shark-repellent" changes to the company charter.[34] Table 33-5 summarizes the principal first and second levels of defense.

Why do managers contest takeover bids? One reason is to extract a higher price from the bidder. Another possible reason is that managers believe their jobs may be at risk in the merged company. These managers are not trying to obtain a better price; they want to stop the bid altogether.

---

[34]Since shareholders expect to gain if their company is taken over, it is no surprise that they do not welcome these impediments. See, for example, G. Jarrell and A. Poulsen, "Shark Repellents and Stock Prices: The Effects of Antitakeover Amendments since 1980," *Journal of Financial Economics*, **19**:127–168 (1987).

Some companies reduce these conflicts of interest by offering their managers *golden parachutes*, that is, generous payoffs if the managers lose their jobs as the result of a takeover. The payoffs can be very large; for example, when Revlon was taken over by Pantry Pride, its chief executive received $35 million. It may seem odd to reward managers for being taken over. However, if a soft landing overcomes their opposition to takeover bids, even $35 million may be a small price to pay.[35]

Any management team that tries to develop improved weapons of defense must expect challenge in the courts. In the early 1980s the courts tended to give managers the benefit of the doubt and respect their business judgment about whether a takeover should be resisted. But the courts' attitudes to takeover battles have changed. For example, in 1993 a court blocked Viacom's agreed takeover of Paramount on the grounds that Paramount's directors did not do their homework before turning down a higher offer from QVC. Paramount was forced to give up its poison-pill defense and the stock options that it had offered to Viacom. Because of such decisions, managers have become much more careful in opposing bids, and they do not throw themselves blindly into the arms of any white knight.[36]

At the same time, state governments have provided some new defensive weapons. In 1987 the Supreme Court upheld state laws that allow companies to deprive an investor of voting rights as soon as the investor's share in the company exceeds a certain level. Since then state antitakeover laws have proliferated. Many allow boards of directors to block mergers with hostile bidders for several years and to consider the interests of employees, customers, suppliers, and their communities in deciding whether to try to block a hostile bid.

New laws and antitakeover devices will keep cropping up. All we can say is, "Stay tuned." However, there is one other takeover defense that we haven't yet stressed. Here is the story of how Phillips Petroleum restructured its balance sheet to keep its independence.

Phillips Restructures to Stave Off Takeover

The main protagonist is once again Boone Pickens of Mesa Petroleum. In 1982 Mesa had been involved in a battle for General American Oil (GAO) Company but had dropped its bid when GAO agreed to sell out to Phillips Petroleum. Two years later Mesa bought 6 percent of Phillips stock at an average price of $38 a share and then bid for a further 15 percent at $60 a share.

Phillips responded in three ways.[37] First, it agreed to buy back Mesa's holding, giving Mesa a profit on the deal of $89 million.[38] Second, it raised its dividend by 25

---

[35]In 1984 popular hostility to the size of golden parachutes led to new legislation. Golden parachutes that are triggered by a change of control attract a 20 percent excise tax, and the payments cannot be deducted for corporate tax.

[36]In 1985 a shiver ran through many boardrooms when the directors of Trans Union Corporation were held personally liable for being too hasty in accepting a takeover bid. Changes in judicial attitudes to takeover defenses are reviewed in L. Herzel and R. W. Shepro, *Bidders and Targets: Mergers and Acquisitions in the U.S.*, Basil Blackwell, Inc., Cambridge, Mass., 1990.

[37]Phillips also devised a poison pill that would make it a less appetizing morsel for future predators. This poison pill gave shareholders the right to exchange their stock for notes worth $62 a share if anyone bought 30 percent or more of Phillips's stock. (The purchaser who triggered this provision would not be entitled to any of the notes.)

[38]Phillips's move to deter Mesa by buying out its holding at a premium is another example of greenmail. But giving in to greenmail can be dangerous, as Phillips soon discovered. Just 6 weeks later a group led by another corporate raider, Carl Icahn, acquired nearly 5 percent of Phillips stock and made an offer to buy the remainder. Phillips responded with a second greenmail payment: it bought out Icahn and his pals, giving them a profit of about $35 million.

TABLE 33-6

Phillips's balance sheet was dramatically changed by its leveraged repurchase
(figures in billions)

	1985	1984		1985	1984
Current assets	$ 3.1	$ 4.6	Current liabilities	$ 3.1	$ 5.3
Fixed assets	10.3	11.2	Long-term debt	6.5	2.8
Other	.6	1.2	Other long-term liabilities	2.8	2.3
			Equity	1.6	6.6
Total assets	$14.0	$17.0	Total liabilities	$14.0	$17.0

percent, reduced capital spending, and announced a program to sell $2 billion of assets. Third, it agreed to repurchase about 50 percent of its stock and to issue instead $4.5 billion of debt. Table 33-6 shows how this leveraged repurchase changed Phillips's balance sheet. The new debt ratio was about 80 percent, and book equity shrank by $5 billion to $1.6 billion.

This massive debt burden put Phillips on a strict cash diet. It was forced to sell assets and pinch pennies wherever possible. Capital expenditures were cut back from $1065 million in 1985 to $646 million in 1986. In the same years, the number of employees fell from 25,300 to 21,800. Austerity continued through the late 1980s. By the end of the decade, long-term debt was reduced to $3.9 billion, and Phillips had regained an investment-grade debt rating. Employment was steady, and capital expenditures were gradually increasing, although not to the levels of the early 1980s. Phillips emerged from the decade leaner but healthy and still independent.

How did this restructuring shield Phillips from takeover? Certainly not by making purchase of the company more expensive. On the contrary, restructuring drastically reduced the total market value of Phillips's outstanding stock and therefore reduced the likely cost of buying out its remaining shareholders.

But restructuring removed the chief *motive* for takeover, which was to force Phillips to generate and pay out more cash to investors. Before the restructuring, investors sensed that Phillips was not running a tight ship and worried that it would plow back its ample operating cash flow into mediocre capital investments or ill-advised expansion. They wanted Phillips to pay out its free cash flow rather than let it be soaked up by a too comfortable organization or plowed into negative-NPV investments. Consequently, Phillips's share price did not reflect the potential value of its assets and operations. *That* created the opportunity for a takeover. One can almost hear the potential raider thinking:

> So what if I have to pay a 30 or 40 percent premium to take over Phillips? I can borrow most of the purchase price and then pay off the loan by selling surplus assets, cutting out all but the best capital investments and wringing out slack in the organization. It'll be a rough few years, but if surgery's necessary, I might as well be the doctor and get paid for doing it.

Phillips's managers did not agree that the company was slack or prone to overinvestment. Nevertheless, they bowed to pressure from the stock market and undertook the surgery themselves. They paid out billions to repurchase stock and to service the $6.5 billion in long-term debt. They sold assets, cut back capital investment, and put their organization on the diet investors were calling for.

When the merger motive is to eliminate inefficiency or distribute excess cash, the target's best defense is to do what the bidder would do, and thus avoid the cost, confusion, and random casualties of a takeover battle.

....

**Divesti-
tures and
Spin-Offs**

Firms not only acquire businesses; they also sell them. In fact, the sales often involve assets which have recently been acquired as part of a merger but which are not essential to the core business.[39] In recent years the number of divestitures has been almost half the number of mergers.

Instead of selling a business to another firm, companies may spin off a subsidiary by distributing its stock to the shareholders of the parent company. For example, in 1995 ITT split itself into three separate firms. One acquired ITT's interests in hotels and gambling, a second took over ITT's electrical businesses, and the third specialized in financial services. Shareholders in ITT received common stock in each of these new companies.

Some spin-offs have tax or regulatory advantages. Others may widen investors' choice by allowing them to invest directly in just one part of the business. However, probably the most common reason for creating spin-offs is that they improve efficiency. Companies sometimes refer to a business as being a "poor fit." By spinning it off, the management of the parent company can concentrate on its main activity. If each business must stand on its own feet, there is no risk that funds will be siphoned off from one in order to support unprofitable investments in the other. Moreover, if the two parts of the business are independent, it is easy to see the value of each and to reward managers accordingly.

Sometimes corporate restructuring involves fundamental changes in the legal structure of the business. For example, some spin-offs have been organized as limited partnerships with a finite life.[40] (Many limited partnerships are found in the oil industry, where producing oil wells have been spun off into partnerships.) In this case the shareholders are replaced by partners in the business, and the firm's revenues and expenses are credited directly to the individual partners' accounts according to a predefined formula.

The management of a corporation has considerable discretion over whether to pay out income as dividends or reinvest it in the business. In a limited partnership there is no such discretion: most income must be paid out. Thus, if you are concerned that managers may be tempted by imprudent investments, you will feel better if the business is a limited partnership.

33-7 LEVERAGED BUY-OUTS

Leveraged buy-outs (LBOs) differ from ordinary acquisitions in two ways. First, a large fraction of the purchase price is debt-financed. Some, perhaps all, of this debt is junk, that is, below investment grade. Second, the LBO "goes private," and its shares no longer trade on the open market.[41] The remaining equity in the LBO is privately held by a small group of (usually institutional) investors. When this group

---

[39]One study calculated that over 30 percent of assets acquired in a sample of hostile merger contests between 1984 and 1986 were subsequently sold. See S. Bhagat, A. Schleifer, and R. Vishny, "Hostile Takeovers in the 1980s: The Return to Corporate Specialization," in *Brookings Papers on Economic Activity: Microeconomics*, 1990.

[40]See Section 14-1.

[41]Sometimes a small "stub" of shares is left over and continues to trade.

is led by the company's management, the acquisition is called a **management buy-out (MBO)**.

In the 1970s and 1980s many management buy-outs were arranged for unwanted divisions of large, diversified companies. Smaller divisions outside the companies' main lines of business often lacked top management's interest and commitment, and divisional management chafed under corporate bureaucracy. Many such divisions flowered when spun off as MBOs. Their managers, pushed by the need to generate cash for debt service and encouraged by a substantial personal stake in the business, found ways to cut costs and compete more effectively.

In the 1980s MBO/LBO activity shifted to buy-outs of entire businesses, including large, mature public corporations. We start with the largest, most dramatic, and best-documented LBO of them all: the $25 billion takeover of RJR Nabisco in 1988 by Kohlberg, Kravis and Roberts (KKR). The players, tactics, and controversies of LBOs are writ large in this case.

RJR Nabisco

On October 28, 1988, the board of directors of RJR Nabisco revealed that Ross Johnson, the company's chief executive officer, had formed a group of investors that was prepared to buy all RJR's stock for $75 per share in cash and take the company private. Johnson's group was backed up and advised by Shearson Lehman Hutton, the investment bank subsidiary of American Express. RJR's share price immediately moved to about $75, handing shareholders a 1-day 36 percent gain over the previous day's price of $56. At the same time RJR's bonds fell, since it was clear that existing bondholders would soon have a lot more company.[42]

Johnson's offer lifted RJR onto the auction block. Once the company was in play, its board of directors was obliged to consider other offers, which were not long in coming. Four days later Kohlberg, Kravis and Roberts bid $90 per share, $79 in cash plus PIK preferred valued at $11. (PIK means "pay in kind." The preferred dividends would be paid not in cash but in more preferred shares.)[43]

The resulting bidding contest had as many turns and surprises as a Dickens novel. RJR's board set up the Committee of Independent Directors, advised by the investment bank Lazard Freres, to set rules for the bidding. Financial projections for RJR were made available to KKR and another bidding group put together by First Boston. The bidding finally closed on November 30, some 32 days after the initial offer was revealed. In the end it was Johnson's group against KKR. KKR offered $109 per share, after adding $1 per share (roughly $230 million) in the last hour.[44] The KKR bid was $81 in cash, convertible subordinated debentures valued at about $10, and PIK preferred shares valued at about $18. Johnson's group bid $112 in cash and securities.

But the RJR board chose KKR. Although Johnson's group had offered $3 per share more, its security valuations were viewed as "softer" and perhaps overstated. Also KKR's planned asset sales were less drastic; perhaps its plans for managing the business inspired more confidence. Finally, the Johnson group's proposal contained a management compensation package that seemed extremely generous and had generated an avalanche of bad press.

---

[42]N. Mohan and C. R. Chen track the abnormal returns of RJR securities in "A Review of the RJR Nabisco Buyout," *Journal of Applied Corporate Finance*, **3**:102–108 (Summer 1990).

[43]See Section 24-7.

[44]The whole story is reconstructed by B. Burrough and J. Helyar in *Barbarians at the Gate: The Fall of RJR Nabisco*, Harper & Row, New York, 1990 (see especially chap. 18), and in a movie with the same title.

But where did the merger benefits come from? What could justify offering $109 per share, about $25 billion in all, for a company that only 33 days previously was selling for $56 per share? KKR and the other bidders were betting on two things. First, they expected to generate billions in additional cash from interest tax shields, reduced capital expenditures, and sales of assets not strictly necessary to RJR's core businesses. Asset sales alone were projected to generate $5 billion. Second, they expected to make the core businesses significantly more profitable, mainly by cutting back on expenses and bureaucracy. Apparently there was plenty to cut, including the RJR "Air Force," which at one point included 10 corporate jets.

In the year after KKR took over, new management was installed that sold assets and cut back operating expenses and capital spending. There were also layoffs. As expected, high interest charges meant a net loss of $976 million for 1989, but pretax operating income actually increased, despite extensive asset sales, including the sale of RJR's European food operations.

Inside the firm, things were going well. But outside there was confusion, and prices in the junk bond market were rapidly declining, implying much higher future interest charges for RJR and stricter terms on any refinancing. In mid-1990 KKR made an additional equity investment, and in December 1990 it announced an offer of cash and new shares in exchange for $753 million of junk bonds. RJR's chief financial officer described the exchange offer as "one further step in the deleveraging of the company."[45] For RJR, the world's largest LBO, it seemed that high debt was a temporary, not permanent, virtue.

RJR, like many other firms that were taken private through LBOs, enjoyed only a short period as a private company. In 1991 RJR went public again with the sale of $1.1 billion of stock.[46] KKR progressively sold off its investment, and its remaining stake in the company was sold in 1995 at roughly the original purchase price.

Barbarians at the Gate?

The RJR Nabisco LBO crystallized views on LBOs, the junk bond market, and the takeover business. For many it exemplified all that was wrong with finance in the 1980s, especially the willingness of "raiders" to carve up established companies, leaving them with enormous debt burdens, basically in order to get rich quick.

There was plenty of confusion, stupidity, and greed in the LBO business. Not all the people involved were nice. On the other hand, LBOs generated enormous increases in market value, and most of the gains went to the selling stockholders, not the raiders. For example, the biggest winners in the RJR Nabisco LBO were the company's stockholders.

We should therefore consider briefly where these gains may have come from before we try to pass judgment on LBOs. There are several possibilities.

THE JUNK BOND MARKETS.   LBOs and debt-financed takeovers may have been driven by artificially cheap funding from the junk bond markets. With hindsight, it seems that investors in junk bonds underestimated the risks of default in junk bonds. Default rates climbed painfully from 1988 through 1991, when 10 percent of out-

---

[45]G. Andress, "RJR Swallows Hard, Offers $5-a-Share Stock," *Wall Street Journal*, December 18, 1990, pp. C1–C2.

[46]Northwest Airlines, Safeway Stores, Kaiser Aluminum, and Burlington Industries are other examples of LBOs that reverted to being public companies.

standing junk bonds with a face value of $18.9 billion defaulted.[47] The junk bond market also became much less liquid after the demise of Drexel Burnham, the chief market maker. Yields climbed dramatically, and new issues dried up. Suddenly junk-financed LBOs became as scarce as great blind dates.

If junk bond investors in 1985 had appreciated the risk of what actually happened in 1990, junk finance would have been dearer. That would have slowed down LBOs and other highly leveraged transactions.

LEVERAGE AND TAXES.   Borrowing money saves taxes, as we explained in Chapter 18. But taxes were not the main driving force behind LBOs. The value of interest tax shields was just not big enough to explain the observed gains in market value.[48] For example, Richard Ruback estimated the present value of additional interest tax shields generated by the RJR LBO at $1.8 billion.[49] But the gain in market value to RJR stockholders was about $8 billion.

Of course, if interest tax shields were the main motive for LBOs' high debt, then LBO managers would not be so concerned to pay off debt. We saw that this was one of the first tasks facing RJR Nabisco's new management, as well as the management of Phillips Petroleum after its leveraged recapitalization.

OTHER STAKEHOLDERS.   We should look at the total gain to *all* investors in an LBO, not just to the selling stockholders. It's possible that the latter's gain is just someone else's loss and that no value is generated overall.

Bondholders are the obvious losers. The debt they thought was well secured may turn into junk when the borrower goes through an LBO. We noted how market prices of RJR Nabisco debt fell sharply when Ross Johnson's first LBO offer was announced. But again, the value losses suffered by bondholders in LBOs are not nearly large enough to explain stockholder gains. For example, Mohan and Chen's estimate[50] of losses to RJR bondholders was at most $575 million—painful to the bondholders, but far below the stockholders' gain.

LEVERAGE AND INCENTIVES.   Managers and employees of LBOs work harder and often smarter. They have to generate cash for debt service. Moreover, managers' personal fortunes are riding on the LBO's success. They become owners rather than organization people.

It's hard to measure the payoff from better incentives, but there is some preliminary evidence of improved operating efficiency in LBOs. Kaplan, who studied 48 MBOs between 1980 and 1986, found average increases in operating income of 24 percent 3 years after the LBO. Ratios of operating income and net cash flow to assets and sales increased dramatically. He observed cutbacks in capital expenditures but not in employment. Kaplan suggests that these "operating changes are due to improved incentives rather than layoffs or managerial exploitation of shareholders through inside information."[51]

---

[47]See E. I. Altman and V. Kishore, "Defaults and Returns on High Yield Bonds: Analysis through 1994," New York University Salomon Center, Leonard N. Stern School of Business, 1995. See also Section 23-5.

[48]Moreover, there are some tax costs to LBOs. For example, selling shareholders realize capital gains and pay taxes that otherwise could be deferred. See L. Stiglin, S. N. Kaplan, and M. C. Jensen, "Effects of LBOs on Tax Revenues of the U.S. Treasury," *Tax Notes*, **42**:727–733 (February 6, 1989).

[49]R. S. Ruback, "RJR Nabisco," case study, Harvard Business School, Cambridge, Mass., 1989.

[50]Mohan and Chen, op. cit.

[51]S. Kaplan, "The Effects of Management Buyouts on Operating Performance and Value," *Journal of Financial Economics*, **24**:217–254 (October 1989).

FREE CASH FLOW.   The free-cash-flow theory of takeovers is basically that mature firms with a surplus of cash will tend to waste it. This contrasts with standard finance theory, which says that firms with more cash than positive-NPV investment opportunities should give the cash back to investors through higher dividends, share repurchases, or other devices. But we see firms like RJR Nabisco spending on corporate luxuries and questionable capital investments. One benefit of LBOs is that they put such companies on a diet and force them to pay out cash to service debt.

The free-cash-flow theory predicts that mature, "cash cow" companies will be the most likely targets of LBOs. We can find many examples that fit the theory, including RJR Nabisco. The theory says that the gains in market value generated by LBOs are just the present value of the future cash flows that would otherwise have been frittered away.[52]

We do not endorse the free-cash-flow theory as an exclusive explanation for LBOs. We have mentioned several other plausible reasons, and we suspect that most LBOs are driven by a mixture of motives. Nor do we say that all LBOs are positive. On the contrary, there are many mistakes, and even soundly motivated LBOs are dangerous (at least for the buyers), as the bankruptcies of Campeau, Revco, National Gypsum, and many other highly leveraged companies prove. However, we do quarrel with those who portray LBOs *simply* as Wall Street barbarians breaking up the traditional strengths of corporate America. In many cases LBOs have generated true gains. In the next section we sum up the longer-run impact of mergers, including LBOs, on the United States economy. We warn you, however, that there are no neat answers. Our assessment has to be mixed and tentative.

33-8   MERGERS AND THE ECONOMY

Merger Waves

Mergers come in waves. The first episode of intense merger activity occurred at the turn of the century and the second in the 1920s. There was a further boom from 1967 to 1969 and then again in the 1980s and 1990s (1994 and 1995 were record years).[53] Each episode coincided with a period of buoyant stock prices, though in each case there were substantial differences in the types of companies that merged and the ways they went about it.

We don't really understand why merger activity is so volatile. If mergers are prompted by economic motives, at least one of these motives must be "here today and gone tomorrow," and it must somehow be associated with high stock prices. But none of the economic motives that we review in this chapter has anything to do with the general level of the stock market. None burst on the scene in 1967, departed in 1970, and reappeared for most of the 1980s and again in the mid-1990s.

Some mergers may result from mistakes in valuation on the part of the stock market. In other words, the buyer may believe that investors have underestimated the value of the seller or may hope that they *will* overestimate the value of the combined firm. But we see (with hindsight) that mistakes are made in bear markets as well as bull markets. Why don't we see just as many firms hunting for bargain acquisitions when the stock market is low? It is possible that "suckers are born every minute," but

---

[52]The free-cash-flow theory's chief proponent is Michael Jensen. See "The Eclipse of the Public Corporation," *Harvard Business Review*, **67**:61–74 (September–October 1989), and "The Agency Costs of Free Cash Flow, Corporate Finance and Takeovers," *American Economic Review*, **76**:323–329 (May 1986).

[53]S. Lipin, "Let's Do It: Disney to Diaper Makers Push Mergers and Acquisitions to Record High," *Wall Street Journal*, January 2, 1996.

it is difficult to believe that they can be harvested only in bull markets. Companies are not the only active buyers and sellers in a bull market. Investors also trade much more heavily after a rise in share prices. Again, nobody has a good explanation of why this should be the case. Perhaps the answer has nothing to do with economics. Perhaps merger booms and stock market trading are behavioral phenomena—human beings, like some animals, are more active when the weather is sunny.

Although we can't explain the timing of merger waves, we can do a bit better in interpreting recent history. We have seen that during the 1980s merger boom, many acquisitions were undertaken to discipline managers rather than to achieve benefits from combining two businesses. During those years few companies were immune from attack from a rival management team. For example, in 1985 Pantry Pride, a small supermarket chain recently emerged from bankruptcy, made a bid for the cosmetics company Revlon. Revlon's assets were more than five times Pantry Pride's. What made the bid possible (and eventually successful) was the ability of Pantry Pride to finance the takeover by borrowing $2.1 billion. The growth of leveraged buy-outs during the 1980s depended on the development of a junk bond market that allowed bidders to place low-grade bonds rapidly and in high volume.[54]

In the 1980s corporations in mature industries, such as oil, tobacco, tires, and forest products, found themselves with limited investment opportunities within their existing businesses. Many of these companies used their cash surpluses to buy into new areas. But they were also themselves the targets of takeovers which obliged them to distribute cash.

We can detect some broad economic forces behind these developments. During the 1980s, rapid changes in technology, deregulation, and higher oil prices and real interest rates required painful adjustments by established United States companies. In many cases leveraged buy-outs or the threat of buy-out served as the mechanism that forced these changes on reluctant management. In other countries such as Japan and Germany, where hostile takeovers are almost unknown, change has come from within and has been more gradual, though not less painful.

This contrast takes us back to our discussion of corporate governance in Chapter 14. In the United States the takeover market provides an important control on management. It is often clumsy and expensive, but if we are to rely less on this *external* control, then we need to ensure that *internal* controls are able to provide effective incentives.

By the end of the 1980s the merger environment had changed. Many of the obvious targets had disappeared, and the battle for RJR Nabisco highlighted the increasing cost of victory. Institutions were reluctant to increase their holdings of junk bonds. Moreover, the market for these bonds had depended to a remarkable extent on one individual, Michael Milken of the investment bank Drexel Burnham. By the late 1980s Milken and his employer were in trouble. Milken was indicted by a federal grand jury on 98 counts and was subsequently sentenced to jail for 10 years and ordered to pay $600 million in fines. Drexel likewise pleaded guilty to six felony counts and paid $650 million in penalties. In early 1990 Drexel filed for Chapter 11 bankruptcy, but by that time the junk bond market was moribund and the finance for highly leveraged buy-outs had largely dried up.[55] Finally, in reaction to the perceived excesses of the merger boom, state legislatures and the courts began to turn against takeovers.

---

[54]Because speed is important in takeovers, most junk bond issues in leveraged buy-outs were private placements. Pantry Pride's public junk bond issue was unusual.

[55]For a readable history of the role of Milken in the development of the junk bond market, See C. Bruck, *The Predators' Ball: The Junk Bond Raiders and the Man Who Staked Them,* Simon and Schuster, New York, 1988.

The decline in merger activity proved temporary; by the mid-1990s stock markets and mergers were booming once again. However, LBOs remained out of fashion, and relatively few mergers were intended simply to replace management. Instead, companies began to look again at the possible benefits from combining two businesses. Cuts in defense spending encouraged major defense firms to consolidate their operations, and new technologies led to a spate of mergers in the communications and entertainment industries. There was also a surge in cross-border, that is, international, acquisitions.

Do Mergers Generate Net Benefits?

There are undoubtedly good acquisitions and bad acquisitions, but economists find it hard to agree on whether acquisitions are beneficial *on balance*. Indeed, since there seem to be transient fashions in mergers, it would be surprising if economists could come up with simple generalizations.

We do know that mergers generate substantial gains to acquired firms' stockholders. Since buyers roughly break even and sellers make substantial gains, it seems that there are positive overall benefits from merger.[56] But not everybody is convinced. Some believe that investors analyzing mergers pay too much attention to short-term earnings gains and don't notice that these gains are at the expense of long-term prospects.[57]

Since we can't observe how companies would have fared in the absence of a merger, it is difficult to measure the effects on profitability. Ravenscroft and Scherer, who looked at mergers during the 1960s and early 1970s, argued that productivity declined in the years following merger.[58] But studies of more recent merger activity suggest that mergers *do* seem to improve real productivity. For example, Paul Healy, Krishna Palepu, and Richard Ruback examined 50 large mergers between 1979 and 1983 and found an average increase of 2.4 percentage points in the companies' pretax returns.[59] They argue that this gain came from generating a higher level of sales from

---

[56]M. C. Jensen and R. S. Ruback, "The Market for Corporate Control: The Scientific Evidence," *Journal of Financial Economics*, **11**:5–50 (April 1983), after an extensive review of empirical work, conclude that "corporate takeovers generate positive gains" (p. 47). Richard Roll reviewed the same evidence and argues that "takeover gains may have been overestimated if they exist at all." See "The Hubris Hypothesis of Corporate Takeovers," *Journal of Business*, **59**:198–216 (April 1986).

[57]There have been a number of attempts to test whether investors are myopic. For example, McConnell and Muscarella examined the reaction of stock prices to announcements of capital expenditure plans. If investors were interested in short-term earnings, which are generally depressed by major capital expenditure programs, then these announcements should depress stock price. But they found that increases in capital spending were associated with *increases* in stock prices and reductions were associated with *falls*. Similarly, Jarrell, Lehn, and Marr found that announcements of expanded R&D spending prompted a *rise* in stock price. See J. McConnell and C. Muscarella, "Corporate Capital Expenditure Decisions and the Market Value of the Firm," *Journal of Financial Economics*, **14**:399–422 (July 1985), and G. Jarrell, K. Lehn, and W. Marr, "Institutional Ownership, Tender Offers, and Long-Term Investments," Office of the Chief Economist, Securities and Exchange Commission (April 1985).

[58]See D. J. Ravenscroft and F. M. Scherer, "Mergers and Managerial Performance," in J. C. Coffee, Jr., L. Lowenstein, and S. Rose-Ackerman (eds.), *Knights, Raiders, and Targets: The Impact of the Hostile Takeover*, Oxford University Press, New York, 1988.

[59]See P. Healy, K. Palepu, and R. Ruback, "Does Corporate Performance Improve after Mergers?" NBER Working Paper No. 3348, 1990. The study examined the pretax returns of the merged companies relative to industry averages. A study by Lichtenberg and Siegel came to similar conclusions. Before merger, acquired companies had lower levels of productivity than did other firms in their industries, but by 7 years after the control change, two-thirds of the productivity gap had been eliminated. See F. Lichtenberg and D. Siegel, "The Effect of Control Changes on the Productivity of U.S. Manufacturing Plants," *Journal of Applied Corporate Finance*, **2**:60–67 (Summer 1989).

the same assets. There was no evidence indicating that the companies were mortgaging their long-term future by cutting back on long-term investments; expenditures on capital equipment and research and development tracked the industry average.[60]

If you are concerned with public policy toward mergers, you do not want to look at only their impact on the shareholders of the companies concerned. For instance, we have already seen that in the case of RJR Nabisco some part of the shareholders' gain was at the expense of the bondholders and the Internal Revenue Service (through the enlarged interest tax shield). The acquirer's shareholders may also gain at the expense of the target firm's employees, who in some cases are laid off or are forced to take pay cuts after takeovers. Andrei Shleifer and Lawrence Summers argue that such activities may involve a loss of trust between employer and employee which can spread throughout the economic system.[61]

Many people worried because the merger wave of the 1980s led to excessive debt levels and left many United States companies ill equipped to survive a recession. Also, many savings and loan companies and some large insurance firms invested heavily in junk bonds. Defaults on these bonds threatened and in some cases extinguished their solvency.

Perhaps the most important effect of acquisitions is felt by the managers of companies that are *not* taken over. For example, one effect of LBOs was that managers of even the largest corporations could not feel safe from challenge. Perhaps the threat of takeover spurs the whole of corporate America to try harder. Unfortunately, we don't know whether, on balance, the threat of merger makes for active days or sleepless nights.

But merger activity is also very costly. For example, in the RJR Nabisco buy-out, the total fees paid to the investment banks, lawyers, and accountants amounted to over $1 billion. Phillips Petroleum spent an estimated $150 million defending itself. And that does not include the amount of time Phillips's management spent on defending rather than running their business.

Even if the gains to the community exceed the costs, one wonders whether the same benefits could not be achieved more cheaply in ways other than acquisition. For example, are leveraged buy-outs really necessary to make managers work harder?

33-9   SUMMARY

A merger generates an economic gain if the two firms are worth more together than apart. Suppose that firms A and B merge to form a new entity, AB. Then the gain from the merger is

$$\text{Gain} = PV_{AB} - (PV_A + PV_B)$$

Gains from mergers may reflect economies of scale, economies of vertical integration, improved efficiency, fuller use of tax shields, the combination of complementary re-

---

[60]Maintained levels of capital spending and R&D are also observed by Lichtenberg and Siegel, op. cit., and B. H. Hall, "The Effect of Takeover Activity on Corporate Research and Development," in A. J. Auerbach (ed.), *Corporate Takeover: Causes and Consequences,* University of Chicago Press, Chicago, 1988.

[61]See A. Shleifer and L. H. Summers, "Breach of Trust in Corporate Takeovers," in A. J. Auerbach (ed.), *Corporate Takeovers: Causes and Consequences,* University of Chicago Press, Chicago, 1988. However, Lichtenberg and Siegel, op. cit., found no evidence showing that, on average, ownership changes lead to layoffs or wage cuts.

sources, or redeployment of surplus funds. In other cases there may be no advantage in combining two businesses, but the object of the acquisition is to install a more efficient management team. We don't know how common these benefits are, but they do make economic sense. Sometimes mergers are undertaken to reduce the costs of borrowing, diversify risks, or play the bootstrap game. These motives are dubious.

You should go ahead with the merger if the gain exceeds the cost. Cost is the premium that the buyer pays for the selling firm over its value as a separate entity. It is easy to estimate when the merger is financed by cash. In that case,

$$\text{Cost} = \text{cash} - PV_B$$

When payment is in the form of shares, the cost naturally depends on what those shares are worth after the merger is complete. If the merger is a success, B's stockholders will share the merger gains.

The mechanics of buying a firm are much more complex than those of buying a machine. First, you have to make sure that the purchase is unlikely to fall afoul of the antitrust laws. Second, you have a choice of procedures: you can merge all the assets and liabilities of the seller into those of your own company; you can buy the stock of the seller rather than the company itself; or you can buy the individual assets of the seller. Third, you have to worry about the tax status of the merger. In a tax-free merger the tax position of the corporation and the stockholders is not changed. In a taxable merger the buyer can depreciate the full cost of the tangible assets acquired, but tax must be paid on any write-up of the assets' taxable value, and the stockholders in the selling corporation are taxed on any capital gains.

Mergers are often amicably negotiated between the management and directors of the two companies; but if the seller is reluctant, the would-be buyer can decide to make a tender offer or engage in a proxy fight. We sketched some of the offensive and defensive tactics used in takeover battles. We also observed that when the target firm loses, its shareholders typically win: selling shareholders earn large abnormal returns, while the bidding firm's shareholders roughly break even. The typical merger appears to generate positive net benefits for investors, but competition among bidders, plus active defense by target management, pushes most of the gains toward the selling shareholders.

The threat of hostile takeover has stimulated corporate restructuring, which usually involves additional borrowing, selling or spinning off businesses, and buying back common stock. In a management buy-out (MBO) or leveraged buy-out (LBO), all public shares are repurchased and the company "goes private." LBOs tend to involve mature businesses with ample cash flows and modest growth opportunities.

LBOs and other debt-financed takeovers are driven by a mixture of motives, including the value of interest tax shields; transfers of value from lenders, who sometimes see the market values of their securities fall as the borrowing firm piles up more debt; and the opportunity to create better incentives for managers and employees, who have a greater personal financial stake in the company but must work harder to service debt. In addition, among such takeovers that have occurred, many were designed to force firms with cash surpluses to distribute cash rather than plow it back. Investors feared that such companies would channel free cash flow into negative-NPV investments.

Mergers seem to generate net economic gains, but they are also costly. Investment banks, lawyers, arbitrageurs, and greenmailers thrived during the 1980s merger and LBO boom. Many companies were left with heavy debt burdens and will have to sell assets or improve performance to stay solvent. By 1990, the new-issue junk bond market had dried up, and the corporate jousting field was strangely quiet. But not for long: As we finish this chapter, at year-end 1995, another merger boom is clearly under way.

APPENDIX: CONGLOMERATE MERGERS AND VALUE ADDITIVITY

A pure conglomerate merger is one that has no effect on the operations or profitability of either firm. If corporate diversification is in stockholders' interests, a conglomerate merger would give a clear demonstration of its benefits. But if present values add up, the conglomerate merger would not make stockholders better or worse off.

In this appendix we examine more carefully our assertion that present values add. It turns out that values *do* add as long as capital markets are perfect and investors' diversification opportunities are unrestricted.

Call the merging firms A and B. Value additivity implies

$$PV_{AB} = PV_A + PV_B$$

where PV_{AB} = market value of combined firms just after merger

PV_A, PV_B = separate market values of A and B just before merger

For example, we might have

PV_A = $100 million ($200 per share $\times$ 500,000 shares outstanding)

and

PV_B = $200 million ($200 per share $\times$ 1,000,000 shares outstanding)

Suppose A and B are merged into a new firm, AB, with one share in AB exchanged for each share of A or B. Thus there are 1,500,000 AB shares issued. *If* value additivity holds, then PV_{AB} must equal the sum of the separate values of A and B just before the merger, that is, $300 million. That would imply a price of $200 per share of AB stock.

But note that the AB shares represent a portfolio of the assets of A and B. Before the merger investors could have bought one share of A and two of B for $600. Afterward they can obtain a claim on *exactly* the same real assets by buying three shares of AB.

Suppose that the opening price of AB shares just after the merger is $200, so that $PV_{AB} = PV_A + PV_B$. Our problem is to determine if this is an equilibrium price, that is, whether we can rule out excess demand or supply at this price.

In order for there to be excess demand, there must be some investors who are willing to increase their holdings of A and B as a consequence of the merger. Who could they be? The only thing new created by the merger is diversification, but those investors who want to hold assets of A *and* B will have purchased A's and B's stock before the merger. The diversification is redundant and consequently won't attract new investment demand.

Is there a possibility of excess supply? The answer is yes. For example, there will be some shareholders in A who did not invest in B. After the merger they cannot invest solely in A, but only in a fixed combination of A and B. Their AB shares will be less attractive to them than the pure A shares, so they will sell part of or all their AB stock. In fact, the only AB shareholders who will *not* wish to sell are those who happened to hold A and B in exactly a 1:2 ratio in their premerger portfolios!

Since there is no possibility of excess demand but a definite possibility of excess supply, we seem to have

$$PV_{AB} \leq PV_A + PV_B$$

That is, corporate diversification can't help, but it may hurt investors by restricting the types of portfolios they can hold. This is not the whole story, however, since investment demand for AB shares might be attracted from other sources if PV_{AB} drops below $PV_A + PV_B$. To illustrate, suppose there are two other firms, A* and B*, which are judged by investors to have the same risk characteristics as A and B, respectively. Then before the merger,

$$r_A = r_{A^*} \quad \text{and} \quad r_B = r_{B^*}$$

where r is the rate of return expected by investors. We'll assume $r_A = r_{A^*} = .08$ and $r_B = r_{B^*} = .20$.

Consider a portfolio one-third invested in A* and two-thirds in B*. This portfolio offers an expected return of 16 percent:

$$r = x_{A^*}r_{A^*} + x_{B^*}r_{B^*}$$
$$= \tfrac{1}{3}(.08) + \tfrac{2}{3}(.20) = .16$$

A comparable portfolio of A and B before their merger also offered a 16 percent return.

As we have noted, a new firm AB is really a portfolio of firms A and B, with portfolio weights of $\tfrac{1}{3}$ and $\tfrac{2}{3}$. Thus it is equivalent in risk to the portfolio of A* and B*. Thus the price of AB shares must adjust so that it likewise offers a 16 percent return.

What if AB shares drop below $200, so that PV_{AB} is less than $PV_A + PV_B$? Since the assets and earnings of firms A and B are the same, the price drop means that the expected rate of return on AB shares has risen above the return offered by the A*B* portfolio. That is, if r_{AB} exceeds $\tfrac{1}{3}r_A + \tfrac{2}{3}r_B$, then r_{AB} must also exceed $\tfrac{1}{3}r_{A^*} + \tfrac{2}{3}r_{B^*}$. But this is untenable: investors A* and B* could sell part of their holdings (in a 1:2 ratio), buy AB, and obtain a higher expected rate of return with no increase in risk.

On the other hand, if PV_{AB} rises above $PV_A + PV_B$, the AB shares will offer an expected return less than that offered by the A*B* portfolio. Investors will unload the AB shares, forcing their price down.

A stable result occurs only if AB shares stick at $200. Thus, value additivity will hold exactly in a perfect-market equilibrium if there are ample substitutes for the A and B assets. If A and B have unique risk characteristics, however, then PV_{AB} can fall below $PV_A + PV_B$. The reason is that the merger curtails investors' opportunity to custom-tailor their portfolios to their own needs and preferences. This makes investors worse off, reducing the attractiveness of holding the shares of firm AB.

In general, the condition for value additivity is that investors' opportunity set—that is, the range of risk characteristics attainable by investors through their portfolio choices—is independent of the particular portfolio of real assets held by the firm. Diversification per se can never expand the opportunity set given perfect security markets. Corporate diversification may reduce the investors' opportunity set, but only if the real assets the corporations hold lack substitutes among traded securities or portfolios.

In a few cases the firm may be able to expand the opportunity set. It can do so if it finds an investment opportunity that is unique—a real asset with risk characteristics shared by few or no other financial assets. In this lucky event the firm should not diversify, however. It should set up the unique asset as a separate firm so as to expand investors' opportunity set to the maximum extent. If Gallo by chance discovered that a small portion of its vineyards produced wine comparable to Chateau Margaux, it would not throw that wine into the Hearty Burgundy vat.

Further Reading

Here are two useful recent books on takeovers:

J. F. Weston, K. S. Chung, and S. E. Hoag: *Mergers, Restructuring, and Corporate Control,* Prentice-Hall, Inc., Englewood Cliffs, N.J., 1990.

L. Herzel and R. Shepro: *Bidders and Targets: Mergers and Acquisitions in the U.S.,* Basil Blackwell, Inc., Cambridge, Mass., 1990.

A good review of the mechanics of acquisitions is provided in:

S. M. Litwin: "The Merger and Acquisition Process: A Primer on Getting the Deal Done," *The Financier: ACMT,* **2**:6–17 (November 1995).

Jensen and Ruback review the extensive empirical work on mergers. The April 1983 issue of the Journal of Financial Economics *also contains a collection of some of the more important empirical studies:*

M. C. Jensen and R. S. Ruback: "The Market for Corporate Control: The Scientific Evidence," *Journal of Financial Economics,* **11**:5–50 (April 1983).

The papers by Kaplan and by Kaplan and Stein provide evidence on the evolution and performance of LBOs; Jensen, the chief proponent of the free-cash-flow theory of takeovers, gives a spirited and controversial defense of LBOs:

S. N. Kaplan, "The Effects of Management Buyouts on Operating Performance and Value," *Journal of Financial Economics,* **24**:217–254 (October 1989).

S. N. Kaplan and J. C. Stein: "The Evolution of Buyout Pricing and Financial Structure (Or, What Went Wrong) in the 1980s," *Journal of Applied Corporate Finance,* **6**:72–88 (Spring 1993).

M. C. Jensen: "The Eclipse of the Public Corporation," *Harvard Business Review,* **67**:61–74 (September–October 1989).

Finally, here are some informative case studies:

G. P. Baker: "Beatrice: A Study in the Creation and Destruction of Value," *Journal of Finance,* **47**:1081–1119 (July 1992).

R. S. Ruback: "The Conoco Takeover and Shareholder Returns," *Sloan Management Review,* **23**:13–33 (Winter 1982).

R. S. Ruback: "The Cities Service Takeover: A Case Study," *Journal of Finance,* **38**:319–330 (May 1983).

B. Burrough and J. Helyar: *Barbarians at the Gate: The Fall of RJR Nabisco,* Harper & Row, New York, 1990.

Quiz

1. Are the following hypothetical mergers horizontal, vertical, or conglomerate?
   (*a*) IBM acquires Compaq.
   (*b*) Compaq acquires Stop & Shop.
   (*c*) Stop & Shop acquires General Mills.
   (*d*) General Mills acquires IBM.

2. Velcro Saddles is contemplating the acquisition of Pogo Ski Sticks, Inc. The values of the two companies as separate entities are $20 million and $10 million, respectively. Velcro Saddles estimates that by combining the two companies, it will reduce marketing and administrative costs by $500,000 per year in perpetuity. Velcro Saddles can either pay $14 million cash for Pogo or offer Pogo a 50 percent holding in Velcro Saddles. If the opportunity cost of capital is 10 percent:
   (*a*) What is the gain from merger?
   (*b*) What is the cost of the cash offer?
   (*c*) What is the cost of the stock alternative?

    (*d*) What is the NPV of the acquisition under the cash offer?
    (*e*) What is its NPV under the stock offer?

3. Which of the following transactions are *not* likely to be classed as tax-free?
    (*a*) A merger undertaken solely for the purpose of taking advantage of tax-loss carry-forwards
    (*b*) An acquisition of assets
    (*c*) A merger in which payment is entirely in the form of voting stock
    (*d*) An acquisition in which firm A acquires all of firm B's shares in a cash tender offer

4. True or false?
    (*a*) Sellers almost always gain in mergers.
    (*b*) Buyers almost always gain in mergers.
    (*c*) Firms that do unusually well tend to be acquisition targets.
    (*d*) Merger activity in the United States varies dramatically from year to year.
    (*e*) On the average, mergers produce substantial economic gains.
    (*f*) Tender offers require the approval of the selling firm's management.
    (*g*) If a merger can be treated as a pooling of interest rather than a purchase, reported earnings are usually increased.
    (*h*) The cost of a merger is always independent of the economic gain produced by the merger.
    (*i*) The cost of a merger to the buyer equals the gain realized by the seller.

5. Which of the following motives for mergers make economic sense?
    (*a*) Merging to achieve economies of scale
    (*b*) Merging to reduce risk by diversification
    (*c*) Merging to redeploy cash generated by a firm with ample profits but limited growth opportunities
    (*d*) Merging to make fuller use of tax-loss carry-forwards
    (*e*) Merging just to increase earnings per share

6. Connect each term to its correct definition or description.

(*a*)	LBO	(A)	Payment to target firm's managers who leave after a takeover
(*b*)	Poison pill	(B)	Attempt to gain control of a firm by winning the votes of its stockholders
(*c*)	Tender offer	(C)	Offer to buy shares directly from stockholders
(*d*)	Greenmail	(D)	Target company buys out shareholders threatening takeover; repurchase price exceeds market price
(*e*)	Golden parachute	(E)	Shareholders issued rights which must be repurchased by acquiring firm or which can be used to acquire shares of acquiring firm
(*f*)	Proxy fight	(F)	Company or business bought out by private investors, largely debt-financed

7. True or false?
    (*a*) One of the first tasks of an LBO's financial manager is to pay down debt.
    (*b*) Shareholders of bidding companies earn higher abnormal returns when the merger is financed with stock than they do in cash-financed deals.
    (*c*) Takeovers are regulated by the SEC and other agencies of the federal government. State governments have little or no influence.
    (*d*) Targets for LBOs in the 1980s tended to be profitable companies in mature industries with limited investment opportunities.
    (*e*) Greenmail payments were outlawed by the SEC after the Gulf Oil takeover.

Questions and Problems

1. Examine several recent mergers and suggest the principal motives for merging in each case.

2. Examine a recent merger in which at least part of the payment made to the seller was in the form of stock. Use stock market prices to obtain an estimate of the gain from the merger and the cost of the merger.

3. The Muck and Slurry merger has fallen through (see Section 33-3). But World Enterprises is determined to report earnings per share of $2.67. It therefore acquires the Wheelrim and Axle Company. You are given the following facts:

	World Enterprises	Wheelrim and Axle	Merged Firm
Earnings per share	$2.00	$2.50	$2.67
Price per share	$40	$25	?
Price-earnings ratio	20	10	?
Number of shares	100,000	200,000	?
Total earnings	$200,000	$500,000	?
Total market value	$4,000,000	$5,000,000	?

Once again there are no gains from merging. In exchange for Wheelrim and Axle shares, World Enterprises issues just enough of its own shares to ensure its $2.67 earnings per share objective.
(*a*) Complete the above table for the merged firm.
(*b*) How many shares of World Enterprises are exchanged for each share of Wheelrim and Axle?
(*c*) What is the cost of the merger to World Enterprises?
(*d*) What is the change in the total market value of the World Enterprises shares that were outstanding before the merger?

4. Explain the distinction between a tax-free and a taxable merger. Are there circumstances in which you would expect buyer and seller to agree to a taxable merger?

5. Identify a few public companies that would not be suitable for an LBO. Then identify a few that would be suitable. Explain why the value of the companies in the second group might be increased by an LBO.

6. As treasurer of Leisure Products, Inc., you are investigating the possible acquisition of Plastitoys. You have the following basic data:

	Leisure Products	Plastitoys
Earnings per share	$5.00	$1.50
Dividend per share	$3.00	$.80
Number of shares	1,000,000	600,000
Stock price	$90	$20

You estimate that investors currently expect a steady growth of about 6 percent in Plastitoys' earnings and dividends. Under new management this growth rate would be increased to 8 percent per year, without any additional capital investment required.

(*a*) What is the gain from the acquisition?

(*b*) What is the cost of the acquisition if Leisure Products pays $25 in cash for each share of Plastitoys?

(*c*) What is the cost of the acquisition if Leisure Products offers one share of Leisure Products for every three shares of Plastitoys?

(*d*) How would the cost of the cash offer and the share offer alter if the expected growth rate of Plastitoys were not changed by the merger?

7. Look again at Table 33-3. Suppose that B Corporation's fixed assets are reexamined and found to be worth $1.2 million instead of $.9 million. How would this affect the AB Corporation's balance sheet under purchase accounting? How would the value of AB Corporation change? Would your answer depend on whether the merger is taxable?

8. Do you have any rational explanation for the great fluctuations in aggregate merger activity and the apparent relationship between merger activity and stock prices?

9. What was the common theme in the Phillips Petroleum restructuring and the RJR Nabisco LBO? Why was financial leverage a necessary part of both deals?

10. Explain why the fall in value of RJR Nabisco bonds that was caused by its LBO represented a gain to the *equity* investors in the LBO. (*Hint:* See Section 18-3.)

11. Read *Barbarians at the Gate* (see Further Reading). Does this story support Michael Jensen's free-cash-flow theory of takeovers?

12. What costs, dangers, and inequities did the boom of the 1980s in LBOs and debt-financed takeovers create? Would you support new legislation designed to restrict such transactions in the 1990s? Can you think of other ways companies could realize the benefits of these transactions without financing at very high debt ratios?

13. In July 1994 the top managers of Sovereign Bancorp were at loggerheads:[62]

   ■ Jay Sidhu, president and chief executive officer of the $5 billion bank, wants to be an acquirer. Only by buying up other banks, he argues, will Sovereign gain the financial clout it needs to survive in the increasingly competitive industry.

   ■ But Fred Jaindl, the bank's chairman and largest stockholder, wants it to *be* acquired. A buy-out, he figures, would deliver big profits to stockholders, including $50 million on his own stock.

   (*a*) Are shareholders generally better off as sellers, rather than buyers, in mergers and acquisitions? Why?

   (*b*) Under what conditions would the active acquisition strategy advocated by Sidhu make sense for Sovereign *and* its shareholders?

14. In December 1995 NatWest, one of the largest British banks, sold its U.S. retail banking operations to Fleet Financial for about $3.5 billion. This price was

---

[62]G. Bruce Knecht, "Nationwide Banking Is around the Corner, but Obstacles Remain," *Wall Street Journal*, July 26, 1994, p. A1.

much less than industry observers had expected, but NatWest's stock price nevertheless sharply increased. "The central explanation [for the stock price rise] was found in the strong hints in NatWest's announcement that it would not rush out immediately and spend the sale money on some ill-judged and overpriced acquisition."[63] NatWest also announced that it was considering re-purchasing shares.

Explain how adherents of the free-cash-flow hypothesis would interpret this episode.

15. Examine a recent hostile acquisition and discuss the tactics employed by both the predator and the target companies. Do you think that the management of the target firm was trying to defeat the bid or to secure the highest price for its stockholders? How did each announcement by the protagonists affect their stock prices?

16. Examine some recent examples of divestitures or spin-offs. What do you think were the reasons for them? How did investors react to the news?

17. How do you think mergers should be regulated? For example, what defenses should target companies be allowed to employ? Should managers of target firms be compelled to seek out the highest bids? Should they simply be passive and watch from the sidelines?

18. In Italy the first firm to bid for a target is allowed to revise its offer, but subsequent bidders may enter only one bid and they are not allowed to revise it. What do you think is the reason for this rule? Do you think that it should be introduced in the United States?

---

[63]George Graham, "NatWest Bids Farewell to an Albatross," *Financial Times*, December 23–24, 1995, p. 2.

34

International Financial Management

So far we have talked principally about doing business at home. But many companies have substantial overseas interests. Of course, your objectives in international financial management are still the same. You want to buy assets that are worth *more* than they cost, and you want to pay for them by issuing liabilities that are worth *less* than the money raised. But when you try to do these things in international business, you come up against some additional problems.

The unique feature of international financial management is that you need to deal with multiple currencies. We will, therefore, look at how foreign exchange markets operate, why exchange rates change, and what you can do to protect yourself against exchange risks.

The financial manager must also remember that interest rates differ from country to country. For example, in 1994 the rate of interest was about 2½ percent in Japan, 8 percent in the United States, and 10,000 percent in Brazil. We will discuss the reasons for these differences in interest rates, along with some of the implications for financing overseas operations. Should the parent company provide the money? Should it try to finance the operation locally? Or should it treat the world as its oyster and borrow wherever interest rates are lowest?

We will also consider how international companies decide on capital investments. How do they choose the discount rate? And how does the financing method affect the choice of project? You'll find that the basic principles of capital budgeting are the same, but there are a few pitfalls to look out for.

34-1 THE FOREIGN EXCHANGE MARKET

An American company that imports goods from Switzerland may need to buy Swiss francs in order to pay for the purchase. An American company exporting to Switzerland may receive Swiss francs, which it sells in exchange for dollars. Both firms make use of the foreign exchange market.[1]

The foreign exchange market has no central marketplace. Business is conducted by telephone or telex, and the principal dealers are the larger commercial banks and investment banks. A corporation that wants to buy or sell currency usually does so

---

[1] Alternatively, trade may take place in dollars. In this case the American importer pays for goods in dollars, and the Swiss exporter sells those dollars to buy Swiss francs. Similarly, the American exporter may demand payment in dollars; in this case the Swiss importer must sell Swiss francs to buy those dollars.

TABLE 34-1

···

Spot and forward exchange rates, January 3, 1995

	Spot Rate*	FORWARD RATE*		
		1 Month	3 Months	1 Year
Europe:				
Austria (schilling)	10.9325	10.925	10.9085	10.811
Belgium (franc)	31.9400	31.918	31.845	31.465
Denmark (krone)	6.1025	6.1032	6.1050	6.0895
France (franc)	5.3578	5.3570	5.3536	5.3218
Germany (mark)	1.5539	1.5528	1.5491	1.5269
Greece (drachma)	241.05	243.55	247.80	264.55
Holland (guilder)	1.7397	1.7385	1.7348	1.7110
Ireland (punt)	1.5464	1.5465	1.5462	1.5464
Italy (lira)	1620.50	1624.05	1631.00	1663.50
Norway (krone)	6.7810	6.7773	6.7715	6.7210
Portugal (escudo)	159.500	160.075	161.125	164.625
Spain (peseta)	131.775	132.030	133.520	134.775
Sweden (krona)	7.4481	7.4593	7.4786	7.5556
Switzerland (franc)	1.3125	1.3101	1.3053	1.2750
United Kingdom (pound)	1.5628	1.5629	1.5625	1.5619
Ecu	1.2244	1.2244	1.2248	1.2309
Americas:				
Canada (dollar)	1.4032	1.4033	1.4046	1.4128
Mexico (peso)	5.3250	5.3260	5.3278	5.3352
Pacific:				
Australia (dollar)	1.2986	1.2993	1.3011	1.3139
Hong Kong (dollar)	7.7378	7.7358	7.7346	7.7423
Japan (yen)	100.340	100.020	99.320	95.435
New Zealand (dollar)	1.5642	1.5651	1.5676	1.5766
Singapore (dollar)	1.4530	1.4515	1.4480	1.4315

*Rates show the number of units of foreign currency per dollar, except for the U.K. pound, Irish punt, and Ecu, which show the number of dollars per unit of foreign currency. *Source: Financial Times,* January 4, 1995.

through a commercial bank. Turnover in the foreign exchange market is huge. In London about $460 billion of currency changes hands each day. New York and Tokyo together account for a further $400 billion of turnover.

Table 34-1 is adapted from the table of exchange rates in the *Financial Times.* Exchange rates are generally expressed in terms of the number of units of the foreign currency needed to buy one United States dollar. This is termed an *indirect quote.* In the first column of Table 34-1 the indirect quote for Swiss francs shows that you can buy 1.3125 Swiss francs for $1. This is often written as SFr1.3125/$.

A *direct* exchange-rate quote states how many dollars you can buy for one unit of foreign currency. To make life confusing, the British pound sterling, the Irish punt, and the Ecu are usually shown as direct quotes.[2] For example, Table 34-1 shows that

---

[2] The Ecu is a basket of currencies of European Union (EU) countries.

£1 is equivalent to $1.5628 or, more concisely, $1.5628/£. If £1 buys $1.5628, then $1 must buy 1/1.5628 = £.6399. Thus the indirect quote for sterling is £.6399/$.

The exchange rates in the first column of Table 34-1 are the prices of currency for immediate delivery. These are known as **spot rates of exchange.** The spot rate for the Swiss franc is SFr1.3125/$, and the spot rate for sterling is $1.5628/£.

The term *immediate delivery* is a relative one, for spot currency is usually purchased for 2-day delivery. For example, suppose that you need 100,000 francs to pay for imports from Switzerland. On Monday you telephone your bank in New York and agree to purchase 100,000 francs at SFr1.3125/$. The bank does not hand you a wad of banknotes over the counter. Instead, it instructs its Swiss correspondent bank to transfer SFr100,000 on Wednesday to the account of the Swiss supplier. The bank debits your account by 100,000/1.3125 = $76,190 either on the Monday or, if you are a good customer, on the Wednesday.

In addition to the spot exchange market, there is a *forward market*. In the forward market you buy and sell currency for future delivery. If you know that you are going to pay out or receive foreign currency at some future date, you can insure yourself against loss by buying or selling forward. Thus, if you need 100,000 francs in 3 months, you can enter into a 3-month *forward contract*. The *forward rate* on this contract is the price you agree to pay in 3 months when the 100,000 francs are delivered.

If you look again at Table 34-1, you see that the 3-month forward rate for the Swiss franc is quoted at SFr1.3053/$. If you buy Swiss francs for 3 months' delivery, you get fewer francs for your dollar than if you buy them spot. In this case, the franc is said to trade at a forward *premium* relative to the dollar, because forward francs are more expensive than spot ones. Expressed as an annual rate, the forward premium is

$$4 \times \frac{1.3125 - 1.3053}{1.3053} \times 100 = 2.2\%$$

You could also say that the dollar was selling at a 2.2 percent *forward discount*.

A forward purchase or sale is a made-to-measure transaction between you and the bank. It can be for any currency, any amount, and any delivery day. You could buy, say, 99,999 Vietnamese dong or Haitian gourdes for a year and a day forward as long as you can find a bank ready to deal. Most forward transactions are for 6 months or less, but banks are prepared to buy and sell the major currencies for several years forward.[3]

There is also an organized market for currency for future delivery known as the currency *futures* market. Futures contracts are highly standardized—they exist only for the main currencies, and they are for specified amounts and for a limited choice of delivery dates.[4]

When you buy a forward or a futures contract, you are committed to taking delivery of the currency. As an alternative, you can take out an *option* to buy or sell currency in the future at a price that is fixed today. Made-to-measure currency options can be bought from the major banks, and standardized options are traded on the options exchanges.[5]

---

[3]Forward and spot trades are often undertaken together. For example, a company might need the use of Japanese yen for 1 month. In this case it would buy the yen spot and simultaneously sell them forward. This is known as a *swap* trade, but do not confuse it with the longer-term interest-rate and currency swaps described in Chapter 25.

[4]See Chapter 25 for a further discussion of the difference between forward and futures contracts and Table 25-2 for a list of currency futures.

[5]Some investment banks have also made one-off issues of currency warrants (i.e., long-term options to buy currency).

Finally, you can agree with the bank that you will buy foreign currency in the future at whatever is the prevailing spot rate *but subject to maximum and minimum prices.* If the value of the foreign currency rises sharply, you buy at the agreed upper limit; if it falls sharply, you buy at the lower limit.[6]

34-2   SOME BASIC RELATIONSHIPS

You can't develop a consistent international financial policy until you understand the reasons for differences in exchange rates and interest rates. Therefore let us consider the following four problems:

- *Problem 1.* Why is the dollar rate of interest ($r_\$$) different from, say, the Swiss franc rate (r_{SFr})?
- *Problem 2.* Why is the forward rate of exchange ($f_{SFr/\$}$) different from the spot rate ($s_{SFr/\$}$)?
- *Problem 3.* What determines next year's expected spot rate of exchange between dollars and Swiss francs [$E(s_{SFr/\$})$]?
- *Problem 4.* What is the relationship between the inflation rate in the United States ($i_\$$) and the Swiss inflation rate (i_{SFr})?

Suppose that individuals were not worried about risk and that there were no barriers or costs to international trade. In that case the spot exchange rates, forward exchange rates, interest rates, and inflation rates would stand in the following simple relationship to one another:

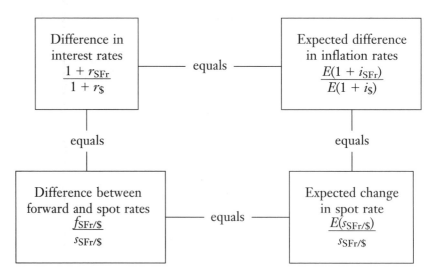

Why should this be so?

---

[6]This contract is equivalent to buying forward currency, buying a put option on the currency with an exercise price equal to the lower limit, and selling a call with an exercise price equal to the upper limit. Here's a chance to review your knowledge of options by checking this out with a position diagram. See Sections 20-1 and 20-2 if you need review.

Interest Rates and Exchange Rates

You have $1 million to invest for 1 year. Is it better to make a dollar loan at an interest rate of 7⅝ percent or a Swiss franc loan at a rate of 4%₁₆ percent? Does the answer sound obvious? Let's check:

- *Dollar loan.* The rate of interest on a 1-year dollar deposit is 7.625 percent. Therefore at the end of the year you get $1,000,000 \times 1.07625 = \$1,076,250$.

- *Swiss franc loan.* The current rate of exchange is SFr1.3125/$. For $1 million, you can buy $1,000,000 \times 1.3125 = \text{SFr}1,312,500$. The rate of interest on a 1-year franc deposit is 4.5625 percent. Therefore at the end of the year you get $1,312,500 \times 1.045625 = \text{SFr}1,372,383$. Of course, you don't know what the exchange rate is going to be in 1 year's time. But that doesn't matter. You can fix today the price at which you sell your francs. The 1-year forward rate is SFr1.275/$. Therefore, by selling forward, you can make sure that you will receive $1,372,383/1.275 = \$1,076,379$ at the end of the year.

Thus, the two investments offer almost exactly the same rate of return. They have to—they are both risk-free. If the domestic interest rate were different from the "covered" foreign rate, you would have a money machine.

When you make the Swiss franc loan, you receive a lower interest rate. But you get an offsetting gain because you sell Swiss francs forward at a higher price than what you pay for them today.

The interest rate differential is

$$\frac{1 + r_{\text{SFr}}}{1 + r_{\$}}$$

And the differential between the forward and spot exchange rates is

$$\frac{f_{\text{SFr/\$}}}{r_{\text{SFr/\$}}}$$

Interest-rate parity theory says that the difference in interest rates must equal the difference between the forward and spot exchange rates:

Difference in interest rates $\dfrac{1 + r_{\text{SFr}}}{1 + r_{\$}}$	equals	Difference between forward and spot rates $\dfrac{f_{\text{SFr/\$}}}{s_{\text{SFr/\$}}}$

In our example,

$$\frac{1.045625}{1.07625} = \frac{1.275}{1.3125}$$

The Forward Premium and Changes in Spot Rates

Now let us think about how the forward premium is related to changes in spot rates of exchange. If people didn't care about risk, the forward rate of exchange would depend solely on what people expected the spot rate to be. For example, if the 1-year forward rate on Swiss francs is SFr1.275/$, that can only be because traders expect the spot rate in 1 year's time to be SFr1.275/$. If they expected it to be, say, SFr1.3/$, nobody would be willing to sell francs forward.

Therefore the *expectations theory* of exchange rates tells us that the percentage difference between the forward rate and today's spot rate is equal to the expected change in the spot rate:

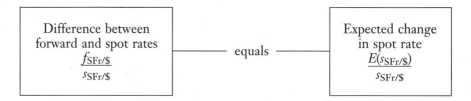

Of course, this assumes that traders don't care about risk. If they do care, the forward rate can be either higher or lower than the expected spot rate. For example, suppose that you have contracted to receive 1 million Swiss francs in 3 months. You can wait until you receive the money before you change it into dollars, but this leaves you open to the risk that the price of francs may fall over the next 3 months. Your alternative is to sell francs forward. In this case, you are fixing today the price at which you will sell your francs. Since you avoid risk by selling forward, you may be willing to do so even if the forward price of francs is a little *lower* than the expected spot price.

Other companies may be in the opposite position. They may have contracted to pay out Swiss francs in 3 months. They can wait until the end of the 3 months and then buy francs, but this leaves them open to the risk that the price of francs may rise. It is safer for these companies to fix the price today by *buying* francs forward. These companies may, therefore, be willing to buy forward even if the forward price of francs is a little *higher* than the expected spot price.

Thus some companies find it safer to *sell* Swiss francs forward, while others find it safer to *buy* francs forward. If the first group predominates, the forward price of francs is likely to be less than the expected spot price. If the second group predominates, the forward price is likely to be greater than the expected spot price.

Changes in the Exchange Rate and Inflation Rates

Now we come to the third side of our quadrilateral—the relationship between changes in the spot exchange rate and inflation rates. Suppose that you notice that silver can be bought in New York for $4.80 a troy ounce and sold in Zurich for SFr7. You think you may be onto a good thing. You decide to buy silver for $4.80 and put it on the first plane to Zurich, where you sell it for SFr7. Then you exchange your SFr7 for 7/1.3125 = $5.33. You have made a gross profit of $.53 an ounce. Of course, you have to pay transportation and insurance costs out of this, but there should still be something left over for you.

Money machines don't exist—not for long, anyway. As others notice the disparity between the price of silver in Zurich and the price in New York, the price will be forced down in Zurich and up in New York until the profit opportunity disappears. Arbitrage ensures that the dollar price of silver is about the same in the two countries.

Of course, silver is a standard and easily transportable commodity, but to some degree you might expect that the same forces would be acting to equalize the domestic and foreign prices of other goods. Those goods that can be bought more cheaply abroad will be imported, and that will force down the price of the domestic product. Similarly, those goods that can be bought more cheaply in the United States will be exported, and that will force down the price of the foreign product.

This is often called the *law of one price* or, in a more general sense, *purchasing-power parity.*[7] Just as the price of goods in Safeway must be roughly the same as the price of goods in A&P, so the price of goods in Switzerland when converted into dollars must be roughly the same as the price in the United States.

The law of one price implies that any differences in the rates of inflation will be offset by a change in the exchange rate. For example, if inflation is 4 percent in the United States and 1 percent in Switzerland, then in order to equalize the dollar prices of goods in the two countries, the number of Swiss francs that you can buy for $1 must fall by $1.01/1.04 - 1$, or about 3 percent. Therefore the law of one price suggests that in order to estimate changes in the spot rate of exchange, you need to estimate differences in inflation rates:[8]

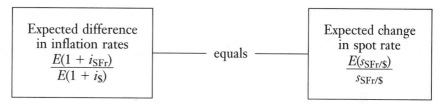

$$\underset{\begin{array}{c}\text{Expected difference}\\\text{in inflation rates}\\\frac{E(1 + i_{\text{SFr}})}{E(1 + i_{\$})}\end{array}}{}\quad\text{equals}\quad\underset{\begin{array}{c}\text{Expected change}\\\text{in spot rate}\\\frac{E(s_{\text{SFr}/\$})}{s_{\text{SFr}/\$}}\end{array}}{}$$

In our example,

Current spot rate × expected difference in inflation rates = expected spot rate

$$1.3125 \quad\times\quad \frac{1.01}{1.04} \quad=\quad 1.275$$

Interest Rates and Inflation Rates

Now for the fourth leg! Just as water always flows downhill, so capital always flows where returns are greatest. In equilibrium the expected *real* return on capital is the same in different countries.

But bonds don't promise a fixed *real* return: they promise a fixed *money* payment. Therefore we have to think about how the money rate of interest in each country is related to the real rate of interest. One answer to this has been provided by Irving Fisher, who argued that the money rate of interest will reflect expected inflation.[9] In this case the United States and Switzerland will both offer the same expected *real* rate of interest, and the difference in money rates will be equal to the expected difference in inflation rates:

$$\underset{\begin{array}{c}\text{Difference in}\\\text{interest rates}\\\frac{1 + r_{\text{SFr}}}{1 + r_{\$}}\end{array}}{}\quad\text{equals}\quad\underset{\begin{array}{c}\text{Expected difference}\\\text{in inflation rates}\\\frac{E(1 + i_{\text{SFr}})}{E(1 + i_{\$})}\end{array}}{}$$

---

[7]Economists tend to use the phrase *law of one price* when they are talking about the price of a single good. The notion that the price level of goods in general must be the same in the two countries is called *purchasing-power parity.*

[8]We are suggesting here that the *expected* difference in the inflation rates equals the *expected* change in the exchange rate. Notice, however, that the law of one price also implies that the *actual* difference in the inflation rates always equals the *actual* change in the exchange rate.

[9]We discussed the Fisher effect in Section 23-1.

In other words, capital market equilibrium requires that *real* interest rates be the same in any two countries. In Switzerland, the real interest rate is about 3.5 percent:

$$r_{\text{SFr}}(\text{real}) = \frac{1 + r_{\text{SFr}}}{E(1 + i_{\text{SFr}})} - 1 = \frac{1.045625}{1.01} - 1 = .035$$

and ditto for the United States:

$$r_{\$}(\text{real}) = \frac{1 + r_{\$}}{E(1 + i_{\$})} - 1 = \frac{1.07625}{1.04} - 1 = .035$$

....

Is Life Really That Simple?

We have described above four theories that link interest rates, forward rates, spot exchange rates, and inflation rates. Of course, such simple economic theories are not going to provide an exact description of reality. We need to know how well they predict actual behavior.

1. *Interest-rate parity theory:* Interest-rate parity theory says that the Swiss franc rate of interest covered for exchange risk should be the same as the dollar rate. In the example that we gave you earlier we used the rates of interest on eurodollar and eurofranc deposits. The eurocurrency market is an international market that is mostly free of government regulation or tax. Since money can be moved easily between different eurocurrency deposits, interest-rate parity almost always holds.[10] In fact, dealers *set* the forward price of francs by looking at the difference between the interest rates on eurofrancs and eurodollars.[11]

The relationship does not hold so exactly for the domestic money markets. In these cases taxes and government regulations sometimes prevent the citizens of one country from switching out of domestic bank deposits and covering their exchange risk in the forward market.

2. *The expectations theory of forward rates:* The expectations theory of forward rates does not imply that managers are perfect forecasters. Sometimes the *actual* future spot rate will jump above previous forward rates. Sometimes it will fall below. But if the theory is correct, we should find that *on the average* the forward rate is equal to the future spot rate. The theory passes this simple test with flying colors.[12] That is important news for the financial manager; it means that a company which always covers its foreign exchange commitments does not pay any extra for this insurance.

Although *on the average* the forward rate is equal to the future spot rate, the forward rate does seem to provide an exaggerated estimate of the likely change in the spot rate. Therefore, when the forward rate appears to predict a sharp rise in the spot rate, the actual rise generally turns out to be less. And when the forward rate appears to predict a sharp decline in the spot rate, the actual decline is also likely to be less.

---

[10]See, for example, T. Agmon and S. Bronfield, "The International Mobility of Short-Term Covered Arbitrage Capital," *Journal of Business Finance and Accounting*, **2**:269–278 (Summer 1975); and J. A. Frenkel and R. M. Levich, "Transactions Costs and Interest Arbitrage: Tranquil versus Turbulent Periods," *Journal of Political Economy*, **85**:1209–1225 (November–December 1977).

[11]The forward exchange rates shown in the *Financial Times* and reproduced in Table 34-1 are simply calculated from the differences in interest rates.

[12]For some evidence on the average difference between the forward rate and the subsequent spot rate, see B. Cornell, "Spot Rates, Forward Rates, and Market Efficiency," *Journal of Financial Economics*, **5**:55–65 (1977).

TABLE 34-2

• •

Price of Big Mac hamburgers in different countries

	Price in Local Currency	Exchange Rate (Currency/Dollar)	Local Price Converted to Dollars
Australia	A$2.45	1.35	1.82
Belgium	BFr109	28.4	3.84
Canada	C$2.77	1.39	1.99
China	Yuan9.00	8.54	1.05
Denmark	DKr26.75	5.43	4.92
France	FFr18.50	4.80	3.85
Germany	DM4.80	1.38	3.48
Holland	FL5.45	1.55	3.53
Hong Kong	HK$9.50	7.73	1.23
Italy	L4500	1702	2.64
Japan	¥391	84.2	4.65
Poland	Zloty3.40	2.34	1.45
Spain	Pts355	124	2.86
Sweden	SKr26.00	7.34	3.54
Switzerland	SFr5.90	1.13	5.20
United Kingdom	£1.74	.62	2.80
United States	US$2.32	—	2.32

Source: "Big MacCurrencies," *The Economist*, April 15, 1995, p. 108. © *The Economist.*

This result is *not* consistent with the expectations hypothesis. Instead, it looks as if sometimes companies are prepared to give up a little return in order to buy forward currency and other times they are prepared to give up return in order to sell forward currency.[13]

We should also warn you that the forward rate does not usually tell you much about the future spot rate. This does not mean that the forward rate is a poor measure of managers' expectations; it just means that exchange rates are very tough to predict. Many banks and consultants produce forecasts of future exchange rates. But Richard Levich found that more often than not the forward rate provided a more accurate forecast than the currency advisory services.[14]

3. *The law of one price:* What about the third side of our quadrilateral—the law of one price? No one who has compared prices in foreign stores with prices at home really believes that the law of one price holds exactly. Look at the first column of Table 34-2, which shows the price of a Big Mac in different countries. Notice, for example, that 5.90 Swiss francs buy as many Big Macs as 2.32 United States dollars. You could say that the Big Mac or *real* exchange rate is SFr5.90 = $2.32, or equivalently

[13]For evidence that forward exchange rates contain risk premia that are sometimes positive and sometimes negative, see, for example, E. F. Fama, "Forward and Spot Exchange Rates," *Journal of Monetary Economics,* **14**:319–338 (1984).

[14]See R. M. Levich, "How to Compare Chance with Forecasting Expertise," *Euromoney,* 61–78 (August 1981).

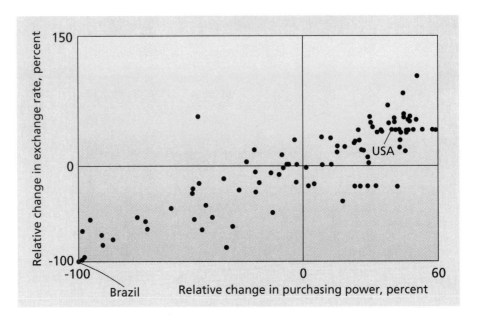

Figure 34-1 A decline in a currency's purchasing power and a decline in the exchange rate usually go hand in hand. In this diagram, each point represents the experience of a different country between 1989 and 1994. The vertical axis shows the change in the value of a foreign currency relative to the average. The horizontal axis shows the change in the currency's purchasing power relative to the average.

SFr2.54 = \$1.[15] This is the exchange rate you would expect to see if the law of one price held for Big Macs. But the actual exchange rate was SFr1.13/\$. At this rate Big Macs are more than twice as expensive in Switzerland as they are in the United States.

This suggests a possible way to make a quick buck. Why don't you buy a hamburger-to-go in (say) China for the equivalent of \$1.05 and take it for resale to Switzerland, where the price in dollars is \$5.20? The answer, of course, is that the gain would not cover the costs. The same good can sell for different prices in different countries because transportation is costly and inconvenient.[16]

On the other hand, there is clearly some relationship between inflation and changes in exchange rates. For example, between 1989 and 1994 prices in Brazil rose about a million times. Or, to put it another way, you could say that the purchasing power of money in Brazil declined by over 99.999 percent. If exchange rates had not adjusted, Brazilian exporters would have found it impossible to sell their goods. But, of course, exchange rates did adjust. In fact, the value of the Brazilian currency also declined by more than 99.999 percent relative to the dollar.

Brazil is an extreme case, but in Figure 34-1 we have plotted the relative change in purchasing power for a sample of countries against the change in the exchange rate. Brazil is tucked in the bottom left-hand corner; the United States is closer to

---

[15]The real exchange rate is usually measured not in terms of Big Macs but in terms of the amount of currency that you would need to buy a representative *basket* of goods and services.

[16]Of course, even *within* a country there may be considerable price variations. The price of Big Macs, for example, differs substantially from one part of the United States to another.

Figure 34-2 Since 1900 sterling has fallen sharply in value against the dollar. But this fall has largely offset the higher inflation rate in the United Kingdom. The *real* value of sterling has been roughly constant. [*Source:* N. Abuaf and P. Jorion, "Purchasing Power Parity in the Long Run," *Journal of Finance,* **45**:157–174 (March 1990).]

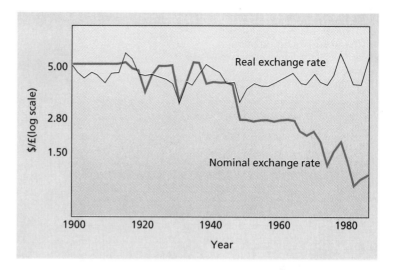

the top right. You can see that although the relationship is far from exact, large differences in inflation rates are generally accompanied by an offsetting change in the exchange rate.

Strictly speaking, the law of one price implies that the differential inflation rate is always identical to the change in the exchange rate. But we don't need to go as far as that. We should be content if the *expected* difference in the inflation rates equals the *expected* change in the spot rate. That's all we wrote on the third side of our quadrilateral. Look, for example, at Figure 34-2. The solid line shows that in 1988 £1 sterling bought about 70 percent fewer dollars than it did at the beginning of the century. But this decline in the price of sterling was largely matched by the higher inflation rate in the United Kingdom. The thin line shows that the inflation-adjusted, or *real*, exchange rate has been roughly constant.[17] If you were a financial manager called on to estimate the long-term change in the value of sterling, you could not have done much better than to assume that it would offset the difference in inflation rates.

4. *Capital market equilibrium:* Finally we come to the relationship between interest rates in different countries. Do we have a single world capital market with the same *real* rate of interest in all countries? Can we even extend the notion and think of a single world market for risk capital, so that the real opportunity cost of capital for risky investments is the same in all countries? It is an attractive idea. Unfortunately, the evidence is scanty.

Since governments cannot directly control interest rates in the international eurocurrency markets, we might expect that in these markets differences between the expected real rates of interest would be small. Governments have more control over their domestic rates of interest, at least in the short run. Therefore, it's possible for a country to have a real rate of interest in the domestic market that is below the real

---

[17]The real exchange rate is equal to the nominal exchange rate multiplied by the inflation differential. For example, suppose that the value of sterling falls from $1.54 = £1 to $1.40 = £1 at the same time that the price of goods rises 10 percent faster in the United Kingdom than in the United States. The inflation-adjusted, or real, exchange rate is unchanged at

$$\text{Initial exchange rate} \times (1 + i_£)/(1 + i_\$) = 1.40 \times 1.1 = \$1.54/£$$

Figure 34-3 Countries with the highest interest rates generally have the highest inflation rates. In this diagram each point represents the experience of a different country.

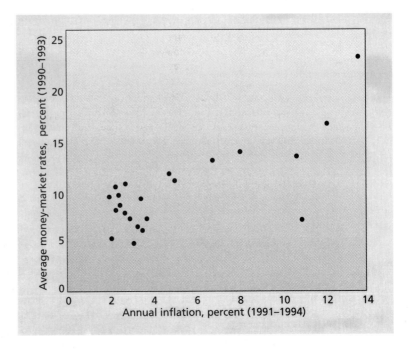

rate in other countries. But it is not easy to maintain this position indefinitely. Individuals and companies are capable of great ingenuity in transferring their cash from countries with low real rates of interest to those with high real rates.

We cannot show the relationship between interest rates and *expected* inflation, but in Figure 34-3 we have plotted the average interest rate in each of 22 countries against the inflation that subsequently occurred. You can see that, in general, the countries with the highest interest rates also had the highest inflation rates. There were much smaller differences between the real rates of interest than between the nominal (or money) rates.

34-3 INSURING AGAINST CURRENCY RISKS

To hedge or not to hedge? Laker Airlines went bankrupt because it didn't hedge. It had borrowed dollars aggressively, when much of its revenue was in sterling. When the dollar "took off" in the early 1980s, Laker could not meet its debt service.

With misfortunes like this in mind, most companies hedge or at least limit their foreign exposures. For example, in 1989 another British company, Enterprise Oil, bought some oil properties from Texas Eastern for $440 million. Since the payment was delayed a couple of months, Enterprise's plans for financing the purchase could have been thrown out of kilter if the dollar had strengthened during this period. Enterprise therefore covered the exchange risk by borrowing pounds, buying spot dollars, and investing the dollars in short-term instruments until the payment date.[18]

At the same time Enterprise also agreed to buy Texas Eastern's North Sea oil assets for $1.03 billion, but in this case the payment date was imprecise. Enterprise's solution was to place a floor on the cost of dollars by paying $26 million for a 90-

---

[18]See "Enterprise Oil's Mega Forex Option," *Corporate Finance*, **53**:13 (April 1989).

day call option to buy the $1.03 billion it needed. The exercise price of the option was, of course, in pounds.

To illustrate how firms can cope with foreign exchange risk, we will now look at a typical company in the United States, Outland Steel, and walk through its foreign exchange problems.

· · · · · · · · · · · · · · · ·

Example: Outland Steel

Outland Steel has a small but profitable export business. Contracts involve substantial delays in payment, but since the company has had a policy of always invoicing in dollars, it is fully protected against changes in exchange rates. Recently the export department has become unhappy with this practice and believes that it is causing the company to lose valuable orders to Japanese and German firms that are willing to quote in the customer's own currency.

You sympathize with these arguments, but you are worried about how the firm should price long-term export contracts when payment is to be made in foreign currency. If the value of the currency declines before payment is made, the company may suffer a large loss. You want to take the currency risk into account when you price the contracts, but you also want to give the sales force as much freedom of action as possible.

Notice that you can insure yourself against this currency risk by selling the foreign currency forward.[19] This means that you can separate the problem of negotiating individual contracts from that of managing the company's foreign exchange exposure. The sales force can allow for currency risk by pricing on the basis of the forward exchange rate. And you, as financial manager, can decide whether the company *ought* to insure.

What is the cost of insurance? You sometimes hear managers say that it is equal to the difference between the forward rate and *today's* spot rate. That is wrong. If Outland does not insure, it will receive the spot rate at the time that the customer pays for the steel. Therefore, the cost of insurance is the difference between the forward rate and the expected spot rate when payment is received.

Insure or speculate? We generally vote for insurance. First, it makes life simpler for the firm and allows it to concentrate on its main business.[20] Second, it does not cost much. (In fact, the cost is zero on average if the forward rate equals the expected spot rate, as the expectations theory of forward rates implies.) Third, the foreign exchange market seems reasonably efficient, at least for the major currencies. Speculation should be a zero-NPV game unless financial managers have information superior to the pros who make the market.

Is there any other way that Outland can protect itself against exchange loss? Of course. It can borrow currency against its receivables, sell the foreign currency spot, and invest the proceeds in the United States. Interest-rate parity theory tells us that in free markets the difference between selling forward and selling spot should be exactly equal to the difference between the interest that you have to pay overseas and the interest that you can earn at home. However, in countries where capital markets are highly regulated, it may be cheaper to arrange foreign borrowing rather than forward cover.[21]

---

[19]Of course, if you don't know the exact payment date, you cannot be sure of the appropriate delivery date for the forward contract. Banks are prepared to deal in forward contracts which allow the company some choice of when to deliver, but such contracts are not common.

[20]It also relieves shareholders of worrying about the foreign exchange exposure they may have acquired by purchase of the firm's shares.

[21]Sometimes governments also attempt to prevent currency speculation by limiting the amount that companies can sell forward.

It is not always so simple to hedge exports against currency fluctuations. Suppose, for example, that Outland has tendered for a large export order. It will not know for several weeks whether it has been successful in getting the order. If it sells the foreign currency forward and doesn't get the order, it stands to lose from a rise in the value of the foreign currency. If it doesn't sell the currency and *does* get the order, it stands to lose from a fall in the value of the foreign currency. When faced with this dilemma, many financial managers limit their downside risk by buying an option to sell the foreign currency at a specified price. That way they know that the most they can lose is the cost of the option.

Our discussion of Outland's export business illustrates three practical implications of our simple theories about forward exchange rates. First, you can use forward rates to adjust for exchange risk in contract pricing. Second, the expectations theory suggests that insurance against exchange risk is usually worth having. Third, interest-rate parity theory reminds us that you can insure either by selling forward or by borrowing foreign currency and selling spot.

Perhaps we should add a fourth implication. The cost of forward cover is not the difference between the forward rate and *today's* spot rate; it is the difference between the forward rate and the expected spot rate when the forward contract matures. There is a corollary to this. You don't make money simply by buying currencies that go up in value and selling those that go down. If investors anticipate the change in the exchange rate, then their expectations will be reflected in the interest-rate differential; therefore what you gain on the currency you will lose in terms of interest income. You make money from currency speculation only if you can predict whether the exchange rate will change by more or less than the interest-rate differential. In other words, you must be able to predict whether the exchange rate will change by more or less than the forward premium or discount.

34-4   INTERNATIONAL INVESTMENT DECISIONS

Outland Steel's export business has risen to the point at which it is worth establishing a subsidiary in Holland to hold inventories of steel. Outland's decision to invest overseas should be based on the same criteria as the decision to invest in the United States—that is, the company must identify the incremental cash flows, discount them at a rate that reflects the opportunity cost of capital, and accept all projects with a positive NPV.

Here are two ways that Outland could calculate the net present value of its Dutch venture:

■ *Method 1.* Outland could follow the practice of many multinational companies and do all its capital budgeting calculations in dollars. In this case it must first estimate the guilder cash flows from its Dutch operation and convert these into dollars at the projected exchange rate. These dollar flows can then be discounted at the dollar cost of capital to give the investment's net present value in dollars.

■ *Method 2.* In order to avoid making forecasts of the exchange rate, Outland could simply calculate the project's net present value entirely in terms of guilders. Outland could then convert this figure into dollars at the current exchange rate.

Each method has three steps, but the order of steps 2 and 3 differs:

	Method 1	Method 2
Step 1	Estimate future cash flow in guilders	Estimate future cash flow in guilders
Step 2	Convert to dollars (at forecasted exchange rates)	Calculate present value (use guilder discount rate)
Step 3	Calculate present value (use dollar discount rate)	Convert to dollars (use spot rate)

Suppose Outland uses method 1. Where do the exchange-rate forecasts come from? It would be foolish for Outland to accept a poor project just because management is particularly optimistic about the guilder—if Outland wishes to speculate in this way, it can simply buy guilders forward. Equally, it would be foolish for Outland to reject a good project just because it is pessimistic about the prospects for the guilder. The company would do much better to go ahead with the project and sell guilders forward. In that way, it would get the best of both worlds.

Thus, as long as the company can alter its exchange exposure, its international capital expenditure decisions should *not* depend on whether management feels that a currency is wrongly valued. Instead of using its own exchange-rate forecast, Outland should base its capital investment decision on cash flows that are hedged against currency risk. In other words, it should convert each cash flow to dollars at the forward exchange rate. Forward exchange rates are usually quoted only for a year or less. But that shouldn't cause a problem: interest rate parity theory tells us that the forward premium or discount is equal to the difference between the interest rates in the two countries.

If Outland uses either of our two methods, its investment decision is also going to be heavily influenced by its assumption about the Dutch inflation rate. Although Outland's financial manager may well have her own views about Dutch inflation, it would again be foolish to let these views influence the investment decision. After all, there are more efficient ways to speculate on the inflation rate than by building (or not building) a steel-distribution depot.[22] So the financial manager of Outland would do much better to assume that in efficient capital markets, the difference between the Dutch and American interest rates reflects the likely difference in the inflation rates.[23]

Does it matter which of the two methods Outland uses to appraise its investment? It does if Outland employs its own forecasts of the exchange rate and inflation rate. However, as long as Outland assumes our simple parity relationships between interest rates, exchange rates, and inflation, the two methods will give the same answer.

Example: NPV Calculations for Outland's Investment

We will illustrate with a simple example. Suppose Outland's Dutch facility is expected to generate the following cash flows in guilders:

---

[22]For example, if the manager believes that investors have underestimated the Dutch inflation rate, she should issue long-term guilder bonds and invest in short-term guilder bonds or notes.

[23]There is a general point here that is not confined to international investment. Whenever you face an investment that appears to have a positive NPV, decide what it is that you are betting on and then think whether there is a more direct way to place the bet. For example, if a copper mine looks profitable only because you are unusually optimistic about the price of copper, then maybe you would do better to buy copper futures rather than open a copper mine.

	YEAR				
	1	2	3	4	5
Cash flow, thousands of guilders	400	450	510	575	650

How much are these cash flows worth today if Outland wants a 16 percent *dollar* return from its Dutch investment?

Outland's financial manager looks in the newspaper and finds that the risk-free interest rate is 8 percent in the United States ($r_\$ = .08$) and 9 percent in Holland ($r_{fl} = .09$). She sees right away that if real interest rates are expected to be the same in the two countries, then the consensus forecast of the Dutch inflation rate (i_{fl}) must be approximately 1 percentage point higher than the inflation rate in the United States ($i_\$$). For example, if the expected rate of inflation in the United States is 5 percent, then the real rate of interest and the expected Dutch inflation rate are calculated as follows:

	1 + Nominal Interest Rate	=	1 + Real Interest Rate	×	1 + Expected Inflation Rate
In dollars	1.08	=	1.029	×	1.05
In guilders	1.09	=	1.029	×	1.06

The financial manager therefore checks that the guilder cash-flow forecasts are consistent with this inflation rate.

Suppose the current spot rate is 2 guilders to the dollar. Since the interest rate in Holland is 1 percent higher than in the United States, the implied forward rate on the guilder must rise by 1 percent a year relative to the spot rate:

$$\text{Forward exchange rate for year } t = \text{spot rate} \times \frac{(1 + r_{fl})^t}{(1 + r_\$)^t}$$

For example,

$$\text{Forward exchange rate for year } 1 = 2 \times \frac{1.06}{1.05} = 2.02 \text{ guilders per dollar}$$

The financial manager can use these forward exchange rates to produce a forecast of the cash flows in *dollars:*

	YEAR				
	1	2	3	4	5
Cash flow, guilders	400	450	510	575	650
Forward exchange rate	2.02	2.04	2.06	2.08	2.10
Cash flow, dollars	198	221	248	276	310

Now she uses method 1 and discounts these *dollar* cash flows at the *dollar* cost of capital:

$$PV = \frac{198}{1.16} + \frac{221}{(1.16)^2} + \frac{248}{(1.16)^3} + \frac{276}{(1.16)^4} + \frac{310}{(1.16)^5} = \$794,000$$

Notice that she discounted at 16 percent, not the domestic interest rate of 8 percent. The cash flow is risky, so a risk-adjusted rate is appropriate.

Just as a check, the financial manager tries method 2. Since the guilder interest rate is lower than the dollar rate, the risk-adjusted discount rate must also be correspondingly lower:[24]

	1 + Risk-Adjusted Discount Rate	=	1 + Nominal Interest Rate	×	1 + Risk Premium
In dollars	1.16	=	1.08	×	1.074
In guilders	1.171	=	1.09	×	1.074

To use method 2, the manager discounts the *guilder* cash flows by the *guilder* discount rate:

$$PV = \frac{400}{1.171} + \frac{450}{(1.171)^2} + \frac{510}{(1.171)^3} + \frac{575}{(1.171)^4} + \frac{650}{(1.171)^5}$$
$$= 1588, \text{ or } 1{,}588{,}000 \text{ guilders}$$

Now convert to dollars at the spot rate, fl2/$:

$$NPV = \frac{1588}{2.0} = 794, \text{ or } \$794{,}000$$

34-5 THE COST OF CAPITAL FOR FOREIGN INVESTMENT

Now we need to think more carefully about the risk of overseas investment and the reward that investors require for taking this risk. Unfortunately, these are issues on which few economists can agree.[25]

Remember that the risk of an investment cannot be considered in isolation; it depends on the securities that the investor holds in his or her portfolio. For example, at one extreme, we can imagine a single world capital market in which investors from each country hold well-diversified international portfolios. In that case, Outland could measure the risk of its Dutch venture by the project's beta relative to the *world* market portfolio. Since Outland would face exactly the same risk on its Dutch project as a local Dutch steel company, it would need to earn exactly the same return.

---

[24]Here is a point that can cause confusion: We *multiply* (1 + nominal interest rate) by (1 + risk premium) in these calculations. In the CAPM we *added* the risk premium to the risk-free rate. Why the difference? Think of it this way: If the inflation rate in the United States is 3 percent, then the *real* cost of capital on a risky investment is $1.16/1.03 - 1 = .126$, or 12.6 percent. If the real cost of capital is also .126 in Holland and the Dutch inflation rate is 4 percent, then the nominal cost of capital in Holland must be $1.04 \times 1.126 = .17$, or 17 percent.

[25]Why not? One fundamental reason is that economists have never been able to agree on what makes one country different from another. Is it just that they have different currencies? Or is it that their citizens have different tastes? Or is it that they are subject to different regulations and taxes? The answer affects the relationship between security prices in different countries. See, for example, F. L. A. Grauer, R. H. Litzenberger, and R. E. Stehle, "Sharing Rules and Equilibrium in an International Capital Market under Uncertainty," *Journal of Financial Economics,* **3**:233–256 (June 1976); B. H. Solnik, "An Equilibrium Model of the International Capital Market," *Journal of Economic Theory,* **8**:500–524 (1974); and F. Black, "International Capital Market Equilibrium with Investment Barriers," *Journal of Financial Economics,* **1**:337–352 (December 1974).

At the other extreme, we can imagine a world in which capital markets are completely segmented so that American investors hold only American stocks and Dutch investors hold only Dutch stocks. In these circumstances, Outland and the Dutch company do not face the same risk. Outland could measure the project's risk by its beta relative to the *United States* market, whereas a Dutch company would want to measure it by its beta relative to the *Dutch* market. An investment in the Dutch steel industry would appear to be a relatively low risk project to Outland's shareholders who hold only United States shares, whereas it might seem a relatively high risk project to a Dutch company whose shareholders are already highly exposed to the fortunes of the Dutch market. In this case Outland would be satisfied with a lower return on the project than the Dutch company would demand.

Here, in summary, are these two scenarios:

A Single World Capital Market	Completely Segmented Capital Markets
Individuals invest internationally	Individuals invest domestically
Risk measured relative to world market index	Risk measured relative to domestic index
No further gains from international diversification	Large gains from international diversification
Outland's Dutch subsidiary has same cost of capital as local Dutch company	Outland's Dutch subsidiary has lower cost of capital than local Dutch company

The truth seems to lie closer to the scenario in the right-hand column. Americans are free to hold foreign shares, but they generally invest only a small part of their money overseas.

Nobody knows quite why investors are so reluctant to buy foreign shares—maybe it is simply that there are extra costs in figuring out which shares to buy. Or perhaps investors are worried that a foreign government will expropriate their shares, restrict dividend payments, or catch them by a change in tax law. However, the world is changing. Large American financial institutions have substantially increased their overseas investments, and literally dozens of mutual funds have been set up for individuals who want to invest abroad. For example, you can now buy funds that specialize in investment in smaller capital markets such as Chile, India, Thailand, or Hungary.

If Americans incur extra costs when they invest in foreign shares, they must be prepared to earn a lower return on these shares than local investors. This suggests a standard for American corporations that are investing abroad. They need at least to match the return that American investors can earn on their own account. But if these investors are willing to pay a shade more for investing in overseas shares, they should be happy to see American corporations invest abroad even if they expect to earn a shade less than local companies.[26]

---

[26]Cooper and Kaplanis have estimated the costs of foreign investments by asking how large the cost would need to be for the American holdings in foreign shares to make sense. A subsequent paper analyzes implications for the cost of capital. See I. Cooper and E. Kaplanis, "Costs to Crossborder Investment and International Equity Market Equilibrium," in J. Edwards et al. (eds.), *Recent Advances in Corporate Finance*, Cambridge University Press, Cambridge, England, 1986, and "Home Bias in Equity Portfolios and The Cost of Capital for Multinational Firms," *Journal of Applied Corporate Finance*, **8**:95–102 (Fall 1995).

**Does
Japan
Enjoy a
Lower
Cost of
Capital?**

If there are costs in investing across national borders, then the cost of capital may not be identical in all countries. For example, you often hear people say that Japanese companies enjoy a lower cost of capital than their United States rivals. This difference, it is argued, shows up in the lower earnings-price ratio of Japanese stocks.[27]

This argument is two parts possible confusion and one part probable truth. What has the earnings-price ratio got to do with the cost of capital? Think back to Section 4-4, where we showed that this ratio, EPS_1/P_0, depends on the cost of equity capital, r, and the present value of growth opportunities, PVGO:

$$\frac{EPS_1}{P_0} = r\left(1 - \frac{PVGO}{P_0}\right)$$

Thus a lower earnings-price ratio for Japanese stocks could mean three things:[28]

1. Japanese accountants measure earnings more conservatively than their United States cousins.[29] Since investors look through book earnings to true economic income, the stock price is unaffected. Thus the ratio of reported income to price is lower in Japan.

2. PVGO is higher; i.e., Japanese firms have more growth opportunities.

3. r is lower; i.e., investors are satisfied with a lower expected return from Japanese companies.

Explanations 1 and 2 remind us that a simple comparison of earnings-price ratios won't tell us whether Japan has the lower cost of capital. But how plausible is explanations 3—that r really is different in the two countries? Notice first that if the cost of capital in Japan is measured in yen and the cost in the United States is measured in dollars, then the two figures are not comparable.[30] For example, you wouldn't say that a 10-inch-high rabbit was taller than a 9-foot elephant. You are measuring their height in different units. In the same way it makes no sense to compare an expected return in yen with a return in dollars. The units are different.

But suppose that in each case you measure r in *real* terms. Then you are comparing like with like,[31] and it does make sense to ask whether the *real* cost of capital may be lower in Japan. Think about the costs of overseas investment. Japan has had

---

[27]At year-end 1989 the earnings-price ratio for the Japanese stock market was about 1.9 compared with 6.7 for the United States. The argument that differences in earnings-price ratios indicate a lower cost of capital in Japan is put forward in R. N. McCauley and S. A. Zimmer, "Explaining International Differences in the Cost of Capital," *Federal Reserve Bank of New York Quarterly Review*, **14**:7–28 (Summer 1989). *Note:* McCauley and Zimmer adjust the ratios for differences in accounting practices.

[28]For a discussion of these possible explanations, see K. R. French and J. M. Poterba, "Were Japanese Stock Prices Too High?", *Journal of Financial Economics*, **29**:337–363 (October 1991).

[29]For example, Japanese companies use accelerated tax depreciation for their reports to shareholders. This practice reduces their reported EPS compared to that of United States firms, most of which use straight-line depreciation.

Of course, choice of depreciation method doesn't affect reported EPS in a no-growth steady rate—although it does affect the book rate of return, as we explained in Section 12-4. However, most firms grow. Many Japanese firms have grown rapidly.

[30]For example, it could be that investors in the United States foresee a high rate of inflation and a depreciating currency. In this case they will demand high dollar returns to compensate.

[31]We assume that the measured inflation rates used to calculate real returns are based on the same basket of goods. If the inflation rate in Japan reflects the price of sushi and the rate in the United States reflects the price of hamburgers, then our measures of real returns will not be comparable.

substantial excess savings that could not be absorbed by Japanese industry and therefore needed to be invested overseas. Japanese investors are not *compelled* to invest overseas: they need to be tempted to do so. If there are costs to buying foreign stocks, then the relative price of Japanese stocks must rise and the expected real return must fall until Japanese investors are happy to hold foreign investments.

There is a general message here. If investors have large surpluses that must be invested overseas, or if they incur unusually large costs to get their money out, then the domestic cost of capital is likely to be forced down and it will no longer be the case that real returns will be the same in different countries.

Avoiding Fudge Factors in International Investment Decisions

We certainly don't pretend that we can put a precise figure on the cost of capital for foreign investment. But you can see that we disagree with the frequent practice of automatically marking *up* the domestic cost of capital when foreign investment is considered. We suspect that managers mark up the required return for foreign investment to cover the risk of expropriation, foreign exchange restrictions, or unfavorable tax changes. A fudge factor is added to the discount factor to cover these costs.

We think managers should leave the discount rate alone and reduce expected cash flows instead. For example, suppose that Outland is expected to earn 450,000 guilders in the first year *if no penalties are placed on the operations of foreign firms.* Suppose also that there is a 10 percent chance that Outland's operation may be expropriated without compensation.[32] The *expected* cash flow is not 450,000 guilders but $.9 \times 450 = 405,000$ guilders.

The end result may be the same when you add a fudge factor to the discount rate. Nevertheless, adjusting cash flows brings management's assumptions about "political risks" out in the open for scrutiny and sensitivity analysis.

34-6 FINANCING FOREIGN OPERATIONS

Outland can pay for its Dutch venture in three ways. It can export capital from the United States, it can borrow Dutch guilders, or it can borrow wherever interest rates are lowest.

Notice that if the guilder is devalued, other things equal, the Dutch assets will be worth fewer dollars than before. In this case, Outland could protect itself against exchange risk by borrowing guilders. It would then have both a Dutch asset and an offsetting Dutch liability. If the guilder is devalued, the dollar value of the asset falls, but that is offset by the fact that Outland now needs fewer dollars to service its guilder debt.

Unfortunately, other things are rarely equal, for the devaluation may be accompanied by changes in the guilder value of Outland's assets. Remember that the law of one price states that any change in the guilder exchange rate will be exactly offset by a change in the relative price of Dutch goods. Of course you know better than to take that theory literally, but it may not be too bad an approximation in the case of readily exportable goods such as steel inventory. In other words, even if the guilder is devalued, Outland's steel inventory may largely hold its value in terms of dollars. Therefore, rather than finance the entire venture by guilder debt, it may be safer to finance it with a mixture of guilders and dollars.

---

[32]Our example is fanciful. Most measures of political risk place Holland as one of the most stable environments for investment.

Managers sometimes think of currency risk as arising only from delays in foreign currency payments. For example, a firm that invoices in foreign currency is at risk if overseas customers do not pay their bills immediately. These *transaction exposures* can be easily identified and hedged. But our discussion of Outland's financing choices suggests that firms need to think more broadly about risk and recognize the impact of a change in the exchange rate on the value of the entire business. This is known as *economic exposure*.[33]

During 1991 and 1992 the value of the deutschemark appreciated relative to that of other major currencies. As a result, Porsche and other German luxury-car manufacturers found it increasingly difficult to compete in the United States. American dealers that had a franchise to sell German luxury cars also took a bath. Thus the German car producers and their dealers in the United States were exposed to exchange-rate changes even though they may have had no fixed obligations to pay or receive dollars. They had economic exposure as well as transaction exposure.[34]

One more example. Suppose that your company sites a plant in Taiwan to produce video recorders. The law of one price predicts that a high rate of inflation in Taiwan will be offset by a change in the exchange rate. So the *United States dollar* cash flows from the Taiwan plant are not affected by the level of inflation in Taiwan.

The problem occurs if the law of one price does *not* hold. For example, suppose that a relatively high rate of inflation in Taiwan coincides with a rise in the value of the Taiwan dollar. In this case there is a rise in the *real* value of the Taiwan dollar and, other things equal, a rise in the plant's cash flows when measured in United States dollars.

There are some other factors that you need to take into account. Because it is now more costly to manufacture in Taiwan, the plant will find it less easy to compete in export markets and profit margins are likely to be cut. This will tend to *reduce* cash flows when measured in United States dollars. You cannot determine how to hedge your exchange risk until you have decided whether on balance the firm gains or loses by a rise in the value of the Taiwan dollar.[35]

Instead of worrying about reducing risk, why doesn't Outland follow our third alternative and borrow wherever interest rates are lowest? For example, instead of borrowing in Holland or the United States, perhaps Outland should borrow in Switzerland, where the rate is (we assume) 5 percent. However, you must ask yourself *why* the Swiss rate is so low. Unless you know that the Swiss government is deliberately holding the rate down by restrictions on the export of capital, you should suspect that the real cost of capital is roughly the same in Switzerland as it is anywhere else. The nominal interest rate is low only because investors expect a low domestic rate of inflation and a strong currency. Therefore, the advantage of the low

---

[33]Financial managers also refer to *translation exposure*, which measures the effect of an exchange-rate change on the company's financial statements.

[34]The German car producers could have hedged their exposure by borrowing dollars. As the deutschemark appreciated, their dollar income fell but the cost of servicing dollar loans would also have fallen. However, we should repeat here a point that we made in Chapter 25: Borrowing dollars would have reduced the risk for German car producers, but it should not have affected their decisions as to where to produce and sell cars.

[35]Notice that it is the change in the *real* exchange rate that you would like to hedge against. In other words, the value of the Taiwan venture would be equally affected by a rise in the exchange rate and by a rise in the Taiwan inflation rate. Unfortunately, it is much easier to hedge against a change in the *nominal* exchange rate than against a change in the *real* rate.

rate of interest is likely to be offset by the additional dollars required to buy the Swiss francs to pay off the loan.[36]

We think that it makes sense for a firm to establish a "passive" or "normal" financing strategy. But sometimes you may come across an opportunity that truly does make it cheaper to depart from your normal strategy and finance in one particular country. For example, here is a deal worked out by Massey-Ferguson, the Canadian farm equipment manufacturer, as described in a paper by Donald Lessard and Alan Shapiro:

> The key to Massey's strategy is to view the many foreign countries in which it has plants not only as markets, but also as potential sources of financing for exports to third countries. For example, in early 1978, Massey-Ferguson had the opportunity to ship 7200 tractors worth $53 million to Turkey, but was unwilling to assume the risk of currency inconvertibility. Turkey, at that time, already owed $2 billion to various foreign creditors and it was uncertain whether it would be able to come up with dollars to pay off its debts (especially since its reserves were at about zero).
>
> Massey solved this problem by manufacturing these tractors at its Brazilian subsidiary, "Massey-Ferguson do Brasil," and selling them to Brazil's Interbras, the trading company arm of Petrobas, the Brazilian national oil corporation. Interbras in turn arranged to sell the tractors to Turkey and pay Massey in cruzieros. The cruziero financing for Interbras came from Cacex, the Banco de Brasil department that is in charge of foreign trade. Cacex underwrote all the political, commercial, and exchange risks as part of the Brazilian government's intense export promotion drive. Prior to choosing Brazil as a supply point, Massey made a point of shopping around to get the best export credit deal available.[37]

Tax and the Financing Method

Outland's choice of initial financing may also depend on how it plans to use the profits of its Dutch subsidiary. In the early years the venture may well run a continuing deficit, but Outland hopes that it will generate a cash surplus eventually. You need to think about how you can best repatriate this surplus.

Broadly speaking, international affiliates make the following payments to the parent company:

- Dividends
- Interest payments and repayment of parent company loans
- Royalties for use of trade names and patents
- Management fees for central services
- Payments for goods supplied by the parent

---

[36]In 1989 several Australian banks, which had induced their clients to borrow at low interest rates in Switzerland, found themselves sued by the same clients for not having warned them of the risk of a rise in the price of Swiss francs. Of course, borrowing in a particular capital market does not commit you to take on that particular currency risk. You can choose to finance in a particular market and then swap your debt into a different currency. See Section 25-4. For a further discussion of financing choices, see D. R. Lessard and A. C. Shapiro, "Guidelines for Global Financing Choices," *Midland Corporate Financial Journal*, **1**:68–80 (Winter 1983).

[37]From the working paper version of "Guidelines for Global Financing Choices," M.I.T., Sloan School of Management, Cambridge, Mass., October 1982, p. 17.

TABLE 34-3

Calculation of United States tax on dividends paid by Outland Steel's Dutch subsidiary (figures in dollars)

	Dutch Corporate Tax = 35%	Dutch Corporate Tax = 30%
Profits before tax	100	100
Dutch company tax	35	30
Net profits	65	70
United States company tax	35	35
Less double-tax relief (maximum 35)	35	30
United States tax payable	0	5
Available for dividend	65	65

The form of payment is important because it affects the taxes paid. Companies are generally subject to local taxes on their local earnings. Therefore Outland's Dutch subsidiary will pay corporate tax in Holland on all profits that it earns there. In addition it is liable to United States corporate tax on any dividends that are remitted to the United States.[38]

Many countries (including Holland) have a double-taxation agreement with the United States. This means that the company can offset the payment of any local taxes against the United States tax liability on the foreign dividends. For example, suppose Outland Steel's subsidiary pays Dutch income tax of 35 percent on its profits plus a withholding tax of 5 percent on any dividends paid to the United States. The left-hand portion of Table 34-3 shows that Outland is, therefore, exempt from any additional tax on these dividends. The right-hand portion shows what would happen if the Dutch income tax rate were changed to 30 percent. In this case Outland could claim double tax relief only to the amount of taxes paid in Holland.

If the subsidiary is operating in a high-tax country with a double-tax agreement, dividend payments are not subject to additional taxes in the United States. On the other hand, in such cases you may do better to arrange a loan from the parent to the subsidiary. The parent company must pay United States tax on the interest, but the foreign subsidiary can deduct the interest before paying local tax. Another way to transfer income from high-tax areas to low-tax areas is to levy royalties or management fees on the subsidiary. Or it may be possible to change the transfer prices on sales of goods within the group. Needless to say, the tax and customs authorities are well aware of these incentives to minimize taxes, and they will insist that all such intergroup payments be reasonable.

---

[38]If Outland's Dutch operation were a branch of the parent company rather than a subsidiary, the tax authorities in the United States would treat the income as part of the parent's income and tax it immediately rather than when it was remitted. That is usually a *disadvantage* when the foreign operation is showing profits but an *advantage* when it is making losses.

34-7 POLITICAL RISK

Think about what the political risk of a foreign investment really is. It is the threat that a foreign government will change the rules of the game—that is, break a promise or understanding—*after* the investment is made. Some managers think of political risk as an act of God, like a hurricane or earthquake. But the most successful multinational companies structure their business to reduce political risk.

Foreign governments are not likely to expropriate a local business if it cannot operate without the support of its parent. For example, the foreign subsidiaries of American computer manufacturers or pharmaceutical companies would have relatively little value if they were cut off from the know-how of their parents. Such operations are much less likely to be expropriated than, say, a mining operation which can be operated as a stand-alone venture.

We are not recommending that you turn your silver mine into a pharmaceutical company, but you may be able to plan overseas manufacturing operations to improve your bargaining position with foreign governments. For example, Ford has integrated its overseas operations so that the manufacture of components, subassemblies, and complete automobiles is spread across plants in a number of countries. None of these plants would have much value on its own, and Ford can switch production between plants if the political climate in one country deteriorates.

Multinational corporations have also devised financing arrangements to help keep foreign governments honest. For example, suppose your firm is contemplating investing $500 million to reopen the San Tomé silver mine in Costaguana, with modern machinery, smelting equipment, and shipping facilities.[39] The Costaguanan government agrees to invest in roads and other infrastructure and to take 20 percent of the silver produced by the mine in lieu of taxes. The agreement is to run for 25 years.

The project's NPV on these assumptions is quite attractive. But what happens if a new government comes to power 5 years from now and imposes a 50 percent tax on "any precious metals exported from the Republic of Costaguana?" Or changes the government's share of output from 20 to 50 percent? Or simply takes over the mine "with fair compensation to be determined in due course by the Minister of Natural Resources of the Republic of Costaguana"?

No contract can absolutely restrain a sovereign power. But you can arrange project financing to make these acts as painful as possible for the foreign government.[40] For example, you might set up the mine as a subsidiary corporation, which then borrows a large fraction of the required investment from a consortium of major international banks. If your firm guarantees the loan, make sure the guarantee stands only if the Costaguanan government honors its contract. The government will be reluctant to break the contract if that causes a default on the loans and undercuts the country's credit standing with the international banking system.

If possible, you should finance part of the project with a loan from the World Bank (or one of its affiliates). Include a *cross-default* clause, so that a default to any creditor automatically triggers default on the World Bank loan. Few governments have the guts to take on the World Bank.

Here is another variation on the same theme: Arrange to borrow, say, $450 million through the Costaguanan Development Agency. In other words, the develop-

---

[39]The early history of the San Tomé mine is described in Joseph Conrad's *Nostromo*.

[40]We discussed project financing in Section 24-6.

ment agency borrows in international capital markets and relends to the San Tomé mine. Your firm agrees to stand behind the loan providing the government keeps *its* promises. If it does keep them, the loan is your liability. If not, the loan is *its* liability.

These arrangements do work. In the late 1960s Kennecott Copper financed a major expansion of a copper mine in Chile using arrangements like those we have just described. In 1970 a new government came to power, headed by Salvador Allende, who vowed to take over all foreign holdings in Chile giving "ni un centavo" in exchange. Kennecott's mine was spared.

Political risk is not confined to the risk of expropriation. Multinational companies are always exposed to the criticism that they siphon funds out of countries in which they do business, and, therefore, governments are tempted to limit their freedom to repatriate profits. This is most likely to happen when there is considerable uncertainty about the rate of exchange, which is usually when you would most like to get your money out.

Here again a little forethought can help. For example, there are often more onerous restrictions on the payment of dividends to the parent than on the payment of interest or principal on debt. So it may be better for the parent to put up part of the funds in the form of a loan. Royalty payments and management fees are less politically sensitive than dividends, particularly if they are levied equally on all foreign operations. A company can also, within limits, alter the price of goods that are bought or sold within the group, and it can require more or less prompt payment for such sales.

34-8 INTERACTIONS OF INVESTMENT AND FINANCING DECISIONS

You cannot entirely divorce the value of an international project from the way that it is financed. For example, the taxes paid on Outland Steel's Dutch venture depend on the form in which it remits profits to the United States. If it lends funds to the subsidiary rather than providing equity, the group will pay more tax in the United States and less in Holland.

Major international investments often have so many financing side effects that it's foolhardy to try to reduce the project analysis to one stream of cash flows and one adjusted discount rate. You need the adjusted-present-value (APV) rule, which we introduced in Chapter 19. Remember that APV is defined as (1) "base-case" project NPV plus (2) the sum of the present values of the project's financing side effects.

The base-case NPV of an international project is usually calculated assuming that the project is all-equity-financed by the parent firm and that all income is paid back as dividends at the first opportunity.

The next step is to value the financing side effects. If you finance the project in part by a loan from the parent rather than completely by equity, you should calculate the value of any tax savings that result. And if the project also allows the firm *as a whole*[41] to borrow more on its own account, you should also calculate separately the value of any tax shields on this debt.

---

[41]Don't confuse a foreign subsidiary's debt with its contribution to the firm's *overall* debt capacity. For example, we spoke of borrowing 80 to 90 percent of the $500 million cost of the San Tomé mine, but we did not assume the mine would support that debt. Instead, we assumed the firm could use relatively more of its overall borrowing capacity in Costaguana and less in the United States. It could finance the project by committing its debt capacity instead of cash.

When you calculated your base-case net present value, you assumed that all funds were exported from the United States and all income was remitted as soon as possible. But you may do better to raise some of the money locally. Or you may already have surplus funds abroad that you are not allowed to repatriate or the you do not wish to repatriate for tax reasons. Instead of remitting all income by the normal channels, you may be able to remit some income more profitably in the form of royalties or management fees, or you may prefer to retain the funds overseas for further expansion. Such benefits should also be valued separately.[42]

There are many other financing side effects. The subsidized financing provided to Massey-Ferguson by Brazil is one example. So make a complete list, value each side effect separately, and add up all the values to get APV.

34-9 SUMMARY

The international financial manager has to cope with different currencies, interest rates, and inflation rates and must be familiar with a variety of different capital markets and tax systems. The most we can hope to do in these pages is to whet your appetite.

To produce order out of chaos, the international financial manager needs some model of the relationship between exchange rates, interest rates, and inflation rates. We described four very simple but useful theories.

Interest-rate parity theory states that the interest differential between two countries must be equal to the difference between the forward and spot exchange rates. In the international markets, arbitrage ensures that parity almost always holds. There are two ways to hedge against exchange risk—one is to take out forward cover, the other is to borrow or lend abroad. Interest-rate parity tells us that the costs of the two methods should be the same.

The expectations theory of exchange rates tells us that the forward rate equals the expected spot rate. If you believe the expectations theory, you will generally insure against exchange risks.

In its strict form the law of one price states that $1 must have the same purchasing power in every country. That doesn't square very well with the facts, for differences in inflation rates are not perfectly related to changes in exchange rates. This means that there may be some genuine exchange risks in doing business overseas. On the other hand, the difference in the inflation rates is just as likely to be above as below the change in the exchange rate.

Finally, we saw that in an integrated world capital market real rates of interest would have to be the same. In practice, government regulation and taxes can cause differences in real interest rates. But do not simply borrow where interest rates are lowest. Those countries are also likely to have the lowest inflation rates and the strongest currencies.

With these precepts in mind we looked at three common problems in international finance. First, we showed how you can use the forward markets or the loan markets to price and insure long-term export contracts.

Second, we considered the problem of international capital budgeting. We warned against making stupid investment decisions simply because you have a strong

---

[42]See, for example, D. R. Lessard, "Evaluating Foreign Projects—An Adjusted Present Value Approach," in D. Lessard (ed.), *International Financial Management: Theory and Application*, 2d ed., John Wiley and Sons, New York, 1986.

view about future exchange rates. And we showed that it makes no difference which currency you use for your calculations as long as you assume that prices, interest rates, and exchange rates are linked by the simple theories that we described above. The main difficulty is to select the right discount rate. If there is a free market for capital, the discount rate for your project is the return that your shareholders expect from investing in foreign securities. This rate is difficult to measure, but we argued against just adding a premium for the "extra risks" of overseas investment.

Finally, we looked at the problem of financing overseas subsidiaries. There are at least three issues that you should think about. First, other things equal, you would like to protect yourself against exchange risk. You may be able to do this by borrowing part of the money in the local currency. Second, you need to think about tax. For example, you can reduce tax by borrowing in high-tax countries and lending in low-tax countries. Third, you should consider whether you can structure the financing to reduce the risk that governments will change the rules of the game.

The cash flow that the parent company receives from its overseas operations depends on the way that they are financed. Therefore an adjusted-present-value approach is needed to analyze international investment proposals.

Further Reading

There are a number of useful textbooks in international finance. Here is a small selection:

D. K. Eiteman and A. I. Stonehill: *Multinational Business Finance*, 7th ed., Addison-Wesley Publishing Company, Inc., Reading, Mass., 1994.

I. H. Giddy: *Global Financial Markets*, D. C. Heath and Company, Lexington, Mass., 1994.

P. Sercu and R. Uppal: *International Financial Markets and the Firm*, South-Western College Publishing, Cincinnati, Ohio, 1995.

A. C. Shapiro, *Multinational Financial Management*, 3d ed., Allyn and Bacon, Inc., Boston, 1989.

Here are some general discussions of international investment decisions and associated exchange risks:

D. R. Lessard: "Global Competition and Corporate Finance in the 1990s," *Journal of Applied Corporate Finance*, **3**:59–72 (Winter 1991).

M. D. Levi and P. Sercu: "Erroneous and Valid Reasons for Hedging Foreign Exchange Exposure," *Journal of Multinational Financial Management*, **1**:25–37 (1991).

J. J. Pringle: "Managing Foreign Exchange Exposure," *Journal of Applied Corporate Finance*, **3**:73–82 (Winter 1991).

A. C. Shapiro: "International Capital Budgeting," *Midland Corporate Finance Journal*, **1**:26–45 (Spring 1983).

Listed below are a few of the articles on relationships between interest rates, exchange rates, and inflation:

FORWARD AND SPOT EXCHANGE RATES

B. Cornell: "Spot Rates, Forward Rates and Exchange Market Efficiency," *Journal of Financial Economics*, **5**:55–65 (1977).

E. F. Fama: "Forward and Spot Exchange Rates," *Journal of Monetary Economics*, **14**:319–338 (1984).

C. P. Wolff: "Foreign Exchange Rates, Expected Spot Rates and Premia; A Signal Extraction Approach," *Journal of Finance*, **42**:395–406 (June 1987).

INTEREST-RATE PARITY

K. Clinton: "Transaction Costs and Covered Interest Arbitrage: Theory and Evidence," *Journal of Political Economy*, **96**:358–370 (April 1988).

J. A. Frenkel and R. M. Levich: "Covered Interest Arbitrage: Unexploited Profits?" *Journal of Political Economy*, **83**:325–338 (April 1975).

LAW OF ONE PRICE

N. Abuaf and P. Jorion: "Purchasing Power Parity in the Long Run," *Journal of Finance*, **45**:157–174 (March 1990).

M. Adler and B. Lehmann: "Deviations from Purchasing Power Parity in the Long Run," *Journal of Finance*, **38**:1471–1487 (December 1983).

R. Roll: "Violations of the 'Law of One Price' and Their Implications for Differentially Denominated Assets," in M. Sarnat and G. Szego (eds.), *International Finance and Trade*, Ballinger Press, Cambridge, Mass., 1979.

INTERNATIONAL COST OF CAPITAL

F. Black: "International Capital Market Equilibrium and Investment Barriers," *Journal of Financial Economics*, **1**:337–352 (December 1974).

F. L. A. Grauer, R. H. Litzenberger, and R. E. Stehle: "Sharing Rules and Equilibrium in an International Capital Market under Uncertainty," *Journal of Financial Economics*, **3**:233–256 (June 1976).

B. H. Solnik: "An Equilibrium Model of the International Capital Market," *Journal of Economic Theory*, **8**:500–524 (1974).

R. M. Stultz, "A Model of International Asset Pricing," *Journal of Financial Economics*, **9**:383–406 (December 1981).

Quiz

1. Look at Table 34-1.
   (*a*) How many German marks do you get for your dollar?
   (*b*) What is the 1-month forward rate for the deutschemark?
   (*c*) Is the dollar at a forward discount or premium on the deutschemark?
   (*d*) Calculate the annual percentage discount or premium on the deutschemark.
   (*e*) If the interest rate on eurodollars is 6.0 percent annually compounded, what do you think is the 1-year euromark interest rate?
   (*f*) According to the expectations theory, what is the expected spot rate for the deutschemark in 3 months' time?
   (*g*) According to the law of one price, what then is the expected difference in the rate of price inflation in the United States and Germany?

2. Define each of the following theories in a sentence or simple equation:
   (*a*) Interest-rate parity theory
   (*b*) Expectations theory of forward rates
   (*c*) Law of one price
   (*d*) International capital market equilibrium (relationship of real and nominal interest rates in different countries)

3. The following table shows interest rates and exchange rates for the United States dollar and French franc. The spot exchange rate is 7.05 francs per dollar. Complete the missing entries:

	3 Months	6 Months	1 Year
Eurodollar interest rate (annually compounded)	11½%	12¼%	?
Eurofranc interest rate (annually compounded)	19½%	?	20%
Forward francs per dollar	?	?	7.5200
Forward discount on franc, percent per year	?	−6.3%	?

4. An importer in the United States is due to take delivery of silk scarves from Italy in 6 months. The price is fixed in lire. Which of the following transactions could eliminate the importer's exchange risk?
    (*a*) Sell 6-month call options on lire.
    (*b*) Buy lire forward.
    (*c*) Sell lire forward.
    (*d*) Sell lire in the currency futures market.
    (*e*) Borrow lire; buy dollars at the spot exchange rate.
    (*f*) Sell lire at the spot exchange rate; lend dollars.

5. A United States company has committed to pay 10 million deutschemarks to a Germany company in 1 year. What is the cost (in present value) of covering this liability by buying deutschemarks forward? The German interest rate is 4.2 percent, and exchange rates are shown in Table 34-1. Briefly explain.

6. A firm in the United States is due to receive payment of 1 million deutschemarks in 8 years' time. It would like to protect itself against a decline in the value of the deutschemark but finds it difficult to get forward cover for such a long period. Is there any other way in which it can protect itself?

7. (*a*) Which of the following items do you need if you do all your capital budgeting calculations in your own currency?
        (*i*) Forecasts of future exchange rates
        (*ii*) Forecasts of the foreign inflation rate
        (*iii*) Forecasts of the domestic inflation rate
        (*iv*) Foreign interest rates
        (*v*) Domestic interest rates
    (*b*) Which of the above items do you need if you do all your capital budgeting calculations in the foreign currency?

8. Company A has two overseas subsidiaries in countries X and Y. The United States has a 50 percent rate of corporate tax, X has a 60 percent rate, and Y a 40 percent rate. Both X and Y have a double-tax agreement with the United States. Suppose that the company earns $100 pretax in both countries.
    (*a*) What taxes would be paid in the United States and overseas if the company remitted all net income in the form of dividends?
    (*b*) What taxes would be paid if it remitted all net income in the form of interest?

Questions and Problems

1. Look at the foreign exchange table in a recent issue of *The Wall Street Journal*.
    (*a*) How many United States dollars are worth one Canadian dollar today?
    (*b*) How many Canadian dollars are worth one United States dollar today?
    (*c*) Suppose that you arrange today to buy Canadian dollars in 90 days. How many Canadian dollars could you buy for each United States dollar?
    (*d*) If forward rates simply reflect market expectations, what is the likely spot exchange rate for the French franc in 90 days' time?
    (*e*) Look in the *Journal's* table of money rates. What is the 3-month interest rate on eurodollars?
    (*f*) Can you deduce the likely 3-month interest rate for eurocurrency French francs?

(g) You can also buy currency for future delivery in the financial futures market. Look in the *Journal's* table of futures prices. What is the rate of exchange for Canadian dollars to be delivered in approximately 6 months' time?

2. Table 34-1 shows the 90-day forward rate on the Swedish krona.
   (a) Is the dollar at a forward discount or a premium on the krona?
   (b) What is the annual *percentage* discount or premium?
   (c) If you have no other information about the two currencies, what is your best guess about the spot rate on the krona 3 months hence?
   (d) Suppose that you expect to receive 100,000 krona in 3 months. How many dollars is this likely to be worth?

3. Look at Table 34-1. If the 3-month interest rate on eurodollars is 6.5 percent, what do you think is the 3-month drachma interest rate? Explain what would happen if the rate were substantially above your figure.

4. Look in *The Wall Street Journal*. How many French francs can you buy for $1? How many deutschemarks can you buy? What rate do you think a German bank would quote for buying or selling French francs? Explain what would happen if it quoted a rate that was substantially above your figure.

5. What do our four basic relationships imply about the relationship between two countries' interest rates and the expected change in the exchange rate? Explain why you would or would not expect them to be related.

6. Ms. Rosetta Stone, the treasurer of International Reprints, Inc., has noticed that the interest rate in Switzerland is below the rates in most other countries. She is, therefore, suggesting that the company should make an issue of Swiss franc bonds. What considerations ought she first to take into account?

7. What considerations should an American company take into account when deciding how to finance its overseas subsidiaries?

8. An American firm is evaluating an investment in Italy. The project costs 2 billion lire and it is expected to produce an income of 300 million lire a year in real terms for each of the next 10 years. The expected inflation rate in Italy is 6 percent a year, and the firm estimates that an appropriate discount rate for the project would be about 8 percent above the risk-free rate of interest. Calculate the net present value of the project in dollars using each of the two methods described in this chapter. Exchange rates are given in Table 34-1. The interest rate was about 9 percent in Italy and 6½ percent in the United States.

9. "The decline in the value of the dollar has made chemical producers in the United States attractive targets for takeover by European companies." Discuss.

10. Suppose you are the treasurer of Lufthansa. How is company value likely to be affected by exchange-rate changes? What policies would you adopt to reduce exchange-rate risk?

11. Suppose that you use your own views about inflation and exchange rates when valuing an overseas investment proposal. Specifically, suppose that you believe that inflation will be 2 percent in Holland and 5 percent in the United States but that the exchange rate will remain unchanged. Recalculate the NPV of the Outland project using both of our methods. Each NPV implies a different financing strategy. What are the two strategies?

12. Companies may be affected by changes in the nominal exchange rate or in the real exchange rate. Explain how this can occur. Which risks are easiest to hedge against?

13. A Ford dealer in the United States may be exposed to a devaluation in the yen if this leads to a cut in the price of Japanese cars. Suppose that the dealer estimates that a 1 percent decline in the value of the yen would result in a permanent decline of 5 percent in the dealer's profits. How should she hedge against this risk, and how should she calculate the size of the hedge position? You may find it helpful to refer back to Section 25-5.

14. You have bid for a possible export order which would provide a cash inflow of 1 million deutschemarks in 6 months. The spot exchange rate is DM1.5/$ and the 6-month forward rate is DM1.4/$. There are two sources of uncertainty— (1) the deutschemark could appreciate or depreciate, and (2) you may or may not receive the export order. Illustrate in each case the profits or losses that you would make if:
    (*a*) You sell 1 million deutschemarks forward.
    (*b*) You buy a 6-month put option on deutschemarks with an exercise price of DM1.4/$.

15. On January 3, 1995, an American investor buys 1000 shares in a Greek company at a price of 500 drachmas a share. A year later she sells the shares for 550 drachmas each. The share does not pay any dividend. Exchange rates for January 3, 1995, are shown in Table 34-1.
    (*a*) How many dollars does she invest?
    (*b*) If the exchange rate at the end of the year is dr255/$, what is the investor's total return in drachmas? In dollars?
    (*c*) Do you think that the investor has made an exchange-rate profit or loss? Explain.

16. If investors recognize the impact of inflation and exchange-rate changes on a firm's cash flows, changes in exchange rates should be reflected in stock prices. How would the stock price of each of the following Swiss companies be affected by an unanticipated appreciation in the Swiss franc of 10 percent, only 2 percent of which could be justified by comparing Swiss inflation to that in the rest of the world?
    (*a*) *SwissAir:* More than two-thirds of its employees are Swiss. Most revenues come from international fares set in U.S. dollars.
    (*b*) *Nestlé:* Fewer than 5 percent of its employees are Swiss. Most revenues are derived from sales of consumer goods in a wide range of countries with competition from local producers.
    (*c*) *Union Bank of Switzerland:* Most employees are Swiss. All non–Swiss franc monetary positions are fully hedged.

17. Suppose that U.S. investors invest largely in the United States and are content to hold only a very small proportion of their portfolios in foreign shares. Suppose also that the average beta of German shares when measured against the portfolios of U.S. investors is .7. The U.S. interest rate is 5 percent, and the expected risk premium on the U.S. market is 8 percent.
    (*a*) What is the expected return on the average U.S. share?
    (*b*) What is the expected return to a U.S. investor from the average German share?

TABLE 34-4

● ●

Comparative data for Australia and the United States, 1980–1993

	Foreign Exchange Rate, A$/US$	INFLATION RATE*	
		Australia	United States
1980	.8776	100	100
1981	.8701	110	110.4
1982	.9829	122	117.1
1983	1.1082	134	120.9
1984	1.1369	140	126.1
1985	1.4269	149	130.5
1986	1.4905	162	133.1
1987	1.4267	176	137.9
1988	1.2752	189	141.2
1989	1.2618	203	146.7
1990	1.2799	218	151.7
1991	1.2835	225	156.4
1992	1.3600	227	159.3
1993	1.4704	231	162.2

*Consumer price index: 1980 = 100.

(c) What is the cost of capital for a U.S. firm investing in a German project that has about the same risk (beta relative to the portfolio of U.S. investors) as the average German share?

18. Table 34-4 shows the foreign exchange rate for the Australian dollar and the Australian and U.S. inflation rates. Using the table's data, plot the nominal and real exchange rates. Which has been the more stable?

19. Look again at Table 34-4. George and Bruce each have an equal share in a trust fund that provides them with an income of US$100,000 a year. George lives in Seattle, but Bruce emigrated to Sydney in 1980. What has happened to George's *real* income since 1980? What was Bruce's income in 1980 in Australian dollars? What was it in 1993? What has happened to Bruce's *real* income?

20. In 1992 a liter of Scotch cost $22.84 in New York, S$69 in Singapore, and 3240 rubles in Moscow.
(a) If the law of one price held, what was the exchange rate between U.S. dollars and Singapore dollars? Between U.S. dollars and rubles?
(b) The actual exchange rates in 1992 were S$1.63 = US$1 and 250 rubles = US$1. Where would you prefer to buy your Scotch?

21. Table 34-5 shows the annual interest rate (annually compounded) and exchange rates against the dollar for different currencies. Are there any arbitrage opportunities? If so, how could you secure a positive cash flow today, while zeroing out all future cash flows?

TABLE 34-5
● ●

Interest rates and exchange rates

	Interest Rate, Percent	Spot Exchange Rate*	1-Year Forward Exchange Rate*
United States (dollar)	3	—	—
Costaguana (pulga)	23	10,000	11,942
Westonia (ruple)	5	2.6	2.65
Gloccamorra (pint)	8	17.1	18.2
Anglosaxophonia (wasp)	4.1	2.3	2.28

*Number of units of foreign currency that can be exchanged for $1.

22. "Although recent currency turmoil will not in itself trigger deals, it will undoubtedly give the mergers and acquisitions market further impetus. The decline of the dollar has made U.S. assets especially cheap for companies in Germany and Switzerland" (*Financial Times*, April 18, 1995). Discuss.

23. Alpha Corporation has a plant in Hamburg which imports components from the United States, assembles them, and then sells the finished product in Germany. Omega Corporation is at the opposite extreme. It also has a plant in Hamburg, but it buys its raw materials in Germany and exports its output back to the United States.
    How is each firm likely to be affected by a fall in the value of the deutschemark? How could each firm hedge itself against exchange risk?

24. In September 1995 interest rates were 5.8 percent in the United States and 10.6 percent in Italy. The spot exchange rate was L1626/$. Suppose that 1 year later interest rates are 8 percent in both countries, while the value of the lira has fallen to L1800/$.
    (*a*) Floria Tosca from Rome invested in an Italian 2-year zero coupon bond in September 1995 and sold it in September 1996. What was her return?
    (*b*) Benjamin Pinkerton from New York also invested in the Italian 2-year bond in September 1995 and sold it in September 1996. What was his return *in dollars?*
    (*c*) Suppose that Mr. Pinkerton had correctly forecasted the price at which he sold his bond and that he hedged his investment against currency risk? How could he have done so? What would have been his return in dollars?

PART eleven

CONCLUSIONS

35

Conclusion: What We Do and Do Not Know about Finance

It is time to sign off. Let us finish by thinking about some of the things that we do and do not know about finance.

35-1 WHAT WE DO KNOW: THE SEVEN MOST IMPORTANT IDEAS IN FINANCE

What would you say if you were asked to name the seven most important ideas in finance? Here is our list.

1. Net Present Value

When you wish to know the value of a used car, you look at prices in the second-hand car market. Similarly, when you wish to know the value of a future cash flow, you look at prices quoted in the capital markets, where claims to future cash flows are traded (remember, those highly paid investment bankers are just secondhand cash-flow dealers). If you can buy cash flows for your shareholders at a cheaper price than they would have to pay in the capital market, you have increased the value of their investment.

This is the simple idea behind *net present value* (NPV). When we calculate a project's NPV, we are asking whether the project is worth more than it costs. We are estimating its value by calculating what its cash flows would be worth if a claim on them were offered separately to investors and traded in the capital markets.

That is why we calculate NPV by discounting future cash flows at the opportunity cost of capital—that is, at the expected rate of return offered by securities having the same degree of risk as the project. In well-functioning capital markets, all equivalent-risk assets are priced to offer the same expected return. By discounting at the opportunity cost of capital, we calculate the price at which investors in the project could expect to earn that rate of return.

Like most good ideas, the net present value rule is "obvious when you think about it." But notice what an important idea it is. The NPV rule allows thousands of shareholders, who may have vastly different levels of wealth and attitudes toward risk, to participate in the same enterprise and to delegate its operation to a professional manager. They give the manager one simple instruction: "Maximize present value."

2. The Capital Asset Pricing Model

Some people say that modern finance is all about the capital asset pricing model. That's nonsense. If the capital asset pricing model had never been invented, our advice to financial managers would be essentially the same. The attraction of the model is that it gives us a manageable way of thinking about the required return on a risky investment.

Again, it is an attractively simple idea. There are two kinds of risk—risks that you can diversify away and those that you can't. You can measure the *nondiversifiable*, or *market*, risk of an investment by the extent to which the value of the investment is affected by a change in the *aggregate* value of all the assets in the economy. This is called the *beta* of the investment. The only risks that people care about are the ones that they can't get rid of—the nondiversifiable ones. This is why the required return on an asset increases in line with its beta.

Many people are worried by some of the rather strong assumptions behind the capital asset pricing model, or they are concerned about the difficulties of estimating a project's beta. They are right to be worried about these things. In 10 or 20 years' time we will probably have much better theories than we do now. But we will be extremely surprised if those future theories do not still insist on the crucial distinction between diversifiable and nondiversifiable risks—and that, after all, is the main idea underlying the capital asset pricing model.

3. Efficient Capital Markets

The third fundamental idea is that security prices accurately reflect available information and respond rapidly to new information as soon as it becomes available. This *efficient-market theory* comes in three flavors, corresponding to different definitions of "available information." The weak form (or random-walk theory) says that prices reflect all the information in past prices. The semistrong form says that prices reflect all publicly available information, and the strong form holds that prices reflect all acquirable information.

Don't misunderstand the efficient-market idea. It doesn't say that there are no taxes or costs; it doesn't say that there aren't some clever people and some stupid ones. It merely implies that competition in capital markets is very tough—there are no money machines, and security prices reflect the true underlying values of assets.

4. Value Additivity and the Law of Conservation of Value

The principle of *value additivity* states that the value of the whole is equal to the sum of the values of the parts. It is sometimes called the *law of the conservation of value*.

When we appraise a project that produces a succession of cash flows, we always assume that values add up. In other words, we assume

$$\text{PV(project)} = \text{PV}(C_1) + \text{PV}(C_2) + \cdots + \text{PV}(C_t)$$

$$= \frac{C_1}{1 + r} + \frac{C_2}{(1 + r)^2} + \cdots + \frac{C_t}{(1 + r)^t} + \cdots$$

We similarly assume that the sum of the present values of projects A and B equals the present value of a composite project AB.[1] But value additivity also means that you

---

[1]That is, if

$$\text{PV(A)} = \text{PV}[C_1(A)] + \text{PV}[C_2(A)] + \cdots + \text{PV}[C_t(A)] + \cdots$$
$$\text{PV(B)} = \text{PV}[C_1(B)] + \text{PV}[C_2(B)] + \cdots + \text{PV}[C_t(B)] + \cdots$$

and if for each period t, $C_t(AB) = C_t(A) + C_t(B)$, then

$$\text{PV(AB)} = \text{PV(A)} + \text{PV(B)}$$

can't increase value by putting two whole companies together unless you thereby increase the total cash flow. In other words, there are no benefits to mergers solely for diversification.

If the law of the conservation of value works when you add up cash flows, it must also work when you subtract them.[2] Therefore, financing decisions that simply divide up operating cash flows don't increase overall firm value. This is the basic idea behind Modigliani and Miller's famous proposition I: In perfect markets changes in capital structure do not affect value. As long as the *total* cash flow generated by the firm's assets is unchanged by capital structure, value is independent of capital structure. The value of the whole pie does not depend on how it is sliced.

Of course, MM's proposition is not The Answer, but it does tell us where to look for reasons why capital structure decisions may matter. Taxes are one possibility. Debt provides a corporate interest tax shield, and this tax shield may more than compensate for any extra personal tax that the investor has to pay on debt interest. Also, high debt levels may spur managers to work harder and to run a tighter ship. But debt has its drawbacks if it leads to costly financial distress.

In everyday conversation we often use the word *option* as synonymous with *choice* or *alternative;* thus we speak of someone as "having a number of options." In finance *option* refers specifically to the opportunity to trade in the future on terms that are fixed today. Smart managers know that it is often worth paying today for the option to buy or sell an asset tomorrow.

If options are so important, the financial manager needs to know how to value them. Finance experts always knew the relevant variables—the exercise price and the exercise date of the option, the risk of the underlying asset, and the rate of interest. But it was Black and Scholes who first showed how these can be put together in a usable formula.

The Black-Scholes formula was developed for simple call options and does not directly apply to the more complicated options often encountered in corporate finance. But Black and Scholes's most basic ideas—for example, the risk-neutral valuation method implied by their formula—work even where the formula doesn't. Valuing the real options described in Chapter 21 may require extra number crunching but no extra concepts.

A modern corporation is a team effort involving a number of players, such as managers, employees, shareholders, and bondholders. The members of this corporate team are bound together by a series of formal and informal contracts to ensure that they pull together.

For a long time economists used to assume without question that all players acted for the common good, but in the last 20 years economists have had a lot more to say about the possible conflicts of interest and how companies try to overcome such conflicts. These ideas are collectively known as *agency theory.*

We devoted at least one chapter of this book to each of the other important ideas in finance. We didn't allocate a chapter to agency theory, but the theory has helped us to think more clearly about several questions, including:

---

[2] If you *start* with the cash flow $C_t(AB)$ and split it into two pieces, $C_t(A)$ and $C_t(B)$, then total value is unchanged. That is, $PV[C_t(A)] + PV[C_t(B)] = PV[C_t(AB)]$. See footnote 1.

- How can an entrepreneur persuade venture capital investors to join in his or her enterprise?
- What are the reasons for all the fine print in bond agreements?
- Why might a bank sometimes be unwilling to lend a firm more money at any price?
- Are LBOs simply attempts to "rip off" the other players, or do they add value by increasing management's incentives to work hard?

Are these seven ideas exciting theories or plain common sense? Call them what you will, they are basic to the financial manager's job. If by reading this book you really understand these ideas and know how to apply them, you have learned a great deal.

35-2 WHAT WE DO NOT KNOW: 10 UNSOLVED PROBLEMS IN FINANCE

Since the unknown is never exhausted, the list of what we do not know about finance could go on forever. But, following Brealey and Myers's third law (see Section 28-2), we will list and briefly discuss 10 unsolved problems that seem ripe for productive research.

1. How Are Major Financial Decisions Made?

Arnold Sametz commented in 1964 that "we know very little about how the great nonroutine financial decisions are made."[3] That is no less true today. We know quite a bit about asset values, but we do not know very much about the decisions that give rise to these values. What is the process that causes one company to make a major investment and another to reject it? Why does one company decide to issue debt and another to issue equity? If we knew why companies made particular decisions, we would be better able to help improve those decisions.

Our ignorance is largest when it comes to major *strategic* decisions. In Section 28-1 we described strategic planning as "capital budgeting on a grand scale." Strategic planning attempts to identify the lines of business in which the firm has the greatest long-run opportunities and to develop a plan for achieving success in those businesses. But it is hard to calculate the NPV of major strategic decisions. Think, for example, of a firm that makes a major commitment to the design and manufacture of computer memories. It is really embarking on a long-term effort which will require capital outlays over many years. It cannot identify all those future projects, much less evaluate their NPVs. Instead, it decides to go ahead because the computer memory business is growing rapidly, because firms already in that business are doing well, and because it has intangible assets—special technology, perhaps—which it thinks will give it a leg up on the competition.

Strategic planning is a "top-down" approach to capital budgeting: you choose the businesses you want to be in and make the capital outlays necessary for success. It's perfectly sensible and natural for firms to look at capital investments that way *in addition to* looking at them "bottom-up." The trouble is that we understand the bottom-up part of the capital budgeting process better than the top-down part.

Top-down and bottom-up should not be competing approaches to capital budgeting. They should be two aspects of a single integrated procedure. Not all firms

---

[3]A. W. Sametz, "Trends in the Volume and Composition of Equity Finance," *Journal of Finance*, **19**:450–469 (September 1964). See p. 469.

integrate the two approaches successfully. No doubt some firms do so, but we don't really know how.

In Sections 21-1 and 28-1 we suggested that option pricing theory might help unravel some of the mysteries of strategic planning. We will have to wait and see whether it does.

2. What Determines Project Risk and Present Value?

A good capital investment is one that has a positive NPV. We have talked at some length about how to calculate NPV, but we have given you very little guidance about how to find positive-NPV projects, except to say in Section 11-2 that projects have positive NPVs when the firm can earn economic rents. But why do some companies earn economic rents while others in the same industry do not? Are the rents merely windfall gains, or can they be anticipated and planned for? What is their source, and how long do they persist before competition destroys them? Very little is known about any of these important questions.

Here is a related question: Why are some real assets risky and others relatively safe? In Section 9-4 we suggested a few reasons for differences in project betas— differences in operating leverage, for example, or in the extent to which a project's cash flows respond to the performance of the national economy. These are useful clues, but we have as yet no general procedure for estimating project betas. Assessing project risk is therefore still largely a seat-of-the-pants matter.

3. Risk and Return— What Have We Missed?

In 1848 John Stuart Mill wrote, "Happily there is nothing in the laws of value which remains for the present or any future writer to clear up; the theory is complete." Economists today are not so sure about that. For example, the capital asset pricing model is an enormous step toward understanding the effect of risk on the value of an asset, but there are many puzzles left, some statistical and some theoretical.

The statistical problems arise because the capital asset pricing model is hard to prove or disprove conclusively. It appears that average returns from low-beta stocks are too high (that is, higher than the capital asset pricing model predicts) and that those from high-beta stocks are too low; but this could be a problem with the way the tests are conducted and not with the model itself. [4]

Meanwhile, scholars toil on the theoretical front. We discussed some of their work in Section 8-4. But just for fun here is another example: Suppose that you love fine wine. It may make sense for you to buy shares in a grand cru chateau, even if doing so soaks up a large fraction of your personal wealth and leaves you with a relatively undiversified portfolio. However, you are *hedged* against a rise in the price of fine wine: your hobby will cost you more in a bull market for wine, but your stake in the chateau will make you correspondingly richer. Thus you are holding a relatively undiversified portfolio for a good reason. We would not expect you to demand a premium for bearing that portfolio's undiversifiable risk.

In general, if two people have different tastes, it may make sense for them to hold different portfolios. You may hedge your consumption needs with an investment in wine making, whereas somebody else may do better to invest in Baskin-Robbins. The capital asset pricing model isn't rich enough to deal with such a world. It assumes that all investors have similar tastes: the "hedging motive" does not enter, and therefore they hold the same portfolio of risky assets.

---

[4] See R. Roll, "A Critique of the Asset Pricing Theory's Tests: Part 1: On Past and Potential Testability of the Theory," *Journal of Financial Economics*, **4**:129–176 (March 1977); and for a critique of the critique, see D. Mayers and E. M. Rice, "Measuring Portfolio Performance and the Empirical Content of Asset Pricing Models," *Journal of Financial Economics*, **7**:3–28 (March 1979).

Merton has extended the capital asset pricing model to accommodate the hedging motive.[5] If enough investors are attempting to hedge against the same thing, the model implies a more complicated risk-return relationship. However, it is not yet clear who is hedging against what, and so the model remains difficult to test.

So the capital asset pricing model survives not from a lack of competition but from a surfeit. There are too many plausible alternative risk measures, and so far no consensus exists on the right course to plot if we abandon beta.

In the meantime we must recognize the capital asset pricing model for what it is: an incomplete but extremely useful way of linking risk and return. Recognize too that the model's most basic message, that diversifiable risk doesn't matter, is accepted by nearly everyone.

4. How Important are the Exceptions to the Efficient-Market Theory?

The efficient-market theory is strong, but no theory is perfect—there must be exceptions. What are the exceptions and how well does the evidence stand up?

We noted some apparent exceptions in Section 13-2. For example, we saw that the stocks of small companies appear to have yielded higher average returns than those of large companies with comparable betas. Thus, whatever your target portfolio beta, you can apparently generate superior average returns by investing in small companies.

Now, this could mean one of several things:

1. The stock market is inefficient and consistently underprices stocks of small firms.

2. The difference between the stock market performances of small and large firms is just a coincidence. (The more researchers study stock performance, the more strange coincidences they are likely to find.)

3. Firm size happens to be correlated with variable x, that mysterious second risk variable that investors may rationally take into account in pricing shares.

In searching for an explanation of the small-firm phenomenon, researchers have uncovered other puzzles. For example, almost all the extra return on small-company stocks has occurred in January. So the mystery deepens. Does the turn-of-the-year effect provide a clue to the explanation of the small-company effect, or is it just a false trail? Sorting out what is really going on in these cases will take considerable work and thought.

If stocks were fairly priced, there would be no easy ways to make superior profits. That is why most tests of market efficiency have analyzed whether there are simple rules that produce superior investment performance. Unfortunately, the converse does *not* hold: stock prices could deviate substantially from fair value, and yet it could be difficult to make superior profits.

For example, suppose that the price of IBM stock is always one-half of its fair value. As long as IBM is *consistently* underpriced, the percentage capital gain is the same as it would be if the stock always sold at a fair price. Of course, if IBM stock is underpriced, you get correspondingly more future dividends for your money, but for low-yield stocks that does not make much difference to your total return. So, while the bulk of the evidence shows that it is difficult to earn high returns, we should be cautious about assuming that stocks are *necessarily* fairly priced.

---

[5]See R. Merton, "An Intertemporal Capital Asset Pricing Model," *Econometrica*, **41**:867–887 (1973).

5. Is Management an Off-Balance-Sheet Liability?

Closed-end funds are firms whose only asset is a portfolio of common stocks. One might think that if you knew the value of these common stocks, you would also know the value of the firm. However, this is not the case. The stock of the closed-end fund often sells for substantially less than the value of the fund's portfolio.[6]

All this might not matter much except that it could be just the tip of the iceberg. For example, real estate stocks appear to sell for less than the market values of the firms' net assets. In the late 1970s and early 1980s the market values of many large oil companies were less than the market values of their oil reserves. Analysts joked that you could buy oil cheaper on Wall Street than in west Texas.

All these are special cases in which it was possible to compare the market value of the whole firm with the values of its separate assets. But perhaps if we could observe the values of other firms' separate parts, we might find that the value of the whole was often less than the sum of the values of the parts.

We don't understand why closed-end investment companies or any of the other firms sell at a discount on the market values of their assets. One explanation is that the value added by the firm's management is less than the cost of the management. That is why we suggest that management may be an off-balance-sheet liability. For example, the discount of oil company shares from oil-in-the-ground value can be explained if investors expected the profits from oil production to be frittered away in negative-NPV investments and bureaucratic excess. The present value of growth opportunities (PVGO) was negative!

Whenever firms calculate the net present value of a project, they implicitly assume that the value of the whole project is simply the sum of the values of all the years' cash flows. We referred to this earlier as the law of the conservation of value. If we cannot rely on that law, the tip of the iceberg could turn out to be a hot potato.

6. How Can We Explain the Success of New Securities and New Markets?

In the last 20 years companies and the securities exchanges have created an enormous number of new securities—options, futures, options on futures; zero coupon bonds, floating-rate bonds; bonds with collars, caps, and droplocks; dual-currency bonds; bonds with currency options . . . the list is endless. In some cases, it is easy to explain the success of new markets or securities—perhaps they allow investors to insure themselves against new risks or they result from a change in tax or in regulation. Sometimes a market develops because of a change in the costs of issuing or trading different securities. But there are many successful innovations that cannot be explained so easily. Why do investment bankers continue to invent, and successfully sell, complex new securities that outstrip our ability to value them? The truth is we don't understand why some innovations in markets succeed and others never get off the ground.

7. How Can We Resolve the Dividend Controversy?

We spent all of Chapter 16 on dividend policy without being able to resolve the dividend controversy. Many people believe dividends are good; others believe they are bad; and still others believe they are irrelevant. If pressed, we stand somewhere in the middle, but we can't be dogmatic about it.

We don't mean to disparage existing research; rather, we say that more is in order. Whether future research will change anybody's mind is another matter. In 1979 Joel Stern wrote an article for the editorial page of *The Wall Street Journal* arguing

---

[6]There are relatively few closed-end funds. Most mutual funds are *open-end.* This means that they stand ready to buy or sell additional shares at a price equal to the fund's net asset value per share. Therefore the share price of an open-end fund always equals net asset value.

for low dividends and citing statistical tests in support of his position.[7] The article attracted several strongly worded responses, including one from a manager who wrote, "While Mr. Stern is gamboling from pinnacle to pinnacle in the upper realms of the theoretical, those of us in financial management are down below slogging through the foothills of reality."[8]

8. What Risks Should a Firm Take?

Financial managers end up managing risk. For example:

- When a firm expands production, managers often reduce the cost of failure by building in the option to alter the product mix or to bail out of the project altogether.
- By reducing the firm's borrowing, managers can spread operating risks over a larger equity base.
- Most businesses take out insurance against a variety of specific hazards.
- Managers often use futures or other derivatives to protect against adverse movements in commodity prices, interest rates, and exchange rates.

All these actions reduce risk. But less risk can't always be better. The point of risk management is not to reduce risk but to add value. We wish we could give general guidance on what bets the firm should place and what the *appropriate* level of risk is.

In practice, risk management decisions interact in complicated ways. For example, firms that are hedged against commodity price fluctuations may be able to afford more debt than those that are not hedged. Hedging can make sense if it allows the firm to take greater advantage of interest tax shields, provided the costs of hedging are sufficiently low.

How can a company set a risk management strategy that adds up to a sensible whole?

9. What Is the Value of Liquidity?

Unlike Treasury bills, cash pays no interest. On the other hand, cash provides more liquidity than Treasury bills. People who hold cash must believe that this additional liquidity offsets the loss of interest. In equilibrium, the marginal value of the additional liquidity must equal the interest rate on bills.

Now what can we say about corporate holdings of cash? It is wrong to ignore the liquidity gain and to say that the cost of holding cash is the lost interest. This would imply that cash always has a *negative* NPV. It is equally foolish to say that, because the marginal value of liquidity is equal to the loss of interest, it doesn't matter how much cash the firm holds. This would imply that cash always has a *zero* NPV.

We know that the marginal value of cash to a holder declines with the size of the cash holding, but we don't really understand how to value the liquidity service of cash. In our chapters on working-capital management we largely finessed the problem by presenting models that are really too simple[9] or by speaking vaguely of the need to ensure an "adequate" liquidity reserve. We cannot successfully tackle the problem of working-capital management until we have a theory of liquidity.

---

[7] Joel Stern, "The Dividend Question," *Wall Street Journal*, July 16, 1973, p. 13.

[8] *Wall Street Journal*, August 20, 1979, p. 16. The letter was from A. J. Sandblute, senior vice-president of Minnesota Light and Power Company.

[9] For example, models based only on the transaction costs of switching between cash and interest-bearing assets. See Section 31-1.

The problem is that liquidity is a matter of degree. A Treasury bill is less liquid than cash, but it is still a highly liquid security because it can be sold and turned into cash easily and almost instantaneously.[10] Corporate bonds are less liquid than Treasury bills; trucks are less liquid than corporate bonds; specialized machinery is less liquid than trucks; and so on.[11] But even specialized machinery can be turned into cash if you are willing to accept some delay and cost of sale. The broad question is therefore not "How much cash should the firm hold?" but "How should it divide its total investment between relatively liquid and relatively illiquid assets?"—holding other things constant of course. That question is hard to answer. Obviously, every firm must be able to raise cash on short notice, but we have no good theory of how much cash is enough or how readily the firm should be able to raise it. To complicate matters further, we note that cash can be raised on short notice by borrowing, or selling other securities, as well as by selling assets. The financial manager with a $1 million unused line of credit may sleep just as soundly as one whose firm holds $1 million in marketable securities.

10. How Can We Explain Merger Waves?

In 1968, at the first peak of the postwar merger movement, Joel Segall noted: "There is no single hypothesis which is both plausible and general and which shows promise of explaining the current merger movement If so, it is correct to say that there is nothing known about mergers; there are no useful generalizations."[12] Of course there are many plausible reasons why two firms might wish to merge. If you single out a *particular* merger, it is usually possible to think up a reason why that merger could make sense. But that leaves us with a special hypothesis for each merger. What we need is a *general* hypothesis to explain merger waves. For example, everybody seemed to be merging in 1995 and nobody 5 years earlier. Why?

We can think of other instances of apparent financial fashions. For example, from time to time there are hot new-issue periods when there seems to be an insatiable supply of speculative new issues and an equally insatiable demand for them. We need better theories to help explain these "bubbles" of financial activity.

35-3   A FINAL WORD

That concludes our list of unsolved problems. We have given you the 10 uppermost in our minds. If there are others that you find more interesting and challenging, by all means construct your own list and start thinking about it.

It will take years for our 10 problems to be finally solved and replaced with a fresh list. In the meantime, we invite you to go on to further study of what we *already* know about finance. We also invite you to apply what you have learned from reading this book.

---

[10]That is, you can realize the asset's true economic value in a quick sale. Liquidity means that you don't have to accept a discount from true value if you want to sell the asset quickly.

[11]It also happens that investments are very liquid except when you want to sell them. In the heyday of the junk bond market, institutions were able to trade these bonds in volume with little impact on prices. But then Michael Milken, the founder of the junk bond market, was indicted for securities fraud, his employer Drexel Burnham Lambert filed for bankruptcy, and a number of junk bond issuers defaulted on their debt. The result: Many investors (including Drexel) found themselves stuck with junk bonds that were unmarketable, on short notice, at almost any price.

[12]J. Segall, "Merging for Fun and Profit," *Industrial Management Review,* **9**:17–30 (Winter 1968).

Now that the book is done, we sympathize with Huckleberry Finn. At the end of his book he says:

> So there ain't nothing more to write, and I am rotten glad of it, because if I'd a'knowed what a trouble it was to make a book I wouldn't a' tackled it, and I ain't a'going to no more.

Present Value Tables

APPENDIX TABLE 1

Discount factors: Present value of $1 to be received after t years $= 1/(1 + r)^t$

Number of years	Interest rate per year														
	1%	2%	3%	4%	5%	6%	7%	8%	9%	10%	11%	12%	13%	14%	15%
1	.990	.980	.971	.962	.952	.943	.935	.926	.917	.909	.901	.893	.885	.877	.870
2	.980	.961	.943	.925	.907	.890	.873	.857	.842	.826	.812	.797	.783	.769	.756
3	.971	.942	.915	.889	.864	.840	.816	.794	.772	.751	.731	.712	.693	.675	.658
4	.961	.924	.888	.855	.823	.792	.763	.735	.708	.683	.659	.636	.613	.592	.572
5	.951	.906	.863	.822	.784	.747	.713	.681	.650	.621	.593	.567	.543	.519	.497
6	.942	.888	.837	.790	.746	.705	.666	.630	.596	.564	.535	.507	.480	.456	.432
7	.933	.871	.813	.760	.711	.665	.623	.583	.547	.513	.482	.452	.425	.400	.376
8	.923	.853	.789	.731	.677	.627	.582	.540	.502	.467	.434	.404	.376	.351	.327
9	.914	.837	.766	.703	.645	.592	.544	.500	.460	.424	.391	.361	.333	.308	.284
10	.905	.820	.744	.676	.614	.558	.508	.463	.422	.386	.352	.322	.295	.270	.247
11	.896	.804	.722	.650	.585	.527	.475	.429	.388	.350	.317	.287	.261	.237	.215
12	.887	.788	.701	.625	.557	.497	.444	.397	.356	.319	.286	.257	.231	.208	.187
13	.879	.773	.681	.601	.530	.469	.415	.368	.326	.290	.258	.229	.204	.182	.163
14	.870	.758	.661	.577	.505	.442	.388	.340	.299	.263	.232	.205	.181	.160	.141
15	.861	.743	.642	.555	.481	.417	.362	.315	.275	.239	.209	.183	.160	.140	.123
16	.853	.728	.623	.534	.458	.394	.339	.292	.252	.218	.188	.163	.141	.123	.107
17	.844	.714	.605	.513	.436	.371	.317	.270	.231	.198	.170	.146	.125	.108	.093
18	.836	.700	.587	.494	.416	.350	.296	.250	.212	.180	.153	.130	.111	.095	.081
19	.828	.686	.570	.475	.396	.331	.277	.232	.194	.164	.138	.116	.098	.083	.070
20	.820	.673	.554	.456	.377	.312	.258	.215	.179	.149	.124	.104	.087	.073	.061
25	.780	.610	.478	.375	.295	.233	.184	.146	.116	.092	.074	.059	.047	.038	.030
30	.742	.552	.412	.308	.231	.174	.131	.099	.075	.057	.044	.033	.026	.020	.015

Number of years		Interest rate per year													
	16%	17%	18%	19%	20%	21%	22%	23%	24%	25%	26%	27%	28%	29%	30%
1	.862	.855	.847	.840	.833	.826	.820	.813	.806	.800	.794	.787	.781	.775	.769
2	.743	.731	.718	.706	.694	.683	.672	.661	.650	.640	.630	.620	.610	.601	.592
3	.641	.624	.609	.593	.579	.564	.551	.537	.524	.512	.500	.488	.477	.466	.455
4	.552	.534	.516	.499	.482	.467	.451	.437	.423	.410	.397	.384	.373	.361	.350
5	.476	.456	.437	.419	.402	.386	.370	.355	.341	.328	.315	.303	.291	.280	.269
6	.410	.390	.370	.352	.335	.319	.303	.289	.275	.262	.250	.238	.227	.217	.207
7	.354	.333	.314	.296	.279	.263	.249	.235	.222	.210	.198	.188	.178	.168	.159
8	.305	.285	.266	.249	.233	.218	.204	.191	.179	.168	.157	.148	.139	.130	.123
9	.263	.243	.225	.209	.194	.180	.167	.155	.144	.134	.125	.116	.108	.101	.094
10	.227	.208	.191	.176	.162	.149	.137	.126	.116	.107	.099	.092	.085	.078	.073
11	.195	.178	.162	.148	.135	.123	.112	.103	.094	.086	.079	.072	.066	.061	.056
12	.168	.152	.137	.124	.112	.102	.092	.083	.076	.069	.062	.057	.052	.047	.043
13	.145	.130	.116	.104	.093	.084	.075	.068	.061	.055	.050	.045	.040	.037	.033
14	.125	.111	.099	.088	.078	.069	.062	.055	.049	.044	.039	.035	.032	.028	.025
15	.108	.095	.084	.074	.065	.057	.051	.045	.040	.035	.031	.028	.025	.022	.020
16	.093	.081	.071	.062	.054	.047	.042	.036	.032	.028	.025	.022	.019	.017	.015
17	.080	.069	.060	.052	.045	.039	.034	.030	.026	.023	.020	.017	.015	.013	.012
18	.069	.059	.051	.044	.038	.032	.028	.024	.021	.018	.016	.014	.012	.010	.009
19	.060	.051	.043	.037	.031	.027	.023	.020	.017	.014	.012	.011	.009	.008	.007
20	.051	.043	.037	.031	.026	.022	.019	.016	.014	.012	.010	.008	.007	.006	.005
25	.024	.020	.016	.013	.010	.009	.007	.006	.005	.004	.003	.003	.002	.002	.001
30	.012	.009	.007	.005	.004	.003	.003	.002	.002	.001	.001	.001	.001	.000	.000

E.g.: If the interest rate is 10 percent per year, the present value of $1 received at year 5 is $.621.

APPENDIX TABLE 2

Future value of $1 after t years $= (1 + r)^t$

| | | | | | | | | Interest rate per year | | | | | | | |
Number of years	1%	2%	3%	4%	5%	6%	7%	8%	9%	10%	11%	12%	13%	14%	15%
1	1.010	1.020	1.030	1.040	1.050	1.060	1.070	1.080	1.090	1.100	1.110	1.120	1.130	1.140	1.150
2	1.020	1.040	1.061	1.082	1.102	1.124	1.145	1.166	1.188	1.210	1.232	1.254	1.277	1.300	1.323
3	1.030	1.061	1.093	1.125	1.158	1.191	1.225	1.260	1.295	1.331	1.368	1.405	1.443	1.482	1.521
4	1.041	1.082	1.126	1.170	1.216	1.262	1.311	1.360	1.412	1.464	1.518	1.574	1.630	1.689	1.749
5	1.051	1.104	1.159	1.217	1.276	1.338	1.403	1.469	1.539	1.611	1.685	1.762	1.842	1.925	2.011
6	1.062	1.126	1.194	1.265	1.340	1.419	1.501	1.587	1.677	1.772	1.870	1.974	2.082	2.195	2.313
7	1.072	1.149	1.230	1.316	1.407	1.504	1.606	1.714	1.828	1.949	2.076	2.211	2.353	2.502	2.660
8	1.083	1.172	1.267	1.369	1.477	1.594	1.718	1.851	1.993	2.144	2.305	2.476	2.658	2.853	3.059
9	1.094	1.195	1.305	1.423	1.551	1.689	1.838	1.999	2.172	2.358	2.558	2.773	3.004	3.252	3.518
10	1.105	1.219	1.344	1.480	1.629	1.791	1.967	2.159	2.367	2.594	2.839	3.106	3.395	3.707	4.046
11	1.116	1.243	1.384	1.539	1.710	1.898	2.105	2.332	2.580	2.853	3.152	3.479	3.836	4.226	4.652
12	1.127	1.268	1.426	1.601	1.796	2.012	2.252	2.518	2.813	3.138	3.498	3.896	4.335	4.818	5.350
13	1.138	1.294	1.469	1.665	1.886	2.133	2.410	2.720	3.066	3.452	3.883	4.363	4.898	5.492	6.153
14	1.149	1.319	1.513	1.732	1.980	2.261	2.579	2.937	3.342	3.797	4.310	4.887	5.535	6.261	7.076
15	1.161	1.346	1.558	1.801	2.079	2.397	2.759	3.172	3.642	4.177	4.785	5.474	6.254	7.138	8.137
16	1.173	1.373	1.605	1.873	2.183	2.540	2.952	3.426	3.970	4.595	5.311	6.130	7.067	8.137	9.358
17	1.184	1.400	1.653	1.948	2.292	2.693	3.159	3.700	4.328	5.054	5.895	6.866	7.986	9.276	10.76
18	1.196	1.428	1.702	2.026	2.407	2.854	3.380	3.996	4.717	5.560	6.544	7.690	9.024	10.58	12.38
19	1.208	1.457	1.754	2.107	2.527	3.026	3.617	4.316	5.142	6.116	7.263	8.613	10.20	12.06	14.23
20	1.220	1.486	1.806	2.191	2.653	3.207	3.870	4.661	5.604	6.727	8.062	9.646	11.52	13.74	16.37
25	1.282	1.641	2.094	2.666	3.386	4.292	5.427	6.848	8.623	10.83	13.59	17.00	21.23	26.46	32.92
30	1.348	1.811	2.427	3.243	4.322	5.743	7.612	10.06	13.27	17.45	22.89	29.96	39.12	50.95	66.21

Interest rate per year

Number of years	16%	17%	18%	19%	20%	21%	22%	23%	24%	25%	26%	27%	28%	29%	30%
1	1.160	1.170	1.180	1.190	1.200	1.210	1.220	1.230	1.240	1.250	1.260	1.270	1.280	1.290	1.300
2	1.346	1.369	1.392	1.416	1.440	1.464	1.488	1.513	1.538	1.563	1.588	1.613	1.638	1.664	1.690
3	1.561	1.602	1.643	1.685	1.728	1.772	1.816	1.861	1.907	1.953	2.000	2.048	2.097	2.147	2.197
4	1.811	1.874	1.939	2.005	2.074	2.144	2.215	2.289	2.364	2.441	2.520	2.601	2.684	2.769	2.856
5	2.100	2.192	2.288	2.386	2.488	2.594	2.703	2.815	2.932	3.052	3.176	3.304	3.436	3.572	3.713
6	2.436	2.565	2.700	2.840	2.986	3.138	3.297	3.463	3.635	3.815	4.002	4.196	4.398	4.608	4.827
7	2.826	3.001	3.185	3.379	3.583	3.797	4.023	4.259	4.508	4.768	5.042	5.329	5.629	5.945	6.275
8	3.278	3.511	3.759	4.021	4.300	4.595	4.908	5.239	5.590	5.960	6.353	6.768	7.206	7.669	8.157
9	3.803	4.108	4.435	4.785	5.160	5.560	5.987	6.444	6.931	7.451	8.005	8.595	9.223	9.893	10.60
10	4.411	4.807	5.234	5.695	6.192	6.728	7.305	7.926	8.594	9.313	10.09	10.92	11.81	12.76	13.79
11	5.117	5.624	6.176	6.777	7.430	8.140	8.912	9.749	10.66	11.64	12.71	13.86	15.11	16.46	17.92
12	5.936	6.580	7.288	8.064	8.916	9.850	10.87	11.99	13.21	14.55	16.01	17.61	19.34	21.24	23.30
13	6.886	7.699	8.599	9.596	10.70	11.92	13.26	14.75	16.39	18.19	20.18	22.36	24.76	27.39	30.29
14	7.988	9.007	10.15	11.42	12.84	14.42	16.18	18.14	20.32	22.74	25.42	28.40	31.69	35.34	39.37
15	9.266	10.54	11.97	13.59	15.41	17.45	19.74	22.31	25.20	28.42	32.03	36.06	40.56	45.59	51.19
16	10.75	12.33	14.13	16.17	18.49	21.11	24.09	27.45	31.24	35.53	40.36	45.80	51.92	58.81	66.54
17	12.47	14.43	16.67	19.24	22.19	25.55	29.38	33.76	38.74	44.41	50.85	58.17	66.46	75.86	86.50
18	14.46	16.88	19.67	22.90	26.62	30.91	35.85	41.52	48.04	55.51	64.07	73.87	85.07	97.86	112.5
19	16.78	19.75	23.21	27.25	31.95	37.40	43.74	51.07	59.57	69.39	80.73	93.81	108.9	126.2	146.2
20	19.46	23.11	27.39	32.43	38.34	45.26	53.36	62.82	73.86	86.74	101.7	119.1	139.4	162.9	190.0
25	40.87	50.66	62.67	77.39	95.40	117.4	144.2	176.9	216.5	264.7	323.0	393.6	478.9	581.8	705.6
30	85.85	111.1	143.4	184.7	237.4	304.5	389.8	497.9	634.8	807.8	1026	1301	1646	2078	2620

E.g.: If the interest rate is 10 percent per year, the investment of $1 today will be worth $1.611 at year 5.

APPENDIX TABLE 3

Annuity table: Present value of $1 *per year* for each of *t* years $= 1/r - 1/[r(1 + r)^t]$

Interest rate per year

Number of years	1%	2%	3%	4%	5%	6%	7%	8%	9%	10%	11%	12%	13%	14%	15%
1	.990	.980	.971	.962	.952	.943	.935	.926	.917	.909	.901	.893	.885	.877	.870
2	1.970	1.942	1.913	1.886	1.859	1.833	1.808	1.783	1.759	1.736	1.713	1.690	1.668	1.647	1.626
3	2.941	2.884	2.829	2.775	2.723	2.673	2.624	2.577	2.531	2.487	2.444	2.402	2.361	2.322	2.283
4	3.902	3.808	3.717	3.630	3.546	3.465	3.387	3.312	3.240	3.170	3.102	3.037	2.974	2.914	2.855
5	4.853	4.713	4.580	4.452	4.329	4.212	4.100	3.993	3.890	3.791	3.696	3.605	3.517	3.433	3.352
6	5.795	5.601	5.417	5.242	5.076	4.917	4.767	4.623	4.486	4.355	4.231	4.111	3.998	3.889	3.784
7	6.728	6.472	6.230	6.002	5.786	5.582	5.389	5.206	5.033	4.868	4.712	4.564	4.423	4.288	4.160
8	7.652	7.325	7.020	6.733	6.463	6.210	5.971	5.747	5.535	5.335	5.146	4.968	4.799	4.639	4.487
9	8.566	8.162	7.786	7.435	7.108	6.802	6.515	6.247	5.995	5.759	5.537	5.328	5.132	4.946	4.772
10	9.471	8.983	8.530	8.111	7.722	7.360	7.024	6.710	6.418	6.145	5.889	5.650	5.426	5.216	5.019
11	10.37	9.787	9.253	8.760	8.306	7.887	7.499	7.139	6.805	6.495	6.207	5.938	5.687	5.453	5.234
12	11.26	10.58	9.954	9.385	8.863	8.384	7.943	7.536	7.161	6.814	6.492	6.194	5.918	5.660	5.421
13	12.13	11.35	10.63	9.986	9.394	8.853	8.358	7.904	7.487	7.103	6.750	6.424	6.122	5.842	5.583
14	13.00	12.11	11.30	10.56	9.899	9.295	8.745	8.244	7.786	7.367	6.982	6.628	6.302	6.002	5.724
15	13.87	12.85	11.94	11.12	10.38	9.712	9.108	8.559	8.061	7.606	7.191	6.811	6.462	6.142	5.847
16	14.72	13.58	12.56	11.65	10.84	10.11	9.447	8.851	8.313	7.824	7.379	6.974	6.604	6.265	5.954
17	15.56	14.29	13.17	12.17	11.27	10.48	9.763	9.122	8.544	8.022	7.549	7.120	6.729	6.373	6.047
18	16.40	14.99	13.75	12.66	11.69	10.83	10.06	9.372	8.756	8.201	7.702	7.250	6.840	6.467	6.128
19	17.23	15.68	14.32	13.13	12.09	11.16	10.34	9.604	8.950	8.365	7.839	7.366	6.938	6.550	6.198
20	18.05	16.35	14.88	13.59	12.46	11.47	10.59	9.818	9.129	8.514	7.963	7.469	7.025	6.623	6.259
25	22.02	19.52	17.41	15.62	14.09	12.78	11.65	10.67	9.823	9.077	8.422	7.843	7.330	6.873	6.464
30	25.81	22.40	19.60	17.29	15.37	13.76	12.41	11.26	10.27	9.427	8.694	8.055	7.496	7.003	6.566

Interest rate per year

Number of years	16%	17%	18%	19%	20%	21%	22%	23%	24%	25%	26%	27%	28%	29%	30%
1	.862	.855	.847	.840	.833	.826	.820	.813	.806	.800	.794	.787	.781	.775	.769
2	1.605	1.585	1.566	1.547	1.528	1.509	1.492	1.474	1.457	1.440	1.424	1.407	1.392	1.376	1.361
3	2.246	2.210	2.174	2.140	2.106	2.074	2.042	2.011	1.981	1.952	1.923	1.896	1.868	1.842	1.816
4	2.798	2.743	2.690	2.639	2.589	2.540	2.494	2.448	2.404	2.362	2.320	2.280	2.241	2.203	2.166
5	3.274	3.199	3.127	3.058	2.991	2.926	2.864	2.803	2.745	2.689	2.635	2.583	2.532	2.483	2.436
6	3.685	3.589	3.498	3.410	3.326	3.245	3.167	3.092	3.020	2.951	2.885	2.821	2.759	2.700	2.643
7	4.039	3.922	3.812	3.706	3.605	3.508	3.416	3.327	3.242	3.161	3.083	3.009	2.937	2.868	2.802
8	4.344	4.207	4.078	3.954	3.837	3.726	3.619	3.518	3.421	3.329	3.241	3.156	3.076	2.999	2.925
9	4.607	4.451	4.303	4.163	4.031	3.905	3.786	3.673	3.566	3.463	3.366	3.273	3.184	3.100	3.019
10	4.833	4.659	4.494	4.339	4.192	4.054	3.923	3.799	3.682	3.571	3.465	3.364	3.269	3.178	3.092
11	5.029	4.836	4.656	4.486	4.327	4.177	4.035	3.902	3.776	3.656	3.543	3.437	3.335	3.239	3.147
12	5.197	4.988	4.793	4.611	4.439	4.278	4.127	3.985	3.851	3.725	3.606	3.493	3.387	3.286	3.190
13	5.342	5.118	4.910	4.715	4.533	4.362	4.203	4.053	3.912	3.780	3.656	3.538	3.427	3.322	3.223
14	5.468	5.229	5.008	4.802	4.611	4.432	4.265	4.108	3.962	3.824	3.695	3.573	3.459	3.351	3.249
15	5.575	5.324	5.092	4.876	4.675	4.489	4.315	4.153	4.001	3.859	3.726	3.601	3.483	3.373	3.268
16	5.668	5.405	5.162	4.938	4.730	4.536	4.357	4.189	4.033	3.887	3.751	3.623	3.503	3.390	3.283
17	5.749	5.475	5.222	4.990	4.775	4.576	4.391	4.219	4.059	3.910	3.771	3.640	3.518	3.403	3.295
18	5.818	5.534	5.273	5.033	4.812	4.608	4.419	4.243	4.080	3.928	3.786	3.654	3.529	3.413	3.304
19	5.877	5.584	5.316	5.070	4.843	4.635	4.442	4.263	4.097	3.942	3.799	3.664	3.539	3.421	3.311
20	5.929	5.628	5.353	5.101	4.870	4.657	4.460	4.279	4.110	3.954	3.808	3.673	3.546	3.427	3.316
25	6.097	5.766	5.467	5.195	4.948	4.721	4.514	4.323	4.147	3.985	3.834	3.694	3.564	3.442	3.329
30	6.177	5.829	5.517	5.235	4.979	4.746	4.534	4.339	4.160	3.995	3.842	3.701	3.569	3.447	3.332

E.g.: If the interest rate is 10 percent per year, the present value of $1 received in each of the next 5 years is $3.791.

APPENDIX TABLE 4

Values of e^{rt}: Future value of \$1 invested at a *continuously compounded* rate r for t years

rt	.00	.01	.02	.03	.04	.05	.06	.07	.08	.09
.00	1.000	1.010	1.020	1.030	1.041	1.051	1.062	1.073	1.083	1.094
.10	1.105	1.116	1.127	1.139	1.150	1.162	1.174	1.185	1.197	1.209
.20	1.221	1.234	1.246	1.259	1.271	1.284	1.297	1.310	1.323	1.336
.30	1.350	1.363	1.377	1.391	1.405	1.419	1.433	1.448	1.462	1.477
.40	1.492	1.507	1.522	1.537	1.553	1.568	1.584	1.600	1.616	1.632
.50	1.649	1.665	1.682	1.699	1.716	1.733	1.751	1.768	1.786	1.804
.60	1.822	1.840	1.859	1.878	1.896	1.916	1.935	1.954	1.974	1.994
.70	2.014	2.034	2.054	2.075	2.096	2.117	2.138	2.160	2.181	2.203
.80	2.226	2.248	2.271	2.293	2.316	2.340	2.363	2.387	2.411	2.435
.90	2.460	2.484	2.509	2.535	2.560	2.586	2.612	2.638	2.664	2.691
1.00	2.718	2.746	2.773	2.801	2.829	2.858	2.886	2.915	2.945	2.974
1.10	3.004	3.034	3.065	3.096	3.127	3.158	3.190	3.222	3.254	3.287
1.20	3.320	3.353	3.387	3.421	3.456	3.490	3.525	3.561	3.597	3.633
1.30	3.669	3.706	3.743	3.781	3.819	3.857	3.896	3.935	3.975	4.015
1.40	4.055	4.096	4.137	4.179	4.221	4.263	4.306	4.349	4.393	4.437
1.50	4.482	4.527	4.572	4.618	4.665	4.711	4.759	4.807	4.855	4.904
1.60	4.953	5.003	5.053	5.104	5.155	5.207	5.259	5.312	5.366	5.419
1.70	5.474	5.529	5.585	5.641	5.697	5.755	5.812	5.871	5.930	5.989
1.80	6.050	6.110	6.172	6.234	6.297	6.360	6.424	6.488	6.553	6.619
1.90	6.686	6.753	6.821	6.890	6.959	7.029	7.099	7.171	7.243	7.316

rt	.00	.01	.02	.03	.04	.05	.06	.07	.08	.09
2.00	7.389	7.463	7.538	7.614	7.691	7.768	7.846	7.925	8.004	8.085
2.10	8.166	8.248	8.331	8.415	8.499	8.585	8.671	8.758	8.846	8.935
2.20	9.025	9.116	9.207	9.300	9.393	9.488	9.583	9.679	9.777	9.875
2.30	9.974	10.07	10.18	10.28	10.38	10.49	10.59	10.70	10.80	10.91
2.40	11.02	11.13	11.25	11.36	11.47	11.59	11.70	11.82	11.94	12.06
2.50	12.18	12.30	12.43	12.55	12.68	12.81	12.94	13.07	13.20	13.33
2.60	13.46	13.60	13.74	13.87	14.01	14.15	14.30	14.44	14.59	14.73
2.70	14.88	15.03	15.18	15.33	15.49	15.64	15.80	15.96	16.12	16.28
2.80	16.44	16.61	16.78	16.95	17.12	17.29	17.46	17.64	17.81	17.99
2.90	18.17	18.36	18.54	18.73	18.92	19.11	19.30	19.49	19.69	19.89
3.00	20.09	20.29	20.49	20.70	20.91	21.12	21.33	21.54	21.76	21.98
3.10	22.20	22.42	22.65	22.87	23.10	23.34	23.57	23.81	24.05	24.29
3.20	24.53	24.78	25.03	25.28	25.53	25.79	26.05	26.31	26.58	26.84
3.30	27.11	27.39	27.66	27.94	28.22	28.50	28.79	29.08	29.37	29.67
3.40	29.96	30.27	30.57	30.88	31.19	31.50	31.82	32.14	32.46	32.79
3.50	33.12	33.45	33.78	34.12	34.47	34.81	35.16	35.52	35.87	36.23
3.60	36.60	36.97	37.34	37.71	38.09	38.47	38.86	39.25	39.65	40.04
3.70	40.45	40.85	41.26	41.68	42.10	42.52	42.95	43.38	43.82	44.26
3.80	44.70	45.15	45.60	46.06	46.53	46.99	47.47	47.94	48.42	48.91
3.90	49.40	49.90	50.40	50.91	51.42	51.94	52.46	52.98	53.52	54.05

E.g.: If the continuously compounded interest rate is 10 percent per year, the investment of $1 today will be worth $1.105 at year 1 and $1.221 at year 2.

APPENDIX TABLE 5

Present value of $1 per year received in a continuous stream for each of t years (discounted at an *annually compounded* rate r) $= \{1 - 1/(1 + r)^t\}/\{\ln(1 + r)\}$

Number of years	1%	2%	3%	4%	5%	6%	7%	8%	9%	10%	11%	12%	13%	14%	15%
1	.995	.990	.985	.981	.976	.971	.967	.962	.958	.954	.950	.945	.941	.937	.933
2	1.980	1.961	1.942	1.924	1.906	1.888	1.871	1.854	1.837	1.821	1.805	1.790	1.774	1.759	1.745
3	2.956	2.913	2.871	2.830	2.791	2.752	2.715	2.679	2.644	2.609	2.576	2.543	2.512	2.481	2.450
4	3.922	3.846	3.773	3.702	3.634	3.568	3.504	3.443	3.383	3.326	3.270	3.216	3.164	3.113	3.064
5	4.878	4.760	4.648	4.540	4.437	4.337	4.242	4.150	4.062	3.977	3.896	3.817	3.741	3.668	3.598
6	5.825	5.657	5.498	5.346	5.202	5.063	4.931	4.805	4.685	4.570	4.459	4.353	4.252	4.155	4.062
7	6.762	6.536	6.323	6.121	5.930	5.748	5.576	5.412	5.256	5.108	4.967	4.832	4.704	4.582	4.465
8	7.690	7.398	7.124	6.867	6.623	6.394	6.178	5.974	5.780	5.597	5.424	5.260	5.104	4.956	4.816
9	8.609	8.243	7.902	7.583	7.284	7.004	6.741	6.494	6.261	6.042	5.836	5.642	5.458	5.285	5.121
10	9.519	9.072	8.657	8.272	7.913	7.579	7.267	6.975	6.702	6.447	6.208	5.983	5.772	5.573	5.386
11	10.42	9.884	9.391	8.935	8.512	8.121	7.758	7.421	7.107	6.815	6.542	6.287	6.049	5.826	5.617
12	11.31	10.68	10.10	9.572	9.083	8.633	8.218	7.834	7.478	7.149	6.843	6.559	6.294	6.048	5.818
13	12.19	11.46	10.79	10.18	9.627	9.116	8.647	8.216	7.819	7.453	7.115	6.802	6.512	6.242	5.992
14	13.07	12.23	11.46	10.77	10.14	9.571	9.048	8.570	8.131	7.729	7.359	7.018	6.704	6.413	6.144
15	13.93	12.98	12.12	11.34	10.64	10.00	9.423	8.897	8.418	7.980	7.579	7.212	6.874	6.563	6.276
16	14.79	13.71	12.75	11.88	11.11	10.41	9.774	9.201	8.681	8.209	7.778	7.385	7.024	6.694	6.390
17	15.64	14.43	13.36	12.41	11.55	10.79	10.10	9.482	8.923	8.416	7.957	7.539	7.158	6.809	6.490
18	16.48	15.14	13.96	12.91	11.98	11.15	10.41	9.742	9.144	8.605	8.118	7.676	7.275	6.910	6.577
19	17.31	15.83	14.54	13.39	12.39	11.49	10.69	9.983	9.347	8.777	8.263	7.799	7.380	6.999	6.652
20	18.14	16.51	15.10	13.86	12.77	11.81	10.96	10.21	9.533	8.932	8.394	7.909	7.472	7.077	6.718
25	22.13	19.72	17.67	15.93	14.44	13.16	12.06	11.10	10.26	9.524	8.877	8.305	7.797	7.344	6.938
30	25.94	22.62	19.89	17.64	15.75	14.17	12.84	11.70	10.73	9.891	9.164	8.529	7.973	7.482	7.047

Interest rate per year

Number of years	16%	17%	18%	19%	20%	21%	22%	23%	24%	25%	26%	27%	28%	29%	30%
1	.929	.925	.922	.918	.914	.910	.907	.903	.900	.896	.893	.889	.886	.883	.880
2	1.730	1.716	1.703	1.689	1.676	1.663	1.650	1.638	1.625	1.613	1.601	1.590	1.578	1.567	1.556
3	2.421	2.392	2.365	2.337	2.311	2.285	2.259	2.235	2.211	2.187	2.164	2.141	2.119	2.098	2.077
4	3.016	2.970	2.925	2.882	2.840	2.799	2.759	2.720	2.682	2.646	2.610	2.576	2.542	2.509	2.477
5	3.530	3.464	3.401	3.340	3.281	3.223	3.168	3.115	3.063	3.013	2.964	2.917	2.872	2.828	2.785
6	3.972	3.886	3.804	3.724	3.648	3.574	3.504	3.436	3.370	3.307	3.246	3.187	3.130	3.075	3.022
7	4.354	4.247	4.145	4.048	3.954	3.865	3.779	3.696	3.617	3.542	3.469	3.399	3.331	3.266	3.204
8	4.682	4.555	4.434	4.319	4.209	4.104	4.004	3.909	3.817	3.730	3.646	3.566	3.489	3.415	3.344
9	4.966	4.819	4.680	4.547	4.422	4.302	4.189	4.081	3.978	3.880	3.786	3.697	3.612	3.530	3.452
10	5.210	5.044	4.887	4.739	4.599	4.466	4.340	4.221	4.108	4.000	3.898	3.801	3.708	3.619	3.535
11	5.421	5.237	5.063	4.900	4.747	4.602	4.465	4.335	4.213	4.096	3.986	3.882	3.783	3.689	3.599
12	5.603	5.401	5.213	5.036	4.870	4.713	4.566	4.428	4.297	4.173	4.057	3.946	3.841	3.742	3.648
13	5.759	5.542	5.339	5.150	4.972	4.806	4.650	4.503	4.365	4.235	4.112	3.997	3.887	3.784	3.686
14	5.894	5.662	5.446	5.245	5.058	4.882	4.718	4.564	4.420	4.284	4.157	4.036	3.923	3.816	3.715
15	6.010	5.765	5.537	5.326	5.129	4.945	4.774	4.614	4.464	4.324	4.192	4.068	3.951	3.841	3.737
16	6.111	5.853	5.614	5.393	5.188	4.998	4.820	4.655	4.500	4.355	4.220	4.092	3.973	3.860	3.754
17	6.197	5.928	5.679	5.450	5.238	5.041	4.858	4.687	4.529	4.381	4.242	4.112	3.990	3.875	3.767
18	6.272	5.992	5.735	5.498	5.279	5.076	4.889	4.714	4.552	4.401	4.259	4.127	4.003	3.887	3.778
19	6.336	6.047	5.781	5.538	5.313	5.106	4.914	4.736	4.571	4.417	4.273	4.139	4.014	3.896	3.785
20	6.391	6.094	5.821	5.571	5.342	5.130	4.935	4.754	4.586	4.430	4.284	4.149	4.022	3.903	3.791
25	6.573	6.244	5.945	5.674	5.427	5.201	4.994	4.803	4.627	4.464	4.314	4.173	4.042	3.920	3.806
30	6.659	6.312	6.000	5.718	5.462	5.229	5.016	4.821	4.641	4.476	4.323	4.181	4.048	3.925	3.810

E.g.: If the interest rate is 10 percent per year, a continuous cash flow of $1 a year for each of 5 years is worth $3.977. A continuous flow of $1 in year 5 only is worth $3.977 − $3.326 = $.651.

APPENDIX TABLE 6

Call option values, percent of share price

SHARE PRICE DIVIDED BY PV (EXERCISE PRICE)

	.40	.45	.50	.55	.60	.65	.70	.75	.80	.82	.84	.86	.88	.90	.92	.94	.96	.98	1.00
.05	.0	.0	.0	.0	.0	.0	.0	.0	.0	.0	.0	.0	.0	.0	.1	.3	.6	1.2	2.0
.10	.0	.0	.0	.0	.0	.0	.0	.0	.0	.1	.2	.3	.5	.8	1.2	1.7	2.3	3.1	4.0
.15	.0	.0	.0	.0	.0	.0	.1	.2	.5	.7	1.0	1.3	1.7	2.2	2.8	3.5	4.2	5.1	6.0
.20	.0	.0	.0	.0	.0	.1	.4	.8	1.5	1.9	2.3	2.8	3.4	4.0	4.7	5.4	6.2	7.1	8.0
.25	.0	.0	.0	.1	.2	.5	1.0	1.8	2.8	3.3	3.9	4.5	5.2	5.9	6.6	7.4	8.2	9.1	9.9
.30	.0	.1	.1	.3	.7	1.2	2.0	3.1	4.4	5.0	5.7	6.3	7.0	7.8	8.6	9.4	10.2	11.1	11.9
.35	.1	.2	.4	.8	1.4	2.3	3.3	4.6	6.2	6.8	7.5	8.2	9.0	9.8	10.6	11.4	12.2	13.0	13.9
.40	.2	.5	.9	1.6	2.4	3.5	4.8	6.3	8.0	8.7	9.4	10.2	11.0	11.7	12.5	13.4	14.2	15.0	15.9
.45	.5	1.0	1.7	2.6	3.7	5.0	6.5	8.1	9.9	10.6	11.4	12.2	12.9	13.7	14.5	15.3	16.2	17.0	17.8
.50	1.0	1.7	2.6	3.7	5.1	6.6	8.2	10.0	11.8	12.6	13.4	14.2	14.9	15.7	16.5	17.3	18.1	18.9	19.7
.55	1.7	2.6	3.8	5.1	6.6	8.3	10.0	11.9	13.8	14.6	15.4	16.1	16.9	17.7	18.5	19.3	20.1	20.9	21.7
.60	2.5	3.7	5.1	6.6	8.3	10.1	11.9	13.8	15.8	16.6	17.4	18.1	18.9	19.7	20.5	21.3	22.0	22.8	23.6
.65	3.6	4.9	6.5	8.2	10.0	11.9	13.8	15.8	17.8	18.6	19.3	20.1	20.9	21.7	22.5	23.2	24.0	24.7	25.5
.70	4.7	6.3	8.1	9.9	11.9	13.8	15.8	17.8	19.8	20.6	21.3	22.1	22.9	23.6	24.4	25.2	25.9	26.6	27.4
.75	6.1	7.9	9.8	11.7	13.7	15.8	17.8	19.8	21.8	22.5	23.3	24.1	24.8	25.6	26.3	27.1	27.8	28.5	29.2
.80	7.5	9.5	11.5	13.6	15.7	17.7	19.8	21.8	23.7	24.5	25.3	26.0	26.8	27.5	28.3	29.0	29.7	30.4	31.1
.85	9.1	11.2	13.3	15.5	17.6	19.7	21.8	23.8	25.7	26.5	27.2	28.0	28.7	29.4	30.2	30.9	31.6	32.2	32.9
.90	10.7	13.0	15.2	17.4	19.6	21.7	23.8	25.8	27.7	28.4	29.2	29.9	30.6	31.3	32.0	32.7	33.4	34.1	34.7
.95	12.5	14.8	17.1	19.4	21.6	23.7	25.7	27.7	29.6	30.4	31.1	31.8	32.5	33.2	33.9	34.6	35.2	35.9	36.5
1.00	14.3	16.7	19.1	21.4	23.6	25.7	27.7	29.7	31.6	32.3	33.0	33.7	34.4	35.1	35.7	36.4	37.0	37.7	38.3
1.05	16.1	18.6	21.0	23.3	25.6	27.7	29.7	31.6	33.5	34.2	34.9	35.6	36.2	36.9	37.6	38.2	38.8	39.4	40.0
1.10	18.0	20.6	23.0	25.3	27.5	29.6	31.6	33.5	35.4	36.1	36.7	37.4	38.1	38.7	39.3	40.0	40.6	41.2	41.8
1.15	20.0	22.5	25.0	27.3	29.5	31.6	33.6	35.4	37.2	37.9	38.6	39.2	39.9	40.5	41.1	41.7	42.3	42.9	43.5
1.20	21.9	24.5	27.0	29.3	31.5	33.6	35.5	37.3	39.1	39.7	40.4	41.0	41.7	42.3	42.9	43.5	44.0	44.6	45.1
1.25	23.9	26.5	29.0	31.3	33.5	35.5	37.4	39.2	40.9	41.5	42.2	42.8	43.4	44.0	44.6	45.2	45.7	46.3	46.8
1.30	25.9	28.5	31.0	33.3	35.4	37.4	39.3	41.0	42.7	43.3	43.9	44.5	45.1	45.7	46.3	46.8	47.4	47.9	48.4
1.35	27.9	30.5	33.0	35.2	37.3	39.3	41.1	42.8	44.4	45.1	45.7	46.3	46.8	47.4	47.9	48.5	49.0	49.5	50.0
1.40	29.9	32.5	34.9	37.1	39.2	41.1	42.9	44.6	46.2	46.8	47.4	47.9	48.5	49.0	49.6	50.1	50.6	51.1	51.6
1.45	31.9	34.5	36.9	39.1	41.1	43.0	44.7	46.4	47.9	48.5	49.0	49.6	50.1	50.7	51.2	51.7	52.2	52.7	53.2
1.50	33.8	36.4	38.8	40.9	42.9	44.8	46.5	48.1	49.6	50.1	50.7	51.2	51.8	52.3	52.8	53.3	53.7	54.2	54.7
1.55	35.8	38.4	40.7	42.8	44.8	46.6	48.2	49.8	51.2	51.8	52.3	52.8	53.3	53.8	54.3	54.8	55.3	55.7	56.2
1.60	37.8	40.3	42.6	44.6	46.5	48.3	49.9	51.4	52.8	53.4	53.9	54.4	54.9	55.4	55.9	56.3	56.8	57.2	57.6
1.65	39.7	42.2	44.4	46.4	48.3	50.0	51.6	53.1	54.4	54.9	55.4	55.9	56.4	56.9	57.3	57.8	58.2	58.6	59.1
1.70	41.6	44.0	46.2	48.2	50.0	51.7	53.2	54.7	56.0	56.5	57.0	57.5	57.9	58.4	58.8	59.2	59.7	60.1	60.5
1.75	43.5	45.9	48.0	50.0	51.7	53.4	54.8	56.2	57.5	58.0	58.5	58.9	59.4	59.8	60.2	60.7	61.1	61.5	61.8
2.00	52.5	54.6	56.5	58.2	59.7	61.1	62.4	63.6	64.6	65.0	65.4	65.8	66.2	66.6	66.9	67.3	67.6	67.9	68.3
2.25	60.7	62.5	64.1	65.6	66.8	68.0	69.1	70.0	70.9	71.3	71.6	71.9	72.2	72.5	72.8	73.1	73.4	73.7	73.9
2.50	67.9	69.4	70.8	72.0	73.1	74.0	74.9	75.7	76.4	76.7	77.0	77.2	77.5	77.7	78.0	78.2	78.4	78.7	78.9
2.75	74.2	75.4	76.6	77.5	78.4	79.2	79.9	80.5	81.1	81.4	81.6	81.8	82.0	82.2	82.4	82.6	82.7	82.9	83.1
3.00	79.5	80.5	81.4	82.2	82.9	83.5	84.1	84.6	85.1	85.3	85.4	85.6	85.8	85.9	86.1	86.2	86.4	86.5	86.6
3.50	87.6	88.3	88.8	89.3	89.7	90.1	90.5	90.8	91.1	91.2	91.3	91.4	91.5	91.6	91.6	91.7	91.8	91.9	92.0
4.00	92.9	93.3	93.6	93.9	94.2	94.4	94.6	94.8	94.9	95.0	95.0	95.1	95.2	95.2	95.3	95.3	95.4	95.4	95.4
4.50	96.2	96.4	96.6	96.7	96.9	97.0	97.1	97.2	97.3	97.3	97.3	97.4	97.4	97.4	97.5	97.5	97.5	97.5	97.6
5.00	98.1	98.2	98.3	98.3	98.4	98.5	98.5	98.6	98.6	98.6	98.6	98.7	98.7	98.7	98.7	98.7	98.7	98.7	98.8

STANDARD DEVIATION TIMES SQUARE ROOT OF TIME

Note: Based on Black-Scholes model. To obtain corresponding European put values, add present value of exercise price and subtract share price.

SHARE PRICE DIVIDED BY PV (EXERCISE PRICE)

1.02	1.04	1.06	1.08	1.10	1.12	1.14	1.16	1.18	1.20	1.25	1.30	1.35	1.40	1.45	1.50	1.75	2.00	2.50	
3.1	4.5	6.0	7.5	9.1	10.7	12.3	13.8	15.3	16.7	20.0	23.1	25.9	28.6	31.0	33.3	42.9	50.0	60.0	.05
5.0	6.1	7.3	8.6	10.0	11.3	12.7	14.1	15.4	16.8	20.0	23.1	25.9	28.6	31.0	33.3	42.9	50.0	60.0	.10
7.0	8.0	9.1	10.2	11.4	12.6	13.8	15.0	16.2	17.4	20.4	23.3	26.0	28.6	31.1	33.3	42.9	50.0	60.0	.15
8.9	9.9	10.9	11.9	13.0	14.1	15.2	16.3	17.4	18.5	21.2	23.9	26.4	28.9	31.2	33.5	42.9	50.0	60.0	.20
10.9	11.8	12.8	13.7	14.7	15.7	16.7	17.7	18.7	19.8	22.3	24.7	27.1	29.4	31.7	33.8	42.9	50.0	60.0	.25
12.8	13.7	14.6	15.6	16.5	17.4	18.4	19.3	20.3	21.2	23.5	25.8	28.1	30.2	32.3	34.3	43.1	50.1	60.0	.30
14.8	15.6	16.5	17.4	18.3	19.2	20.1	21.0	21.9	22.7	24.9	27.1	29.2	31.2	33.2	35.1	43.5	50.2	60.0	.35
16.7	17.5	18.4	19.2	20.1	20.9	21.8	22.6	23.5	24.3	26.4	28.4	30.4	32.3	34.2	36.0	44.0	50.5	60.1	.40
18.6	19.4	20.3	21.1	21.9	22.7	23.5	24.3	25.1	25.9	27.9	29.8	31.7	33.5	35.3	37.0	44.6	50.8	60.2	.45
20.5	21.3	22.1	22.9	23.7	24.5	25.3	26.1	26.8	27.6	29.5	31.3	33.1	34.8	36.4	38.1	45.3	51.3	60.4	.50
22.4	23.2	24.0	24.8	25.5	26.3	27.0	27.8	28.5	29.2	31.0	32.8	34.5	36.1	37.7	39.2	46.1	51.9	60.7	.55
24.3	25.1	25.8	26.6	27.3	28.1	28.8	29.5	30.2	30.9	32.6	34.3	35.9	37.5	39.0	40.4	47.0	52.5	61.0	.60
26.2	27.0	27.7	28.4	29.1	29.8	30.5	31.2	31.9	32.6	34.2	35.8	37.4	38.9	40.3	41.7	48.0	53.3	61.4	.65
28.1	28.8	29.5	30.2	30.9	31.6	32.3	32.9	33.6	34.2	35.8	37.3	38.8	40.3	41.6	43.0	49.0	54.0	61.9	.70
29.9	30.6	31.3	32.0	32.7	33.3	34.0	34.6	35.3	35.9	37.4	38.9	40.3	41.7	43.0	44.3	50.0	54.9	62.4	.75
31.8	32.4	33.1	33.8	34.4	35.1	35.7	36.3	36.9	37.5	39.0	40.4	41.8	43.1	44.4	45.6	51.1	55.8	63.0	.80
33.6	34.2	34.9	35.5	36.2	36.8	37.4	38.0	38.6	39.2	40.6	41.9	43.3	44.5	45.8	46.9	52.2	56.7	63.6	.85
35.4	36.0	36.6	37.3	37.9	38.5	39.1	39.6	40.2	40.8	42.1	43.5	44.7	46.0	47.1	48.3	53.3	57.6	64.3	.90
37.2	37.8	38.4	39.0	39.6	40.1	40.7	41.3	41.8	42.4	43.7	45.0	46.2	47.4	48.5	49.6	54.5	58.6	65.0	.95
38.9	39.5	40.1	40.7	41.2	41.8	42.4	42.9	43.4	44.0	45.2	46.5	47.6	48.8	49.9	50.9	55.6	59.5	65.7	1.00
40.6	41.2	41.8	42.4	42.9	43.5	44.0	44.5	45.0	45.5	46.8	48.0	49.1	50.2	51.2	52.2	56.7	60.5	66.5	1.05
42.3	42.9	43.5	44.0	44.5	45.1	45.6	46.1	46.6	47.1	48.3	49.4	50.5	51.6	52.6	53.5	57.9	61.5	67.2	1.10
44.0	44.6	45.1	45.6	46.2	46.7	47.2	47.7	48.2	48.6	49.8	50.9	51.9	52.9	53.9	54.9	59.0	62.5	68.0	1.15
45.7	46.2	46.7	47.3	47.8	48.3	48.7	49.2	49.7	50.1	51.3	52.3	53.3	54.3	55.2	56.1	60.2	63.5	68.8	1.20
47.3	47.8	48.4	48.8	49.3	49.8	50.3	50.7	51.2	51.6	52.7	53.7	54.7	55.7	56.6	57.4	61.3	64.5	69.6	1.25
48.9	49.4	49.9	50.4	50.9	51.3	51.8	52.2	52.7	53.1	54.1	55.1	56.1	57.0	57.9	58.7	62.4	65.5	70.4	1.30
50.5	51.0	51.5	52.0	52.4	52.9	53.3	53.7	54.1	54.6	55.6	56.5	57.4	58.3	59.1	59.9	63.5	66.5	71.1	1.35
52.1	52.6	53.0	53.5	53.9	54.3	54.8	55.2	55.6	56.0	56.9	57.9	58.7	59.6	60.4	61.2	64.6	67.5	71.9	1.40
53.6	54.1	54.5	55.0	55.4	55.8	56.2	56.6	57.0	57.4	58.3	59.2	60.0	60.9	61.6	62.4	65.7	68.4	72.7	1.45
55.1	55.6	56.0	56.4	56.8	57.2	57.6	58.0	58.4	58.8	59.7	60.5	61.3	62.1	62.9	63.6	66.8	69.4	73.5	1.50
56.6	57.0	57.4	57.8	58.2	58.6	59.0	59.4	59.7	60.1	61.0	61.8	62.6	63.3	64.1	64.7	67.8	70.3	74.3	1.55
58.0	58.5	58.9	59.2	59.6	60.0	60.4	60.7	61.1	61.4	62.3	63.1	63.8	64.5	65.2	65.9	68.8	71.3	75.1	1.60
59.5	59.9	60.2	60.6	61.0	61.4	61.7	62.1	62.4	62.7	63.5	64.3	65.0	65.7	66.4	67.0	69.9	72.2	75.9	1.65
60.9	61.2	61.6	62.0	62.3	62.7	63.0	63.4	63.7	64.0	64.8	65.5	66.2	66.9	67.5	68.2	70.9	73.1	76.6	1.70
62.2	62.6	62.9	63.3	63.6	64.0	64.3	64.6	64.9	65.3	66.0	66.7	67.4	68.0	68.7	69.2	71.9	74.0	77.4	1.75
68.6	68.9	69.2	69.5	69.8	70.0	70.3	70.6	70.8	71.1	71.7	72.3	72.9	73.4	73.9	74.4	76.5	78.3	81.0	2.00
74.2	74.4	74.7	74.9	75.2	75.4	75.6	75.8	76.0	76.3	76.8	77.2	77.7	78.1	78.5	78.9	80.6	82.1	84.3	2.25
79.1	79.3	79.5	79.7	79.9	80.0	80.2	80.4	80.6	80.7	81.1	81.5	81.9	82.2	82.6	82.9	84.3	85.4	87.2	2.50
83.3	83.4	83.6	83.7	83.9	84.0	84.2	84.3	84.4	84.6	84.9	85.2	85.5	85.8	86.0	86.3	87.4	88.3	89.7	2.75
86.8	86.9	87.0	87.1	87.3	87.4	87.5	87.6	87.7	87.8	88.1	88.3	88.5	88.8	89.0	89.2	90.0	90.7	91.8	3.00
92.1	92.1	92.2	92.3	92.4	92.4	92.5	92.6	92.6	92.7	92.8	93.0	93.1	93.3	93.4	93.5	94.0	94.4	95.1	3.50
95.5	95.5	95.6	95.6	95.7	95.7	95.7	95.8	95.8	95.8	95.9	96.0	96.1	96.2	96.2	96.3	96.6	96.8	97.2	4.00
97.6	97.6	97.6	97.6	97.7	97.7	97.7	97.7	97.8	97.8	97.8	97.9	97.9	97.9	98.0	98.0	98.2	98.3	98.5	4.50
98.8	98.8	98.8	98.8	98.8	98.8	98.8	98.8	98.9	98.9	98.9	98.9	98.9	99.0	99.0	99.0	99.1	99.1	99.2	5.00

STANDARD DEVIATION TIMES SQUARE ROOT OF TIME

Hedge ratios for call options, percent of share price

SHARE PRICE DIVIDED BY PV (EXERCISE PRICE)

	.40	.45	.50	.55	.60	.65	.70	.75	.80	.82	.84	.86	.88	.90	.92	.94	.96	.98	1.00
.05	.0	.0	.0	.0	.0	.0	.0	.0	.0	.0	.0	.1	.6	1.9	5.0	11.3	21.4	35.2	51.0
.10	.0	.0	.0	.0	.0	.0	.0	.2	1.5	2.7	4.5	7.2	11.0	15.8	21.7	28.5	36.0	44.0	52.0
.15	.0	.0	.0	.0	.0	.3	1.1	3.3	7.9	10.6	13.8	17.6	21.9	26.5	31.5	36.8	42.2	47.6	53.0
.20	.0	.0	.0	.2	.7	2.0	4.6	9.0	15.5	18.6	22.0	25.7	29.5	33.5	37.6	41.7	45.9	50.0	54.0
.25	.0	.1	.4	1.2	2.8	5.5	9.7	15.3	22.1	25.2	28.4	31.6	35.0	38.3	41.7	45.1	48.5	51.8	55.0
.30	.2	.6	1.5	3.3	6.0	9.9	14.9	20.9	27.6	30.4	33.3	36.2	39.1	42.0	44.9	47.8	50.6	53.3	56.0
.35	.7	1.8	3.6	6.3	9.9	14.6	19.9	25.9	32.2	34.8	37.3	39.9	42.5	45.0	47.5	49.9	52.3	54.7	56.9
.40	1.8	3.6	6.3	9.8	14.1	19.0	24.5	30.2	36.0	38.4	40.7	43.0	45.2	47.5	49.7	51.8	53.9	55.9	57.9
.45	3.5	6.1	9.4	13.5	18.1	23.2	28.5	33.9	39.3	41.4	43.5	45.6	47.6	49.6	51.6	53.5	55.3	57.1	58.9
.50	5.7	8.9	12.8	17.2	22.0	27.0	32.2	37.2	42.2	44.2	46.1	47.9	49.8	51.6	53.3	55.0	56.7	58.3	59.9
.55	8.2	12.0	16.2	20.8	25.7	30.6	35.4	40.2	44.8	46.6	48.3	50.0	51.7	53.3	54.9	56.5	58.0	59.4	60.8
.60	11.0	15.1	19.6	24.3	29.1	33.8	38.4	42.9	47.1	48.8	50.4	51.9	53.5	55.0	56.4	57.8	59.2	60.5	61.8
.65	13.9	18.3	22.9	27.6	32.2	36.8	41.1	45.3	49.3	50.8	52.3	53.7	55.1	56.5	57.8	59.1	60.3	61.6	62.7
.70	16.9	21.5	26.1	30.7	35.2	39.5	43.7	47.6	51.2	52.7	54.0	55.4	56.6	57.9	59.1	60.3	61.5	62.6	63.7
.75	19.9	24.5	29.1	33.6	38.0	42.1	46.0	49.7	53.1	54.4	55.7	56.9	58.1	59.3	60.4	61.5	62.6	63.6	64.6
.80	22.8	27.5	32.0	36.4	40.6	44.5	48.2	51.6	54.8	56.0	57.2	58.4	59.5	60.6	61.6	62.7	63.6	64.6	65.5
.85	25.7	30.3	34.8	39.0	43.0	46.7	50.2	53.4	56.5	57.6	58.7	59.8	60.8	61.8	62.8	63.8	64.7	65.6	66.5
.90	28.5	33.1	37.4	41.5	45.3	48.9	52.1	55.2	58.0	59.1	60.1	61.1	62.1	63.0	64.0	64.8	65.7	66.6	67.4
.95	31.2	35.7	40.0	43.9	47.5	50.9	54.0	56.8	59.5	60.5	61.5	62.4	63.3	64.2	65.1	65.9	66.7	67.5	68.3
1.00	33.9	38.3	42.3	46.1	49.6	52.8	55.7	58.4	60.9	61.9	62.8	63.7	64.5	65.3	66.2	66.9	67.7	68.4	69.1
1.05	36.4	40.7	44.6	48.2	51.5	54.6	57.4	59.9	62.3	63.2	64.0	64.9	65.7	66.4	67.2	67.9	68.7	69.3	70.0
1.10	38.9	43.0	46.8	50.3	53.4	56.3	58.9	61.4	63.6	64.4	65.2	66.0	66.8	67.5	68.2	68.9	69.6	70.3	70.9
1.15	41.2	45.2	48.9	52.2	55.2	57.9	60.4	62.7	64.8	65.6	66.4	67.1	67.9	68.6	69.2	69.9	70.5	71.1	71.7
1.20	43.5	47.4	50.9	54.1	56.9	59.5	61.9	64.1	66.1	66.8	67.5	68.2	68.9	69.6	70.2	70.8	71.4	72.0	72.6
1.25	45.7	49.4	52.8	55.8	58.6	61.0	63.3	65.4	67.2	67.9	68.6	69.3	69.9	70.6	71.2	71.8	72.3	72.9	73.4
1.30	47.8	51.4	54.6	57.5	60.1	62.5	64.6	66.6	68.4	69.1	69.7	70.3	70.9	71.5	72.1	72.7	73.2	73.7	74.2
1.35	49.9	53.3	56.4	59.2	61.7	63.9	65.9	67.8	69.5	70.1	70.7	71.3	71.9	72.5	73.0	73.5	74.0	74.5	75.0
1.40	51.8	55.2	58.1	60.8	63.1	65.3	67.2	69.0	70.6	71.2	71.8	72.3	72.9	73.4	73.9	74.4	74.9	75.4	75.8
1.45	53.7	56.9	59.8	62.3	64.5	66.6	68.4	70.1	71.6	72.2	72.7	73.3	73.8	74.3	74.8	75.2	75.7	76.1	76.6
1.50	55.5	58.6	61.3	63.7	65.9	67.8	69.6	71.2	72.6	73.2	73.7	74.2	74.7	75.2	75.6	76.1	76.5	76.9	77.3
1.55	57.3	60.3	62.8	65.1	67.2	69.0	70.7	72.2	73.6	74.1	74.6	75.1	75.6	76.0	76.5	76.9	77.3	77.7	78.1
1.60	59.0	61.8	64.3	66.5	68.5	70.2	71.8	73.2	74.6	75.0	75.5	76.0	76.4	76.9	77.3	77.7	78.1	78.4	78.8
1.65	60.6	63.3	65.7	67.8	69.7	71.4	72.9	74.2	75.5	76.0	76.4	76.8	77.3	77.7	78.1	78.5	78.8	79.2	79.5
1.70	62.2	64.8	67.1	69.1	70.9	72.5	73.9	75.2	76.4	76.8	77.3	77.7	78.1	78.5	78.8	79.2	79.6	79.9	80.2
1.75	63.7	66.2	68.4	70.3	72.0	73.5	74.9	76.1	77.3	77.7	78.1	78.5	78.9	79.2	79.6	79.9	80.3	80.6	80.9
2.00	70.6	72.6	74.3	75.8	77.2	78.4	79.4	80.4	81.3	81.6	81.9	82.2	82.5	82.8	83.1	83.4	83.6	83.9	84.1
2.25	76.4	77.9	79.3	80.5	81.5	82.5	83.3	84.1	84.8	85.0	85.3	85.5	85.7	86.0	86.2	86.4	86.6	86.8	87.0
2.50	81.2	82.4	83.5	84.4	85.2	85.9	86.6	87.2	87.7	87.9	88.1	88.3	88.5	88.6	88.8	89.0	89.1	89.3	89.4
2.75	85.1	86.1	86.9	87.6	88.3	88.8	89.3	89.8	90.2	90.4	90.5	90.7	90.8	90.9	91.1	91.2	91.3	91.4	91.5
3.00	88.4	89.1	89.8	90.3	90.8	91.3	91.6	92.0	92.3	92.4	92.5	92.6	92.7	92.9	93.0	93.0	93.1	93.2	93.3
3.50	93.2	93.6	94.0	94.3	94.6	94.8	95.0	95.2	95.4	95.5	95.5	95.6	95.7	95.7	95.8	95.8	95.9	95.9	96.0
4.00	96.2	96.4	96.6	96.8	96.9	97.1	97.2	97.3	97.4	97.4	97.5	97.5	97.5	97.6	97.6	97.6	97.7	97.7	97.7
4.50	98.0	98.1	98.2	98.3	98.4	98.4	98.5	98.6	98.6	98.6	98.6	98.7	98.7	98.7	98.7	98.7	98.7	98.8	98.8
5.00	99.0	99.0	99.1	99.1	99.2	99.2	99.2	99.3	99.3	99.3	99.3	99.3	99.3	99.3	99.3	99.4	99.4	99.4	99.4

STANDARD DEVIATION TIMES SQUARE ROOT OF TIME

Note: Based on Black-Scholes model. Subtract 1.0 to obtain corresponding hedge ratios for European puts.

SHARE PRICE DIVIDED BY PV (EXERCISE PRICE)

1.02	1.04	1.06	1.08	1.10	1.12	1.14	1.16	1.18	1.20	1.25	1.30	1.35	1.40	1.45	1.50	1.75	2.00	2.50	
66.3	79.1	88.3	94.1	97.3	98.9	99.6	99.9	100.	100.	100.	100.	100.	100.	100.	100.	100.	100.	100.	.05
59.8	67.1	73.7	79.4	84.2	88.2	91.3	93.8	95.6	96.9	98.9	99.6	99.9	100.	100.	100.	100.	100.	100.	.10
58.2	63.2	67.8	72.2	76.1	79.7	82.9	85.6	88.1	90.2	94.1	96.6	98.1	99.0	99.5	99.7	100.	100.	100.	.15
57.9	61.6	65.2	68.6	71.8	74.8	77.5	80.0	82.3	84.4	88.8	92.1	94.5	96.3	97.5	98.3	99.8	100.	100.	.20
58.1	61.1	64.0	66.7	69.4	71.8	74.2	76.4	78.4	80.4	84.6	88.0	90.7	92.9	94.6	96.0	99.1	99.8	100.	.25
58.6	61.1	63.5	65.8	68.0	70.1	72.1	74.0	75.9	77.6	81.4	84.7	87.5	89.8	91.8	93.3	97.8	99.3	99.9	.30
59.2	61.3	63.4	65.4	67.3	69.1	70.9	72.5	74.1	75.7	79.2	82.2	84.9	87.2	89.2	90.9	96.2	98.4	99.7	.35
59.9	61.7	63.5	65.3	66.9	68.6	70.1	71.6	73.0	74.4	77.6	80.4	82.9	85.1	87.1	88.8	94.5	97.3	99.4	.40
60.6	62.3	63.9	65.4	66.9	68.3	69.7	71.0	72.3	73.6	76.5	79.0	81.4	83.5	85.3	87.0	92.9	96.1	98.8	.45
61.4	62.9	64.3	65.7	67.0	68.3	69.6	70.8	71.9	73.1	75.7	78.1	80.2	82.2	84.0	85.6	91.5	94.9	98.1	.50
62.2	63.5	64.8	66.1	67.3	68.5	69.6	70.7	71.8	72.8	75.2	77.4	79.4	81.2	82.9	84.4	90.2	93.8	97.4	.55
63.0	64.3	65.4	66.6	67.7	68.8	69.8	70.8	71.8	72.7	74.9	77.0	78.8	80.5	82.1	83.5	89.1	92.7	96.6	.60
63.9	65.0	66.1	67.1	68.1	69.1	70.1	71.0	71.9	72.8	74.8	76.7	78.4	80.0	81.5	82.9	88.2	91.8	95.9	.65
64.7	65.8	66.8	67.7	68.7	69.6	70.4	71.3	72.1	72.9	74.8	76.6	78.2	79.7	81.1	82.4	87.5	91.0	95.1	.70
65.6	66.5	67.5	68.4	69.2	70.1	70.9	71.7	72.4	73.2	74.9	76.6	78.1	79.5	80.8	82.0	86.9	90.3	94.5	.75
66.4	67.3	68.2	69.0	69.8	70.6	71.4	72.1	72.8	73.5	75.1	76.7	78.1	79.4	80.6	81.8	86.4	89.7	93.9	.80
67.3	68.1	68.9	69.7	70.4	71.2	71.9	72.6	73.2	73.9	75.4	76.8	78.2	79.4	80.6	81.6	86.1	89.3	93.4	.85
68.2	68.9	69.7	70.4	71.1	71.8	72.4	73.1	73.7	74.3	75.7	77.1	78.3	79.5	80.6	81.6	85.8	88.9	92.9	.90
69.0	69.7	70.4	71.1	71.7	72.4	73.0	73.6	74.2	74.8	76.1	77.4	78.5	79.6	80.7	81.6	85.6	88.6	92.5	.95
69.8	70.5	71.2	71.8	72.4	73.0	73.6	74.2	74.7	75.2	76.5	77.7	78.8	79.9	80.8	81.7	85.5	88.4	92.2	1.00
70.7	71.3	71.9	72.5	73.1	73.7	74.2	74.7	75.3	75.8	77.0	78.1	79.1	80.1	81.0	81.9	85.5	88.2	91.9	1.05
71.5	72.1	72.7	73.2	73.8	74.3	74.8	75.3	75.8	76.3	77.4	78.5	79.5	80.4	81.3	82.1	85.5	88.1	91.7	1.10
72.3	72.9	73.4	74.0	74.5	75.0	75.5	75.9	76.4	76.8	77.9	78.9	79.8	80.7	81.5	82.3	85.6	88.1	91.5	1.15
73.1	73.7	74.2	74.7	75.2	75.6	76.1	76.5	77.0	77.4	78.4	79.4	80.2	81.1	81.8	82.6	85.7	88.1	91.4	1.20
73.9	74.4	74.9	75.4	75.8	76.3	76.7	77.1	77.6	78.0	78.9	79.8	80.7	81.4	82.2	82.9	85.8	88.1	91.3	1.25
74.7	75.2	75.6	76.1	76.5	76.9	77.4	77.8	78.2	78.5	79.4	80.3	81.1	81.8	82.5	83.2	86.0	88.2	91.2	1.30
75.5	75.9	76.4	76.8	77.2	77.6	78.0	78.4	78.7	79.1	80.0	80.8	81.5	82.2	82.9	83.5	86.2	88.3	91.2	1.35
76.2	76.7	77.1	77.5	77.9	78.3	78.6	79.0	79.3	79.7	80.5	81.3	82.0	82.6	83.3	83.9	86.4	88.4	91.2	1.40
77.0	77.4	77.8	78.2	78.5	78.9	79.3	79.6	79.9	80.3	81.0	81.8	82.4	83.1	83.7	84.2	86.7	88.6	91.3	1.45
77.7	78.1	78.5	78.9	79.2	79.5	79.9	80.2	80.5	80.8	81.6	82.2	82.9	83.5	84.1	84.6	86.9	88.7	91.3	1.50
78.5	78.8	79.2	79.5	79.9	80.2	80.5	80.8	81.1	81.4	82.1	82.7	83.4	83.9	84.5	85.0	87.2	88.9	91.4	1.55
79.2	79.5	79.9	80.2	80.5	80.8	81.1	81.4	81.7	82.0	82.6	83.2	83.8	84.4	84.9	85.4	87.5	89.1	91.5	1.60
79.9	80.2	80.5	80.8	81.1	81.4	81.7	82.0	82.3	82.5	83.2	83.7	84.3	84.8	85.3	85.8	87.8	89.3	91.6	1.65
80.6	80.9	81.2	81.5	81.8	82.0	82.3	82.6	82.8	83.1	83.7	84.2	84.8	85.3	85.7	86.2	88.1	89.6	91.8	1.70
81.2	81.5	81.8	82.1	82.4	82.6	82.9	83.1	83.4	83.6	84.2	84.7	85.2	85.7	86.2	86.6	88.4	89.8	91.9	1.75
84.4	84.6	84.8	85.0	85.3	85.5	85.7	85.9	86.1	86.2	86.7	87.1	87.5	87.9	88.2	88.5	90.0	91.1	92.8	2.00
87.2	87.3	87.5	87.7	87.8	88.0	88.2	88.3	88.5	88.6	89.0	89.3	89.6	89.9	90.1	90.4	91.5	92.4	93.7	2.25
89.6	89.7	89.9	90.0	90.1	90.2	90.4	90.5	90.6	90.7	91.0	91.2	91.5	91.7	91.9	92.1	93.0	93.7	94.7	2.50
91.7	91.8	91.9	92.0	92.1	92.2	92.3	92.3	92.4	92.5	92.7	92.9	93.1	93.3	93.4	93.6	94.3	94.8	95.6	2.75
93.4	93.5	93.6	93.6	93.7	93.8	93.9	93.9	94.0	94.1	94.2	94.4	94.5	94.7	94.8	94.9	95.4	95.8	96.4	3.00
96.0	96.1	96.1	96.2	96.2	96.3	96.3	96.3	96.4	96.4	96.5	96.6	96.7	96.8	96.8	96.9	97.2	97.4	97.8	3.50
97.8	97.8	97.8	97.8	97.9	97.9	97.9	97.9	97.9	98.0	98.0	98.1	98.1	98.1	98.2	98.2	98.4	98.5	98.7	4.00
98.8	98.8	98.8	98.8	98.8	98.9	98.9	98.9	98.9	98.9	98.9	99.0	99.0	99.0	99.0	99.0	99.1	99.2	99.3	4.50
99.4	99.4	99.4	99.4	99.4	99.4	99.4	99.4	99.4	99.4	99.5	99.5	99.5	99.5	99.5	99.5	99.5	99.6	99.6	5.00

STANDARD DEVIATION TIMES SQUARE ROOT OF TIME

Glossary*

Abnormal return Part of return that is not due to systematic influences, e.g., marketwide price movements.

Absolute priority Rule in bankruptcy proceedings whereby senior creditors are required to be paid in full before junior creditors receive any payment.

Accelerated cost recovery system (ACRS) Schedule of *depreciation* rates allowed for tax purposes.

Accelerated depreciation Any *depreciation* method that produces larger deductions for depreciation in the early years of a project's life.

Accounts payable (*payables, trade debt**) Money owed to suppliers.

Accounts receivable (*receivables, trade credit*) Money owed by customers.

Accrued interest Interest that has been earned but not yet paid.

ACH *Automated Clearing House.*

Acid-test ratio *Quick ratio.*

ACRS *Accelerated cost recovery system.*

ACUs *Asian currency units.*

Adjusted present value (*APV*) *Net present value* of an asset if financed solely by equity, plus the *present value* of any financing side effects.

ADR *American depository receipt.*

Adverse selection A situation in which a pricing policy causes only the less desirable customers to do business, e.g., a rise in insurance prices that leads only the worst risks to buy insurance.

Agency theory Theory of the relationship between a principal, e.g., a shareholder, and an agent of the principal, e.g., the company's manager.

Aging schedule Record of the length of time that *accounts receivable* have been outstanding.

AIBD Association of International Bond Dealers.

*Italicized words are listed elsewhere in the glossary.

AIRS *Amortizing interest rate swap.*

All-or-none underwriting An arrangement whereby a security issue is canceled if the *underwriter* is unable to resell the entire issue.

American depository receipt (*ADR*) A security issued in the United States to represent shares of a foreign company.

American option *Option* that can be exercised any time before the final exercise date (cf. *European option*).

Amex American Stock Exchange.

Amortization (1) Repayment of a loan by installments; (2) allowance for *depreciation.*

Amortizing interest rate swap (*AIRS*) *Swap* in which the *principal* amount rises (declines) as interest rates rise (decline).

Annual percentage rate (*APR*) Annual interest rate calculated using *simple interest.*

Annuity Investment that produces a level stream of cash flows for a limited number of periods.

Annuity due *Annuity* whose payments occur at the start of each period.

Annuity factor *Present value* of $1 paid for each of t periods.

Anticipation Arrangements whereby customers who pay before the final date may be entitled to deduct a normal rate of interest.

Appraisal rights A right of shareholders in a *merger* to demand the payment of a fair price for their shares, as determined independently.

Appropriation request Formal request for funds for a capital investment project.

APR *Annual percentage rate.*

APT Arbitrage pricing theory.

APV *Adjusted present value.*

Arbitrage Purchase of one security and simultaneous sale of another to give a risk-free profit.

"Arbitrage" or "risk arbitrage" Often used loosely to describe the taking of offsetting positions in related securities, e.g., at the time of a takeover bid.

Articles of incorporation   Legal document establishing a corporation and its structure and purpose.

Asian currency units (*ACUs*)   Dollar deposits held in Singapore or other Asian centers.

Asian option   *Option* based on the average price of the asset during the life of the option.

Ask price (*offer price*)   Price at which a dealer is willing to sell (cf. *bid price*).

Auction-rate preferred   A variant of *floating-rate preferred* stock where the dividend is reset every 49 days by auction.

Authorized share capital   Maximum number of shares that a company can issue, as specified in the firm's articles of incorporation.

Automated Clearing House (*ACH*)   Private electronic system run by banks for high-volume, low-value payments.

Availability float   Checks deposited by a company that have not yet been cleared.

Aval   Bank guarantee for debt purchased by *forfaiter*.

BA   *Banker's acceptance.*

Backwardation   Condition in which *spot price* of commodity exceeds price of future.

Balloon payment   Large final payment (e.g., when a loan is repaid in installments).

Banker's acceptance (*BA*)   Written demand that has been accepted by a bank to pay a given sum at a future date (cf. *trade acceptance*).

Barrier option   *Option* whose existence depends on asset price hitting some specified barrier (cf. *down-and-out option, down-and-in option*).

Basis point   0.01 percent.

Basis risk   Residual risk that results when the two sides of a hedge do not move exactly together.

Bearer security   Security for which primary evidence of ownership is possession of the certificate (cf. *registered security*).

Bear market   Widespread decline in security prices (cf. *bull market*).

Benefit-cost ratio   One plus *profitability index.*

Best-efforts underwriting   An arrangement whereby *underwriters* do not commit themselves to selling a security issue but promise only to use best efforts.

Beta   Measure of *market risk.*

Bid price   Price at which a dealer is willing to buy (cf. *ask price*).

Bill of exchange   General term for a document demanding payment.

Bill of lading   Document establishing ownership of goods in transit.

Blue-chip company   Large and creditworthy company.

Blue-sky laws   State laws covering the issue and trading of securities.

Boilerplate   Standard terms and conditions, e.g., in a debt contract.

Bond   Long-term debt.

Book entry   System whereby only one global certificate is issued for *bond* and evidence of ownership is receipt showing interest in this certificate.

Book runner   The managing *underwriter* for a new issue. The book runner maintains the book of securities sold.

Bought deal   Security issue where one or two *underwriters* buy the entire issue.

Bracket   A term signifying the extent of an *underwriter's* commitment in a new issue, e.g., major bracket, minor bracket.

Break-even analysis   Analysis of the level of sales at which a project would just break even.

Bridging loan   Short-term loan to provide temporary financing until more permanent financing is arranged.

Bull-bear bond   *Bond* whose *principal* repayment is linked to the price of another security. The bonds are issued in two *tranches:* In the first the repayment increases with the price of the other security; in the second the repayment decreases with the price of the other security.

Bulldog bond   *Foreign bond* issue made in London.

Bullet payment   Single final payment, e.g., of a loan (in contrast to payment in installments).

Bull market   Widespread rise in security prices (cf. *bear market*).

Buy-back   *Repurchase agreement.*

Call option   Option to buy an asset at a specified *exercise price* on or before a specified exercise date (cf. *put option*).

Call premium   (1) Difference between the price at which a company can call its *bonds* and their *face value;* (2) price of an *option.*

Call provision   Provision that allows an issuer to buy back the *bond* issue at a stated price.

Cap   An upper limit on the interest rate on a *floating-rate note.*

Capital budget   List of planned investment projects, usually prepared annually.

Capitalization   Long-term debt, plus *preferred stock*, plus *net worth.*

Capital lease   *Financial lease.*

Capital market   Financial market (particularly the market for long-term securities).

Capital rationing   Shortage of funds that forces a company to choose between worthwhile projects.

Capital structure   Mix of different securities issued by a firm.

CAPM Capital asset pricing model.

CAR Cumulative *abnormal return*.

CARDs (Certificates for Amortizing Revolving Debt) *Pass-through securities* backed by credit card *receivables*.

CARs (Certificates of Automobile Receivables) *Pass-through securities* backed by automobile *receivables*.

Cash and carry Purchase of a security and simultaneous sale of a *future*, with the balance being financed with a loan or *repo*.

Cash budget Forecast of sources and uses of cash.

Cash-deficiency arrangement Arrangement whereby a project's shareholders agree to provide the operating company with sufficient *net working capital*.

CD *Certificate of deposit*.

CEDEL A centralized clearing system for *eurobonds*. Also *Euroclear*.

Certainty equivalent A certain cash flow that has the same future value as a specified risky cash flow.

Certificate of deposit (*CD*) A certificate providing evidence of a bank time deposit.

CFO Chief financial officer.

CHIPS *Clearing House Interbank Payments System*.

Clean price *Bond* price excluding *accrued interest* (cf. *dirty price*).

Clearing House Interbank Payments System (*CHIPS*) An international wire transfer system for high-value payments operated by a group of major banks.

Closed-end mortgage Mortgage against which no additional debt may be issued (cf., *open-end mortgage*).

CMOs *Collateralized mortgage obligations*.

Collar An upper and lower limit on the interest rate on a *floating-rate note*.

Collateral Assets that are given as security for a loan.

Collateralized mortgage obligations (*CMOs*) A variation on the mortgage *passthrough security*, in which the cash flows from a pool of mortgages are repackaged into several *tranches* of *bonds* with different maturities.

Collateral trust bonds *Bonds* secured by *common stocks* that are owned by the borrower.

Collection float Customer-written checks that have not been received, deposited, and added to the company's available balance (cf. *payment float*).

Commercial draft (*bill of exchange*) Demand for payment.

Commercial paper Unsecured *notes* issued by companies and maturing within nine months.

Commitment fee Fee charged by bank on an unused *line of credit*.

Common stock Security representing ownership of a corporation.

Compensating balance Non-interest-bearing demand deposits to compensate banks for bank loans or services.

Competitive bidding Means by which public utility *holding companies* are required to choose their *underwriter* (cf. *negotiated underwriting*).

Completion bonding Insurance that a construction contract will be successfully completed.

Compound interest Reinvestment of each interest payment on money invested, to earn more interest (cf. *simple interest*).

Compound option Option on an *option*.

Concentration banking System whereby customers make payments to a regional collection center. The collection center pays the funds into a regional bank account and surplus money is transferred to the company's principal bank.

Conditional sale Sale in which ownership does not pass to the buyer until payment is completed.

Conglomerate merger *Merger* between two companies in unrelated businesses (cf. *horizontal merger*, *vertical merger*).

Consol Name of a perpetual *bond* issued by the British government. Sometimes used as a general term for *perpetuity*.

Contingent claim Claim whose value depends on the value of another asset.

Contingent project Project that cannot be undertaken unless another project is also undertaken.

Continuous compounding Interest compounded continuously rather than at fixed intervals.

Controller Officer responsible for budgeting, accounting, and auditing in a firm (cf. *treasurer*).

Convenience yield The extra advantage that firms derive from holding the commodity rather than the *future*.

Conversion price *Par value* of a *convertible bond* divided by the number of shares into which it may be exchanged.

Conversion ratio Number of shares for which a *convertible bond* may be exchanged.

Convertible bond *Bond* that may be converted into another security at the holder's option. Similarly convertible *preferred stock*.

Correlation coefficient Measure of the closeness of the relationship between two variables.

Cost company arrangement Arrangement whereby the shareholders of a project receive output free of charge but agree to pay all operating and financing charges of the project.

Cost of capital *Opportunity cost of capital*.

Coupon (1) Specifically, an attachment to the certificate of a *bearer security* that must be surrendered to collect interest payment; (2) more generally, interest payment on debt.

Covariance Measure of the comovement between two variables.

Covenant Clause in a loan agreement.

Credit scoring A procedure for assigning scores to borrowers on the basis of the risk of default.

Cross-default clause Clause in a loan agreement stating that the company is in default if it fails to meet its obligation on any other debt issue.

Cum dividend *With dividend.*

Cum rights *With rights.*

Cumulative preferred stock Stock that takes priority over *common stock* in regard to dividend payments. Dividends may not be paid on the common stock until all past *dividends* on the *preferred stock* have been paid.

Cumulative voting Voting system under which a stockholder may cast all of his or her votes for one candidate for the board of directors (cf. *majority voting*).

Current asset Asset that will normally be turned into cash within a year.

Current liability Liability that will normally be repaid within a year.

Current ratio *Current assets* divided by *current liabilities*—a measure of liquidity.

DCF *Discounted cash flow.*

Debenture Unsecured *bond.*

Decision tree Method of representing alternative sequential decisions and the possible outcomes from these decisions.

Defeasance Practice whereby the borrower sets aside cash or *bonds* sufficient to service the borrower's debt. Both the borrower's debt and the offsetting cash or bonds are removed from the balance sheet.

Delta *Hedge ratio.*

Depository transfer check (*DTC*) Check made out directly by a local bank to a particular company.

Depreciation (1) Reduction in the book or market value of an asset; (2) portion of an investment that can be deducted from taxable income.

Derivative Asset whose value derives from that of some other asset (e.g., a *future* or an *option*).

Diff *Differential swap.*

Differential swap (*diff, quanto swap*) Swap between two *LIBOR* rates of interest, e.g., yen LIBOR for dollar LIBOR. Payments are in one currency.

Dilution Diminution in the proportion of income to which each share is entitled.

Direct lease *Lease* in which the *lessor* purchases new equipment from the manufacturer and leases it to the *lessee* (cf. *sale and lease-back*).

Direct quote For foreign exchange, the number of U.S. dollars needed to buy one unit of a foreign currency (cf. *indirect quote*).

Dirty price *Bond* price including *accrued interest*, i.e., the price paid by the bond buyer (cf. *clean price*).

Discount bond Debt sold for less than its *principal* value. If a discount bond pays no interest, it is called a "pure" discount, or *zero-coupon*, bond.

Discounted cash flow (*DCF*) Future cash flows multiplied by *discount factors* to obtain *present value.*

Discount factor *Present value* of $1 received at a stated future date.

Discount rate Rate used to calculate the *present value* of future cash flows.

Disintermediation Withdrawal of funds from a financial institution in order to invest them directly (cf. *intermediation*).

Dividend Payment by a company to its stockholders.

Dividend reinvestment plan (*DRIP*) Plan that allows shareholders to reinvest dividends automatically.

Dividend yield Annual *dividend* divided by share price.

Double-declining-balance depreciation Method of *accelerated depreciation.*

Double-tax agreement Agreement between two countries that taxes paid abroad can be offset against domestic taxes levied on foreign *dividends.*

Down-and-in option *Barrier option* that comes into existence if asset price hits a barrier.

Down-and-out option *Barrier option* that expires if asset price hits a barrier.

DRIP *Dividend reinvestment plan.*

Drop lock An arrangement whereby the interest rate on a *floating-rate note* or *preferred stock* becomes fixed if it falls to a specified level.

DTC *Depository transfer check.*

Dual-currency bond *Bond* with interest paid in one currency and *principal* paid in another.

Duration The average number of years to an asset's *discounted cash flows.*

EBIT Earnings before interest and taxes.

Economic exposure Risk that arises from changes in real exchange rates (cf. *transaction exposure, translation exposure*).

Economic income Cash flow plus change in *present value.*

Economic rents Profits in excess of the competitive level.

ECU *European currency unit.*

Efficient market Market in which security prices reflect information instantaneously.

Efficient portfolio Portfolio that offers the lowest risk (*standard deviation*) for its *expected return* and the highest expected return for its level of risk.

Employee stock ownership plan (*ESOP*) A company contributes to a trust fund that buys stock on behalf of employees.

EPS Earnings per share.

Equipment trust certificate Form of *secured debt* generally used to finance railroad equipment. The trustee retains ownership of the equipment until the debt is repaid.

Equity (1) *Common stock* and *preferred stock*. Often used to refer to common stock only. (2) *Net worth*.

Equivalent annual cash flow *Annuity* with the same *net present value* as the company's proposed investment.

ESOP *Employee stock ownership plan*.

Eurobond *Bond* that is marketed internationally.

Euroclear A centralized clearing system for *eurobonds*. Also *CEDEL*.

Eurodollar deposit Dollar deposit with a bank outside the United States.

European currency unit (*ECU*) A basket of different European currencies.

European option *Option* that can be exercised only on final exercise date (cf. *American option*).

Evergreen credit *Revolving credit* without maturity.

Exchange of assets Acquisition of another company by purchase of its assets in exchange for cash or shares.

Exchange of stock Acquisition of another company by purchase of its stock in exchange for cash or shares.

Ex dividend Purchase of shares in which the buyer is not entitled to the forthcoming *dividend* (cf. *with dividend, cum dividend*).

Exercise price (*striking price*) Price at which a *call option* or *put option* may be exercised.

Expected return Average of possible returns weighted by their probabilities.

Ex rights Purchase of shares in which the buyer is not entitled to the rights to buy shares in the company's *rights issue* (cf. *with rights, cum rights, rights on*).

Extendable bond *Bond* whose maturity can be extended at the option of the lender (or issuer).

External finance Finance that is not generated by the firm: new borrowing or an issue of stock (cf. *internal finance*).

Extra dividend *Dividend* that may or may not be repeated (cf. *regular dividend*).

Face value *Par value*.

Factoring Arrangement whereby a financial institution buys a company's *accounts receivable* and collects the debt.

Fair price provision *Appraisal rights*.

FASB Financial Accounting Standards Board.

FCIA Foreign Credit Insurance Association.

FDIC Federal Deposit Insurance Corporation.

Federal funds Non-interest-bearing deposits by banks at the Federal Reserve. Excess reserves are lent by banks to each other.

Fedwire A wire transfer system for high-value payments operated by the Federal Reserve System (cf. *CHIPS*).

Field warehouse Warehouse rented by a warehouse company on another firm's premises (cf. *public warehouse*).

Financial assets Claims on *real assets*.

Financial engineering Combining or dividing existing instruments to create new financial products.

Financial lease (*capital lease, full-payout lease*) Long-term, noncancelable *lease* (cf. *operating lease*).

Financial leverage (*gearing*) Use of debt to increase the *expected return* on *equity*. Financial leverage is measured by the ratio of debt to debt plus equity (cf. *operating leverage*).

Fiscal agency agreement An alternative to a bond *trust deed*. Unlike the trustee, the fiscal agent acts as an agent of the borrower.

Flip-flop note *Note* that allows investors to switch backward and forward between two different types of debt.

Float See *availability float, payment float*.

Floating lien General *lien* against a company's assets or against a particular class of assets.

Floating-rate note (*FRN*) *Note* whose interest payment varies with the short-term interest rate.

Floating-rate preferred *Preferred stock* paying dividends that vary with short-term interest rates.

Floor planning Arrangement used to finance inventory. A finance company buys the inventory, which is then held in trust by the user.

Foreign bond A *bond* issued on the domestic *capital market* of another country.

Forex Foreign exchange.

Forfaiter Purchaser of promises to pay (e.g., *bills of exchange* or *promissory notes*) issued by importers.

Forward cover Purchase or sale of forward foreign currency in order to offset a known future cash flow.

Forward exchange rate Exchange rate fixed today for exchanging currency at some future date (cf. *spot exchange rate*).

Forward interest rate Interest rate fixed today on a loan to be made at some future date (cf. *spot interest rate*).

Forward rate agreement (*FRA*) Agreement to borrow or lend at a specified future date at an interest rate that is fixed today.

FRA *Forward rate agreement*.

Free cash flow Cash not required for operations or for reinvestment.

FRN *Floating-rate note*.

Full-payout lease *Financial lease*.

Full-service lease (*rental lease*) *Lease* in which the *lessor* promises to maintain and insure the equipment (cf. *net lease*).

Fundamental analysis   Security analysis that seeks to detect misvalued securities by an analysis of the firm's business prospects (cf. *technical analysis*).

Funded debt   Debt maturing after more than one year (cf. *unfunded debt*).

Future   A contract to buy a commodity or security on a future date at a price that is fixed today. Unlike forward contracts, futures are generally traded on organized exchanges and are *marked to market* daily.

GAAP   Generally accepted accounting principles.

Gearing   *Financial leverage.*

General cash offer   Issue of securities offered to all investors (cf. *rights issue*).

Golden parachute   A large termination payment due to a company's management if they lose their jobs as a result of a merger.

Goodwill   The difference between the amount paid for a firm in a *merger* and its book value.

Gray market   Purchases and sales of *eurobonds* that occur before the issue price is finally set.

Greenmail   Situation in which a large block of stock is held by an unfriendly company, forcing the target company to repurchase the stock at a substantial premium to prevent a takeover.

Greenshoe option   *Option* that allows the *underwriter* for a new issue to buy and resell additional shares.

Growth stock   *Common stock* of a company that has an opportunity to invest money to earn more than the *opportunity cost of capital* (cf. *income stock*).

Harmless warrant   *Warrant* that allows the user to purchase a *bond* only by surrendering an existing bond with similar terms.

Hedge ratio (delta, option delta)   The number of shares to buy for each *option* sold in order to create a safe position; more generally, the number of units of an asset that should be bought to hedge one unit of a liability.

Hedging   Buying one security and selling another in order to reduce risk. A perfect hedge produces a riskless portfolio.

Hell-or-high-water clause   Clause in a *lease* agreement that obligates the *lessee* to make payments regardless of what happens to the *lessor* or the equipment.

Highly leveraged transaction (*HLT*)   Bank loan to a highly leveraged firm (formerly needed to be separately reported to the Federal Reserve Board).

HLT   *Highly leveraged transaction.*

Holding company   Company whose sole function is to hold stock in other companies or subsidiaries.

Horizontal merger   *Merger* between two companies that manufacture similar products (cf. *vertical merger, conglomerate merger*).

Horizontal spread   The simultaneous purchase and sale of two *options* that differ only in their exercise date (cf. *vertical spread*).

Hurdle rate   Minimum acceptable rate of return on a project.

IBF   *International Banking Facility.*

IMM   *International Monetary Market*

Immunization   The construction of an asset and a liability that are subject to offsetting changes in value.

Imputation tax system   Arrangement by which investors who receive a *dividend* also receive a tax credit for corporate taxes that the firm has paid.

Income bond   *Bond* on which interest is payable only if earned.

Income stock   *Common stock* with high *dividend yield* and few profitable investment opportunities (cf. *growth stock*).

Indenture   Formal agreement, e.g., establishing the terms of a *bond* issue.

Indexed bond   *Bond* whose payments are linked to an index, e.g., a consumer price index.

Index fund   Investment fund designed to match the returns on a stockmarket index.

Indirect quote   For foreign exchange, the number of units of a foreign currency needed to buy one U.S. dollar (cf. *direct quote*).

Industrial revenue bond (*IRB*)   Bond issued by local government agencies on behalf of corporations.

Initial public offering (*IPO*)   A company's first public issue of *common stock*.

In-substance defeasance   *Defeasance* whereby debt is removed from the balance sheet but not canceled (cf. *novation*).

Intangible asset   Nonmaterial asset, such as technical expertise, a trademark, and a patent (cf. *tangible asset*).

Integer programming   Variant of *linear programming* whereby the solution values must be integers.

Interest cover   *Times interest earned.*

Interest equalization tax   Tax on foreign investment by residents of the United States (abolished 1974).

Interest-rate parity   Theory that the differential between the *forward exchange rate* and the *spot exchange rate* is equal to the differential between the foreign and domestic interest rates.

Intermediation   Investment through a financial institution (cf. *disintermediation*).

Internal finance   Finance generated within a firm by *retained earnings* and *depreciation* (cf. *external finance*).

Internal growth rate   The maximum rate of firm growth without *external finance* (cf. *sustainable growth rate*).

Internal rate of return (*IRR*) *Discount rate* at which investment has zero *net present value*.

International Banking Facility (*IBF*) A branch that an American bank establishes in the United States to do eurocurrency business.

International Monetary Market (*IMM*) The financial futures market within the Chicago Mercantile Exchange.

Interval measure The number of days that a firm can finance operations without additional cash income.

In-the-money option An *option* that would be worth exercising if it expired immediately (cf. *out-of-the-money option*).

Inverse FRN *Floating-rate note* whose payments rise as the general level of interest rates falls and vice versa.

Investment banker *Underwriter.*

Investment-grade bond *Bond* rated at least Baa by Moody's or BBB by Standard and Poor's.

Investment tax credit Proportion of new capital investment that can be used to reduce a company's tax bill (abolished 1986).

IPO *Initial public offering.*

IRB *Industrial revenue bond.*

IRR *Internal rate of return.*

IRS Internal Revenue Service.

ISDA International Swap and Derivatives Association.

Issued share capital Total amount of shares that are in issue (cf. *outstanding share capital*).

Junior debt *Subordinated debt.*

Junk bond Debt that is rated below an *investment-grade bond.*

Kiretsu A network of Japanese companies organized around a major bank.

LBO *Leveraged buyout.*

Lease Long-term rental agreement.

Legal capital Value at which a company's shares are recorded in its books.

Legal defeasance *Novation.*

Lessee Us r of a leased asset (cf. *lessor*).

Lessor Ow er of a leased asset (cf. *lessee*).

Letter of credit Letter from a bank stating that it has established a credit in the company's favor.

Letter stock Privately placed *common stock*, so-called because the *SEC* requires a letter from the purchaser that the stock is not intended for resale.

Leverage See *financial leverage, operating leverage.*

Leveraged buyout (*LBO*) Acquisition in which (1) a large part of the purchase price is debt financed and (2) the remaining *equity* is privately held by a small group of investors.

Leveraged lease *Lease* in which the *lessor* finances part of the cost of the asset by an issue of debt secured by the asset and the lease payments.

Liabilities, total liabilities Total value of financial claims on a firm's assets. Equals (1) total assets or (2) total assets minus *net worth*.

LIBOR *London interbank offered rate.*

Lien Lender's claims on specified assets.

Limited liability Limitation of a shareholder's losses to the amount invested.

Limited partnership *Partnership* in which some partners have *limited liability* and general partners have unlimited liability.

Linear programming (*LP*) Technique for finding the maximum value of some equation subject to stated linear constraints.

Line of credit Agreement by a bank that a company may borrow at any time up to an established limit.

Liquid asset Asset that is easily and cheaply turned into cash—notably cash itself and short-term securities.

Liquidating dividend *Dividend* that represents a return of capital.

Liquidator Person appointed by unsecured creditors in the United Kingdom to oversee the sale of an insolvent firm's assets and the repayment of debts.

Liquidity premium (1) Additional return for investing in a security that cannot easily be turned into cash; (2) difference between the *forward interest rate* and the expected *spot interest rate*.

Liquid yield option note (*LYON*) *Zero-coupon*, callable, putable, *convertible bond.*

Load-to-load Arrangement whereby the customer pays for the last delivery when the next one is received.

Lock-box system Form of *concentration banking*. Customers send payments to a post office box. A local bank collects and processes the checks and transfers surplus funds to the company's principal bank.

London interbank offered rate (*LIBOR*) The interest rate at which major international banks in London lend to each other. (LIBID is London interbank bid rate; LIMEAN is mean of bid and offered rate.)

Long hedge Purchase of a *hedging* instrument (e.g., a *future*) to hedge a short position in the underlying asset (cf. *short hedge*).

Lookback option *Option* whose payoff depends on the highest asset price recorded over the life of the option.

LP *Linear programming.*

LYON *Liquid yield option note.*

Maintenance margin Minimum margin that must be maintained on a *futures* contract.

Majority voting   Voting system under which each director is voted upon separately (cf. *cumulative voting*).

Management buyout (*MBO*)   *Leveraged buyout* whereby the acquiring group is led by the firm's management.

Margin   Cash or securities set aside by an investor as evidence that he or she can honor a commitment.

Marked-to-market   An arrangement whereby the profits or losses on a *futures* contract are settled up each day.

Market capitalization rate   *Expected return* on a security.

Market risk (*systematic risk*)   Risk that cannot be diversified away.

Maturity factoring   *Factoring* arrangement that provides collection and insurance of *accounts receivable*.

MBO   *Management buyout.*

MDA   *Multiple-discriminant analysis.*

Medium-term note (*MTN*)   Debt with a typical maturity of 1 to 10 years offered regularly by a company using the same procedure as *commercial paper.*

Merger   (1) Acquisition in which all assets and liabilities are absorbed by the buyer (cf. *exchange of assets, exchange of stock*); (2) more generally, any combination of two companies.

MIP   *Monthly income preferred security.*

Mismatch bond   *Floating-rate note* whose interest rate is reset at more frequent intervals than the rollover period (e.g., a note whose payments are set quarterly on the basis of the one-year interest rate).

MMDA   *Money-market deposit account.*

Money center bank   A major U.S. bank that undertakes a wide range of banking activities.

Money market   Market for short-term safe investments.

Money market deposit account (*MMDA*)   In return for maintaining a minimum balance, the depositor receives both interest on the account and limited checking privileges.

Money-market fund   *Mutual fund* that invests solely in short-term safe securities.

Monte Carlo simulation   Method for calculating the probability distribution of possible outcomes, e.g., from a project.

Monthly income preferred security (*MIP*)   *Preferred stock* issued by a subsidiary located in a tax haven. The subsidiary relends the money to the parent.

Moral hazard   The risk that the existence of a contract will change the behavior of one or both parties to the contract; e.g., an insured firm may take fewer fire precautions.

Mortgage bond   *Bond* secured against plant and equipment.

MTN   *Medium-term note.*

Multiple-discriminant analysis (*MDA*)   Statistical technique for distinguishing between two groups on the basis of their observed characteristics.

Mutual fund   Managed investment fund whose shares are sold to investors.

Mutually exclusive projects   Two projects that cannot both be undertaken.

Naked option   *Option* held on its own, i.e., not used for *hedging* a holding in the asset or other options.

NASD   National Association of Security Dealers.

Negative pledge clause   Clause under which the borrower agrees not to permit an exclusive *lien* on any of its assets.

Negotiated underwriting   Method of choosing an *underwriter*. Most firms may choose their *underwriter* by negotiation (cf. *competitive bidding*).

Net lease   *Lease* in which the *lessee* promises to maintain and insure the equipment (cf. *full-service lease*).

Net present value (*NPV*)   A project's net contribution to wealth—*present value* minus initial investment.

Net working capital   *Current assets* minus *current liabilities.*

Net worth   Book value of a company's *common stock*, surplus, and *retained earnings.*

Nominal interest rate   Interest rate expressed in money terms (cf. *real interest rate*).

Nonrefundable debt   Debt that may not be called in order to replace it with another issue at a lower interest cost.

Normal distribution   Symmetric bell-shaped distribution that can be completely defined by its mean and *standard deviation.*

Note   Unsecured debt with a maturity of up to 10 years.

Novation (*legal defeasance*)   *Defeasance* whereby the firm's debt is canceled (cf. *in-substance defeasance*).

NPV   *Net present value.*

NYSE   New York Stock Exchange.

Odd lot   A trade of less than 100 shares (cf. *round lot*).

Off-balance-sheet financing   Financing that is not shown as a liability in a company's balance sheet.

Offer price   *Ask price.*

OID debt   *Original issue discount debt.*

Old-line factoring   *Factoring* arrangement that provides collection, insurance, and finance for *accounts receivable.*

On the run   The most recently issued (and, therefore, typically the most liquid) government *bond* in a particular maturity range.

Open account   Arrangement whereby sales are made with no formal debt contract. The buyer signs a receipt, and the seller records the sale in the sales ledger.

Open-end mortgage   Mortgage against which additional debt may be issued (cf. *closed-end mortgage*).

Operating lease   Short-term, cancelable *lease* (cf. *financial lease*).

Operating leverage Fixed operating costs, so-called because they accentuate variations in profits (cf. *financial leverage*).

Opportunity cost of capital (*hurdle rate, cost of capital*) *Expected return* that is forgone by investing in a project rather than in comparable financial securities.

Option See *call option, put option*.

Option delta *Hedge ratio*.

Original issue discount debt (*OID debt*) Debt that is initially offered at a price below *face value*.

OTC *Over-the-counter*.

Out-of-the-money option An *option* that would not be worth exercising if it matured immediately (cf. *in-the-money option*).

Outstanding share capital *Issued share capital* less the *par value* of shares that are held in the company's treasury.

Oversubscription privilege In a *rights issue*, arrangement by which shareholders are given the right to apply for any shares that are not taken up.

Over-the-counter (*OTC*) Informal market that does not involve a securities exchange. Specifically used to refer to the NASDaq dealer market for *common stocks*.

Partnership Joint ownership of business whereby general partners have unlimited liability.

Par value (*face value*) Value of a security shown on the certificate.

Pass-through securities *Notes* or *bonds* backed by a package of assets (e.g., mortgage pass-throughs, *CARs*, *CARDs*).

Path-dependent option *Option* whose value depends on the sequence of prices of the underlying asset rather than just the final price of the asset.

Payables *Accounts payable*.

Payback period Time taken for a project to recover its initial investment.

Pay-in-kind bond (*PIK*) *Bond* that allows the issuer to choose to make interest payments in the form of additional bonds.

Payment float Company-written checks that have not yet cleared (cf. *availability float*).

Payout ratio *Dividend* as a proportion of earnings per share.

PBGC Pension Benefit Guarantee Corporation.

P/E ratio Share price divided by earnings per share.

PERC *Preferred equity redemption cumulative stock*.

Perpetuity Investment offering a level stream of cash flows in perpetuity (cf. *consol*).

PIK *Pay-in-kind bond*.

PN *Project note*.

Poison pill An issue of securities that is convertible, in the event of a *merger*, into the shares of the acquiring firm or must be repurchased by the acquiring firm.

Poison put A *covenant* allowing the *bond*holder to demand repayment in the event of a hostile *merger*.

Pooling of interest Method of accounting for *mergers*. The consolidated balance sheet of the merged firm is obtained by combining the balance sheets of the separate firms.

Position diagram Diagram showing the possible payoffs from a *derivative* investment.

Postaudit Evaluation of an investment project after it has been undertaken.

Preemptive right Common stockholder's right to anything of value distributed by the company.

Preferred equity redemption cumulative stock (*PERC*) *Preferred stock* that converts automatically into equity at a stated date. A limit is placed on the value of the shares the investor receives.

Preferred stock Stock that takes priority over common stock in regard to *dividends*. Dividends may not be paid on *common stock* unless the dividend is paid on all preferred stock (cf. *cumulative preferred stock*). The dividend rate on preferred is usually fixed at time of issue.

Prepack *Prepackaged bankruptcy*.

Prepackaged bankruptcy (*prepack*) Bankruptcy proceedings intended to confirm a reorganization plan that has already been agreed to informally.

Present value Discounted value of future cash flows.

Present value of growth opportunities (*PVGO*) *Net present value* of investments the firm is expected to make in the future.

Primary issue Issue of new securities by a firm (cf. *secondary issue*).

Prime rate Benchmark lending rate set by U.S. banks.

Principal Amount of debt that must be repaid.

Principal-agent problem Problem faced by a principal (e.g., shareholder) in ensuring that an agent (e.g., manager) acts on his or her behalf.

Privileged subscription issue *Rights issue*.

Production payment Loan in the form of advance payment for future delivery of a product.

Profitability index Ratio of a project's *NPV* to the initial investment.

Pro forma Projected.

Project finance Debt that is largely a claim against the cash flows from a particular project rather than against the firm as a whole.

Project note (*PN*) *Note* issued by public housing or urban renewal agencies.

Promissory note Promise to pay.

Prospectus Summary of the *registration* statement providing information on an issue of securities.

Proxy vote Vote cast by one person on behalf of another.

Public warehouse (*terminal warehouse*) Warehouse operated by an independent warehouse company on its own premises (cf. *field warehouse*).

Purchase fund Resembles a *sinking fund* except that money is used only to purchase bonds if they are selling below their *par value*.

Put option *Option* to sell an asset at a specified *exercise price* on or before a specified exercise date (cf. *call option*).

PVGO *Present value of growth opportunities.*

q Ratio of the market value of an asset to its replacement cost.

Quadratic programming Variant of *linear programming* whereby the equations are quadratic rather than linear.

Quanto swap *Differential swap.*

Quick ratio (*acid-test ratio*) Measure of liquidity: (*current assets* − inventory) divided by *current liabilities*.

Range forward A *forward exchange rate* contract that places upper and lower bounds on the cost of foreign exchange.

Real assets *Tangible assets* and *intangible assets* used to carry on business (cf. *financial assets*).

Real estate investment trust (*REIT*) Trust company formed to invest in real estate.

Real interest rate Interest rate expressed in terms of real goods, i.e., *nominal interest rate* adjusted for inflation.

Receivables *Accounts receivable.*

Receiver A bankruptcy practitioner appointed by secured creditors in the United Kingdom to oversee the repayment of debts.

Record date Date set by directors when making dividend payment. *Dividends* are sent to stockholders who are registered on the record date.

Recourse Term describing a type of loan. If a loan is with recourse, the lender has a general claim against the parent company if the *collateral* is insufficient to repay the debt.

Red herring Preliminary *prospectus.*

Refunding Replacement of existing debt with a new issue of debt.

Registered security Security whose ownership is recorded by the company's *registrar* (cf. *bearer security*).

Registrar Financial institution appointed to record issue and ownership of company securities.

Registration Process of obtaining *SEC* approval for a public issue of securities.

Regression analysis In statistics, a technique for finding the line of best fit.

Regular dividend *Dividend* that the company expects to maintain in the future.

Regulation A issue Security issues of under $1.5 million; partially exempt from *SEC registration* requirements.

REIT *Real estate investment trust.*

Rental lease *Full-service lease.*

Repo *Repurchase agreement.*

Repurchase agreement (*RP, repo, buy-back*) Purchase of Treasury securities from a securities dealer with an agreement that the dealer will repurchase them at a specified price.

Residual risk *Unique risk.*

Retained earnings Earnings not paid out as *dividends.*

Return on equity Usually, equity earnings as a proportion of the book value of equity.

Return on investment (*ROI*) Generally, book income as a proportion of net book value.

Revolving credit Legally assured *line of credit* with a bank.

Rights issue (*privileged subscription issue*) Issue of securities offered to current stockholders (cf. *general cash offer*).

Rights on *With rights.*

Risk premium Expected additional return for making a risky investment rather than a safe one.

ROI *Return on investment.*

Roll-over CD A package of successive *certificates of deposit.*

Round lot A trade of 100 shares (cf. *odd lot*).

RP *Repurchase agreement.*

R squared (R^2) Square of the *correlation coefficient*—the proportion of the variability in one series that can be explained by the variability of one or more other series.

Rule 144a *SEC* rule allowing qualified institutional buyers to buy and trade unregistered securities.

Sale and lease-back Sale of an existing asset to a financial institution that then *leases* it back to the user (cf. *direct lease*).

Salvage value Scrap value of plant and equipment.

Samurai bond A yen *bond* issued in Tokyo by a non-Japanese borrower (cf. *bulldog bond, Yankee bond*).

SBIC Small Business Investment Company.

Seasoned issue Issue of a security for which there is an existing market (cf. *unseasoned issue*).

Season datings Extended credit for customers who order goods out of the peak season.

SEC Securities and Exchange Commission.

Secondary issue (1) Procedure for selling blocks of *seasoned issues* of stock; (2) more generally, sale of already issued stock.

Secondary market Market in which one can buy or sell *seasoned issues* of securities.

Secured debt   Debt that, in the event of default, has first claim on specified assets.

Securitization   Substitution of tradable securities for privately negotiated instruments.

Security market line   Line representing the relationship between *expected return* and *market risk*.

Self-liquidating loan   Loan to finance *current assets*. The sale of the current assets provides the cash to repay the loan.

Self-selection   Consequence of a contract that induces only one group (e.g., low-risk individuals) to participate.

Semistrong-form efficient market   Market in which security prices reflect all publicly available information (cf. *weak-form efficient market* and *strong-form efficient market*).

Senior debt   Debt that, in the event of bankruptcy, must be repaid before *subordinated debt* receives any payment.

Sensitivity analysis   Analysis of the effect on project profitability of possible changes in sales, costs, and so on.

Serial bonds   Package of *bonds* that mature in successive years.

Series bond   Bond that may be issued in several series under the same *indenture*.

Shark repellant   Amendment to company charter intended to protect it against takeover.

Shelf registration   A procedure that allows firms to file one *registration* statement covering several issues of the same security.

Shogun bond   Dollar *bond* issued in Japan by a nonresident.

Short hedge   Sale of a *hedging* instrument (e.g., a *future*) to *hedge* a long position in the underlying asset (cf. *long hedge*).

Short sale   Sale of a security the investor does not own.

Sight draft   Demand for immediate payment (cf. *time draft*).

Signal   Action that demonstrates an individual's unobservable characteristics (because it would be unduly costly for someone without those characteristics to take the action).

Simple interest   Interest calculated only on the initial investment (cf. *compound interest*).

Simulation   *Monte Carlo simulation.*

Sinker   *Sinking fund.*

Sinking fund (*sinker*)   Fund established by a company to retire debt before maturity.

Skewed distribution   Probability distribution in which an unequal number of observations lie below and above the mean.

Special dividend (*extra dividend*)   *Dividend* that is unlikely to be repeated.

Specific risk   *Unique risk.*

Spin-off   Distribution of shares in a subsidiary to the company's shareholders, so that they hold shares separately in the two firms.

Spot exchange rate   Exchange rate on currency for immediate delivery (cf. *forward exchange rate*)

Spot interest rate   Interest rate fixed today on a loan that is made today (cf. *forward interest rate*).

Spot price   Price of asset for immediate delivery (in contrast to forward or futures price).

Spread (*underwriter's* spread)   Difference between the price at which an *underwriter* buys an issue from a firm and the price at which the underwriter sells it to the public.

Standard deviation   Square root of the *variance*—a measure of variability.

Standard error   In statistics, a measure of the possible error in an estimate.

Standby agreement   In a *rights issue*, agreement that the *underwriter* will purchase any stock not purchased by investors.

Step-up bond   *Bond* whose *coupon* is stepped up over time (also step-down bond).

Stock dividend   *Dividend* in the form of stock rather than cash.

Stock split   "Free" issue of shares to existing shareholders.

Straddle   The combination of a *put option* and a *call option* with the same *exercise price*.

Straight-line depreciation   An equal dollar amount of *depreciation* in each period.

Striking price   *Exercise price* of an *option*.

Stripped bond   *Bond* that can be subdivided into a series of *zero-coupon bonds*.

Strong-form efficient market   Market in which security prices reflect instantaneously *all* information available to investors (cf. *weak-form efficient market* and *semistrong-form efficient market*).

Structured debt   Debt that has been customized for the buyer, often by incorporating unusual *options*.

Subordinated debt (*junior debt*)   Debt over which *senior debt* takes priority. In the event of bankruptcy, subordinated debtholders receive payment only after senior debt is paid off in full.

Sum-of-the-years'-digits depreciation   Method of *accelerated depreciation*.

Sunk costs   Costs that have been incurred and cannot be reversed.

Supermajority   Provision in a company's charter requiring a majority of, say, 80 percent of shareholders to approve certain changes, such as a *merger*.

Sushi bond   A *eurobond* issued by a Japanese corporation.

Sustainable growth rate   Maximum rate of firm growth without increasing financial leverage (cf. *internal growth rate*).

Swap   An arrangement whereby two companies lend to each other on different terms, e.g., in different currencies, or one at a fixed rate and the other at a floating rate.

Swaption   *Option* on a *swap.*

Swingline facility   Bank borrowing facility to provide finance while the firm replaces U.S. *commercial paper* with eurocommercial paper.

Systematic risk   *Market risk.*

Take-up fee   Fee paid to *underwriters* of a *rights issue* on any stock they are obliged to purchase.

Tangible asset   Physical asset, such as plant, machinery, and offices (cf. *intangible assets*).

Tax-anticipation bill   Short-term bill issued by the U.S. Treasury that can be surrendered at *face value* in payment of taxes.

T-bill   *Treasury bill.*

Technical analysis   Security analysis that seeks to detect and interpret patterns in past security prices (cf. *fundamental analysis*).

TED spread   Difference between U.S. *treasury bill* rate and eurodollar rate.

Tender offer   General offer made directly to a firm's shareholders to buy their stock.

Tenor   Maturity of a loan.

Terminal warehouse   *Public warehouse.*

Term loan   Medium-term, privately placed loan, usually made by a bank.

Term structure of interest rates   Relationship between interest rates on loans of different maturities (cf. *yield curve*).

Throughput arrangement   Arrangement by which shareholders of a pipeline company agree to make sufficient use of pipeline to enable the pipeline company to service its debt.

Tick   Minimum amount the price of a security may change.

Time draft   Demand for payment at a stated future date (cf. *sight draft*).

Times interest earned (*interest cover*)   Earnings before interest and tax, divided by interest payments.

Tombstone   Advertisement listing the *underwriters* to a security issue.

Trade acceptance   Written demand that has been accepted by an industrial company to pay a given sum at a future date (cf. *banker's acceptance*).

Trade credit   *Accounts receivable.*

Trade debt   *Accounts payable.*

Tranche   Portion of a new issue sold at a point in time different from the remainder or that has different terms.

Transaction exposure   Risk to a firm with known future cash flows in a foreign currency that arises from possible changes in the exchange rate (cf. *economic exposure, translation exposure*).

Transfer agent   Individual or institution appointed by a company to look after the transfer of securities.

Translation exposure   Risk of adverse effects on a firm's financial statements that may arise from changes in exchange rates (cf. *economic exposure, transaction exposure*).

Treasurer   Principal financial manager (cf. *controller*).

Treasury bill (*T-bill*)   Short-term discount debt maturing in less than one year, issued regularly by the government.

Treasury stock   *Common stock* that has been repurchased by the company and held in the company's treasury.

Trust deed   Agreement between trustee and borrower setting out terms of *bond*.

Trust receipt   Receipt for goods that are to be held in trust for the lender.

Underpricing   Issue of securities below their market value.

Underwriter (*investment banker*)   Firm that buys an issue of securities from a company and resells it to investors.

Unfunded debt   Debt maturing within one year (cf. *funded debt*).

Unique risk (*residual risk, specific risk, unsystematic risk*)   Risk that can be eliminated by diversification

Unseasoned issue   Issue of a security for which there is no existing market (cf. *seasoned issue*).

Unsystematic risk   *Unique risk.*

Value additivity   Rule that the value of the whole must equal the sum of the values of the parts.

Value-at-risk model (*VAR model*)   Procedure for estimating the probability of portfolio losses exceeding some specified proportion.

Vanilla issue   Issue without unusual features.

Variable rate demand bond (*VRDB*)   Floating rate *bond* that can be sold back periodically to the issuer.

Variance   Mean squared deviation from the expected value—a measure of variability.

Variation margin   The daily gains or losses on a *futures* contract credited to the investor's margin account.

VAR model   *Value-at-risk model.*

Venture capital   Capital to finance a new firm.

Vertical merger   *Merger* between a supplier and its customer (cf. *horizontal merger, conglomerate merger*).

Vertical spread   Simultaneous purchase and sale of two options that differ only in their *exercise price* (cf. *horizontal spread*).

VRDB   *Variable rate demand bond.*

WACC   *Weighted average cost of capital.*

Warehouse receipt   Evidence that a firm owns goods stored in a warehouse.

Warrant   Long-term *call option* issued by a company.

Weak-form efficient market   Market in which security prices instantaneously reflect the information in the history of security prices. In such a market security prices follow a random walk (cf. *semistrong-form efficient market* and *strong-form efficient market*).

Weighted average cost of capital (*WACC*) *Expected return* on a portfolio of all the firm's securities. Used as *hurdle rate* for capital investment.

White knight A friendly potential acquirer sought out by a target company threatened by a less welcome suitor.

Wi. When issued.

Winner's curse Problem faced by uninformed bidders. For example, in an *initial public offering* uninformed participants are likely to receive larger allotments of issues that informed participants know are overpriced.

With dividend (*cum dividend*) Purchase of shares in which the buyer is entitled to the forthcoming *dividend* (cf. *ex dividend*).

Withholding tax Tax levied on *dividends* paid abroad.

With rights (*cum rights, rights on*) Purchase of shares in which the buyer is entitled to the rights to buy shares in the company's *rights issue* (cf. *ex rights*).

Working capital *Current assets* and *current liabilities*. The term is commonly used as synonymous with *net working capital*.

Workout Informal arrangement between a borrower and creditors.

Writer *Option* seller.

Yankee bond A dollar *bond* issued in the United States by a non-U.S. borrower (cf. *bulldog bond*, *Samurai bond*).

Yield curve *Term structure of interest rates*.

Yield to maturity *Internal rate of return* on a *bond*.

Zero-coupon bond *Discount bond* making no *coupon* payments.

Z score Measure of the likelihood of bankruptcy.

Answers to Quizzes

Chapter 1

1. (*a*) Real
   (*b*) Executive airplanes
   (*c*) Brand names
   (*d*) Financial
   (*e*) Bonds
   (*f*) Investment
   (*g*) Capital budgeting
   (*h*) Financing

2. *a*, *c*, and *d*.

3. *c*, *d*, *e*, and *g* are real assets. Others are financial.

4. (*a*) Advantage: simplicity. Disadvantages: unlimited liability, only accommodates one owner.
   (*b*) Advantage: allows shared ownership and control by partners. Disadvantage: unlimited liability.
   (*c*) Advantages: allows dispersed ownership, public trading of shares, separation of ownership and control, limited liability. Disadvantages: double taxation.

5. (*a*) corporation
   (*b*) proprietorship
   (*c*) corporation
   (*d*) corporation
   (*e*) public company

Chapter 2

1. (*a*) Negative
   (*b*) $PV = \dfrac{C_1}{1 + r}$
   (*c*) $NPV = C_0 + \dfrac{C_1}{1 + r}$
   (*d*) It is the return forgone by investing in the project rather than the capital market.
   (*e*) The return offered by default-free U.S. Treasury securities.

2. $DF_1 = .867$; discount rate $= .154$, or 15.4 percent.

3. (*a*) .909
   (*b*) .833
   (*c*) .769

4. (*a*) $\text{Return} = \dfrac{\text{profit}}{\text{investment}} = \dfrac{132 - 100}{100}$
   $= .32$, or 32 percent
   (*b*) Negative (if the rate of interest *r* equals 32 percent, $NPV = 0$).
   (*c*) $PV = \dfrac{132}{1.10} = 120$, or \$120,000
   (*d*) $NPV = -100 + 120 = 20$, or \$20,000

5. Net present value rule: Invest if NPV is positive. Rate-of-return rule: Invest if the rate of return exceeds the opportunity cost of capital. They give the same answer.

6. (*a*) $12 million
   (*b*) +50 percent
   (*c*) Z offers a 20 percent expected return. Its payoffs are proportional to the project, so the two investments have the same risk. The $8 million required for the project could have been invested in Z by your company or its stockholders. Therefore Z's return is the opportunity cost of investing in the project.
   (*d*) NPV $= 8 + \dfrac{12}{1.2} = +2$ million. The project is worthwhile because it adds $2 million to the market value of the firm.

7. (*a*) $1 + r = 5/4$. Therefore $r = .25$, or 25 percent
   (*b*) $2.6 - 1.6 = \$1$ million
   (*c*) $3 million
   (*d*) Return $= (3 - 1)/1 = 2.0$, or 200 percent
   (*e*) Marginal return $=$ rate of interest $= 25$ percent
   (*f*) PV $= 4 - 1.6 = \$2.4$ million
   (*g*) NPV $= -1.0 + 2.4 = \$1.4$ million
   (*h*) $4 million ($2.6 million cash + NPV)
   (*i*) $1 million
   (*j*) $3.75 million

8. They will vote for (*a*) only. The other tasks can be carried out just as efficiently by stockholders.

Chapter 3

1. $1.00

2. $125/139 = .899$

3. $596 \times .285 = \$170$

4. $\dfrac{374}{(1.09)^9} = \$172$

5. PV $= \dfrac{432}{1.15} + \dfrac{137}{(1.15)^2} + \dfrac{797}{(1.15)^3}$
   $= 376 + 104 + 524 = 1004$

6. $100 \times (1.15)^8 = \$305.90$

7. $232 \times (1 + r)^2 = 312.18$ implies $r = .16$, or 16 percent

8. NPV $= -1548 + \dfrac{138}{.09} = -\$14.67$

9. Find g so that NPV $= 0$.
   NPV $= -2590 + \dfrac{220}{.12 - g} = 0$ implies $g = .035$, or 3.5 percent.

10. PV $= \dfrac{4}{.14 - .04} = \$40$

11. PV of $502 at $t = 1, 2, \ldots, 9$, at 13 percent $= 502 \times 5.132 = 2576$. Future value $= 2576 \times (1.13)^9 = \$7738$.

12. (*a*) Let S_t = salary in year t

$$PV = \sum_{t=1}^{30} \frac{S_t}{(1.08)^t} = \sum_{t=1}^{30} \frac{20,000\,(1.05)^{t-1}}{(1.08)^t}$$

$$= \sum_{t=1}^{30} \frac{20,000/1.05}{(1.08/1.05)^t} = \sum_{t=1}^{30} \frac{19,048}{(1.029)^t}$$

$$= 19,048 \left[\frac{1}{.029} - \frac{1}{.029\,(1.029)^{30}} \right] = 378,222$$

(*b*) PV (salary) × .05 = 18,911.
Future value = 18,911 × $(1.08)^{30}$
= 190,295.

(*c*) Annual payment = initial value ÷ annuity factor; 20-year annuity factor at 8 percent = 9,818; annual payment = 190,295/9,818 = 19,382.

13.

Period	Discount Factor	Cash Flow	Present Value
0	1.0	−400,000	−400,000
1	.893	+100,000	+ 89,300
2	.797	+200,000	+159,400
3	.712	+300,000	+213,600
		Total = NPV =	$ 62,300

14. (*a*) PV = 1/.10 = $10

(*b*) PV = $\dfrac{1}{.10\,(1.10)^7} = \dfrac{10}{2}$ = $5 (approx.)

(*c*) PV = 10 − 5 = $5 (approx.)

(*d*) PV = $\dfrac{C}{r-g} = \dfrac{10,000}{.10-.05}$ = $200,000

15. (*a*) From Appendix Table 1, $1/(1.05)^5$ = .784. You therefore need to set aside 10,000 × .784 = $7840.

(*b*) From Appendix Table 3, the present value of $1 a year for 6 years at 8 percent is $4.623. Therefore you need to set aside 12,000 × 4.623 = $55,476.

(*c*) From Appendix Table 2, 1.08^6 = 1.587. Therefore, at the end of 6 years you would have 1.587 × (60,476 − 55,476) = $7935.

(*d*) From Appendix Table 2, $1 grows to $1.762 by year 5 at an annually compounded rate of 12 percent. From Appendix Table 4, $1 grows to $1.762 by year 5 at a continuously compounded rate of about 11.4 percent.

Chapter 4

1. $P_0 = \dfrac{10+110}{1.10}$ = $109.09

2. $r = \dfrac{5}{40}$ = .125

3. $P_0 = \dfrac{10}{.08-.05}$ = $333.33

4. By year 5, earnings will grow to $18.23 per share. Forecasted price per share at year 4 is $18.23/.08 = \$227.91$.

$$P_0 = \frac{10}{1.08} + \frac{10.50}{(1.08)^2} + \frac{11.03}{(1.08)^3} + \frac{11.58}{(1.08)^4} + \frac{227.91}{(1.08)^4} = 203.05$$

5. $\dfrac{15}{.08} = \text{PVGO} = 333.33$; therefore PVGO = \$145.83

6. (b) and (c); (a) ignores the cost of the investments needed to produce the earnings.

7. If present value of growth opportunities (PVGO) is zero.

8. Free cash flow is the amount of cash generated by a project or business net of all costs, taxes, and positive-NPV investments. Free cash flow can be negative if investment outlays are large. A business with positive free cash flow can pay it out as dividends.

9. Z's forecasted dividends and prices grow as follows:

	Year 1	Year 2	Year 3
Dividend	10	10.50	11.03
Price	350	367.50	385.87

Calculate the expected rates of return:

From year 0 to 1: $\dfrac{10 + (350 - 333.33)}{333.33} = .08$

From year 1 to 2: $\dfrac{10.50 + (367.50 - 350)}{350} = .08$

From year 2 to 3: $\dfrac{11.03 + (385.87 - 367.50)}{367.50} = .08$

Double expects 8 percent in *each* of the first 2 years. Triple expects 8 percent in *each* of the first 3 years.

Chapter 5

1. The opportunity cost of capital is the expected rate of return investors could earn at a given level of risk.

2. (a) A = 3 years, B = 2 years, C = 3 years
   (b) B
   (c) A, B, and C
   (d) B and C (NPV$_B$ = \$3378; NPV$_C$ = \$2405)
   (e) False
   (f) True
   (g) It will accept no negative-NPV projects but will turn down some with positive NPVs. A project can have positive NPV if all future cash flows are considered, but still not meet the stated cutoff period.

3. $\dfrac{1000}{4000} = .25$, or 25 percent

4. (a) True, because the time value of money is ignored.
   (b) False; they will turn down good projects with returns less than the company average.

5. (*a*) $15,750; $4250; $0
   (*b*) 100 percent

6. (*a*) (i) Both (IRR is greater than the cost of capital). (ii) The *incremental* cash flows on B are: −2000, +1100, +1210. The IRR on these incremental flows is 10 percent. Since this is greater than the cost of capital, the incremental investment in A is worthwhile.
   (*b*) NPV of incremental investment = 690 − 657 = $33

7. C (if both projects have NPV = 0 at the same discount rate, the project with the later cash flows must have the higher NPV if we use a lower discount rate).

8. No (you are effectively "borrowing" at a rate of interest higher than the opportunity cost of capital).

9. 1, 2, 4, and 6

10. Soft rationing means provisional capital constraints imposed by management as an aid to financial control. This doesn't rule out raising more money if necessary. Firms facing hard rationing can't raise money from capital markets.

Chapter 6

1. *a, b, d, g, h*

2. Real cash flow = 100,000/1.1 = 90,909; real discount rate = (1.15/1.1) − 1 = .0455
   $$PV = \frac{90,909}{1.0455} = 86,953,$$ four francs short because of rounding error.

3. The suggested procedure is not accurate. Not all prices and costs increase at the general inflation rate. For example, prices of personal computers have been falling (for the same performance) despite continued inflation. Also, tax depreciation is not inflation-adjusted, so the present value of depreciation tax shields decreases as inflation accelerates.

4. The longer the recovery period, the less the present value of depreciation tax shields. This is true regardless of the discount rate. If, say, r = .10, then 35 percent of the 5-year schedule's PV is .271. The same calculation for the 7-year schedule yields .253.

5. Forecasts of cash flows usually start with sales and cost of goods sold. However, a sale does not generate an immediate cash flow if the customer pays later. Cost of goods sold does not mean a cash outlay at the time of sale: The company will have paid out cash for raw materials and production. Also, a part of cost of goods sold may represent bills due to suppliers.

   Sales and cost of goods sold are converted to cash flows by tracking changes in working capital (inventory and accounts receivable and payable).

   If sales and cost of goods sold are not considered, and only cash inflows and outflows are forecasted, there is no need to track changes in working capital.

6. Comparing present values can be misleading when projects have different economic lives and the projects are part of an ongoing business. For example, a machine that costs $100,000 per year to operate and lasts 5 years is not necessarily more expensive than a machine that costs $125,000 per year to operate but lasts only 3 years, even though the present value of the first machine's lifetime costs may be higher. Calculating the machines' equivalent annual costs allows an unbiased comparison.

7. (*a*) $\text{NPV}_A = \$100,000$; $\text{NPV}_B = \$180,000$
(*b*) Equivalent cash flow of A $= 100,000/1.736 = \$57,604$; equivalent cash flow of B $= 180,000/2.487 = \$72,376$
(*c*) Machine B

8. Replace at end of 5 years ($\$80,000 > 72,376$).

Chapter 7

1. (*a*) About 12 percent
(*b*) 8–9 percent
(*c*) 0–1 percent
(*d*) About 20 percent (less in recent years)
(*e*) Less (diversification reduces risk)

2. Standard deviation of returns, correlated, less, unique market.

3. Expected payoff is $100 and expected return is zero. Variance is 20,000 (percent squared) and standard deviation is 141 percent.

4. Mr. Interchange had a lower average return than the S&P (6.0 percent versus 9.3 percent) but also had a lower standard deviation (12.4 percent versus 14.9 percent). (Following footnote 6, the answers are 13.8 percent and 16.6 percent.)

5. (*a*) False
(*b*) True
(*c*) True
(*d*) True
(*e*) False

6. A: 1.0; B: 2.0; C: 1.5; D: 0; E: -1.0

7. (*a*) 26 percent
(*b*) zero
(*c*) .75
(*d*) Less than 1.0 (the portfolio's risk is the same as the market, but some of this risk is unique risk).

8. 1.3 (Diversification does not affect market risk.)

9. (*d*)

10.

$x_1^2 \sigma_1^2$	$x_1 x_2 \sigma_{12}$	$x_1 x_3 \sigma_{13}$
$x_1 x_2 \sigma_{12}$	$x_2^2 \sigma_2^2$	$x_2 x_3 \sigma_{23}$
$x_1 x_3 \sigma_{13}$	$x_2 x_3 \sigma_{23}$	$x_3^2 \sigma_3^2$

11. False. Corporations can reduce risk by diversifying, but so can investors. Therefore they will not be prepared to pay extra for the stocks of diversified companies.

Chapter 8

1. (*a*) Figure 8-15: Diversification reduces risk (e.g., a mixture of portfolios A and B would have less risk than the average of A and B).

(*b*) Those along line *AB* in Figure 8-14.
(*c*) See Figure 1.

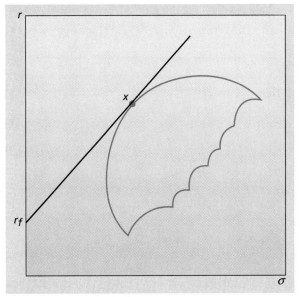

Figure 1   Chapter 8, Quiz question 1(c).

2. (*a*) Portfolio A (higher expected return, same risk)
   (*b*) Cannot say (depends on investor's attitude toward risk)
   (*c*) Portfolio F (lower risk, same expected return)

3. *a, b*

4. (*a*) See Figure 2.

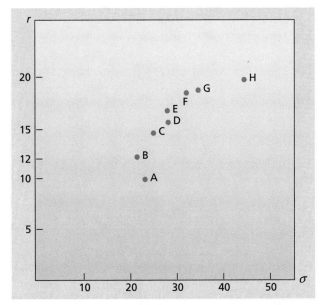

Figure 2   Chapter 8, Quiz question 4(a).

(*b*) A, D, G

(*c*) F

(*d*) 15 percent in C

(*e*) Put 25/32 of your money in F and lend 7/32 at 12 percent:
Expected return = 7/32 × 12 + 25/32 × 18 = 16.7 percent
Standard deviation = 7/32 × 0 + 25/32 × 32 = 25 percent
If you could borrow without limit, you would achieve as high an expected return as you'd like, with correspondingly high risk, of course.

5. (*a*) True

(*b*) False (it offers twice the market *risk premium*)

(*c*) False

6. (*a*) 11.3 percent

(*b*) 17.2 percent (Biogen)

(*c*) 7.1 percent (Exxon)

(*d*) lower (10.7 versus 11.1 percent)

(*e*) higher (9.7 versus 9.5 percent)

7. (*b*)

8. (*a*) .5 × 23 + .5 × 13 = 18 percent

(*b*) Variance = $(.5 \times 40)^2 + (.5 \times 24)^2 + 2(.5 \times .5 \times .8 \times 40 \times 24) = 928$.

Standard deviation = $\sqrt{928}$ = 30.5 percent

(*c*) β_A = average covariance/market variance
= $((.5 \times 40^2) + (.5 \times .8 \times 40 \times 24))/928 = 1.28$;
$\beta_B = ((.5 \times 24^2) + (.5 \times .8 \times 40 \times 24))/928 = .72$

(*d*) No (according to CAPM, expected return is 20.2 percent on *A* and 15.8 percent on *B*).

9. $r - r_f = b_1(r_{\text{factor 1}} - r_f) + b_2(r_{\text{factor 2}} - r_f) + \cdots$
r = expected return on stock
r_f = risk-free interest rate
$r_{\text{factor } j}$ = expected return on portfolio of stocks that is exposed only to the *j*th economic factor
b_j = sensitivity of stock to returns on *j*th factor

10. (*a*) 7 percent

(*b*) 7 + 1(5) + 1(−1) + 1(2) = 13 percent

(*c*) 7 + 0(5) + 2(−1) + 0(2) = 5 percent

(*d*) 7 + 0(5) + (−1.5)(−1) + 0(2) = 8.5 percent

Chapter 9

1. It will tend to overinvest in risky projects, and pass valuable safe projects by.

2. Suppose r_f = 7 percent.

$r = r_f + \beta(r_m - r_f) = 7 + 2.0\ (8.5) = 24$ percent

$\text{NPV} = -100{,}000 + \dfrac{150{,}000}{1.24} = +20{,}970$

3. BETA = market risk measure. Average risk would imply beta = 1.0
ALPHA = average price change on stock when market return was zero
R-SQR = ratio of market risk to total risk of stock—that is, proportion of variance of stock return attributable to market risk

RESID STD DEV-N = stock's unique risk, measured as a standard deviation
STD ERR OF BETA = measure of extent of possible error in beta estimate
STD ERR OF ALPHA = measure of extent of possible error in alpha estimate
ADJUSTED BETA = beta estimate adjusted for fact that high estimated betas tend to be overestimates of the true betas, and low estimated betas tend to be underestimates
NUMBER OF OBSERV = number of monthly returns used to estimate beta and alpha

4. $\beta_{\text{ASSETS}} = 0 \times .40 + .5 \times .60 = .30$
$r = 10 + .30(18 - 10) = 12.4$ percent

5. (a) $r_f + \beta(r_m - r_f) = 8 + 1.5 \times 9 = 21.5$ percent

(b) $\beta_{\text{ASSETS}} = \beta_{\text{DEBT}}\left(\dfrac{\text{debt}}{\text{debt} + \text{equity}}\right)$

$+ \beta_{\text{EQUITY}}\left(\dfrac{\text{equity}}{\text{debt} + \text{equity}}\right)$

$= 0 \times \dfrac{4}{4 + 6} + 1.5 \times \dfrac{6}{4 + 6}$

$= .9$

(c) $r_f + \beta_{\text{ASSETS}}(r_m - r_f) = 8 + .9 \times 9$
$= 16.1$ percent

(d) $r = 16.1$ percent

(e) $r_f + \beta(r_m - r_f) = 8 + 1.2 \times 9 = 18.8$ percent

6. (a) Expected daily production $= .2(0) + .8(.4 \times 1000 + .6 \times 5000) = 2720$ barrels. Expected annual revenues $= 2720 \times 365 \times \$18 = \$17.9$ million.

(b) The possibility of a dry hole is a diversifiable risk and should not affect the discount rate. This possibility should affect forecasted cash flows, however. See part (a).

7. (a) A (higher fixed cost).

(b) C (more cyclical revenues).

8. $\text{CEQ}_t/[(1 + r_f)^t]$; less than; $r_f + \beta(r_m - r_f)$; declines at a constant rate

9. (a) $\text{PV} = \dfrac{110}{1 + r_f + \beta(r_m - r_f)}$

$+ \dfrac{121}{[1 + r_f + \beta(r_m - r_f)]^2}$

$= \dfrac{110}{1.10} + \dfrac{121}{1.10^2} = \$200$

(b) $\dfrac{\text{CEQ}_1}{1.05} = \dfrac{110}{1.10}$, $\text{CEQ}_1 = \$105$

$\dfrac{\text{CEQ}_2}{1.05^2} = \dfrac{121}{1.10^2}$, $\text{CEQ}_2 = \$110.25$

(c) $\text{Ratio}_1 = \dfrac{105}{110} = .95$

$\text{Ratio}_2 = \dfrac{110.25}{121} = .91$

Chapter 10

1. (a) Detailed analysis of capital investment projects, to identify what cash flows depend on, what can go wrong, whether the project could be abandoned if performance is disappointing, and so on.
   (b) Analysis of how project profitability and NPV change if different assumptions are made about sales, cost, and other key variables.
   (c) Determines the level of future sales at which project profitability or NPV equals zero.
   (d) An extension of sensitivity analysis which explores all possible outcomes and weighs each by its probability.
   (e) A graphical technique for displaying possible future events and decisions taken in response to those events.
   (f) The additional present value created by the option to bail out of a project, and recover part of the initial investment, if the project performs poorly.
   (g) The additional present value created by the option to invest more and expand output, if a project performs well.

2. −$30 million

3. (a) NPV = old NPV

$$- \begin{array}{c} \text{additional} \\ \text{investment} \end{array} + \begin{array}{c} \text{reduction in} \\ \text{net variable} \\ \text{costs} \end{array}$$

$$+ \begin{array}{c} \text{increase in} \\ \text{depreciation tax} \\ \text{shield} \end{array}$$

$$= 34.3 - 150 + \sum_{t=1}^{10} \frac{(.5 \times 40)}{(1.10)^t}$$

$$+ \sum_{t=1}^{10} \frac{(.5 \times 15)}{(1.10)^t}$$

$$= \$53 \text{ million}$$

   (b) See Figure 3.
   (c) Figure 3 shows that expected sales have to be at least 85,000 for the project to have a positive NPV.

4. (a) "Optimistic" and "pessimistic" rarely show the full probability distribution of outcomes.
   (b) Sensitivity analysis changes variables one at a time; in practice, all variables change, and the changes are often interrelated. Sensitivity analysis using scenarios can help in this regard.

5. (a) False
   (b) True
   (c) True
   (d) True
   (e) True
   (f) False
   (g) True
   (h) True

6. (a) Describe how project cash flow depends on the underlying variables.
   (b) Specify probability distributions for forecast errors for these cash flows.
   (c) Draw from the probability distributions to simulate the cash flows.

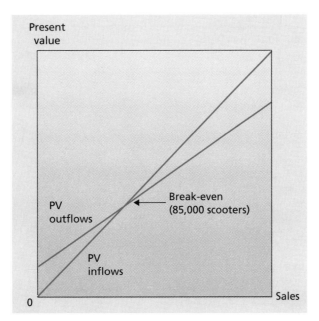

Figure 3   Chapter 10, Quiz question 3.

7.

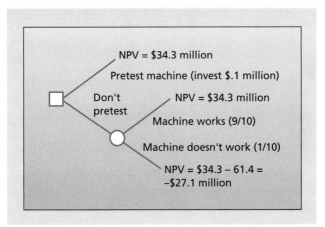

NPV (pretest) = 34.3 − .1 = $34.2 million

NPV (don't pretest) = .9 × 34.3 + .1 × (−27.1) = $28.2 million

8. See Table 1, page AN12. The decision tree shows the probability of finding oil earlier. At 2000 feet, the expected payoff to further drilling is (.25 × 1) + (.75 × −3) = −$2 million. This is greater than the payoff to stopping. Therefore Big should drill to 3000 feet. At 1000 feet the expected payoff to drilling to 2000 feet is .8 × [(.25 × 1) + (.75 × −3)] + (.2 × 2) = −$1.2 million. This is greater than the payoff to stopping. Therefore Big should drill to 2000 feet. The expected payoff to drilling to 1000 feet is (.5 × 3) + (.5 × −1.2) = $.9 million. As long as the certainty equivalent value of this payoff is positive, Big should drill to 1000 feet.

TABLE 1
Chapter 10, Quiz question 8.

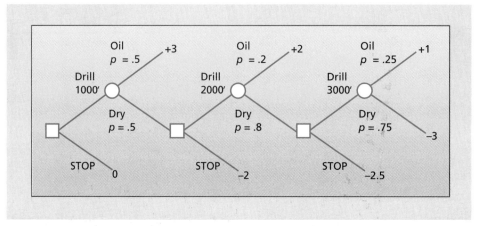

Chapter 11

1. To a baby with a hammer, everything looks like a nail. The point is that financial managers should not mechanically apply DCF to every problem. Sometimes part or all of a valuation problem can be solved by direct observation of market values. Sometimes careful thought about economic rents will clarify whether NPV is truly positive.

2. Your best estimate is $1000 per acre, the actual market value. Why do a discounted-cash-flow analysis to estimate market value when you can observe it directly?

3. (*a*) False
   (*b*) True
   (*c*) True
   (*d*) False

4. $15

5. DC-8s should have been valued at market prices for used airplanes. The low *book* depreciation charge was irrelevant. Alitalia should have compared the total costs of operating 747s and DC-8s, in which the DC-8s' cost includes the opportunity cost of capital on, and depreciation of, their actual secondhand value. *Note:* If 747s and DC-8s were perfect substitutes in terms of range, passenger comfort, and so on, we would expect the DC-8s' secondhand value to adjust until their total operating costs per seat mile were the same as the 747s'.

6. It depends first on competition among capital equipment producers. If other producers can quickly match the new machine, its advantages are passed on to its buyers. But then the buyers will compete to pass on the machine's advantages to their customers. In the end, users will realize positive NPVs from buying the machine only if they are in a position to make better use of it than their competitors.

7. Product prices tend to equilibrium levels at which efficient producers see capacity expansion as zero-NPV. Calculating NPV from the point of view of a European competitor allowed estimation of this equilibrium price.

8. First consider whether *renting* the building and opening the Taco Palace is positive NPV. Then consider whether to buy (instead of renting) based on your optimistic view of local real estate.

9. The present value of the future price of gold is equal to today's price. Just multiply production volume by today's gold price.

Chapter 12

1. (*a*) False
   (*b*) False—top management usually makes the final decision on major projects.
   (*c*) True
   (*d*) False. They may look at several criteria.
   (*e*) False
   (*f*) True

2. (*a*) Can lead to investment in negative-NPV project.
   (*b*) Confuses the relative NPVs of projects proposed by different business units.
   (*c*) Project interactions may be ignored. Some opportunities, such as the closing or sale of a division, will not be considered. Strategic investments may be missed.
   (*d*) Creates a bias in favor of quick payback projects and against long-lived projects that may have large NPVs.
   (*e*) This just encourages project sponsors to make more optimistic assumptions.

3. Cash flow, economic, less, greater.

4.

	Year 1	Year 2	Year 3
Cash flow	0	78.55	78.55
PV at start of year	100.00	120.00	65.46
PV at end of year	120.00	65.46	0
Change in value during year	+ 20.00	− 54.54	−65.46
Expected economic income	+ 20.00	+ 24.00	+13.09

5. (*a*) False; the biases rarely wash out. For example, steady-state *income* may not be much affected by investments in R&D, but book asset value is understated. Thus book profitability is too high, even in the steady state.
   (*b*) True. All biases in book profitability can be traced to accounting rules governing which assets are put on the balance sheet and the choice of book depreciation schedules.

Chapter 13

1. *c*

2. Weak, semistrong, strong, fundamental, strong, technical, weak

3. *c* and *f*

4. (*a*) Decline to $200
   (*b*) Less

    (c) A slight abnormal fall (the split is likely to have led investors to expect an above-average rise in dividends)

5. (a) False
    (b) True
    (c) False
    (d) True
    (e) False
    (f) True (a small change in price *in the absence of new information* causes a large increase in demand)

6. $6 - (-.2 + 1.45 \times 5) = -1.05$ percent

7. (a) True
    (b) False
    (c) True
    (d) True
    (e) True

8. Decrease. The stock price already reflects an expected 25 percent increase. The 20 percent increase conveys bad news relative to expectations.

Chapter 14

1. (a) $40,000/.50 = 80,000$ shares
    (b) 78,000 shares
    (c) 2000 shares are held as Treasury stock
    (d) 20,000 shares
    (e)

Common stock	$ 45,000
Additional paid-in capital	25,000
Retained earnings	30,000
Common equity	100,000
Treasury stock	5,000
Net common equity	$ 95,000

2. (a) 80 votes
    (b) $10 \times 80 = 800$ votes

3. (a) Funded
    (b) Eurobond
    (c) Subordinated
    (d) Debentures
    (e) Sinking fund
    (f) Call
    (g) Prime rate
    (h) Floating rate
    (i) Private placement, public issue
    (j) Lease
    (k) Convertible
    (l) Warrant; exercise price

4.

Internally generated cash	72
Financial deficit	28
Net share issues	−6
Debt issues	17

5. (*a*) False
   (*b*) True
   (*c*) True
   (*d*) True
   (*e*) True
   (*f*) True
   (*g*) True
   (*h*) True
   (*i*) False
   (*j*) False
   (*k*) False
   (*l*) True
   (*m*) True

6. (*a*) Agents act in their own interests rather than maximizing market value of the firm.
   (*b*) Principals incur costs to monitor agents and constrain their actions.

7. This separation occurs when managers own only a small minority of outstanding shares. This raises concerns about agency costs.

8. In the United States, banks cannot hold shares of nonfinancial corporations. In Japan, banks can hold no more than 5 percent of a nonfinancial company's shares, but banks stand at the center of networks of companies (kiretsus) linked by cross-holdings of shares and various business relationships. In Germany, banks often hold large blocks of shares and vote other shares by proxy. Thus, in Germany, banks can have effective voting control of nonfinancial companies.

Chapter 15

1. (*a*) Issue of seasoned stock
   (*b*) U.S. bond issue by foreign corporation
   (*c*) Bond issue by industrial company
   (*d*) Bond issue by large industrial company
   (*e*) Issued outside United States

2. A (*d*); B (*f*); C (*c*); D (*a*); E (*b*); F (*g*); G (*e*)

3. (*a*) A large issue
   (*b*) A bond issue
   (*c*) A large competitive bond issue
   (*d*) A small private placement of bonds

4. (*a*) False
   (*b*) True
   (*c*) False
   (*d*) True
   (*e*) False

5. (*a*) 50,000 shares
   (*b*) Primary: 500,000 shares
        Secondary: 400,000 shares
   (*c*) $15 or 19 percent, which is the same as observed by Ibbotson, Sindelar, and Ritter.

(*d*)

	Millions
Underwriting cost	$ 4.5
Administrative cost	.82
Underpricing	13.5
Total	$18.82

6. (*a*) Net proceeds of public issue = 10,000,000 − 150,000 − 80,000 = $9,770,000
Net proceeds of private placement = $9,970,000

(*b*) PV of extra interest on private placement = $\sum_{t=1}^{10} \dfrac{.005 \times 10,000,000}{1.085^t} =$ $328,000, i.e., extra cost of higher interest on private placement more than outweighs saving in issue costs. N.b. We ignore taxes.

(*c*) Private placement debt can be custom-tailored and the terms more easily renegotiated.

7. (*a*) Number of rights needed to purchase one share: 2
(*b*) Number of new shares: 50,000
(*c*) Amount of new investment: $500,000
(*d*) Total value of company after issue: $4,500,000
(*e*) Total number of shares after issue: 150,000
(*f*) Rights-on price: $40
(*g*) Ex-rights price: $30
(*h*) Price of a right: $10

Chapter 16

1. (*a*) A, e; B, d; C, c; D, a; E, b
(*b*) November 27 = ex-dividend date
(*c*) .80/65 = .012 or 1.2 percent
(*d*) .80/3.96 = .202 or about 20 percent
(*e*) The price would fall to 65/1.1 = $59.09.

2. (*e*) (they are taxed on 30 percent of dividends received)

3. (*a*) False. The dividend depends on past dividends and current and forecasted earnings.
(*b*) True. This target does reflect growth opportunities and capital expenditure requirements.
(*c*) False. Dividends are adjusted gradually to a target. The target is based on current or forecasted earnings multiplied by the target payout ratio.
(*d*) True. Dividend changes convey information to investors.
(*e*) False. Dividends are "smoothed." Managers rarely increase regular dividends temporarily. They may pay a special dividend, however.
(*f*) False. Dividends are rarely cut when repurchases are being made.

4. (*a*) .34
(*b*) .23

5. A dividend increase signals management's optimism about future earnings (the company is putting its money where its mouth is).

6. Before the Tax Reform Act investors paid up to 50 percent tax on dividends versus a maximum 20 percent on capital gains. After the act, individuals were

taxed equally on dividends and realized capital gains. Because capital gains can be deferred, individuals still had a tax reason to prefer gains.

Because effective tax rates on dividends and capital gains are now more alike, individual investors are less motivated to hold low-payout stocks. This would induce a *relative* fall in the price of low-payout stocks and a *relative* rise in their required pretax return.

7. A two-tier system taxes dividends twice, once at the corporate level before the dividend is paid, and again at the personal level when the investor receives the dividend. An imputation system removes part or all of the corporate-level tax by giving the investor a credit for the corporate tax. The imputation system reduces the total tax on dividends and so encourages payout.

8. (*a*) $127.25
   (*b*) Nothing; the stock price will stay at $130. 846,154 shares will be repurchased.
   (*c*) The with-dividend price stays at $130. Ex-dividend it drops to $124.50; 883,534 shares will be issued.

Chapter 17

1. (*a*) .10P
   (*b*) Buy 10 percent of B's debt + 10 percent of B's equity
   (*c*) .10(P − 100)
   (*d*) Borrow an amount equal to 10 percent of B's debt and buy 10 percent of A's equity

2. Note the market value of Copperhead is far in excess of its book value:

	Market Value
Common stock (8 million shares at $2)	$16,000,000
Short-term loans	$2,000,000

Ms. Kraft owns .625 percent of the firm, which proposes to increase common stock to $17 million and cut short-term debt. Ms. Kraft can offset this by (*a*) borrowing .00625 × 1,000,000 = $6250, and (*b*) buying that much more Copperhead stock.

3. Expected return on assets is

$$r_A = .08 \times 30/80 + .16 \times 50/80 = .13$$

The new return on equity will be

$$r_E = .13 + 20/60(.13 - .08) = .147$$

If stockholders pass on more of the firm's risk to debtholders, expected return on equity will be *less* than 14.7 percent.

4. (*a*) (i) $\beta_A = \left(\dfrac{D}{D + E} \times \beta_D\right)$

$$+ \left(\dfrac{E}{D + E} \times \beta_E\right)$$

$$1.0 = (.5 \times 0) + (.5 \times \beta_E)$$

$$\therefore \beta_E = 2.0$$

(ii) $\beta_D = 0$

(iii) $\beta_A = 1.0$

(b)   (i) .10

(ii) $r_A = \left(\dfrac{D}{D + E} \times r_D\right)$

$+ \left(\dfrac{E}{D + E} \times r_E\right)$

$.10 = (.5 \times .05) + (.5 \times r_E)$

$r_E = .15$

(iii) $r_D = .05$

(iv) $r_A = .10$

(c)   (i) 50 percent

(ii) 6.7 (i.e., the P/E ratio falls to offset the increase in EPS)

5. (a)

Operating income, dollars	500	1000	1500	2000
Interest, dollars	250	250	250	250
Equity earnings, dollars	250	750	1250	1750
Earnings per share	.33	1.00	1.67	2.33
Return on shares, percent	3.3	10	16.7	23.3

(b) $\beta_A = \left(\dfrac{D}{D + E} \times \beta_D\right) + \left(\dfrac{E}{D + E} \times \beta_E\right)$

$.8 = (.25 \times 0) + (.75 \times \beta_E)$

$\beta_E = 1.07$

6. (a) True, so long as the market value of "old" debt does not change.

(b) False. MM's Proposition I says only that overall firm value ($V = D + E$) does not depend on capital structure.

(c) False. Borrowing increases equity risk even if debt is default-risk free.

(d) False. Limited liability affects the relative values of debt and equity, not their sum.

(e) True. Limited liability protects shareholders if the firm defaults.

(f) True—but the required rate of return on equity and the firm's assets are the same only if the firm holds risk-free assets. In this case r_A, r_D, and r_E all equal the risk-free rate of interest.

(g) False. The shareholders could make the same debt issue on their own account.

(h) True. To put it more precisely, it assumes that the expected rate of return to equity goes up, but stockholders' required rate of return goes up proportionately. Therefore, stock price is unchanged.

(i) False. The formula $r_E = r_A + D/E(r_A - r_D)$ does not require $r_D = $ a constant.

(j) False. The clientele has to be willing to pay extra for the debt, which they will not do if plenty of corporate debt issues are already available.

7. See Figure 17-5.

8. (a) $r_A = .15$, $r_E = .175$

(b) $\beta_A = .6$ (unchanged), $\beta_D = .3$, $\beta_E = .9$

(c) 18.3

9. (a) 10 percent

(b) 13.3 percent

10. (*a*) Not affected
    (*b*) 16 million
    (*c*) $250 million
    (*d*) D/V = 160/250 = .64
    (*e*) No one

11. (*a*) It rises by $2 per share or $30 million.
    (*b*) 5 million
    (*c*) $250 million (unchanged)
    (*d*) 130/250 = .52 (using market values)
    (*e*) Shareholders gain; investors in old debt lose.

Chapter 18

1. (*a*) PV tax shield
$$= \frac{T_C(r_D D)}{1 + r_D} = \frac{.35(.08 \times 1000)}{1.08}$$
$$= 25.93$$
   (*b*) PV tax shield
$$= \sum_{t=1}^{5} \frac{T_C(r_D D)}{(1 + r_D)^t}$$
$$= \sum_{t=1}^{5} \frac{.35(.08 \times 1000)}{(1.08)^t} = \$111.80$$
   (*c*) PV tax shield $= T_C D = \$350$

2. (*a*) PV tax shield $= T_C D = \$16$
   (*b*) $T_C \times 20 = \$8$
   (*c*) New PV tax shield
$$= \sum_{t=1}^{5} \frac{.40(.08 \times 60)}{(1.08)^t} = \$7.67$$
   Therefore, company value $= 168 - 24 + 7.67 = \$151.67$

3. (*a*) Relative advantage of debt
$$= \frac{1 - T_P}{(1 - T_{PE})(1 - T_C)}$$
$$= \frac{.69}{(1)(.65)} = 1.06$$
   (*b*) Relative advantage $= \dfrac{.69}{(.69)(.65)} = 1.54$

4. (*a*) Direct costs of financial distress are the legal and administrative costs of bankruptcy. Indirect costs include possible delays in liquidation (Eastern Airlines) or poor investment or operating decisions while bankruptcy is being resolved (Penn Central). Also the *threat* of bankruptcy can lead to costs.
   (*b*) If financial distress increases odds of default, managers' and shareholders' incentives change. This can lead to poor investment or financing decisions.
   (*c*) See the answer to 4(*b*). Examples are the "games" described in Section 18-3.

5. Not necessarily. Announcement of bankruptcy can send a message of poor profits and prospects. Part of the share price drop can be attributed to anticipated bankruptcy costs, however.

6. A firm with no taxable income saves no taxes by borrowing and paying inter-est. The interest payments would simply add to its tax-loss carry-forwards. Such a firm would have little tax incentive to borrow.

7. (*a*) Stockholders win. Bond value falls, since the value of assets securing the bond has fallen.
   (*b*) Bondholder wins if we assume the cash is left invested in Treasury bills. The bondholder is sure to get $26 plus interest. Stock value is zero, be-cause there is no chance that firm value can rise above $50.
   (*c*) The bondholders lose. The firm adds assets worth $10 and debt worth $10. This would increase Circular's debt ratio, leaving the old bondholders more exposed. The old bondholders' loss is the stockholders' gain.
   (*d*) Both bondholders and stockholders win. They share the (net) increase in firm value. The bondholders' position is not eroded by the issue of a junior secu-rity. (We assume that the preferred does not lead to still more game playing, and that the new investment does not make the firm's *assets* safer or riskier.)
   (*e*) Bondholders lose because they are at risk for longer. Stockholders win.

8. Specialized, intangible assets such as growth opportunities are most likely to lose value in financial distress. Safe, tangible assets with good secondhand mar-kets are least likely to lose value. Costs of financial distress are thus likely to be less for, say, real estate firms or trucking companies than for advertising firms or high-tech growth companies.

9. More profitable firms have more taxable income to shield and are less likely to incur the costs of distress. Therefore the trade-off theory predicts high debt ratios. In practice the more profitable companies borrow least.

10. Firms have a pecking order of preference for new finance. Internal finance is preferred, followed by debt and then external equity. Each firm's observed debt ratio reflects its cumulative requirements for external finance. The more prof-itable companies borrow least because they have sufficient internal finance.

11. When a company issues securities, outside investors worry that management may have unfavorable information. If so the securities can be overpriced. This worry is much less with debt than equity. Debt securities are safer than equity, and their price is less affected if unfavorable news comes out later.

    A company that can borrow (without incurring substantial costs of financial dis-tress) usually does so. An issue of equity would be read as "bad news" by investors, and the new stock could be sold only at a discount to the previous market price.

12. Value is increased if the cash would otherwise be plowed back into negative-NPV investments. If this possibility worries investors, a high debt ratio may reassure them by committing the firm to pay out cash flows.

13. Financial slack is most valuable to growth companies with good but uncertain investment opportunities. Slack means that financing can be raised quickly for positive-NPV investments.

14. Chapter 7 is designed to liquidate the firm's assets and pay out as much as pos-sible to creditors. Chapter 11 is designed to rehabilitate the firm. Under Chapter 11, management (or perhaps other parties) is given time to propose a plan for fixing the firm's problems and maintaining it as a going concern. The creditors must approve the plan, however.

15. (*a*) False
    (*b*) True

(c) True

(d) True

(e) False. Tax-loss carry-forwards do not survive liquidation.

16. There is always a chance that the company's fortunes will improve during bankruptcy, allowing creditors to be paid off and leaving something for shareholders. Also, shareholders may retain some interest in a firm reorganized under Chapter 11.

Chapter 19

1. Market values of debt and equity are $D = .9 \times 75 = \$67.5$ million and $E = 42 \times 2.5 = \$105$ million. $D/V = .39$.

$r^* = .09(1 - .35).39 + .18(.61) = .1325$, or 13.25 percent

The key assumptions: stable capital structure (D/V constant); Federated will pay taxes at 35 percent marginal rate in all relevant future years; use r^* as discount rate for projects with same risk as average of firm's assets.

2. (a) $r^* = r - Lr_D T_C\left(\dfrac{1 + r}{1 + r_D}\right)$

$\qquad = r - .39(.09)(.35)\left(\dfrac{1 + r}{1.09}\right) = .1325$

$\qquad r = .1454$, or about 14.5 percent

(b) $r^* = .1454 - .25(.09)(.35)\left(\dfrac{1.1454}{1.09}\right) = .137$, or 13.7 percent

$\qquad r^* = .09(1 - .35).25 + r_E(.75) = .137$

$\qquad r_E = .163$, or 16.3 percent

3. If the bank debt is treated as permanent financing, the capital structure proportions are:

Bank debt ($r_D = 10$ percent)	$ 280	9.4%
Long-term debt ($r_D = 9$ percent)	1800	60.4
Equity ($r_E = 18$ percent, 90×10 million shares)	900	30.2
	$2980	100.0%

$r^* = .10(1 - .35).094 + .09(1 - .35).604 + .18(.302)$

$\quad = .096$, or 9.6 percent

4. Forecast after-tax incremental cash flows as explained in Section 6-1. Interest is not included—the forecasts assume an all-equity financed firm.

5. Calculate APV by subtracting $4 million from base-case NPV.

6. APV = base-case NPV ± PV financing side effects

(a) APV = $0 - .15(500,000) = -75,000$

(b) APV = $0 + 175,000 = +175,000$

(c) APV = $0 + 76,000 = +76,000$

(d) APV = $0 - .15(500,000) + 76,000 = +1000$

7. Miles-Ezzell $r^* = .12 - .5(.08)(.35)\left(\dfrac{1.12}{1.08}\right) = .1055$

$$\text{NPV} = -10 + \sum_{t=1}^{10}\frac{1.8}{(1.1055)^t} = .804, \text{ or } \$804,000$$

MM $r^* = .12(1 - .35(.5)) = .099$

$$\text{NPV} = -10 + \sum_{t=1}^{10}\frac{1.8}{(1.099)^t} = 1.108 \text{ or } \$1,108,000$$

The MM formula gives a lower adjusted discount rate, because it assumes that future tax shields are fixed. The tax shields are implicitly discounted at a lower rate, so project NPV is higher.

8. (*a*) 12 percent, of course

   (*b*) $r^* = .12 - .30(.075)(.35)\left(\dfrac{1.12}{1.075}\right)$

   $= .112$, or 11.2 percent
   $r^* = .075(1 - .35).30 + r_E(.70) = .112$
   $r_E = .139$, or about 14 percent

9. PV tax shield $= (.10/.34)\,561{,}000 = \$165{,}000$
   APV $= 170{,}000 + 165{,}000 = \$335{,}000$

10. (*a*) Base-case NPV $= -1000 + \dfrac{1200}{1.20} = 0$

    (*b*) PV tax shield $= \dfrac{.1 \times .2 \times .3(1000)}{1.10} = \$5.45$

    APV $= 0 + 5.45 = \$5.45$

11. No. The more debt you use, the higher rate of return equity investors will require. (Lenders may demand more also.) Thus there is a hidden cost of the "cheap" debt: It makes equity more expensive.

12. The after-tax borrowing or lending rate.

13. PV lease $= \displaystyle\sum_{t=0}^{5} \dfrac{(1 - .35)\,100{,}000}{[1 + (1 - .35).09]^t}$

    $= \$339{,}925$

14. Below both lines. WACC is less than the opportunity cost of capital as long as interest tax shields add to the market value of the firm.

Chapter 20

1. Call; exercise; put; European; call; assets; bondholders (lenders); assets; promised payment to bondholders

2. (*a*) Call
   (*b*) Put
   (*c*) Call
   (*d*) Call
   (*e*) Put
   (*f*) Call
   (*g*) Call
   (*h*) Put

3. Figure 20-11*a* represents a call seller; Figure 20-11*b* represents a call buyer.

4. (*a*) The exercise price of the put option (i.e., you'd sell stock for the exercise price).
   (*b*) The value of the stock (i.e., you would throw away the put and keep the stock).

5. Buy a call and lend the present value of the exercise price.

6. The lower bound is the option's value if it expired immediately: either zero or the stock price less the exercise price, whichever is larger. The upper bound is the stock price.

7. (*a*)   Zero
   (*b*)   Stock price less the present value of the exercise price.
8. The call price
   (*a*)   Increases
   (*b*)   Decreases
   (*c*)   Increases
   (*d*)   Increases
   (*e*)   Decreases
   (*f*)   Decreases
9. True. The beta and standard deviation of an option always exceeds its stock's. The risk of an option decreases as the stock price increases.
10. First, estimating expected cash flows from an option is difficult, although not impossible. Second, the risk of an option changes every time the stock price changes, so there is no single, well-defined risk-adjusted discount rate.
11. With an exercise price of 60,

$$\sigma \times \sqrt{t} = .06 \times \sqrt{3} = .10$$

$$P/PV(EX) = 60/(60/1.03) = 1.03$$

   (*a*)   Call price = approximately $.056 \times 60$
   $$= 3.4$$
   (*b*)   Put price = call price + PV(EX) − stock price
   $$= 3.4 + 58.23 − 60$$
   $$= 1.6 \text{ (approximately)}$$
   (*a*)   From Appendix Table 7 call option delta = .6. Thus replicating portfolio is .6 shares (cost = $.6 \times 60 = \$36$) and borrow balance ($36 − 3.4 = \$32.6$).
   (*b*)   Put option delta = $.6 − 1 = −.4$. Replicating portfolio is *sell* .4 shares (cash inflow = $.4 \times 60 = \$24$) and lend balance ($24 + 1.6 = \$25.6$).
12. (*a*)   The option payoffs are either $86.67 − 65 = \$21.67$ or zero. These payoffs can be replicated by buying .5715 shares and borrowing $27.18.
   The option is worth $.5715 \times 65 − 27.18 = 9.97$.
   (*b*)   Let p = risk-neutral probability of rise.
   $$.333p − .25(1 − p) = .025$$
   $$p = .472$$
   $$\text{Value of option} = \frac{.472(21.67)}{1.025} = 9.98$$
   The slight difference from (*a*) is due to rounding.
   The call is worth more because its "upside" payoff increases. The "downside" payoff remains at 0.
13. Your stock options are worth more under the riskier alternative.
14. (*a*)   See Figure 4, page AN24.
   (*b*)   Zero. From put-call parity,
   Value of call + PV(exercise price) = value of put + share price
   Since in this case PV(exercise price) = share price, the cost of the call must equal the proceeds from selling the put.
15. (*a*)   2/3
   (*b*)   PV = $2/3 \times 100 − 30.30 = 36.36$
   (*c*) $p = .4$
   (*d*)   PV = $\dfrac{.4 \times 100 + .6 \times 0}{1.1} = 36.36$

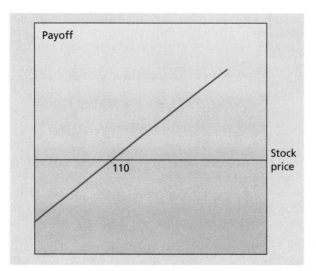

Figure 4   Chapter 20, Quiz question 14.

   (*e*) No. The price of an option does not depend on the expected return of the security on which the option is written.

16. Sell the stock short for 200, buy the call for 75, invest 125. After one year recover the 125 (plus interest) and exercise the call if it's in the money. This gives a guaranteed profit.

Chapter 21

1. (*a*) Backwoods has an in-the-money call option on expansion.
   (*b*) Project provides call option on further projects.
   (*c*) Standard equipment contains valuable abandonment (put) option.
   (*d*) Phoenix has the option to exchange one asset (a passenger plane) for another (a freight plane).

2. (*a*) Using risk-neutral method

$$(p \times 20) + (1 - p)(-16.7) = 1$$

$$p = .48$$

$$\text{Value of call} = \frac{(.48 \times 8) + (.52 \times 0)}{1.01}$$

$$= 3.8$$

   (*b*) $\text{Delta} = \dfrac{\text{spread of option prices}}{\text{spread of stock prices}} = \dfrac{8}{14.7}$

$$= .544$$

   (*c*)

	Current Cash Flow	Possible Future Cash Flows	
Buy call	−3.8	0	+8.0
equals			
Buy .544 shares	−21.8	+18.2	+26.2
Borrow 18.0	+18.0	−18.2	−18.2
	−3.8	0	+8.0

(*d*) Possible stock prices with call option prices in parentheses:

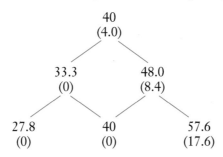

Option prices were calculated as follows:

Month 1: (i) $\dfrac{(.48 \times 0) + (.52 \times 0)}{1.01}$

$= 0$

(ii) $\dfrac{(.48 \times 17.6) + (.52 \times 0)}{1.01}$

$= 8.4$

Month 0: $\dfrac{(.48 \times 8.4) + (.52 \times 0)}{1.01}$

$= 4.0$

(*e*) Delta $= \dfrac{\text{spread of option prices}}{\text{spread of stock prices}}$

$= \dfrac{8.4}{14.7} = .57$

3. The period to expiration is subdivided into an indefinitely large number of subperiods (and when there is no incentive to early exercise).

4. (*a*) Yes (earn interest on exercise money)
   (*b*) No (dividend gain is less than loss of interest)
   (*c*) Yes (if the dividend becomes sufficiently larger than loss of interest to justify killing the option)

5. (*a*) $(p \times 15) + (1 - p)(-13) = 10$
   $p = .82$
   Put value if exercised now $= \text{EX} - 60$

   Put value if not exercised now $= \dfrac{(.82 \times 0) + .18(\text{EX} - 52.2)}{1.1}$

   $\therefore$ You are indifferent if $\text{EX} = 61.5$
   (*b*) Higher interest rate reduces break-even exercise price (i.e., the benefit of the higher interest rate offsets the disadvantage of the lower exercise price).

6. A *commitment* to invest in the Mark II would have negative NPV. The *option* to invest has positive NPV. The value of the option more than offsets the negative NPV of the Mark I.

7. (**i**) Keep gold stocks and buy put option with exercise "price" of £500,000.
   (**ii**) Sell gold stocks, invest £472,000 in 6-month time deposit, and use balance of £128,000 to buy call option on gold stocks with exercise price of £500,000.

Chapter 22

1. (*a*)   (**i**) 0
         (**ii**) 0
        (**iii**) 0
        (**iv**) $10
         (**v**) $20

   (*b*)

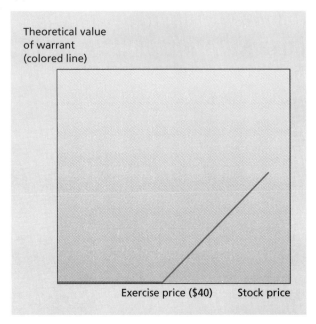

Theoretical value
of warrant
(colored line)

Exercise price ($40)   Stock price

   (*c*)   Buy the warrant and exercise, then sell the stock.
         Net gain = −5 − 40 + 60 = +$15.

2. (*a*) No
   (*b*) No
   (*c*) 1/3 × 70 = $23.33
   (*d*) No
   (*e*) Zero
   (*f*) More
   (*g*) (**i**) less; (**ii**) less; (**iii**) more; (**iv**) more; (**v**) more
   (*h*) When the dividends on the stock outweigh the interest on the exercise
         price.

3. (*a*) EPS = $2.00
   (*b*) Diluted EPS = $1.33

4. (*a*) 1000/47 = 21.28
   (*b*) 1000/50 = $20.00
   (*c*) 21.28 × 41.50 = $883.12, or 88.31 percent
   (*d*) 650/21.28 = $30.55
   (*e*) No (not if the investor is free to convert immediately)
   (*f*) $12.22, i.e., (910 − 650)/21.28
   (*g*) (47/41.50) − 1 = .13, or 13 percent
   (*h*) When the price reaches 102.75

5. Convertibles give investors in small or risky companies an "upside" to offset the risk of default. Assessing or monitoring risk and the likelihood of default is not as important as for straight debt. Also, the low coupon rate of convertibles is a convenience to cash-short, rapidly growing companies.

Chapter 23

1. (*a*) Figure 5 shows that an increase in the demand for capital increases investment and saving. The rate of interest also rises.

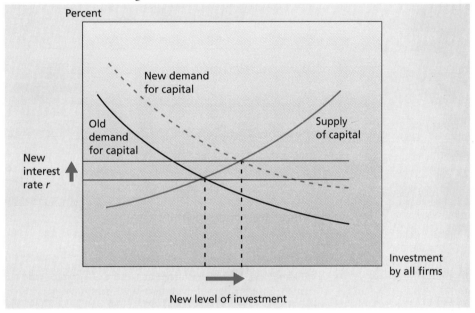

Figure 5   Chapter 23, Quiz question 1(a).

(*b*) Figure 6, page AN28, shows that an increase in the supply of capital also increases investment and saving. The rate of interest falls.

2. (*a*) $PV = \dfrac{50}{1 + r_1} + \dfrac{1050}{(1 + r_2)^2}$

(*b*) $PV = \dfrac{50}{1 + y} + \dfrac{1050}{(1 + y)^2}$

(*c*) Less (it is between the 1-year and 2-year spot rates).

(*d*) Yield to maturity; spot rate

3. (*a*) Fall

(*b*) Less than 100

(*c*) Less than the coupon

(*d*) Higher prices, other things equal

4. (*a*) 12 percent

(*b*) 82.52 (interpolated)

(*c*) 68.22, 87.54

5. (*a*) $(1 + r_2)^2 = (1 + r_1)(1 + f_2)$

$1.03^2 = 1.01 \times (1 + f_2)$

$f_2 = .05,$ or 5 percent

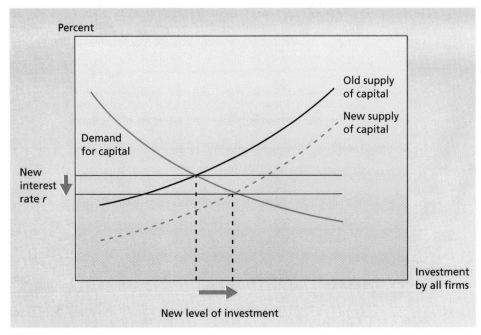

Figure 6   Chapter 23, Quiz question 1(b).

(b)   The expected 1-year spot rate at time 1, $E(_1r_2)$, equals the forward rate f_2.
(c)   Against (unless one believes that investors have generally expected interest rates to rise).
(d)   The forward rate equals the expected spot rate *plus* a liquidity premium.
(e)   Long-term bonds.
(f)   Short-term bonds.
(g)   The forward rate equals the expected spot rate plus a premium for the inflation risk.

6. (a)   Aaa, Aa, A, and Baa
   (b)   (i) Increase
         (ii) Increase
         (iii) Increase (*Note:* The value of the stockholders' call on the firm's assets increases with the interest rate.)
         (iv) Increase

7. (a)   Value of guarantee = value of put (i.e., shareholders' option to put the company to the bondholders for the face value of the bond).
   (b)   Put option: exercise price is face value of bond.

8. (a)   False. Duration depends on the coupon as well as the maturity.
   (b)   False. Given the yield to maturity, volatility is proportional to duration.
   (c)   True. A lower coupon rate means longer duration and therefore higher volatility.
   (d)   False. A higher interest rate reduces the relative present value of (distant) principal repayments.

9.

	Year	C_t	$PV(C_t)$	Proportion of Total Value	Proportion × Time
Security A	1	40	37.04	.359	.359
	2	40	34.29	.333	.666
	3	40	31.75	.308	.924
		V	= 103.08	1.0	
				Duration = 1.949 years	
Security B	1	20	18.52	.141	.141
	2	20	17.15	.131	.262
	3	120	95.26	.728	2.184
		V	= 130.93	1.0	
				Duration = 2.587 years	
Security C	1	10	9.26	.088	.088
	2	10	8.57	.082	.164
	3	110	87.32	.830	2.490
		V	= 105.15	1.0	
				Duration = 2.742 years	

Volatilities: A, 1.80; B, 2.40; C, 2.49.

10. The semiannual discount rate was 6.65/2 = 3.325 percent. Coupon rate = 10.75/2 = 5.375 (percent of face value). There are 16 semiannual periods.

$$PV = \sum_{t=1}^{16} \frac{5.375}{(1.03325)^t} + \frac{100}{(1.03325)^{16}} = 125.12$$

Chapter 24

1. (*a*) High-grade utility bonds
   (*b*) Short-dated notes
   (*c*) Industrial holding companies
   (*d*) Industrial bonds
   (*e*) Railroads

2. ■ Indenture or trust deeds—agreement between the borrower and a trust company representing bondholders.

   ■ Notes—short- or medium-term debt securities—debentures have longer maturities.

   ■ Mortgage bonds—debt secured by property.

   ■ Call provision—company has right to call and pay off debt.

   ■ Sinking fund—provision for repayment of part or most of principal prior to maturity.

   ■ Foreign bond—bond sold in another country's market.

   ■ Eurobond—bond sold simultaneously in several markets.

   ■ Defeasance—buying the government securities sufficient to cover debt service. The government securities are put in a trust and the debt is removed from the company's balance sheet.

- Negative pledge clause—limits additional secured debt.
- Affirmative covenant—borrower accepts certain duties; e.g., to maintain minimum working capital or to supply accounting statements.
- Negative covenant—borrower is prohibited from taking certain actions; e.g., increasing dividends or taking on additional debt.

3. (*a*) Decreases
   (*b*) Impossible to say
   (*c*) Increases

4. (*a*) You would like an issue of junior debt.
   (*b*) You prefer it not to do so (unless it is also junior debt). The existing property may not be sufficient to pay off your debt.

5. (*a*) First Boston, Goldman Sachs, Shearson Lehman, Stifel Nicholas
   (*b*) Continental Bank
   (*c*) $967.25
   (*d*) Registered
   (*e*) 104.26 (percent of par)
   (*f*) No

6. (*a*) Issue price + approximately 1 month's interest = 976.00 + 95/12 = $983.92
   (*b*) December 1, 1986; $47.50
   (*c*) Sinking fund designed to pay off all but $8.64 million of principal. The company must pay off at least $13.5 million.
   (*d*) 2002

7. (*a*) False. Lenders usually retain some recourse; e.g., they may demand a completion guarantee.
   (*b*) The first sentence is true, but some new securities (e.g., zero-coupon bonds) survive even when the original motive for issuing them disappears.
   (*c*) False. The borrower has the option.
   (*d*) True. But debt issues with weak covenants suffered in such takeovers.
   (*e*) True. The costs of renegotiation are less.

Chapter 25

1. (*a*) True
   (*b*) True
   (*c*) False (depends on coupon)
   (*d*) False
   (*e*) False
   (*f*) False
   (*g*) True

2. Sell short $1.2 million of the market portfolio. In practice rather than "sell the market" you would sell futures on $1.2 million of the market index.

3. (*a*) The calculations for A and C are given for Quiz question 9, Chapter 23. For B, the calculations change to:

Year	C_t	$PV(C_t)$	Proportion	Proportion × Time
1	120	111.11	1.0	1.0
2	0	0	0	0
3	0	0	0	0
		$V = 111.11$	1.0	Duration = 1.0 years

(**b**) A has a duration of 1.949 years. So does a portfolio with 45.5 percent invested in B and 54.5 percent invested in C. To hedge A sell $4.55 million of B and $5.45 million of C.

(**c**) Sell $5.13 million of A, borrow $10 - 5.13 = \$4.87$ million short-term. Alternatively, sell $3.65 million of C and borrow $6.35 million.

4. $\dfrac{\text{Value of future}}{1.049} = 95 - 4$

∴ Value of future $= 95.46$

5. $\dfrac{2408}{1.12} = 2550 + 100 - \text{PV (convenience yield)}$

∴ PV (convenience yield) $= \$500$

6. (**i**) A promise to make a series of payments in one currency in exchange for receiving a series of payments in another currency.

(**ii**) A promise to make a series of fixed-rate payments in exchange for receiving a series of floating-rate payments (or vice versa). Also exchange of floating-rate payments linked to different reference rates (e.g., LIBOR and commercial paper rate).

Swaps may be used because a company believes it has an advantage in borrowing in a particular market or in order to change structure of existing liabilities.

7. (**a**) A shortage of heating oil increases net convenience yield and reduces the futures price relative to spot price.

(**b**) Spot and futures prices decrease. The futures price rises relative to spot because convenience yield falls and storage costs rise.

8. Basis risk is highest in (*a*), because Disney stock has considerable nonmarket risk. In (*b*) basis risk is likely to be small, and in (*c*) it should disappear.

9. Insurance companies have the experience to assess routine risks and advise companies how to reduce the frequency of accidents. These advantages are less likely for infrequent events with large losses. The stock market can be an efficient risk-absorber for large but diversifiable events.

10. ■ Moral hazard—having an insurance policy makes the policyholder less careful and increases the odds of loss.

■ Adverse selection—when an insurance company offers policies at a set price, it will get more high-risk customers than low-risk ones.

Moral hazard and adverse selection both increase the insurance company's losses and increase the premium it must charge to break even.

Chapter 26

1. A, c; B, d or i; C, b or e; D, f; E, a; F, h; G, g

2. a, b, d, f, and h (though there may be other ways to reduce AMT)

3. (a) The lessor must charge enough to cover the present value of the costs of owning and operating the asset over its expected economic life. In a competitive leasing market the present value of rentals cannot exceed the present value of costs. The competitive rental payment ends up equal to the lessor's equivalent annual cost.

(b) The user's equivalent annual cost is the annual cost to the user of owning and operating the asset. If the operating lease rate is less than this cost, it pays to lease.

4. (a) True
(b) True
(c) True
(d) True
(e) True
(f) True
(g) True

5. The present value of depreciation tax shields on the $3000 desk, using the 5-year schedule from Table 6-5, is:

$$\text{PV (at 9 percent)} = .35 \times \text{PV (5-year schedule)} \times 3000$$
$$= \$832$$

After-tax administrative costs are $400(1 - .35) = \$280$ per year for 6 years. If the first costs are incurred immediately, their present value is $1369. Thus the present value of all costs is $3000 - 832 + 1369 = \$3537$. The break-even lease rate is about $724. In other words, the present value of six payments of $724, with the first payment due immediately, is about $3537.

6. Administrative costs drop to $200 per year, so the present value of total costs is $2853. Moreover, the lease payments are a fixed commitment of the blue chip company. The six lease payments are discounted at the after-tax rate at which Acme would lend money; that is, $6(1 - .35) = 3.9$ percent. The break-even lease rate falls to about $522.

7. (a) $59,307; the present value of the lease cash flows from $t = 1$ to $t = 3$, discounted at $r(1 - T_c) = .10(1 - .35) = .065$

(b) $62,000 - 59,307 = 2693$

(c) It should not invest. The lease's value of +2693 does not offset the machine's negative NPV. It would be happy to sign the same lease on a more attractive asset.

Chapter 27

1.

(a) $\dfrac{3904}{3904 + 2620} = .60$

(b) $\dfrac{1025 + 746}{453} = 3.9$

(c) $\dfrac{1862}{2325} = .80$

(d) $\dfrac{53 + 566}{2325} = .27$

(e) $\dfrac{1025 - 246}{12,738} = .061$

(f) $\dfrac{9881}{.5(1209 + 1202)} = 8.2$

(g) $\dfrac{326}{.5(2620 + 2402)} = .13$

(h) $\dfrac{145}{326} = .44$

2. The illogical ratios are a, b, c, f, and i. The correct definitions are:

$$\text{Debt-equity ratio} = \frac{\text{long-term debt} + \text{value of leases}}{\text{equity}}$$

$$\text{Return on equity} = \frac{\text{earnings available for common}}{\text{average equity}}$$

$$\text{Payout ratio} = \frac{\text{dividend}}{\text{earnings per share}}$$

$$\text{Current ratio} = \frac{\text{current assets}}{\text{current liabilities}}$$

$$\text{Average collection period} = \frac{\text{average receivables}}{\text{sales} \div 365}$$

3. (a) False
   (b) True
   (c) False
   (d) False
   (e) True (as a general rule)
   (f) True
   (g) False
   (h) False
   (i) False—it will tend to increase the price-earnings multiple

4. (a) Shipping company
   (b) United Foods
   (c) Paper mill
   (d) Mail order company
   (e) Fledgling Electronics
   (f) Pharmaceutical company

5. $365,000; 12.2

6. (a) 12 percent
   (b) 16 percent

7. .25

8. 3.65 percent; .73

9. (a) 1.47
   (b) Net working capital = 40. Total capitalization = 540. Debt to total capitalization = .52.

10. $10 million

11. $82 million

12. (*a*) Intangible assets, off-balance sheet debt, pension assets and liabilities (if the pension plan has a surplus), derivatives positions.

   (*b*) The value of intangible assets does not show up on the company's books. This affects accounting rates of return, because book assets are too low. It can also make debt ratios seem high, again because assets are undervalued.

   (*c*) Inventory profits increase. Depreciation is understated, as are asset values. Equity income is depressed because this inflation premium in interest payments is not offset by a reduction in the real value of debt.

Chapter 28

1. (*a*) False (it is a process of deciding which risks to take).

   (*b*) False (financial planning is concerned with possible surprises as well as expected outcomes).

   (*c*) True (financial planning considers both the investment and financing decisions).

   (*d*) False (a typical horizon for long-term planning is 5 years).

   (*e*) True (investments are usually broken down by category).

   (*f*) True (perfect accuracy is unlikely to be obtainable, but the firm needs to produce the best possible consistent forecasts).

   (*g*) False (excessive detail distracts attention from the crucial decisions).

2. Pro forma financial statements (balance sheets, income statements, and sources and uses of cash); description of planned capital expenditure, and a summary of planned financing.

3. Most financial models are designed to forecast accounting statements. They do not focus on the factors that directly determine firm value, such as incremental cash flow or risk.

4. (*a*) $2900

   (*b*) $225

   (*c*) .25

5. Dividend; $350

6. (*a*) 8.6 percent

   (*b*) 13.75 percent

Chapter 29

1. See Table A2.

2. Month 3: $18 + (.5 \times 90) + (.3 \times 120) + (.2 \times 100) = \$119,000$

   Month 4: $14 + (.5 \times 70) + (.3 \times 90) + (.2 \times 120) = \$100,000$

3. (*a*) Long-term financing, cumulative capital requirement, marketable securities

   (*b*) Cash, cash, cash balance, marketable securities

   (*c*) Trial, error, financial models

4. (*a*) Inventories go up (use).

   (*b*) Accounts receivable go up (use).

   (*c*) No change shown on the firm's books.

   (*d*) Decrease in assets (source).

TABLE A-2
· ·

Chapter 29, Quiz question 1

Cash	Working Capital
1. $2 million decline	$2 million decline
2. $2500 increase	Unchanged
3. $5000 decline	Unchanged
4. Unchanged	$1 million increase
5. Unchanged	Unchanged
6. $5 million increase	Unchanged

    (e) Net worth declines (use).
    (f) Retained earnings fall (use).
    (g) Long-term debt increases (source), short-term debt falls (use).
5. (a) Table 29-2: Bank loans = 3, Cash = 8, Current assets = 58, Current liabilities = 30, Total assets = Total liabilities and net worth = 118. Table 29-4: Repaid short-term bank loan = 2, Increase in cash balance = 4. Tables 29-5 and 29-6 unchanged.
    (b) Table 29-2: Long-term debt = 22, Gross investment = 82, Net fixed assets = 52, Cash = 3, Total assets = Total liabilities and net worth = 125. Table 29-4: Issued long-term debt = 17, Total sources = 21, Invested in fixed assets = 26, Total uses = 42, Increases in cash balance = −1. Table 29-5: Fixed and Total assets change as in Table 29-2, as do Long-term debt and Total liabilities and net worth. Table 29-6: same changes as in Table 29-4, except Increase in net working capital = 6.
    (c) Table 29-3: Operating costs = 289, Pretax income = 56, Net income = 28, Retained earnings = 27. Table 29-2: Net worth = 92, Total liabilities and net worth = Total assets = 131; Inventory = 22.5, Accounts receivable = 27, Cash = 10.5. Table 29-5: Net worth = 92, Long-term liabilities and net worth = Total assets = 104. Table 29-6: Net income = 28.
    (d) Table 29-7: Third quarter, Total collections = 120.1, Ending receivables = 26.6. Fourth quarter, Total collections = 129.5, Ending receivables = 28.1. Table 29-8, Third quarter: Sources minus uses and Cash at end of period increase by 11.6, Cumulative financing required decreases by 11.6. Fourth quarter: Sources minus uses increase by 1.5, Cumulative financing required decreases by 13.1 to −12.6.
    (e) Table 29-8: Labor, etc. = 26, Sources minus uses decrease by 4 in each quarter. Cumulative financing required decreases by 4 in first quarter, 8 in second, etc.
    (f) Table 29-8: Other sources of cash increase by 10 in the second quarter, increasing Sources minus uses and decreasing Cumulative financing required.
    (g) Table 29-8: Minimum operating cash balance = 2, Cumulative financing required decreases by 2 in all quarters.
6. (a) 19.2, 16.8, 15, 13.2, 12, 12
    (b) 26.5, 23.2, 20.6, 18.2, 16.4, 16

Chapter 30

1. (*a*) 1 percent of $1000 = $10
   (*b*) 1 percent for 30 days = 12 percent per annum simple interest or 12.7 percent compound interest.
   (*c*) (i) Shorter
   (ii) Longer
   (iii) Shorter

2. (*a*) Due lag decreases, therefore pay lag decreases.
   (*b*) Due lag increases, therefore pay lag increases.
   (*c*) Terms lag increases, therefore pay lag increases.

3. Open account, promissory note, commercial draft, shipping documents, trade acceptance, the customer's, banker's acceptance, letter of credit, the customer's, his or her own, letter of credit, shipping documents, shipping documents

4. Reject because PV of Q's order
   $$= \frac{7.5 \times 50}{1.10^{1/2}} - 40$$
   $= -\$4.25$ per iron, or $-\$4250$ in total

5. (*a*) Expected profit $= p(1200 - 1050) - 1050\,(1 - p) = 0$
   $$p = .875$$
   Therefore, grant credit if probability of payment exceeds 87.5 percent.
   (*b*) Expected profit from selling to slow payer:
   $.8(150) - .2(1050) = -90$. Break-even point for credit check: $(.05 \times 90 \times$ units$) - 12 = 0$. Units $= 2.67$.

6. Total expected profit on initial order $= -40 + \dfrac{.8[(p_2 \times 200) - 1000(1 - p_2)]}{1.2} = 0$
   $p_2 = .88$, or 88 percent

7. (*a*) False
   (*b*) True
   (*c*) False
   (*d*) False—should be collection agency or attorney
   (*e*) True

Chapter 31

1. (*a*) Carrying cost per book/2 = $1
   (*b*) $(200 \times 2)/Q^2 = 1$
   $Q = \sqrt{400} = 20$ books
   (*c*) $200/20 = 10$ orders
   (*d*) $Q/2 = 10$ books

2. (*a*) Carrying cost/2 = $.01
   (*b*) $(20{,}000 \times 2)/Q^2 = \$.01$
   $Q = \sqrt{4{,}000{,}000} = \$2000$
   (*c*) $20{,}000/2000 = 10$ orders
   (*d*) $Q/2 = \$1000$

3. (*a*) Interest rate, cost of each transaction, and variability of cash balance.
   (*b*) It should restore it to one-third of the distance between the lower and upper limits.

(c) By holding a lower cash balance, the firm increases the transaction frequency but earns more interest.

4. (a) Less
   (b) Less
   (c) Invest the same amount
   (d) More

5. (a) Payment float = $25,000. Availability float = $75,000
   (b) It can earn interest on these funds.
   (c) Payment float increases. The bank's gross ledger balance and available balance increase by the same amount.

6. (a) The $.40 per check fee is cheaper at 300 × .40 = $120 per day. The cost of putting up $800,000 of compensating balances is .09 × 800,000 = $72,000 per year, or 72,000/365 = $197 per day.
   (b) The lock-box system costs $120 per day, or $43,800 per year. You would need $487,000 additional cash to generate this much interest. Thus, the lock-box system must generate at least this much cash. The cash flow is 300 × 1500 = $450,000 per day. Thus the lock box must speed up average collection time by 487,000/450,000 = 1.08 days.

7. Because the bank can forecast early in the day how much money will be paid out, the company does not need to keep extra cash in the account to cover contingencies. Also, since zero-balance accounts are not held in a major banking center, the company gains several days of additional float.

8. Payment float; availability float; net float; concentration banking; wire transfer; depository transfer check; lock-box banking

Chapter 32

1. (a) Repurchase agreements
   (b) Commercial paper
   (c) U.S. certificates of deposit
   (d) Finance company commercial paper
   (e) Medium-term notes
   (f) Treasury bills
   (g) Treasury bills
   (h) Treasury bills

2. 5.66 percent simple interest or 5.74 percent compound interest

3. Line of credit; clean-up provision; prime rate; compensating balance; floating lien; collateral; with recourse; public warehouse; field warehouse; warehouse receipt; trust receipt; floor planning; commercial paper; medium-term notes

4. Only 30 percent of the floating-rate preferred dividend is taxed versus 100 percent of bond interest. The fixed-dividend preferred also has this tax advantage but its price fluctuates more than the floating-rate preferred's.

5. (a) 1 year
   (b) Often
   (c) No
   (d) Floating rate (e.g., linked to prime)
   (e) A larger fraction of the loan is repaid at maturity.
   (f) A legally assured line of credit that can be converted into a term loan

Chapter 33
1. (*a*) Horizontal
   (*b*) Conglomerate
   (*c*) Vertical
   (*d*) Conglomerate

2. (*a*) $5 million (We assume that the $500,000 saving is an after-tax figure.)
   (*b*) $4 million
   (*c*) $7.5 million
   (*d*) +$1 million
   (*e*) −$2.5 million

3. *a, b, d*

4. (*a*) True
   (*b*) False
   (*c*) False
   (*d*) True
   (*e*) False (They may produce gains, but "substantial" is stretching it.)
   (*f*) False
   (*g*) True (assuming that the purchase price exceeds the value of the tangible assets acquired)
   (*h*) False
   (*i*) True

5. *a* and *d*; *c* can also make sense, although merging is not the only way to redeploy excess cash.

6. ■ LBO—buyout by private investors
   ■ Poison pill—shareholders issued rights . . .
   ■ Tender offer—offer to buy shares directly from stockholders
   ■ Greenmail—target buys out shareholders threatening takeover
   ■ Golden parachute—payment to target firm's managers
   ■ Proxy fight—attempt to gain control by winning stockholders' votes

7. (*a*) True
   (*b*) False
   (*c*) False
   (*d*) True
   (*e*) False

Chapter 34
1. (*a*) 1.5539
   (*b*) 1.5528
   (*c*) Premium
   (*d*) $\dfrac{1.5539 - 1.5269}{1.5269} = 0.177$, or 1.77 percent
   (*e*) $\dfrac{1 + r_{DM}}{1 + r_{\$}} = \dfrac{f_{DM/\$}}{s_{DM/\$}}$

   $\dfrac{1 + r_{DM}}{1.06} = \dfrac{1.5269}{1.5539}$

   $r_{DM} = .042$

(*f*) 1.5491

(*g*) $\dfrac{E(1 + i_{DM})}{E(1 + i_\$)} = \dfrac{f_{DM/\$}}{s_{DM/\$}} = .983$

That is, inflation in Germany was expected to be 1.7 percent less than in the United States.

2. (*a*) The interest rate differential equals the forward premium or discount, i.e.,

$$\frac{1 + r_x}{1 + r_\$} = \frac{f_{x/\$}}{s_{x/\$}}$$

(*b*) The expected change in the spot rate equals the forward premium or discount, i.e.,

$$\frac{f_{x/\$}}{s_{x/\$}} = \frac{E(s_{x/\$})}{s_{x/\$}}$$

(*c*) Prices of goods in different countries are equal when measured in terms of the same currency. It follows that the expected change in the spot rate equals the expected inflation differential; i.e.,

$$\frac{E(1 + i_x)}{E(1 + i_\$)} = \frac{E(s_{x/\$})}{s_{x/\$}}$$

(*d*) Expected real interest rates in different countries are equal; i.e.,

$$\frac{1 + r_x}{1 + r_\$} = \frac{E(1 + i_x)}{E(1 + i_\$)}$$

3.

	3 Months	6 Months	1 Year
Eurodollar interest rate (percent)	11.5	12.25	12.5
Eurofranc interest rate (percent)	19.5	19.7	20
Forward francs per dollar	7.17	7.28	7.52
Forward discount on franc, percent per year	−6.7	−6.3	−6.3

Note: Spot dollars per franc = 1/7.0500 = .1418.

4. (*b*)

5. $\dfrac{10}{1.042} \div 1.5539 = \$6.17$ million

6. It can borrow the present value of 1 million DM, sell the deutschemarks in the spot market, and invest the proceeds in a 2-year dollar loan.

7. (*a*) Foreign inflation rates to produce cash-flow forecasts
Future exchange rates to convert cash flows into domestic currency
Domestic interest rate to discount domestic currency cash flows
(*b*) Foreign inflation rates to produce cash-flow forecasts
Foreign interest rate to discount foreign currency cash flows

8. (a)

	Overseas	U.S.
X	60	0
Y	40	10*
	100	10

*$50 less double-tax relief of $40.

(b)

	Overseas*	U.S.
X	0	50
Y	0	50
	0	100

*Interest in most countries is deductible for corporate tax.

Index

SOME USEFUL FORMULAS

(The section number indicates the principal reference in the text.)

Perpetuity (3-2)

The value of a perpetuity of $1 per year is:

$$PV = \frac{1}{r}$$

Annuity (3-2)

The value of annuity of $1 per period for t years (t-year annuity factor) is:

$$PV = \frac{1}{r} - \frac{1}{r(1 + r)^t}$$

A Growing Perpetuity (the "Gordon" model) (3-2)

If the initial cash flow is $1 at year 1 and if cash flows thereafter grow at a constant rate of g in perpetuity,

$$PV = \frac{1}{r - g}$$

Continuous Compounding (3-3)

If r is the continuously compounded rate of interest, the present value of $1 received in year t is:

$$PV = \frac{1}{e^{rt}}$$

Equivalent Annual Cost (6-3)

If an asset has a life of t years, the equivalent annual cost is:

$$\frac{PV(\text{costs})}{t\text{-year annuity factor}}$$

Measures of Risk (7-2 to 7-4)

Variance of returns $= \sigma^2$
$$= \text{expected value of } (\tilde{r} - r)^2$$

Standard deviation of returns $= \sqrt{\text{variance}} = \sigma$

Covariance between returns of stocks 1 and 2
$= \sigma_{12} = $ expected value of $[(\tilde{r}_1 - r_1)(\tilde{r}_2 - r_2)]$

Correlation between returns of stocks 1 and 2 $=$

$$\rho_{12} = \frac{\sigma_{12}}{\sigma_1 \sigma_2}$$

Beta of stock $i = \beta_i = \dfrac{\sigma_{im}}{\sigma_m^2}$

The variance of returns on a portfolio

The variance of returns on a portfolio with proportion x_i invested in stock i is:

$$\sum_{i=1}^{N} \sum_{j=1}^{N} x_i x_j \sigma_{ij}$$

Capital Asset Pricing Model (8-2)

The expected risk premium on a risky investment is:

$$r - r_f = \beta(r_m - r_f)$$

Capital Asset Pricing Model (Certainty-Equivalent Form) (Chapter 9 Appendix)

The present value of a one-period risky investment is:

$$PV = \frac{C_1 - \lambda \text{Cov}(\tilde{C}_1, \tilde{r}_m)}{1 + r_f}$$

where

$$\lambda = \frac{r_m - r_f}{\sigma_m^2}$$

Value of Right and Ex-Rights Price (Chapter 15, Appendix A)

If N is the number of rights required to buy 1 share, the value of a right is:

$$\frac{\text{Rights-on price} - \text{issue price}}{N + 1}$$

$$= \frac{\text{ex-rights price} - \text{issue price}}{N}$$

The ex-rights price is:

$$\frac{1}{N + 1} (N \times \text{rights-on price} + \text{issue price})$$

Adjusted Cost of Capital (19-2 and 19-3)

If r is the cost of capital under all-equity financing, the adjusted cost of capital is:

MM formula:

$$r^* = r(1 - T_c L)$$